Neil Sheehan was a Vietnam War correspondent for United Press International and *The New York Times* and won a number of awards for his reporting. In 1971 he obtained the Pentagon Papers, which brought *The Times* the Pulitzer Prize gold medal for meritorious public service. He lives in Washington, D.C. *A Bright Shining Lie* won the National Book Award and the Pulitzer Prize for Nonfiction.

Neil Sheehan

A BRIGHT
SHINING LIE

John Paul Vann and America in Vietnam

PICADOR

in association with Jonathan Cape

First published in Great Britain 1989 by Jonathan Cape Ltd
This Picador edition published 1990 by Pan Books Ltd,
Cavaye Place, London SW10 9PG
in association with Jonathan Cape Ltd
Grateful acknowledgement is made to Fall River Music, Inc.,
for permission to reprint excerpts from the lyrics to
"Where Have All the Flowers Gone?" by Pete Seeger.
© Fall River Music 1981
9 8 7 6 5 4 3 2 1
© Neil Sheehan 1988
Cartography © Jean Paul Tremblay 1988
ISBN 0 330 31304 5
Printed and bound in Great Britain by
Richard Clay Ltd, Bungay, Suffolk

Once Again and Always for Susan
A First Time for Maria and Catherine
And for my Mother and Kitty

We had also, to all the visitors who came over there,
been one of the bright shining lies.

—John Paul Vann
to a U.S. Army historian,
July 1963

CONTENTS

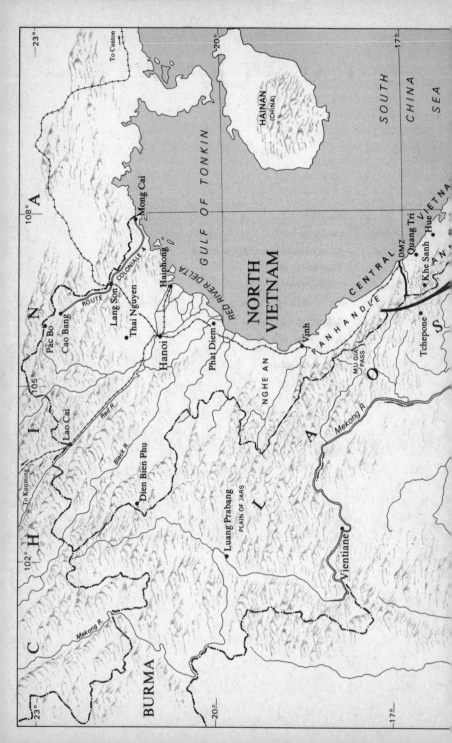

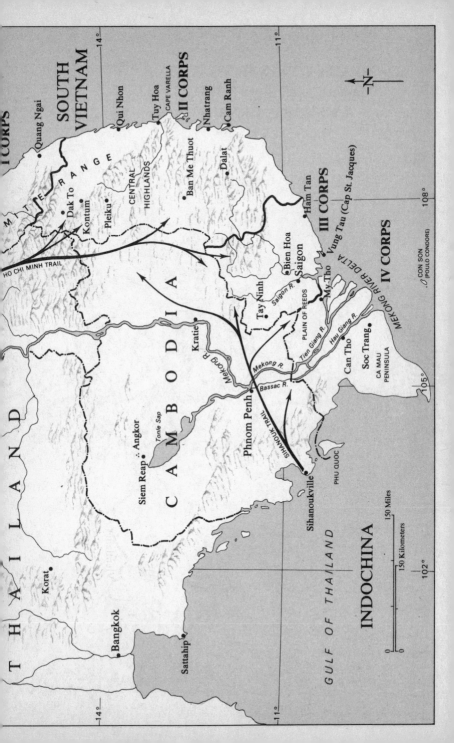

JOHN VANN COMES TO VIETNAM
March 22, 1962–April 3, 1963
AND HE RETURNS
March 20, 1965

Kratie

Phnom Penh

Mekong R.

Bassac R.

-N-

C A M B O D I A

TAY NINH
WAR ZONE C
NUI BA DEN
(BLACK VIRGIN MOUNTAIN)

Tay Ninh   BI

PARROT'S
BEAK   Bau Trai
(Khiem Cuong)

Chau Doc (Chau Phu)   Moc Hoa
KIEN TUONG

SEVEN MOUNTAINS   CHAU   KIEN PHONG   PLAIN OF REEDS   29
DOC

Tien Giang R.   DINH TUONG
T A
My Tho   4

AN GIANG   SA DEC   Vinh Long   Ben T
VINH LONG   (Truc Gia

PHU
QUOC   8A   Rach Gia   KIEN   Can Tho
GIANG   PHONG   Hau Giang R.
DINH

Vi Thanh   VINH BINH
(Duc Long)   4

GULF   OF   CHUONG   Soc Trang
THIEN   (Khanh Hung)
THAILAND   BA XUYEN   IV CORPS

U MINH   CA MAU
FOREST   PENINSULA
BAC
Bac Lieu (Vinh Loi)

Ca Mau   LIEU
(Quan Long)

+ Airfield   AN XUYEN
—— Principal road
---- Provincial boundary
—·—· International boundary
—— Corps boundary   0   50 Miles
                       0   50 Kilometers

The original III Corps region mentioned in book I encompassed all of the post-December 1962 III and IV Corps.

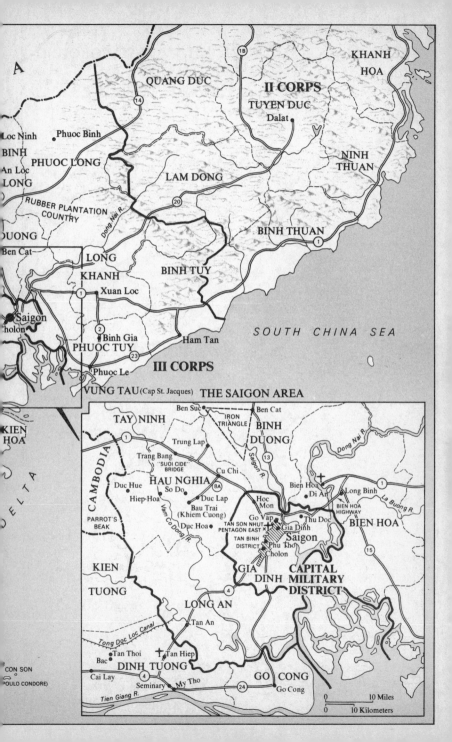

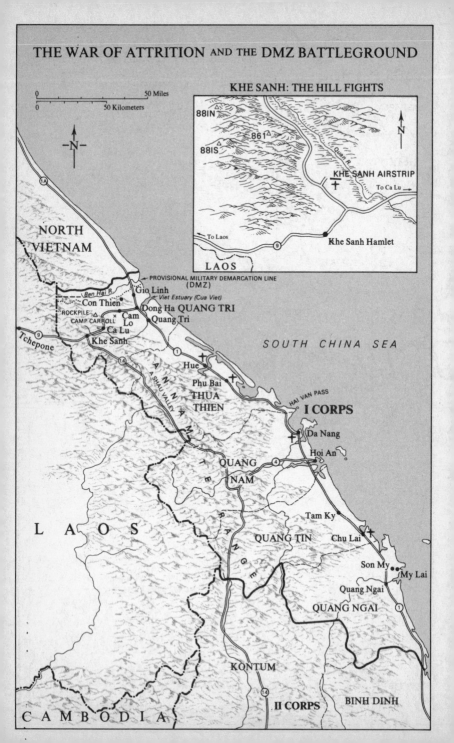

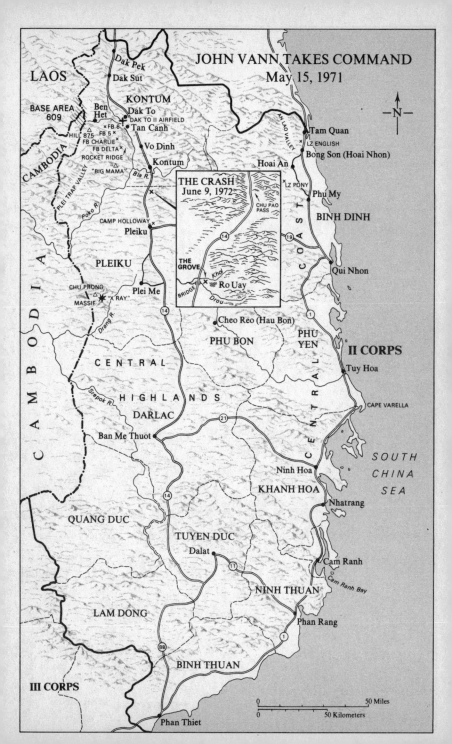

JOHN VANN TAKES COMMAND
May 15, 1971

LAOS

Dak Pek
Dak Sut

KONTUM

BASE AREA 609
Ben Het
Dak To
DAK TO II AIRFIELD
HILL 875 ×FB 6
FB 5 ×
FB CHARLIE
FB DELTA ×
ROCKET RIDGE
Tan Canh
Vo Dinh

△ "BIG MAMA"

CAMBODIA

Bla R.
Kontum

Poko R.

PLEI TRAP VALLEY

CAMP HOLLOWAY ×
Pleiku

PLEIKU

CHU PRONG
MASSIF △ "X RAY"
Plei Me

Drang R.

CENTRAL

Srepok R.

HIGHLANDS

DARLAC

Ban Me Thuot

CAMBODIA

QUANG DUC

14

TUYEN DUC
Dalat

LAM DONG

8B

BINH THUAN

III CORPS

Phan Thiet

AN LAO VALLEY

Tam Quan
LZ ENGLISH
Bong Son (Hoai Nhon)
Hoai An
× LZ PONY
Phu My

BINH DINH

THE CRASH
June 9, 1972
CHU PAO PASS
14
19
THE GROVE
BRIDGE × Ro Uay
Kha
Drou

Qui Nhon

Cheo Reo (Hau Bon)

PHU BON

PHU YEN

II CORPS

Tuy Hoa

CAPE VARELLA

CENTRAL

21

COAST

SOUTH CHINA SEA

Ninh Hoa

KHANH HOA

Nhatrang

Cam Ranh
Cam Ranh Bay

NINH THUAN

11

Phan Rang

1

—N—

0   50 Miles
0   50 Kilometers

A
BRIGHT
SHINING
LIE

THE FUNERAL

★ I T WAS a funeral to which they all came. They gathered in the red brick chapel beside the cemetery gate. Six gray horses were hitched to a caisson that would carry the coffin to the grave. A marching band was ready. An honor guard from the Army's oldest regiment, the regiment whose rolls reached back to the Revolution, was also formed in ranks before the white Georgian portico of the chapel. The soldiers were in full dress, dark blue trimmed with gold, the colors of the Union Army, which had safeguarded the integrity of the nation. The uniform was unsuited to the warmth and humidity of this Friday morning in the early summer of Washington, but this state funeral was worthy of the discomfort. John Paul Vann, the soldier of the war in Vietnam, was being buried at Arlington on June 16, 1972.

The war had already lasted longer than any other in the nation's history and had divided America more than any conflict since the Civil War. In this war without heroes, this man had been the one compelling figure. The intensity and distinctiveness of his character and the courage and drama of his life had seemed to sum up so many of the qualities Americans admired in themselves as a people. By an obsession, by an unyielding dedication to the war, he had come to personify the American endeavor in Vietnam. He had exemplified it in his illusions, in his good intentions gone awry, in his pride, in his will to win. Where others had been defeated or discouraged over the years, or had become disenchanted and had turned against the war, he had been undeterred in his crusade to find a way to redeem the unredeemable, to lay hold of victory in this doomed enterprise. At the end of a decade of struggle to prevail, he had been killed one night a week earlier when his helicopter had crashed and burned in rain and fog in the mountains of South Vietnam's Central Highlands. He had just beaten back, in a battle at a town called

Kontum, an offensive by the North Vietnamese Army which had threatened to bring the Vietnam venture down in defeat.

Those who had assembled to see John Vann to his grave reflected the divisions and the wounds that the war had inflicted on American society. At the same time they had, almost every one, been touched by this man. Some had come because they had admired him and shared his cause even now; some because they had parted with him along the way, but still thought of him as a friend; some because they had been harmed by him, but cherished him for what he might have been. Although the war was to continue for nearly another three years with no dearth of dying in Vietnam, many at Arlington on that June morning in 1972 sensed that they were burying with John Vann the war and the decade of Vietnam. With Vann dead, the rest could be no more than a postscript.

He had gone to Vietnam at the beginning of the decade, in March 1962, at the age of thirty-seven, as an Army lieutenant colonel, volunteering to serve as senior advisor to a South Vietnamese infantry division in the Mekong Delta south of Saigon. The war was still an adventure then. The previous December, President John F. Kennedy had committed the arms of the United States to the task of suppressing a Communist-led rebellion and preserving South Vietnam as a separate state governed by an American-sponsored regime in Saigon.

Vann was a natural leader of men in war. He was a child of the American South in the Great Depression, a redneck born and raised in a poor white working-class district of Norfolk, Virginia. He never tanned, his friends and subordinates joked during that first assignment in Vietnam. Whenever he exposed himself to the sun by marching with the South Vietnamese infantrymen on operations, which he did constantly, his ruddy neck and arms simply got redder.

At first glance he appeared a runty man. He stood five feet eight inches and weighed 150 pounds. An unusual physical stamina and an equally unusual assertiveness more than compensated for this shortness of stature. His constitution was extraordinary. It permitted him to turn each day into two days for an ordinary man. He required only four hours of sleep in normal times and could function effectively with two hours of sleep for extended periods. He could, and routinely did, put in two eight-hour working days in every twenty-four and still had half a working day in which to relax and amuse himself.

The assertiveness showed in the harsh, nasal tone of his voice and in the brisk, clipped way he had of enunciating his words. He always knew what he wanted to do and how he wanted to do it. He had a genius for solving the day-to-day problems that arise in the course of moving forward a complicated enterprise, particularly one as complicated as the art of making war. The genius lay in his pragmatic cast of mind and in his instinct for assessing the peculiar talents and motivations of other men and then turning those talents and motivations to his advantage. Detail fascinated him. He prized facts. He absorbed great quantities of them with ease and was always searching out more, confident that once he had discovered the facts of a problem, he could correctly analyze it and then apply the proper solution. His character and the education the Army had given him at service schools and civilian universities had combined to produce a mind that could be totally possessed by the immediate task and at the same time sufficiently detached to discern the root elements of the problem. He manifested the faith and the optimism of post–World War II America that any challenge could be overcome by will and by the disciplined application of intellect, technology, money, and, when necessary, armed force.

Vann had no physical fear. He made a habit of frequently spending the night at South Vietnamese militia outposts and survived a number of assaults against these little isolated forts of brick and sandbag blockhouses and mud walls, taking up a rifle to help the militiamen repel the attack. He drove roads that no one else would drive, to prove they could be driven, and in the process drove with slight injury through several ambushes. He landed his helicopter at district capitals and fortified camps in the midst of assaults to assist the defenders, ignoring the shelling and the antiaircraft machine guns, defying the enemy gunners to kill him. In the course of the decade he acquired a reputation for invulnerability. Time and again he took risks that killed other men and always survived. The odds, he said, did not apply to him.

A willingness to take risks in his professional life was another quality he had in great measure. He displayed it during his first year in Vietnam, from March 1962 to April 1963, and showed it often in later years. While serving as senior advisor to a South Vietnamese infantry division in the Mekong Delta that first year, Vann saw that the war was being lost. The ambassador and the commanding general in South Vietnam were telling the Kennedy administration that everything was going well and that the war was being won. Vann believed then and never ceased to believe that the war could be won if it was fought with sound tactics and strategy. When the general and his staff in Saigon did not listen to him, and his reports aroused their displeasure, he leaked his meticulously documented assessments to the American correspondents in the country. He was reassigned to the Pentagon at the end of his tour, and he conducted a campaign there to try to convince the nation's military leadership that corrective action had to be taken if the United States was not to be defeated in Vietnam. He was rebuffed. Having completed twenty years of active duty, he chose to retire from the Army on July 31, 1963. His retirement was interpreted by most of his friends and associates as an act of protest so that he could speak out publicly on the war. Vann proceeded to do precisely that in newspaper, magazine, and television interviews and in speeches to whatever groups would listen to him.

He went back to Vietnam in March 1965 as a provincial pacification representative for the Agency for International Development (AID). He was never to return to the United States, except for occasional home leaves, until his death. He distinguished himself as pacification representative in one of the most dangerous provinces in the country just west of Saigon and by the end of 1966 was made chief of the civilian pacification program for the eleven provinces in the corps region surrounding the capital. In his reports to his superiors during those years, Vann denounced as cruel and self-defeating the indiscriminate bombing and shelling of the countryside which the U.S. high command was conducting to try to deprive the Vietnamese Communists of their population base. Large sections of the peasantry were driven into slums in the cities and into refugee camps near the district capitals and larger towns. Vann never hesitated to use whatever level of force he felt was required to further his cause, but he considered it morally wrong and stupid to wreak unnecessary violence on the innocent.

In 1967 his professional boldness again put him in disfavor with those in authority. He warned that the strategy of attrition being pursued by Gen. William Westmoreland with a 475,000-man American army was not succeeding, that security in the countryside was worsening, that the Vietnamese Communists were as strong as ever. Vann was vindicated when, on January 31, 1968, the Communists took advantage of Tet, the Vietnamese Lunar New Year holiday, to launch a surprise offensive against installations in cities and towns throughout the country, penetrating even the U.S. Embassy compound in the middle of Saigon. The war-of-attrition strategy was discredited. Westmoreland was relieved as commanding general in Vietnam.

Although Vann hurt his family and others close to him in his personal life, his loyalty to friends, associates, and subordinates seemed limitless over the years. After the Tet Offensive his best Vietnamese friend, a former lieutenant colonel and province chief who had left the South Vietnamese Army to go into politics, launched a complicated scheme to negotiate a settlement to the war and started to denounce the Saigon regime. Several senior U.S. officials suspected Vann's friend of seeking to form a coalition government with the Communists in the hope of securing a prominent place for himself. Vann disapproved of his friend's negotiating scheme, but he risked his career again in a vain attempt to save his friend from jail. He was nearly dismissed and sent home. Vann also parted over the war with his best American friend, Daniel Ellsberg, who had earlier been a comrade in the struggle to make the Vietnam endeavor succeed. Ellsberg began an antiwar crusade in the United States while Vann continued his crusade to win the war in Vietnam. Their friendship remained intact. When Vann was killed, Ellsberg was preparing to go on trial in the Federal District Court in Los Angeles for copying the Pentagon Papers. Vann had told Ellsberg that he would testify in his behalf. Ellsberg wept at the loss of the man to whom he had been closest in life.

Despite his maverick behavior, Vann had gradually risen in the system. His leadership qualities and his dedication to the war had assisted his promotion, as had a realization by those in power in Saigon and Washington that his dissent over tactics or strategy was always meant to further the war effort, not to hinder it. In May 1971 he was made senior advisor for the corps region comprising the Central Highlands and the adjacent provinces on the Central Coast. He was given authority over all U.S. military forces in the area, along with control of those civilians and military officers assigned to the pacification program. The position made him, in effect, a major general in the U.S. Army. The appointment was unprecedented in the history of American wars, as Vann was technically a civilian employed by AID. In addition, he covertly shared command of the 158,000 South Vietnamese troops in the corps because of a special relationship he had developed with the South Vietnamese general who was his counterpart. The influence he wielded within the U.S. civil-military bureaucracy and the Saigon government structure made him the most important American in the country after the ambassador and the commanding general in Saigon. His accumulated expertise and aptitude for this war made him the one irreplaceable American in Vietnam.

Vann's political credo was the set of beliefs characteristic of the United States that had emerged from World War II as the greatest power on earth, the view of self and the world that had carried America to war in Vietnam in the fullness of this power. To Vann, other peoples were lesser peoples: it was the natural order of things that they accept American leadership. He was convinced that having gained the preeminence it had been destined to achieve, the United States would never relinquish the position. He did not see America as using its power for self-satisfaction. He saw the United States as a stern yet benevolent authority that enforced peace and brought prosperity to the peoples of the non-Communist nations, sharing the bounty of its enterprise and technology with those who had been denied a fruitful life by poverty and social injustice and bad government. He assumed that America's cause was always just, that while the United States might err, its intentions were always good. He was simplistic in his anti-Communism, because to him all Communists were enemies of America and thus enemies of order and progress.

He saw much that was wrong about the war in Vietnam, but he could never bring himself to conclude that the war itself was wrong and un-winnable. To admit this would have been to admit the inevitability of defeat, and at a certain point in him intellect stopped and instinct took over. He could not abide defeat, defeat for himself or for his vision of America. He believed that America had staked that vision in Vietnam and he knew that he had made his stake there. That spring, when many around him had despaired at the height of the North Vietnamese Army offensive, he had said no, they would not retreat, they would stand and fight. He had fought and won the battle and then he had died. This was why some of those who had assembled at Arlington on June 16, 1972, wondered if they were burying with him more than the war and the decade of Vietnam. They wondered if they were also burying with him this vision and this faith in an ever-innocent America.

The man who had been the attending physician at the birth of South Vietnam, Maj. Gen. Edward Lansdale, was standing on the steps beneath the portico, saying hello to friends and acquaintances as they passed him on their way into the chapel. He had retired from government service four years earlier. He was a widower and alone because of the death of his wife that spring. "I'm sorry about your wife, Ed," one man said, shaking his hand. "Thanks," Lansdale replied with his habitual smile and a throaty voice that was now tired and old.

It was difficult to imagine that this ordinary-looking man of sixty-four had been the legendary clandestine operative of the Central Intelligence Agency, the man who had guided Ramón Magsaysay, the pro-American Filipino leader, through the campaign that had crushed the Communist Hukbalahap rebels in the Philippines in the early 1950s; that this un-stylish man in a light brown business suit had been the famed missionary of American democracy in the Cold War era, the "Colonel Hillandale" of a best-selling novel of the period, *The Ugly American*. In an ironic play on its title, the novel told how imaginative Americans filled with the ideals of their own Revolution could get Asians to defeat the dark ideology of Communism in the Orient.

Lansdale had arrived in Saigon eight years before Vann. He had gone there in 1954 after his triumph in the Philippines, when the United States was tentatively but openly extending its power into Vietnam to replace the French, whose will had been broken by their defeat at Dien Bien Phu. America's new hope in Saigon, a Catholic mandarin named Ngo Dinh Diem, had faced more enemies than it seemed possible to vanquish. Arrayed against him were rival politicians, pro-French dissidents in the South Vietnamese Army, and two religious sects and a brotherhood of organized criminals. The religious sects and the organized-crime society also had their own private armies. Lansdale had arranged the defeat of them all. He had denied the Vietnamese Communists the chaos that would have permitted them to take over Vietnam south of the 17th Parallel without another war. He had convinced the Eisenhower administration that Diem could govern and that South Vietnam could be built into a nation that would stand with America.

Waiting just behind Lansdale, a step above him, was Lt. Col. Lucien Conein, the best-known member of the team Lansdale had employed to help him preside over the creation of South Vietnam. Conein was a rough and sentimental man, an adventurer born in Paris and raised in Kansas. He had enlisted in the French Army at the beginning of World War II. After the fall of France and the entry of the United States into the war, he had joined the Office of Strategic Services, the World War II forerunner of the CIA. He had first landed in Indochina by parachute in 1945, under the pseudonym Lieutenant Laurent, to conduct raids against the Japanese Imperial Army. He had been of considerable assistance to Lansdale ten years later because of his felicity for what the intelligence trade calls "dirty tricks." When Lansdale had returned to the United States in 1956, Conein had stayed on in South Vietnam, and in 1963 he had accomplished the act that is one of the highest professional aspirations for a man of Conein's calling—setting up a successful coup d'état. He had been the liaison agent to the South Vietnamese generals who had been encouraged to overthrow the man whose position Lansdale had taken such pains to consolidate. Ngo Dinh Diem had outlasted his usefulness to the United States in the intervening years. He and his family had been getting in the way of the Kennedy administration's campaign to suppress the Communist-led rebellion. Diem and his brother, Ngo Dinh Nhu, had been assassinated in the coup.

Joseph Alsop, the newspaper columnist and journalist of the American Establishment, was already inside the chapel. He was sitting in one of the center pews on the left, dressed in a sober blue suit made by his English tailor, with a matching polka-dot bow tie and a white shirt. John Kennedy had once displayed his esteem for Alsop's advice and friendship by stopping at Alsop's Georgetown home for a bowl of turtle soup on the night of his inauguration in 1961. It was fitting that Alsop should attend Vann's funeral. He was a grandnephew of Theodore Roosevelt, an instigator and captain in battle in the Spanish-American War at the turn of the century. That "splendid little war," as a friend and collaborator of Roosevelt had pronounced it at the time, had gained the United States the Philippines, made America a power in the Pacific, and started the nation on the course to Vietnam. Alsop was a faithful scion of the Anglo-Saxon elite of the Northeast that had determined the standards of taste, morality, and intellectual respectability for the rest of the country. He had given his professional life to public battle for the expansionist foreign policy his forebears had conceived. He regarded Vietnam as a test of the will and ability of the United States to sustain that policy and had been undeviating in his advocacy of the war. At sixty-one he remained the man of contrasts he had always been. A bulldoggish face belied his slight frame, and the many lines and wrinkles of his face were exaggerated by large, round, dark horn-rimmed glasses. He was an aesthete who collected French furniture and antique Chinese porcelain and Japanese lacquer; an accomplished amateur historian of art and archaeology and the ancient civilizations of Greece and the Middle East; a man of kindness, loyalty, and consideration to his friends and relatives—the godfather of nearly thirty of their children. In his professional life, however, he was the ferocious combatant his granduncle had been. He did not see those who disagreed with him as merely incorrect or misguided. He depicted them as stupid men who acted from petty or selfish motives. In the final years of Vann's life, Alsop had been his principal champion in the press. Alsop had come to have a singular affection for this Virginia cracker who so differed from him in background and personality. He had felt toward Vann a sense of comradeship.

Beside Alsop, wearing the three silver stars of a lieutenant general on the epaulets of his dark green Army tunic, was another warrior whom Alsop admired, William DePuy. Bill DePuy was also a slight man, but his features at fifty-two were the tawny, hard ones of a soldier who enjoys his trade and keeps himself fit for it. He had been a model of the generation of majors and lieutenant colonels who had led the battalions in Europe during World War II and then gone to war in Vietnam as generals accustomed to winning. He combined intelligence and skill at articulating his ideas with an impetuous self-confidence and courage. He had been convinced of the invincibility and universal application of the system of warfare the U.S. Army had derived from World War II. The system consisted of building a killing machine that subjected an enemy to the prodigious firepower that American technology provided. DePuy had been the main architect of the building and deployment of the machine in Vietnam. He had been chief of operations on West-moreland's staff in 1965 when Lyndon Johnson had persevered in Ken-nedy's commitment and embarked upon a full-scale war. DePuy had planned the strategy of attrition that was supposed to achieve victory over the Vietnamese Communists. The machine was going to decimate the Viet Cong guerrillas and kill off the troops of the North Vietnamese Army faster than the men in Hanoi could send them down the Ho Chi Minh Trail into the South. The machine was going to make the Viet-namese soldiers on the Communist side die until the will of the survivors and their leaders was broken. Westmoreland had rewarded DePuy for his talent at strategic planning with the leadership of the 1st Infantry Division, "the Big Red One." DePuy had set himself apart from his fellow generals by turning the firepower of the machine loose with even more lavishness than they did and by ruthlessly dismissing any subor-dinate commander who did not meet his standard of aggressiveness in battle. He and Vann had clashed because Vann had considered the war-of-attrition strategy the cause of needless death and destruction and a waste of American soldiers and munitions. Vann had been particularly contemptuous of DePuy's practice of it. From Washington in 1972, however, DePuy watched Vann wield the firepower of the artillery, the helicopter gunships, the jet fighter-bombers, and the B-52 Stratofor-tresses to beat back the North Vietnamese Army at Kontum. When Vann was killed, DePuy paid him a DePuy tribute. "He died like a soldier," DePuy said, and came to sit at his funeral alongside their mutual advocate, Joseph Alsop.

Senator Edward Kennedy was late. He got to the funeral shortly before the service was to begin at 11:00 A.M. He entered the chapel as unostentatiously as was possible for a Kennedy—by having one of the ushers seat him in a pew in the back. The last of the Kennedy brothers had turned against the war that his elder brother John had set the nation to fight. He had not kept the faith, as Vann had, with the call of his brother's inaugural address, which was engraved on the granite of John Kennedy's tomb at Arlington: "Let every nation know, whether it wishes us well or ill, that we shall pay any price, bear any burden, meet any hardship, support any friend, oppose any foe, in order to insure the survival and success of liberty." Liberty as defined by John Kennedy and the statesmen of his Presidency had meant an American-imposed order in Kennedy's "New Frontier" beyond America's shores. The price of trying to organize the world had been the war in Vietnam, and that price had gone too high for Edward Kennedy to bear. His brother Robert had also begun to turn against the war before he too had been assassinated and buried in a simple grave near John's elaborate tomb. Edward Kennedy and John Vann had become friends, because Edward Kennedy had shared Vann's concern for the anguish of the Vietnamese peasantry and had, like Vann, attempted to persuade the U.S. government to wage war with reason and restraint. Edward Kennedy had made it his special mission to alleviate the suffering of the civilian war wounded and the peasants who had been reduced to homeless refugees. He had traveled to Vietnam to see their plight, had held Senate hearings, and had brought political pressure to bear for more humane conditions in the refugee camps, for adequate hospitals, and for an end to the indiscriminate bombing and shelling of the countryside. He and Vann had corresponded, and Vann had briefed him in Vietnam and passed him information to help exert more influence on the administration in Washington.

Daniel Ellsberg, the turncoat knight of the crusade, was sitting in the second pew just behind Vann's family at the right front of the chapel. He had flown to the funeral from Los Angeles, where his lawyers were engaged in pretrial maneuvering. He was a pariah to those within the closed society of government secrecy, who had once considered him a valued member of their order. He was a traitor who had violated their code of morality and loyalty. Some resented the conspicuous seat he occupied in the chapel. He did not appear the pariah. He still dressed like one of them, as he had learned to do at Harvard. His suit was a conservative three-button model, a blue pinstripe with a matching striped shirt and an equally conservative foulard tie in a narrow knot. At forty-one he had let his hair grow from the crew-cut style he had worn when he had first met Vann in Vietnam seven years earlier. The frizzly, gray-black curls framed his high forehead and gentled the angular features of his lean and tanned face.

Ellsberg was a complicated man. The son of middle-class Jewish parents who had converted to Christian Science, he was an intellectual and a man of action. His mind had surpassing analytical ability. His ego was so forceful it sometimes got out of control. His emotions were in conflict. He was at once a florid romantic and an ascetic with a pained conscience.

What he believed, he believed completely and sought to propagate with missionary fervor. He had benefited from the social democracy practiced by the American Establishment by obtaining an education that had qualified him for a position of eminence in its new state, the great web of military and civilian bureaucracies under the presidency that World War II had created. A competitive scholarship funded by the Pepsi-Cola Company had put him through Harvard. He had graduated in 1952 *summa cum laude*, and had been given a fellowship to continue his studies for a year at Cambridge University in England. He had then demonstrated his militancy by serving the better part of three years as an infantry officer in the Marine Corps. Harvard had selected him while he was still in the Marines to be a junior member of its Society of Fellows, the most illustrious assemblage of young scholars in American academia, so that he could earn his doctorate. From Harvard he had joined the Rand Corporation in Santa Monica, California, the brain trust of the Air Force, and had helped to perfect plans for nuclear war against the Soviet Union, China, and the other Communist states. He had been permitted to learn the nation's most highly classified secrets. His performance at Rand had been rewarded by a position in Washington as the special assistant to the Pentagon's chief for foreign policy, the assistant secretary of defense for international security affairs.

In 1965 his intense desire for confrontation in the American cause had led him to volunteer to fight in Vietnam as a Marine company commander. When told that he ranked too high in the bureaucracy for such mundane duty, he had found another way to the war. He had gone as a member of the new team Lansdale had organized when Lansdale had returned to Vietnam in 1965 to try to reform the Saigon regime and devise an effective pacification program. Two years later, Ellsberg had gone back to the Rand Corporation from Vietnam dispirited by an unhappy love affair and ill from an attack of hepatitis. He had been discouraged too by the repetitive violence of the war of attrition Westmoreland was pursuing and by the unwillingness of the U.S. leadership to adopt an alternative strategy that he believed was the only way to justify the death and destruction and to win the war. The Tet 1968 Offensive had turned discouragement into disillusion. His inability to bring about a change had destroyed his faith in the wisdom of the system he served. He had concluded that the violence in Vietnam was senseless and therefore immoral. His conscience had told him that he had to stop the war. During the fall of 1969 he had begun covertly photocopying the top-secret 7,000-page Pentagon Papers archive on Vietnam and started an antiwar crusade with a public letter to the press demanding the withdrawal of U.S. troops from South Vietnam within a year. After the *New York Times* had published the secrets of the Pentagon archive in a series of articles in June and July 1971, Ellsberg had been indicted at the order of Richard Nixon, who intended to send him to prison for as many years as possible. Ellsberg, the man who had staked his life on a career in the service of a power he had thought was innately good, had come to see buried the friend he had also lost to this war.

Ellsberg was sitting with the family because Mary Jane, Vann's wife of twenty-six years until their divorce eight months earlier, had asked him to do so. She needed the strength of his friendship at this time and she valued the calming influence he had on Jesse, her twenty-one-year-old son, who was sitting next to Ellsberg in the second pew. She had also asked Ellsberg to sit with the family as an act of defiance. She intended to have her gesture say to those in the chapel who resented Ellsberg's presence that she admired his actions against the war and shared his views. The previous year she had said as much to two agents of the Federal Bureau of Investigation, who had come to the family home in Littleton, Colorado, a suburb of Denver, to question her about Ellsberg's relationship with Vann.

Mary Jane considered herself John Vann's widow despite the divorce. The divorce had been a gesture of frustration, a self-defeating attempt to strike back at him for a marriage that had become one of form rather than substance after Vann had gone back to Vietnam in 1965, this time to stay. He had been the love of her youth, her first man, the father of her five children—four sons who were with her in the chapel and a married daughter who could not come to Washington because she had just given birth to Vann's first granddaughter. Mary Jane had clung to the marriage as long as she could. She could not imagine loving any other man the way she had loved him. The raising of their children and the keeping together of a marriage had been a calling as central to her background and character as this war had been to his.

Her father had been a proper family man, the chief court reporter in Rochester, New York. Her mother had possessed a sense of respectability that had approached a passion. When Mary Jane had married John at the age of eighteen, the year after her graduation from high school, she had been slightly plump, yet quite attractive. Her brunette hair had been lovely in the wavy set of the day, her hazel eyes pleasing, her mouth nicely formed. Her values had been those of family, church, and country, as defined for her by her parents and the other figures of authority in her middle-class world. A calm marriage and a warm family life had been the dream of her maiden years. Because she had known nothing but security in her childhood, she had expected to find it as well in marriage and motherhood. She had not found security in marriage, however hard she had sought it. The war and the want of a father who was there when needed had also profoundly disturbed Mary Jane's second son, Jesse. The conventions of patriotism and the socially approved behavior that she had thought beyond question had threatened Jesse and clashed with her vocation of motherhood.

At forty-four, Mary Jane Vann was still a pleasant woman to look at when she took the trouble to dress nicely and to make up her face and set her hair, as she had done on this funeral morning. It was ironic, she thought, that Christmas was the last time John had come home. Christmas was always when she most wanted him to be at home, because they had met at Christmas and their first son, John Allen, had been born on a Christmas morning. She remembered all the Christmas days when he had not been there and she had needed him. The day she learned of the crash she had looked through the house for his dress uniform, that dark blue uniform with the gold trim that the soldiers of the honor guard were wearing today. He had once told her to dress his body in it if he was killed. She had not been able to find it. Perhaps he had taken it to Vietnam. When she got to Washington they had told her that the casket was sealed and that she would not have been able to bury him in his dress blues anyway. She remembered that he had kissed her on the cheek that last Christmas, even though they were divorced, instead of shaking hands when he said goodbye as he had been doing for a number of years before.

There was silence in the chapel now. The organist had stopped playing. It was time for the service to begin. From outside, Mary Jane heard the shouts of commands and the sounds of rifles being slapped by white-gloved hands as the honor guard came to present arms. This was her first military funeral, but she had been an Army wife. She knew what those shouts and those sounds meant. They were bringing John into the chapel in his coffin. He really is dead, she thought. She began to sob quietly.

The coffin, shrouded in a flag and resting waist-high on a wheeled frame, was rolled down the center aisle by two soldiers from the honor-guard regiment who were acting as ushers. Eight official pallbearers followed it in two columns of four. Ellsberg looked at them. Three he did not know. Two of these were civilian officials from AID, and the third was a South Vietnamese army colonel who was the military attaché at the embassy and was representing his government. Ellsberg recognized the other five prominent men. In his grief and bitterness he remarked to himself that they were appropriate pallbearers for Vietnam.

Three of them were generals in white summer dress uniforms. The first was Westmoreland, now chief of staff of the Army, a position to which President Johnson had elevated him in 1968 after relieving him of the Vietnam command. He walked at the front of the right file, the place of highest rank, as protocol required. When the United States Army had gone to war in Vietnam in full array in 1965, Westmoreland had seemed, in his handsomeness and proud demeanor, to represent the Army's pride and accomplishment. Today, seven years later, still outwardly the model of a general at fifty-eight, he represented as chief of staff the institution of the Army, which was claiming Vann in death as one of its own. It was an Army that sensed its defeat in Vietnam, although it did not understand the reasons for its defeat. Westmoreland would never understand. The Army had spent so much of its pride in Vietnam that it could not help but hope for the ultimate vindication of its aims there. Vann had implicitly been seeking to vindicate those aims. In his last battle in the mountains of the Central Highlands he had been trying to accomplish with the South Vietnamese Army, the protégé of the U.S. Army, what the Army had been unable to accomplish by itself. The Army also knew that Vann had never left it in spirit. He had finally become the fighting general he had always wanted to be, despite his nominal civilian status, and in his refusal to accept defeat he had embodied the Army's ideal of leadership.

Gen. Bruce Palmer, Jr., the vice chief of staff, a contemporary of Westmoreland—a fellow member of the West Point class of 1936—walked at the head of the left file of pallbearers. He had served in Vietnam as one of Westmoreland's deputies, after having commanded the expeditionary force that President Johnson had dispatched to the Dominican Republic in 1965 to prevent that small Caribbean country from going the way of Fidel Castro's Cuba. The paratroopers and Marines under Palmer's command had made it possible for Ellsworth Bunker, currently the U.S. ambassador in Saigon, to reimpose on the Dominican Republic a government that would function as a surrogate for American interests. Palmer had been one of Vann's Army patrons since the mid-1950s, when Palmer had been a colonel commanding the 16th Infantry Regiment in Germany and Vann had been a captain in charge of his heavy mortar company. Vann had been the best of his company commanders, if the most difficult to handle, Palmer remembered. Four days prior to Vann's death, Palmer sent him a note praising his leadership at Kontum. Vann received and read the note just before he died.

The third general in dress whites was the Army's deputy chief of staff for military operations, fifty-five-year-old Lt. Gen. Richard Stilwell. Dick Stilwell had been one of those who had not been sorry to see Vann leave the Army in 1963. He had arrived in Saigon in April of that year just as Vann was departing for Washington and his unsuccessful campaign at the Pentagon to try to persuade the ranking military leadership that the United States was failing in Vietnam and had to change its strategy. In 1963, Stilwell had been a brigadier general and chief of operations for Gen. Paul Harkins, Westmoreland's predecessor in the Saigon command. Stilwell had applied his high intelligence to rebutting the arguments of Vann and those other field advisors who had also believed that the war was being lost. Stilwell's behavior in 1963 had been predictable to those who knew him. He had an unwavering trust in authority that led him to place loyalty to superiors above other concerns. He aspired to gain the pinnacle of chief of staff, an aspiration he was to be denied. He had graduated near the top of his class at West Point, two years after Westmoreland and Palmer, and had chosen the traditional route for a graduate of academic stature, a commission in the Corps of Engineers. His ambition and his talent as a staff officer had led him to switch to the infantry during World War II, when he and DePuy, who was sitting in the chapel next to Alsop, had served together in the same infantry division in Europe. Two wars later, in mid-1964, Stilwell had moved up in Saigon and become chief of staff to Westmoreland, the new commanding general. DePuy had arrived to assume Stilwell's former duties as chief of operations, and Stilwell had then overseen DePuy's work in planning the war-of-attrition strategy that was to have brought victory. Stilwell had gradually realized that he had been wrong about Vann and had come to admire him. As Stilwell was also a man of sentiment, he had asked to be a pallbearer at Vann's funeral.

The pallbearer who walked behind Westmoreland was a civilian, a slim and erect man in a navy-blue suit. He wore glasses with clear plastic frames that added a further touch of plainness to his pinched and undistinguished features. One had to notice the unusual steadiness of the myopic pale blue eyes behind the glasses to sense the sternness in this man's character. The civilian was William Colby of the CIA, covert warrior, soon to be named the Agency's deputy director for plans, the euphemism for clandestine operations, and then spymaster-in-chief as the director of central intelligence.

Had William Colby been born in the sixteenth century, his character and mindset might have led him into the Society of Jesus and a life as a Jesuit soldier of the Counter-Reformation. Having been born in the twentieth, he had joined the CIA and become a soldier of the Cold War. A need to serve and a desire to serve in secret were dominant traits in his personality. He had parachuted into German-occupied France in August 1944 as a twenty-four-year-old major in the OSS, schooled in the arts of sabotage and terrorism at an English country estate (Lucien Conein had been one of his classmates there), to lead a French Resistance group against the Nazis. The war had not ended for him with the surrender of Germany nine months later. Godless Communism, a term that meant just what it said to Colby, had replaced Fascism as the menace to humankind. The Roman Catholicism he had inherited from his father, an Army colonel who had been a convert, and from his Irish mother had made him from his student days at Princeton as fervently anti-Communist as he had been anti-Fascist. The question had simply been which menace to fight first.

In contrast to Lansdale, Bill Colby had been an unsung member of the clandestine service. His way had been quiet and sustained. He had carried out the desires of the U.S. government in Vietnam over much of the previous twelve years, beginning in early 1959 as deputy and subsequently chief of the CIA station in Saigon and then in the same promotion pattern as deputy and chief of the Far East Division of clandestine operations. He had supervised the Agency's first counterguerrilla programs in the South. On President Kennedy's order, he had resumed the covert warfare against the Communist North that had been allowed to lapse after Lansdale's years. He had infiltrated by parachute and boat teams of Vietnamese terrorists and saboteurs trained by the CIA to try to start a guerrilla war against the Hanoi authorities like the one the Viet Cong were waging in South Vietnam. In 1967 he had helped Robert Komer, a former CIA officer and the fifth pallbearer Ellsberg recognized, to set up the Phoenix Program to kill, jail, or intimidate into surrender the members of the secret Communist-led government the guerrillas had established in the rural areas of the South. The program had resulted in the death or imprisonment of tens of thousands of Vietnamese. The antiwar movement had condemned Colby as an assassin and war criminal. "Wanted for Murder" posters with his picture on them had been plastered on the buildings of college campuses in Washington. None of the accusations had unsettled Colby's faith in his cause and his conviction that the work he was doing was necessary and good. His manner had remained as gentle and as friendly and—not without some calculation—as disarming as it had always been. In 1968, Komer had departed and Colby had taken over the entire pacification program and become Vann's superior. He had appreciated Vann's talents. Vann, who sought klieg lights and center stage, and Colby, who preferred to perform in the shadows, had come to respect each other.

The two soldiers positioned the flag-draped coffin at the end of the center aisle before the altar. The official pallbearers took their places in the pews at the left front of the chapel where William Rogers, the secretary of state, and Melvin Laird, the secretary of defense, were already seated. After the Army chaplain had read from the scripture and given his sermon, Robert Komer rose from the first pew and walked up onto the altar to deliver the eulogy.

Komer had been the general of the pacification campaign, what the newspapers had called "the other war in Vietnam." A man of medium height and build, balding in middle age, he had been noticeable among the pallbearers. Unlike the other civilians in suits of dark colors, he was dressed in light gray. His suit had been made for him by a proper London tailor during his CIA years back in the 1950s. He had worn it today because Komer felt that the etiquette of a eulogy demanded a vest and it was the only summer suit he owned that had one.

President Johnson had once regarded Komer as an extraordinary problem solver. The president had sent him to Vietnam in May 1967 to pull together into a single, cohesive organization the fragmented pacification programs of the military and the various civilian agencies. Komer had created the organization and had done his best to pacify Vietnam. He had a terrierlike personality. He had dashed into the task with spirited confidence and abrasive vigor. He had taken joy in violating bureaucratic decorum and had been pleased with the nickname that friends and enemies alike had applied to him—"the Blowtorch." Vann had given Komer his most valuable advice on how to build the organization and had been his most accomplished subordinate at translating plans into action.

The Vietnamese Communists had spoiled Komer's career in government with their Tet 1968 Offensive. Prior to the offensive he had mistakenly believed that the United States was winning the war, had told the president so, and had publicly predicted that victory was assured and imminent. After Tet he had been something of an embarrassment to the Johnson administration, and he had left Saigon toward the end of 1968. He had continued to coach from Washington, however, making occasional trips to Vietnam and writing upbeat reports which said that Vann and his comrades in the hard core still committed there might just be able to pull it off, might just succeed in keeping South Vietnam going long enough to exhaust the Communists and persuade them to give up.

This morning the 300 persons assembled at the funeral heard the reedy, tough-guy voice of the old Komer carry through the chapel as he stood over the coffin and praised Vann.

He spoke of "the courage, the spirit, the exuberant energy, the earthy vitality, the sheer gutsiness of the John Vann we knew." He praised Vann in the same unstinting fashion in which the old Komer had given himself to the war.

"To us who worked with him, learned from him, and were inspired by him, he was that scrawny, cocky little red-necked guy with a rural Virginia twang—always on the run like a human dynamo, sleeping only four hours a night, almost blowing a fuse at least twice a day, knowing more than any of us about what was really going on, and always telling us so. And any of us with his head screwed on right invariably listened.

"That's the John Vann we remember. He was proud to be a controversial character, a role he played to the hilt.

"I've never known a more unsparingly critical and uncompromisingly honest man. He called them as he saw them—in defeat as well as victory. For this, and for his long experience, he was more respected by the press than any other official. And he told it straight to everyone—not just to them [the press] or his own people, but to presidents, cabinet officers, ambassadors and generals—letting the chips fall where they may. After one such episode I was told, and not in jest, to fire John Vann. I replied that I wouldn't, and couldn't; that in fact, if I could only find three more John Vanns we could shorten the war by half."

Mary Jane, who had not heard anything the chaplain had said, found herself listening to Komer. His voice and words restored her composure. The meaning of what he said was less important to her than the pleasure of hearing John praised by a man who spoke in the same bold way he had.

"If John had few illusions," Komer said, "he also had no torturing doubts about why he was in Vietnam—to help defend the right of the South Vietnamese people, whom he loved, to live in freedom. He probably knew more Vietnamese and worked more closely with them, sharing their trials as well as their joys, than any other American. He was more at home in the hamlets, where he so often spent the night, than in the offices of Saigon.

"In uniform or out, he was a born leader of men. Personally fearless, he never asked anyone to do what he wouldn't do himself. To him the role of a leader was to lead, regardless of the risk. He was the epitome of the 'can do' guy. And I've never met one among the thousands of men who served with or under John who didn't admire him. He educated and inspired a whole wartime generation of Vietnamese and Americans—as our teacher, our colleague, our institutional memory, our hairshirt, and our friend."

Komer was swept up by the occasion and by what he was saying. His voice rose into a high pitch it acquired whenever he felt great emotion. He spoke his words sharply and distinctly. He said it was fitting that Vann should be buried in Arlington.

"For he was the highest type of professional soldier, whose last tour fulfilled his secret longing to be back in command of American troops. But John was more than a professional soldier. He understood well that firepower alone was not the answer to Vietnam's travail.

"Let us hope," Komer said, trying to be positive even on this day, "that his real monument will be the free and peaceful South Vietnam for which he fought so well.

"Yet whether or not this tragic conflict ends with that aim fulfilled, all of us who served with Vann will long remember him. He is not a man who will be easily forgotten. So we salute one of the authentic heroes of a grim and unpopular war, who gave all of himself to the cause he served, finally even his life. No, we shan't forget you, John. You were the best we had to give."

Ellsberg, who had worked with Komer and had once been friendly with him, did not feel any friendship toward him today, even at Komer's praise of the friend they had shared. He felt alienated from Komer and others in the chapel who still supported the war. "Yes," he said to himself in an angry play on Komer's last words, "he was the best we had to give away."

The chaplain said the concluding prayers and a benediction, and then the head usher announced: "Everyone please rise." The assembly stood up. The organist began to play a hymn. The coffin was wheeled back down the aisle, this time preceded by the official pallbearers. They formed two lines of honor, one along each side of the green canvas archway leading out from the center door of the portico, for the coffin to pass through as it followed them from the chapel. The generals and the South Vietnamese Army colonel saluted and the civilians placed their right hands over their hearts when the coffin was lifted off the wheeled frame and placed on the caisson trimmed in black bunting and hitched to the six gray horses that had been waiting in the sun. The drum major raised his silver mace high into the air and brought it down sharply. The band struck up a march for the procession to the grave three-fifths of a mile away through the gate and down the cemetery road.

The band led the way, playing the march that Mary Jane had requested for Vann because it had been his favorite. It was a tune of unbroken will, "The Colonel Bogie March" from the film *The Bridge on the River Kwai*. He had bought a record of the march after he had seen the movie and had never seemed to tire of listening to it. The honor guard, the color bearers, the pallbearers in two files, and the chaplain marched in sequence behind the band. Next came the horses drawing the caisson, followed by the family in black Cadillac limousines lent by an armaments and aerospace firm for which Vann had briefly worked as an executive in between his retirement from the Army and his return to Vietnam. Despite the heat and the distance, many in the assembly chose to walk behind the limousines out of respect for Vann rather than to ride in their own cars.

They passed, most without noticing them, the monuments to the "splendid little war" with Spain in 1898 which had thrust the western frontier of the United States across the Pacific from San Francisco to Manila and inaugurated the American imperial age whose confident enthusiasm this gathering was symbolically laying to rest today. The first monument was the memorial to the 385 men killed in action in the whole of that war, less than a week's battle deaths at the height of the war in Vietnam. It was a tall memorial, a round column of buff marble topped by a globe, and it conveyed the ambition of that beginning. A bronze band of stars from "Old Glory" ringed this globe of 1898. An eagle sat astride it and surveyed the earth, holding the arrows of war in its talons, ready to loose them at a challenge. As the procession moved along, a second monument rose in the near distance off to the left. It was the mast of the USS *Maine*, salvaged from the hulk of the battleship that had mysteriously blown up and sunk in Havana harbor, killing 266 of her officers and crew and giving an eager America the opportunity to seize what an old and corrupt Spain was no longer able to defend. A bit farther down the cemetery road the procession passed another monument, this one low and spike-shaped and hewn with deliberate roughness out of gray stone. It was the memorial to the dead of the 1st U.S. Volunteer Cavalry Regiment, the "Rough Riders" Alsop's granduncle had recruited and helped lead to glory in that all too easy commencement.

There was no fresh earth at Vann's grave to remind one of the battlefields in Vietnam. The grave had been dug in a grove of maples on a rise that looked down toward the white marble of the Memorial Amphitheater and the Tomb of the Unknown Soldier where the Unknowns of World War I and World War II and the Korean War lay. The succession of wars had made the American military practiced at rites for the living and the dead. When ceremonies were held on the front lawn of the Pentagon in winter, the frost-browned grass was dyed green. The authorities had taken care to make certain that everything here at Arlington was also presentable. The gravediggers had covered the dirt with carpets of what is called cemetery grass, an ersatz grass like the Astroturf that is used for artificial playing fields. Two rows of folding steel chairs with green slipcovers had been set up off to the right side of the grave for the family and close relatives.

Mary Jane was sitting next to a door in the backseat of the first limousine in the procession. When Edward Kennedy had walked over to the air-conditioned Cadillac in front of the chapel to give her his sympathy, she had opened the door window to let him speak to her. She had forgotten to close the window, and so she heard another tune as soon as the band started to play it after the horses pulling the caisson halted before the grave. She had not expected to hear this song. During the flight from Denver to Washington two days earlier she had asked the Army liaison officer to have the band play it beside the grave. She had repeated the request several times since, most recently this morning on the way to Arlington. She had thought that the authorities would consider the song inappropriate for the state funeral of a hero of the war and would forbid it. But the drum major set the band to playing the song at the moment when eight sergeants in dress blues, four on each side, grasped the handle railings of the coffin and lifted it off the caisson. Mary Jane was moved when she heard it. She wondered if the drum major and the men in the band shared her feelings about the war and what the war had done and if this was why they were fulfilling her wish. She thought that anyone else at the funeral who heard the song and knew it would understand much of the message she was trying to convey.

The song was called "Where Have All the Flowers Gone?" It had originated in the antiwar movement. Then it had caught on among the American soldiers in Vietnam and had eventually become a popular song of the era, perhaps the best-known song of Vietnam, a song that made one think of the war whenever it was played. The verses and refrain were simple and cumulative, and the band played through them while the sergeants carried the coffin to the grave.

> Where have all the flowers gone?
> Long time passing.
> Where have all the flowers gone?

Long time ago.
Where have all the flowers gone?
Gone to young girls every one.
When will they ever learn?
When will they ever learn?

This was Mary Jane's song, as "The Colonel Bogie March" had been John's. It was a song of the sadness she felt as a mother for all of the young men who had died in the war; it was a song of the ravaging of her son Jesse by the structure of authority that had made the war, because he had opposed that authority and the war; it was a song of the ruined hopes of the marriage she had dreamed of in her youth; it was a song of the death of a man she had not wanted to die, because she had loved him despite all that had happened between them.

Where have all the young girls gone?
Long time passing.
Where have all the young girls gone?
Long time ago.
Where have all the young girls gone?
Gone to young men every one.
When will they ever learn?
When will they ever learn?

Where have all the young men gone?
Long time passing.
Where have all the young men gone?
Long time ago.
Where have all the young men gone?
Gone to soldiers every one.
When will they ever learn?
When will they ever learn?

The chaplain led the way to the grave now, walking before the eight sergeants carrying the coffin. The sergeants turned in step after they had lifted the coffin from the caisson, the steel plates on the toes and heels of their pristine black imitation-leather shoes clicking on the pavement until they reached the grass. The lieutenant in command of the honor guard stood at attention with his saber unsheathed, the blade held out at an angle from his side, the tip pointing toward the ground. The troops behind him held their rifles high and straight before their faces at present arms. A color bearer dipped the Army flag and the battle streamers in salute to the coffin as the band played.

> Where have all the soldiers gone?
>> Long time passing.
> Where have all the soldiers gone?
>> Long time ago.
> Where have all the soldiers gone?
> Gone to graveyards every one.
> When will they ever learn?
> When will they ever learn?

Peter Vann received the flag from the coffin. The sergeants folded it into a triangle with the stars showing. Peter had asked his mother if he could be the one to accept it, and she had consented, because, at sixteen years, he was the youngest child. He stood up to receive it. The chaplain handed it to him at the end of the graveside service, after the firing party had fired three volleys, the bolts of the rifles working harshly, metal on metal, in the stillness between each volley; after the bugler had sounded the taps; after the chaplain had said the last prayer and a final benediction.

Peter had been six years old when his father had first gone to Vietnam. He had not felt any genuine grief until the moment he accepted the flag, because he had hardly known his father and knew even less about what his father had done. Peter was not an intellectual. His interest was tinkering with cars. The war had been going on so long that he had forgotten which side was the enemy. When the family had been driven to the South Vietnamese Embassy the previous day to receive the posthumous award to his father of the Saigon government's highest honor, Peter had wondered whether it was the South Vietnamese or the North Vietnamese Embassy. He hoped, as he took the flag and started to cry, that his father had not died hating him for all of the arguments they had had when Vann was home. He also hoped that his father would not be ashamed of him for crying. His father had always ridiculed his sons when they had wept, telling them it was a sign of weakness.

John Allen, twenty-four, Vann's oldest son, deliberately did not stand at the end of the service, as was customary, to receive the condolences from Rogers, the secretary of state, who was representing President Nixon at the funeral; from Laird, the secretary of defense; from Westmoreland and the rest of the official pallbearers; and from several other dignitaries who filed by the front row of chairs where the family was seated. He knew that if he remained seated the rest of the family would. His acquaintance with these men was limited to television and newspapers. He had agreed to the state funeral at Arlington because he thought that the occasion would vindicate his father. He felt that his father would have taken satisfaction from this pomp and circumstance. Some of these men, or others like them, he said to himself, had probably been involved in forcing his father to retire from the Army in 1963. He thought he would even the score a bit by letting them bend over to shake his mother's hand, and his, and those of his brothers, and thus make amends to his father in death.

Ellsberg had been standing to the right front of the grave near the family. His position was as conspicuous as it had been in the chapel. The pallbearers and the dignitaries had to pass close by him after they shook hands with the family. Rogers glanced over at him out of curiosity. Laird ignored him, looking straight ahead. Ellsberg did not see either of them. He was staring at the coffin, thinking of a night in early March 1971. Vann had been in Washington on leave, and Ellsberg had waited vainly until well after midnight for Vann to return to his hotel so that they could talk. Ellsberg had finally despaired and come to my house to spend the night. I had been a reporter then for the *New York Times*. We had stayed up into the predawn hours talking for the first time about the Pentagon Papers he had clandestinely copied. The conversation had led to my obtaining a copy of the papers, to their publication by the *Times*, and to Ellsberg's being put on trial and his life changed forever.

Jesse had been thinking about the war again since his father's death. His father's death had made him realize that the war was as alive as ever and that he and the other people had started to accept its existence. Passively accepting the war was wrong, Jesse thought, and he was not going to tolerate this complicity in himself any longer. Jesse was the son most like his father in his refusal to endure anything that denied him the freedom to live life as he wanted to live it. He stood out at the funeral, with his blond hair falling defiantly over his shoulders, unfurled from the ponytail in which he customarily wore it. He had learned how to put his hair up into a hairnet and hide it under a wig when he had to in order to find a job and earn a living. Today he flaunted its length. Jesse's beard was also unkempt. A year or two earlier his father had mailed him a blue polyester suit from Hong Kong. His elder brother, John Allen, had asked him to wear the suit to the funeral, but Jesse disliked suits, regarding them as uniforms. He was wearing only the coat of the suit, with a pair of purple knit slacks he had selected in a Denver store and his mother had paid for before they had flown to Washington. His shoes were a two-tone white-and-black pair that had been his late grandfather's golf shoes. His grandmother had supplied them as a substitute for the dirty brown canvas crepe-soled shoes that he normally wore.

Jesse decided he would give his father a parting gift, the gift of his own honesty and his willingness to take a stand for what he believed to be right. He would leave half of his draft card on the coffin with his father as a token of the gift. Then he would complete the gift by handing the other half of the card to Richard Nixon when the family drove to the White House in a little while for a ceremony at which Nixon was to honor his father with a posthumous award of the Presidential Medal of Freedom. Jesse had always refused to accept the draft, but there was no longer any need for him to go to jail because of his refusal, other than to be honest and to take a stand. He was immune now from actually being drafted. Several years earlier, he had been in danger of going to prison for draft resistance. Jesse's draft board in Colorado had classified him as delinquent then for his refusal to cooperate. Delinquent status meant that he would shortly have been faced with the choice of prison or induction into the Army. (He had ruled out fleeing to Canada.) John Allen had put on his college ROTC uniform, gone to the draft board office, and told the middle-aged woman who was the clerk that their father was serving in Vietnam in an important position. He had talked her into changing Jesse's status to 1-Y, temporarily unfit for service, because Jesse was seeing a psychiatrist. John Allen had acted without consulting either Jesse or their father. He had by then assumed the role of the man in the family because of Vann's absence. John Allen had known that Jesse would continue to resist the draft and that their father was unsympathetic to Jesse's argument that his conscience forbade him to serve in Vietnam. A few months before his father's death, Jesse had received a new draft card in the mail. The board had reclassified him as 4-F, permanently unfit for service. Jesse didn't know why the board had exempted him in this way. He had stopped seeing the psychiatrist after a few months in 1969, and he had no physical or mental disability.

Someone handed Jesse a rose to leave on the coffin. He took out his draft card, ripped it in half, put Nixon's half back into his pocket, and tucked the half he was giving his father under the rose, between the bloom and a branch of the stem, to try to conceal what he was doing. He laid both on top of the silver-gray coffin alongside the other roses his mother, his brothers, and his father's relatives had placed there. "Here, this is all I can give you now; this is all I can do," he said to his father. He turned away and went over to talk to Dan Ellsberg for a few minutes before it was time to leave for the White House. Jesse thought of what he would do when the family walked into the Oval Office for the ceremony and Nixon put out his hand to shake Jesse's. Instead of shaking hands, Jesse would silently present Nixon with his half. Half of a draft card would speak for him. It was a crime to refuse to carry one's draft card and an additional crime to mutilate one. Jesse wondered if it was a third crime to present a mutilated half to the president. He did not look forward to going to jail, but he believed his act of protest would be worth it. One of his friends had already gone to a federal prison for refusing to be drafted.

Jesse's younger brother, Tommy, eighteen, saw him tear the draft card in two and asked him what he was doing. Jesse reluctantly explained what he had in store for Nixon. Tommy could not keep Jesse's exciting plan to himself and told Peter about it on the way to the White House. The sirens of two police motorcycles cleared the way for the limousines to run the red lights, because the ceremony was scheduled to begin at noon and the men in charge of the funeral did not want to keep the president waiting. Tommy approved of Jesse's scheme. He had a theory that Nixon was not bothered by the dying and the maiming and the other suffering of the war because none of it had ever personally touched Nixon or anyone close to him. Nixon had never experienced the war as the Vanns and other families Tommy knew had felt it, families who had lost a son or a father to death, or feared for one wounded, or grieved over a son who had made the opposite choice of resistance and jail or exile. Neither of Nixon's sons-in-law had gone to Vietnam to fight as Johnson's sons-in-law had done. He was anticipating the expression on Nixon's face when Jesse handed him half of a mutilated draft card. The war might at last come home to Richard Nixon, Tommy thought.

Peter said that Jesse's plan was stupid. Peter had been looking forward to this opportunity to meet the president.

At the White House the family was shown to the Roosevelt Room, about five paces across the hall from the Oval Office, for what was supposed to be a wait of a few minutes. Nixon was finishing a high-level discussion of welfare reform begun while the funeral was taking place at Arlington. Vann's half sister, Dorothy Lee, a housewife from Norfolk, Virginia, and his half brothers, Frank, a carpenter and construction supervisor, and Eugene, a senior master sergeant in the Air Force, had also ridden over from Arlington to witness the award of the medal.

Jesse tried to ease the strain within himself by inspecting the rust-colored wall-to-wall carpet. He was currently earning his livelihood on his knees laying carpets in Texas. He was observing that the Roosevelt Room carpet had been shoddily installed and that he could have done a better job when John Allen confronted him. Jesse's older brother had also noticed him doing something odd beside the coffin. The conversation between Tommy and Peter in the limousine, which John Allen had overheard, had given him the explanation.

"Don't do it, Jesse!" he said.

"Why not?" Jesse asked.

"This day is not for you, Jesse," his brother said, keeping his voice low and controlled to try to prevent anyone else in the room from overhearing them. "This is for Dad. This is what Dad lived for and what he died for. Don't belittle him by doing this."

The day that John Allen saw as the vindication of their father would be destroyed. The White House press corps would be covering the ceremony. The spectacle of the long-haired son of a legendary American warrior in Vietnam handing the president half of his draft card, after leaving the other half with his father on top of the coffin, would make quite a story.

Tommy guessed what they were arguing about and came over to defend Jesse. "But this is what Jesse believes in," he said. The three of them began to argue over whether Jesse's right to express his opposition to the war took precedence over the public vindication of their father's career. Jesse's uncles overheard the argument and joined in the attempt to dissuade him.

"If you're thinking of doing that, I won't go in there," his Uncle Frank, a balding, stocky man, said.

"Well, you do what you want," Jesse replied. "I have to do what I have to do."

His Uncle Eugene, the Air Force senior master sergeant with the seven stripes of his rank on the sleeves of his tunic, resembled Jesse's father in the way his face got red when he was angry. He was called Gene in the family. "Jesse," he said, "your father was my brother and I've known him a hell of a lot longer than you have. He believed so strongly in what he was fighting for that to do this to him would be a slap in his face."

"Leave me alone," Jesse said to them all. "I have my own conscience to obey."

John Allen walked over to his mother. After a trip to the powder room, Mary Jane had been chatting in another corner of the Roosevelt Room with Dorothy Lee. She had taken a small dose of Valium at the hotel before the funeral to try to control her emotions. The drug was having only a partial effect. She looked composed in a simply tailored slate-blue dress. She was wearing her glasses, however, to hide her red-rimmed eyes.

"Mom," John Allen said, "Jesse wants to give Nixon half of his draft card. We can't let this happen."

Mary Jane started sobbing again as she had in the chapel when they wheeled in the coffin. She went to Jesse and pleaded with him. "Please Jesse, please, for your father, don't do this. This is your father's day, not yours, or mine, or anybody else's. You would disgrace him." His mother's pleading troubled Jesse, but he would not relent.

The Department of the Army civilian official who was supervising the funeral and a captain assisting him rushed out of the room to find someone on the White House staff. They met Lt. Gen. Brent Scowcroft, an Air Force officer who was then a brigadier general and the president's military assistant, in the hallway. He was heading toward the Roosevelt Room to see if the family was ready, because one of his duties was to supervise such ceremonies. He had known Vann slightly and liked him. They warned Scowcroft what was happening and then one of them brought out John Allen to relate what Jesse intended.

"That's impossible," Scowcroft said.

"We really don't know how to stop him," John Allen said. "He's determined to do it."

Scowcroft walked into the Oval Office, gave the president the briefest possible explanation of what was occurring, and said there would be a slight delay while he handled the problem. A career staff officer, Scowcroft was known for his businesslike approach to crises large and small.

He went into the Roosevelt Room and drew Jesse aside from the group that was haranguing him. Scowcroft spoke to Jesse in a calm voice.

"Listen," he said, "whatever you think about the war and whatever you want to do about it, this ceremony is to honor your father. There is no way you can do this and not ruin the ceremony. Unless you promise us you won't give your draft card to the president, unless you promise us you won't do this, we'll have to cancel the ceremony."

Jesse had already begun to weaken under his mother's continued pleading and because his Uncle Frank, in contrast to the others, had quieted down and tried to reason with him in similar fashion. The calm tone of this man made a further impression on him. He decided that he might be exploiting for his own ends a situation in which he was present only because of his father. He might not have a moral right to do that. Since he couldn't act with a clean conscience, he wouldn't act at all. Anyway, he wasn't being given much choice. "Okay, okay," he said to Scowcroft, "I promise not to do it."

Scowcroft squeezed Jesse's forearm and gave him one of those "Good boy!" looks. He turned to John Allen. "Will he or won't he?" Scowcroft asked.

"If he says he won't do it, he won't do it," John Allen answered.

Scowcroft returned to the Oval Office and told the president that the ceremony could go forward.

John Allen escorted his mother into the Oval Office, followed by his brothers and his aunt and two uncles. As the family entered, the president was sitting at his desk, which had been cleared of work except for a single looseleaf folder he had been reading. He closed the folder, rose, walked around the desk, and met them halfway into the room. The cleared desk, the last bit of work put aside to give full attention, the rising and the meeting halfway were Richard Nixon's ritual for greeting visitors to the president's office. He expressed his sympathy to Mary Jane and John Allen and then shook hands with each in turn. Tommy overheard Nixon say "Thanks" to Jesse when the president shook his hand. Jesse was so disturbed by the sensation of actually touching the hand of Richard Nixon that he did not hear this word of presidential gratitude. He noticed only that Nixon had a large hand.

Rogers and Laird followed them into the president's office. Mary Jane was surprised to see Alsop with them and wondered, because she did not understand Alsop's position in the Washington constellation, why a newspaper columnist was being treated like family. Knowing of Alsop's affection for Vann, Nixon had invited him to join the ceremony ahead of the ordinary press and to hear Nixon's private remarks to the family.

The White House photographer lined up everyone except Alsop for the official photograph. He arranged them in a semicircle in front of the drapes of the bay windows behind the desk where the Stars and Stripes and the presidential flag rested on poles topped by gilded eagles. The president stood between John Allen and Mary Jane. At the moment the photographer pressed the shutter button, he smiled slightly, but he looked a bit queasy in the subsequent photograph.

After the official photograph had been taken, the president spoke briefly to the family. He said that Vann's death had been a personal loss to him as well as a loss to the country. He extended sympathy to them on behalf of the entire nation. He had felt friendship toward Vann, he said, and great respect and appreciation for Vann's work in Vietnam. The last time he had seen Vann had been right here in this office during one of Vann's home leaves. Nixon said there had been a shared understanding of the war in that meeting and that Vann had given him new insights into the conflict and into the desires of the people of South Vietnam.

Peter had read Dale Carnegie's *How to Win Friends and Influence People*. Carnegie recommended sincerity in dealing with others. Peter did not give Nixon a high score for sincerity. Richard Nixon was attempting to be gracious to the Vanns. His apparent nervousness over Jesse and his personal mannerisms got in the way. As he talked, he smiled too much for what was not a happy occasion. His eyes moved constantly, without ever focusing on anyone in particular. John Allen had acquired his father's habit of wanting to look someone he was meeting directly in the eyes. The president's eyes seemed to avoid his, sliding off whenever their glances met. The family's impression of insincerity was heightened by the makeup Nixon was wearing to cover his heavy beard for the television cameras that were shortly to appear. They had never seen a man wearing makeup before except on a stage and were surprised to go to the White House and be greeted by a president with pancake makeup on his face. The family got the feeling that this was some sort of theatrical performance, that Vann's death had created an opportunity for Richard Nixon to do some public relations work as the bestower of a medal on a war hero.

The president irritated them most by saying twice in the course of his remarks that he had wanted to give Vann the nation's highest award, the Congressional Medal of Honor, but that the law prevented this because Vann had technically been a civilian official. Therefore, Nixon said, he was reluctantly limited to bestowing the second-highest honor on Vann, the Presidential Medal of Freedom. No one in the family believed that John Vann rated anything less than the highest award. Peter thought that the president should either have made a special arrangement to give his father the Congressional Medal of Honor or have had the good taste not to mention it.

The president's aides let the reporters and television cameramen into the room. John Allen received the medal for his father, because Mary Jane was no longer Vann's legal wife. He stood in front of the president at the right side of the desk, where the colors and battle streamers of the country's armed services hung from another row of flag poles crested by gold-plated eagles.

Scowcroft kept his eyes on Jesse.

Before handing the medal to John Allen, the president read the citation praising Vann:

"Soldier of peace and patriot of two nations, the name of John Paul Vann will be honored as long as free men remember the struggle to preserve the independence of South Vietnam.

"His military and civilian service in Vietnam spanned a decade, marked throughout by resourcefulness, professional excellence and unsurpassed courage; by supreme dedication and personal sacrifice.

"A truly noble American, a superb leader," the president read, "he stands with Lafayette in that gallery of heroes who have made another brave people's cause their own."

Mary Jane resented being forced to watch from the side. She resented more the staged manner of the ceremony. She resented most that Nixon was giving Vann a second-best medal.

"This is a dirty damn shame, John," she said silently to him now, just as she had told him she loved him when she put a rose on his coffin. "He's going to bury you second. The whole bag is still keeping you down."

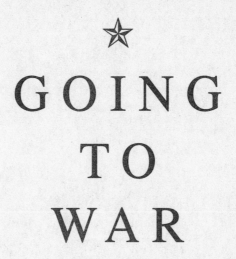

BOOK ONE

GOING
TO
WAR

★ H E DIDN'T SEEM like a man anyone could keep down when he strode through the swinging doors of Col. Daniel Boone Porter's office in Saigon ten years earlier, shortly before noon on March 23, 1962. Porter soon had the feeling that if the commanding general were to tell this junior lieutenant colonel in starched cotton khakis and a peaked green cap that he was surrendering direction of the war to him, John Vann would say, "Fine, General," and take charge. In light of the figure he was to become, it was a small irony that he almost hadn't made it to Vietnam. The plane he should have taken to Saigon in March 1962, with ninety-three other officers and men, had disappeared over the Pacific. He had missed the flight because, in his eagerness to go to war, he had forgotten to have his passport renewed. A clerk had noticed that the passport had expired during the final document check, and he had been instructed to step out of the boarding line. Shortly after the plane vanished, the Red Cross had telephoned Mary Jane to inform her that her husband had been lost in the Pacific. Mary Jane had said that he was all right, that he had telephoned and was taking a later flight. She must be mistaken, the Red Cross worker had persisted. Her husband was missing. Passenger rosters didn't lie.

Everything was in the flux and confusion of commencement then. President Kennedy had just created the new U.S. Military Assistance Command Vietnam (MACV) in Saigon in February 1962, and appointed Gen. Paul Harkins to head it. Harkins had made his reputation as the principal staff aide to George Patton, the battlefield genius of World War II. The president was to nearly quadruple the number of American military men in South Vietnam that year, from 3,200 at the beginning of 1962 to 11,300 by Christmas. Far more of Porter's time than he wanted to spend was being taken up with interviewing and assigning these newcomers. His office was in an old French cavalry compound hidden behind the trees along a wide boulevard, noisy with traffic, that connected downtown Saigon with its Chinese suburb of Cholon. The compound was the headquarters of a corps of the Saigon government's army, formally known as the Army of the Republic of Vietnam (ARVN) and colloquially as the Arvin, following the American military's penchant for converting initials into acronyms. Porter was the advisor to the Vietnamese brigadier general in command of the corps, and the other officers in his detachment worked with the corps' staff sections. In Vietnam in 1962, air conditioners were not yet as routine fixtures as typewriters in every U.S. Army headquarters. Porter and the advisors under him had their desks, as the French had before them, in high-ceilinged offices that opened onto verandas erected at each level of the three-story buildings of brick and stucco. The verandas looked out over a neglected parade ground of weeds and dirt, but viewing was not their primary function. They had been designed as walkways and as reflectors to catch any rare freshet of cool air and move it past the swinging louver doors—like the saloon doors in cowboy movies—to the outsized electric fans hanging from the ceilings.

This short lieutenant colonel standing in front of Porter had an ability to convey self-confidence. He had also managed to keep his khaki shirt and trousers unrumpled, despite the heat, and he gave a brisker salute than most officers would have before he accepted Porter's invitation to sit down. Otherwise, there was little that was impressive about him. He reminded Porter of one of those banty roosters Porter used to watch darting among the hens in the farmyards around Belton, in central Texas, where Porter's father had owned a feed and farm merchandise store. When he took off his cap as he sat down one could see better what a homely man he was. His straight-ribbed nose was too large for his narrow face. The nostrils flared over a wide and equally straight mouth. These features were accentuated by a high forehead and by his habit of wearing his sandy hair close-cropped on the sides and on top in the fashion of American military men of the 1950s and '60s. His gray-blue eyes caught one's attention and gave an indication of his character. They were the eyes of a falcon, narrow and deep-set under bushy brows. His body was lithe, all muscle and bone, and wonderfully quick. He had been a gymnast and a track star in school and in his early Army years. He prized his body; he did not smoke and rarely drank, and kept fit with basketball and volleyball and tennis. At thirty-seven he could still perform a backflip somersault.

Vann responded without hesitation to Porter's questions about his career experience. When he had volunteered to go to Vietnam he had requested one of the sought-after positions as chief advisor to an ARVN infantry division. There were nine divisions in the country, three of them in Porter's corps region. (A corps is a military organization composed of two or more divisions.) Vann had been a lieutenant colonel only ten months, however, and by date of rank, which could be waived at Porter's discretion, there were other officers who stood ahead of him.

He was cocky about his ability to handle the job as he and Porter now discussed it. The cockiness of this bantam did not put off Porter, a senior colonel of infantry, large-boned in build and white-haired at fifty-two, whose restrained manner tended to obscure his knowledge of his profession and the firmness of his own character. Since being commissioned a second lieutenant in the Texas National Guard thirty years earlier, he had learned that cockiness was useful provided the officer also knew what he was doing. He was looking for a bold and unconventional man to replace Lt. Col. Frank Clay, son of the former proconsul in occupied Germany, Gen. Lucius Clay, and the current senior advisor to the most important division in the corps, the 7th Infantry Division in the northern Mekong River Delta. Clay's tour was due to end that summer.

Porter had read Vann's record of previous assignments and schooling carefully. He had noticed that Vann had commanded a Ranger company on behind-the-lines operations during the Korean War and had also displayed a capacity for management in a number of staff assignments. He was a specialist in logistics, unusual for an infantry officer who had proved his ability to lead in combat, and had a master's degree in business administration from Syracuse University. Porter wanted an officer who was an organizer and a fighter, because both talents were required to put together a coordinated war effort in the northern part of the Mekong Delta. The more they talked, the more Porter thought that Vann might do. His boldness and the likelihood that he would take an imaginative approach counted with Porter. Although Porter had been in South Vietnam less than three months himself, he had traveled widely and had gone out on a number of operations against the Communist-led guerrillas. Everything he had seen had convinced him that if the Vietnamese on the Saigon side were going to prevail, they needed Americans who would show them how to fight their war and also find a way to goad them into fighting it.

He told Vann that he could consider himself the prospective replacement for Clay, but that Porter was going to reserve a firm decision until shortly before Clay left. In the meantime Vann would be on probation, undergoing seasoning and doing odd jobs.

After lunch, Porter gave Vann his first odd job. He explained that some idiot who had preceded them—who had mentally never left a Pentagon office and had since probably gone back to one—had set up a computerized supply system for the ARVN divisions and the territorial forces in the corps. The Vietnamese lieutenant colonel who was the corps G-4 (the designation for the assistant chief of staff for logistics) and his officers had no idea of how to send a supply request to a computer. Neither did the American lieutenant colonel who was the current G-4 advisor. Instead of spare parts and other equipment they needed, they had received this large stack of unintelligible paperwork, which Porter proceeded to hand to Vann. Could Vann try to make some sense out of it? He took Vann down to the G-4 advisory section, introduced him to the American officers working there, and arranged for them to give him a desk.

Toward the end of the afternoon Vann returned to Porter's office with a memorandum several pages long, which he had typed. It translated the computerese into layman's language, described the concept of the system simply, and laid out a practical method through which the Vietnamese G-4 officers and their American advisors who were not computer specialists could use the system to order the spare parts and other matériel required. Porter was taken aback. He had no more than a passing knowledge of computerized systems, but he was certain that he had given Vann enough work to keep an ordinary officer with an expertise in logistics occupied for two days. This man was back in half a day with a far better solution than he had expected. What was the next odd job that Porter wanted him to do? Although Porter did not tell Vann then, he decided that afternoon that the rooster was going to the 7th Division.

For the next two months, Porter took advantage of Vann's diverse talents and prepared him for his task. Of the three ARVN corps regions, that of Porter's III Corps (the ARVN used the U.S. Army system of designating a corps by Roman numerals) was the largest in the country, and most of the fighting was taking place within it. The III Corps zone extended from the tip of the Ca Mau Peninsula at the bottom of the Mekong Delta up through a belt of provinces that ringed Saigon on the north. To acquaint Vann with as much of this war as he could, Porter sent him on helicopter assault missions with the division stationed in the rubber-plantation country north of the capital, where the teak and mahogany rain forests edged down from the foothills of the Central Highlands. He let Vann range south through the expanse of rice lands nourished by the Mekong, the great river of Indochina. Vann marched on operations with the two divisions there and visited the main province towns and the rural district centers where the district chiefs lived with their families and had their offices in little compounds fortified with bunkers and barbed wire. To familiarize Vann with the weaknesses of the ARVN staff system, Porter also put him to work in the corps G-3 (operations) and G-2 (intelligence) sections.

On the morning of May 21, 1962, Vann shook hands with Porter and climbed into a jeep. He drove out of the old French cavalry camp and then maneuvered in his impatient way through Saigon's vehicular extravaganza of trucks and gaudily painted buses coming and going from the countryside, Vespa scooters and Lambretta motorbikes, cyclos (a bicycle version of the rickshaw), motorcyclos (a wildly dangerous motorcycle version of the rickshaw), modest French and British sedans, an occasional and immodest swan-fendered Mercury or Chevrolet from the 1950s; and everywhere tiny yellow-and-blue Renault taxis of a vintage no one could remember, driven with an abandon equal to their durability. At last, at a place called Phu Lam, he cleared the southwestern edge of the city. A construction crew was at work there starting to raise giant antennas over land that had been rice paddies until American bulldozers had recently drained and filled them. A high-frequency radio station at Phu Lam already tied General Harkins's Saigon headquarters into the communications network that reached out over the globe from the telephones and teletypes of the National Military Command Center at the Pentagon. The antennas, the latest in communications technology, bounced electronic signals off the troposphere through a technique called Troposcatter. They would extend the span of General Harkins's command into the Southeast Asian mainland—north along the peaks and plateaus of the Annamite chain of the Highlands and up the narrow rice basins of the Central Coast to the other principal ports and airfields of South Vietnam, and then over the mountains to the military air base at Ubon in Thailand, a second ally that America had given its word to protect in this part of the world.

Vann turned the jeep's engine loose and sped south down the two-lane tarmac road that was the main route into the Mekong Delta, the wind against his face in the open vehicle an added pleasure. He was on his way to the 7th Infantry Division headquarters at My Tho thirty-five miles away. Porter had given him the best assignment in the country. He was putting Vann in command of the American effort in the cockpit of the war.

The 7th Division's zone of responsibility covered most of the northern half of the Delta, where the course of the war was going to be decided. The 6,000 square miles and five provinces swung across South Vietnam from the swamps of the Plain of Reeds on the Cambodian border on the west to the South China Sea on the east. The division zone held more than 2 million people, a seventh of South Vietnam's population of 14 million in 1962, who grew more than a seventh of the country's food. The Saigon government had already forfeited most of the southern half of the Delta to the guerrillas. The northern half was still being contested. Approximately 38,000 of Saigon's troops faced an estimated 15,000 guerrillas there. The government that the United States was depending on to hold South Vietnam could hardly survive if it lost a region so rich in manpower and resources on the edge of its capital.

The challenge and the responsibility did not intimidate Vann. Rather, he welcomed them with an exhilaration that held no little arrogance. In his American mental universe of 1962 there were no unknowables and no unattainables. What he did not know, he could discover. He had no experience with guerrilla warfare beyond the unconventional operations with his Ranger company in Korea, but he had spent the past nineteen of his thirty-seven years learning how to make war. A counterguerrilla war was simply another form of warfare, and he would learn how to wage it successfully. The previous year, on instructions from President Kennedy, the Army had begun to publish doctrine for its officers on how to suppress guerrillas. Porter had developed some specific ideas on ways to apply these vague concepts to the context of the war in Vietnam as a result of his observations in the field. Porter's ideas made sense to Vann on the basis of what he had been able to see over the previous two months.

Vann also knew nothing of the Vietnamese and their culture and history. He did not consider this ignorance any more of an impediment to effective action than his lack of knowledge of counterguerrilla warfare. He was convinced from his experiences as a junior officer in Korea and Japan that Asians were *not* inscrutable orientals. Lansdale was one of his heroes for this reason. He had read *The Ugly American* and liked it. Lansdale knew how to operate in Asia. Lansdale understood that Asians were people, that you could discern their desires and play upon those desires to your advantage. Vann was sure that he would be able to see what motivated the Vietnamese officers with whom he would be working and persuade them to do what was in their best interest and in the interest of the United States. The fact that the French had been defeated in Indochina was irrelevant to him. Americans were not colonialists as the French had been, and the French were, in any case, a decadent people whose time had passed. Their army had never recovered from the humiliation of being beaten by the Germans in World War II. Vann had seen the U.S. Army lose battles in Korea but never a war. History had not shown Americans to be fallible as other peoples were. Americans were different. History did not apply to them.

Vann had no moral qualms about killing Vietnamese Communists and those who fought for them, nor was he troubled by the fact that he would be getting Vietnamese who sided with the United States killed to achieve American aims in Vietnam. He had been trained to kill Germans and Japanese in World War II, although the war had ended before he could. During the Korean War he had killed Koreans on the Communist side and, with a clear conscience, had helped send Koreans who were fighting with him to their deaths in his cause. He assumed that he and his fellow Americans had a right to take life and to spend it, as long as they did so with discretion, whenever killing and dying were necessary in their struggle. His assumptions were buttressed by his pride in being one of the best officers in the U.S. Army, the finest army that had ever existed, but he was also conscious that he and the Army represented a greater entity still, an entity in which he took even more pride. He was a guardian of the American empire.

America had built the largest empire in history by the time John Vann reached Vietnam in 1962. The United States had 850,000 military men and civilian officials serving overseas in 106 countries. From the combined-services headquarters of the Commander in Chief Pacific on the mountain above Pearl Harbor, to the naval base at Subic Bay in the Philippines, to the shellproof bunkers along the truce line in Korea, there were 410,000 men arrayed in the armies, the fleets, and the air forces of the Pacific. In Europe and the Middle East, from the nuclear bomber bases in the quiet of the English countryside, to the tank maneuver grounds at Grafenwöhr on the invasion route from Czechoslovakia, to the attack aircraft carriers of the Sixth Fleet waiting in the Mediterranean, to the electronic listening posts along the Soviet frontier in Turkey and Iran, there were another 410,000 soldiers, sailors, and airmen deployed. When the diplomats from the State Department, the agents from the CIA, and the officials of the sundry other civilian agencies were counted, together with all of their wives and children, the United States had approximately 1.4 million of its servants and their families representing it abroad in 1962. John Vann saw himself as one of the leaders of the expeditionary corps of infantry advisors, helicopter crews, fighter-bomber pilots, and Special Forces teams whom President Kennedy had decided in November 1961 to dispatch to South Vietnam, the threatened Southeast Asian outpost of this empire. With the wind in his face on the road to My Tho, he did not intend to let the Communist-led guerrillas win the battle for the northern half of the Mekong Delta.

The Mekong Delta was a deceptive place in late May 1962. It had the appearance of a land of milk and honey. The onset of the monsoon early in the month had quickened the rice seeds into shoots that were pushing green from the seedbeds and would soon be ready for the second event in a Vietnamese peasant's year—the transplanting of the seedlings into the earth waiting beneath the gray water of the paddy fields that stretched out in an expanse from both sides of the road. The landscape looked flat, but it kept the eye busy. Narrow dikes to trap the water for the rice plants checkered the paddy fields. The checkerboard of the paddy fields and the dikes was in turn crisscrossed by the straight lines and sharp angles of canals for irrigation and transport. The lines and angles of the canals were occasionally interrupted by the wide bend of one of the rivers that fed them. Stands of bamboo and a species of water palm whose fronds stood twenty feet high edged the canals and rivers. Taller coconut palms also grew in profusion, singly and in clusters, along the banks. There were large groves of the most common Vietnamese fruit trees—bananas and papayas. There were smaller groves and sep- arate trees of mangos, grapefruits, limes, tangerines, oranges, peaches, and jackfruit. The list of others was so various that a horticulturist would have puzzled at trying to identify all of the local subspecies. Peasant boys wearing conical straw hats to ward off the sun rode the backs of the buffalos that pulled the plows and harrows to prepare the paddy fields for the rice. Rangy black hogs rooted among the thatched houses in the hamlets. Although the houses seemed insubstantial, they were adequate for this climate. They were made by erecting a frame of logs and bamboo poles over a pounded earth floor. Dried and split fronds of the water palm were then used to thatch the fairly steep ridge roof and the sides and to partition the interior into rooms. The roof overhung the sides so that its thatch carried off the monsoon torrents and also shaded the house against the sun. Chickens shared the yards with the hogs. The ducks were usually kept in flocks, with their wings clipped so that they could not fly. They were herded by children or by landless agricultural laborers to keep them out of the paddy fields and vegetable gardens of neighbors. The canals and the rivers knew no limit of fish, shrimp, crabs, and eels. When the monsoon reached its height in July and August, and the fish could swim into the paddy fields, these too became fish ponds.

Every once in a while a soldier stopped Vann's jeep at a bridge to let a line of traffic from the opposite direction cross over. The bridges were one-lane structures erected by the French out of Eiffel steel beams that arched overhead. Peasant children posted at these checkpoints would come up to hawk, for the equivalent of a few pennies in Saigon government piasters, chunks of coconut meat and sugar cane, and slices of fresh pineapple sprinkled with large grains of salt to contrast with the sweetness. Material want seemed to be the least of concerns in this land.

The concrete blockhouses at the bridges were the warning that this was not a land of contentment. While he bought a piece of pineapple from one of the insistent children, Vann had time to study the block-houses, encircled with rusting barbed wire, and to observe the soldiers walking guard along the sides of the bridges. He had time to think that the green line of water palm fronds along a canal bank he had passed five minutes earlier might suddenly have quickened with the muzzle flashes of an automatic weapon reaching at the jeep. He could see that the rains would make the fields of sprouting sugar cane high and dense enough in a few months to conceal a battalion. He had time to wonder if a guerrilla might be waiting, across the river and farther down the road, for a jeep such as his. Jeeps were the most satisfying targets, because they usually carried officers. If a guerrilla was waiting he would probably be squatting behind a tombstone in one of the small peasant graveyards set on mounds among the paddy fields. He would be a patient man, not one to waste an opportunity if he could avoid doing so. He would be keeping himself alert, his hands over the detonator connected by wires to a mine dug into the road the night before—the cut tarmac set carefully back into place to conceal the explosive—ready to send the jeep and its occupants twisting into the air.

This land had known war for most of the seventeen years prior to Vann's arrival. The older children among the groups selling coconut and pineapple at the checkpoints could remember the final years of the first war. It had begun in 1945 when the French had attempted to reim-pose their colonial rule on Vietnam and the neighboring countries of Cambodia and Laos. There had been only three years of intermittent peace after the first war had ended with the humiliation of the French and their Vietnamese troops in the mountain valley of Dien Bien Phu in North Vietnam in 1954. Then war had resumed in 1957 between the guerrillas and the Saigon regime of Ngo Dinh Diem, the mandarin whom Lansdale had secured in power. By 1961 the guerrillas had become so strong that President Kennedy had had to commit the arms of the United

States to prevent Diem's government from being overthrown. The Americans and the Saigon government called the guerrillas the Viet Cong, an abbreviation of the words for Vietnamese Communists. (The advisors had shortened the term to VC for everyday usage, except in the lingo of field radio traffic, in which the VC became Victor Charlies.) The guerrillas referred to themselves as the Liberation Army and called this second war the Liberation War. They said that both wars were part of the Vietnamese Revolution—this second war a renewal of the struggle to achieve the original goals of the war against the French.

There was no guerrilla with a mine on the way to My Tho on May 21, 1962. Vann reached the new quarters of the 7th Division Advisory Detachment on the main road half a mile north of the town without incident. The Saigon soldier guarding the iron grillwork gate swung it open and let his jeep into the courtyard. The place had been a school for aspiring men of God and then briefly an orphanage before its recent conversion to the profane work of war. The advisors called their quarters the Seminary because of its original purpose, and two white masonry crosses atop the former chapel at the far end of the courtyard still proclaimed this holy intent to passersby. The American military authorities, who had become the major renter and bankroller of construction in the country, had leased the building from a Roman Catholic diocese in exile from North Vietnam and in need of funds. When Frank Clay, whom Vann was to succeed, had arrived in My Tho the year before, the detachment had consisted of only seven officers and a sergeant, with three of the officers living with the division's component regiments in other provincial towns. A large house in My Tho had been more than sufficient. After Clay had learned that the detachment was to multiply twentyfold in the spring of 1962 and to keep growing (it would slightly exceed 200 officers and men by the end of 1962), he had arranged for the leasing and renovation of the Seminary as the best available building in the area.

The main two-story structure was pleasant if undistinguished French colonial architecture of brick sheathed in white stucco and roofed with red tile. It was roughly L-shaped, with the long back of the L running down beside a narrow river. The first floor at the base of the L had been remodeled into an office section. The rest of the ground floor had then been renovated into sleeping rooms for the officers, a mess hall, showers and toilets, and a bar and service club. The mess hall doubled as a theater for the movies every second night that, with charcoal-broiled steaks on Sunday and bargain-priced liquor every evening, were among the privileges of American military life overseas. Vann and a few of the senior officers rated small bedrooms on the second floor above the office section. The remainder of the second floor was divided into dormitory bays for the enlisted men. The advisors used the courtyard as a parking lot for their jeeps and three-quarter-ton trucks. The courtyard was also the scene of the volleyball contests that Vann started right after his arrival. He had a net erected over a basketball court the seminarians had laid out there.

The Viet Cong had come a few nights after the advisors had first moved into the Seminary in early May to tell the Americans they were not beyond the guerrillas' reach. A group had sneaked through the banana groves across the road and started shooting at the mess hall in the middle of a movie. The sergeants, some of whom were old enough to have been through World War II or Korea, had been amused at the sight of captains who had never before been under fire running around in undershorts, T-shirts, and steel helmets, waving .45 caliber service pistols, with which it is difficult to hit a man in the daytime. Periodically the guerrillas would repeat the exercise, usually from the concealment of a stand of water palm on the opposite bank of the river behind the building. Several guerrillas would fire a string of shots at the generator or water-purification equipment and withdraw into the night. No damage was ever done beyond some pockmarks on the stucco. The next morning the advisors would see a Viet Cong flag, a gold star on a horizontally split field of red over blue, flying from a tree.

A determined guerrilla company could probably have overrun the Seminary in a few minutes. The two dozen territorial troops from the province, called Civil Guards, who were responsible for defending the compound were friendly but seemed to take a casual attitude toward safeguarding the foreign advisors. The Americans could not protect themselves, because there were not enough men to do the job of advising the 7th Division during the day and also mount a guard each night sufficiently strong to hold off the attackers while the rest snatched up their weapons and ran to their stations. Nearly half of the officers and men did not live full-time at the Seminary. They were instead dispersed throughout the division zone with the battalions and regiments, stayed in the province capitals advising the province chiefs and their staffs, or worked at the training centers for the territorial forces. Vann chose to take what precautions he could without interfering with advisory duties and to accept the risk of an attack in order to fulfill the detachment's mission. The behavior of the guerrillas indicated to him that they did not actually intend to shoot the advisors in their beds. He guessed correctly. The Americans were privileged people in South Vietnam in the early 1960s. The Vietnamese Communists limited terrorist attacks against Americans in these first years because they did not wish to provoke greater intervention. They were hoping that forbearance would elicit sympathy for their cause from the American public.

The 7th Division headquarters was in the former French Army caserne in the safety of My Tho. The place was a community of about 40,000 people in 1962, the major population center for the northern Delta, a provincial city by Vietnamese standards, a large town by American ones. Like most of the important Delta towns it was located beside a big canal or river for easy access by sampan or barge. This one was a spur off the upper branch of the Mekong as it flowed to the sea, appropriately called Tien Giang for Upper River. My Tho had been founded in the latter half of the seventeenth century by Chinese refugees fleeing the collapse of the Ming dynasty and the Manchu conquest of their homeland. The Vietnamese, who were completing their centuries-long migration by conquest down the Indochinese Peninsula by seizing the Delta from the original Cambodian inhabitants, had welcomed these immigrant allies. The French had enlarged My Tho after they had in turn conquered the Delta in the 1860s. The town had become a garrison and administrative center and a place of commerce to process rice for the export trade to China and other rice-deficit countries of East Asia, and to Europe and Latin America. The plantations of thousands and tens of thousands of acres organized out of the fertile soil and landless peasantry of the Delta, first with the encouragement of the Vietnamese emperors and then on a grand scale by the French and upper-class Vietnamese who had benefited from colonial rule, had been broken up during the first war and its aftermath. My Tho had otherwise changed little physically from the French era by the time Vann arrived. The town was still a busy community that battened off the labor of the peasantry in the surrounding region. Most of the rice produced in the Delta was now consumed within South Vietnam. The warehouses and mills kept occupied storing and processing it for shipment to Saigon and the provinces to the north.

For the Americans the town could be a diversion on an evening or a Sunday afternoon. Groups of advisors occasionally came to the Chinese restaurant beside the river for a meal, or sat and drank at the open-air tables set up around kiosks that sold beer and soft drinks, enjoying the breeze that cooled the Delta landscape at dusk, comparing the merits of the girls on the street, and watching the boats haul produce to the riverfront dock. The enterprising Chinese still ran the small shops that offered everything from bolts of cheap cotton cloth, out of which the peasants sewed the pajamalike blouses and pants called *ao babas*, to aphrodisiacs. There was a central market with all of the pungent smells of this land. Among the stalls of the fish and fruit sellers were those of the acupuncture artists, whose needles promised an end to pain, and the sorcerers, who peddled ancient herbal medicines and the ancient and modern hokum of magic cures. The Vietnamese and Chinese merchants and landowners lived in solid masonry houuss. The poor made do with wooden shacks. One of the more impressive houses in the town was the villa that the French had built for their provincial governor. It was on the main avenue, with handsome if somewhat neglected gardens around it and a tennis court that the American officers were permitted to use. The villa was occupied by an ARVN major who had been appointed province chief by President Diem. Vann's counterpart, Col. Huynh Van Cao, the commander of the 7th Division, was forced for want of an established prerogative of office to occupy a more modest whitewashed house, carefully guarded, in a small compound behind a row of flame trees on a side street a few blocks away. He lived there alone and kept his wife and seven children in Saigon.

Vann felt it urgent to reverse the trend of the war in the northern Delta. As matters stood in May 1962, the Viet Cong had the strategic and tactical initiative. It was the Communists who were determining the course of the war by deciding when and where and on what terms to fight. The Saigon side was on the defensive, reacting to guerrilla moves rather than carrying the war to the enemy. Only the main road that went south from Saigon to My Tho and then split into two roads that ran west and south into the lower Delta could be traveled in the daytime in a single jeep and at night by a pair. In large areas of the five provinces the guerrillas had rendered the secondary roads impassable to vehicles by organizing the peasants to dig ditches across them and to dismantle the bridges. They had not yet gotten around to removing the roads entirely by having the peasants dig up the beds bit by bit and scatter the dirt across the rice paddies, as they had in much of the lower Delta. They would get around to it if they were not stopped in time. On those secondary roads that were usable, an escort of at least a reinforced platoon was considered a necessity by the Saigon officers, and then there was no guarantee that the vehicles would not be ambushed. While all of the peasantry in the northern Delta did not sympathize with the guerrillas, the majority either favored the Viet Cong cause or tacitly aided the Communists through the silence of a neutrality that worked against the Saigon government. Whether the neutrality was created by fear of guerrilla terrorism or by sympathy made no practical difference: the Saigon government lacked the cooperation of the peasantry, and cooperation was necessary to suppress the Communist-led insurrection. South Vietnam in 1962 was an overwhelmingly rural society; 85 percent of the population dwelt in the countryside. With his training in statistics, Vann was struck by the potential for the growth of the Communist guerrilla power in a society with this sort of profile. All of the 2 million people in the division zone, except for the 15 percent who lived in My Tho and the other towns, were currently or potentially within the reach of the Viet Cong. There was no question of who still had the raw military power. Vann estimated that two companies of ARVN regulars, about 180 men, with their American infantry weapons and artillery and fighter-bombers at their call, could go anywhere in the five provinces. In a metaphor he drew for one of his staff officers that summer, however, he observed that the passage of Saigon's troops through the countryside was like the movement of a ship through the sea. While the ARVN troops were in a given area, their presence pushed the guerrillas into hiding or flight, in the way a ship displaced water. The moment they departed, the guerrillas flowed back.

Prior to leaving Saigon, he and Porter had agreed on a number of goals they saw as the foundation blocks for a strategy to reverse this losing course and win the war. As soldiers, their first priority was to develop offensive operations that would corner and destroy the main striking forces of the guerrillas. The current ARVN operation was appropriately known as "the sweep." It consisted of marching several battalions across the countryside in dispersed columns. Porter had noted that the scheme of maneuver might be adequate for moving an armored division across North Germany, but it was hardly effective against guerrillas in rice-delta country. He wanted Vann to take advantage of the dexterity that the helicopter offered for landing and shifting assault troops and devise tactics that would stampede the best Viet Cong units into engagements in which they could be annihilated. To initiate these unconventional operations Vann was in turn to persuade Colonel Cao to accept a face-saving ploy that would give the Americans proxy control over the division. The euphemism for the ploy was "joint planning." Under "joint planning," Vann and Cao and their staffs would ostensibly plan operations together. In fact, the intent was to persuade Cao to carry out operations that Vann and his staff conceived.

Vann was supposed to work as Clay's deputy for a month so that he could fully orient himself to the job prior to Clay's return home near the end of June. He did not have to wait that long. During an operation on the Plain of Reeds west of My Tho on May 23, 1962, two days after Vann's arrival, Clay attempted to drive a platoon of about twenty fleeing guerrillas back toward the Saigon troops by strafing them from a pair of helicopters. The Viet Cong paused long enough to shoot up the lead helicopter in which Clay was riding with another lieutenant colonel from Porter's advisory staff. The pilot received a bullet in the foot; Clay, the other lieutenant colonel, and the copilot were all superficially wounded by fragments of Plexiglas and aluminum sent flying by the bullets that smashed through the cockpit canopy and the control panel. Vann took charge while Clay was flown up to Saigon for treatment and then left for a delayed eight-day rest leave in Hong Kong. Vann was again in acting command through much of June. Clay was off on a tour of the Central Highlands and the central coastal provinces north of Saigon. He had been selected to be the guerrilla warfare specialist on the faculty of the National War College in Washington and wanted to acquaint himself with the differing conditions of the war in these areas.

When Vann formally took charge toward the end of the month, there was no change-of-command ceremony and trooping of the colors in the courtyard of the Seminary as is the custom at the passing of the baton in the U.S. Army. Clay would have forbidden a ceremony, because he was an emotional man and knew that he embarrassed himself on such occasions by turning misty-eyed. In this case he would not have had a choice. The advisors were forbidden to fly the Stars and Stripes over their compounds in 1962. They were also not authorized any combat decorations. Clay and the others wounded on the helicopter were not even entitled to a Purple Heart, and had they been killed their families would not have been given one. (The medal is routinely awarded for wounds and posthumously for death.) President Kennedy hoped that by keeping the horizon of the American presence in South Vietnam as low as possible he could avoid the political consequences of having the public at home understand that the United States was at war there.

Clay had brought the detachment by late May to the point where it could begin to function. Vann put his extraordinary energy into the task of turning promise into accomplishment. The battle in which Clay had been wounded on May 23 gave Vann a fortunate start with Colonel Cao in "joint planning." The success had resulted from Clay's persistence, luck, and the talent at operational planning of Capt. Richard Ziegler, thirty years old, from the West Point football line of the class of 1954. Clay had become exasperated at Cao's refusal, always genially stated, to let the Americans have a role in planning operations. He had become further exasperated with the fiascos Cao had planned himself. In mid-

May he had denied Cao use of the helicopters until he let the Americans participate. Porter, who had been pressuring Clay all the while to achieve joint planning, had backed his decision, with Harkins's consent. At that Cao had relented and agreed to a trial. Clay had now needed an officer for the task of drawing up detailed plans. The one officer he had with any experience at the work was Ziegler, who had been training Ranger companies in the countryside since his arrival at the Seminary in early April. Ziegler's experience had been limited to three months as assistant operations officer for an infantry battalion in Japan. To plan the operation he had been given French Army maps of a 1954 series and an intelligence report that was weeks old and probably no longer valid. The report said that a Viet Cong battalion was training somewhere within a ten-square-kilometer area on the Plain of Reeds.

Ziegler turned out to have a gift for matching a particular scheme of maneuver to a particular military problem. Moreover, he could distill his ideas into a map overlay, a sketch on tracing paper of broad arrows and other military symbols to show the timing and placement of assault troops and the directions and objectives of their advance. The sketch is drawn to the same scale as a map and then laid over the area of the operation so that the unit commanders can see how to maneuver.

In this case Ziegler provided the logical answer for ignorance. He decided that the best chance of finding guerrillas in those ten square kilometers lay in an operation that was a sequence of probes, each from a different direction. If one of the probing units struck Viet Cong, the helicopters could land the division reserve troops or shift others already on the ground to drive the guerrillas into what Ziegler's instructors in the advanced course for infantry officers at Fort Benning had called "the killing zone."

The intelligence report was outdated. The guerrillas from the battalion of Viet Cong mentioned in the report had left the area. They returned at 2:00 A.M. on the morning of the 23rd. Guerrillas from a second battalion not mentioned in the report had also been tarrying in the vicinity. Ziegler's probing task forces flushed an astonishing number of guerrillas out into the open, where the fighter-bombers slaughtered them. Ninety-five Viet Cong were killed and twenty-four captured, including one of the Communist battalion commanders. The other battalion commander was killed. Thirty-three weapons, more highly prized than lives in this guerrilla war, were also seized. Among them was an American-made machine gun, a 60mm mortar, and several Thompson submachine guns. The guerrillas who returned at 2:00 A.M. suffered the worst losses.

Cao was beside himself with happiness at this first genuine success for his division. With the behind-the-arras approach that the advisory system took, he could claim all of the credit in public.

Vann was also impressed. He had been looking over Clay's staff to decide whom to keep in what job. He drew Ziegler aside in the temporary headquarters the division had set up beside a dirt airstrip. "You're going to be my planner," Vann said. He described to Ziegler how they would seize on the self-interest this success had aroused in Cao to institutionalize joint planning and gain proxy control over the division. "We're going to get this thing organized and run it just like an American outfit. We'll have an American on the ground with every unit. I will work with Cao and you will work with the operations officer and we will get done what we want done."

When Vann suggested that Ziegler and the ARVN captain who was Cao's G-3 (operations) officer plan all future actions together, Cao said he thought it was a good idea. He also consented to other steps that Vann had in mind to stitch his advisors so thoroughly into the structure of the division that the question of who was telling whom what to do would be forgotten. Cao agreed to let Vann's intelligence advisor, Capt. James Drummond, a self-contained North Carolinian of thirty-four years, who was, like Ziegler, seemingly custom-made for his assignment, work on the same sharing basis with his G-2 (intelligence) officer. Previously Cao had forbidden his G-2 to give the Americans any useful information.

Vann settled on a bluff extrovert from San Antonio, Maj. Elmer "Sandy" Faust, thirty-six, as his chief of staff to supervise the work of Ziegler and the other younger staff advisors and to run the advisory side of the division field headquarters while Vann was off marching with a battalion or up in a helicopter or observation plane. Faust's husky frame and open, pleasing features matched his temperament. He was attractive to the opposite sex and refused to conform to the Army crewcut, still combing his blond hair up from his forehead in the pompadour wave fashionable in the 1940s. Cao raised no objection to having Faust act as a counterpart to Lt. Col. Bui Dinh Dam, his own chief of staff. He likewise agreed to integrate Vann's advisors into the other staff sections, G-1 (personnel and administration) and G-4 (logistics). He accepted Vann's proposal to organize a Tactical Operations Center to monitor military activity in the five provinces, to inform Cao and Vann of any emergency, and to maintain liaison with the military headquarters of each province chief and coordinate requests for fighter-bombers to support beleaguered outposts and similar calls for help. The TOC was manned on a twenty-four-hour basis. The radios and maps were set up in a large office on the first floor of Cao's two-story house. Because he kept his family in Saigon, Cao had no need for most of the rooms and had turned all of the two stories except for a bedroom and kitchen into a miniature division headquarters. Ziegler and his counterpart used the TOC as a place to plan operations. It became another funnel through which the Americans could gain knowledge.

A briefing by the staff for the commanding general is a daily ritual at division-level and higher headquarters in the U.S. Army. Vann suggested that they have a joint "command briefing" at 4:00 P.M. on every afternoon the division was not in the field. Cao offered to convene it in what he called his War Room on the second floor of the house. He had furnished this office elegantly in comparison to the one downstairs that was converted into the TOC. It was lined with maps, and he had constructed a podium at the front for the briefer. Ziegler and the division operations officer would report on significant actions anywhere in the zone. Drummond and the G-2 captain would brief on the intelligence outlook and the G-1 and G-4 officers and their advisors would also report whenever they had something worth announcing. Cao would sit in a chair at the front near the podium, with Vann beside him, and Faust and Dam behind. Prior to Ziegler and the operations officer getting together to plan a helicopter assault on the guerrillas, Vann would insist on a session in the War Room at which Cao would give "command guidance" to everyone on what he wanted to achieve.

In the beginning Ziegler wondered about the usefulness of these daily briefings and command guidance sessions. They were artificial in their formality, like training models of the same at the Infantry School at Fort Benning. He soon saw that Vann was using them to encourage Cao's ego to flower. Cao liked to forget that he was a colonel and to put on the airs of a general. He enjoyed expounding in broad strategic terms at the command guidance sessions. When he got carried away with himself at one of the first ones, Vann whispered to Ziegler: "Don't worry about what he's saying—I'll tell you what to do after we get back to the Seminary." That is what Vann did, outlining a plan for a helicopter assault into a guerrilla area on the wall-length map in the Seminary's combined operations and intelligence office. The map was covered with transparent acetate so that one could write on it with a grease pencil. Ziegler wove Vann's ideas and his own into the finished plan. Vann approved it; Cao accepted it. They killed more guerrillas; Cao was happier still. Ziegler suspected that the success of the May 23 action had made Cao like a gambler who goes into a casino one day wearing a certain tie and wins big. From that day forward, unless there is some compelling reason not to do so, the gambler is going to wear that tie whenever he goes back to the casino. The plans that Vann had Ziegler draw up were Cao's lucky tie.

Cao reacted in the same positive manner to Vann's proposals for training the Saigon troops in squad and platoon tactics of fire and maneuver, a prerequisite to besting the guerrillas at the small-unit combat characteristic of this war. The state of training of the 10,000 ARVN regulars in the division zone would have sufficed had there been no war. (There were 8,500 regulars in the division and an attached armored regiment and 1,500 in independent Ranger companies.) They could march well enough for a parade. The majority of the 28,000 territorial troops would have had trouble parading. Despite more than $1.65 billion in American military aid between 1955 and mid-1961 and the supposed guidance of a 650-man training mission for most of those years, Vann had discovered that few of the regulars or territorials knew how to adjust the sights of their rifles and carbines well enough to hit a target, let alone a guerrilla. The ARVN and the territorials had been formed by the French. The Americans had then tinkered with their organization. The ARVN was an amalgam of Vietnamese officers and men from the regular French colonial army and a predecessor Vietnamese National Army that France had created in 1948 for Bao Dai, the former emperor who had collaborated with the colonial power. The ARVN was currently organized on the triangle model of the old American infantry division— three regiments to a division, three battalions to a regiment, three companies to a battalion.

The better of the two territorial forces, the Civil Guard, or Bao An in Vietnamese, had originated in a pre–World War II colonial formation called La Garde Indigène (the Native Guard) and in a militia created under Japanese sponsorship near the end of the world war. It was a province-level force, the rough equivalent in Saigon's military structure of a state National Guard in the United States, formed into companies and battalions under the control of the province chiefs except when assigned to the division for specific operations. There were approximately 10,000 Civil Guards in the division zone. The second territorial group was a raggedy militia recruited by the French to man the brick watchtowers and mud-walled outposts that the French had built during their war to reimpose colonial rule and that the Saigon government was now trying to defend. It was organized into squads and platoons that operated at the district level and below and was called the Self-Defense Corps, or Dan Ve in Vietnamese, and commonly referred to by the advisors as the SDC. The SDC was the most numerous (about 18,000 men) and the most poorly armed force in the five provinces. The militiamen had to make do with the bolt-action rifles the French had given them. Theoretically the SDC was the equivalent of the early American village and town militia, because the men were local residents who wore no uniform. They dressed in the same pajamalike blouse and trousers of black calico that their fellow peasants wore as work clothes. There was an important difference from the early American militia: the SDC militia, like the Civil Guard, fought for pay.

Vann moved to remedy the lack of training by laying out a three-week "refresher course" for the division regulars at an old SDC training camp, which Clay had improved, near Tan Hiep village center about six miles up the road toward Saigon. The airstrip for My Tho was located there. Cao agreed to put all of the division's nine battalions through the course one by one. They were also to conduct marksmanship and small-unit training at their home bases when not out on operations. Clay had already started training courses for the territorials. Vann increased the course capacity to bring the Civil Guard and the SDC up to par more rapidly. To measure progress, he established specific training and operational goals for every division battalion and for the territorials under each province military headquarters. Every advisor had to submit a "Monthly Critique," with a copy to his Vietnamese counterpart, stating whether the goals were being attained.

Cao did not listen happily to the arguments Vann made for another priority that Vann and Porter had agreed upon—halting the growth of the Communist-led insurrection by depriving the Viet Cong of the freedom of the night. Cao's face would go blank or he would frown as Vann explained why they had to teach the troops to patrol and lay ambushes after dark. "It is not safe to go out at night," Cao would say. Most of the five province chiefs regarded night activity with the same fear that Cao did. They and Cao had their units report night patrols and ambushes to fob off the Americans. No one went out, or if anyone did go out he did not go farther than the nearest canal for a nap on the bank. When persuasion failed, Vann turned to bravado. He issued an order requiring all American officers and any sergeant involved in combat training to go out on at least one night patrol or ambush a week. Cao and the province chiefs could have ignored the requirement and made a fool of Vann. The advisors could not, after all, venture out on their own. Cao knew that Porter was behind Vann on the issue, and Harkins had also been preaching the virtue of night activity to Diem. After an outburst the previous November when the Kennedy administration had tried to push him into political and administrative reforms as the price for U.S. military intervention, Diem's relations with senior American officials had improved. The guidance from the presidential palace was to accommodate the Americans where it would do no harm. Cao and the province chiefs acquiesced. A consistent if limited pattern of night patrols and ambushes began. Vann set the example by traveling to a different regular or territorial unit at least once and sometimes twice a week for a night foray. With his ability to function on a couple of hours of sleep, being up most of the night did not bother him.

He made it a point, over the objection of Cao, who was fearful that he might be killed or captured, to go out with squad-size groups of about a dozen men. Vann knew there was a better chance of laying a successful ambush with a small unit and also less chance of being counterambushed in the dark. To his chagrin he was rarely able to ambush guerrillas. He learned that the reason was not a lack of Viet Cong moving about the countryside at night. He told Porter they had a lot of work ahead of them with this army. These soldiers, the regulars and the territorials, had a sense of inferiority toward the enemy. They were afraid to risk a fight on a man-to-man basis with the guerrillas. He noticed that almost every time he heard the approach of what might be a bunch of Viet Cong walking down the trail and into the snare, one of the Saigon soldiers would give the ambush away by coughing, or snapping the bolt of a weapon, or making some other noise. This occurred too often to be accidental. Porter had suspected an attitude of inferiority. He was glad that for the first time in this war the United States had an infantry officer with experience and perspective who insisted on working at the cutting edge. To solve any of these problems they needed information and understanding. Vann was giving him both, because Vann had rank and credentials. What he reported could not be dismissed by the generals and the headquarters staff colonels as the imaginings of a green captain.

Vann fulfilled his vow to Ziegler that every unit participating in an operation would have an American advisor attached to it. The advisors serving with the territorials were assigned to various training centers and not to specific units. The division battalions taking part were also usually split into two task forces each, to increase the chances of running into guerrillas. The American captain advising the battalion commander obviously could not be with both. Vann overcame the problem by calling for volunteers before an operation. His purpose went beyond acquiring proxy control. He thought that the Saigon troops might behave more aggressively if the commander always had an American officer or sergeant by his side to encourage and assist him. American élan, he hoped, would prove infectious.

John Vann's élan was infectious within the advisory detachment. The atmosphere had been enthusiastic under Clay. He was the sort of brave, considerate, and hardworking officer who is admired and liked in any army. (He had twice won the Silver Star, the nation's third-highest decoration, leading tanks against the Germans in North Africa and Italy.) Under Vann the atmosphere became supercharged. When the advisors returned to the Seminary, exhausted after a couple of days in the sun and the muck of the paddies, the familiar voice would call out in a high-pitched rasp: "Come on, let's get those volleyball teams out there." He had rested less than anyone, but in a few minutes he would have them all out in the courtyard in front of the net. If his team began to lose, he would yell and bang his fist against one of the posts holding up the net in frustration and to goad his side to greater effort. He would never give up trying to outjump a six-foot, 185-pound Hawaiian captain named Peter Kama, who was to serve under him ten years later in the Central Highlands.

The war was still an adventure in 1962—"the greatest continuing war games we've ever come up with," as one officer put it—no matter what problems Vann and his detachment faced in trying to improve the fighting qualities of the Saigon troops. The frequent presence of danger and the occasional shooting created the tension and zest of war without the unpleasantness of dying. The Vietnamese were doing the dying almost exclusively. Fewer than twenty Americans had been killed in Vietnam by late May 1962 when Vann reached My Tho, and no one in the 7th Division Advisory Detachment had been unlucky enough to die. The older men were hoping to retrieve the excitement of wars past. The young men were eager to prove themselves worthy of their first. Maj. Gen. Charles Timmes was chief of the original Military Assistance and Advisory Group (MAAG) in South Vietnam, now a subordinate command responsible for training and equipment programs. Timmes had earned his Distinguished Service Cross leaping into Normandy on D-Day at the head of a battalion of paratroops. He summed up the prevailing attitude in a pep talk at the Seminary: "It isn't much of a war, but it's the only war we've got, so enjoy it."

Timmes was also reflecting more than the excitement of an adventure in his remark. These men were the regulars of an Army that had chafed for eight years under President Eisenhower's strategy of "massive retaliation." The mission of the Army had seemed reduced to occupying the radioactive rubble of Eastern Europe, Russia, and China after the

Air Force and the Navy had won World War III by loosing their planes and missiles in a thermonuclear holocaust. The military budget had been apportioned accordingly. The Army had become a mendicant. Now the Army had a president in John Kennedy who was intent on making "the sword . . . an effective instrument of foreign policy," in the words of his military mentor, the distinguished general Maxwell Taylor. Kennedy wanted a military establishment that would enable him to apply whatever level of force was necessary to have his way wherever the United States was challenged. He saw an expanded Army, revitalized with the latest in mobility and weapons, as the principal means of wielding the sword under his strategy of "flexible response." Taylor had minted the term to contrast the apparent rationality of this approach with the irrationality of Eisenhower's strategy of massive retaliation. The strategic concept was the logical application of Taylor's doctrine of "limited war." He had retired as chief of staff of the Army in 1959 to preach the doctrine in a much-praised book called *The Uncertain Trumpet*. Kennedy had adopted Taylor's ideas enthusiastically, exploiting them during his 1960 campaign for the presidency. He had made the doctrine, with Taylor's catchy name for it, the national strategy after his election. He had also appointed Taylor as his White House military advisor.

The new American president and the men around him saw the guerrilla insurgency that Vann was determined to crush in the northern Delta as the most insidious form of challenge that the Communists had yet devised. Fidel Castro had come to power in Cuba with a guerrilla revolution, and similar insurrections were expected elsewhere throughout the so-called Third World—the poor countries of Asia, Africa, and Latin America. It was for this reason that Kennedy had instructed the Army to use Vietnam as a laboratory to develop techniques of "counterinsurgency." The Pentagon had composed an acronym for this mission of suppressing revolutions—COIN. The Soviet dictator of the day, Nikita Khrushchev, had announced the guerrilla war strategy to a Moscow conference of Communist parties in January 1961. Khrushchev had said that the Soviet Union would avoid an atomic war with the United States but would support "liberation wars and popular uprisings" in the poor nations of the Third World. The Chinese had vowed what appeared to be like intentions. Kennedy had condemned such revolutions as "wars of subversion, covert aggression." The war in Vietnam was more than a test of the feasibility of Taylor's doctrine of limited war, in which the Army had such a stake. Vietnam in 1962 was a test of whether the "Free World" or the "Communist World" would prevail.

Americans of the early 1960s, paid little attention to the animosity between the Soviet Union and China and to other cracks in the monolith they called "International Communism." The enmity between Moscow and Peking had been evident and growing for quite a while. In the summer of 1960, Khrushchev had cut off all aid to China and withdrawn thousands of Soviet technicians working on development projects there. The implication of Yugoslavia's break with Russia in 1948, that a nationalist movement could be led by native Communists, was not a matter to which Americans gave serious thought. Vann and the Americans of his time were mentally habituated to a globe halved between darkness and light. Their thinking was governed by their own ideology, and this vision of the world accommodated and reinforced that ideology. The Army's security-clearance forms reflected the vision by grouping all Communist countries together in "the Sino-Soviet bloc."

While no one in the detachment displayed quite as much self-assurance as Vann did in this adventure that had the moral fervor of a crusade, these men were a confident crowd. The captains were a cock-of-the-walk bunch. Most displayed both the wings of a parachutist and the gold-lettered tab of a Ranger on their combat fatigue shirts. Ziegler was typical. He had been an instructor at the Ranger School at Fort Benning for two years before being told one morning that the Army personnel branch at the Pentagon had just selected 150 outstanding captains to be field advisors in Vietnam and that he was one of them. The son of a salesman, he had been a star on the high school football team in East Greenville, Pennsylvania. He had gone on to West Point because he had wanted, he recalled, "to be a big fish in a big pond" on the West Point football team and because he had needed a free education. Two famous coaches of the era, Earl "Red" Blaik and Vince Lombardi, had thought enough of his skill at handling his six feet of brawn to make him a varsity middle linebacker and running guard as soon as he had completed his plebe year.

Having a leader with Vann's charisma made these men cockier still and gave a special verve to this adventure. Soldiers respect a leader who is competent. They admire a leader who is competent and bold. When he is an accomplished student of war, leads boldly, and also savors gambling his own life, he acquires a mystique. Cautious officers shake their heads at this love of danger and condemn it as daredeviltry, which it often is. They secretly admire it and wish they had as much faith in their luck and the power to lead lesser men that the mystique confers. Vann's luck was so good it was called "the Vann luck."

Vann knew which of the secondary dirt roads the Viet Cong had ditched and which were still usable because he explored them in a jeep

on his frequent trips to the district centers and to outposts and hamlets
that interested him. The normal American method of surveying roads
was from a helicopter or an observation plane. It was safer. The sky
was free of mines and ambushes. Vann claimed that surveying by aircraft
was not good enough. To find out how much of the countryside the Viet
Cong controlled and how much was still accessible it was necessary to
go out on the ground and test. "Hell, you can drive these roads with a
ninety-five percent chance of survival if you just use your head," he
would say in his penchant for a statistic. He avoided patterns, trying
not to return by the same route. He did not linger in one place too long
and give the guerrillas in the area time to come after him or to organize
an ambush farther down the road. He refused to take along the reinforced platoon of troops considered the minimum escort, because an
escort would slow him down. He drove fast, and he always drove himself.
He would put the ARVN soldier Cao had assigned to him as a driver
in the backseat with a carbine. If there was a scrape and a Vietnamese
driver was wounded or lost his nerve, he might stop. Vann wanted to
make sure this could not happen, because he was convinced that salvation lay in movement and he was determined never to be taken
prisoner.

Porter did not try to restrain him. Porter knew that if he ordered
Vann not to take such risks, Vann would take them without telling him.
As with Vann's night patrols, Porter was getting observations he would
otherwise never have received from a man whose experience he could
trust. Instead of trying to stop Vann, he would kid him about his daredeviltry on visits to the detachment when Vann would mention some
place he wanted to see and invite Porter to ride with him. "Is this another
of your suicide drives, John?" Porter would ask.

The advisors at the Seminary learned to look forward to a trick Vann
played on staff officers who came down from Saigon to "see the war."
These visitors were referred to derisively as "Saigon commandos" or
"straphangers," slang for supernumeraries which derives from stand-up
passengers who grip the overhead straps to steady themselves on a
subway or bus. The staff officer often came outfitted in a panoply of
combat regalia, complete to a wide-brimmed bush hat and a hunting
knife strapped to his pants leg. He would announce that he was not
going to be content with briefings at the Seminary and was determined
to "get out where the action is." Vann would smile and say that there
was some action underway in a nearby province and instruct the visitor
to be ready to depart at 4:30 A.M. the next morning for a "little reconnaissance mission" en route to the operation.

At 4:20 A.M., while the staff officer was still lacing his boots in one of the bedrooms in the senior officers' suite on the second floor, Vann would have had his coffee and be standing at the bottom of the stairs, shouting up at him to hurry. "All right, we're ready to go," he would holler. "Get your butt down here." As Vann turned on a flashlight and led the straphanger to his jeep in the darkness of the courtyard, he would explain that the two of them were going to "check out the security" on the road to Ben Tre, the next province capital, about ten miles to the south, from which they would then drive "to the action." Vann would climb in behind the wheel and carefully place a fast-firing new rifle called the Armalite and a couple of grenades beside his seat so that he could easily grab one. All the while he would be instructing the staff officer on how to play dead if they were ambushed and the man was fortunate enough to be wounded rather than killed outright, because the guerrillas executed prisoners too injured to march with a bullet through the back of the head. Then he would rev up the jeep motor, yell at the Vietnamese guard to open the gate, and dash out and down the road toward Ben Tre.

The staff officer would have assumed that they would have an ARVN squad or a platoon to escort them, or at least another jeep of advisors along for company. Here he was in a lone jeep with the black mass of the foliage rushing by, here and there the light of a candle or a kerosene lamp flickering from a peasant's house, and this wild man behind the wheel shouting at him above the wind to be prepared to open fire with his own weapon if they hit a Viet Cong roadblock, because he, Vann, was going to smash through; he had no intention of being taken alive to be exhibited in a cage like a monkey. There was a ferry crossing on the way, which stretched the nerves of the visitor a bit further. The crossing was guarded, and the Vietnamese on the boat were just travelers or farmers going to market in Ben Tre. The visitor would not notice the guards, and he had probably never stood in a crowd of Vietnamese country folk before. The whole experience usually sufficed to persuade the staff officer to stay in Ben Tre until he could catch a helicopter back to Saigon. If he turned out to be a kindred sort who laughed at this initiation, he was welcomed on his next visit to the Seminary. Actually, the predawn trip was somewhat dangerous. Vann was shot at a couple of times by a stay-awake sniper. He had deduced, however, that any guerrillas manning a roadblock would probably have gone home to sleep by 4:30 A.M.

Maj. Herbert Prevost was the one man in the detachment who seemed to love danger as much as Vann did, whose luck appeared just as phenomenal, and who summed up the nostalgia for the excitement of wars past. Prevost, an impish-looking thirty-eight-year-old pilot, was the Air Force liaison officer to the 7th Division. The U.S. Air Force might have decided as an institution that strategic bombing was the proper way to win wars. Herb Prevost was not the sort to go along with the crowd. He had remained a small-plane man who liked to keep his wars personal. During World War II in Europe he had managed to get several P-47 Thunderbolt fighter-bombers shot up under him while blasting Germans who impeded the advance of armored and infantry columns. His Distinguished Service Cross had come the day Prevost and his wingman in another P-47 had taken off loaded with a new incendiary weapon called napalm and had seen a pack of German tanks lying in wait in a woods to surprise an American column advancing up a road. The wingman was shot down and killed by Germans firing machine guns from the tanks. Prevost's plane was struck so many times that the mechanics decided to junk it after he somehow flew it back to the airfield. The Germans' surprise had been spoiled and five of the tanks and their crews incinerated.

In Vietnam it appeared that Prevost had been tamed. The Air Force had assigned him the smallest aircraft in its inventory, a Cessna observation plane called the L-19 (also designated the O-1) Bird Dog. It was a single-engine two-seater, the seat in front for the pilot and the one behind for the observer. The L-19 had no guns. Prevost's job was to coordinate requests for fighter-bomber and transport plane support for the 7th Division and the territorial forces in the five provinces with the 2nd Air Division in Saigon, the Air Force component of General Harkins's command. He had been given the L-19 to enable him to keep in touch with three Air Force captains who worked for him in the provinces.

Prevost was an imaginative gladiator of the air. He persuaded Vann to give him a pair of the new lightweight Armalite rifles, officially designated the AR-15 and later to be designated the M-16 when the Armalite was adopted as the standard U.S. infantry rifle. The Army was experimenting with the weapon and had issued Armalites to a company of 7th Division troops to see how the soldiers liked it and how well it worked on guerrillas. (The Armalite had a selector button for full or semiautomatic fire and shot a much smaller bullet at a much higher velocity than the older .30 caliber M-1 rifle. The high velocity caused the small bullet to inflict ugly wounds when it did not kill.) Prevost strapped the pair of Armalites to the support struts under the wings of the L-19 and invented a contrivance of wire that enabled him to pull the triggers from the cockpit to strafe guerrillas he sighted. He bombed the Viet Cong by tossing hand grenades out the windows. Occasionally he dropped twenty-pound antipersonnel bombs, whenever he could talk some out of acquaintances assigned to an air commando squadron operating from the former French air base at Bien Hoa fifteen miles north of the capital.

Herb Prevost's acquaintances referred to their squadron by its unofficial code name, Jungle Jim. (The official code name was Farm Gate, a play of gallows humor on the World War II expression for the passage into eternity: "He bought the farm.") The squadron was equipped with propeller-driven planes of World War II and the Korean War—twin-engine A-26 Invaders designed for low-level bombing and strafing with six to ten .50 caliber machine guns in the nose, and T-28 Trojan trainers converted into fighter-bombers by fitting .50 caliber machine guns and racks for bombs, rockets, and napalm canisters into the wings. Although the planes belonged to the U.S. Air Force, they had been repainted with the markings of the Vietnamese Air Force, called the Veenaf, from the abbreviation VNAF, by the Americans. The repainting was not difficult, because the VNAF had, in deference to its more recently acquired patron, done away with its original French-inspired system of marking military aircraft with roundels in the national colors on the sides of the fuselage. The Saigon aviators had adopted the U.S. insignia of a white star in a blue circle, and where American military aircraft had bars in red, white, and blue going off to each side of the circle, the VNAF had bars in red and yellow, the colors of the Saigon government. With a bit of red and yellow paint, the planes of the air commando squadron became Vietnamese. The pilots also never flew without a junior officer or noncom from the VNAF in the backseat. If one of these planes with VNAF markings and a Vietnamese in the backseat was shot down or crashed, the Kennedy administration could claim, as it did on occasion, that the American pilots were merely "conducting training in a combat environment." Other American aviators were assigned directly to the VNAF with the mission of training and advising the Saigon airmen in the employment of their fighter-bombers—T-28s and AD-6 (also designated A-1) Skyraiders, a Navy plane of the Korean era. These American trainers functioned as extra pilots for air strikes against the guerrillas, again with a Vietnamese in the backseat. The small foreign press corps in Saigon was not permitted into the Bien Hoa base to describe at first hand how the system worked.

Except at critical times during operations when he was tied to the command post summoning air support for the division, Prevost was eager to take Vann, or Ziegler, or Jim Drummond, the intelligence advisor, out on reconnaissance missions in his miniature fighter-bomber. Army observation pilots who flew ordinary, unarmed L-19s out of Tan Son Nhut were on call to the detachment for reconnaissance work, but Prevost was the ready alternate and, if available, the preferred choice. Vann liked to fly low to study the countryside as much as possible. Prevost preferred to stay lower still, practically shearing the tops off the rice stalks until he had to hop over a tree line. The Air Force liaison officer who replaced him when Prevost was reassigned many months later was new to the country. He asked Vann if Major Prevost normally flew at 1,500 feet, considered a height of acceptable risk from small-arms fire. "Major Prevost didn't accumulate fifteen hundred feet of altitude in his entire time with this detachment," Vann replied.

This mood of the war as an adventure was reinforced by the sentimental attachment many of the advisors developed for the Vietnamese for whose benefit, along with that of their own country, they believed they had come to fight. The captains advising the battalion commanders stayed with their battalions whether in base camps or on the march, eating Vietnamese food and accepting the other conditions of life of the ARVN captains they had been sent to help. So did the sergeants teaching weaponry to the soldiers. The advisors to the Civil Guards and the SDC militia lived near the training centers and accompanied their territorial troops on local day-to-day actions against the guerrillas. These shared circumstances evoked a natural affection from the Americans.

The Vietnamese soldiers would pull at the hair on the forearms of the Americans out of curiosity, because their bodies were smooth. They would cadge cigarettes; giggle when an American recoiled at the strong-smelling fish-oil sauce, called *nuoc mam,* which the Vietnamese used as seasoning (it added concentrated protein to their diet in the process); and laugh when one of the big foreigners teetered and toppled off one of the palm logs the peasants laid across the canals for bridges.

Vann took a particular liking to the common soldiers, who were peasants like their guerrilla opponents, whether ARVN regulars or territorials. Perhaps the fact that he was also slightly built and did not tower above their average height of about five feet two inches also made them appeal to him. Their American equipment was invariably too big and too heavy. The helmets swamped their heads; the U.S. Army's semiautomatic M-1 rifle was too heavy for them at nine and a half pounds and its stock was too long for their arms; and the Browning Automatic Rifle (BAR) the light machine gunners carried was much too hefty at sixteen pounds for men who averaged 105 pounds in weight to tote through a day. What Vann admired most about them was their cheerfulness and their endurance. They were as deceptive in appearance as their country. Their bodies were strong despite their slightness, because their diet was good by Asian standards. One could not see their strength because the American-style fatigues hid their wiry build. Their peasant upbringing had also hardened them psychologically to physical labor, so they did not complain on marches in the heat. They smiled often and joked among themselves, and they did not scream or lose control when wounded. The stoic bearing of pain seemed to be part of their culture. They would lie still and moan or clench their teeth against the hurt. They were potentially good soldiers, Vann concluded, who deserved to win their war and not have their lives wasted.

Because he saw the solution to the conflict primarily in military terms during his first year in Vietnam, Vann focused on the initial priority that he and Porter had agreed upon—the destruction of the main striking forces of the Viet Cong through surprise helicopter assaults. These troops were the Communist equivalent of the ARVN and the Civil Guard. They consisted of the elite guerrilla battalions, called the Main Force by the Communists and the "regulars" or the "hardcore" by the Americans, and the provincial battalions and companies known as the Regionals. The Main Force battalions each ran about 250 to 300 men strong in late May 1962. They ranged over a territory of two to three provinces. The Regionals usually kept to their home province. The advisors tended to group both together, calling them "hard hats" because they wore turtle-shaped sun helmets, an imitation of the colonial sun helmet that one saw in Kiplingesque movies of British India on late-night television, and that the French had worn in Indochina. The Viet Cong made their sun helmets by stretching green canvas or plastic over a frame of bamboo. Both the Main Force and the Regionals were full-time soldiers. Their uniforms, homemade by their families or the women of sympathetic peasant hamlets from cloth that was available in nearby markets, varied in these early years. They usually fought in the black *ao baba* of the peasants or in a khaki shirt and trousers, but the regulars also sometimes wore a green battle outfit. The Viet Cong dress uniform, which the guerrillas carried in their knapsacks for ceremonial occasions, was fairly standardized—a shirt and trousers of a deep blue cloth that was commonly sold in country towns. The Main Force had the highest level of combat proficiency and political motivation and the best of the captured weapons. All of the officers and most of the noncoms were Party members. They were called "cadres." (The Vietnamese Communists used the term "cadre" for anyone in a leadership position, whether officer, noncom, or administrative official, and for specialists such as medical personnel.) Several of the provincial battalions approached those of the Main Force in fighting quality.

There were about 2,000 Viet Cong regulars operating within the five provinces of the division zone, as well as Jim Drummond could estimate with the information available to him by the end of May, and about 3,000 Regional guerrillas. The way matters stood, the Communist strategy was succeeding. The guerrillas were capturing more and more weapons, which enabled them to launch more and bigger attacks. The Saigon government's Civil Guard and SDC militia were in turn becoming more intimidated and keeping closer to their outposts and the district centers, ceding more and more of the peasantry to the guerrillas. The quickest way to halt the momentum of this revolution, Vann believed, was to break the point of the spear. If the regular and provincial guerrillas were killed off or scattered, the Communists would no longer be able to mass a force for big ambushes of road convoys and of Saigon's territorial troops as they marched through the countryside during the day trying to assert the regime's authority. The Viet Cong would not be able to overrun outposts at night with quite their current ease. Security would start to return and progress toward an enduring pacification could begin. "Security may be ten percent of the problem, or it may be ninety percent, but whichever it is, it's the first ten percent or the first ninety percent," Vann would say. "Without security, nothing else we do will last."

Once the process of decimating the Main Force and Regional guerrillas was well underway, the cycle of the war would turn against the Viet Cong, Vann thought. This conclusion was based on a conviction he shared with virtually all Americans in Vietnam in this early period— a conviction that the Vietnamese peasants were essentially apolitical. The fact that the majority of the peasants in the division zone appeared to be either sympathetic to the Viet Cong or neutral did not mean they were expressing a political value judgment, according to American thinking: the peasantry lacked the political sophistication to make such a judgment. Except for a minority who had specific grievances against local officials of the regime, the peasants were simply responding to whichever side was stronger where they lived. Vann held this conviction with more than ordinary firmness because he had observed on intelligence-gathering missions with his Ranger company in Korea that the Korean peasants he questioned seemed to have no political values. They had appeared just to respond to the side that was dominant at the moment. What all Asian peasants wanted most, he was certain, was peace and security in which to till their land. They did not care whether those who established the law and order were Communists or capitalists.

When the farmers saw the regular and provincial guerrilla battalions and companies being destroyed one after another, they would realize that the Communists were not going to win. Provided the Saigon side also stopped abusing them, the peasants would begin to lean toward the regime. Intelligence would improve because more and more peasants would be willing to talk. It would become easier to target and decimate the rest of the Viet Cong's main striking forces. The Communists would also lose the broad base of their armed strength—the local guerrillas on the hamlet and village levels. (The Vietnamese village is not a single population center but rather a cluster of hamlets. The village government has its offices in one of the hamlets. The hamlet chiefs and their assistants are executors who carry out the decisions of the village government.) These local guerrillas were called the Guerrilla Popular Army by the Viet Cong. They were part-time soldiers, farmers during the day, fighters at night, on orders from above or when the spirit moved them. Drummond estimated that there were about 10,000 local guerrillas throughout the division zone. They were of immense value to the Main Force and Regional guerrillas and to the clandestine government of the Viet Cong. The local guerrillas were a pool of manpower in training for the higher forces, an omnipresent intelligence network, a source of scouts and guides who knew the terrain and the attitudes of their neighbors and the militia in the nearest Saigon outpost, a waiting assembly of porters to haul ammunition and to carry away the wounded and the dead during battle, and an ever-present arm to enforce the desires of the hidden Communist administration.

These part-time local guerrillas would "fade back into the woodwork," Vann reasoned, and become full-time peaceful farmers again. The Saigon authorities, with American assistance, could then start the slow task of identifying and arresting the secret Communist agents who had fomented this insurrection and who directed the clandestine government in its daily activity of marshaling the peasantry to support the guerrilla fighting units. The economic and social aid the United States was providing would further influence the allegiance of the farmers. The gift of drilled wells for clean drinking water and lessons in how to build latrines on solid ground were going to liberate the farmers from the parasites and intestinal diseases that afflicted them. They would be given dispensaries for regular medical care, elementary schools to eliminate illiteracy among their children, fat Yorkshire hogs to replace the lean black native variety, and better rice yields with improved seed and chemical fertilizer. Vann thought that it would probably require ten years to create a healthy rural society of satisfied peasants and effective local government which would be impervious to Communist attempts to renew the insurgency. It should not take him more than six months to smash the Main Force and Regional guerrillas in the northern Delta and start this cycle of returning peace in the most vital part of the country.

Vann had been as fortunate in the assignment of Jim Drummond to the detachment as its intelligence officer as he had been in finding Ziegler available as an operations planner. He had again demonstrated his talent for leadership by recognizing Drummond's qualities and giving him rein to exercise them, while at the same time directing Drummond so that his work meshed with that of Ziegler. The two were the team Vann needed to conduct his six-month campaign.

Secrecy shielded the Viet Cong fighting forces in the same way that it protected the activities of the Communist administration. As long as their location and movements were secret, the guerrillas could train and prepare undisturbed and strike with surprise. For the first time in this war they were being deprived of this secrecy. Drummond was taking away their shield with the skills of intelligence gathering that the U.S. Army had accumulated through two world wars and the Korean conflict. In Drummond's case, the skills were fortified by an unusual affinity for his craft.

Drummond displayed a passion for knowledge of his quarry. Everything about the guerrillas interested him. He collected the homemade shotguns the Viet Cong turned out in their thatched-roof arsenals for the local guerrillas along with the crude but functioning copies of sophisticated small arms like the Thompson submachine gun. He even examined the seams and cut of uniforms to see if they differed in one province or region from another. Vann was struck by this fascination. He saw there would be no need to remind Drummond, as he would have had to remind some intelligence officers, that it was not enough to interrogate prisoners and to read translations of captured documents at headquarters, that one had to venture into the field to gain insights about the enemy and to gather the myriad details that could never be obtained from an office. Drummond, who had twice won the Bronze Star for Valor as an infantryman in Korea, had begun marching on operations as soon as he had arrived in late April, and Vann often ran across him in the field after he reached the Seminary in May.

For all their cleverness, the Viet Cong had a weak point. They had fallen into regular patterns of behavior. They had done so, despite a

doctrine that said they must never lapse into such dangerous predicta-
bility, because they were human and human beings are creatures of
habit. These guerrillas had been fighting the same war against the same
enemy in the same rice paddies too long not to succumb to their humanity. Drummond had spotted the weakness early, and he and Vann
had talked about it in one of their first discussions. Vann's haste in
persuading Cao to let his intelligence officer cooperate with Drummond
had been motivated as much by eagerness to exploit this weakness as
by the need to gain proxy control over the division. Ever since, Drummond had been organizing a system to produce information for Vann's
six-month campaign of destruction.

He and his assistant, an Army sergeant who was an intelligence specialist, showed Cao's G-2 and his staff how to compose a "profile" for
each regular and provincial guerrilla battalion and company. The sergeant, who was a patient man, taught the Vietnamese to sort the captured Viet Cong reports, messages, diaries, letters, maps, and sundry
other material by unit and to extract anything potentially useful. All the
available data on a unit were then assembled and broken down into
categories with file folders and charts and cross-reference cards. The
system was designed to permit new material to be added constantly in
order to increase knowledge of the unit and ability to predict its behavior. Distinguishing characteristics were carefully noted, because
these were like fingerprints that helped Drummond to track a unit with
fragmentary reports that would otherwise be worthless.

In this early period, all of the Viet Cong battalions were greatly
inferior in firepower to their ARVN opposites, their weaponry an arms
bazaar of French and American manufacture captured from the Saigon
troops. Some of the battalions had a mortar, while others had none; a
couple had two .30 caliber machine guns and the rest were fortunate to
have one. The catalogue of weaponry measured the threat the battalion
posed and was also a distinguishing characteristic. Drummond and his
sergeant started rosters on the personnel strength of each battalion and
its components and created biographical files for the officers and noncoms. The Viet Cong cadres used aliases for protection, but because
they were local men and not Northern Communists, it was at times
possible to learn who they were and to obtain some knowledge of their
personalities and attitudes. Their aliases alone were useful as fingerprints
of the unit. In some cases Drummond was able to obtain photographs
taken from dead guerrillas or seized in raids on camps. The Vietnamese
are a sentimental people, and despite the risk of compromise the Viet
Cong liked to take souvenir photographs of each other. Whole platoons

would line up to have their picture taken, as if they were a high school class. Another separate file was established to delineate the normal operating area of each battalion and company. Their movements were charted to learn the customary routes the guerrillas took and the hamlets in which they stopped while making their assigned rounds to overrun outposts and stage ambushes. Drummond was just as interested in the escape routes they were likely to follow if attacked in a given vicinity.

Drummond discovered that his counterpart, Capt. Le Nguyen Binh, a Catholic from North Vietnam who had fled south after the French collapse in 1954, was a conscientious officer whose performance had been underestimated by Cao and the Americans. He was friendly and eager to share his information. One reason Binh had been so little heeded in the past was that there had been no professional intelligence officer on the American side to work with him, even if Cao had permitted cooperation. No one whose expertise Cao could recognize had told him of Binh's worth. The unit profiles that Drummond and his sergeant put together with Binh and his staff were rudimentary and had great gaps. Nonetheless, Drummond was surprised at how much relevant information Binh's raw files contained. He was also surprised to learn that Binh had a useful network of secret informants. Binh had established the network after being assigned to the division a year earlier and ran it himself out of fear that one of his staff might be a Communist penetration agent. He paid his spies with nonaccountable funds he was given for the purpose in imitation of the *caisse noire* ("black chest") system of the French colonial army. The most useful informant was a jobber of water buffalo, who had the perfect excuse to travel all over the northern Delta buying and selling these work animals of the Vietnamese peasantry, moving in and out of guerrilla-dominated sections without arousing any suspicion. He could be sent on missions to verify reports from other informants or to obtain a specific piece of information.

Vann cultivated another source of intelligence—the American Protestant missionary who lived in My Tho. Like most American missionaries in Asia, he believed in promoting anti-Communism along with Christianity. Clay had told Vann of his attitude, and Vann took to calling on him regularly. He was happy to pass along what he could gather from the Vietnamese pastors of his congregations in the outlying towns.

In their quest for security, the Viet Cong would give themselves away. When they assembled in a hamlet, or in a cluster of hamlets, to rest, to propagandize the peasantry, or to launch an attack, they usually restricted the movements of the population. If anyone responsible on the Saigon side was alert, the fall-off in the number of peasants coming to market was a tip of the Viet Cong's presence.

Like all good military organizations, the guerrillas wanted to operate in an efficient manner. Over the years they had configured the decks of their sampans to utilize the available space to best advantage. Their packs, cook stove, rice, stack of wood or charcoal, and crock of *nuoc mam* were placed in specific spots toward the bow to leave maximum room for sitting and sleeping toward the stern. Once one learned the arrangement, it was not difficult to tell that these sampans did not belong to farmers.

The guerrillas' permanent training camps and hospitals were well hidden in patches of woods in remote areas of the Plain of Reeds near the Cambodian border on the western side of the division zone or in mangrove swamps and water palm jungles that were difficult to penetrate in the populated provinces to the east. They could also conceal themselves in woods and swamps when they stopped to sleep while on the march, because each regular and provincial guerrilla carried a hammock he could sling between two trees. But sleeping in the open in a malaria-ridden country that has a monsoon climate and numerous other biting insects besides mosquitos is neither healthy nor comfortable. The guerrillas' doctrine also said that they could not survive if they did not live among the peasants. For these reasons they slept in hamlets whenever they could and built way stations and "safe houses" in populated regions so as not to impose on the peasantry. The ditched roads advertised the strongholds of population under their control and thus the hamlets where they slept and where such way stations and safe houses were most likely to be found. At first glance these structures also seemed to be just more peasant houses. On second look there were no animals around them and no cultivation except perhaps a small garden.

Although the Viet Cong did not know it, they were also sending an invisible tracer of their movements to a tracker in the sky. The Army's electronic espionage organization, the U.S. Army Security Agency, had begun functioning in earnest in South Vietnam in 1962 under the innocuous-sounding code name of the 3rd Radio Research Unit. By June there were 400 ASA technicians in the country. The majority worked out of the military side of Tan Son Nhut Airport in planes as innocent-appearing as their code name. The aircraft were built by De Havilland of Canada and had originally been designed for bush flying. They were a long and boxy, single-engine propeller type called the Otter, which could carry a communications intercept team and its sophisticated monitoring and direction-finding equipment and loiter for hours high over suspect areas while the team picked up and tape-recorded Viet Cong radio traffic. The guerrillas had older American radios of the World War II generation which they had captured from the Saigon forces or from the French before them. They used voice radios for short distances and the rudimentary but reliable Morse-code method of sending dots and dashes with a telegraph key (a different combination of dots and dashes for each of the letters in the romanized script of their language) for long-range communications. They transmitted sparingly and encrypted everything, so they thought they were reasonably safe.

They did not realize, until an Otter with an intercept team aboard crashed about a year later, that not only were the Americans breaking their codes, but that the transmissions themselves gave them away. Every Morse operator strikes the key with a different rhythm, called his "fist" in the electronics spy trade. Voices can also be tape-recorded, compared, and identified. The "fist" or the voice became the distinguishing characteristic of the radio. The electronic emissions likewise vary from one radio to another. The highly advanced ASA methods of interception and analysis collected and sorted this "special intelligence," as it is known. The results came to Drummond in a separate pouch. By putting the findings of this electronic espionage together with what he received from the human network, Drummond was often able to confirm that a particular radio belonged to a specific company or battalion. Because the ASA technicians could also frequently determine the general location from which the radio was transmitting, the unit could be followed and its pattern of movement outlined on the map.

With all of this information coming to him from these varied sources, Drummond started filling out the profiles and providing Vann with fresh tactical intelligence on the location and apparent intentions of a number of the regular and provincial guerrilla units. His limited knowledge often made his information imprecise, but there was enough hard information for Vann to begin systematic attacks in June.

The same American technology that tracked the guerrillas from the sky enabled Vann to launch effective assaults. The Vietnamese Communists no longer had the protection of time and space that the geography of their country had provided them during the war against the French and against Diem's regime prior to Kennedy's intervention. In the past the guerrillas had been able to shelter in natural fortresses that were impregnable to surprise attack. The largest and most famous one in Vann's area was the Plain of Reeds. Its expanse of swamp, fields of waist-high reeds, and clumps of brush and woods covered most of two provinces at the northwestern corner of the Mekong Delta adjacent to

Cambodia. The plain was nearly roadless and thinly populated, because the acid soil of black clay made rice cultivation difficult despite annual flooding by the Mekong. To reach one of the guerrilla havens on the plain required an enervating two- to three-day march. The smaller fortresses the Viet Cong had created in the populated regions had also been immune to surprise. The ditched roads and a warning network of pickets and sympathetic peasants had given days or at least hours of notice that the Saigon troops were coming.

The helicopter leaped the barrier of terrain and shrank time and effort from enervating days to exhilarating minutes. Almost all of the guerrillas' havens were within twenty miles in point-to-point distance from a province capital or a district center held by the Saigon government. The helicopter the Army had sent to Vietnam, the H-21 Shawnee, was an ungainly-looking machine of Korean War vintage, shaped like a fat bent pipe with large rotors fore and aft and appropriately named the Flying Banana by its crews. Nevertheless, it was a helicopter. A Flying Banana could pick up a squad of a dozen soldiers and move them, at eighty miles an hour, twenty miles in any direction in fifteen minutes. The newer H-34 Choctaw of the Marines, also called the HUS-1 Sea Horse, somewhat resembled a tadpole turned sideways. It could carry the same squad twenty miles in thirteen minutes at slightly over ninety miles an hour. A mere fourteen helicopters sufficed to carry the standard assault task force of half an ARVN battalion, about 165 men, with all of their weapons, ammunition, and food for a couple of days. Half an hour later the machines could return with a second task force and drop it along a route that the fleeing guerrillas had hoped to use for an orderly escape. There would be no warning beyond a minute or two if the pilots flew "contour"—that is, at treetop level—for the last few miles, which they did whenever they could. The whirling rotor blades drove the sound of the engines into the earth.

U.S. industry furnished Vann another machine that terrified the guerrillas every time they encountered it. The thing was a movable box of aluminum-alloy armor, rectangular, with sundry hatches and doors. A powerful engine mounted within turned caterpillar tracks on both sides. It was properly known as an armored personnel carrier, officially designated the M-113, and called an APC, a "track," or a "carrier" in the slang of armor officers. A company of twelve of these machines joined the division in June. Each had a .50 caliber heavy machine gun mounted in front of the command hatch on top. A reinforced company of 140 infantrymen also rode inside the protection of the boxes. The behemoth weighed ten tons and was amphibious. When the monster struck flooded rice paddies it churned across them at ten to twenty miles an hour, crashing into the small dikes of the fields with its tracks and bouncing over them. The armor was impervious to the bullets of the guerrillas' rifles and machine guns, and the Viet Cong had no antitank weapons worth mentioning. The company of infantrymen were trained to dismount through the rear hatches on signal and to attack under the formidable firepower of the dozen .50 caliber machine guns.

As guerrillas were killed and weapons were captured with regularity, Colonel Cao became still more pleased and cooperative. Vann was sure he would be able to set in place the last element of his plan to run the 7th Infantry "just like an American division" and launch it on a ruthlessly executed campaign to destroy the Main Force and Regional Viet Cong battalions in the northern Delta. This final element was the transformation of Cao into an aggressive leader in Vann's U.S. Army image. To attain the degree of proxy control necessary for a campaign of this magnitude, Vann needed to turn Cao, as Vann put it, into "the Tiger of South Vietnam."

The difficulty was that Cao did not have a tigerish personality. What resemblance he bore to a cat was a certain plump sleekness of body and craftiness of character. He lacked claws. Vann thought he saw a way around that deficiency. He would emulate his hero, Lansdale.

The Ugly American, the novel by Eugene Burdick and William Lederer that had embellished Lansdale's legend and made good sense to Vann when he had read it, was a political tract, "written as fiction . . . based on fact," to warn Americans that the United States was losing to Communism an ideological battle for the minds of Asians. The book was a primer on how Americans could win this battle if they would learn how to get Asians to do what was good for America and Asia. *The Ugly American* was not only a best-seller and the basis of a movie after its publication in 1958, it was accepted well into the 1960s as an example of serious political thought. In the novel, Col. Edwin B. Hillandale is sent from the Philippines, where he has recently outwitted the Communist Hukbalahap guerrillas and helped his friend Ramón Magsaysay win the presidential election by a landslide vote, to the kingdom of Sarkhan, "a small country out toward Burma and Thailand," where the United States is engaged in a contest with the Russians and the Chinese Communists for the friendship of the Sarkhanese leaders and people. One of Hillandale's hobbies is reading palms and casting horoscopes. He has a diploma from the "Chungking School of Occult Science." He observes during a walk through the capital city, Haidho, that palm readers and astrologers are accorded the same respect in Sarkhan as "fashionable physicians in America" and that no one of importance makes any decision of importance without a palm reading and a horoscope. After a bit of spying and dossier reading to familiarize himself with the personalities and backgrounds of the Sarkhanese leaders and the latest intrigues, Colonel Hillandale is soon manipulating political events in the country by convincing the prime minister that he is the world's greatest palm reader and astrologer. "Every person and every nation has a key which will open their hearts," Hillandale tells the American ambassador to Sarkhan. "If you use the right key, you can maneuver any person or any nation any way you want." As Hillandale had employed palm reading and horoscopes in Sarkhan, so Vann was going to use ego appeal to metamorphose Cao into a tiger and have the Vietnamese Communists suffer the consequences.

Huynh Van Cao was thirty-four years old in the summer of 1962 and had been promoted to command of a division when he was twenty-nine, an extraordinarily rapid rise in any army. Once asked by an American correspondent to explain his rocket ascent, Cao had pointed his swagger stick at himself and said: "Leadership!" He had designed the briefing office on the second floor of his house, his "War Room," to be an exact replica of the map room of Napoleon. He had to settle for a partial replica when it turned out that imitating Napoleon to perfection would entail having the door open through the middle of the most important province on Cao's enlarged map of the division zone. He had written a transparently disguised autobiography in the form of a novel entitled *He Grows Under Fire*. The book held up his career as a model for aspiring military leaders. He had a tendency to strut and he was never without his swagger stick, a gnarled and highly polished piece of exotic dark wood.

The title of Cao's autobiographical novel was somewhat misleading. He had not seen a great deal of combat and should not have chosen the profession of soldiering because he had no vocation for making war. He lacked the nerves of a soldier. During one operation when nervous strain undid him he ran out of the command tent, vomited, and ordered the artillery to stop firing a barrage in support of an infantry unit engaged with the guerrillas. The noise upset him too much, he said. He did possess a semblance of military competence, as distinguished from combativeness, as a result of superficial schooling by the French and U.S. armies. With his intelligence and glibness, he was able to make this semblance pass for actual competence with visiting American generals because they never saw him under stress.

Competence had, in any case, little to do with his double-time promotions and the fact that he held command of the 7th Division astride the main road thirty-five miles below the capital. He had been appointed division commander because he was a Central Vietnamese and a Roman Catholic who had been born and educated in the former imperial capital of Hue, Diem's home city, where his family had been known to the Ngo Dinhs, the president's family. Like many sons of Vietnamese mandarin families who had taken the side of the French during the first war, he had gone into the military because it had offered status in an employment-starved society, not because he had wanted to fight.

He had begun in 1946 when it was still respectable in the milieu in which Cao grew up for a young Vietnamese of decent family to serve as a noncom. He had joined the French-sponsored regional militia for Central Vietnam, a post–World War II equivalent of the Civil Guard, as a staff sergeant. The French secondary education that had qualified him for a job in the operations section of a headquarters (the church had put him through its Lycée Pellerin in Hue) had also kept him out of harm's way most of the time. He had thus been around two years later to obtain a place in the first class of a cadet school the French had opened in Hue to train officers for the new Vietnamese National Army they were raising for Bao Dai. In 1949, at the end of the six-month course, Cao had been commissioned a second lieutenant. He had then shuttled upward over the succeeding years of the early 1950s from platoon leader to company commander to staff officer of a battalion. The positions were more pro forma than real in terms of leadership and combat experience, because the French, under pressure from the United States to organize a native army, did not season and test these young men.

Cao had come to Diem's notice in 1954 when he was on the staff of a battalion that had taken Diem's side while Lansdale was guiding Diem to victory in the power struggle with his non-Communist rivals. Diem had brought Cao to the palace to work on his personal military staff for two years, making him its chief within a few months. To Diem's way of thinking, two years of service at the palace and Cao's family background were the best preparation for the responsibility of a division. He had given Cao one of the lesser divisions in 1957 and then, after Cao had completed a series of three-month courses in the United States at the Army's Command and General Staff College at Fort Leavenworth, Kansas, and other schools, had put him in charge of the 7th.

His first duty was to be prepared at all times to rush his troops to Saigon to save the president and his family should dissident elements of the armed forces launch another coup d'état like the one that a group of paratroop officers had attempted unsuccessfully in November 1960. Diem had a special radiotelephone network that reached directly from the palace to Cao and the other division commanders and to most of the province chiefs. The fact that Cao kept his family in the security of Saigon was not the primary reason he had turned his house into a second headquarters, with another set of communications like the radios at the division headquarters in the old French caserne. The headquarters at the house was meant to serve as an alternate command post should disloyal subordinates seize the main one.

Cao theoretically took his orders from the brigadier general who was Porter's counterpart at the corps headquarters in Saigon. In practice, Cao reported directly to Diem and ignored or appealed to the president any orders that did not suit him. "He is my king," Cao would say when he spoke of his devotion to Diem. Cao's king was a wily man who had rigged numerous fail-safe devices. While Cao was a trusted officer, unlike the brigadier general, who had no direct control over the troops in the three divisions that composed his corps, Cao too was not beyond question from another officer of nominally lower rank. The major who was the province chief in My Tho simultaneously commanded the armored regiment attached to the division. Diem had made the appointment just in case Cao might acquire strange ideas or fail Diem and his family for some other reason. Tanks could be president keepers or president killers. The major was from one of the landowning families of the Mekong Delta who had allied themselves with the Ngo Dinhs. He was a distant cousin but close associate of another division commander who had come to Diem's rescue with troops in 1960 and had displayed his own loyalty by joining his relative in the crisis. Like the rest of the province chiefs, the major in My Tho also reported directly to the president, supposedly in his capacity as civil governor of the province.

In the summer of 1962, Vann felt confident that the flaws in Cao, to the extent he could then perceive them, and related problems like this deliberate muddling of authority, would not prevent him from turning Cao into an aggressive military leader. He believed that if he made Cao appear to be a tiger often enough Cao's vanity would force him to play the part, even if he was a pussy cat.

Through June and into July, whenever the division killed a score or two of guerrillas in an operation, Vann would flatter Cao by telling him what a fine commander he was. He would praise Cao in the same way to me and the other reporters who came down to cover these engagements while Cao stood by listening and smiling. (I had arrived in South Vietnam as a freshman foreign correspondent in April 1962, about a month after Vann, to serve as Saigon bureau chief for the UPI. The Kennedy administration had lifted its prohibition against newsmen riding along on helicopter assaults and accompanying the advisors on operations in late May, just as Vann reached My Tho.) Nothing Vann said in public ever betrayed his game. Instead, after dinner in the Seminary mess hall the night before an operation he would give the assembled correspondents a pep talk on "emphasizing the positive" in our stories in order to encourage our ally. "Sandy" Faust, the outgoing major who was Vann's chief of staff, and Ziegler and the other officers at the command post were amused when they watched Vann work on Cao during an operation. To try to get Cao to direct the action the way he wanted, Vann would resort to little devices such as: "I know what you're going to do next because you're that kind of a commander." Before Cao had a chance to ask what Vann meant, Vann would pretend that he had heard Cao ask and describe the move. Often Cao would smile and say, yes, that was exactly what he had in mind, and issue the order. If Cao did not like the proposal, he would smile just as cheerfully and tell Vann that he had a better idea. Vann did not approve of all of Cao's ideas, but he took care never to contradict Cao in front of the American or Vietnamese staffs. Later in private he would explain his objections.

Cao's attitude gave every evidence that Vann's puppeteering was having the desired effect. He strutted a bit more and his manner became more pompous, but he also clearly saw advancement of his career in the hero image that Vann was projecting of him and in the fact that his division was killing Viet Cong on a scale that none of the other divisions was attaining. Vann told Ziegler he was sure that his handling of Cao would pay off soon in the first "big kill" of the series of hammer blows with which he intended to smash the guerrillas. At the rate they were harrying the Viet Cong, the guerrillas were going to make a truly serious mistake one of these days while attempting to escape a helicopter assault. When that moment came he was going to kill or capture an entire battalion of Viet Cong or its equivalent in separate companies that had banded together to train or fight.

He saw the possibility of such a victory in an unorthodox attack that his innovative mind had conceived in June and that he gradually stiffened Cao's nerve to launch in the latter half of July. He intended to show the guerrillas that the darkness did not belong entirely to them. He would stage the first night helicopter assault of the war to rouse the Viet Cong from their sleep in the twilight just before dawn.

Vann was doubly encouraged about this operation because Cao had become sufficiently confident of his advice to take risks that Cao would ordinarily not have accepted. When Vann had initially proposed the idea at the beginning of July, Cao, whose favorite admonition was "We must be prudent," had gone along with the concept but had insisted on an alternative to the target Vann wanted. Prevost had flown Vann out to inspect Cao's alternative. It turned out to be a couple of thatched huts where a squad of local guerrillas might assemble on occasion. Vann had to look at several other bunches of huts, or rice paddies next to large outposts, before he had cajoled and challenged enough in private to batten down Cao's fear that the landing force would suffer serious casualties. Cao's timidity was greater than usual because the sites Vann had selected for the predawn landing and a sequence of daylight landings to follow were all beyond the range of artillery. The troops would be dependent on fighter-bombers for support. Vann's expectations went up several more degrees after he finally pushed Cao to this unprecedented level of risk-taking.

He was hoping to catch and this time annihilate the 504th Main Force Battalion, one of the two regular units that had been hurt in the first operation that Ziegler had planned on May 23. A group of guerrillas from the 504th who had survived the terror of that day had offered at the end of May to surrender in return for amnesty. Diem did not grant amnesty to Communists and their followers, and their offer had not been answered. Drummond had tracked the battalion to a far section of the Plain of Reeds. There were indications that elements of the second regular battalion that had been cut up on May 23 might be with the 504th. The troops of the 504th and this second battalion were mainly engaged in refitting and training, according to Drummond's information, but one company from the 504th was reported to be harboring with the sympathetic inhabitants of several hamlets at the confluence of two small rivers about nine miles from the Cambodian border. They were preparing to stage out of these hamlets some night soon and attack an outpost that protected a large agricultural settlement of Catholic refugees from North Vietnam. Drummond thought it likely that a second company of regulars or provincial guerrillas was in the vicinity of these hamlets to reinforce the first for the planned attack and that there was a good chance of discovering other units from either battalion during the follow-up landings in daytime.

Vann selected the river junction for the predawn landing because the report of the company there was the freshest and most detailed intelligence Drummond had and because the Y where the two streams joined should be easy for the pilots to distinguish from the air in the dim light. To verify his judgment, Vann did the final reconnaissance in a helicopter with Drummond, instructing the pilots to make two passes at 1,500 feet and to fly off and circle for ten minutes in between so that the guerrillas would think the aircraft was on some routine mission and not realize they were under surveillance. Drummond crouched in the open door and held his Leica camera steady against the wind to get sharp pictures of the target while Vann questioned the pilots as to whether the river junction would stand out enough for an aviator in predawn conditions. They thought it would.

Binh was friendly with the owner of a photography shop in My Tho. He arranged for Drummond's film to be developed and printed in eight-by-ten-inch photographs. These were distributed to the pilots and to the leader of the landing task force and his company commanders to help them recognize their objective. A sequence of five other landings was planned after this first predawn one. The subsequent landings would initially try to snare any guerrillas who fled north up the larger stream that the two smaller ones formed and then probe at suspect spots along a canal that ran west from the river junction to Cambodia. Cao would have his command post in a hangar beside the dirt airstrip at Moc Hoa, a huddle of shoddy wooden and thatched houses around a church, a pagoda, and a province chief's house about forty miles northwest of My Tho. Vann would hold three more companies in reserve there.

He and Cao agreed that as soon as they flushed guerrillas they would drop the reserves in front of the Viet Cong and wipe them out. They would have nearly thirty helicopters to give them ideal flexibility with all of the troops at their disposal in the open terrain of reed fields and swamps. Some of the landings were certain to prove fruitless. These task forces could then be converted into more reserves for the helicopters to pick up and shift to wherever they were needed to trap fleeing guerrillas. They would use the newer Marine H-34 Choctaws for the first landing, because the H-34s had instruments for night flying.

At 5:00 A.M. on the morning of July 20, 1962, sixteen Marine helicopters circled in the darkness and descended one behind the other toward an airfield outlined by dots of flame below. Vann's advisors had placed pails of sand soaked with oil around the edges of the field and set them afire. The airfield was southeast of the target on a direct flight line from the World War II Japanese fighter airstrip at Soc Trang in the lower Delta where the Marine squadron was based. Two companies of troops, one the experimental company armed with the fast-firing Armalites, had been assembled there a day and a half before. The soldiers were ready. The advisors had reorganized them into three assault groups and lined them up at intervals down the runway in squads of a dozen men for each helicopter. As soon as the pilots leading the three flight groups had conferred with the advisors, the engines cranked again and the gold-and-blue flames of the exhaust speckled the darkness once more.

Curling up their arms to shield their faces from the dirt and pebbles whirled into the air by the blast from the rotor blades, the diminutive Vietnamese infantrymen climbed into the big machines. The interiors were faintly lit by the instrument panels and the amber of the cabin lights. The soldiers sat on the floors and reached out with one hand to grab hold of each other or of the nylon webbing attached to the cabin walls. With the other hand they tried to keep their rifles from falling back and bashing them in the face as the pilots turned the engines up to full power. The cabins reverberated with a noise that made the teeth vibrate in the jaw. The helicopters shook and swayed, and then tilted forward and lifted off one by one in a string formation, the outside navigation lights blinking through the night.

The Vietnamese soldiers were afraid. One could see the fear on their faces. Vann's captains were excited by the anticipation of action. Their thoughts were those of Vann and the other Americans in Vietnam in that first year: they were fighting now and someday they would triumph and make this a better country.

Forty-five minutes later the flight leaders spotted the Y-shaped sheen of water that cut through the deeper blackness of the trees around the houses along the banks. The aircraft plummeted toward the three designated sites at the river junction, the pilots shutting off the outside navigation lights in order not to help any Viet Cong gunners who might be awake. The Saigon officers and the American captains shouted above the racket of the engine, and the troops pulled themselves to their feet and faced the open door. The wheels of the helicopters splashed into the flooded rice paddies just beyond the trees at 6:03 A.M., fifteen minutes before dawn, and nearly 200 men leaped out into the knee-high water and muck and began sloshing toward the houses. As the Marine aviators lifted off and turned back east toward the field at Moc Hoa fifteen miles away to refuel and join thirteen Army H-21 Flying Bananas from Tan Son Nhut for the subsequent landings, a twin-engine C-47 transport that Prevost had arranged for arrived overhead and the crew chief tossed out a parachute flare that consumed what was left of the darkness in the glare of an artificial sun.

Vann seemed out of luck. The hamlets contained only women, children, and old men. In the backseat of an Army L-19, where he spent the early part of the morning searching for guerrillas and talking to his advisors over the radio, Vann cursed that the first night helicopter assault of the war, executed with such finesse by the Marines, should come to naught. The company of the 504th Main Force Battalion that Drummond had thought was at the river junction had pulled out the day before. A separate platoon of provincial guerrillas who were in one of the hamlets managed to get away to the north up the larger river into which the two smaller streams flowed because the Army helicopters were half an hour late coming from Saigon and so threw off schedule the landing of the Ranger company that was supposed to sever this escape route. Vann then flew back to Moc Hoa to try to resolve an unforeseen problem in refueling the aircraft. He was unable to do anything, and the next assault was delayed by nearly two and a half hours. It too proved to be an empty target. Vann began to wince at the embarrassment of turning up a large zero.

The fourth landing was designed to search the vicinity of two hamlets seven and a half miles farther up the canal that ran west from the river junction to Cambodia. Vann had selected these two hamlets on the assumption that the Viet Cong might have established base camps near them because of the convenience of the canal for transport. Employing all twenty-nine helicopters, he simultaneously dropped two task forces north of the hamlets at 9:50 A.M. The troops ran right into an estimated 150 guerrillas. Vann had remained at the command post for this lift. The radio reports that some of the Viet Cong were firing automatic weapons and that many were dressed in khaki uniforms indicated that they were almost certainly regulars. Drummond's information had been essentially correct after all. Vann had made up for its lack of precision by letting terrain suggest to him where guerrillas might be located and by using Ziegler's probe technique to test his hunch.

The Viet Cong had seen the illuminating flares during the predawn assault and had watched the helicopters make the subsequent daylight landings. They had assumed that the net would not spread far enough to touch them and that they were safe staying where they were instead of breaking down into small groups and disappearing across the border into Cambodia, only four and a half miles away in a northerly direction and just a couple of miles farther west along the canal. They compounded this first mistake with one of war's unforgiving errors. They ran to the killing ground that their enemy had prepared for them.

In attacking this close to the border, Vann knew that he would be tempting any guerrillas who might be in or near the hamlets to run for Cambodia. The Viet Cong had dug foxholes, and expertly camouflaged them, in the higher ground of trails that cut through clumps of woods and brush where the troops had landed just above the hamlets. Instead of taking advantage of these fortifications to try to defend themselves until night gave them an opportunity to escape, they panicked after a few moments of shooting, as Vann had thought they would, abandoned the cover of brush and trees, and fled in disorder toward the hope of sanctuary.

Five minutes after this fourth landing, a VNAF observer pilot in an L-19 spotted a mob of about 100 Viet Cong start the rush across the open fields of reeds, flooded at midpoint in the monsoon season. The reeds were two to six feet tall. The soft ground underneath was covered with one to three feet of water. Some of the guerrillas were foolishly attempting to wade through the reeds, while others were poling small sampans that held half a dozen men. The observer asked permission to call in the fighter-bombers. It was the moment for which Vann had been waiting since May. He advised Cao to let the planes go to work until they could refuel the helicopters again and drop the first reserve task force ahead of the guerrillas to start the process of encircling and annihilating them. Cao was never averse to an air strike. He issued the order.

The observer, known as a FAC after the acronym for forward air controller, radioed the planes on station overhead and then banked his wisp of an aircraft to sweep over the guerrillas and mark them by tossing down a white smoke grenade. It was hardly necessary. The pilots, Vietnamese trained in France or the United States and "Farm Gate" Americans from the air commando squadron at Bien Hoa, could easily see the sampans and the bunches of tiny figures pushing in a frenzy through the reeds. The sun was high in the sky now and had burned away the ground fog that might earlier have given some concealment to the movements of these fear-crazed men. The sun's rays glinted off the silver fuselages when the pilots dove.

The bullets from the .50 caliber machine guns and 20mm cannons churned the water in the strafing runs. The rockets exploded on the sampans, breaking them apart. The shiny aluminum canisters of napalm tumbled end over end and burst on the reed fields, engulfing a group of guerrillas in a great orange flower. From the air the scene had beauty to it. In the cool clarity of the midmorning sky there was no consciousness of the sweat and terror in the heat below. Instead there was the sensation of grace as the planes responded to the controls and the intoxication of omnipotence in the power of these weapons. The pilots had rarely had such good shooting. The radio frequencies of this hybrid air force were alight with a mixture of Vietnamese, French, and English as they talked excitedly with each other and the observer directing their runs. Their propeller-driven AD-6 Skyraiders and converted T-28 Trojan trainers were better than jets for this work, because the pilots could dive more slowly and see better to strafe and rocket. With the wind rushing past the cockpit canopy in the descent, the fuselage shuddering from the recoil of the guns, and the whoosh of the rockets darting out from under the wings, the drama was like one of those World War II movies when the Army Air Corps gave the Germans and the Japs what they deserved. The little figures jumped out of the sampans as the bullets raced up the water toward them, wild to get away. Out in the open like this, escape was pure chance, a chance that was often missed. Soon moving figures lay still and bodies floated among the reeds. Vann's advisors later counted more than forty dead here. The Saigon troops also blasted away at the panicked guerrillas with their rifles and automatic weapons, cutting down some, but the advisors afterward concluded that the planes had done the biggest portion of the killing.

While the pilots made run after run and the helicopters were refueled, Vann got Cao organized to reap the full harvest of this opportunity toward which so much preparation had gone. He created two more reserve task forces to supplement the one they already had. With three reserves they could cut off the escape of these guerrillas and any others who might be flushed no matter which way they turned. The airmen had forty-five minutes of exuberant shooting before the helicopter refueling was completed and the first reserve of two companies lifted off from Moc Hoa airstrip to be dropped farther north between the Viet Cong and the border. The assault troops who had landed at 9:50 A.M. were ordered to stop and hold in a "blocking position." The two-company reserve task force was to drive south in the classic "hammer and anvil" tactic. Those guerrillas who had managed to escape the planes by hiding in the reeds were to be killed or captured by the descending "hammer" of the reserve or caught on the "anvil" of the troops in the block if they fled back south. Vann took off in a separate helicopter to encourage the Saigon commanders and to see for himself what was happening so that he could guide Cao accurately now that the action had reached the critical stage.

As the helicopters descended with this first reserve, the pilots saw more guerrillas heading toward the border farther away to the west. Vann wasn't worried about how to deal with them. He and Cao had discussed what to do before he had left the airstrip. Just to make sure, he radioed Faust, who was in charge of the advisory side of the command post in his absence, and told him to recommend that Cao commit the second reserve northwest of these guerrillas with similar instructions to drive down onto the "anvil." Faust said he already had made the recommendation and that Cao had agreed.

The turning of Vann's anticipated triumph into an unanticipated nightmare began in a puzzling way. He flew over the scene of the air strikes and verified the evidence of the planes' success floating among the reeds. He then stopped to see the battalion commander in charge of the assault troops who were holding in place as the "anvil." Everyone was jubilant. They had found an 81mm mortar to add to the numerous small arms abandoned by the terrified guerrillas. He congratulated them and took off again to check on the progress south of the first reserve task force. He was surprised to see as soon as the helicopter gained altitude that they had not moved from the spot where they had jumped out of the helicopters. He landed to find out why and was told by the ARVN captain that he had been ordered by the regimental commander to "maintain a blocking position." That didn't make sense, Vann said. The assault troops were already blocking and Colonel Cao had ordered the captain to push south as fast as he could before the reserve had left Moc Hoa. The regimental commander had just instructed him over the radio to block and not advance, the captain replied. Where in hell did the major running the regiment get the authority to overrule Colonel Cao? Vann demanded. The captain looked at him blankly and said nothing. Didn't he realize that the Viet Cong he was supposed to be killing and capturing were escaping while he dawdled? Vann yelled. The captain shrugged. Vann asked him to call the regimental headquarters, explain the situation, and ask permission to move. Vann flew back to the assault troops to see if the regimental commander had instructed them to attack north instead. No, they were supposed to hold in place. He returned to the reserve. The captain said he had contacted regiment as Vann had asked and had again been ordered to stay put. Vann radioed his advisor at the regimental headquarters set up in a village center south of the operation and also called Faust to have Cao dispel this confusion right away. He got no results. He tried to argue the reserve captain into advancing on his, Vann's, responsibility. The captain refused. Vann flew back to the assault troops again and attempted to persuade the captain there to advance, also to no avail. Forty minutes of this maddening routine went by, and every few minutes the Viet Cong got that much closer to the border. In the meantime the helicopters did not return to drop the second reserve to the northwest. When Vann radioed Faust for an explanation, Faust said that Cao seemed to be reneging on his earlier agreement. Cao would not issue the order. Vann flew back to Moc Hoa to set matters right himself.

He jumped from the helicopter, ran into the headquarters in the hangar, and told Cao that he had to get the first reserve in motion and load the second into the waiting helicopters right away or the Viet Cong were going to escape. Cao said he couldn't do that.

"Why not?" Vann asked.

"Because the commander of the Tenth Regiment does not wish to share his big victory with another regiment," Cao said. The 10th Regiment commander was the major who had ordered the reserve not to move. One of his battalions, split into two task forces, had made the original landing. The reserves were from other regiments.

Vann was so astonished he was at a rare loss for words. "What?" he said, staring into Cao's face.

Cao repeated what he had said with a calm expression. He smiled.

Vann had to strain hard to control himself. He drew Cao off to one side to avoid openly embarrassing him in front of their subordinates. Cao could not let the vanity of some major stop them from winning the war, he said. Cao was the division commander. He could simply override his subordinate by issuing an order. There were no risks. They far outnumbered the Viet Cong. Cao had lost a mere two men killed and a dozen wounded. Vann estimated that there were probably 200 guerrillas still alive and heading for Cambodia. Cao could not allow the Communists to escape like this to fight another day. He had a reputation to uphold as an aggressive commander. Today was his opportunity to accomplish an unprecedented feat. He could bag a whole battalion. If he didn't act, he would look like a coward.

Cao was unmoved. He said he was not going to upset his regimental commander.

Vann eventually argued Cao into marching the first reserve south, but they did not start until 2:00 P.M., almost three hours after they had landed. As a result of Vann's persistence, Cao obtained a rare prize. The reserve troops found a heavy .50 caliber machine gun abandoned by the Viet Cong. Seven guerrillas hiding under the water and breathing through hollow reeds were also discovered and shot as they vainly tried to run, and more small arms were captured. Cao was not at all hesitant about gathering up the weapons. He had already sent helicopters out to bring in the 81mm mortar and small arms seized in the original assault by the time Vann returned and had called the Joint General Staff in Saigon to boast of his treasure. Vann nearly regretted gaining Cao the .50 caliber when the ARVN general who was chief of staff of the JGS and a colonel flew out to ooh and ah over the mortar and machine gun and the twenty-seven small arms captured, most of them French bolt-action rifles. Cao had soldiers stack the weapons in front of the hangar on tables covered with white sheets like trophies at a banquet.

The headquarters ceased to function as Cao in his ecstasy abandoned further direction of the operation and most of his staff did the same. "It was only with the greatest of difficulty that the interest of the division commander and his staff could be refocused on continuing," Vann said later in the temperate language of his official report. He was flabbergasted that the Saigon general saw nothing wrong with the way Cao behaved and acted no better himself. Cao had also let another 80 to 100 guerrillas escape on the eastern end of the operation while Vann was out flogging himself into useless frustration trying to get the reserve to advance. These Viet Cong were probably the company of the 504th Battalion that Vann had just missed catching by one day at the river junction. Neither of the two Saigon battalions that flushed the guerrillas would pursue them, despite the pleas of their advisors. Cao also would not respond when Vann called for pursuit after his return. An A-26 Invader from the air commando squadron had been on station overhead, and Cao had loosed an air strike with his customary alacrity the moment the guerrillas had been sighted. The pilots claimed to have killed twenty-five. Vann carefully inspected the scene from a helicopter. This time the airmen had blasted reeds and bushes. There were no bodies.

Vann received worse news the next day. Cao had forfeited an opportunity to destroy a resource more valuable to the Vietnamese Communist cause than a battalion of guerrilla regulars. The clumps of woods above the hamlet had hidden the most important Viet Cong training camp in the northern Delta. Interrogation of the eleven prisoners captured disclosed that one of the units hit was a specialized company of instructors. Drummond had not known of its existence before. The second unit was another company of the 504th Battalion assigned to protect these training cadres. The rest of the Viet Cong were youths from provincial units all over the region who had been selected for assignment to the Main Force battalions. They had been in the camp for four months receiving advanced instruction in weapons, tactics, and camouflage and other techniques of guerrilla warfare. Drummond found four thatched-hut classrooms furnished with blackboards under the trees, as well as two other groups of huts used for medical training.

The pilots shuddered at the sight of the American-manufactured .50 caliber, because the big machine gun can be a lethal antiaircraft weapon in skilled hands, and its appearance was evidence that the guerrillas were beginning an intelligent program to counter the helicopters. This first impression was confirmed. In his eagerness for more captured arms to display, Cao brought out two teams with mine detectors the next day. They discovered the tripod mount for another .50 caliber underwater. The barrel and action could not be found. The prisoners said the training company had three .50 calibers and had been teaching a select group of the recruits how to shoot them against aircraft. Drummond and Binh found instruction booklets in the camp describing how the gunner should fire ahead of the fighter-bomber or helicopter in order to compensate for its speed. One captured document listed the serial numbers of the three machine guns, which had probably either been lost by the French or captured from an ARVN unit in some other region, as Binh knew of none taken in the 7th Division zone. The prisoners said that some of the braver guerrillas had tried to shoot down the fighter-bombers with the .50 calibers before they were killed or fled.

The fiasco was the more painful for Vann because it was so unexpected. It had been inconceivable to him twenty-four hours earlier that after he had prepared so meticulously by orchestrating the talents of Ziegler and Drummond and every other means at his disposal, Cao would nullify all. It had been just as inconceivable to him that Cao would confound his theory of human nature by sidestepping the burden of the role Vann had assigned to him. In Vann's code of an officer it was unthinkable to throw away the lives of one's soldiers by permitting an enemy to escape as Cao had done. The Viet Cong had been badly hurt, but since approximately 300 of them had gotten away, there were plenty of survivors to reconstitute the units. The training cadres would be back to breed more guerrillas, and the 504th Main Force Battalion would return to overrun more outposts and lay more ambushes.

Raising a public fuss would have ended Vann's game with Cao, which he was determined to pursue despite this defeat, and would have led to his dismissal by General Harkins, because policy was to display a front of cordiality between the advisors and their counterparts. When Malcolm Browne, then with the Associated Press, hitched a ride out to Moc Hoa on a helicopter from Saigon, Vann gave him the impression that all had gone precisely according to plan right from the start. The predawn landings by the Marines had been "a beautiful job," he said. "They landed exactly on schedule, and for a change, it looks as if we caught the Viet Cong completely off guard." After Cao announced that his troops and the planes had killed a record 131 Viet Cong in the biggest success of the war and that one of the eleven prisoners was the Party representative for a district, Vann did not quietly enlighten the correspondents. (He estimated in his confidential report to Porter and Harkins that the number of guerrillas slain "did not exceed 90.") He had to watch, seething, while Cao received a hero's laurels, unable to let truth tarnish his creation.

Diem was so pleased that he gave Cao the most elaborate victory parade in Saigon since 1955, the year the ARVN paratroopers delivered the *coup de grâce* to the private army of the organized crime society, the Binh Xuyen, which had been one of Diem's rivals. Radio Saigon and the controlled newspapers of the capital exulted in "the greatest victory of the war." The parade was held on a Saturday so that as many civil servants and their families as possible could be recruited to fill the crowds. Pretty girls in the traditional Vietnamese woman's dress, the *ao dai*, a tight-fitting tunic that becomes a split skirt at the waist and unfurls over pantaloons, met Cao and his officers at the outskirts and bedecked them with garlands of orchids and other flowers. He rode into the city to the parade marshaling point standing up in a jeep, waving and saluting right and left, and then marched at the head of his officers and men down one of the main avenues to the former French opera house where Diem's National Assembly met. Everyone had on combat fatigues, boots, and steel helmet, except Cao, who took a general's prerogative of calling attention to himself by wearing the baseball-type field cap coming into fashion in the U.S. Army. He carried his fancy swagger stick and had a Colt .45 on his hip in a leather holster. All of the captured weapons were displayed for the public to see on a stage erected in the square in front of the opera house. Scores of medals were awarded to officers and soldiers, and the acting minister of national defense pinned a medal for heroism to the 7th Division flag. In the climax to the day, Cao was driven to the palace and decorated by Diem for gallantry.

The contrast between this public chicanery and the honesty of Vann's confidential after-action report to Porter and Harkins made the alarm Vann sounded in secret for his leaders all the more resonant. By this time he had seen enough of the flaws in the leadership of the Saigon forces, noting them individually in previous after-action reports, to begin to understand the dimensions of the problem that confronted the whole advisory mission. He and his colleagues were charged with waging a war of infantry combat against a guerrilla enemy with an army that suffered from an institutionalized unwillingness to fight. Vann owed his premature assumption of command at the Seminary to this unwillingness. Clay's helicopter had been shot up and he had been wounded on May 23 because the ARVN lieutenant leading the company he was with had refused to pursue or even fire at a platoon of guerrillas running across the dikes of a rice paddy in plain sight, and so Clay had chased after them with a pair of helicopters. Now the division commander was letting fifteen times as many guerrillas run free. The timidity amounted to a phobia against risks and casualties. "A deplorable condition . . . exists," Vann wrote, "because commanders at all levels who do nothing can still retain their command, and even advance, while those who are aggressive may be relieved if they suffer a setback or sustain heavy losses." The ARVN officers also did not understand the purpose of their existence. "Petty jealousies among battalion and regimental command-ers take precedence over, and detract from, the primary mission of closing with and destroying the enemy. Regimental and battalion com-manders obey orders that suit them, ignore or change those that do not." If the advisors were to fulfill their mission of winning the war with the ARVN, the magnitude of these failings had to be recognized and adequate measures taken to overcome them. "Unless the entire ARVN can be retrained to function on a chain of command, orders *will* be obeyed basis, then an acceptable degree of combat effectiveness will not be achieved," he warned Porter and Harkins.

A U.S. Army officer is taught to do the best he can with what he is given. To recognize the possibility of failure is never to concede it but rather to persevere all the harder on the assumption that if one does persevere with imagination, failure will not occur. This attitude was more pronounced in Vann than in most officers because he prided him-self on never permitting a challenge to defeat him. He also partially believed Cao's excuse that the 10th Regiment commander had prevented Cao from trapping the Viet Cong. He did not absolve Cao of respon-sibility, but he knew that Cao had his problems with the province chiefs and Vann thought that the major in charge of the regiment might be some other favorite of Diem's.

In addition, Cao talked a good war. He spoke of his desire to prevent the Communists from imposing a dour tyranny on the South. They would repudiate their promises of land and other benefits to the peasants once they had seized control, he said. They would massacre all genuine and potential opponents in a bloodbath, collectivize the land, suppress re-ligion, destroy Vietnamese traditions, and ban those personal freedoms that Vietnamese in the South did have under Diem in order to regiment the society with their Marxist totalitarianism.

Vann believed that the Communists would commit all of these crimes if they won the war. He concluded that Cao, whatever his faults, was a Vietnamese patriot, a sincere nationalist who wanted to give his country the decent alternative of an anti-Communist government in Saigon and gradual modernization under American guidance. He assumed that Cao cared as much about a country called South Vietnam as Vann did about the United States and that with time he could still flatter and coax and shame Cao into acting like the kind of military leader South Vietnam needed to protect it.

The fiasco of July 20 thus became for Vann a setback but not the failure of his plan. In August he sent Mary Jane a snapshot of himself and Cao standing side by side in front of the headquarters tent during an operation. He had the photo shop in My Tho tint the black-and-white photograph with life tones to turn it into a color shot. In the photo, Vann was looking at the camera and Cao was looking at Vann. On the back Vann wrote in ball-point for Mary Jane:

VANN & CAO
AUGUST, 1962

"The best US-Vietnamese team for fighting Communists."

Had Vann wanted to throw up his hands over Cao, he could not have done so in any case. By the early fall of 1962 he was snared in his "Cao the Tiger" game because of the sheer number of Viet Cong being killed through the level of planning and intelligence he had attained and with the shock effect on the guerrillas of American technology—the helicopters, the M-113 armored personnel carriers, and the fighter-bombers. Vann was, in effect, trapped by his own outward-seeming success. During the first four months after his arrival, as many Viet Cong were reported killed by ground and air action in the 7th Division zone as in the rest of the country combined—4,056, including village and hamlet guerrillas. (The figures were those of the Saigon officers and encompassed the separate, province-level operations by the Civil Guard and the SDC when Americans were often not on the ground to estimate casualties.) Even when Vann subtracted 50 percent for exaggeration, a factor that he and the senior advisors to the other ARVN divisions believed was common to the reporting of enemy casualties throughout South Vietnam, 2,000 dead in four months was a punitive rate of loss for the Viet Cong in the northern Delta. None of the Main Force or Regional battalions had been destroyed—that is, had had so many men killed that there were not enough survivors to reconstitute the unit with time and replacements. A number had been hit so hard that they were incapable of combat for the moment. Indeed, Vann began to hope that if he could somehow maintain the current pace of operations the cumulative impact could still break the striking arm of the Viet Cong despite Cao's refusal to pay the price of infantry combat. For six straight operations in August and September the guerrillas suffered 100 or more dead. Another operation on the Plain of Reeds on September 18 against a Main Force battalion, this one the 502nd, was a greater success in fact than the July 20 "greatest victory" had been on paper. One company of the 502nd and about 100 provincial guerrillas with it were literally wiped out by the M-113 armored personnel carriers.

The Viet Cong regulars tried to organize a defense behind the low dikes of a flooded paddy field, but the squat tracked monsters bounded right over the dikes and charged into them, the bullets of the guerrillas ricocheting off the aluminum-alloy armor. The infantry riding inside the carriers stood up in the open hatches and fired over the sides, shooting guerrillas in the water a few yards away. The machine gunners manning the big .50 calibers mounted in front of the top hatches raked down others who insanely attempted to run through the waist-high water and gray muck underneath that sucked at their feet. The Viet Cong who managed to keep their heads amid this terror sought to escape by hiding under the water of the paddies and nearby reed fields, breathing through hollow reeds or by holding only their nostrils at the top of the water. The carrier drivers defeated this ruse by rocking their ten-ton boxes back and forth to make waves, which exposed the guerrillas. The Saigon infantrymen on the M-113s also threw grenades into the water to blast them to the surface. As soon as a Viet Cong was spotted the driver would turn the carrier toward him and run him down, if he did not die first in a storm of bullets before the vehicle could crush him.

The guerrillas lost 158 killed and 60 captured that day. Vann sent Mary Jane a clipping of the lead front-page article on the Communist debacle in Saigon's English-language newspaper, the *Times of Vietnam*. He wrote across the top of the double-decker headline: "Biggest single kill of whole war in Vietnam!" Diem awarded the 7th Division the ARVN fourragère, a braided, multicolored cord worn around the left shoulder as a citation of an entire unit for gallantry. It was copied from a French decoration of the same type which has also been imitated by the U.S. and other western armies. This was the first time the fourragère had been given to a whole ARVN division. Cao was informed that Diem had in mind promoting him to general and elevating him to command of a corps.

Vann had also become General Harkins's favorite advisor. The reason was not that Vann's after-action reports had become optimistic. They continued to be written with the coarse-grained honesty of his July 20 report. Where the ordinary lieutenant colonel might have shaped events positively in the success-oriented atmosphere of the Army, Vann did not polish the rough edges. The recurrent theme of his reports was that he and his advisors were getting no closer to solving the long-term problem of turning the ARVN into an army capable of fighting and winning the war against its guerrilla opponent. Harkins did not seem to be disturbed by the bad-news side of Vann's reporting. Instead he seemed to focus on the stacks of bodies that Vann was piling up. The general and his staff had decided that in this war of no fronts the essential measure of progress was the number of Viet Cong killed, the "body count" in the jargon of the bureaucracy. "In a war without battle lines, perhaps the best overall index of progress is that of casualties," the briefing officer at the Saigon headquarters put it in less macabre fashion in his standard orientation lecture for newcomers and visitors.

Harkins's press officers encouraged correspondents to visit Vann's detachment and to cover 7th Division operations. Touring congressmen and generals and civilian officials from the Pentagon were invariably flown down for a briefing by the Vann-Cao team that was shooting record numbers of guerrillas. As part of his strategy, Vann had coached Cao to the point where he was a model briefer who radiated offensive-mindedness from the podium in the War Room of his villa. Vann also had his staff compose colored charts and graphs and produce slides for Cao that were on a par with anything displayed in the Pentagon. While he always gave Cao center stage in these performances, Vann would take the podium to cap them with a short presentation of his own. He had learned the art of briefing while a young major on the U.S. Army Europe headquarters staff in Heidelberg, rehearsing until he had mastered the weaving together of gesture, statistic, and personal anecdote to convey dramatic effect and conviction to his audience. Long after he had left he was remembered at the Heidelberg headquarters as the best briefer who had served there. He invariably impressed his audience in Vietnam. If there was time, which there often was not, Vann would draw the Pentagon general or civilian official aside or take him over to the sitting room on the second floor of the Seminary for a private and different briefing. Otherwise, he left it to Harkins's headquarters to pass along what he was reporting confidentially. This occasional privilege of privately imparted perspective from Vann did not apply to congressmen and journalists.

Cao reveled in the acclaim and the prospect of a general's stars. "I kill fifty Viet Cong today," he would announce to reporters coming to the command post. He began to learn the public relations game perhaps too well. Whenever a particularly large body count had been achieved, Harkins's headquarters or the presidential palace would lay on a special flight to make certain that all of the press, including the French correspondents and the Vietnamese from the Saigon newspapers, advertised this evidence of who was winning the war. Horst Faas, a German-born photographer for the Associated Press who was to win the Pulitzer Prize twice during ten years in Vietnam, arrived earlier than the reporters were expected on one occasion. He found Cao reconstructing the battlefield. ARVN soldiers were dragging the cadavers of guerrillas into fighting positions and placing captured weapons in front of them. Cao was striding about giving directions with his swagger stick.

Several of Vann's captains were offended after Cao also took to wearing a bush hat around the headquarters tent as the fancy struck him. They thought the hat was a bit much, even for Cao. He would rub his hands together when the fighter-bombers or the armored personnel carriers were running up an excellent score and talk about how he had the guerrillas in a trap.

But he would never spring the trap. Each time the moment came, he and Vann would have the same clash they had had at the decisive point in the July 20 operation. The reserve troops would be ready, the helicopters would be fueled and waiting, and Cao would refuse to block the guerrillas' escape. He stopped giving Vann bizarre explanations of the sort he had on July 20 that a regimental commander did not want to share the "victory." Instead Cao began pulling what Ziegler called his "general's act." He would listen to Vann for a while, say something about being prudent, listen to Vann a bit more, and then pout and say that he did not want to discuss the subject any further. If Vann continued to press him, he would draw himself up and announce: "You are an advisor. I am the commander. I make the decision."

Vann held his temper, but his staff noticed how difficult it was becoming for him to control himself. His face would flush and the normal harshness of his nasal voice would get harsher with the stress. Back at the Seminary afterward he would scream out his frustration, cursing Cao with a profanity that had the fluent vileness of the poor-white Norfolk neighborhood of his youth.

During one argument he gestured to Faust and the other advisors to walk away to the far side of the command-post tent. He grasped Cao by the arm and led him to the map. The staff watched him jab again and again at the opening through which the guerrillas were running.

They could hear him tell Cao in a low voice that tamped down the fury inside him that Cao had to face up to his moral responsibility as an officer and a soldier. He had to bar the gate and wipe out that Viet Cong battalion so that those guerrillas would not live and learn how to fight better another day and come back and kill his people. Vann's staff waited for Cao to issue the order to load the reserve into the helicopters. Their chief really had his dander up, and surely he was going to prevail this time. Cao did not pull his "general's act" on this occasion. He simply walked out of the tent. Faust started to wonder if Cao might secretly be a Communist agent.

John Vann was in such excellent graces with General Harkins because of the casualty toll he was inflicting on the guerrillas that when Maxwell Taylor returned to South Vietnam in September for a brief survey, Vann was one of the officers invited to have lunch with him at Harkins's residence in Saigon. It had been nearly a year since Taylor's mission of inquiry in the fall of 1961 had hastened Kennedy's decision to commit the arms of the United States to this war. Taylor's purpose on the current trip was to see whether there had been any progress in the intervening year. Vann was chosen to represent the division-level advisors at the luncheon the day after Taylor's arrival on September 10, 1962. Three other advisors who were more junior, a major and two captains, were also invited. They were all supposed to give Taylor a frank appraisal of the situation as they saw it in the field where the war was being fought.

Vann was thrilled with this opportunity to state his worries to a man who had the power to influence high policy and set matters right. Kennedy, who had brought Taylor out of retirement in 1961 to be his military advisor, had in July once more demonstrated his confidence in Taylor by naming him to be the new chairman of the Joint Chiefs of Staff. When his turn came to speak, Vann intended to present Taylor with an appraisal as rudely honest as his confidential reports to Harkins. He was disappointed that his reports had not aroused the sense of urgency in Harkins that he had thought they would. Porter had been upset by them, but Porter had also been unable to stir Harkins. The John Vann who had driven down the road to My Tho in May so confident of how he was going to win the war was by September uncertain that he could accomplish what he was expected to achieve within the limitations imposed on him, and he was apprehensive about the future.

His seeming success tended to buffer him against his worries, but not to eliminate or even diminish them. While he could and did hope that he would destroy the Viet Cong regular and provincial battalions in spite of Cao, it would have been irresponsible of him to count on doing so. The likelihood was that the guerrillas would sooner or later learn not to panic and to fight more intelligently, and when they did the days of easy killing would end. In the meantime he was not accomplishing the minimum tasks he and Porter had agreed on. After an initial show of enthusiasm, Cao was not cooperating in a matter as elementary as training the division's battalions in marksmanship and infantry tactics. He never allowed any of the battalions to complete the three-week refresher course that Vann had set up at the SDC training center at Tan Hiep, and none of the battalions did anything fit to be called training at their home bases. The "Monthly Critiques" by the advisors were monotonous in reporting that the battalions spent most of their time "resting." When a battalion did get to Tan Hiep and had been training for a few days, Cao would pull it out, often to pursue a guerrilla band that had overrun an outpost or staged an ambush. Vann was certain Cao knew as well as he did that it was impossible to catch the Viet Cong after such attacks; they planned their withdrawal in advance. Cao would never acknowledge this. Vann suspected Cao sent the battalions chasing long-gone foxes because he wanted to give the presidential palace the impression he was on the alert. Afterward he would order the battalion back to its base to "rest" instead of returning it to the training center. Training his men for combat was not one of Cao's priorities. He pretended they were already well trained.

Cao was also thwarting Vann's effort to foster night patrols and ambushes that would hinder the growth of the insurgency by denying the Viet Cong the freedom of the night. Cao had only acquiesced in night operations in the first place because of Diem's instruction to get along with the Americans where it cost nothing and because he had wanted to show generosity to his new advisor. Having demonstrated that he was amiable, Cao had become intent on returning to what he considered sanity. He had just finished breakfast one recent morning when his staff had informed him that Vann had been out all night with less than half a squad this time—a five-man patrol. Cao had sent for Vann in a fury and had shouted that unless Vann stopped this madness he, Cao, was going to request another advisor. Didn't Vann realize that if an American officer as senior as a lieutenant colonel were captured or killed on an adventure like this, President Diem would hold Cao responsible and never forgive him the embarrassment to the government? Cao's career would be ruined. Diem might even throw him into jail. Vann had said that he was under orders from Porter to provoke night actions and someone had to push the troops. He had reminded Cao that he was not an amateur and had learned in Korea that one was safer at night with a small group than with a large one. Cao had been so angry and fearful that Vann had decided he would have to compromise in order to retain any ability to employ American officers and sergeants as a possible catalyst for night patrols and ambushes. He had let Cao argue him into an agreement that he and the other field-grade officers in the detachment would not go out at night with less than a company. The junior officers and sergeants could continue to go out with small groups. Once Cao had Vann and the senior Americans reined in, he had begun to squeeze. Vann's junior officers and sergeants were finding it increasingly difficult to round up men willing to accompany them. Cao had passed the word.

Vann had much more on his mind than training and night patrols and ambushes. He was troubled by the resilience the Viet Cong were demonstrating against the battering he was giving them. He had heard from Drummond that some of the battalions they had decimated were already receiving replacements to start rebuilding. Drummond had also discovered that despite all of the Viet Cong reported killed in the division zone since the beginning of the year, the total number of Main Force and Regional Viet Cong in the five provinces remained unchanged. Those units Vann had not yet caught up with had increased in size and offset the numerical losses in the ones he had crippled. Worse, Drummond had learned that there were a lot more local—that is, village and hamlet—guerrillas in the region than the 10,000 they had originally estimated. He did not yet know how many more existed, but the difference was substantial. This meant that the Communists had a much wider manpower base in the Guerrilla Popular Army from which to replace their casualties in the Main Force and Regionals than Vann had thought at the beginning.

During the jeep drive from My Tho to Saigon on the morning of September 11, 1962, Vann rehearsed, with the intensity he had rehearsed his first briefings for VIPs at U.S. Army Europe headquarters in Heidelberg in 1956, how he was going to grasp Taylor's attention at the luncheon table and keep the conversation focused while he made his points. He was going to be careful not to sound alarmist to Taylor. One did not influence generals by talking like a Cassandra. They concluded that you were unprofessional. Vann could truthfully say to himself that he did not feel alarmist. He was both encouraged and worried, and he intended to convey this balance of hope and apprehension to Taylor. Once Taylor knew the truth, he would tell Kennedy the truth, and once Kennedy understood what was happening in Vietnam, he would exert the necessary pressure on Diem, and Taylor would simultaneously exert it on Harkins, and Vann's worries would end.

When he walked up the front steps of the commanding general's residence a couple of minutes before 12:30 P.M., he was the same spiffy figure in starched cotton khakis, peaked green cap, and glass-shined shoes who had reported to Porter that first day in March. His invitation was handwritten on a card embossed with a general's flag of four white stars on a field of red. The residence was a white mansion in the best quarter of Saigon, where the French dignitaries had formerly lived. It had an elegantly kept lawn and a circular drive in front. The butler was an American sergeant. The lesser servants were Vietnamese. The mansion and grounds were encircled by a high wall for privacy and security, but there was company to be had not far away at the pool and tennis courts of the Cercle Sportif, the gathering place of Saigon's foreign community and the Vietnamese upper class.

Two days after the lunch, Maxwell Taylor returned to the United States. He gave a press conference in the VIP lounge at Tan Son Nhut on the morning of his departure. He dismissed questions by some of the correspondents about reports of tension between American advisors and their Saigon counterparts.

"One has to be here personally," he said, "to sense the growing national character, the resistance of the Vietnamese people to the subversive insurgency threat. My overall impression is of a great national movement, assisted to some extent, of course, by Americans, but essentially a movement by Vietnamese to defend Vietnam against a dangerous and cruel enemy."

Vann had driven back to My Tho with his worries intact. He explained why in a summary of the luncheon discussion he wrote with a ball-point pen on the back of his invitation card before he filed it among his papers:

> Opportunity to present views to Gen Taylor as one of four advisors so selected (2 Capt's & 1 Maj & myself). Luncheon lasted 1 hr 15 min. General tenor of conversation such that Gen Harkins presented views and/or overrode key points I tried to present.

His gravest immediate worry was that although the Viet Cong were being killed in unprecedented numbers, the United States was at the same time removing the basic limit on the expansion of the guerrillas— the availability of captured weapons. The advisory mission was inadvertently equipping the Viet Cong with U.S. arms. Since the spring of 1962 the 28,000 Saigon territorials in the division zone had been turning in their bolt-action French rifles for fast-firing American weaponry as quickly as they could be trained to shoot the U.S. arms. The 10,000 Civil Guardsmen were being equipped with a full bristle of infantry weapons from M-1 rifles to machine guns and mortars. The 18,000 Self-Defense Corps militiamen were being armed more selectively but still quite handsomely with semiautomatic .30 caliber carbines, Thompson submachine guns, and the BAR, the clip-fed light machine gun. What Harkins and his staff had failed to foresee prior to ordering the program full speed ahead was that no weapons should be handed out until the little outposts garrisoned by the territorials had been dismantled and consolidated. Otherwise the Saigon territorials would serve as a conduit to channel this American arms largess to the Communists, which was exactly what was happening. The Civil Guards and the SDC were the troops most frequently ambushed, and they manned the 776 outposts in the northern Delta which were the prime targets of the guerrillas. The great majority of these outposts inherited from the French (there were about 2,500 in the whole of III Corps) were easy marks, because the masonry watchtowers, which Vann called "brick coffins," were garrisoned by half a dozen SDC and the little triangular-shaped forts of mud walls surrounded by a moat were held by no more than a reinforced squad. The elimination of most of these "VC supply points," as Vann and his advisors referred to the outposts in general, had been another of the priorities that Vann and Porter had agreed on. Vann had ordered a survey done that had entailed an inspection of every post in the zone by his province advisors. He had checked out many himself on his jeep forays. Afterward he had recommended to Cao and the province chiefs that they consolidate the 776 outposts into 216 camps of company size or larger capable of defending themselves until help could arrive. These defensible posts could then function as bases from which to patrol and initiate local operations. Cao and the province chiefs had all replied that it was impossible to eliminate the outposts, that they were symbols of the government's authority and Diem would never permit their removal. Vann had argued that they ought to tell the president it was irrational to hold on to symbols that were undermining his government, and that in addition to being militarily stupid the outpost system was cruel. Many of the militiamen kept their families in the little forts because they could not house them outside where the guerrillas could capture them and blackmail the garrison into surrendering. The dead or mangled bodies of women and children caught in the crossfire during attacks made propaganda material for the Vietnamese photographers employed by the U.S. Information Service (the U.S. Information Agency was called the U.S. Information Service overseas), but surely there were enough genuine atrocities by the guerrillas so that no one needed to generate them. Neither of Vann's arguments got him anywhere. He could see that Cao and the province chiefs had the same irrational attachment to the outposts that Diem did. The only posts dismantled were those the guerrillas overran and had the peasants tear down before they withdrew, and the province chiefs rebuilt these as fast as they could.

The Vietnamese Communists were clearly able to recruit all of the peasant guerrillas for whom they could obtain arms. Substituting newly captured automatic and semiautomatic American weapons for the previously captured French bolt-action rifles that were still the standard weapon of the regular and provincial guerrillas would also mean a manifold improvement in Viet Cong firepower. That the guerrillas were attempting such a quantum upgrading was evident in the M-1s, carbines, and Thompson submachine guns which were starting to show up in arms seized from Main Force and Regional units. If nothing was done to stop this drain of American arms through the outposts—and Harkins and his representatives were always prodding the training advisors to hand out weapons faster despite the warnings from Vann and other division senior advisors—then Vann would encounter increasingly better-armed Viet Cong in his shakily led campaign to destroy the Main Force and provincial guerrilla units. If his campaign was ever interrupted or lost momentum for some reason and the Communists were able to fully reconstitute their striking force and go on the offensive with impunity, the guerrillas would capture many more American weapons, build their strength far beyond current numbers, and become a foe more formidable than Vann cared to imagine.

There was an ugly side to this war and to his Vietnamese allies that went far beyond the everlasting problem of the Saigon troops treating their peasantry like an occupied population, stealing the chickens and ducks and rice and molesting the women. Vann had learned about beating and murder of prisoners in Korea. During the first months of that war the North Koreans had often killed Americans they captured. The American troops had taken revenge when they could. Vann had considered it stupid to beat or kill a man who might have information that one could exploit to kill or capture a lot more of the enemy if the prisoner was interrogated skillfully, but he had understood how infantrymen, angered beyond reason by combat or the loss of friends, could commit such atrocities. Nothing he had seen or heard of in Korea would have prepared him for the cultivated sadism with which the Saigon troops treated captives.

The worst offender he knew was, oddly, a brave officer, a captain of Cambodian descent named Thuong who led the division's Ranger company. Thuong's troops, the majority of whom were also ethnic Cambodians, were the one competent group of soldiers the 7th had. Thuong's position was equivalent to that of a battalion commander, because his company served the division and he was often given a second Ranger company to control on operations. The Ranger companies were designed to operate alone, but most were simply ordinary infantry companies that had been renamed Rangers and detailed to the province chiefs. Cao showed his special confidence in Thuong and his men by sending them off on their own without hesitation, which Vann could never persuade him to do with any of the division's regular companies.

Captain Thuong meant his appearance to be menacing, and it was. Ziegler, who had initially worked with Thuong's company on Ranger training and who continued occasionally to go out with him on operations, remembered how husky and relatively tall he was for a man of his race. His skin was the dark one of a Cambodian, his nose flat and wide and the lips beneath it pronounced. He wore prescription sunglasses in thick frames of black plastic and silver-colored metal. He carried his Colt .45 in a leather shoulder holster with a string of extra bullets in loops up the strap that ran across his chest. Thuong had been taught how to soldier in the French colonial paratroops long before the Americans had persuaded Diem to form Ranger companies to fight the guerrillas, and he was proud of his antecedents. The snarling tiger's face that the Americans had invented as the Ranger insignia was sewn in a patch on the left shoulder of his shirt, but on the right above his breast pocket were his French parachutist's wings. He often wore the distinctive reddish-brown camouflage fatigues of the French airborne, and he was never without the red beret or the small-brimmed forage cap of *les paras*. In a scabbard on his belt, however, Thuong carried a distinctly American weapon that was his favorite instrument. It was a Bowie knife, a heavy, fifteen-inch blade made famous in knife fighting by James Bowie, the frontiersman who was killed at the Alamo.

Ziegler made a partial list in his diary of the techniques used by Thuong and his Rangers, cataloguing a dozen. Ziegler printed the title "Strong Methods" above the list in a translation of a French euphemism for methods of torture:

1. Wrap in barbed wire.
2. Strip skin off back.
3. Rack by use of vehicle or water buffalo.

4. Head in mud—1½ minute.
5. Shoot thru ear.
6. Hook up to EE8. [EE8 was the designation of the American-supplied battery-powered field telephone. The common method was to tape the ends of two wires from the phone to the genitals of a man or to a woman's vagina and a breast. Shock was then administered as desired by turning the crank handle on the phone.]
7. Sit on entrenching tool. [The entrenching tool was the folding pack shovel the U.S. Army supplied the ARVN for use in digging foxholes. The shovel blade was thrust firmly into the ground. The prisoner was stripped of his pants and made to sit on top of the end of the shovel handle. He was then forced down on the handle.]
8. Knife strapped to back. [Thuong would tie the prisoner's hands behind his back and lash the Bowie knife to the wrists with the blade pointing inward toward the back. He would have the prisoner hauled up against a tree, place his hand on the victim's chest, and start pressing as he asked questions.]
9. Water treatment. [Water was forced into the mouth until the stomach swelled painfully, when it was beaten to induce more pain, or a wet rag was held over the nostrils while water was poured down the throat to create the sensation of suffocating.]
10. Calves beaten.
11. Knee in back, face down, dislocate shoulders.
12. Beat stomach until it collapses and indiv. vomits it out.

Ziegler penned an asterisk next to technique 11 and a matching asterisk between two photographs he had taken and Scotch-taped to the facing page of the diary. The photographs showed a Ranger first dislocating a prisoner's shoulders and then kicking him in the testicles as he lay on the ground. Three more captives, their arms bound, guarded by other Rangers, were standing by for their turn should chance not spare them. It was amazing how the prisoners kept their composure during the agony of their companion. They looked away stoically as if they had expected these soldiers to inflict a death of pain on them and seemed to be trying to summon courage for the ordeal that might begin for them in a few minutes. Whenever Ziegler attempted to stop Thuong and his Rangers, they ignored him. He felt his greatest sense of helplessness and anguish when suspected guerrillas were found in hiding places in their hamlet. The wives and children would cling to the fathers, pleading with the Rangers not to take the men away, until they were cuffed off by the soldiers. If the torment and murder then began right in front of the families, as it sometimes did, the screams and wails of the women and children unnerved Ziegler and nauseated him even more than the sight of the tortures.

Dick Ziegler had told Vann of these experiences. The Rangers were not an exception. Vann had heard similar accounts from some of his battalion advisors and the captains and lieutenants working with the Civil Guard and the SDC. He had been disturbed that prisoners reported captured had disappeared before they reached Drummond and Binh at division level. Because of his tendency to doubt what he did not witness himself, he had wondered whether these horror stories were the exaggerations of young men who had never seen war before. One night in mid-July he had gone out with Thuong's company on an ambush in Cai Lay District about seventeen miles west of My Tho. Ziegler had also gone along. There had been a good possibility of action because the region was a guerrilla stronghold where the majority of the peasantry had sympathized with the Communist cause since the French war.

At dawn a group of seven Viet Cong, thinking they were in a safe area, came walking right across the dikes of a rice field in front of the company. They were local guerrillas, young farmers in black shirts and work shorts. Thuong waited until they were less than a hundred yards away before giving the order to fire, pinned them down, and captured them by sending a platoon to circle around behind. Three were slightly wounded.

Thuong lined up the prisoners, unsheathed his Bowie knife, and began playing the game he liked best of all. He walked back and forth in front of his captives, speaking quietly to them, telling them that he wanted the truth and that he would not tolerate anyone lying to him, holding the Bowie knife in his hand, flicking the big blade in the air with a snap of his wrist. All of a sudden his dark arm shot forward. He snatched a young farmer by the hair, jerked the man's head back, and slashed with the Bowie knife. Then he resumed walking back and forth, talking softly again about telling the truth and not lying while the guerrilla who had lost to Thuong's whimsy writhed on the ground, clutching at his throat, kicking away the last spasms of his life. The rest of the prisoners began to tremble, which is what Thuong wanted. Vann had assumed that Thuong would not dare to murder prisoners in his presence. He had thought Thuong was just threatening them until Thuong slashed the first throat.

"Hey, tell him to cut that shit out," Vann yelled, so taken aback that he shouted first at Ziegler instead of at Thuong.

"That's his way of interrogating," Ziegler replied, shuddering as Thuong cut another throat.

"Goddam you," Vann screamed, leaping toward Thuong with menace in his voice this time, "I said to cut that shit out!"

Thuong quickly slit a third throat to show that he was not intimidated by Vann's screaming and turned, waved his knife at the four surviving guerrillas, and shouted back into Vann's face: "You want 'em. You take 'em." He paid no heed as Vann cursed him for a stupid, murdering bastard. He wiped the blood off the knife onto his pants leg, slid the blade back into the scabbard, and walked away.

One of the four surviving guerrillas had been shot in the leg. The pilots of a Marine helicopter that Vann summoned to evacuate the prisoners hovered just above the flooded paddy instead of landing. Because of a problem with spare parts in these early years, the pilots tried to avoid the stress on the engine of pulling the wheels out of the muck. Vann had picked up the guerrilla with the leg wound and was lifting him into the machine when the pilots tipped the aircraft sideways, tossing Vann and the Viet Cong back into the water. The guerrilla jumped up despite his injured leg, grabbed Vann, shoved him into the machine, and climbed in behind him. His three companions and Ziegler followed.

The episode compelled Vann to conclude that the other stories he had been told were not exaggerations and that torture and murder were a common practice. As an American officer he had resisted making a judgment like this about his ally. At the next general meeting of his advisors he lectured them never to discuss this filth with outsiders, but to report to him every instance they witnessed and always to try to stop it.

He confronted Cao with his conclusion and argued that Cao had to confront the problem and take disciplinary measures to demonstrate to his officers and men that he did not condone what they were doing. A soldier had to learn that he existed to uphold law and order, not to undermine it. Torture and wanton killing were not only morally corrupting, they corrupted discipline in a military organization. If a commander allowed his officers and men to fall into these vices, those like Thuong would pursue them for their own sake, for the perverse pleasure they drew from them. Everyone had to be taught the immense stupidity of these perversions. The guerrillas Thuong had killed might have been the ones with the most useful information.

Cao listened to Vann and agreed that he had to do something, but he took no disciplinary measures against Thuong or anyone else and issued no new instructions on the proper treatment of prisoners. The sole result Vann could discern was that Cao let his officers know he did not wish the Americans to see these regrettable acts. Some of the units took to committing the atrocities when they thought the advisors were not looking. Most, including Thuong and his men, carried on as usual.

Vann had reported this loathsome business to Porter and Harkins in the hope that Harkins would take action against it at the Saigon level. He had planned to keep mention of it to a minimum with Taylor, because to do otherwise could be self-defeating. A visiting general would not welcome tidings of torture and murder. There was an understandable tendency to recoil because of concern about a scandal in the press. Vann had intended to save his words for another horror that troubled him more because it was harming a lot more people. This was the indiscriminate air and artillery bombardment of peasant hamlets. The bombing and shelling were alienating the population by killing and wounding large numbers of noncombatants and destroying farm homes and livestock. Vann also had a particular reason to want to raise this issue with Taylor. He had become convinced that only someone at the top in Washington could put an end to the evil. Harkins and the senior U.S. Air Force officer in South Vietnam were part of the problem.

Porter had alerted Vann to this killing of noncombatants in a conversation shortly after Vann's arrival in March. Porter was haunted by his own first encounter with these deaths a week after he had landed in Vietnam in January. He had joined a helicopter raid out of Moc Hoa against a cluster of thatched houses on the Plain of Reeds. He had been told the place was a "Viet Cong hamlet." Shortly before the helicopters set down, the fighter-bombers made a "prestrike" to demoralize the expected guerrilla resistance. The tactic, also known as a "preliminary bombardment," was a traditional one, reemphasized in the positional fighting of the last phase of the Korean War.

When Porter jumped from the helicopter with the assault troops he did not meet any guerrillas on whom to expend the adrenaline he had built up for the attack. Instead he found the corpses of several older men and women among the houses that the napalm had set ablaze. He then heard a sound he thought he recognized amid the snapping of the burning wood and thatch. He followed it and found a baby lying in the mud, crying hysterically for his mother. Porter was unable to locate her. She was apparently dead or hiding somewhere. He had the baby flown out to an orphanage. No guerrillas were contacted in the vicinity, and there were no foxholes or other evidence that they had been in the hamlet recently. The place probably had been under Viet Cong control, because of its location in a guerrilla-dominated region and the fact that young men were nowhere to be seen. Just as obviously there had been no Viet Cong in the hamlet when the fighter-bombers had struck, or the guerrillas had been experienced enough to sidestep harm as soon as they spotted the L-19 of the forward air controller overhead. The planes had killed the people whom Porter thought he had come to South Vietnam to protect from the Communists.

Vann shared Porter's ideal of the soldier as the champion of the weak. A soldier who valued his honor and understood the purpose of his profession did not deliberately kill or wound ordinary people. His trips around the corps region prior to taking charge at the Seminary and his experience with the division taught Vann that Porter had not been exaggerating. On at least fifteen occasions during his first year in Vietnam, Vann was to see old men, women, and children killed by air and artillery bombardments. In each case their deaths were unnecessary.

Captain Binh, Drummond's counterpart, remembered an incident one day during an operation in Kien Hoa Province south of My Tho. A number of peasants had been killed in an air strike, and an elderly woman had been gravely wounded. Vann radioed for a helicopter to evacuate her to the province hospital. Binh watched him pick her up and carry her to the aircraft, cradling her in his arms and lifting her carefully into the door for the two crewmen to take her from him and lay her on a stretcher. As the pilots opened up the engine's throttle for takeoff and Vann turned and jogged out from under the rotor blades, Binh noticed that his fatigue shirt and pants were smeared with blood from the woman's wound. "That American really cares," Binh said to himself. "No Vietnamese officer would do that." He walked over to Vann to tell him that he too was sorry, but when he reached Vann they looked at each other and Binh was unable to say anything.

The willy-nilly killing and maiming enraged Vann, not only because it contradicted his ideal of his profession, but also because it struck him as the worst conceivable way to fight this war. A counterguerrilla war surely required the strictest possible controls on air and artillery. He wondered how any American could think that Vietnamese peasants who lost family members and friends and homes would not be as angry as American farmers would have been, and these Vietnamese farmers had an alternative army and government asking for their allegiance and offering them revenge.

Vann had initially found it difficult to believe the utter lack of discrimination and capriciousness with which fighter-bombers and artillery were turned loose. A single shot from a sniper was enough to stop a battalion while the captain in charge called for an air strike or an artillery barrage on the hamlet from which the sniper had fired. Vann would argue with the captain and later with Cao that it was ridiculous to let one sniper halt a whole battalion and criminal to let the sniper provoke them into smashing a hamlet. Why didn't they send a squad to maneuver around the sniper and scare him off or kill him while the battalion continued its advance? If they did that they would lose a soldier to a sniper every once in a while, but death was the risk of an infantryman's trade. People hired an army to protect them, not to blow them up.

The province and district chiefs kept their 105mm artillery pieces and large 4.2-inch mortars, the equivalent of artillery, positioned freely so that they could rotate them 360 degrees and shoot in any direction. During one of his first operations in another division area, Vann had stayed late in the command-post tent to work on some notes of the day's events and had been alone with the Vietnamese duty officer and a few enlisted men. A voice came up on the radio. The duty officer picked up the microphone and, after a brief exchange with whoever was calling, walked over to the map, checked something on it, and then returned to the radio to give a quick reply.

"What's going on?" Vann asked.

"That was the district chief. He wanted to know if we have any troops in this hamlet over here," the duty officer said, pointing at the place on the map. "He says he's got a report from an agent that VC are in the hamlet and he wants to shoot at them."

"What did you tell him?" Vann asked.

"I told him we don't have anybody out there," the duty officer replied.

"But what about the people who live in that hamlet?" Vann asked. The duty officer shrugged. Several miles away a howitzer began to sound in the night.

Vann discovered that the same practice held throughout the 7th Division zone. A province or a district chief was liable to start tossing artillery shells in any direction at any hour of the day or night. They did not even need an unverified report from a clandestine agent that yesterday or the day before some guerrillas had gathered in a neighboring hamlet. (Vann noticed that these agents, whom the province and district chiefs recruited with their secret funds and paid for each report, did not provoke shellings or air strikes on hamlets where their families lived.) The Saigon officers supplemented these agent reports with their own version of an artillery tactic called harassment and interdiction fire, or H&I as it was commonly known, which had originated in the static trench fighting of World War I. As the spirit moved them day or night, the province and district chiefs and the major ARVN unit commanders would pick out places on the map—the ford of a canal or stream, a crossing of trails, a clump of water palm jungle, any place they guessed some Viet Cong might conceivably be at that particular moment—and would shoot at these spots. No air or ground observer zeroed the guns beforehand or adjusted the shelling after it started. The gunners calculated the direction and range from the grid coordinates on the map. The fact that the firing was done by the map, without being observed and adjusted, was a small gain for the peasantry. It is difficult to shell effectively from map coordinates alone, and the copies of French Army maps that the ARVN used were so outdated that the hamlet or other target might no longer be located where the map showed it. The irrationality of shooting artillery this way also did not seem to bother the Saigon officers, because nothing was done after a puzzled Vann pointed out this failing too.

With the exception of a few men like Binh, there was no remorse when, as so frequently happened, the shells and bombs hit noncombatants instead of guerrillas. Vann had managed to persuade Cao to forgo preliminary air or artillery bombardments before helicopter landings with the argument that they gave away surprise and were unnecessary because of the shock effect of the helicopters on the guerrillas. Otherwise, all of his reasoning and pleading and cursing went for naught. Cao and the other officers would tell Vann that the victims were bad people—the families of guerrillas. The battalion commanders whom Vann shouted at for tearing up a hamlet and its inhabitants would lead him over to a tree and show him a Viet Cong flag nailed to it or a propaganda slogan on the wall of a house that was still standing. John Vann had come to Vietnam to wage war on other men, not on their mothers and fathers or on their wives and children. That these people were relatives of guerrillas, and undoubtedly did sympathize with the Viet Cong and helped them, did not strip them of their noncombatant status and make them fair game in his mind. Rather, they were people whom the Saigon government ought to be seeking to win over by fair treatment so that they would talk their sons and husbands into deserting the Communist ranks.

Cao and the other Saigon officers, Vann concluded, wanted to kill these people and destroy their homes and slaughter their livestock, not on a systematic basis, but often enough to intimidate them. Their theory of pacification apparently was to terrorize the peasants out of supporting the Viet Cong. For this reason Cao and the province and district chiefs also did nothing to stop the torture and murder. They thought it useful. Their attitude was: "We'll teach these people a lesson. We'll show them how strong and tough we are." The only coherent reply he could ever get out of Cao when they argued about the air strikes and shellings was that the planes and the artillery flaunted the power of the government and made the population respect it. Vann had also been puzzled at first as to why Cao and most of his fellow Saigon officers did not feel any guilt over this butchery and sadism. He had come to see that they regarded the peasantry as some sort of subspecies. They were not taking human life and destroying human homes. They were exterminating treacherous animals and stamping out their dens.

When Porter and Vann appealed to Harkins to stop this self-defeating slaughter, he turned out to be as dense in his own way as the Saigon commanders. Instead of using his influence to put a halt to the bombardments, he was furthering them. It had been dismaying for Vann to watch himself and Porter lose the argument.

The general came to the Delta reasonably often, on flying trips with stops for briefings at major headquarters and a couple of the province capitals. His favorite plane was one of those executive aircraft that were assigned to high-level officers, a twin-engine Beechcraft. The fuselage was painted tastefully in white and contrasting Army green. The cabin seated eight at folding desks for work or lunch and had a little coffee bar at the back. Harkins was punctilious in observing military courtesies. Porter was almost always invited along as the ranking American officer for the area. Harkins would also normally bring a senior Vietnamese officer from Saigon, and if he was visiting the 7th Division zone, Vann and Cao would be asked to join him.

As they flew across the countryside and passed over a Viet Cong-controlled area, Vann and Porter would call Harkins's attention to the marks of recognition—the ditched roads, the dirt barriers blocking the canals, the ruins of an outpost. When they stretched out the map between the seats on the plane or during the briefing at the stop ahead, Cao and the Vietnamese officer from Saigon would point to a "Viet Cong hamlet" here and a "VC arms factory" there. "We must bomb it," Cao would say.

Having heard so many complaints from Vann and Porter, Harkins would ask if the place was not filled with ordinary people.

"No, no, they are all Viet Cong," Cao would answer.

"Absolutely, all of them have been corrupted by the Communists," the officer from Saigon would add.

The moment they were alone afterward, Porter and Vann would explain to Harkins that the "Viet Cong hamlet" was just like many other peasant hamlets in the Delta. The Viet Cong occasionally used it to stay in overnight, and it had a pesky squad of local guerrillas who gave the district chief trouble. The squad would probably escape unscathed if the place was bombed. They had hideaways into which they would jump as soon as the planes appeared. The several hundred other inhabitants would not be so well prepared, and some of them might also panic and get killed out in the open. The Viet Cong taught the peasants to dig cave shelters under the sleeping platforms rural Vietnamese cover with mats of woven straw and use as beds. This expedient gave the peasants a handy shelter right inside the house, unless that house happened to be one of those set afire by the napalm or the white phosphorus, called Willy Peter in U.S. military idiom. The family inside the little cave would not have the time or the battle training to evacuate the shelter. They would be asphyxiated. As for the "VC arms factory" Cao had also put his finger on, Vann and Porter would explain that they had intelligence reports that the Viet Cong were fabricating shotguns out of galvanized pipe in that particular hamlet. The "factory" consisted of one house indistinguishable from those of the peasants. Whether it would be one of the houses hit if the hamlet was bombed was a roll of the dice.

Harkins would resist accepting what they had to say. He would look at them with disbelief when they said that Cao and the senior Saigon officer were not telling him the truth. They got the impression that the words "Viet Cong hamlet" and "VC arms factory" conjured up in his mind World War II images of a German barracks and a munitions plant. Harkins's trips out of Saigon did not extend to marching with the infantry. He therefore never saw anything to contradict these preconceived images. Nor could Vann and Porter get Harkins to agree that, as Vann summed up for Ziegler, the bombing and shelling "kills many, many more civilians than it ever does VC and as a result makes new VC." Vann and Porter would usually be overruled and the hamlets would be bombed. Harkins also did not stop the abuse of artillery. He could have forced restrictions on the Saigon officers by rationing shells.

The senior advisors to the other two divisions in the corps agreed with Porter and Vann that the bombardments were politically damaging and militarily useless. One of them was the sort of lieutenant colonel whose opinion a general customarily notes, Lt. Col. Jonathan "Fred" Ladd, forty-one, the senior advisor to the 21st ARVN Infantry Division in the southern half of the Delta. His father, the late Brig. Gen. Jesse Ladd, had been a well-liked if not prominent figure in the small officer corps of the old Regular Army, a friend and former superior of Eisenhower, and was remembered by some of the men who wore stars in the Army of 1962. Maj. Gen. William Westmoreland, one of the Army's most promising generals in the freshness of the early 1960s, had briefly served as Jesse Ladd's chief of staff when Jesse Ladd had commanded the 9th Infantry Division near the end of his career. Fred Ladd was expected to go far in the Army because of his own exceptional record. He had been an aide to Gen. Douglas MacArthur at the outset of the war in Korea, won a Distinguished Flying Cross there while working for MacArthur's chief of staff, and later served in the infantry. His captains at the 21st ARVN Division were the same high-spirited crowd as Vann's. Among them was Paul Raisig, Jr., who, years later as a colonel, was to play a major role in the reorganization of the Army.

Harkins had shown some interest in Ladd's judgment on other matters, but not on this issue of civilian casualties from artillery and air strikes. The discussions had acquired a way of ending with Harkins giving his *de facto* consent when Cao or another Saigon officer would raise the subject of a "VC arms factory" or some similar "target." The general would ask with a tone more of decision than inquiry: "Then why don't you blast it off the map?" He indicated to Porter and Vann that he was tired of hearing about civilian casualties. He did continue to listen to their complaints with civility.

Not so Brig. Gen. Rollen "Buck" Anthis, the handsome pilot who led the U.S. Air Force component of Harkins's command. The name Porter was a bad word at the headquarters of Anthis's 2nd Air Division at Tan Son Nhut. The Air Force had gained more influence than any of the other services over its Saigon counterpart and had formed what amounted to a Vietnamese-American air force with the VNAF. The Joint Air Operations Center at Tan Son Nhut, which controlled fighter-bomber missions throughout South Vietnam, was staffed and run, for all practical purposes, by American officers. General Anthis had answered Porter's first complaints by saying that Porter must be exaggerating or seeing isolated incidents. Porter had been unacceptably direct with a general officer. He had invited Anthis to come down and take a look at the corpses of the women and children his pilots were killing. Porter renewed the invitation every time Vann's harping on the issue moved him to protest to Anthis again. Anthis reacted with irritation to the first invitation and with increased hostility each time Porter renewed it. They went round and round over the same arguments. Well, perhaps some innocent people were getting hurt, but this was an inevitable tragedy of the war, Anthis would concede in the time-tested "War is hell" theme. It was not a question of *some* noncombatants, it was a question of *mostly* noncombatants, and this was not an ordinary war, Porter would counter. Porter had to be exaggerating, Anthis would say;

the commander of the VNAF and the ARVN officers he met told him that most of the casualties were guerrillas and that the bombing was hurting the Communists a great deal. He was being deceived, Porter would tell Anthis, and try to set him straight with the latest report from Vann on how the bombing was driving "these people right into the arms of the Viet Cong." Anthis would refuse to accept the possibility that his bombs could be a boon to the Communists. Porter would challenge again, if Anthis wasn't afraid of the truth, why didn't he come down and see for himself who his planes were hitting? Anthis would fall back on a legal argument. He and his people didn't initiate any of the bombings. The air strikes were all conducted at the request of the country's legal authorities—the responsible ARVN officers and the province and district chiefs.

"But you wouldn't honor the request for the strike if you thought you would kill women and kids and old folks, would you?" Porter would ask.

"No, but we don't request the strikes, the Vietnamese do," Anthis would reply. He would stay in this circle of legal absolution, refusing to budge as Porter tried to force him out of it, until he got angry enough to end the argument. He had yet to accept Porter's invitation.

Porter had enough seniority as a full colonel and a corps advisor to take on an Air Force general and get away with it. Vann did not. He was fortunate never to have had an opportunity to confront Anthis or he might not have remained at 7th Division long enough to become Harkins's star advisor. He understood what Porter was up against with Anthis. Every service wanted as big a role as possible in Vietnam as soon as Kennedy committed the United States to the war. The more the Air Force bombed, the bigger its role. If air power was restricted the way it ought to be, the Air Force would not have much to do in Vietnam. It was in Anthis's personal interest and the interest of his institution to believe that the bombing furthered the war effort, and so he believed it. Letting himself be confronted with the corpses of women and children would inhibit his ability to bomb with enthusiasm. Vann did not blame the Air Force for being the institutional creature it was. The fault lay with Harkins for not grasping the nature of the war and curbing institutional proclivities.

The bombing was worsening with each month as Anthis and his staff steadily built the power of their hybrid Vietnamese-American air force. At the end of 1961 the VNAF had owned about seventy aircraft. By September 1962, Saigon's air force had twice that number of planes, although the pilot was as likely to be an American as a Vietnamese, and the U.S. Air Force itself had more than a third again as many Farm Gate aircraft, about sixty, in the air commando squadron at Bien Hoa and other units. The number of American airmen in the country had increased apace. There had been 400 Air Force personnel in South Vietnam in December 1961. By September 1962 there were more than 2,000, bringing the U.S. Air Force contingent to a third the size of its Saigon protégé, which had about 6,500 officers and men in 1962. The subterfuges of painting the B-26s and the T-28s of Farm Gate with VNAF insignia and of keeping the correspondents off the main military airfield at Bien Hoa by claiming that it was a "Vietnamese air base" and that the Saigon government did not want them entering it had kept the growth of this American-injected air power from being as publicly noticeable as it might have been. Vann had been watching it rise in the rapidly expanding number of attack sorties (a sortie is a round-trip flight by a single aircraft) and thus the rapidly increasing tonnage of bombs, rockets, and napalm the planes were releasing on the countryside. The sorties had nearly quadrupled, from 251 in January 1962 to 985 by August, and the upward curve gave no indication of leveling off.

In predictable bureaucratic fashion, Anthis and his staff had been inventing targets to keep the growing number of planes busy. With opportunities for air strikes against positively identified groups of guerrillas limited because of the nature of the war, an expandable category of "preplanned targets" had been devised to accommodate the multiplying air raids on "known VC concentrations, headquarters, storage areas, communications and control centers, arms manufacturing facilities"—the official terminology for Cao's "Viet Cong hamlets." All buildings were called "structures" in the reports of the raids. This term removed the distinction between a hut that had been erected by the guerrillas and the home of a peasant family or, for that matter, a pigsty. At the same time the term fulfilled the bureaucratic need to demonstrate that the air strikes were achieving tangible results, i.e., "structures" blown up or burned down. The official reports naturally presented all "structures" as guerrilla "structures." By September the fighter-bombers were blasting away an average of more than a hundred "structures" a week, and as far as Vann could determine from the evidence in his area the majority of them were peasant homes.

The Rules of Engagement, the regulations governing what, where, and when the aircraft could attack, permitted the Vietnamese forward air controllers in the L-19s to decide that anyone on the ground who ran was a Viet Cong. The threatening sensation of a spotter plane buzzing them for a look caused many peasants of both sexes and varying ages to run. Few of the FACs had ever seen a guerrilla dead or alive from the proximity of the earth. The FAC would radio the fighter-bombers that he had "VC in sight" and guide them in for the kill. After the strafing runs the FAC and the fighter-bomber pilots would tally a score sheet of how many "KBAs" the planes had dispatched. The initials stood for "killed by air." Once dispatched, or reported as having been dispatched, a KBA was *ipso facto* a dead guerrilla for Harkins's head-quarters to add to the body count that was the fundamental measure of progress in the war. Vann coined a term of contempt for the forward air controllers. He called them "Killer Kings."

He and everyone else on his side could benefit from studying the Viet Cong, Vann felt. The Vietnamese Communists seemed to him cruel and ruthless. He had initially been told that they tortured and murdered prisoners with the same caprice the Saigon forces did. He had discovered this was not true, that while they were hypocritical enough to frequently violate their own doctrine forbidding torture, they were selective. The guerrillas' philosophy on prisoners was simple. They shot seriously wounded men, as Vann warned the terrified straphangers on his predawn rides to Ben Tre, because their medical facilities were limited. Un-harmed or lightly wounded prisoners were marched off and divided by interrogation into two groups: those whom the Viet Cong thought they could convert to their cause or at least neutralize, and those who they decided would always oppose them. The latter, generally officers and noncoms, were killed. These prisoners were also the ones who might be tortured before being put to death. The Viet Cong "reeducated" the other prisoners at clandestine prison camps in remote areas with in-doctrination courses that consisted of work, lectures, political study, and primitive diet. The average confinement was three to six months, after which the prisoners were released.

The guerrillas also dispensed terror with relative discrimination. They could be indiscriminate—tossing grenades into crowds watching prop-aganda films the U.S. Information Service provided the Saigon govern-ment, killing and wounding bystanders when they blew up village offices, deliberately shooting wives and children of militiamen during an attack on an outpost. The main pattern of Viet Cong terrorism, however, was the selective assassination of rural officials and active sympathizers of the regime. Again the Viet Cong were sufficiently hypocritical to often break their rule that no one was to be killed in the ways that Thuong made people die. It was "forbidden to execute the accused savagely," one typical Viet Cong directive on terror specified. All death sentences were to be "carried out correctly," that is, by shooting or beheading.

Police agents and spies, whether men or women, nevertheless ran the risk of dying from multiple stab wounds, or being beaten to death, or disemboweled. The Viet Cong were consistent in attempting to explain all killings to the population. They would pin a "death notice" to the body which listed the alleged "crimes" of the victim and stated that in the course of committing these crimes the victim had "amassed many blood debts to the people" and therefore had to be condemned. The notice would be in the name of some legal-sounding entity that was unmistakably the Viet Cong and at the same time untraceable: "The People's Court of Cai Lay District." Guerrilla propagandists would later elaborate on the reasons for the death at night meetings in the hamlets and in leaflets and local mimeographed news sheets. The Vietnamese Communists sought to convince the peasants that they, rather than the Saigon government, represented the true force of law and order. The killings were intended to look like executions, not assassinations. This main pattern of Viet Cong terrorism had the dual aim of demoralizing their Saigon opponents while simultaneously making it appear that the Communists would not harm those who did not oppose them, that they were judicious men who resorted to killing when persuasion was of no avail. The code of behavior of the guerrilla fighting men tended both to form a bond with the farmers and to give the peasants a sense of security when the Viet Cong were present. Whenever a Main Force or Regional unit stayed in a hamlet, the troops conducted themselves impeccably, never stealing or molesting the women as the Saigon soldiers did, paying for their food and helping in the rice fields.

John Vann wanted his country to denounce the cruelties of the Viet Cong but to adopt their restraint. He had urged Herb Prevost and Prevost's three captains working as air liaison officers at province capitals in the 7th Division zone to walk through the countryside on operations. As a result, Prevost and his captains had become perhaps the only Air Force officers in South Vietnam who knew "where it was necessary to have air strikes and where we were losing money," as Vann phrased his combination of principle and pragmatism. They were trying to help Vann inhibit air strikes in the northern Delta. A major and three captains were not the Air Force. The number of bombing missions they could stop without being fired was small indeed.

Vann had thought prior to the lunch with Taylor that Harkins would let him speak honestly about the bombing and shelling, even though Harkins had virtually said he considered the issue settled, and about the loss of weapons through the outposts, and about the dilemmas Vann was encountering in trying to make the ARVN fight. Vann's after-action reports had been candid to the point of irritation, bordering at times on dissent, yet Harkins had still invited him to the lunch. Vann had schemed to take advantage of the general's goodwill toward him, but he had not, of course, intended to criticize Harkins personally. He had simply assumed that Harkins felt an obligation to expose the new chairman of the Joint Chiefs of Staff to a range of views and meant the lunch to be a serious discussion, not one of those "dog and pony shows," as they were called in service parlance, which Vann put on with Cao for guided tours through My Tho.

Paul Harkins was Maxwell Taylor's man. At fifty-eight, he was only three years younger than his mentor, but he had graduated from West Point seven years behind Taylor, in the class of 1929, because he had flunked out of Boston Latin School and entered West Point late. A cavalryman and former polo player, Harkins was a tall officer with a distinctive profile. Porter, who was somewhat in awe of Harkins, thought that he resembled John Wayne. Harkins had established himself as one of Taylor's protégés soon after the death of his World War II patron, George Patton, and ever since he had been lofted upward by Taylor's rise. In December 1961, Taylor had obtained for Harkins the fourth star of a full general by urging Kennedy to name him head of the new Saigon military command that was about to be created.

By the code of the Army as Vann understood it, Harkins owed Taylor a particular forthrightness in all of their dealings. Vann had therefore been surprised when Harkins had transformed the lunch into a dog and pony show. He had been more surprised at Taylor, because Taylor had a reputation for having such an incisive mind. Taylor had allowed Harkins to pull rank and monopolize the conversation. He could have stopped Harkins and handed Vann an opening at any point merely by asking him a question and not letting Harkins interfere with the answer.

Vann had misjudged Harkins's intent in sending him the invitation. He had misjudged the extent of Taylor's curiosity about the details of the war. Vann had not been invited to the lunch in order to disturb the chairman of the Joint Chiefs of Staff with problems. He had been invited to sit at the table on September 11, 1962, as an animated exhibit for General Taylor of how General Harkins was killing Communists in Vietnam.

The following month, Vann's ability to kill Communists for General Harkins was curtailed. The trouble began on October 5, 1962, three weeks after Taylor had returned to Washington, duly impressed with progress over the year since he had helped send the United States to war in Vietnam. The division launched an operation that day into a guerrilla-dominated district near the edge of the Plain of Reeds west of My Tho to search for the Viet Cong's 514th Regional Battalion. The 514th was the home battalion for Dinh Tuong Province, of which My Tho was the capital.

The helicopter landings occurred without incident. A forty-man platoon from the division Ranger company of Captain Thuong was advancing across flooded paddies toward a suspicious hamlet. The company was one of Ziegler's probes in the larger scheme of maneuver to try to panic the guerrillas into running out into the open once more. Thuong had broken the company down into platoons to search as wide an area as he could. The hamlet in front of the platoon was a typical Delta settlement, built behind a large irrigation ditch that fed water to the rice fields. A substantial dike ran along the outer edge of the ditch to wall it off from the flooded paddies. There was a strip of trees and dense shrubbery growing on top of the dike. When the lead squad of the Ranger platoon got within about thirty yards of the dike, a fusillade crashed out. The Rangers could not see the guerrillas who were shooting them. The Viet Cong were firing from foxholes dug into the dike amid the shrubbery under the trees. The foxholes were camouflaged so that they were not visible from the rice field in front or from the spotter planes above.

The majority of the forty Rangers were killed or wounded by the initial fusillade. The guerrillas then sortied out of the tree line along the narrow little dikes that crisscrossed the paddies to finish off the platoon. Only the bravery of the American advisor to the company, Capt. James Torrence, the twenty-nine-year-old son of an Army colonel, a husky officer who had played goalkeeper on the West Point varsity lacrosse team in the class of 1955, saved the platoon from being wiped out. Thuong happened to be with another platoon that day. Torrence rallied the survivors and the wounded who could still fire a weapon behind a low paddy dike and beat back several attempts to outflank them.

Vann flew in with reinforcements right away, but other elements of the 514th Battalion in the vicinity of the hamlet supported the group who had ambushed the Rangers by shooting up the helicopters. Two of the aircraft were hit so many times while making their approach that they were forced to crash-land. One was the helicopter in which Vann was riding. His machine was torn by bursts of automatic-weapons fire that killed the U.S. Army crew chief who was manning the machine gun at the front exit and also killed or wounded most of the dozen

ARVN infantrymen aboard. Vann escaped with a nick from a fragment of metal spun through the air by a bullet. He emptied the clip in his Armalite at the guerrillas and, shouting at the few soldiers who were unhurt, got them to help him pull the wounded from the helicopter. He then had to climb back inside—a Viet Cong rifleman was trying to kill him, the bullets were ripping through the aluminum shell of the fuselage around him again—to shut down the engine because the inexperienced pilots had lost their heads and abandoned the aircraft without cutting it off. He later sent Mary Jane a clipping of the front-page story from *Pacific Stars & Stripes*, the armed forces newspaper for the Far East. "31 bullets. I was in the 1st one shot down," he scribbled next to the paragraph on the helicopters. When he reached the platoon he discovered that Torrence and six Rangers were the only men who had come through unscathed. Fourteen of the Rangers were dead and twenty others wounded. (Vann's initial recommendation to award Torrence the Bronze Star for Valor was denied because of President Kennedy's prohibition against combat decorations in 1962. It took Vann nearly three years to obtain for Torrence the medal he rightfully won that day. Torrence was to die as a lieutenant colonel, nine years after the ambush and once more working for Vann, in a helicopter crash in this same Mekong Delta.)

The fighter-bombers struck with bombs, napalm, and rockets. The guerrillas did not panic on this day. They stayed in the shelter of the foxholes until they could withdraw in good order. They used other tree lines for concealment along their route of retreat. They carried their dead and wounded with them and picked up the expended cartridges around the foxholes so that they could reload the brass cases with fresh powder and bullets.

Their performance seemed ominous to Vann. Some of the Viet Cong leaders were teaching their troops not to let fear overcome judgment, to maneuver, and to take advantage of the terrain. The time of easy killing was coming to an end. The 7th Division would have to begin to fight an infantry war. David Halberstam, who had just arrived in Vietnam as the correspondent for the *New York Times*, had been with a division battalion close enough to hear the shooting and to see the planes dive-bombing. Back at the Seminary that night Vann explained to him that the engagement showed how the guerrillas were learning to reduce the advantage American technology gave to the Saigon side. The most recent deserters from the Viet Cong had said the officers were stressing that if every man took the helicopters under fire, they could knock them down. The officers had made their point. The rank-and-file guerrillas would start to look at the helicopters with less awe in the future, Vann said. The incident would also raise the prestige of the Viet Cong with the peasants in the area of the battle. The peasantry called the helicopters "the great iron birds."

In all about twenty men from the division were killed in the fight and another forty wounded. The casualties were light by the measure of subsequent years of the conflict and were not grave by the standards of infantry combat in any war. They were serious in comparison to the negligible casualties the division had taken on previous operations when the guerrillas had conveniently run to the slaughterhouse.

Cao reacted better than Vann anticipated he would. He assured Vann he would not permit the incident to interrupt the pace of offensive operations. They would simply have to be "more prudent" in the future. Vann agreed on the need for caution where tree lines were concerned. From now on, every unit would have to keep skirmishers out in front to probe them. Vann told himself that Cao would learn from the incident and be less nervous the next time they got into a rough fight. He would remember that his career had survived this one. It would also be a while before the rest of the Viet Cong battalions learned to fight as well as the 514th clearly could. The massacre by the M-113s on September 18, only two and a half weeks before this ambush, would retard the learning process because it was bound to have worsened the general morale problem the guerrillas had been having.

Three days after the ambush of the Rangers a Civil Guard company in another province ran into a company of guerrillas from a Main Force battalion and suffered eighteen killed. The Civil Guards gave as good as they took and counted the bodies of eighteen Viet Cong afterward. Cao was not upset. The action had not occurred during a division operation and thus he was not responsible.

Then the calamity came. Cao suddenly called Vann to his house the next day. He was frightened. He said that he had been summoned by Diem to appear at the palace in the morning and explain the losses in both engagements. Vann had him briefed that night by Torrence and the advisor to the Civil Guards. They prepared explanations that Cao rehearsed before he flew up to Saigon at daybreak. Vann assumed that Cao would be able to defend himself adequately. The ambush had been the sort of lesson that soldiers have to learn the hard way in war. Cao had done nothing for which Diem could reproach him in the case of the Civil Guards.

Cao told Vann afterward that he never had an opportunity to explain. He arrived in the anteroom outside the president's office before Diem's first appointment. An aide told him to wait. He sat. Others came to see the president and departed. Cao was left to sit. He sat all day. No one offered him lunch. Late in the afternoon the aide beckoned him into the presence of the man Cao called "my king."

Diem was capable of a discussion when he thought one was to his advantage. He was famous for his monologues. He used the technique on subordinates who caused him problems and on American officials who might ask him unwelcome questions. He talked for hours, ignoring any attempt by his captive to interrupt. All the while he chain-smoked a local imitation of Gauloises Bleues, a pungent French cigarette. In this way he could not be contradicted. The experience was so painful that the victims were eager to describe it to others, which was how he had acquired a reputation for these performances. Cao got the monologue treatment. He was told that he was listening to his American advisors too much and was taking too many risks on offensive operations. These were resulting in too many casualties. If he wanted to be promoted to general and to be given command of a corps, as he had been informed might happen, he would have to show more caution. He was dismissed with no supper.

Cao put an end to Vann's elaborately contrived system of joint planning after he returned to My Tho. He no longer had any interest in Ziegler's talents or the folderol of the command briefings he had enjoyed so much. He resumed the planning of all operations himself, down to the minor details. Vann did not see the plans until they had been completed. Cao planned so prudently that during the next fourteen operations from mid-October through most of December only three of his soldiers were killed and the reports indicated that these three died accidentally from "friendly fire." He put intelligence to a purpose that Vann and Drummond had not foreseen when they had taken such pains to develop a professional system for him. He used the information to go where there were no guerrillas. As further insurance, he planned an easily perceived opening in his scheme of maneuver through which the guerrillas could escape in case any should unexpectedly happen to be in the area. Sandy Faust dubbed it "the gap." There was the potential problem of enemy casualties. Cao solved that by inventing even larger kills from air strikes than he had in the past.

At last Vann understood why Cao had always refused to commit the reserve to trap and annihilate a whole battalion of guerrillas. Cao knew that once the guerrillas were trapped, they might well attack straight into the reserve or turn and try to burst through whichever side of the box was nearest to them in their desperation to escape. There would

be fighting at close quarters. A battalion of the best troops the Communists had would die or be captured, because if the reserve buckled
under the assault, Cao and Vann could always reinforce with more
troops, which the Communists could not do. Cao would also take casualties. If he took casualties he would get into trouble with Diem. He
would not be promoted and he might be dismissed. Once the helicopters
and the armored personnel carriers had terrified the Viet Cong and the
fighter-bombers had stacked up a few cords of bodies for him, he was
no longer interested in taking risks. He had a fine score, and that was
all he needed to look good and get promoted. The order telling the
reserve not to advance on July 20 had come from Cao, not the regimental
commander. He had instructed the regimental commander to issue it in
order to hide its origin from Vann. There had been an explanation for
his baffling attitude, as there was for so many things the Vietnamese
did that the Americans thought were the offspring of stupidity, ignorance, or that inscrutable something called the "Oriental mind."

Vann probed further and discovered that Diem had long ago secretly
issued a verbal order to Cao and his other commanders not to conduct
offensive operations that resulted in serious casualties, particularly to
the regular army, as had occurred on October 5 with the Rangers. Vann
did not yet know enough about the history of the regime to discern the
specific reasons for the order. The explanation, it would turn out, was
again not an especially complicated one.

Diem and his family believed that casualties suffered on offensive
operations against the Viet Cong had been a major cause of the abortive
coup d'état in November 1960. The Ngo Dinhs were convinced that the
ARVN paratroop officers who had led the attempt had plotted with
oppositionist politicians because they had been disgruntled over these
losses. Actually, the paratroop officers had concluded, as had the politicians, that the Ngo Dinhs were creating the conditions that caused
the Communists to thrive. They had also been disgusted at seeing the
lives of their fellow officers and troops wasted by men like Cao whom
the president and his family had promoted to senior command positions.
The Ngo Dinhs had never investigated sufficiently to learn the real
reasons for the 1960 coup, and they could not have accepted the reasons
had anyone dared to confront them with the facts. South Vietnam's
ruling family combined in their outlook the mentality of the Bourbons
of postrevolutionary France and George III, who managed to drive
thirteen colonies in America out of the British Empire. They never
learned anything, they never forgot anything, and they fervently believed that whatever they desired was innately correct and virtuous.

They did not want another attempt at a coup, and therefore they did not want the army to suffer casualties on offensive operations.

The president and his family were also unwilling to commit the ARVN to a war because the army was the mainstay of their rule. The Americans saw the ARVN as an army with which to defend South Vietnam. The Ngo Dinhs, on the other hand, saw the ARVN primarily as a force-in-being to safeguard their regime. The first priority of the Ngo Dinhs was the survival of their rule. To hazard the ARVN in a war was to hazard their regime, and that was unthinkable. Control of the army had enabled them to crush their non-Communist opponents in the young years of the regime in the mid-1950s. They thought that even if most of the South was ultimately lost to the Communists, an intact ARVN would enable them to hold on to Saigon and the other major population centers long enough for Washington to send the U.S. Army and the Marines to rescue them. They assumed that the United States, as the preeminent power in the world, could not afford to let their anti-Communist government fall to Hanoi's guerrillas. John Stirling, the Saigon correspondent of *The Times* of London in 1962, who was, like some Englishmen, more sophisticated about these matters than the Americans, had correctly discerned the attitude of Diem and his family. "The principal export of this country," he was fond of saying, "is anti-Communism." That their attitude could prove expensive in the blood of Vietnamese was another of those thoughts that did not occur to the Ngo Dinhs. They were willing to accept casualties in defensive actions because they saw these as unavoidable to maintain the outpost system that was the substance of their rule in the countryside. Most casualties in defensive actions were also inflicted on the SDC militiamen who manned the posts. The Ngo Dinhs were not troubled by the deaths of these peasants. The stability of the regime was not affected, and the lives of the militiamen were cheap. They could be replaced by other peasant hirelings at the equivalent of $10 a month in Saigon piasters. Diem thought so little of them that he did not allow wounded militiamen to be treated in military hospitals. They had to go to the provincial hospitals, charnel houses where surgery for nonpaying cases like militiamen was crude and medicines scarce, because so much was stolen and sold by the Vietnamese doctors and staff. Infection was common from the vermin and open sewers. An intact regular army, however, was insurance for the president and his family that they would endure come what may.

Vann argued to Cao that Diem's prohibition against casualties was militarily absurd, that the Communists would win the war if the ARVN did not fight, and that it was Cao's duty to tell his president this. Vann had still not fully reckoned with Cao's capacity to rationalize whatever benefited Cao, and Vann was hoisted by his ego-building scheme. Cao transmogrified his refusal to fight into the stuff of military genius. He issued a message to his officers and men on October 31, 1962, the seventh anniversary of the organization of the division, comparing his leadership in the northern Delta to that of Vo Nguyen Giap at Dien Bien Phu. Giap suffered by the comparison. "In the Dien Bien Phu battle of 1954, the tactics employed by Vo Nguyen Giap were so poor and so badly conceived that thousands of troops and people were killed needlessly in obtaining the victory," Cao proclaimed.

When Vann told Porter and Harkins of Diem's secret order, and Harkins went to Diem to ask if he had issued it, Diem was prepared for him. He had heard arguments from the Americans before about aggressiveness. It was the American philosophy. Diem had convinced himself it was a poor approach. He refused to accept the proposition that he had a choice of risking his army or seeing the Communists win the war. He considered airplanes and artillery more effective instruments against guerrillas than infantry. The fact that none of his officers ever repeated the American argument to him strengthened his conviction. (Those who privately agreed with the advisors did not, of course, dare to say so.) He was also convinced that he had already started to win the war with a wise strategy that was in accord with the ideas he and his family had on how to rule the peasantry. He was gaining control over the peasants by herding them into "strategic hamlets." Thousands of these fortified places, surrounded by barbed-wire fences, were being built in the countryside. The Americans were financing this national pacification program and supplying the barbed wire and other materials. Diem thought that he was separating the peasants from the Communists, drying up the sea in which the guerrilla fish of Mao Tse-tung's metaphor swam. With the Strategic Hamlet Program well launched, there was no need to seek out infantry battles.

Their relationship with the Americans was the one area in which Diem and his family had learned new lessons in craftiness. They did not hesitate to disagree with the Americans if they saw that confrontation was to their advantage. They had discovered that the Americans were susceptible to verbal bullying and blackmail. They had also found that frequently the best way to handle the American ambassadors and generals and senior CIA agents was to agree with them, to tell them what they wanted to hear, even if it was a lie. The Ngo Dinhs had learned that these important Americans would more often than not go away content, report what they had been told to Washington, and not inquire to see if it was the truth.

When Harkins asked Diem if it was true that he had ordered his officers not to take casualties, Diem lied. It certainly was not true, Diem said. On the contrary, he had lectured the ARVN commanders and his province chiefs to be aggressive. He had ordered them to attack the Viet Cong without hesitation wherever they could be found. Harkins did not question Diem further. He began to accept Cao's faked body counts and to pass these reports of Communist losses on to Washington with no warnings attached. Vann asked Porter for permission to deny Cao the use of American helicopters to try to put a halt to these farcical operations. Porter told him that Harkins forbade it.

The relationship between the manipulated and the manipulator is a two-way exchange. Vann had thought that he was manipulating Cao, but Cao had gotten his way. Two American presidents, Eisenhower and Kennedy, had sent men of high reputation to Saigon to manipulate the Ngo Dinhs in the interest of the United States and the Ngo Dinhs had gotten their way.

Through November and December, Vann watched the Communist-led guerrillas overrun more outposts, seize more modern American weapons, and build their battalions in the northern Mekong Delta. He got nowhere with Cao or Harkins. Vann became a frustrated and angry man. He had made the same mistake with Cao that his hero, Lansdale, had made with Diem at the commencement of this venture that had brought Vann to South Vietnam.

BOOK TWO

ANTECEDENTS TO A CONFRONTATION

LOOK, THEY STEPPED all over my shoes," Diem said with wonder on the return plane ride to Saigon, staring down at his scuffed and dusty shoes, which had been a lustrous black at the outset of the day. He had been reluctant to go, content to govern from his office in the palace. Now he was glad that he had listened to Lansdale and the Americans around Lansdale. Everet Bumgardner, a Virginian like Vann from the small town of Woodstock on the western edge of the Shenandoah Valley, began working his trade of propaganda and psychological warfare in Vietnam in the mid-1950s as a photojournalist for the U.S. Information Service. He remembered how enthusiastic he and the other Americans on the plane had been after this trip, one of the first visits by Diem in 1955 to what had been a Communist-controlled area, a "liberated zone" in the language of the guerrillas. They had flown up to the small port of Tuy Hoa on the Central Coast that morning. The French had always been unwilling to spare the manpower necessary to permanently occupy Tuy Hoa and the rice-farming hamlets in the valley leading into the mountains behind it. Ho Chi Minh's Viet Minh guerrillas had held the region undisturbed, except for occasional French forays, during the nine years of the first war. The guerrillas had only recently withdrawn, marching up the coast to the larger port of Qui Nhon, where they had boarded Polish and Russian ships to redeploy north of the 17th Parallel as agreed to at Geneva.

The CIA pilots had to put the old twin-engine C-46 down in an open field. The Viet Minh had destroyed the local airstrip. As soon as the plane stopped, a mass of peasants rushed to it, jostling around it so wildly that Bumgardner was afraid some of them might be killed by the propellers before the pilots could shut off the engines. When Diem emerged, the peasants overwhelmed his guards and almost trampled this short, plump figure dressed in the correct attire for senior officials—a white linen suit and a black tie. In their eagerness to see him and to touch his hand, some of the peasants accidentally stepped on his shod feet with their bare ones, imprinting the evidence of this frenzied welcome which he was now regarding in happy amazement.

Although Diem's brother and chief political advisor, Ngo Dinh Nhu, had sent organizers to Tuy Hoa several days earlier to arrange a reception, no one in Saigon had expected anything like this. The drive into town was an unfolding cheer of more peasants and townsfolk. The children and the young people waved miniature paper replicas of the flag of Diem's Saigon government—a yellow banner with three horizontal red stripes across the center. Bumgardner was unable to make an accurate estimate of the crowd at the town soccer field where Diem spoke because the people were jammed into a mass that extended back from the small speaker's stand set up for Diem at one end. There were at least 50,000 and possibly 100,000 persons. The size of the crowd astonished Bumgardner. Diem gave a speech on the evils of Communism and attacked Ho and the Viet Minh as puppets of the Russians and the Chinese. He accused Ho of seeking to destroy Vietnamese traditions and to impose an atheistic tyranny on the country. The stilted tones of his Hue accent did not seem to hinder his ability to communicate. The crowd shouted its approval and applauded each time he paused after making a point. Bumgardner photographed the enthusiastic faces and took notes for a story to accompany the pictures in *Free World*, a magazine published and distributed free by USIS in special editions in Vietnamese and the languages of the other non-Communist countries of Asia. USIS also made his photographs and stories available to friendly newspaper editors in Vietnam and elsewhere round the world.

Listening to Diem marvel at his reception while riding back on the plane, Bumgardner decided that the peasants and townspeople were overjoyed to be freed from the oppression of Communism and welcomed this man as their liberator. He was convinced that he and other Americans in Vietnam would be able to promote Diem into a national hero to compete with the leader of the other side. Lansdale intended to turn Diem into another Ramón Magsaysay, the Filipino paragon of an anti-Communist and progressive Asian leader, and to transform South Vietnam into another Philippines of the mid-1950s, the model of the kind of working democracy the American empire preferred to foster in Asia.

The men who ran the American imperial system—men like Dean Acheson, who had been Truman's principal secretary of state, and the Dulles brothers in the Eisenhower administration, John Foster at the

State Department and Allen at the CIA—were not naive enough to think they could export democracy to every nation on earth. The United States had established democratic governments in occupied West Germany and Japan and in its former colony of the Philippines. If American statesmen saw a choice and high strategy did not rule otherwise, they favored a democratic state or a reformist-minded dictatorship. Their high strategy was to organize the entire non-Communist world into a network of countries allied with or dependent on the United States. They wanted a tranquil array of nations protected by American military power, recognizing American leadership in international affairs, and integrated into an economic order where the dollar was the main currency of exchange and American business was preeminent.

The United States did not seek colonies as such. Having overt colonies was not acceptable to the American political conscience. Americans were convinced that their imperial system did not victimize foreign peoples. "Enlightened self-interest" was the sole national egotism to which Americans would admit. The fashionable political commentators of the day intended more than a mere harkening back to the imperial grandeur of Britain and Rome when they minted the term "Pax Americana." Americans perceived their order as a new and benevolent form of international guidance. It was thought to be neither exploitative, like the nineteenth-century-style colonialism of the European empires, nor destructive of personal freedom and other worthy human values, like the totalitarianism of the Soviet Union and China and their Communist allies. Instead of formal colonies, the United States sought local governments amenable to American wishes and, where possible, subject to indirect control from behind the scenes. Washington wanted native regimes that would act as surrogates for American power. The goal was to achieve the sway over allies and dependencies which every imperial nation needs to work its will in world affairs without the structure of old-fashioned colonialism.

Communists and other radicals claimed that this American imperial system was a more insidious form of colonialism than the old European variety. They termed it "neocolonialism." Most Americans of the 1950s and early '60s were untroubled by the accusation. They viewed the Communists as the true practitioners of neocolonialism. Communist leaders, especially Asian Communists, were, by American definition, traitors to their homelands. They were converts to the alien European philosophy of Marxism-Leninism and agents of foreign—i.e., Soviet—power. Lansdale likened Ho to Benedict Arnold, the great traitor of the American Revolution. "The tragedy of Vietnam's revolutionar for independence was that her 'Benedict Arnold' was successful," he wrote. "Ho Chi Minh, helped by . . . a small cadre of disciplined Party members trained by the Chinese and the Russians, secretly changed the goals of the struggle. Instead of a war for independence against the French colonial power, it became a war to defeat the French and put Vietnam within the neocolonial Communist empire."

Viewed from the American imperial perspective, the Philippines of 1954 was the best of surrogates. The islands had been an American colony until 1946, when the Philippines had celebrated its independence day. In exchange for the grant of independence, the United States had received a ninety-nine-year lease on twenty-three military bases, including the important naval station at Subic Bay and Clark Air Base. The Philippines military and intelligence services continued to function as auxiliaries to the American ones; the Filipino government was more anti-Communist in its foreign policy than the Dulles brothers; and the islands provided a source of trained manpower for the United States to use in fighting Communist movements elsewhere in Asia.

The achievement in the Philippines had been in jeopardy a few years before. Nourished by peasant discontent with landlordism and by resentment in the countryside and the cities against a corrupt and reactionary central government, the Communist-led Hukbalahap rebellion had grown to formidable proportions by the end of 1949. The Huks were able to field about 15,000 guerrillas and to claim another million sympathizers. The most important section of their politburo operated clandestinely right in Manila; mayors and police chiefs all over the main island of Luzon were in collusion with the Huks out of fear or genuine sympathy; the Philippines Army and Constabulary were ineffective; and elections were a jest of fraud and intimidation which lent logic to the Huk slogan that the way to change the government was with bullets, not ballots. The Huks predicted that they would win control of the Philippines within two years.

It was a time of crisis when men's reputations were made or broken. Lansdale made his. He was the catalyst and the behind-the-scenes manager of the rescue operation. He recognized in Ramón Magsaysay precisely the kind of honest and charismatic leader needed to rally those Filipinos who did not want a Communist government, but who were now leaderless and adrift. The son of a farmer and blacksmith who was also a teacher, Magsaysay had started World War II running a bunch of buses as makeshift transport for the American and Filipino defenders of Bataan and had finished it commanding thousands of guerrillas against the Japanese. In 1950, when the job was hardly a sought-after one with the Huk rebellion at its height, he had resigned his seat in the Philippines House of Representatives to accept appointment as secretary of defense. He was an extrovert with abundant if frequently ill-directed energy, an inquisitive mind that also tended to run off in tangents, and a social conscience. He needed a brain trust to organize him.

Lansdale became the brain trust. He had developed some practical ideas on how to suppress the rebellion from a previous tour in the islands as an Air Force intelligence officer assigned to study the Huks. He had returned to the Philippines on detail to the CIA. An affable man who made friends easily, Lansdale was soon sufficiently close to the new secretary of defense to persuade Magsaysay to share his house in the American military compound so that they could spend evenings sorting out Magsaysay's problems. They made a superb team. The Huks suffered the consequences in a brilliantly led counterrevolution. With Lansdale to coach him, Magsaysay created an excellent intelligence service and reformed the army and the paramilitary constabulary into disciplined organizations with esprit and a sense of mission. He fired lazy and corrupt officers and promoted those who could lead and fight and who understood the importance of convincing the population that the military was their protector and not their despoiler. The troops started to treat the populace with civility and kindness rather than abuse. Civilians wounded in a crossfire received the same treatment as soldiers and constabulary men in military hospitals. Magsaysay saw to it that tenant farmers began obtaining justice in the courts. He assigned army lawyers to defend them against their landlords. Anyone in the Philippines could send a telegram to the secretary of defense for a few centavos and the complaints were acted upon. He convinced a majority of Filipinos that he and their government cared about them. He enforced the election laws and returned to Filipinos the right to change their government. He also gave the Huks a choice. They could surrender and obtain amnesty, or they could face increasingly certain imprisonment or death. By 1953 the rebellion was broken, the guerrillas reduced to small bands being swept up in police actions. Magsaysay was elected president of the Philippines the same year.

Lansdale returned to CIA headquarters in Washington as a big man. The Agency had not yet built its modernistic rival to the Pentagon among the fields and woods of Langley, Virginia, and still had its headquarters in the city across the street from the State Department in a cluster of gingerbread brick Victorian buildings with a sign at the gate reading:

"Department of the Navy, Medical Research." Lansdale became the Agency's expert on guerrilla warfare and countersubversion. He also acquired something more important in government than recognized expertise: a mystique, a reputation for being able to perform miracles.

He was sent to Vietnam amid the despair after the fall of Dien Bien Phu on May 7, 1954. At a meeting in Washington four months earlier, when it had initially been decided that he would go to Saigon, he had asked John Foster Dulles what he was to do there. "Do what you did in the Philippines," the secretary of state told him. Lansdale was given the special privilege government grants to a miracle worker. He was to cooperate with but to be independent of the U.S. ambassador and the general in charge of the military assistance group. He was to have his own team. He was to report directly to Washington through CIA channels.

The night of his arrival on June 1, 1954, the Viet Minh celebrated their victory over the French by blowing up the ammunition dump at Tan Son Nhut, "rocking Saigon throughout the night," Lansdale noted afterward in his secret account of the first year of his mission. It was not an auspicious commencement for a man who employed astrology, but Lansdale was not discouraged by the mood of "deepening gloom" he found in Saigon. By the time the French agreed to surrender the North to the Viet Minh with the conclusion of the Geneva Conference on July 21, 1954, he had decided on concrete steps to attain the goal of repeating his accomplishment in the Philippines. He was going to plant "stay-behind" resistance groups in the North to impede the ability of the Communists to govern and reconstruct their half of the country and thus delay the turning of their attention to the South. Simultaneously, he would do all he could to strengthen the position of Diem for the "nation-building" task in South Vietnam.

The CIA maneuvered Bao Dai into offering the prime ministership to Diem that June of 1954. Although the former Vietnamese emperor had retreated to the safety of the Riviera in April, he was still head of state. Diem's appointment was announced the day he landed in Saigon, July 7, 1954, five weeks after Lansdale and two weeks before the settlement at Geneva. The Eisenhower administration was in a hurry to find a Vietnamese leader whom it could trust now that American power would have to move directly into Vietnam and take over from the demoralized French. There were not many candidates from among whom to choose, and Diem seemed the best. His ardent Catholicism gave him impeccably anti-Communist credentials with Americans. Unlike most non-Communist Vietnamese politicians with whom the Americans were acquainted, he was also thought to be a nationalist who had not been tainted by collaboration with the French, since he had not served in any of Bao Dai's previous cabinets. He had impressed those American public figures whom he had met—Senator Mike Mansfield, Francis Cardinal Spellman, John Kennedy (then a first-term senator from Massachusetts), and Kennedy's influential father, Joseph. Justice William O. Douglas had been sufficiently taken with him to write in 1953 that Diem "is a hero . . . revered by the Vietnamese because he is honest and independent and stood firm against the French influence." Assessments of Diem like this one by Douglas were accepted at face value. Americans lacked the knowledge of the country necessary to gain a sophisticated perspective on Diem's background. Even if they had been inclined to inquire much about him (which they were not), there was little time for inquiry in these fear-filled months when it seemed that the Communists would pause only long enough to consolidate their hold on the North before seizing all of the South as well.

"Ev" Bumgardner recalled that the trip to Tuy Hoa was just one of many endeavors that Lansdale and those Americans helping him conceived to turn Diem into another American-style leader like Magsaysay and South Vietnam into a Philippines of the mid-1950s. Bumgardner had also arrived in the months right after Dien Bien Phu. While he was not a member of Lansdale's team, he saw a great deal of him, because the USIS staff in Vietnam was under instructions to assist Lansdale and did so enthusiastically. One could hardly miss Lansdale. He was constantly in motion—the catalyst and organizer, as he had been in the Philippines. He sometimes put on his Air Force uniform, but never one of those formal white suits with a black tie that were *de rigueur* attire for French officialdom and that Diem and the diplomats at the U.S. Embassy wore. Instead, he usually dressed in a short-sleeved sport shirt and slacks. Bumgardner noticed that the Vietnamese respected Lansdale because he cared about them, he was one of the few Americans who could speak the language of guerrilla and counterguerrilla warfare, and he was a man of action who got things done. If you wanted to know what was happening or you needed something out of the ordinary, you went to Lansdale or to one of his senior team members, like Lucien Conein, the French-born roughneck, then a CIA agent posing as an Army major. "Lou" Conein had been brought back to Indochina from Germany, where he had been running undercover agents in and out of the East European countries, to organize the stay-behind resistance network in the North. Lansdale had wanted him because Conein was the only former OSS officer still on active service who had fought against the Japanese in Indochina with a commando of French and Vietnamese colonial troops. He had formed connections among the Vietnamese who had since risen to become officers under the French. (The other OSS men in Indochina during World War II had ended up working primarily with Ho and his Viet Minh guerrillas and would have been useless to Lansdale.)

Haiphong, the main port in the North, was the first place Bumgardner encountered Lansdale. Operation Exodus, the movement to the South of 900,000 refugees, was beginning there in the summer of 1954. The migration of almost a million people from the soon-to-be Communist North was an event of the greatest significance for Diem's future and for the future of South Vietnam. Lansdale stimulated it. He propelled everyone else into concerted action. Diem had attempted to set up a refugee organization, and it had mired in committee meetings. The French and the U.S. Embassy had dawdled. Lansdale drew up a plan; got Diem, the U.S. military, and the French all working together; arranged for the Navy to provide a Seventh Fleet amphibious task force for sea evacuation (it brought down more than a third of the refugees); and had the French award Civil Air Transport, a CIA airline run by Gen. Claire Chennault from Taiwan, a profitable contract to assist in the air evacuation. CAT in turn smuggled stay-behind guerrillas and arms and ammunition into the North for Lansdale. Edward Lansdale also brought in volunteers of his own, paid by the CIA, from the Philippines. One character Bumgardner remembered well was a half-American, half-Filipino priest who ran an organization to help the refugees make their way through Viet Minh lines and then to feed them in Haiphong until they could be moved to the South. The priest dispensed counterfeit French and Viet Minh piasters to pay for their food and to bribe any susceptible guerrillas who might hinder the refugees' flight from their home villages. The Communists became sufficiently annoyed to try to assassinate the priest. His office in Haiphong had shotguns and submachine guns stacked here and there within handy reach.

Bumgardner was sent to Haiphong to produce stories and photos to demonstrate that the refugees leaving the North, in what Washington called "a convincing tribute to the Free World and an indictment of the Communists," were not all Roman Catholics. This was not easy to do, because two-thirds of the refugees, over 600,000 *were* Catholics. Most of the remaining 300,000 also had a special reason to flee. They were the families of Vietnamese officers and soldiers in the colonial armed forces; the families of colonial police and civil servants; Chinese who had Nationalist sympathies or businesses they were afraid would be seized in a Communist state; the Nung tribal minority that had sided with France; and Vietnamese who were French citizens. The Catholics had fought with the French in exchange for autonomy under their bishops in the bishoprics of Phat Diem and Bui Chu in the southeastern section of the Red River Delta. Many of them thus had reason to fear retaliation and wanted to go to a refuge governed by a coreligionist.

Lansdale took measures to see that those Catholics who were undecided had their minds made up for them. Diem flew north and conferred with the bishops. The priests began to urge their peasant parishioners to flee. One favorite sermon was that the Blessed Virgin had gone South and they had to follow her. Lansdale had his team launch a black propaganda campaign in the North to portray forthcoming conditions under Viet Minh rule as grimly as possible. His men distributed leaflets carefully forged to make it appear that they had been issued by Ho's revolutionary government, generated rumors, and passed out an almanac of the kind that was popularly sold in Vietnam. "Noted Vietnamese astrologers were hired to write predictions about coming disasters to certain Vietminh leaders and undertakings," Lansdale's secret account of his mission said. The day after distribution of an especially grim counterfeit leaflet, "refugee registration tripled," his account noted. According to one effective rumor, the Americans were going to drop atomic bombs on the Viet Minh after the Geneva deadline for evacuation from the North ran out in May 1955. Some refugees appeared in Haiphong with leaflets, purportedly printed by the Viet Minh, which showed three concentric circles of nuclear destruction imposed on a map of Hanoi.

The ships of the Seventh Fleet task force evacuated whole villages of Catholics. In all, 65 percent of the North's Catholics went South. The U.S. government contributed $93 million for their resettlement in 1955 and 1956. The exodus of Catholics provided Diem with a hard core of fanatic followers who had no place left to go. The first reliable troops he acquired to guard his palace in Saigon in September 1954 were Catholic militiamen from the North.

The work of Lansdale during the pivotal years of 1954 and 1955 proved that one man and his vision can make a difference in history. Without him the American venture in Vietnam would have foundered at the outset. Diem might have been Washington's choice in Saigon, but he could not have survived without Lansdale at his side. The French were no longer an alternative. They would not have held on in the South indefinitely with their Expeditionary Corps, regardless of the willingness of the United States to underwrite the financial aspect of the burden.

The French were emotionally exhausted, and the Arab population of Algeria, where France had nearly a million European settlers living, began to rebel in 1954, thrusting the French into a new colonial war. The likelihood is that the French would have kept the commitment they had made at Geneva to carry out the southern portion of an all-Vietnam election in July 1956. The election was to decide whether a French-sponsored government in Saigon or Ho's government in Hanoi was to rule a unified Vietnam. The final declaration of the conference carefully stated that the Geneva accords were not an agreement to permanently divide the country and that "the military demarcation line [at the 17th Parallel] is provisional and should not in any way be interpreted as constituting a political or territorial boundary." No one has ever disputed that the Communists would have won the election, either honestly or by rigging the vote more adeptly than their opponents in the South because of their superior organization and the larger population of the North. Eisenhower acknowledged in 1954 that if a free election should then be held in North and South Vietnam, Ho Chi Minh would win 80 percent of the vote as the father of the country in the eyes of most Vietnamese. (In any case there never had been, and never was to be, an honest election in either part of Vietnam.) A Communist victory in the 1956 election would have given the French a face-saving means to withdraw their Expeditionary Corps. They could have taken along their nationals and many of the Vietnamese who had sided with them. Had the 1956 election not sufficed, France would undoubtedly have found some other excuse to abandon the South. As painful as this outcome would have been, the United States would have had no alternative but to accept a unified and Communist Vietnam. Eisenhower had already decided that he was not going to send U.S. troops there to replace the French. Gen. Matthew Ridgway, the Army chief of staff, had convinced him that intervention was not practical because of the nature of the country and the political problems, that he would be ordering American soldiers into a morass. With the Korean War just over, the public mood in the United States was also keenly set against American involvement in another Asian war.

Lansdale prevented the conflict in Vietnam from ending with a total victory by Ho and his followers in 1956, or sooner had the French abdicated their role before then. South Vietnam, it can truly be said, was the creation of Edward Lansdale. He hoodwinked the pro–Bao Dai officers in the Vietnamese National Army who were about to overthrow Diem in the fall of 1954 and engineered their removal. He masterminded the campaign that began in the spring of 1955 to crush the Frenchsubsidized armies of the two religious sects, the Cao Dai and the Hoa Hao, and the troops of the Binh Xuyen organized crime society. (Originally a band of river pirates, the Binh Xuyen had purchased a franchise on the rackets in Saigon and had been given control of the police in exchange for suppressing Viet Minh terrorism in the city, a task that the Binh Xuyen had fulfilled efficiently.)

Gen. J. Lawton "Lightning Joe" Collins, the new ambassador who arrived in the fall of 1954, told Diem to proceed slowly and to compromise with the sects. Lansdale urged Diem to follow his own inclination to smash them all and to assert the authority of the central government, using bribes and trickery to neutralize some of the sect leaders and force to snuff out those who could not be bribed or tricked. Conein helped Lansdale bring the Vietnamese National Army over to Diem's side through his acquaintances among the officers. His message was simple and compelling: in the future the United States was going to pay and supply them and their troops directly, not through the French. If they wanted to keep their army and get promoted, they had better follow instructions from Lansdale and Diem, because Lansdale had the ear of the men who counted in Washington. Conein's courage and his OSS training also made him one of the more useful members of a special action group Lansdale organized to pull off "dirty tricks" on Diem's behalf during the height of the fighting with the Binh Xuyen in Saigon. From the beginning of March 1955 and on into May, Lansdale was at the palace almost every day and spent many of the nights with Diem— encouraging him, planning their moves, calling the plays with the tactical expertise that he had learned in the Huk war and that Diem lacked. Without Lansdale's guile, his intuition for the bold stroke, and the reputation he had acquired with the powerful in Washington because of the apparent miracle in the Philippines, Diem would have been swept away.

It was a near thing. Collins decided that Lansdale was a romantic visionary and Diem a crank. He flew back to Washington that April of 1955 and almost persuaded John Foster Dulles to get rid of both Lansdale and Diem and to resume cooperation with the French, who despised Diem and Lansdale and who were encouraging the sects and the Binh Xuyen to resist. Had Collins prevailed, there seems little doubt in retrospect that the French would have followed the predictable course of events and sooner or later turned the South over to the Communists. Allen Dulles took the renowned Frank Wisner, Lansdale's boss as the CIA's chief of clandestine operations, along to the meeting with Collins and his brother, John Foster. Wisner remembered the argument and later told one of his sons about it. Wisner had watched the Red Army and Stalin's secret police take over Rumania as an OSS officer in World War II. The ugliness of the experience had made him a combatant like Lansdale in the struggle against Communism.

Collins said that Lansdale was mad in claiming they could build a stable government around Diem in South Vietnam. Diem had absolutely no ability to govern and he was alienating everyone, refusing to be reasonable with the sects and to broaden his regime with other non-Communist politicians. America's best hope was to replace Diem with another non-Communist acceptable to the French and pray that he could put some kind of government together. The possibilities of success were grim, given the chaos of the South, but at least there would be some hope. With Diem and Lansdale there was none.

Wisner spoke up in Lansdale's defense. Afterward he recalled thinking just before he raised his voice that he knew next to nothing about Vietnam and little more about Asia, but Americans had succeeded elsewhere and why shouldn't they succeed in Vietnam too? He said that he had been to the Philippines, had met Magsaysay, and had seen what Lansdale had done there. The prospects in Vietnam certainly were poor: Lansdale admitted as much in his reports. There was a fighting chance nonetheless, and Lansdale had shown he had an intuition for these situations that defied everyone else. They ought to back his judgment.

John Foster Dulles did not share Wisner's faith. He sent a cable to the embassy on April 27, 1955, instructing the acting chief of mission to find another prime minister for the Saigon government. At the palace the next day, before the embassy could start putting the instructions into effect, Diem asked Lansdale about the message. He had heard about Dulles's decision from his embassy in Washington. Lansdale assured him that whatever he might have heard, Vietnam still needed a leader and the United States was behind him. He persuaded Diem to order a counterattack that afternoon against the Binh Xuyen, who had started mortaring the palace and shooting at the soldiers of the Vietnamese National Army again to try to intimidate Diem. The 2,500 troops of the organized crime society were no match for the battalions Lansdale had arrayed on Diem's side with Conein's assistance once the battle began in earnest. The Binh Xuyen in central Saigon were broken in nine hours and fled to the Chinese suburb of Cholon. With the Binh Xuyen defeated, the religious sects did not appear as formidable as before. Dulles quickly countermanded his instructions. The embassy burned his earlier cable. There were no further lapses of faith in Lansdale. The United States had made up its mind, as Dulles put it, to "take the plunge" with Diem.

In October 1955, Lansdale sealed the commitment. He helped Diem rig a plebiscite to depose Bao Dai as head of state and establish Diem as president of the new Republic of Vietnam. (The occasional rigging of an election was permissible in the just cause.) Diem won 98.2 percent of the vote, a fraction more than Ho usually claimed for himself in national elections in the North. The resistance groups that Conein helped Lansdale to plant in the North were soon discouraged or wiped out by the Viet Minh, but Lansdale accomplished his mission in the South. He consolidated the position of Diem and his family and created what seemed to be a stable central government. His achievement was to bring on the second war that Vann was sent to fight seven years later.

During a moment of clarity long afterward, Bumgardner suddenly understood how erroneously they had interpreted the reception Diem received at Tuy Hoa that day in 1955. He remembered that the crowd at the soccer field did not seem to be paying much attention to what Diem was saying when they cheered and applauded. The faces smiled, the voices shouted, but the eyes were vacant. The truth came to him. The crowd had not been listening to Diem.

The whole thing had simply been a holiday for the peasants and the townspeople. They had attended enough Viet Minh rallies during the first war to know that when the cadres in the crowd gave the signal, they were supposed to cheer and applaud. The organizers whom Diem's brother, Nhu, had sent ahead to Tuy Hoa had been in the crowd giving similar signals. The peasants responded obligingly. Diem was not well known to ordinary Vietnamese then, and these peasants and provincial townsfolk could not have had the faintest idea who he was. They were bored, extremely bored, by all the years of isolation from the outside world. They were full of joy that the war was over. The landing of a plane—a real airplane—with an exalted visitor to speak to them was a marvelous thrill and an occasion for a celebration. They would have run out and nearly trampled Diem to death had he been the prime minister of Nepal.

Many of these same peasants and townsfolk had relatives among the guerrillas who went to the North. When the second war began, the Tuy Hoa valley turned into one of the strongest guerrilla bases in the South, with a population thoroughly antagonistic to Diem's government in Saigon. Bumgardner realized how foolish it had been of him and other Americans to think that they could promote Diem into a national hero to compete with Ho Chi Minh. Diem had no following beyond the Catholics, and with his personality and political and social attitudes, he had no hope of acquiring one. His rule could only turn out to be destructive.

Lansdale was a victim in Vietnam of his success in the Philippines. Men who succeed at an enterprise of great moment often tie a snare for themselves by assuming that they have discovered some universal truth. Lansdale assumed, as much as his superiors did, that his experience in the Philippines applied to Vietnam. It did not. The Filipinos Lansdale befriended in the 1940s and '50s were a unique people, quite atypical of most Asians. Lansdale's Filipinos were brown Americans. Except for the color of their skin and other physical features, they bore about as much resemblance to the Vietnamese as Lansdale did. Their Independence Day was the Fourth of July. They spoke English with a slightly out-of-date American slang. They liked jazz and much else in American popular culture; they had national organizations like the Philippines Veterans Legion and the Jaycees; they bore names like Col. Mike Barbero, Magsaysay's first assistant for psychological warfare, who was succeeded by a Maj. Joe Crisol, both of whom worked with another Magsaysay assistant, "Frisco Johnny" San Juan. They staged operations against the Huks with code names like Four Roses, for their favorite whiskey, and Omaha, after the D-Day beachhead at Normandy. The CIA was notorious for hiring Filipinos to staff its Asian operations because they were so Americanized. Their presence in an office or a maintenance shop announced that the CIA owned the place.

What guidance Lansdale provided had no impact on forming the values and attitudes of these Filipinos of the early postwar years. He had manipulated a people whose outlook on life had already been shaped by nearly half a century of American tutelage and by the westernizing influence of more than three hundred years of Spanish colonization prior to the seizure of the islands by the United States in 1898. Almost 95 percent of the population was Christian, the great majority Roman Catholic, making the Philippines the sole Christian nation in Asia. During the war against Japan these Filipinos and the Americans of their time had formed the bond whose strength is known only to men who have faced death together in battle. There were more Filipino than American heroes in the defense of the Bataan Peninsula. (The garrison numbered 15,000 Americans and 65,000 Filipinos.) On the Bataan Death March to the prison camps afterward, three Filipinos perished for every American—2,300 Americans and 5,000 to 7,600 Filipinos. (No one knows the exact number.) When Gen. Douglas MacArthur's assault troops leaped from their landing craft into the surf of Leyte Gulf on October 20, 1944, to liberate the islands, two soldiers of the 24th Infantry Division, one an American and one a Filipino, raised the Stars and

Stripes and the red-white-blue-and-gold sunburst banner of the Philippines over Red Beach. The sight of the Stars and Stripes brought forth in Lansdale's Filipino friends the same emotions as that of their own flag. To them the star-spangled banner represented the spirit of independence and freedom from tyranny. Lansdale's Filipinos knew what they wanted to achieve. They were like eleven football players who understood how to play and had a star halfback and yet could not form themselves into a team because they lacked a coach. Lansdale became their coach, and he was a brilliant coach, but he won because his players were so suited to the game.

When Diem told Lansdale that he had resisted the French and spoke of his abhorrence of godless Communism, Lansdale let his preconceptions lead him to false assumptions, as Vann was later to do with Cao. He also thought it was perfectly all right for a Vietnamese leader to be publicly supported by the United States and to associate with high-ranking Americans. After all, he had just come from an Asian country in which the secretary of defense had shared a house in the American military compound with a CIA agent and had lost none of his political integrity as a result. Lansdale thought the Catholic refugees from the North were Vietnamese patriots who had "fought for their country's freedom from the French" until they discovered that they were being hoodwinked in a Communist conspiracy and so were fleeing south to "Free Vietnam" to create a new life of liberty there. Haiphong in the final months of their evacuation was "reminiscent of our own pioneer days," he said in his secret report. He saw nothing wrong with the United States singling out these Catholics for special assistance. He saw nothing inappropriate about having a Catholic as president of what he perceived to be a "Free Vietnam."

Roman Catholics were a tainted minority in Vietnam. Lansdale was anxious to draw a distinction between Americans and French "colonialists." What he did was to make the distinction one without a difference. His actions were now being seen in the perspective of Vietnamese, not Filipino, history. By singling out the Catholics for help, and by putting a Catholic in office in Saigon, he announced that the United States was stepping in to replace the French. Vietnamese converts to Catholicism had been used by the French as a fifth column to penetrate precolonial Vietnam and then had been rewarded by the colonizer for their collaboration. They were popularly regarded as a foreign-inspired, "un-Vietnamese" religious sect. With the French leaving, the Catholics were naturally seeking another foreign protector. They told Lansdale what they sensed he wanted to hear.

Ngo Dinh Diem did not believe in representative government, although he had learned enough about Americans during two and a half years of exile in the United States to give Lansdale the impression that he did. He was also not interested in social justice. He did not want to alter the traditional Vietnamese social structure that the French had preserved in desiccated form. Diem was a fervent reactionary, intent on founding a new family dynasty in a country where most other thinking people thought that dynasties were anachronisms. There had once been a Ngo dynasty, a brief one, in the tenth century. Diem saw himself heading a second one to replace the Nguyen dynasty that had been discredited by the degenerate Bao Dai. His family would help him to rule in the traditional dynastic manner. His concession to modernity would be to call himself a president. Diem's quarrel with the French had been an angry but narrow one, and what dimmed claim to nationalist credentials he once held was besmirched the moment he became Bao Dai's prime minister. At that moment Diem inherited Bao Dai's quisling administration and the Vietnamese element of the French colonial army, police, and civil bureaucracy, and he let the Americans make him their surrogate. The attitudes that held in the Philippines held in reverse in Vietnam. It was not patriotic in Vietnam to collaborate with the Americans. To many Vietnamese, the Americans stood for colonialism, oppression, and social injustice.

With so much of the imagery of the American Revolution in his head, Lansdale could not imagine that he could join the wrong side or become the wrong side in an Asian country in the midst of its national revolution. The strength of their American ideology also made it impossible for men like Bumgardner and Vann to accept this possibility. Yet this was precisely what had happened in Vietnam. There was a national revolution going on in Vietnam, and the United States was not part of it. America had first joined the wrong side by equipping and financing the French in their venture to reimpose colonial rule. America was now becoming the wrong side by moving directly into Vietnam to install Diem and his family as the representatives of its power.

Col. Alfred Kitts was to hold a province capital for Vann against a three-day Communist assault during the Tet 1968 Offensive. Long afterward, from the perspective of retirement on a horse farm in Pennsylvania, Kitts thought that he might not have had to fight that battle if the United States had acted differently at the very beginning. Born to a soldier's and a horseman's life, "Bud" Kitts was the son of an officer in the field artillery who was a distinguished Army equestrian, riding on the U.S.

Olympic team at both the 1932 and 1936 Olympics. Kitts had enlisted a month after graduation from high school in 1943, served in the Philippines, and then, while a first lieutenant in January 1946, had been transferred to Haiphong. There he was a member of a twenty-six-man U.S. Army team in charge of shipping home disarmed Japanese soldiers, cramming them stockyard-fashion into small Liberty Ship transports. Kitts spoke some French and was able to communicate with the Viet Minh officers whose troops were in control of the city. The Vietnamese were friendly to him and the other Americans. They did not mention Communism, only their desire for independence from France and their hope for American assistance in gaining it. This was the period when Ho Chi Minh was playing down his Communist beliefs and the leadership role of the Party in the national revolution in order to form a broad political front within the country and win acceptance and protection from the United States to prevent a French return.

Kitts watched the first French troops who entered the North come ashore at Haiphong on March 6, 1946. They looked like the U.S. Army. They were wearing American helmets, packs, ammunition belts, fatigues, and boots. The landing craft from which they unloaded were American-made, and so were their heavy weapons, vehicles, and the other equipment the United States had originally given Charles de Gaulle's Free French under the Lend-Lease Act to fight the Nazis and the Japanese.

The Viet Minh officers and troops were angered at the arrival of the French. Ho had agreed to let the French station garrisons in Haiphong, Hanoi, and the other major towns of the North only because he otherwise faced an invasion. He had received in exchange a promise of limited independence. The French had quickly begun to dishonor that promise. There were incidents of shooting almost immediately. The Vietnamese officers remained friendly to Kitts and his fellow Americans. They did not yet blame the Americans, as the Viet Minh would later do, for arming and supplying the French. They still seemed to regard Kitts and his teammates as their allies, as different from the colonialists. The Vietnamese believed the pronouncements the United States had made on why it was fighting World War II. There was also a holdover of goodwill from the alliance against the Japanese. The OSS had found the Viet Minh the only Vietnamese resistance group sufficiently well organized and widespread within Vietnam to provide good intelligence on the Japanese, to rescue American pilots, and to conduct sabotage and other behind-the-lines operations. (The colonial army survivors whom Conein's team worked with had proved mainly interested in preparing for postwar reconquest.) The OSS had parachuted a training mission to one of Ho's wartime headquarters in the rugged jungle country north of the Red River Delta and had provided thousands of carbines, submachine guns, and other weapons to arm the original Viet Minh formations.

The Vietnamese officers ordered their troops to try to distinguish Kitts's team from the large number of French in the city and not to shoot at the Americans. This became increasingly difficult for the average Viet Minh soldier, despite the U.S. Army markings and American flags on the teams' vehicles, as more French troops arrived, the French demands grew proportionately, and the shooting incidents proliferated. "How do you tell a Frenchman from an American when the Frenchman is driving the same jeep and wearing the same uniform?" Kitts said. One evening the jeep Kitts and a couple of other officers were driving back to their quarters came under fire from a Viet Minh roadblock. They managed to tumble out in time to avoid being shot, but the vehicle was mangled. The next day Kitts found the young Viet Minh captain responsible for the area. Kitts explained that he and his teammates had to drive these particular streets to and from the harbor and would the captain please ask his men to look more carefully before shooting in the future? The captain apologized and promised to alert his men once more to the route that Kitts and his companions took. He would instruct them to use more restraint and be sure they were not mistaking Americans for Frenchmen. "But my men are so eager," he said. Kitts laughed. He had no sympathy for the French. The Vietnamese captain laughed too.

By July 1946, the skirmishes had become so frequent that it was highly dangerous to keep the team in Haiphong. Kitts and his teammates were instructed to turn over responsibility for repatriating Japanese soldiers to the French and were evacuated. Three words some Vietnamese who knew English had painted on the wall of a building in the harbor stayed with Kitts down the years. The letters spelled out: "We Want America."

America did not want them. For Ho Chi Minh the years of 1945 and 1946 were a repetition of the disappointed hope and frustration he had experienced from the Americans right after World War I. Then the president of the United States had been Woodrow Wilson. This time the president was Harry Truman. Their names were different, and another war and a quarter of a century had passed, but they behaved in the same way.

When Wilson announced his Fourteen Points, Ho took the man and his proclamation seriously. Wilson said that subject peoples had a right

to self-determination and that in the settlement "of all colonial claims
. . . the interests of the populations concerned must have equal weight"
with the claim of the colonial power. The American people had joined
the peoples of Britain and France and the other Allies in this "culmi-
nating and final war for human liberty," Wilson declared, because the
Allied Powers stood for the "evident principle" that ran throughout his
Fourteen Points: "It is the principle of justice to all peoples and nationalities and their right to live on equal terms of liberty and safety
with one another, whether they be strong or weak." The League of
Nations that he was founding would perpetuate this just treatment of
all peoples, Wilson said.

Ho was sufficiently impressed to spend some of the sparse wages he
earned painting fake Chinese antiques and retouching photographs in
a Paris studio to rent a set of formal attire and present himself at the
Paris Peace Conference, where Wilson and the other Allied statesmen
were negotiating the Treaty of Versailles and the Covenant of the
League of Nations the treaty contained. In the Paris of the day, he was
a ridiculous figure, this twenty-eight-year-old Vietnamese with the oddly
intense eyes aping a European gentleman in white tie and tails. Ho
carried with him a petition he had drawn up listing the grievances of
the Vietnamese against the French colonial regime. He had also mim-
icked Wilson in his petition by organizing it into an eight-point program
that would give the Vietnamese an opportunity to recover from the
wrongs done them in an autonomous state within the French empire.
He was not asking for independence, just autonomy. No one from the
American delegation or any of the other Allied delegations would receive him. Ho discovered that Wilson's self-determination applied only
to the Czechs and Poles and other white peoples of Eastern Europe
who had been under German and Austro-Hungarian domination, not
to the brown and yellow peoples of Asia or to the blacks of Africa.
Wilson's fifth point on "colonial claims" meant in practice the divvying
up among the victors of the German colonies in Africa and Asia.

On August 15, 1945, the day Emperor Hirohito announced the surrender of his country over Radio Tokyo, Ho began asking Truman to
make good on his wartime rhetoric and on the pronouncements of his
deceased predecessor, Franklin Roosevelt. He had the Viet Minh representative in Kunming, China, send Truman a message through the
OSS station there asking "the United States, as a champion of democracy" to make Vietnam an American protectorate "on the same status
as the Philippines for an undetermined period" before full independence. Two weeks later, on September 2, 1945, the day the Japanese

delegates were bending over a green-baize-covered table on the deck of the battleship *Missouri* to sign the documents of unconditional surrender, Ho read the Vietnamese declaration of independence and proclaimed the establishment of the Democratic Republic of Vietnam to a crowd of 500,000 people assembled in Ba Dinh Square in Hanoi. He began with words from the declaration Jefferson had written for the Thirteen Colonies: "All men are created equal . . ." In the midst of his proclamation a flight of U.S. P-38 fighter planes appeared high overhead. The curious pilots swooped down for a look. The crowd mistook the coincidence of the pass-over for an American salute to the Vietnamese nation.

There was no reply to Ho's request that the United States make Vietnam a temporary protectorate, but Truman's public words encouraged him to keep trying. The president's first major postwar foreign policy statement in a Navy Day speech on October 27, 1945, was a twelve-point declaration in the best Wilsonian tradition. "The foreign policy of the United States is based firmly on fundamental principles of righteousness and justice," Truman said. He then listed the twelve "fundamentals" of his foreign policy. Three seemed to apply directly to the Vietnamese:

—We believe in the eventual return of sovereign rights and self-government to all peoples who have been deprived of them by force.

—We believe that all peoples who are prepared for self-government should be permitted to choose their own form of government by their own freely expressed choice, without interference from any foreign source. That is true in Europe, in Asia, in Africa, as well as in the Western Hemisphere.

—We shall refuse to recognize any government imposed upon any nation by the force of any foreign power.

Ho therefore protested to Truman in another communication after the United States arranged for France to represent the Vietnamese and the Cambodian and Laotian peoples on the newly formed United Nations Advisory Commission for the Far East. France, Ho said, had lost any moral or legal claim to sovereignty over Indochina because the World War II Vichy government "had ignominiously sold Indochina to Japan and betrayed the Allies" in 1940, cooperating with the Japanese until the occupiers had decided to oust the French colonial administration and rule directly in March 1945. The Viet Minh, in contrast, had "ruthlessly fought against Japanese fascism" in alliance with the United States. Ho sent Truman and Truman's first secretary of state, James Byrnes, eleven telegrams and letters of appeal over an eighteen-month period after his establishment of a Vietnamese government in Hanoi. None was acknowledged. He made similar pleas for rescue to Clement Atlee, the new prime minister of Britain; to Generalissimo Chiang Kai-shek of Nationalist China; and to Joseph Stalin, the dictator of the Soviet Union. They also did not answer.

By September 1946, with the French Army in the North, Ho was reduced to a conversation with the first secretary of the U.S. Embassy in Paris. He was in Paris to make a last attempt at negotiating a compromise with the confident and ever more belligerent French. He offered to turn Vietnam into "a fertile field for American capital and enterprise." He hinted that he would give the United States a naval base at Cam Ranh Bay, one of the finest natural deep-water harbors in the world—where the U.S. military was to build a massive air base, port, and warehousing and maintenance complex to fight the second war in Vietnam—if only the United States would protect the Vietnamese from the French. He signed a "modus vivendi" with France on September 14, 1946, and returned to Hanoi.

In October the French reneged on the agreement by asserting control over customs inspection and the collection of revenues at Haiphong. Their intent was to discredit the sovereignty of Ho's Viet Minh government. Twenty French soldiers were killed in an ensuing dispute in November over the goods of a Chinese trader. The French general in command, Jean Etienne Valluy, decided to take advantage of the incident to teach "a severe lesson . . . and so bring the leaders of the Vietnamese to a better understanding of the situation." He had the local commander, a Colonel Debes, whom the U.S. vice-consul in Hanoi described in a report to the State Department as "notorious for graft and brutality," subject the city on November 23, 1946, to a daylong bombardment by French warships, American-supplied planes, and artillery. Six thousand Vietnamese civilians were killed. The Viet Minh studied the lesson carefully and prepared in secret their "understanding of the situation." Ho summed up, in a remark during this last year in which he reached out to the Americans, what the Vietnamese had finally been forced to conclude: "We apparently stand quite alone; we shall have to depend on ourselves."

At 8:04 P.M. on the night of December 19, 1946, Viet Minh commandos stormed the central power station in Hanoi and threw the city into darkness. The extinction of the lights in the capital was the signal for full-scale assaults on the French garrison there and those in the other cities and towns of the North and in Central Vietnam. There was no turning back now from the first war for Vietnamese independence.

Ho had been sending his letters and telegrams to a file drawer for historians. The United States had abandoned the Vietnamese and the other peoples of Indochina to the French well before he cited the American Declaration of Independence and the P-38s dipped low over Ba Dinh Square in Hanoi. The fact that Ho and his disciples were Communists had nothing to do with the original American decision. Popular history has it that the United States opposed European colonialism in Asia. The belief is a myth. The fable grew out of the Wilsonian rhetoric of Roosevelt and Truman, the private thoughts of Roosevelt, and the personal antipathy of a number of American leaders, such as Douglas MacArthur, to old-fashioned colonialism. The United States as a nation, expressing itself through its government, did not attempt to dismantle the European colonial empires in Asia at the end of World War II.

Franklin Roosevelt wanted to free the Indochinese peoples through a slow process that was to begin by placing the colony under a twenty-five-year trusteeship after the war. As late as January 1944 he remarked to Cordell Hull, his Secretary of State: "France has had the country—thirty million inhabitants for nearly one hundred years, and the people are worse off than they were at the beginning. . . . The people of Indochina are entitled to something better than that."

Churchill and much of the British Establishment could not see that the sun was setting on the lands of Rudyard Kipling. They feared that trusteeship for Indochina would undermine their hold over India and the rest of their empire, which was precisely what Roosevelt also had in mind. De Gaulle, traumatized by the defeat of 1940 and the collusion of most of the French armed forces and the middle and upper classes of France with the Nazis and the Japanese under the Vichy regime, was obsessed with his vision of restoring the glory of the French empire and continuing France's *mission civilisatrice* in Indochina. British opposition and de Gaulle's insistence persuaded Roosevelt to give up his trusteeship scheme. On January 5, 1945, he indicated to Lord Halifax, the British ambassador in Washington, that he would not object to Britain's reinstalling the French in Indochina. He simply wanted to be relieved of having to publicly approve a French reoccupation. At the Yalta Conference a month later he went another step by accepting as official policy a State Department proposal for the restoration of French rule.

After Roosevelt's death on April 12, 1945, Harry Truman facilitated the French venture of reconquest. The new president and those who advised him thought they had sufficient reason to sacrifice the Vietnamese, the Cambodians, and the Lao to French notions of the white man's burden. Although the United States was courting the assistance of the Soviet Union for the final campaign to crush Japan in April 1945, Truman and his associates already saw Russia as a future menace. W. Averell Harriman, another of the architects of the postwar foreign policy, who was then ambassador to Moscow, rushed home in a B-24 bomber specially outfitted for him as a long-range transport plane to alert Truman that they might well face a "barbarian invasion of Europe." To construct a postwar Western Europe where Soviet power would be excluded and American power firmly entrenched, Truman and his statesmen needed the cooperation of France. They wanted the use of French ports, airfields, and military bases to counter the presumed threat from Stalin's Red Army. They believed that France's nineteenth-century colonialism was probably unworkable in the postwar world. They felt morally uneasy about their connivance in its return to Indochina, and they were worried that France might be stepping into a conflict of indefinite duration and cost. Nevertheless, Truman confirmed Roosevelt's decision. In May 1945, four months before anyone could know what sort of Vietnamese government would appear in Hanoi, he permitted Georges Bidault, de Gaulle's foreign minister, to be told that the United States had never questioned, "even by implication, French sovereignty over Indochina." Truman followed FDR's inclination and let the British take the public onus for bringing back the French. They were happy to do so in the hope of stabilizing their own possessions. It was a joke among American officers in the China-Burma-India Theater that the initials of Vice Admiral Lord Louis Mountbatten's Southeast Asia Command (SEAC) stood for "Save England's Asian Colonies." This was, in fact, the command's main purpose.

Maj. Gen. Douglas Gracey arrived in Saigon on September 13, 1945, with a mixed force of Gurkhas, other Indian Army troops, and French parachutists. He freed and rearmed the French soldiers of the Vichy garrison, whom the Japanese had disarmed and imprisoned that March after four and a half years of collaboration, and ordered the Japanese to join with his forces and the French to drive the Viet Minh out of the city. The disarming of the 17,000 Japanese troops in the South was postponed for several months so that they could assist in suppressing the Vietnamese. Everything was done in the name of "restoring order." At the beginning of October, more French soldiers sailed up from Trincomalee, the Royal Navy base on Ceylon, in British transports, accompanied by the French battleship *Richelieu*, which would lend the men ashore the support of her big guns, and a destroyer aptly named to inspire confidence at such a moment, *Triomphant*. Gen. Jacques Philippe Leclerc, the liberator of Paris, flew to Saigon to take charge. He started pushing out of the city in mid-October, reinforced by the British Indian troops and the Japanese, and penetrated far enough into the Mekong Delta to seize My Tho on October 25. Can Tho, the main city in the Delta, fell at the end of the month. By the beginning of December 1945, Leclerc had 21,500 French troops in the South, including the 2nd Armored Division and its American tanks, which he had used to liberate Paris. Truman approved a British request to turn eight hundred Lend-Lease jeeps and trucks over to the French. He claimed that it would be impractical to remove them from Vietnam. The French also obtained through U.S. Lend-Lease most of the many landing craft and a number of the large warships that they deployed to Indochina to launch the reconquest. The first French aircraft carrier to bomb the Viet Minh, the *Dixmunde*, was an American vessel and her pilots flew American planes—Douglas Dauntless dive-bombers made famous by the U.S. Navy during World War II. In the fall of 1945 the U.S. Navy helped open the way for the French landing at Haiphong and the penetration of the North that Kitts was to witness in the spring of 1946. Employing Japanese minesweepers and crews for part of the work, the Navy cleared the Haiphong harbor channel of American mines that had been sown during the war to block Japanese and Vichy French shipping.

With seized German aircraft and other matériel to add to their World War II American gear, the French had enough implements of combat to carry them through 1946. Three weeks after the war of no return began in Hanoi that December, the State Department informed the French government that it could buy what arms it wished in the United States, "except in cases which appear to relate to Indochina." This meant that France could divert all of the weapons and ammunition it still held in Europe and elsewhere to Indochina and replenish stocks with new American armament. In 1947, Truman granted France a $160 million credit to buy vehicles and related equipment explicitly for Indochina. That same year the Marshall Plan began to revive France's economy with hundreds of millions of dollars in aid, making the colonial war less of a strain. The State Department classified all of Ho Chi Minh's letters and telegrams and the memorandum of his last conversation with a first secretary at the Paris embassy Top Secret and locked them away. They were not to be published until a quarter of a century later in the Pentagon Papers.

Requirements of high strategy were not the full explanation for American behavior. There were other, less seemly reasons. Yellow and brown men forgot in listening to the rhetoric of American presidents that the United States was a status quo power with a great capacity to rationalize arrangements that served its status quo interests. The emergence of the United States as the world's leading status quo power with its victory in World War II had enlarged this capacity to rationalize beyond any apparent limits. Hopeful Asians who looked to the United States for protection also did not understand that American attitudes toward them were influenced by a racism so profound that Americans usually did not realize they were applying a racist double standard in Asia. The lyrics of the World War II ditty sung on the assembly lines of America had been:

> Whistle while you work
> Hitler is a jerk
> Mussolini is a weenie,
> But the Japs are worse.

The Japs were not worse; the Germans were. The Germans were the dangerous and fiendish enemy. Japan never possessed the military potential to threaten the existence of the United States; Germany did. The urgency behind the Manhattan Project to build the atomic bomb came from the realization of the American and émigré European scientists that Hitler might be ahead in a race to construct these "superbombs" with which to give the United States and Britain the choice of surrender or annihilation. Japan's World War II technological capacity was so limited that its navy was forced to fight blind at night and in bad weather because the development of radar, let alone nuclear weapons, was beyond Japanese wartime science and industry. In contrast to the satanic planning and efficiency with which the Nazis used the facilities of an industrialized society to liquidate 12 million persons in the concentration camps (6 million Jews and an equal number of non-Jews from the occupied countries), the Japanese atrocities, however barbarous and cruel, were haphazard.

Americans feared and hated the two foes in inverse proportion to the threat each posed. The market-research pollsters in the Treasury Department discovered that advertising that relied on racist hate propaganda against the Japanese sold more war bonds than anti-German hatemongering. Their polls showed that the average American viewed Japanese as "ungodly, subhuman, beastly, sneaky, and treacherous." The war-bond drives therefore concentrated on toothy "Nips." The FBI arrested some of the more prominent American Nazis in the Bund. Otherwise, German-Americans were not disturbed, except for the heckling of neighborhood children.

After Pearl Harbor there was a wave of hysterical rumors in California and the other West Coast states, encouraged by the press and the Army, that Japanese-Americans were signaling submarines, sending secret radio transmissions to invasion fleets, caching arms, and drawing maps with which to guide the Nipponese hordes after they landed. An attempt to organize a program of voluntary resettlement inland failed because no one would have the Japanese. The reply of the governor of Idaho was typical: "The Japs live like rats, breed like rats, and act like rats. We don't want them." The Army rounded up more than 110,000 Japanese-Americans in the spring of 1942, 60,000 of whom were U.S. citizens by birth, and herded them into concentration camps in barren and arid federal reservations in the West. The governor of California tried to have them employed on their way to the camps as menial agricultural labor. The Supreme Court approved what has since been recognized as the greatest violation of civil liberties in the history of the Republic.

Not a single case of espionage or other disloyal conduct was ever discovered among Japanese-Americans. The Army had the gall to ask the Nisei of military age (Nisei is the Japanese-American term for those born in the United States) to fight. Their families still had to remain in the camps for the duration of the war. Surprisingly, 1,200 Nisei did volunteer to prove their patriotism. Others permitted themselves to be drafted without complaint. Their 442nd Regimental Combat Team, formed around a Nisei battalion recruited in Hawaii, became one of the most highly decorated regiments in the Army and won four Presidential Unit Citations for valor in Italy and France. The regimental motto, chosen by the men, was "Remember Pearl Harbor." The Army permitted them to kill Caucasian Germans, but otherwise segregated these Japanese-Americans from white men, just as it then segregated blacks.

Had the Vietnamese been white Europeans, Roosevelt and Truman would not have consigned them so readily to the tortures of colonial conquest. Human considerations would have mitigated strategic ones. Truman's high-minded warning in his October 1945 Navy Day speech that the United States would refuse to "recognize any government imposed on any nation by the force of any foreign power"—the twelve-point Wilsonian declaration that had encouraged Ho to appeal to him for protection against the French—showed that the racist double standard of the American statesman had not changed since Wilson's time. Truman's words were directed at the Soviet Union for imposing its rule on the white nations of Eastern Europe. He was upset by Soviet atrocities in Eastern Europe. There is no indication he was disturbed by the atrocities the French had been committing for a month in their campaign to reconquer the Saigon region and the Mekong Delta. Nor is there any evidence that he or anyone else in a senior position in the U.S. government became seriously upset about the greater atrocities, such as the November 1946 slaughter of 6,000 Vietnamese civilians in Haiphong, which the French were to commit during their subsequent campaign in the North.

Ho and his Communist-led Viet Minh were a happenstance that was not without some benefit to American statesmen. The emergence of Communists at the head of the Vietnamese Revolution gave the leaders of the United States a conscience-salving reason to do in Vietnam what Washington had intended to do there in any case. The men in Washington swiftly forgot the original circumstances and told themselves, to justify inflicting on the Vietnamese the sufferings of a war that was to endure for seven and a half more years, that they were preventing the spread of Soviet (soon to be Sino-Soviet) imperialism in Southeast Asia. Succeeding generations of American statesmen, who never examined the past because they too were so certain of what they wanted to do, were to tell themselves the same thing.

Ho Chi Minh and his disciples became Communists through an accident of French politics. They were mandarins, Vietnamese aristocrats, the natural leaders of a people whom foreigners have repeatedly sought and failed to conquer and pacify. There are a small number of such peoples on the earth. The Irish are one. The Vietnamese are another. The violence of their resistance forms history and legend to remind the living that they must never shame the dead.

The Vietnamese derived their precolonial system of government from China. The country was ruled by an emperor who governed through a hierarchy of mandarins. The Vietnamese emperor was a replica in miniature of the Chinese "Son of Heaven," and his mandarins were scholar-administrators who acquired their positions by demonstrating proficiency in the Confucian classics through a national examination system modeled on the Chinese one. As in China, the mandarins also developed into a class, the scholar-bureaucracy becoming a scholar-aristocracy, because landless peasants and poor farmers were unable to afford the cost of educating their sons for the examinations.

French colonialism corrupted the Vietnamese mandarin class. In order to keep their places, the majority of the mandarin families served the French, became agents of the foreigner, and lost the legitimacy of their claim to national leadership. They became socially depraved too. With its state monopolies to encourage the sale of alcohol and opium, forced-labor conditions on the rubber plantations, and other abuses, French colonialism was highly exploitive. The mandarins who collaborated had to participate daily in crimes against their own people. After a time they and their families no longer felt the sense of guilt that such atrocities would normally have aroused in them. A minority among the mandarins refused to bow their heads to the European barbarians. Their refusal brought about their humiliation and impoverishment, but it was later to be the salvation of family and country. They preserved their pride and a conviction that they were the spiritual heirs of the heroes of the Vietnamese past. They kept their place as the natural leaders of the society in the eyes of a peasantry which also retained a memory of national resistance to foreign rule. They aroused in themselves and passed on to their descendants an anger that would not be satisfied until the nation was rid of outside domination. The leadership of the Vietnamese Communist Party came chiefly from these families and from mandarin families that splintered under the ordeal of colonialism, with some members collaborating while others held true.

The family background and political journey of Ho Chi Minh were representative of the Vietnamese who became his followers. He was the youngest son of a Confucian scholar-aristocrat, born in 1890 in Nghe An, a coastal province in the northern part of Central Vietnam noted for anti-French agitation. The family was impoverished after his father, who had been a district magistrate in Binh Dinh, later a province of the South, was dismissed for nationalist activity. The political context of the colonial power inevitably influenced the politics of colonized Asians. Lansdale's Filipinos had American democracy, where elements of both major parties believed in anticolonialism, as their political model. Jawaharlal Nehru and a number of the leaders of Indian independence were British Socialists in their politics. After Ho had made his way to France and settled in Paris during World War I, he joined the French Socialist Party, because its more radical members were the only French political grouping that seriously advocated independence for the colonies.

In 1920, the French Socialist Party became entangled in one of the most important political debates of modern French history—whether to remain with the socialist parties allied under the Second International convened at Paris in 1889, or to join the far more revolutionary Third International (subsequently known as the Communist International or Comintern) that Vladimir Lenin had organized in Moscow in 1919 to rally support for the Bolshevik cause. Ho recalled in an article forty years later that he attended the initial debates, listened carefully, did not understand many of the issues, but did notice that the question of colonialism was not being argued. He therefore asked: "What I wanted most to know. . . . Which International sides with the peoples of the colonial countries?" He was told that the Third International did. That spring one of his French friends gave him a copy of Lenin's "Thesis on the National and Colonial Questions," which had been published in *L'Humanité*, later the official newspaper of the French Communist Party. He described his reaction on reading it in his scruffy hotel room:

> There were political terms difficult to understand in this thesis. But by dint of reading it again and again, finally I could grasp the main part of it. What emotion, enthusiasm, clear-sightedness, and confidence it instilled in me! I was overjoyed to tears. Though sitting alone in my room, I shouted aloud as if addressing large crowds: "Dear martyrs, compatriots! This is what we need, this is the path to our liberation!"

During future debates he was not silent. He ridiculed the opponents of Lenin with a single question: "If you do not condemn colonialism, if you do not side with the colonial people, what kind of revolution are you making?" At the Socialist Party congress at Tours in December 1920, he voted with the radicals and became a founder of the French Communist Party.

Within five years he was in Canton in southern China founding another organization that was the forerunner of the Vietnamese Communist Party—the Vietnam Revolutionary Youth League. The French Party had sent him to Moscow in the summer of 1923 as its delegate to the Congress of the Peasant International. He was elected to its executive committee and stayed on, studying Marxism-Leninism and revolutionary tactics for a year at the University of Toilers of the East. At the end of 1924 the Comintern dispatched him to Canton as an interpreter with its political and military training mission to the party of China's national revolution—Sun Yat-sen's Kuomintang, in which the Chinese Communists and Chiang Kai-shek's faction were then still allied. Shortly after his arrival he wrote an enthusiastic report saying that he had formed the first secret Communist organization in the history of Vietnam. It was the first chapter of the Youth League and consisted of himself and eight other Vietnamese in Canton, most of whom were from his home province. He traveled to Hangchow and Shanghai and other cities, talking up among Vietnamese exiles who had led abortive revolts and then fled to China the need to give the national cause better organization.

As word of his activities passed down the exile's resistance grapevine into Vietnam, young Vietnamese made their way to the house on Wenming Street in Canton where Ho established a school of revolution for his Youth League. Some found his ideas too radical. Those who accepted him and Communist economic and social concepts did so for the same reason that he had followed Lenin. Through his lessons on Leninist revolutionary strategy and tactics they heard the message he had heard— that while a Communist society was the ultimate salvation, the way to it lay through the achievement of national independence. Most of those who did find what they were seeking in Ho, either in Canton or later as his ideas spread through Vietnam, were also sons, and some daughters too, of disenfranchised scholar-gentry. One of the first to come to him in Canton was a seventeen-year-old student named Pham Van Dong, the son of a mandarin who had been chief secretary to the youthful Emperor Duy Tan. Dong's father had lost his position when the French had deposed Duy Tan at the age of eighteen and exiled him to the island of Reunion in the Indian Ocean for plotting a revolt among Vietnamese troops recruited by the French Army for World War I battlefields. Dong was to become one of Ho's closest associates, to lead the Viet Minh delegation to the Geneva Conference of 1954, and to serve as prime minister of the North. He was also to spend six of his young years on the penal island of Con Son, also known as Poulo Condore. The French had constructed a prison there of sunken cells, barred across the top, that were to become notorious during the American war as "tiger cages" when they were used to confine Viet Cong insurgents.

A proletarian political institution led by an indigenous aristocracy made the Vietnamese organization an oddity among Communist parties. Alexander Woodside, the Canadian historian whose pioneering scholarship discerned the nature of the Vietnamese leadership, invented a term for these men. He called them "Marxist mandarins." Truong Chinh, the senior theoretician of the party; Le Duc Tho, the deft negotiator whom Henry Kissinger was to meet at the table in Paris; and Vo Nguyen Giap, the great military leader of modern Vietnam and the best-known of Ho's disciples to Americans were all from scholar-gentry families. The absence of men of worker or peasant origin among the senior leadership was notable by the conspicuousness of those few who could genuinely claim it. One was Giap's friend and protégé Van Tien Dung, who was to lead a division in the war against the French and then to serve as the chief of staff of the armed forces in the North. Dung started life as a weaver at a textile mill in Hanoi. In 1963 the Party officially admitted that the majority of its members traced their parentage to "petit bourgeois elements."

The turn of this uncorrupted core of the Vietnamese aristocracy to respond to the need of their nation came on February 8, 1941, when Ho Chi Minh crossed the South China border into Vietnam after thirty years of exile. With World War II underway and the Vichy French colonial administration alienated from the Allies by its cooperation with the Japanese forces occupying Indochina, Ho had decided that the time was propitious for a successful revolt. The Central Committee of the Vietnamese Communist Party that he convened at the remote hamlet of Pac Bo in May 1941 was by now composed of canny men mature in the school of struggle. They agreed to adopt the sophisticated strategy he advocated. They toned down the Party's proposals for social revolution in order to form the broadest possible alliance with non-Communist groups and individuals in a national front organization. They named the new organization the Vietnamese Independence Brotherhood League (Viet Nam Doc Lap Dong Minh Hoi), henceforth to be known by its Vietnamese abbreviation—the Viet Minh. The task of the Viet Minh, Ho's proclamation announcing its formation said, would be to wage a war "of national salvation" and "overthrow the Japanese and French and their [Vietnamese] jackals."

Over the next four years these Communist mandarins accomplished a prodigy of revolutionary preparation. Their common heritage was one of the major reasons they were able to do so much in so short a time. It gave them a special cohesiveness and led them to reach back into their history for guidance on how to adapt Marxist-Leninist concepts to the peculiar conditions of Vietnamese society and make their revolution a Vietnamese one. Unlike many small peoples who have been victimized by large neighbors, the Vietnamese have more than martyrs to inspire them. They have historical examples of victorious resistance to foreign domination which they can imitate. They can say to themselves that if their ancestors prevailed, they will prevail too.

It took the Vietnamese a millennium of revolt and sacrifice to win their independence from China in A.D. 938. During the next near millennium, from 938 until the arrival of the French in the 1850s, every new dynasty that came to power in China invaded Vietnam. The recurrent necessity to drive out big invaders from the north, and incessant warfare with less menacing neighbors in the course of their expansion southward down the Indochinese Peninsula, lent a martial cast to Vietnamese culture. Chinese civilization, as it developed in later centuries, did not admire the soldier. China produced the intellectual who was also a man of action—the Confucian mandarin-governor. He was a figure worthy of emulation because of his learning and the ethical standards of his conduct. The warrior was regarded as an inferior human being, to be tolerated when he was necessary, but never to be admired. There was nothing intrinsically good in his art of war. This Chinese ideal underwent a mutation in Vietnamese society. The Vietnamese ideal became the intellectual and man of action who was also a great soldier, a mandarin-warrior. The Vietnamese had few gentle heroes like Lincoln. Their heroes, as a foreigner might notice after studying the porcelain figurines on shelves and tables in Vietnamese homes, were men on horseback or elephants, clad in armor, swords in hand. The same held true for their legendary women heroes, the Trung Sisters, who drowned themselves in A.D. 43 rather than submit after their rebel army was defeated by the Chinese. Physical courage was highly prized for its own sake in Vietnamese culture. Le Loi, the mandarin who overthrew two decades of Chinese domination in a nine-year war in the fifteenth century and consequently founded a new dynasty, made an observation that was often repeated: "We have been weak and we have been strong, but at no time have we lacked heroes."

The wars with the big power to the north also led the Vietnamese to elaborate a particular idea as the central concept of their military thought. The concept is that an ostensibly weaker force, properly handled, can defeat a stronger one. This idea is hardly unique to universal military thought, but in Vietnamese doctrine it became the main arch. Vietnamese military teaching emphasized historically that to bring this concept to fruition, the more powerful enemy had to be worn down by protracted warfare. The Vietnamese forces had to employ hit-and-run tactics, delaying actions, and the ravages of ambush and harassment by guerrilla bands. The enemy had to be lured into wasting his energy in the rain forests and mountains and other formidable terrain of the country, while the Vietnamese used the same terrain as shelter in which to build their strength. Finally, when the enemy was sufficiently drained and confused, he was to be finished off by sudden shock offensives delivered with flexible maneuver and maximum surprise and deception. The most famous of the early Vietnamese generals, Tran Hung Dao, used this strategy to destroy the Mongols, the warrior race that burst out of the Gobi to terrorize the world from Korea to Hungary and subdue China under Genghis Khan and Kublai Khan, when they invaded Vietnam in 1284 and again in 1287. A manual on the art of war which Tran Hung Dao wrote for the training of his officers became a Vietnamese military classic. Le Loi employed similar means to break the Ming-dynasty generals nearly 150 years later.

Another three and a half centuries passed, and the lessons were not lost. In 1789, the year of the French Revolution, the general admired by Giap and his disciple Dung as the most accomplished Vietnamese practitioner of the swift maneuver and the surprise blow smashed the last premodern invasion out of China, this one by the Manchus. Nguyen Hue, the Tay Son leader who later ruled under the imperial name Quang Trung, advanced up the central coast into the Red River Delta by a series of forced marches and violated the sanctity of Tet, the lunar New Year holiday observed by both Vietnamese and Chinese. He caught unawares and shattered a much larger Manchu army encamped near modern Hanoi. He attacked at midnight on the fifth day of the holiday, while the Manchus were sleeping off the food and wine of the day's feasting. His victory was henceforth celebrated on the fifth day of every Tet as the finest single feat of arms in the history of Vietnam.

This martial prowess and tradition of resistance to outside aggression was institutionalized in precolonial Vietnam, ingrained in the folklore and mentality of the peasantry as much as it was in the heritage of the mandarin class. Colonies of soldier-farmers were an important element in the Vietnamese expansion south from the Red River Delta and the settlement by conquest of Central Vietnam and the Mekong Delta. This other victorious epic of Vietnamese history, the "Southward Advance" (Nam Tien), took place over a period of more than 450 years, from the beginning of the fourteenth until late in the eighteenth century. The ancestor worship that Vietnamese peasants practiced along with animism and Buddhism included cults devoted to the spirits of famed mandarin-warriors. Temples dedicated to these heroes were common in the village centers, and the performance of the worship rites was part of the cycle of peasant life. An office in the hero cult was one of the most prestigious positions a farmer could hold in the village. The Vietnamese peasant might appear submissive to a foreigner watching him bent over in a rice paddy. The foreigner mistook restraint and work discipline for submissiveness. Once enthused with a cause and trained, the Vietnamese peasant was a formidable combatant, and not much was required to turn him into a soldier. His farmer's life fitted him to endure the rigors of campaigning, and the group discipline necessary for the cultivation of irrigated rice fields prepared him for the group discipline of the battlefield. He was tenacious and cunning in combat, and he was driven by the value his culture placed on physical courage to demonstrate his bravery if he wanted respect from his comrades.

The French could overwhelm this people in the nineteenth century with superior European organization and modern technology and weapons at a time when Vietnamese civilization, like its Chinese parent, was stagnant. They could not erase the history of the Vietnamese. The rebellions, one after another, were the evidence that the French had never broken the will of this people. The symbols and patterns of the past were waiting for the moment when a new generation of Tran Hung Daos and Le Lois and Nguyen Hues could recall them to life and use them to rouse the nation.

Once Ho Chi Minh and his followers began to rejuvenate the past and relate it in a meaningful way to the present, the scenes and figures of the French colonial period and those of the revolutionary war to come took on a different but familiar perspective to many Vietnamese. Those scenes and figures had all occurred before in Vietnamese history. Vietnamese could begin to cope with what they saw because their past told them what it was and what to do about it. The French were not a superior European race. The French were just another foreign invader who could be destroyed. The mandarins who collaborated with the French and the sundry lesser social types who had risen to positions of power by service to the colonial regime were no longer privileged people whose authority had to be obeyed. They were the same "jackals," as Ho called them in his proclamation of the Viet Minh, who had been the pawns of the invaders from China. There had always been mandarins willing to become the native henchmen of foreign aggressors out of venality, or because they belonged to dissident factions, or because they thought that the conquest would endure and they had best accept it and find places in the new order for themselves and their families. Vietnamese history was full of such "traitors and country-sellers," to cite two other favorite epithets the Communists adopted. The peasants and lower-class men from the towns and cities who tortured and killed their countrymen for the French in the colonial police, militia, and army were also figures with a precedent. The Chinese had recruited Vietnamese "puppet troops" to supplement their forces. In lands like China and Vietnam such men could always be hired out of the mass. The atmosphere of vice, petty intrigue, and mustiness at the court in Hue of Bao Dai and his high mandarins was the classic symptom of a decayed dynasty that could no longer safeguard the country and had to be swept away by patriotic mandarin-warriors.

Working out of the clammy rain forests and mountains of the borderlands below China, these men expanded the Viet Minh during World War II into the nearest thing Vietnam had to a national movement. Ho named the extension of the movement into the rice farming villages of the Red River Delta "Southward Advance" to recall the epic migration. The mountain bases bore the names of Le Loi, Quang Trung, and other spirits of resistance. By the end of 1944, the Viet Minh were able to claim half a million adherents, three-quarters of them in North and Central Vietnam. These half million were directed by a Vietnamese Communist Party of no more than 5,000 members. The appeal was always to nationalism and to tactical social grievances that would arouse the peasantry, but not frighten off those rich farmers and landlords who were patriotic.

The Japanese correctly judged in the spring of 1945 that the Vichy French were about to turn coat on them and become "Free French" now that Japan was losing the war. The ensuing *coup de force* loosed by the Imperial Army throughout Indochina at 9:30 P.M. on March 9, 1945, accomplished more than the dissolution of the colonial administration and the disarming of the French troops. The Japanese administered a deathblow to French colonialism in Indochina. The awe in which many ordinary Vietnamese held their European masters was dispelled by the sight of them being shot and beaten and hauled off to prison camps and their women raped by a race of short yellow men. The hold of central authority over the countryside suddenly vanished at a time when the rural areas of the North were afflicted with the worst famine in memory, a hunger in which 400,000 to 2 million peasant men, women, and children starved to death between late 1944 and the spring and early summer of 1945. (The number of deaths cannot be more accurately determined because there was no administration capable of keeping statistics after March 1945. The Japanese made no attempt to substitute themselves for the French in the countryside and kept mainly to the cities and towns.) The famine resulted from the seizure of rice by the French, beginning in 1943 at the behest of the Japanese, to burn as fuel in Indochinese factories serving the Imperial Army and to ship to Japan as food. The tenant farmers, who made up the majority of the peasantry in the North, were first bankrupted by the seizures and then forced into starvation because they could neither buy seed to plant new rice nor buy food for their families. The seizures were carried out by the lowest level of French authority—the Vietnamese village and canton chiefs (a canton consists of several villages)—backed by the colonial militia. In a fascinating example of the moral corruption wrought by colonialism, these Vietnamese officials continued to seize rice for the foreigner right up until the Japanese *coup de force*, even though their own people were dying around them.

By the time the guerrilla formations Vo Nguyen Giap had newly organized moved into this rural world bereft of central authority, the peasants had been driven into a paroxysm of desperation and hatred by the famine. The Viet Minh made "Destroy the Paddy Granaries and Solve the Famine" a rallying cry of equal importance with "National Independence." (Paddy is unhusked rice; when harvested in large quantities it is stored in granaries until it can be sent to a mill for processing.) The guerrillas demolished the granaries of landlords and rural agents of the French and Japanese and distributed the rice to the starving. The hungry and landless then helped them to depose or arrest village and canton chiefs and to substitute as the governing authority local Viet Minh "People's Committees" whose writ was enforced by "Self-Defense" units of peasants armed with knives, scythes, reaping hooks, and any other handy weapons. When the surrender of Japan was announced on August 15, 1945, Giap had more than 5,000 men under arms, most of them equipped with American weapons provided by the OSS, and the famine had enabled the Viet Minh to win the unquestioning allegiance of the majority of the peasantry in the North and in the upper provinces of Central Vietnam.

The climax came in a torrent. Two days after the Radio Tokyo broadcast, the Viet Minh "Uprising Committee" in Hanoi unfurled the flag of the revolution, a five-pointed gold star centered on a field of red, at a rally called at the municipal theater by Vietnamese colonial civil servants to express support for a puppet regime the Japanese had set up under Bao Dai. No sooner had a civil servant read the agenda for the rally than Viet Minh flags appeared all over the packed theater, including one above the speaker's rostrum. A Viet Minh agitator, backed by others with drawn pistols, grabbed the microphone and called on Vietnamese to revolt and "win back our ancestral land." The militia protecting the theater defected and the rally was transformed into a tumultuous pro–Viet Minh demonstration and parade through the streets which lasted well into the night. Thousands of peasants were marched into the city from the surrounding countryside over the next couple of days. Bao Dai's viceroy fled. The garrison of the Garde Indigène was seized and the weapons in its arsenal distributed among the insurgents. The 30,000-man Japanese garrison in Hanoi, which could easily have dispersed the Viet Minh, declined to defend their puppet regime. They protected only the Bank of Indochina building and their own cantonments.

Near the end of August, Bao Dai abdicated at the imperial capital of Hue in a ceremony that was filled with significance for Vietnamese. The emperor, the personification of the Vietnamese nation until the French had corrupted the symbol, transferred his authority and his claim of legitimacy to the representatives of Ho Chi Minh. Wearing a golden turban, dressed in his imperial robes, and standing on the battlement above the Zenith Gate to his palace within the Hue Citadel—the battlement from which his precolonial ancestors had watched captured rebels paraded by below—Bao Dai handed over to the Viet Minh delegates the dynastic seal and the imperial sword. Bao Dai's flag was hauled down from the giant flagpole that towered above the gate and the gold-starred red banner of the Vietnamese Revolution was raised in its place. The last of the Nguyen-dynasty emperors became Citizen Vinh Thuy (he had been called Prince Vinh Thuy prior to inheriting the monarchy) and was appointed "supreme political advisor" to Ho's government until Ho let him leave the country in early 1946.

Contrary to the subsequent assumption of American statesmen, other Communist parties did not help the Vietnamese during the years of the war with France that truly mattered. The Chinese Communists were preoccupied in North China with the civil war against Chiang Kai-shek. Their original French allies abandoned the Vietnamese. Hoping to win power through the ballot box in 1945 and 1946, the French Communist Party was anxious to avoid any unpopular action and suppressed its historic advocacy of independence for the colonies. The Vietnamese were advised by Ho's old French comrades not to resist the reimposition of colonial rule because a war for independence would obstruct the Soviet Union's foreign policy.

The French Communists were correct about the Soviet attitude. The Vietnamese got no assistance from Moscow, because Stalin was not interested in furthering their revolution. It was not because he shared the hopes of the French Communist leadership. He appears to have shrewdly assumed that the United States would not permit a Communist government in Paris, popularly elected or otherwise. Nonetheless, he wanted to increase the popularity of the French Party for the general political advantage that a strong Communist position in France would give the Soviet Union in Europe. He also wanted the right-wing politicians of France to turn their heads while he consolidated the Soviet hold on Eastern Europe, the German invasion route to Russia in two wars and Stalin's first security concern.

Indeed, the French Communists did worse than refuse to help. They too connived in the French venture of reconquest. Maurice Thorez, the French Party chief at the time, was a vice-premier in the coalition government that embarked on full-scale conflict with the Viet Minh in December 1946. He saw to it that his deputies in the National Assembly did not block, as they could have, the voting of emergency measures and military appropriations to make war on the Vietnamese.

These conditions were to change under the influence of the Cold War and the arrival of Mao Tse-tung's armies on the frontier of Indochina at the end of 1949, but during the first four years of the war against France the Vietnamese were, as Ho said, "quite alone." The building of their Viet Minh army was an act of military ingenuity in keeping with the feats of their ancestors. They had already progressed a substantial distance when Ho despaired of negotiating a compromise with the French and the Viet Minh commandos stormed the central power station in Hanoi on the night of December 19, 1946. In the year and four months since the August 1945 revolt, Giap and his associates in the military leadership had turned 5,000 guerrillas into a force of 100,000 men. This array varied in quality from guerrilla bands in the Mekong Delta to self-styled "regular" battalions in Central Vietnam and the North. The arms the troops carried would have delighted a weapons collector and driven to desperation a U.S. Army quartermaster charged with supplying the bewilderment of ammunition required. The Viet Minh had French arms of sundry vintages and calibers from the colonial arsenals, Japanese weapons seized from the Imperial Army, American Lend-Lease arms bribed out of the Nationalist Chinese to expand the nucleus of OSS weapons, and rough-hewn copies of American carbines and British Sten submachine guns made at arsenals that had also been improvised with machine tools from French factories and railway repair shops. They had even sent divers down to the hulks of Japanese ships sunk during World War II in the Gulf of Tonkin to retrieve weapons and equipment from the cargo holds. Several thousand Japanese officers, soldiers, and technicians deserted to the Vietnamese rather than be shipped home. They provided most of the staff for the arsenals and the instructors to drill the aspiring regulars and train them in combat tactics. The Japanese deserters were supervised by Giap and those few Viet Minh leaders who had acquired experience in the Chinese Communist army or were graduates of the military academy the Comintern mission had set up at Whampoa in China in the 1920s. However motley the result, the Vietnamese had a national army. The French had to battle for three weeks to regain control of Hanoi and for nearly three months to relieve all of their besieged garrisons in the North and in Central Vietnam.

The recruiting, training, and experience of battle never ceased after that decisive night in Hanoi. More and better weapons came steadily through capture from the French and purchase in China and Thailand. The Nationalist warlords in southern China and on Hainan Island in the Gulf of Tonkin were always ready to exchange for cash more of the weapons the United States gave them to fight their own Communists. The Viet Minh maintained an arms-purchasing mission in Bangkok on the same street as the USIS office right up to the Korean War. Money exuded no unpleasant political odor for Thai officialdom. Much of the arms buying was financed by trading opium from the hill tribes of Laos to the Chinese merchants in French-held Hanoi for hard currency. The weapons were transported by pack animals, bicycles, and ox carts over the roads and trails into the Viet Minh's redoubt in the northern borderlands. Others were smuggled by junks and fishing trawlers from Hainan to the innumerable bays and inlets of the northern coast or to the Viet Minh stronghold in the 225-mile stretch of Central Vietnam, where Ev Bumgardner was to observe Diem's visit to a "liberated zone" at Tuy Hoa. Giap actually began forming his regulars in the North into division-size units before the Chinese Communists reached the frontier at the end of 1949 and opened the prospect of extensive help. This man who had earned his living as a history teacher at a lycée in Hanoi, lecturing on the French Revolution and the campaigns of Napoleon, demonstrated that he was a classic Vietnamese scholar-general who could employ the classic Vietnamese strategy against the French.

In a series of offensives from late 1949 to the fall of 1950 in the mountains ringing the Red River Delta, Giap drained and exhausted the French forces. The befuddled French commander, Gen. Marcel Carpentier, panicked and committed the mistake the Vietnamese had been anticipating. He ordered an emergency evacuation of the remaining frontier towns in October 1950. The French columns tried to retreat down a two-lane dirt road known as Route Coloniale 4 that wound a tortured way amid the limestone crags and rain forests of the borderlands. Giap's troops were waiting, and the road the French empire built became a road to the empire's death throes. Six thousand French colonial troops disappeared. The Viet Minh captured sufficient weapons, ammunition, trucks, armored vehicles, and other equipment to outfit an entire division. The debacle was the worst overseas defeat in French history since a British army under James Wolfe beat Louis Montcalm

at Quebec in 1759 and France lost Canada. Giap's victory was a pre-
cursor to Dien Bien Phu. The psychological shock of the disaster would
probably have precipitated negotiations to end the war had France been
left to its own resources, but the Truman administration, which had
recently started direct and generous military assistance, encouraged the
French to persist.

From 1950 onward, the task of Giap and his commanders was essentially one of equipping their seasoned army with the Soviet artillery,
antiaircraft guns, and other heavy weapons that arrived rapidly with
Chinese instructors, and of completing its organization into a modern
fighting force. The work was to require additional years, and there were
to be mistakes and setbacks. The task was, however, the finishing of a
structure that was already well underway. The army that was to triumph
to the attention of the world in 1954 and to establish another epic in
Vietnamese history had been created before the first truck with the first
crates of Soviet weapons crossed the China border.

Leadership of the war for independence by Ho Chi Minh and his disciples
engraved certain popular images in the minds of Vietnamese and established certain fundamental equations in Vietnamese political life.
Virtually the entire population was touched—from boys and girls old
enough to spy and carry messages, to their grandparents able to lie
cunningly with the dignity of age. Vietnamese were confronted with
three alternatives: to join the Communists to win the liberation of their
country, as many did; to collaborate with the French for a variety of
reasons, as many others did; or to avoid participating in the most important moral and political conflict of their time, as a minority, including
Ngo Dinh Diem, did. The war made Ho the father of modern Vietnam
and defined a Vietnamese patriot as a Communist or someone who
fought with the Communists. The war defined someone who collaborated with the French as the Vietnamese equivalent of a Tory in the
American Revolution. The war made political figures like Diem who
declined to participate irrelevant to the struggle. The act of waiting,
attentisme as the French called it, became a passage to obscurity.

The leaders of the United States were unable to accept these Vietnamese realities. Although Ho ceased direct appeals to the Americans
after the war that would end at Dien Bien Phu began with France, he
was careful to leave an opening in the hope of one day reaching an
arrangement. In early 1949, George Abbott, the diplomat who had
spoken to Ho as the first secretary at the Paris embassy in that last,

pathetic conversation in September 1946, tried to interest Dean Acheson in the idea that Ho might be an Asian Tito. The break between Stalin and Tito had become public the previous year, and by 1949 it was accepted in Washington that the Soviet Union and Yugoslavia were in a state of hostility just short of war. In an analysis written that February, Abbott pointed out an oddity in the behavior of the Vietnamese Communists:

> One peculiar thing about Vietnam Communism is that there has been very little anti-American propaganda. It is obvious that this is not due to ignorance of the current party line. It apparently represents a hope on the part of Ho Chi Minh that he may still obtain American support for or at least acceptance of a Viet Minh government under his leadership.

Dean Acheson had been involved in U.S. policy toward Indochina almost from the beginning, first as Truman's under secretary of state and then as secretary for the last four years of the Truman administration. He was another of the founders of the post–World War II system abroad; he entitled his autobiography *Present at the Creation*. Acheson was not prompted by Abbott's observation to taking another look at the Vietnamese Communists. He and Truman and other American figures like them in both political parties assumed that all Communist movements were pawns of a centralized superstate directed from the Kremlin and that Joseph Stalin was another Hitler bent on world conquest. Despite the evidence of Tito's behavior, they could not believe that a Communist leader might have as his basic goal the independence of his country. They helped Tito, but they were never comfortable with him and thought of him as an aberration. Part of the explanation for their failure to take seriously the existence of national Communism (and to perceive that Stalin, monster though he was and responsible for the deaths of millions in the Soviet Union, was in his foreign policy a Russian imperial statesman with limited goals) seems to lie in the fact that they did not want to see the world as a complicated place. If Tito and Ho and Mao Tse-tung were nationalists as well as Communists, if differing cultures and histories might lead Communist nations to develop along distinct lines, then the world was far more complex than these American leaders imagined it to be. Their own inclinations were easier to follow in a simple Manichaean world of Good and Evil.

Acheson was intent on finding an anti-Communist alternative to Ho. He was convinced that the fundamental error of French policy was

France's old-fashioned colonialism. If the French would set up a native government and declare Vietnam independent, that government would have a chance to attract a popular following to rival Ho's. In effect, Acheson wanted the French to apply to Vietnam the American imperial system of surrogate regimes. The search for an anti-Communist alternative was pressed harder after Mao Tse-tung's forces began to move toward victory in the civil war in China. The Truman administration held out the bait of direct economic and military aid for the war if only France would abandon its nineteenth-century mysticism and adopt this sensible policy. The fruit of this American initiative to turn a colonial conflict into a just war of anti-Communism was the so-called Bao Dai solution.

Bao Dai returned to Vietnam from self-imposed exile in Hong Kong in mid-1949 under French and American sponsorship to reassume his status as emperor. It is difficult for a discredited emperor who has abdicated to unabdicate himself and acquire a popular following, particularly for one with the character of Bao Dai. In his own odd way Bao Dai respected his abdication to the revolution of 1945. He was commonly referred to as the emperor, maintained the status and prerogatives of the office, and was addressed as "Your Majesty." He carefully left unchallenged that ceremony so full of symbolism for Vietnamese when he had stood on top of the Zenith Gate in the Citadel at Hue and handed Ho's representatives his imperial sword and dynastic seal. He never attempted to formally reclaim the throne. He called his government a "state," the State of Vietnam, as distinct from an "empire," and he took for his official title Head of State. His government, he said, was a *de facto* successor of the Democratic Republic of Vietnam that Ho had proclaimed in 1945.

Truman and Acheson recognized Bao Dai's regime as the legal government of Vietnam in early 1950. It represented "true nationalist spirit," Acheson said. Ho was "the mortal enemy of native independence in Indochina." (Acheson's national leader had difficulty with his native language. Having been educated by French tutors at Hue and in France, where he had spent three years of his youth, Bao Dai could not speak, read, or write Vietnamese well.) In May 1950, Acheson announced the direct military and economic assistance for the war that the French had been promised in exchange for Bao Dai.

The same year that he was recognized by the United States, Bao Dai sold a gambling, prostitution, and opium concession in Cholon to his friend Bay Vien, the chief of the Binh Xuyen organized crime society, in exchange for a share of the profits. He also appointed Bay Vien a general in the Vietnamese National Army that the French were organizing and the Americans were equipping for him. This "neurasthenic voluptuary," as one French journalist of the period described Bao Dai, displayed more understanding than Acheson did of his role in life. He was informed one day that his favorite of the moment, a buxom peroxide blonde he had flown over from the Côte d'Azur, had been seen drunk in public with several Frenchmen she was amusing. "Yes, I know," he said. "She is only plying her trade. Of the two, I am the real whore."

There was no anti-Communist alternative in Vietnam. The French and the shortcomings of the non-Communist nationalists cleared the way for the Communists to lead the struggle for independence back in the 1930s. The French political police in Indochina, the Sûreté Générale, decimated the largest non-Communist nationalist party, the Vietnam Kuomintang, modeled on the Chinese party, after an uncoordinated uprising in 1930. Its leaders were sent to the guillotine. The survivors fled to China. The non-Communists failed to rebuild their movements in the face of French repression because most of them were urban elitists who lacked the interest in social change necessary to marshal a following. The Communists were also badly hurt by a similarly ill-conceived rebellion in 1930 and 1931, organizing peasant soviets for the Foreign Legion to crush. A second peasant revolt fomented in the Mekong Delta in November 1940 was suppressed by the insecure Vichy authorities with unusual ferocity. The Communists recovered and learned, because their concern with social goals always took them back to the bottom, where there was discontent on which to build.

Ho and the hard-bitten men around him (Pham Van Dong was not the only one among them to know the pain of French prisons; Giap's first wife, also a party activist, perished in a French jail in 1943) then gave the final blow to the non-Communist nationalists after they took power in Hanoi. During the period right after World War II the survivors of the Vietnam Kuomintang and several other non-Communist factions attempted to set up rival administrations and militias in the North to contest the Viet Minh. Ho crushed them. About a hundred of the leaders were rounded up and executed. The Vietnamese Communists also conducted a campaign of selective assassination against non-Communist nationalists during the sixteen months between August 1945 and the outbreak of uninterrupted war with France. About forty Vietnamese political figures were murdered. One was Ngo Dinh Khoi, Diem's eldest brother, a Catholic leader and the governor of Quang Nam Province in Central Vietnam until the French replaced him in 1942 because he was intriguing against them with the Japanese.

The Communists did not seek to eliminate all non-Communist politicians. They killed their most active opponents or those who they suspected might later go over to the French. Most of the survivors did collaborate with France. None of the Vietnamese were democrats, and the non-Communists were as quick to try to eliminate the Communists as the Communists were to succeed in eliminating them. Diem often told Americans how the Communists murdered his brother. He did not add that his brother was scheming with the Japanese to assassinate Viet Minh leaders. The Communists learned of the scheme and murdered Khoi and his son first. In addition to these planned assassinations, Viet Minh adherents in the countryside committed much more widespread and uncontrolled killing of persons suspected of sympathy for the returning French. There is no accurate record of these murders. They ran into the thousands. The killing was especially severe during the French reconquest of the Saigon region and the Mekong Delta in 1945–46.

Collaboration with the French, which Truman and Acheson encouraged through Bao Dai, was a kind of sordid anticlimax for those non-Communist nationalists who were still alive after all of this ravaging by the prewar colonial regime and then by the Communists. In the years to come, American journalists and U.S. Embassy political officers continued to take seriously the shells of these non-Communist factions. Their leaders had pretensions and were adept at giving the impression that they counted for something. Thousands of words were devoted to their activities. Everything that was written could have been summed up in a paragraph. None of these political parties amounted to more than what the French call *une douzaine de messieurs*—a dozen gentlemen.

The American role made the United States as responsible as France for the suffering of the first war, whatever washing of hands over French stubbornness and stupidity was performed from time to time. A quarter of a million to a million Indochinese civilians perished during the nine years; 200,000 to 300,000 Viet Minh died in the fighting, taking 95,000 French colonial troops—Vietnamese, French, Algerians, Moroccans, Senegalese, Germans, and other Foreign Legionaries from sundry Eastern European lands, Cambodians, and Laotians—with them. By the time of Dien Bien Phu, when Eisenhower sat in the Oval Office, the United States was paying 80 percent of France's war costs in Indochina. American statesmen did not recognize their responsibility. Their ability to blame whatever went wrong on the French left them unfeeling of the moral burden they carried.

* * *

After the United States and Edward Lansdale put Ngo Dinh Diem in charge of the Vietnamese residue of the French colonial system, Diem deposed Bao Dai but adopted Bao Dai's flag of three red stripes on a field of yellow, the imperial color, as the flag of his Republic of Vietnam. Diem took Bao Dai's national anthem for his own. He fired the Binh Xuyen chief of police. He kept the same police and Sûreté. The changes Diem did make were not for the better. This man whom Lansdale installed as the leader of "Free Vietnam" provoked the second war in Indochina.

Ho and his Communist mandarins were preoccupied for the first four years after the Geneva Agreements of 1954 with more problems than they could manage in the North. They had a devastated countryside to reconstruct, a population estimated at 14 million to feed in a rice-deficient region cut off from its traditional source of imports in the South, a scarcity of technicians of every kind, and a small and antiquated industrial plant they wanted to enlarge and refurbish as an essential step to modern nationhood. All the while they were engineering a social revolution to transform the North into a Marxist state.

Their mistakes compounded their preoccupations. Truong Chinh, the secretary-general of the Party, inflicted a horror on the country by letting the land-reform campaign get out of hand in his zealotry. The terror caused the deaths of thousands of large and small landholders, including a considerable number of Party members who were purged and executed after trials on trumped-up charges before so-called People's Agricultural Reform Tribunals. The army had to put down an insurrection in November 1956 by Catholic peasants in Ho's home province of Nghe An, killing many farmers in the process. These Catholics, who had not fled to the South like the other two-thirds of their pro-French community, had been singled out for vengeance by Chinh's land-reform cadres. (No reliable statistics are available on the deaths resulting from the land-reform campaign and the suppression of the Catholic peasant rebellion. What precise figures have been published, especially the often-cited one of 50,000 deaths, are largely CIA propaganda. It is clear that thousands died.) Ho apologized for the crimes, abolished the tribunals, ordered the release of all who had been imprisoned, and launched a "Campaign for the Rectification of Errors" to try to quiet the furor. Chinh was dismissed from his post as Party secretary-general. In a speech to a Central Committee meeting in the fall of 1956, Giap admitted that among other "errors," "we . . . executed too many honest people . . .

and, seeing enemies everywhere, resorted to terror, which became far too widespread. . . . Worse still, torture came to be regarded as a normal practice."

The Soviets, as they had in 1945, betrayed the Vietnamese again for their overriding big-power interests. The Eisenhower administration was intent on perpetuating the division of Vietnam by turning the Geneva Conference's "provisional military demarcation line" at the 17th Parallel into an international boundary. The National Security Council had taken a secret decision to sabotage the Geneva Agreements a few days after they were reached. Washington used Diem, with his enthusiastic co-operation, to block the all-Vietnam election the Final Declaration of the conference had scheduled for July 1956. (While Diem was anxious to stop an election he knew he would lose, neither Vietnamese side ever relinquished a claim to sovereignty over the entire country. The three horizontal red stripes on Bao Dai's and Diem's flag stood for North, Central, and South Vietnam.) The Soviet Union was cochair with Britain of the Geneva Conference. Khrushchev was pursuing his policy of "peaceful coexistence" in the latter half of the 1950s. To placate the United States, he declined to make an issue of Hanoi's demands that the election be held. During a UN Security Council debate in early 1957 over an American request to admit South Vietnam to the United Nations, the Soviet delegate proposed that the dispute be resolved by admitting both North and South because "in Vietnam two separate States existed."

Ho protested all of this without energy. His internal troubles were so great and he was so dependent on Soviet assistance to rebuild the North that he seems to have become resigned to the division of the country for the time being, at least. The extent of his resignation showed, perhaps more than he intended, in a public letter he addressed in mid-1956 to the 130,000 Viet Minh soldiers, administrative cadres, and their dependents who had withdrawn to the North after the Geneva Conference. The Party had told them when they left that they would be able to return after the 1956 election. Ho tried to explain why they could not go home. "Our policy is to consolidate the North and to keep in mind the South," he wrote. Diem resolved Ho Chi Minh's dilemma.

Jean Baptiste Ngo Dinh Diem (Vietnamese Catholics often gave their children a French first name as well as their Vietnamese one) was fifty-three years old and almost as ignorant as Lansdale was of the political and social realities of his country when he returned to Vietnam on July 7, 1954, after nearly four years of exile. His ignorance was willful. He was a mystic. He lived in a mental cocoon spun out of a nostalgic reverie for Vietnam's imperial past. The manner in which he rode into Saigon from the airport on the day of his arrival was characteristic. He sat in the back of a curtained car. None of the curious Saigonese who had gathered along the route for a glimpse of the new prime minister could see him, and he was not interested in looking out. "He comes from another planet," a member of his family once said of him.

He claimed to Americans that his family had been high mandarins since the sixteenth century. In fact, his grandfather had been of lowly birth, a fisherman according to some reports, which helped to explain why Diem was a Confucian caricature, more mandarin than the mandarins of old had ever been. The family owed its fortune to Diem's father, Ngo Dinh Kha, who had been selected by French missionaries to study for the priesthood and to learn French at a mission school in Penang, Malaya. While Kha had been in Malaya, most of his family had been herded into a church and burned to death. The killing had been one of the many revenge massacres of Vietnamese Catholics by non-Christian mobs instigated by the precolonial court at Hue during the French conquest of Indochina, a lengthy struggle of twenty-nine years from 1859 to 1888.

France utilized Christianity more systematically than any other European power in its colonial expansion. French missionaries came to Vietnam for the greater glory of God and France, and their converts played an essential role in the seizure of the country. When the Vietnamese emperors persecuted the missionaries and their converts as a subversive foreign sect, France used the pretext of "freedom of religion" to justify military intervention. The expeditions provoked more persecutions and massacres, which provided an excuse for more ambitious intervention and permanent occupation. Most of the early converts who had owned land were pauperized by the persecutions, and many of the later ones were lower-class Vietnamese. They saw in the coming of the French an opportunity to rise in the world and feared the consequences if the French did not prevail. They put themselves in the service of the foreigner, breaking the isolation of the European in this Asian land. The French recruited them as soldiers, employed the educated ones as interpreters, and appointed them to positions in the mandarinate (lack of proficiency in Confucian studies was conveniently overlooked) because they could be trusted. Vietnamese parish priests helped to perpetuate colonial rule by nominating lower-level officials for the French authorities. Individual Catholics were to resist the French as patriotically as other Vietnamese, but the role the community played in the conquest and the colonial aftermath was to stigmatize it with an aura of subversion and treachery and to give Catholics in general a complex of insecurity and dependence on foreigners. Folklore said that their churches and cathedrals were erected with lands stolen from patriots and martyrs. The Catholics were especially resented by disenfranchised scholar-gentry families like Ho's. In his best-known indictment of colonialism, *French Colonization on Trial*, a book written in French and published in Paris in 1925, Ho portrayed Vietnamese Catholic priests as rapacious land thieves.

Baptism in the Holy Roman Church and a knowledge of the foreigner's language brought Diem's father the robe of a mandarin soon after his return from Malaya, eventually carrying him to a high place in Hue as minister of rites and grand chamberlain to the Emperor Thanh Thai. Kha was forced to retire when the French deposed Thanh Thai in 1907 on suspicion of intriguing against them, but through his connections at court and in the church, he rescued a future for his sons in the colonial world. In addition to Khoi, who rose to the governorship of Quang Nam Province, Diem's next-older brother, Thuc, was ordained a priest and by the end of World War II had become the leading Vietnamese prelate in the South as bishop of Vinh Long. It was characteristic of the ambivalent attitude of the family that Thuc declined to join the three other Vietnamese bishops in the country when they had initially supported Ho Chi Minh's declaration of independence in the patriotic fervor of 1945.

Diem graduated at the top of his class from the French school for colonial administrators in Hanoi and began his career as a district chief. He had his first clash with the Communists in 1930 and 1931 when he was governor of a minor province in Central Vietnam and helped the French to crush the first peasant revolts the Party fomented during those years. Diem took the trouble to do some reading on Marxism-Leninism. The doctrines of social revolution and atheism struck him as anathema, a manifestation of the anti-Christ. By 1933, when he was only thirty-two years old, his record of hard work and honesty and his political reliability were so well established that the French agreed to his appointment as minister of the interior to Bao Dai, then just eighteen. Diem interested the young emperor, not yet a debauché, in reforming the corrupt mandarinate and attempted to persuade the French to grant the monarchy more autonomy to run the country through a purged and effective bureaucracy. The French refused to disturb what to them was a satisfactory status quo. Bao Dai forgot about reform and found amusements. Diem, who was distinctly unpliable and who as a child had often been beaten by his father for his willfulness, resigned.

For the next twenty-one years he held no public office or other gainful employment. Until the final years of World War II, he lived off the modest landholdings of the family and passed his time at hunting and horseback riding, photography, and a rose garden, remaining celibate, going to mass and receiving communion every morning, writing and talking of politics—never taking any action. The convulsions set off by the world war moved him back into politics, always on the periphery. He negotiated unsuccessfully with the Japanese for the premiership of the puppet regime they set up under Bao Dai; hid from the Viet Minh and was arrested and imprisoned by them; refused an offer from Ho Chi Minh of a place in a coalition government and fled back into hiding; negotiated, once again unsuccessfully, with the French and Bao Dai; and finally went into exile in 1950, first in the United States and then in Belgium and France, because he feared the Viet Minh and the French declined to give him protection. The twenty-one years of waiting carved deeper his eccentricities, hardened his stubbornness, and wrapped him more tightly in his reactionary vision of an imperial past that had never existed. Within Vietnam, except among the narrow circle of anti-Communist nationalists, he gradually passed into the obscurity from which the United States extracted him in 1954.

As Lansdale guided Diem to success in crushing the sects on the theory that Diem was the Magsaysay to form a new and strong central government, it would never have occurred to Lansdale that Diem was beginning his rule by eliminating the most effective opponents of the Communists in the South. The Viet Minh had not been nearly as strong in the Saigon area and in the Mekong Delta as they had been in Central and North Vietnam. The French had been able to stymie the Communists in the region because the society there was so faction-ridden. The Binh Xuyen crime organization and the Cao Dai and Hoa Hao religious sects were much more interested in autonomy within their individual territories than they were in national independence. By 1954 the Binh Xuyen had risen to such a height of rotten glory that any new government with a claim to decency would have had to suppress them. The two religious sects were a different matter.

Cao Daiism was a zany melange of Christianity, Buddhism, Confucianism, and Taoism, of spiritualist seances and various other occult rites; it had a pantheon of saints that included Joan of Arc, Victor Hugo, and Sun Yat-sen. Its cathedral at its Holy See in the province town of Tay Ninh northwest of Saigon would have dumbfounded Walt Disney. Human credulity seems to be limitless in religion, however, and Cao Dai doctrines were no zanier than some of the religious cults that have drawn millions of supposedly educated and enlightened Americans. Whatever its imaginative theology and architecture, the political and military force of the sect was real. With their 1.5 to 2 million peasant adherents and a French-sponsored army of 15,000 to 20,000 men, the Cao Dai pope and his hierarchy of cardinals and generals exercised authority over much of the populated region northwest of Saigon and enclaves in the Delta to the south, including My Tho and its immediate environs.

The Hoa Hao was a militant Buddhist sect founded in 1939 by a faith healer named Huynh Phu So. The Communists had foolishly murdered him in 1947 because he would not ally the sect with the Viet Minh. Huynh Phu So's 1.5 million peasant followers, under the leadership of his disciples, had begun killing Viet Minh from that day forward. The Hoa Hao army of 10,000 to 15,000 men dominated the six provinces of the western Mekong Delta.

A wise ruler would have compromised with the Cao Dai and the Hoa Hao. They could have been talked into an arrangement. Diem had, in fact, intrigued with them from abroad, using his family in Vietnam as a contact, and with the Binh Xuyen too, when he was angling to have Bao Dai name him prime minister. He also owed the Hoa Hao a debt. Diem was one of the anti–Viet Minh politicians to whom Huynh Phu So had given shelter. Once in power, Diem would tolerate no potentially independent sources of authority. He was so morbidly suspicious that he could share real authority only with his family. By 1956 he had smashed the sects in a series of campaigns with the ARVN battalions now being paid directly by the Americans rather than through the French as in the past. The Cao Dai pope fled to Cambodia. One of the Hoa Hao leaders was captured and publicly guillotined in Can Tho. The stretches of countryside the sects had controlled became vacuums of authority inhabited by disaffected peasants and the remnants of the sect armies that continued to resist sporadically in guerrilla bands. Had good government been substituted for the shattered theocracies of the sects, their destruction might have been justified. Instead the reign of the Ngo Dinhs began.

Ngo Dinh Nhu, Diem's younger brother, bore the title of counselor to the president. He was an intellectual with a corrosive wit, as slim and handsome as Diem was plump and waddling, and a bit daft in his love of power and scheming. In addition to being a chain smoker like Diem, Nhu was a heavy user of opium. His skin had a special yellow hue Vietnamese claimed was characteristic of serious opium smokers. If you pinched the skin, it was said, opium would pop out. No one dared to pinch Nhu. He was the second most powerful man in the country and overseer of numerous intelligence and police agencies he put together to protect the family. At the height of the regime he had thirteen different security agencies operating with the power to arrest and imprison or execute without trial. Nhu had been educated in Paris as an archivist at the Ecole des Chartes, a school for super-librarians, and employed until 1945 at the Imperial Archives in Hue. He had then gone into anti-Communist politics in the 1950s by organizing a Catholic labor union modeled on a counterpart French Catholic labor federation. The connection proved a momentous one for the Ngo Dinh family. The CIA was financing the French federation. When the Dulles brothers began to lose hope that Bao Dai would ever turn into an anti-Communist alternative to Ho, the Agency financed Nhu's agitation to have Diem named prime minister by channeling money to him through the French union.

Nhu was responsible for the hodgepodge of ersatz Fascist and Communist techniques that the regime resorted to in its efforts at political motivation and control. Totalitarianism fascinated him. There had been numerous enthusiasts of Mussolini and Hitler in the France of his student years, and Fascist organizations had flourished under the Vichy regime. Nhu had become an admirer of Hitler. Lou Conein stayed on in Vietnam after Lansdale went home in December 1956, serving as CIA liaison officer to Diem's Ministry of Interior. He nicknamed Nhu "Smiley" because of the mask of a smile Nhu often wore and his grin when he joked at the expense of others. During plane trips to the countryside, Nhu would hold forth to Conein on the magnificence of Hitler's charisma in stirring up the German people and keeping them entranced. Nhu had also read some of Marx's and Lenin's writings, as Diem had, and he envied the discipline of the Vietnamese Communists and their ability to mobilize the masses. The result was that Nhu borrowed promiscuously from both right-wing and left-wing varieties of totalitarianism. The regime's principal political party, which he created, was a clandestine society called the Can Lao, designed to covertly penetrate, and so better manipulate, the officer corps of the armed forces, the civil bureaucracy, and business and intellectual circles. During the secret initiation ceremony, new members knelt and kissed a portrait of Diem.

A proper state also needed a mass organization, and Nhu set up one of these too. He called it the Republican Youth, even though most of the members were civil servants and many of them were not young, and patterned it on Hitler's storm troopers, the so-called Brown Shirts. Nhu dressed his troopers in blue shirts, with blue berets and trousers. (He probably took the precise model for his organization from another of his sources of inspiration—Chiang Kai-shek's Kuomintang. Chiang had formed a Blue Shirts organization during the 1930s after he acquired German military advisors.) Nhu tried to employ his Blue Shirts in the same way that Hitler had used the storm troopers, as an extralegal national apparatus to shape the loyalties of their neighbors and to spy and police. He was fond of convening mass meetings of his Republican Youth in Saigon and at the provincial capitals, because Diem allowed him to play the role of supreme national leader within the organization. He would often arrive dramatically at the stadium or soccer field in a small French helicopter called an Alouette that the family had purchased for their personal use. Before Nhu gave his speech from a high podium, the assemblage of Blue Shirts would drop to one knee in obeisance, thrust a stiff arm into the air in the Fascist salute, and shout allegiance to the leader.

Nhu's wife, Madame Nhu, or Madame Ngo as she preferred to be called for its more regal sound, dominated her husband and her brother-in-law. To interview her at the presidential palace was to enter the mental as well as the physical world of the family. In her youth she had been a petite beauty, the daughter of a wealthy family. Her father, Tran Van Chuong, had been a prominent landowner and lawyer during the French years and had held the post of foreign minister in the short-lived Japanese puppet regime. Her adult years of eagerly grasping and yielding authority gave her features a certain aggressiveness, and she carried herself a bit stiffly. She was still an attractive woman, however, and liked to show off her good looks. She would enter the reception room for the interview wearing an *ao dai* of delicately patterned silk which had been cut with a V-neck rather than the traditional high collar. The V-neck was a modest one but striking nonetheless. Her shoes had stiletto heels to make her taller. She would sit in a brocaded armchair and lecture on the need for sacrifice to defeat the Communists. As she talked, her lacquered fingernails would toy with a diamond-encrusted crucifix on a neck chain. (She had converted from Buddhism to Catholicism after marrying Nhu.) From time to time a servant would enter to bring a fresh pot of tea or to answer her summons for some errand that suddenly came to mind. The servants were all men. They would shuffle in bent over in a bow, bow lower, and acknowledge her commands with a long "Daaa . . ." (the D pronounced like a Z), a servile form of "yes" for servants in old, aristocratic households; then they would shuffle back out still bent over.

Publicly, Madame Nhu asserted herself with an exhibitionist feminism. She formed a counterpart women's organization to her husband's Republican Youth, calling it the Women's Solidarity Movement, played the same role of maximum leader within it, and also used her women to spy and police. The younger members were recruited into a female militia, armed with U.S. Army carbines, and dressed in a uniform like the men's of blue shirts and slacks but with more flamboyant headgear— wide-brimmed bush hats of a matching blue instead of berets. Madame Nhu also appointed herself arbiter of South Vietnam's morals. In a country where polygamy was common, she pushed through Diem's tame National Assembly a "Family Law" that made divorce virtually impossible and at the same time rendered illegitimate *ex post facto* the children born of second wives and concubines. Another of her measures, a "Law for the Protection of Morality," banned sentimental songs and dancing "anywhere at all," forbade "spiritualism and occultism" of the kind practiced by the Hoa Hao and the Cao Dai and in less organized forms by most other Vietnamese, and declared the use of a contraceptive a crime punishable by five years imprisonment for repeat offenders. One ambitious legislator suggested that the law also ban the wearing of "falsies" by Vietnamese women, but others pointed out that this would create an unduly complicated problem of enforcement for the police. The resentment she aroused often expressed itself in scurrilous rumors. Vietnamese women would suggest it was not a coincidence that the Saigon bar girls also favored V necklines on their *ao dais*. (There is no evidence her relationship with Diem involved anything physical.) She became a favorite of Communist propagandists, who always referred to her by her maiden name, an insult to a married woman's virtue in Vietnamese culture. Her maiden name was Tran Le Xuan, which means "Tears of Spring."

The Ngo Dinhs proceeded to impose on South Vietnam what amounted to their own alien sect of Catholics, Northern Tories, and Central Vietnamese from their home region. (Once in the South, many of the non-Catholic Northerners who had fought with the French quickly allied themselves with the Catholics as the group with access to the regime and the new foreigner.) Diem and his family filled the officer corps of the army and the civil administration and the police with Catholics, Northerners, and Central Vietnamese they trusted. The peasants of the Mekong Delta found themselves being governed by province and district chiefs, and by civil servants on the province and district administrative staffs, who were outsiders and usually haughty and corrupt men. Diem intruded further. He did away with the village oligarchies of prominent peasants who had traditionally dominated the village councils—collecting taxes, adjudicating disputes, and performing the basic functions of government. The poorer peasants often did not like these men, but they knew them, and the council members had a sense of how far they could safely push people. In mid-1956, to try to prevent Viet Minh sympathizers and other dissidents from clandestinely controlling village governments, Diem decreed that the province and district chiefs would appoint the village chiefs and council members in the future. The family's alien sect of outsiders started penetrating right down to the village level, subjecting the Southern peasants to abuses and exactions in their daily lives which they had never known before. Lansdale was so naive about the implications of what he set in train that he formed civic action teams of Northern Catholics to propagandize against the Viet Minh among the Delta peasants. He was disappointed by his lack of success. Lansdale was also upset to discover before he went home at the end of 1956 that as Diem's position became consolidated, he acted increasingly counter to Lansdale's advice on political and social issues.

Diem turned next to the land. In the areas they had held south of the 17th Parallel—the 225-mile stretch of Central Vietnam and their enclaves in the Mekong Delta—the Viet Minh had seized French rice plantations and the holdings of "Vietnamese traitors" who sided with the colonial regime. These lands had been distributed to tenant farmers. The peasants had also conducted an *ad hoc* land reform themselves in much of the rest of the country, including regions that had been under sect domination. Many of the landlords had abandoned their rice fields to seek safety from the fighting in the towns and cities. The peasants had divided up these holdings or had ceased paying rent on those they were working. With 85 percent of the population living in the countryside and drawing a livelihood from agriculture, it was difficult to find a single issue of more profound social, economic, and political sensitivity than land.

Lansdale and other senior Americans pressed Diem to launch a land-reform program of his own in order to undercut the Communists by fully ending the injustices of landlordism in the South. The American desire would at first glance appear to create a conundrum for Diem, because he was opposed to any alteration of the traditional social structure. He wanted to return to the landlords of the South as much of their land as was practical and have them act as a buttress to his regime. He wanted the peasants to remain peasants. The trip to Tuy Hoa in 1955 taught him that he liked trips to the countryside, although the excitement of having his feet stamped on once was enough. He was a man who needed decorum, and he saw to it that future occasions were orderly. He would chat in friendly fashion with groups of farmers as well as give

formal speeches. What he never did was to question the peasants seriously in order to learn their desires. He believed that his duty was to
tell them what to do and their duty was to obey. He disposed of the
conundrum by announcing that he was conducting a land-reform program while accomplishing something else.

Diem took away all of the land that the Viet Minh had distributed to
tenant farmers by invalidating the land titles these peasants had been
given. He then confiscated the former French property for his "agrarian
reform" program, and he did distribute much of this land, but he gave
a lot of it to the Northern Catholic refugees rather than to Southern
farmers. Most of the rest of the land he seized went back to the original
Vietnamese landlords who had sided with the French or to other supporters of the regime who could buy it. (Diem's land-reform act specified
a ceiling of 247 acres for an individual holding, quite generous by Vietnamese standards, but the Ngo Dinhs encouraged their officialdom to
smile at subterfuges to get around the ceiling. The minister for agrarian
reform was a landlord. The entire holding of a landlord family would
be disguised by splitting it up among family members.) The regime also
confiscated and returned to its former owners the abandoned land the
peasants had taken for their own. The small minority of Southern tenant
farmers who did receive land discovered that they had to pay for it in
yearly installments. When the Viet Minh had given them land they had
been told it was theirs by right. They were not nearly as angry as all of
the other former tenant farmers who were now tenants again as a result
of Diem's "reform." By 1958, Diem attained his objective. Through
unstinting resort to the armed forces and the police, he reversed the
pattern of land ownership in the Mekong Delta back toward one re-
sembling the prewar pattern, when 2 percent of the owners had held
about 45 percent of the land and approximately half of the farmers had
been landless.

Disorder came with loss of land. In his ignorance and his concern for
the protection of his power to the exclusion of anything else, Diem paid
no heed to the Civil Guards and the SDC militia. When he first returned
in 1954, Diem thought that he could do without large numbers of infantry
and substitute fighter-bombers. (To the end of his days he advocated
indiscriminate air and artillery bombardments and was forever urging
the Americans to bring in more planes and howitzers.) The civil war
with the Binh Xuyen and the sects taught him the value of a regular
army as a bastion, or a sledgehammer. The unwieldy, road-bound
ARVN that the U.S. Army generals in the Military Assistance and
Advisory Group (MAAG) then built for him (on the rationale, an un-

likely one, that the Viet Minh would next resort to a Korea-type invasion across the 17th Parallel) therefore got all of his attention. It did not occur to him that good territorial formations were equally important to his long-term survival. He allowed the forces that were supposed to provide local security to become instead the principal source of insecurity for the inhabitants of the countryside, a daily manifestation of the "capricious lawlessness" of Diem's regime, as one atypical American observer of the period put it. The Civil Guards received some care from the province chiefs, who needed them, but were ill equipped and often unpaid. They used their guns to extort a salary. The SDC militia were treated with such relentless shabbiness that the majority became indistinguishable from bandits. The militiamen caused most rural crime. They were constantly robbing and raping and beating up farmers who dared to protest. Many of the peasants remembered that the last time they had known any security and decent government had been under the Viet Minh or their sect theocracies.

Because of the sufferings of the war against the French, the population of the South might still have put up with the Ngo Dinhs for quite a while had it not been for the Denunciation of Communists Campaign that Diem let loose in the summer of 1955 with U.S. encouragement and help.

Not all Viet Minh withdrew to the North after the Geneva Conference. Ho and the Communist leadership left in the South in covert status an estimated 8,000 to 10,000 military and civilian cadres. U.S. intelligence referred to these cadres by the same term Lansdale used for the anti-Communist guerrillas he hid in the North—"stay-behinds." A large number were Party members. The stay-behinds had access to hidden arms, but they were under orders not to use violence or to foment an insurrection against the Ngo Dinhs. Instead, they were to maintain their cover occupations as farmers and village and hamlet officials, and in the towns and cities as everything from lowly cyclo drivers to teachers and other professionals, while they secretly agitated to foster popular demand for the holding of the all-Vietnam election in 1956. They were to wage the "political struggle" Ho was subsequently to refer to in his June 1956 letter to the 130,000 Viet Minh and their dependents who were withdrawn to the North.

Ev Bumgardner recalled that in 1955 the Viet Minh actually did abandon their bases in the swamps and rain forests and ceased armed resistance. One day late that year while driving back to Saigon from Cambodia in a jeep, he and a friend decided in a moment of self-dare to detour through one of the most famous Viet Minh bases, War Zone C (also called the Duong Minh Chau War Zone) in the rain forest north of the Cao Dai's Holy See at Tay Ninh town. Using a prewar map as a guide, they turned off down a dirt road into the base region before second thoughts of caution could stop them. The experience was more haunting that it was frightening. This forest that they had feared might still be a haven of guerrillas (they told themselves that the guerrillas would probably let them pass because the war had officially ended) was a desolate place. The signs of a recent Viet Minh presence were there. The Eiffel bridges along the road, which had shrunk to little more than a track from nine years of disuse, were all dismantled, the steel spans dropped into the stream beds to impede French columns. Because it was the dry season, Bumgardner was able to put the jeep into four-wheel drive and navigate around the bridges and up the opposite banks. The paths running off the road into the forest of sixty-foot-high teak and mahogany trees, whose canopy of branches blocked the sunlight from the dense hardwood underbrush below, also announced that this had been a guerrilla base. Bumgardner and his friend saw no one during the entire trip.

The 8,000 to 10,000 trusted cadres who had been instructed to stay in the South were by no means the only Viet Minh there. The country was full of men and women who had fought as regional and part-time village and hamlet guerrillas, served as administrators in the local Viet Minh governments, or worked as intelligence agents, messengers, or guides for the revolutionary forces. There were also the Viet Minh sympathizers, most obviously the families and relatives of those who had gone North, or who had died fighting the French. These people were not Communists. They were the non-Communist majority who had followed the Communists out of nationalism. In addition, there had always been a romantic side to the "Resistance War," as the Vietnamese named their struggle in conscious equation with "La Résistance" against the Nazis in occupied France. (On the last night of Dien Bien Phu the Viet Minh played over the radio frequencies of the garrison the "Song of the Partisans," the theme song of the French Resistance, to taunt the defenders that this time they were fighting for an unjust cause: "Friend, can you hear the black flight of the crows in the plain?/ Friend, can you hear the muffled cry of the country being loaded with chains?") All sorts of Vietnamese had been addicted to "Resistance songs." The Binh Xuyen gangsters who murdered Viet Minh liked to play recordings of "Resistance songs" in their dens. Rebellions usually get better with the telling, and after Dien Bien Phu the appellation "Viet Minh" acquired a greater aura of romantic pride. Vietnamese who had stood aside out of timidity suddenly developed memories of having been "Resistance fighters." It was difficult not to take pride in the humbling that men of their race had inflicted on the Europeans who had been their masters for so long.

Diem did not understand that if he persecuted the Viet Minh he would be persecuting a great mass of non-Communist Vietnamese who looked back on what they had done with the emotions of patriotism. Nor did he realize that he would be arousing revulsion in still other Vietnamese who had come to regard the Viet Minh as patriots. He had sat out the war in hiding or in exile, and he and his family did not share these emotions. In his loathing of Communism, Diem regarded all Viet Minh as evil. The majority who were not Party members had been contaminated by Communism. Madame Nhu liked to use the French term—they had been "intoxicated" with Communism. The covert 8,000 to 10,000 stay-behinds were going to stir up a cry for the 1956 election, and they might try to foment guerrilla warfare in the future. The stay-behinds therefore had to be identified, arrested, and shot. Some of the other Viet Minh adherents who seemed to genuinely repent their collusion with the Communists could be allowed to confess their sins as a public example. The rest had to be isolated in "reeducation camps" until their minds could be scrubbed clean of subversive thoughts by indoctrination. Known and likely sympathizers, such as the families of those who had gone North or who had been killed in the war, had to be segregated from the uncontaminated elements of the population and watched so that they did not have an opportunity to cause trouble.

The U.S. government was as eager as its new surrogate in Saigon to get the Viet Minh stay-behinds "cleaned up," in Lansdale's euphemism, and to intimidate the other adherents and sympathizers into permanent submission. American thinking roughly paralleled that of the Ngo Dinhs. The Vietnamese Communist Party had controlled the Viet Minh; *ipso facto*, all Viet Minh were Communists for practical purposes. Those who were not Party members were "dupes" of the Communists and had to be treated like Communists. The National Intelligence Estimates of the period put together by the CIA and the rest of the U.S. intelligence community recognized that the Viet Minh cadres in the South were behaving themselves. One estimate noted that "the Communists in South Vietnam have remained generally quiescent. They have passed by a number of opportunities to embarrass the Diem regime." The currently peaceful behavior of the stay-behinds was of no consequence in American reasoning. "The Viet Minh, despite their relative quiescence, represent the greatest potential threat to Diem," another estimate said. It went on to state American intentions in the simple and unemotional language that bureaucracies of all nations seem to favor for the description of violent acts. The United States needed "a strong, stable anti-Communist government" in Saigon. One of the "fundamental problems" to be solved in reaching this objective was "the suppression of Viet Minh military and political capabilities remaining in South Vietnam."

A team of CIA specialists knowledgeable in solving such "fundamental problems" arrived in Saigon in June 1955. They were part of the first group of civilian advisors sent to the Diem regime. They came under the cover of a Michigan State University advisory group ostensibly financed for development work by the International Cooperation Administration, the predecessor agency of AID. Their task was to teach the police and intelligence services more efficient American methods to "expose and root out Communists."

The CIA team did not have to teach the men of the regular police, the Sûreté, and the security agencies Nhu was starting to form how to repress. They had been well schooled by the French. They might repress the wrong people and let genuine Communists escape with their bungling and enthusiastic brutality (the Americans had little success in persuading them to keep precise dossiers, to cross-reference, and to share information between the various services in order to build up an encyclopedic profile of the Communist Party organization and membership in the South), but they did know how to repress. Women arrested were normally raped as well as tortured. The torturers considered rape a perquisite of their job. Torture produced names. Those named were quickly arrested and tortured. They named others whose arrest and torture led to still others in geometric progression. Not everyone arrested was tortured. The torturers lacked the time to attend to every prisoner, but it was frequent enough to be a common fate. Anyone arrested could be certain of receiving a bullet (Diem authorized the province chiefs to execute on suspicion alone, without even a hearing) or a sentence to a concentration camp. Release was rare. Arrest was presumption of guilt.

No one knows how many real Communist cadres and others suspected of being Party members were killed while the campaign gained momentum during the latter half of 1955 and reached a summit of violence in 1956 and 1957. Those doing the killing were not accustomed to keeping an accurate tally of the lives they extinguished, and after a time the murdering accelerated to the point where, as in the land-reform campaign in the North, no one would have been able to keep score or afterward to reconstruct the number of victims with any precision. The extent of the killing can be documented well enough to say with certainty that thousands died. The arrests often took place at night. Plainclothes police agents, accompanied by Civil Guards or SDC militia, would surround the house and seize the man or woman they wanted. If the victim was to be executed out of hand, as sometimes happened after the campaign was well under way and the security services had enough names to satisfy them for the moment, the condemned would be taken to a road or path near the hamlet and gunned down. The corpse would be left for the family to find the next day. The sight of the body was meant as an admonition to others.

At least 50,000 more fortunate victims were sent to concentration camps. The regime officially admitted to imprisoning that many people for "reeducation" in camps around the country by the time the campaign ended in 1960. Unofficial estimates put the number of people sentenced to concentration camps at approximately 100,000. Again given the lack of accurate record-keeping, no one will ever know precisely how many tens of thousands were put behind barbed wire and how many of these tens of thousands perished in the camps. The police and other forces of the regime, having served the French, naturally applied the same test of loyalty they had in the past. All those who had opposed the French were automatically suspected of disloyalty to the Ngo Dinhs.

The recantation ceremonies, which Nhu patterned after what he had read of Communist "people's tribunals," were staged everywhere amid the shooting and sentencing to concentration camps as a psychological device designed to demonstrate the regime's capacity for mercy to those who merited it. In the hamlets, peasant men and women with Viet Minh records were permitted, at the whimsy of province and district officials, to save themselves by humiliation. They were often rehearsed to make the recantations more dramatic. Their neighbors would be assembled to hear them describe atrocities they had committed for Ho Chi Minh and his Communist devils. They would be required to beg a compassionate President Ngo for forgiveness, and to trample and throw into a fire the red banner with the five-pointed gold star that had become for them during the long war against France the flag of a reborn Vietnamese nation. In the cities and towns the ceremonies tended to be grander affairs with simultaneous group recantations. Portraits of Ho, letters of commendation that had been a frequent form of praise for men in the Viet Minh fighting units, and any other souvenirs of the Resistance were fed to the flames as well. In Saigon in February 1956 a large crowd of civil servants and their families were assembled to watch 2,000 former Viet Minh recant.

Around this time, Bumgardner remembered, USIS discovered that "Viet Minh" was an appellation of patriotism and that Diem was doing the Communists a favor by identifying all Viet Minh as Reds. The American psychological warriors invented the term "Viet Cong," an abbreviation of "Vietnamese Communists," and persuaded the Saigon newspapers to start substituting it for "Viet Minh" later in 1956. Bumgardner recalled how difficult it was to get Diem to say "Viet Cong" consistently instead of "Viet Minh." (Americans assumed the new term was derogatory because in their dictionary "Communism" was a synonym for "evil.") Diem was not the only one who had difficulty growing accustomed to the USIS artifice. As late as the spring of 1959, Maj. Gen. Samuel Myers, the returning deputy chief of the MAAG, spoke with satisfaction of the Denunciation of Communists Campaign to a hearing of the Senate Committee on Foreign Relations. He boasted that "the Vietminh guerrillas . . . were gradually nibbled away until they ceased to be a major menace to the Government." The term "Viet Cong" eventually did come into common usage within the American community and the Saigon government by the early 1960s, as a result of hard work by Bumgardner and his colleagues. Like so many of the other cosmetic manipulations the Americans tried in their world of good intentions, it could not alter the history of the Vietnamese. The Viet Minh by any other name was still the Viet Minh.

The Ngo Dinhs were not content to imprison, torture, and murder the living veterans of the Resistance in the South. Their persecution reached out to the dead. In the most severe insult possible in Vietnamese culture, Diem ordered the desecration of all Viet Minh war memorials and cemeteries. Ancestor worship, filial piety, and the other strong bonds of family have combined in Vietnamese culture to make the rites of burial and the tending of graves particularly sacred. Elderly peasants who can afford to do so buy their coffins to ensure themselves respectable burials. Vann and his fellow American advisors in 1962 assumed that the guerrillas carried off their dead whenever they could in order to hide their casualties. This was not the principal reason. The living brought away the dead, often at risk, because they knew how important it was to their fallen comrades to be buried properly. The vilest scorn one can pour upon a Vietnamese is to deliberately violate the graves of his ancestors. The dynasty of the hero Nguyen Hue was defeated by rivals following his death. They humiliated his son, before torturing him to death, by forcing him to watch while they had Nguyen Hue's bones disinterred and made common soldiers urinate on them. The French opened the family tombs of Phan Dinh Phung, the most tenacious of the monarchist rebels at the end of the nineteenth century, and exhibited the remains of his ancestors in the nearest town in an unsuccessful attempt to break his spirit.

The Geneva Agreements specified that graves registration teams from the Viet Minh, the French Army, and the Vietnamese National Army had the right to travel in both zones of the country in order to seek the remains of those missing in action and to assemble the graves of their war dead into permanent cemeteries. The French undertook to turn the valley of Dien Bien Phu into a hallowed ground for the 8,000 Viet Minh and the more than 3,000 French colonial troops, many of them Vietnamese, who had died there. In May 1955, a joint team from the French Army and the Vietnamese National Army, soon to be redesignated the ARVN, were at Dien Bien Phu identifying their dead and doing preliminary work, with laborers provided by Giap, for a massive ossuary to hold in honor together the bones of 5,000 of the dead from both sides. Diem chose instead to symbolically urinate upon the bones of the Viet Minh in the South. He denied the Viet Minh graves registration teams the right to travel in the South and issued his order for the obliteration of the Viet Minh war memorials and cemeteries there. While they did not raze any cemeteries, the Communist leaders retaliated by canceling travel permits for the French and VNA teams in the North. The dead of Dien Bien Phu were left to lie. In his loathing of Communism, Diem denied an honored burial to the fallen of his own army in the North.

Little was printed in the United States about the Denunciation of Communists Campaign at the time it was being prosecuted in South Vietnam, and little has been published about it since. The American press was not much interested in the country in those years. The CIA officers in the Saigon station, the diplomats, and the generals at the military mission might have expressed some distaste had they looked into the torture. They feigned ignorance. They regarded all of this killing and the concentration camps as a cleansing of Southern society and were not disposed to attract attention to the unpleasant side. They did call attention to the atrocities in the North and made propaganda out of the candor with which Giap and other Vietnamese Communist leaders admitted their crimes. Because candor like Giap's had disappeared from the American system after World War II, it was interpreted as evidence of weakness and not understood for the strength it actually reflected.

I first ran across evidence of the Denunciation of Communists Campaign while in the field with ARVN battalions reporting on operations against the guerrillas in 1962 and 1963. The hamlets in the Communist-dominated areas frequently had war memorials erected by the guerrillas.

They were usually simple, upright slabs of masonry or wood, like those one saw in the parks of small American towns in the 1950s listing the dead of World War II and Korea, with the dead of Vietnam still to come. Beside the name inscribed on the hamlet monument would be the words "Killed by the Puppet Forces" and the date the man or woman had died. I noticed that the first dates were in 1955 and 1956. Those were supposed to have been years of peace in South Vietnam, before Hanoi had allegedly instigated a second war there, and my curiosity was aroused. I inquired and was told that Diem had conducted an early campaign against clandestine cadres whom Hanoi had left behind after Geneva as part of its conspiracy to foment a rebellion, and that not much was known about the campaign, except that the deaths had reached into the thousands. I did not dwell on the matter. In those years, like almost all Americans, I saw nothing wrong with shooting Communists and their "dupes." Not until much later did I learn enough about the campaign to understand its significance for the second war and the enormous consequences of the act that the United States committed in collusion with Diem and his family.

By the beginning of 1957, not many of the original stay-behind cadres were left in the South. The killings, the concentration camps, and desertion had driven their numbers down to an estimated 2,000 to 2,500 from the 8,000 to 10,000 of 1955. Secret Party histories captured by the U.S. Army during the latter half of the 1960s and interviews with old-line Viet Minh who were taken prisoner or who defected during the second war were to tell the tale of what then happened. Ho and the senior Communist leaders in the North, still preoccupied with repairing the devastation wrought by the French and with the aftereffects of the land-reform disaster, did not want another war on their hands in 1957. They instructed the cadres remaining in the South to continue to refrain from armed insurrection and to adopt a strategy of "lying low for a long time" while keeping up political agitation. But the Denunciation of Communists Campaign drove the Southern cadres into disobeying their orders and "violating the Party line," as one secret history captured in 1966 revealed. They were forced for their physical survival to instigate a rebellion against the Ngo Dinhs and the Americans. "In opposing such an enemy, simple political struggle was not possible. It was necessary to use armed struggle. . . . The enemy would not allow us any peace," the history explained.

The dissident Southern cadres who decided to fight back discovered that the Ngo Dinhs and the Americans had made the South ripe for revolution. They went to non-Communists who had been their Viet

Minh comrades in the Resistance War and found these comrades willing to join them in a new resistance because they too were being hounded by Diem's campaign. The guerrilla-band remnants of the armies of the Cao Dai and the Hoa Hao were ready to forget the past and make common cause. Most important of all, much of the peasantry was so angry that the farmers were prepared to face the agony of another war to rid the country of this foreigner who had replaced the French. This regime the Americans had imposed on them was more than they could bear. The Southern cadres who had made up their minds to disobey Hanoi's orders and lead a revolt explained that the Americans, being richer and more powerful than the French, practiced a new and more rapacious form of colonialism. This was why, the cadres explained, the Americans had selected this particularly vicious "traitor," Diem, and his family and clique of "country-sellers" as their henchmen in Vietnam. The cadres named this regime "My-Diem." *My* (pronounced like the pronoun "me") is the Vietnamese word for "American." Many of the peasants believed what they were told because the explanation made sense to them. Their memories of the French had dimmed. They did recall that the French had never harried them as this "My-Diem" did.

(When Vann and other Americans in Vietnam would later read Communist propaganda describing Diem as a "puppet" and the ARVN as "puppet troops," they would dismiss the terms as nonsense, because Diem so often did what the U.S. government did not want him to do and his army did not take orders from U.S. officers. Americans did not understand the meaning of the word "puppet" in the Vietnamese historical context. To Americans the word meant a puppet on a string responding to direct control. To the Vietnamese the word meant a ruler and his Vietnamese soldiers and administrators who represented alien interests, who acted on behalf of a foreigner. In this sense, the word "puppet" accurately described Diem and his government and army. One afternoon in 1962 at a U.S. Army Special Forces camp I questioned a young guerrilla who had been wounded and captured in a skirmish nearby. The American sergeant who was the Special Forces team medic had dressed his wound gently and expertly. He was relaxed, having lost, for the moment, his fear that he was going to be tortured and killed. I asked him why he had joined the guerrillas. "To liberate my country," he said. From whom? I asked. "From the Americans and Diem," he said. But how could he liberate his country from Diem, since Diem was already independent and did not take orders from the Americans? "No," he said, "Diem is the same as the Americans." I argued that Diem could not be the same as the Americans because he often did things that were against the wishes of the U.S. government. "No," he repeated, "Diem is the same as the Americans." I dismissed his answer as that of a brainwashed peasant and began to question him on another subject.)

The Southern cadres, with their old comrades from the Resistance and their newfound allies from the sects, first began striking back at the Ngo Dinhs and the Americans in early 1957, assassinating detested village police agents and village chiefs appointed by Diem's officials. By the beginning of 1958 they had a campaign of counterterror fully launched and were starting to form guerrilla units on a systematic basis. Bernard Fall, the Franco-American scholar of Vietnam, estimated that about 700 village-level officials were killed during the first year of the rebellion, from the spring of 1957 to the spring of 1958, and that the assassinations nearly doubled during the following year. In September 1958, the chief of a district adjacent to My Tho, a secure Cao Dai area during the French war, was ambushed and killed in the daytime on the main road to Saigon. By late 1958 the dissident cadres had succeeded in presenting the Party leadership in Hanoi with a *fait accompli*—a major guerrilla revolt in South Vietnam.

Ho and his disciples in Hanoi were prepared to assume control of it. As Diem's South had been moving toward renewed war, Ho's North had been stabilizing. By 1959 the capacity to learn from error had enabled the Communist mandarins to restore much of the confidence in their regime that had been destroyed by the land-reform campaign. Rice and other agricultural products were limited in the chronically deficient North, but enough was being grown by then to feed the population. Reconstruction with Soviet and Chinese economic assistance had brought French-originated industries back to World War II levels of production by the end of 1957, and a Three-Year Plan launched in 1958 was creating a nucleus of heavy industry for the future. A new steel works, the only one in Southeast Asia, was to begin rising in 1960 beside the vast iron-ore deposits at Thai Nguyen, forty miles north of Hanoi. A Vietnamese government that made Vietnamese mistakes and sought to correct them in a Vietnamese way was granted a tolerance for abuse by its public which would have been denied to any foreign-sponsored regime. Vann and other Americans looked at photographs of the North and saw a poor country where life seemed drab and regimented and assumed that the regime was hated. There was hatred of the regime and opposition, but nothing similar to what existed in the South. The majority of the Northern population was loyal to its government. The photographs held a clue to the attitude of ordinary Vietnamese in the North which Americans always missed. The clue was the absence of barbed wire. The entrances to the police stations and other government buildings in Hanoi and in the smaller towns and villages of North Vietnam were not protected by the barbed-wire barricades and bunkers that guarded every government building in Saigon and the rest of the South. The Vietnamese Communists were not afraid of their people.

Toward the end of 1958, Ho sent Le Duan, the man he was soon to name secretary-general of the Party, on a secret trip to South Vietnam to determine whether the rebellion was as widespread and self-sustaining as the reports claimed it was. Duan, a Central Vietnamese by birth, had fought almost the entire French war in the South, rising to become a senior leader of the Viet Minh in the Saigon area and the Mekong Delta. (As the one national party in Vietnam, the Communists were able to overcome regionalist divisions.) Duan returned to Hanoi in early 1959 and urged the Party leadership to reverse policy and resume the unfinished revolution. Ho and the rest of the Politburo agreed. The full Central Committee was convened in May and ratified the leadership's decision. The second war formally began.

That fall, when the monsoon rains ended and the trails through Laos started to dry, the first few hundred infiltrators marched south. They were the first of the thousands to follow in the coming years from among the Southern Viet Minh who had been withdrawn to the North after Geneva. The cadres who had stayed in the South and disobeyed and led the revolt distinguished themselves from the newcomers. They named the infiltrators "autumn cadres" and called themselves "winter cadres." The nickname did not derive from the season in which the newcomers arrived. Rather it was drawn from the pride of the cadres who had stayed in surviving alone the winter of Diem's terror. Many years later an old-line Viet Minh who had been a winter cadre explained to his American interrogators why he and his comrades had been able to fire this second rebellion so quickly: "The explanation is not that these cadres were exceptionally gifted. . . . The people were like a mound of straw, ready to be ignited."

Replicas of the Resistance War started coming to life clandestinely in the South. The old Nam Bo (South Region) Central Committee, which had directed the Viet Minh from the tip of the Delta through the rubber plantation country above Saigon, was revived and resumed its former mission under a new name—the Central Office for South Vietnam (COSVN). The Interzone Five Headquarters reappeared to command a second generation of guerrillas in the provinces where the Annamite Mountains meet the sea along the Central Coast. The infiltrators joined the cadres who had stayed as a framework of experienced officers and noncoms around which to organize fighting units and as political agitators and administrators in the secret revolutionary government the Party began to erect in imitation of the Viet Minh government of the French years.

By the end of 1960 the insurrection had gathered sufficient momentum for Ho and his associates to create another replica, one they were to display publicly. (The guerrilla fighting forces quintupled from the roughly 2,000 surviving cadres of 1957 to about 10,000 fighters who captured at least 5,000 weapons from the Saigon side in 1960. By the time Kennedy made his decision to intervene in November 1961, they were to grow to more than 16,000 fighters and to capture another 6,000 weapons.) This replica was a copy of the Viet Minh League. Formally organized on December 20, 1960, it was called the National Liberation Front of South Vietnam (NLF). The difference between this new national front organization and its predecessor model Ho had headed was that most of its announced leaders were carefully chosen nonentities. Its chairman, Nguyen Huu Tho, was a left-wing Saigon lawyer with strong nationalist convictions who had cooperated with the Party in the past. He had been arrested during the Denunciation of Communists Campaign and later escaped with Communist help. Like most of those whose names appeared on the "Central Committee" of the NLF (including a representative of a purified Binh Xuyen), Tho had no authority. The front was run by clandestine or relatively unknown Party members inserted among the nonentities.

Their experience with the Viet Minh League had taught the Vietnamese Communists the value of a national front organization, and the NLF fulfilled several needs of this second war. It made joining the rebellion easier for non-Communists in the South. They did not have to join the Communist Party itself. As an institution, the NLF was also the mechanism for waging guerrilla warfare and simultaneously conducting social revolution that the Viet Minh had been. At the same time, it was a sham organization behind which the leaders in Hanoi could shelter while directing the conflict below the 17th Parallel. The United States had rhetorically converted the Provisional Military Demarcation Line of the Geneva Agreements into a national boundary, and the voice of the greatest power on earth had weight. A number of non-Communist countries that subsequently recognized the NLF as the official representative of the Southern guerrillas would have found this difficult to do had the front been run openly by Hanoi. Many of the American intellectuals who were to participate in the peace movement during this second war, and Europeans who were also to agitate against

U.S. intervention, would have had problems of conscience supporting a rebellion in South Vietnam publicly controlled by the Vietnamese Communist Party. Clandestine control permitted anyone to believe what he or she wished to believe.

With the passage of years and the repetition of the denials, the NLF was to acquire a credibility of its own. American and European authors were to devote books to it. The U.S. government was finally to recognize its "independent" existence by granting its delegation, headed by Mrs. Nguyen Thi Binh, a secret Party member whose mandarin grandfather had fought the French in the early twentieth century, a seat at the peace table in Paris on an equal basis with Washington's Saigon surrogate. When pretense was no longer necessary, Huynh Tan Phat, the secretary-general of the NLF, a Saigon architect who became a secret Party member after joining the Viet Minh during World War II, was to settle the argument with an example of the candor that Vietnamese revolutionaries could display in equal measure with duplicity: "Officially, we were separate [Hanoi and the NLF], but in fact we were the same thing all the time; there was a single party; a single government; a single capital; a single country."

The Vietnamese on both sides of the war in the South were not fooled by this stage managing. They knew that the Viet Minh had returned and that they were participating in a historic replay. The guerrillas called themselves by the original name the Viet Minh had used—Giai Phong Quan (Liberation Army). The flag of this new national front was a slightly altered copy of the Viet Minh flag. In the middle of its split field of red and blue was the five-pointed gold star of the Vietnamese Revolution. The fear the U.S. intelligence officers had expressed back in the mid-1950s had come true, but as another of those prophecies about Vietnam that Americans made self-fulfilling. The United States had sought to destroy the old Viet Minh and had renamed it the Viet Cong. In the process the United States had created a new Viet Minh, far more formidable than the old Viet Minh the French had faced in the South.

On my first helicopter assault operation in the early summer of 1962 with a battalion from Vann's 7th Division, I hoped, as young reporters will, for action to write about, hoped that I would witness a fight that day between the ARVN and the Viet Cong. In my mind, as in the minds of other Americans recently come to Vietnam like Vann, the Viet Minh were a distinctly different generation of guerrillas from the Viet Cong. The Viet Minh of my thoughts had been patriots, by and large nationalist revolutionaries who happened to have been led by Ho and his lieutenants because the Communists had "captured" the independence movement during the war against France. That war had ended and the French had gone. The United States had then intervened in South Vietnam to pro-mote nationalism. The Viet Cong guerrillas were misguided peasants who had been gulled into following the wrong side by Communists who were the enemies of good men everywhere.

A Marine helicopter I was riding in was the fourth or fifth in the flight. Our objective was a Viet Cong base area on the Plain of Reeds. I heard bursts of automatic-weapons fire from the door gunners on the aircraft ahead as mine was settling into a field of waist-high reeds. Looking out the open door over the gunner's shoulder, I saw half a dozen figures bounding away through the reeds less than a hundred yards beyond. They had weapons in their hands and small packs on their backs, and were wearing some sort of green uniform and dark sun helmets with a turtle-shell shape, like those I had seen Viet Minh guer-rillas wearing in photographs of the French war. These were Viet Cong regulars from one of the Main Force battalions. The aim of the Marine gunners was poor. All of the guerrillas managed to escape toward a woods along a canal about half a mile away.

The ARVN captain commanding the battalion dallied for at least fifteen minutes, studying his map and talking over the radio to higher headquarters, before he ordered the troops to move out from the landing zone. He was an older officer. He spoke French and carried a cane, an affectation of French field commanders. The battalion stopped at a cluster of peasant huts a few hundred yards from the woods. An old man and some children were the only people present. The parents of the children were apparently hiding. The ARVN captain started ques-tioning the old man, obviously about the guerrillas. He kept using the term "Viet Minh," over and over again. The old peasant replied with the same term. "Why is he calling the guerrillas the Viet Minh?" I asked a Vietnamese reporter for one of the foreign news agencies who was with me. "I thought we were after the Viet Cong."

"The Americans and the government people in Saigon call them the Viet Cong," he said, "but out here everyone still calls them the Viet Minh."

"Why?" I asked.

"Because they look like the Viet Minh, they act like the Viet Minh, and that's what these people have always called them," he said.

The ARVN captain knew that the Viet Minh were back; that was why he had been so cautious. Cao knew that the Viet Minh were back;

that was why he was more afraid than he would normally have been. Diem knew that the Viet Minh were back; that was another reason why he wanted to keep his army intact. Only the Americans knew neither the Vietnamese they were depending on to work their will, nor the Vietnamese enemy they faced.

In his innocence of the antecedents of this war he had been sent to Vietnam to win, Vann still thought at the end of 1962 that the solution was a military one—forcing the ARVN to attack and break up the battalions of guerrilla regulars like those I had seen on the Plain of Reeds. He also could not yet bring himself to abandon his scheme to manipulate Cao into a fighting general who would serve this task.

On December 22, 1962, Diem announced a restructuring of the ARVN command system. The country had previously been divided into three army corps regions. Diem split the third corps region into two sections. He left Saigon and the belt of provinces that ringed the capital from the west to the north and east under the original III Corps headquarters. He established a new IV Corps to cover the Mekong Delta itself, with a headquarters at Can Tho in the center of the Delta. He gave Cao the twin stars of a brigadier general for his prudence in holding down casualties (the ARVN followed the French system in which general-officer ranks begin with two stars) and put him in charge of the new IV Corps. The change also raised the stakes for Vann. Diem enlarged the 7th Division's zone by adding two provinces to the five the division already had. The effect was to make the division responsible for the entire northern half of the Delta, where an estimated 3.2 million people lived.

Vann heard what was coming and drove up to Saigon a few days before Diem's announcement with a memorandum for General Harkins. He asked for an appointment and personally delivered his message, explaining that he had written it for the commanding general's eyes alone. The memorandum was phrased in the diplomatic language that Vann could use well when diplomacy suited him. He reminded the general of the gambit that he had, with Harkins's approval, employed on Cao—building "a 'military leader image' in the eyes of news reporters, subordinate commanders, and visiting U.S. VIPS." Unfortunately, Vann continued, "General Cao has not yet developed a real aggressive attitude on his own. He needs a strong advisor to stimulate him." Vann came to his point. Dan Porter, the wise and persistent Texan, was moving to Can Tho to become Cao's new advisor there but was scheduled to end his tour and go home in February. Harkins had designated Col. John Powers Connor, who was shortly due from the United States, to replace Porter. Colonel Connor was a gracefully built and pleasantly conventional man. His Army nickname was "Poopy." Vann did not think that he would "stimulate" Cao. He also observed that Connor's lack of experience in Vietnam would put him at a disadvantage. Vann proposed another advisor for Cao, an officer he had served under as an instructor at the Ranger Command at Fort Benning in 1951 after leading his Ranger company in Korea. "At the risk of seeming impertinent, I suggest that your efforts this spring will be materially improved if Colonel Wilbur Wilson becomes the Senior Advisor to General Cao," Vann wrote. "Colonel Wilson's experience and personality are tailored to bring out the best in General Cao, and the Delta area offers the best opportunity to break the back of the Viet Cong."

The thought of subjecting Cao to the stimulation of Wilbur Wilson must have amused Vann, as serious as he was in his suggestion. He admired Wilson, as he did Porter, but for different qualities. Wilbur Wilson was a legend in the U.S. Army of his time. He was a strapping, lantern-jawed paratroop officer, fifty-three years of age in 1962, known as "Coal Bin Willie," a nickname he had gained from one of his eccentricities of discipline. When inspecting barracks he insisted that the coal stacked in the bins at the back slope down at a perfect angle. He would not tolerate a single piece out of line. This was one of several tricks he had put together over the years to train and discipline troops to perfection. He was not a martinet, despite his eccentricities. He had the good commander's knack for instilling pride in his troops, and he showed them kindness and consideration. His rough side, a frankness to the point of brutality, was reserved for his equals and his superiors. He had spent the past year as senior advisor in the corps region that encompassed the mountains of the Central Highlands and several coastal provinces of Central Vietnam. There had been comparatively little fighting there in 1962 and no opportunity for Wilson to apply his full talents. Oddly enough, his ARVN counterpart in that corps region, a whiskey-drinking ex-paratrooper in the colonial forces, had grown tired of American officers being hypocritically nice to him and appreciated Wilson's directness.

Harkins thanked Vann for his memorandum and ignored it. The mild-mannered Colonel Connor was assigned to be Cao's advisor. During his first nine months, Vann had met and been frustrated by the Vietnamese he thought he was supposed to help. In two and a half weeks, at a hamlet called Bac, in the first great battle of the American war in Vietnam, he was to learn the mettle of the Vietnamese he had been sent to defeat.

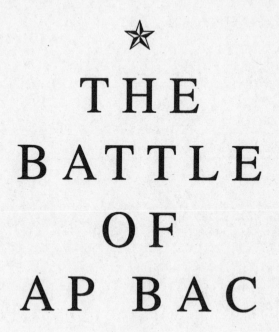

BOOK THREE

★

THE
BATTLE
OF
AP BAC

T HREE DAYS after Christmas 1962, the 7th Infantry Division received an order from the ARVN Joint General Staff to seize a Viet Cong radio transmitter that was operating from the hamlet of Tan Thoi fourteen miles northwest of My Tho. The order originated with General Harkins's headquarters. The United States had brought the unobtrusive side of its technology to bear on the revolt in the South again. An Army Security Agency team from the 3rd Radio Research Unit at Tan Son Nhut, eavesdropping from on high in one of those boxy Otters built for Canadian bush flying, had intercepted and pinpointed the guerrilla radio with its monitoring and direction-finding equipment.

Vann and his staff were enthusiastic about the attack. The operation was the first of the new year, the first under a new division commander, and, most important of all, an opportunity to make a new beginning. Cao's chief of staff, Lt. Col. Bui Dinh Dam, had succeeded him after Cao's elevation to general and move to Can Tho to head the just-established IV Corps. Dam was an unwilling successor. A diminutive and mild-mannered individual, Dam considered himself a competent administrator but doubted his ability to cope with the emotional burden of command. Cao persuaded him to take the job because Cao did not want to create an opening for a potential rival and knew that he could control Dam. Bui Dinh Dam was a North Vietnamese Catholic and politically reliable, so Diem acceded to Cao's wish. He promoted Dam to full colonel and gave him the 7th to lead.

Dam preferred honesty in his personal relationships when possible, and he wanted to cooperate with the Americans. When Vann urged a resumption of the system of joint planning that Cao had aborted after the Ranger platoon had been decimated in October, Dam consented. Vann cabled Capt. Richard Ziegler, the former West Point football

lineman who was his talented planner, to break off a Christmas leave
at the Teahouse of the August Moon Hotel in Hong Kong and return
on the next flight. Everyone, including Cao, who reviewed the plan in
Can Tho, was satisfied with the result of Ziegler's work. Dam made
only one change. He postponed the attack by twenty-four hours from
its originally scheduled starting time of New Year's morning. It would
be unwise, he said, to wake the American helicopter pilots at 4:00 A.M.
to fly with a night's celebration still in their heads.

At dawn on January 2, 1963, the scene so often repeated in this war
took place at the division's dirt airstrip at Tan Hiep six miles up the
road toward Saigon. The calm and freshness of the Delta at daybreak
was fouled by the racket, the engine exhaust, and the whirling dust of
helicopters as the squads of infantrymen lined up to climb aboard the
flying machines. Vann took off at 6:30 A.M. in the backseat of an Army
L-19 spotter plane to observe the landing of the first company of a
division battalion north of Tan Thoi.

General Harkins and his Saigon staff regarded the Viet Cong with
the contempt conventional soldiers from great powers usually display
toward the guerrillas of small nations. They referred to the Viet Cong
as "those raggedy-ass little bastards." At Vann's level in the field there
was a contrasting respect for the Communist-led guerrillas. Vann and
his field advisors and Harkins and his headquarters staff did share a wish
common to American officers in Vietnam. They hoped that the guerrillas
would one day be foolish enough to abandon their skulking ways and
fight fairly in a stand-up battle. The desire was expressed wistfully. No
American officer, Vann included, expected to see it fulfilled. The destruction of the Ranger platoon in October had essentially been an
ambush followed by an effective withdrawal under strafing and bombing.
The guerrillas had not tried to trade blows all day with the Saigon side.
Frustrated as he was by Cao's refusal on so many occasions to close the
trap, Vann could not help but hope that the guerrillas would someday
display such foolhardy temerity. It seemed to be the only way he would
ever succeed in annihilating a whole battalion. He and other American
officers would muse with pity on the fate of any Viet Cong battalion
that risked a set-piece battle. The slaughter the Saigon troops would
inflict on the lightly armed guerrillas with their M-113s, artillery, and
fighter-bombers would be unsporting by U.S. Army standards.

As Vann watched ten H-21 Flying Bananas carrying the company of
infantry descend to the gray waters of the paddies at 7:03 A.M. and land
the troops without incident, he had no way of knowing that he was to
be the recipient of the common wish. One of those rare events in a

conflict of seemingly endless engagements, no one of which appeared to have any intrinsic meaning, was about to occur—a decisive battle that would affect the course of the war. Today the Viet Cong were going to stand and fight.

The commander of the 261st Main Force Battalion completed his preparations by 10:00 P.M. on the night before the battle. His name and those of almost all of his officers and noncoms remain unknown because of the clandestine traditions of their revolution. A copy of the secret Viet Cong account of the battle and the events preceding it, captured in an unusual night ambush two months afterward, mentions the names of only one junior officer who led a sortie and some of the lower-ranking men who fought with courage worthy of special note.

Radio intercepts from the eavesdroppers in the Otters and other information gathered by Jim Drummond, Vann's intelligence officer, and his counterpart, Capt. Le Nguyen Binh, indicated that Tan Thoi hamlet was being used as some sort of headquarters location. The transmitter was reported to be guarded by a reinforced company of Viet Cong regulars, about 120 men in all. Ziegler's plan had attack elements converging on Tan Thoi from three directions. The 7th Division infantry battalion of approximately 330 men being landed to the north by the helicopters was to press down on the hamlet. Simultaneously, two battalions of Civil Guards were to march up from the south in separate columns. A company of thirteen M-113 armored personnel carriers, with an infantry company mounted in the tracked, amphibious vehicles, was also to thrust up from the south along the west flank of the operational area. The M-113s were positioned so that they could be shifted to the point of contact once the guerrillas began to retreat. Each of the three marching elements—the division battalion and the two Civil Guard battalions—was capable of handling a reinforced company of guerrillas with the support of the artillery and fighter-bombers. In case there was trouble, the M-113s and their mounted infantry constituted a mobile reserve as well as a striking force, and Dam had two other infantry companies in reserve at Tan Hiep which he could dispatch as reinforcements by helicopter. No one expected to find more than 120 Viet Cong. Dick Ziegler privately wondered if there would be that many. They had received intelligence this precise before to discover after they attacked that the guerrillas had moved the radio a couple of days prior to the operation.

The intelligence was incorrect on this occasion. Nearly three times that many guerrillas had been assembled in Tan Thoi and the hamlet of Bac just below it. (The battle was to become known as the Battle of Ap Bac rather than the Battle of Bac because the news dispatches of the fighting included the word *ap*, which means "hamlet," as part of the place name.) The commander of the 261st Battalion and his head-quarters group had a defending force that amounted to a mixed battalion of about 320 Main Force and Regional guerrillas. They were augmented by approximately thirty village and hamlet guerrillas to assist as scouts, emergency replacements, and bearers for ammunition and the wounded.

The battalion commander and the Viet Cong committee for the prov-ince, with whom he was in contact by radio, knew that an attack was coming on the morning of January 2, 1963. They did not know the precise target because they did not realize that one of their main radios had been located, but they knew that it would be somewhere in the vicinity of Tan Thoi and Bac. They had anticipated a campaign, once the dry season started, against a belt of villages they controlled along the eastern edge of the Plain of Reeds. The two hamlets belonged to one of these villages. The hamlets were two miles from a large canal called the Tong Doc Loc, which formed the eastern boundary of the plain. The Viet Cong intelligence agents in My Tho had first tipped the province leadership to the operation by reporting the arrival of seventy-one truckloads of ammunition and other supplies from Saigon. By New Year's Day the province committee had received enough information to deduce that the attack would begin the next morning.

Vann would have taken satisfaction at the reason for the decision by the guerrilla leaders to stay and fight. They believed they had to do so in order to restore the confidence of their troops and the peasantry who supported them. Vann had thrown their revolution in the northern half of the Delta into crisis the previous summer and fall by the savaging he had given the Viet Cong with the shock effect of the helicopters and the armored carriers and with his shrewd orchestration of the planning skill of Ziegler and the aptitude for intelligence of Drummond. The mass killings had led the rank-and-file guerrillas to question the ability of their officers to teach them how to survive and win against this lethal American technology that kept surprising them in their once-safe ha-vens. A number had requested discharge to return to their families. A lot of the peasants had also been asking whether the Americans were so much more powerful and ferocious than the French that this revived Viet Minh could not succeed against them. The secret Viet Cong account of the battle spoke of the way these unanticipated defeats had imperiled the Party's hold over the "liberated areas" that were the basis for the expansion of the revolution into the disputed regions beyond. The peasants needed to be convinced that the Party's clandestine government had come back to stay and that its guerrilla forces could give them some protection against the depredations of the Saigon troops and the machines of the Americans.

The Viet Cong battalion commanders and the provincial leaders were men in their forties with records going back to the resistance against the French colonial administration and the Japanese during World War II. They could not turn back, whatever the outcome of the war. They could not flee to the North, even had they wished to do so; disheartened cadres were not welcomed there. They did not think of fleeing, because they were unwilling to accept the possibility that their revolution might fail. A passage in one of their clandestine writings of the period, which discussed the need to teach young men and women in junior leadership positions not to be daunted by a prolonged struggle filled with hardships, summed up their own attitude as well: "We should teach them to win without arrogance and to lose without discouragement until we have achieved the liberation of the South and the reunification of our ancestral land."

They studied the American machines, devised tactics they hoped would overcome them, and worked hard at seeking to convince their junior officers, noncoms, and troops that if they did not panic, and skillfully employed the arts of fortification and camouflage, the terrain of the Delta would provide ample protection and concealment in which to fight and maneuver. The first result of their efforts had been the ambush of the Rangers at a hamlet just a few miles northwest of Tan Thoi and the shooting down of two of the helicopters ferrying reinforcements, including the one in which Vann had been riding. The unit chiefly responsible for that small but significant success, the 1st Company of the 514th Regional Battalion, was waiting in Tan Thoi on this second day of the New Year.

Diem's reaction to that counterstroke, Cao's bootlicking acceptance of his leader's self-defeating strategy, and the refusal of Harkins to believe Vann and to challenge Diem had given the Viet Cong a two-and-a-half-month respite. The guerrilla battalion and company commanders had taken full advantage of the time to replace losses and to train their men in the new tactics and in the use of captured American arms. By January 1963, the Main Force and Regional guerrillas had seized enough modern American weapons from the outposts that Harkins had neglected to have dismantled before commencing his arms largess to be able to pass down to the district and local guerrillas their bolt-action French rifles. Most of the Viet Cong infantrymen now carried semiautomatic M-1 rifles, carbines, or Thompson submachine guns. Each company had a standard .30 caliber machine gun that was fed with a belt of ammunition, and virtually all of the platoons had a pair of the Browning Automatic Rifles (BARs) named for John Moses Browning, the American firearms genius who had designed these clip-fed light machine guns and the bigger belt-fed types for the U.S. Army. There were plenty of bullets and grenades. The United States and its surrogate regime in Saigon had brought about a qualitative advance in the firepower of their enemy.

Ironically, the Party leadership in the northern Delta had not discovered that Cao had been faking operations. They thought that the Saigon forces were still trying to encircle and destroy their units as Vann had vainly sought to do earlier. They noticed that the individual assault elements suddenly became larger, from a battalion broken down into two task forces to a whole battalion. They assumed that the ARVN commanders and their American advisors were simply being more cautious in the way they were attempting encirclement.

The hamlets of Tan Thoi and Bac were in one of the most important "liberated zones" in the northern Delta. The best way to discourage forays by the Saigon forces into the "liberated zones" was to make them unpleasant and unprofitable by effective resistance. The Viet Cong leaders did not intend simply to stand and hold ground. They were accepting battle in the expectation that they would be able to fight and maneuver on their terms. They felt they had progressed to the point where they could risk a test. The risk had to be run sooner or later, and this was as good an opportunity as any. The terrain was advantageous. Despite the fact that it was the dry season, there were so many streams and canals in this section of the province that the farmers kept the paddies flooded all year.

The Viet Cong in the two hamlets would also have the advantage of fighting in familiar surroundings with the spirit of local men defending their land. The guerrillas were all men of the Delta, including the officers and the noncoms, who were Communist Party members. The 514th Regional, whose 1st Company was in Tan Thoi, was the home battalion of Dinh Tuong Province. About half of the troops in the 1st Company of the 261st Main Force Battalion, who were waiting in Bac hamlet, were from the My Tho vicinity and another quarter were from the environs of Ben Tre just across the upper branch of the Mekong.

This was historically fitting ground for a decisive battle. The peasants in this belt of villages along the eastern edge of the Plain of Reeds had followed the Communists since the first insurrection the Party had raised against the French in the Delta in November 1940. The French had crushed that rebellion by razing many of the hamlets with artillery and bombs. The prisoners had been taken up to Saigon on river barges and unloaded on the docks at night under searchlights. They had been strung together in long lines by wires pushed through the palms of their hands. The peasantry of the region had not been intimidated. During the nine years of the Resistance War they had responded to the call of the Viet Minh.

At 4:00 A.M. some of the scout teams of local guerrillas, dispersed in a net for miles around the two hamlets, passed the word through runners that they could hear truck and boat engines. The battalion commander issued the alert order. The troops, who had rehearsed where they were to go the night before when the battalion commander had decided how to dispose his force, picked up their weapons and hurried to the foxholes the peasants had helped them to dig and camouflage under the trees.

Tan Thoi was connected to Bac right below it by a creek with tree lines on both banks which permitted concealed movement in daytime. The hamlets thus constituted two mutually supporting positions. The battalion commander deployed the stronger half of his force, the 1st Company of his own battalion, reinforced by a couple of rifle squads, and his battalion weapons platoon with a second .30 caliber machine gun and a 60mm mortar, in Bac hamlet because it was the most difficult to defend. His intelligence indicated that if an attack was made against Bac, it would probably come from the south or the west. Just south of the hamlet a branch of the creek ran off to the west, and a tree line jutted out along it. He placed a platoon of infantry under this tree line in foxholes on the far bank of the stream, where they had an unobstructed view of the rice paddies to the south.

The western boundary of Bac hamlet was a big irrigation ditch that ran in a north-south direction. A large dike followed the outer edge of the ditch, and trees grew on top of the dike. The battalion commander positioned the rest of his company of regulars and his weapons platoon in foxholes dug into the dike under the trees. The dike, which was four feet thick in its narrowest sections and thicker elsewhere, was built up above the paddies in front like a levee. Because of their crazy-quilt patterns of land ownership, the peasants had neither dug the ditch nor built the dike straight. The result was that the dike zigzagged out into the rice fields at several points. Firing across the paddies to the west of Bac from foxholes in this dike was comparable to shooting across a high school football field from the third or fourth row of bleachers. The zigzags of the dike out into the paddies also enabled the guerrillas to catch in crossfires anyone or anything approaching. The battalion commander sited his two machine guns and his BARs at these outcroppings to achieve what the U.S. Army calls "interlocking fields of fire." He deployed the second half of his force, the 1st Company of the 514th Regionals strengthened by a separate provincial platoon, in similar fashion in the irrigation dikes that edged the three exposed sides of Tan Thoi.

From the air and from the rice fields outside, these hamlets gave no indication that they were the twin bastions of a fortress. The tree lines were the usual Delta profusion of banana and coconut groves, assorted fruit trees, stands of bamboo and water palm, and the hardwoods the peasants let grow to pole height to use for construction. The undergrowth at the bottom was thick. Under the supervision of the officers who had learned this technique during the war against the French, the peasants and the troops dug the foxholes without disturbing the foliage above or at the front and back. The excess dirt was carried away and dispersed. Where the original foliage did not seem dense enough, fresh branches were cut and erected over and around the foxholes. Even from a low-flying L-19 spotter or a helicopter, all appeared natural.

The foxholes were dug sufficiently deep for a man to stand up inside. The machine-gun and BAR positions had foxholes that were wider than the others so that two men, the gunner and the loader, could stand in them. The depth of the foxholes enabled the guerrillas to duck down and escape harm from the fighter-bombers and the artillery. To kill a man crouched down inside one of these foxholes required a direct hit from an artillery shell or a bomb, or a napalm strike close enough to burn or asphyxiate him. Airburst artillery might kill him, but only if the shell was guided with precision to explode it directly above the foxhole or at a sufficiently close angle. Unless the guerrilla was reckless enough to raise himself out of the hole when the aircraft passed overhead, strafing with machine guns and rockets was virtually useless.

The irrigation ditch behind the foxhole line became a communications trench. Men could move up and down it out of sight and shot of anyone in front of the dike and the trees on top. The ditch was about six feet across and was flooded waist-deep. The guerrillas could wade in it or shuttle quickly back and forth in one of the wooden sampans the peasants made by burning and hewing out a log. When a plane came over, any Viet Cong in the ditch could hide by ducking beneath the water or under the foliage on either side. The irrigation ditch permitted the troops in the foxholes to be resupplied with ammunition as needed, the wounded to be evacuated, replacements to be sent into the line, and the officers and noncoms to circulate in relative safety while they controlled and encouraged their men.

Most of the women and children and old men among the approximately six hundred inhabitants of Bac, and a like number in Tan Thoi, fled to nearby swamps to hide as soon as the alert order was issued. Some of the adults stayed behind to help with the wounded and to serve as runners.

The ground fog that morning was the element of chance in the battle. The fog was bad all over the region. It obscured the landscape from the air, suspending itself above the paddies and enveloping the trees and thatched roofs of Tan Thoi and Bac and most of the other hamlets. Vann had not been given the approximately thirty transport helicopters required to lift a whole ARVN battalion in one move. The Army was having trouble maintaining the Korean-era H-21s in flying condition. Harkins had also assigned priority to an elaborate operation that same morning code-named Burning Arrow—1,250 paratroopers jumping and a battalion of infantry landing from helicopters after prodigious bombing—to surprise and wipe out the main Communist headquarters, the Central Office for South Vietnam (COSVN), in the rain forests of War Zone C, the old Duong Minh Chau bastion northwest of Saigon that Bumgardner had driven through eight years earlier. (Burning Arrow was a failure. The headquarters was not found.) With the ten H-21s that he was able to obtain, Vann had to shuttle the division battalion to the landing zone north of Tan Thoi a company at a time.

The fog was especially thick around Tan Hiep airstrip. The helicopter pilots managed to lift off through it with the first company not long before 7:00 A.M. and to find an open area above the hamlet in which to set down the troops. (This was the initial landing Vann watched from the spotter plane.) Then the fog thickened still further and the pilots objected to running the risk of a midair collision or getting lost with the second and third companies of the battalion. Vann and Dam therefore had to postpone the second and third lifts for nearly two and a half hours, until 9:30 A.M., when the sun was high enough to dissipate the fog. In the meantime the first company had to mark time. Had the movement of the division infantry battalion to Tan Thoi not been delayed, the fight might have begun there and the battle unfolded differently. The delay brought the Civil Guards marching up from the south into action first with the platoon of guerrillas positioned in the tree line along the creek branch just below Bac. That happenstance exploded the battle into the dramatic and illuminating clash that was to have such an impact on the war and to influence Vann's life so keenly.

The guerrillas knew the Civil Guards were coming. The Viet Cong battalion commander warned the company leader in Bac that his platoon dug in on the far side of the stream was going to fire the first shots. The battalion radio operators, whose radios were captured American models, were following the movements of the Saigon troops by monitoring the frequencies they were using. The ARVN did not practice communications security and transmitted in uncoded language map coordinates that the Viet Cong staff could easily plot on its own maps. Scouts and a platoon of district guerrillas fleeing ahead of the Civil Guards confirmed the radio intelligence. The guerrilla infantrymen in the foxholes under the trees finally saw the troops of the first Civil Guard battalion walking up toward them in files along the dirt trails and on narrow paddy dikes. The district guerrillas were hurriedly placed in a coconut grove off to the right. They were instructed to rake the Civil Guards from that flank after the Viet Cong regulars had surprised them from the front.

Alert to the possibility that tree lines can hold such surprises, the captain in charge of the Civil Guard battalion became more prudent as his troops got closer. He stopped at a paddy dike about 150 yards away and sent part of one company ahead into the open rice field to reconnoiter. The guerrillas let the Civil Guardsmen get within thirty yards before they started shooting. As the Saigon troops lurched back through the muck and water toward the security of the dike, the district platoon in the coconut grove opened a fusillade from the right. The Civil Guard company commander and his executive officer were killed within a few seconds. The rest of the Civil Guard battalion at the dike should have given their comrades protecting fire. Instead, many cowered down behind the low mud wall and others stuck their weapons over the top and pulled the triggers without looking, so that those retreating were being shot at from both directions. It was 7:45 A.M.

For the next two hours the captain leading the Civil Guard battalion attempted to dislodge the guerrillas with inconclusive flanking maneuvers. His artillery observer was either incompetent or the field command post of the province military headquarters would not let him adjust the fire, because the occasional salvos he called for landed behind the guerrillas rather than on their foxhole line. The maneuvering ended shortly before 10:00 A.M. when the captain was wounded slightly in the leg.

Vann did not know about the fight at the southern tree line until it had almost ended. Maj. Lam Quang Tho, the Dinh Tuong Province chief, who was in charge of these provincial forces and who was theoretically functioning as one of Dam's regimental commanders for the operation, did not bother to inform Dam that it was occurring. Tho was the man whom Diem had also made commander of the armor regiment at My Tho as additional anticoup insurance because his family was among the landowning class of the Delta who had allied themselves with the Ngo Dinhs. Tho did not order his second Civil Guard battalion to hurry to the assistance of the first once the shooting started, so that they could attack together, nor did he do anything to correct the faulty artillery after an American lieutenant accompanying the Civil Guards borrowed a radio to warn him about it. He did not come forward to organize an assault himself, although the scene of the action was less than a two-mile walk from the main road to the south where he had set up his field headquarters. After the casualties reached eight killed and fourteen wounded and the Civil Guard captain was hit in the leg, he did what was normal for a Saigon commander: he asked someone else to fight his war. He radioed a request to Dam to land the two infantry companies Dam was holding at Tan Hiep airstrip as a division reserve in the rice fields behind the southern tree line. Theoretically, dropping the reserve in their rear would force the guerrillas to abandon their positions. Tho did not realize it would also mean landing troops in the open paddies in front of the western tree line of Bac where the rest of the guerrilla regulars were waiting in the foxholes dug into the irrigation dike.

Vann was in an L-19 north of Tan Thoi, following the movements of the third company of the division battalion which had landed ten minutes before, when Ziegler came up on the radio from the command-post tent at the airstrip. He described Tho's request and said that Dam wanted Vann to fly down to Bac and select a landing site for the reserve. Vann was suspicious of Bac as soon as he saw the hamlet. It occurred to him that the guerrillas opposing the Civil Guards from the southern tree line might be part of a larger force that had retreated ahead of the advancing provincial troops. If so, Bac would be the logical assembly area for them. For the next fifteen minutes he searched the hamlet and the tree lines around it from the backseat of the spotter plane. The Army pilot up front slid the little aircraft back and forth in wide swoops at an altitude of a few hundred feet with the grace of a hawk riding a strong current of air. Occasionally, when Vann requested it, the pilot would shove the throttle forward and nose the plane down for a high-speed pass right over the trees.

As practiced as his eye was by this time, Vann could not see any of the guerrillas. He could tell there were Viet Cong in the southern tree line only because he could see the impact of their bullets striking around the Civil Guards. The guerrillas in the irrigation dike that formed the western tree line watched from their foxholes and let the small green plane make swoop after swoop with impunity, resisting the temptation to fire because they knew what the game was. Despite the tranquillity of Bac, Vann remained suspicious of the western tree line. He had his pilot contact another L-19 that was leading the flight of ten H-21s with the first reserve company from the airstrip. The ungainly H-21s were being escorted by a platoon of five of the new "gunship" helicopters the Army had deployed to Vietnam the previous fall. These were graceful machines with a trim, aerodynamic shape, fast in maneuver because of a powerful shaft turbine engine. Built by Bell and officially designated the HU-1 Iroquois, the gunship had been affectionately renamed the Huey by the Army airmen. The Huey had an electrically rotated 7.62mm machine gun mounted beneath the fuselage on each side and pods of 2.75-inch rockets above the machine guns. The copilot aimed the machine guns with a cross-hair device and fired them and the rockets with buttons on the device. Vann relayed instructions to the command pilot of the ten H-21s to land the reserve company at a spot three hundred yards from both the western and southern tree lines. He also gave the helicopters a flight route in and out of the landing zone that would minimize their exposure.

Command relationships among the Americans were not firmly established in 1963. The helicopter companies saw themselves as independent of the senior advisors. Vann was disliked by many of the ranking pilots because, with his domineering temperament and experience in aviation, he was always trying to assert control over them. They might have disregarded instructions from any advisor, but there was a tendency to go out of their way to show Vann that they knew more than he did about how to fly helicopters and where to land troops in a combat area. The senior H-21 pilot in the lead machine ignored Vann's instructions and headed for a landing spot about two hundred yards from the western tree line. The three hundred yards specified by Vann is the distance at which .30 caliber small-arms fire is regarded as minimally effective. Because of the drop of a bullet in flight, visibility, and other factors, the one-hundred-yard difference can be infinity—the difference between hitting and missing.

While Vann was relaying his instructions, the Viet Cong battalion commander was alerting his troops to prepare to shoot down helicopters.

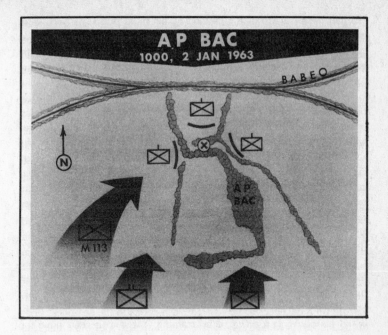

This is John Vann's sketch map of the Battle of Ap Bac, which he drew for the Joint Chiefs of Staff. He reproduced the map on a colored slide so that he could cast the tree lines of Bac and Tan Thoi on the screen in the Pentagon conference room of the American military leaders. He left the slide in his papers.

The X in the circle marks the original target of the operation—the radio transmitter operating from Tan Thoi. The three companies of the 7th Division infantry battalion are shown closing on that hamlet. Vann has used an alternate name, Babeo, for the Tong Doc Loc Canal that forms the boundary of the Plain of Reeds. The arrow on the lower right shows the first Civil Guard battalion engaged with the guerrilla platoon in the tree line along the creek branch just south of Bac. The next arrow to the left designates the second Civil Guard battalion still moving up from the south, while the company of M-113s is shown sweeping along the outer west flank of the operational area. The time preceding the date is twenty minutes before the helicopters were to land the reserve company in the open rice paddies between the western edge of Bac, where the company of the 261st Main Force Viet Cong Battalion was waiting, and another tree line Vann has sketched along a canal farther to the west.

He had been warned of the landing by his radio operators, who were monitoring the ARVN frequencies. It was 10:20 A.M. and the fog was gone. The large, dark green silhouettes of the "Angle Worms," as the guerrillas called the bent-pipe H-21s, and the "Dippers," their nickname for the Hueys, would stand out clearly in the sunshine.

Sgt. 1st Class Arnold Bowers, twenty-nine years old, from a Minnesota dairy farm and the 101st Airborne Division, heard the bullwhip crack of the first bullet burst through the aluminum skin of the helicopter while the machine was still fifty feet in the air. Bowers's helicopter was the second in the flight. Vietnam was his first war. During his previous eight and a half months in the country he had experienced no combat beyond a few skirmishes with snipers. The whip cracked again and again over the din of the H-21's engines before the wheels of the machine settled into the paddy and Bowers jumped out into the knee-high water with a squad of infantry and the ARVN first lieutenant commanding the company.

His ears free of the clangor of the engines, Bowers could hear a roaring of automatic weapons and rifles from the curtain of green foliage in front. The bullets were snapping all around, buzzing close by his ears and splitting the air overhead. He plunged forward, the gray ooze sucking at his boots, in a reflex of his training that said the best hope for survival lay in moving and shooting until you could get on top of your opponent and kill him. The lieutenant and the ARVN infantrymen thought otherwise. They threw themselves down behind the first paddy dike they could reach about fifteen yards from where the helicopter had landed.

Sergeant Bowers yelled at the lieutenant that they had to return fire and maneuver to get out of the open or they would all die in the paddy. The lieutenant said that he couldn't understand Bowers. Back at the airstrip the lieutenant had understood Bowers's English perfectly as they had waited to board the helicopters. The Vietnamese was a graduate of the company-level officers' course at the Infantry School at Fort Benning. Bowers was the staff operations sergeant for the advisory detachment, but he was always volunteering for patrols and assaults. Vann, who liked his spunk, had asked him that morning if he wanted to go with the reserve, should it be committed, because the unit lacked a regular advisor, and Bowers had said yes. He shouted at the lieutenant again. The lieutenant stared at Bowers, his eyes communicating fear, and pressed his body lengthwise against the low dike and down into the water and muck to expose as little of himself as possible to the bullets.

Bowers glanced to the right and saw one of the ARVN sergeants from a helicopter farther back in the flight string leading a squad toward the tree line on the south. They were bent over in a crawl behind the dike. Bowers jumped up, ignoring the bullets, and did the best imitation of a sprint the muck would permit, flinging himself down into a quick crawl the moment he passed the sergeant. He intended to keep the squad going before they had a chance to hesitate and stop. Bowers had noticed on earlier operations that the ARVN noncoms, unlike their officers, seemed to welcome help and thought an American sergeant enough of a cut above them so that they could blame him if things went wrong. He had also observed that they were not literate city types, as the officers were, but ex-peasants who were more willing to fight.

He thought through his next move as he crawled. He would push into the southern tree line with the squad and try to turn the flank of the guerrillas in the western tree line in front. Once they got an initiative underway, other squads might maneuver too. At least he could lay down a base of fire from the protection of the tree line to relieve some of the pressure on the company in the paddies. The guerrillas were concentrating their fire on the main element of the company back toward the lieutenant. The farther they crawled, the fewer bullets cracked overhead or slapped into the dike. They had gone about 150 yards and were close to the tree line. Bowers saw a figure run through the trees and assumed it was a guerrilla messenger. The man was intent on his business and did not see them. Bowers had not been briefed on the situation at Bac hamlet before climbing aboard the helicopters and did not realize there were guerrillas on the far side of the stream toward which he was heading. The sight of the runner was an indication to him that some might be there. He was not concerned, even though he was not well armed himself. He had only a carbine and two thirty-round clips of ammunition. Once in the woods the squad could use the trees for cover just like the Viet Cong.

Suddenly the sergeant, who was about fifteen to twenty yards behind, started yelling at him in a mixture of Vietnamese and pidgin English. Bowers looked over his shoulder. The sergeant was gesturing at him to turn back. The Vietnamese pointed to his radio and then back toward the lieutenant, indicating that he had an order to return. "Damn!" Bowers cursed to himself. He thought he would have a try at overriding the lieutenant. "*Di, di!*" he shouted, Vietnamese for "Go!" American advisors also used it for "Come on!" He waved the sergeant forward with his arm and turned and crawled toward the trees again. After a few yards Bowers glanced over his shoulder. He was making a one-man flanking maneuver. The sergeant and the squad were crawling back toward the lieutenant.

Vann watched helplessly from the L-19 as the helicopters were shot down. The Viet Cong officers had been training their troops for months in the hope of an opportunity like this. During an assault landing late the previous summer an H-21 crew chief had been surprised by the sight of a guerrilla kneeling in the open about seventy-five yards away. The Viet Cong had his rifle pointed right at the American standing in the door of the helicopter. As the crew chief brought up his carbine to fire, the guerrilla, rather than shooting the American while he had the advantage, swung his rifle in front of the helicopter, shot into the air, brought the rifle back again, swung it in front of the helicopter again, and shot into the air once more. At that moment the astonished crew chief recovered his senses and shot the guerrilla. The story made the rounds of the helicopter crews, and the advisors and everyone laughed. After today those who recalled the story would realize they should have shivered. This guerrilla had made a poor beginning. Others would make better ones. He had been engaged in a skewed version of the technique that wildfowlers use to bring down flighting geese and ducks with a shotgun. It is called "lead." Applied in war, the idea is to make flying machine and bullets intersect by shooting ahead so that the aircraft, in effect, flies into the bullets. The training cadres whom Vann had found near the Cambodian border on July 20 had been teaching the technique to selected crews for .50 caliber machine guns. The Viet Cong leadership had simultaneously begun to teach all of their troops to use their individual weapons in the same way. Mimeographed pamphlets were distributed which explained how one calculated the length of lead by the angle of approach and speed of the aircraft—the wider the angle and greater the speed, the greater the lead. The slow H-21 required the shortest lead, the faster Huey somewhat more, and the fast, fixed-wing fighter-bombers—which the officers assured their men were also vulnerable—the longest length ahead. The best time to start shooting at the H-21s was when they were at their slowest coming in for a landing. "Usually the proper lead is two-thirds of the fuselage when the aircraft is landing," one Viet Cong instruction pamphlet said.

The mathematical errors of this guesswork did not matter. What counted was to inculcate the habit of shooting ahead. The officers and noncoms drilled the men constantly to make this something that was done without hesitation. To conserve ammunition and to practice with the least chance of discovery, almost all of the drill consisted of dry-firing exercises in the training camps on the Plain of Reeds and in other havens. Cardboard models of H-21s, Hueys, and fighter-bombers were pulled along a string between two poles to simulate an aircraft in flight. The guerrilla was taught to keep swinging and firing in front once he had begun to shoot ahead, gauging how well he was doing from the paths of the red and green tracer bullets placed every few rounds in the clips of captured American ammunition and in the belts of bullets for the machine guns. The Viet Cong machine gunners and BAR men, whose weapons could knock down fighter-bombers if handled properly, were given the most careful training.

The guerrilla officers emphasized to their troops that they had to restrain themselves until an entire squad or platoon or company could open up at once. Massed fire offered the best chance of putting enough bullets into an aircraft to cripple or destroy it. A helicopter on the ground unloading troops required no lead, of course.

The H-21 flight leader could hardly have obliged the Viet Cong more in the way he disregarded Vann's instructions. Having been warned that there were "Victor Charlies" in the southern tree line, he assumed there were none in the western one. He first brought the string of helicopters low over the western edge of Tan Thoi. Some of the guerrillas of the 514th Regionals there cut loose, raising the adrenaline of their comrades in Bac at the anticipation of the "iron birds" coming into their guns next. The ten H-21s continued low over the western tree line on top of the irrigation dike at Bac and then turned and landed in a rough sequence of ones and twos in the flooded paddies about two hundred yards directly in front. The guerrillas had plenty of time to bring their initial excitement and fear under control and to adjust their fire until they were hitting the machines consistently.

The pilots of the five escorting Hueys flung their aircraft down at the guerrillas the moment the shooting began, the copilots lining up the cross hairs of the aiming devices on the trees and pressing the buttons to turn on the machine guns and launch rockets. Normally a strafing pass by the Hueys suppressed ground fire, but this time the Viet Cong gave tit for tat. The tracer bullets from their machine guns and BARs started reaching for a "Dipper" as soon as one of the Hueys dove for a strafing pass and kept reaching, swinging with the helicopter and following it when the pilot pulled up at the end of the run. Much of the firepower of the Hueys was wasted on the southern tree line. (The guerrillas on the far side of the stream there were not shooting at the H-21s landing the reserve because the trees blocked their view.) The Huey copilots also could not see precisely where to aim their machine guns and rockets, because they could not make out the foxholes in the dike through the treetops and the foliage underneath, and they were shaken at this unexpected opposition and the bullets walloping into their own machines.

Every H-21 took multiple hits. The helicopters farther back in the flight string were punished the most severely, as the Viet Cong had fewer aircraft to shoot at and could concentrate their fire more effectively. A helicopter, especially one with an aluminum fuselage as large as the H-21, can absorb many bullets and still fly, provided that none strikes a vital component. All of the aircraft managed to take off except one. The pilot radioed that its controls would no longer respond. He said that he was shutting down the engine and that he and his copilot and their two enlisted crewmen would join the ARVN in the paddy.

In the short era of innocence when the war was still an adventure—an era that was ending on this day—the helicopter crews adhered to a strict code of camaraderie. The code said that a crew on the ground had to be rescued immediately, even if there were Saigon troops around them. One of the H-21s circled back to pick up the downed crew. The pilots landed in the worst possible place, between the helicopter already in the paddy and the dike. The would-be rescuers had their aircraft immediately shot out of commission.

The code called for another rescue attempt, now to pick up two crews. The command pilot of the Huey gunship platoon announced over the radio circuit that he was going in for them. Vann the risk-taker, orbiting overhead in the L-19, was angry at the uncalculating recklessness of this chivalry, but he did not try to stop it. He knew that the pilots would not heed him. The lead Huey circled low over the two H-21s so that the two pilots and the crew chief (the Hueys had three-man crews) could locate the men on the ground. The four other Hueys strafed and rocketed both tree lines in another desperate and confused attempt to suppress the Viet Cong fire. The Huey platoon leader turned his aircraft and banked for a landing in the rear of the two H-21s, seeking to obtain what protection he could by putting the downed machines between his helicopter and the tree line that marked the dike. As he was ending his approach, his airspeed fell off toward a hover, and the guerrillas were able to hit most consistently; they put round after round through his machine until a bullet struck the main rotor blade on top. The Huey flipped over onto its right side and crashed into the paddy about fifty yards behind the two H-21s. The Viet Cong had set a new record for the war. In approximately five minutes of shooting they had brought down four helicopters. (A third H-21 had been so badly damaged that it had been forced to land in a rice paddy a little over a mile away where the crew had been picked up unharmed.) The guerrillas had hit every helicopter out of the fifteen except for one Huey.

Bowers leaped to his feet and ran to the crashed Huey. The water was shallower over to the right where he had gone with the squad and the paddy was not much more than damp back where the Huey lay, so he was able to make good time. When he reached the wreck the turbine engine was screaming crazily. With the weight of the main rotor blade knocked free it was running amok. Bowers was afraid that at any moment it would heat red-hot, blow up, and ignite the fuel tanks. The pilot in the left seat had managed to climb out and was staggering toward a nearby mound in the paddy which seemed to offer some shelter from the Viet Cong bullets. Bowers shouted at the man, but he did not reply. Bowers assumed that he was too dazed to help him rescue the other pilot and the crew chief, who were still inside.

The machine was almost over on its back against the ground. The door on the right side had been partially crushed into the paddy, but Bowers was able to push the sliding window open enough to unbuckle the pilot's seat belt and pull him through. The man was also dazed and had a cut in his leg from the crash. He had enough wits left to put his arm around Bowers's shoulder and hobble while Bowers helped him over to the mound.

Bowers rushed back for the crew chief, an older black sergeant named William Deal. The engine was still screaming, and an occasional Viet Cong bullet cracked into the fuselage. Deal was strapped into a side seat behind the extra machine gun he had been firing at the guerrillas. He was hanging almost upside down because of the angle of the fuselage. The only hope he had of getting Deal out before the aircraft blew up, Bowers thought, was to drag him through the front. He kicked in the Plexiglas of the cockpit windshield and climbed inside. He assumed that Deal had been knocked unconscious by the impact. The plastic crash helmets the pilots and other helicopter crewmen wore were equipped with internal earphones and a mike for the intercom and radio. The wire from Deal's helmet was tangled. Bowers released the chin strap and removed the helmet in order to be able to haul Deal free once he had unbuckled the seat belt. The moment he took off the helmet, Bowers discovered that he was trying to save a dead man. Deal had been shot in the head and apparently killed instantly.

The engine had stopped screaming, having evidently burned itself out without blowing up. Bowers decided he would pull Deal from the wreck anyway. Bowers was strong from the farm and the Army and he looked like a country boy. His people were third-generation Irish and Germans who had migrated to Minnesota from Iowa via the coal mines of North Dakota. He was taller than Vann, with angular features and long arms, but was built in the same slight and wiry way Vann was at

150 pounds. Deal was a big man. Dragging him was hard work. Bowers had him out in the paddy and was pulling him toward the mound, his hands under Deal's armpits and his fingers gripping the tough nylon of the gray flight suit Army aviators then wore. The explosion of what sounded like a bazooka rocket fired by the guerrillas at the helicopters told Bowers that he was behaving stupidly. "Hell, I can't do anything for him. He's dead," Bowers said to himself. He laid Deal's body down in the paddy. He felt no sense of disrespect, because the ground was not flooded here.

In this first of America's televised wars, Deal's seven-year-old son back home in Mays Landing, New Jersey, saw his daddy in action on television the day he learned that his father was dead. The family was watching a news broadcast, and a film clip of an earlier helicopter operation was shown. "Look, that's my daddy!" the boy yelled to his mother. Six hours later a telegram came from the Pentagon.

Bowers crawled forward toward the second H-21 that had been downed. He could see one of the crew lying in the water next to a wheel of the aircraft, which was standing in the paddy like its partner. The explosion Bowers had taken for a bazooka rocket announced an attempt by the Viet Cong battalion commander to cap the success of his men. He was trying to burn the carcasses of the helicopters in the rice field. He had sent a squad out along another tree line that ran parallel to the helicopters on the north side, hoping that the squad would be able to set the helicopters ablaze with rifle grenades. These are fired by mounting the grenade on the end of the barrel and launching it with the propellant force of the powder in a blank cartridge. Bowers had heard the first of these grenades blow up. To the chagrin of the guerrillas and their leader, the helicopters were out of range. The few grenades they fired detonated harmlessly in the air. To burn the helicopters would be another act of great psychological value, and the battalion commander did not want to surrender the opportunity lightly. He parted with half a dozen precious shells from the 60mm mortar of his weapons platoon, the heaviest armament he had. These missed the helicopters too, raising no more than showers of muck and water, because the mortarmen were still amateurs in 1963. By the time Bowers reached the H-21 the mortaring had also ceased.

The young man hunkering down in the water beside the wheel was the rear-door machine gunner, a private first class. He said that the pilots were with the ARVN behind the paddy dike and had abandoned him and his buddy, the crew chief, Spec. 4 Donald Braman, twenty-one years old, who was still inside and wounded. "I can't get him out.

Every time I try to climb back in there they start shooting at me," he said, pointing toward the guerrillas in the tree line in front. Bowers told the soldier to crawl over to the dike where the pilots were lying near the Vietnamese lieutenant and said that he would look after his friend.

As Bowers popped up and pulled himself through the door, several of the guerrilla riflemen saw him and started firing. The silhouette of the H-21 standing in the paddy made the Viet Cong tend to shoot high. They also naturally lost sight of Bowers once he was inside. The strings of bullets tearing through the upper part of the fuselage were frightening, but Bowers reasoned that he had a good chance of not being hit as long as he stayed down on the aluminum floor where Braman was lying between the two doors. In a few minutes, the guerrillas ceased wasting their ammunition on a dead machine.

Braman was coherent and did not appear seriously hurt. He had been shot while quixotically firing his carbine at the Viet Cong from the helicopter door when the H-21 landed. He had emptied one clip and was bending over to reload when he had been struck in the shoulder. Ironically, all four crewmen from the first H-21 disabled, whom Braman's helicopter had been trying to rescue, had escaped into the paddy unhurt. Bowers cut away Braman's flight suit and examined the wound. It did not seem grave. The full-metal-jacketed bullet, apparently captured American ammunition, had made a clean wound, entering at the top of the shoulder and exiting just below the shoulder blade. There was some bleeding from the exit hole, but not much. The soldiers of most armies carry a first-aid bandage in a pouch on their belt. Bowers used Braman's bandage to dress the top of the wound. He took his own bandage and also dressed the bullet's exit below the shoulder blade, tying the cotton thongs of the bandage around Braman's neck and shoulders so that they would hold the pad in place. He then made Braman lie on his back to put pressure on this lower bandage and stop the bleeding. Bowers decided that Braman would be just as safe inside the helicopter as he would be in the paddy and better off because the filthy water would not get into the wound and infect it. He explained this to Braman. The youth said he understood.

Bowers gave Braman a drink from his canteen and then lay beside him for a few minutes chatting. He could see that Braman was trying to keep up his nerve and he wanted to help him. Braman had taken his wallet out of his pocket and placed it on the floor at his side. He picked it up with his good arm and showed Bowers a snapshot of his wife in one of the plastic photo holders.

"Gee, I sure hope I get home to see her again," Braman said. Bowers assured him that he would. "Don't worry, you're not hurt bad," he said. "You'll be all right and we'll get you out of here soon." He told Braman that he had to go, but would stay nearby and not desert him. He crawled back to the door on the far side and rolled out into the paddy, drawing another flurry of shots.

The Vietnamese lieutenant had recovered his ability to speak English when Bowers returned to him. Why had he stopped the flanking movement into the southern tree line? Bowers asked. The lieutenant said that it was too dangerous to divide the company in a situation like this, that they all had to stay together. While crawling back, Bowers saw he had been correct in his original judgment that the company would take a lot more casualties lying out in the paddy field than they would if they maneuvered. Staying put had allowed the guerrillas to first concentrate on the helicopters and then to turn to the company at their leisure. A number of the dead and wounded had been shot in the back and buttocks. Bowers guessed that some of the guerrillas had to be up in the trees to obtain plunging fire that would hit men behind the paddy dike like this. He did not realize that the irrigation dike was sufficiently high to give the Viet Cong a perspective down into the rice field. The guerrilla squad that had worked out along the tree line on the north to try to burn the helicopters had also taken a toll from that left flank. The ARVN survivors, wounded and unwounded, were all now pressing themselves up against the dike lengthwise as the lieutenant was doing. Most of them were not returning the guerrillas' fire, which had slackened to intermittent shooting. The Viet Cong discouraged those hardier souls who, in imitation of the Civil Guardsmen in the morning, would stick a rifle above the dike wall and pull the trigger a few times blindly. Ten to fifteen well-aimed shots that slapped into the dike or clipped the top were enough to bring the rifle down in a hurry with no threat that it would be raised again.

Bowers had in mind a way to extricate them all from their predicament and get Braman and the Vietnamese wounded evacuated. He would blast the Viet Cong out of the irrigation dike with artillery or air strikes. Bowers could not see the guerrillas (throughout the whole day he had glimpses of only three Viet Cong, the first the figure running through the southern tree line and later two others on the dike), but from the sound of their weapons and the path of the bullets they obviously had to be under the trees on the dike. The lieutenant had a multichannel field radio. Before boarding the helicopter, Bowers had been given, as a normal precaution, the frequency on which Vann, who was carrying a similar field radio in the L-19, communicated with Ziegler at the division command post, and Vann's call sign, Topper Six. Bowers was going to contact Vann over the lieutenant's radio, explain the plight of the company and the helicopter crews, and have Vann relay Bowers's instructions to the artillery fire direction center or to a forward air controller. Bowers was experienced at such work. He had been trained as a forward observer for an 81mm mortar company and had later served as a mortar platoon sergeant before transferring to staff operations. Batteries of 105mm howitzers and heavy 4.2-inch mortars had been set up along the main Delta road to the south and on a canal to the east so that they could hurl shells out over the entire area of potential action. Bowers told the lieutenant he needed to use his radio, explaining why. Borrowing a radio from the Vietnamese had never been a problem in the past, which was why Bowers had not brought one himself. The lieutenant refused, saying that he had to keep the radio tuned to his frequency to receive orders from division. Artillery or air strikes would save them, Bowers argued. The Viet Cong might sally out of the tree line and overrun the company, he warned. The lieutenant still refused.

The artillery forward observer assigned to the company, a second lieutenant who had control of the only other multichannel radio, was lying about ten yards from the company commander. He was in contact with the fire direction center at the division command post back at Tan Hiep airstrip, which relayed instructions to the batteries. The observer was sporadically calling in shells, but he was too frightened to raise his head and see where they were landing in order to correct the range and walk them down the guerrillas' foxhole line as Bowers intended to do. Bowers watched the shells fall into the paddy between the guerrillas and the company. He had been on previous operations with the same observer and knew that his English was limited. Bowers kept his instruction as simple as possible: "Add one hundred meters," he called. In his fear, the observer did not seem to hear or understand. Bowers shouted the instruction. Then he asked the company commander to translate his directions into Vietnamese. This Fort Benning graduate again lost his ability to speak English. Bowers crawled over to the observer. "Give me the radio," he said. "I'll adjust the fire." The observer and the company commander both replied in English that Bowers could not have the radio. The observer had to talk to the artillery, the company commander said. It became clear to Bowers that the two lieutenants were afraid that if he got on the radio, the end result might be that they would receive orders to do something, which might mean getting up from behind the dike. After eight shells had been called in to no effect, a bullet wounded the soldier who had the observer's radio strapped to his back. Another bullet knocked out the radio. The observer burrowed deep into the ooze.

When they had been in the paddy about half an hour, the prospect of rescue appeared in the form of two AD-6 Skyraider fighter-bombers. The planes first dropped napalm. It did not land on the guerrillas. The pilots instead struck the thatched houses behind the irrigation dike, some of which had already been set afire by the rockets from the Hueys. The heat of the napalm was so intense just the same that for a few minutes it was oppressive to breathe all the way out in the rice field. If it was this bad where he was, Bowers wondered how the Viet Cong could bear the heat and suffocating effect of the jellied gasoline. He rose to a crouch to see if the guerrillas would run. Many of the Saigon infantrymen assumed that their ordeal was over and stood up to watch the spectacle of the planes dive-bombing with conventional bombs and strafing and rocketing the flaming houses. Suddenly two soldiers next to Bowers fell dead, hit by rifle fire from the tree line. The others threw themselves back down. Bowers remained in his crouch for another moment or two, not yet convinced the Viet Cong were staying. He searched the tree line for a sign of movement. There was none. The guerrillas were apparently not retreating. For the first time since he had come to Vietnam, Bowers felt some admiration for the Viet Cong. "Come on, give me that radio," he called to the ARVN lieutenant, who had not moved from behind the dike. "We'll burn them out. I'll get the planes to put the napalm right on top of that tree line." The lieutenant shook his head. "No, no," he said. "Napalm too close; too close to us."

Bowers thought of shooting the lieutenant and taking the radio, as he would have done to a cowardly American officer who was endangering a company of paratroopers, and instantly dismissed the possibility. He was a good noncom who obeyed orders. The Army had told him that in Vietnam he was a mere advisor, that he did not have command authority, that this was "their war." During a week's orientation course at the Special Warfare Center at Fort Bragg, North Carolina, prior to departure the previous March, he had been instructed to use "tact and diplomacy" with the Vietnamese. The downed helicopter pilots had not been of any help to him in dealing with the Vietnamese lieutenant. This fighting on the ground was not their game. He looked down the dike. The petrified infantrymen were pressed up against it. He reflected that if the guerrillas did sortie out of that tree line, he would never be able to rally these men to return fire. The company would be overrun and they would all be killed. While he was in the helicopter dressing Braman's wound he had spotted a packet of cigarettes and some matches in an open C-ration box and picked them up and put them into the breast pocket of his fatigue shirt. He had stopped smoking a month before and had bet another sergeant a fifth of whiskey that he would beat the habit. Now he decided he might as well have a smoke. He lay back with his head resting against the dike and lit up.

Vann was a prisoner in the backseat of the spotter plane, almost manic with anger and frustration. He had an advisor and three helicopter crews on the ground, whether dead or wounded he did not know. These Americans and the ARVN infantry they were with were all in danger of being overrun, and he could not get anyone to come to their rescue.

As soon as the Huey crashed he turned the dial on the portable field radio he had wedged between his legs in the cramped quarters of the L-19 to the frequency of Capts. James Scanlon and Robert Mays, who were with the company of M-113 armored personnel carriers that Vann had previously seen about a mile to the northwest. Scanlon, thirty-one, short and square built, was the advisor to the armored regiment at My Tho commanded by Major Tho, the province chief. Mays, thirty-two, a loose-limbed Texan with a measured way of speaking, was Scanlon's deputy and the regular advisor to Capt. Ly Tong Ba, the commander of the M-113 company. Although Scanlon's job was to advise the whole regiment, Ba's company and another M-113 unit attached to the 21st Division in the southern half of the Delta were the most active armored units, and so Scanlon spent most of his time in the field with them.

"Walrus, this is Topper Six, over," Vann said, releasing his finger from the button on the telephone-type microphone and earpiece so that Mays or Scanlon could reply. (Walrus was the coded radio call sign for the advisors with the M-113s.)

"Topper Six, this is Walrus, over," Scanlon replied.

"Walrus, I've got three repeat three choppers down and a rifle company pinned in the paddies due southeast of you at X-Ray Sierra three zero niner five three niner." Vann repeated the map coordinates to be certain that Scanlon heard them correctly. "Tell your counterpart"—it was clear in the context of the conversation that Vann was referring to Captain Ba—"to get his tracks over here as fast as he can. Make damn sure he understands the urgency of the situation."

"Roger, Topper Six," Scanlon replied.

Vann acknowledged Scanlon's response with a "This is Topper Six, out" (in U.S. Army radio procedure the initiator of the conversation ends it), and told the pilot of the L-19 to nose down for a landscape-level pass over the wrecked Huey and the infantry of the reserve company cowering behind the dike. He could see that the ARVN were making no attempt to return what he described in one report of the battle as "withering fire" from the western tree line of Bac. The banging of the guerrillas' automatic weapons and the occasional tracers flashing past the fuselage made it apparent that the Viet Cong were trying to add the spotter plane, a much more difficult target than the helicopters because of its short and narrow silhouette, to their bag. Vann had the Army pilot brave the fusillade for several more passes in order to ascertain as best he could the situation of the company and the helicopter crews. The little aircraft was not hit.

While they were regaining altitude after the last pass, Scanlon came back on the air with bad news. "I've got a problem, Topper Six," he said. "My counterpart won't move."

"Goddammit, doesn't he understand this is an emergency?" Vann asked.

"I described the situation to him exactly as you told me, Topper Six, but he says, 'I don't take orders from Americans,' " Scanlon answered.

"I'll get right back to you, Walrus," Vann said. He switched frequencies and raised Ziegler at the command-post tent beside the airstrip. He gave Ziegler a capsule account of what had occurred and told him to ask Dam to order Captain Ba to head for Bac immediately with his M-113s. "This situation is absolutely critical," Vann said. The command post already knew of the downed helicopters from monitoring the radio. Ziegler returned in a few moments. He said that Dam agreed and was issuing the order through the division's radio channels.

From where he was circling about 1,000 feet over Bac, Vann could see the rectangular shapes of the thirteen carriers. He instructed the pilot to head for them, and as soon as they reached the armored vehicles, he switched frequencies and called Scanlon again. He directed his attention to the column of white smoke beginning to rise above Bac from the houses set afire by the rockets and tracer bullets of the Hueys. "You tell your counterpart that I am relaying an order from his division commander," Vann said. "He is to head for that column of smoke right away. He is to move out now!"

Captain Ba started the M-113s toward Bac. Almost immediately they were confronted by a canal with high banks. High-banked canals, streams, and rivers were the sole obstacles that seriously impeded movement of the M-113s across the Delta landscape. The amphibious vehicles had no trouble swimming them, but the tracks could not get sufficient grip in the soft mud of the steep bank on the opposite side to pull the ten-ton carriers out of the water. The company of mounted infantry who rode in the M-113s and the crews would have to climb out and hand-cut brush and trees until the canal was filled high enough for one or more of the carriers to cross. The ten-ton weight would quickly crush the brush down into the canal bottom. The last carrier across would then have to tow the next one over by cable and so on until all of the vehicles had traversed the canal. This canal that now confronted them would take about an hour to cross. The alternative was to try to locate another spot where the banks were not so high and the tracks could get a firm grip on the opposite bank. Captain Ba did not move to go and find one. Instead he spent several minutes speaking in Vietnamese over the radio. To Scanlon, who understood some of the language, he seemed to be seeking instructions from his superiors. Then he balked again. He did not want to go. The canal would take too long to cross. "Why don't they send the infantry?" he said, pointing to lines of riflemen marching along the paddy dikes near them. These infantrymen were the third company of the division battalion that was descending on Tan Thoi from the north and had landed a bit over an hour earlier. Because the lifts of the second and third companies had been delayed for two and a half hours, Vann had arranged for the helicopters to drop them farther south than originally planned and to link up with the first company, which had landed at 7:03 A.M. Scanlon was surprised that Ba was balking. His aggressiveness had been a pleasing contrast to the excessive caution of most ARVN officers.

Ly Tong Ba was a contemporary of his American counterparts, ten months younger than Scanlon. He was fighting with them rather than resisting them and their machines because he was the son of a prosperous Delta farmer who had served the French empire and believed in it. Ba's father had been conscripted into the French Army and shipped to France near the end of World War I. The Armistice of November 11, 1918, had saved him from death in the trenches, and he had come home to rise to sergeant major in the Garde Indigène. In his later years, he had settled down to farm on a comfortably large, if not grand, scale with two of Ba's uncles. Together they had owned about 2,500 acres of rice land in the southern Delta. Ba's playmates had been the sons of the landless agricultural laborers who depended on his father for a livelihood. He had guarded his father's water buffalos with them, riding the wide backs of the beasts in a conical straw hat to ward off the sun as the peasant boys did in the fields through which he now drove his metal behemoths. He had lost touch with his playmates after his father had sent him to the lycée in Can Tho for a French education. From the lycée he had gone in 1950 to the French-sponsored officer candidate school at Hue. His boyhood friends had been taken in a different direction by their origins. A good many of them had joined the Viet Minh. His father had kept track of the families of his workers until this second Communist-led insurrection had forced him to abandon his lands entirely and seek safety in Can Tho. He sometimes mentioned the names of several of Ba's "buffalo boy" playmates who had become officers in the Viet Cong.

Ba was an intelligent man, and in a nati~ ¬ whose women are often remarked on for their beauty but whose men are not considered good-looking, he was handsome. His ancestry was that common to the people of the Delta—mainly Vietnamese with some Chinese blood and probably a tinge of Cambodian as well to account for the slightly duskier hue of the skin. His nature was cheerful and he genuinely enjoyed soldiering. He was a bit given to exaggeration and there was some bravado about him, which was perhaps why he had joined the armored cavalry and spent the last years of the French war commanding a platoon of armored cars in North Vietnam. In the interval between the French war and this one he had been well instructed in France and the United States. First there had been a year at the French armored cavalry officers' school at Saumur in the valley of the Loire and then another year in 1957–58 at the Armor School at Fort Knox, Kentucky.

Scanlon was so surprised because Ba had never shown any hesitancy on past occasions. Whenever guerrillas had been sighted, Ba had headed straight for them. The M-113 company was regarded by everyone as a virtually invincible combination of armored mobility and firepower. The Viet Cong were supposed to possess a few 57mm recoilless cannons (technically called recoilless rifles), which could knock out the armored carriers, but none had ever been encountered in action. The .50 caliber heavy machine gun mounted in front of the command hatch on top of twelve of the thirteen carriers in the company was another achievement of John Browning. It was a formidable weapon, capable of plowing through earth parapets and cutting down trees with its big steel-jacketed slugs. The thirteenth carrier, a recent addition, had a flamethrower in a turret in place of the .50 caliber on a swing mount. Each M-113 also carried a squad of a dozen infantrymen, armed with BARs and M-1s, who were trained to dismount and attack in unison with the armored vehicles. Ba had been sent off on a number of independent missions because his unit was considered capable of handling anything the Viet Cong might put up against it. His spirited leadership and the shock effect the machines had on the guerrillas, as the slaughter of September 18 had demonstrated, had led to the M-113 company's killing and capturing more Viet Cong than any other organization in the 7th Division.

Ba's announcement that he was not going and that the infantry ought to go instead set off half an hour of emotional confrontation. A brief reconnaissance on foot by Mays and Ba after the carriers encountered the first canal revealed a second high-banked canal behind it. The M-113s were up against a double canal that would require two hours to cross at this spot. Ba grasped at this as an excuse to do nothing. He seemed unimpressed by appeals from Scanlon and Mays to his humanitarian instinct—there were three helicopter crews and a company of ARVN infantry who might all be killed or captured. "We can't get across the canal," he would say, and repeat that the infantry battalion could reach Bac much faster. Within a few minutes Scanlon and Mays, who were standing with Ba on top of his carrier, were shouting at him and he was shouting back. Vann, circling overhead in the spotter plane, was raging at all three of them, trying to goad the two advisors into moving Ba and attempting to shame Ba into action at the same time. Ba's English was good, and he could hear everything Vann was saying, because the portable radio Scanlon and Mays were using was not the telephone type. It had a loudspeaker for incoming calls and a push-button microphone with which to answer.

Scanlon could measure the rise in Vann's rage from the way his voice went up a quarter of an octave in shrillness with each exchange. "I told you people to do something and you're not doing it," he berated Scanlon. "Why can't you get the lead out of that son of a bitch's ass? He's got his order from the division commander." Scanlon in turn berated Ba.

"Are you afraid to go over there?" he asked. Ba said no. "Then why won't you go?" Scanlon shouted. "We're just sitting here staring at two canals. I know we can find a place to get across somewhere else if we'd start looking for one." Ba repeated his excuses.

"Jesus Christ, this is intolerable," Vann's nasal shrill broke in again from the radio. "That bastard has armored tracks and .50 cals and he's afraid of a bunch of VC with small arms. What's wrong with him?"

"We're doing the best we can, Topper Six," Scanlon replied.

"Your best isn't worth a shit, Walrus," Vann cursed back. "This is an emergency. Those people are lying out there exposed. I want you to make that son of a bitch move."

Scanlon knew that Vann was given to tantrums when thwarted. Vann had always seemed to think well enough of Scanlon not to subject him to this verbal lashing before, but this was an unprecedented situation.

Scanlon could picture Vann in the backseat of the little plane gritting his teeth, the redness of the rage in his face merging into the redness of the sunburn on his neck, the veins in his neck bulging from the fury within. Scanlon was professional enough to assume that much of the anger was not directed personally at him and Mays, that Vann was making no effort to control his temper because he thought that his only chance for success lay in shaming Ba and in stinging the two advisors into putting more pressure on the Vietnamese captain. Ba was correct, Scanlon noted to himself, in arguing that the infantry could reach Bac sooner than the M-113s. He thought that Vann, like most officers who were not armor specialists, had a poor notion of how time-consuming it was for the carriers to cross canals at the best of fords, and there would be more canals between this one and Bac. Knowing Vann, however, Scanlon guessed that he had other reasons for demanding that the carriers perform the rescue. Scanlon was correct in this guess and wrong in thinking that Vann was ignorant of the problem the carriers had in traversing the canals.

Vann's knowledge of the extent to which canals could impede the M-113s was one of the factors adding to his rage. He had asked the previous September for portable bridging equipment for the company so that the crews and the mounted infantry would not have to stop to cut trees and brush. Like almost all of his requests, it had gone unfulfilled by Harkins's headquarters. He had to send the armored vehicles to Bac because he knew that it was futile to try to use the division infantry battalion. Once the battalion commander realized that he was being asked to make a frontal assault on entrenched Viet Cong, which he would soon discern if given the rescue mission, he would see to it that his battalion never reached Bac. By diverting the battalion from its advance on Tan Thoi, Vann would not save the Americans and the pinned-down reserve. All he would accomplish would be to open a covered route of retreat for the guerrillas to the north along the tree lines that ran in that direction. He was damned if he was going to let these Viet Cong escape. They had downed four helicopters and had his blood up. Ba's armored tracks were the one means he had of both saving the men in front of Bac and destroying the guerrillas.

He was trying to goad Scanlon and Mays and shame Ba into going to Bac, but this was just one of the reasons for his rage. All of this bile was pouring down on them because he was unable to contain any longer the anger and frustration that had been building in him for five and a half months since the fiasco of July 20. His sense of fury at his helplessness had risen each week after Cao had begun to fake the operations outright in mid-October. He had warned that there would be a day of reckoning if Harkins did not make Cao fight and allowed the Communists to continue to harvest American weapons from the outposts. None of this would have happened if the command in Saigon had held up its end of this war. Now the day of reckoning had come and the captain in charge of the M-113s, who had been one of the few decent officers in this stinking army, was behaving like the rest of the cowardly bastards. He, John Vann, was supposed to move thirteen ten-ton carriers across a mile of rice paddies and canals and redeem this disaster by waving a wand from the back of a spotter plane. He kept checking with Ziegler to see if Dam had issued the order to Ba. Dam kept confirming that he had. You never could be certain what these people were saying over the radio. They lied to you and they lied to each other.

What Vann did not realize, because in his fury he was not thinking clearly enough to guess at the cause of Ba's reluctance, was that the coup phobia of Diem and his family had put Ba in a dilemma. Getting Dam to order Ba to move wasn't enough. Vann needed to have Major Tho issue the order, but no one on the Saigon side was going to tell him that. Prior to December, Ba's company had been assigned directly to the 7th Division. Diem had then come to see that although armored personnel carriers were not as useful in a coup as tanks, they were potentially effective tools to help overthrow his regime, or to protect it. He had therefore decided to purchase more anticoup insurance. During his reorganization of the armed forces in December he had removed the two companies of M-113s in the Delta from divisional command and assigned them to the armored regiment under Tho. Dam had ordered Ba to proceed to Bac. Ba could not raise Tho on the radio to find out what Tho wanted him to do, and he was afraid to go without Tho's approval. From what he could gather, the presidential palace was not going to be pleased with the events at Bac. Tho for Tho's sake might not want any of his subordinates to get involved. If Ba went and Tho disapproved, Ba was liable to a reprimand and dismissal. His career had already been set back for political reasons. He was a Buddhist and he had been unjustly accused of sympathy with the leaders of the abortive 1960 paratrooper coup. Although he had cleared himself, Diem was watching him and holding up his promotion to major.

Beneath Ba's bravado, he was a conservative man. He did not lack courage. Neither was he a professional risk-taker like Vann. He had been an officer in a colonial army that had lost its war. He was fighting this second war for the Tory regime of his class. He was doing precisely what could be expected of a man who had grown up in a system where, when in doubt, the best thing to do was to do nothing. He was stalling.

Vann's bullying over the radio made matters worse. He was increasing Ba's resistance. Ba had come, out of his pride, to resent the superiority complex of these Americans. Vann had been cordial to him, and their relations had been bluff and easy, except on those occasions when Vann's manner had become overbearing. Ba had then found him singularly grating. Ba could not know the pent-up emotions that were the larger source of Vann's abusive language and the extent to which Vann was in turn a prisoner of the American system. In the U.S. Army, when a combat emergency occurred and a senior officer took charge, he issued brisk orders and everyone obeyed instantly. Vann could not help reverting to this procedure in his current predicament.

At the end of the half hour of shouting, Ba relented to the extent of giving Scanlon a carrier to return south and find a crossing site that Scanlon had seen on the way up to this spot where they had met the infantry and been blocked by the double canal. Vann flew off to try to get the Civil Guards to maneuver and dislodge the Viet Cong at Bac.

He had the L-19 pilot make a couple of passes over the first Civil Guard battalion, which had opened the battle by walking into the guerrillas on the far side of the stream south of the hamlet. He could see the Civil Guardsmen lolling around, heads back against the paddy dikes in repose or in a snooze. If there were any Viet Cong left under the trees in front of them, they had clearly stopped shooting, and the Saigon troops were rendering a like courtesy. Vann concluded that the guerrillas in the southern tree line, having halted the Civil Guards, had turned their attention to the reserve company as soon as it had landed behind them. In any case, the Civil Guards were now perfectly situated to flank around to the right and unhinge the position of the Viet Cong along the irrigation dike on the western edge of Bac. Vann radioed Ziegler with a recommendation that Dam have Tho order the Civil Guards to assault around this vulnerable flank.

Vann's lieutenant on the ground with the Civil Guards, who now also could not get access to a radio with which to talk to his chief overhead, had been attempting since the helicopters landed the reserve at 10:20 A.M. to persuade the Vietnamese captain in charge of the battalion to do precisely this. The guerrillas in front of them had stopped firing the moment the helicopters had arrived. The lieutenant had drawn the same conclusion as Vann. He had been urging the Civil Guard commander, whose slight leg wound was not incapacitating, to push his troops up through the coconut grove on the right where the district guerrilla platoon had lain in ambush and, using it for cover, to turn the tables on the Viet Cong. The Vietnamese captain kept replying that Major Tho had instructed him to stay where he was in a "blocking position." The term had lost any connotation of the "hammer and anvil" tactic that Vann had sought to employ on July 20 and had become a euphemism among the Saigon commanders for doing nothing. Tho did not want any more casualties among his Civil Guards. When Dam called him at Vann's behest and told him to have his troops execute the flanking movement, he ignored the order.

From the plane Vann could see the second Civil Guard battalion still marching up from the southwest, searching hamlets along the way. Tho was in no hurry for it to arrive at Bac. The division infantry battalion moving down from the north had also not yet reached the hamlet of Tan Thoi above Bac.

A voice speaking English with a Vietnamese accent, probably the lieutenant cowering behind the dike at Bac, suddenly came up on Vann's portable field radio and said that two of the helicopter crewmen were seriously wounded. Vann tried to keep the conversation going and obtain more information. The voice did not reply to his questions.

He told the L-19 pilot to return to the M-113s and circled low over them. The armored tracks were in the same place he had left them. It was 11:10 A.M., forty-five minutes since the Huey had flipped over on its side and crashed and he had radioed Ba to come to the rescue at once with his mobile fortresses. Ba's refusal to cooperate in this emergency was incredible to Vann. Just before flying off ten minutes earlier to attempt to maneuver the Civil Guards, he had, through Ziegler, appealed to Dam to repeat his order to Ba and this time to raise Ba on the radio himself and personally to order him to head for Bac immediately. Orders from the division commander were normally relayed down through whichever regiment had contact with the M-113s. Dam had confirmed that he had done as Vann had asked. Orbiting just above the vehicle now, Vann could see Mays standing beside Ba on top of Ba's carrier.

"Walrus, this is Topper Six, over," he called. Mays acknowledged.

"Is that goddam counterpart of yours going to respond, Walrus?" Vann asked.

"Negative, Topper Six," Mays replied. "He still says we can't get across the canal in time and division ought to send the infantry."

Vann had endured all he could bear. "Walrus, can you take that company over there? Can you? Can you, goddammit?" His voice coming over the loudspeaker of Mays's radio was a shriek.

Mays was puzzled that Vann would ask him if he could assume command of the company. Yes, he could get the M-113s across the canals to Bac, although he knew the men would not follow him without Ba telling them to do so. He was fearful of Vann in his rage and decided to treat the question hypothetically. "Roger, Topper Six, I could do that," he replied.

"Then shoot that rotten, cowardly son of a bitch right now and move out," Vann screamed back.

Mays did not answer. He looked at Ba. The two men liked each other. They had become friends over the four months that Mays had been the company's advisor. Ba also said nothing, but the expression on his face asked: "Would you shoot me?" Mays reminded Ba that they had crossed a canal earlier in the morning which was probably this double canal at a point where it was still a single one. Why didn't they drive back, recross it, and work their way east to Bac from that point? Ba agreed.

Ba slipped on his radio headset and transmitted an order to the company. The drivers started the engines and the tracks of the carriers churned through the muck and water on the way to Bac.

Vann turned his attention to the plight of the aviators in the rice paddy. The information that two of them were seriously wounded made it imperative, he concluded, to attempt another helicopter rescue, this one better calculated. He flew back to Tan Hiep to refuel the L-19 and discuss the plan with Ziegler and the senior helicopter pilots. The situation of the reserve company might be easing, Vann thought. As far as he could discern from the air, they were being shot at only every once in a while. Since the Civil Guards on the south were not being fired on, it was possible that the Viet Cong were withdrawing and endeavoring to infiltrate out of the area. Vann had the division communications section try to find out if Bowers was alive and instruct the lieutenant to put him on the radio in order to obtain some reliable information. He was unsuccessful, apparently because the lieutenant did not respond to the regimental headquarters that relayed the instructions to him. Vann still felt they owed it to the wounded aviators to act on the possibility that the Viet Cong might be disengaging.

He described his plan. He and the L-19 pilot would be the decoy to learn whether the guerrillas remained in force. They would make several treetop passes to draw fire. The spotter-plane pilot told Vann he was crazy and wanted to commit suicide, but he agreed to fly. Three of the Hueys were capable of strafing. (A fourth had taken a hit in a critical area and was considered unsafe to fly until repaired.) If the spotter plane attracted little or no shooting and the guerrillas were apparently no longer at Bac in force, the Hueys would machine-gun and rocket the western and southern tree lines to suppress the fire of any Viet Cong who might have stayed behind while an H-21 went in for the pickup. A second H-21 would stay aloft in case of some unforeseen emergency. At this point Vann was still under the misimpression that the guerrillas in the southern tree line had helped to shoot down the helicopters that morning and that they remained a menace. The helicopter pilots, also wanting to save their wounded, accepted the plan.

Bowers did not realize it was Vann in the L-19 that appeared all of a sudden and began buzzing the downed helicopters and the tree lines. He assumed it was that daredevil major from the Air Force, Herb Prevost, who was always taunting the Viet Cong to shoot him down. Perhaps they would today, Bowers thought. He knew that the Viet Cong were still in the western tree line to his front, because Braman had made a racket inside the fuselage of the H-21 where he was lying a little while before and the guerrillas had immediately fired at it. Bowers had crawled to the helicopter and attracted another burst of shots as he pulled himself through the door and slid over to Braman. He asked him what was wrong. Braman said everything had become so quiet that he thought they had gone off and abandoned him. He did not want to raise himself off his back for fear of causing the wound to bleed, so he had banged the heels of his boots against the aluminum floor to try to attract the attention of someone. Bowers assured him that no one had gone anywhere and that he was attracting the attention of the wrong people, who were, as he could hear, still around too. Braman had fortunately not been hit a second time. The large silhouette of the H-21 had again performed the optical trick of causing the guerrillas to shoot high, and the top part of the fuselage had more perforations.

Braman's physical condition seemed to be holding stable. Bowers examined his wound. There was no fresh bleeding, and Braman did not appear to be going into shock. He was starting to become emotional because the lonely waiting was weakening his nerve. Bowers gave him another drink of water and once more lay beside him for a while to comfort and calm him. Help must be on the way, Bowers said, and Braman really was safer inside the helicopter as long as he kept quiet. He definitely wouldn't thank Bowers later if the sergeant carried him out into the paddy where he might take another bullet and the filthy water would infect his wound. Before he left, Bowers placed a canteen at Braman's side where he could reach it whenever he got thirsty. For some reason the Viet Cong did not fire at Bowers when he rolled back out the door for the return crawl to the dike, but he was certain they were watching him.

Vann and the L-19 pilot dangled as tempting a bait as they could in front of the guerrillas. Vann was not satisfied to just buzz the treetops, a reconnaissance tactic that gives some protection because it is difficult to see and shoot up through the foliage at an object flying directly overhead. Instead, he had the pilot fly twice right over the downed helicopters on a course parallel to the western tree line, presenting the easiest of targets. Then they made a third pass at a 45-degree angle over the helicopters, which exposed the little plane to fire from the southern tree line as well. "You son of a gun, Prevost, you sure are looking for it," Bowers said to himself.

Not a shot was fired. The Viet Cong had resumed their discipline of not shooting at spotter planes and waited to see what the game was. Bowers picked up the sound of a helicopter approaching from behind and turned to see an H-21 flying directly toward him up the rice field. The pilot was trying to put the downed machines between his aircraft and the western tree line, as the pilot of the crashed Huey had sought to do. Simultaneously the three Hueys appeared and started machine-gunning and rocketing the western and southern tree lines. At that moment Bowers heard the deadly percussion of automatic weapons and rifles begin from under the trees on the irrigation dike as the Viet Cong battalion commander also saw the H-21 and gave the order to open fire. The Hueys were again wasting half of their firepower on the southern tree line. This mistake and the inefficacy of their light 7.62mm machine guns and rockets against troops entrenched beneath trees and foliage meant there was no interruption in the torrent of bullets that rent the air over Bowers's head on their way toward the H-21 flying up the paddy. The pilot landed about thirty yards behind the wrecked Huey, but immediately radioed that he was pulling out because he was taking so many hits. Some of his controls were shot away, and he had great difficulty keeping his craft in the air. With guidance from Vann's pilot he was able to turn and fly back about three-quarters of a mile to where Ba's M-113s were crossing a canal.

It was almost noon, and the Viet Cong guerrillas had set a new record for the war. They had knocked out five helicopters in a single day. They had also foxed Vann a second time. He was more determined than ever to make these men pay for making him look foolish.

Vann might have taken some comfort had he known that things were not going so well on the other side. The commander of the 261st Main

Force Battalion and the province committee had intended to punish the Saigon army and then maneuver into an orderly retreat. They had wanted to repeat on a bigger scale the ambush of the Ranger platoon on October 5. As the action unfolded, they lost the option of withdrawal. By midday the guerrilla battalion commander had his 350 men locked into an unequal contest from which there was no possibility of retreat until darkness fell at 7:30 P.M. He had hesitated to pull back through Tan Thoi after downing the four helicopters in the morning because, as a result of Vann's decision, the 7th Division troops approaching that hamlet from the north were not deflected to rescue the reserve company and the helicopter crews. At 12:15 the division battalion finally reached Tan Thoi. Instead of making a careful reconnaissance and then an assault, the ARVN commander let his infantry blunder into a firefight with the company of the 514th Regionals entrenched in the dikes around the edges of the place. The provincial guerrillas had the ARVN stymied, but the Tan Thoi escape route was blocked nonetheless. The only unobstructed side of the battlefield at this point was on the east, and this area was open rice paddy and swamp. Any attempt to cross it in daytime was bound to end in another massacre by the fighter-bombers.

The positions of the two reinforced guerrilla companies in Bac and Tan Thoi were mutually supporting. They were also mutually dependent. Men running from one hamlet would probably cause the troops in the other to panic too. Even if the men in the second hamlet did not panic, they would come under too much pressure from too many sides in too confined a space to resist effectively. Both Vann who was trying to destroy them and the guerrilla battalion commander who was attempting to save his men knew what the alternatives were. The 350 guerrillas could stand and fight and some of them would die, but if they held until darkness most of them would live. Or they could break and run and most of them would die. It takes the experience of having fought against superior odds and a capacity for clear thought amid violence and confusion to see the alternatives of a battle this starkly. Vann and the guerrilla battalion commander had that experience and that capacity. Vann was doing his best to make these men break and run so that he could kill them. The Viet Cong leader was using every skill he had learned from his years against the French and from his study of the earlier battles of this war to inspire his men to stand and fight and survive to fight again.

Ordinary men see their immediate peril rather than the larger one to come. The platoon of guerrilla regulars on the far side of the stream south of Bac and the district platoon with them began to crack before noon. The platoon leader of the regulars was slightly wounded during the morning's fight and was carried back to the company first-aid station in Bac. While the platoon was not bothered again by the Civil Guards after they beat back the initial flanking maneuver, they felt exposed with the reserve company at their rear. They apparently did not realize that their comrades along the irrigation dike had rendered the reserve company harmless by killing or wounding more than half of its 102 men. They knew from the local guerrilla scouts that another Civil Guard battalion was marching northeast toward them. One of their BARs malfunctioned and they could not repair it. They reported to their company commander in Bac that their position was "in bad shape" and asked to withdraw with the district platoon which had joined them. He gave permission, planning to place both platoons in new foxholes at the bottom end of the irrigation dike, where they could still protect his flank to the south. The men did not exercise good camouflage discipline in retreating. A VNAF air controller in an L-19 saw some of them and called in a fighter-bomber. Although few of the men were killed or wounded by the strafing, it dispersed them, and most started up the stream toward the seeming safety of Tan Thoi rather than reporting to the company commander at Bac. A scout team sent to locate and lead them back succeeded in finding them, but the men were frightened and refused an order to return. The company commander had to weaken his main line of defense in the irrigation dike toward which the M-113s were slowly moving by withdrawing a squad to provide some cover on the south flank. He assumed, as Vann and the American lieutenant had been urging, that Major Tho's Civil Guards would push into the southern tree line vacated by the two platoons and attack him. A single squad is scant protection against a battalion. Had the Civil Guards assaulted with any vigor they undoubtedly would have turned this flank and pushed into the rear of the foxholes along the irrigation dike, rendering the position in Bac untenable.

The worried company leader in Bac requested reinforcements from the company in Tan Thoi to replace his lost platoon of regulars. The battalion commander refused. The province guerrillas in Tan Thoi might have the ARVN battalion stalled, but they were one reinforced company confronted by three companies of a battalion. The battalion might be strengthened at any moment by a fourth company, a Ranger unit that was another element of the 7th Division reserve and that was just a ten-minute march away from the hamlet. In view of these odds the guerrilla battalion commander could not bring himself to do anything that might unsettle the men in Tan Thoi. The entire situation was so precarious and the two positions so interdependent that he did not dare risk any action that might trigger the loss of one of them. Bac would have to be held, he told his company commander there, by the men who had stayed.

The guerrillas in the irrigation dike at Bac had suffered a mere five wounded in the whole morning's fight, but their resolve was also eroding under the air and artillery bombardment and the prospect of having to accomplish what seemed impossible—stopping the armored carriers with the weapons they held in their hands. The artillery had resumed firing again, and again inaccurately, around noon. The nearest ground observer was with the battalion at Tan Thoi. He could do no more than adjust into the general area of Bac by watching the smoke columns of an occasional white-phosphorus round. Since the abortive helicopter rescue, Vann was no longer under any illusion as to where the guerrillas were entrenched, and he repeatedly tried to have the high-explosive shells adjusted onto the western tree line. Despite reiterated promises from division headquarters that a correction was about to be made by a VNAF observer in an L-19, the division artillery officer never got the observer to accomplish it. The shells landing within the hamlet were mainly smashing the peasant houses.

Vann had the theoretical option of sending the captain who was his artillery advisor to take charge of one of the firing batteries and then to direct the shells himself from the spotter plane. It was an option that even Vann did not dare try to exercise. Seizing control of the artillery would have meant removing a major weapon from the hands of the Saigon officers. Dam, his chief artillery officer, and the battery commander concerned would all have refused and Vann would have had to back down, which was why he never seriously considered the option as an alternative. At this early stage of the war the advisors were under too many strictures from above to remain advisors and not reach openly for command functions, and their Saigon counterparts knew it, to attempt a radical step like this. Vann had no choice but to keep demanding that the division artillery officer contact the VNAF observer in the L-19. The rub was that he couldn't make the Vietnamese on his side make their system work. What was true of the artillery also held for air power on this day when Vann needed it most.

The Vietnamese forward air controllers (FACs) in other L-19s and the Vietnamese and American fighter-bomber pilots of the hybrid air force created by General Anthis and his 2nd Air Division staff had been doing all day what they always did when told that the infantry were receiving fire from a hamlet. They were attacking the thatched-roof dwellings of Bac and Tan Thoi and the smaller livestock shelters beside the peasant houses, shattering the frail structures with their bombs and rockets and burning them down with napalm. Having never been on the ground to learn how the guerrillas fought, they had no sense that they were engaged in a futile exercise. A man in an airplane does not easily grasp the logic of a landscape beneath him. He does not naturally deduce that if the guerrillas are in the houses inside the hamlet, they will not be able to shoot at the infantry out in the rice field: the foliage around the hamlet will block their view. The optical relationship between a man in a diving plane and the profusion of a rural landscape also seems to automatically focus a pilot on the largest man-made structure he can see. The French Air Force had done the same thing during its war, bombing the peasant houses while the Viet Minh watched from foxholes under the trees on the dikes. When the U.S. Air Force was to bomb North Vietnam in the later years of this war the pilots were also inadvertently to blow up schools and pagodas, because these were normally the largest buildings in a rural Vietnamese community.

Vann had not thought to appeal to Prevost for help to get the planes to hit the dike because he was under the misimpression that Prevost had left for the corps headquarters in Can Tho to set up a regional air control center. Prevost had actually been packing to leave when he heard the news of the helicopters being shot down. He had immediately driven to the command post at Tan Hiep and borrowed a VNAF L-19 sitting on the airstrip to survey the battlefield. With Vann also in the air, the two men had missed contact. Vann could not simply guide an air strike himself by talking directly to an American pilot. He was forbidden to do so. Because the VNAF had been zealous to guard its prerogatives and Anthis and his staff in Saigon had supported their protégé, Harkins had not responded to Vann's urging that they adopt a workable system to allow Americans to take charge when the fighter-bomber pilots were American, as was the case with many of the pilots today. The Vietnamese FACs retained sole authority to control the strikes. Vann implored Dam to tell the VNAF FACs to stop incinerating houses and to have the fighter-bombers lay the napalm down the tree line. Words in any language did not seem to influence the automatonlike behavior of the airmen.

What Vann scorned as ineffective was not easy for the guerrillas to endure. The rushing through the air of the incoming artillery, the shaking earth from the explosions of the shells and bombs, the heat from the flaming thatch, the way the napalm did make it difficult to breathe by suddenly sucking the oxygen out of the air, the devil's din of .50 caliber machine guns, 20mm rapid-fire cannon, salvos of rockets, and the roaring of aircraft engines when the fighter-bombers swept overhead on their strafing runs—all of this was hard on the nerves as well as on the ears. And shortly before 1:00 P.M. the guerrillas saw the M-113s slowly approaching across the rice fields. It was nearly seven hours until darkness, so there was no avoiding a fight with these terrifying machines. The men in the foxholes began reliving in their minds the scenes of killing the behemoths had wrought in past battles.

Their predicament was that, lacking antitank weapons, the Viet Cong leadership had not been able to devise any sound tactics for dealing with the M-113s. To attempt to give their troops enough courage to stand up to the armored tracks with small arms and grenades, they had developed a list of the supposed weaknesses of the carriers and had lectured on these in training classes. All of their observations were fallacious with the exception of two: they had noticed that the machine gunner was unprotected from the waist up when he stood in the command hatch on top to fire the .50 caliber, and they thought that the driver could be shot through his visor slit. There was no visor slit, but this observation still had a valid application. The drivers habitually drove with their heads sticking out of the hatch in front because it was easier and more fun, they could go faster, and the risk of being hit in previous actions had not been great enough to persuade them to "button up." If they drove fully shielded with the hatch down, they had to look out through a reflecting mirror device. The device was bulletproof. Driving with it took practice, however, and vision was limited to about 100 degrees to the front. This meant that the driver had less freedom of maneuver and had to go more slowly. The Viet Cong leaders had also lectured their troops on the importance of subjecting the M-113s to massed fire, exactly as with aircraft. Each squad or platoon was to pick out the nearest carrier and to bring all of its weapons to bear simultaneously.

The M-113 had been sent to Vietnam by American armor officers imbued with the U.S. Army doctrine of superior firepower. The .50 caliber gunner did not need a protective shield, they thought, because he would be able to suppress any opposition with a few bursts from this most lethal of machine guns. The .50 caliber had twice the effective range and three times the destructive force of the .30 caliber weapons the guerrillas possessed. The theory was reasonable provided that the gunner could see his intended target and could handle the machine gun well enough to hit consistently. The difficulty is that firing a .50 caliber is like riding an unruly horse. The recoil tends to drive the barrel up into the air and off the target. The problem is accentuated for a lightly built Vietnamese gunner. Unless the M-113 gunner was carefully trained to brace a foot against the hatch rim and rear back on the gun to keep the barrel pointed down, his shooting tended to be erratic. Most of Ba's gunners had not been adequately trained.

The Viet Cong battalion commander had about seventy-five men and his two .30 caliber machine guns in the foxholes along the section of the irrigation dike toward which the M-113s were headed. He had sited one machine gun at the southern corner—at the right end of the tree line as one faced the hamlet—where the dike was high. He had sited the second machine gun on the left, about three-quarters of the way up toward the northern end, at another point where the dike jutted out into the rice field. The two machine guns could catch anything in between in a crossfire.

To try to keep up the resolve of his troops, he had been resorting all morning to mutual encouragement. When the company in Bac shot down the helicopters, he passed the news of their "victories" to the company in Tan Thoi to raise their confidence for the imminent engagement with the 7th Division battalion. After the men at Tan Thoi stopped the battalion, he circulated word of their "victory" to the men getting ready to battle the M-113s at Bac. The company commander at Bac and the platoon and squad leaders there had been controlling their men by using the six-foot-wide irrigation ditch behind the dike as their communications trench. They now waded once more from foxhole to foxhole through the waist-deep water, hugging the bank to stay out of sight of the planes, and briefed each man again on the supposed weaknesses of the armored tracks, seeking to convince the men that they could beat the machines if they used their heads as well as their weapons. In any case, they emphasized to each guerrilla, there was no place to go until dark. If they must die, they said, it was preferable to die with dignity, to perish fighting, rather than to run and be chopped down like buffalo. They had every man inspect his weapon to be certain it was functioning. Porters brought more boxes of captured American ammunition down the ditch in small sampans to replenish the company's supply. A couple of wounded infantrymen were evacuated in the boats, and volunteers from the local guerrillas took their places. The three remaining wounded from the morning's action were cadres and apparently Party members, as were all of the officers and most of the noncoms in the company. To set an example, they refused to leave the line and go to the first-aid station. The cadres composed a slogan and had the men repeat it from foxhole to foxhole: "It is better to die at your post. It is better to die at your post."

* * *

The carriers were taking so long to negotiate the remaining canals between them and Bac that Bowers, who was watching them from behind the paddy dike in front of the guerrillas, asked himself if they were taking a break for lunch. From overhead Vann fretted at their slow progress too. He wondered if he was ever going to get the M-113s to Bac. In between discouraging looks at the stalemated battalion at Tan Thoi and the sluggish movement of the second Civil Guard battalion up from the southwest, he circled over the armored tracks in the L-19, haranguing Mays, who had kept the radio he and Scanlon had been sharing, to hurry Ba along. Easy fords over the canals could not be found, and brush and trees had to be cut to fill each one. The troops took their time. Because they fought for pay, they had no desire to risk their lives unnecessarily. Unless prodded, their normal work pace was like a permanent slowdown strike, based on the usually sound assumption that if they tarried long enough, the Viet Cong would go away. Ba, in no hurry today for his own reasons, did not push them. It was not until 1:00 P.M. that he was able to raise Major Tho on the radio and obtain an order to attack the Viet Cong at Bac.

As the carriers neared the last canal, about five hundred yards from the helicopters and seven hundred from the irrigation dike, the guerrilla battalion commander decided to risk half a dozen of his carefully hoarded 60mm mortar shells to try to stop them. Several shells exploded close enough to two of the M-113s to frighten the crews and the mounted riflemen sitting on top next to the open main hatch, but none hit their mark. A mortar is an indirect-fire weapon that throws its projectile up in an arc. It obviously was not going to be of much use against these machines. If the guerrillas were to survive, they would have to perform with small arms and grenades a feat that had never been achieved before.

Mays thought the mortar shells were coming from another ARVN unit overshooting a target. "Topper Six, request you shut off friendly mortar fire," he radioed.

"I'd like to, Walrus, but they're not ours," Vann said, in a bit of the gallows humor he always seemed to be able to summon up at such moments.

When Mays passed along Vann's answer a few minutes later to Scanlon, who was on another carrier, he appreciated the humor, but thought Vann must be mistaken in thinking the shells had come from the guerrillas. Scanlon did not believe there were any Viet Cong left at Bac. From the top of his vehicle, the scene there appeared tranquil. There was no shooting around the helicopters, and off to the right, just below the southern tree line where the guerrilla platoon had been that morning, he could see the lunch fires of the Civil Guardsmen cooking the rice and chicken they had looted from the peasants. "Well, it's all over now," Scanlon thought to himself. "All we have left to do is to police up those chopper crews and the wounded."

The troops of the M-113 company seemed to have the same thought. They were even more dilatory than before in cutting trees and brush to fill this last canal. Scanlon got the impression that this time it was less the calculated shunning of combat than the conclusion that their earlier delaying and the usual tactic of the Viet Cong in withdrawing had brought them the unspoken accommodation with their enemy that they sought. Instead of setting to work, most of the crews and the rifle squads stood on the canal bank and watched an air strike by a couple of planes that had just arrived. Planes bombing hamlets the guerrillas had evacuated was still a spectacle worth seeing. With the wounded Americans and Vietnamese at Bac on his mind, Scanlon walked up to one group of soldiers and told them to get busy. The men smiled at him. He went to his vehicle, took out an ax, and handed it to one of them. They reluctantly began to cut trees.

Seeing that it was going to take another forty-five minutes to bring all of the carriers across the canal, Mays asked Ba to turn the company of mounted infantry over to his command. He could strip a couple of .50 caliber machine guns off the carriers and double-time over with the infantry in five minutes. The expedient would get Vann off their backs. If any guerrillas were tarrying in the hamlet, two .50 calibers and a company of infantry could handle them. Ba consented. He was no longer tense. Having reached Tho, he had the authorization he needed, and it also appeared to him that the Viet Cong had, in any case, departed.

Mays thought there still were guerrillas at Bac. Knowing how Vann kept track of who was doing what on a battlefield, he did not believe that Vann would have incorrectly identified the source of the mortar fire. Because the mortaring had ceased so quickly, Mays assumed it was merely a delaying tactic to cover a withdrawal. He could not conceive that any sizable number of guerrillas would stay in the hamlet with the M-113s so long in view during the slow approach.

He was surprised at Vann's answer when he called him on the radio and proposed dismounting the infantry and a couple of machine guns. "No, goddammit," Vann said in exasperation. "Get the carriers over there!" Vann did not have to explain to another professional soldier what else was in his mind. Mays understood him. Vann thought the Viet Cong remained at Bac in force, and he wanted Mays to hurry the M-113s over there and flush them out so that he could kill them as they tried to flee across the open ground to the east. There was no question in Mays's mind, and he knew there was none in Vann's, that once the M-113s reached the hamlet and assaulted, any guerrillas in Bac would fire a flurry of shots and run.

It was 1:45 P.M., three hours and twenty minutes since Vann had originally sent his emergency call to this company of armored tracks a mile away, before three carriers—Ba's command vehicle and two others—were across the last canal. One of the other two carriers was that of Lieutenant Cho, the most aggressive of Ba's platoon leaders. Mays climbed onto Cho's vehicle and set off toward the helicopters with these first two M-113s while Ba was towing a fourth across with a cable. He wanted to get the wounded American helicopter crewmen inside the safety of the armored hulls in case there was any shooting. The guerrilla battalion commander issued an order for every man to give his weapon a final check. The fight that had been so slow in coming began quickly.

As this first pair of carriers swept across the rice field toward the downed helicopters, the guerrilla mortar crew fired their last three shells at the two machines. Mays dismissed the explosions and spouts of paddy water as another spastic delaying tactic. "We've put the fear of God into them and they're moving out," he thought. Cho was up manning the .50 caliber machine gun, and Mays was sitting beside him on top of the M-113. He sighted three of the pilots behind the paddy dike in front of the H-21 nearest the tree line, the one in which Braman had been wounded. He motioned to Cho to have the carrier driver swing the machine around to the right front of the aircraft and pull up beside the pilots. He leaned over and asked them where their wounded and their enlisted crewmen were. Officers are naturally expected to assume responsibility for their men and the wounded in an emergency. Two of the pilots, the survivors of the Huey, seemed dazed, and the third, a warrant officer from one of the H-21s, said that he didn't know, which angered Mays. Just then Sergeant Bowers splashed over through the paddy and said that he had a wounded crewman to evacuate from the helicopter right behind them. Mays vaulted off the M-113. He had taken a step through the paddy when the Viet Cong battalion commander gave the order to fire. The tree line crashed with the opening volley. Bowers did not pause, and Mays controlled his nerves and stayed right behind him despite the cracks of the incoming bullets. Cho's .50 caliber and the heavy machine gun on the other M-113 slammed like jackhammers in response to the guerrillas' fire. Mays could make out amid the din the answering drumrolls of defiance from the Viet Cong machine gunner at the right-hand corner of the irrigation dike.

He and Bowers climbed into the helicopter to carry Braman to safety after his nearly three-and-a-half-hour wait for rescue. The boy was dead. Bowers was stunned and could not believe it at first. He turned Braman over and examined his body. The boy had not been hit a second time, and his shoulder wound showed no sign of having hemorrhaged. A couple of hours later, when things calmed down again, Bowers was to be overcome by the thought that perhaps he had made a mistake in leaving Braman in the helicopter, whatever the risk of another wound or infection from the paddy water. "Maybe if I'd given him some company we might have kept up his hope and he'd still be with us," he was to think. The notion that he was somehow responsible for Braman's death was to haunt Bowers in the years ahead.

A rash movement by Mays brought Bowers out of his shock. Mays stood up in the helicopter. A guerrilla rifleman spotted him through one of the windows and nearly caught him with a couple of quick shots. Mays shouted that they had better get the three pilots into the M-113. They plunged back through the paddy to the vehicle, and Bowers helped Mays hustle the aviators into the armored hull through the rear hatch, which dropped down like a clamshell door. Mays decided it was foolish to try to rescue any others at this point. Bowers had told him of Deal's death and had said that except for Braman, none of the airmen had suffered wounds that required immediate evacuation. Bowers declined Mays's offer of safety in the M-113, saying that he was going to attempt to rally the survivors of his Vietnamese infantry company, and took off at a crouch down the dike.

When Mays stepped back inside, he learned that they had lost the driver to a bullet through the head. Cho had come down from the .50 caliber to talk to Ba on the radio. Had Cho not relinquished the gun, Mays thought, he would probably be dead like the driver. The aluminum-alloy armor of the M-113 muffled the sound of the strings of bullets ricocheting from the sides of the hull. They bounced off with a bung, bung, bung. Mays called Vann, who was circling overhead in the L-19, on his portable radio. He reported that he had rescued three of the pilots and that two of the helicopter crewmen were dead. The radio then went silent. A Viet Cong bullet had clipped away the aerial where Mays had attached it on top of the carrier.

The second pair of M-113s were on their way from the canal with instructions from Ba to drive around to the left side of the helicopters in order to give the men in the paddy cover from that flank. Scanlon had grabbed a hook on the back while the second machine was pulling away and swung himself aboard.

Vietnam was Scanlon's first war too. Like Bowers and Mays, he had been pushed into the military by the Korean War. Again as with Bowers and Mays, the desire of the Army to build up its forces in Europe to meet the perceived Soviet challenge there had kept him from seeing any combat in Korea. He had stayed in because the life of an American officer in the 1950s, with its sense of mission and travel, was a lot more interesting and meaningful than his civilian life as a dividends clerk in a St. Louis brokerage. Scanlon was a paratrooper as well as a tanker, and he was flush with the faith of the U.S. Army that the best defense is an offense and that aggressiveness wins battles and wars. This faith was the reason he now found himself in a rice paddy with his .45 caliber service pistol in his hand and bullets from guerrilla weapons he could not see ricocheting off the M-113 beside him.

Scanlon's pair of armored tracks swung around the left side of the helicopters as Ba had ordered them to do and drove directly toward the guerrilla machine gun dug in on the point three-quarters of the way up to the left where the irrigation dike jutted out into the rice field. When the M-113s came abreast of the aircraft the .50 caliber gunners loosed a couple of bursts at the tree line and were answered by the same concentration of raking fire that had opened on Mays's two vehicles over on the right. The carriers stopped, the clamshell rear hatches dropped down, and the infantry squads piled into the paddy and fanned out. The drivers started again, and men and machines began an assault, the infantrymen holding their rifles at their hips and spraying clips of ammunition like water from a hose, guiding their aim by the path of the tracer bullets. The maneuver was automatic. The Saigon troops had been trained to do it by Scanlon and the other American instructors. They had done it in the past on several occasions when a bunch of guerrillas had been unlucky enough not to be able to flee before the carriers arrived and had then been sufficiently foolhardy to shoot at the M-113s. The maneuver was designed to supplement the machine guns by bringing to bear the full firepower of the infantry squad. Scanlon was one of the first out the door, unholstering his pistol as he cleared the hatch and began to slog forward through the paddy next to the armored track. He didn't intend to shoot anyone himself. The pistol was merely an officer's accouterment and a means of self-defense. Pulling it from the holster was just another reflex action. His job was to teach these men how to fight, and he wanted to be out there where he could see what was happening.

One of the riflemen a couple of steps farther from the carrier was knocked down by a bullet. The .50 caliber gunner was initially confused by the guerrillas' fusillade and thought that most of the fire was coming from a banana grove higher up on the left which also extended out into the paddy and where there were, in fact, no Viet Cong. He sprayed it with the machine gun while the last of the infantrymen were clearing the rear hatch. The recoil immediately bucked the barrel up into the air, and Scanlon saw the slugs cutting the tops off banana trees. The bullets lashing the front of the M-113 in another burst from the Viet Cong machine gun made the gunner realize his error, and he swung to the tree line on the irrigation dike ahead again, sweeping along it and cutting some of the saplings there in half. "The bastard is just spreading the stuff around in the air over their heads," Scanlon cursed.

The trouble was that neither the gunner, nor Scanlon, nor anyone else could see any guerrillas. Scanlon couldn't see anything in front except a wall of green. The only logical place for the guerrillas to be was at the base of the wall, but the foliage was so thick there that his eyes couldn't even pick up the muzzle flashes that would normally have given away the positions of the machine gun and the other weapons.

A BAR man firing from beside the .50 caliber on top of the carrier was also hit before the assault had advanced many yards. The machine gunner lost his nerve, ducked down inside the hatch, and began shooting at the clouds. These guerrillas whom Scanlon had not expected to find at Bac were not behaving in the fashion he had come to expect Viet Cong to behave when confronted by M-113s. The sight of them fleeing panic-stricken before the armored tracks in previous actions had always reminded him of a covey of quail flushing from cover when the hunters walked in past the pointing dogs with their shotguns at the ready. It dawned on him that he and all of the infantry were going to be killed and wounded unless they returned to the shelter of the armored hulls right away. Scanlon spoke rudimentary Vietnamese. He called to the driver to stop, shouted and gestured to the infantrymen to return, and hurried back inside himself through the rear hatch.

The reflex of aggressive action and the virtue of firepower were so ingrained in Scanlon by his training that it was beyond him to think the best thing to do was to back off, analyze the situation, and come up with a more sensible solution than a bull-headed assault. He had always been taught that when you couldn't see the other fellow, the answer was to lock horns with him. In the jargon of the tactical instructors, the solution was to "resolve the firefight." He thought that if he could get the .50 caliber gunners to work over the base of the tree line they could intimidate the Viet Cong while the drivers took the vehicles close enough for them to locate the guerrillas' automatic weapons. Once located, these mainstays of the Viet Cong defense could be knocked out by the .50 calibers and the infantry could make another assault from the protection of the armored hulls. The rest of the guerrillas would then "bust like a covey."

The .50 caliber gunner wouldn't stand up and aim the gun again when Scanlon told him to do so. "Get up, goddammit, and aim at the base of the tree line," Scanlon screamed. He grabbed the man by his fatigue shirt and pulled and hauled at him, yelling these instructions in the best Vietnamese he could muster until he had the gunner up behind the .50 caliber firing it once more.

The driver of the second M-113 began to back up. Scanlon saw that this crew was abandoning one of their infantrymen who had fallen wounded into the paddy. He shouted and waved his arms. The driver of the other vehicle heard him and pulled forward again, but no one would get out to pick up the wounded soldier. Scanlon sprang over the side of his M-113 and ran to the man. As he reached him, one of the infantrymen from the second M-113, braver than the rest, reached him too and helped Scanlon to pick him up and carry him in through the rear hatch and lay him on the floor. While they were rescuing this wounded soldier, yet another infantryman who was still in the paddy was hit and a BAR man on this second M-113 was struck. The .50 caliber gunner on the second M-113 had also lost his nerve and was cowering in the hatch and perforating the sky. After they had carried in the other wounded soldier, Scanlon pulled and yelled at this gunner too until he had him up and trying to aim the machine gun. "Shoot at the bottom of the tree line," Scanlon shouted.

These two M-113 crews had been intimidated. The drivers backed up behind the fuselages of the two H-21s to hide from the punishment of the guerrillas' bullets. The Viet Cong ceased firing as soon as the machines retreated. At first the drivers headed toward the right side of the helicopters, where the M-113s Mays was with were engaged. Hearing the heavy firing over there, they thought better of it and turned tail for the canal. Scanlon hollered at them to stop. He motioned to the driver of the carrier he was on to move forward of the helicopters again. The driver shook his head. Scanlon argued with the sergeant who was the vehicle commander and with the other crewmen that they had to go back and attack the Viet Cong, that there were pinned-down infantry and wounded from the reserve company who were depending on them. The sergeant said they already had three wounded among their own people on the carrier and that was enough. The driver resumed the retreat to the canal. Scanlon wanted no part of a "bugout." He saw Bowers crouched nearby at the corner of a dike, gesturing to him. Scanlon leaped off to join him.

Bowers had decided that he might as well link up with one of the officer advisors, because he had no further hope of doing anything useful with the unhurt survivors of his reserve company. He had tried to inspire an assault a few minutes before and felt foolish for having done so. As Scanlon's pair of M-113s had arrived on the left flank of the helicopters, he had sought to lead the survivors in one of those classic tank-infantry team maneuvers in which he had been trained. The motto of the Infantry School at Fort Benning is "Follow Me!" Bowers in its best tradition had run down the paddy dike bent over and shouting "Attack!" in Vietnamese, stood up, waved with his carbine at the Saigon infantrymen to follow, and started forward with the armored tracks against the guerrillas in the tree line. He had gone about twenty paces before he had the feeling for the second time that day that he was alone. He looked behind. He was. Just then the M-113s began to back up, and Bowers hurried back to the dike, glad that he had not inspired anyone to follow him. He might have gotten more of these Vietnamese soldiers killed accomplishing nothing, which was how they had been dying around him all day. He told Scanlon that Braman and Deal were dead and that Mays had picked up three of the pilots. Scanlon asked him where the other aviators were, and Bowers led him over to the spot where they were lying behind the dike in front of the helicopters, watching the unfolding of the decisive struggle that had begun between the guerrillas and the armored machines.

At about the same time that Scanlon was jumping off the retreating pair of M-113s to join Bowers in the paddy, Ba was arriving on the right flank where Mays was located with another pair. He had used his carrier to tow two more across the canal and, leaving one behind to continue the towing process, had rushed off with the other to take charge of the fight. Ba was in the lead M-113 of his pair, sitting up against the open cover of the command hatch behind the .50 caliber. He normally directed the company from that position. His vision was unobstructed and he liked to fire the gun when he had an opportunity. Mays saw him coming and reached down for the push-button microphone on the radio in Cho's carrier. He intended to tell Ba that they should not attack frontally but should instead maneuver far around to the right and approach the guerrilla foxhole line from that end of the irrigation dike. Although they would still face the machine gun and the guerrilla squad deployed there, they would be coming up against a small number of weapons rather than a whole line. (Mays could not see the squad. He had by now spotted the machine gun and a rifleman in a foxhole behind it, because the vegetation on the dike was thinnest at that point.) The maneuver would be like "crossing the T" in a naval battle. They would be reducing the guerrillas' firepower drastically while taking maximum advantage of their own, and in the same stroke they would minimize their exposure. Once they had killed the machine-gun crew, Mays believed, they could bring the foxhole line under flanking fire from this right end and drive the guerrillas out of it.

When Ba's carrier drew near and Mays was about to speak to him, Ba stepped down into the hatch for a moment, probably to make an adjustment to the radio. Cho had told him of the resistance they were receiving, and Ba was talking to him and to the other vehicle commanders over his radiophone headset to coordinate all four machines for an assault. His carrier happened to hit a mound or to jolt its way across one of the low paddy dikes just as Ba stepped down. The .50 caliber gun swiveled on its mount and the heavy barrel smacked Ba on the forehead, knocking him half-conscious into the vehicle.

The company was temporarily leaderless. Ba's executive officer, a competent and experienced man who could have assumed command immediately and with whom Mays could have communicated because he spoke English, was in the hospital at the time with typhoid fever. Cho, despite his aggressiveness in individual actions, was apparently incapable of taking charge, because he did not do so. Since Mays had also been unable to speak to Ba before the machine-gun barrel struck him, Ba had not given Cho any instructions to flank around the right end. Cho's English was limited to a few words, and Mays's Vietnamese was of similar non-fluency. Mays knew words like "assault" and "together" and repeated them to Cho with gestures in body Vietnamese, but for the next twenty minutes no coordinated action was taken. The four carriers and three or four others that joined them during that time (the crews of the pair Scanlon had been with and two or three others stayed back at the canal out of cowardice) made individual sorties against the tree line, all of which were beaten back.

The twenty minutes were critical. The men most often killed or wounded during these confused actions were the .50 caliber gunners. They were the easiest for the Viet Cong to hit, because they were silhouetted against the sky on top of the armored tracks. The gunners also usually happened to be the sergeants who commanded both the carrier crew and the rifle squad. The system had been designed by the

Americans so that machine and infantry would function smoothly in a team. The noncoms had taken to commanding their vehicles and rifle squads from behind the machine gun for the same reasons of unob-structed vision and the fun of firing the gun that had led Ba to choose this perch as the place from which to direct the company. Since the Americans had told them they could put unlimited faith in the efficacy of the .50 caliber and earlier actions had not been that dangerous, the sergeants had not learned to command the vehicles and squads from a more protected spot. Once the shooting started, everyone acted out of training with no thought of the consequences until it was too late. The company first sergeant, who was Ba's closest friend in the unit, climbed up behind the .50 caliber as soon as he had done what he could for his dazed captain. He ordered the M-113 forward into an attack on the machine gun at the right corner of the tree line and after a few moments of firing fell back into the vehicle mortally wounded, shot through the throat. During the twenty minutes that Ba was too stunned to command his company he was progressively losing the capacity to control the individual carriers. The dead and wounded vehicle commanders were replaced by less experienced men, and the morale of the crews began to crack.

The moment had come for American technology to fill the human gap. The M-113 with the flamethrower mounted on top in place of a .50 caliber churned forward, the long tube sticking out from the rotating turret like a cannon. "Hey, this is going to be it. This guy will just hose down that tree line and burn them out," Scanlon bragged to one of the helicopter pilots lying beside him behind the paddy dike. The flame-thrower carrier drove up to within a hundred yards of the tree line, sufficiently close for the burning jet of jellied gasoline to reach the frightened men whose bullets were bouncing off this armored fire-spitter. The operator rotated the tube from side to side ominously and then focused it straight ahead to begin roasting the guerrillas. He turned on the device. A spout of flame shot out twenty to thirty yards and expired in the air. The crew had not mixed enough of the jelling agent with the gasoline to keep the jet of flame burning properly.

"Oh God, the force and effect of a Zippo lighter," Scanlon moaned. (Zippo is the brand name of a popular cigarette lighter.)

The pilot, who had been wounded in the arm, was more philosophical. "It figures," he said. "Everything else went wrong, so what the hell."

Vann was nearly out of his mind with frustration as he circled overhead in the rear seat of the spotter plane, watching the guerrillas shoot the gunners off the carriers, the machines back away one by one, and the flamethrower fail too. It was the most maddening moment in this utterly maddening day. He was cursing Ba for not assembling all of his M-113s for a simultaneous assault and cursing Harkins for making it impossible for him to influence the course of the battle. He was as surprised as everyone else at the refusal of the guerrillas to break and run from the armored tracks; what was unbearable was his inability to recoup from this unexpected setback. He wanted to tell Mays and his jackass of a counterpart that if they were getting too much fire for the .50 caliber gunners to expose themselves, they should button up the hatches and charge into the tree line, dumping out the infantry to kill the guerrillas in the foxholes as soon as they ran up the dike. With Mays no longer responding to his calls over the field radio, Vann had no alternative means of talking to him or Ba. The radios installed in the M-113s had different frequencies than the regular radios in the L-19s, which was why Vann and the advisors had been using portables. Vann had been fruitlessly asking Saigon for months for an L-19 equipped with a radio matching those in the carriers.

The Viet Cong in the foxholes could not afford to curse. They were battling now to avoid annihilation. Ba had finally recovered enough from the concussion of the .50 caliber barrel slamming into his forehead to pull seven to eight carriers together and begin a coordinated assault on the right front of the guerrillas' foxhole line. Still dazed from the blow and shocked by the death of his first sergeant and by his surprise that the guerrillas were standing and fighting, he could not think clearly enough to respond to Mays's repeated calls over the radio to flank around the right end. He was too stunned to even realize that he ought to force the four or five carriers hanging back at the canal to come forward and bolster his attack. He could not think beyond making the frontal assault he had been taught most often to do. He instinctively rejected the tactic that Vann wanted him to take of buttoning up the hatches and charging into the tree line. Vann did not know that as an armor officer Ba had been taught, with good reason, never to attempt this tactic that would appear intelligent to an infantryman. The instructors at Saumur and Fort Knox had warned him that fools ran armored vehicles blindly into a woods. The enemy infantry could swarm all over the vehicles the moment they were in the trees, toss a grenade inside as soon as someone opened a hatch to get out, or shoot the crew like rats popping out of holes in a box as they tried to climb free. It was also obvious to Ba that there was water on the far side of the dike. If he charged up the near side, the carriers would acquire enough momentum to run over the dike and plunge into the irrigation ditch. The water would rush in through the air-intake vents and flood the engines, and the carriers would be stuck at a crazy angle, unable to use their machine guns, with guerrillas all around them. In his befuddled state the only solution that occurred to Ba was to shoot his way into the tree line with the .50 calibers and the BARs, and with what firepower the rifle squads could add by banging away over the armored sides; mount the dike carefully enough not to run across it into the irrigation ditch; and then roll up the guerrillas' foxhole line if they did not break once their perimeter had been breached.

The armored tracks ground forward through the muck and water of the paddy in a ragged line. The twenty minutes of confused individual actions and the loss of so many sergeants told in indecisiveness when resolve was needed most. Ba had difficulty coordinating the vehicles, and the crews showed their weakened morale. The assault was hesitant, the attackers uncertain. The drivers would not stick up their heads anymore. They were all down inside, trying to steer through the bulletproof reflecting mirrors. The lack of practice and the limited vision made them go more slowly than they should have and increased the exposure to the guerrillas' fire of the .50 caliber gunners and the infantrymen hammering away from on top with clip after clip of ammunition from their BARs and M-1 rifles. The unaccustomed handicap was also making it impossible for the drivers to keep the vehicles abreast of each other and thus bring the combined firepower of the seven or eight carriers to bear at once. A couple of the substitute .50 caliber gunners would not stand up behind their weapons. They crouched in the hatch and fired the guns by sticking up their arms, punishing the clouds again.

Bowers's admiration for the soldierly stuff of his enemy was rising with each second. He was fascinated at the way the guerrillas were keeping their heads and fighting wisely as the squat, dark green brutes closed with them. They did not disperse their fire along the entire line of armored tracks. Instead they focused their weapons on whichever vehicle happened to be foremost. He watched the bullets dance off the hull when the two machine guns and the other weapons held an M-113 in a crossfire until they had killed or wounded the crewman manning the .50 caliber or hit a BAR gunner or a rifleman. The driver would hesitate and stop at the casualty. The Viet Cong would then cease fire for a few moments to conserve ammunition or shift their torrent of bullets to the next machine that had pushed to the forefront. "By God, you have to hand it to them," Bowers thought to himself. "They are really hanging in there." The assault faltered. Some of the drivers began to back up. Even the aggressive Cho, in whose vehicle Mays was riding, let his crew pull away after the .50 caliber gunner was hit.

Ba's carrier and one or two others kept pressing forward, despite casualties, and were within fifteen to twenty yards of the irrigation dike. Ba's mercenaries had not bargained for a fight like this, but they were Vietnamese and some of them were brave enough once they were in the midst of it. The nerve of the guerrillas was cracking. In a few moments one of the ten-ton behemoths was going to climb the dike and the guerrillas' will to resist would snap. The crews of every carrier that had been beaten off would take heart and surge forward. The Viet Cong officers and noncoms would not be able to shout down the panic. Their men would jump out of the foxholes and run and the butchery would begin again as it had so often in the past.

Squad Leader Dung stopped the machines. He leaped from his foxhole and stood up right in front of the metal beasts. Their ugliness was part of the terrifying effect these evil contrivances had always had on him and his comrades. The fore ends angled down into broad snouts with popeyes on top where the two headlights for night driving protruded. Yanking a grenade from his belt, he pulled the pin, cocked his arm, and hurled it at one of the monsters. The grenade landed on top of the M-113 and erupted with a great bang and flash. Carried beyond their fear by his courage, the men of his squad abandoned the protection of their foxholes to join him, throwing their grenades at the carriers too. A guerrilla over on the left named Son also sprang up on the dike and shot a rifle grenade down the line at the armored tracks. From where he was lying out in the paddy, Bowers saw two of the grenades burst in the air just above the carriers. Dung was apparently unhurt, but three of his comrades were killed, and all the other members of his squad were wounded by bullets from the armored tracks or by shrapnel from their own grenades. Whether the shrapnel also killed or wounded any more men aboard the machines is unknown. It did not matter. The deafening clap and the flare of the exploding grenades were enough to shatter what spirit the crews had left. Ba allowed the driver of his carrier to back up, and the one or two vehicles persevering with him followed. The assault had failed. Ba was too stunned and emotionally drained to organize another attack. His crews were so demoralized they would not have obeyed him had he tried to do so. Mays made two last attempts with Cho's carrier to turn the guerrillas' flank by killing the machine-gun crew on the right end. Both sorties were driven back with the loss of two more .50 caliber gunners and riflemen. It was about 2:30 in the afternoon. The Viet Cong had accomplished the impossible.

* * *

The anticlimax was a macabre farce staged by Cao. He had flown to Tan Hiep airstrip from his new corps headquarters at Can Tho at 11:30 A.M. that morning, right after hearing the news that four helicopters had been downed. He arrived alarmed at the publicity that would ensue from the helicopter losses and became increasingly distraught over what Diem might do to him as the radio brought in reports of more and more casualties. Diem would hold him responsible, because Dam was his man. He was furious with Vann and Dam for putting him into what was, from his point of view, the worst possible predicament. They had thrust him into a situation where he was being forced to fight the Viet Cong. When the information from Ba's company indicated that the machines were also failing to flush the guerrillas and give him easy killing, he began scheming to extricate himself from this battle and shift the blame for the losses to someone else.

Vann first heard of Cao's plan to rescue Cao in a radio call from Dan Porter while he was still circling over Bac, watching the final sortie by Cho's carrier against the machine gun at the right corner. Porter had flown to Tan Hiep with Cao that morning. He informed Vann in voice code that Cao had requested a battalion of paratroops from the Joint General Staff reserve in Saigon. Vann asked Porter to have Cao drop the paratroops in the rice fields and swampland on the east side of Tan Thoi and Bac, the one open flank that the guerrilla battalion commander could not retreat across during the day, but that would become the logical escape route after dark.

"Topper Six, I've already told him to do that and he says he's going to employ them on the other side," Porter replied.

"I'll be right there, sir," Vann said, and instructed the pilot to return to the airstrip as fast as possible. He knew instantly what Cao's game was. As he was to put it in his after-action report for Harkins, Cao intended to use the airborne battalion not to trap and annihilate the Viet Cong but rather "as a show of force . . . in hopes that the VC units would disengage and the unwanted battle would be over."

Vann clambered out of the little plane and strode into the command-post tent. He told Cao that on this day he could not spend all of this blood for nothing. He had to close the box around the guerrillas and destroy them. Porter supported him, both of them arguing that Cao had no choice as a responsible commander. "You have got to drop the airborne over there," Vann said, poking his finger at the big operations map where it showed the open flank on the east side of the two hamlets.

He became so angry and was jabbing so hard at the map that he almost toppled over the easel on which it rested.

Cao would have none of this soldier's logic. "It is not prudent, it is not prudent," he kept replying. It was better, he said, to drop the paratroops on the west behind the M-113s and the Civil Guards where they could tie in with these other units. "We must reinforce," he said.

Vann was later to sum up Cao's logic with the tart remark: "They chose to reinforce defeat."

He lost his temper one more time. "Goddammit," he shouted, "you want them to get away. You're afraid to fight. You know they'll sneak out this way and that's exactly what you want."

Embarrassed at being driven into a corner, Cao pulled a huffy general's act on Vann, the lieutenant colonel. "I am the commanding general and it is my decision," he said. Brig. Gen. Tran Thien Khiem, the chief of staff of the Joint General Staff, who had flown down from Saigon at Cao's request and was present during the argument, did not object. Harkins had not come down to find out why an unprecedented five helicopters had been lost, nor had any of his subordinates appeared, so there was no American general in the tent to brandish his stars for Vann and Porter. Cao then attempted to mollify Vann by pretending to move up the drop time. He said, "We will drop at sixteen hundred hours"— 4:00 P.M. civilian time. Knowing that it was useless to argue further and hoping that he might at least get a paratroop battalion early enough to be of some use, Vann went back to his spotter plane.

He spent the rest of the afternoon asking when the paratroops were going to arrive and attempting to persuade Cao and Dam and Tho to turn what was about to become the biggest defeat of the war so far into its biggest victory. They still had the opportunity to redeem the day. All they had to do was to pull the two Civil Guard battalions and Ba's company together for a combined attack on Bac. As demoralized as Ba's men were, they could have at least supported the Civil Guards with their .50 calibers, and the guerrillas could not have withstood the total force. Neither Cao nor Tho, who were the men in control, could see that the sensible and moral course was to press ahead and accept the further and proportionately minor casualties that would be necessary to give meaning to the sacrifice of those who had already been killed and maimed.

The second Civil Guard battalion had, in fact, arrived at Bac in the midst of Ba's attempt at an organized assault. The commanding officer was a young man, a competent lieutenant. He saw that he could come to Ba's relief immediately by flanking around to the right and working in behind the guerrillas' foxhole line from the south as the first battalion should have done. He radioed Tho for permission to attack and, anticipating approval, positioned one of his companies forward to begin as soon as he alerted Ba to his move. Tho ordered him to wait. As the afternoon wasted away, after Ba had been beaten and the guerrillas were being left undisturbed except for air and artillery bombardments, the lieutenant asked permission to attack three more times.

Prevost cleared the way for him by knocking out the machine gun at the right-hand corner of the dike in the single effective air strike of the battle at 3:40 P.M., more than an hour too late to help Ba, but with hours left to spare for the Civil Guards. Vann had encountered Prevost at the airstrip right after his argument with Cao over the paratroop drop. He had asked Prevost to do something about the air-control fiasco and, before returning to his own spotter plane, had gone back to the map and shown Prevost where the foxholes were dug under the trees on the dike and the location of the machine gun. Vann had noticed the gun during the abortive helicopter rescue at the end of the morning. Prevost borrowed another VNAF L-19, and Dam instructed a Vietnamese FAC waiting at the airstrip to ride in the backseat and direct a Farm Gate A-26 Invader on its way down from the air commando squadron at Bien Hoa.

At first Prevost stayed within the rules and let his Vietnamese FAC control the twin-engine bomber. The result was that the FAC and the American pilot wasted the two canisters of napalm the plane was carrying and four of its 100-pound bombs. Prevost then bent the rules by persuading the FAC to give him control of the A-26. He directed it through several strafing runs, walking the streams of .50 caliber bullets right along the tree line. The pilot of the A-26 was initially irritated with Prevost for coaching him to take a low and shallow approach and to keep the stick forward as he strafed. The pilot was diving too steeply and then pulling out of his dive too soon. The bullets from the .50 calibers in the nose were missing the machine-gun foxhole. The staff at the Joint Air Operations Center at Tan Son Nhut were monitoring the radio traffic. One of the older officers knew Prevost and recognized his voice. "Listen," he said to the others, "Herb's telling the guy how to make an attack." After the pilot had learned to hold down the nose, Prevost had him fire a salvo of rockets precisely into the corner of the dike. The Viet Cong machine gun went silent, the crew killed or wounded. The fire direction center at the Tan Hiep command post then mistakenly called off the A-26 so that the artillery could resume shooting, but it was not the mistake of the division artillery officer that rendered

Prevost's achievement another accomplishment in the void. Each time the Civil Guard lieutenant asked permission to attack, Tho ordered him to wait. Three men in the forward company were killed and two were wounded while waiting.

Whenever Vann radioed Ziegler to ask why the airborne battalion had not yet been dropped, and Ziegler inquired of Cao, Cao would look out the door of the tent at the sky and say: "They're supposed to be here. Saigon is late." He had actually arranged for the paratroops to be dropped at 6:00 P.M., an hour and a half before darkness. He thought this would be convenient, that they would have just enough time to regroup and set up a perimeter defense for the night and no time to get into a fight. Cao was to convenience the Viet Cong.

The paratroops began jumping at 6:05 P.M. from seven U.S. Air Force twin-engine transports, whale-shaped C-123 Providers. By monitoring the ARVN radio traffic, the guerrilla battalion commander had known for two hours that they were coming. The important piece of information he had been unable to obtain was the exact location of the designated drop zone. He therefore ordered the company commander at Tan Thoi to prepare to shift some of his troops to counter the landing if the airborne proved threatening.

Unlike the exhausted regulars at Bac, the regional guerrillas at Tan Thoi were relatively fresh. Their fight with the 7th Division battalion had never developed into anything more than an exchange of fire. Vann's favorite battalion advisor and the most popular officer in the detachment, Capt. Kenneth Good, a thirty-two-year-old Californian, West Point class of 1952, had perished because he had gone forward on a reconnaissance to try to get the stalled battalion moving. He had been wounded and needlessly bled to death because the ARVN captain he was with failed to report that he was hit. It was two hours before he was accidentally discovered by another advisor and Vann could have him evacuated to the airstrip, where he died in a few minutes. Two and a half hours after Good's death, when the paratroops arrived, the troops of his battalion cheered and the bugler blew a rousing call. No one advanced or fired a shot to assist the airborne.

Either the flight leader of the American transport planes or the Vietnamese jumpmaster—the source of the mistake was never explained—committed the error that made Cao accommodate the guerrilla battalion commander. The paratroops started leaping from the planes at the end, rather than at the beginning, of their drop zone. The mistake put them off by more than half a mile. Many of them landed in front of the Viet Cong positions on the west and northwest sides of Tan Thoi, instead of safely behind the Civil Guards and the M-113s at Bac as Cao had planned. There was always the risk of such an error in airborne operations, which was another reason why Porter and Vann had wanted the drop made much earlier in the afternoon. The guerrillas were able to take the paratroops under fire as they were still descending in their chutes.

In contrast to the regular ARVN, the Saigon airborne were hardy soldiers. The French parachute officers had been the doomed knights of the colonial army, romantic men who exalted comradeship and a brave death as somehow redeeming whatever stupidities accompanied their lot. Their Vietnamese men-at-arms who stayed behind kept the memory, and these paratroops tried to react with the pluckiness of their French ideal. Cao had inadvertently committed them to combat under the worst of circumstances. It was impossible to get organized in the thickening dusk while being shot at by an enemy close by. They were unable to do more than launch piecemeal attacks in small units before darkness put an end to the fighting. The guerrillas made short work of them and inflicted substantial casualties. Nineteen of the paratroops were killed and thirty-three wounded, including the two American advisors to the battalion, a captain and a sergeant.

To make certain the guerrillas withdrew during the night, Cao would not permit a C-47 flare plane that Prevost summoned to drop its flares and illuminate the Viet Cong's retreat route. Vann wanted to light up the rice fields and swamps all along the east flank of Tan Thoi and Bac and to keep them under regular bombardment with 500 rounds of artillery. Cao agreed to fire 100 shells. He then ordered the batteries to shoot four shells per hour. His excuse for banning flares was that the paratroops did not want their night defensive positions revealed to the guerrillas. It was doubtful that the airborne ever made such a request, and Vann protested that the flares would not illuminate the paratroops because they were on the other side of Tan Thoi. Cao's logic of facilitating his personal disengagement from this disaster prevailed. The C-47 dropped no flares.

The "raggedy-ass little bastards" had obliged the Americans. The 350 guerrillas had stood their ground and humbled a modern army four times their number equipped with armor and artillery and supported by helicopters and fighter-bombers. Their heaviest weapon was the little 60mm mortar that had proved useless to them. They suffered eighteen killed and thirty-nine wounded, light casualties considering that the

Americans and their Vietnamese protégés subjected them to thousands of rifle and machine-gun bullets, the blast and shrapnel of 600 artillery shells, and the napalm, bombs, and assorted other ordnance of thirteen warplanes and five Huey gunships. The Hueys alone expended 8,400 rounds of machine-gun fire and 100 rockets on the tree lines at Bac. With the weapons they held in their hands the guerrillas killed or wounded roughly four of their enemies for every man they lost. They inflicted about 80 killed and well over 100 wounded on the Saigon forces and also killed three Americans, wounded another eight, and accounted for five helicopters. (The Saigon side later officially admitted to 63 killed and 109 wounded, holding down their losses by misstating the number of casualties suffered by the reserve company in front of Bac.) The guerrillas managed to cause all of this damage while still conserving their own bullets. From the first shots at the Civil Guards through the last fight with the paratroops they fired about 5,000 rounds of rifle and machine-gun ammunition.

The battalion commander fixed the departure hour for 10:00 P.M. and the assembly point as the house of a peasant named Muoi at the southern end of Tan Thoi. Since dawn he had been performing the indispensable role of battlefield leader, making the decisions affecting the fate of all that only a soldier of his experience and judgment could make, spending the lives of his men conscientiously to win. Now with the same care he organized their escape to fight again. He had the two reinforced companies shift their units to the vicinity of the house in stages. The company at Bac, which had begun evacuating the foxholes in the section of the tree line facing Ba's M-113s by late afternoon, worked its way up the stream connecting the two hamlets. During the fall-back to the assembly point, one platoon of each company was assigned the role of rear guard just in case the ARVN attempted an uncharacteristic night attack. About two hours before departure the battalion commander dispatched local guerrilla scout teams to reconnoiter the retreat routes to the east and to arrange for sampans to be waiting at a canal to transport the wounded to a thatched-hut hospital in one of the nearest base camps. He and the company commanders conferred after the scout teams reported back and selected the safest route. He also sent a squad back down to Bac to recover the bodies of Dung and his comrades so that they could be carried to the battalion base and buried with honors. The man to whose courage they owed their lives had been killed by an air strike or an artillery barrage while his company was withdrawing through an orchard inside the hamlet. The squad returned without the bodies. They said they had been unable to find Dung and his companions in the darkness and were fearful of making any noise within the hamlet because Ba's M-113s were bivouacked for the night on the edge of the tree line. "Comrade Dung could not come," the Viet Cong account of the battle said.

At 10:00 P.M. the two companies set off in a column for the base camps on the Plain of Reeds. The village and hamlet guerrillas and the peasants from Bac and Tan Thoi who had stayed to help during the fight left by a different route for their separate hideouts in the water palm jungles in the vicinity. The regulars of the 261st Main Force who had held Bac led the way. The men of the weapons platoon marched in the middle of the column, carrying the wounded and the bodies of other dead who had been retrieved for burial. The province guerrillas of the 514th Regionals followed, with one of their platoons forming a rear guard. These men were in friendly country, and they were accustomed to marching at night. The sampans were waiting at the canal by the time the column reached it. The wounded were transferred to the boats. The column continued down the canal to a fording place, waded across, and kept marching until well after daybreak without being detected, reaching the camps safely at 7:00 A.M. They had done more than win a battle. They had achieved a Vietnamese victory in the way of their ancestors. They had overcome the odds.

Vann paid them a tribute at about the time they were beginning their march to safety from the peasant Muoi's house. It was fitting that the tribute should come from him. He had been the vehicle of destiny in this battle. Without him, Ba might have delayed long enough to have reached the hamlet after it was too late to fight. In his determination to destroy these men, Vann had goaded the armored personnel carriers to Bac. He had forced the battle to its climactic humiliation of the Saigon side and had consummated the triumph of the Viet Cong.

With Nicholas Turner, a New Zealander who was the Reuters correspondent in South Vietnam, and Nguyen Ngoc Rao, the Vietnamese reporter for the UPI, I had driven down to Tan Hiep that night to find out what was happening. The news we had received in Saigon of five helicopters lost and an airborne battalion dropped in the midst of a battle, all so extraordinary, had made us decide that we had to get to Tan Hiep despite our fear of being stopped and taken prisoner or killed at one of the roadblocks the guerrillas sometimes set up along the route at night. We had probably taken a greater risk in racing Turner's little Triumph sedan along the two-lane tarmac at seventy miles an hour.

Cao was incapable of talking to us. I found him pacing to and fro in front of the command-post tent, running both of his hands back over his hair again and again in a kind of nervous crisis. When I walked up to him and asked a question, he stared at me for a moment and then said something incoherent and turned away.

One of Vann's captains located him for us. Vann drew us off into the darkness at the edge of the airstrip, away from the dim light cast out of the headquarters tent by the naked bulbs that hung inside on wires from the generator. He did not want Cao and Dam and the other ARVN officers to see him talking to us. He was frank, but he was still struggling that night to conceal the full measure of his anger from us because of the consequences if we published the worst details of this debacle. He spoke of how the guerrillas had stood and held despite the assault of the armored tracks and all of the pounding and burning from the air and the artillery. He looked out across the darkness toward Bac, as the token artillery fire sounded in the muffled way that artillery always seems to sound on battlefields at night and an occasional star shell from the batteries illuminated the sky despite Cao's ban on flares.

"They were brave men," he said. "They gave a good account of themselves today."

BOOK FOUR

TAKING ON THE SYSTEM

H E WAS NOT SUPPOSED to accept defeat. He was a lieutenant colonel in the United States Army. He might be just an advisor with no authority to command, but this war had become his war emotionally, and emotionally he could not understand why he was being forced to lose it. His pride in himself and his institution and in the majesty of his nation and its preeminence in the world was being trod on more than he could endure. Ap Bac was a decisive battle both for the Vietnamese Revolution in the South and for John Vann. It propelled him down a course toward which he had gradually been moving. He set out to convince Harkins in Saigon, and if Harkins would not listen then to reach over his head and to convince the military and political leadership in Washington, that the only way the United States could avoid being beaten in Vietnam was to drastically change strategy and coerce the Saigon side into accepting direction from him and the other American officers in the field. Harkins was unwittingly preparing a catastrophe for the American enterprise in South Vietnam and for those Vietnamese who had thrown in their lot with the United States. Vann saw the elements of that catastrophe with more clarity than anyone else in Vietnam at the time, and he was determined to do everything he could to prevent it. His undertaking was an ambitious one for a lieutenant colonel. He did not realize how ambitious it was when he began it because he took each step as events confronted him. He was prepared to break the rules the Army had conditioned him to obey in order to change policy and to win his war. The first indication that he was ready to kick over the traces was his abandonment the morning after the battle of any attempt to conceal his anger and the extent of the debacle from reporters he knew.

Just as the U.S. military presence had not yet escalated by January 1963 to the hundreds of thousands of troops it was to reach after 1965, so the foreign press corps had not yet burgeoned to the hundreds of both sexes and all nationalities—newspaper, television, and radio correspondents, still photographers, television cameramen, sound technicians, and sundry war groupies posing as free lances—who were to descend on Vietnam to cover "the big war." When the Battle of Ap Bac occurred there were about a dozen resident correspondents in Vietnam, including the French journalists, who were relatively inactive because it was no longer their war. The U.S. expeditionary force had grown to 11,300 by then, but the field advisors numbered only about a quarter of the total, approximately 3,000 officers and men. The dimensions of the war were still such that the reporters and the most important advisors and many of their subordinates could get to know each other.

The reporters had not needed encouragement from Harkins's senior public affairs officer, as impressed as his chief was by Vann's high "body counts," to cover the 7th Division and its advisory detachment. Reporters follow a story: the story in 1962 and 1963 was the pivotal fighting for the northern half of the Delta. Vann had reinforced a natural relationship. He had welcomed reporters to the Seminary. He liked publicity; it flattered him. At the beginning he also saw publicity as useful in his campaign to turn Cao into the "Tiger of South Vietnam," always brandishing the clipping of the story to Cao whenever he conned a reporter into writing that Cao was aggressive. The forthright side of his personality, on the other hand, permitted us journalists to see and hear much that did not further this chicanery. He made certain that his staff officers gave us what briefings we wanted and that we got out on operations with his captains and lieutenants. Vann's subordinates took their cue from him; the junior officers advising the combat units were candid about the flaws in the Saigon forces.

Once a reporter had demonstrated that he would endure discomfort and expose himself to danger by marching through the paddies and spending nights in the field—that he would take this soldier's baptism—he was accepted by these amiable and sincere men, and frank discussion followed. On his next trip the exchange was freer. The advisors also noticed, from wire service dispatches printed in *Pacific Stars & Stripes*, the armed forces newspaper in the Far East, and from clippings mailed by their wives and families, that the reporters protected them by quoting anonymously or otherwise disguising the source when the remark or information was derogatory. By the time of Ap Bac, I and the half dozen other American correspondents had been out on numerous operations with the 7th Division and were friendly with Vann and his men. (Nick Turner of Reuters, and Peter Arnett, a New Zealander who worked for the Associated Press, counted as Americans because they held essentially the same attitude as their American colleagues.) The American reporters shared the advisors' sense of commitment to this war. Our ideological prism and cultural biases were in no way different. We regarded the conflict as our war too. We believed in what our government said it was trying to accomplish in Vietnam, and we wanted our country to win this war just as passionately as Vann and his captains did.

Turner and Rao and I drove back to Saigon after talking to Vann on the night of the battle, cabled our dispatches, and then showered and ate and returned to Tan Hiep in the darkness in order to fly to Bac as soon as the helicopters resumed operations at dawn. Merton Perry, then with *Time* magazine, a rotund man of 220 pounds whose cheerfulness and energy were as great as his girth, came with us. We arrived shortly after sunrise, in time to watch Cao drive up in a jeep, its olive-green paint waxed to a sheen, from My Tho, where he had spent the night. He had regained some of his composure and was dressed in freshly starched fatigues with the twin stars of his new rank attached in French Army style to the front of his shirt. Dam had called out the division honor guard for the corps commander. The soldiers were drawn up in a line in front of the headquarters tent—white helmets, white web belts, shined brass buckles, and white laces in their black boots. The honor guard came to attention and presented arms as Cao alighted from the jeep. He acknowledged their salute with a wrist snap of his swagger stick and strode into the tent, smiling nervously at us in greeting, clearly still not wanting to talk. Vann pointed out two H-21s that were about to fly to Bac to pick up the dead. Turner and I climbed aboard one while Mert Perry stayed behind to talk to Vann and Rao remained at Tan Hiep to learn what he could from the Vietnamese junior officers.

The rubble of the houses was still smoking, and the H-21 pilots circled cautiously to the west of the hamlet. They stayed well away from the tree line, landing in a paddy not far from the last canal that Ba's company had been so slow to cross the day before. Turner and I could see Ba's M-113s parked over by the tree line. There was no shooting, and we walked along a paddy dike toward the downed helicopters. I counted about twenty dead in the largest group of corpses stacked on top of other dikes. These Vietnamese soldiers lay on their backs, their fatigues bloodied, the toes of their small boots pointing up into the air.

Scanlon approached with two M-113s to load the bodies and carry them to the helicopters. He said that the guerrillas had withdrawn from the tree line the previous afternoon, but despite the absence of the Viet Cong, the pilots had orders not to land any closer. The infantrymen on Ba's two carriers were so demoralized they did not want to touch the corpses of their comrades. Scanlon shouted at them and pulled several off the machines to force them to load the bodies. Turner and I helped pick up the dead, including Braman and Deal. At the helicopters Scanlon had the same trouble making the living show their fellow soldiers the decency of returning the bodies to the families for burial. He again had to shout and manhandle Ba's troops to force them to lift the corpses into the aircraft. By now Turner and I were also angry at their behavior, and we started yelling at them too. We had never seen an American advisor and ARVN soldiers behave like this. We wondered at the dimensions of the debacle that had occurred here.

Brig. Gen. Robert York, forty-nine years old, from the red-dirt town of Hartselle in the hill country of northern Alabama, who commanded a special detachment the Pentagon had established in Vietnam to experiment with weapons and tactics, landed at Bac in a third helicopter soon after we had finished loading the bodies. York was another member of that Depression generation of Southerners who had initially been attracted to the military academies by the opportunity for a free education and had then discovered that soldiering was a profession that suited them. He had been a boxer at West Point and carried his alert, muscular figure into midlife. York was envied by his contemporaries for one of the finest infantry combat leadership records in the Army. He had led a battalion, originally in the renowned 1st Infantry Division, "the Big Red One," and then a regiment flawlessly for more than two years from the first testing battles against the Germans in Tunisia through Sicily, Italy, and D-Day in Normandy to the mopping up in the rubble of the Third Reich.

Of the twelve American generals in Vietnam in January 1963—a third more general officers than the entire Saigon forces had on active service—only York felt an obligation to fly to Bac and personally find out what had happened there. His desire to learn the truth was unusual, and Vann was one of the reasons for it. Since his arrival in Saigon the previous October, York had been using the freedom of his position (Harkins's headquarters exercised only nominal control over York and his detachment) to roam about the countryside so that he could form his own estimate of how the war was going. Vann had understood the seriousness of York's purpose and had tried to give him a feeling for the people and the terrain and the particular problems of this conflict, like the outpost system Vann was making no progress in dismantling, by boldly taking York on jeep tours through areas that York had sensed were dangerous. As they talked, York had been struck by Vann's capacity to become emotionally involved and yet to stand back, to see the Vietnamese on his side objectively and to acknowledge their faults. Vann had not been tempted into the error some advisors had committed of conjuring up success for their Vietnamese because progress by their counterparts would help to advance their own careers. One was fortunate to find a young lieutenant colonel who thought creatively at his own echelon. Vann could think creatively at Harkins's level.

York was able to follow Vann's arguments because a special experience in his career set him apart from his peers. The only American general to fly to Bac was also the only American general in Vietnam with any firsthand knowledge of a Communist-led guerrilla insurgency in Asia. In 1952, York had by chance been assigned for three and a half years as the U.S. Army observer of the British campaign to suppress the guerrilla revolt by the Chinese minority in Malaya. The lessons he had learned there led him to suspect prior to coming to Vietnam that the task of defeating the Viet Cong was going to be a lot more difficult than his fellow generals thought. The British had held a twenty-to-one advantage in police and troops against a guerrilla force that never numbered more than 10,000, including its civilian support apparatus, a fraction of the Viet Cong armed strength and civilian adherents, and they had had the racial antagonism of the Malay majority toward the Chinese in their favor as well. The war had still lasted twelve years.

There was also a personal reason to bring General York to Bac. He and his relatives had been one of the first American families to be hurt by the war in Vietnam. In July 1962, three months after his arrival, a nephew he regarded with pride and affection, Capt. Donald York, one of Ziegler's classmates at West Point, who had volunteered to advise a paratroop battalion, had been killed in an ambush on Route 13 where the road ran through an old Viet Minh redoubt in the rubber-plantation country just north of Saigon. When York heard the news of Ap Bac late the previous day, he had made up his mind to fly to the scene at the first opportunity in the morning.

York and Turner and I, and York's aide, Lt. Willard Golding, found only three bodies while walking down the foxhole line and then through the hamlet. In the irrigation ditch behind the main dike, half sunken from a rocket hit, was one of the hollowed-log sampans the guerrillas had used to evacuate the wounded and to replenish their ammunition. Standing among the foxholes on top of the dike, we could appreciate for the first time the football-field view the Viet Cong had held of the rice fields to the front where the helicopters had landed. The whole position had been so perfectly chosen and prepared that Scanlon was later to remark that it was the Fort Benning "school solution" of how an outnumbered infantry unit ought to organize a defense. We noticed that despite the stress of retreating under air and artillery bombardment, the Viet Cong had practiced their usual frugality by collecting most of the brass shell cases to reload with new powder and bullets in the base camps.

I had acquired enough experience by this time to know what the evidence meant, but a reporter is supposed to have an authority draw judgments for him. York was a handy authority, and so I asked him how he thought the guerrillas had fared. "What the hell's it look like?" he said, a bit exasperated by the silliness of the question. "They got away—that's what happened."

Turner, York, Lieutenant Golding, and I thought for a while that we were not going to be as lucky as the guerrillas. Cao, who claimed to have killed the same Viet Cong general several times over, always forgetting that he had made the boast before, almost bagged a genuine American general, his aide, and two reporters. The four of us were standing on a paddy dike near the downed helicopters watching a fresh battalion of 7th Division infantry who had arrived that morning march into the hamlet. Turner and I had been at Bac for over four hours. We knew that this was the biggest story we had ever encountered in Vietnam. We were eager to get a fuller explanation of the battle from Vann and his staff at Tan Hiep and then drive back to Saigon to file another dispatch and tell the world what we had learned. York had consented to give us a ride to the airstrip in his helicopter, which was scheduled to return soon. A howitzer sounded from the south, and a smoke shell threw up a shower of mud on our side of Bac a short distance inside the tree line, where a column of infantry from the new battalion had just disappeared into the foliage.

"Hey, that's pretty damned close," Golding shouted. As he shouted, two howitzers boomed. The high-explosive shells rushed through the air toward us with that unnerving, fast-train-in-the-night hustle; they crashed beside another column of infantry walking toward the hamlet on a dike about seventy-five yards away. The concussion and flying shrapnel knocked several soldiers off the dike, and the rest tumbled into the paddy yelling with fear.

"Let's get the hell out of here!" York shouted while more shells exploded in the paddy about thirty yards from us. With York in the lead, we ran away from the hamlet down the narrow, sun-baked top of the dike, trying to escape from the impact area. The shells followed us. We had sprinted only a short distance when one exploded close by and the blast almost knocked us off our feet. "Get down!" York yelled. We threw ourselves into the slime and huddled up against the dike with the shells crashing all around us.

Cao had decided to fake an attack on Bac now that the Viet Cong were gone. He wanted the palace to think that he was doing something to recoup. For this reason he had ordered the additional infantry battalion to Bac to make the attack along with some of Ba's troops. He had then taken a helicopter over to Tho's field command post on the main Delta road to the south and instructed Tho to fire a barrage to soften up the enemy for "the assault." Cao had not flown over Bac to see whether any of his men were inside the hamlet. Tho in turn had simply told his deputy to order the batteries to open fire. Cao and Tho might have been stopped had the ARVN second lieutenant who was the artillery forward observer with the new division battalion been more proficient at reading a map. The artillery officer had been worried and had radioed the lieutenant to check on the position of the battalion. The lieutenant had replied with map coordinates that had put the battalion about three-quarters of a mile southwest of Bac.

Unlike Cao and Tho, the second lieutenant paid for his error. Enraged at the shells killing and wounding his men, the battalion commander pulled his service pistol and shot the lieutenant in the head as soon as the barrage began. Before the lieutenant's radio operator could again make contact with the artillery officer to halt the bombardment, four soldiers had been killed and twelve wounded by the nearly fifty shells fired. There would have been more casualties had the mud and water not limited the bursting range of the shrapnel. Some or all of us four would also have been killed or wounded had York not shouted at us to jump up and run farther down the dike during a lull of about thirty seconds at one point. The next two shells exploded right where we had been lying. As it was, a shard of shrapnel as big as a fist sliced into the dike ten feet in front of Turner.

I located one of Ba's sergeants who spoke French from his days in the colonial forces and translated York's instructions to radio the airstrip for helicopters to evacuate the wounded. Ba and the advisors and Herb Prevost, who had also flown in for a look, were off in the hamlet with the infantry. York supervised the loading of all of the wounded and dead the troops could gather.

At the airstrip we found General Harkins. He had flown down from Saigon for a briefing by Vann. I had seen him and spoken to him many times previously and nothing about his appearance was unfamiliar, but the sight of him suddenly took me aback on that day after Ap Bac, perhaps the more so because I, like Turner and Golding, was covered with filth. I was twenty-six years old, and Turner and Golding were also in their twenties. The bombardment was our first experience at the wrong end of artillery, and we had burrowed into the ooze in terror to try to hide from the shells. York was the only one who was still presentable. In a feat of self-control, he had propped himself up on his elbows and kept the front of his fatigue shirt clean. "I didn't want to get my cigarettes wet, son," he said when I noticed his unsoiled shirt right after the shelling and asked him how he had managed it.

Harkins was a world apart from the four of us. He was dressed in his office uniform, a short-sleeved shirt and trousers of tan tropical worsted, an outfit called "suntans." The tabs of his shirt collar were held in place by matching bands of four silver stars. The brim of his parade-ground cap was covered with gold braid. He was wearing street shoes, carrying a swagger stick, and using the long white cigarette holder he favored. He questioned York about the shelling incident before boarding his twin-engine Beechcraft to fly back to Saigon. David Halberstam of the *New York Times* and Peter Arnett of the AP told me that they had approached Harkins a little earlier and asked him what he thought of the battle. "We've got them in a trap and we're going to spring it in half an hour," he said. Halberstam and Arnett had looked at Harkins in amazement. They had just come back from circling over Bac and Tan Thoi in a helicopter. They could see that the hamlets were quiet. They had also learned from reports the pilots were receiving over the radio and from Vann and the advisors at the airstrip that the Viet Cong were long gone.

There was something obscene about all of this to me and the other reporters. Amid this maiming and dying, a Vietnamese general who should have been serving in an opera company rather than an army was heaping macabre farce upon macabre farce while an honor guard waited upon him. An American general with a swagger stick and a cigarette holder, whose four stars on his collar tabs said that he commanded the fighter-bombers and helicopters and the flow of arms and ammunition that made this battle and this war possible, but who would not deign to soil his suntans and street shoes in a rice paddy to find out what was going on, was prattling about having trapped the Viet Cong.

As soon as Harkins had left, Vann came over to say that he was sorry about the shelling. "Jesus Christ, John," I asked, "what in the hell happened?"

Vann had not yet learned that Cao was principally to blame for the bombardment. "It was that goddam poltroon Tho," he said. This last idiocy seemed to break the restraint he had always imposed on himself with reporters. He went into a tirade at the stupidities and acts of cowardice of the last two days.

"It was a miserable damn performance," he said. "These people won't listen. They make the same goddam mistakes over and over again in the same way." He railed on about the escape that Cao had arranged for the Viet Cong. "We begged and pleaded and prayed for the paratroops to come in on the east, but when they finally came in they were deliberately put on the western side."

What Vann did not say, his subordinates said for him. The level of indiscretion was commensurate with the level of disgust. The helicopter pilots also talked freely. They were equally incensed because the lives of their people had been thrown away and their aircraft squandered.

Like the other reporters, I tried to shield Vann and his advisors and the pilots by quoting them anonymously. I attributed Vann's remarks to "one American officer." A headline writer for the *Rochester Democrat & Chronicle*, the hometown newspaper of Vann's wife, Mary Jane, picked up his forthright description of how the Saigon forces had disgraced themselves. The newspaper ran my dispatch across the top of its front page under the headline "A Miserable Damn Performance." Mary Jane's mother, Mary Allen, who still lived in Rochester, recognized her son-in-law's flair for the candid phrase. Vann had been stationed at Fort Bliss, Texas, adjacent to El Paso, prior to volunteering for Vietnam. Mary Jane was living there with the children. Her mother mailed her a clipping of the article with a notation over the headline: "This sounds like a remark John would make."

Harkins almost cut short Vann's ambitious endeavor to change policy on the war. When the general returned to Tan Hiep the next morning, January 4, for another briefing, he wanted to fire Vann. The "playbacks" of our dispatches as they had been printed and broadcast in the United States had come in over the teletype. Prior to Ap Bac, the Kennedy administration had succeeded in preventing the American public from being more than vaguely conscious that the country was involved in a war in a place called Vietnam. The public had been focused on places like Berlin, Cuba, Laos, and the Congo as the scenes of the nation's foreign policy crises. Ap Bac was putting Vietnam on the front pages and on the television evening news shows with a drama that no other event had yet achieved. Harkins was embarrassed and enraged by the stories. The dispatches, replete with details of cowardice and bungling and salty quotations like Vann's "miserable damn performance" remark, were describing the battle as the worst and most humiliating defeat ever inflicted on the Saigon side and as a dramatic illumination of all of the flaws in Diem's armed forces. President Kennedy and Secretary McNamara wanted an explanation. Harkins was also under pressure from the regime to make Vann a scapegoat. Diem and his family and their trusted adherents were in a fury over the loss of face. Cao's excuse to the reporters when he finally talked to us on January 3 was that Vann and Dam had drawn up a faulty plan and failed to show it to him beforehand so that he could correct it. In his excuse to the palace he blamed the whole debacle on Vann. Madame Nhu said that everything would have gone splendidly had it not been for an American colonel who had flown around the battlefield all day in a little plane, countermanding the orders of her brother-in-law's senior officers.

"We've got to get rid of him," Harkins said to Maj. Gen. Charles Timmes, his principal Army subordinate as chief of the Military Assistance and Advisory Group. Timmes had been on a tour of the northern part of the country on the day of the battle, and the morning of the fourth was his first opportunity to fly to Tan Hiep. He had arrived shortly after the commanding general. Harkins took him aside right away and ordered him to replace Vann immediately as senior advisor to the 7th Division. Vann technically worked for Timmes. The field advisors were still being assigned to the MAAG in these early years, even though they took their operating instructions from Harkins's headquarters. Timmes had served Harkins loyally and earned his confidence. Harkins therefore did not feel a necessity to maintain the bland and courteous exterior he normally preserved in personal dealings. He let Timmes see how angry he was.

Timmes was alarmed at Harkins's order. The son of a doctor in Queens, Charlie Timmes had always wanted to be a soldier and had repeatedly tried and failed to gain admission to West Point as a youth. He had instead gone to Fordham and unhappily practiced law for a meager livelihood during the Depression until he could turn a reserve commission into active duty as a lieutenant with the Civilian Conservation Corps in 1939, finally transferring to the Army itself three months before Pearl Harbor. Although he had amply proved himself as a paratroop battalion commander during World War II, he tended to be awed by the West Point insiders like Harkins, perhaps because of his rebuffed attempts to enter their fraternity. He was convinced that Harkins's optimistic view of the war was the correct one and that Vann's reports were too grim. Yet as a fighting soldier himself, he liked Vann. Outbursts were part of the man's character. Timmes was ready to forgive Vann's flaws in order to profit from his other qualities. It also struck him that if he relieved Vann in these circumstances, he would undermine the morale of the rest of the division advisors. They would conclude that if they took risks to win the war and trouble with the Vietnamese resulted, he and Harkins would discard them and ruin their careers. Above all he wanted to stop Harkins from committing a rash act that would provoke a new scandal in the press.

"You can't do it," he said to Harkins. "They'll crucify you." He reminded Harkins that the MACV public affairs officers had promoted Vann as the "hotshot" of the advisory effort and that Vann also had a flair for handling the press and that the reporters were fond of him. They would be certain to leap on his dismissal, whether justified or not, as a craven act of surrender to the Saigon regime. It would be a public relations disaster.

Timmes saw that his argument was having the desired effect. Harkins had calmed down and was listening to him. Timmes mentioned the danger of also undermining the morale of the other advisors, but he stressed the certainty of a scandal. "Please, let me handle it," he urged. Vann had just three months left to serve in Vietnam. Timmes proposed leaving him at My Tho for a decent interval and then relieving him and sending him off to tour the Central Highlands and the Central Coast region on the pretext that Timmes needed an independent estimate of how the war was going there. Harkins agreed.

A few days later, Timmes tested Porter's attitude by telling him that Harkins was furious at Vann and wanted Porter to dismiss him. Timmes and Porter had known each other for years and were friends. Porter became extremely upset. "I'd fire myself before I fired John Vann," he said. The implicit threat was that if he was told to relieve Vann, he would ask to be relieved himself. That would give the reporters further grist for a scandal, and as Porter was not scheduled to leave until mid-February, Vann had some protection for the immediate future.

Vann also defused some of Harkins's anger with the duplicity he could employ convincingly when it suited his purpose. He swore that he had not talked to us. We had overheard his briefings for Harkins and others, he said, but through no fault of his because he did not control access to the command-post area. Access was a responsibility of the Saigon officers, and they had been "too polite" to order us to leave. He claimed that our unwelcome presence had also allowed us to eavesdrop on his transmissions from the spotter plane by listening to the headquarters radios during the battle. No one in Harkins's entourage had the wit to call Vann's bluff by checking to find out if any reporters had been present at the command post during the battle to overhear him on the radio.

Harkins's displeasure eased. He did not veto a recommendation by Porter to award Vann the Distinguished Flying Cross for braving Viet Cong fire in the spotter plane. (In mid-December 1962, President Kennedy had relented on his fiction of the nonwar in Vietnam to the extent of authorizing combat decorations up to the third-highest award—the Bronze Star for Valor. The Distinguished Flying Cross was the equivalent award for heroism in the air.) Harkins also tried to indicate to Vann that he realized he had not given Vann a band of fearless Gurkhas to advise and that he was willing to forgive Vann's impolitic behavior. One of Harkins's staff officers passed him a newspaper clipping of a cartoon on Ap Bac by Bill Mauldin, the creator of the archetypal GIs of World War II, Willie and Joe. In the cartoon an ARVN infantryman was huddled down inside a foxhole. An American sergeant, exposing himself to Viet Cong bullets, knelt beside the foxhole with his hands stretched out in supplication. "When I say attack, don't just lean forward," the sergeant said to the cowering Saigon soldier. "Send it to Col. Vann," Harkins wrote on the memo routing slip, initialed it, and had the slip and the cartoon dispatched to Vann at My Tho.

Had he been able to understand what a complicated man he was dealing with and what grief Vann was to cause him, Harkins undoubtedly would have fired Vann, let Porter go in the bargain, and accepted crucifixion by the news media as the lesser evil. Vann had no intention of behaving himself in the future. He would dissemble only to win. His professional conscience would not permit him to fake the score if he thought that lying would bring defeat for his country.

Vann's first step was to attempt to turn the Battle of Ap Bac to his advantage. He held up the debacle as proof that this army he had been sent to help guide was ludicrously inadequate to the task of holding South Vietnam for the United States. He put together an after-action report on Ap Bac that was the longest and most detailed report of its kind in the history of the war thus far.

He had each of the advisors write accounts of their experiences to append as testimony to the main body of his report. Scanlon surpassed Vann's expectations with six and a half pages of single-spaced type.

Together with the reports of Mays and Bowers, Scanlon's narrative made for unsettling reading. The advisor to Major Tho wrote five pages on the nonperformance of the province chief and attached a copy of a separate two-page letter he had sent to Tho the day after the battle, with Vann's permission. It amounted to a sarcastic letter of reprimand, enumerating Tho's acts "for your [Tho's] further convenience, enlightenment and corrective training." Prevost produced fourteen pages of observations.

After Ziegler had edited all sixteen of these individual accounts to be sure they were as crisp as possible, Vann topped them with the main body of his report—twenty-one pages of descriptive chronology and analysis. He communicated his "miserable damn performance" feelings without using words like "debacle" or "defeat." He knew that any display of emotion would weaken his report and permit Harkins and other superiors who did not wish to hear this bad news to point to the emotion as evidence that his judgment was impaired. He wrote in the restrained language mandatory for Army reports. The authenticity of the personal accounts by the advisors and the hour-by-hour recitation of bumble after bumble and wretched act after wretched act in his chronology and analysis broke the bonds of this bland Army language and conveyed what he wished to say. He signed the finished product— ninety-one pages with map overlays of the action—and sent it off to Porter at Cao's IV Corps headquarters in Can Tho a week after the battle. Army procedure called for Porter to write a memorandum of comment, officially referred to as an indorsement, on the report before forwarding it to Harkins's headquarters.

Porter's memorandum to Harkins was an astonishing document for a white-haired colonel of his sobriety. The memorandum read like a charge sheet for a court-martial, to which Porter was attaching Vann's report as evidence for the prosecution. "The subject after-action report is possibly the best documented, most comprehensive, most valuable, and most revealing of any of the reports submitted . . . during the past 12 months," he began. "The conduct of this operation revealed many glaring weaknesses," he said, and reminded Harkins that Vann and his fellow division senior advisors had already called attention to "most" of these weaknesses on an individual basis in their reports on "the bulk of other operations" by the 7th Division and its two associate ARVN divisions in the Delta and the belt of provinces that ringed Saigon on the north. Porter next abstracted from Vann's report the worst flaws in the performance of Diem's forces during the battle and listed them in a string of alphabetized subparagraphs. The list was a quick-step march through almost every mortal sin known to the profession of arms. It went on in a litany of:

Failure . . .
Unwillingness . . .
Futility . . .
Failure . . .
Failure . . .

Porter did not have a single redeeming comment to make. He warned in his conclusion that there was no sense fooling themselves about the leadership of the Saigon army. "Many of the weaknesses enumerated above are characteristic of virtually all of the senior officers of the Vietnamese armed forces," he wrote.

To start the process of reformation, Porter recommended that Harkins obtain Diem's consent to "a series of joint US/VN conferences or seminars at the national level for all Vietnamese general officers, the key members of the corps and higher staffs, and division and brigade commanders" and their advisors. At these meetings the Americans would "openly and frankly discuss" with their Saigon counterparts what needed to be done. The agenda for discussion and subsequent reform that Porter then laid out again encompassed practically every attribute of a respectable army, from "principles of shock action" to a reform that had immediate application to Cao and Tho—"the necessity to eliminate ineffective commanders." In short, they would have to begin from scratch.

General York, whose escape from Cao's "friendly fire" at Bac lent a certain keenness to his estimate of ARVN leadership, obtained the first indication of how Harkins viewed the battle and how he would react to Vann's report and to Porter's judgment and recommendation. York had also decided that Ap Bac illuminated so many flaws in the Saigon side and was so portentous of the future that it merited a special report to the commanding general. He assumed that his personal analysis would prove useful to Harkins because it would carry the credibility of his record as an infantry combat leader in World War II and the knowledge of guerrilla warfare, rare among general officers in the U.S. Army, that he had acquired in Malaya. He returned to the Seminary a few days after the battle, questioned Vann again, and interviewed a number of the advisors. His analysis for Harkins made, briefly, many of the same points that Vann and Porter laid out in detail. He had only two copies typed, one for his files and the original, which he personally delivered to Harkins. That same night the two men happened to have dinner together. Harkins said that he had not yet had an opportunity to read York's report, but he was looking forward to doing so. Harkins then started talking about Ap Bac. As York listened he began to realize with astonishment that Harkins had apparently been serious when he had claimed, in another encounter with the reporters a week after the battle, that Ap Bac had been a "victory" for the Saigon forces. Harkins seemed to have truly convinced himself that when everything was taken into account, Ap Bac had been a gain for his Vietnamese wards. York said that Harkins was not going to like his report, because he had reached a different conclusion. Harkins looked at him for a moment and passed on to another subject.

We reporters would also have been astonished had we heard what York just had, because none of us thought that Harkins actually believed the Saigon side had won the battle. "I consider it a victory. We took the objective," he had said to us. We had assumed that his remark was another maladroit attempt to put the best face on things. We took it for granted that he privately viewed the war with a modicum of reality, however flawed with false optimism his vision might be.

We were wrong. Harkins had genuinely believed that the Viet Cong were still in Bac and Tan Thoi hamlets when he said to Halberstam and Arnett, "We've got them in a trap and we're going to spring it in half an hour." Despite Vann's having told him that they were gone, he had believed Cao's lie that they were still there and that Cao was going to snare them. In the same way he now really believed that the battle had not been a defeat for the Saigon troops. He was convinced of the truth of these assertions that angered us because we interpreted them as an insult to our intelligence. All of us—and Vann, Porter, and York—had been profoundly underestimating Harkins's capacity for self-delusion. He was not the only one of his rank and station whom we had been underestimating.

Harkins was to become an object of ridicule by the time he returned to the United States to retire in a year and a half. To "pull a Harkins" was to become a slang term among younger American officers in Vietnam for committing an egregiously stupid act. Harkins was to be regarded as an aberration among American military leaders, a fatuously optimistic General Blimp. In fact, as the years were to reveal, Harkins was a representative figure of the American military hierarchy of the 1960s, a man whose values and preconceptions were shared by the majority of the armed forces leadership. Harkins only seemed to be an aberration because he was the first to be noticed. The years were to demonstrate that it was Vann and Porter and York who were members of an atypical minority.

Time magazine, whose editors, under Henry Luce's guidance, almost invariably portrayed American generals in heroic dimension in the 1960s, had favorably compared Harkins to George Patton, his World War II patron, in a profile in May 1962. The two men had been outwardly dissimilar—"Patton, a shootin' cussin' swashbuckler; Harkins, quiet, firm, invariably polite." Nonetheless, *Time* continued, quoting an anonymous acquaintance of Harkins, " 'I really think that inside he and Patton were the same.' "

The two men were dissimilar outwardly and inwardly. Patton had not led simply by charging up to the front. The "Old Blood and Guts" image that *Time* was perpetuating was one he had helped the newsmen cultivate (he coined the nickname himself) because it appealed to his neurotic ego and he thought the troops liked it. Patton had been a reflective man, an extraordinarily well-read student of wars and military leaders, ancient and modern, with a curiosity about his war to match his energy. No detail had been too minor or too dull for him, nor any task too humble. Everything from infantry squad tactics to tank armor plate and chassis and engines had interested him. To keep his mind occupied while he was driving through a countryside, he would study the terrain and imagine how he might attack this hill or defend that ridge. He would stop at an infantry position and look down the barrel of a machine gun to see whether the weapon was properly sited to kill counterattacking Germans. If it was not, he would give the officers and men a lesson in how to emplace the gun. He had been a military tailor's delight of creased cloth and shined leather, and he had worn an ivory-handled pistol too because he thought he was a cavalier who needed these trappings for panache. But if he came upon a truck stuck in the mud with soldiers shirking in the back, he would jump from his jeep, berate the men for their laziness, and then help them push their truck free and move them forward again to battle. By dint of such lesson and example, Patton had formed his Third Army into his ideal of a fighting force. In the process he had come to understand the capabilities of his troops and he had become more knowledgeable about the German enemy than any other Allied general on the Western Front. Patton had been able to command with certainty, overcoming the mistakes that are inevitable in the practice of the deadly art as well as personal eccentricities and public gaffes that would have ruined a lesser general, because he had always stayed in touch with the realities of his war.

Harkins lacked curiosity about his war. He had not refrained from going to Bac because he was a physical coward: he never walked through the rice paddies. When Horst Faas, the German photographer for the Associated Press, asked to take pictures of him in the field with ARVN troops, Harkins said: "I'm not that kind of a general." The fact that he did not go down into the muck to learn what was happening reinforced his aversion to bad news. His habit of seeing the Vietnamese countryside from the air was symptomatic of his attitude. His mind never touched down in Vietnam.

Harkins's laziness and complacency and chronic staff-officer habits did not, however, explain similar attitudes toward the war by generals who did not share his personal characteristics. These were the fighting generals with combat records who were to come to Vietnam after him. They were to exhibit abundant energy and to venture constantly into the field. They were to shoot guerrillas and get shot at themselves, and a few of them were to be killed, but most of them were to operate from assumptions that were essentially the same as those of Harkins. They were always to see what they had thought they would see before they ever got near a battlefield in Vietnam.

By the second decade after World War II, the dominant characteristics of the senior leadership of the American armed forces had become professional arrogance, lack of imagination, and moral and intellectual insensitivity. These are the kinds of traits that cause otherwise intelligent men like Harkins to behave stupidly. The attributes were the symptoms of an institutional illness that might most appropriately be called the disease of victory, for it arose out of the victorious response to the challenge of Nazi Germany and imperial Japan. The condition was not limited to the armed services. It had also touched the civilian bureaucracies—the Central Intelligence Agency, the State Department, and the lesser civilian agencies—that joined the armed services in managing American overseas interests for the president. The attitudes had spread as well to the greater part of the political, academic, and business leadership of the United States. World War II had been such a triumph of American resources, technology, and industrial and military genius, and the prosperity that the war and the postwar dominance abroad had brought had been so satisfying after the long hunger of the Depression, that American society had become a victim of its own achievement. The elite of America had become stupefied by too much money, too many material resources, too much power, and too much success.

In February 1943, the U.S. Army of World War II had met the Germans for the first time at the Kasserine Pass in the mountains of western Tunisia. The Americans had run. A British general had had to take charge to stop the rout. Eisenhower had telephoned Patton, who was in the occupation backwater of Morocco, to fly over and meet him at Algiers airport. Their conversation at the airport had been hurried. Eisenhower had told Patton to rehabilitate the demoralized troops and prepare to counterattack the Germans. He had scribbled a note in pencil giving Patton authority to assume command of the four American divisions in Tunisia the moment he landed there, and Patton had taken off again directly for the front. Eisenhower had followed up his note with a memorandum of instructions. Patton was not to keep "for one instant" any officer who was not up to the mark. "We cannot afford to throw away soldiers and equipment . . . and effectiveness" out of unwillingness to injure "the feelings of old friends," Eisenhower had written. Ruthlessness of this kind toward acquaintances often required difficult moral courage, Eisenhower continued, but he expected Patton "to be perfectly cold-blooded about it." The first old acquaintance to go had been the general who had commanded at Kasserine, a man whom Eisenhower had rated, prior to the start of the serious shooting, as his best combat leader after Patton. This general had been shipped home to spend the rest of the war exercising his top-notch paper qualifications as an elevated drill instructor.

The Eisenhower who had written that memorandum was a general with four new stars who had been a lieutenant colonel three and a half years earlier in the army of "a third-rate power," to quote the description of its newly appointed chief of staff, Gen. George Marshall. It had been an army inferior in numbers to the army of Portugal, its best armor twenty-eight obsolescent tanks built between the wars. The Eisenhower who had written that memorandum had also been a nervous man, because if Patton did not restore Eisenhower's damaged reputation for selecting able subordinates by winning a victory for him against the Germans, General Marshall was going to take back Eisenhower's freshly issued title of Commander in Chief of Allied Forces. The recipient of the memorandum, Patton, was an amateur boxer who had trained superbly, but who had yet to fight his first professional match. That first match was going to be in the ring at Madison Square Garden against the world heavyweight champion: the Afrika Korps of "the Desert Fox," Field Marshal Erwin Rommel. Field Marshal Rommel was succeeded by another German general as commander of the Afrika Korps just before Patton fought it, but Patton did not know that at the time. Eisenhower and Patton and their United States Army of 1943 had been small men in a world of big men. Their personal survival, the survival of their army, and the survival of their nation had been at stake. And they had been afraid that they might lose.

Twenty years after the debacle at the Kasserine Pass, it was hard to find a general in the U.S. Army who worried that he or his colleagues might squander resources and waste the lives of soldiers. The junior officers of World War II, now the generals of the 1960s, had become so accustomed to winning from the later years of that war that they could no longer imagine they could lose. (The failure in Korea they rationalized away as the fault of a weak civilian leadership which had refused to "turn loose" the full potential of American military power against China.) They assumed that they would prevail in Vietnam simply because of who they were.

By telling Harkins the truth about what had happened at Bac and urging him to demand that Diem reform his army before Diem's regime and the United States were defeated, Vann and Porter and York were asking Harkins to submit a "fail report." No such form existed among the tens of thousands printed by the U.S. armed forces. A Vietnamese Communist leader could report that he was failing to attain success without necessarily jeopardizing his position, as long as he was seeking alternative means to overcome his problems. His system encouraged self-criticism, criticism of colleagues and subordinates, and analysis of what the Party called the "objective conditions" that confronted the revolution in any given situation. The Vietnamese Communists were fighting a war of national independence and survival. They had to be able to record dark hours and to learn from them if they were to live to see sunny ones. The post–World War II American system was receptive only to the recording of sunny hours. All reports were by nature "progress reports." Harkins's weekly report to the Joint Chiefs and McNamara, for example, was entitled "Headway Report." He had no "Lostway Report" for a contingency like Ap Bac.

In keeping with this mentality Harkins had, long before Ap Bac, devised a strategy that he was convinced was bringing him victory in Vietnam. It was an attrition strategy that relied on a plentitude of American-supplied resources and firepower. Harkins thought that he was building the Saigon forces into a killing machine that would grind up the Viet Cong the way Patton had minced the Wehrmacht in Europe. He was monitoring the effectiveness of his strategy with measurements the Army had evolved out of World War II and elaborated in Korea. Numbers that Vann regarded as meaningless or indicators of counterproductive activity had great significance to Harkins. Harkins focused on the body count for this reason, deriving it from an older measurement the Army continued to use in Vietnam called the "kill ratio," the number of friendly versus enemy killed in action. He focused for the same reason on the total number of operations reported launched, on the number of aircraft sorties flown and the tonnage of bombs dropped, and on the training and equipping of additional troops to increase the momentum of this drive to victory that he imagined he had set in motion. The generation of Eisenhower and Patton had not fought World War II simply by building a killing machine and turning it loose in the expectation that it would bring them victory. They had been generals of maneuver. Attrition had been only one component of their strategy. Time and the bureaucratization of the officer corps had distorted the memory of how World War II had been won. Harkins's strategy was a fantasy of the past, but the fantasy was real because it had been institutionalized and he and most of his fellow generals had faith in it.

Harkins had described his strategy to Maxwell Taylor in a briefing at his Saigon headquarters during Taylor's September 1962 visit. Had Vann been present at the briefing he would have understood why Harkins overrode everything he attempted to say at the subsequent luncheon for the chairman of the Joint Chiefs. Harkins stressed in the briefing what he called his "Three M's"—men, money, and matériel. Lots of all three were being fed into the war. The ARVN was being expanded by nearly 30,000 men and would soon be fielding two new infantry divisions. The Civil Guard and the SDC were undergoing similar expansions. The United States was currently spending $337 million a year in military and economic aid, not counting the cost of its expeditionary corps, in contrast to $215 million the year before. The quadrupling of the fighter-bomber sortie rate, which so upset Vann because of the concomitant rise in civilian casualties, was another statistic that Harkins boasted about. There was no doubt that the Communists were feeling the weight of his Three M's, Harkins assured Taylor. He pointed to the steadily increasing body count.

By the end of 1962, Harkins said, all of these programs he had set in motion would mature. He described how he would then mesh them into a coordinated campaign to achieve final victory over the Communists. Harkins's plan was code-named Operation Explosion. Phases I and II, Planning and Preparation, were in the process of completion, and he had presented the concept to Diem. The detonation date was mid-February 1963. This was when "Phase III—EXECUTION" would begin: a nationwide offensive by these sharply honed Saigon forces and their reinforcing American elements, an offensive that would continue nonstop until the Viet Cong had been broken as an organized force and ground down to a fraction of their current size. "Phase IV—FOLLOW-UP AND CONSOLIDATION" would end the war by mopping up the guerrilla remnants and restoring the authority of Diem's regime throughout the country.

The adjunct of Harkins's attrition strategy, the Strategic Hamlet Program, was also going well, Taylor had been told at the September briefing. The isolation of the guerrillas from the peasantry that the Strategic Hamlet Program was achieving would enable Harkins's killing machine to mince the Viet Cong faster when Phase III of his nonstop offensive began in February. More than 2,800 strategic hamlets had been built by the date of the briefing. The senior embassy officer overseeing the plan said that the Country Team, an American executive council consisting of Harkins, Ambassador Frederick Nolting, Jr., the CIA station chief, and the heads of the other U.S. agencies in Vietnam, was confident that the program had progressed too far for the Viet Cong to interfere with it successfully.

Secretary McNamara, who personified the hubris of the senior civilian leadership with his cocksureness and naive acceptance of his generals at face value, had put the self-fulfilling success machine in motion when the American war effort was only five months old. At the end of his first visit to Vietnam in May 1962, he gave a press conference in the living room of Nolting's Saigon residence. He had been in the country just two days, and he was in a hurry to board his four-engine jet and fly back to Washington to report to President Kennedy. Running the world was a big job, and high American officials of McNamara's generation were always in a hurry, hurrying to make decisions so that they could hurry on to more decisions. McNamara was admired for his capacity for decision-making at a trot. His staff once calculated that he made 629 major decisions in a single month. The fact that he never seemed to worry about the possibility of a mistake and never looked back afterward was also regarded as a virtue.

He was unshaven at the press conference, because he had not wanted to waste time using a razor that morning. His khaki shirt and trousers were rumpled and his hiking boots dusty from touring the countryside. His notebooks were filled with figures he had gathered by incessantly questioning every American and Vietnamese officer or official he met at each stop. The reporters asked him what impression he was carrying back to the president. "I've seen nothing but progress and hopeful indications of further progress in the future," he said. The reporters pressed him. Surely he could not be this optimistic this soon? He would not yield under the questioning. He was a Gibraltar of optimism. I assumed that he had gained an unfortunate notion of what constituted good advertising in his years at the Ford Motor Company. I caught him outside as he was getting into his car. I said that I was not quoting him, that the question was off the record because I wanted to know the truth. How could a man of his caliber be this sanguine about a war we had barely begun to fight? He gave me the McNamara look, eyes focusing boldly through rimless glasses. "Every quantitative measurement we have shows that we're winning this war," he said. He sat down on the backseat of the sedan. A Marine guard slammed the door shut and the driver sped off to the airport.

At a strategy conference in Honolulu on July 23, 1962, three days after the fiasco on the Plain of Reeds when Cao dismayed Vann by letting 300 guerrillas escape into Cambodia—including the company of training cadres, who would return to germinate more Viet Cong—McNamara asked Harkins how long it would take "before the VC could be eliminated as a disturbing force." The question followed a briefing by Harkins on the current state of the war. Prior to leaving Saigon for Honolulu, Harkins had requested and received from Vann a special after-action report on the July 20 engagement. The top-secret record of the conference shows that he did not permit anything Vann told him to interfere with what he wished to tell the assemblage of dignitaries. He gave them an extremely optimistic estimate of the situation characterized by his favorite briefing fare:

> Contact is being made with the VC every day. During April 434 ground operations were mounted. This was increased to 441 in May. Over 1,000 air sorties were flown in June. The GVN still needs to work on their organization but progress is being made. PRES DIEM has indicated that he plans that his troops will get out into the field more often and stay out longer.

The general ended his briefing with a pronouncement that would have astounded Vann: "There is no doubt that we are on the winning side."

McNamara was understandably pleased. "Six months ago we had practically nothing and we have made tremendous progress to date," he remarked to the gathering. Harkins then replied to McNamara's question as to how long it would take to defeat the Viet Cong: "One year from the time that we are able to get [the Saigon forces] fully operational and really pressing the VC in all areas." He indicated that the start of this one-year period would be early 1963 when his Operation Explosion was scheduled to go off.

The secretary of defense thought it unwise to be so optimistic. "We must take a conservative view and assume it will take three years instead of one year," McNamara said. "We must assume the worst and make our plans accordingly." He was worried that American public opinion and Congress might force the administration to withdraw from Vietnam after Americans began to die there. "We must line up our long-range programs as it may become difficult to retain public support for our operations in Vietnam," he explained. "The political pressure will build up as U.S. losses continue to occur."

With this worst-case scenario of three years to victory settled, McNamara instructed Harkins to draw up a plan to phase out the U.S. expeditionary corps and hand over what was left of the mopping up to the Saigon forces by the end of 1965. In the meantime, Harkins was to train enough Vietnamese to man the fighter-bombers, helicopters, and other gear that would be left behind. Harkins's staff obligingly formulated a withdrawal plan, entitled "Comprehensive Three-Year Plan for South Vietnam." It called for reducing the number of American military personnel in South Vietnam to 1,600 by December 1965. This would not meet the 685-man limit allowed by the Geneva Agreements of 1954, but the level would be low enough for the American public to lose interest and would be insignificant by comparison with South Korea, where 40,000 American troops remained nine years after the conclusion of that war.

Harkins may have consciously deceived McNamara and Taylor and others above him. He may have thought that since he was going to win anyway, what was the harm in fudging the score a bit to keep his superiors happy? If so, he gave no indication of this to anyone around him, including men he trusted like Charlie Timmes. The more likely explanation seems to be that Harkins was not lying, that he willed himself to believe what he wished to believe and to reject what he wished to reject.

The after-action report on Ap Bac that Vann compiled with such passion and concern and the judgment that Porter rendered with the logic and insight of an old infantry officer merely angered the commanding general. Harkins placed Porter and Vann in a category that was above, but not far above, the reporters who exasperated him for the same reason. They were all denying the truth of the approaching victory that he could so plainly see. York warned Porter that Harkins was so incensed that Porter should not be surprised if he found himself being fired along with Vann. Porter and York had become friends while serving together in the 1950s at Fort Benning. Another brigadier general who was also a friend of Porter's from Benning years separately passed him the same warning. The fear of a scandal that had prevented Harkins from dismissing Vann and the imminence of Porter's departure provided Porter with equivalent protection, although Porter was not aware of this protection at the time. He quickly noticed the commanding general's displeasure. Harkins came to the Delta on another flying tour and did not invite Porter to ride along in the twin-engine Beechcraft. While Harkins continued otherwise to be polite to his face, Porter sensed the irritation beneath.

Harkins saw no reason to postpone the start of his Operation Explosion. On the contrary, he wanted to move up its scheduled detonation from mid-February to the end of January. On January 19, 1963, three days after Porter had forwarded Vann's report and his own warning of disaster to Saigon, Harkins also sent to Adm. Harry Felt, Commander in Chief Pacific, in Honolulu, the final draft of the program for victory by the end of 1965—the Comprehensive Three-Year Plan for South Vietnam that McNamara had requested. Harkins continued to believe that he would not require three years.

Paul Harkins need not have had the last word at this moment when the war was at the meeting of two trails. The Joint Chiefs voted to dispatch an investigating team of six generals and an admiral, assisted by sundry colonels and lieutenant colonels, from the three major services and the Marine Corps. They were to spend as much time as necessary in South Vietnam, and they had the broadest possible mandate. The team was instructed "to form a military judgment as to the prospects for a successful conclusion of the conflict in a reasonable period of time" and to recommend in its report any "modifications to our program which appeared to be desirable." The head of the team, an Army general, stated simply the question the mission was to answer: "Are we winning or are we losing?"

The Joint Chiefs' team was a distinguished group that was presumably capable of rising to its task. The team chief was one of the Army's most prominent generals. The other members were drawn from among the ranking officers in the Pentagon or were designated heirs to leadership. The delegations from the three major services were each headed by the deputy for operations who also acts as a proxy for his service head within the organization of the Joint Chiefs. The deputies meet as regularly as the chiefs do to dispose of ordinary business and to fight the exploratory skirmishes on issues that are scheduled to come before the service heads themselves. The Marines, as the ostensibly junior service, settled for a brigadier general who was a well-regarded aviator. In fact, the Corps was more than amply represented in an unofficial capacity by the team member with the greatest potential for influencing the mission's report. Maj. Gen. Victor Krulak was a fifty-year-old bantam Marine who had won the Navy Cross, an award that ranks just below the Congressional Medal of Honor, for heroism against the Japanese in the Pacific. Krulak was the only general on the team who had been to Vietnam before. He had accompanied McNamara there on the secretary of defense's first visit in May 1962, and he had been back again in the late summer of 1962 when Vann was still inflicting fearsome casualties on the Viet Cong in the northern Delta. The war in Vietnam was Krulak's business. He was its inspector-general in Pentagon heraldry, overseeing the conflict from Washington on a day-to-day basis for the Joint Chiefs and Mc-Namara as their special assistant for counterinsurgency and special activities (SACSA). He was going this time as the delegate from the Joint Staff that served the Joint Chiefs.

If one were to select any man in the hierarchy of the U.S. armed forces in 1963 with the imagination to grasp the importance of this moment and not let it escape him, Victor Krulak would probably have been that man. During his twenty-eight and a half years of service he had displayed a capacity for innovative military thinking that could be described without exaggeration as genius. The war with Spain and the turn-of-the-century drive for empire had transformed the Marines from shipboard soldiers into an amphibious assault force that prided itself on anticipating the needs of the next war to fulfill a mission of expanding American power through the Caribbean and Central America and across the Pacific into Asia. Krulak's career reflected this spirit of the Corps. The son of a Denver gold-mine manager who mined enough to retire and let his son grow up in the tranquillity of San Diego, Krulak gained admission to the Naval Academy in 1930 at the age of sixteen—the year after his father lost his fortune in the crash of the stock market and returned to Denver and mining—by passing the entrance examination with just a ninth-grade education. His fellow midshipmen at Annapolis nicknamed him "Brute" to poke fun at his undernourished appearance. He was slighter than Vann. He stood five feet five inches and weighed 138 pounds; he needed an exemption from the regulations to obtain his commission in the Marines.

As a fresh-caught first lieutenant in the intelligence section of the 4th

Marine Regiment at Shanghai in 1937, Brute Krulak made a contribution to the winning of World War II that reserved him a place of note in the history of the Corps. The Marines lacked an essential tool for the war they were anticipating with imperial Japan: landing craft capable of rapidly unloading infantry, vehicles, and heavy weapons like artillery and tanks onto a beach. The Japanese militarists set out to conquer all of China in 1937. By the fall of that year they reached Shanghai, China's main seaport, and were about to seize the city (except for the International Settlement, a privileged commercial enclave the Marines were guarding) with an assault landing. Krulak knew from intelligence reports that the Japanese were also experimenting with amphibious operations. He decided that they might reveal something valuable and that he would watch. He persuaded a fleet intelligence officer to lend him a Navy tugboat and a Navy photographer equipped with a telephoto lens. The captains of the Japanese destroyers rendered the courtesy of the sea to the little tug carrying this Marine spy bent on their future destruction. As the boat drew abreast of one of the destroyers bombarding the shore, the guns would go silent, the Japanese destroyer crew would give the traditional salute from one navy to another—the American tug crew returning it—and the destroyer would then resume firing when the tug passed.

Not long after the landing commenced, Krulak spotted the answer to the Corps' quest. One type of Japanese landing craft had a square bow that was also a retractable ramp. When the craft reached shore, the crew would drop the bow. The infantrymen inside would charge right out or the vehicles in the boat would drive across the ramp and onto the beach. The boat crew would then raise the ramp and return to a transport ship for more troops or vehicles. Nothing had to be laboriously hoisted over the sides as with the landing craft the Marines were then using. Krulak told the photographer to concentrate on the ramp-bow craft and made it the principal subject of his report. He selected photographs that best illustrated it and supplemented the photographs with sketches that further explained how well this simple design solved the problem of rapid unloading. The report was relayed up through channels to Washington with praise from his superiors.

Lieutenant Krulak did not let the matter rest on applause. Reassigned to the Washington area nearly two years later, he learned that Marine Corps Headquarters had referred his report to the Navy's Bureau of Ships. The two civil servants in a broom-closet office that was the small-craft section of "Buships" had decided that Krulak was such a green lieutenant he did not know a bow from a stern. (The stern of the Japanese landing craft was somewhat pointed, as a bow normally is.) They had tucked his discovery away in a filing cabinet as a curiosity. "Some nut out in China," a marginal comment read.

Krulak retrieved his report and took it and a balsa-wood model he made of the Japanese craft to one of the most farsighted officers ever to command Marines, then Brig. Gen. Holland M. "Howling Mad" Smith, the father of modern amphibious warfare, who was to lead the way across the Pacific and watch the men of the Corps raise the Stars and Stripes over Mount Suribachi on Iwo Jima. The Marines had found the hull design they needed in a craft originally created for rum-running during Prohibition by a New Orleans boat builder named Andrew Jackson Higgins. The retractable ramp-bow turned Higgins's boat into an assault vehicle.

The result was the LCVP (Landing Craft, Vehicle and Personnel), the standard landing craft of World War II. A larger version to bring a thirty-ton Sherman tank ashore became the LCM (Landing Craft, Mechanized). Krulak's inspiration carried American and Allied troops and the tanks and trucks and artillery and ammunition and other supplies and equipment they needed to prevail onto every beachhead from Saipan to Normandy. The 1937 report from the lieutenant in Shanghai and his sketches and the photographs of the Japanese landing craft were one day to be displayed in a glass case at the Marine Corps Museum in the Washington Navy Yard.

World War II did not diminish Krulak's imagination. In 1948, when the helicopter was regarded as a toy, he foresaw the rapidity with which its technology would mature into large and powerful machines. He prompted the Corps into staging the first helicopter assault maneuver in history on May 23, 1948, with first-generation Sikorskys, each capable of carrying only three Marines, from an aircraft carrier anchored off Camp Lejeune, North Carolina. The helicopter tactics that were considered so new in 1963 had been sketched out fifteen years earlier by Krulak when he was a lieutenant colonel on the staff of the Marine Corps Schools at Quantico, Virginia, near Washington. All the basic elements of the Army's current helicopter operations manual were copied from a Marine manual he shaped then.

The originality of Krulak's mind was not the sole reason for his potential to influence the mission of inquiry the Joint Chiefs were sending to Vietnam. He had also formed an enviable relationship that gave anything Brute Krulak said unusual credibility with the president of the United States and others at the top. He had chanced upon the opportunity to form it while demonstrating during World War II that he could fight as well as he could think. Holland Smith had appointed Krulak his aide, and when Pearl Harbor occurred he was a captain on Smith's staff in San Diego. He decided that the quickest way to get out of staff work and into the shooting was to volunteer for the first dangerous and unorthodox assignment he heard about. This turned out to be parachute training. By the fall of 1943, Captain Krulak was a lieutenant colonel leading the 2nd Marine Parachute Battalion in the South Pacific. Krulak's "ParaMarines" never had an opportunity to jump into battle. Instead they fought as an independent amphibious assault unit for Adm. William "Bull" Halsey.

In late October 1943, Krulak was ordered to conduct a series of night amphibious raids on the island of Choiseul in the Solomons to trick the Japanese into thinking that Halsey was trying to capture the place and divert Japanese reinforcements from the garrison at Bougainville, the largest island in the chain, where a landing by 14,000 Marines was to take place on November 1, 1943. During a fighting withdrawal after one of the raids, a landing craft carrying about thirty of Krulak's men, a number of them wounded, struck a coral reef and began to sink. A torpedo boat from a Navy squadron assigned to support the landings dashed in and took many of the Marines aboard, including three severely wounded. The rescue was a courageous act. The reef was close to the beach, and the Japanese were shooting at the torpedo boat while its captain and crew held it alongside the landing craft to take off the Marines. Had they not been picked up, some of the Marines would have been killed by the Japanese and the wounded would certainly have drowned. As it was, one of the gravely wounded men died shortly afterward in the bunk of the torpedo boat's skipper, a twenty-six-year-old Navy lieutenant. When the torpedo boat pulled up to Krulak's headquarters ship to transfer the rescued Marines, Krulak wanted to express his gratitude. Privileges were rare in the Solomons in 1943. Whiskey was especially hard to come by. Krulak had a fifth of the popular brand Three Feathers stored in his duffel on Vella Lavella, another island his battalion had captured earlier. "If we ever get back to Vella Lavella alive, that bottle of Three Feathers is yours," he told the lieutenant.

The lieutenant had a long wait for the whiskey. Krulak's diversion worked a bit too well. As he and his approximately 600 Marines made their last raid they found several thousand Japanese whom they had attracted from Bougainville waiting for them. It was nip and tuck getting back into the landing craft. Krulak was wounded twice. He was awarded the Navy Cross for refusing to relinquish command and accept treatment until the evacuation was completed. During a lengthy recovery at hospitals in the United States, he forgot about his promise of the bottle of whiskey.

He remembered it when the lieutenant was elected president of the United States. Not long after John Kennedy's inauguration in January 1961, Krulak, by then a major general, bought a fifth of Three Feathers and left it at the White House with a note that said, as well as he could recall years later:

> Dear Mr. President,
>   You've probably forgotten about this, but I've remembered it and here is the bottle of whiskey I promised you.

The president was delighted. Kennedy remembered the promised whiskey and the heroic Marine lieutenant colonel he had looked up to when he was a junior naval officer with the same nostalgia he recalled all his experiences in World War II. He was fond of talking about those adventures and would do so at any opportunity. He came home a war hero himself. He was awarded the Navy and Marine Corps Medal after another torpedo boat he commanded, PT-109, was rammed and sunk by a Japanese destroyer and Kennedy pulled one of his injured sailors four miles through the water to safety, gripping the ties of the man's life jacket with his teeth so that he could swim. The story of PT-109 and her brave skipper helped elect him to Congress during his first campaign in Massachusetts in 1946, but these adventures meant much more to John Kennedy than grist for political advancement. World War II had also been his formative experience. Those simple and glorious years were a time when he had tested his manhood and the values of the Anglo-Saxon culture of the Northeastern United States in which he had grown up. The PT boats were the roughest riding vessels in the U.S. Navy and Kennedy had volunteered for them despite a chronically bad back that lesser men would have used to avoid the war altogether. He was the first of the junior officers of World War II to rise to commander in chief. He brought to the presidency the attitudes toward life and the world molded by that war and he tended to hold in special regard those who had shown their mettle in the same test. He invited Krulak to the White House. They enjoyed a ceremonial drink of the Three Feathers while they reminisced. Kennedy then screwed the cap back on the bottle and put the whiskey away as a keepsake.

In February 1962, when a general had been needed for a Kennedy innovation, a counterguerrilla warfare specialist on the staff of the Joint

Chiefs, the president instructed his brother Robert, his attorney general and also his overseer of the government, to see that the post went to Krulak. Most generals would have been disappointed at the assignment, because guerrilla warfare is out of the mainstream and unlikely to further their careers over the long run. Krulak was not unhappy. He understood how much the president feared a wave of Communist-led "wars of national liberation," and he knew that he had been chosen for the job because he was the president's favorite Marine general. Performing well at a task of particular interest to the president could lead to other things.

During the year since Krulak had been appointed special assistant for counterinsurgency he had also become the favorite Marine general of Robert Kennedy. Bobby Kennedy and Brute Krulak hit it off easily because the two men admired in each other qualities that they esteemed in themselves. Krulak was struck by what a "quick study" Bobby Kennedy was, and he liked the iron the president's brother could display when a situation called for it.

As the four-engine jet transport carrying Krulak and the other members of the Joint Chiefs' mission set down at Tan Son Nhut on the morning of January 18, 1963, Krulak was conscious that the president and his brother would expect him to assure them if they were still on the right course, or, if they had gone wrong, to warn them of what they ought to do differently in order to win. McNamara, who had also come to value Krulak, had not hidden his concern. He was troubled over the press reports of how the Saigon forces had behaved at Bac, and the downing of five helicopters in one battle had shaken him. Before the team left the Pentagon, he told Krulak that the administration had to have a fresh appraisal of the war. Krulak had noted to himself that if McNamara was worried, he could be certain that the president and Bobby Kennedy were worried too.

The four-star Army general who was the team leader followed the custom of the era and let Harkins and his staff arrange the itinerary in South Vietnam. Harkins knew the team's purpose from the cables that preceded it. Most of the fighting was taking place south of Saigon. Harkins had the team spend most of its time in the capital or north of Saigon in the mountains of the Central Highlands and in the coastal provinces of Central Vietnam. He believed that he was making progress more rapidly there because, except in some sections of the Highlands, he was encountering less resistance. Harkins was encountering less resistance in Central Vietnam because the Viet Cong already held clandestine control of so much of the peasantry there that they did not feel the same need to contest the population. They preferred to concentrate their effort in Vann's area, where the issue was still in doubt.

One day out of the eight the team spent in the country was allotted to the Delta. That day did not include a visit to My Tho or anywhere else in the 7th Division zone to question Vann and his advisors about the events that had provoked the Joint Chiefs, with encouragement from the White House, to send this august group to Vietnam. The Delta portion consisted instead of briefings at Cao's IV Corps headquarters at Can Tho and then a visit to Fred Ladd's 21st Division area in the southern half of the Delta, which had largely been lost to the Communists. There is no indication in the records that any member of the mission, including Krulak, felt that this was perhaps not the best way to conduct an investigation. (Nor could anyone afterward remember feeling uneasy.) It was not lack of time that kept the group from visiting My Tho or that limited them to one day in the Delta. Their stay in Vietnam was doubled from an originally projected four days because the prominent Army general heading the team came down with the flu. He was still too ill to go to Can Tho on the appointed day. His senior aide, a highly regarded colonel who had spent a year in Vietnam as an advisor at the Saigon command level from 1958 to 1959 and who was one day to attain three-star rank himself, went as the team chief's representative. Krulak and the lieutenant general who was then chief of operations for the Army also flew down for briefings by Porter and Cao.

Asked about his briefing many years later, Porter could not recollect details. He was certain he would not have hidden anything from these generals. His commentary and recommendation to Harkins had already put him into more professional disfavor than he had ever previously dared to incur in his career. There would have been no reason for him to be coy. Two days before the team's arrival in Vietnam he had forwarded to Saigon Vann's report and his summing up of all that was wrong with Diem's armed forces. He would have assumed at the time of his briefing that Harkins would not conceal the report from a mission like this. He was sure he must have spoken frankly, believing that these generals were familiar with his views and would question him on anything they wished to explore further. He was able to recall that no one interrogated him to any degree. The issues were so emotional that if anyone of this rank had questioned him closely, he would have remembered it.

Bob York also happened to be at Can Tho then. To the best of his memory, no one on the mission asked him on that day or on any other the main question the Joint Chiefs had posed: "Are we winning or are we losing?" York had previously briefed the team on the experimental work with weapons and tactics that he was supervising for the Pentagon. He had described the role of the Hueys at Bac because they were in his domain. Otherwise he had not elaborated on the battle. York had the strength and weakness of Porter. He was an individualist with an inquiring mind, and his character was beyond reproach. He was also a man molded by his institution who put faith in its mores. He was not the sort to violate the chain of command by starting to preach out of turn to these senior officers. He had provided Harkins, who was responsible as the commanding general, with his confidential analysis of the battle and his warning of what it portended. The choice of whether to share this analysis with the members of the team belonged to Harkins. For York to have made copies and distributed them on his own would have been going behind Harkins's back. York did not behave that way. He would have been free to give his opinions had any of the visitors asked for them. None did. He recalled that the conversation at the luncheon after the briefings by Porter and Cao was nonchalant. These generals from the Pentagon were not anxious about anything.

After lunch Fred Ladd took Krulak, the team leader's aide, and the general who was the Army's deputy chief of staff for operations into the southern Delta to view an operation by his 21st Division and to visit an SDC outpost on the coast of the South China Sea. Ladd's diary entries indicate the trip was what is called a "look-see" in the military. He took a photograph of the outpost and pasted it into the diary. Ladd could not remember being questioned at any length about the state of the war.

Porter was correct in assuming that Harkins would not conceal from the mission Vann's after-action report and his catalogue of the flaws in the Saigon forces. Harkins made both available to the members of the team. The team leader's aide, a considerably more perceptive officer than the starred man for whom he worked, read them carefully and showed them to his general. He also called Vann up to Saigon and had Vann brief him on the battle and on Vann's assessment of the war. He remembered that Vann's estimate was the antithesis of what they were hearing from Harkins. Krulak did not talk to Vann, but he recalled reading the after-action report and Porter's indictment. In addition, the colonel probably filled him in on what Vann said in the private briefing because it had already been decided that the colonel and Krulak would draft the mission's written report to the Joint Chiefs.

These generals were therefore confronted with the truth in Vietnam, despite wasting most of their time on Harkins's tourist excursions. They received more than the fallible opinions of Vann and Porter. They were given, in the appendices to the main report, eyewitness accounts by sixteen of the advisors who witnessed the shambles. Their minds rejected what their eyes read. Krulak, for example, had only a vague memory of the report. He recalled deciding that Vann and his field advisors and Porter were being unduly harsh in their appraisal of the performance of the Saigon army because they were comparing it to the standards of their U.S. Army model. One could not expect such standards of Diem's forces, he remembered thinking, and the important thing was that the Saigon troops were out in the field.

To conclude that any army could behave as badly as Diem's forces had in the Battle of Ap Bac and win a war against a competent and dedicated opponent was manifestly absurd. Yet this was precisely what the Joint Chiefs' mission, urged on by Harkins and Krulak, concluded.

At a top-secret "debrief" (military jargon for an oral report) convened shortly after the group landed in Hawaii for the admirals and generals at the headquarters there of Commander in Chief Pacific, the Army general heading the team was enthusiastic about the course of the war in Vietnam. Admiral Felt was away, but his chief of staff attended for him, and a transcript was made from a tape recording for the benefit of other senior officers who might be absent. "There is no question," the team leader said in summarizing the mission's findings, "that in the military field in the past year we have established what I would call the human and matériel infrastructure which can be the basis for a successful military operation." He attributed this encouraging state of affairs to inspired generalship by Harkins. "If it were not for General Harkins things would not be in the state we found them by any manner of means," he said. "It would be pretty deplorable. His own attitude and leadership have permeated the whole command. . . ."

The head of the team was also impressed with the man Lansdale had installed in Saigon. "Mr. Diem struck me as being both an energetic and knowledgeable man, and most articulate." If anything, the general went on to explain, Diem was too articulate. Harkins had taken him to a two-and-a-half-hour meeting with Diem, and the four-star visitor from the Pentagon had found it difficult to say much himself. "The great problem with the president is getting an opportunity to say something to him, because he is a pretty fast man with the words." Nevertheless, the team chief concluded that Diem "certainly knows his country and I think knows his people. He is a leader in the same sense that we think of political leadership to a high degree of success." Diem's government was "immature" and "fumbling in carrying out significant programs," but the general suspected that these shortcomings were due primarily to the social and intellectual backwardness of "the Asiatic or the Vietnamese character," rather than to any lack of capability by Diem.

One device the regime was using for population control fascinated this Army general because he had been told it had the side benefit of gaining the goodwill of the peasantry. It was the requirement that everyone in a strategic hamlet carry an ID card with the person's photograph and thumbprint on the card. Having to obtain and carry an ID card "certainly would not be appealing . . . to the American population," the general said, but Vietnamese peasants were different. "The people think that this is the finest thing since canned beer because it indicates to them that the government loves them, has an interest in them. . . . They don't regard this as harassment or as a means of keeping tabs on them, which, of course, it is; but here you are."

Krulak kept any doubts from entering the discussion after a general at CINCPAC headquarters asked when Harkins was going to start his Operation Explosion offensive to reduce the Viet Cong to remnant bands. The team leader said that Harkins had been "pretty cagey on this one," that when he had asked about it Harkins had replied: "I'm not going to tell anybody when I start this campaign." (Harkins had reason to be cagey. He had apparently not informed the team chief that Diem was stalling him. He and his staff had drawn up a plan and had had it translated into Vietnamese, but he was unable to persuade Diem to have the Joint General Staff issue the plan as their own. Although Diem thought he had Harkins well tamed, his painfully suspicious nature still led him to worry that Harkins might be trying to entice him into big engagements with the Viet Cong. Ap Bac exacerbated his fear. Despite continued pleas from Harkins, the paper offensive was not to begin on paper until July 1, 1963.) "It might be useful to approach it [Harkins's offensive] from the viewpoint that it's already begun—and it has," Krulak said. "They are doing so very much more than they were a year ago that I think you might lay the 'Explosion' ghost [to rest] by saying that there is no beginning. It is a natural outgrowth of what has been going on for a year." The team leader underscored Krulak's logic. "I had them [Harkins and his staff] give me a rundown the other day of operations going on in Vietnam the length and breadth of the country . . . and Harkins told me an average of four hundred and fifty a month. . . . Now this is a step in the right direction, you see. It's an offensive operation."

"Even if they don't find them it's good," said the CINCPAC general.

(In an ironic footnote to this parody of high strategy, the meeting was being held in a headquarters named Camp H. M. Smith in memory of Krulak's World War II patron and idol. The place had once been the Pearl Harbor naval hospital. The Navy had abandoned the hospital back in the 1950s and wanted to sell it to a developer who would tear it down and build a tourist hotel. Krulak had persuaded his superiors to rehabilitate the place for headquarters use and dedicate the installation to Holland Smith.)

After the session at Camp Smith the group moved over to several VIP cottages at Fort de Russy, a small military enclave that existed at the time on Waikiki Beach in Honolulu, to give Krulak and the team leader's aide tranquillity in which to write the report. The aide's contribution naturally reflected the views of his general. The other members of the team approved the draft before the final typing.

The report of the Joint Chiefs' mission provided an unequivocating response to the question of whether the United States and its Saigon surrogate were winning or losing. "The situation in South Vietnam has been reoriented, in the space of a year and a half, from a circumstance of near desperation to a condition where victory is now a hopeful prospect." There was no need for any drastic alternatives. "We are winning slowly on the present thrust, and . . . there is no compelling reason to change." The specifics of the report were as cheerful as its broad statements. Where Harkins's Explosion offensive was concerned, Krulak managed to get in his opinion that it had "already begun" and "offers reasonable prospects for improving greatly the military situation." The separate three-years-to-victory plan that Harkins's staff had composed at McNamara's request was also "a generally sound basis for planning the phase-out of United States support" by the end of 1965. The newspaper reports the president and Robert Kennedy and McNamara had been reading of advisors' complaints that the Saigon officers ignored their advice were at best exaggerations and at worst false. "United States advice will be increasingly followed as Government of Vietnam confidence in themselves and their advisors continues to grow."

Ap Bac was mentioned only once in the twenty-nine pages of the report. This was to warn that the resident newsmen in Vietnam had become unwitting saboteurs of a fruitful policy:

The unfortunate aftermath of reports of the fight at Ap Bac on 2 January 1963 is a prime instance of the harm being done to the war effort [by the resident correspondents]. Press members . . . insist that the stories were derived from United States sources. The latter is true, but only to the extent that the stories were based on ill-considered statements made at a time of high excitement and frustration by a few American officers.

"The principal ingredients for eventual success have been assembled in South Vietnam," the report concluded. "Now, perseverance in the field, and at home, will be required in great measure to achieve that success."

A few of the men who counted in Washington—W. Averell Harriman, then assistant secretary of state for Far Eastern affairs, was one—were skeptical of this reassurance. President Kennedy and his counselor-brother believed it, and so did McNamara, and Dean Rusk at the top of the State Department, and most of the rest of the civilian and military hierarchy. John Kennedy had confidence in the system that had given him a world to guide. Brute Krulak had also been on that mission, and Kennedy had seen Krulak lead in war and knew he was a man to be trusted.

Another Marine general who had watched Krulak rise reflected long afterward that ambition might explain his behavior. He had a reputation for the flair at self-promotion he exhibited in sending John Kennedy the note and the bottle of Three Feathers. He wanted, of course, to consummate his career by adding the name Krulak to the roll of commandants of the Corps. The current commandant, Gen. David Shoup, who had won his Congressional Medal of Honor at Tarawa, was due to retire at the end of 1963. There was a chance that the president, out of esteem for Krulak, might pass over more senior candidates and name Krulak as the new commandant. The addition of Robert Kennedy to Krulak's admirers had raised his prospects. If he could not attain his goal on this occasion because he was still too junior within the Marine hierarchy, the favor of the Kennedy brothers could give it to him on the next one. John Kennedy's defeat of Richard Nixon had been extremely close in 1960, but by January 1963 he was a popular president. The common assumption was that he would easily win a second term. In 1967, it would again be time to select a commandant of the Corps, and by then Krulak would have seniority to his credit as well. Krulak's colleague therefore thought he had probably not wanted to risk his career at this moment by challenging the established optimism and bringing down on himself the wrath of Maxwell Taylor, the fashionable military savant whom the Kennedy brothers and McNamara considered the ultimate source of wisdom on war, and that of Harkins, Taylor's protégé. (Robert Kennedy named one of his sons Matthew Maxwell Taylor Kennedy.)

"Brute Krulak is too smart not to have seen what was happening in South Vietnam," his colleague said. "He could think circles around those Army and Air Force generals." Ambition may have influenced Krulak's behavior, perhaps unconsciously, but ambition alone was not an adequate explanation. For all of his ambition and gift for self-promotion, Krulak was not a cynical man and he did not lack moral courage. He was later to take a stand on the war that was to seriously jeopardize his chance of fulfilling his ambition.

The mission of inquiry the Joint Chiefs sent to South Vietnam in January 1963 demonstrated that the military institutions of the United States were so overcome by their malady of victory that they could not respond to events and adjust themselves to reality even when reality took them by the shoulders and shook them. That a thinker and fighter of Krulak's stature had also been so affected by the arrogance that he could not free himself when he knew that the president, the president's brother, and the secretary of defense wanted him to find the truth and bring it back to them told, as only personal example can, the true dimension of the change in the once superbly led armed services of the United States. When John Kennedy had had Krulak appointed special assistant for counterinsurgency, Krulak had said to himself that he would learn this new kind of war by applying logic and imagination as he had in the past. He had instead taken the word of another big man, Paul Harkins, during his earlier trips to Vietnam and had allowed Taylor's faith in Harkins to reinforce illusion. Despite the warning flares of Ap Bac, he clung to his preconceptions and helped to implant them in the other members of the Joint Chiefs' mission. This was not difficult to do. They were inclined to listen to him anyway because of who he was and who he knew.

President Kennedy would have been better served if he had remembered from his days as a junior officer in the Navy that the closer one gets to a fight, the more one learns of its essence. He could then have spared the public purse the expense of carrying this distinguished mission 20,000 miles round trip in a four-engine jet transport and simply sent for one of the helicopter men who had flown into the guns of the Viet Cong regulars at Bac. Any pilot or crewman would have done. His one qualification would have been an ability to sing, on or off key. After the battle a pilot or crewman—later no one could recall the author's name—had composed a ballad about the fight. It was being sung in the evenings over gin and whiskey and vodka and cold beer in the clubs at Soc Trang, and at the Seminary, and at Tan Son Nhut. Ziegler first heard a sergeant singing it and made the man repeat it slowly while he wrote down the words for his diary. The verses were flawed by a number of factual inaccuracies. Ballads of battles composed by the men who fight them often do suffer from factual inaccuracies because of the confusion of war, but the inaccuracies do not detract from truth. The ballad—called "Ap Bac" and sung to the tune of "On Top of Old Smokey"—would have told the president what he needed to know:

> We were called into Tan Hiep
> On January 2,
> We would never have gone there
> If we'd only knew.
> We were supporting the ARVNs,
> A group without guts,
> Attacking a village
> Of straw-covered huts.
> A ten-copter mission,
> A hundred-troop load,
> Three lifts were now over
> A fourth on the road.
> The VC's start shooting,
> They fire a big blast,
> We off-load the ARVNs
> They sit on their ass.
> One copter is crippled,
> Another sits down,
> Attempting a rescue,
> Now there are two on the ground.
> A Huey returns now
> To give them some aid,
> The VCs are so accurate
> They shoot off a blade.
> Four pilots are wounded,
> Two crewmen are dead,
> When it's all over
> A good day for the Red.
> They lay in the paddy
> All covered with slime,
> A hell of a sunbath
> Eight hours at a time.
> An armored battalion
> Just stayed in a trance,

One captain died trying
To make them advance.
The paratroops landed,
A magnificent sight,
There was hand-to-hand combat,
But no VCs in sight.
When the news was reported
The ARVNs had won,
The VCs are laughing
Over their captured guns.
All pilots take warning,
When tree lines are near,
Let's land those damn copters
One mile to the rear.

One of the vestiges of the Geneva Agreements of 1954 was a tripartite organization called the International Commission for Supervision and Control. The commission had been created to monitor observance of the accords by all parties and had therefore been balanced by delegations from Communist Poland, anti-Communist Canada, and then neutral India, which held the chairmanship permanently and was supposed to referee. By 1963, the ICSC had long ceased to serve any purpose, but the delegations still maintained offices and living quarters in Hanoi and Saigon, commuted back and forth on a special plane, and, because of their diplomatic status, circulated with relative freedom in both capitals. The delegates were thus thought to be informed about opinion on both sides of the war.

The senior Polish delegate in 1963 was an inquiring man, a Jewish intellectual named Miecyslaw Maneli, who taught international law at the University of Warsaw when he was not on diplomatic assignment. He had helped the Vietnamese as a member of an ICSC inspection team in 1954, and they liked him. At a reception in Hanoi one evening he was taken aside by another man of inquiring mind with rough, homely features, the sort one would expect in a rice-paddy Vietnamese and not in the son of the chief secretary to the last of the Nguyen emperors to be deposed and exiled by the French—Pham Van Dong, Ho Chi Minh's prime minister. There was no need for an interpreter; both men spoke French.

"Tell me something," the prime minister said. "The American generals are always boasting of how they are winning the war in the South. Do they believe it?"

"Yes," Maneli replied. "As far as I can discover they do."

"You're joking," Pham Van Dong continued, his eyes studying Maneli. "Perhaps they boast for propaganda, but the CIA must tell them the truth in its secret reports."

"I don't know what the CIA tells them," Maneli said. "All I can find out is that they seem to believe what they say."

"Well, I find it hard to believe what you say," the prime minister said. "Surely the American generals cannot be that naive."

When the Vietnamese Communist leaders proceeded to exploit Ap Bac as a catalyst to transform the revolution in the South, they were to discover that Ambassador Maneli was correct. They were to discover more. They were to learn that their American opponents were supplying them with the wherewithal to fundamentally alter the balance of military force in South Vietnam, that virtually everything the United States and its Saigon ally were doing would facilitate their task.

By January 1963, the United States had potentially furnished the Vietnamese Communists with enough weapons to create an army in the South capable of challenging and defeating the ARVN. The Americans had distributed more than 130,000 firearms—carbines, rifles, shotguns, submachine guns, BARs, machine guns, mortars, and recoilless cannon, along with copious quantities of ammunition and grenades and thousands of radios—to Saigon's Civil Guard and Self-Defense Corps militia and to a menagerie of irregular units financed and equipped by the CIA. As the training and equipping programs for the Civil Guard, the SDC, and these irregular units were carried forward, the number of weapons potentially stocked for the Communists in the countryside was to nearly double by mid-1963, to approximately 250,000. The ARVN was another possible source of captured arms, of course, but its weapons were not conveniently arrayed in the outposts that Diem refused to dismantle and in vulnerable hamlets.

With a modest portion of this quarter of a million American arms, Ho Chi Minh and his confederates could double or triple their main striking forces in the South, the regular and provincial guerrillas, estimated in January 1963 at about 23,000 men. With a more generous share of this weapons bonanza, the Vietnamese Communists could formidably enhance the Guerrilla Popular Army, the roughly 100,000 village and hamlet guerrillas who were the local enforcers and intelligence gatherers for the clandestine Viet Cong government and the reserve manpower pool for the regular and provincial units. The local guerrillas would have no further need for the homemade shotguns of galvanized pipe that were as much a threat to the user as to the target. For the first time in the war, every local guerrilla could be armed with a modern weapon. The end result could be an immense expansion of Communist control in the countryside and the turning of the Main Force and Regional guerrillas, now organized into units no larger than companies and battalions, into regiments and divisions.

The basic infantry weapons for this second Viet Minh army were not all that was in place or was unwittingly being prepared. The soldiers to fill its ranks and the political climate within the rural population to sustain it with vigor were also being created by the constant bombing and shelling and by a still more enraging act: the forced relocation of millions of peasants into the new strategic hamlets. A peasantry already alienated by the exactions and indignities inflicted on it by the regime was being roused into a fury by an abuse beyond any it had previously experienced from this foreign-rooted government.

Cao had shown the common sense to oppose the Strategic Hamlet Program. The religion of the majority of the Delta peasants was a meld of Buddhism, ancestor worship, and animism—devotion to the spirits that were thought to dwell in the streams, rocks, and trees around their hamlets. Cao pointed this out to Vann and explained that many of the Delta farmers had comfortable homes by their standards. His government would profoundly anger the peasants, he said, if it systematically destroyed their houses and made them leave their fields and the graves of the ancestors they worshiped. He was bold enough to tell Robert (subsequently Sir Robert) Thompson, the British pacification specialist who had played a major role in suppressing the Chinese insurgency in Malaya and had come to Saigon to be the brain truster of pacification in this war, that the scheme would not work in South Vietnam. (Cao then, in character, became one of the most enthusiastic herders into the barbed wire after Diem and Nhu informed him that the program was the centerpiece of their strategy and they expected him to support it.) The forced relocations were particularly massive in the Delta, not simply to move peasants out of guerrilla-dominated regions, but also to reduce many hamlets to a physical area small enough to be encircled with barbed wire and fortified. The larger Delta hamlets sprawled out along the canals and streams, often on both banks, for the best part of a mile or more. This meant that roughly half of the houses—starting at both ends and squeezing in toward the middle—had to be demolished in order to shrink the area to the desired size.

Two groups of peasants were infuriated. The first consisted of the farm folk who had seen their houses torn down or burned and been forced to build new ones, inferior to their former homes, with their own labor and at their own expense. Those relocated to entirely new hamlets to take them out of areas controlled or contested by the Viet Cong were often subjected to the further indignity of having their homes blown up and burned down by bombs and napalm. Although the technique was an expensive way to destroy thatched housing, Anthis liked it because it kept up the sortie rate of his fighter-bombers and added more "structures" to the statistics reported to Washington. The corruption endemic to the regime worsened the relocation ordeal. The local officials customarily "sold" the peasants the galvanized sheet-metal roofing and other building materials provided free by the United States. Vann sent a report to Harkins on the entrepreneurship one province chief was exhibiting with the most common item provided gratis by the U.S. government—the barbed wire. "He was putting a price on it and then charging each peasant for the amount of barbed wire that was strung in front of his quarters," Vann said, using the military term, "quarters," for the new homes of the peasant families. (The practice turned out to be common.) The second group of angry peasants were those who were permitted to keep their original homes, but now lived in crowded conditions they found distasteful, with neighbors squatting in houses built on *their* land. Both groups shared a common anger at the long days of compulsory labor they had to put in digging a moat around the place, erecting the barbed-wire fence, raising a firing parapet for the militia, and cutting and planting sharpened bamboo stakes—the "pungee stakes" the Viet Minh had taught them to set out for the French and which the Viet Cong had had them conceal in foot traps to impede the Saigon troops. The more prosperous peasants paid bribes to evade the work. This placed a larger burden on the poor farmers. The prosperous ones still resented having to pay the bribes. What little the peasants received in the way of free medicine, Yorkshire hogs, and other amenities in exchange for this misery was hardly likely to persuade them to forgive their tormentors.

In the competition to kowtow to the palace, the province chiefs were erecting strategic hamlets willy-nilly everywhere. The regime had no priority as to which section of the country should be pacified first. The CIA and AID, which were financing the program, and Robert Thompson had wanted to pacify areas of strategic and economic value and then proceed to less important ones in the "spreading oil spot" (*tache d'huile*) method of pacification originated by the French. Diem and Nhu had decided to proceed simultaneously all over the South. Harkins's staff believed that about half of the thousands of strategic hamlets reported constructed by January 1963 had gone beyond the rudiments of fortification to become functioning communities.

The rub was for whose benefit the strategic hamlets were functioning. The Americans and Diem and Nhu were not gaining the communities of controlled peasants they sought. They were instead fostering temporary encampments of peasants motivated as never before to support the Viet Cong. By day the hamlet might appear to be controlled by the regime. The outward calm reinforced in Americans their false conviction that the Vietnamese peasants were essentially passive, seeking security above all else. The appearance of control existed because the Vietnamese had learned to be devious in combating the French and because officials on the Saigon side from hamlet chief to province chief lied to those above them on what they controlled in order to keep their jobs. The CIA and AID officials involved also fooled themselves with devices of constraint like the plastic-covered identity cards they encouraged the regime to issue to everyone. What actual control existed during the day was tenuous. The farmers, their wives, and the older children had to be released in the morning to go back and cultivate their fields, a walk of a mile to half a dozen miles from the strategic hamlet. They were out of sight and hearing until they returned at sunset. As soon as darkness came, the garrison of Self-Defense Corps militiamen retreated with the hamlet chief into their mud-walled fort at one corner of the place. The Viet Cong cadres would then often emerge to take charge. The new "volunteer" hamlet militia would also have taken shelter in the outpost for the night, or they might turn out secretly to be local guerrillas who were pleased with the five-shot pump shotguns and carbines and grenades the CIA had presented to them.

Ap Bac came at the most propitious moment and was a drama ready-made for the purposes of Ho Chi Minh and his disciples. It was exactly the sort of event they needed to infuse the building of a Viet Cong army with the patriotic emotion they had aroused and poured into the creation of the original Viet Minh. In March, with their assessment completed and their preparations made, they seized on the battle and turned Ap Bac into the rallying cry of the revolution in the South. Posters, professionally printed in color, began to appear in the Delta extolling the victory and the fighters who had attained it. The Hanoi Politburo had the Central Committee of the National Liberation Front announce the first three-month round of "the Ap Bac Emulation Drive" that was to continue for the next two years. Everything started to move ahead full speed. Harkins's intelligence section thought that infiltration from the North during the 1962–63 southwest monsoon dry season was running at approximately the same level as the 1961–62 season, about 6,000 infiltrators on an annual basis. (The southwest monsoon dry season extends for seven months from October, right after the rains end and the trails through southern Laos and the Highlands become passable once more, until the monsoon returns in late April or early May.) Subsequent evidence showed that in an act of faith rewarded by Ap Bac, Hanoi had doubled the flow from an average of 850 men coming down the trails each month during the 1961–62 season to about 1,700 a month during the current season. The infiltrators were more former southern Viet Minh who had gone to the North in 1954, more "autumn cadres" to join the "winter cadres" who had survived Diem's terror and launched the rebellion in 1957. Almost all of the infiltrators were military personnel who had been serving since 1954 in the Vietnam People's Army, the regular army of the North. They would provide additional officers and noncoms for the second Viet Minh army; specialists in communications, intelligence, heavy weapons and other fields; and training groups like the one Cao had permitted to escape. A minority were civilians who had been in the Northern administration and who would now assist in expanding the secret Viet Cong government or practice specialties for which they had been trained like propaganda, mass organization, counterintelligence, and terrorism. The distinguishing characteristic of the infiltrators was that all of them were skilled. They and the veteran cadres awaiting them in the South were akin to the steel beams that form the framework of a modern building. The southern peasants being recruited as fast as possible were the concrete to raise the walls. Every cadre would be needed. In Kien Hoa Province, for example, just south of My Tho across the upper branch of the Mekong (Ben Tre was its capital), 2,500 young farmers volunteered in the spring of 1963. Diem's province chief there was a favorite of the CIA officials involved in the Strategic Hamlet Program, because he had fought the French with the Viet Minh for almost four years before deserting, could talk the language of guerrilla warfare, and took pacification seriously. The Viet Cong cadres recruited most of the 2,500 volunteers they needed from Kien Hoa right out of his strategic hamlets.

Skilled manpower was not all that was secretly entering the South at a quickened pace. Hanoi also decided after Ap Bac to begin smuggling in earnest the heavy weapons for a Viet Cong army. Prior to 1963, Ho and his colleagues had kept the smuggling of all weapons to a minimum because experience had taught them that to become viable a guerrilla movement must learn to sustain itself with captured arms. What was happening to the American arms illustrated a social truism that tends to confound an imperial power intervening in the affairs of a smaller nation: resources put into a society at odds with itself do not necessarily benefit the intended recipient, but rather end up aiding the faction best organized to profit by them. Crew-served heavy weapons could not be captured in the quantities needed, however, and so Hanoi had always intended to supply these. The second Viet Minh would need 12.7mm antiaircraft machine guns, the Soviet-designed equivalent of John Browning's .50 caliber, to further intimidate the helicopter pilots and to force the fighter-bombers to fly higher and become less effective than they already were; 81mm mortars to unnerve its Saigon opponents, who were not accustomed to being shelled (the 81mm and an 82mm Soviet variant hurl seven and a half pounds of shrapnel and high explosive more than two miles); and 57mm and 75mm recoilless cannon to break open outpost bunkers and turn tanks and armored personnel carriers into hulks.

There was a standing joke among American staff officers in Saigon about the Viet Cong porter who spends two and a half months toting three mortar shells down the mountain and rain-forest tracks of the Ho Chi Minh Trail. He finally reaches a battle and hands them to a mortarman, who fires them off faster than the porter can count and says: "Now go back and get three more." The joke was on those who told it. The trails through Laos were useful for marching men into the South; they were an inefficient way to smuggle heavy weapons and the ammunition for them. The efficient way was by sea in ocean-going fishing trawlers—one can handily transport 100 tons of arms and assorted munitions in a 120-foot steel-hulled trawler—that sailed to night rendezvous with guerrillas at any of the hundreds of small bays, lagoons, and river outlets along the South's 1,500 miles of coastline. Prior to Ap Bac, the trawlers had made a few voyages to the South. After the battle, they started sailing a regular schedule.

The voyage was often difficult and required superlative seamanship, because the coast of the Delta, where many of the landings were made, lies flat against the horizon with no identifiable promontories. There was the further handicap that the landings were made on moonless nights to reduce the risk of detection. Smuggling has always been a sophisticated profession in Asia, and the Vietnamese Communists had had a lot of practice at arms smuggling during the nine years of war against France. The trawlers loaded at one of the southern Chinese ports if China was supplying the arms and ammunition. (Chinese arsenals were retooled after 1949 to manufacture copies of Soviet weapons like the 12.7mm machine gun, and China had large quantities of American arms captured from the Nationalists and in Korea.) The skipper would sail down past Hainan Island and then tack toward the Vietnamese coast, staying out to sea yet close enough to gain anonymity among the thousands of fishing craft and coastal freight junks. The steel-hulled trawlers were of local manufacture and looked the same as the trawlers of the seagoing fishermen from the South. These smugglers also had removable registration plates. As soon as they got below the 17th Parallel the crew slid in a plate with numbers matching those of a similar trawler registered with the Saigon authorities. On the day of the landing the skipper, with only a compass to steer by, would set a course timed to take the trawler to a predesignated point near the shore in the middle of the night. A sampan carrying a pilot would be waiting there. The pilot would climb on board and guide the trawler into a bay or lagoon or up one of the river mouths to a spot where teams of Viet Cong porters were standing by. The trawler would be camouflaged while it was unloaded. On the following night—or a night later if the unloading took longer—the pilot would guide the skipper back out to sea and then switch to the sampan again while the trawler sailed free, to make another trip on the next moonless night. The antiaircraft machine guns, mortars, and recoilless cannon and the ammunition for them were transported inland and hidden carefully. Hanoi gave orders that they were not to be issued until units yet to be formed had been trained to employ them properly. Their first appearance was intended to come with surprise at the commencement of the next phase of the war.

Ho and his followers were not alone in seizing on Ap Bac. The resident newsmen in South Vietnam also seized on it. We reacted as if we had been waiting for it because, beleaguered as we felt, we *had* been waiting for it. The contradiction between the press reporting of the war and the official version being propounded by Harkins and Ambassador Nolting had grown into an embittered confrontation.

The controversy was another issue of these years that had its origin in World War II. There had been little to argue about once the shooting had started in that war. The threat to national survival was beyond question, and the generals and admirals were sometimes brilliant and normally capable—or they were dismissed. Reporters became habituated to a role that was characterized more by support than skepticism. With some exceptions, the ability to stand aside and exercise independent and critical judgment of basic policy and of authority was lost as a result. In the postwar period the American press remained the most vigorous on earth, but where foreign affairs was concerned the reporting, while often gifted, was weighted toward the furthering of the anti-Communist crusade. When the press did cause trouble the argument was over detail, not substance. The news media were also being manipulated by government to an extent they did not realize.

At the outset of the 1960s, the relationship was essentially unchanged. The military institutions, and those associated with the military in the running of American overseas interests like the State Department, were continuing to receive credit for a competence and perspicacity they no longer possessed. The reporters of the period were not accustomed to thinking of their military leaders and diplomats as deluded men, and the military leaders and diplomats were not accustomed to reporters who said that they were consistently wrong. The secrecy that shielded the meetings and written communications of the men at the top helped to perpetuate the false impression that they sought and weighed facts in their discussions. The secrecy that in the 1940s had protected the nation was by the 1960s concealing the fact that the system was no longer rational.

The resident correspondents in Vietnam were also questioning detail, not substance. We thought it our duty to help win the war by reporting the truth of what was happening in order both to inform the public and to put the facts before those in power so that they could make correct decisions. (Our ignorance and our American ideology kept us from discerning the larger truths of Vietnam beneath the surface reality we could see. Professionally, we were fortunate in our ignorance. Had any reporter been sufficiently knowledgeable and open-minded to have questioned the justice and good sense of U.S. intervention in those years, he would have been fired as a "subversive.") The confrontation had occurred because of the unprecedented consistency with which we were questioning details.

Our critical faculty did not come from any genius. One of the regular complaints Harkins and Nolting made about us was that we were "immature and inexperienced." Our youth and inexperience made it possible for us to acquire what critical faculty we were displaying. Vietnam was our first war. What we saw and what we were told by the men we most respected and most closely identified with—the advisors in the field like Vann—contradicted what we were told by higher authority. We were being forced at the beginning of our professional lives to come to grips with a constant disparity between our perception of reality and higher authority's version of it, the opposite of the experience of the World War II generation of journalists.

The contrast between what we saw and what authority saw was caught succinctly in an exchange in early 1962 between Nolting and François Sully, a Frenchman who was then the correspondent for *Newsweek*. The American war was not Sully's first. He had emigrated to Indochina in 1949 and covered the French war as a stringer (a press term for a local correspondent without staff status) for *Time*. The errors of his own country gave him a sharp perspective on the errors the United States was making, and his reporting was considerably bolder than that of the other correspondents in early 1962. He enraged the ambassador with an article he did on Operation Sunrise, the first forced relocation for the Strategic Hamlet Program, accompanied by photos he took of the peasants' homes being burned. Nolting sallied into him about it at a dinner shortly afterward.

"Why, Monsieur Sully, do you always see the hole in the doughnut?" the ambassador asked sarcastically.

"Because, Monsieur l'Ambassadeur, there is a hole in the doughnut," Sully replied.

(Diem expelled Sully in September 1962, to the ambassador's public protests and private relief.)

Harkins and Nolting never ceased complaining about the rest of us, hoping that our editors would fire us and replace us with more cooperative types. They claimed that our articles were bizarre snapshots that did not reflect the wider reality of the war, as they could prove with the "big picture" they were able to assemble from the information flowing to them from a multitude of sources.

Ap Bac was a big picture that discredited the big picture Harkins and Nolting were projecting. We exploited the battle as much as we dared for this reason, and when Vann, out of his anger and a shared interest, tacitly offered an alliance afterward, we entered it eagerly. Vann did not offer the alliance without pausing and calculating. Prior to Vietnam, he had never dealt with the press on a regular basis, and all of his institutional conditioning was to use the news media in the service of his superiors, not against them as he had been doing since the battle. He did not realize that the words of his after-action report and Porter's commentary had run off the minds of the generals of the Joint Chiefs' mission as rapidly as rain off a steep roof. He did know, from his sources on the Saigon staff, what Harkins was telling Washington, and he decided he was not going to let Harkins bar his way any longer. In his urgency to alert authority and prevent the catastrophe, he made up his mind to reach over Harkins's head by influencing the reporters to speak with his voice.

There were other American advisors and Vietnamese on the Saigon side who taught us important lessons about the war. We learned much from our own observations. Vann taught us the most, and one can truly say that without him our reporting would not have been the same. Because of Vann, Ap Bac had been, for better or worse, a decisive battle. Looking back at the other dramatic events that were to follow in 1963, one can see his will at work in the impact of our dispatches. He gave us an expertise we lacked, a certitude that brought a qualitative change in what we wrote. He enabled us to attack the official optimism with gradual but steadily increasing detail and thoroughness. He transformed us into a band of reporters propounding the John Vann view of the war.

Vann was a natural teacher. He enjoyed the role. Indeed, he found it difficult not to impart something he had learned to others when he knew they were interested in his subject. He had already been providing us before Ap Bac with an education in "the essentials of guerrilla warfare," as David Halberstam was to call Vann's early lessons in his 1965 book *The Making of a Quagmire*. One of Vann's most famous maxims, often quoted down the years, came from those first lessons: "This is a political war and it calls for discrimination in killing. The best weapon for killing would be a knife, but I'm afraid we can't do it that way. The worst is an airplane. The next worst is artillery. Barring a knife, the best is a rifle—you know who you're killing."

The most prominent graduate of the Vann school on the war and the reporter with whom Vann formed his closest relationship in these early years was Halberstam of the *New York Times*. Through Halberstam, Vann was to achieve his greatest impact on events during this opening phase of the American war. What Halberstam learned from Vann was to help make him one of the famous journalists of his time. Halberstam was in turn to create Vann's public legend with a long profile in *Esquire* magazine in November 1964 and the following spring with *The Making of a Quagmire*. (The magazine article was an excerpt from the book manuscript.)

The two men were attracted to each other because they were uncommon spirits with uncommon backgrounds, but Vann's singling out of Halberstam for special attention was also no more of an accident than his original decision to use the reporters to go over Harkins's head. Halberstam's dispatches were his surest means of reaching President Kennedy and everyone else in Washington. There were reporters and then there was the correspondent of the *Times*. Like *The Times* of London when a quarter of the globe had been tinted red with the scarlet tunics of a British monarch's soldiery, the *New York Times* was the most prestigious newspaper in the world in this bright era of the American empire. President Kennedy read Halberstam's dispatches with as much care as he did cables from Nolting and Harkins. He did not expect to find more truth in Halberstam's reports. He had faith in his ambassador and his general. Although the popular belief was that "sooner or later everything comes out in the *New York Times*," anyone living within the secret world of the upper reaches of the American state in 1963 could not help but be aware of how much he and those around him regularly kept hidden from the *Times*. This did not lessen Kennedy's concern with what the *Times* published. The reporters and editors of the paper tried to keep the *Times* honest. They did not knowingly allow themselves to be manipulated. Most of the paper's readers believed that what the *Times* printed was the truth or a reasonable approximation of the truth. Halberstam's reporting influenced domestic and international opinion, and no American government could afford to ignore it.

The friendship between Halberstam and Vann grew quickly. Both were outsiders trying to become somebody in a society dominated by the WASP culture of the Northeast. Vann was conscious of his white-trashy origins in Norfolk. Halberstam had been born in New York City the son of a doctor, but in the Bronx, not in Manhattan where the families of prosperous Jewish doctors lived, and he had grown up in the Bronx, in Yonkers, and in towns in Connecticut where his mother had worked as a schoolteacher to support him and his brother after his father had died prematurely of a heart attack when Halberstam was sixteen. He had an enduring sense of Jewish apartness. He was unable to forget that he was two generations from the ghettos of Poland and Lithuania. His insecurity showed, as Vann's did, in his compulsion to be recognized and in his need to test himself.

At twenty-eight, David Halberstam was on his second overseas assignment for the *Times*. He had volunteered to go to Vietnam in September 1962 after fourteen months in the Belgian Congo. (The Belgian Congo took the name Republic of the Congo after independence and was renamed Zaire in 1971.) That country had fragmented into chaos and civil conflict after Belgium had granted it independence in mid-1960. Halberstam had made an auspicious beginning of a career in the way he handled the dangerous and physically taxing job of making what sense was possible out of the melee. He had won an Overseas Press Club Award, and the *Times* had nominated him for the Pulitzer Prize for international reporting. (He lost out to the late Walter Lippmann, the doyen of columnists. Lippmann flattered him after his return by inviting him to lunch to question him about Africa.) Halberstam saw in Vietnam an even more significant story with which he could turn this fortunate beginning into a reputation as a leading foreign correspondent.

Halberstam was a physical contrast to Vann. He stood six feet two inches and weighed about 180 pounds, none of it fat. His fellow reporters were in awe of his appetite and stamina. He would put away a lunch of soup, two filet mignons, french fries, salad, and pie à la mode, and then burn off every calorie in un-Kiplingesque activity through the heat of the tropical afternoon. His long arms, big hands, and broad shoulders, which he tended to hunch forward a bit as he walked, and a coiled-spring quality to his gait gave one the impression of a boxer or a football player. The impression was strengthened by his features. He had a square jaw and a ridge of a nose. Both were accentuated by a five-o'clock shadow and black hair close-cropped in imitation of the military crewcut. He wore glasses with thick lenses. The frames were heavy and unfashionable plastic ones of contrasting black and neutral tint. The glasses tended to hide his dark brown eyes, which were the softest element in his features and which laughed first when he was amused.

He used this aggressive-looking body to communicate his mental combativeness. His hands and arms and shoulders were always in motion when he talked. To emphasize his points he would stab out with a finger. If he suddenly discovered something he had missed or if he felt satisfaction at the phrasing of his words, he would ball his right fist and slap it into the palm of his left hand with a quick laugh. When he was explaining a complicated matter he had a way of arching his hands with his fingers together in the shape of bent wings and flashing them back and forth through the air, like a plane weaving and diving in a dogfight. All the while his hunched shoulders would roll with his arms and hands. One had the feeling that he was mentally boxing with a situation as he talked, convincing himself of what he thought was true at the same time that he battled off ideas he saw as false.

This mental combativeness was the manifestation of other qualities that were to make Halberstam an ideal reporter for Vann's endeavor. They were also qualities that were to make Halberstam one of those rare journalists who put a personal imprint on the opinions of their time, instead of simply reporting information of interest that disappears into the newspaper archives of libraries. He was a man who saw the world in light and dark colors with little shading in between. A capacity for outrage at injustice and wrongdoing was one of his guiding motivations. The capacity had been enlarged by five years spent on Southern newspapers, witnessing and writing about the early civil rights movement, after his graduation from Harvard in 1955. Articles on the struggle that he had written in his spare time for the *Reporter*, a magazine that preached the synthesis of domestic liberalism and foreign intervention and anti-Communism that was fashionable to the era, had gained him an invitation to join the *Times* from James "Scotty" Reston, the columnist who was then also chief of the newspaper's Washington bureau.

A certain ruthlessness in Halberstam's character also shaped his reporting. At Harvard he had been inadvertently pitted in competition against a friend for the managing editorship of the *Crimson*, the college's daily newspaper. The competition had become so savage that Halberstam had sickened of it emotionally by the time he won the job. He was asked why he had continued the competition if having to humiliate his friend to win the editorship had upset him so. "I guess I'm a killer," he answered quietly after a moment's thought. His answer was unjust to himself in that it left unmentioned his support and kindness to friends and colleagues in any other circumstances, but there was truth in it nonetheless. The ruthlessness showed in a fondness for metaphors drawn from war and the gladiator's arena. A good reporter, he would say, had to have "a jugular instinct" to go for what was vital in a situation he was covering; a reporter had to hold his fire until he had built up credibility with his readers and then, when events gave him an opportunity, to overwhelm them with the truth in a series of dispatches delivered with the force of a rolling barrage of artillery shells.

Halberstam was capable of changing his conclusions with time and differing circumstances. If his outrage at injustice and wrongdoing and the certainty that he had at last learned the truth of a situation came together, his zeal to communicate that truth infused his reporting with firm moral judgments about everybody and everything involved. He left his readers with no doubt as to which was the good and which was the evil side, and his "instinct for the jugular" brought thrusts at anyone impeding his just cause.

David Halberstam's generation, the generation of the 1950s and the momentous confrontation known as the Cold War, was the last generation of Americans to go so naively into the world. It was destined to lose its innocence in the war and be forced to grapple with the consequences of disillusionment. Halberstam was to end the decade in 1972 denouncing in his popular book *The Best and the Brightest* the very men—Robert McNamara, Maxwell Taylor, Dean Rusk, McGeorge Bundy, and Walt Rostow—whose worldview he subscribed to so emotionally in these opening years of the Vietnam era when he met Vann. In 1963, Halberstam was still one with Vann—another janissary for the

American system. He and Vann and so many like them were examples of the genius of the Anglo-Saxon society of the Northeast for co-opting the talents and loyalty of outsiders with its social democracy. A society that would give an uncouth redneck a place of respect in the officer corps of its army and the grandson of immigrant Jewish peddlers a Harvard education and a job on the *New York Times* was innately good, incapable of perpetrating evil in other lands. They were full of gratitude to that society and wanted to spread its good.

As the two men saw more and more of each other in the weeks and months after Ap Bac, Halberstam was struck by Vann's remarkable career promise and by how recklessly Vann was disregarding that promise. At thirty-eight, Vann was relatively young for his rank and position as one of the nine division senior advisors, and with his flair for leading men in war he stood out as the obvious star among his peers. His attributes indicated that this was a man who would go far in the Army. As Halberstam was to write in his *Esquire* profile in the fall of 1964, "Vann was . . . clearly on his way to a colonelcy, and with a very good chance for promotion to a general['s] star . . . clearly a man about to take off in his career, one of those men who reaches his mid-thirties and then begins to pull away from many of his contemporaries." That Vann would recklessly disregard this career promise made him stand out still more sharply from his peers. It is precisely at this takeoff point in his career that an officer has the most at stake and, having also been molded by his profession, finds it impossible to be genuinely indiscreet with reporters. The majority of the lieutenant colonels heading the advisory detachments at the other eight divisions shared Vann's views to varying degrees, but they spoke with discretion. For example, Fred Ladd at the 21st Division, the colleague closest to Vann in his thinking, was frank yet exercised some reserve in communicating his worries to us. Vann, who seemed to have more to lose than any of his peers, was alone among them in being heedless of the professional consequences.

Not long after Ap Bac it became common knowledge that Vann was the principal source behind the harsher press criticism of official strategy. In order to bluff Harkins out of taking formal action against him, Vann resorted to the same loud denials he had made in claiming that he had not talked to the reporters about the battle. Otherwise Vann did not attempt to hide his game. Instead of restricting contact with Halberstam and the other resident correspondents as the level of irritation rose at Harkins's headquarters, he made himself and his subordinates available to us with more freedom than ever. He did nothing to protect himself against the informal and effective means of revenge that powerful men like Harkins can exact against lesser beings who cross them in an institution like the Army. Despite the value of what Vann was doing, Halberstam began to feel guilty over the probable career consequences for him. He urged Vann to be more circumspect. Vann told him not to worry and to keep coming down. He seemed to want a confrontation with Harkins. Halberstam could think of no explanation for Vann's recklessness other than moral heroism. The rest of us reached the same conclusion. Vann would give us an identical answer when we cautioned him. We decided he was deliberately sacrificing his career in order to alert the nation to the danger of defeat in this war.

Vann's behavior had special meaning to Halberstam, because he drew a parallel with his late father's conduct during World War II. Charles Halberstam's practice of internal medicine and surgery in the Bronx had only recently started to prosper with the end of the Depression when the Japanese attacked Pearl Harbor on December 7, 1941. The draft began conscripting doctors, but Charles Halberstam did not have to go. He was beyond the draft age limit, forty-five years old. He had also done his turn in World War I, prior to medical school, enlisting in the Army and serving as a corpsman at a field evacuation hospital in France, where he had risen to sergeant and had been encouraged by the doctors to go into medicine. To the disappointment of Halberstam's mother, Blanche, who had been looking forward to a substantial income after the hardship of the Depression years, Charles Halberstam quickly volunteered for service as an Army field surgeon. He was shipped overseas in 1943 and did not emerge from the Army until the fall of 1946 as a lieutenant colonel. He then died of a heart attack less than four years after resuming his practice in New York. Halberstam's family had suffered for his father's patriotism. They had also drawn pride from it. To Halberstam, being the son of a doctor did not make you legitimate in American society, if you were a Jew, but being the son of a lieutenant colonel in the United States Army did help to legitimize you. Even though Halberstam could not shake his feeling of apartness as a Jew, he had grown up with the sense that his father had earned the Halberstams a right to a place in America. He saw what Vann was doing in the light of what his father had done. Vann's actions were patriotism and self-sacrifice of the highest kind.

Halberstam became convinced that Vann, for all of his analytical powers, was at bottom a simple man whose professional integrity was so diamond-hard and whose moral courage was so unyielding that he could not compromise on a matter of fundamental right and wrong. Vann confirmed his conclusion by once remarking to Halberstam that the trouble with compromise was that you put a right and a wrong together and you ended up with neither. War, Vann said, was much too serious a business for that. Vann appeared almost puritanical to Halberstam in his dedication to his mission of winning this war. He had a habit of staying overnight with one of the province chiefs at the end of a swing he made every week by jeep and light plane through the seven provinces of the zone. Dinner and an evening of talk were an opportunity for him to get to know and to size up each province chief. Halberstam found out what day he was going one week and arranged to accompany him. As they landed in the province capital where Vann had chosen to spend the night, Vann spoke to him in that intense way he did when he was giving a lesson: "You know, Halberstam, every time I spend a night with one of these province chiefs, they put women in front of me. I always refuse. It lowers our prestige in their eyes. They're trying to get something they can hold over you. Too damn many Americans in this country are sleeping with Vietnamese women. It's bad for our image. The Vietnamese don't like it. It arouses their resentment." Halberstam felt a rush of guilt. He had a Vietnamese girlfriend in Saigon. "Jesus," he thought. "Am I undermining the war effort?"

Although Vann had decided to turn to the press, he did not give up working within his own system. Nearly twenty years in the Army told him to persist. Each month Drummond sent a report to Harkins's headquarters on the competing degrees of control exercised within the division zone by the Viet Cong and the Saigon regime. The report consisted of two parts: a colored tracing-paper overlay for the map accompanied by a written description that went into such details as which roads were safe or unsafe at what hours. The overlay was colored in blue for Saigon-controlled areas and in red for those controlled by the guerrillas. Drummond sent up the January report at the beginning of February. A couple of days later a major on Harkins's intelligence staff called and said that Drummond had too much red on his map overlay. Other information available to the headquarters, the major said, claimed that a number of the areas Drummond had colored in red were still controlled by the Saigon authorities. The major told Drummond to review his information and submit a new report.

Drummond knew right away what the rub was. He had been having trouble with these reports since Cao began to fake operations in October and the guerrillas started to recover. Harkins did not want to admit to

Washington that his intelligence information showed a deterioration in the regime's position in the northern half of the Delta. The complaint was always the same, that Drummond had too much red on his map overlay. On the previous occasion he had asked the major to identify some of the areas that were supposed to be under Saigon's control. Drummond had checked and found out that Dam and the province chiefs would not go into them with less than a battalion. To be able to say he had looked himself, Drummond reconnoitered in a spotter plane. He returned with bullet holes in the plane. He informed Harkins's headquarters that they were listing these areas as secure for the wrong people, but he doubted that his information had changed any listing. A couple of his acquaintances on Harkins's staff let slip that because he had refused to dilute this previous report, it had been suppressed. The overlay forwarded to Washington had reflected a far greater degree of Saigon control. Drummond was determined not to back down on the report for January, because it recorded the most serious deterioration yet.

The Viet Cong had become bolder and more active and were doing things in the daytime, such as harassing outposts, that they had usually dared only at night in the past. Two advisors driving back from Tan Hiep airstrip had almost been killed by a guerrilla standing alongside the road in front of a banana grove right near the Seminary. They had been fortunate enough to notice in time that this loitering farmer was armed with a carbine and had ducked as he raised it and blasted the windshield out of the jeep. The chief of the hamlet at the fork in the road above the Seminary had not been so lucky. An assassination squad walked into the hamlet on another day and gunned him down. The Viet Cong had criticized themselves in their after-action report on Ap Bac for having been too "passive in opposing the enemy" and had spoken of the need to better coordinate actions by all levels of fighters from local guerrillas to regulars in order to transform the countryside into a hell for their opponents. Drummond was seeing the first results of that self-criticism. The deterioration was especially marked between My Tho and Saigon along Route 4, the main road out of the Delta and the route by which the capital received most of its food.

After the call from the major, Drummond contacted the captains serving as intelligence advisors in the province capitals throughout the division zone and asked if they or their counterparts wished to retreat from anything they had told him. No one wanted to soften anything, and some felt they had understated the increase in guerrilla control. With Vann's permission, Drummond had all of the province intelligence advisors and their counterparts meet with him and Binh at My Tho. The new map overlay for Harkins's headquarters that emerged from the meeting had more red on it than the original one, and the written section of the report was grimmer.

Vann decided to time its arrival with a disconcerting message of his own. On February 8, 1963, he sent a secret three-page memorandum to Porter in Can Tho, as the chain of command required, but dispatched an "information copy" directly to Saigon so that Harkins would receive the memorandum immediately. Vann was hoping that his memorandum and the additional red on Drummond's overlay might at last embarrass Harkins into accepting facts. He told Harkins that Drummond and Binh had reliable information locating Viet Cong regular or Regional companies at ten different sites and just as sound information on thirty-five locations where guerrillas were operating at platoon strength. He had tried to persuade Dam to attack them, but Dam, apparently on orders from Cao, refused to go near any of these forty-five Viet Cong units. Dam was instead imitating Cao's farces of the previous fall and was staging one large operation after another of 1,000 to 3,000 troops in areas where the intelligence showed there were no Viet Cong or at most a smattering of local guerrillas. Vann proposed that Drummond draw up a list of priority targets in consultation with Porter's intelligence officer and that Harkins then present the list to the Joint General Staff with a demand that JGS order Dam to attack these guerrillas.

The memorandum sent Harkins into a renewed state of high dudgeon. He ordered his intelligence chief, Col. James Winterbottom of the Air Force, to go down to My Tho with a team of his subordinates. They were to interrogate Vann and Drummond, compare the intelligence files at the Seminary and the 7th Division headquarters with the February 8 memorandum and Drummond's control report, and search carefully for discrepancies. If anything had been exaggerated, Harkins was going to fire Vann.

Harkins had an Air Force officer as his intelligence chief because the bureaucratization of the American military hierarchy had led to a treaty arrangement decreeing that every service had to have a share of the action. Winterbottom's specialty had been photo interpretation for the Strategic Air Command, odd credentials for counterguerrilla war. Nevertheless, Drummond had discovered in prior dealings that the worst impediment to Winterbottom's performance was not his pre-Vietnam experience but the fact that he worked directly for Harkins. Winterbottom had turned out to be a decent man who would often listen. He and his team spent eight hours in My Tho being briefed by Drummond, questioning him and Vann, and examining the files. (One of the staff officers let slip to Drummond how provoked the commanding general was by the red on his overlays.) When Winterbottom and his team returned to Saigon, Vann and Drummond had reason to hope that they might at last have forced some truth into the system. "There is no question in my mind," Winterbottom assured Drummond, "that you have the necessary data to back up your report." He told Vann that he thought the February 8 memorandum had also been accurate and fair.

Vann was hoping too that Porter would arouse something beyond anger with his final report as corps senior advisor, which Porter was going to submit to Harkins shortly before his departure on February 17 to take up a staff post at Fort Hood, Texas. Vann knew the essentials of what Porter would say, because Porter had discussed them with him and Fred Ladd when he had called them to Can Tho to write a preliminary draft for a section on the views of the division senior advisors. The subsequent drafts and the shaping of the report as a whole were entirely Porter's work. He wanted to make this record so that he could leave Vietnam and the Army with a clear conscience. He had requested Fort Hood because his hometown of Belton was nearby. He had an elderly mother to take care of there, and he expected the assignment at Hood to be his last before he retired to the place where he had been born.

Porter designed his last report to be more alarming than his commentary on Vann's chronicle of Ap Bac. He delineated the major fallacies in the entire U.S.-Saigon war effort in the Delta and the provinces of the rubber-plantation country north of the capital. (He had a right to speak of this region too because it had been part of his responsibility under the old III Corps boundaries.) He omitted nothing, including the illusion that the Strategic Hamlet Program was isolating the population from the guerrillas. He took additional care to ensure that the report could not be dismissed as the personal opinion of Dan Porter. Vann and Ladd were not the only advisors he consulted. He also tested his conclusions with the senior members of his staff, the senior advisor to the 5th Division north of Saigon, and with all of the regimental advisors. He said this in the report, stating that the conclusions therefore represented the consensus of the advisors. To translate Porter's message into Harkins's World War II terms, the majority of Harkins's commanders at the most critical sector of the front were warning him that his estimate of the situation was a pipe dream.

Because they were old friends and he knew how General York felt, Porter showed him a nearly final draft. Was he being too blunt? Porter asked. Bob York said that he had encountered a concrete wall in his continued attempts to influence Harkins, but Porter was speaking with the authority of a year in the country and the report was a consensus. No, Porter was not being too blunt, York said. He urged Porter to hurry the report to Harkins.

Harkins was outwardly cordial when Porter stopped by for a short farewell chat. A recommendation to award Porter the Legion of Merit for a year of distinguished service was going forward, the general said. He did not mention Porter's final report. Several members of Harkins's staff had not been so evasive before Porter went in to see the general. They told Porter that Harkins was disgusted with him and considered him a disloyal member of the team. Porter could sense the anger beneath Harkins's politeness. He knew what Harkins was thinking: "Who in the hell does this country bumpkin of a Reserve colonel think he is, telling me how to fight a war?" Being in the presence of a four-star general usually made Porter slightly nervous, even when the general was as friendly as Harkins had been to him in easier days. On this occasion Porter was calm. For the first time in the nearly thirty-one years since he had earned his second lieutenant's bars in the Texas National Guard, Dan Porter was not worried about the approval of a general. If he had to make Harkins mad to force him to see the truth, then that was the way it had to be. He had done his job and he was going home.

Scrupulous nicety of behavior can be counterproductive in large bureaucracies governed by manipulative individuals. Porter's honesty cost him the record he wished to leave. He was so afraid that someone might leak a copy of his final report to the press because of the growing resentment among the field advisors over Harkins's attitude that he typed the last draft himself, destroyed his earlier drafts, had Winterbottom classify the report Top Secret, and personally delivered it in a sealed envelope to Harkins's chief of staff. Porter's scruples also forbade him to retain a copy for himself, as officers of his rank frequently do when they write a report of this moment. As soon as Porter left the country, Harkins checked to see whether he had every copy. He satisfied himself that he did and announced to his staff that if Porter's final report ever went to Washington, it would go in properly sanitized form. The final report vanished. Porter was also not called to the Pentagon on his way to Fort Hood for a debriefing on his experience as was supposed to be done with senior advisors. Harkins arranged that too.

Winterbottom reported honestly on Vann's February 8 memorandum. "The only thing wrong with what he wrote," Winterbottom told the commanding general at a staff conference, "is that all of it is true." He said he had also seen ample evidence to justify Drummond's overlay revealing the deterioration in the northern Delta. The information did not change Harkins's mind, and he still wanted to fire Vann. His relationship with Dam had to be unsatisfactory if he was having so much trouble, Harkins said. This time Brig. Gen. Gerald Kelleher, Harkins's chief of operations, came to Vann's defense. Kelleher was a rough-hewn infantryman who had won his single star through bravery and battlefield leadership. (He had twice been awarded the Distinguished Service Cross, in World War II and in Korea leading a regiment.) Kelleher was cantankerous and narrow-minded on most subjects, but Vann had recently begun to convert him to Vann's view of the war. Kelleher was the only senior member of Harkins's staff ever to adopt it actively. York also defended Vann, and Timmes, who kept lengthening the decent interval he had told Harkins he needed to relieve Vann, again urged forebearance to avoid an outcry. Harkins relented.

By now there was considerable dissent within the middle level of the staffs at Harkins's headquarters and at Timmes's MAAG. Vann soon learned the fate of Porter's report and the outcome of Winterbottom's trip to My Tho. One of Drummond's sources also informed him that while Winterbottom might have agreed in My Tho that Saigon's control was deteriorating in the countryside, "that isn't what went back to Washington." Harkins had Winterbottom discard Drummond's overlay and compose another showing far less red and more blue for a gain in the area Saigon held. A report altered like this was not called a false report in the parlance of the American military of the 1960s. It was called a "directed" report. The commander accepted responsibility, and the subordinate concerned supposedly had the moral burden lifted from him.

Unlike Porter, Vann had a way of rationalizing his actions to fit the exigencies of a fight. He was not going to permit Harkins to stop him from sounding the alarm by manipulating the rules. He made up his mind to violate the rules wholesale, and he made Halberstam his instrument. On Halberstam's next visit to the Seminary in late February, Vann took him into the operations room, closed the door, and sat him down in front of the map of the division zone that covered most of one wall. "Halberstam," he announced, "I may be a commissioned officer in the United States Army who's sworn to safeguard classified information, but I'm also an American citizen with a duty to my country. Now listen carefully." He briefed Halberstam on his February 8 memorandum to Harkins, using the map to point out the locations of the

Viet Cong units and to demonstrate how Cao and Dam exploited the improved intelligence Drummond provided them to go where there were no guerrillas. Vann said his ability to do anything about the problem was exhausted. He told Halberstam of Harkins's refusal to confront Diem and force Diem to reverse his self-defeating policy and how Harkins got mad himself when anyone attempted to confront him with the facts and provoke him into action. Vann laid out the whole tale of Winterbottom's trip to My Tho and the reception the truth had received after Winterbottom had brought it back to Saigon. The situation must not be allowed to drift, Vann said. The Viet Cong were becoming more formidable every day. If nothing was done the United States and the Vietnamese on the U.S. side were going to pay dearly for this moral cowardice.

"Jesus Christ, have I got a hell of a story," Halberstam shouted that afternoon as he burst though the door of the makeshift office we shared in the front room of my apartment on a side street in Saigon. (Halberstam and I had formed a working partnership. A reporter for a wire service, as I was then for the UPI, and a correspondent for a newspaper did not compete with each other because of their differing outlets.) The dispatch he cabled on February 28 began by telling readers of the March 1, 1963, edition of the *Times* that senior ARVN commanders were using intelligence to fake operations and avoid the guerrillas in the entire stretch of country from the 5th Division zone north of the capital down through the whole of the Mekong Delta. (Vann said the fakery was general, and Halberstam and I were able to confirm this by questioning Ladd and his team and sources in the 5th Division advisory detachment.) As the story went on, it narrowed to specific details that made the source of this unusual dispatch obvious to anyone familiar with the message traffic out of the Seminary. Halberstam gave the precise numbers of the Viet Cong company- and platoon-size units that Vann had stated in his secret memorandum. He wrote that the Americans were unable to get Diem's army to attack any of these units "even with a 7 to 1 advantage, or greater," and described the most recent phony assault in Vann's area: "In one of these operations last week, 2,000 troops were used. One guerrilla was killed; one woman and one child were killed in air strikes, and another woman and child seriously wounded by aircraft fire.

"One American advisor," Halberstam continued, had become so upset over these murderous farces and the consequences for the future of refusing to fight the guerrillas that he had sent "a sharply critical report" to Saigon. The report had been "so controversial" that an investigation had been ordered. Halberstam then quoted verbatim Winterbottom's response to Harkins: "The only thing wrong with what he wrote is that all of it is true." He concluded his story by repeating Vann's accusation that Harkins was, in effect, more interested in staying on friendly terms with Diem and his family than in winning the war.

Vann would have been fired for this outrage had an instance of the "Vann luck" not occurred. Porter's recommendation to award Vann the Distinguished Flying Cross for his heroism in the spotter plane at Bac had by chance been approved in Washington in late February. Two days before Halberstam cabled his dispatch, Timmes pinned the medal on Vann's starched khaki shirt in a ceremony at the MAAG head-quarters. Firing Vann right after decorating him was awkward and would certainly make the scandal in the press that much worse. With Timmes continuing to counsel restraint, Harkins made the mistake of temporizing once more.

John Vann was not deterred in the least by the narrowness of his escape, and he did not waste the month remaining to him in Vietnam. He maintained his newfound role of principal critic of policy via the news dispatches, continuing to educate us and to shape our reporting, arousing in us ever greater admiration for his moral heroism. To keep him out of trouble for a week, Timmes finally did gingerly follow through on the solution he had originally proposed to Harkins and sent Vann on a tour of the Central Highlands and the coastal provinces on the pretext that Timmes wanted a private assessment. Vann was delighted at the opportunity to see the war in the rest of the country. Timmes then sent him off for a two-day visit to the British Jungle Warfare School in Malaya. Vann came back with a tale of how he had managed to get himself assigned to the Gurkhas on the ambushing side. Perhaps the U.S. Army could use some Gurkha advisors, he said. He made sure he found time for the additional task he had set himself this last month. It was to organize material for a briefing campaign he was planning to conduct at the Pentagon to convince every Army general there who would listen to him that Harkins was deceiving the nation's leadership and that the radical change in policy Vann wanted had to be adopted to avoid defeat. He was scheduled to begin the full ten-month course at the Industrial College of the Armed Forces at Fort McNair in Washington in mid-August 1963. From late May until his classes began he was to be assigned to the Army's Directorate of Special Warfare at the Pentagon, and it was during this time that he intended to wage his personal crusade.

As a format for these anticipated briefings, he was summarizing his views in a four-and-a-half-page document that was officially his final report to Harkins as division senior advisor. The report was a precisely worded and often witty assault on official policy and optimism. He calculated the level of effort the Diem regime was putting into the war in comparison to the level it could expend if it prosecuted the war seriously: "The counterinsurgency effort in this tactical zone is approximately 10–20% of what could reasonably be expected in view of the personnel and resources available." One of the documents appended to the report as supporting evidence was an analysis, replete with more statistics, to show that the distribution of regular and territorial troops among the seven provinces of the northern Delta bore no relationship to population density, economic and geographic importance, and enemy threat. Instead the allocation—"misallocation" might be a more accurate term—was governed entirely by Diem's obsession with anticoup measures and by his personal regard for the province chief concerned. Vann was also carrying home with him a file of his earlier after-action reports, including the Ap Bac account and Porter's commentary, and other reports he had submitted or that his advisors had sent up to him. He intended to use all of this material to write a thesis someday for a doctorate in public administration, a project that he would always be too busy to undertake in subsequent years.

On the morning of April 1, 1963, his first year in Vietnam at an end, Vann turned over command of the advisory detachment to his successor in the same manner that he had received it—without ceremony—and drove out the Seminary gate to spend a couple of days in Saigon before flying home. He had said his goodbyes and shaken hands with Dam and the 7th Division staff the previous day. In mid-March he had also written a farewell message to the division, had it translated into Vietnamese and mimeographed, and distributed it to the division staff, to each of the regimental and battalion commanders, and to all of the province chiefs. There was no reproach for the angry exchanges of the past. The message, a long one that ran four legal-length pages, was warm and tactful, a bit touching in the way he let through some of the emotional attachment that had built up in him toward the country and its people. He wanted to part from these Vietnamese whom he had come to know in a moment of friendliness and hope. He said that he was "proud to have shared with you, even in a small way, a part of the burden of limiting and driving back the spread of communism." He spoke of "your wonderful children and young people" and said he was certain that they would achieve "peace, prosperity, and freedom" someday. As always, there was purpose behind his diplomacy. Most of his message consisted of polite but forceful summaries of each of the lessons he had spent the last ten months seeking without success to impart. A copy of his English original went to all of his advisors as a précis of what they should strive to teach. (A decade later in the mountains of the Central Highlands, an Army lieutenant colonel who had served as a captain in Vietnam during Vann's first year, and who was back fighting with an ARVN Ranger group, took a frayed copy of the original mimeographed message from his fatigue shirt pocket and showed it to me. He said that a friend had sent it to him in 1963, and he had been so struck by its distilled knowledge that he had preserved it and always carried it with him, reading it over every once in a while to remind himself of what he had to try to attain.)

Bowers, who was also going home, rode up to Saigon with him in the jeep at Vann's invitation. He knew that Vann was leaving under a career shadow, but it was not etiquette for a sergeant and a lieutenant colonel to discuss the lieutenant colonel's dispute with the commanding general, and so they reminisced about their ten months together in the Delta. Vann had said to Ziegler, just before Ziegler's own departure two weeks earlier, that he was going to have to decide whether he had spoiled his prospects in the Army by defying Harkins so boldly.

Early in the afternoon of April 3, 1963, a small crowd gathered in the second-floor restaurant of the passenger terminal at Tan Son Nhut to say goodbye. There were a number of his captains from My Tho, the commanding officers and a few of the pilots from two of the helicopter companies, and Halberstam and I and others from the handful of correspondents who had learned so much from him. We were proud and sad for him, proud for the man and what he had sought to achieve, sad for what we were afraid he was going to have to pay for his patriotism. Halberstam had proposed that we give him a memento to express our gratitude for his lessons and to show our admiration for his moral heroism and professional integrity. Vann did not smoke, but a shop on Tu Do, Saigon's main street, still called Rue Catinat from its name in French days, sold handsome round cigarette boxes fashioned by Cambodian silversmiths for coffee tables. We all contributed, and Halberstam arranged for the shop to engrave our names on the side of the box under the inscription:

> *To Lt. Col. John Paul Vann*
> *Good Soldier, Good Friend*
> *From His Admirers in the American Press Corps*

Halberstam presented the box to Vann with some emotional remarks about how much we and the public who read our reports owed to him. The Saigon customs and passport-control officers were casual in those years. Everyone walked downstairs and out onto the field to the plane with Vann when it was time to board. Halberstam said he had one last thing to tell him: every time we had cabled a story we had worried about hurting his career. We hoped that Vann would pull through professionally. Vann looked up at him quickly. Halberstam remembered his small, tight smile. "You never hurt me any more than I wanted to be hurt," Vann said.

By chance I flew home with Vann, and he was not discouraged about his future in the Army in all of the talking we did during a long flight to San Francisco. I had decided to spend a month's leave in the United States, because I had not been back to Massachusetts to see my parents in three years. Neither Vann nor I had thought to bring a book, so there was not much to do except talk and sleep. Vann said he would not permit himself the luxury of letting what had happened during his ten months in the Delta get him down. He had done his best and he had learned a lot. He was looking forward to his year at the Industrial College of the Armed Forces and then to promotion to full colonel early in his next assignment. (The Industrial College is in the topmost rung of institutional schools that a career officer can attend, the equivalent of the National War College or the Army War College for officers with the logistics speciality that Vann had adopted seven years earlier while a major in Germany to obtain accelerated promotion.) He showed me his farewell message to the division and let me have a copy; I asked for it because I was impressed at what a catechism it was. At the end of the message he conveyed the same intention of persevering in the Army. He invited any of the advisors or Vietnamese officers who wished to do so to write to him at Fort McNair and to visit him and Mary Jane and their family if they happened to pass through Washington. Normally, he said to me, an officer who was marked as a troublemaker never went beyond a full colonel's eagles. He was game to see if he could become an exception. The Army was his life, he said, and he was not about to let Harkins push him out of it. Time and events, he thought, would vindicate him. In the meantime, he was going to convert every general he could to his point of view in the hope of gaining high-level allies to discredit Harkins.

In mid-May 1963, after six weeks of leave in El Paso to let the children finish the school term, he and Mary Jane sold their house there, packed and shipped their furniture as they had in so many previous Army moves, and took the family off to Washington. Patricia and John Allen, the eldest, had the treat of flying ahead to Baltimore to meet Mary Jane's sister and her husband for a week of sightseeing in Virginia at Williamsburg and Jamestown. The three youngest, Jesse, Tommy, and Peter, had to ride all the way from Texas in the family station wagon. Vann initially put the family up in the Washington suburb of McLean, Virginia, with a Methodist minister who had been his boyhood patron in Norfolk. They then crowded into an apartment in Alexandria until he rented a house on the Chesapeake Bay shore about twenty-five miles east of the capital. He had a long commute to the Pentagon, but the rent was low and the area was semirural, with lots of room for the boys to play and to fish and net crabs.

I got back to Vietnam in time to watch the regime provoke rebellion in the cities and towns with the same abuse and arrogance that had maddened the population of the countryside. On May 8, 1963, the Ngo Dinhs set off what was to become known as the Buddhist Crisis. A company of Civil Guards, commanded by a Catholic officer, killed nine persons, some of them children, and injured fourteen others in a crowd in the former imperial capital of Hue. The crowd was protesting a new decree that forbade the flying of the Buddhist flag on Buddha's birthday, his 2,587th. The edict had been issued by Diem at the instigation of his elder brother, Thuc, archbishop of Hue and the South's leading Catholic prelate in 1963. When Thuc had celebrated the twenty-fifth anniversary of his elevation to bishop a few weeks earlier, the Catholics of Hue had flown Vatican flags all over the home city of the Ngo Dinhs. After the killings, Diem and his family behaved in character. They did not attempt to mollify the chief monks, who were antagonized by nine years of discrimination. Instead, they maneuvered to crush the Buddhist leaders as they had crushed the Cao Dai and Hoa Hao sects and the Binh Xuyen organized crime society in 1955.

The monks fought back in a Vietnamese way. On the morning of June 11, 1963, a seventy-three-year-old monk named Quang Duc sat down in the middle of a Saigon intersection a few blocks from Ambassador Nolting's residence. He crossed his legs in the lotus position of meditation while another monk poured gasoline from a five-gallon plastic container over his shaven head, soaking his orange robe. The old monk's hands moved swiftly when he lifted them from his lap to strike the match, lighting his body into a symbol of anger and sacrifice and setting ablaze the tinder of resentment in the urban centers of the South.

The Buddhist movement became a rallying point for all of the discontent that had been accumulating against the ruling family among urban Vietnamese since 1954. While the monks were able to draw on the ill will against Catholics as a foreign-serving minority that was a reflex in Vietnamese society, the Ngo Dinhs had made themselves so repugnant by early 1963 that some Catholics clandestinely aided the Buddhist leaders. A photograph of Quang Duc's suicide taken by Malcolm Browne, the Saigon bureau chief of the Associated Press, astonished the American public and international opinion and embarrassed the Kennedy administration.

The Ngo Dinhs applied tear gas and billy clubs and attempted to seal off the pagodas with barbed wire barricades in the streets. They spurned appeals to compromise from Nolting, who cut short a vacation in Europe to try to persuade Diem to see reason, and from Kennedy himself. "If the Buddhists wish to have another barbecue," Nhu said at the end of a dinner with Nolting and a number of other senior American officials in July, "I will be glad to supply the gasoline and a match." Madame Nhu said in press interviews that the monks were all Communists and dupes of the Communists, that the demonstrators "should be beaten ten times more" by the police, and that "I shall clap my hands" at another suicide. She preempted Richard Nixon by nearly a decade in the use of a term that he was to make famous. The family was supported by a "silent majority," she announced. The Ngo Dinhs assumed that the Americans would gradually acquiesce in the crushing of the Buddhist leaders as Washington had welcomed the suppression of the sects and the Binh Xuyen in 1955. The one member of the family who argued for a settlement, Ngo Dinh Can, another younger brother of Diem who lived in Hue and was the overlord of Central Vietnam, was deprived of much of his authority by Diem for his common sense. The police swung the truncheons harder, as Madame Nhu wished, and threw more tear-gas grenades and stretched more barbed wire, but the monks instigated more self-sacrifices by fire, the anger against the family grew fiercer, and the demonstrations spread from the cities to the smaller towns.

John Mecklin, a career foreign correspondent who had taken a leave from *Time* for the experience of a stint in government and who was chief of the USIS in Vietnam in 1963, had a nightmare. In his nightmare he went to a play in which the members of the U.S. Embassy gradually discover that the local government they have been dealing with for years is composed of madmen, whose words are meaningless, and everything the Americans thought had happened in this strange dream country has actually never occurred. He woke up before he found out how the play ended.

Vann had his campaign at the Pentagon going within a few days of reporting for duty to the Directorate of Special Warfare on the morning of May 24, 1963. He looked up the "debriefing officer" responsible for interviewing returned advisors for the "Lessons Learned" program on Vietnam. Vann said that he wanted to be debriefed. The officer replied that at "Saigon's wish" he was not going to be interviewed. Vann had been expecting that response. (Kelleher, his one senior convert on Harkins's staff, had returned in April to retire, and he, like Porter, had also not been debriefed at "Saigon's wish.") Vann began to brief on his own. He started out by just talking to fellow officers in the directorate and showing them copies of his final report, his February 8 message, the Ap Bac account, and like documentation to substantiate his arguments. His official job at the directorate was to devise new procedures to handle financing and procurement for the worldwide counterinsurgency mission of the Special Forces, a small chore for a man with Vann's training in fiscal management. He therefore had lots of time for his serious task. Over the next month he gradually worked his way up through the Army hierarchy; his conversations formalized into briefings for senior officers and their staffs, complete with statistical charts and maps he would cast on a screen with a slide projector, and anecdotes of his experiences in Vietnam for authenticity and a human touch. Vann's dramatic briefing techniques helped him put his arguments across, but they did not gain him his listeners. What attracted Vann's audience was that he had so much of substance to say and that he was saying it in 1963. A U.S. Army officer in Washington then could still regard the war as a foreign affair and look upon the performance of the Saigon forces with a certain amount of objectivity generated by distance and his feeling that they were not his own army.

By late June, Vann had briefed several hundred officers in the Pentagon, almost all Army men, including half a dozen generals in staff positions. One of the few officers he briefed from another service was an Air Force major general named Lansdale. It was the first meeting between Vann and his hero. Lansdale listened and did not react, because there was nothing he could do. He was in disfavor with the circle of power. After his enemies in the bureaucracy had sabotaged a proposal to name him ambassador to South Vietnam in late 1961—Diem had requested his return and Kennedy had told him he would be going—

the president had put him in charge of an ultrasecret project that was of intense emotional concern to John Kennedy because of his humiliation at the Bay of Pigs. The project was called Operation Mongoose. The task was to get rid of Fidel Castro, coiled in defiance and threatening to breed other Communist reptiles in the Caribbean and Latin America, by fomenting a revolution against him or by some other, more direct means. The president and Robert Kennedy were not particular about propriety. They wanted results. The pressure had risen after the Cuban missile crisis of October 1962. Lansdale had failed to fulfill his reputation as a magician of clandestine operations and conjure up a Rikki-Tikki-Tavi to dispose of the cobra in Havana. He was about to be driven into retirement. His Filipino friend Ramon Magsaysay had died prematurely in a plane crash in 1957, without instituting the social and economic reforms that might have brought a lasting peace to the Philippines.

Toward the end of June, Vann finally reached an officer who did have influence, Maj. Gen. Harold Johnson, the Army's assistant deputy chief of staff for operations. (Johnson was to be made chief of operations and then to be promoted to full general and appointed chief of staff within a little over a year.) He listened to Vann and sent him to Gen. Barksdale Hamlett, the vice chief of staff. Hamlett found Vann's presentation sufficiently upsetting to arrange for him to brief the assembled Joint Chiefs of Staff on July 8, 1963.

Vann was thrilled and awed that he was at last coming within touch of victory in his battle to get the truth about the war to those with the power to make use of it. Hamlett's response reaffirmed a conviction that Vann had held to in Vietnam despite all of his frustrations with Harkins—the conviction that Harkins was an aberration, that bad strategies came from ignorance and misguided intentions, that in the final analysis his system was founded on reason.

When Vann briefed the Joint Chiefs on July 8 he was going to cross paths again with Victor Krulak, who returned at the beginning of July from another inspection trip to South Vietnam. Krulak briefed McNamara and Taylor and the other members of the Joint Chiefs on his week-long visit. The distribution list for copies of his 129-page report has been lost, but documents such as this were widely distributed at the top in Washington. In all likelihood Krulak's report went up to his admirer at the White House through McGeorge Bundy, Kennedy's special assistant for national security affairs, and to his other admirer in the attorney general's office.

"The shooting part of the war is moving to a climax," Brute Krulak announced. The boys would be coming home on McNamara's three-year schedule with another war behind them. "General Harkins considers that a reduction of 1,000 men could be accomplished now, without affecting adversely the conduct of the war." Had the report not been classified Secret because of its intelligence data and discussion of Hanoi's use of Cambodia and U.S.-Saigon forays into Laos, it would have qualified as an immediate press release. Krulak had personally written only the fifteen-page introduction. The remainder consisted of questions submitted by Krulak and answers prepared under the guidance of then Brig. Gen. Richard Stilwell, who had arrived in Saigon in April to replace Kelleher as chief of operations. His habitual confidence in authority had immediately led him to start promoting the views of the commanding general and suppressing dissent within Harkins's staff and anywhere else in the command he could find it. Krulak made Stilwell's answers his own by ornamenting them with the enthusiasm of his introduction.

The Viet Cong were not proliferating and growing into a more formidable foe, as Vann said. On the contrary, Harkins's attrition strategy was turning them into an endangered species of Vietnamese. "Captured documents have revealed that many Viet Cong are already on short rations and are in dire need of drugs. . . . Prisoners of war have also stated that Viet Cong morale is deteriorating due to lack of logistics and popular support," one of Stilwell's answers read. The latest intelligence data showed that the total number of Communist-led insurgents in the country had declined from a peak of 124,000 guerrillas of all types in January 1963 to a "reasonably reliable" estimate of 102,000 to 107,000 Viet Cong by June.

What made the Communist-led guerrillas so vulnerable to this attrition process? It was the Strategic Hamlet Program, "the heart of the counterinsurgency strategy," Krulak said. By mid-June 1963, 67 percent of the rural population of the South was living in the 6,800 strategic hamlets built since the first had been erected in Operation Sunrise in April 1962. Most of the peasantry "appears favorably disposed" to the program. By the end of 1963, when the United States and the Diem regime had constructed all 11,246 strategic hamlets planned for the South, the Viet Cong would be complete outsiders. Although the United States had persuaded Diem to permit an amnesty program for the guerrillas, the number of defectors was going to fall off dramatically because "there will actually not be a very great number of people available for the amnesty program to attract," Krulak wrote.

(The intelligence section of Krulak's report did contain some significant information. The Viet Cong were creating regiments in skeletal form in the rain-forest war zones north of Saigon. The numerical designation the guerrillas had given one regiment was mentioned. "Artillery specialists" were also being grouped into "heavy weapons battalions." Other and unconfirmed information said that the Viet Cong had received 75mm recoilless cannon and 12.7mm antiaircraft machine guns which "allegedly are to be kept 'secret' until the proper time arrives for their employment." Neither Krulak nor Stilwell understood the importance of these details, apparently assuming, as Harkins did, that guerrillas in regiments would be bigger and easier targets.)

Several days before July 8, Krulak's staff began calling the Army's Directorate of Special Warfare for a copy of Vann's briefing. The Pentagon grapevine had apparently alerted Krulak to Vann's campaign to discredit Harkins's version of the war. As Vann was now to brief the Joint Chiefs, the normal course was being followed of leaving nothing to chance. Vann was preparing a text of what he would say, along with slides of the statistical charts and maps he was going to display on the screen in the "Tank," the irreverent nickname for the conference room of the Joint Chiefs at the Pentagon. He rehearsed the briefing before his colleagues in the directorate, editing his text at their suggestion so that it would startle his august audience into attention and yet not put them off by sounding too radical or seeming to attack Harkins personally. Vann's immediate superior, Lt. Col. Francis Kelly, a one-time New York policeman who was later to command the Special Forces in Vietnam, and others advised him to stall Krulak as long as possible.

Vann's briefing would strike anyone who was enthralled by Harkins's illusion as outrageous. His twelve-page narrative and his accompanying charts and maps might well impress someone whose mind was not made up as a deftly crafted presentation of the war by a man who had spent most of a year at its center in the struggle for the northern Delta. Vann was confining the briefing to his experience and specific area of responsibility so that his personal knowledge could not be challenged.

The Joint Chiefs would first see a map of South Vietnam cast on their screen with the northern Delta colored to stand out in relation to the rest of the country. Vann would explain to them what was at stake in the people, the geography, and the economic resources of the half of the South's rice bowl that touched Saigon itself. Then he would display some statistical charts while he sought to dispel myths and attempted an education in "the fundamentals of guerrilla warfare" as John Vann had learned them and passed them on to the newsmen. For example, he would display a chart showing a total of 9,700 Viet Cong "reported killed" in the 7th Division zone during the ten months that he had been senior advisor. (He would not mention the body-count figures in Harkins's "Headway" reports. The Joint Chiefs were familiar with these.) "I use the term 'reported killed,' " he would say. "Actually the number [9,700] is highly misleading. With over 200 advisors in the field, we estimate, and I stress this can only be an estimate, that the total number of people killed was less than two-thirds of those claimed. Additionally, we estimate that from 30 to 40 percent of the personnel killed were merely bystanders who were unfortunate enough to be in the vicinity of a combat action." The Joint Chiefs would be told that "we never had intelligence that was good enough to justify prestrikes by air, artillery, or mortars" but that as weapons went "a rifle . . . is the last one that was preferred for use." They would tour the outposts in the 7th Division zone where the garrisons were "shot in their beds," follow Cao's campaign of the fall of 1962—"plans so prudently made that we had only three friendly troops killed"—and see the tree lines of Bac and Tan Thoi as Vann cast a colored sketch on the screen and gave a brief account of the disastrous consequences to which make-believe leads in war.

John Vann was not going to conclude his briefing for the Joint Chiefs with a dirge. He knew this would not help him with these generals, and he did not feel that way in any case. There was still time to win if corrective action was taken. If policy was changed and the Saigon side was forced to accept American advice it would be possible to "break the back of the Viet Cong military forces [in the northern Delta] within six months." The complete pacification of the region would take years, but a war effort that exploited the full potential of the Saigon side and a hard-fought six-month campaign could reduce "the military capability of the Viet Cong . . . from battalion-size operations of regular forces to platoon-size harassments by local guerrillas."

He had Mary Jane send a uniform to the cleaners especially for the Monday of the briefing. "There wasn't a wrinkle near him," she remembered later, as he left for the Pentagon in the morning. He was scheduled to address the Joint Chiefs at 2:00 P.M. He stalled as long as he dared on letting Krulak have a copy of his text, until four hours before the briefing, and then sent one over and walked to the outer office of Gen. Earle Wheeler, the current chief of staff of the Army, to wait there just in case there were any last-minute questions from Wheeler's aides. They had already been given a copy.

At about 11:00 A.M., an hour after he had sent the text to Krulak's office, the phone rang on the desk of one of Wheeler's aides. Vann heard the aide ask the officer at the other end of the line: "Who wants the item removed from the agenda?" The answer was apparently confusing.

"Is it the secretary of defense or the chairman's office?" the aide continued. He seemed to get some clarification. "Is that an order or a request?" he asked. There was further explanation from the other end of the line. "Let me get this right," the aide said, summing up the conversation to be certain he had it correctly. "The chairman requests that the item be removed." The aide answered that he would convey Taylor's request to the chief of staff and call back. He hung up.

"Looks like you don't brief today, buddy," he said to Vann. He walked into the inner office where Wheeler worked, came back in a short time, and telephoned the caller at Taylor's office. "The chief agrees to remove the item from the agenda," he said.

Krulak had clearly alerted Taylor to this incredible briefing as soon as he read Vann's text, and Taylor acted. Taylor did not bear professional contradiction lightly. He was quick to show irritation when he encountered opposition on military matters. Neither Krulak nor Taylor believed it was possible that Vann could be correct. He was obviously a disgruntled upstart of a lieutenant colonel. They had other reasons to stop him. They did not want to expose all of the Joint Chiefs to dissent of this magnitude and have it go on the record. To attack Harkins was first of all to attack Krulak. He was by this time identified in the eyes of the Washington establishment with Harkins's position. It was also to attack Taylor. He too had been consistently sanguine in his reports to McNamara and the president. In addition, Taylor was responsible by proxy for the performance of his protégé in Saigon. When the question had come up in December 1961 of a general for the new command in Vietnam, Kennedy had not wanted to entrust the war to Harkins. He had considered Harkins too regular. He had wanted to reach down for a younger man with an unorthodox background in the hope of imaginative performance. Taylor had persuaded the president to accept Harkins, assuring him that Harkins had exactly the talents they needed.

They would not have encountered any resistance to silencing Vann from Wheeler. He was the prominent Army general who had headed the Joint Chiefs' mission, the man who had conducted the most important inquiry of the war thus far by submitting himself to a guided tour arranged by the officer he was supposed to be investigating, Harkins, and by listening to Krulak, a like-thinking acquaintance of Harkins. Wheeler had apparently known nothing of the contents of Vann's briefing before July 8 because Hamlett, the vice-chief whom Vann had briefed, a general at the end of his career and soon to retire, had scheduled it on his own authority. Wheeler also happened to be another of Taylor's protégés. He owed his position as chief of staff to Taylor, who had influenced the president to name him head of the Army the previous summer. Wheeler was fifty-five years old and lean and urbane in the Taylor image. He was without Taylor's aloofness and was well liked by his peers in the other services for his genial and even-handed attitude in professional relations. His nickname was Bus. Wheeler was the competent staff officer type who is a benefit to any army as long as he has someone above him to do the original thinking. When he was launched on his own, the limitations of the paperwork soldier showed in his reflex orthodoxy and in a credulity that was easily aroused by documents labeled Top Secret with red borders around the pages and by confident words from another man in stars and gold braid.

In his rage and despair, Vann blamed Krulak and Taylor for his defeat, but he also blamed himself. He blamed himself for helping Harkins create the myth of imminent victory by staging those "dog and pony show" briefings with Cao for the visiting generals and officials from Washington when he had still thought he could imitate Lansdale and make Cao his instrument to destroy the Viet Cong. "We had also, to all the visitors who came over there, been one of the bright shining lies," he said to an Army historian in a tape-recorded interview two weeks after the cancellation of his briefing for the Joint Chiefs. The interview was classified Top Secret and the transcript and the tape put away in a locked filing cabinet.

Krulak could not recall the briefing incident when he was asked about it much later, but he was convinced that he would not have done anything to interfere with Vann. He did not appear to be lying. Rather, he seemed to have genuinely forgotten the role he played, as busy men of affairs often forget such episodes in their pasts.

They did not succeed in silencing him. The students he left behind in Vietnam spoke for him. He did not have to do any long-distance leaking. We had absorbed his lessons well enough to proceed on our own. Halberstam thanked him for them when Vann wrote in July and remarked on how daringly critical of the regime we had become in our coverage of the Buddhist crisis. "This was the time to go for broke and use all our ammo—while people were really watching," Halberstam agreed in his letter of reply. "We think and talk about you all the time," Halberstam said, "and often when we write it is with you in mind. But more important, I think you ought to know that what you taught us about the Mekong Delta remains of crucial importance in covering this story, that it is almost impossible to kid us now, that we . . . know exactly what to look for and what the heart of the matter is. In the face of the monumental effort here to con us, we have mental flak jackets you gave us."

We picked up news of the dimensions of the Viet Cong buildup in the Delta—in retrospect, the first stage in the creation of the second Viet Minh—at the beginning of August. We would have learned about it sooner but we had all been unable to leave Saigon for a look at the war since June because of the Buddhist street demonstrations and the constant threat of another suicide. Mert Perry of *Time* heard of a big fight in Kien Hoa Province in July in which eleven helicopters had been hit. I knew the captain who was the advisor to the 7th Division battalion involved in the battle from a march through the rice paddies long before. He came to Saigon at the beginning of August for a weekend leave, and I ran into him by chance on the street. The guerrillas his unit had clashed with had been like no Viet Cong battalion he had ever previously encountered. They seemed to outnumber the approximately 300 men his battalion fielded, and they certainly outgunned their ARVN opponent. He had never heard such a drumfire of automatic weapons. The guerrillas pinned down the Saigon troops immediately and kept them pinned down until the Viet Cong broke off the fight at dark, despite the machine guns and rockets of the Huey gunships and half a dozen strikes by the fighter-bombers. Had the guerrillas been daring enough to sally out of their positions in the tree lines and maneuver, they definitely would have overrun all or part of his battalion, the captain said. The ARVN captain who was his counterpart had been timid before, but the experience with these new Viet Cong had astonished and thoroughly cowed him.

At around the same time, an ARVN colonel whose professional ability we and almost all of the advisors respected, Pham Van Dong, who bore the same name as the prime minister in Hanoi, returned in alarm from a tour of the Delta. The Viet Cong were starting the cycle against his army and the United States that the Viet Minh had worked against the French, he said. Colonel Dong was from one of the minority peoples in the North. He had earned his commission in the French Army, as distinct from Bao Dai's Vietnamese National Army, and was one of two officers in the ARVN who had commanded a brigade-size unit in the regular French Expeditionary Corps. (Harkins had inadvertently gotten him dismissed in December as deputy commander of III Corps by writing a letter to Diem recommending that he be promoted to brigadier general. "Now Diem will fire me for sure," Colonel Dong had said when he received a carbon of the letter Harkins sent to him, thinking he would be pleased. "Diem will think that if the Americans like me this much, they might use me to make a coup." A couple of weeks later Diem had appointed Colonel Dong an inspector of strategic hamlets.)

These portents obviously required a story. Because the Buddhist crisis so monopolized our time and energy, Halberstam and I decided to pool our reporting with Perry's for the major research effort entailed. Colonel Dong was one of our most helpful informants. He obtained statistics we needed and details of how the Viet Cong were creating their new big battalions through a general at Joint General Staff headquarters who had been one of his subordinates in the North during the French war. I spent an evening at his house transcribing the information. For all of Cao's lies, the ARVN intelligence officers in the Delta were still managing to push quite a bit of sound information up through their system. The JGS was apparently not passing the data along to the presidential palace because it was not welcome there. Harkins's intelligence staff was ignoring the information because the U.S. intelligence officers knew that it was similarly unwelcome to their chief. There was a sense of *déjà vu* in Colonel Dong's comparison of what was happening in the Delta with the French war. Over the year from late 1949 to the fall of 1950 while Giap had been turning his first Viet Minh into full-size divisions and readying an execution ground for the French garrisons along Route Coloniale 4 on the China border—the disaster that was the harbinger of Dien Bien Phu—the French high command had scoffed at reports of "a new Viet Minh" boldly challenging their troops in that limestone-crag country of the far north where Colonel Dong's ancestors rested.

We cross-checked and supplemented the JGS information through our other American and Vietnamese sources. Halberstam drove down to the Seminary for an afternoon with several of the captains who were nearing the end of their tours and who had watched the change taking place in the Delta. The CIA and AID men running the U.S. side of the Strategic Hamlet Program were also more candid now because they were worried. The Viet Cong had begun to literally dismantle the hated stockades. The guerrilla technique was to concentrate on destroying the SDC outpost inside or adjacent to the strategic hamlet. Simultaneously, the unpaid hamlet militia were being disarmed, won over, or emerging as what they had been all along—clandestine local guerrillas. The peasants were then told they were free to return to their native hamlets. Before leaving, the farmers would strip off the sheet-metal roofing to use in rebuilding their old homes. If metal roofing had been unavailable and the Saigon authorities had forced them to use thatch to roof the houses in the strategic hamlet, the Viet Cong cadres would have had the farmers pull down the roofs to render the place uninhabitable. The cadres would also have the peasants chop the barbed wire off the posts—the "American spaghetti" as some Saigon wags had taken to calling it—and cut it up into short strips. The roof-tearing and barbed-wire-chopping exercises had psychological meaning and were a visual demonstration that the cause of Ho Chi Minh had triumphed over this scheme of the Americans and their Vietnamese surrogates. The cut-up barbed wire was not being thrown away. It was being put into mines and booby traps as shrapnel.

As events turned out, Perry and I did some volunteer work for Halberstam, because he was the only one who managed to get our findings into print right away. As a wire-service reporter, I had to cable news as fast as it occurred, because I was reporting for news outlets all over the world rather than for a single newspaper or magazine. There was an outbreak of fiery suicides and more demonstrations right after we finished reporting, and I could not stop long enough to write the Viet Cong buildup story. Halberstam was naturally in a hurry to write and unable to wait. I had to be satisfied with using the material for subsequent analytical articles. Perry's dispatch to *Time* was read and filed away. The late Henry Luce and the managing editor of his magazine, Otto Fuerbringer, were as unhappy about the reporting out of Vietnam as Harkins was.

On August 15, 1963—a little over five weeks after Vann's day of rage and despair at the Pentagon—an updated version of Vann's view of the war appeared on the front page of the *New York Times* under Halberstam's byline. Halberstam did not dare to state flatly that the Viet Cong were winning the war. None of the resident correspondents dared write this boldly yet. He knew that his editors in New York were already frightened by his reporting. A straightforward assertion that the Viet Cong were winning would make them more nervous and they would say that it was subjective and refuse to print it. He therefore arranged the facts to make the statement for him. The headline writer saw the point and set it over the story: VIETNAMESE REDS GAIN IN KEY AREA.

"South Vietnam's military situation in the vital Mekong Delta has deteriorated in the last year, and informed officials are warning of ominous signs," Halberstam's dispatch began. He piled fact upon fact to describe the Communist buildup in the artillery-barrage fashion he liked to recommend as good reporting. A year ago, he wrote, the guerrillas had been assembling in formations no larger than 250 men. Now they were massing in groups of "600 and even 1,000," a reference to reports of two reinforced battalions moving through the countryside together. A year ago the Viet Cong had avoided the ARVN and concentrated on the inferior Civil Guards and SDC militia. Today, because of their "new strength . . . in captured United States weapons," they were "picking fights" with Saigon's regulars. "They are almost cocky about it," he quoted an unnamed American advisor as saying. Saigon commanders "have sighted battalions in their areas that they cannot identify." And "what is more ominous," Halberstam went on, "the Vietcong are creating standardized battalions" of 400 men each in three rifle companies and a heavy weapons unit. "Increasing quantities of Communist-made weapons and ammunition" were being smuggled into the South to supplement the captured American arms of these battalions, and the guerrillas were also acquiring "better [radio] communications than ever." The objective of these preparations was still more alarming. Halberstam quoted an "expert source" as warning that the Hanoi leadership was building toward a strategy of "fast, hard-hitting mobile warfare" to overwhelm the ARVN.

Halberstam and I and the other correspondents had seized on the Buddhist crisis as we had on Ap Bac. We had been holding it up as proof that the regime was as bankrupt politically as it was militarily. Harkins had retreated to the argument that although the Buddhist movement had marshaled discontent in the cities and towns, it had not interfered with the successful prosecution of the war against the guerrillas in the countryside. Krulak had endorsed Harkins's argument in his July report on his latest trip to Vietnam just before sabotaging Vann's scheduled briefing for the Joint Chiefs. Halberstam's August 15 story was truth revealed with a hidden motive. The story was meant to be a mine of facts to blow up this newest stage set of Harkins and compel the administration to face the reality that it was losing.

The dispatch did detonate in Washington with the blast of a mine, but the force of the explosion did not blow away the fantasy as Halberstam, Perry, and I had hoped it would. Kennedy demanded to know if there was any truth in the story. Krulak appealed to Harkins, and Stilwell teletyped a lengthy memorandum rebutting the article point by point. Thanks to Stilwell and Krulak and to their own hubris, Kennedy and the majority of those at the top of his administration retained confidence in the generals. Dean Rusk went out of his way to denounce Halberstam's article as false at a State Department press conference the day after it was published.

There was great irony in Krulak's role in perpetuating Harkins's fantasy. Krulak's talent for making war was too large for him to remain forever stupid about the war in Vietnam. In a couple of years he was to see the fatuousness of the attrition strategy that obsessed the Army generals. He was then to attempt to make this system he served behave rationally, and he was then to know the anguish Vann had long felt.

The claim that young reporters on the scene were inventing bad news had become more ludicrous than ever by the late summer of 1963, because by now the majority of the established correspondents in Asia who regularly visited Vietnam saw the war in essentially the same terms that we did. They included Peter Kalischer and Bernard Kalb of CBS, James Robinson of NBC, Stanley Karnow, formerly with *Time* and in 1963 with the *Saturday Evening Post*, Pepper Martin of *U. S. News & World Report*, and Charles Mohr, *Time*'s chief correspondent for Southeast Asia. These men were not the sort to be hoodwinked by a bunch of cubs. The embassy, Harkins's headquarters, and the regime had, in fact, never been happy with the reporting of most of the regular visitors. Diem had expelled Robinson the month after the family had thrown out François Sully of *Newsweek* and had not let Robinson into the country again for nine months.

For every one of the regular visitors who saw the war as we did, there were others in the United States anxious to accept and defend the official view. The lack of precedent for such a wholesale failure by the military and political leadership of the country was too much for them to overcome. A famous foreign correspondent who had the professional stature that Halberstam lacked in 1963—Marguerite Higgins of the *New York Herald Tribune*—was an example. She had won a Pulitzer Prize in 1951 for her reporting in Korea, writing bravely of the debacles at the beginning of that war. The Joint Chiefs team had recommended encouraging "mature and responsible news correspondents" to go to Vietnam in order to correct the hysterical stories by the local reporters. Miss Higgins accordingly flew to Saigon in August at the urging of the Pentagon. During the approximately four weeks she spent in South Vietnam she filed a series of dispatches saying, in sum, that the Buddhist crisis was the invention of Machiavellian monks and gullible reporters, that General Harkins and the Diem regime were defeating the Viet Cong; and that "reporters here would like to see us lose the war to prove they're right."

Joseph Alsop, who had not yet met Vann in 1963 and would not have approved of him if he had, flew out in September to accuse us of undermining Diem as some of the World War II correspondents in China had supposedly helped to undermine Chiang Kai-shek by calling attention to the corruption and incompetence in his regime. Our coverage amounted to "another of these egregious crusades," Alsop wrote in one of his columns. "The constant pressure of the reportorial crusade against the government has also helped mightily to transform Diem from a courageous, quite viable national leader into a man afflicted with a galloping persecution mania, seeing plots around every corner, and therefore misjudging everything." Alsop accepted the Harkins-Krulak line that while the Buddhist crisis had caused political turmoil in the cities, the war in the countryside was progressing unaffected. We had, he said, erroneously painted "a dark, indignant picture" of the military situation. He suggested that we spend less time at the demonstrations and suicides and more at the "fighting front." Halberstam thought his term a quaint one for the war we knew.

Nevertheless, Halberstam was in serious trouble with his editors in New York. He was fighting for his professional life as well as to win a war. The *Times* did not believe in crusading journalism, and while Halberstam might have convinced some of the paper's readers that he was correct about the regime and the war, he had not convinced his own superiors. The two senior news editors in New York, Turner Catledge, the managing editor, and his deputy, Clifton Daniel, who had married Margaret Truman, were Southerners and newspapermen of the Depression and World War II generation. They had no wish to see the *Times* used as a propaganda platform by the U.S. government. They enjoyed an occasional scrap with whichever administration was in office. Halberstam had forced the paper into a consistently adversarial position with the Kennedy administration. The decade of Vietnam was to change the attitudes of Catledge and Daniel. Both men were to become advocates of an aggressive and rigorously independent press, but in 1963 the adversarial role was new and they did not like it at all. The *Times'* executives were also still feeling the pain of the controversy over Herbert Matthews's sympathetic reporting of the pre-Communist phase of Castro's revolution in Cuba. They were afraid that Halberstam might be bringing a similar scandal upon them. Diem's supporters in the press, like Alsop with his echo of Chiang and the "Who Lost China?" witch-hunts of the 1950s, did not hesitate to probe this fear. In early September the *New York Journal-American* and the other Hearst newspapers began to accuse Halberstam of being naive about Communism and preparing the way for a Vietnamese Fidel Castro.

The doubts about Halberstam's reporting grew as one descended the news-editing chain of command at the *Times*, and at the lower level irritation reinforced the doubt. Halberstam's strengths as a journalist were his total commitment of time and energy to a story, the weight and quality of information that flowed from this commitment, and the speed with which he could write under deadline. During a three-week period in August and September the regime effectively denied us use of the telegraph office by imposing a censorship that let through nothing except propaganda. We had to send out all of our dispatches on commercial airliners and have them cabled from other Southeast Asian cities. On one morning four different articles totaling about 4,000 words came whirling out of Halberstam's typewriter in time to make a noon flight from Tan Son Nhut—the main news story of the day, an article on a related development, a personality profile of a figure in the news that day, and an analysis for the "News of the Week in Review" section of the Sunday *Times*. The *Times'* foreign news editor in 1963, Emanuel Freedman, and his senior copy desk editor, Nathaniel Gerstenzang, were clerkly men who had never been reporters. They had no sense of the tensions under which Halberstam was working, and instead of seeing Halberstam's strengths, they saw his chronic shortcomings as a journalist—his run-on sentences, his mixed-up syntax, and his cabling at greater length than they thought a story warranted. Their own predilection for neatness led them to focus on the weaknesses, and so did the complaints from the copy desk editors, who had to struggle every evening to ready Halberstam's dispatches for print. ·

Strengthened by the irritation, the doubts came out in a rush when Marguerite Higgins arrived in Saigon and began to contradict everything Halberstam was saying. The foreign news desk badgered him with cables about her stories, the inquiries implying that she might be right and that he ought to hedge or correct what he had been reporting. Halberstam was furious and heartsick that after all these months his own editors did not believe him. He lost his temper completely. "Gerstenzang, if you mention that woman's name to me one more time I will resign repeat resign and I mean it repeat mean it," he cabled in response to yet another maddening inquiry. The New York editors did not want to transfer Halberstam out of Saigon or have him resign while the paper might be accused of moral cowardice, and so the inquiries about Miss Higgins's stories stopped, but the doubts remained.

A measure of how low Halberstam's credibility was with his New York editors—and how high they held the credibility of government in 1963—came in late August when the regime staged a series of mass arrests and the U.S. Embassy and the CIA station gave the administration a version that was the opposite of what Halberstam reported. The State Department released the official version in Washington. The New York editors wanted to print the official version on the front page and to put Halberstam's story inside the paper. His patron on the *Times* and the man who had hired him, Scotty Reston, then running the Washington bureau as well as writing his column, stopped them. He argued that they should not second-guess the man in the field. He persuaded them to run both versions side by side on the front page under the same headline with a statement below the headline explaining that the conflict reflected "the confused situation in South Vietnam." The *Times* had never done anything like that before. Three days later other events forced the State Department to admit that the official version had been wrong.

Halberstam's personal behavior upset Catledge and Daniel in New York as much as the adversarial quality of his reporting. They heard about it through the newspaper grapevine and through informal complaints from officials in the State Department and the Pentagon. Adolph Ochs, the man who bought a bankrupt newspaper in 1896 and founded the modern *New York Times*, had consciously imitated *The Times* of London to the extent of creating a paper that provided respectable, as well as comprehensive and reliable, news. ("All the News That's *Fit* to Print.") In the early 1960s the newspaper as an institution still reflected the spirit of the apocryphal story of the English butler informing his titled employer that half a dozen reporters have arrived to interview him: "My lord, there are five men from the press waiting and a gentleman from *The Times*." The *New York Times* did not attempt to control the private lives of its correspondents. The paper did want them to behave in public with a certain decorum. *Times* men were not supposed to carry on in Halberstam's tempestuous manner.

We all personalized the struggle, but Halberstam personalized it more than anyone else. While everyone felt contempt for Harkins, the rest of us observed civility and were polite to him. Halberstam was openly contemptuous. At the annual Fourth of July reception at the embassy residence, he refused to shake hands with the general, embarrassing Harkins, who was accustomed to a world where one concealed one's hostilities.

Richard Holbrooke, who was to become the youngest man ever to hold the office of assistant secretary of state for Far Eastern affairs, in the Carter administration fourteen years later at the age of thirty-five, remembered Halberstam on the subject of Harkins at dinner in a French restaurant in Saigon one night in the summer of 1963. Holbrooke was then a freshman Foreign Service officer assigned to a southern Delta province as a pacification advisor. Several of us had invited him to join us at one of the late dinners we often had after a long day. Halberstam began holding forth on what a swine Harkins was for faking reports and throwing away American and Vietnamese lives. As he talked he got angrier and his voice rose. He raised his big fist, banged it down on the table, and shouted his prosecutorial summation: "Paul D. Harkins should be court-martialed and shot!" Holbrooke looked slowly around the restaurant to see if anyone at another table might know him.

There were no American conventions to restrain our confrontation with the regime. The Ngo Dinhs wanted to beat the monks and the Buddhist faithful who took to the streets with them, as Madame Nhu said, but they wanted to do their beating in the dark. The presence of foreign reporters gave the Buddhist leaders hope that if they continued their campaign, sympathetic officers in the ARVN might eventually move against the regime, or the revulsion in the United States and the rest of the world might drive the Kennedy administration into encouraging a coup. They knew by July that peace with the family, which had always seemed to be impossible, was certainly impossible now, and if enforced tranquillity was restored they would be imprisoned one by one. The monks and their ever-growing number of followers were, in any case, prepared to die to bring down the regime. "There is blood on the orange robes," a monk would cry with one of the battery-powered portable loudspeakers which, along with mimeograph machines to print pamphlets, these antique-looking figures quickly caught on to using. The crowd would shout back its willingness to shed more for the cause.

The Ngo Dinhs did not understand that each act of repression bred more followers for the Buddhists. They did understand that photographs, television film, and news stories of the repression and the fiery suicides were the worst kind of publicity for their interests. When the moment of truth came at a demonstration the monks and nuns and their lay followers would kneel in prayer on the pavement. The companies of special Combat Police in helmets and camouflage uniforms, trained and armed by the CIA to hunt down guerrillas in the hamlets, would storm into the kneeling figures, kicking and flailing. They would grab the girls in the white *ao dais* by their long black hair and smash their faces with billy clubs and pistol butts before tossing them into trucks to haul them off to jail. The family was reluctant to expel us as a group for fear of an outcry in Congress that might disrupt the military and economic aid on which the South depended and trigger a coup by desperate ARVN officers. They decided to try to frighten us into staying away from the demonstrations.

We were waiting for a scheduled demonstration to begin at one of the small pagodas in the city on the morning of July 7 when half a dozen plainclothesmen from the Sûreté jumped the AP's Peter Arnett. The place was perfect for an ambush, because we were crowded, with the plainclothesmen and the uniformed Saigon police, into a narrow dirt alley that led from the main street to the pagoda. The Sûreté men threw Arnett to the ground so that they could kick him in the kidneys with the pointed-toe shoes they wore in the Saigon-French fashion of the day. Halberstam charged with a bellow before they had an opportunity to hurt Arnett seriously. He knocked and tossed the lightly built Vietnamese aside and stood over Arnett, his grizzly-bear shoulders hunched and his great fists poised, yelling: "Get back, get back, you sons of bitches, or I'll beat the shit out of you." Several of us who were close to Arnett pulled him to his feet. Malcolm Browne managed to take a photograph of Arnett standing behind Halberstam for protection a moment later, just before another plainclothesman sneaked up behind Browne and smashed his camera with a rock. The rock did not damage the film inside. The Sûreté men backed off. They apparently had orders not to use clubs, and they decided Halberstam was too much for them hand to hand. The uniformed police did not intervene to protect us. Arnett escaped with some cuts and bruises.

He and Browne were summoned to a precinct headquarters the next day and interrogated for four hours before being released. The interrogators kept alleging that they had "attacked" the Sûreté men. Several sources in the regime explained that the family was now considering the possibility of exploiting the incident to arrest Arnett and Browne and prosecute them for assault. The CIA picked up the same report from the police. A number of the regular visitors like Kalischer of CBS had also been in the alley leading to the pagoda and had seen the beating. They joined us in a telegram of protest to President Kennedy. The president responded by sending out Robert Manning, a former *Time* correspondent who was then assistant secretary of state for public affairs. A friendly, patient man who was to become editor-in-chief of *Atlantic Monthly* after his tour in government, Manning listened to our complaints about the assault and our other grievances and persuaded Diem not to proceed with any charges.

The family temporarily stopped beating reporters and switched to the more sinister tactic of threatening assassination. With the Ngo Dinhs, especially Nhu and his wife, one could never be certain whether they were bluffing in a war of nerves or meant to carry out the threat. When Madame Nhu told an English correspondent, "Halberstam should be barbecued, and I would be glad to supply the fluid and the match," one could know that her wish, at least, was genuine.

Our first tip came from the police. The disaffection that had spread through most of the bureaucracy had also touched them. They would still execute orders from the palace to keep their jobs, but many were fearful of the future and, despite their acquaintanceship with moral filth, guilt-ridden. At a demonstration one day in late July a plainclothesman walked up to the Vietnamese television cameraman who worked for me, taking film for UPI Movietone News. "Tell your boss to be careful when he goes out at night," he said. "We may get orders to kill him and make it look like the VC did it."

By this time Nguyen Ngoc Rao, the Vietnamese reporter in the UPI bureau, had developed excellent police sources. They told him that the Nhus had drawn up an assassination list. It included a number of reporters and senior ARVN officers and civilian Vietnamese intelligence officials who were considered disloyal and potential coup plotters. The Nhus were serious, the police said, and they might soon be instructed to carry out the killings. Halberstam and I were on the list. As they had nothing against us personally, the police officials advised Rao to warn us to take precautions. A couple of CIA sources passed along the same information, saying that several of their people were also on the list because the Nhus suspected them of fomenting plots.

Halberstam and I were still reluctant to accept the threat as genuine, because we were already living with so much tension, when one of the Vietnamese intelligence officers on the list (he was ostensibly the regime's deputy director general of information) confirmed it for us. He was a bachelor and a womanizer who frequented a nightclub that was a hangout for some of Saigon's gangsters. They said they had been hired by the Nhus to conduct possible assassinations and that he was one of their potential targets. Would he please be careful, the gangsters said. He was a friend and they would not like to have to kill him.

The White House announced in July that Henry Cabot Lodge, Jr., would replace Frederick Nolting as ambassador at the end of the summer. By the time Nolting departed in mid-August, the broadcasts of "Radio Catinat"—as Saigon's rumor mill was called for the gossip gatherings in the coffee shops and cafés of the main street—said that the arrival of Lodge meant an end to the U.S. policy of supporting the Ngo Dinhs. "I do not think that Mr. Cabolodge will be President Diem's cup of tea," the witty monk who was the press spokesman for the Buddhist leadership said to Halberstam in his best pronunciation of Lodge's name. On Sunday, August 18, the Buddhists displayed their mounting strength as if to impress the soon-to-arrive Lodge through the news reports. They assembled about 15,000 people at the main Xa Loi Pagoda, one of the largest and most enthusiastic crowds they had ever summoned, for hours of speeches by the monks denouncing the regime for its tyranny and its outrages against Vietnamese Buddhism. Prayers alternated with the speeches, and occasionally the monks broke the tension with a favorite intermission—a scurrilous joke about Madame Nhu. This time the palace did not order the police to intervene, despite the provocation, and the demonstration ended peacefully.

The restraint was ominous. Two nights later, half an hour after midnight on the 20th, Diem and Nhu took a brutal gamble to end the Buddhist crisis in a stroke and force the Kennedy administration and "Mr. Cabolodge" to drink their cup of tea. Thousands of police and ARVN Special Forces troops simultaneously assaulted the pagodas in Saigon, Hue, and the other cities and towns where the Buddhists were strongest. Thanks to Mert Perry's ability to understand French, Halberstam and I reached the main Xa Loi Pagoda with the raiders. Perry and his wife, Darlene, lived in the apartment just above mine, and we shared the same phone number. (Telephones were scarce in Saigon in 1963.) An anonymous tipster, probably a police or intelligence officer, called shortly before midnight. Perry had just undressed for bed. The caller asked for me. Perry said that I was not there. (I had dropped off Halberstam after checking the pagodas with him and was on my way back in one of the city's little rattletrap Renault taxis.) "Tell him they will arrest all of the monks right after midnight," the tipster said in French.

Perry shouted the message down to me as I was climbing out of the taxi a moment later. I jumped back inside and yelled at the driver to race for Halberstam's house. He had no phone at home. There was a police precinct headquarters a couple of blocks before his house. When the taxi passed it I could see that the floodlit compound was filled with the U.S. Army model two-and-a-half-ton trucks the military aid program provided and that soldiers in battle gear and police were climbing into them. We met the raiding convoy a few minutes later as the trucks were pulling out of the compound and starting for Xa Loi and the taxi, with Halberstam now inside, came hurtling back in the same direction. By gesturing to the driver and shouting at him in a mixture of French and pidgin Vietnamese, Halberstam and I browbeat him into slipping the tiny Renault between the second and third trucks in the convoy. He was understandably terrified. We assumed that the police at the tail end of the convoy would block the street as soon as the trucks reached the pagoda.

The raid on Xa Loi, like those on the pagodas elsewhere in South Vietnam, was flawlessly executed. It reminded me of a scene from a movie of the French Resistance—the scene when the Gestapo arrive at the Resistance hideout in Paris. As the drivers of the trucks in our convoy slammed to a stop beside the pagoda compound, two more convoys converged on the place from opposite directions. The police and troops in the trucks vaulted to the pavement, and the officers shouted orders and formed up their units. The gong at the top of the pagoda started to clang an alarm into the night. The monks added to this din of helplessness by beating on pots and pans. The police battered open the pagoda gate and then squads of ARVN Special Forces troops, in trim camouflage fatigues and berets, with submachine guns held high, pranced up before the gate to lead the assault.

The ARVN Special Forces were another creation of the CIA that the Ngo Dinhs had turned to their private purpose. The CIA had trained and armed this elite unit for commando operations against the guerrillas and for forays into Laos and the North. The Ngo Dinhs had always had another goal in mind, which explained why the ARVN Special Forces had been held back and never employed effectively against the Viet Cong. The family had hoodwinked the CIA into forming a Praetorian Guard for them. They had made certain that the Special Forces troops were recruited mainly from Central and North Vietnamese Catholic families and had put them under command of a man they trusted absolutely, Lt. Col. Le Quang Tung, another Central Vietnamese Catholic.

There was enough illumination from the streetlamps and the headlights of the trucks for Halberstam and me to see the shoulder patches of the troops from the convoys as they assembled. None of them were regular ARVN soldiers or paratroopers. They were all Tung's men. Diem and Nhu did not trust the regular army for this internal cleansing. For this work they were using their household troops. Colonel Tung was literally a man of their household. He had been a family servant of the Ngo Dinhs before becoming a noncom in the French Expeditionary Corps. Diem had given him his officer's commission. The rest of the raiders were the Combat Police the CIA had also created, in their own distinctive camouflage uniforms, and the French holdovers—the ordinary, white-uniformed National Police.

An officer shouted a command, and the first of the prancing squads charged through the pagoda gate, followed by more Special Forces troops and police. The crash of breaking glass began, and the splintering of doors giving way to boot heels and the butts of submachine guns. Shots interspersed with the screams of the monks being dragged from their rooms, and there were bursts of automatic-weapons fire from other Special Forces troops stationed behind the pagoda who were shooting BARs to stop any of the monks from escaping over the rear wall. Trucks with canopies of dark green canvas erected over the beds to conceal the cargo backed up to the gate. The police hurled figures in orange robes inside. When one truck was filled and pulled away for Saigon's Chi Hoa Prison, another backed up in its place.

The drama went on for two hours, because some of the monks barricaded themselves in their rooms with stacks of furniture. Two monks managed to escape over the rear wall despite the bullets from the BARs and took shelter in a U.S.-owned building right next to the pagoda. It was the four-story Saigon headquarters of AID. The most militant of the Buddhist leaders, Thich Tri Quang (Thich is the Vietnamese honorific for a monk), who had organized the first protest meeting in Hue and who knew that he was marked for death, stole out of the pagoda just before the raid with two fellow monks and went into hiding. Approximately 1,400 monks and nuns at Xa Loi and other pagodas in South Vietnam were arrested that night, including some lay followers who had gone to the pagodas as an act of faith. Thirty of the monks at Xa Loi were wounded, and seven were never heard from again. They were apparently killed and their bodies disposed of secretly. The raids were bloodiest in Hue. About thirty monks and student followers were shot or clubbed to death there, and the great statue of Buddha in Hue's main Tu Dam Pagoda was smashed.

Diem declared martial law. He put Saigon under Brig. Gen. Ton That Dinh, a boisterous ex-French paratrooper, given to Scotch and loyal to the Ngo Dinhs. A 9:00 P.M. curfew was imposed. The troops and police had orders to shoot to kill anyone on the streets after curfew who did not have a pass and tried to flee arrest. Under the cover of night and curfew the police ransacked houses and apartments and rounded up more suspected opponents of the regime. Fear was as tangible in Saigon as touching one's skin. The dissident intelligence officer who had passed on the warning from his gangster acquaintances—and who was involved in an abortive coup plot and had arranged for Halberstam to witness the coup from its command post if the plot went forward—fled for his life. A lycée classmate who owned several freighters shipped him to Yokohama with a load of fertilizer.

Halberstam and I no longer dared to sleep at home. We slept every night for the next three weeks at the house of John Mecklin, the USIS chief, who was kind enough to give us shelter. I took Nguyen Ngoc Rao to Mecklin's house with me. He had courageously refused to quit and hide, despite pleas from his family. While Mecklin's house did not have diplomatic immunity, it was U.S. property, and we assumed that at night we were safer there from arrest or worse. Tran Van Chuong, Madame Nhu's father and the regime's ambassador in Washington, resigned, announcing that now there was "not one chance in a hundred for victory" over the Communists with his daughter and her husband and brother-in-law in power. Her mother, Saigon's official observer at the UN, resigned with him, as did most of the embassy staff.

The press spokesman for the Foreign Ministry, who never had anything to announce, telephoned in hysteria. The foreign minister, a meek man named Vu Van Mau, had also resigned, shaved his head like a monk, and asked Diem for permission to go on a pilgrimage to India. Diem gave consent. The press and the diplomatic corps assembled at Tan Son Nhut to see him off. He never arrived. Nhu had General Dinh arrest Mau on his way to the airport. Another general persuaded Dinh to put the former foreign minister under house arrest, not in a cell, and to let him keep his passport. "Tomorrow you may be given the order to have me arrested," the other general said to Dinh. "Be good to me, eh? Get me a nice cell and put a pretty girl in it."

The Saigon University students rioted. Hundreds were beaten and arrested. Diem closed the university. (He had already closed the South's other university at Hue because of demonstrations there.) The high school students then rioted. The schools that rioted first were the best Vietnamese high schools, many of the students the sons and daughters of civil servants and military officers.

At Trung Vuong, a famous girls' school, the police were met in the yard by long lines of young ladies, dressed in the pale blue *ao dai* that was their school uniform, holding hands and chanting in high-pitched voices: "*Da Dao* Ngo Dinh Diem!" (Down with Ngo Dinh Diem!), "*Da Dao* Ngo Dinh Nhu!" "*Da Dao* Tran Le Xuan!" (Madame Nhu in the insulting form of her maiden name). The boys were violent. They smashed the windows with their desks and chairs and hung banners on the outside walls that were more explicit in their insults to Madame Nhu.

The Ngo Dinhs proceeded to arrest the children of the people who ran the country for them. One morning the trucks hauled more than 1,000 high school students off to jail. As the police burst into the school-yards, jeeps and staff cars would pull up and officers would dash in and try to rescue their children. This prolonged suicide of the dynasty that Lansdale had founded became a theater of the bizarre. At a high school one morning a plainclothesman was pushing a boy toward a van and kicking him hard. A senior police officer in uniform went manic at the sight. He grabbed the plainclothesman and beat him wildly with a truncheon. Diem closed the high schools too.

General Dinh boasted in French to Lou Conein, his old CIA acquaintance from earlier years: "I, Dinh, am a great national hero. I have defeated the American, Cabot Lodge. He was on his way here to pull a coup d'état, but I, Dinh the hero, have foiled him."

He arrived at Tan Son Nhut in a drizzling rain two nights after the raids on the pagodas. He looked a bit old-fashioned when the door of the plane opened and he emerged into the glare of the television spotlights with a straw hat in his hand. As he walked down the steps of the gangway, one saw that he was too long of limb at nearly six feet three inches to be called lanky. He was, rather, the lean and angular man that popular legend said New England Yankees were supposed to be. His profile was cut precisely, the jaw pronounced, the nose large and slightly hooked. Sixty-one years had rounded his shoulders, brought his neck and head forward, and grayed his hair. Otherwise one could still recognize the man in the photographs of his prime—the freshman senator from Massachusetts in 1936, the one Republican star in Franklin Roosevelt's landslide against Alfred Landon; the Army lieutenant colonel on the Western Front in World War II; a leading Republican senator of the postwar era, the national political strategist who had persuaded Eisenhower to run for president and had been Ike's campaign manager in 1952; Eisenhower's ambassador to the United Nations when the post had truly been second in rank and prestige to that of the secretary of state; the man Eisenhower had trusted to escort Nikita Khrushchev on his historic tour of the United States in 1959; and then what had seemed an unsatisfactory end to his public life, Nixon's running mate in the 1960 election against Kennedy.

The straw hat was a clue to the man. Henry Cabot Lodge, Jr., was an anachronism in American public life by the 1960s—a man of character and lineage with independent political stature. He had modeled himself on the grandfather after whom he had been named, Senator Henry Cabot Lodge, Republican senator from Massachusetts for thirty-one years, closest friend and collaborator of Theodore Roosevelt, and one of the founders of the American empire. If any two men could claim principal responsibility for the seizure of the Philippines and the transformation of the United States into a power abroad, the elder Lodge and Theodore Roosevelt would be those two men. Lodge's grandfather had been at his most brilliant as an orator when he had been calling the country to its new destiny on the eve of the war with Spain that had started the imperial venture. The Senate galleries would fill to hear him speak. He had been the author of the famous description of the commencement: "It has been a splendid little war." It was yet another irony of this war in Vietnam that sixty-five years after that beginning the grandson of one of the founders should be sent to Saigon to resolve a major crisis of the overseas order, a crisis that was eventually to challenge the American role in the world that the grandfather had initiated and the grandson had helped bring to maturity.

Halberstam and I and the other correspondents would have felt less beleaguered had we been privy to the secret debate in Washington. We did not realize that our dispatches had been arming Averell Harriman, who had moved up to become under secretary of state for political affairs, and Roger Hilsman, who had replaced Harriman in the Far Eastern affairs post at State, in their attempt to persuade Kennedy to authorize the overthrow of Diem and his family. We would have been still more encouraged had we known how much our reporting—and Vann's view of the war as it was reflected in that reporting—had contributed to shaping the judgment of this man who was to take the power of the United States into his hands in Vietnam in the late summer and fall of 1963 and wield it as he saw fit.

Shortly after his arrival, Halberstam, Browne, and I were invited to have lunch, individually, with the new ambassador and his wife, Emily, a lady from the Boston merchant family of Sears, whose sprightliness and wit leavened the marriage. We were told that the lunches were to be private, that Mr. Lodge wanted our "advice." When my turn came he questioned me about the regime, the Buddhist crisis, and the war for about an hour at the table and over coffee afterward in the drawing room of the embassy residence. He put the questions matter-of-factly. I watched his face to see what he thought of the answers, but his expression stayed blandly uncommunicative. I told him, in sum, that the Ngo Dinhs were so mad and hated that they were incapable of governing, that the Viet Cong were gaining rapidly in the countryside, and that if Diem and his family stayed in power the war was certain to be lost. If they were replaced by a military regime there was no guarantee that a junta of generals would do better, but there was hope that they might. With the Ngo Dinhs one could look forward only to defeat.

We had been warned that Lodge was to do the questioning, that we were not to attempt to pry anything out of him. I did not want to leave, however, without obtaining something. "And what's your impression, Mr. Ambassador?" I asked as it was time to go.

He was sitting on the couch beside his wife, his legs crossed lazily and his arm extended behind her. He smiled. "About the same as yours," he said.

I was skeptical of his proffered frankness. I wondered if this was more flattery, as inviting reporters in their twenties to give "advice" to Henry Cabot Lodge had been, regardless of how sincerely he might be seeking information.

In retrospect, I was wrong to be skeptical, and the other reporters and I soon ceased to be. Lodge's public behavior and the secret cables in the Pentagon Papers disclose that he had virtually made up his mind before he arrived. "We are launched on a course from which there is no respectable turning back: the overthrow of the Diem government," he told Kennedy in a top-secret cable just a week after he landed in the rain at Tan Son Nhut and prior to any luncheon interrogations. He gave the president the "fundamental" reason that the United States could not shrink from this intimidating business: "There is no possibility, in my view, that the war can be won under a Diem administration."

Our reporting and Vann's investment in it might have been wasted on most of the other important figures in the U.S. government. The effort had not been wasted on Lodge. The explanation was not that he had spent most of his twenties as a reporter and editorial writer, first for the *Boston Transcript* and then for the *New York Herald Tribune*. The explanation was in the peculiar mix of the man—the self-containment of the aristocrat, the sensitivity of the politician to human factors, and a perspective on the military leaders of the 1960s that reached back into the pre–World War II era. Unlike Kennedy, McNamara, and Rusk, he did not think that these generals were necessarily more competent to judge wars than he was. Taylor and Harkins, an old military acquaintance of Lodge's as another Bostonian, had been his contemporaries in the Army. He had followed the martial tradition of his family by joining the Cavalry Reserve in Boston in 1923, had gone on maneuvers every summer, and had progressed with the Army of the '20s and '30s from horses to the tanks of Patton's new 2nd Armored Division in the maneuvers of 1941. He had been in the first tank fighting of the war to involve Americans in mid-1942 when Marshall and Eisenhower had arranged for him to lead an exploratory mission to the British Eighth Army in Libya and Rommel had unexpectedly attacked. Henry Stimson, the secretary of war, had managed to keep Lodge in the Senate as the Army's unofficial representative there until the beginning of 1944. With the battle for Europe coming, Lodge had been unable to resist any longer. He had resigned his seat to serve as a lieutenant colonel, the first senator to do so since the Civil War. After World War II he had maintained his interest in military affairs and in 1963 was a major general in the active reserve.

Lodge had been assured in briefings at the Pentagon and at Admiral Felt's headquarters in Honolulu that the reporters were contriving stories about flaws in the Saigon forces and Viet Cong gains. He had thought it unlikely that reporters as a group would consistently invent such information. He had also decided that a regime as grotesque as Diem's in its political behavior could not be expected to win a war. He had known that his invitations to lunch would flatter. He went out of his way in his dealings with all of the reporters to gain as good a press as possible for himself. He had also been interrogating us to take our measure and to see if we had anything of further use to him in the enterprise he had begun.

He was two months bringing his task to fruition. Publicly, he isolated Diem and his family and made them vulnerable to a coup by implying repeatedly in word and gesture that the United States, in the person of Henry Cabot Lodge, would like nothing better than to see them overthrown. On his first morning in Saigon he insulted the Ngo Dinhs by ostentatiously driving to the AID headquarters next to the Xa Loi Pagoda where the two monks were sheltering, telling them they were welcome, and ordering fresh vegetables bought daily for the vegetarian diet to which Buddhist monks adhere. When the chief Buddhist leader, Tri Quang, and the two other monks who had slipped out of Xa Loi and into hiding with him ahead of the raids ran into the embassy lobby a couple of days later and asked for asylum, Lodge granted it to them and gave them a new conference room as temporary living quarters.

Secretly, Lodge put Lou Conein to work as his liaison to three dissident ARVN generals. To remove the Ngo Dinhs, Lodge utilized some of the same senior ARVN officers whom Conein had worked with at Lansdale's direction in 1955 to install Diem as America's man in Saigon. They had been colonels then, and Diem had made them generals for coming over to his side. He and his family had later alienated them. They were all members of the small Franco-Vietnamese elite the colonial system had created and had been French citizens until 1955. They would have left with the French Expeditionary Corps had they not been encouraged by American power and money and its representatives like

Lansdale and Conein to stay and attempt to preserve in the South the colonial society in which they had been reared.

The leader of the plot was the second-ranking general in the ARVN, Maj. Gen. Duong Van Minh, forty-seven, "Big Minh" as he was called for his six-foot build. He was from a well-to-do Southern family, born at My Tho, and had attended the best French lycée in Saigon as a youth, Jean Jacques Rousseau, the same school where Prince Sihanouk of Cambodia had been educated. Prior to 1945 he had belonged to the exclusive group of fifty Vietnamese who held a commission in the French Army. Minh's height and broad shoulders were not the only reason for his unusual appearance. His two upper front teeth had been broken by the interrogators of the Kempeitai, the dreaded Japanese military police, when the Imperial Army suddenly disarmed the Vichy French forces in Indochina in 1945. He refused to have the teeth replaced. In early 1955, during the street fighting with the Binh Xuyen and the maneuvering of the pro–Bao Dai officers to oust Lansdale's man, Minh had been able to help Diem as commanding officer of the Saigon garrison. Later he had been put in charge of destroying the army of the Hoa Hao sect in the Delta. By 1963, Diem had sidetracked him into the fictitious post of military advisor to the president. ("Since Diem accepts no advice, Minh has lots of time to scheme," Colonel Dong remarked.)

Minh's most important associate in the plot was another officer who had rallied to Diem's support at Lansdale's and Conein's behest in the spring of 1955 and who had been more adept at holding some of Diem's trust in the intervening years—Maj. Gen. Tran Van Don, forty-six, chief of staff of the ARVN in 1963. Don was the unusually handsome son of an aristocratic family; he had been born in France, near Bordeaux, and had attended the Hautes Etudes Commerciales in Paris before World War II and the French Army.

Don's brother-in-law, Brig. Gen. Le Van Kim, forty-five, was the third plotter. Kim had been a general without an assignment for nearly three years by 1963, having been fired as head of the Military Academy by Diem on suspicion of complicity in the abortive 1960 paratrooper coup. He had studied mathematics and philosophy in Marseilles, joined the French Army in 1939, fought against the Germans, and then been commissioned after the war. His bookish manner had given Kim a reputation as the intellectual of the ARVN.

Lodge had a talent for selecting subordinates with the credentials to perform a particular task for him. In Conein he had the perfect liaison to the plotters. These men trusted Conein as they would not have trusted another CIA agent. He was an old comrade, and his French birth fortified the relationship. When he was with them he saw that his French side came out, because he lived in both cultures in spirit and he knew that it put them at ease. Conein had been bored for the last several years with his job as pacification advisor to the Ministry of the Interior, and from his vantage point the stakes were far higher this time than in 1955. Few secret agents are ever given an opportunity to scale the professional summit by arranging the overthrow of a government. Conein was transmitting the power of the United States to influence these generals to do its bidding. The clandestine meetings, the passing back and forth of messages between Lodge and the plotters, the coaxing along of the generals, all had the emotional lift of a strong amphetamine. Lives were being risked, including Conein's, and, he believed, the destinies of two nations were in the balance.

Harkins was opposed to a coup. He did not want to disrupt the war he thought he was winning. He regarded Diem as a satisfactory local ruler and viewed the Buddhist crisis as a passing intrigue. The raids on the pagodas were an unfortunate loss of temper. The Nhus were to blame for the raids, and Diem might be coaxed into parting with them in time. Harkins had other allies in Washington besides Taylor. McNamara and Rusk also saw the situation essentially as he did.

Lodge knew that he would lose if he confronted Harkins and the system, despite the additional weight with Kennedy that his independent political stature gave him. He therefore handled Harkins by indirection, and Harkins, who thought himself a master bureaucrat, was outwitted at his game. Lodge was always polite in his personal dealings with Harkins, and when he had to refer to him in a cable he called him "a splendid general and an old friend of mine." He then hid from Harkins his cables to Washington about Conein's meetings with the generals (sent for greater security through the CIA's separate communications system) until it was too late for Harkins to interfere effectively. Minh and Don helped Lodge by confusing Harkins even then as to whether there was a plot. Because they were afraid that he would betray them to Diem, they lied and told the general they were not planning a coup. Lodge also undercut Harkins's judgment on the war. He sent Kennedy independent assessments (again without copies to the general) that contradicted Harkins's optimism. Once more Lodge was careful not to confront. He did not assert baldly that the war was being lost. He said this by filling his reports with the bad news that Harkins was suppressing and by letting others say it for him. The plotters were of help here too. These Saigon generals knew they were losing the war, which was another reason they were so eager to overthrow the Ngo Dinhs. On September

19, Lodge sent a top-secret cable marked "for President only" giving Minh's view that

> the Viet Cong are steadily gaining in strength; have more of the population on their side than has the GVN [Government of Vietnam—the Saigon regime]; that arrests are continuing and that the prisons are full; that more and more students are going over to the Viet Cong; that there is great graft and corruption in the Vietnamese administration of our aid; and that the "Heart of the Army is *not* in the war." [Emphasis Lodge's]

This assessment by "Vietnamese No. 1 general" (Minh was considered by Americans, including Harkins, to be the most professional of the Saigon generals) was being "echoed" by Diem's faithful acting minister of defense, Nguyen Dinh Thuan, "who wants to leave the country," Lodge went on to tell Kennedy. He also warned in other cables against Harkins's claim that Diem was a good man who was being victimized by the Nhus and might eventually be persuaded to rid the regime of them. He pointed out that the brothers did not see the world differently and that Diem was convinced he needed Nhu's skill at manipulating the police and intelligence services in order to keep the army in check. Diem "wishes he had more Nhus, not less," Lodge said.

Kennedy was uncertain and wavered. He had virtually no understanding of political and social revolution in modern Asia and little feeling for the realities of counterguerrilla warfare. He feared a wave of Communist-inspired guerrilla wars in the underdeveloped countries and was determined to build a capability to crush them, but he lacked knowledge of what he feared. Had he possessed sensitivity on the subject, he would have stopped Harkins and Anthis from bombing and shelling the Vietnamese peasantry. He was constantly issuing instructions and suggestions for counterguerrilla warfare to the Army through his military aide, Maj. Gen. Chester Clifton, Jr. His ideas never went much beyond employing Special Forces men, popularly known as Green Berets because of their headgear, in "Terry and the Pirates" ventures and the sort of technological gimmickry and superspy intrigues that filled the James Bond novels he liked to read. It was Kennedy who had given the Special Forces their romantic headgear to mark them as the shock troops of his "wars in the shadows."

At a National Security Council meeting at the White House on Friday, September 6, 1963, he accepted a suggestion from McNamara to fly Krulak out in a jet to "get the facts" and report back to the NSC by Tuesday. Hilsman interjected that a State Department representative should also go along for an independent viewpoint. Kennedy agreed. McNamara tried to outsmart Hilsman by putting Krulak in the air to Vietnam within minutes of the end of the meeting. Hilsman telephoned and made him hold the plane until he could get his man, Joseph Mendenhall, the former political counselor of the embassy, out to Andrews Air Force Base near Washington. The plane was a windowless Boeing 707, an Air Force tanker version of the four-engine passenger jet, converted for the ferrying of important men by the installation of desks and bunks. The type had been nicknamed the McNamara Special because of the secretary's fondness for fly-and-sprint trips. Twenty thousand miles and four days later Krulak and Mendenhall read diametrically opposed reports to another NSC meeting at the White House on Tuesday, September 10.

"You two did visit the same country, didn't you?" Kennedy asked.

"I can explain it, Mr. President," Krulak said. "Mr. Mendenhall visited the cities and I visited the countryside and the war is in the countryside."

"I want to see you after this in my office," Kennedy said to Krulak.

McNamara accompanied Krulak into the Oval Office when the meeting had ended. The president looked up from something he was reading. "I just wanted you to know that I understand," he said to Krulak, indicating by his manner that he was preoccupied and did not wish to talk. Krulak and McNamara left. In the limousine on the way back to the Pentagon, McNamara and Taylor were pleased. They interpreted Kennedy's remark in the Oval Office as meaning: "I understand what happened and I agree with you." Krulak was also happy. He interpreted the president's remark similarly and was convinced that he had put down Mendenhall.

Kennedy may have agreed with Krulak, but he sent McNamara and Taylor to Vietnam two weeks later for more "facts." One of Lodge's independent assessments may have prompted him, perhaps the cable relaying Minh's frightening views. By the end of September, when the jet carrying McNamara and Taylor lifted off from Tan Son Nhut with another report for Kennedy, one could drive down to My Tho and see the ghosts of the strategic hamlets along the road. The lines of steel fence posts with shreds of chopped-off barbed wire hanging from the notches announced who owned most of this main route into the Delta. From a helicopter the sense of the guerrillas' power was greater and the sight of these ghost hamlets stranger. The rows of roofless houses looked like villages of play huts that children had erected and then whimsically abandoned.

McNamara and Taylor assured Kennedy that "the military campaign has made great progress and continues to progress," despite "serious political tensions in Saigon," and that the war would still be won by the end of 1965. Harkins should win it sooner in the rubber-plantation country and in the Highlands and the Central Coast provinces north of Saigon, they said in their top-secret memorandum of October 2. He should crush the Viet Cong there by the end of 1964. The slower progress in the Delta would delay the defeat of the guerrillas south of the capital until the end of 1965, and "it should be possible to withdraw the bulk of U.S. personnel by that time." They recommended pulling out 1,000 Americans by the end of 1963 in order to demonstrate how well the plans for victory were being implemented. The White House announced a forthcoming withdrawal of this first 1,000 men.

The president gained no peace of mind. The analysts at the CIA told him that Saigon's military position was deteriorating, and the State Department's Bureau of Intelligence and Research said that there had been "an unfavorable shift in the military balance" since July and that the regime would have been in trouble in the countryside even without the Buddhist crisis.

Kennedy showed how confused he was and how angry he had become at the messenger who most annoyed him when Arthur Ochs Sulzberger, who had recently become publisher of the *Times*, paid a courtesy call at the White House on October 22. As soon as the pleasantries were over Kennedy asked: "What do you think of your young man in Saigon?" Sulzberger said that he thought Halberstam was holding up well. "Don't you think he's too close to the story?" Kennedy asked. No, Sulzberger said, he did not. Kennedy pushed harder. Had Sulzberger thought about transferring Halberstam? he asked. Sulzberger said that he had no plans to do so. If Kennedy had not been so upset, he probably would not have taken such a crude approach. Sulzberger was reacting defensively, as publishers almost always do when their reporters are attacked. Catledge, the managing editor in New York who had been so upset by Halberstam, was with Sulzberger on the White House visit. He would have been happy to transfer Halberstam out of Saigon, but he could not do so while the paper might lose face.

Halberstam, without knowing that the president had personally requested his transfer, thought that the Ngo Dinhs were going to grant Kennedy's wish. He told Vann in a letter on October 29 that he suspected they would throw him out of Vietnam in a couple of weeks. His visa expired in mid-November. He was writing to thank Vann for having defended our reporting in letters to the editors of *Newsweek* and *Time*. (*Newsweek* published Vann's letter in its October 21, 1963, issue. *Time* declined to print it.) "We all still miss you and refer to you as the Bible," Halberstam wrote. "There's damn little joy in covering something which has such a sour meaning for your country," he said. "The brightest spot is Lodge, whose performance for my money has been near perfect. He's tough and intelligent and he has few illusions about this situation; he doesn't intend to see the U.S. kicked around, and he . . . doesn't think this Ngo outfit is worth a tinker's damn." The weaponry and firepower of the Viet Cong battalions in the Delta was getting "better and better . . . very ominous," Halberstam told Vann. "And watching a police state in action, particularly an American-financed one, is a sad experience. But we still have a chance, I guess, and I like the way Lodge handles himself."

Kennedy ended by deferring to Lodge's judgment. Lodge had exacted what he needed from McNamara and Taylor during their late-September visit. In response to his arguments they had conceded in their memorandum to Kennedy that "further repressive actions by Diem and Nhu could change the present favorable military trends" and had recommended the suspension of economic aid and the cutting off of military and CIA support for Tung's Special Forces as a way of exerting pressure for conciliation and reform. Lodge had wanted both measures in order to hold up the largest possible "Go" sign to the dissident generals. Kennedy decided on October 5 to let Lodge have his way. The plotting, which had been in hiatus, resumed in earnest. Kennedy asked only that Lodge guarantee him a successful coup, that he not be forced to endure the disgrace of another Bay of Pigs. Lodge would not mislead the president. He said that he thought the plot would succeed, but he could give no guarantee. "Should the coup fail," he cabled, "we will have to pick up the pieces as best we can at that time."

Diem and Nhu erected their own scaffold. Toward the end of October they discovered the plot that Lodge had been fomenting and decided to take advantage of it to spring a scheme they had conceived. They summoned General Dinh to the palace. He had continued to rule Saigon for them as its military governor since the sacking of the pagodas. The brothers instructed Dinh to draw up troop movement plans for a "false coup." The phony coup had two purposes. The long-range purpose was to scare the Americans out of ever again attempting to interfere with their rule. This objective was to be achieved by making the false coup appear to be a "neutralist coup." Since the surprise coup d'état in Laos in 1960 by Kong Le, the neutralist paratroop commander, Washington had feared the possibility of a similar occurrence in Saigon by some hostile or opportunistic group who would demand a U.S. withdrawal.

The demand would make a mockery of the American claim that the United States was in Vietnam at the invitation of a Vietnamese government to defend the South against "outside aggression." The National Liberation Front was calling for the replacement of the Ngo Dinhs by a neutralist coalition. Charles de Gaulle, then President of France, was also promoting the idea as a solution to the war. The Kennedy administration regarded it, accurately, as a face-saving arrangement for a takeover by Ho Chi Minh. Nhu had been playing on Washington's fear by feigning negotiations with Hanoi through Maneli, the senior Polish delegate to the ICSC, and the French ambassador. He had also been talking about the possibility of asking the Americans to withdraw and of turning South Vietnam into a country like Yugoslavia which would accept aid from both Communist and non-Communist nations.

Nhu had been mistaking for independence the slack in the string to which he and Diem were tied. He had not realized that his blackmail had played into Lodge's hands by further alarming Kennedy. When the brothers had sacked the pagodas they had put out a cover story to try to shift the blame from themselves by having Radio Saigon and the government press agency announce that the raids had been carried out by the army and that the generals had requested Diem to declare martial law. Under their false-coup scheme they were going to have the radio and their press agency announce the formation of a neutralist coalition and broadcast a demand that the United States pull out of the country. They would have Dinh occupy the streets and main public buildings with troops and armor and emerge and announce that they had saved South Vietnam by crushing a neutralist plot. During the confusion they planned to carry out the second and immediate purpose of their false coup—a small bloodbath. They were going to have Tung's Special Forces and Nhu's hired gangsters murder Minh, Don, Kim, and a number of other generals and senior ARVN officers they suspected of involvement in the plot, civilian accomplices of the generals like Diem's titular vice-president, Nguyen Ngoc Tho, and some Americans. They would later blame the killings on "neutralist and pro-Communist elements." How many and precisely which Americans were to be killed has never been ascertained. Lodge was supposed to have been marked, but there will never be any way of knowing. Conein was an obvious target, as Diem and Nhu had by now learned of his role in the plot. Nhu code-named the scheme Operation Bravo One.

What Diem and Nhu did not realize was that in drawing up the movement order for Bravo One, Dinh was actually bringing into Saigon the troops and tanks and armored personnel carriers to conduct a second scheme code-named Operation Bravo Two. Except for Cao, who sat in Can Tho in ignorance of the plot, Diem and Nhu had run out of generals. Their faithful Dinh—the same Dinh who had boasted two months earlier to his old CIA friend Conein that he had made himself "a great national hero" by foiling "the American, Cabot Lodge"—had turned traitor. Minh and Don had tricked Diem into offending him. They had told Dinh that he was a great national hero and that he should ask Diem to reward him by appointing him minister of the interior. When Dinh had tried to claim his reward, Diem had refused. (He and Nhu had already paid Dinh a large cash reward.) Dinh had gone off in a sulk and the plotters had then recruited him, promising him the ministry in their government. As insurance they also recruited the officers under him, so that they could shoot him and seize command of the troops and armor if he changed his mind at the last moment and tried to turn traitor on them.

Bravo Two began at 1:30 P.M. on November 1, 1963, with the storming of the National Police headquarters by a battalion of Saigon marines. Three hours later Diem telephoned Lodge from the palace. By the time of the call, which was tape-recorded, Diem knew enough to realize that his position was hopeless. Tan Son Nhut and all of the city other than the palace and the nearby Presidential Guards Barracks were in the hands of the coup forces. Diem had learned that Dinh was a traitor; that his other pillar, Tung, had been tricked into a meeting with the generals at JGS headquarters and shot; and that Cao was blocked from coming to the rescue with troops from Can Tho. Minh and Don had told Diem over the phone from JGS that they would give him and Nhu safe conduct out of the country if he surrendered and resigned the presidency. They had then put all of the other generals who had joined them on the line one by one so that he would understand the futility of resistance. They had also broadcast the offer over Radio Saigon. The offer might be a trick. If Diem surrendered, he and Nhu might be murdered. He would, however, save the lives of the soldiers holding out at the palace and the Presidential Guards Barracks.

"Some units have made a rebellion and I want to know, what is the attitude of the U.S.?" Diem asked Lodge.

The ambassador evaded the question. He told Diem, "I am worried about your physical safety," and asked a question himself: "I have a report that those in charge of the current activity offer you and your brother safe conduct out of the country if you resign. Had you heard this?"

Lodge had wanted the generals to make the safe-conduct offer in order to avoid the bad publicity of an assassination. His question carried a question within it that Diem could not have failed to hear after nine years of dealing with American and other foreign statesmen. By raising the safe-conduct offer in these circumstances, Lodge was extending the offer himself and saying that it was not a trick. The American ambassador was telling Diem that the U.S. government would fly him and his brother to safety if Diem would formally relinquish authority.

Diem gave Lodge an answer in the language of implication that statesmen use when they wish to say clearly what they do not want to say literally. No, Diem replied, he had not heard of the safe-conduct offer.

Lodge carefully left the offer open should Diem later change his mind. "If I can do anything for your physical safety, please call me," Lodge said.

"I am trying to reestablish order," Diem answered. He did not call back.

He was at the end what he had been at the beginning, a self-willed anachronism, an obstinate pseudo-mandarin lost in his reverie of an imaginary past. While there was life in his body he would never resign and abdicate the role of emperor that Lansdale had made it possible for him to assume. "After all, I am a chief of state," he said to Lodge earlier in their phone conversation. "I have tried to do my duty . . . I believe in duty above all."

The Presidential Guards Barracks was overrun before midnight in an assault by a paratroop battalion. The palace fell at dawn. Diem and Nhu had secretly fled from it during the night to hide in the house of a Chinese businessman in Cholon who had grown wealthy on their favors. The brothers apparently deluded themselves into thinking that Cao might still come to their rescue from the Delta. Cholon is on the south side of Saigon. The loyal Presidential Guards holding the palace had not realized until they discovered Diem's absence at dawn that they were dying for a shell. With the fall of the palace, the symbol of Diem's authority was also gone, and the value of his resignation fell accordingly.

He also angered Minh by telephoning early on the morning of November 2 to say that he would meet Minh at the palace to surrender and resign. The preparations for the abdication ceremony had been ready since the previous afternoon. The generals had a table set up and covered with a green baize cloth in a conference room in the main headquarters of the JGS compound. There was a chair waiting in front of it for Diem to sit in when he signed the document of resignation. Minh went to the palace. Diem failed to appear. Later in the morning the brothers were traced to a church in Cholon where they had gone to hear mass and were seized.

Minh had had enough of Diem's trickery, and he feared the fox alive. He decided that safe conduct for him was to murder both brothers. He sent his aide, a major, to be the executioner. The major shot them with his pistol while they were being brought to JGS inside an armored personnel carrier with their hands bound behind them. The soldiers mutilated Nhu's corpse by stabbing it repeatedly with bayonets.

For the first time in the history of the war, crowds in Saigon spontaneously cheered ARVN soldiers. Girls gave them bouquets of flowers. Men bought them beer and soda. Women carried pots of tea and food to the parks and schools where they were bivouacked.

Madame Nhu escaped because she was in the United States on a publicity tour to try to drum up support for the regime. She had been notably unsuccessful. Public opinion polls showed disapproval of her statements by thirteen to one. Lodge saw that her children, who were at the family's villa at the mountain resort of Dalat when the coup occurred, were protected and flown to her in Rome.

Diem's older brother, Archbishop Thuc, also escaped. The Vatican had called him to Rome in an effort to disassociate the church from the regime's behavior toward the Buddhists.

Can, the younger brother and overlord of Central Vietnam—the one member of the family who had vainly urged conciliating the monks— was not as fortunate. He took refuge in the U.S. Consulate in Hue with an airlines bag full of gold leaf and greenbacks. Lodge had him tricked out of the consulate and onto an American plane on the assumption that he would be flown to asylum in the Philippines. The plane stopped at Tan Son Nhut. Can was handed over to the generals. He was later shot by a firing squad. Cao thought that he was going to be shot too, but he was merely fired.

Lodge was not unhappy that Diem and Nhu had declined the offer of safe conduct out of the country. "What would we have done with them if they had lived?" he said to Halberstam. "Every Colonel Blimp in the world would have made use of them."

The hope that Halberstam had expressed in his letter to Vann three days before the coup was misplaced. The overthrow of the Ngo Dinhs came too late to save the Delta and to avert the catastrophe that Vann had feared. Within a week of the coup the Viet Cong launched an offensive across the entire northern half of the Delta and in the rubber-plantation provinces of the 5th Division above Saigon. There were also assaults of unprecedented scale in the southern half of the Delta, but these attracted less attention, because the Vietnamese Communists had already solidified so much of their control south of the Bassac. The temporary interruption in the line of authority from Saigon caused by the coup facilitated the offensive. The hiatus did not prompt the Viet Cong to strike the blow or explain the offensive's success. Ho and his associates had been building toward this opportunity over the ten months since Ap Bac (or more than a year if one took Vann's view that Saigon's decline had started in mid-October 1962, when Cao had begun faking operations), and the regime's position had been eroding all the while. The Hanoi leaders had scheduled the opening of the offensive independent of who was in office in Saigon. The National Liberation Front called it the Second Phase of the Ap Bac Emulation Drive. When the new Viet Cong battalions attacked the week after the coup, the structure of the regime in the countryside was like a beam that has been eaten from inside by wood-boring beetles. The instant the beam is stressed it snaps in two and reveals the powdered residue within.

The violence began suddenly, and it was unremitting. Outposts were being assaulted all over the place, hardly any stretch of road seemed safe from an ambush, one was constantly being shot at by snipers, and to ride in a convoy was hard on the nerves because the norm was no longer whether the convoy might run into a mine, but which truck or jeep would be blown up. Merely to drive to My Tho in the daytime in a civilian car—not a high risk a year before—became dangerous because of the groups of guerrillas who set up shifting roadblocks along the highway.

Outposts fell by the dozen that November. In Dinh Tuong Province surrounding My Tho, twenty-five outposts fell that month, many of them large forty-to-fifty-man garrisons. From a distance across the rice paddies in the morning one could detect the evidence of the night's harvest by the guerrillas. The Viet Cong would burn the posts after overrunning them, and smoke would still be rising when the light returned to show the ruins and the corpses. It became difficult to sleep at the Seminary, because the howitzers crashed all night in response to radio appeals from terrified garrisons, and if the artillery was silent the planes were bombing to try to save some post.

The Seminary itself now buttoned up like an outpost at night. The advisors were forbidden to drive the quarter of a mile into town after dark. Toward the end of the month the Viet Cong grew so bold that they began assaulting outposts close to My Tho in the daytime. One afternoon in late November while I was in the club at the Seminary questioning several of the advisors the planes began bombing so close that the ice cubes rattled in the glasses. The guerrillas hardly bothered anymore with the small posts and tiny watchtowers. Their garrisons fled, and those that stayed and survived did so because the Viet Cong left them in place to serve as quartermasters for fresh ammunition. A standard price for a month's survival was 10,000 rounds. The demoralized militiamen would turn it over and requisition 10,000 more to survive next month by telling the district chief that they had been attacked and fired it off themselves.

What happened in Dinh Tuong occurred all over the northern Delta and in the ring of provinces above Saigon. Most of the thousands of strategic hamlets that Harkins listed on his charts ceased to exist. By the end of the year, except for Catholic hamlets and other isolated communities that had always opposed the Viet Cong for some particular reason, the regime held little beyond the district centers and the province capitals. The Saigon troops could venture into the general countryside only at a price, a price that the guerrillas raised steadily to discourage intrusions. Areas into which the Saigon side had been able to go before with a company now required a battalion reinforced by armored personnel carriers with artillery and air cover standing by. On many mornings the main road out of My Tho running west and south into the Delta would itself be cut and the ARVN would have to send a battalion-size convoy to open it. The task was laborious. The troops had to search for mines and carefully dig them up and fill in the ditches that guerrillas had ripped across the road during the night with ease. The Viet Cong would simply stuff a culvert under the road with an explosive compound of potassium chlorate and red phosphorus that Hanoi smuggled to them through Cambodia as agricultural fertilizer and touch it off with a detonator. From other towns other convoys would be pushing out in this morning ceremony that was familiar to those who had fought in the French war. With their bent for formality, the French had given the ceremony a name. They had called it *L'Ouverture de la Route*, the Opening of the Road. Behind the shield the guerrilla fighters erected, the Viet Cong cadres could go unmolested about their work of marshaling the peasantry for the final phase of the revolution in the South.

The American leadership had furthered the goal of Ho and his followers to a degree they could not have imagined. The combined distributive powers of Harkins's command and the CIA had exceeded the midyear figure of a quarter of a million weapons. About 300,000 American arms had been passed out to the Civil Guard, the SDC, the strategic hamlet militia, and the other irregulars by the beginning of November. Precisely how many of these weapons the Viet Cong captured is impossible to determine. The guerrillas had already seized enough before

November to acquire the strength they displayed then, and in November they tipped the cornucopia and weapons began to flow to them by the tens of thousands. The evidence indicates that if one counts the period before November and from then through the first half of 1964, the Vietnamese Communists obtained about 200,000 U.S. arms. With the exception of the heavy weapons specialists, the U.S. government armed virtually every fighter—right down to the local hamlet guerrillas—on the Communist side. The galvanized-pipe shotguns and other homemade arms that had been so common became curiosities for collectors. Hanoi seems to have reduced shipments of Soviet-designed semiautomatic carbines and other small arms that it had started to smuggle into the South to be sure the second Viet Minh did not lack for infantry weapons. There was no need for them, and they required different ammunition. The Viet Cong commanders wanted to keep their supply procedures as simple as possible by standardizing on American ammunition.

Washington's reflex was to apply more force. Another Honolulu conference convened at Camp H. M. Smith on November 20 to assess strategy in post-Diem Vietnam recommended that the president adopt a scheme Krulak had devised for large-scale clandestine warfare against the North. The idea had occurred to Krulak because of his experience as a Marine raider. The coast of North Vietnam appeared to him to be open and vulnerable to hit-and-run operations. Krulak wanted to substitute his big program for a sparely tailored scheme William Colby had devised to foment a guerrilla war in the North with Vietnamese infiltrators trained by the CIA. (Colby had ended three and a half years as CIA station chief in Saigon in the summer of 1962 and by late 1963 was chief of the Far East Division of clandestine operations.)

McNamara sponsored Krulak's idea at the November 20 conference. Thinking on the American side continued to be governed by the presumption that the war in the South could be controlled—kept a "limited war"—by exerting military and psychological pressure on the North. The American civilian and military leaders of the 1960s tended to see force as a panacea and thought there was no bottom to the reservoir of force they held. They believed that the men in Hanoi could be frightened into abandoning the Viet Cong and that an end to infiltration and other support from the North would substantially reduce the violence in the South. No one looked closely enough to see that the insurrection drew its main sustenance from the Saigon government and the United States.

Colby was opposed to Krulak's scheme. His own program had been, by his subsequent admission, "notoriously unsuccessful." All of the teams he had parachuted into the North or smuggled in by boat had either ceased radio communication within a short time or were known to have been captured. One or two were being "doubled" by their Hanoi captors and were sending messages designed to lure more teams to capture or death. The previous May, McNamara had told Colby to increase the number of teams he was parachuting into the North and to concentrate on sabotage groups. They had perished one after another just like the earlier teams. Colby had concluded that such World War II–style commando and underground operations were futile and that it would be "unconscionable" to waste any more lives on them. He said as much to McNamara.

The secretary had been undeterred by the losses in May, and he was undeterred now. "He listened to me with a cold look and then rejected my advice," Colby recalled. McNamara was influenced by Krulak's belief that the flaw in Colby's program was that it was too small and that a major program run by the military would work. He was also unheeding because Kennedy wanted to try Krulak's scheme. The idea appealed to Kennedy's romantic notions about covert operations. McNamara was performing a role he often fulfilled, that of being the president's straw man. He was seeing that the president received the moral support of a formal recommendation from his advisors for a decision he wanted to make anyway.

Two days after the November Honolulu conference, John Kennedy was assassinated in Dallas by a psychotic sharpshooter named Lee Harvey Oswald. The war in Vietnam that Lyndon Johnson inherited was not much of an American war by comparison with what was to follow. There were 17,000 U.S. servicemen in the South. Less than 120 had been killed, and the number of men wounded seriously enough to require hospitalization had not yet reached 250. Nonetheless, it was an American war. John Kennedy had raised the Stars and Stripes and shed blood and enveloped in the protection and self-esteem of the United States that half of Vietnam below the 17th Parallel which the 1954 Geneva Agreements had said was just a truce zone, but which American statesmen had pronounced a sovereign state and called South Vietnam. Lyndon Johnson was no more willing than Kennedy would have been to become the first president to lose a war. The record also indicates that had he been the president-elect in 1960 rather than Kennedy, he probably would not have handled the war up to this point any differently than Kennedy had. Four days after Kennedy's death, Johnson formally recorded his intention to carry on the war in a top-secret National Security Action Memorandum and accepted the recommendation of the November 20 conference to begin large-scale clandestine warfare.

McNamara gave the new president a self-serving excuse for the failure to perceive the erosion in the Saigon position and Viet Cong progress before the coup. He flew to South Vietnam again in the latter half of December for a two-day trip. In his report to Johnson on December 21 he blamed the Ngo Dinhs and their servants like Cao. McNamara said it was "my best guess . . . that the situation has in fact been deteriorating in the countryside since July to a far greater extent than we realized because of our undue dependence on distorted Vietnamese reporting." His acceptance of July as the start of the decline was an acknowledgment of the analysis the State Department's Bureau of Intelligence and Research had made the previous October to try to warn Kennedy. No effort was made by anyone at the top of the U.S. government to look back further than July and see what sort of reports Vann and Porter and Ladd and other prescient field advisors had been submitting prior to the coup.

The men at the top could not afford to investigate Harkins, because McNamara and Taylor were nearly as guilty as he was. He was not relieved and sent home in disgrace like the general whom Patton had replaced after the rout at the Kasserine Pass in 1943. He was not officially blamed at all. McNamara and Taylor gradually undercut him in private, they gave him less and less protection from the public ridicule that built up against him, and they finally insulted him professionally by not inviting him to one of the strategy conferences in Honolulu, asking instead his new deputy, William Westmoreland, whom they sent out in January 1964. They did not remove him. They kept him in command in Vietnam for nearly eight months after the coup, until late June 1964. When they did bring him home he was taken to the East Room of the White House, where the president decorated him with the Distinguished Service Medal in order "to say on behalf of a grateful Nation, 'Well done,' to a good and faithful servant."

The plan for the major campaign of clandestine warfare, code-named Operation Plan 34A, was presented to the president at the beginning of January 1964 in a memorandum from Krulak. He referred to the raids as "destructive undertakings" and said they were designed "to result in substantial destruction, economic loss and harassment." Their tempo and magnitude were intended to rise in three phases through 1964 to "targets identified with North Vietnam's economic and industrial well-being." The raids were to be prepared and controlled by Harkins's headquarters rather than the Saigon regime. Johnson approved, and the strikes began on February 1, 1964, using Vietnamese, Chinese, and Filipino mercenaries. As the attacks unfolded, fast PT boats bombarded radar sites and other coastal installations, commandos were landed by sea to blow up rail and highway bridges near the coast, and teams of saboteurs were parachuted to try to destroy targets farther inland. Groups of Vietnamese trained in psychological warfare were also dropped into the night to attempt to undermine the confidence of the population in Hanoi's rule. Northern fishing boats were seized. The civilian fishermen were kidnapped, taken South to be interrogated for intelligence purposes, and then released off the coast of the North again.

Lodge was in a wider sea than he knew how to navigate after the coup. The situation in the South was probably irretrievable for any government in Saigon by November 1, 1963, but "Big Minh" proved more talented at plotting a coup than governing. He was indecisive. Nothing was done to organize a coherent war effort. He and Don and Kim (they brought in General Dinh as the fourth member of their junta and gave him the Ministry of the Interior as they had promised) also suffered from the lack of roots among their people and other flaws common to the Tory mandarin class.

Henry Cabot Lodge did not think, as Vann did, that the United States should take over the direction of the war. He had grown up with the surrogate system, had seen it succeed elsewhere, and believed that the Saigon government should retain command of its own armed forces and war effort. He stated what he sought in an unintentional description of the surrogate system in a cable prior to the coup. He wanted a regime that was on a par with one of "the very unsatisfactory governments through which we have had to work in our many very successful attempts to make these countries strong enough to stand alone." He had not gained this minimum standard in Minh's junta. He permitted Minh and his associates to be overthrown at the end of January 1964 in a second coup by a more ambitious general—Nguyen Khanh, thirty-six, another member of the Franco-Vietnamese elite.

Khanh made an ostentatious start in his paratrooper's red beret. (He had graduated from the French Army Airborne School at Pau in the Pyrenees in 1949 and been a company commander in the first battalion of *parachutistes* formed for Bao Dai's army.) He soon showed himself as indecisive and incapable of governing as his predecessors. All of his energy went into counterintrigues against the generals and colonels who wanted to replace him as he had replaced Minh's junta. "Every one of these sons of bitches drives by the palace and thinks about how he'd like to shack up in there with his mistresses," Conein said in disgust at the plots and counterplots.

The lack of coherence was just as bad on the American side. Lodge and Harkins hardly communicated, because there was so much rancor between them from the coup and because Harkins sheltered in new fantasies of victory to come as the Viet Cong built on their gains from the November-December offensive and absorbed more and more of the country.

The Central Highlands went the way of the northern Delta and the rubber-plantation country in the spring of 1964. The CIA's organizing work among the Montagnards in the Highlands and the efforts of the Special Forces teams operating there had been wasted because Diem had refused to grant the tribes any of the local autonomy that the minority peoples possessed in the North. He had insisted on "assimilating" them, precisely what the Montagnards did not want because it meant permanent victimization in a Vietnamese-dominated society. At the beginning of 1964 the Viet Cong also dispensed with clandestine control and started to assert themselves openly in the coastal rice deltas of Central Vietnam that had been Viet Minh redoubts during the French war. They began there to repeat the pattern of sweeping Saigon's presence from most of the densely populated countryside as they had in the big Delta to the south. Lodge could hoodwink the commanding general and organize the American elements of a coup by himself. He needed the commanding general to organize the American elements of a war effort. After William Westmoreland arrived to be Harkins's deputy, Lodge offered him an office in the embassy so that they could work together. A surprised Westmoreland replied that he was an Army officer and his boss was Harkins.

As the intelligence advisors colored their maps with more red each month of 1964, those Americans most responsible retained their positions of influence within the circle of power or were promoted. Johnson's confidence in McNamara became greater, perhaps, than Kennedy's had been. Krulak was given the third star of a lieutenant general in early 1964 and put in charge of all of the Marines in Holland Smith's ocean as Commanding General Fleet Marine Force Pacific. The Air Force laid bureaucratic claim to his job as watchman of counterguerrilla warfare to ensure that air power would gain a larger share and brought Anthis home from Vietnam to be the new special assistant for counterinsurgency and special activities. No one reread Wheeler's report on his mission of inquiry after Ap Bac. In late June on the advice of McNamara and Taylor, Johnson promoted Wheeler from chief of staff of the Army to chairman of the Joint Chiefs. Taylor gave up the chairmanship to replace Lodge in Saigon. (Lodge came home at the beginning of July ostensibly to try to stop Barry Goldwater from gaining the Republican nomination and leading the party to defeat in the fall and actually because he was a tired and frustrated man who had run out of ideas. He recommended bombing North Vietnam.)

Johnson had no less confidence in Taylor than he did in McNamara. An agreement between the Pentagon and the State Department that had made Harkins the equal of the ambassador was abrogated. Taylor went to Saigon with the full civil and military authority of a proconsul. Westmoreland succeeded Harkins as commanding general, but he was Taylor's subordinate. Taylor was supposed to use his unhampered authority to organize an effective prosecution of the war. Only Harkins had to retire, with honor, at the beginning of August.

Colby was correct in predicting that Krulak's major campaign of clandestine warfare would be a waste of lives. Operation Plan 34A was as ineffective as Colby's small program. The raids did not intimidate the leaders in Hanoi, nor did they reduce the level of violence in the South. The officers in the Studies and Observations Group in Saigon (the covert section of Harkins's and then Westmoreland's headquarters), who readied the attacks and supervised their execution after Washington had approved each raid in advance, were never able to escalate the program to the destruction of industrial targets as Krulak had envisioned. The task was beyond the capability of their teams of Vietnamese and mercenary Asian saboteurs. Had they succeeded in sabotaging some industries in the North, it would not have made any difference.

The sole tangible result of Krulak's scheme was to facilitate the commencement of the larger war in which Krulak was to suffer the rage and despair of Vann. The 34A raids provoked the Tonkin Gulf incident of August 1964, the clashes between torpedo boats of Hanoi's navy and U.S. Navy destroyers, which Johnson used to trick the Senate into giving him an advance declaration of war for the far higher level of force he had decided by then he was probably going to have to employ to bend Hanoi to his will. McNamara and Dean Rusk helped him by deceiving the Senate Committee on Foreign Relations about the clandestine attacks in secret testimony before the committee. The president thought that his deception was in the best interest of the nation, as did McNamara and Rusk in misleading the senators. Johnson did not want to incur the blame Truman had received for going to war in Korea without a Senate resolution, and at the same time he wished to avoid a public debate that might bring the Vietnam policy into question. He was sufficiently confident of prevailing to think that he could get by with the form of a declaration and that his trickery would not be discovered.

The statesmen and military leaders of the United States did not understand that their Vietnamese opponents had passed beyond intimidation by 1964 and were willing to risk whatever punishment the greatest power on earth might inflict on them. Walt Rostow, the interventionist intellectual who was then counselor for policy planning at the State Department, assured Rusk in a memorandum in February that the Hanoi leaders were extremely vulnerable to the blackmail of bombing. Ho Chi Minh "has an industrial complex to protect: he is no longer a guerrilla fighter with nothing to lose," Rostow said. At the urging of Lodge, Rusk arranged for the senior Canadian delegate to the ICSC to call at the prime minister's office in Hanoi on June 18, 1964. The Canadian diplomat transmitted a secret message designed to reinforce what Washington was trying to communicate through the 34A strikes and preparatory military deployments it was making in Asia at the time and publicizing so that Hanoi would not miss them. He told Pham Van Dong that the patience of the United States was running out and that if the war kept escalating "the greatest devastation would of course result for the DRV itself." (DRV means Democratic Republic of Vietnam, i.e., North Vietnam.) On August 10, after Johnson had also used the Tonkin Gulf incident as a pretext to conduct a preliminary round of bombing raids on the North and demonstrate his readiness to punish with the awesome force the United States possessed, the Canadian was sent back with a more detailed threat. He received the same response he had on the first occasion. "Pham Van Dong showed himself utterly unintimidated and calmly resolved to pursue the course upon which the DRV was embarked to what he confidently expected would be its successful conclusion," a Pentagon historian wrote from the report of the Canadian messenger.

By 1964, Ho Chi Minh and Pham Van Dong and the other Vietnamese revolutionaries in Hanoi were prepared to lose the industries they had constructed with hope and sacrifice. They were prepared to risk having every city and town in the North bombed into rubble and worse. They were willing to risk anything. Ho and his disciples were not engaged in a "limited war," Maxwell Taylor's rationalization to find employment for an unemployed U.S. Army. They were committed to a total war. There were no limits for them. They could be physically destroyed and the will of their people broken if the United States turned its air power loose on the North without restraint, targeting the flood-control system of the Red River Delta and the population itself, killing millions as Curtis LeMay, the chief of staff of the Air Force, wanted to do. "Bomb 'em back into the Stone Age," he said. The men in Hanoi were willing to take that risk too. The one thing that the United States could not do was to deter them.

The Communist mandarins had strayed from their destiny in the mid-1950s when they had been distracted by the fashioning of their Marxist society in the North and in undoing the damage caused by the disastrous fanaticism of their Land Reform Campaign. The Southern cadres who survived Diem's terror and disobeyed them in 1957 by rebelling against the Ngo Dinhs and the Americans had recalled them to their destiny. Men like Squad Leader Dung had kept them in the war. By 1964 it was too late to retreat, whatever the Americans threatened, whatever the Americans did. The men in Hanoi knew that if they did order the Viet Cong cadres to halt, they would lose control, because many would defy them and persist in a war that was being won. But they would never issue such an order. To do so would be to deny the central purpose of their lives. "Vietnam is one nation," their constitution proclaimed.

Their actions were the proof of their refusal to be deterred. They pressed ahead throughout 1964 with the creation of the second Viet Minh to complete the revolution in the South. The heavy weapons the trawlers had brought in on moonless nights made their first appearance in battle that spring. The 12.7mm Soviet-model antiaircraft machine gun was more accurate against helicopters and fighter-bombers than the Browning .50 caliber, because the gun rested on a tall and hefty mount that steadied the weapon and permitted the gunner to swing it more freely. The Viet Cong commanders staged a regimental-size action in April in the southern half of the Delta, a safe place to perform this first test of simultaneously maneuvering three battalions in combat. The fighting and training and organizing went on all through the summer and fall of 1964, and by the end of the year the Hanoi leaders were close to their goal. On January 2, 1963, the Viet Cong had been a hesitant force of approximately 23,000 regular and Regional guerrillas assembled in twenty-five battalions of varying strengths from 150 to 300 men and sundry provincial companies and district platoons. By December 1964, these 23,000 guerrillas had grown twice over and then some into an army of 56,000 confident and well-trained troops. The twenty-five catch-all battalions and assorted companies and platoons had been transformed into seventy-three uniformly strong battalions, sixty-six infantry units, and an additional seven heavy weapons and antiaircraft machine gun battalions. The infantry battalions were formidable task forces of 600 to 700 men each. (The JGS intelligence information had said in the summer of 1963 that the Viet Cong were moving toward 600-man battalions, but Halberstam, feeling so much pressure, had settled in his August 15 dispatch for a more conservative report that spoke of 400-man formations. They had seemed menacing enough at the time.) Most of the battalions had been organized into regiments complete with communications, engineer, and other combat support units, and the Viet Cong commanders were in the process of forming the regiments into divisions. This army of 56,000 fighters was backed by another 40,000 men in base-echelon training, supply, medical, and related services.

Nearly six years of pain and dying had been necessary to raise the desperate remnant of 2,000 Viet Minh in the spring of 1957 to the 23,000 uncertain guerrillas of the day of Ap Bac. It had taken less than two years, with the help of Diem and the Americans, to form the sledge-hammer battalions of December 1964.

The hammers began to break the ARVN into pieces that month. On December 9 an unprecedented ambush occurred on a road in the rubber-plantation country forty miles east of Saigon. An entire company of fourteen M-113s was destroyed, all of the armored personnel carriers smashed into hulks by 57mm and 75mm recoilless cannon. An L-19 and two of the Huey gunships that came to their assistance were shot down. Although no one in Saigon knew it, the ambushers were two battalions from one of the new Viet Cong regiments. At the end of the month the Viet Cong commanders baited the Saigon side into battle in the same area by repeatedly attacking a district center and overrunning the out-posts protecting a neighboring hamlet of Northern Catholic refugees called Binh Gia. On December 31, 1964, an elite Saigon marine battalion of 326 officers and men was decimated in a giant ambush amid the rubber trees near Binh Gia. Almost two-thirds of the Saigon marines were killed, wounded, or captured. Twenty-nine of the battalion's thirty-five officers died. Another elite Saigon battalion was operating close by that day, one of the new Ranger battalions Westmoreland had formed to try to strengthen the ARVN. It suffered a worse fate in a second giant ambush and was literally wiped out. Nearly 400 officers and men became casualties. The two guerrilla regiments responsible for the ambushes were part of a still larger unit whose existence was also unknown to Westmoreland and the ARVN generals—the 9th Viet Cong Division, the first division of the second Viet Minh to become operational in the South.

Only the intervention of the regular armed forces of the United States could now prevent the collapse of the Saigon regime and the unification of Vietnam by the men in Hanoi. The alternative that Vann had been convinced was not an alternative—the big American air and ground war in Vietnam—had become inevitable. Ziegler remembered what Vann would say when the subject came up of bringing the U.S. Army and the Marine Corps out to take over the war. It would be the worst possible move, Vann said. They had to find a way to make the ARVN fight, because waging the war with a Vietnamese army was the only course that made sense. The Viet Cong were so intermingled with the peasantry that the Saigon troops had difficulty distinguishing friend from foe. Think, Vann said, how much more difficult it would be for Americans. The American soldiers would soon start to see the whole rural population as the enemy. The Army and the Marine Corps would create a bloody morass into which they and the Vietnamese peasantry would sink. "We'd end up shooting at everything—men, women, kids, and the buffalos," Vann said.

There was obviously no satisfaction to be drawn from the catastrophe, but Halberstam and I and Vann's other friends regretted that he was no longer in the Army to obtain at least the professional vindication he deserved now that the truth was so large some of it would have to be conceded sooner or later. The letter we had received from him in July 1963 had said that he was going to retire at the end of the month to accept a job as an executive with the Aerospace Division of Martin-Marietta in Denver. He said that the Army personnel officers refused to give him the troop-command assignment he was entitled to after his classes at the Industrial College of the Armed Forces ended in June 1964, and that he could not face the three to four years of elevated clerkdom they insisted he would then have to accept in a logistics job at the Pentagon. He wrote us a capsule account of his campaign at the Pentagon and the cancellation of his briefing for the Joint Chiefs three hours before he was to give it. He sent a similar letter to the advisory team at My Tho. His emotion showed at the end of the letter to his captains. He signed it, "Your brother officer, John." We, and Vann's Army friends, all assumed that he was retiring in disgust after being refused a hearing before the Joint Chiefs so that he could gain the freedom to speak out about the war in public. He confirmed our assumption in press interviews after he left the Army by saying that this had been the real reason for his retirement.

The failure of his briefing campaign at the Pentagon would not have hurt Vann's odds at overcoming the clash with Harkins had he subsequently behaved himself by taking up his studies at the Industrial College until ruffled dignity settled and events began to vindicate him. He had gained the disapproval of Wheeler, who was to succeed Taylor as chairman of the Joint Chiefs, but one of the numerous admirers he had simultaneously gained was Harold Johnson, who was to succeed Wheeler as chief of staff. With the chief of staff as an admirer, one can afford some ill will in other quarters. Vann's retirement raised still higher our admiration for his moral courage.

Vann's moral heroism became the core of his legend. An account of the cancellation of his briefing for the Joint Chiefs first appeared at the end of September 1963, two months after he retired, in a long, front-page article with a photograph of Vann and Cao in the *New York Journal-American*. Vann provided the details and the photograph to an editor of the paper who had heard rumors about the incident and telephoned him in Denver.

Halberstam, whose reporting was vindicated by a Pulitzer Prize after his return to the United States in December 1963, gave the real life to Vann's legend by putting it into print prominently, first with his profile of Vann in *Esquire* magazine in November 1964, and then with his book *The Making of a Quagmire* in 1965. When Halberstam flew out to Denver in the spring of 1964 to interview him for the book, Vann recounted his crusade at the Pentagon and how Krulak and Taylor had aborted the briefing. He said that he could not bear to stay in the Army after that disappointment. The denouement was the perfect high-drama ending to the epic of Lt. Col. John Paul Vann, the officer of surpassing career promise, who had renounced a general's stars to alert the nation to the truth about the war in Vietnam because he was also a man of surpassing principle. The ending appealed as well to Halberstam's hero-villain style of journalism. While writing the book, Halberstam thought of Vann's retirement so much in terms of a resignation of protest that he used "retired" and "resigned" interchangeably:

> So he retired and took a job with an aircraft company in Denver. . . . He had . . . done what no other American official had done in that land where there was such a disparity between theory and practice: he had thought that the failures and the mendacity were serious enough to merit a resignation, the traditional American protest.

Vann emerged as the one authentic hero of this shameful period. The heroism stayed with him, the heroism of the David who had stood up to the Goliath of lies and institutional corruption. It was repeated in subsequent articles written about him. It was cited in 1969 when the secretary of state, then William Rogers, presented him an award from the Association of the Foreign Service for "extraordinary accomplishment involving creativity, intellectual courage and integrity." If you asked a friend why he had left the Army, he would reply that Vann had resigned in protest.

The memory of Vann's moral heroism was the foundation of his reputation in later years in Vietnam for candor and willingness to grasp the brambles of fact however they might hurt. Even though he always drew back from condemning the war itself, this reputation for truth-telling lent credibility to what he had to say about the war to those who might differ with him on the fundamental issue of whether the United States ought to be waging war in Vietnam at all. The memory was in the chapel the day he was buried at Arlington. His old professional enemies and friends like Ellsberg who had since come to oppose his war—all paid homage to a man who had given up what he loved most, the Army, rather than be a party to lies and delusions.

The story wasn't true. He had not renounced his career and retired in protest in order to warn the country of impending defeat. He did have moral courage. He had defied Harkins, fought to gain acceptance of the truth at the Pentagon, and had his briefing for the Joint Chiefs canceled by Krulak and Taylor just as he was within reach of the hearing he wanted, but these were not the reasons he left the Army. He lied to Halberstam and manipulated him, doing so naturally with the same talent he sought to work on Cao. He had deceived everyone in Vietnam. We had interpreted his career recklessness as self-sacrifice and had worried about our stories hurting him because we had thought that he was sacrificing a general's stars. He had wanted us to think this. He had wanted his captains like Ziegler and his enlisted men like Bowers to think this too—otherwise he would not have told Ziegler he was worried that he might have spoiled his prospects in the Army by defying Harkins. All the time he was deceiving us he knew that he had no career to ruin and no stars to throw away. He had known before he went to Vietnam in March 1962 that he would probably retire after he came home. He had meant more than Halberstam could have realized when he said at the airport farewell with his small, tight smile: "You never hurt me any more than I wanted to be hurt." He also said more about himself than he meant to say when he told the Army historian: "We had also, to all the visitors who came over there, been one of the bright shining lies."

He had left the Army because a dark compulsion in his personality had led him to commit an act that he was convinced would bar him forever from promotion to general. There was a duality in the man, a duality of personal compulsions and deceits that would not bear light and a professional honesty that was rigorous and incorruptible. Two years before he had marched through the swinging doors of Dan Porter's office in the old French cavalry compound in Saigon, he had nearly been court-martialed because of his secret vice. By maneuvering with cunning he had managed to get the charges dismissed. The system through which the Army maintained an officer's personnel record had permitted him to hide the incident from everyone in Vietnam. There was much else about his life that he always kept hidden or repressed.

He had known that he could not hide the black spot from a board considering colonels for promotion to general officer. A promotion board would have access to his entire record, including a file with his name on it that was preserved permanently by the criminal investigation division of the Military Police and a copy of the pre-court-martial proceedings that might still exist in the records of the Office of the Judge Advocate General. He had tried and failed before going to Vietnam to steal those records and destroy them in order to remove the stain. He had been convinced that any promotion board that saw that stain would decide the Army could not afford to risk having an officer accused of his crime among its generals. He had sworn to himself when he was a boy that he would go places and be somebody. He could not stand being relegated to Number Two. He had to be in on the scramble to be Number One. Once he had determined that he was barred from the opportunity to climb to the top in the Army, he told himself that he would have to leave when he was still young enough at thirty-nine to begin another career.

Yet while he left the Army for his own hidden reasons, he did not want to leave and he regretted leaving as soon as he had done so. He felt rejected in Denver, as if the Army had cast him out. The feeling was one he knew well. He had been born an outcast. His mother had not wanted him, nor had she had a rightful name to give him, nor any love.

BOOK FIVE

ANTECEDENTS
TO
THE MAN

H E WAS ILLEGITIMATE. His father's name was not Vann, it was Spry, Johnny Spry, and he was named John Paul after him. His mother's name was Myrtle Lee Tripp. She was just short of nineteen years old when she gave birth to him on July 2, 1924, in a run-down brick mansion that had been cut up into apartments in an old section of the port of Norfolk, Virginia. He was the offspring of one of the few genuine attachments his mother was to have in a lifetime of shoddy liaisons until the effects of alcoholism and a beating when she was drunk one night on the Norfolk beachfront carried her off at the age of sixty-one.

Johnny Spry was in his mid-twenties in 1924 and drove a trolley car. His formal name was John Paul, but everyone who knew him called him Johnny. Even if he had wanted to marry Myrtle Tripp someday, it would have been inconvenient. Johnny Spry already had a wife, a three-year-old son named John Paul, Jr., and another son of nine months when the boy who could not bear his family name was born. This John Paul was a "love child" in the phrase of the South of his birth, a euphemism that was never to help alleviate his shame.

When her son was four, Myrtle Tripp met Aaron Frank Vann, a city bus driver. He had migrated to Norfolk from a farm in North Carolina just as Myrtle and most of her family had done in her childhood. She decided to marry him after she became pregnant with the daughter who was to be Vann's half sister, Dorothy Lee. The marriage was to endure in form, if not in fact, for twenty years, and Frank Vann, as he was called, eventually adopted the boy Myrtle brought to him.

John Paul Vann was an original white Southerner. His lineage reached back centuries to the beginnings of the South, and his birth was in keeping with his ancestry: the majority of his forebears had been social illegitimates.

The Puritans who settled in New England to escape religious persecution were a community of farmers, craftsmen, and scholar-preachers. The settlements they founded tended to attract others in their image, skilled and literate people who joined in starting the village-to-town-to-city civilization that was to make America an industrial colossus.

The white settlers of the South were mainly the condemned and the desperate of seventeenth- and eighteenth-century England and Ireland, with a passel of troublesome Scots tossed in for good riddance. Tobacco was the principal reason for their coming. It had been discovered being grown by the native inhabitants of the South, the Indians, who were being exterminated. Britain and the rest of Europe were demanding the new narcotic in such quantities that the slave traders could not bring over those other original settlers of the South; the black men and women of Africa, fast enough to meet the labor needs of the colonial planters along the coasts of what are now Maryland, Virginia, the Carolinas, and Georgia.

Ireland was a garrisoned colony then, with a truculent peasantry kept in check by the gun and the noose. The countryside of England was a battleground of class warfare. The gentry were expanding their estates by gradually expropriating the common lands, ruining small farmers, evicting tenants, and driving down the survival wages of agricultural laborers. The poor and the victimized fought back by organizing strikes and burning barns and mills and with riots to loot grain storehouses during the recurrent famines. The atmosphere encouraged lawlessness of every kind. In the cities there was the added peril of dying from one of the many diseases bred by the filth. Life was so precarious in eighteenth-century London that deaths outnumbered baptisms by two to one.

The gentry of Britain took advantage of the planters' need for labor to rid themselves of their undesirables. Parliament passed statutes authorizing judges to commute death sentences to exile (the euphemism was "transportation") to the colonies for life. With men and women being hanged for rioting to get something to eat or stealing half a pound of tobacco (approximately 200 offenses were punishable by hanging), there was no dearth of sentences to commute. Transportation was also made a general punishment for noncapital offenses. The minimum sentence was for seven years, the usual number these unfortunates had to labor in the tobacco fields to repay the planter the cost of having a "convict servant" shipped across the Atlantic in chains.

Except for the chains, the greater part of the other white migrants to the South were hardly distinguishable from the convict men and women. The coast of the colonial South, with its malaria and yellow fever and cholera, was not a place that would attract the settlers who went to New England. The majority of those who came were the orphans, the ruined farmers, the evicted tenants, the destitute rural laborers, and their women and children. After hunger had so bereft them of hope that they were willing to face the terror of the two-to-three-month voyage in the frail sailing ships and the grimness of work in the plantation fields, they sold themselves to a planter to pay for their passage to America. Their bondage was called "indenture." It was the same as that imposed on the convicts but for a shorter term, normally about four years. They too were chattel property of the planter for the duration of their contract. They could be pursued and returned by force if they ran away, and they could be whipped if they refused to work.

Half to two-thirds of all the white people who came to the South prior to the Revolution were convicts or indentured laborers. Their good fortune was that they were not brought as the black people were to labor in permanent bondage. A few had sufficient ambition and cunning to complete their terms of servitude and go on to acquire large lands of their own, to buy slaves, and to bring more of their compatriots across the Atlantic to cultivate their tobacco. These planter families prospered sufficiently over the generations to gain learning and manners and to mimic the British gentry who had cast out their ancestors. They became the grandees of the old South and the cavaliers of the Confederacy.

The crowd of farmers beneath the planter aristocrats remained more representative of those who got off the ships. These original white Southerners were a distinct people among the many peoples who were to make up America. The social conditions in the mother country that influenced who would be forced to emigrate and the harshness of their introduction to the new world gave them certain qualities that set them apart. They tended to be a hardy people. The weaker among them perished on the ships, in the fields from the long days and bad food, or from the epidemics. They also had a kind of wildness. The Victorian era and industrialization tamed the masses of Britain. Nothing ever quite tamed these people whom Britain had discarded. The hellfire-and-brimstone fulminating of their Methodist and Baptist and Presbyterian preachers could not burn away a strain of hedonism. There was a strain of violence in them as well. It showed in the value they placed on physical prowess, on a man's ability to ride and shoot and use his fists, and in their impetuous love of a fight. They followed their planter captains eagerly into the Civil War, and amid defeat and occupation by a Northern army they drew solace from how bravely they had fought. To outsiders there seemed to be something about them that harked back to what they must have been like in that turbulent Britain of long ago.

John Vann's ancestors did not go far from the coast where they had landed. Little information is available about the Spry side, from which Vann seems to have obtained most of his physical traits and his high nervous energy. (Johnny Spry rarely slept more than four or five hours a night, and he had to keep himself busy all the time he was awake.) Clarence Spry, Vann's paternal grandfather, followed the familiar job-seeking route from North Carolina to Norfolk. He married a young woman named Olive Savells, whose people had been farmers and fishermen in the tidewater country just below Norfolk.

His mother's family, the Tripps and the Smiths, seem to have given Vann much of his character, especially his will to dominate. He appears to have taken after his maternal grandmother, Queenie Smith, and his mother's older sister, Mollie, both independent and venturesome women. From his Aunt Mollie, a handsome woman with long legs, he also got the two physical traits that gave a hint of his character—his narrow, bird-of-prey eyes and the straight mouth with the firm upper lip.

There have been Tripps and Smiths in the piney lowlands of northeastern North Carolina since the region was first settled during the latter half of the 1600s and the early 1700s. The Tripps and Smiths who were Vann's immediate forebears had their lands in Pitt County near the modern city of Greenville, where the coastal plain picks up from the swampy tidewater country and stretches out in a level and gently rolling expanse to the foothills of the Appalachians. Their holdings were not large enough to rank them as planters, but they were big farmers, with hundreds of acres and slaves to raise their tobacco and then the cotton that followed as the source of wealth in the South. The sandy loam of the upper coastal plain of North Carolina is one of the finest soils in America. Almost anything will grow well in it, and the Tripps and the Smiths prospered until the Civil War.

Defeat brought Northern exploitation that ground Southern farmers down into poverty. A worldwide depression in agricultural commodities began in the 1880s and continued through the turn of the century. The price of cotton fell from fourteen cents a pound in 1873 to four and a half cents a pound by 1894. The value of tobacco plummeted too. The

North took advantage of the situation to shackle the conquered South into the classic relationship of an agricultural colony to an industrialized power. The Northern-dominated Congress passed prohibitive tariffs to keep competing European manufactures out of the country. Northern industry bought cheap raw materials from the South and then pegged the prices of the manufactured goods it sold there artificially high.

Henry Tripp, Vann's great-grandfather on his mother's side, was the last Tripp to know the pride of owning a big farm. He had eight children who needed land, and with crop income so low there was no way he could generate cash to help them buy ground of their own. He began parceling up his farm. In 1902 when Vann's maternal grandfather, John William "Bill" Tripp, married Inelline Smith, who preferred her nickname of Queenie, Henry Tripp gave Bill forty acres, a mule, and enough timber from the farm woods for a house, a barn, and a hog shed.

Queenie endured the marriage and the existence it entailed for a dozen years and five children—four daughters and a son. They were all born in the iron double bed she and Bill shared in the largest of the four rooms in the pine-plank farmhouse his brothers had helped him build. That room also served as the dining and living room for the family. Everyone gathered there in the evening until it was time to go to sleep. There was no electricity and no plumbing. Light came from kerosene lamps, water from a well in buckets, and there was a privy. Nothing inside or outside of the house was painted: paint was an unnecessary expense. The babies were delivered by a midwife. A doctor cost more money and was reserved for a more serious medical problem than a birth. Myrtle Lee, Vann's mother, was the third-born child on July 18, 1905. There were no Lees in the Tripp or Smith family lines as far as anyone could remember. Myrtle acquired her middle name for the same reason so many Southern children received it—to honor Robert E. Lee.

Bill Tripp's tobacco and cotton and corn never brought enough money to pay off the "supply merchant," as the owner of the local general store was called. Each year Bill would have to borrow again at interest rates never lower than 30 percent for the fertilizer and plowpoints and other necessities of farming. For the family to survive, Queenie also had to have flour and salt and a bit of molasses and sugar, kerosene for the lamps, and bolts of cloth to cut and sew into clothes. As soon as the fresh vegetables from the garden were gone in the fall the Tripps subsisted on the pellagra-and-rickets diet that was one of the curses of the post–Civil War South—hog meat and gravy with biscuits for one meal and hog meat and gravy with corn bread for the next. Myrtle and Mollie and the three other Tripp children were lucky enough not to contract either disease from the vitamin deficiency. Tens of thousands of white and black children across the South were less fortunate.

The poverty made so much else that was difficult to bear still more difficult. Dying, for example. There were no fancy caskets or wakes at funeral homes to allay grief. The family washed the body, dressed the deceased in the best clothes he or she had owned or the living would spare, and placed the body in a pine coffin and nailed down the top. The next morning the preacher came, the relatives and friends assembled, and the body was buried.

Epidemics of dysentery from the bad sanitation struck like late frosts to cull the young. Vann's uncle, William Arthur "Buddie" Tripp, the only son of Queenie and Bill, remembered when his cousin Moses took sick during one epidemic. Moses was Buddie's best playmate, and he went over to Moses's house to cheer him up. Moses was too ill to talk. He just lay in the bed and looked at Buddie. The doctor rode by every day in a horse and buggy and gave Moses medicine. It didn't do any good. Moses was a strong boy. He lay in the bed at least a week before he went. Mollie came down with dysentery during the same epidemic. She was older than Moses and perhaps hardier. Her body fought off the disease. No one had told her that Moses was sick. She was surprised one morning to look out the bedroom window and see a procession of relatives passing by the house.

She got out of bed and found her mother. "Momma, what's happenin'? I know somethin's wrong," she said.

"Your cousin Moses died, Mollie," Queenie told her. "They're buryin' him in the cemetery up next to the woods."

The Tripps had their own family cemetery in a field near the woods behind the grandparents' house, another relic of the years before defeat. Buddie walked with the procession. He remembered that there were no flowers on Moses's coffin. The pine box with his playmate in it rode to the grave on top of a flatbed farm wagon.

Queenie kept badgering Bill to abandon farming and move the family to Norfolk. He could do carpentry and was a competent mason, and there was work to be found in Norfolk. The port had become one of the islands of relative prosperity in the South. Norfolk had picked up considerable traffic from the new east-west railroads hauling coal and cotton for export to New England and Europe. The modern, deep-draft ocean freighters had to load at Norfolk, because they could not sail up the James River to Richmond as their smaller precedessors had been able to do.

Bill Tripp was a taciturn man with little capacity for love, another reason the marriage was difficult. He did love his land and he wouldn't leave it, so Queenie left him. In 1914 she put the five children up with her parents while she went to Norfolk to get a job. She told Bill she would earn enough to support all of them better than he had.

Vann's grandfather did not farm long for an empty house. Shortly after Queenie left and before future events might have rescued him, Bill Tripp learned that the owner of the general store was foreclosing on his debt. The county judge issued a writ, and the sheriff sold the forty acres and everything on it at auction to pay off the loan. Bill loaded his shotgun and went to the sheriff's house to kill him. He was not mad at the sheriff for handling the auction; an auction was a sheriff's job. He was mad at the sheriff for arranging to auction the farm to himself. Perhaps the sheriff had schemed for it and persuaded the supply merchant to foreclose.

Bill was intercepted and arrested before he could shoot the sheriff. The judge gave him two years on a chain gang building roads. A blacksmith fastened irons around his legs above the ankles. A guard ran the chain through the loops on the irons to shackle Bill to the other prisoners. The men worked chained together all day long, ate and performed their bodily functions together, and slept chained together at night. The chain and the leg irons were not removed until Bill was released and banished from the county for another two years because the sheriff was still afraid. When Bill returned, one of his brothers staked him to a lease as a sharecropper. He was never again to have his own land.

Queenie picked the right time to leave the farm. The armies of Europe marched against each other in August 1914, and the carnage on the Marne and at Verdun and on the Somme was as expensive in resources as it was wasteful in lives. The extravagance of Europe's self-destruction gave life back to the South. There were profits to be had on a scale that had not been seen since the Cotton Kingdom, and nowhere were the good times of World War I to come in greater lavishness than in Norfolk.

Cotton boomed. The constricting of the textile mills of Britain, France, and Germany, with warfare on the oceans as well as on the Continent, meant that America soon had a corner on the world's cotton trade. Vann's grandmother found a job in a mill that was producing long cotton drawers and undershirts, the "long johns" that men wore in cold weather until the advent of central heating. This mill paid by the piece rather than by the hour. Queenie brought Mollie to Norfolk to help her turn out more underwear. Mollie was ten years old at the time. She remembered that she was not yet tall enough to reach the top of the seaming machine and had to stand on a box to be able to flip over the undershirts and drawers so that her mother could sew them faster.

Mother and daughter between them sewed long johns so swiftly that in less than a year Queenie had saved enough to bring the other four children up from North Carolina and to open a boardinghouse. She rented a three-story place of about twenty rooms in the oldest section of Norfolk, near the wharves on the Elizabeth River. The house had been a mansion in the pre–Civil War era. (It was torn down during urban renewal in the 1960s.) A boardinghouse is a sensible business for a country woman who knows how to cook and care for men. Queenie's choice was also shrewd; housing for workmen is a prime commodity in wartime. After Woodrow Wilson persuaded Congress to enter the fight by declaring war on Germany in April 1917, Queenie's problem became one of trying to find space for an extra bed and for another chair at the tables in her dining room.

"Mars Moulds a Great City" was the title an enthusiastic historian of Norfolk chose for his chapter on World War I. In a period when millions of dollars had the economic impact of billions, tens of millions in military construction projects were literally started overnight and whipped forward with spare-no-money speed. Norfolk was "swept down upon by a tidal wave of progress" and forced to "ride upon the flood of prosperity," as a local newspaper phrased it. The Navy seized the moment to obtain funds for an 800-acre base beyond any of the admirals' peacetime reveries on the end of the peninsula just north of the city. Rows of piers for battleships, cruisers, and destroyers, a submarine basin, a seaplane lagoon, an airfield, hangars, multistory concrete warehouses, barracks, machine shops, and hundreds of other buildings began to appear. The old Norfolk Navy Yard at Portsmouth across the Elizabeth River was torn apart and modernized with a battleship dry dock that was the largest and most complicated example of concrete construction in American history up to that point. The Army looked at the congestion in the ports of Boston, New York, and Philadelphia and decided that Norfolk was the best alternative from which to ship troops and supplies for the expeditionary force it was creating in France. The result was the wharves and rail marshaling yards and assorted facilities of the biggest Army transport base in the country. The troop trains steamed into Norfolk, and every day and through the night thousands of men embarked for France. Everything from socks to mules to locomotives was shipped off with them to help defeat the Kaiser's gray-clad soldiery. Norfolk's population doubled from a prewar 68,000 to 130,000 as men and women from all over the South and from Texas and Kansas and even Minnesota came to labor in the war effort. Within the year and a half before the Armistice of November 11, 1918, Norfolk was transformed from a modest city beside the sea into a port of significance and the greatest naval base in the Western Hemisphere.

Queenie gave up the boardinghouse in 1921 when the last of the base construction was done and the money tree was no longer bountiful. With her profits, she bought a small house in another section of the city, and she found work as a ship stewardess on overnight passenger steamers that plied between Norfolk and New York. Her children had begun to spin off during the boardinghouse years, which did not trouble her, because she saw Norfolk as an improvement for them. Mollie had eloped at the height of the good times in 1918 with a ship welder who was staying at the boardinghouse. She was just fourteen (her welder was nineteen), but young marriage was common then and she wanted a home of her own. Her older sister, Lillian, also married a boarder, who had a job at a dry-cleaning establishment; she divorced him after a son, and married a Norfolk policeman.

Mertie, as Vann's mother was called within the family, did not find the kind of providers her sisters married, nor did she settle into a job. The practical choices she faced were to marry a workingman who wanted a family or to seek a relatively pleasant job like her mother's. Her education did not fit her for anything else. It had stopped after the elementary years in North Carolina, because Queenie had needed the girls to help her with the waiting on table and bedmaking and other chores of the boardinghouse. Myrtle had sufficient looks to have found a provider had she set her mind to it. Her features were somewhat homely— her mouth slightly crooked and her nose too big. Her long brunette hair was attractive, her smile appealing, and her trim figure more appealing still, especially her pretty legs. She was also sufficiently intelligent to have found a job like her mother's had she wanted to stay single. Myrtle disliked making practical choices. "I'm Myrtle and there's not another one in the world like me. I love myself," was Mollie's way of summing up her sister's character.

Myrtle was a dreamer. She never thought about tomorrow. She liked to dance, to laugh, to drink, and to make love, and she did not worry about the consequences for herself and others. When she found a job, she did not keep it long. When she made some money, she spent it right away on clothes and makeup. In the spring of 1923, three months before she turned eighteen, she struck up a romance with a French merchant sailor named Victor LeGay and took a train to Elizabeth City, North Carolina, just below the Virginia border to marry him there in a hasty ceremony. They shared quarters for six months. LeGay had been gone about a month when Myrtle got pregnant by Spry. The indications are that she had started seeing him before LeGay's departure.

Johnny Spry's pleasures were gambling and chasing women. He had known Myrtle when she was a girl, having grown up in the same neighborhood in old Norfolk where Queenie had her boardinghouse. One of the benefits of his job as a city trolley driver was the opportunity to meet women. He and Myrtle may have renewed acquaintance that way. She seems to have loved him as much as Myrtle could love any man. She staked out her claim by riding on the seat behind him when he drove his trolley. Spry's wife, who was aware of his habits, quickly spotted the affair. She leaped onto the trolley one day and lit into Myrtle to try to scare her off—the two women screeching, slapping, and pulling hair in an old-fashioned catfight. Spry was amused at being fought over and recounted the scene to a son many years later. Myrtle was not deterred. She intended to divorce LeGay as soon as she could (she subsequently did obtain a divorce in the Circuit Court in Norfolk, charging LeGay with adultery) and seems to have let herself get pregnant in the hope that a child would persuade Spry to divorce his wife and marry her. Johnny Spry did not believe smart men married women like Myrtle. He had ended the affair by the time the child was born on July 2, 1924.

Myrtle's son need not have been illegitimate. She was still legally married. To avoid embarrassing herself with the doctor who delivered the baby, she lied and said that LeGay was the father. The lie gave the boy a pro forma last name on his birth certificate. Although her family knew about the affair and also knew that LeGay had been gone too long to be the father (Lillian was renting the apartment next door to Myrtle's), they would have kept the secret if only for the child's sake. The boy could have grown up ignorant of his true parentage.

Myrtle made her son illegitimate. She told everyone she knew who his real father was. She also told her son as soon as he was old enough to ask about a daddy. Spry always said that she named the boy John Paul after him "out of spite."

With the·purpose of his conception gone when he was born, Myrtle did not want the baby. She left him in Lillian's custody while she went off in search of amusement and another man. Lillian put him into the crib with the first son of her second marriage, Vann's cousin George

John Paul Vann's mother, Myrtle Lee Tripp, in her self-indulgent finery. "I'm Myrtle and there's not another one in the world like me. I love myself," said her sister Mollie in summing up Myrtle's character.
Courtesy Dorothy Lee Cadorette.

His father, Johnny Spry, in a moment of brief prosperity before his bootleg whiskey still was raided. Myrtle named the boy John Paul after him.
Courtesy John Paul Spry, Jr.

Dillard, who had been born two weeks earlier and had been delivered by the same doctor. Vann and his cousin also shared the same bottle, and Lillian gave him the care and affection she gave her George. Myrtle took him back several months later after she found another man to pay the rent on another apartment for a while. He experienced his first pain then from the neglect and rejection his mother inflicted on him with her egocentricity and the instability of her life. Mollie decided to check up on the baby one day. "I know my sister; she's not takin' care of him right," she remembered thinking. She found him deserted. He was lying in a crib in his own filth, crying from hunger. She took him home, cleaned him up, and began raising him with her two infant sons. Periodically Myrtle would come back and claim him. Her ego made her want to pretend to be a mother. Vann's aunts would watch her and retrieve him as soon as she wandered off again. He spent most of his first four and a half years with Lillian or Mollie—until Myrtle became pregnant with his half sister, Dorothy Lee, and married Aaron Frank Vann in January 1929. His aunts bought him new clothes or saw that he got decent hand-me-downs from his cousins, and he never wanted for food.

The appearance of a stepfather who would presumably give him a home seemed fortunate; little Johnny, as he had been nicknamed, was losing the protection of his aunts. Mollie moved to New York in 1928, and Lillian and her family followed in 1929 after her husband lost his job on the Norfolk police force. They arrived before the Great Depression started that October with the Black Tuesday crash of the stock market. Queenie instigated the moves. She had become familiar with New York as a stewardess on the coastal steamships. She told Mollie it was a marvelously exciting place with all sorts of opportunities and persuaded Mollie to take a trip up on a steamer to see the city. "We're movin' to New York," Mollie announced to her husband as soon as she returned to Norfolk. Her shipyard welder had by this time graduated to well-paid work as a loading-crane operator at one of the Norfolk coal piers. He became a mechanic with the New York subway system. Lillian's husband was hired as a security guard at the main branch of the Irving Trust Company at 1 Wall Street.

Mollie dyed her flowing black hair blond, hired baby-sitters for her two boys, and became a hostess in the tearoom of the Hotel Taft, then known as the Menger. The hotel was next to the Roxy Theater, the grandest of the movie palaces in those years of cinema glory. The Roxy's patrons would go to the hotel tearoom for a snack and a light meal after screenings of first-run movies and the four stage shows daily that were accompanied by the Roxy's own 110-piece orchestra. The headwaiter in the hotel grill downstairs was a handsome Italian who resembled a fellow immigrant, Rudolph Valentino, the lover-idol of the silent-film era of the 1920s. He was so proud of the resemblance that he had people call him Valentino. Mollie fell in love with him, divorced her Norfolk man, and became Mrs. Terzo Tosolini. She retained custody of her two sons. "My mother was a very progressive woman," Mollie said of the quality in Queenie, and in herself, which had taken them both on the journey from Bill Tripp's forty acres.

Frank Vann seemed to be a responsible man. He was thirty, seven years older than Myrtle was, when he married her in 1929. His home country on the Carolina coastal plain was the Murfreesboro region close by the Virginia line. His father was an unusually clever and industrious tenant farmer who had raised nine children and, with help from the Baptist Church and what they could earn on their own, sent a number of them to teacher-training colleges. Frank Vann had completed high school and clerked in a country store prior to moving to Norfolk. He was a well-meaning man, kind and gentle in his dealings with others. It was his weakness and passivity that hurt those who depended on him.

The first four years of the marriage were probably the most tolerable, despite Frank Vann's recurring unemployment. He was laid off by the city bus company, found a job on the assembly line at the Ford plant in Norfolk, and then lost that too as the Depression worsened. He and Myrtle had two more children following the birth of Dorothy Lee in 1929. Vann's first half brother, Aaron Frank, Jr., or Frank Junior as he was called, was born at the end of 1931. Eugene Wallace came in the spring of 1933. Frank Vann moved the family down to North Carolina shortly after Gene's birth, because he was able to obtain work in a zipper factory at a place called George not far from his father's farm. Myrtle made him quit and bring them back to Norfolk in a few months. She did not like living in the country, and she did not get along with his family. Grace was said before every meal at the farmhouse table of Frank's father, and his sisters and their families were also active in the local Baptist church. They were shocked by Myrtle's contempt for house-keeping and child-rearing and they wondered about her morals.

In the Norfolk to which they returned, Johnny and his sister and brothers were subjected to a level of deprivation that made Myrtle's childhood in Pitt County seem comfortable by comparison. Frank Vann worked at the Ford plant when there was a spate of production in

NORFOLK, VIRGINIA

Frank Vann, John Paul's stepfather, did the cooking; he tried to make the monotonous fried potatoes and biscuits as tasty as possible. Young Johnny in Frank Vann's hat, Frank Junior, Dorothy Lee, little Gene in his big brother's Boy Scout hat as cowboy gear.
Courtesy Dorothy Lee Cadorette.

Gene was the victim of the vitamin-deficient diet. Rickets bowed his legs grotesquely. The surgeons at a charity hospital broke his legs to set them straight and he wore a body cast for eight months.
Courtesy Dorothy Lee Cadorette.

ESCAPE TO FERRUM

A rich Norfolk oyster dealer outfitted him in sport coat and slacks and wrote a check for a scholarship at Ferrum Training School and Junior College in the foothills of the Blue Ridge Mountain.
Courtesy Dorothy Lee Cadorette.

A happy Johnny Vann in *The Beacon*, the Ferrum yearbook for the class of 1943: "Intelligent, clear-eyed — of such as he,/Shall Freedom's young apostles be." *Courtesy The Parker Studio, Roanoke, Virginia.*

Myrtle and Frank Vann came
to visit him at a processing center in
Nashville, Tennessee, before he went
on to flight training. Myrtle wore her
grey-squirrel coat.
Courtesy Dorothy Lee Cadorette.

The eve of the wedding:
John Vann between Myrtle
and Mary Jane.
Courtesy Mary Jane Vann.

THE AIR CORPS AND A GIRL

Lt. John Paul Vann and Mary Jane Allen on their wedding day, October 6, 1945.
Courtesy Mary Jane Vann.

FAMILY DAYS

The halcyon time in Osaka, Japan, before the outbreak of the Korean War, with Patricia, their first-born, and John Allen on his mother's lap.
Courtesy Mary Jane Vann.

West Germany in the mid-1950s: Tommy listening to his father during a bicycle excursion along a dirt road through a forest. Tow-headed Jesse at left, John Allen behind Tommy, blond boy beside him is the child of a family friend.
Courtesy Mary Jane Vann.

VIETNAM: THE FIRST YEAR

Vann and Cao, August 1962.
*"The best U. S.-Vietnamese
team for fighting
Communists."*
Courtesy Mary Jane Vann.

Capt. Thuong, the Cambodian who
commanded the Rangers and
who wielded a Bowie knife.
John Paul Vann Papers.

Col. Daniel Boone Porter in civies.
John Paul Vann Papers.

Dick Ziegler's war diary opened to facing pages on the battle.

Top: Planning an earlier operation: Ziegler, standing; Maj. Essex, left; Lt. Col. Bui Dinh Dam, center; Capt. Linh, 7th Division operations officer, right.
Center: The paratroops are dropped too late and in the wrong place.
Bottom: An A-26 Invader hitting Bac hamlet with napalm.

THE BATTLE OF AP BAC

Ziegler's sketch map of the battle. Bac is at the place where he has penned the number 3 in a circle. *Courtesy Lt. Col. Richard Ziegler, U. S. A. (Ret.).*

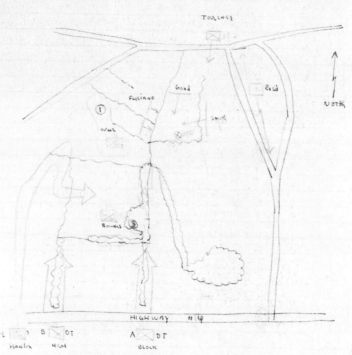

Jim Scanlon and Ly Tong Ba on top of Ba's M-113 APC during an operation prior to the battle. *Courtesy Lt. Col. James Scanlon, U. S. A. (Ret.).*

Downed helicopters: the two H-21s stand forlornly in the paddy field in front of Bac. The crashed Huey is behind to the left.
Courtesy Lt. Col. James Scanlon, U. S. A. (Ret.).

David Halberstam of *The New York Times* fording a stream, or, "Knee-deep in the Big Muddy," as he later put it.
Horst Faas/Associated Press.

Lt. Gen. Victor "Brute" Krulak of the Marine Corps became a rarity among the American military leaders. He learned to think like the men in Hanoi.
U. P. I./Bettmann Newsphotos.

Paul Harkins, right, takes Gen. Earle Wheeler in hand when Wheeler is sent out after Ap Bac to investigate Harkins's direction of the war.
U. S. Army.

BACK IN VIETNAM

Hau Nghia Province, 1965: Doug Ramsey, the cheerful, lanky Westerner who was the perfect assistant and partner for Vann in this most insecure of provinces west of Saigon after Vann's return to Vietnam.
Mert Perry.

Dan Ellsberg, right, who replaced Ramsey as Vann's companion in the field after Ramsey was captured by the Viet Cong. Vann, showing Ellsberg Hau Nghia, has stopped to talk to the local Vietnamese official at left.
John Paul Vann Papers.

John Vann with Gen. Fred Weyand, the friend who was to help Vann get his stars and who saved Saigon during the Communist Tet Offensive, at Weyand's headquarters at Long Binh. *Dick Swanson, Life Magazine,* ©*Time, Inc.*

The author, then a correspondent for *The New York Times*, talking to Brig. Gen. Du Quoc Dong, commander of the ARVN Airborne Division, during the fighting in Da Nang between two factions on the Saigon side. *Paul Avery.*

The civilian general of the mountains of the Highlands and the rice deltas of the Central Coast with his staff at II Corps headquarters at Pleiku. To Vann's left is his chief of staff, Col. Joseph Pizzi; to Vann's right is his military deputy, Brig. Gen. George Wear. *U. S. Army.*

John Vann, in the golf jacket he wore to ward off the chill of flying in his helicopter, at the command post of an ARVN airborne brigade battling the North Vietnamese Army for control of Rocket Ridge between Tan Canh and Kontum. *Matt Franjola.*

John Vann strides through Bong Son town in a vain effort to encourage the defenders as it and the rest of northern Binh Dinh Province on the coast collapse before the Communist forces. *Matt Franjola.*

Calling in the B-52s: John Vann telling U. S. military advisors in Kontum at the height of the siege of the town how he will defeat the NVA. At right is Brig. Gen. Nguyen Van Toan, the new ARVN II Corps commander, who had been instructed to listen to Vann. *Matt Franjola.*

Camp Holloway Airstrip, June 10, 1972: John Vann's casket is carried to a C-130 transport for the flight to Saigon. *Matt Franjola.*

DEATH OF A SOLDIER

June 16 1972: In the Oval Office of the White House after the funeral at Arlington National Cemetery. Left to right: Aaron Frank Vann, Jr., Eugene Wallace Vann, Dorothy Lee Vann Cadorette, Jesse Vann, Thomas Vann, Peter Vann, Mary Jane Vann, President Richard Nixon, John Allen Vann, Secretary of Defense Melvin Laird, Secretary of State William Rogers. *Official White House Photo.*

between layoffs. He also drove a taxi now and then. The Works Progress Administration started by Franklin Roosevelt gave him occasional employment at building parks and other public projects. Most of the time he was out of a job. There was no unemployment compensation in those years, and no welfare payments worth mentioning. The family moved constantly for failure to pay the rent, and yet they moved nowhere. They simply shifted to one more dark and grimy house within the dingy world of two white working-class sections—the Lamberts Point area behind the coal-shipping piers of the Norfolk and Western Railroad at the mouth of the Elizabeth River and a former cotton and lumber mill district nearby called Atlantic City—where someone else was also going to be evicted and Frank Vann could talk his way into another house.

The neighborhood where the family lived in Lamberts Point in 1936 at the height of the Depression, when Vann was twelve, and the house they occupied there were typical of their other neighborhoods and houses. The city had paved the streets, laid sewers and strung electric lines on poles overhead, and built a large elementary school of brownish-red brick beyond a vacant lot across the street. Then everything had stopped. There were no sidewalks, only dirt paths in front of the houses and more dirt paths and alleys in between. Here and there at odd intervals a tree, like the big locust before the Vanns' house, had been left for shade. Few of the families bothered to cultivate the small front yards and plant grass for lawns. They were content with the patches of weeds that remained where the children and the dogs did not wear the ground bare. All of the buildings, including the school, were low-lying, and many of the wooden ones had not been painted for so long that they had acquired the dun color of naturally weathered wood.

The Vanns' house fell into the dun-colored category and was of a construction so common to the poor districts of pre–World War II Southern cities that it might be called Southern urban working class. It was two stories high under a peaked roof. The siding was clapboard. The house was narrow, gaining its space by running back to the rear. There was no basement. The roofed porch across the front was only about a foot and a half above the ground. The porch railing had fallen away for want of repair, and no one bothered to build a new one, as it was more convenient to step directly off the porch and into the yard. The narrow design contributed to the dark interior of the house by reducing the amount of light that could penetrate. Age and accumulated filth added to the darkening effect. Someone had once painted all of the interior doors black. The wooden floors were barren of carpets or linoleum and had dips worn into them from use and grit. They stayed dirty, because

Frank Vann, who did what cleaning was done, wasn't fussy about them.

The first room off to the left of the entrance hallway was the living room. It was furnished with a sofa of considerable age and unknown origin, a wooden rocker as scratched as another rocker on the porch, and a couple of straight-backed wooden chairs. An empty Prince Albert pipe tobacco can rested on the floor beside the rocker. Frank Vann used it as a spittoon. He chewed tobacco at first and then switched to another country habit called "dipping snuff." He would put a pinch of snuff between his lip and his front teeth and let it sit there to melt. A potbelly stove in the living room also served him as a spittoon. The stove was the principal heating system for the house in winter. Vents had been cut into the ceilings to let the warm air drift upward to the bedrooms above. Frank Vann burned coal in the stove when he could pick some up around the Norfolk and Western loading piers, otherwise scrap wood, and when neither was available the rooms stayed cold. The kitchen was at the end of the hallway. The wood-fired cooking stove there, square and of black iron like Queenie's in North Carolina, made the kitchen and the bedroom above it the last rooms in the house to go cold. A single light bulb hung from a wire in the ceiling over the table and chairs in the center of the kitchen. The sink had one brass spigot that gave cold water. Hot water had to be heated on the stove. If anyone wanted a bath the hot water had to be carried in pails to the bathroom upstairs and poured into the old-fashioned tub that stood on legs.

Frank Vann did the cooking too, as Myrtle also refused to do any of that. He was an early riser and would get up at 5:00 A.M. to wash and make breakfast for himself and the children, whistling and singing hymns as he heated water with which to shave. (He was not religious. He and Myrtle sometimes sent the children to Baptist Sunday school but never went to church themselves.) In the most empty-handed months of winter on Bill Tripp's farm, Myrtle had always had some hog meat and gravy to eat with the biscuits or cornbread Queenie baked. The basic diet of Myrtle's children was biscuits for breakfast, fried potatoes and biscuits for lunch (it was called dinner in country fashion), and more fried potatoes and biscuits for supper. They drank coffee with their meals, although milk would have been more nourishing, because coffee is a Southern taste and Frank Vann seemed to find money for it no matter how hard times became. Potatoes were the cheapest vegetable he could buy. He carried them home on his shoulder in fifty-pound burlap sacks.

He was not a bad cook. He tried to make the potatoes as tasty as possible by peeling them carefully and slicing them across and extremely thin like potato chips. He would also buy a few onions to dice and toss in with the potatoes for flavor. He varied the biscuits with something he called "flour bread," biscuit dough spread out in the frying pan and baked into unleavened bread. He also frequently served something he called "tomato gravy" to pour over the biscuits or unleavened bread. Tomatoes were the cheapest canned vegetable at three or four cents for a large can. Frank Vann turned the canned tomatoes into a gravy by whipping some flour into them in the frying pan. On rare occasions he brought home cans of salmon, which he mixed with flour to bake salmon cakes, and on those still rarer occasions when his pocket was flush he appeared with eggs to scramble with the salmon, or served fried pork brains and scrambled eggs. His most common good supper, one the children looked forward to with anticipation, was "cheese biscuits." He would buy a small portion of cheese, cut it up, and bake the biscuits with a piece of cheese hidden inside every third one. Frank Junior learned to watch for a biscuit that had revealed its prize by leaking a bit of melted cheese in the oven so that he could snatch it from the pile on the platter before somebody else spotted it. Johnny's cribmate, George Dillard, came down to Norfolk every year with his parents during his father's vacation from security-guard work at Irving Trust on Wall Street. He chummed around with his cousin and often spent the night at Johnny's house. He recalled the whooping at the table whenever anyone grabbed a biscuit with a piece of cheese in it. "Then you got the treat," he said. "Otherwise you were out of luck. You got the plain biscuit." At most meals the Vann children were out of luck with plain biscuits and fried potatoes. Dorothy Lee sprinkled salt and pepper on a biscuit one evening to try to make it taste better.

This urban variation of the pellagra-and-rickets diet was more dangerous than the rural one, because Frank Vann did not plant a garden in the backyard to provide the children with fresh vegetables in the spring and fall. Gene became its victim. He was the most vulnerable to vitamin deficiency as the youngest, just three in the spring of 1936. He developed a severe case of rickets, which causes defective bone growth. The disease left him grotesquely bowlegged. "That boy could have stepped around a keg of nails and never known it," Frank Junior reflected.

A charity hospital in Norfolk sent a public health nurse around periodically to examine children in poor neighborhoods. The Vann children knew her as a kind and imposing lady who arrived in a chauffeur-driven car wearing a blue uniform and spoke with an accent that sounded German or Scandinavian. Her name was Miss Landsladder, and she rescued Gene from a cripple's life. She arranged for the surgeons at the hospital to see him. They first broke and set the left lower legbone, and when it healed well, they brought him back and broke and properly aligned the rest of the major bones in both legs in a single operation. For eight months afterward he was encased in a plaster cast that began at the upper half of his chest and extended over his thighs and down each leg to his feet. His legs were held apart in a wide V by a splint set into the plaster at knee level. Among the many things he could not do was to turn over in bed, but his brother Johnny made that problem fun once the bones had fused and Gene was no longer in pain. He would put his arms under the cast and flip Gene over in the bed. Johnny also did not abandon Gene at home when there were ballgames and other excursions. He toted Gene on his back, carrying him on and off the trolley cars that way and joking with the conductors so that they would not be asked for the fare they did not have. The surgeons gave Gene a pair of straight legs. In that era of primitive skin grafting they did not attempt to repair the wide scars they created from his thighs to his shins. The disease also stunted the growth of his legs, making Gene the shortest in the family at a shade under five feet seven inches in adulthood, and the long-term effects of the operation caused painful osteoarthritis in his hips in later years.

Shame accompanied the hunger and pain and raggedy clothes. The Vann children knew the neighbors knew that Myrtle sold herself and had plenty of money. She was clever about it. She did not walk the streets. The police would have arrested her right away if she had. Prostitution was regulated in Norfolk until the 1950s by an unofficial arrangement that profited politicians, police, and organized criminals and kept moral ugliness from the eyes of children. There was a red-light district in old Norfolk, with bordellos in a spectrum of amenities and prices. One was a tourist attraction. A visitor could bed down with a whore in the same room in which Lafayette was supposed to have slept when he visited Norfolk in 1824.

Myrtle discovered an unoccupied niche. She specialized in middle-class men who would have been embarrassed to be seen going to a brothel. As a professed amateur, Myrtle was less intimidating, and she soon had a string of regulars. She had her clients come to the house or met them at some other spot where they felt secure. One of her customers was a lay leader and Sunday-school superintendent at a Norfolk church. Dorothy Lee remembered another of her mother's clients because he met Myrtle every week outside the same hot dog stand downtown to arrange the time of their rendezvous. He was a well-dressed man in late middle age. He would smile and hand Dorothy Lee some coins. "Go into the hot dog stand," Myrtle would then say, and Dorothy Lee would buy herself a hot dog while her mother and the gentleman talked. When he subsequently appeared at the house, normally on a Wednesday afternoon, Myrtle would order Dorothy Lee to play outside. She seems to have taken Dorothy Lee along to the meetings because the child was protection. A woman who had her daughter with her was unlikely to be arrested for soliciting. (Myrtle was apparently known to the police, but there is no record of her having been prosecuted, probably because the police did not want to expose her clients.)

Had she sold herself for the sake of her children, they might have been less troubled by shame, given the grimness of the times. Except for Dorothy Lee's weekly hot dog treat, the only sight of the money they ever had was on Myrtle. She spent it all on herself—for stylish clothes, for jewelry and makeup, and for whiskey. A wardrobe in the bedroom she shared with Frank Vann was full of pretty dresses and suits, and she had hats and shoes and silk stockings and handbags to match. One of her suits was in black velvet with a fox-fur collar. At a time when rent for a whole house was $6 a month, its cost would have paid the rent for several months. She also had an evening gown and enough jewelry to have kept the family in rent and groceries for many months—a solitaire diamond ring (the stone was large, almost a carat), a diamond-studded wristwatch and band to go with the ring, a gold-and-diamond bracelet for her other arm, and a white-gold dinner-ring set with diamonds and contrasting black stones. Eventually she completed her outfit with a fur coat and hat of gray squirrel. More money went to the hairdresser to keep her hair in a permanent wave. She did not want to be bothered setting it herself. She painted her fingernails and toenails while sitting in the rocker on the porch. She would also move the rocker into the front yard to tan herself in the sun. The porch and front-yard sitting had another purpose; she was attracting more clients. A woman posed in fancy clothes before a shabby house is an advertisement that requires no caption.

Frank Vann not only acquiesced in what Myrtle did, he also gave her most of the money he earned when he was working, and she spent it too. This and his passive pattern of behavior helped to explain why the Vann children suffered so grievously. There was more and better food available from charity organizations than he brought home, and there was more work to be had than he found. One of Johnny's acquaintances whose father was also often without a job wondered why the Vanns didn't have more food until it struck him that his father was constantly foraging at the relief centers and searching for work of any kind, while

Frank Vann could usually be found at home. He liked to sit and read in his rocker in the living room. The explanation was not that he was physically lazy. He would work when work was offered to him. (During the manpower shortage of World War II he held down two jobs simultaneously—as a carpenter at the Norfolk Naval Base by day and a city fireman by night—and Myrtle managed to spend both salaries as fast as he could hand her his paychecks.) What he would not do was aggressively seek work. He never attempted to use his education to better himself with a white-collar position, instead gravitating to manual labor and ultimately retiring in the mid-1960s with a medical disability from his carpentry job at the naval base. He did seem to have a craving to be humiliated, and Myrtle satisfied that.

She would curse him for not finding more work and bringing her more money and taunt him with her promiscuity. She ordered him about like a servant, and he obeyed. She addressed him as Vann rather than Frank. For a wife to call her husband by his last name was a custom in the South of the period. Myrtle's tone when she said "Vann!" was what made the difference. Dorothy Lee was given to nightmares and leg cramps. If she woke her mother with her cries at night, Myrtle would call to her husband from her twin bed: "Vann, get up and see what's the matter with Dorothy Lee." She never nursed the children when they were ill. Frank Vann was a compassionate nurse. He turned Myrtle's empty whiskey bottles into hot-water bottles, wrapping them in cloth and placing them next to Dorothy Lee's legs to ease the cramps. The children feared Myrtle's rages; her temper and tongue were also of the gutter. Frank Vann normally sat silent while she cursed him. His silence enraged her further. Her voice became shriller and her language viler as she tried to provoke him into reacting. Only rarely did he fight back. Once he picked up a hatchet and shouted at her to get out. She left, but returned in a couple of days and the relationship resumed. She apparently strengthened her hold on him by letting him make love to her once in a while.

Frank Vann's passivity exposed Johnny and his sister and brothers to the full extent of Myrtle's cruelty. The Vann children grew up without ever having a Christmas tree. Frank Junior and Gene found a discarded tree one year about a week after Christmas in an alley where another family had left it for trash. They dragged it home, determined to put it up in the living room. The tree still had bits of tinsel the other family had not bothered to remove amid the green needles on the boughs. Myrtle caught them while they were trying to figure out how to get the tree to stand up on the floor and shouted and cursed and made them drag it back to the alley. The boys in other families kept the street noisy with their new cap pistols on Christmas morning and paraded in their new cowboy suits. The girls had dolls to show off. Christmas morning for the Vann children was four stockings Frank Vann hung behind the potbelly stove, each holding an apple, an orange, some nuts, and a few pieces of hard Christmas candy. Not until the end of the 1930s when he began working more did the boys get a cowboy suit and Dorothy Lee a doll.

At Thanksgiving there was never a turkey. If the family was lucky, Myrtle might bake a cake at Thanksgiving or Christmas. She could bake delicious ones when she took a rare notion to buy the ingredients. She covered them with a thick chocolate icing. She baked no cakes for birthdays, because nobody's birthday was celebrated. Dorothy Lee got the next-best thing to a cake on one birthday when she was sick with scarlet fever. Miss Landsladder came to see her and brought a chocolate cupcake and lit a candle on it.

Myrtle's cruelty could also be sudden and physical. She slapped fast, across the face and hard up against the side of the head, at the slightest hesitation in response to one of her commands or at any back talk.

She was not fully conscious of her cruelty. Her selfishness was so consuming that it protected her from understanding what she did to others. Her vanity led her to buy a Kodak camera, one of the early box models, to have photographs taken of herself in her finery. She also took pictures of her children in their cast-off clothes, of the squalid houses in which they lived, of little Gene with his crooked legs, of Gene in the body cast he wore for a year after the second operation. She pasted all of the photographs into scrapbooks and displayed them freely during her lifetime. She had no awareness that what she recorded as souvenirs others might see as something else. Her ego similarly protected her from the disgrace of her trade. Being paid by men made her feel young and desirable. "Men tell me I've got the prettiest legs in the city of Norfolk," she would say to her daughter in a sprightly voice.

The shame was often harder for the Vann children to bear than the deprivations. The white working-class sections of Norfolk in the 1930s were not like the urban slums that were to grow in the decayed cities of the North after World War II. They were not places of crime and moral filth, where many of the children were fatherless and had sisters and mothers who were part-time or full-time prostitutes. Many of the fathers were heavy drinkers. On Friday and Saturday nights the children would gather to watch the fistfights in front of the taverns. Some of the women also drank, battled noisily with their husbands, and strayed to other beds like their men. Nevertheless, these poor and grubby Norfolk neighborhoods were family neighborhoods. They were safe. Rape and mugging and other street crimes were rare. Hardly anyone locked a door at night. There was also a social stratum. A few middle-class families had chosen to stay behind rather than move to better sections. They were people to look up to and normally provided the leadership in church and civic affairs. Divorce was not uncommon. One or both parties then usually married someone else. Even the less respectable women tended to be wives and mothers in between drinking bouts, and the majority of the women took their roles seriously. They busied themselves running households and caring for their husbands and offspring. Myrtle was the exception. In the Norfolk of the 1930s the Southern term "white trash" was not applied to a family on the basis of poverty alone. The term connoted a way of living more than it did income. Myrtle made the Vanns white trash.

The weight of shame was double for Johnny because of his illegitimacy. As Myrtle did not hide the circumstances of his conception, he assumed that most people he was acquainted with knew about it. The working class of Norfolk had carried the values of rural Southern culture with them to the city. To be illegitimate was to have no family, to be nothing. His birth certificate said that he was John Paul LeGay. A French sailor named Victor LeGay had never had anything to do with him. He wanted to have a real name and be a member of a real family and have a daddy. Any family and any daddy were better than none. He wanted to be called John Paul Vann.

His mother would not let him escape the disgrace of his birth. She refused to allow Frank Vann to adopt him. Had she not prevented it, Frank Vann probably would have adopted the boy at the outset of the marriage when Johnny was four and a half. He treated Myrtle's boy with the same gentleness he showed toward his own children. He referred to Johnny as his son, never as his stepson, and saw to it that Dorothy Lee, Frank Junior, and Gene called him their brother. Although rejection is one of love's opposites, it evokes responses as powerful as those that love arouses. Spry's rejection of Myrtle seems to have evoked in her a need to stop any other man from claiming her "love child" with his name, because the boy was all that she had retained of the affair. She would repeatedly warn Frank Vann that he was not to try to control or discipline her Johnny. "He doesn't belong to you," she would say. "He's my son. He's not your son."

That other need that made her attack the masculinity of her men by taunting them with her promiscuity also led her to sense how vulnerable her son was about his birth. She used it as an additional weapon with which to wound him. He gave her lots of opportunities, because he would not let the argument rest, constantly begging her to permit Frank Vann to adopt him. "He's the only daddy I've ever had and Vann's the only name I've ever wanted," he would say.

Myrtle would point a finger at her husband and sneer. "He's not your daddy," she would say. "Your name ain't Vann. You don't have a daddy."

He didn't have a daddy. Myrtle was right. He liked Frank Vann, despite his weakness, because Frank Vann was never mean to him, but Frank Vann couldn't ever be a real daddy. If Frank Vann were capable of being a real daddy he would have somehow found them food and clothes and paid the rent and tamed Myrtle or thrown her out of the house. The boy's ambivalence toward Frank Vann was reflected in the way he spoke of him. Within the family the boy addressed him as Daddy. To cousins and other outsiders the boy called him Vann. There was no one to whom he could turn for the kind of help that a father is supposed to give.

Spry was still in Norfolk, but he was of little comfort. The boy called him Johnny. Spry had abandoned trolley-car driving toward the end of the 1920s for the big money to be made in the Prohibition era distilling "white lightning" for bootleggers. He had also divorced his first wife. After his whiskey still was raided and he spent six months in jail, Spry decided that bootlegging was not for him. He married another young woman he had fallen in love with and curbed his wenching and gambling sufficiently so that they did not ruin his second marriage. By the latter half of the 1930s he had a steady job driving a bakery truck and was raising a new family of three boys. He was a good father to them. The requirements of this second family and what wenching and gambling he still allowed himself left him scant time or money for the two sons of his first marriage or for this other John Paul. When the boy came to him once in a while for money to buy food, he gave it to him. Spry was also occasionally able to let him earn a little by working as a helper on the bakery van. Otherwise he left the boy to survive with Frank Vann and Myrtle.

Something in the son did not let Myrtle destroy him. He told his grammar school teachers so often and so insistently that his name was John Vann, not John LeGay, that they came up with the compromise under which he was registered at school: John LeGay Vann. His high spirits showed in his enthusiasm for basketball and track and tumbling, the last another talent he seems to have acquired from Spry, who was so strong and limber he could chin himself with one arm and walk on his hands. Johnny would amuse his sister and brothers by rolling cartwheels along the dirt paths and also by walking on his hands up and down the stairs. He would amaze visiting cousins by tossing himself off the porch roof in a backflip somersault to the ground.

He turned to anyone who offered a temporary escape from the prison of his family life. One man who did was an eccentric Salvation Army captain, a former bandmaster in the Navy, who was well liked by the youngsters in the area. He preferred not to dress in the blue-and-maroon uniform of his new religious ranks. Instead he wore a spiffy suit and a wide-brimmed soft hat of the sort favored by the Chicago gangster Al Capone. He organized and coached a basketball club to give poor boys some fun and keep them out of trouble. His best team won the championship in the Norfolk Central YMCA Junior League with five straight victories. The *Virginian-Pilot* published a photograph of the winners. The shortest member of the team was a blondish-haired boy who looked straight into the camera. His sweater had "SA" for Salvation Army lettered crudely on the front. The buckle of the man's belt that held up his pants was so big it stuck out askew from under the sweater.

The Boy Scouts offered more hours of escape. He joined a troop that met at his grammar school in the Lamberts Point neighborhood where the family was living when he was twelve. Within four months he had climbed to assistant patrol leader, and the scoutmaster arranged for him to be given a secondhand uniform. He posed for Myrtle's scrapbook in front of a furniture repair shop next to the house, pushing the pancake-brim campaign hat the Scouts wore back over the clipped hair above his forehead for a jaunty look. His happy eyes and smile indicate he was too proud of his uniform to think that there was anything inappropriate about the khaki shirt and flared riding breeches that enveloped his slip of a body, seventy-one pounds and four feet seven inches tall according to his Scout identification card, issued in the name of John Paul Vann.

The family moved again in the fall of 1937, this time back to Atlantic City, the other working-class section where Frank Vann could find a house. Johnny was thirteen and about to enter the eighth grade in junior high school. The move brought him his first best friend. He seems to have been a loner before. The need to hide so much, to struggle against the want and the torment, and the frequent moves appear to have prevented him from forming close friendships with anyone except his brothers and visiting cousins. This first friend was a boy quite different in temperament and childhood experience. In adult life the friend was to content himself with a brief career on the Norfolk police force and then an air-conditioning business in Florida. His name was Edward Crutchfield, called Gene for his middle name of Eugene. He was six months younger than Vann and a grade behind. Crutchfield's memory was that they somehow fell into conversation one day on the street. He suspected there were several reasons that they became friends: Crutchfield knew nothing of Vann and his family before they met, and Crutchfield's home was a real one in contrast to Vann's; they did not compete in sports (Crutchfield was huskier and played baseball) or clash in any other way; and Crutchfield was a good listener.

Crutchfield called him John rather than Johnny, because he had introduced himself as John Vann and seemed to prefer being addressed by his formal first name. As they saw more of each other, Crutchfield noticed that although John washed and was always clean, he wore virtually the same clothes day after day. He apparently did not have enough to change. His shoes were not the sort a boy would have chosen and looked like hand-me-downs. John also appeared thin for a boy so remarkably fit, Crutchfield thought. Crutchfield's mother gave Gene two apples shortly after they met, and he passed one on to his new acquaintance. John thanked him and then wolfed down the apple as though it were going to disappear if he did not eat it instantly.

He ate politely if quickly when Crutchfield invited him home for supper. Crutchfield was proud of his home and especially of his mother, and he could tell that John was impressed. The Crutchfields were one of the few working-class families in Atlantic City who could afford to own a house rather than rent. Crutchfield's father was the diesel engineer on a small vessel the Army Corps of Engineers operated out of Fort Norfolk for coastal surveys and related projects. He drank, but not enough to lose his job or deprive the family of groceries. Crutchfield's mother compensated for her husband's vice with a strength of character and the affection with which she practiced the art of motherhood. She tried to serve a particularly fine supper whenever one of her sons was going to bring home a chum, and she did not disappoint Gene the first evening he invited John.

The two boys developed a habit of playing at a lumberyard in Atlantic City when the place was deserted after working hours, because John could practice tumbling on a huge sawdust pile there. Crutchfield was fascinated by the intensity with which his friend drove himself to achieve perfection in backflips and other tumbling exercises for the competitions at school. John would climb to the top of the sawdust heap, fling his body into the air and spin end over end to land at the bottom, clamber up the sawdust slope and hurl himself into the air again, and do it again, and again.

Late one afternoon the boys spotted a car parked on a narrow road that ran through the lumberyard, hidden from the view of anyone outside by the work sheds and stacks of boards. The license plate displayed the MD letters of a doctor. The movements they could see inside the car from a distance indicated that a couple were making love. They sneaked up to watch the performance. As they slowly raised themselves alongside a door and peeked through a window, they were both surprised. Myrtle was entertaining a client her son had not known about. They crept away without disturbing the assignation. John did not attempt to hide how profoundly upset he was. His friend knew who the woman inside the car was, because John had taken Crutchfield to his house a few days before and introduced him to Myrtle. He had pretended that she was just like Crutchfield's mother. He had also introduced Crutchfield to Frank Vann, making believe that Frank Vann stood in the same relationship to him as the natural father he had met at Crutchfield's home. Crutchfield had observed how shabby the house was, but John had been careful not to give the game away by inviting Crutchfield to supper.

After his mortification in the lumberyard, John ceased to pretend and shared his pain. "Why couldn't I have a nice mother like yours, Gene?" he asked.

"I'm sorry, John, I don't know what to say," Crutchfield replied.

"I appreciate your being the good friend to me that you are," John said. "I really appreciate it."

Crutchfield wanted to comfort him but didn't know how.

On another day they were walking through the alley beside the house when John stopped in front of an empty whiskey bottle that Myrtle had discarded. He kicked it. "There'd be more food in the house if she didn't spend the money on that," he said. He explained how Frank Vann handed Myrtle almost all of his money. He cursed Frank Vann for his weakness. His face got angrier. He kicked the bottle again. "She never did want me anyway," he said.

Each time that depression overcame John, Crutchfield would hear those words. Vann never admitted his illegitimacy to his friend. Crutchfield discovered it from one of his own cousins who knew of Spry. The discovery gave John's words more meaning.

Crutchfield began to understand too why his friend practiced backflips with such intensity on the sawdust heap. He was releasing some of the rage that Myrtle built up in him. Other boys also felt the anger in him. They would snicker about Myrtle "messin' around" with men—but not to John's face. They were afraid to provoke him. He had a reputation as a fighter that said you couldn't land a punch on Johnny Vann. The fistfights Crutchfield saw did not last long. Some boy who did not know John would decide to test his reputation. The other boy would swing and John would duck and hit him hard. John's opponent would swing again and find more air and then panic and flail wildly as John's fists kept flashing and striking. He also had a way of tripping his opponent after the other boy had swung and landing another punch as the opponent went down. Crutchfield was amazed at the speed of John's reactions. He seemed to sense danger. Some of the boys who knew the family attributed his speed to practice at dodging Myrtle. In one fight John whipped a bigger boy who was a grudge-keeper. A few days later Crutchfield and John were walking around the corner of a building when the boy lunged out of a narrow indentation in the wall. John was on the inside, close to the wall, and the boy was well hidden until he leaped. It should have been impossible for him to miss, but John dodged and tripped him and punched him as the boy pitched to the ground. "You dumb son of a bitch, don't you ever learn?" John shouted at the prostrate grudge-keeper.

John did not provoke fights, Crutchfield observed. While he was assertive, he wanted to be accepted by his contemporaries. He seemed to relish a challenge only if the other boy was bigger or was a bully who had picked on one of his brothers. He sought out any older boy who bothered Frank Junior, or Gene and beat them if a warning did not suffice. One bully whom he punished made friends with his brothers after the fight and became an additional protector. Crutchfield never saw him lose a fight and never knew him to lack confidence in the outcome beforehand. "He doesn't worry me," John would say of his opponent as a scrap threatened in the schoolyard or a neighborhood lot.

He played a game that frightened Crutchfield. He would run halfway across the street and jump right in front of an oncoming vehicle, bluffing the driver into slamming on the brakes to avoid hitting him. Before the startled driver could shout a curse, he would have dashed the rest of the way across.

"Stop it, John, you're going to get killed," Crutchfield yelled at him the first time he saw the game.

John laughed. "It's lots of fun," he called from the other side of the street. He leaped in front of a bus on the way back to Crutchfield. He liked trucks and buses best and would pick a big bus out of the traffic.

One evening in the fall of 1938 when they had been friends about a year, Crutchfield came by to pick up John. He was waiting on the porch. Crutchfield could hear Myrtle inside the house screaming obscenities at Frank Vann. "Let's get out of here," John said. "She's raising hell."

He told Crutchfield that he was in despair. He couldn't stand living at home any longer. He didn't know what to do. He was thinking of running away. It seemed to be the only alternative. Crutchfield had seen enough to be convinced that John would run away, and if he did there was no knowing what would happen to him. Even if he did not run away, Crutchfield thought, the anger that Myrtle kept building within him would sooner or later burst out in self-destructive acts that would get him into trouble with the law. A young minister had taken over the Methodist church to which Crutchfield and his family belonged. He was stirring the whole congregation with his energy and ideas. Crutchfield took John to see him.

The minister's name was Garland Evans Hopkins. He was a man of charisma and contradictions, and he became the closest figure to a father Vann ever knew. Hopkins was a scion of one of those antique Virginia families—the Evanses on his mother's side—who were rich in pedigree and short in coin. He saw himself as an aristocratic champion of the downtrodden. He was to attain a reputation of sorts before his premature death twenty-seven years later. The Methodist Church sent him to Palestine in 1947 to assess the conflict between the Palestinian Arabs and the Zionist Jews who were creating the state of Israel. Hopkins came away from the experience convinced that the victims of Hitler's Holocaust were in turn victimizing the Palestinian Arabs. He became the principal American advocate of Palestinian rights in a period when it was fashionable to sympathize only with Israel and built the first major organization to lobby for the Arab cause and to promote relations with the Arab states—the American Friends of the Middle East. The CIA clandestinely financed the organization but Hopkins ran it.

When Gene Crutchfield brought his troubled friend to Hopkins in 1938, Hopkins was twenty-four years old and in charge of LeKies Memorial, the Methodist church in the Atlantic City neighborhood. He had taken over the parish the year before and wore a mustache to try to make himself look older. It complemented his horn-rimmed glasses and added a bit of distinction to an otherwise unimpressive medium height and build. Hopkins's father and grandfather had been Methodist ministers, but tradition was not the reason he had dropped out of law school and entered the ministry. He had been attracted by the ideas then being promoted within the Methodist Church in Virginia. They were ideas of the kind that are now taken for granted in American life—nutrition and welfare support for dependent children; free medical care for the impoverished and the aged; the right of workers to organize a union, to receive a minimum wage, to strike; interracial cooperation. In the Virginia of Hopkins's youth all of these ideas were new and "liberal," and they were radical where labor and race were concerned. His first assignment in the ministry had been as social-work director at a church in a Richmond slum which was being used as a center to experiment with relief and welfare programs. He had then been sent to LeKies to put his experience to work in Atlantic City.

The Depression had fostered receptivity to change at the lower level in the urban South. The working-class congregations of the period liked having a minister who was "progressive." The content of Hopkins's sermons was not the only innovation that had made him so popular at LeKies. His dynamism suffused every aspect of church life from worship to social work, and he led in whatever he did. The choir improved, because Hopkins was an accomplished pianist and taught its members to sing better. The church did not have a Boy Scout troop, and so he started one, made himself the scoutmaster, took the boys on camping trips, and joined them in earning merit badges for lifesaving and other skills. He told terrifying ghost stories around the campfire. The boys were as enthusiastic about him as their parents were.

It is apparent from what Crutchfield saw and from the subsequent relationship between Hopkins and Vann that the fourteen-year-old boy unburdened himself to the young minister as he had not done to any other man. Crutchfield had been struck by the high intelligence Vann displayed in understanding the relationship between Myrtle and Frank Vann and wanting to break free. Another boy caught in his predicament might not have been able to perceive the source of his troubles so clearly. Hopkins saw that this was not only a boy who wanted to be rescued, but one whom it would be particularly sad to lose. In a letter written not long after they met he spoke of what "an exceptionally bright boy" Vann was. He brought Vann into his congregation toward the end of 1938 by having him join eleven other young people and adults who stood up at a Sunday service and professed Christian faith. Hopkins also persuaded him to enter the LeKies Boy Scout troop. Vann's troubles had led him to drop out of the first troop he had joined at his grammar school.

The question of whether he would survive emotionally until Hopkins could separate him from Myrtle hung in the balance for a while. Crutchfield recalled that in his roller-coaster emotional state John would appear at a Scout meeting one week and then fail to show up for the next and have some irrational excuse. Hopkins's counseling summoned up more of the strength within him, and Hopkins held out the possibility of going away to a Methodist boarding school the following fall if he successfully completed ninth grade at the junior high in Norfolk. Vann's prowess at athletics also helped bring him through his trial. In the spring of 1939 he won first place for his age and weight class in the junior high sports carnival, a medley of track and tumbling events. He brought home his gilded cup and ribbons. Myrtle kept them. She was beginning to take pride in her eldest son. She photographed the cup for her album. Under the picture Vann proudly lettered the words MY CUP.

That fall Hopkins turned into Vann's genie from the magic lamp. He lifted his hand and a rich Norfolk oyster dealer who shared his wealth with the church because he believed in its good works took the boy down to the Hub, the city's most prestigious men's clothing store. Young John was outfitted with a sport coat and slacks, shoes, shirts, ties, and a sweater. Hopkins lifted his hand again and the businessman wrote a check for a scholarship that sent the boy to Ferrum Training School and Junior College in the foothills of the Blue Ridge Mountains in southwestern Virginia. Ferrum was a Methodist-run school that had been founded just prior to World War I as a "mountain mission" to bring basic education to the children of the isolated Blue Ridge communities. The same World War I prosperity that had briefly revived the economy of the South and given Norfolk a public education system from which poor children like Vann could benefit had also enabled the Methodist Church in Virginia to expand Ferrum into a small coeducational preparatory school and junior college. In mid-September 1939, two weeks after Hitler invaded Poland, Vann entered the tenth grade of the training school, Ferrum's high school division.

His four years at Ferrum were the first good years of his life. He had occasional lapses into despondency, and these showed in slumps in his grades. Most of the time he was happy, because Ferrum was a different world, a world that gave him hope of permanent escape into a life of respectability and accomplishment. The school was built in a bowl amid the foothills south of Roanoke. The beauty of oak and maple forests surrounded him. The classroom buildings and dormitories were red brick in that imitation Georgian style that is commonplace and yet appealing. He slept in a room that was warm with steam heat in winter;

the sheets on his bed were clean; he had eggs for breakfast and fresh milk to drink, rolls and bread warm from the oven and butter to put on them, and meat and vegetables every day.

There were few of the class distinctions among the students at Ferrum that had made him feel inferior at the junior high in Norfolk. Most of the thirty-five other boys and girls in his class were on full or partial scholarship. Norfolk was also the most sophisticated place anyone could call home. The majority of his classmates were from the inland towns and hamlets of Virginia and North Carolina. Each of the students was also assigned a job fifteen hours a week so that the school could keep overhead costs to a minimum by dispensing with clerical help and labor. Only a few supervisors were needed. The students did the cooking, waited on tables, mopped floors, washed clothes, clerked in the offices, and milked the cows and fed the chickens and shoveled the manure at the school farm that provided much of the food. Vann was put to work in the laundry for the first couple of years until the lady who was the guidance counselor discovered that he liked to lead and could teach. She gave him a job as a teacher's assistant at a country elementary school in a nearby hamlet. Ferrum was still running several of these for the mountain children of the region.

His happiness showed in his disposition. The Johnny Vann his teachers and classmates at Ferrum saw was not the same youth Crutchfield had known. He was like a bowstring that has been eased. When the dean described him she wrote that he was "a pleasing personality . . . very likable . . . makes friends easily . . . an 'all-round' man." His classmates remembered how much fun he was, how quick he was to joke. One of the girls recalled that he had a mischievous smile and used to tease her about another boy she dated. He gave no hint of what he had endured. He never discussed his family or home life, and when he returned from summers in Norfolk and Christmas and spring vacations he did not speak of how he had spent them.

Nothing changed at home. In fact, things got worse. Myrtle became infatuated with an alcoholic taxi driver, spent her earnings and Frank Vann's on her boyfriend, and kept him at the house for extended periods. Frank Vann would then sleep in another bedroom. Her son was now buffered against her by the prospect of flight each fall, and he stayed busy during his summers. Johnny Spry was by this time in a position to help him earn spending money for school. Spry had risen to chief shipping clerk at the bakery and could assign young John to a truck as a helper. The boy and his natural father became better friends. Hopkins saw to it that the wealthy businessman who was paying the scholarship kept him in proper clothes with a new suit or sports outfit and shoes and other accessories each September. Hopkins also tutored him in European history and in English composition and literature during his first summer at home in 1940 so that he could skip the eleventh grade and complete three years of high school in two. He had Vann do the reading prescribed by the Ferrum curriculum and write the term papers and gave him exams at the parsonage where Hopkins and his family lived a couple of blocks from LeKies Memorial Church. He graded his protégé generously in a letter to the school certifying that Vann had passed both courses: a 96 in history and a 94 in English. Vann graduated from Ferrum Training School in June 1941 and entered the junior college that fall.

Myrtle finally allowed Frank Vann to adopt John in June 1942, two weeks before his eighteenth birthday. John Paul LeGay became John Paul Vann by order of the Circuit Court of Norfolk. He had warned his mother that if she stopped the adoption proceedings, he would change his name to Vann himself as soon as he reached his twenty-first birthday. He was registered at Ferrum as he had been at public school under the makeshift name John LeGay Vann. Myrtle was becoming proud enough of him now to be willing to give him his way. She told Mollie that she had arranged the scholarship to Ferrum. Twenty-eight years later Myrtle's son had to mention his adoption in the autobiographical section of a government security-clearance form. He moved the adoption date back ten years to 1932.

He had not wanted to wait to finish junior college after the Japanese attacked Pearl Harbor in December 1941. Garland Hopkins seems to have persuaded him to do so. Vann wanted to go to war right away. No one he knew regretted that the Japanese had at last given the United States just cause to enter the fight. In his part of the country there was little of the isolationism that had forced Woodrow Wilson to take the nation tardily into World War I and that made Franklin Roosevelt maneuver Japan into striking the first blow of this war, not realizing it would fall as close as Hawaii. While the majority of the country was opposed to going to war again, much of what World War II historians were to interpret as isolationism was not a reflection of George Washington's admonition to stay out of Europe's quarrels. It was rather the ethnic factor in American politics—the resistance of German-Americans who continued to remember the Fatherland as the advanced and mildly authoritarian Germany of the Kaisers and the hatred of Britain among the Irish. The latter were especially strong in the cities of the Northeast that Roosevelt needed. Their memories of the five-year revolution that had rewarded centuries of struggle and gained southern Ireland its independence after World War I were vivid. Their politicians railed against spending American blood a second time to save the British Empire.

In Vann's Virginia, with its predominantly English stock, sympathy for Britain had been the popular attitude long before the dive bombers and torpedo planes of the Japanese Navy settled the argument for everyone. The voice of Winston Churchill rallying his people and reaching across the sea to other free men and women through the still-fresh miracle of the radio aroused Americans of all backgrounds who understood the threat to civilization. Those of Vann's Virginia felt more than a stirring. The sentimentalizing of their roots in the mother country gave them a feeling of kinship with Britain as an island alight with hope and defiance off a continent darkened by the barbarism of the Nazis.

One of Vann's contemporaries in Vietnam, Samuel Vaughan Wilson, grew up in a family that had raised tobacco and corn from the red earth of southern Virginia since the 1700s. Over the radio at the family farmhouse one day in June 1940, Wilson heard Churchill's address to the House of Commons as Britain awaited invasion and its army had just been forced to abandon almost everything except the rifles and machine guns the soldiers could carry to escape Hitler's panzer divisions in the epic evacuation at Dunkirk. The static of the shortwave heightened the drama of the words and the gruff majesty of the voice: "We shall fight on the beaches, we shall fight on the landing grounds, we shall fight in the fields and in the streets . . . we shall never surrender."

The local unit of the Virginia National Guard met on Monday nights in a drill hall at the town of Farmville seven miles away. The next Monday night, Sam Wilson, who was to fight with Merrill's Marauders in Burma, to see the war in Vietnam too, and to retire from the Army as a lieutenant general, walked seven miles through rain over the dirt roads to raise his right hand in the oath of enlistment.

The Depression had also readied the people of Vann's Virginia for a war. They were as bored as they were hungry after a dozen years of famine. The war swept away boredom and destitution. Suddenly the humblest among them, who had had to work before at wasting time, were making lots of money and participating in a holy cause. In early 1942, Frank Vann got his first steady job since 1930 as a carpenter helping to build the biggest amphibious assault training base in the country at the Little Creek inlet on the seaward side of Norfolk. No one would have wanted to start a war to make money. That prosperity and foreign wars went together was an accident, but who could be upset when the fountain of money was erupting in another gusher after having stood dry for so many years?

Young John's summer job in 1942 was hustling cold drinks and sandwiches at his Aunt Mollie's share of the gusher. His grandmother, Queenie, had been proud of the stake she had made with her board-inghouse during the base-building boom of World War I. Mollie, to her greater pride, outdid Queenie. She met an old boyfriend while in Nor-folk on a brief visit from New York in the spring of 1942. He had become a contractor and had a portion of the massive construction project un-derway at the Little Creek inlet. He asked her how much she was earning a week as a hostess in the tearoom at the Hotel Menger. Mollie told him.

"Hell, you could make that in an hour if you came out and ran a canteen for my men," he said. He explained that his workers had no place to buy sandwiches and milk and soda for lunch.

"Well, I'll try it," Mollie said.

The next morning she bought cold cuts, bread, and pies. She made sandwiches and cut up the pies into pieces. She drove out at noon and sold everything as fast as she could hand out the sandwiches and pieces of pie and take in the money from the men who flocked around her car. Her contractor friend had been right. She counted the money when she got back to town and discovered that she had made a profit of $38. She telephoned the handsome Italian headwaiter she had divorced her Nor-folk husband to marry in New York, Terzo Tosolini, and told him he was going to have to watch over her two sons by her first marriage, Vann's cousins Joseph and Melvin Raby, while she stayed in Norfolk to try the venture for a couple of weeks.

The following day she doubled the number of sandwiches and slices of pie and her profit. The contractor had his carpenters convert an old shack that fishermen had once used to store bait into a canteen, putting a counter and flap window in the front to serve the white workers and a smaller counter and flap window at the rear for the "colored." Mollie sold sandwiches, pie, soda, milk, cigarettes, and other odds and ends. She used fifty-five-gallon drums filled with water and ice to keep the bottles of soda and half-pints of milk cold. As a barracks was completed, sailors and Marines would move in and they would buy at her canteen too. Her volume rose to about 1,000 half-pints a day in milk alone. She remembered she had to work so fast that the bills would get wadded up into balls and she wouldn't have time to unfold the money until she got back to Norfolk at night. "I didn't have a cash register," she recalled thirty-three years later. "I had a cigar box for change and the bills went under it and your hands were wet from gettin' the sodas out and the milk—cuz we had no refrigeration, cuz it was fast-turnover stuff. The bills would be so wet and when you were tryin' to put 'em in your pocket they'd get pushed in there, so when you'd go home you'd carry a bag of money. You really had a bag of money, I'm tellin' you! You wouldn't want to walk around with it today."

Every few weeks Mollie would drive up to New York to spend a weekend with Tosolini and her boys, driving through the night in her Buick to get there by dawn, with $6,000 to $7,000 in bills of large denominations pinned into her underclothing. She stashed the money away in a house in Jackson Heights that she and Tosolini had bought with a mortgage when times were still hard. Her contractor friend ("He put me wise") told her: "Now don't put too much money in the bank." That might attract the curiosity of the Internal Revenue Service.

After eighteen months, the Navy decided to open an official post exchange. The admiral in command ordered Mollie to shut down. She refused. He had to send the Shore Patrol to close her canteen shack. By that time Mollie had felt her profits crinkling in her lingerie often enough on the road to New York to be content. She invested the money in a luncheonette in Jackson Heights. She and Tosolini then sold their house there and Mollie bought another one in Great Neck, Long Island. It was a large house, the sort that only mill managers had been able to afford in the South when Mollie had stood on a box to reach the long johns and flip them for Queenie to sew faster.

Toward the end of 1942, halfway through his second year of junior college at Ferrum, Vann decided that he could wait no longer. Some of his classmates had already quit and gone to fight. They felt that the country was in danger and they could not delay. Most young men who had turned the draft age of eighteen, as he had in July 1942, and were not in uniform began to feel ashamed. He had delayed because he wanted to be a fighter pilot, and Hopkins had apparently convinced him that he had a better chance of being selected for flight school if he completed junior college before enlisting.

To become a paladin of the air was a dream Vann shared with many of his generation. The fabled men of the last war in Europe had been the aviators, and they were the romantic figures of this war too. Vann saw them in the newsreels at the movies: the immortals of the Royal Air Force in their white scarves and sheepskin jackets climbing into their Spitfires to humble the arrogant Luftwaffe. To fly was to fight among the elite. Vann's fascination with flying also went beyond the reflection of a popular fantasy. Mollie thought it was the same urge that led him to seek the freedom he felt when his body was hurtling through the air in a backflip off a porch roof. When he had earned a dime as a boy he had often chosen not to spend it on food; instead he had bought a model airplane kit of balsa wood. He would carve out the parts and glue them together and carefully follow the directions on how to paint the replica with the original colors and insignia of one of the primitive aircraft in which the pilot heroes of World War I had dueled. His model airplanes had been the sole possession he would not share with Frank Junior and Gene.

His dream was to become one of those smiling, thumbs-up pilots he also saw in the newsreels revving their engines on the decks of the aircraft carriers to lift into the wind and face the Zeros over the Pacific. When he came home on Christmas vacation in 1942 he was carrying a letter from the president of Ferrum recommending him for the Naval Air Service. He seems to have been disappointed by the response he received at the recruiting office in Norfolk. He returned to Ferrum to finish enough of his coursework so that the junior college would make the common exception of the wartime emergency and credit him for the full two years even if he left early to put on a uniform. In March, with his eligibility fortified, he took a train to Richmond and tried the Army Air Corps recruiter there. This time the response was not discouraging. There were too many would-be heros of the air for the Army to make promises, but he was an excellent candidate for flight school if he enlisted. Perhaps to have an excuse for Myrtle, who was afraid he would be killed and was urging him to find a civilian job that would entitle him to a deferment, he allowed himself to be drafted with the proviso that he was entering for the Air Corps.

Early on the morning of March 10, 1943, he took the train to Richmond again for his physical examination at the induction center there. He was eighteen years and eight months old. The Army record of his physical shows that he stood five feet six and a half inches and weighed 125 pounds. An examining physician recorded his complexion as "ruddy." He spent several hours in a line with other youths who had likewise stripped to their shorts to be questioned about their childhood ailments and drinking habits; made to read an eye chart; ordered to bend over and poked embarrassingly by a finger in a rubber glove; stuck with a needle for a blood test and type determination (his was A); and given a chest X-ray to see if they had tuberculosis (his test was negative). Then he was allowed to dress again and was led into a large room with the other recruits to take the oath to obey all lawful orders from his superiors. He was given a train ticket back home to Norfolk and mimeographed orders instructing him to report to Camp Lee, Virginia, a week later. The induction station also thoughtfully provided him with a voucher for the train ticket from Norfolk to Camp Lee. He spent his last week of civilian life passing out more sandwiches and cold drinks at Mollie's canteen and sticking the wet bills under her cigar box. He would need the money he earned. The pay of an Army private in 1943 was fifty dollars a month.

On arrival at Camp Lee he signed "Johnny Vann" to a statement saying that he was in the same physical condition as when he had enlisted the week before. His youth seems to have ended with his initiation into the way of a soldier. Henceforth he was to sign all statements with a formal "John P. Vann."

During his first day at Camp Lee and for four days afterward the Army hit him with the psychological shock of disorientation and beginning anew that facilitates the transformation of boys into fighting men. He was made to shed his civilian clothing, including his underwear, and handed Army khaki and olive green; his head was shaved; he was given another medical examination to verify that he had been telling the truth when he had signed the arrival statement; and he was revaccinated for smallpox and vaccinated for typhoid and tetanus. A sergeant shouted him and his fellow recruits out of the barracks and into formation for frequent roll calls and, with more shouts and curses, marched them in a column to and from meals and wherever else they went. The Army also examined everyone's mind. He and his comrades took a series of aptitude tests that would supposedly determine how the Army could best utilize their skills. Vann scored 97 on the aptitude test for flight training. A notation was put on his record that he was "Qualified for Aviation Cadet Appointment." The clerk also noted that he had received the Army's "Sex Morality Lecture" on the day after his arrival.

Despite his score on the aptitude test and the original notation the Norfolk induction center had made on his record that he was entering the service for the Air Corps, Vann was a long way from a plane, and he learned what could be in store for him if his wish to fly was not granted. Camp Lee (subsequently Fort Lee) was the chief quartermaster training center for World War II. The assignment section there put him in the Army Service Forces and designated him to spend the war repairing jeeps and trucks. On March 22, 1943, he was shipped by train to the Atlanta Ordnance Depot for basic infantry training and then rudimentary instruction in automotive mechanics.

He wrote to Ferrum for additional letters of recommendation and submitted a request for flight school. The application and the letters got him a hearing before the officers of the Aviation Cadet Examining Board in Atlanta. The guidance counselor at Ferrum who had made him a teacher's assistant in the country grade school because she noticed that he liked to lead and teach told the board that she looked forward to "outstanding accomplishments" from Vann. "I *expect* him to go beyond the ordinary call of duty," she wrote.

On June 19, 1943, nearly three months after he arrived in Atlanta, Pvt. John P. Vann of the 3037th Auto. Maint. Co., 139th Auto. Maint. Bn., received a letter from the second lieutenant who was the secretary of the board. "We are pleased to inform you that you have been fully qualified for Air Crew training in the Army Air Corps," the letter said. It told Vann he would soon be transferred. (The Air Corps was officially renamed the Army Air Forces in 1942 but continued to be referred to popularly and in official correspondence as the Air Corps.)

"Soon" in the Army meant another month in Atlanta and then two months at an Air Corps processing center in Miami Beach before he obtained what he wanted: orders directing him to the 51st College Training Detachment (Air Crew) at Rochester, New York. The Air Corps had taken over part of the Rochester Business Institute and was using it as a preflight center to instruct cadets in elementary knowledge of aviation prior to more detailed schooling and actual air crew training for those who passed this preliminary course.

Vann arrived in Rochester on September 18, 1943, and thrived at his course work. His instructors also quickly recognized his leadership ability and appointed him one of the cadet officers in the detachment. That June the administrator at Ferrum had mailed him his junior college diploma and his copy of the yearbook of the Class of 1943, *The Beacon*. Quotations were printed beside the photographs of each member of the class. The quotation beside the photograph of the smiling boy who had been Johnny Vann at Ferrum read:

Intelligent, clear-eyed—of such as he,
Shall Freedom's young apostles be.

They met in Critic's ice cream parlor on the Sunday before Christmas, 1943. It was around 3:00 in the afternoon. Mary Jane and her girlfriend, Nancy, always went there for a sundae after the matinee at the movies. Being well-bred young women, they sat in a booth for two. He was sitting in the booth opposite with five other Air Corps cadets. She overheard him ask the waitress for apple pie, which Critic's did not serve but which her mother made well, before he turned and started a conversation with her. He said he had noticed her standing on the sidewalk during a Saturday-afternoon parade the previous weekend when he had been marching at the head of his group of cadets.

Although she remembered him right away, because she had noticed him too, she didn't answer at first. She had never replied to a sally from a strange young man before. She was sixteen years old and in the middle of her senior year at West High School. His Virginia twang, which had strength to it and was not unpleasant to her ear, was not the only thing that made him different from any of the boys she had dated at school. His hair, still blondish then, was combed up high on his forehead in a wave that was the fashion of the day. His dark green cadet uniform was attractive with its small silver wings at the jacket lapels and the round wing-and-propeller badge of an aspiring aviator sewn on the lower left sleeve. He smiled and leaned forward as he spoke. She got a feeling that he knew a lot more about women than she did about men. He was what she and her girlfriends would call a "wolf." Everything she had been told to beware of in a young man, she liked about him. So she broke the rule her mother had sworn her to and answered him by acknowledging that she had been standing on the sidewalk and that she did recognize him now. The rest of the conversation passed from memory over the years, except that he ended it by asking her for a date. She refused. Her mother, she told him, did not permit her to go out with strangers.

The next afternoon he appeared in the picture-frame section of Sibley's department store at the corner of Main Street and Clinton, where she was working part time as a sales clerk after school. He used the purchase of a frame for a photograph as a pretext to ask her again for a date. She couldn't accept, she said, but her mother might let her date him if he came to her house and met her parents. Why didn't he come for Christmas Eve dinner and bring another cadet for her girlfriend? She saw that smile she liked so much. Where did she live and what time should he come?

He arrived promptly with a friend and impressed her parents with his politeness and the fact that he answered their questions about his cadet training directly and knowledgeably, not like some nineteen-year-olds they knew. Her mother served him apple pie for dessert. Mary Jane had asked her mother to bake it. After dinner the grown-ups left the two couples to trim the tree, and he flirted with her while they talked and laughed. When it was time for him and his friend to leave he told her mother that it was the best Christmas Eve he had ever had. Her older sister, Doris, offered to drive the two cadets back to the hotel where they were being billeted. He flirted with Mary Jane some more in the car on the way.

They did not see each other again for well over a year. His preflight course at Rochester had ended, and he had to spend Christmas Day on a train to an Air Corps classification center at Nashville, Tennessee. He telephoned to say goodbye on Christmas morning. He called her "honey" on the phone and said a number of other endearing things. At Nashville he was given a ride in a Piper Cub liaison plane, his first opportunity to fly. He sent her a love letter enclosing a snapshot of himself as the storied figure he hoped to become. He was standing beside the little plane in a sheepskin flight jacket with a parachute strapped on behind, his gloved right hand resting on a wing strut. His cap was cocked to the side of his head and his hair rippled over his forehead. He signed the snapshot as he had the letter: "Love, Johnny."

She replied encouragingly, and the romance thrived as the letters and photographs went back and forth in the months that followed. To her he was the impulsive vitality, the excitement, the adventure she had never known in her stable life. To him she was not only physically attractive, she was the world of middle-class respectability and family love and absence of shame that he had dreamed about when he had walked through the prosperous sections of Norfolk on his way to junior high school and looked at the well-groomed houses and thought that life must indeed be wondrous within them.

Her name was Mary Jane Allen. She had known everything that he had been denied. She had been one of those little girls whom Norman Rockwell idealized in his covers for the *Saturday Evening Post*. Her father, Justus Smith Allen, was a man of modest but worthy position in Rochester. He was the senior court reporter for the city and corresponding secretary of the Justices and Magistrates Association of Monroe County, New York. His branch of the Allen family were originally Mainers. They claimed ancestry to Ethan Allen of Vermont, who had liberated Fort Ticonderoga during the American Revolution in the name of "the Great Jehovah and the Continental Congress." Justus Allen (he was called "Jess" by his wife and friends) was a pleasant-looking, even-tempered man, short, slightly stocky, and of firm jaw. He wore a vest with his suits and rimless glasses, parted his hair down the middle, and came home every afternoon at 5:30 to read his newspaper before dinner.

Mary Jane's mother was Mary Andrews, the daughter of Solomon and Catherine Eleck, Rumanian immigrants who had assimilated quickly into American life by changing the family name and converting to Presbyterianism in Gary, West Virginia, a coal town in the southeastern part of the state, where Solomon found work in the mines. He had shifted the family to Detroit when Mary was eleven to take a job on the assembly line at the Ford plant. She had met Jess on a June afternoon at an amusement park on the outskirts of Detroit. She had also been just sixteen when she met her man. Jess had been twenty-seven and a steno-grapher at General Motors then. They courted a year and married the following June. Perhaps in part because of her immigrant background, Mary Andrews had a passion for upright Protestant ways and the sanctity of marriage and family. She and Jess moved to Rochester the fall after they were married when an opening occurred for a court reporter. Jess had spent much of his youth in the upstate New York city and had a brother living there. He had found a better stenographic position at Ford since meeting Mary, but he disliked punching a time clock in Detroit. He felt that court reporting would be more interesting and secure.

He was correct on both counts. The human folly of crime and lawsuits is secure from economic collapse, and Jess's occupation shielded the Allen household from the misery that pained millions of other families across the land after 1929. While Mary Jane was in grammar school and the Depression was at its worst, the family moved upward from a plain house in a suburb of Rochester to a spacious home within the city. The city government was conscientious about repairing the sidewalks and tending the big shade trees that lined Elmdorf Avenue and its neigh-boring streets. The Allens' home, like the others on the avenue, sat back behind a box hedge and a deep lawn. It was a two-story house with white siding on the ground level—the boards precisely joined and neatly painted, none of the slipshod clapboarding of the South—and green shingles on the second story. The front porch was a pleasure to sit on of a day or an evening. Mary Allen had awnings made to shelter it from sun and rain and furnished it with rockers and swings. Jess kept the lawns thriving and planted shrubbery alongside the two-car garage at the back where he parked his Chrysler and stored his gardening tools. There were four bedrooms on the second floor and an enclosed sleeping porch for summer nights. The dining room on the ground floor had bay windows, exposed oak beams, and a chandelier. Jess had the basement converted into a recreation room with a hand-crank victrola and a Ping-Pong table. Although Rochester summers are not particularly hot, the Allens rented a cottage every July and August on one of the Finger Lakes of upstate New York, Lake Conesus, about an hour's drive from the city. Mary Allen would go there at the end of June with the children. Jess would drive out for the weekend after Friday's court session and then spend his summer vacation at the lake.

The Allens were able to give each child a separate bedroom in the house on Elmdorf Avenue and still have a guest room to spare, because they had only two children. Mary Jane, the second daughter, was born on August 11, 1927. She was bright but lacked the intellectual curiosity to be an outstanding student. Her interests were in domestic and traditionally feminine pursuits—dolls and doll houses, sewing, and playing at keeping house.

As a little girl she was a sugar-and-spice of smiles and curls and bows and fashion-plate dresses. Shirley Temple was the child movie star of the day, and the age was one in which the public admired and imitated movie stars somewhat more naively than it would later. Every little girl wanted to look like Shirley Temple. Those with mothers who had the patience to do the curling wore their hair coiled in the style that Shirley Temple made popular. Not many little girls also had enough of the Shirley Temple charm to go with the curls and be chosen by the Rochester department stores to model Shirley Temple clothes. Mary Jane Allen did. On April 23, 1934, Shirley Temple's sixth birthday, Mary Jane and eight other mini-models displayed "exact copies of dresses that were made for Shirley herself" at McCurdy's department store. "The juvenile fashion revue was attended by nearly 500 interested mothers and excited little boys and girls," the *Rochester Times-Union* reported. Mary Jane had an appropriately wide-eyed look in the photograph above the story. By Shirley Temple's seventh birthday, Mary Jane was modeling at B. Forman Company and appeared in the *Rochester Journal-American* smiling and crinkling up her nose in a way she often did if something amused her. This time she also had an oversized bow pinned into her brunette hair. And when the Westminster Presbyterian Church, where her family attended 11:00 A.M. services and she went to Sunday school, staged a Christmas pageant, it seemed natural to choose Mary Jane Allen to play the part of Mary.

Her parents raised her to mirror their values of family and church and country, and she never questioned anything. Her Grandmother Allen had a particular effect on her. They seemed to have much in common. Whenever Jess's mother, a small, pale woman, visited the Allens in Rochester or came to the lake cottage for a few weeks in the summer, Mary Jane wanted to spend every moment she could with her grandmother. Grandmother Allen taught her to sew well, and to knit and crochet, and she told Mary Jane stories about her own younger years. Two of her ten children had died in infancy during an influenza epidemic. Grandfather Allen had then died when Jess Allen was still a boy. There had not been much money, and Grandmother Allen had had to struggle to raise her surviving children. She was proud of what she had accomplished, of how well Jess and his seven brothers and sisters had turned out. A woman should take pride in being a mother, she said.

Even though the man might be the provider, raising the family was ultimately the woman's responsibility. In a time of trouble, a woman should sacrifice for her children, holding them firmly to her and nurturing them into adulthood. If a woman fulfilled her duty to her family, she would also be fulfilling her duty to God and her country, for without the family, the church and the nation could not exist, Mary Jane's grandmother said.

Mary Jane had been keeping a hope chest for the marriage she dreamed of even before she met John. She started it as soon as she began working part-time in the picture-frame and toy departments at Sibley's. She bought tablecloths and napkins and pretty ashtrays and other knickknacks. Her mother never objected to the purchases, because Mary Jane had innate good taste. Most of her friends also kept hope chests. After she met John the question of the man was settled. Except for her high school graduation in June 1944, when she went to the prom with a boy who had been a childhood friend, she dated no one during the year and nearly four months until she saw John again. It was romantic to be in love with a serviceman who was fighting, or was preparing to fight, this war for the salvation of the world. Hardly a week passed without the photo of a "war bride" in the society sections of the Rochester newspapers. Mary Jane's graduation ceremony at West High School was in keeping with this spirit. One of the boys read his essay, "What I Am Fighting For," and a girl read hers, "Hands Across the Sea." Another young woman sang a solo entitled "British Children's Prayer."

At the classification center in Nashville, Vann had been lucky enough to be selected for pilot training, despite slightly higher scores on the aptitude tests for bombardier and navigator. He passed the winter, spring, and summer of 1944 shifting through the South from one stage of flight training to another—to Primary School at Bainbridge, Georgia, where he survived his initial flying test, a solo after eight to ten hours of instruction; to a faster trainer aircraft, his first formation flying, and instrument training in the simulated cockpits of the Link Trainers at the Basic School at Maxwell Field, Alabama; finally to the thrill of Advanced Flying School at Dorr Field, Florida.

His exuberance and the love of freedom in flight that had drawn him to aviation in the first place then denied him his dream of becoming a pilot. He flew a trainer through some forbidden stunt maneuvers one day in early August. He was punished by dismissal from the school. The language of bureaucracy hid the precise nature of his sin. His record said only: "Eliminated from further Pilot training due to Flying Deficiency." He was crestfallen by the penalty for his foolishness and fibbed to his worshipful youngest brother, Gene, saying that the flight surgeons had found a spot on a lung from a childhood case of tuberculosis. (He told Mary Jane the truth years later.) His instructors noted his ability and exemplary behavior most of the time (he had been nominated for the Good Conduct Medal at Maxwell Field) and recommended him for Navigation School at San Marcos Army Air Field in Texas. He was transferred there in October, graduated in late January 1945, and was awarded his navigator's wings and the gold bars of a second lieutenant in mid-February.

He sent Mary Jane a photograph of himself in his new officer's uniform, with a short, tight-fitting tunic called the "Ike jacket" because General Eisenhower liked to wear it. The quickie studio where he had the photograph taken had a canvas backdrop painted in sea and clouds. He crushed in his cap at the sides for a rakish aviator effect, put a hand on his hip, and stared off at destiny to the left of the camera. "So help me Hon," he wrote on the back, "The guy that took this (at a 2 bit carnival)—*made* me stand like this—looking off into the *wild* blue yonder—and Lord alone knows for what."

John telephoned long-distance in April. He had been granted a short leave in the course of being transferred to Lincoln, Nebraska, and he was coming to see her for the first time since the Christmas Eve dinner. He hitched plane rides from one airfield to another and arrived in Rochester on April 12, 1945. Mary Jane remembered the date because it was the day Franklin Roosevelt died and Harry Truman became president. They went downtown to a jewelry store and he bought her an engagement ring. He didn't propose marriage, and she did not mention it prior to getting the ring. It was just assumed between them that they would be married.

Mary Allen forced them to agree to wait two years. The Allens liked their glimpse of the young man, but they wanted to see more before he took their daughter. Mary Allen's concern with family also made her wish to learn whether his family were her kind of people. She was anxious as well to have her daughter obtain a better education than she had, to have at least two years of college before marrying. After her high school graduation in 1944 Mary Jane had attended Miss McCarthy's Business School to learn typing and shorthand and had since been working as a secretary. Her mother had set aside money for her to enter the University of Rochester in the fall of 1945.

For the first time in her life, Mary Jane became rebellious. John called that summer from New Mexico, where he had been sent for three months of specialized radar navigation training on the B-29 Superfortress, the four-engine monarch of the World War II bombers, and invited her to come down on a train for a visit. She accepted without obtaining her parents' permission. They were away on a trip and difficult to reach. She persuaded her older sister, Doris, to act as her chaperon. John arranged for the two girls to stay at a guest house on the air base and found a date for Doris. Both girls had a grand time swimming at the pool and going to parties. In August she pressured her mother into announcing the engagement. The *Rochester Times-Union* carried the notice in its evening edition of Saturday, August 18, 1945, with a studio portrait of Mary Jane.

In September, John telephoned again. He was being assigned to a regular B-29 squadron at Smoky Hill Army Air Field near Salina, Kansas. Although Japan had surrendered on August 14, his term of service was being continued indefinitely because he had had no overseas duty. (Men were being discharged through a point system based on time overseas and in combat.) He could take two weeks of leave at the beginning of October and be in Rochester by October 3. They could be married as quickly as they could get a license and Mary Jane could return with him to Kansas, where they would live in an apartment near the base. Mary Jane said yes. She asked her mother if she would like to spend the money she had been saving for the university on a wedding. When her mother objected, Mary Jane announced that if her parents refused to let her marry John in Rochester, she was going to take the train to Kansas and marry him at the air base. She was eighteen now and no longer needed her parents' permission. John was twenty-one. There wasn't time to arrange a proper wedding by early October, her mother argued. They would have to make do, Mary Jane insisted. Her mother agreed because she had no choice. They set the wedding day for October 6 so that the ceremony could be held on the conventional Saturday afternoon when it would be convenient for their friends to attend. Mary Jane called John back and gave him the date. He'd be there in plenty of time, he said.

John was so impressed by the wedding invitation printed in fancy Gothic type that he mailed Mary Jane a list of people who could not come but to whom he wanted invitations sent for pride's sake. One was his rescuer, Garland Hopkins, who was serving as an Army chaplain in Southeast Asia at the time. John was to have only three people from his side at the wedding: Mollie; her older son, Joe Raby, whom he asked to be his best man; and Myrtle. He did not want to arouse the suspicions of the Allens by not having anyone from his family. (He invented an excuse for Frank Vann, who stayed in Norfolk because of the usual shortage of money.)

As Mollie remembered it, her nephew was blunt in his instructions to her: "I leave my mother in your hands, Aunt Mollie," he said. "You keep her straightened up and don't let her get drunk or anything like that." He was afraid alcohol would stir the meanness in her. "She could get to talkin' if she took too much," Mollie recalled. " 'Well, you know, Vann is not his real name, you know.' That was the sort of thing she might say."

Mollie kept Myrtle sober, but her vanity caused a small crisis. Myrtle took the train from Norfolk to New York and then drove to Rochester with Mollie and Joe Raby the day before the wedding. Mary Allen insisted that John's mother and aunt stay at her house. John and Joe put up at a hotel. While Myrtle and Mollie were riding to the church the next afternoon with Mary Allen for the 4:30 ceremony, Myrtle discovered a run in her stocking. "I can't go," she said to Mollie. "I have a run in my stockin'."

"You have to go," Mollie replied. "We can't get stockin's now. Weddin's take place. They go, you know. We've got to get there."

"Mollie, I am not goin' in that church with a run in my stockin'," Myrtle insisted.

"No one will ever notice, because they're so excited by the bride," Mollie said. "They're not lookin' at you. They're lookin' at the bride."

Myrtle was adamant.

"Don't worry, we'll get stockings somewhere, Mrs. Vann," Mary Allen intervened. "We'll get the stockings for you."

No one could remember how Mary Allen produced the stockings, whether she stopped at a store or they drove back home for another pair. In any case, Myrtle did a quick change before entering the church.

It was John who held up the ceremony for half an hour. He and Joe Raby got lost driving Mollie's car to the chapel of the Colgate-Rochester Divinity School. The neo-Gothic chapel was a romantic setting, and like many Rochester brides, Mary Jane had chosen to be married there rather than at her own church. The bridal consultant whom the Allens had hired to oversee the flower arrangements and to tend to Mary Jane's gown and other fine points of the wedding became convinced she had a jilted bride on her hands and almost lost her self-control. Mary Jane's pastor from Westminster Presbyterian, who was to perform the ceremony, kept the guests calmer than he was by announcing that they would have to wait a bit because the groom had been delayed. Mary Jane recalled that she seemed to be the only one who was not worried. She was certain that she and John were meant for each other and that he would come to marry her. The chapel was a difficult place for a stranger to find, and Vann's knowledge of Rochester was limited to the downtown area. The rehearsal the day before had been held at Westminster Presbyterian. He and Joe finally managed to hail a motorcycle policeman. The arrival of the groom was announced by a siren.

Despite the rush their son-in-law-to-be imposed on them with his sudden-turn ways, the Allens gave their daughter a wedding that was decidedly not an Atlantic City, Norfolk, affair. The altar was lit by candelabra and flanked on both sides by large baskets of pink and white gladiola set against a background of palms. Mary Jane wore the long-sleeved gown of white satin she had liked best at Sibley's Bridal Shop. It had a heart-shaped neckline traced by rows of seed pearls. Her necklace was a string of pearls. The skirt of her gown swept behind her in a long train; her full-length veil fell back from a tiara of orange blossoms. Doris was the maid of honor in rose taffeta. Three of Mary Jane's girlfriends were bridesmaids, and the bride and her attendants carried bouquets of pink pompons, roses, daisies, and snapdragons. Jess, in a formal double-breasted suit with a striped silver morning tie and a carnation in his lapel, gave the bride away.

The groom and the other servicemen among the guests in the chapel lent the wedding its World War II aura, for the war was still in the air even though Japan had surrendered. John was elegant in the semidress uniform of an Army officer of the period. It was called "pinks and greens" and consisted of a long belted jacket of dark green and contrasting trousers of tan cavalry twill with a pinkish hue. Mary Jane noticed that John was nervous during the ceremony and the reception that followed when they cut a four-tiered wedding cake. His nervousness shows in the pictures taken by the photographer the Allens hired to record the wedding. Perhaps he was a bit intimidated by all of this middle-class pomp and satin and worried whether Mollie would succeed in keeping his mother in line. The photographs also show that he was a happy young man, pleased with the prize he had gained in this young woman. Mary Jane looked a prize worth winning that day. She was a pretty bride. The dark red lipstick women wore in the 1940s emphasized the symmetry of her mouth and her fine, even teeth. The fullness of her brunette hair, set in graceful waves, called attention to her hazel eyes and matched, in its sheen, the satin of her gown.

John Vann had learned a lot in two and a half years in the Army. The most important thing he had learned was that he was a different person in this uniform. When he had this uniform on he wasn't little Johnny

Vann or LeGay or what's-his-name, the bastard kid of that good-timer Myrtle down at the end of the bar. He was Lieutenant John Paul Vann of the U.S. Army Air Corps. The Army and the war had freed him in a way that Ferrum could not do from that trash-filled house in Norfolk, and he wasn't ever going back into it again. No matter what he did in Norfolk, if he became richer than the millionaire oyster dealer who had bought him his first good clothes, he still couldn't achieve the respectability he felt as a second lieutenant in the Army. In Norfolk, somebody would always remember and point. In this uniform, no one could tell. He was indistinguishable from decent folk as long as he kept it on.

The proof was this woman he had gained for a wife. Her parents had accepted him because he was an Army officer. They would never have let him have her if they had been able to see through that uniform and recognize who he was and where he had come from. (Mary Allen did learn a few years later that John's family were not her kind of people, but Jess shielded her from the details. One day when the Allens were passing through Norfolk on a trip, Jess stopped by the police headquarters and, using his credentials, got the police to tell him what they knew. He was so upset by what he found out that he refused to let Mary know what it was. The police apparently gave him an earful about Myrtle. Jess and Mary did not hold John's beginnings against their son-in-law. Rather, they decided they had to admire him for going so far.)

He intended to go much further, and the Army seemed to him the place in which to do it. He had also discovered during these two and a half years that he was smarter than most of his contemporaries, and tougher too, and that he could work twice as hard as they could, three times as hard if necessary. He could become one of those awesome colonels with eagles on their shoulders and the power of command over lines of men and machines. He might someday wear the stars of a general. It seemed hardly possible that anything so grand could happen to him, but he could hope.

Spry sensed what the Army meant to him. After John bought Mary Jane her engagement ring in April 1945, he went down to Norfolk for a triumphal visit. He appeared at Spry's house in his pinks and greens to better display his new lieutenant's bars and navigator's wings. Spry had been in the Coast Guard during World War I but had not risen beyond ordinary seaman. Spry mentioned the visit to another son who was also in the service and who intended to return to Norfolk after the war. "We won't be seeing much of Johnny around here anymore," Spry said.

He and Mary Jane had been married only a few months when he was transferred from Kansas to Guam to recover B-29s from Saipan and other Pacific island bases and fly them to storage parks in Hawaii and the United States. She went back to Rochester to stay with her parents until his return. He wrote her from Guam in the spring of 1946 to say that he had decided to give the military a trial as a career and was taking an examination for a permanent, or Regular Army, commission. His original commission was in the Army Reserve, and under it he could be demobilized at any time. He said that he could finish his college education free at government expense and could always resign his commission later.

Mary Jane was pregnant at the time with their first child, Patricia. He had not consulted her before making his decision. She wondered about it at first. Most people she knew would not have considered Army service a fit way to earn a living and raise a family, but she felt that the choice of career had to be his and she wanted him to do something he enjoyed. She did not see why a military career for him should deny her the family life she envisioned the marriage as bringing. She could adjust to the periodic separations as she was adjusting to this one. Vann received his Regular Army commission in July 1946. It was his first victory on the road he had set himself. Ten reserve officers had applied for every Regular Army commission available.

Educational credentials are important for an officer who wants to move ahead. Vann got himself sent to Rutgers University in New Jersey in the fall of 1946 on a program available to new Regular Army officers for a two-year course in economics to complete requirements for his bachelor's degree. Mary Jane made what home she could for the two of them and little Patricia in one of the tiny trailers the university provided for married students. Then in May 1947 he suddenly announced that he was suspending his studies and transferring to the infantry. The Air Corps was in the course of breaking away from the Army to form an independent Air Force under the National Security Act of 1947. Vann was one of the relatively few Air Corps officers who elected to stay with the Army. He guessed accurately that pilots, not navigators, were going to dominate an independent Air Force and that he would have a better chance of advancement in the infantry. It had room for maneuver, and the opportunity to command men would give him a challenge on the ground that would be greater than that of piloting a plane in the air. If and when another war came the infantry would also mean maximum risk and maximum possibility of distinction in combat and promotion.

That June he sold their first car, a worn Chevy coupe he had bought for $200, because its radiator boiled over constantly and he did not think it would carry them far on the journey they had to make. He invested in a Ford of more recent vintage. Mary Jane laid eight-month-old Patricia in a traveling crib on the backseat and they set out for Georgia and the Infantry School at Fort Benning, where John was to take the three-month course every infantry lieutenant receives in the fundamentals of leading a platoon and a company in battle. He had also decided to take parachute and glider training so that he could command airborne troops. Again he had not consulted her, and again she had not objected. She had not expected life with him to be normal. She had expected it to be an adventure, and so far the adventure had been a good one.

The odor of drying fish startled her. There were thousands drying on open-air racks along the docks. She had never smelled anything so strange and pungent before, nor had she ever seen oranges and reds as rich as those in the sunset across the harbor as the ship maneuvered up to the dock in Yokohama in April 1949. John was waiting at the end of the gangplank to take charge of her life again, to kiss and hug her and lift the children in his arms. He had asked her if she would join him in Japan when he had been sent there after nine months with the American occupation forces in Korea. (With some exceptions, military families were not permitted in Korea, even though no one of importance anticipated a war there.)

Vann's career as an officer of infantry had not begun auspiciously. While his instructors at the airborne training center at Fort Benning had been so impressed with him they had urged assigning him to a regular paratroop unit as a platoon leader, the personnel officers at the Pentagon had ruled otherwise. They had shipped him to Korea to be a special services officer—the man in charge of service clubs and entertainment for the troops. His job in Japan was also hardly one that an ambitious infantry officer would choose, although his duty station was certainly pleasant. He was the purchasing and contracting officer at the headquarters of the 25th Infantry Division in Osaka, another port city on the main Japanese island of Honshu, 240 miles southwest of Tokyo. His task was to procure supplies through the Japanese administration that served the occupation forces and to manage seized buildings and other real estate the division was using.

She was glad she had not known how harrowing the journey to Japan would be or she might not have had the courage to say yes. The Army of the late 1940s regarded travel in comfort as an officer's right and travel by his family as an unnecessary nuisance. When John had sailed the Pacific to Korea he had shared a ship's cabin with another officer. They had played bridge and read to pass the time. After her train trip across the country with Patricia, who was now two and a half, and John Allen, their first son, born on Christmas morning of 1947 in the garrison hospital at Fort Benning, she had waited three weeks in Seattle to board a troop ship, the USS *Darby*. She was the only officer's wife to sail on this trip, but the distinction entailed no privilege. She spent the three weeks in Seattle living dormitory-fashion in a barracks with the wives and children of enlisted men. A measles epidemic broke out. Neither Patricia nor John Allen caught measles, but John Allen came down with an ear infection and tonsillitis. There was more dormitory living on the *Darby* in a compartment with several enlisted families. The door to the communal toilet was of heavy steel and slammed shut whenever the ship rolled in the trough of the waves. One child lost a finger to it. The banging of the door kept Mary Jane in fear that one of her children was going to be similarly maimed. She held on to fourteen-month-old John Allen with one hand while restraining Patricia in a harness and leash with the other. The boy continued to run a high fever and to suffer from diarrhea aboard ship. Most daylight hours during the two-week voyage she seemed to be either in the ship's dispensary with him or waiting with him on line to get into the dispensary.

Mary Jane's anger over the hardships disappeared in her surprise at the sights and smells of this country and at the Japanese themselves. She had expected to find wicked little monsters who were surly under American rule. She saw cheerful and industrious people, the porters at the Yokohama docks smiling at the children as they hustled the luggage into a taxi John hired to drive them to the railway station for the train to Osaka and their new home.

He took her to a paradise on a hill in a suburb south of Osaka. She could not believe at first that she was to be the mistress of such a house, she who had trimmed her dreams to a trailer and then to a cottage outside Fort Benning that had formerly been a tenant farmer's shack. She did not yet understand that to be an American in Japan in these years of the occupation was to be a demigod. A mere first lieutenant was entitled to a mansion, and it was acquired simply by evicting the Japanese owners. This mansion had, in fact, previously been given to a warrant officer without children. He and his wife had found it too big and so they had passed it to John in order to move to a smaller place.

The house was white. It was built near the base of the hill at a level spot where the slope evened out briefly. A high stone wall at the front and sides gave privacy, reserving the perfection of the azalea bushes and ornamental trees that landscaped the grounds for the eyes of those who dwelt within. The gate opened to a path of flat stones in irregular shapes fitted together to form a walk that curved to the house entrance. The gardener had placed a sentinel beside the three steps leading up to the front door of dark wood. The sentinel was a cultured Japanese pine tree called a *mugo*, this one tall, with a gently crooked trunk and boughs that reached out in sculptured spreads of gray-green needles. When John opened the door, Mary Jane was stopped again by more of the beauty these Japanese created with such sureness. The servants—another privilege for a conqueror's wife—had filled a vase with azalea blossoms and placed it on a stand at the far end of the entrance alcove to welcome their new mistress. On the wall behind the vase a scroll of calligraphy was hung. The red of the azalea blossoms seemed to illuminate the Chinese characters sketched on the scroll in jet-black ink and made them stand out more sharply on the yellowed parchment.

The interior of the house was U-shaped. The right wing was Westernized, with a carpeted dining room, a living room, and bedrooms on the second floor equipped with European-type plumbing. The left wing, where the kitchen was located, was traditional Japanese, the floors covered with straw tatami mats. The open space between the two wings had once been an interior garden. The warrant officer and his wife had converted it into a patio and hung floodlights for entertaining at night. Mary Jane was glad to have it, because for the first time in their marriage, she needed a home in which she could entertain. At Fort Benning their social life had been limited because John had been a transient as a student. Now, with John an officer on the 25th Division staff, she had added responsibilities.

Japan was Mary Jane's initiation into Army garrison life and into a group the Army quaintly referred to as the "distaff side"—the corps of officers' wives. She discovered that she liked this life and membership in this special circle for the same reasons that she had enjoyed growing up in the middle-class world of Rochester. The hierarchy and the structured, busy, group-oriented atmosphere appealed to her and gave her a feeling of security and place. The officers' wives had a sense of belonging to a service of their own, because responsibility for most of the social activities of the garrison and its community and welfare work fell to them by tradition. The women liked the arrangement because it gave them authority and something to do. The Army liked it because the government got their talents and labor free. The belief that a wife's attitude and behavior reflected on her husband and either helped or hindered his career also contributed to this sense of membership in an inner group. The rank structure within the corps of wives paralleled the official one. The commanding general's wife headed it. The wives of the more senior officers acted like den mothers toward the younger women, coaching them in the same way that older officers were supposed to counsel their juniors. Mary Jane found the wives of the major and the lieutenant colonel who were John's superiors to be warm and caring women, and she responded in kind. She was ambitious for John and wanted to help him advance. She tried to be just as "ready, willing, and able" to entertain with cocktail parties and dinners in their paradise on the hill and to participate in arranging the dances and bridge parties and in the fund-raising and volunteer work for organizations like the Red Cross as John was at his duties for the division. She had bought a book at Fort Benning entitled *The Army Wife*, and she studied it to be certain that she behaved properly.

She decided her initial suspicion that the Army was an unfit place in which to raise a family had been unwarranted. The twin demands of family and garrison activities kept her days and nights filled, and the opportunity to observe this remarkable country and people in the most privileged of circumstances gave life a distinction it could never have had at home. The Army appeared to her like an international bank or some other large firm with overseas branches. Her husband was required to work abroad periodically, and in return he and his family were rewarded with adventure and this gracious existence. One of the American women with whom she made friends in Japan was the wife of the Coca-Cola representative. He was about John's age, and he and his wife lived as comfortably as the Vanns did. John was adapting to occupation duty by learning golf. By Christmas 1949, Mary Jane was pregnant with their third child, Jesse.

Paradises, it seemed, were nevertheless mixed as well as difficult to reach. Her house on the hill was infested with cockroaches, centipedes, and rats. The Army exterminators fumigated the insects, and Mary Jane learned to live with those that persisted. She found the rats much harder to tolerate. She was not aware of them at first because they lived inside the walls and normally waited until the house was still at night to come out and forage. She learned of them when she got up at dawn one morning to get John some breakfast before he left for an unusually early appointment. A big gray rat was crouched under the kitchen table. It looked at her and did not run. She screamed for John. He came bounding downstairs in his shorts and bare feet, and the rat took off toward the den. Most men would have been content to run the rat out of the kitchen and let it go back to its nest, because rats get viciously aggressive when cornered. Not Vann. He grabbed a small steel kitchen stool and a cane and, while Mary Jane watched, aghast, chased the rat and drove it into a corner of the den. When the terrified rat leaped at him with its teeth chattering, he knocked it down with the stool and slashed at it with the cane to force it back into the corner, thrusting and slashing, as the rat kept leaping at him, until he finally had it pinned to the wall with the stool. Then he beat the rat to death with the cane. Mary Jane was trembling afterward. Vann was out of breath, but not frightened. He seemed satisfied.

The rats defied the best efforts of the Army exterminators to get rid of them with traps and poisoned bait. Mary Jane tried to ignore them, because she did not want to leave the house, but they disturbed her peace of mind. She could hear them scurrying inside the walls in the daytime. She walked warily whenever she got up at night or again at dawn, and she was watchful of Patricia and John Allen at night too to make sure neither of them would be bitten.

One of the Japanese maids set the house on fire in the spring of 1950 while melting some floor wax in a pan on an electric hot plate. The blaze started as John was coming home from a game of golf. He seized a fire extinguisher and tried unsuccessfully to put out the flames as Mary Jane grabbed the children and their family papers and ran to the nearby house of another Army couple to summon help. Although the local Japanese and Army fire teams arrived quickly, much of the house was damaged or ruined by smoke and water, as well as by the fire itself, and the fire fighters chopped great holes in the walls to soak them and prevent the fire from creeping through the entire structure. The holes exposed the nests of dozens of rats.

The division engineers inspected the house the next day and decided it was not worth repairing because of the extent of the damage and the infestation of rats. The Vanns moved closer to the center of Osaka to a house that Frank Lloyd Wright had designed for a wealthy Japanese family before World War II. This house was even larger, three stories. It had fine wood paneling, a sunken bathtub of blue tile large enough for four, and a kitchen tiled throughout—floor and walls and counters. There was also a small swimming pool in the garden. The opulence of the place kept Mary Jane from complaining, but she did not like the severity of the architecture, and the house tended to be dark. She missed the banks of azaleas and the Japanese light and charm of her house on the hill.

Then, in the middle of the night, John went off to war. Ninety thousand North Korean soldiers, their columns led by Soviet-built tanks, crossed the 38th Parallel and invaded South Korea in the predawn of another historic Sunday, June 25, 1950. Patricia was old enough in the summer of 1950 to remember her mother waking her and John Allen to say goodbye. Her father was carrying his helmet and wearing a pistol on his belt. Her mother was crying. He crouched down to take her and John Allen in his arms and kiss them. He said he was going to be away for a while. Patricia laughed. She felt happy that he was leaving, because this figure of authority who demanded perfect behavior would be gone. Her mother asked why she was laughing. Patricia did not answer. In later years, when she realized that he might not have come back, she had a sense of guilt about her reaction.

Trains and ships were John Vann's preoccupation during the first weeks after the 25th Infantry Division was ordered to move to Korea as rapidly as possible and join the forces Douglas MacArthur was assembling there to stop the advance of the North Korean Army down the peninsula. First Lieutenant Vann was appointed assistant supply and evacuation officer—i.e., the man in charge of transportation. Overnight he found himself coordinating the train and ship schedules and expediting the loading and unloading of 15,000 officers and men and the artillery, trucks, tanks, armored half-tracks, and sundry other combat gear of the 25th Infantry. The capacity to refresh himself in an hour or two of sleep was to prove helpful, for he was to get no more than that a night for the next two months. Eighty trains were required to move the three infantry regiments and the associated division units from their occupation bases dispersed around the southern third of the island of Honshu to the ships at Yokohama. The task was not simply one of loading men and equipment onto trains and then ships. The logistics section of the division staff, G-4, to which Vann was assigned, had to load enough ammunition, food, and other supplies with the troops to sustain them during their initial days in combat. Once across the Korea Strait, Vann again had to help keep order amid seeming chaos during the unloading at the port of Pusan at the bottom of the Korean peninsula. Everything had to be done on the run, and everything had to be improvised, because no one in authority at MacArthur's headquarters in Tokyo or in Washington had anticipated the North Korean invasion.

Vann's job as trainmaster and stevedore-in-chief was more important under the circumstances than the leadership of a company in battle that he immediately craved. (He knew a staff assignment would not look impressive on an infantry officer's record when the war was over, regardless of how vital it might be.) The problem was to get American troops into South Korea while there was still a South Korea to save. MacArthur's field commander, Lt. Gen. Walton Walker, was racing the tank-led columns of North Koreans to try to organize a defensive perimeter above Pusan before the enemy overran all of Korea. Vann won his first Bronze Star Medal for the imagination and drive he displayed in hurrying the division on and off the trains and ships and into the war during those initial all-or-nothing weeks. Although the 25th Infantry received its movement order on June 30, the day after MacArthur flew to Korea to see the fighting and reported to Washington that the South Korean Army was falling apart, it took a week of planning and assembling units before Vann was given his first trainload to send to Yokohama and then two more weeks until the last elements of the division unloaded at the Pusan docks on July 19. The next day the North Koreans seized the town of Taejon, halfway down the peninsula from the 38th Parallel.

The war in Korea was to cause the deaths of 54,246 Americans and to take millions of Korean and Chinese lives. An estimated 120,000 civilians were to die in South Korea in the first year of the war alone. Ironically, the leaders of the United States had not wanted to keep South Korea until they saw they were going to lose it. They had also helped to bring on the war by communicating their lack of interest to opponents they did not understand.

The conflict originated in the division of the country at the end of World War II along the 38th Parallel line into separate Soviet and American occupation zones. Japan had previously held all of Korea as a colony. The Soviets organized a regime in the North under Kim Il Sung, an anti-Japanese guerrilla leader who had gravitated to Communism because the Chinese Communists and the Russians had been his natural allies. The United States set up a rival regime in the South under Syngman Rhee, a right-wing Korean patriot who had led an exile movement from Hawaii and the American mainland. While Rhee and Kim had antithetical ideas on Korean society, they were both fervid nationalists intent on reunifying the country. They constantly harassed each other with subversion and violent incidents and plotted civil war to decide who would rule a united land.

Korea has a tragic history because of its position as a way station between the Japanese archipelago and China and Russia on the Asian mainland. The proximity of northeastern Korea to Russia's Far Eastern naval base at Vladivostok gave Stalin an interest in the country. The Truman administration, on the other hand, twice formally decided that

South Korea was one of the few places on the rim of the "Soviet bloc" that the United States would not defend. The second decision was made by the National Security Council and approved by the president just fourteen months before the war began. It affirmed the original reasoning that American air and naval dominance was sufficient to protect Japan and that South Korea was thus of "little strategic interest."

Although these decisions were made in secret, their content was publicized. MacArthur first placed South Korea outside the American defense perimeter in Asia in an interview with a British correspondent in early 1949. Acheson then did so in a speech to the National Press Club in Washington in January 1950. American actions spoke consistently, especially in contrast with Soviet behavior. The last of the U.S. occupation troops were withdrawn in mid-1949. Rhee's army was left with secondhand infantry weapons, outmoded artillery, and a 482-man American military advisory group. Rhee asked for up-to-date artillery, tanks, and fighter-bombers, which the Russians were investing in his enemy in the North. He was denied them. He asked for a guarantee that the United States would come to the rescue of South Korea if it was invaded. He was denied that too. The Joint Chiefs of Staff drew up a secret contingency plan, again approved by the president, to withdraw all Americans if there was an invasion.

During the winter of 1949 and the spring of 1950, Kim gradually convinced Stalin that he could finish off his rival with minimal risk of American intervention. Kim was so certain the United States would not intervene that his military commanders were told they did not have to consider the possibility. MacArthur's headquarters, which was responsible for intelligence in Northeast Asia, failed to take note of the increased skirmishing between the two sides that spring and the buildup of North Korean assault troops and tanks along the 38th Parallel. The surprise may have contributed to the complete reversal of policy in Washington.

The moment the invasion occurred, Truman and Acheson overlooked the local rivalry that was the immediate cause of the war and forgot about the signals they had been sending. They saw the attack across the 38th Parallel, as Acheson described their reaction in his memoirs, "in its worldwide setting of our confrontation with our Soviet antagonist." Kim was a mere hireling and his assault on Rhee's South Korea was the first truly bold move in a master plan by Stalin for world conquest. "To back away from this challenge, in view of our capacity for meeting it, would be highly destructive of the power and prestige of the United States," Acheson wrote. "By prestige I mean the shadow cast by power, which is of great deterrent importance." As events were to show, transforming shadow into substance was to prove more difficult than Acheson imagined, and at the moment the soldiers were struggling with the shortfall between ultimate capacity to meet the challenge and current preparedness.

That Kim Il Sung was stopped before he achieved his goal demonstrated the resourcefulness in adversity of Americans like Vann whom World War II had lifted out of their obscure worlds and set to work at the cutting edge of the nation's newest frontier. They had to hold the line until the higher echelons of the Army caught up with the needs of this war, and they had little indeed to hold it with during those first months. The experience forged Vann's attitude toward war. Korea taught him that war was not an enterprise in which one neatly calculated applications of force. War was a hurly-burly of violence in which men prevailed through imagination and the fortitude to struggle on despite reverses.

Much of the unpreparedness of the Army was later to be blamed on the meager military budgets of the late 1940s and on the spending priority given to the Air Force and the Navy for an atomic striking force to annihilate the cities and industries of the Soviet Union, Eastern Europe, and China (added to the target list after the Communist victory there in 1949) in the event of a third world war. The Army had adequate weapons, however, and more than enough manpower in its nearly 600,000-man force of mid-1950 to have halted and smashed the North Koreans in a matter of weeks. The blame lay with the leaders of the Army. They had been neglecting their primary obligation of maintaining an Army that was ready to fight. The troops were not trained and organized. The weapons they needed were in disrepair or in warehouses and storage parks. Of the Army's ten active divisions, only the one in Europe was up to strength. The other nine lacked the normal third battalion in their infantry regiments and also had just two instead of three firing batteries in the artillery battalions.

The deterioration had been severe among the four divisions in Japan, with MacArthur focused on his proconsul's task of restructuring Japanese society into a democratic mold. Walton Walker had headed MacArthur's ground forces in Japan since 1948 as commanding general of the Eighth Army, but he had idled on his reputation as Patton's best corps commander during World War II. His training program had not progressed much beyond the mimeograph machines at his headquarters. His troops had not been unduly distracted from what most, in these years without the draft, had enlisted to enjoy—submissive Japanese women and cheap whiskey—and many were now to die simply because they did not have the physical stamina to march and fight.

Vann's division commander, Maj. Gen. William Kean, had been less complacent than some of his contemporaries. General Kean was one of those unsung workaday generals who rise to an emergency. The 25th Division suffered from all the equipment deficiencies typical of the Eighth Army—trucks that would not start, radios that would not transmit, rifles that jammed, no extra machine-gun barrels to replace barrels that burned out in combat, no maps for a country where no one had expected to fight. (Copies of old Japanese maps had to be airdropped to the troops after they reached Korea.) One of Kean's battalions left Japan with only the battalion commander's radio working; another battalion had exactly one recoilless cannon. Nevertheless, after he had taken charge of the division in 1948 Kean had insisted that his units do a minimum of training. His troops were in better physical condition than the average soldier in the Eighth Army and, with the exception of one regiment, they had some confidence in themselves and their officers.

The exception was the 24th Infantry, a black regiment. (Most of the officers were white.) The 24th might have been Kean's best regiment but for the racist policies of the still-segregated Army of 1950. The regiment was the only one outside Europe that was up to strength in June 1950, with all three infantry battalions and a third firing battery in its artillery battalion. The Southerners who had dominated the Army officer corps since their return during the Spanish-American War had been denigrating black combat units for half a century. (Black fighting units had first been organized by the Union side during the Civil War and had performed well then and during the Indian Wars and the war with Spain.) Decades of forcing black soldiers into quartermaster and transportation units to fetch and carry for white warriors had exacted its price. Many of the troops of the 24th believed the myth of inferiority and repeatedly ran before the North Koreans. The regiment was finally disbanded in 1951. While numerous black Americans fought gallantly in Korea, black soldiers as a group were to have to wait for the changes brought about by integration and the civil rights movement to prove in Vietnam that courage has no color.

Kean's two other regiments, the 27th and the 35th, steadied after their initial encounters. Vann's superior, Lt. Col. Silas Gassett, a brisk, task-oriented artilleryman who was the division G-4, harassed the Eighth Army supply officers for more and better weapons and equipment. In the meantime the officers and noncoms made do with what they had. The companies and platoons without functioning radios fell back on the most ancient form of military communication—a runner with a message.

The regiments were soon strengthened with third battalions stolen from another division in Eighth Army. The 27th Regiment performed so well under the leadership of Lt. Col. John Michaelis that General Walker made it the fire brigade for Eighth Army. He sent Michaelis rushing across the peninsula at the end of July to block a flanking move by the North Koreans that might have captured Pusan, severed the channel of supply and reinforcement, and driven the Americans to evacuate Korea. Marguerite Higgins was to turn "Mike" Michaelis and his 27th Infantry "Wolfhounds" into an Army legend in her dispatches to the *New York Herald Tribune*, and Michaelis was to leave the Army a general.

Walton Walker was as resolute as the bulldog he resembled. He was to redeem himself in Korea and to give a lieutenant an example to carry to Vietnam, an example of how a military leader stands and fights back when the battle runs against him. MacArthur's plan was to have Walker keep a foothold on the peninsula while he got ready to cut off and destroy the North Korean Army with an amphibious landing far in its rear at Inchon, the port for Seoul. He flew to Korea in late July and told Walker there could be no question of an evacuation. Walker had, in fact, already chosen the ground on which he intended to stand. The day before MacArthur's visit he had warned Kean and his other American division commanders, and the Korean officers leading the units of Rhee's army that Walker had salvaged, to prepare for withdrawal to it soon. The ground was a rectangle that ran north up the peninsula for about a hundred miles and inland from the east coast for fifty to sixty miles all along its length. It was to become known as the Pusan Perimeter, because the port was its anchor at the bottom. Walker had selected the ground because most of it is bounded by the Naktong River, a natural obstacle behind which he could maneuver his troops to mass and counterattack wherever the North Koreans penetrated in force.

At the end of July, as the time neared to fall back for a last time, Walker appeared at a dusty schoolhouse in a town called Sangju where the 25th Division had temporarily established a headquarters. He spoke alone to Kean first and then had him assemble the whole staff. One of the officers took notes of the general's speech and wrote a summary afterward for the division's war diary. Lieutenant Vann stood at the back of the room behind the majors and lieutenant colonels. "We are fighting a battle against time," General Walker explained, and they had run out of space. "There is no line behind us to which we can retreat." Nor could they contemplate escape or surrender:

> There will be no Dunkirk, there will be no Bataan, a retreat to Pusan would be one of the greatest butcheries in history. We must fight until

the end. Capture by these people is worse than death itself. We will
fight as a team. If some of us must die, we will die fighting together.
Any man who gives ground may be personally responsible for the death
of thousands of his comrades.

I want you to put this out to all the men in the Division. I want
everybody to understand that we are going to hold this line. We are
going to win.

Walker gave the 25th the worst sector of the line to hold. It was the
bottom corner of the southwest, where Michaelis had momentarily
stopped the North Koreans from thrusting to Pusan. The enemy now
began to batter much harder at this door to victory in the fight to the
death between the two armies. The terrain on the southwest, a series
of hills, was also more favorable to the North Koreans, because the
Naktong offered no obstacle there. The river turns from its southerly
course and starts to flow east about fifteen miles above the coast. The
battle quickly became a slugging match in which the outcome was as
dependent on the supply officers on both sides as on the courage and
stamina of the infantry. The North Koreans were at the end of a long
supply line. They would build up stocks and assault, but then run low
on ammunition after a couple of days and lose momentum. In the meantime the Americans would also have run low on ammunition from having
thrown everything they had at their opponents to try to contain the
attack. Vann and the other supply officers under Gassett would work
frantically to replenish fast enough for the troops to counterattack and
regain the hill positions just lost or to hold on to those they had retained
when the next assault came in a week or so, as it surely would. The
American riflemen were able to hold against the greatly superior odds
because of the superb artillery and air support they were receiving by
August, but the supply situation was so confused that there was constant
danger of an interruption in the flow of shells to the artillery. Gassett
gave a lieutenant a further lesson, this one in how to short-circuit the
bureaucracy when it gets in the way of winning. Instead of simply arguing
with the Eighth Army G-4 officers who were responsible for supplying
the shells, Gassett wangled out of their headquarters copies of the cargo
manifests and sailing dates of freighters coming from the United States.
The length of the voyage to Pusan from the various U.S. ports was
known; it averaged sixteen days from the West Coast. Gassett would
send Vann or another officer with a convoy of trucks to meet the ship
as soon as the freighter docked and seize what the 25th Division needed.

It was the boy who had leaped in front of the buses and trucks in his
street game in Norfolk who kept many of the riflemen in the fight and

saved scores and possibly hundreds of lives when the climax of the battle came at the beginning of September. By late August, Kim Il Sung and his generals were wild to break down Walker's Pusan Perimeter and grasp the victory that was so close and yet might be so quickly denied them and replaced by the destruction of their army. Although they did not know where MacArthur might stage an amphibious landing, and never guessed that it would be at Inchon, they knew that he had a counterstroke like this in mind, because he boasted of it in interviews with correspondents in Tokyo. They did not have the manpower to prepare to defend the numerous places where MacArthur might land and still pursue their main chance against Walker, and so they concentrated on Walker. They sent every bullet and grenade and shell they could down the peninsula by train and truck, in fishing boats along the coast, and then on A-frame packs on the backs of peasant men and women to the fighting units beyond the roads. This time they intended to sustain the attack until Walker's troops buckled.

The offensive began half an hour before midnight on August 31, 1950, with the whistling and crashing of the most intense mortar and artillery bombardment of the war thus far against the positions of the 35th Infantry Regiment northwest of the town of Masan. General Kean had set up his division headquarters in Masan in the classrooms of another schoolhouse. The North Korean infantry assaulted by the thousands behind the barrage. By dawn on September 1 an estimated 3,000 enemy troops had surged past the company strongpoints on the hilltops in the front line of the 35th and penetrated through the rest of the regiment six to seven miles into its rear. The only impediment that kept the North Koreans from reorganizing and resuming their advance on September 1 was the refusal of any element of the 35th to budge. The men of the 35th Infantry were resisting with a gallantry that was matched only by the desperate valor of their North Korean opponents. The cannoneers at the artillery batteries became their own infantry, lowering their pieces and firing point-blank into the North Koreans and radioing other batteries to lay barrages around them. There was hand-to-hand fighting at a number of places with grenades and the bayonet.

Many of the soldiers in the 35th Infantry had initially resented Walker's order to "stand or die." They had thought the general was commanding them to "stand *and* die." They were veterans now, understood the wisdom of the order, and fought in its spirit. They had learned that when the North Koreans enveloped both flanks and the rear in a favorite tactic to make an opponent panic, the worst option was to try to withdraw. Only a few would escape then. If they held until a relief column could reach them, some would die but some would live and they would avoid having to abandon their wounded comrades to certain death and possibly torture and mutilation beforehand by the enraged North Korean soldiery. The rub was that on this occasion Kean had no way of pushing relief columns through to the surrounded front-line companies of the 35th before some of them would run out of ammunition and perish.

Vann had been pondering the problem from earlier battles and had come up with an idea for resupply in just such an extremity. Vann's scheme was for him to toss ammunition to the infantrymen from the back of an L-5 observation plane, the World War II predecessor of the L-19 in which he was to win the Distinguished Flying Cross at Bac a dozen years later. The L-5 had a less powerful engine than its successor but was highly maneuverable and had the same tandem seating arrangement of pilot in front and observer behind. Two days before the offensive, Vann had persuaded Gassett to let him test the idea to resupply a company that was under pressure from a preliminary North Korean move, and the technique had worked.

On the morning of the offensive the division aviation section refused to provide the planes. The pilots said that Vann's scheme was suicidal. The American mortar and artillery crews were dropping shells around the encircled riflemen to help them hold off their attackers while the North Koreans were simultaneously bombarding them to weaken resistance. The pilots would have to fly through the trajectories of all these shells as well as expose their aircraft to small-arms fire from the enemy infantry. Vann said the pilots were being too cautious. Gassett appealed to Kean, arguing that the risk was acceptable, given the stakes. Kean agreed and ordered L-5s put at the disposal of Lieutenant Vann. Because of their protest, the pilots were assigned to one mission each in the sequence in which they would normally have come up for duty on the roster that day. A mission consisted of three ammunition drops. One pilot volunteered for a second flight, six drops in all, and then he quit. The other pilots would fly only a single mission.

Vann flew every mission, and he displayed no nervousness after returning. He was calm as he went about packaging ammunition and loading a plane for the next flight. He selected boxes big enough to hold about 100 pounds in clips of bullets for the M-1 rifles, belts for the machine guns, and hand grenades. After he filled a box he wrapped and tied a blanket around it to prevent it from bursting and spewing out its contents on impact. Although a 100-pound box weighs almost four-fifths of what Vann did at the age of twenty-six, he was strong enough to manhandle one. He wedged two of the boxes into the back of the plane where he sat and held the third in his lap. The locations of the companies were known. Before they took off, Vann spread out his map and briefed the pilot on where they were going to make the drops and how he wanted the approach flown. Three hundred pounds of ammunition overloaded the plane, but Vann's lightness compensated somewhat and the dirt airstrip near the Masan schoolhouse was sufficiently long and the engine sufficiently powerful to get the L-5 into the air. Once they were aloft, Vann gave the pilot further directions over the intercom.

A major from the division intelligence section who was flying over the battlefield that morning to assess the situation and to drop propaganda leaflets on the North Koreans urging them to surrender could hardly believe what he was watching. He saw another L-5 suddenly dive to ground level and start flying right over the heads of the North Korean infantrymen straight for one of the hills where an American company was holding out. The enemy soldiers could shoot at the plane from all sides. There were no clumps of woods or rows of trees the pilot could fly alongside to partially obscure the aircraft on the approach to the hill. The terrain was completely open, either barren or grassy. The plane did gain some concealment from the clouds of smoke and dust rising from the mortar and artillery shells crashing into the ground just beneath it, but this could hardly be comforting, the major thought, given the danger of being blown up by one of the shells. Right before the base of the hill the pilot pulled back on the stick, skimmed up the slope, and clipped over the American position at the top. As the plane cleared the hilltop by twenty to thirty feet the major saw a box sail out and land among the foxholes below. He realized then that Vann was in the L-5. He had seen Vann loading the boxes at the airstrip, had asked out of curiosity what was going on, and had been told about the novel resupply method.

Vann was ordering the pilots to take this straight, ground-skimming approach to be sure that he did not miss with the box of ammunition. Most of the perimeters had by this time shrunk to only about 100 feet across, a difficult target for an airdrop. The companies had originally been deployed in platoon-size strongpoints—mutually supporting foxhole perimeters fortified with barbed wire and minefields. These had gradually become weaker as the riflemen had been killed and wounded. At some places the platoons had consolidated, the survivors of one platoon moving to a neighboring position during a lull or under the cover of an artillery barrage. They carried the wounded with them. Wounded men who could walk were counted as effectives. One company had been reduced to the equivalent of a platoon. It had twenty-two men capable of resistance.

After the pilot had climbed up to altitude and was orienting himself for another run at the same position—or at an adjacent one if the platoons were still separated—Vann would grab hold of the next box and prepare to toss it out the door as he had the first. Then he would have the pilot return to deliver his third box of sustenance to the infantry.

The major from the intelligence section watched in awe as the aircraft made the second and third runs. The little plane sped across the valley floor through the dust and smoke, racing ahead of the bullets of the North Korean soldiers trying to knock it out of the sky. A contour path was actually the most intelligent way to fly in the circumstances, given the tendency of a soldier, unless he is carefully trained to do otherwise, to misjudge the speed of an aircraft flying close by and shoot behind it. If the plane was crippled at this low altitude, however, the pilot would have no margin for maneuver, and if Vann and the pilot survived the crash the North Koreans would kill them anyway. The major could see that the pilot was having trouble holding true for the hill. The blasts from the mortar and artillery shells exploding on the ground jolted the plane and knocked it off course. The pilot would straighten it and keep running for the hill, and each time he cleared the top a box would fly out and down to the foxholes.

A hundred pounds of bullets and grenades is a lot of ammunition to riflemen who used it as frugally as those American soldiers did in the hills beyond Masan, Korea, on September 1, 1950. Vann brought them 100 pounds twenty-seven times that day, persisting until the approach of darkness forced him to stop. Some of the units had almost exhausted their ammunition. The men had started stripping bullets for their rifles from the last of the machine-gun belts.

Relief columns dispatched by General Kean fought through the North Koreans to the company positions as rapidly as possible over the next several days, reinforced the survivors, and brought out the wounded in armored personnel carriers. Vann kept the surrounded infantrymen in ammunition until a column could reach them. He made forty-two more drops over the three days following September 1. He got in his own thumps too from an extra bag of grenades he carried at his side. He pitched them at the North Koreans on the far slope of the hill as the pilot was pulling away after the drop. There is no record of damage to any of the planes he used. Apparently none took more than a few bullets through the fuselage. The pilots did not know they had "Vann luck" riding in the back. Vann resumed the aerial resupply whenever necessary until MacArthur's counterstroke at Inchon on September 15 threw the North Koreans into disarray by severing their main line of supply and retreat. John Vann had been promoted to captain two days earlier.

Vann's contribution did not, of course, decide the battle for the Pusan Perimeter. Walker had sufficient reserves by the end of August to have stopped a North Korean advance to Pusan even if the 35th Infantry Regiment had broken and the enemy had been able to reorganize and surge ahead again. Walker's stalwart generalship and the resolution of the soldiers of the 35th and the other fighting units of the Eighth Army won the victory. The lonely battle of the riflemen on the hilltops had been different. Their lives had hung on the fearlessness of one man.

The war in Korea was a prelude to the war in Vietnam. It was the first war in American history in which the leaders of the Army and the nation were so divorced from reality and so grossly underestimated their opponent that they brought disaster to the Army and the nation. Mac-Arthur now wasted Walker's achievement in the Pusan Perimeter by sending his army into the mountains of North Korea, and the highest civilian and military leaders in Washington acquiesced in MacArthur's gamble. MacArthur threw away the heroism and resourcefulness of Vann and others who had behaved so nobly, squandering the lives of the thousands of men who had died for the victory and the thousands more who would die in a defeat they did not deserve.

Vann's involvement in the disaster in North Korea became part of his legend in Vietnam. He often cited the episode as a lesson in why it made no sense to attempt to fight a war of attrition on the Asian mainland with American soldiers. Vann told me the story not long after I met him at My Tho. He described how he had organized and led the Eighth Army Ranger Company, the first such commando and reconnaissance unit to be formed in the Army since the disbanding of the famous Ranger battalions after World War II, and then how he lost his Rangers to a night of human-wave assaults when the Chinese Army fell on MacArthur's forces in November 1950 in the mountains below the Yalu. He repeated the story often to others. One person who heard it was President-elect Richard Nixon in a letter Vann wrote in another November in the midst of the war in Vietnam:

On the night of 26 November 1950, I commanded a Ranger company which took the brunt of the opening Chinese campaign in the Korean War. By 3:00 A.M. on the morning of the 27th, my 8th Army Ranger Company had received three assaults by Chinese forces employing human-wave tactics. We had excellent artillery support and good fighting positions and killed them by the hundreds. I realized, however, after the third assault, that I was going to lose my company. On the sixth assault just before dawn, I did lose my company. Myself and fifteen men, most of them wounded, were all that were left when the sixth human-wave attack ran through us. We got off the hill by going down the way the Chinese had come up. On the way down the hill, I estimated that there were over five hundred dead Chinese soldiers in front of our positions.

John Vann did at one point command the Eighth Army Ranger Company while in Korea, but the truth of what happened was different and more interesting than the legend.

For some time prior to November 1950, Vann had been envious of a twenty-three-year-old lieutenant named Ralph Puckett, Jr. Puckett commanded the Eighth Army Ranger Company attached to the 25th Division. He and Vann were fond of each other, because both were crackers and both loved soldiering. Puckett was a Georgia boy, West Point class of 1949, and as innocent as he was gung ho. He had volunteered for Korea right out of the parachute training course at Fort Benning because he thought that going to war was like going to a football game and his only fear was that the war would be won before he got to the fight. Vann liked to tease Puckett whenever he came to the supply section at division headquarters to request something for his company. Puckett still retained enough of the West Point cadet spirit to enjoy the "RA" (for Regular Army) game of saluting briskly, holding himself at attention before a mere captain, and saying "Sir!" in a drill-field voice each time he answered a gibe.

"What's with you Rangers and where've you been, Puckett?" Vann would ask with a grin.

"Out operatin' sir!" Puckett would reply with a grin in kind.

"Aw, bullshit," Vann would say. "You guys have been out goofin' off."

When Puckett had stated his request in the crispest Armyese he could summon, Vann would pass him to Gassett, so that Gassett could also have the fun of razzing Puckett before they gave him whatever he wanted.

Puckett's Ranger company, the object of Vann's envy, had been formed the previous summer at the initiative of a colonel on the Eighth Army staff. The colonel had intended to use it to infiltrate and reconnoiter a salient the North Koreans had pushed into the northeastern side of the Pusan Perimeter. The colonel had selected Puckett to organize the Rangers because Puckett's record indicated that he was aggressive and the colonel thought a lieutenant fresh from West Point might operate with more daring than an officer who had been shot at. Puckett confirmed the colonel's impression in an interview. The colonel asked if he would like to command a Ranger company. "Colonel, I've wanted to be a Ranger all my life," Puckett said. "I'll do anything to be a Ranger. You can make me a squad leader or a rifleman if you want."

Puckett found kindred spirits among the cooks, clerk typists, and mechanics of the Eighth Army. He was forbidden to recruit trained riflemen, because the fighting in the Perimeter was at its height and there was a severe shortage of replacements for the regular line companies. He therefore went around the service units back in Japan asking for volunteers to go to Korea for "a secret and dangerous mission involving operations behind enemy lines." Puckett was surprised at how quickly he gathered the seventy-four enlisted men he was authorized. He enrolled two of his West Point classmates to be his platoon leaders. By the time he finished training the company near Pusan, the Inchon landing had dissolved the reason for its creation, and the North Korean Army was attempting to flee back across the 38th Parallel with the Eighth Army in pursuit. Puckett's Rangers were then attached to the 25th Division. General Kean employed them on searches for North Korean stragglers trying to escape through the countryside as the Eighth Army moved north rapidly during the fall, seized Pyongyang, the North Korean capital, and then regrouped on the edge of the mountain range below the Yalu River border with China. Puckett's Rangers had been in a few skirmishes, but they had not seen any serious action prior to MacArthur's order on November 24, 1950, to drive through the mountains to the Yalu and end the war.

In retrospect, Inchon was the sign that MacArthur's egomania had grown beyond tolerable bounds. An amphibious landing far in the enemy's rear was an act of sound generalship taken from his World War II experience. His insistence on Inchon as the site was a grave and needless risk, a gamble with lives and the nation's interest prompted by vanity. He chose Inchon because it was the port for Seoul, but a preliminary examination of the place showed, as one of the officers on the naval planning staff remarked, that Inchon had "every conceivable and natural handicap" to an amphibious assault. The approach channels were twisting and narrow and had a number of "dead-end" points where a ship disabled by shore batteries or a mine would block all those behind and trap all those in front. The Marines would be storming a city whose buildings and quays and high stone seawall made it more defensible than an open beach. Before they could seize the city they would have to secure a fortified island that fronted the harbor. The rise and fall of the tides is so severe at Inchon (approximately thirty-two feet on September 15, 1950) that the Marines would have to take the island at dawn and then wait until dusk before the water rose high enough again to carry their landing craft to the city. They would thus lose tactical surprise, and the attacking regiments would have just two hours of daylight to get ashore. The tides would then prevent reinforcement until the following dawn. If Inchon happened to be well garrisoned, or the North Koreans learned of MacArthur's target and prepared a trap, the landing could be repulsed in a spectacular shambles.

The Navy and Marine commanders involved and the Joint Chiefs of Staff argued with MacArthur to select an alternate site. The Marines found a place about thirty miles south of Inchon that had none of its risks, and the possible delay of a few days in reaching Seoul would be militarily insignificant. MacArthur would not yield. Having put his finger on Inchon, Inchon it had to be. He dismissed risks and obstacles with a theatrical mysticism. "I can almost hear the ticking of the second hand of destiny," he said as he neared the end of a forty-five-minute soliloquy to a war council in Tokyo in August that included two members of the Joint Chiefs. "We must act now or we will die. . . . Inchon will succeed. And it will save 100,000 lives." The success of the gamble on September 15 increased his sense of infallibility and inhibited those who might contradict him.

The second hand of destiny was ticking again in November 1950. MacArthur could not hear it this time because it was ticking for him. He had long ago lost interest in the details of the battlefield, that compass by which all military leaders must guide themselves. His mind was on loftier things. Dean Acheson later observed that MacArthur had become "practically a chief of state . . . the Mikado of Japan and Korea." The description was almost accurate. When Truman summoned him to a meeting at Wake Island that October, MacArthur did not salute his commander in chief as military courtesy said he should. Instead he shook hands as between equals. He was not simply the ruler of Japan, he was a ruler venerated by the Japanese people. There were other MacArthurs within this haughty five-star general of the Army. The MacArthur the Japanese saw was the civil libertarian and missionary for the American way of life. They had expected harshness in 1945 and he had given them magnanimity and wisdom, introducing the democratic government and social reforms they were eager to accept after the horrors that militarism had brought them. At seventy, he was determined to bring his life of glory to a culmination worthy of previous achievements. He was going to fulfill Acheson's description by winning total victory and extending his beneficent rule to the whole of Korea right up to the frontiers of China and Russia.

The men in Washington were willing to settle for four-fifths of Korea. They did see the country as an important way station now, and they wanted to repulse the challenge they perceived from the Soviets. Yet their main concern was Europe, where they had an unrealistic but genuine fear of a big military adventure by Stalin. The Korean War was providing the rationale for a huge rearmament program. By early 1951, aircraft production was to start returning to the World War II peak of 1944. The benefits of the program were going to a buildup of the NATO alliance rather than to Korea. MacArthur was warned that he would have to win his war with the equivalent of the eight divisions he had received by the time of Inchon. The Joint Chiefs instructed him to avoid provoking the Chinese and Stalin by halting at a line about fifty miles above Pyongyang. The northernmost fifth of the country, the mountainous provinces along the Yalu and the section on the northeast corner where Korea borders the Soviet Union, was to be left as a buffer zone.

MacArthur ignored the restriction. He was convinced that he knew how to deal with the Chinese. During a press briefing aboard the command ship *Mount McKinley* on the way to Inchon, a reporter asked whether he feared China would enter the war. "If the Chinese do intervene," he said, "our air will turn the Yalu River into the bloodiest stream in all history." In mid-October at the Wake Island conference, Truman asked him what chance there was of Chinese intervention. "Very little," he replied. He said that his air force could, in any case, prevent the Chinese from bringing more than 50,000 to 60,000 men south of the Yalu and that not many of them would survive subsequent air attacks. "If the Chinese tried to get down to Pyongyang there would be the greatest slaughter," he said. No one accompanying the president from Washington, including Omar Bradley, the chairman of the Joint Chiefs and the other five-star general then on active service, contradicted MacArthur. He took their silence for agreement. He told Truman that "formal resistance" would end throughout Korea by Thanksgiving and that he hoped to bring the Eighth Army back to Japan by Christmas. He promised Bradley a division for Europe in January 1951.

When the appearance of Chinese units within the once-contemplated buffer zone at the end of October prolonged "formal resistance,"

MacArthur sent the B-29s of his Far East Air Forces to demolish the bridges from Manchuria and fighter-bombers to interdict the roads south. He ordered his air commanders to burn with incendiaries "every installation, factory, city and village" in northern Korea that might assist or shelter the Chinese. He held to the judgment he had given Truman at Wake Island, and no message came from Washington telling him to stop. On November 24, 1950, he flew to Walker's command post on the Chongchon River along the southern edge of the mountain range to witness the launching of his final offensive to end the war. He assured his soldiers in a communiqué that they need not fear "the new Red Armies" facing them in Korea. They would be advancing to the Yalu as part of a "massive compression envelopment," he said. "The isolating component of the pincer, our air forces of all types," had essentially cut off the Chinese and prepared them for destruction. He was also not troubled at ordering his troops into these pine-covered mountains in the lethal cold of a Manchurian winter. If everything continued according to plan, he said, they could be "home by Christmas."

By the late afternoon of November 25, 1950, Ralph Puckett and his company of Rangers were settled into the foxholes of a perimeter they had dug out of the frozen earth on Hill 205, a ridge about fifteen miles north of the Chongchon. (The U.S. Army designates hills by height in meters.) Their mission was a standard precaution during a phased movement forward. They were holding the high ground on the right flank of Task Force Dolvin, a two-battalion composite of tanks and infantry under Lt. Col. Welborn Dolvin that was the point element of the division's advance. In the morning the task force was to secure a place called Unsan a bit farther up the road and then to press on in these deliberate stages with the rest of the division following until they reached the Yalu.

Lieutenant Puckett wondered why the 25th Division was advancing. At a briefing for Puckett and the other unit leaders of the task force the previous day, an intelligence officer from one of the battalion staffs had warned that there were 25,000 Chinese soldiers "in the immediate area" of the division. If the intelligence officer was correct, then the 25th should be digging in and preparing to defend rather than going forward in an offensive. Puckett had been taught in the Basic Course for infantry officers at Fort Benning that you needed odds of two or three to one in your favor in order to attack. By the intelligence officer's estimate the Chinese had two-thirds again as many men as the 25th

Division, which was running at about 15,000 men in November 1950 because of sickness and accumulated casualties. One of Puckett's men owned a Zenith Transoceanic radio. The shortwave news broadcasts also kept reporting that hordes of Chinese "volunteers" were coming down from Manchuria to oppose MacArthur's army.

The Rangers had, nevertheless, occupied Hill 205 virtually unopposed on the afternoon of November 25. Dolvin's tanks had carried them up the road and dropped them off at a point abreast of the ridge. While they were walking toward the slope across some iced-over rice paddies, scattered automatic-weapons fire opened on them from the crests of a couple of nearby ridges. They were able to sprint through it and climb the hill at a cost of a couple of wounded. There was no opposition amid the thin pines at the top where they dug their foxhole perimeter, Puckett carefully positioning the machine guns and the BARs to give them the best fields of fire. He did lose a platoon leader. The nerves of one of his West Point classmates cracked at the prospect of running across the paddies through the bullets. The man deserted to the task force command post in the valley and refused to come to the hill. No one shot at Puckett later in the afternoon when he walked back to the command post to see the artillery officer and arrange a fire-support plan just in case they were attacked that night. Nor was he fired at on the return trip to the hill. A fire-support plan was a routine precaution, but one that Puckett always observed.

He was glad the afternoon's casualties had been so light. Although Puckett's Rangers had seen no serious combat, illness and the skirmishing on the way up the peninsula from the Pusan Perimeter had also taken a toll on his company, and it was down a third in strength. He had about fifty enlisted men left of the seventy-four he had recruited in Japan four and a half months earlier, along with the other lieutenant and classmate whose nerves were, like Puckett's, those of a soldier. He would need them all for the hard fight with the Chinese that he felt was certain to come.

Puckett was not frightened at the prospect of encountering 25,000 Chinese. After all, this was the U.S. Army, not Mussolini's rabble, and there must be a sound reason for what they were doing. He merely felt a sense of wry amusement that the generals would order an offensive at these odds, in view of what the Army taught its lieutenants, and he was puzzled as to how this strange maneuver was going to unfold. As the last of the light disappeared on the ridges around him, he assumed from the token opposition they had received in the afternoon that the fight with the Chinese would come on some other hill farther up the road.

* * *

Three hundred thousand Chinese soldiers, not the 60,000 of Mac-Arthur's imagination, were waiting in the mountains of North Korea to fall upon his army. As night came on November 25, 1950, the assault columns that had not yet reached their jump-off points were trotting down the trails along the stream beds to attack on time. The Chinese had not been seriously inconvenienced by MacArthur's air force. One of the juniormost staff officers attached to the main headquarters group of Gen. Peng Teh-huai was a nineteen-year-old lieutenant from North China named Yao Wei. He was to become a specialist in American studies after the war and to come to Washington thirty years later on a research fellowship. Yao Wei remembered that the headquarters group suffered more casualties from truck accidents than from bombs. They were told before crossing the Yalu that the planes would not trouble them if they stayed out of the towns and villages and drove at night. This turned out to be true enough, but the drivers had difficulty steering on the twisting dirt roads with the headlights off.

The Chinese infantry did not have trucks. The trucks of the Chinese Army, other than a small number assigned to the senior headquarters groups, were reserved for hauling supplies and towing artillery. The Chinese infantry marched. Their pace was almost as fast as the twenty miles in five hours of marching time that Caesar's legions set on an average day in Gaul, and the Chinese were traversing rougher country and doing it in the dark. Their day began at 7:00 in the evening. They marched, with time out for meals and rest breaks, until 3:00 A.M., when they made camp again. By 5:30 A.M., as dawn was approaching, every man, all the weapons and equipment, and the Manchurian ponies and horses and carts used to haul the mortars and ammunition were camouflaged against detection from the air. No one moved in daylight except small scouting parties sent ahead to select the next day's bivouac. In this fashion, thirty Chinese infantry divisions, a total of about 300,000 men with the attached artillery and support units, marched into Korea and positioned themselves in front of MacArthur's army by the end of the third week in November without being detected by the U.S. Air Force reconnaissance planes that flew overhead while the Chinese slept below. When MacArthur was telling Truman at Wake Island in mid-October that China could send 60,000 troops at most into North Korea, twice that number were already there or on the way.

Mao Tse-tung, Chou En-lai, and the other leaders of the Chinese Communist Party had just completed a twenty-eight-year revolution to win China independence and freedom from foreign exploitation and to build their country into a modern nation. They regarded the United States as a grave menace to everything they had achieved. The failed champion of the Truman administration, Chiang Kai-shek, had fled to Taiwan with the remnants of his Kuomintang army and administration. The warships of the Seventh Fleet were protecting him there by blocking the Formosa Strait, and the United States was continuing to recognize his regime as the legitimate government of China. The CIA was smuggling spies and guerrillas into China. Periodically some prominent American politician spoke of having the U.S. Navy bring Chiang's army back to reconquer the mainland. Now the Americans were sending an army up through the Korean peninsula toward the Yalu. A secret initiative the year before by Chou En-lai offering to resolve differences and asking the United States to help China preserve its independence from the Soviet Union had been rebuffed. Chou and his colleagues, like Ho and his associates, could fit into the American world vision only as tools of the Russian menace. To accept an American army on their frontier was more than the Chinese could bear. Stalin also encouraged them to resist because of his concern for the security of Vladivostok, secretly promising to back them with Soviet arms and matériel.

The Chinese did not want war and tried to deter the Americans. Chou issued a warning at the beginning of October through the Indian ambassador in Peking. (The United States had no direct diplomatic relations with China.) The chief of staff of the Chinese Army passed an identical warning through a Dutch diplomat. The Chinese explained that they were not going to be intimidated into compromising their independence by the threat of atomic bombs. When the secret diplomacy brought no response, Radio Peking started to broadcast the warnings and, with the Chinese press, began to prepare its public for a war against the United States in Korea. Despite the failure of the aerial reconnaissance, there was also enough intelligence by late November to have sounded an alarm on the extent of the Chinese buildup in the mountains. The information came from the interrogation of prisoners captured during preliminary fighting with Chinese units and from the interception and decoding of Chinese communications.

The warnings all went unheeded, and the intelligence was always misinterpreted or ignored. There was some worrying, never enough to change the attitude reflected in Acheson's reaction to Chou's October warning. "We should not be unduly frightened," he told the British, who were frightened, "at what was probably a Chinese Communist bluff." Afterward he and Omar Bradley said they and their staffs (Dean

Rusk was Acheson's assistant secretary of state for Far Eastern affairs) concluded that Peking would not dare to seriously challenge the United States. Truman felt the same way. These American statesmen and generals thought that Chinese statesmen and generals would endure, because they were Chinese, what Americans would never have endured in like circumstances. As in Vietnam the American leaders also confused their venal Chinese on Taiwan with the Chinese they were facing. On the eve of the blow, Maj. Gen. Charles Willoughby, MacArthur's chief of intelligence, cabled the Joint Chiefs that the Chinese in Korea were running out of food and ammunition. Willoughby did not expect Peking to do much to sustain its army. "The Chinese have always been, by Western standards, notoriously poor providers for their soldiers," he said.

MacArthur magnified the calamity by easing the task of his Chinese opponents. He divided his army into the equivalent of five divisions under Walker on the west side of the peninsula and an independent corps of the 1st Marine Division and two Army divisions on the east under his chief of staff, Lt. Gen. Edward Almond. He also parceled out the South Korean divisions to both subordinates. Walker and Almond did not communicate with each other. MacArthur took it upon himself to coordinate their movements from his headquarters across the Sea of Japan eight hundred miles away. His rhetoric and his aura of infallibility hypnotized almost all of the generals under him. Walker showed his state of mind by agreeing to a suggestion from the Pentagon that it reduce the number of men being shipped to him from the United States as replacements for combat losses. When the commander of the 1st Marine Division told Almond that he would need to build an airstrip at a place called Hagaru-ri to resupply his men and evacuate casualties, Almond asked him: "What casualties?"

Douglas MacArthur's "home by Christmas" talk made him a Pied Piper to his soldiers. With the war over in their minds, the men lightened their physical burden. Many were no longer wearing helmets when they marched toward the Yalu. They wore wool pile caps instead. The caps gave warmth. The helmets were useful only for fighting and so were discarded as unnecessary weight. For the same reason, many also threw away the folding shovels called entrenching tools that they normally carried to dig foxholes. As for ammunition, a lot of the soldiers had just a few clips and a grenade or two, rather than the waistbelt full of bullets and an extra bandolier slung around the shoulder and the ample supply of grenades they would have been carrying had they been expecting a battle.

By waiting in the mountains the Chinese accomplished the twin purposes of delaying war as long as possible in the hope that the Americans might heed their warnings and then of being certain that if war did come the opening battle would be fought on their terms. The mountains deprived the Americans of their mechanical advantage in tanks, artillery, and fighter-bombers. The "massive compression envelopment" that MacArthur envisioned his army as executing was actually a series of isolated, road-bound columns wending their way through the defiles. In the mountains the Chinese could bring to bear their advantage in superior numbers and in the fighting quality of their infantry. Their plan was to employ some of their assault elements to strike the heads of MacArthur's columns and fix them in place while they launched the main body of their infantry down from the high ground and into the valleys to outflank the Americans and attack with greatest force deep in the rear. As the amateurs on this occasion, the Chinese generals were of the mindset of Eisenhower and Patton in North Africa in 1943. They played for keeps and arrayed their best army in front of Walker, who represented MacArthur's main battle line. It was the Fourth Route Army under Gen. Lin Piao—eighteen divisions, 180,000 strong.

China had not fielded an army the equal of Lin Piao's in centuries. It was a product of the talent and energy that a country pours out during a national revolution. Its like was not to be seen again, because this army was also to be sacrificed in the subsequent years of the war after the Chinese became exposed to American firepower. Yao Wei remembered the Fourth Route Army as it was in November 1950. He had joined it as a youth and served with it until detailed to the staff of Gen. Peng Teh-huai's main headquarters just before the move to Korea. Most of the soldiers were older than he was, in their late twenties. They had fought in the civil war without a major defeat all the way from Manchuria, where the Fourth Route Army had been organized, down through China to the capture of Hainan Island off the southern coast in an amphibious landing in the spring of 1950. As North China troops they had adequate clothing for a winter campaign in Korea—heavy quilted cotton uniforms and fleece-lined caps with flaps to protect the ears from frostbite. When the soldiers were told they might have to fight the Americans they were not afraid, Yao Wei remembered. They knew that fighting the Americans would not be like fighting the Kuomintang, but they were veterans with the confidence of battles past.

Puckett and his Rangers got no warning on top of Hill 205. Fifteen minutes before midnight a shower of sparks flashed across the darkness of the forward slope below. Grenades exploded among the foxholes. Chinese infantrymen had crawled silently up the slope close enough to toss their missiles. The sparks were from the arming devices on the grenades. Then mortar shells crashed on the Americans in a quick barrage. Then the Chinese rushed, hoping to crack the Americans with a headlong assault as they had become accustomed to overwhelming their Kuomintang opponents.

Ralph Puckett had trained his cooks and clerk-typists well. They did not fall for the Chinese trick and cower down in their foxholes from the blast of the grenades and the mortar shells. Instead they raised their heads, picked out the figures running up at them through the night, and killed them as they came. Puckett helped them to aim and to fling their own grenades down at the attackers by dispelling the darkness with a radio call to the artillery for flare shells. In the light of the flares, he could see more groups of Chinese soldiers running up the slope behind the lead squads. He dropped the next rounds of high explosive from the 105mm and 155mm howitzers right into them. Because Puckett was a conscientious lieutenant and because he had anticipated a fight farther up the road, his men did not have to stint on their fire. He had made sure that every man was carrying a basic load of ammunition and then some to spare, and lots of grenades. The hilltop was a bedlam of carbines, rifles, BARs, and machine guns savaging the Chinese, while the volleys from the howitzers ripped them with shrapnel and tossed bodies into the air.

The Chinese soldiers faltered. The combination of the artillery and the drumfire from Puckett's men was too much for them. Soon there were fewer figures running up the slope to join those already dead or wounded there, and then there were none as the survivors withdrew into the darkness beyond the illumination flares. The Americans were left undisturbed except for an occasional shot. Puckett crawled around the perimeter from foxhole to foxhole to encourage his men and see how they had fared. The company had escaped lightly, with only half a dozen wounded, and they refused evacuation to the task force headquarters, insisting they could still fight. Puckett learned that this enemy was persistent. One of the Chinese survivors managed to sneak to the edge of the foxholes and throw a grenade. A fragment from it wounded Puckett in the arm. He could not yet know that the night was just beginning and that he and his classmate and their half a hundred Rangers were the target of a force that was later judged to be an entire Chinese battalion of approximately 600 men.

The sequence was repeated three times over the next two hours—the shower of sparks, the grenades, the mortars, the rush—and each time the Rangers dreaded it more than they had the last. They always managed to break the Chinese with the help of the artillery, but a few of them were wounded every time, or killed after the first assault, and they were gradually expending their ammunition.

The fifth assault at 2:45 A.M. was worse than the previous four. There were more grenades. The mortar barrage was longer and more intense. When Puckett called for help from the howitzers the officer at the artillery fire-direction center said that he couldn't give it to the Rangers right away. "We're firing another mission," he told Puckett. "We'll give it to you as soon as we can." Puckett was on his knees facing one end of a two-man foxhole he was sharing with his classmate, bent over with the radiophone against one ear under his helmet and his free hand cupping the mouthpiece so that he could hear and speak amid the din. Even with the wounded who could still prop themselves up continuing to resist, there were gaps in the foxhole line. Puckett's men were also nearly out of ammunition. He had only one clip of eight bullets for his own carbine. "We really need it now," he said to the artillery officer. "We've just got to have it."

At that moment two mortar shells, one followed a fraction of a second by another, exploded behind Puckett in the foxhole. His classmate was killed instantly, and by the odds Puckett should have died too. He had Vann's odds that night and was instead wounded severely in both feet and in the left shoulder and arm by the shrapnel. His right foot was slashed so badly that he later had difficulty persuading the surgeons not to amputate it.

As soon as he recovered enough of his senses to talk again on the radio, Puckett started to laugh. Things were so bad there wasn't anything else to do. The Chinese were coming from two directions this time, he told the artillery officer, and there seemed to be more of them than ever before and he had to have the barrage right away if they were going to hold. When the officer said the guns were still busy helping somebody else who was also under attack, Puckett looked up out of the foxhole and saw that it was too late anyway. Chinese soldiers were running into the perimeter. He told the officer to pass the word to Colonel Dolvin that his company was being overwhelmed.

Those of his Rangers who could still do so jumped out of their foxholes and ran past Puckett down the hill. Partway down, three of them, all privates first class, had second thoughts about leaving their lieutenant behind. They went back up the hill to get him. "Lieutenant, how are you?" one of them asked, crouching on the edge of Puckett's foxhole.

There were Chinese all around. Puckett saw one Chinese soldier about fifteen yards away fire a burst from a submachine gun into a foxhole to finish off another of his Rangers. Only the confusion and the darkness were keeping him and his would-be rescuers from being killed too. "I'm hurt bad," he said. "Let's get off this hill." The man asked if Puckett could walk with help. "No, drag me," he said. He was getting groggy from the loss of blood and shock.

Two of the men pulled him out of the foxhole and carried him down the hill and across the frozen rice paddies while the third trailed behind ready to cover them with the few bullets he had left. The two men carrying Puckett heard him muttering to himself: "I'm a Ranger. I'm a Ranger."

MacArthur's overreaching and the failure of his civilian and military superiors in Washington to restrain him precipitated the longest retreat in the history of American arms. Walker was stunned by the onslaught. Before he could recover and maneuver, the Chinese crushed the entire right flank of his army. The main Chinese flanking drive first scattered a South Korean corps of three divisions and then struck the U.S. 2nd Infantry Division. Its general decided to withdraw the bulk of his division directly south in a single column of tanks and vehicles down a road through a mountain gorge. He was in such a hurry that he neglected to first take the heights above the road. This was the rash decision his Chinese opponents had hoped he would make. They were waiting on the heights when the Americans started down the road. The 2nd Division retreated into a massive ambush.

Walker fell back down the peninsula through Pyongyang 155 miles before he dared attempt to hold along the original 38th Parallel line above Seoul. After he was killed there in a jeep accident on an icy road in late December, the Eighth Army was driven another fifty-five miles down the peninsula and Seoul was lost for the second time in the war, until his successor, Matthew Ridgway, could reorganize and begin a series of counteroffensives.

The independent corps that MacArthur had sent up the east side of North Korea under his chief of staff, Almond, was evacuated by sea, but not before it too lost several of its South Korean divisions and much of the U.S. 7th Infantry Division to the 120,000 troops of the Chinese Third Route Army who fell on it. Almond, as recklessly imperious as his mentor, had ordered the 7th Division to rush all the way to the Yalu by itself. The Chinese let the 7th reach the border and then appeared. Those soldiers who survived the new enemy and the cold did so by

breaking out of the encirclement and retreating back south fast enough
to join up with the Marines.

The Marines alone wrought glory from the disaster, because their
commander, Maj. Gen. Oliver Smith, was the one general in Korea to
perceive the madness of MacArthur's scheme and to have the moral
courage to act on his conviction to save his men. Smith had apparently
become suspicious of MacArthur during the argument over the landing
at Inchon. He decided that the risk MacArthur was taking in North
Korea amounted to military insanity. He therefore prepared his retreat
as he advanced. Smith slowed the movement of his 1st Marine Division
to a mile a day during November, despite the anger of Almond, while
he had the Marine engineers improve the road back through the mountains to the coast and build a base and an airstrip at Hagaru-ri on the
southern end of the Changjin Reservoir. (The reservoir is also known
as the Chosin Reservoir from its Japanese name.) When the Chinese
struck and swung behind the Marines to block a withdrawal, Smith was
ready to turn and literally attack in the opposite direction. The retreat
of the 1st Marine Division from the Changjin Reservoir became another
epic in the roll call of the exploits of the Corps.

The perspicacity and moral courage of Smith and the disciplined gallantry of his Marines could not alter the fact that MacArthur had provoked and lost the decisive battle of the Korean War. The United States
was to settle for half, rather than four-fifths, of Korea, and at five
times the cost in American dead. Of the 54,246 Americans who died in
Korea, the battle of the Pusan Perimeter and the pursuit of the remnants
of the North Korean Army cost the lives of approximately 10,000 men.
The other 44,000 perished in the catastrophe in the mountains below
the Yalu and during the two and a half years of seesaw fighting that
followed until the conflict ended in July 1953, at a truce line roughly
along the 38th Parallel where the war had begun.

Of the fifty-two men who climbed Hill 205, Puckett and nineteen
others came back. Many of the other nineteen survivors were also
wounded, but they had been able to walk or stumble down the hill by
themselves. Puckett was the only seriously wounded man to live. The
rest of the wounded Rangers who could not walk died on the hill. Those
who were not finished off by the Chinese—as Puckett saw one of his
Rangers die—were probably killed by the barrages of white phosphorus
shells and the air strikes that Colonel Dolvin laid on the crest to prevent
the Chinese from exploiting this dominant terrain against the rest of his
task force. Dolvin changed direction the next morning on orders from
General Kean and began withdrawing down the road.

Puckett was to spend a year in Army hospitals in Japan and the United States undergoing surgery to repair his feet and shoulder. When he first woke up at one of the forward casualty centers in Korea he noticed an Asian working as an orderly and wondered if he really had been saved.

"Is that guy Chinese or Korean?" Puckett asked a nurse.

"He's Korean," the nurse said.

As soon as Vann heard what had happened to the Rangers he asked Gassett's permission to see Kean and said, as insistently as a captain could to his general, that he thought he had earned an opportunity to rebuild the company around the survivors with new volunteers. This was not the first time Vann had come to Kean in quest of a company. He had never stopped pestering Gassett to release him, and to silence him on an earlier occasion Gassett had let him see Kean to ask for a company in the 24th Infantry Regiment. Garland Hopkins and Ferrum had freed Vann of racism toward blacks. He was convinced that black soldiers would fight as well as whites if someone showed them that they could. The general had disappointed Vann then by telling him that he was making the most valuable contribution he could on the division staff. At the moment, Kean was preoccupied with saving the 25th Division, but he did not have the heart to say no a second time. Gassett also felt it was no longer fair of him to stand in Vann's way. Vann got the Rangers. He had to recruit and organize amid the turbulence of the retreat, but Kean also gave him a haven within which to work by extricating the 25th relatively intact and conducting a withdrawal that was orderly, given the circumstances. While Kean did not have Oliver Smith's independence of mind, he had been more cautious than his fellow Army generals. Instead of aligning most of the division forward on a thin front for MacArthur's offensive, he had disposed his units in considerable depth. The Chinese maneuver to rush around the end of the 25th and envelop the division therefore encountered resistance. Kean used the time the resistance bought to pull back Task Force Dolvin and other lead elements before they were too badly hurt. He thus consolidated strength as he withdrew and kept the division balanced and able to fight its way free of the attackers.

Mary Jane learned of her husband's first command when his next letter instructed her to go to the Osaka post exchange and have the tailor shop there make up shoulder tabs with the word RANGER embroidered on them for the men to sew on their uniforms. He felt the same pride Puckett had of distinction from ordinary infantry and used the shoulder tabs as one of many ways to impart it to his men. He was overjoyed with his first command precisely because the Rangers were an independent unit; Vann was always happiest as top man. The Korean War and the general expansion for Europe had led to an Army decision to create a number of permanent Ranger companies. Vann was allowed to recruit from within the 25th Division and the general pool of replacements coming to Korea and to expand the company by adding a third platoon, increasing its strength to five officers, including himself, and 107 enlisted men. His enthusiasm brought him far more volunteers than he could accept.

There was no time for formal training. Vann had to develop the skill of his Rangers in whatever free moments he could find and in the fashion the Army calls OJT, the military abbreviation for on-the-job training. In mid-December 1950, as soon as he had brought the company up to strength and rushed it through a couple of exercises to enable the men to function more or less as a unit, Vann and his Rangers were carried by Navy landing craft to the island of Kangwha close to the west coast of Korea in the mouth of the Imjin River. The river mouth was the western end of the defense line Walker was trying to establish along the 38th Parallel. Vann was assigned two missions. The first was to give warning if the Chinese attempted an amphibious landing behind the Eighth Army. The second was more enterprising and dangerous. Vann and his Rangers crossed the river mouth to the mainland in small boats at night and reconnoitered behind Chinese lines to gather intelligence.

The Rangers were evacuated from Kangwha when the Eighth Army retreated again after Walker's death, but were sent on new behind-the-lines operations to obtain intelligence for the first counteroffensive launched by General Ridgway in late January. Vann had to avoid anything more serious than a skirmish during these missions. An encounter with a large Chinese force would have doomed his men to no purpose. He thought he might have an opportunity to show his mettle on February 10, 1951, when the Rangers teamed up with the tanks of the 25th Division's mechanized reconnaissance company to help recapture Inchon. There were only stragglers to fight. The Chinese abandoned the city.

Vann did not steal the tale of Puckett's valor right away. On the contrary, he behaved with the loyalty he always showed toward a brave fellow officer. He was responsible for Puckett's receiving the Distinguished Service Cross. He interviewed survivors of the night on Hill 205, collected affidavits of Puckett's courageous leadership, and submitted a recommendation for the award along with a proposed citation to accompany the medal. He also obtained decorations for the enlisted men who rescued Puckett. When he and Puckett met later at Fort Benning, Vann asked to see the citation and said how pleased he was that it had been approved exactly as he had written it.

The theft of Puckett's story was to come a dozen years later in Vietnam. Vann appropriated it for a number of reasons. The John Vann of Vietnam could not have been the John Vann he wanted to be and not have led his Ranger company through a night of heroic resistance when the Chinese attacked in Korea. He knew he would have behaved just as courageously as Puckett had, and so he wove the story into his legend. He recalled the details fairly well from having written the citation, and he added a few others to give the episode broader meaning—for example, the "over 500 dead Chinese soldiers" he had seen by the dawn's light "going down the way the Chinese had come up." (Puckett didn't know how many Chinese they had killed. There had been no way to count.)

The picture of hundreds and hundreds of bodies and Vann's description of the Chinese "human-wave tactics" were useful for his argument in Vietnam that Americans could never win a war of attrition on the Asian mainland. There would always be more of them than of us no matter how much firepower we had, he would say, and then cite what had happened to him and his Ranger company. The way he modified the details in his mind—"when the sixth human-wave attack ran through us"—also reflected the image of China he was to bring to Vietnam. To Vann, China's millions were not a transitory military asset and a permanent impediment to achieving true power through modernization. Rather, they were an ever-expanding menace to be contained. The image was shared by most Americans of this time. Korea made the image vivid and tangible to Vann.

Like many Army officers of his generation, Vann had a tendency as well to rationalize what happened in North Korea. The Army was too close to its World War II victory to admit that its leaders had been outgeneraled and that, with some exceptions like Puckett's Rangers and the Marines, the American soldier had been outfought by his Chinese opponents because he was so unprepared and misinformed. Vann told Mary Jane afterward that MacArthur had made a terrible mistake in doing battle with the Chinese, but he was inclined to excuse the defeat by attributing it to numbers. MacArthur's accomplishments were too large, he had wrapped himself too artfully in the flag and in the pride of the nation, and his excuses were too eloquent for Americans like Vann to see his flaws of character and his loss of touch with his profession. It was to take Truman four and a half months to fire him, and the president dismissed MacArthur then only because the general, in his craving to vindicate his military reputation, insisted on publicly lobbying for all-out war with China. When he came home MacArthur received a hysterical welcome from a country that still loved him.

Ironically, Vann was never to receive the decoration he deserved for saving the rifle companies in the Pusan Perimeter. The major from the intelligence section who witnessed the fights from another spotter plane was preoccupied with his own work and did not mention what he saw to Gassett. Vann's calm demeanor while loading the ammunition and the luck that none of the planes was seriously damaged gave Gassett the misimpression that the pilots really were exaggerating the risk. Vann was not shy about letting Gassett know that he shuttled trains and truck convoys and moved men and supplies faster than any other division transportation officer in the Eighth Army. (He received a second Bronze Star for his skill at this work during the pursuit of the routed North Koreans up the peninsula after Inchon.) He boasted of these accomplishments to Gassett in the same way he had boasted to Crutchfield about the athletic awards he won at the junior high school in Norfolk. He measured his worth by his achievements. He never gave Gassett any indication of how dangerous the ammunition drops to the surrounded companies had been. His silence did not come from lack of desire for a medal. He told Mary Jane afterward how much he had wanted to win an impressive decoration in Korea. He knew that he would appear to be asking for a medal if he described the flights to Gassett. A medal for bravery was one of the few things he valued so highly that he would not ask or scheme for it. If it did not come his way by itself, he did not want it. He said nothing, and Gassett, a conservative man who believed that an officer took the risks necessary to do his job, only recommended that Vann be given an Air Medal with Oak Leaf Cluster, the equivalent of receiving the medal twice. An Air Medal is a mundane award for a specific number of flights in a combat area, without regard to the degree of hazard involved. The recommendation was lost by the clerks somewhere along the chain of command.

(Eight years later in Heidelberg, Germany, the intelligence officer met Gassett again and told him the extraordinary daring he had witnessed. The two men wrote a description of Vann's exploit, the intelligence officer attached an affidavit of what he had seen, and Gassett recommended that Vann be decorated with the Silver Star for Gallantry. Vann was denied the medal on one of those Catch-22 technicalities that military bureaucrats seem to have a gift for inventing. The law would have permitted him to receive the award by raising Gassett's original recommendation for an Air Medal with Oak Leaf Cluster to a recommendation for the Silver Star. The law even provided for the consideration of lost recommendations if evidence could be found that they had once been submitted. The evidence in Vann's case was a carbon of the original recommendation in his personnel file and Gassett's word that he had submitted it. The Office of The Adjutant General ruled that this evidence was insufficient and that separate evidence had to be found in its records to prove that the recommendation had been "placed in military channels" prior to being lost. Separate evidence could not be found, because the recommendation had been lost. Vann would have to wait for Ap Bac to receive his first medal for valor in the Distinguished Flying Cross.)

Vann might still have won the high decoration he wanted in Korea if he had been able to lead his Ranger company long enough to run into a hard fight with the Chinese and distinguish himself. He kept the company only two and a half months. Jesse, who was to object so much to his second war, ended his first one prematurely.

John Vann had never seen his second son. Jesse had been born on August 5, 1950, while his father and the 25th Division were in desperate battle to hold the southwest corner of the Pusan Perimeter. The Army hospital at Osaka was in such turmoil that the nurse was unable to find clean sheets for the bed when Mary Jane went there with labor pains. The obstetrician was in surgery helping with the latest group of wounded to arrive on the planes from Korea and rushed over to the delivery room just before Mary Jane started to give birth.

Jesse was a pretty baby, with light blond hair and large blue eyes, but sickly, without much appetite. Mary Jane blamed his weakness on her foolishness in listening to another obstetrician at the prenatal clinic who had instructed her to diet during her pregnancy. Instead of eating for two, according to her Grandmother Allen's old saying, as she had done with Patricia and John Allen, she had often eaten little but celery and carrots. In early February 1951, when Jesse was six months old, his breathing became shallow and his eyes began to protrude. He kept moving to the foot of the crib, another old-wives'-tale symptom of illness in a child. Mary Jane couldn't understand what might be wrong with him, because he was not running a temperature. The pediatrician who examined him at the hospital happened to have worked with meningitis prior to being sent to Japan. He did a spinal tap. The analysis of the fluid showed that Jesse had a form of meningitis, attacking the layer of tissue covering the brain. The pediatrician told Mary Jane that he might be able to save the baby with a recently developed treatment, but that Jesse's chances were not good. As she walked down a corridor in shock, Mary Jane met a friend, another officer's wife who was working at the hospital as a Red Cross volunteer. Mary Jane broke down and told her friend the news. The friend sent an urgent message to Korea through Red Cross channels. Vann found himself on a plane with emergency-leave papers in his pocket.

He surprised her by arriving unexpectedly at the house. The friend had called to say that he was on his way, but he had to change planes in Tokyo and Mary Jane had not known when he would reach Osaka. She was overcome at the joy of having him home again and having him embrace her, despite the reason for his return. He was dressed in clean fatigues he had been given at the delousing station at the Tokyo airfield. He took off his cap to show her how his head had also been shaved to deprive the lice of their best hiding place. He was amused at his bald pate. "Don't worry about catching any from me," he said, explaining how thoroughly he had been fumigated.

They drove to the hospital immediately. In the couple of days it had taken for the message to reach the division headquarters and for Vann to return to Osaka, Jesse had started to hold his own against the disease. The doctor was encouraged. Vann comforted Mary Jane. They had been lucky with Patricia and John Allen, he said, and Jesse would recover and someday be as healthy as they were.

When the child survived the crisis and the doctor wanted Vann sent home because Jesse had a long period of recuperation ahead and could get better treatment in the United States, Vann resisted going. The division headquarters was informed of the doctor's wish and sent Vann a message at the end of February, as his two-week leave was almost over, telling him that he was being given a compassionate transfer. He telephoned Korea and said there was no need for him to go home, that Mary Jane could take Jesse and the two older children to her parents in Rochester by herself. He said he wanted to return to his company. The headquarters assumed he was trying to behave like a good soldier and refused to listen. He was told that as a captain he would be coming up for rotation during the summer in any case to attend the next Advanced Course at the Infantry School at Fort Benning. In the meantime an officer with his experience was needed at the new Ranger Training Command there. His reassignment orders were being cut. He had no choice.

Mary Jane sensed how much he resented giving up the war and his

Ranger company. His attitude hurt her badly. She had looked forward eagerly to having him return and to sharing things with him again. Physically nothing was different between them. The physical attraction had always been strong and they renewed the relationship undiminished, but John did not reminisce when they were together and reveal his thoughts as he had before. She tried to talk to him about the life that she and the children had led while he had been away. He did not respond. She could tell that his mind was still in Korea with his company. She may also have sensed a change in him because they had reacted so differently to the war. For him the war had been the most fulfilling experience of his life. No time had hung on his hands. Nothing had been trivial or dull. Every day had been meaningful, every act important and urgent. He had been fascinated to learn how he excelled at war's demands, how far he could rise above other men in its test. Intellectually she had accepted the justification of the war at face value, as she did everything else she was told. Emotionally she had rejected it, because the war had taken John away and what she saw of it frightened her.

General Kean had asked all of the officers' wives to work either as nurse's aides and Red Cross volunteers at the hospital or in helping sort the wounded at the airfield when they were flown in from Korea. Mary Jane had chosen to work at the airfield, because she lived closer to it. The walking wounded were escorted into a hangar and sat on benches while a doctor and several medical corpsmen assigned them to buses that took them to different sections of the hospital, depending on their wounds. The serious cases with shattered limbs and grave intestinal, chest, or head injuries were carried directly from the planes to ambulances. Before they served coffee and cocoa to the walking wounded and assisted them onto the buses, Mary Jane and the other wives would go into the ambulances and try to comfort the badly wounded men. The sight of this human wreckage coming off the planes stunned her. She had never imagined such brutality. For the rest of her life she was to recall the faces of these young men and the way their bodies were broken. After she overcame her initial reaction, the dread that one of the figures on a stretcher might be John, she could not help seeing the wounded as boys. At twenty-three she was not much older than most of these soldiers of eighteen and nineteen and twenty, but she was a mother with two sons of her own. It seemed so wrong to her that this should be happening to these boys. They should be in college, or working at their first jobs, or out on a date, not getting mangled. She wondered if someday one of her sons would be taken and torn apart like this in some other war. She was struck at how naive she had been to think that the Army was like Coca-Cola or some other big corporation that periodically sent husbands and families to pleasant overseas stations. Now she realized that the business of the Army was making war.

John's resentment at being forced to leave the war would pass, Mary Jane felt, but there was something else between them that time did not seem to change, despite their physical attachment. It was John's sexual compulsion. She had learned of it before he left for Korea. It was another of the unsettling discoveries she had made in the house on the hill. He was making love to the two Japanese housemaids. At first she was outraged that he would betray her and magnify the indignity by doing so in her home. Then she became fearful because she thought that if she confronted him openly, it might destroy their marriage, and every action she took to show her disapproval silently only brought firmer resistance from him. The maids, who were sixteen to eighteen years old, could hardly refuse him, with jobs and food so scarce for Japanese in 1949–50. She nevertheless decided to fire the maid he seemed most actively involved with and hoped that he would get the message. He ignored it and took up with the new maid she hired. When Mary Jane fired her and did not replace her, he hired another second maid himself without informing her. She could tell that he had selected this latest girl and brought her into the house in order to make love to her. When Mary Jane fired this girl too, he got still another. His activity with the maids did not seem to affect his ability or desire to make love to her. It seemed that John had plenty of sexual energy to spare. Mary Jane had remained silent, but for the first time in the marriage there had been tension between them. He made clear that he was going to have his harem and that he expected her to accept his behavior. He showed no sign of guilt.

At Fort Benning, which the Vanns reached in early May 1951 after the voyage home and a long visit with the Allens in Rochester, John substituted American women for the Japanese maids. The family lived in one of the new garden-apartment complexes the Army had constructed on the post with funds flowing from the Korean War. John often went out in the evening after dinner, saying that he had a basketball game or had to study at the post library. Mary Jane continued to say nothing. Instead she retaliated by becoming bitchy with him when she could not contain her anger, but she usually controlled herself and endured his infidelities. The parachute jumping and other rigorous exercise at the Ranger Training Command and then the eight months of studying his profession in the Advanced Course at the Infantry School kept him in good humor. He was attentive to her need for diversion from the children and took her to parties and bridge games with fellow officers and their wives. They frequently got together with Ralph Puckett and his fiancée to charcoal-broil steaks while the men talked about the war. (Puckett's shoulder and feet were being rebuilt by the surgeons at the Fort Benning Hospital.)

On many evenings when John was off pursuing women, Mary Jane was also preoccupied with nursing Jesse through bouts of pneumonia, which kept recurring during his first three years. To relieve the congestion in Jesse's lungs the doctors had her improvise a steam tent by draping a sheet over his crib and putting a vaporizer underneath. Afraid to leave him, she would sit for hours by the crib. His head was too big for his little body. His eyes still bulged from the pressure on the brain, and the doctors had to tap the skull cavity once to remove fluid. The meningitis also caused lesions on the brain. They gradually scarred over, but the constant illness delayed Jesse's mental and physical development. He walked late and did not speak his first word until he was two.

When Vann finished his course at the Infantry School in the spring of 1952 and was assigned to Rutgers University as an ROTC instructor, a crueler time began for Mary Jane. He requested the assignment so that he could take his bachelor's degree in business administration through spare-time and night classes. He needed at least a bachelor's degree for career purposes, and given his talent at mathematics and statistics and his earlier year at Rutgers in economics, business administration was a logical subject. He drove to New Jersey ahead of time and rented a house for the family in Parlin, a small town east of New Brunswick where the university is situated. The location made sense to him, because the rent for a house large enough for a wife and three children was cheaper in Parlin than in other communities nearer the campus and yet he was still within commuting distance.

For Mary Jane, Parlin was sudden isolation after the closeness of garrison living at Fort Benning and the camaraderie of the 25th Division families in Japan. The house he rented was in a predominantly Polish neighborhood composed of people who had immigrated long before World War II. Most of Mary Jane's neighbors were elderly couples who did not speak English well and whose children had grown up and moved away. Her next-door neighbor happened to be a widow of Anglo-Saxon heritage who was always cooking and sending over pies and casseroles and offering to help with the children. One kindly neighbor is not a community or a social life. John would leave at 8:00 A.M. after breakfast and Mary Jane would rarely see him until late at night.

Had she wanted to hire a baby-sitter and take a bus to go bowling, or to the movies, or window-shopping in a more prosperous section, she would not have had the money. John bought her a secondhand car for herself and the children, but it was such a jalopy that it did not run most of the time. He used the family's new car to commute to the university. He controlled all of the money, paying the major bills like the rent himself and keeping Mary Jane on a tight budget. On Saturdays he would drive her to the commissary at an Army installation to buy groceries and then dole out money during the week for whatever additional food she had to buy and for the children's clothing and other essentials. If she protested to him about rising prices, he would retort that he had gone without shoes when he was a boy and by God his children could make do with a pair that cost no more than such-and-such—citing a price that had prevailed when he was in his teens or during World War II. Because he did not shop for the family himself, he had little idea of the rise in the cost of living.

When Mary Jane complained of her loneliness he said that he did not have time to spare for her and the children at this point in his career. He took the position that he was fulfilling his obligation by supporting the family. He also refused to move them to a house closer to the campus, saying that he could not afford it. He was genuinely busy. He taught ROTC courses, took day and night classes for his own degree, and was the detachment's supply officer. In his ambitious way he later volunteered to coach the demonstration drill team, called the Scarlet Rifles, and to serve as a physical education instructor. By now Mary Jane knew that he always made time for what he wanted to do and that on nights when he could be at home he was chasing women instead. She also began to realize that he was miserly with her and the children because he wanted money to spend on his extracurricular pastime.

She started checking up on him through acquaintances she made at the few social gatherings of ROTC officers and their wives and friends to which he did take her. She discovered that, among more fleeting adventures, he was having an affair with a secretary. Mary Jane had met the woman at one of the social gatherings. They were about the same age. She was not worried that John was going to leave her to marry the secretary. The woman was the sort of good-time party girl whom men pick up and discard. Yet somehow knowing her made it harder to tolerate his unfaithfulness. After the children were asleep at night she would imagine him making love to the secretary and drive herself into fits of depression and weeping.

Mary Jane refused to consider the possibility of leaving him. Raising three children on what she could expect to earn as an unskilled woman intimidated her, and she regarded divorce as a public admission to her parents and friends that she had failed at the one enterprise in life at which she most wanted to succeed. She told herself that she would not be able to bear the shame of it. She could not even bring herself to take revenge by having an affair.

If he had given her the semblance of the marriage she wanted, she might have learned to accept his promiscuity. She would plead with him to come home for dinner after classes on a given evening. He would promise and she would cook a special meal, put candles on the table, buy some wine—everything just for the two of them and the expectation of making love afterward—and he would fail to show up. She would be hysterical by the time he did return well after midnight, railing at him in tears that she was his wife, that he had taken marriage vows, that it was his duty to come home to her. One evening he promised to return early to eat with her and the children because it was Patricia's birthday. Mary Jane baked a cake. Midnight came and went without Patricia's father coming home. Patricia remembered her birthday cake sitting on the table uncut, the candles unlit, and her mother lying on her parents' bed sobbing uncontrollably.

Mary Jane began to pick fights with him over his stinginess, his lack of attention to the children, his running around, or any grievance that came to mind. The arguments became steadily more vicious. When she had worked herself into a fit she would shriek and throw plates or anything else she had in her hand at him. Her impulses were self-destructive. The fights made the marriage more hellish than it already was and gave John yet another excuse not to come home. He took to staying out all night frequently, saying that he had to study late and would sleep in the car and shave and shower at the gym the next morning. She would deny him her body when he did come home to try to punish him. The denials would not last long because of her desire for him. In the summer of 1953, as the marriage was entering one of its worst stages, she became pregnant again.

During earlier and happier years of the marriage, John had told her more about his childhood than he was ever to tell anyone. He had told her that he was illegitimate and had taken her to meet Johnny Spry during a stopover in Norfolk in 1947 on their first trip to Fort Benning. She was struck by his resemblance to his natural father and listened to him reminisce about riding on kegs of bootleg whiskey as a little boy when Spry had taken him along on delivery runs before Spry's still had been raided. She heard how Mollie had rescued him from the crib in which his mother had abandoned him, of Frank Vann's perpetual fried potatoes and biscuits, of how Garland Hopkins had given him an escape by sending him to Ferrum. They had driven over to Ferrum so that he could show her the school and introduce her to his teachers. At the time Myrtle had taken up with a chief petty officer in the Navy for whom she was soon to leave Frank Vann. Mary Jane had gathered from what John said of his mother that she was altogether egocentric, a drinker and a loose woman who had rejected him and her other children. His first memory of his mother, he had said, was of her sitting in front of her dresser brushing her hair.

For every fragment of his childhood John revealed to her, he concealed many more. He was too ashamed of the memories to speak of them even to her, or he suppressed them. At this unhappy time in her marriage she had no way of knowing why John behaved as he did. She had no way of understanding the magnitude of the insecurity that Myrtle had created in him. The boy who had to prove to himself that he had the courage of a male by feats of daring was the man who had to keep assuring himself of his masculinity by a never-ending marathon of seduction. What was a penchant for womanizing in Spry was a hunger that no number of women could satisfy in John. Using women to give himself fleeting assurance was also not enough for him. He had to victimize women too, as he was victimizing Mary Jane in a kind of revenge on his mother.

He also had not told her that Garland Hopkins was another man with a dark side and that Hopkins had exacted a price for liberating him. Hopkins's tragic flaw was pedophilia, a homosexual attraction to boys. Hopkins did not recite ghost stories around the campfire simply to entertain his Boy Scouts. He would pick out a boy who had been frightened by his tales and crawl into the boy's sleeping bag later that night saying that he wanted to comfort him. Hopkins's particular compulsion did not involve sodomy or other advanced acts of homosexuality. It was the fondling of the genitals that little boys commonly engage in with each other as sex play. (He had a normal relationship with his wife and fathered three children.) Men like Hopkins are most attracted to the blond-slip-of-a-youth sort that Vann was at fourteen. There is no doubt there was a relationship between them. It is not unusual in such cases for the sexual relationship to end as the boy grows older and for the two men to wind up being friends. This is apparently what happened in the case of Vann and Hopkins. Vann admired Hopkins's qualities as a social reformer and political activist and was immensely grateful to him. The relationship does seem to have aggravated the insecurity that Myrtle created, making Vann even more ferociously heterosexual.

There was so little warmth in the marriage in the spring of 1954 that John abandoned Mary Jane and the children the night that Tommy was born. He took her to the hospital in the afternoon when she had labor pains. She thought he then returned to stay with the children. The kind widow who was her neighbor had come over to watch them while John drove her to the hospital. When she called the house that night to tell him that he had a fourth child and a third son, her neighbor answered the phone. John had not reappeared. Mary Jane was unable to reach him until late the next morning at the ROTC office at the university.

He left for a new assignment with the 16th Infantry Regiment at Schweinfurt, Germany, after his Rutgers graduation that June, promising to send for Mary Jane and the children as soon as he could find a place for them to live. The Army's family housing project in Schweinfurt was temporarily full. At John's suggestion they moved in with the Allens in Rochester to wait. This expedient saved money; Vann lost his Army allowance for food and house rent in New Jersey after he went overseas. His promise seemed sincere when he left. He took with him Mike, the family dog, a friendly blend of cocker spaniel and miscellaneous that he had saved from execution at the Fort Benning pound when he decided that the children ought to have a pet.

Once he was in Germany, the temptation to keep an ocean between himself and the burden of Mary Jane and her brood was too much for him to resist. In his letters John did not say or imply that he wanted a separation or a divorce. He gave officers he met in Germany the impression that he missed Mary Jane and the children, as he was to give David Halberstam the same impression in Vietnam by calling attention to the large colored photograph of his sons that he kept on his desk at My Tho. Mary Jane thought that he wanted the marriage to continue because Army promotion boards were said to look with greater favor on family men. Actually, his motivations were more complicated. He played roles as much to satisfy himself as to impress others. He liked to think of himself as a husband and father and to talk about his children—from a distance.

Months went by as he stalled with the excuse that no housing was available. Mary Jane moved to an apartment that her sister, Doris, and her brother-in-law, Joseph Moreland, found for her in the small upstate New York town where they were living. She was embarrassed to remain with her parents in Rochester as a married woman with four children, and the checks that John was sending the Allens for room and board were not generous. Her sister and brother-in-law were childless, but her brother-in-law was a big, warm Irishman who loved children. He was

Uncle Joe to the young Vanns and was always taking them on excursions. Joe and Doris knew from what they saw and from what Mary Jane admitted that she did not have a marriage. They offered to help her make another life for herself and the children. She thought about divorce again, as she had in New Jersey, and once again, she couldn't face it.

She telephoned John from her parents' house on Christmas Day, 1954. She and the children were in Rochester to spend the holidays with the Allens. She was full of emotion at the memories of the day and thought that he might be moved too. She wept on the phone, told him how much she loved and missed him, and said that six months was too long and that he had to let her and the children join him. He gave her hell. There was no family housing open in Schweinfurt yet, he said. She was being her usual emotional self. She would have to be patient and wait. She stopped crying and got tough too. She had heard differently about housing, she said. She was going to borrow money for the tickets and she and the children would be on the first plane to Germany they could get out of New York.

John seemed happy to see his family again when he met the Pan American flight at Frankfurt. Mary Jane had sent him a telegram with their arrival time. His mood was a good omen. The next two and a half years were one of the better periods in the marriage, and they were years when his career filled with promise.

The U.S. Army in Germany in the mid-1950s was an Army that could appreciate a John Vann. It was an Army on the qui vive, honing itself for the clash with the Russians that every man from general to private was certain would come. The John Vann who went to Germany was an officer maturing professionally from the combination of his military and civilian education and lessons learned in the most adverse of circumstances in combat. His performance in an Army actually at peace, but emotionally at war, therefore stood out all the more prominently.

His initial assignment on arrival at the 16th Infantry Regiment in June 1954 was to be acting executive officer of a battalion. Then, for a week, he was acting battalion commander. The bold and astonishingly competent way in which he handled himself caught the attention of a man who was to become one of Vann's Army patrons, Bruce Palmer, Jr., at that time a colonel commanding the regiment. When Palmer needed a new leader for the regiment's 4.2-inch mortar company a couple of weeks later, he chose Vann. Heavy Mortar Company, as the unit was called, was the ideal assignment for a captain in an infantry regiment because it was a separate command, the closest a captain could get to a lieutenant colonel's job of leading one of the infantry battalions. The 4.2-inch is the biggest of the American mortars; it throws a shell approximately equivalent to a 105mm artillery round about two and a half miles. There were twelve mortars in a company. They were carried to position on trucks and served as the regiment's integral artillery. Palmer selected his subordinates carefully. He had shaped the 16th Infantry into the best of the three regiments in the 1st Infantry Division, which was stationed in central Germany across the presumed main invasion route of the Soviets from East Germany and Czechoslovakia.

Heavy Mortar Company reflected the second-to-none attitude of its commanding officer. Palmer noted on an efficiency report that Vann's inclination to discipline his men severely did not interfere with his ability to gain their loyalty, because "he drives himself at a terrific pace and expects the same standard of performance from his subordinates." During maneuvers on the plain of Grafenwöhr near the Czech border, Vann had his mortars in position and ready to fire the moment the infantry called for a barrage. The shells landed on target; the mortar fire was meticulously coordinated with that of the artillery; the gun emplacements were so perfect they could have been used as demonstration models. At inspections in garrison the weapons and equipment were in faultless condition; the records were kept precisely according to regulation; the appearance of the company commander and his platoon leaders and men was a perfection of spit and polish.

The mortar company and its commanding officer also excelled at those other activities that keep an army prepared. The company won more athletic awards than any other in the regimental competitions and contributed members to the regimental basketball team, which Vann coached to a victory over the teams from the other two regiments in the 1st Infantry Division championship. "I was particularly impressed with the fighting spirit and will to win evidenced by all members of the team," Palmer said in his letter of commendation to Vann. "They might have been outplayed at times, but they were never outfought."

When Vann was transferred to Headquarters U.S. Army Europe at Heidelberg in June 1955, after a year with the regiment (he had been promoted to major that April), Palmer went out of his way to alert future promotion boards and selection boards for schooling to Vann's potential. He rated Vann on a final efficiency report as "one of the few highly outstanding officers I know." Palmer urged that Vann be given "an early opportunity" to attend the Command and General Staff College at Fort Leavenworth, Kansas, a virtual requirement for promotion to lieutenant colonel. To drive home his assessment of Vann's talent, Palmer added a special letter of commendation to Vann's file:

> You have been an outstanding company commander and all-around leader of men. Under your leadership, I have had the utmost confidence in Heavy Mortar Company to accomplish any mission assigned.
>
> On all occasions, Heavy Mortar Company has reflected the highly competitive, aggressive, and enthusiastic spirit which you have provided. . . . I feel that much credit for the success of your company is due to your integrity, tenacity, and singleness of purpose.

At the headquarters in Heidelberg, where Vann joined the Logistical Management Section of the G-4 Division, his superiors were soon praising him with similar exuberance. "I consider this officer to be one of the Army's outstanding young men," his immediate superior said on his first efficiency report.

Vann's private life did not affect the esteem in which his superiors held him. These superiors, Palmer among them, uniformly praised Vann's "high moral character" on his efficiency reports. In professional terms, Vann was a highly moral man. He believed wholeheartedly in the ideals of the American officer—in caring for his troops, in leading by example, in reporting honestly to those above him—because the fulfillment of those ideals was bound up with his sense of self-respect. The Army also does not concern itself with the private lives of its officers as long as the officer avoids scandal and his private life does not include such things as homosexuality, which can easily lead to blackmail. The frequent separations of military life tend to reduce adultery to the mere transaction on a couch that Napoleon claimed it to be. Those marriage partners who remain faithful, as Mary Jane did, do so because monogamy is an emotional preference or need. A number of Vann's contemporaries knew of his off-duty activity, because he boasted of his sexual prowess. Most found his tales amusing or envied his virility. He also made appearance count in his favor. One of Vann's friends at Schweinfurt noticed that although Vann quickly acquired a bevy of German girlfriends, he was discreet. He never brought his girlfriends to the officers' club, even before Mary Jane arrived, as some of the other officers who were away from their wives did. Vann's superiors undoubtedly heard something about his extramarital activities through the grapevine. They could see that he was being careful, and discretion was equivalent to personal morality in their set of values. Vann also seemed to be an upright man in his other habits. He never drank to excess; in fact, he hardly drank at all. Nor did he run up debts. For her own reasons, Mary Jane did not betray him with tales or scenes outside the family.

Life in Germany was much happier than she could have anticipated after her ordeal in New Jersey. John's good mood at being in an overseas unit tended to make him give her a semblance of the marriage she wanted. He showed an interest in the children and on Sundays frequently took the family on bicycle trips along the dirt roads through the evergreen forests. Mary Jane would put the newest baby, Peter, who was born at Heidelberg in November 1955, in the basket of her bicycle. John carried little Tommy in the basket of his bicycle, and five-year-old Jesse rode in a seat on the back. Patricia, who became nine in the fall of 1955, and John Allen, who became eight that Christmas, followed on their small bikes. Mary Jane packed a lunch, and she and John strapped badminton rackets and poles and a net to their bicycles to set up a game at a picnic clearing. Every six months or so John went on leave and loaded the family into the car for a vacation. They drove to the Bavarian Alps on one occasion, toured Holland on another, and visited West Berlin, which bustled with a freedom that defied the Soviets, who kept it isolated.

Patricia remembered that Christmas was always the best time of the year, because her father made such a fuss about it. One year he even painted a panorama of Santa Claus and his reindeer across the picture window in the living room of their apartment in Patrick Henry Village, the Army housing complex at Heidelberg. He insisted that they have a big tree and helped decorate it lavishly. A couple of days before Christmas he bought everyone lots of presents at the PX. Mary Jane later told Patricia that he would not let her go along, that he wanted to do all of the Christmas shopping by himself. John and Mary Jane would wrap the presents after the children had gone to sleep on Christmas Eve. They would then rouse Patricia and her brothers at 4:00 A.M. or so and watch the children rush to the tree and whoop as they tore open their gifts.

One afternoon in Heidelberg when Mary Jane was home and Peter and Tommy were having their naps, the door buzzer sounded. She opened the door to a German girl who spoke English. The girl said that she wanted to speak to Mary Jane about a private matter. Mary Jane took her into the living room and offered her a cup of coffee. The girl's hand shook. She spilled some of the coffee on her dress as she tried to sip it. She started to sob and told Mary Jane a long tale of how John had seduced her by saying that he loved her and was going to divorce his wife and marry her. After a few weeks he suddenly dropped her;

he was having his secretary at the office tell her that he was out whenever she telephoned, and he would not answer her letters pleading to see him. At first she had not wanted to confront Mary Jane, the girl said, but then she had decided it was the only way to learn the truth. She was so much in love with John that she had to know. He had seemed so sincere, and that was why she had gone to bed with him. Was it true that he and Mary Jane no longer loved each other and were going to be divorced?

Mary Jane felt pity for the girl. John had probably used this same technique on dozens of girls, she thought; for all she knew, perhaps hundreds, at the rate he went through women. She told the girl that she believed John still loved her in his own way and there had been no discussion of divorce. If there was, she would fight a divorce, she said. She advised the girl to be more careful with men in the future. Mary Jane gave her a handkerchief to blow her nose and wipe her eyes and said that she would have to leave now because the older children were about to return from school. The girl did not mention her age, but was clearly still in her late teens.

John did not deny sleeping with her. He did deny that he had said he loved her and had promised to marry her. He had better learn to control himself, Mary Jane said, before he made some young woman pregnant or ran across one who raised a stink when he dropped her and he hurt his career and his family. He told Mary Jane to leave him alone, that he knew how to handle himself.

His success in the G-4 Division at the Heidelberg headquarters was even grander than the acclaim he had won at the 16th Infantry. If Vann's degree of energy and verve is rare in the world of the fighting soldier, it is that much rarer in the world of the quartermaster. "Major Vann is a virtual dynamo in getting work done," one of his superiors remarked on an efficiency report. "It would take the production of three or four average officers to equal his daily work production anywhere—in an office, on a staff study, or in the field."

Vann's job in the Logistical Management Section was to analyze the Army supply system in Europe and recommend improvements. He approached it, as he did all professional tasks, by seeking the basics. He got authorization to travel. He went to the depots and found out what they had in stock and how they were issuing their supplies. He went to the combat units and found out what they needed and whether they were receiving it. Major Vann soon knew more than anyone else in the G-4 Division of U.S. Army Europe about how the supply system was actually functioning. He wrote up his findings in reports that were simple and incisive in their reasoning, full of facts that were surprising because no one else had thought to look for them, and illustrated with statistical tables that complemented his logic instead of cluttering it.

He presented a plan to reorganize the entire system and eliminate many of the bottlenecks and other shortcomings. His plan was accepted by the two-star general in charge of the G-4 Division and by the four-star commander of U.S. Army Europe. Vann was appointed the action officer to implement his plan. The reorganization uncovered further problems. Vann again won acceptance of his views on how to solve them and was once more put in charge of carrying out the solution. He was promoted to chief of the Logistical Management Section and made the briefing officer for the G-4 Division. Whenever a civilian VIP or a touring general or admiral appeared in Heidelberg, Major Vann got out on the high wire in the briefing room to dazzle the eminent visitor with what a remarkable job the G-4 Division of U.S. Army Europe was doing. Wilbur Brucker, President Eisenhower's secretary of the Army, came to the headquarters in July 1956 on an inspection trip. Major Vann briefed him on supply operations in Europe. The G-4 Division did work hard in those years of tension, and Vann was, in any case, convinced its performance was exemplary because his own was so good. Brucker and the other visitors wrote letters of appreciation afterward that went into Vann's file, and his grateful superiors saw to it that his other accomplishments were also recorded for future promotion boards. He was twice sent as a special escort officer with newly arrived generals on orientation tours of the units the generals were to command. The trips were a compliment to a young major. He advised the generals on what questions to ask and also on the usefulness of the answers.

"Vann is an . . . officer with a bright future ahead of him," Bruce Palmer had predicted. Major Vann's future was bright indeed. He and Mary Jane and the children sailed home from Germany in the summer of 1957 for a long leave before he started classes in the fall at the Command and General Staff College at Fort Leavenworth. He had been selected to attend it that spring as he was nearing completion of his two years at Heidelberg. His superiors at Heidelberg gave him the highest possible efficiency rating: "an outstanding officer of rare value to the service," equally adept at staff or command. "He represents a great potential to the Army as a future leader of the Army."

John Vann fulfilled their expectations at Fort Leavenworth. His standing in the class there reflected the extent to which he had grown in his profession by diligence down through the years. He had graduated from the Basic Course at the Infantry School in 1947 in the bottom half of his class. He had completed the Advanced Course there in 1952 in the upper 20 percent. He graduated from the nine-month course at the Command and General Staff College in June 1958 in the top 2 percent, eleventh out of 532 officers in his class.

The college had to mail him his diploma. He and the family left a week before the graduation ceremony in a Volkswagen bus he had bought in Germany and drove east to Syracuse, New York, so that he could start the summer session at the university there. While at Heidelberg he had agreed to a career specialty in logistics, because specialization was the most certain route to early promotion for an officer who was not a West Pointer. The Army had in turn approved his request for civilian postgraduate study at Syracuse University to obtain his master's degree in business administration. By early May 1959, he was within three months of his MBA. He had also crammed in enough additional courses in public administration so that he would leave Syracuse with two courses and a thesis left to do for a doctorate in that field. He planned to take the two courses and write the thesis in Washington during a three- to four-year logistics staff assignment he was scheduled to begin at the Pentagon in the summer of 1959. He wanted the civilian degrees for their own sake, but also because they would help him win accelerated promotion to lieutenant colonel and beyond. He did not intend to stay in logistics. It bored him on a steady basis. He intended to work his way to command of an infantry battalion as quickly as possible after he became a lieutenant colonel, turn in another of his spectacular performances, and by then be far enough ahead of his contemporaries to win further accelerated promotions within the infantry itself. His future was assured. He could see his stars. Then his other life caught up with him.

An agent from the criminal investigation division of the Military Police appeared in Syracuse on the morning of May 7, 1959, and called Vann out of class. The agent informed him of his Constitutional right not to incriminate himself, because he was going to be questioned about an accusation that could become a formal charge of statutory rape. He had been accused by another officer of having an affair with a fifteen-year-old girl while a student at Fort Leavenworth. Statutory rape is a felony under military law. If convicted, Vann could be sentenced to fifteen years in prison. Because of his record, a court-martial would most likely show mercy and dismiss him from the Army. Dismissal for an officer is the equivalent of dishonorable discharge for an enlisted man. He would be ruined in civilian life as well if that happened. Former soldiers with dishonorable discharges had a hard time finding decent low-level jobs in the pre-Vietnam atmosphere of the 1950s and early '60s. What business firm would hire a dishonored officer as an executive?

Vann was cagey. He said the agent's questions did not surprise him. The girl had told a chaplain at Fort Leavenworth that he had had an affair with her, he said. He had received a letter from the chaplain about it shortly after reaching Syracuse and had written back to say that it wasn't true. It was all a fantasy, he said. The girl was emotionally disturbed. At the agent's request he signed and swore to a statement saying that he had not slept with her.

Mary Jane was sewing when he came home in the afternoon. He told her the truth. When he told her who the girl was she screamed and threw a box of buttons at him. The girl had done some baby-sitting for Mary Jane. She had been an overweight fifteen-year-old, not pretty, and emotionally withdrawn and unhappy with her family life. Men as sexually insecure as Vann are sometimes drawn to girls like this. Mary Jane was already full of worry and didn't know how she was going to stand any more. Peter had been in the hospital at Rome Air Force Base, thirty-five miles from Syracuse, for the last four months. Vann had driven him there at Mary Jane's request for an examination in early January, about a month and a half after Peter's third birthday, because his skin had started to turn yellow. The doctors said he had hepatitis. He got worse in the hospital. He lost weight, and the skin all over his body became deeply jaundiced. The doctors didn't seem to know how to make him well. She and Vann had been having terrible arguments over the boy's illness. He accused her of bringing on the hepatitis by neglecting Peter. She had become suspicious of the Air Force doctors and wanted to transfer Peter to a civilian hospital. The Rome unit was the only military hospital in the area. Government regulations required officers and enlisted men to pay for civilian medical treatment for themselves and their families if they chose it when military facilities were available. Vann was unwilling to pay the possibly large sums involved. He said that the civilian doctors would not be any better.

Three days after the appearance of the CID agent, the Air Force doctors decided to release Peter from the hospital. They claimed that his condition had stabilized. The weight loss had recently stopped and the jaundice had diminished. Peter didn't look that much better to Mary Jane, but she was glad to get him away from the Air Force doctors. He wasn't home long before the jaundice returned in all of its gruesome hue and his stomach swelled up. Now Vann also became alarmed for

Peter and did not object when Mary Jane said she was taking the boy to Strong Memorial Hospital in Rochester, where she had been treated as a child. The doctors at Rochester confirmed the hepatitis diagnosis of the Air Force physicians and put Peter on the same cortisone medication, with the same lack of success.

By mid-June, Mary Jane was convinced that she was going to lose her son. With his swollen stomach and his spindly arms and legs sticking out from his body, Peter reminded her of child victims she had seen in photographs of Nazi concentration camps. Someone on the hospital staff at Rochester was also apparently convinced that Peter was going to die soon and tipped off an enterprising representative of a funeral home. He approached Vann and Mary Jane while they were visiting one evening and asked if he could ease their burden. She went berserk and raved at the man. As angry as he was himself, Vann had to restrain her. They drove Peter to the hospital at Syracuse University Medical School. The doctors there said that Peter might have a blood disorder, but they really didn't know what was wrong. Their advice was to take him to the Children's Hospital in Boston, the best pediatric medical center in the world. Vann carried Peter out of the hospital wrapped in a blanket and laid him on the backseat of the car. He dropped Mary Jane off at the house to stay with the other children and drove straight through the night to Boston.

He returned to Syracuse a day later and told her he had had a horrible experience getting Peter admitted to the Children's Hospital. When Vann had walked in carrying Peter early in the morning the clerk at the admissions desk had said the hospital's services were in such demand that it could not take patients right off the street. Vann needed an appointment to have one of the staff doctors examine his son. There were no beds available at the moment. The best the clerk could do was to put Peter on a waiting list. Vann said he barged past the admissions desk and roamed the corridors with Peter in his arms until he found a doctor whom he talked into examining the boy. He told the doctor that he didn't care about the fees, that he would pay whatever the hospital wanted—just please save his son. The doctor said that Peter's chances did not appear good, but that he would do his best, and he arranged Peter's admission to the hospital. A bed opened up because another child who had been one of the doctor's patients had just died. Peter might need surgery to try to find out what was wrong with him, Vann said. Mary Jane immediately closed down the house they were renting in Syracuse—sending the other children to her mother in Rochester and putting her furniture in storage—and moved into a rooming house in

Boston to be with Peter. Vann stayed in Syracuse to finish his courses.

After a week of tests, the doctors at the Children's Hospital decided that exploratory surgery was necessary. Peter didn't have hepatitis. The cortisone the Air Force doctors and the civilian physicians at Strong Memorial had been giving him for this presumed liver infection had been aggravating the problem he did have. He also was not as close to death as he looked, but the condition from which he was suffering and continued mistreatment of it would eventually have killed him. The exploratory surgery revealed that a temporary disorder of the pancreas gland had caused an obstruction in the duct leading from the pancreas to the small intestine. (The pancreas secretes an alkaline solution that is required for the digestive process.) The disordered pancreas and the obstructed duct had in turn caused all sorts of other abnormalities, including a malfunctioning liver. Peter's body was in such disarray that he had the highest cholesterol count in the history of the Children's Hospital. The surgeon who did the exploratory work and diagnosed the problem also removed the obstruction in the same operation and sent Peter back to his bed, a child ready to mend. The hospital released him in the first part of July, two weeks after the surgery, although Peter was to be many months recovering fully. Vann came down and picked up Mary Jane and his son and drove them to her parents.

The story of how Vann saved Peter's life by begging a doctor at the Children's Hospital to accept him became part of the family lore. Peter thought of it as he stood beside the grave at Arlington and the chaplain handed him the folded flag from the coffin. Vann did save his son's life by acting immediately on the advice of the Syracuse University doctors. Mary Jane had also saved the boy by goading Vann into letting her take Peter to civilian hospitals. The truth was that Vann hadn't had any difficulty getting Peter admitted in Boston. The Children's Hospital never turns away a child in need of care. The pediatrician on duty in the hospital's emergency room when Vann arrived had examined Peter and ordered him admitted, and a staff pediatrician and a surgeon had been assigned to his case. Vann had invented the drama because he wanted Mary Jane to think well of him at a time when she had reason to think otherwise.

The CID had been pressing ahead with its investigation. Agents checked details of the girl's story that could be independently verified, such as a claim that she had visited a doctor in Leavenworth, Kansas, the garrison town next to the fort, at one point in the affair when she had feared she was pregnant. The details checked out. The girl agreed to be questioned about her story with a lie detector. The machine said that she was telling the truth. The CID agents offered Vann an opportunity to take a lie-detector test to confirm his denials. He refused. When he received his M.B.A. from Syracuse University at the end of July, he was kept in a holding pattern instead of being sent to the Pentagon as scheduled. Two weeks later the CID submitted a lengthy report recommending that he be court-martialed for statutory rape and adultery. The adultery charge was a misdemeanor tossed in to buttress the felony count. It was taken from the catchall article of military law that forbids "conduct unbecoming an officer and a gentleman." Mary Jane, who had not been questioned by the agents, was listed as the "victim" under the adultery charge.

First Army Headquarters, then at Fort Jay, New York, appointed an officer to conduct a second investigation known as an Article 32 proceeding, the equivalent of the grand jury process in civilian law. If the investigating officer found that there was sufficient evidence to convict, Vann would be formally charged and court-martialed. Until his fate could be decided, he was assigned as deputy comptroller at Camp Drum (later Fort Drum), then a training base for reservists and National Guardsmen in the snow belt of northern New York State off Lake Ontario. He rented the first floor of a large farmhouse in a hamlet near the post for Mary Jane and the children.

Vann knew that Mary Jane would lie for him. She had rallied to him after her initial anger had passed and out of gratitude for what he had done for Peter. She had also seen the threat from the beginning as directed as much at her and the children as at him. What kind of a future would she and the children have with John in prison or ruined? With her potential role as a corroborating witness in mind, he had already created a framework in which she could lie effectively for him. Prior to another interrogation by a CID agent at Fort Jay in mid-July he composed a story of befriending an emotionally disturbed girl who expressed her unhappiness at her home life by having affairs with older men. The girl happened to tell him of her troubles because he was willing to listen. He did not inform her parents because she confided in him and asked him not to betray her. He implied that her parents were too insensitive to understand in any case. In her depression the girl finally turned on him too and falsely claimed to the chaplain that he was having an affair with her. The agent at Fort Jay asked him to write down his story. He did so in a seventeen-page account in longhand. The story was filled with incidents that Mary Jane could witness. In one incident Mary Jane overheard the girl talking to one of her adult lovers on the Vanns' phone. Vann instructed his wife not to let the girl use the phone anymore. He disposed of incidents from the girl's story like the visit to the doctor in Leavenworth (the CID had questioned him about this and other details of her account) by writing that the girl's mother had asked Mary Jane for the name of a gynecologist for her daughter.

The lie detector seemed a more formidable obstacle to him. Mary Jane's testimony would be viewed with suspicion. In order to cast serious doubt on the girl's veracity he would eventually have to accept the CID's challenge and submit to a lie-detector test. Then he would have to fool the machine. After the Article 32 investigation began in August the regulations entitled him to divert to his defense what time he wished from his duty as deputy comptroller at Camp Drum. He gathered all of the technical literature he could and turned himself into an amateur specialist on the polygraph, the most common form of lie detector and the type that is used by the investigative branches of the military services, the CIA, and other government agencies. The polygraph measures blood pressure, pulse, breathing, and perspiration of the hands. It detects lying if a pattern of change in these vital signs occurs under the emotional tension of trying to deceive.

Vann finagled tranquilizers and drugs to lower blood pressure. He bought a physician's instrument for measuring blood pressure. He timed the rate of his pulse beats with his watch. He drew up lists of questions about his affair with the girl. He arranged the questions in the sequence he believed a polygraph operator would follow. He put himself through mock interrogations, changing the questions and the sequence from one interrogation to another so that he would not be surprised. He interrogated himself with and without the various medications. He took notes on his bodily reactions. He finally decided that he seemed best able to slow down his reactions, and not run the risk of appearing to have drugged himself, simply by staying awake for forty-eight hours and answering the questions in a confident manner.

On the day she appeared before the officer conducting the Article 32 investigation, Mary Jane wore a tweed skirt with a blouse and jacket. The fall had come by then and she knew the outfit made her look her most attractive. The investigating officer was probably also a family man, she thought. He would see that she was a respectable woman and might be tempted to believe her. Although she did not reveal it, showing only a superficial nervousness, she was filled with dread as she put her hand on the Bible and swore to tell the truth. Unlike Vann, she was religious. The Bible gave her emotional comfort during the most trying periods in the marriage. During the worst of Peter's illness she had read the

Bible several times every day and at night when she prayed for him to live. She hoped that this blasphemy would be understood and forgiven. She answered the questions as John had rehearsed her to do, corroborating the events in his story. She also told the investigating officer on her own that she and John loved each other and had a happy marriage.

Vann then volunteered to take the lie-detector test. He fooled the machine. Like a civilian jury, a group of officers sitting on a court-martial must find that the accused is guilty beyond a reasonable doubt. Vann's success at beating the lie detector brought the case down to his word against the girl's. No court-martial would convict on that basis. The investigating officer recommended dropping the charges.

First Army Headquarters took until mid-December to concur in the finding of the investigating officer. The snow and the cold that blew off Lake Ontario were hard on Mary Jane. She developed a cough and went to the dispensary at Camp Drum after she started spitting up blood too. The tests showed that she had tuberculosis.

The afternoon they received the news that the charges had been dropped was a warm day for a change. Mary Jane went for a walk with John down the road from the farmhouse, the packed snow soft under their feet from the sun. He talked on and on about how relieved he was. He was ready to do backflips in the snow he was so happy over his victory.

"I guess you've learned your lesson now," she said.

"I sure as hell have," he said. "Next time I'll make goddam sure they're old enough."

John Vann was assigned to the Army's antiaircraft missile center at Fort Bliss in El Paso, Texas, as chief of the program and budget section in the comptroller's office. He resumed his life-style in El Paso, and the marriage took another of its turns for the worse. At the office Vann always appeared enthusiastic, and he received superlative efficiency reports. Privately he was desperate with boredom over his work as a super-accountant. He had never complained to Mary Jane before about his Army job. He complained now. He felt doubly trapped, first by the Army bureaucracy he had thought he was outwitting in agreeing to specialize in logistics so that he could obtain graduate degrees and accelerated promotions and second by this woman and her children. Although he was never to know it, Mary Jane did snare him into the two years and two months he was to spend in El Paso. A friend in Army personnel at the Pentagon had telephoned while they were still awaiting the outcome of the Article 32 investigation and asked if there was anything he could do. Mary Jane described how the Lake Ontario weather was destroying her health. If the charges against John were dropped, would the friend please not give him any choice in his next assignment and send him directly to a warm and dry climate. The friend, who understood the circumstances of the Vanns' marriage, said that her wish would be granted.

Vann won early promotion to lieutenant colonel in May 1961, and he knew that he could also look forward to receiving the eagles of a full colonel ahead of his contemporaries. No matter how superlatively he performed in the future, he would always be held back from the leap to general if any mention of the statutory rape charge existed in his records. There are more candidates for stars than stars to give, and the Army does not want its generals to have personal habits that could cause scandal. A promotion board for general officers would feel obliged to hold to the opposite standard of court-martial. The possibility of guilt would suffice to condemn him to rejection.

Nevertheless, he tried to salvage his career. One of his former superiors in Germany sent him to a mutual acquaintance who had recently retired from the Army to join a missile division of Martin Marietta. The acquaintance was Col. Francis Bradley, who was subsequently to become one of the leading executives of the weapons and aerospace firm. He was a close friend of Vann's former superior and had also met Vann briefly in Germany. Frank Bradley's last job in the Army had been as an assistant in the chief of staff's office. He still had good connections there. When Vann came to see him and told his story, Bradley was struck by his lack of guilt at having slept with the girl. His regrets were confined to getting caught and spoiling his career. He boasted to Bradley of how he had fooled the lie detector. Vann said that unless he could make the evidence of the scandal disappear, he was going to leave the Army in 1963 when he reached twenty years of service and could retire on half pay. He asked Bradley to arrange for him to see his entire personnel file in a room at the Pentagon where he could be alone. He did not say that he intended to steal the records of the CID investigation and the Article 32 proceeding, but his implication was as open as the rest of his conversation. Bradley put Vann off with a vague reply.

Vann and Bradley met again in El Paso in early 1962 as Bradley was passing through there on business. Vann was preparing to go to Vietnam. He reiterated his intention to retire. Bradley was impressed with what he had previously heard of Vann's talent and he trusted the praise of

Vann's former superior in Germany. He was also a forgiving man about the personal habits of others. Bradley offered Vann a job with Martin Marietta, and Vann said that he was interested.

Less than two months later, John Vann walked through the swinging doors of Dan Porter's office in Saigon to start his first year in Vietnam, to struggle with Huynh Van Cao and the other straw men of Diem's army, to meet his Viet Cong enemy at Bac, to try to prevent the defeat of the Saigon side and the calamity of a big American war by fighting the battle of truth with Paul Harkins and Victor Krulak and Maxwell Taylor, and to cope with the arrogance and professional corruption of the American military system of the 1960s. A man like John Vann might well have sacrificed a career to fight that larger battle. A might-well-have is still an uncertainty. The only certainty is that Vann fought that battle in the luxury of believing his career was already lost and he was decorated for conspicuous moral gallantry while deceiving Halberstam and me and all his other admirers.

In the early fall of 1962, before Cao had begun to systematically fake operations against the guerrillas and when Vann was still Harkins's star advisor, he wrote Frank Bradley to confirm that he planned to retire in the coming year. In May 1963, shortly after his return to the United States, Vann flew to Denver for an interview at Martin Marietta's main aerospace complex. He accepted a position as the executive in charge of sales presentations. At the end of May, just as Vann was beginning his briefing campaign at the Pentagon to warn of the disaster that Harkins was brewing in Vietnam, he submitted a formal request to be retired on July 31, 1963. When Taylor canceled his scheduled briefing for the Joint Chiefs on July 8, he had three weeks left on active duty.

In Denver, Vann had barely started his intended climb to the top in the world of industry when he realized what a terrible mistake he had made in leaving the Army. Permanent consignment to second place in the Army was superior to anything he could attain in business. There were no stars to be won in the business world. What happened in business really didn't matter.

Bob York, who had recently been promoted to major general, wrote from Vietnam just before Christmas 1963 to say that he was coming home to take charge of the 82nd Airborne Division at Fort Bragg, North Carolina. Not knowing the true reason, York had been sickened at the loss to the Army when he had heard of Vann's retirement. He offered Vann command of a battalion in the 82nd if he would return to the service. Vann was overjoyed.

The Army wouldn't let him return. The general in charge of officer personnel at the Pentagon told York that he would not request Vann's recall to active duty because he knew that Taylor or McNamara would disapprove. Vann appealed to Bruce Palmer, by then a major general senior to York. He could not help either.

Outwardly, John Vann was an active and successful man. His progress at Martin Marietta was steady, and he went into politics, leading the Colorado movement to draft Henry Cabot Lodge as the Republican presidential candidate in 1964 and then organizing Republican support for Lyndon Johnson after Barry Goldwater became the candidate and split the party. When he was not occupied with business or politics, Vann was traveling to lecture or do newspaper and television interviews on the war in Vietnam. He gave scores of lectures and interviews on Vietnam all over the country between his retirement in mid-1963 and the end of 1964.

Inwardly, Vann was a man being crushed by the boredom of his job and by the concerns of Mary Jane and the children. She was an embittered woman by now, and she took out her bitterness in constant squabbles with him. He avoided the house he had bought for the family in Littleton, a Denver suburb near the Martin Marietta plant, as much as he could, leaving early in the morning and not returning until late at night. Mary Jane remarked to him one day that the marriage certainly must be finished when he wouldn't eat her cooking anymore. "Yeah," he said. "You're right."

In the summer of 1964, after the failure of another attempt by York to persuade the Army to let him return, Vann approached officials at the Far East Bureau of the Agency for International Development in Washington. The White House had assigned AID principal responsibility for the civilian pacification program in Vietnam, and the agency was having trouble recruiting men for the work. Most of its career economic development officers were unsuited to the tasks involved. Many of them also did not want to live apart from their families and get shot at in the Vietnamese countryside. AID was therefore starting to turn toward retired military officers as the most logical source of manpower. The officials at the Far East Bureau were delighted at the prospect of a man with Vann's experience and talent. At the moment, like almost all Washington agencies every fourth year, AID was in a holding pattern until after the presidential election. Vann was told to come back in November if he was still interested.

He did, as soon as he had finished making his small contribution to the landslide defeat of Goldwater, and was offered the post of regional director of pacification for the Mekong Delta. He accepted and flew home to tell Mary Jane: "I will never live with you again." Maxwell Taylor, who had resigned the chairmanship of the Joint Chiefs of Staff in mid-1964 to replace Lodge as the ambassador in Saigon, vetoed the appointment. A cable from the embassy informed AID that Vann was "too controversial." Vann offered to go as a simple province pacification representative. The embassy replied that Vann was not wanted in any capacity. He said that he would go to Thailand, where a minor insurgency was then underway, if he couldn't go to Vietnam. The officials at the Far East Bureau said they would think about his offer.

Mary Jane realized that he had to return to Vietnam for his own survival. She had never seen him as despondent as he became during the winter of 1964–65. He "took to the bed," as the old Southern expression has it. He lay on the couch in the living room for hours at night and on weekends, staring at nothing. He no longer walked the way her John had always done, swinging a leg forward as he strode into life. He walked more slowly that winter and let his head droop. He was, she could see, losing his self-respect and his faith in himself.

As usual, he did not give up entirely. He appealed to Lodge and York to intervene for him. He persuaded the officials at the Far East Bureau to ask Taylor to reconsider. He even wrote Taylor a friendly letter describing his efforts to maintain public support for the war with his lectures and interviews on Vietnam.

He was rescued by a fellow Virginian who admired him—the Sam Wilson who had heard Churchill's voice over the farmhouse radio in 1940 defying the Nazis and walked seven miles through the rain to join the National Guard. Twenty-five years later Wilson was an Army colonel in Vietnam, detailed to AID as chief of its pacification program. He had been Lansdale's assistant at the Pentagon during Vann's briefing campaign there in 1963. Wilson had been amazed then by the brilliance of Vann's critique, and the two men had immediately liked each other. He did not learn Vann was attempting to return to Vietnam until he saw a copy of the message from the Far East Bureau asking Taylor to reconsider. Wilson went to Taylor and said they could not afford to reject a man of Vann's qualities. Taylor relented. Vann could come as an ordinary province pacification officer.

Vann had a cruel encounter with his youth just before he left. While in Washington in February and March for three weeks of processing and orientation lectures at AID headquarters, he stayed with Garland Hopkins at Hopkins's house in the Virginia suburb of McLean. Hopkins had been destroyed by his pedophilia. The CIA had fired him as head of the American Friends of the Middle East, the pro-Arab lobby that he had built and that the CIA secretly funded. He had then been dismissed as pastor of a prominent church in Arlington and also removed from the Virginia Conference of Methodist ministers, in which his father and grandfather had held honored places. His wife had divorced him because he had taken to beating her and their youngest son under the stress of his disgrace. He still could not control his obsession and molested some boys in his neighborhood. The parents complained to the police, and this time he was going to be prosecuted. He could not bear the shame. He wrote out his will and an obituary listing his accomplishments. He also wrote a note to Vann, and then he took a rat poison containing strychnine, inflicting a painful death on himself—strychnine kills with convulsions. Vann found Hopkins's body when he returned to the house on a Sunday night. The note asked Vann to distribute the obituary to the newspapers, listed family members and friends for Vann to notify, and also asked him to see to it that Hopkins's body was cremated. Vann called the police and then did as his boyhood mentor asked. "Let these few chores be a last token of our long and splendid friendship," the note said. The horror of it made Vann more eager than ever to be gone.

Martin Marietta put him on a leave of absence, because his AID appointment was a temporary one. Washington did not expect the war to last long. His conscience was clear about Mary Jane and the children. He had them settled in the house in Littleton, and his contract with AID entitled him to fly home once a year at government expense to visit them for thirty days.

He took the Pan American jet west out of San Francisco along the route that the nation had followed into Asia in the previous century—to Honolulu, to Guam, then to Manila, and then on to Saigon, this new and contested place. Shortly after 11:00 A.M. on Saturday, March 20, 1965, his plane circled high over the city and then banked down sharply to the runway at Tan Son Nhut to avoid the guerrilla snipers who were now all around Saigon. He walked out of the air-conditioned cabin and down the ramp into the heat and humidity, which were at their worst just before the monsoon season. The discomfort felt good to him. He had been gone almost two years—twenty-three months and two weeks. He would never be away from the war that long again. He was back in Vietnam, where he belonged.

BOOK SIX

A
SECOND
TIME
AROUND

★ T HE VIETNAM to which John Vann returned in late March 1965 was a nation
on the threshold of the most violent war in its history. At the beginning
of the month, Lyndon Johnson had started Operation Rolling Thunder,
the bombing campaign against North Vietnam. Two U.S. Marine battalions, the first of many to follow, had landed at Danang to secure the
airfield there as one of the staging bases for the bombing raids. At
MACV headquarters in Saigon, William DePuy, then a brigadier general
and Gen. William Westmoreland's chief of operations, had taken the
first step in the planning that was to bring hundreds of thousands of
U.S. troops into South Vietnam with artillery and armor and fleets of
fighter-bombers for a new American war to destroy the Vietnamese
Communists and their followers. "We are going to stomp them to
death," DePuy predicted.

The phone in the room of the Saigon hotel where Vann was temporarily staying rang early on the first day after his return, Sunday,
March 21, 1965. It was Cao. In his complicated way, Vann kept friendships with the Vietnamese he got to know, despite the worst of quarrels.
Cao was no exception. He was grateful for an offer of financial help
Vann had made from Denver in the months immediately after Diem's
demise when it appeared that Cao might be thrown out of the ARVN
and lose the means to support his wife and many children. Vann had
known that Cao had little in the way of personal savings, because one
of Cao's few professional virtues was relative honesty in the handling
of funds. Vann had asked Lodge's assistant and Bob York to do what
they could for Cao and to let Cao know that he could count on Vann
for money until he found another livelihood. As it turned out, Cao had
not needed the help. He had managed to ingratiate himself with a
number of his fellow Saigon generals amid the political turmoil that had

set in after Lodge had despaired of the lackadaisical junta that had overthrown Diem and had permitted them to be overthrown in turn by Lt. Gen. Nguyen Khanh, the ambitious graduate of the French Army paratroop school. Khanh too had finally been driven from power (his plane had literally run out of gas over Nhatrang while he was trying to stay aloft to avoid resigning) and forced into exile only a month before Vann's return. The group currently on top was the so-called Young Turk faction of generals dominated by Air Vice-Marshal Nguyen Cao Ky, the commander of the VNAF.

Huynh Van Cao's principal asset was that he did not threaten any of the other generals. The second-ranking member of the Young Turk faction, Brig. Gen. Nguyen Van Thieu, also happened to be another Central Vietnamese Catholic. Cao had been serving as director of psychological warfare for the Joint General Staff. He told Vann excitedly that just the day before the council of generals had chosen him to be the new chief of staff of the JGS, the second-ranking position after the chief. He wanted to know if Vann could come out to his house in the JGS compound near the airport for dinner that evening. Vann said he would be happy to come.

Cao spent much of the dinner filling Vann in on the couping and countercouping by the generals and their civilian political allies of the moment and on the street riots by the Buddhist and Catholic factions that had occupied the capital for the last two years while the Viet Cong had grown ever more menacing in the countryside. Despite his elevation the day before by the other Saigon generals, Cao remained Cao. He was fearful that as chief of staff he might be drawn into an intrigue against his will. Absence had not diminished Vann's capacity to observe his former counterpart. "It is evident that Cao never has and never will participate in a coup," Vann wrote that night in the diary he kept intermittently for the first six months after his return. "He is deathly afraid and does his best to straddle the fence on all issues." (Cao was relieved when the military council changed its mind shortly afterward and he was allowed to stay chief of psychological warfare.)

Vann got a contrasting reception on Monday morning at the Saigon office of the U.S. Operations Mission (USOM), as AID was then called in Vietnam. While AID's Washington headquarters was eagerly recruiting retired military men to staff its pacification program, its civilian bureaucrats in Vietnam were fearful that their agency was going to be taken over by the military. Retired officers like Vann were regarded as infiltrators. The only man to welcome him was the infiltrator on loan from the Army to run the program, Col. Sam Wilson, who had persuaded Taylor to let Vann return. AID Washington had managed to bring Vann into government as a Grade 3 in the Foreign Service Reserve, a rank between lieutenant colonel and colonel in the Army, sufficiently senior for him to be a director of USOM operations in one of the South's four corps regions. Wilson informed Vann that in addition to Taylor's instruction that Vann serve as an ordinary province representative, the chief of AID in Vietnam, James Killen, had reserved all of the regional directorships for civilian career men like himself. Vann would have to display his worth in the field and then move upward, possibly to become deputy director of a region in summer. The previous fall, Westmoreland had designated the six provinces surrounding Saigon as the priority area for pacification. With Vann's talents in mind, Wilson was thinking of sending him to a relatively new province, Hau Nghia, the most insecure of the six.

Hau Nghia, west of Saigon between the capital and the Cambodian border, was approximately 500 square miles of wild reeds, rice paddies, and fields of sugar cane. Nearly a quarter of a million Vietnamese peasants lived there. Diem had established the province as one of his last official acts by putting together the four most troublesome districts of three adjoining provinces. His hope had been to eradicate trouble by consolidating it. The result for his successors had been a whole province that mocked the name Diem had given it—Hau Nghia, a Vietnamese literary term, means Deepening Righteousness. The province was considered strategic because the so-called Parrot's Beak section of Cambodia thrust into South Vietnam at this point and put central Saigon less than thirty-five air miles east of the border. Hau Nghia was also a natural route of north-south movement for the Viet Cong. It lay between the rice lands and the Plain of Reeds in the Mekong Delta and the rubber-plantation country and the beginning of the rain forest of the Annamite foothills above Saigon.

A week after his initial meeting with Wilson, when his assignment had been confirmed and he had finished his processing, Vann went to the embassy for a political briefing on the province. The political section could not find its sparse file on Hau Nghia, and he left. Ten minutes later, two Viet Cong terrorists arrived under the CIA office on the second floor to retaliate for the bombing of the North. The terrorists had 350 pounds of plastic explosive packed into an old gray Peugeot sedan. Embassy officials had been warned repeatedly over the last couple of years to block the streets around the building to traffic and to take other simple precautions, such as substituting shatterproof Plexiglas for the ordinary glass of the windows. Neither Lodge nor Taylor had done anything effective, afraid that showing fear might cause the United States to lose face. The plastic explosive was the best American kind, called C-4, captured or bought from the Saigon side, as was the detonator, a quick-fuse type known as a "time pencil." The old car became a massive grenade, sending shards of metal in every direction along with bits of concrete from a four-foot hole blown out of the pavement. The windows of the six-story building burst inward in myriads of fragments along with the plaster and the wood and metal fixtures on the walls facing the street.

Vann rushed back at the sound of the explosion to help evacuate the injured. Most of the twenty dead were innocent Vietnamese—passersby and patrons and workers in an open-air restaurant and commercial offices across the street. Another 126 Vietnamese were wounded. (The Vietnamese Communists were now ignoring the carnage such urban terrorism caused among their own people, rationalizing it with warnings they regularly gave the population in leaflets and radio broadcasts to stay away from American buildings.) The two terrorists were killed as well as several of the Saigon policemen guarding the building. One of the two Americans killed was a Navy petty officer; the other was a young woman who was a secretary to the CIA station chief. The station chief himself was gravely hurt and nearly lost both eyes. Two of his CIA officers were permanently blinded. A number of the other fifty-one men and women hurt inside the embassy were also horribly wounded, their faces torn. Vann noticed that one hunk of concrete or metal was hurled up all six stories and ripped a large hole through the American flag on the roof.

John Vann left for Hau Nghia the day after the attack on the embassy. He drove right through the province capital of Bau Trai before he realized that he had missed it and turned around. The place was, he wrote in his diary, "the most unlikely looking province capital in all Vietnam." The last time he had seen Bau Trai had been during an operation in early 1963. (Two of Hau Nghia's four districts had been part of Long An Province in the old 7th Division zone.) It had been a Viet Cong-controlled hamlet of about 1,000 people then. Diem had selected it as the province capital because it happened to be at the junction of the dirt roads connecting three of the district centers. The population had nearly doubled with the arrival of soldiers for a garrison and wives and children and camp followers. Bau Trai had also gained a handful of buildings that were used as offices and housing for the province officials and their American advisors. Diem had tried to abolish the plain country name (Bau Trai means Round Farm) by bestowing one of his literary titles, Khiem Cuong, which means Modest But Vigorous. The fancy name had not taken. Everyone continued to call the place Bau Trai. Despite the near doubling in population, Bau Trai was just about 200 yards across at the widest point where it straddled both sides of the road. Vann looked again and recognized the hamlet of two years before.

Closer inspection brought more discouragement. At a small compound in the center of town where the military advisors lived, he asked directions to the USOM office. He was sent down a lane to a long tinroofed warehouse and walked inside to "a completely disheartening sight." The warehouse was bursting with "disorderly stacked piles of bulgur wheat, corn, shovels, paint, clothing, medical supplies, cooking oil, cement, dried milk, pitch forks, mattresses, chairs, chests, saws, angle iron lengths, nails, rice hullers, and miscellaneous items I later found came from the salvage yard." The man he was replacing, William Pye, a fifty-two-year-old Army Reserve lieutenant colonel who had volunteered for AID and who was a brave and decent man, but extremely tense and disorganized, was standing in the midst of this magpie's delight, pad and pen in hand, "apparently inventorying some item." The USOM office consisted of a couple of desks in a corner of the warehouse. Vann could see that the papers on the desktops were in as much disarray and covered with as much dust as everything else.

He asked where the living quarters were and walked a short distance to a new bungalow of the inevitable masonry and stucco construction. On the outside, except for some useless barbed wire strung around it, the house was trimly built, with wooden shutters. On the inside, it was the same grubby warren as the warehouse. There was no electricity for lights and fans, just gasoline lanterns that made the house hotter at night. Nor could Vann look forward to relaxing at a meal. He had told himself that to be effective he was going to have to live with the Vietnamese. He had therefore decided not to take his meals with the U.S. military advisors at their mess. But when eating at the one restaurant in Bau Trai, Vann wrote to a friend in Denver, it was "very difficult to stick a bite of food in the mouth without the flies riding in with it."

Flies were not the primary threat to the health of an American or Saigon official in Hau Nghia. The USOM motor-pool officer in Saigon had grumbled about letting Vann borrow a station wagon to drive to Bau Trai. The man had been worried about getting his vehicle back. Vann was the first Vietnamese or American official to drive unescorted from Saigon in many months. Everyone else traveled to and from Saigon and on all of the roads still open within the province in armed convoys.

As the convoys were also frequently mined or ambushed, they traveled above the roads in helicopters whenever possible. The majority of the province was, in any case, no longer in contact with the Saigon side. The four districts had been reduced to three in mid-1964 when the fourth one, the northeast corner of the Plain of Reeds across the Vam Co Dong River, had been abandoned entirely to the guerrillas. (The district chief had been given three villages in another district to administer.) By early 1965 when Vann arrived, the direct roads between Bau Trai and two of the three remaining district centers had also been cut. It was likewise no longer possible to drive directly to Bau Trai from Saigon, even though the place was a mere twenty miles from the city. Vann had been forced to take an indirect way that circled to the northwest up Route 1, the main road from Saigon to Cambodia, and then south down a secondary road from the town of Cu Chi, the third district center in the province.

Hau Nghia was such a "Siberia assignment," as Vann put it, that the regime was currently unable to find a chief for the province. The last province chief had been jailed for complicity in the most recent abortive coup in February. The job had since been offered to two other ARVN officers, and both had refused it. With the exception of Bau Trai and the district towns, half a dozen hamlets, and the outposts that still existed at the sufferance of the guerrillas, Hau Nghia had been ceded to the Viet Cong.

Although Vann's job for USOM was to supervise school building, hog raising, refugee relief, and similar civilian pacification projects, a vacuum of leadership and a confrontation were precisely the circumstances in which he thrived. He immediately began scheming to take Hau Nghia back from the Viet Cong. He started organizing on his first night, convening a meeting with the acting province chief, a civilian Saigon official who was the deputy for administration, to work out the province budget requirements for the coming fiscal year. The next morning he was off to begin a tour of the district centers to meet the district chiefs and their American advisors and be briefed. Westmoreland had arranged in mid-1964 for the headquarters of the ARVN 25th Infantry Division and two of its regiments to be transferred to Hau Nghia from Central Vietnam. Vann also stopped at the division headquarters and at one of the regimental command posts on his first morning. He learned that despite Westmoreland's priority designation, no one had drawn up a pacification plan for Hau Nghia. They had to have one, Vann said, and he initiated the process. He got USOM's Vietnamese work crew in Bau Trai busy bringing order to the warehouse and told the acting province chief that he had to have a respectable office in the province headquarters. The headquarters building, with a large veranda, was the only structure in town of any vague distinction.

He told the assistant he found waiting for him in Bau Trai, Douglas Ramsey, a thirty-year-old Foreign Service officer who had reached the province a month earlier, that they could not afford to surrender access to the population as the guerrillas wanted by staying off the roads and riding helicopters. Ramsey was a cheerful, gangling Westerner of six feet three inches with black hair and a round-the-clock five o'clock shadow. He was a rarity among Americans in 1965—fluent in spoken and written Vietnamese. Convoys would not permit them the freedom of movement they needed either, Vann said, and he thought they would actually be in less danger driving alone. The Viet Cong interdicted all official traffic and, whenever they wished, set up roadblocks to collect taxes from commercial trucks and to kidnap individual soldiers riding civilian buses. Otherwise they permitted civilian vehicles to move freely on the roads that were still open.

All of the USOM vehicles were civilian types. In addition to several large cargo trucks with Vietnamese drivers for hauling supplies, there were two smaller vehicles for Ramsey and Vann to use. One was an International Harvester Scout with armor concealed in the body. The other was an unarmored pickup truck, also an International, painted a canary yellow. Vann preferred the pickup, because it was fast. The weight of the armor slowed down the Scout. He believed they would be able to drive when and where they wanted and have a reasonable chance of staying alive if they kept their pattern as irregular as possible and checked with the local police or militia before starting down a stretch of road. Most of Ramsey's previous work in Vietnam had not been dangerous, but he had done some operating in the countryside, and he was game.

Within a week and a half, Vann no longer had to do battle with the flies in Bau Trai's restaurant. He and Ramsey were invited by the province officials and military officers to join the communal Vietnamese mess. (The officials and officers had organized a mess because the lack of decent housing and the insecurity kept them from bringing their families to Bau Trai.) The inclusion of the Americans meant that the Vietnamese would eat better; Vann and Ramsey could purchase food from the commissary in Saigon. The invitation would not have been extended, however, had the Vietnamese decided they did not like Vann. He was delighted, because mealtimes were an opportunity to settle problems and talk up new programs. Vann also did not anticipate any conflict with the senior American military advisor in the province, a young lieutenant colonel named Lloyd Webb, who knew Vann by reputation and respected his experience.

Near the end of April, a new province chief arrived—Maj. Nguyen Tri Hanh, a Southern Catholic who had previously been a deputy province chief in the rubber-plantation country. He had been promised a quick promotion to lieutenant colonel to induce him to accept Hau Nghia. He was a husky man of forty-five years with a stolid temperament, and he was a surprise. Hanh was straightforward in manner, appeared honest, and seemed sincerely committed to governing the province well. "I'll have him in the palm of my hand in thirty days," Vann predicted to Ramsey.

Two nights later the Viet Cong reminded Vann that goodwill and hard work would not by themselves suffice to rescue Hau Nghia or to win the war in the rest of South Vietnam. He had understood this, but in the strongly positive mood in which he approached any new task he had not faced up to the implications of what he had been seeing around him. At 2:30 A.M. on April 28, 1965, the guerrillas brought him to fuller awareness. They started firing 81mm mortar shells into Bau Trai to discourage the artillerymen there from supporting an ARVN Ranger company the Viet Cong were assaulting at that same moment at a hamlet two miles away. Radio contact with the company was lost immediately.

When Vann drove to the hamlet early in the morning he found the company annihilated—thirty-five Rangers dead, sixteen missing and captured, and eleven wounded survivors left behind by the attackers. The assault force was one of those armed-by-Harkins nightmares Vann had had at 7th Division, elements of a regional guerrilla battalion rich in American machine guns and other automatic and semiautomatic weapons, its heavier recoilless cannons and mortars smuggled in by sea from the North. (The Viet Cong, who had been fortunate to possess a couple of machine guns for a battalion in 1962, now had three in each platoon, the same as in the U.S. Army.)

The guerrillas had hardly needed to employ their heavy armament. Despite the fact that another Ranger company had been lost at the same hamlet the previous October, the officers and noncoms of this company had not taken the most elementary precautions. No outer listening posts had been organized or trip flares set up, and no foxholes had been dug for a perimeter defense. The company had simply bedded down for the night around a house near the elementary school at one end of the hamlet. The peasants said that the Rangers had been asleep. Vann had already surmised this, because most of the dead wore only undershorts and he counted eleven men who had been shot in the face while they were apparently still lying unawares. Women and children from the hamlet had come with torches as soon as the attack was over, Vann learned, and picked up the weapons of the Rangers for the guerrillas. The women and children had also helped to carry off several wounded guerrillas and two Viet Cong who had been killed by the few Rangers who woke up in time to fight. The Rangers were detested by the population in the vicinity for their abuse. Vann noticed that the guerrillas were careful not to harm any of the other houses in the hamlet with their fire. Only the one house near the school and the school itself were damaged.

The deterioration on the Saigon side was far beyond anything Vann could have imagined in Denver. Bau Trai was not a dangerous place to live simply because the Viet Cong menaced it. The demoralized Saigon soldiery were a closer peril. Four soldiers from the 25th Division's M-113 company got drunk and started a rumpus at the town's restaurant. At midnight the police attempted to quiet them down. The soldiers scattered the cops with a fusillade from Thompson submachine guns and several other weapons they had with them. They then decided it was fun to frighten policemen and higher figures of would-be authority too. For the next three and a half hours, until they got bored and went to sleep, the four soldiers staggered around Bau Trai firing in every direction. They yelled challenges to Hanh, the new province chief; to the major who was his military deputy; and to every other officer in town to come out and try to stop them.

The USOM bungalow was a mere thirty yards from the restaurant. Ramsey was in Saigon for the evening, but the area police advisor was spending the night with Vann. They lacked the authority to halt the rampage and could only take shelter on the floor and curse whenever a soldier swung a weapon their way. The next morning Vann counted the pockmarks of about twenty bullets on the stucco of the outside walls of the bungalow. He was incredulous that no Saigon officer had taken action to stop four drunks from shooting up a town. At breakfast he did not hide his contempt from Hanh. To Vann's further amazement, Hanh and his military deputy pretended that nothing had happened. Vann would soon learn that Hanh and his deputy believed there was nothing they could do. The soldiers were in a state of despair. They had lost respect for their officers and would mutiny if anyone tried to discipline them.

Sandy Faust had wondered at 7th Division if Cao was a Viet Cong agent. The intelligence advisor on the province military advisory staff was absolutely convinced that the commander of the 25th Division in Hau Nghia, Col. Phan Trong Chinh, was a Communist agent. The previous intelligence advisor had reached the same conclusion. It did not seem possible to behave so consistently for the benefit of the enemy out of mere incompetence or cowardice, and Chinh appeared to be a smart man. He had a reputation as an amateur poet. Chinh forbade ambushes at night and in the day too except in "friendly" territory. He not only did everything he could to avoid attacking the guerrillas himself, he went to pains to keep anyone else from doing so. He interfered so frequently with province operations, altering the plans and forcing Hanh to send the troops where there was no enemy, that Hanh too began to suspect that Chinh was working for the other side. When Chinh ordered airburst artillery fire, even the time fuses on the shells would be set to go off high above the ground and vitiate the effect of the shrapnel.

Chinh, of course, was not a Communist agent, no more than Cao had been, and looking back a decade later, Ramsey decided that Chinh was probably just terrified of the Viet Cong and thought that his troops would be torn apart if they seriously engaged the enemy. Chinh was too cruel to the peasantry, targeting hamlets for air strikes and shelling them with point-detonating ammunition that did blow up houses and blast away people, to have been a genuine Communist sympathizer. In Hau Nghia in 1965, Vann and Ramsey, while not as convinced as the intelligence advisor, also suspected Chinh's motives. They had a standing joke between them that he must report nightly to Hanoi.

If Chinh's purpose was to save the lives of his men, he kept it well hidden. He and his regimental commanders were forever marching columns up and down roads with no troops out on the point and the flanks for security. The result was a monotonous series of slaughters. Between these ambushes and the guerrillas' night attacks, Chinh was losing an average of a company a month. The Viet Cong had no need to tear his division apart. He was bleeding it to death for them.

The question of where incompetence and stupidity ended and treachery and sabotage began was a real one. Viet Cong penetration of the Saigon side had always been a major problem, and it became an ever graver one as the fortunes of the regime declined and men and women turned their coats to hedge against the future. The suspicion the subversion bred was even more corrosive. No one trusted anyone. In the village headquarters of Trung Lap north of Bau Trai, where a Ranger training center was located, the village chief, the local militia commander, and the head of the training center all accused each other of

being Viet Cong agents. The village chief moved elsewhere in fear for
his life after a guerrilla commando squad walked into the place one day
disguised in Ranger uniforms and shot seven genuine Rangers.

It was hardly surprising that the soldiers would despair in this atmosphere. During Vann's first year in Vietnam, Saigon soldiers had
used alcohol sparingly while outside of town and in potential danger.
Many now drank heavily at night on bivouac in the countryside. They
had also taken to smoking marijuana, another reason they may have
continued to sleep soundly after the Viet Cong arrived. Their desperation seemed to aggravate the vicious cycle in which they were caught.
It magnified their sense of alienation from their own people. Their
predatory habits worsened and they provoked more of the peasantry
into conniving with the Viet Cong to kill them, as had happened to the
Ranger company. In their hopelessness the soldiers seemed almost to
offer themselves up to death to end the suspense. Less than two weeks
after the Ranger company died while sleeping at the hamlet two miles
from Bau Trai, another company perished in identical fashion while
camped at a hamlet four miles south of the town. The habit of falling
asleep without security precautions had formerly been confined to militiamen in outposts. It had now become common to almost all of the
Saigon forces.

In these circumstances, the Viet Cong could behave with near impunity. One night a twenty-man commando invaded Cu Chi district
town to kidnap or assassinate two members of the district intelligence
squad who had been sufficiently conscientious to irritate the guerrillas
in the area. The two intelligence men had the unusual good luck to flee
their houses as the guerrillas were breaking inside. The annoyed Viet
Cong chased their quarry through the town, across rooftops, and down
dirt lanes with shouts and shots. The intelligence men eluded them, but
the guerrillas did not feel any need to leave. They searched the town
for two hours in a vain attempt to find their intended victims. None of
the Civil Guards, now called the Regional Forces or RF and referred
to derisively by the advisors as "Ruff Puffs," who were supposed to be
protecting Cu Chi, stirred. The district chief was not disturbed by the
guerrillas, and he returned the courtesy by doing nothing to help his
intelligence men. Nor did any officer appear with a rescue force from
the headquarters of a regiment of Chinh's division less than half a mile
away in a rubber plantation on the edge of Cu Chi. Vann and Ramsey
later determined that the regimental headquarters had become fully
aware of what was occurring.

On another evening a Viet Cong propaganda troupe decided to en-

tertain the population of a large village center just off the main road to
Saigon a few miles west of Cu Chi. The troupe set up its show in the
village movie theater right across the street from a school where an
ARVN company was bivouacked. The propaganda troupe was armed
and had a small escort. The lieutenant in charge of the company ordered
his men to attack the guerrillas. They refused. He got in his jeep and
drove to Cu Chi to ask the district chief what to do. They discussed the
problem for a while and then both of them went out and got drunk.

After the death of the first Ranger company at the hamlet two miles
from Bau Trai, Vann wrote a friend in Denver not to hold out any hope
that the bombing of the North would alter events in the South because
"regrettably, we are going to lose this war."

> We're going to lose because of the moral degeneration in South
> Vietnam coupled with the excellent discipline of the VC. This country
> [South Vietnam] has pissed away its opportunities so long it is now
> force of habit—and apparently nothing is going to change them.
>
> I'm bitter . . . not at these ridiculous little Oriental play soldiers—
> but at our goddam military geniuses and politicians for refusing to
> admit and act on the obvious—to take over the command of this op-
> eration lock, stock, and barrel—but maintaining Vietnamese front
> men. It is such a hopeless situation that nothing else will work. The
> little bastard, General Ky, made a speech today demanding that we
> invade the North and liberate North Vietnam—the goddamn little fool
> can't even drive a mile outside of Saigon without an armed convoy and
> he wants to liberate the North! How damned ridiculous can you get?

During his first year in Vietnam, Vann had seen the solution to the war
primarily in military terms—the destruction of the regular Viet Cong
battalions in order to create enough security to gradually pacify the
countryside. The means of destruction was an ARVN that would fight.
The way to attain such an ARVN was through a junta in Saigon or a
strongman who would willingly take American advice or who could be
dragooned into accepting American direction by the threat of with-
holding the military and economic aid that kept South Vietnam alive.
In Hau Nghia, Vann was learning that the task facing the United States
was a much more complicated and intractable one. He was finding out
how parasitic and moribund the Saigon side was, some of the reasons
for its condition, and how profoundly Saigon society would have to be
changed if it was ever to survive against its Communist opponent.

The worst of the ills he was encountering, the one from which these other ills of demoralization and indiscipline seemed to rise, was corruption. He had not known before exactly how pervasive it was. He was discovering in Hau Nghia that corruption infected the whole of Saigon society, from Ky and almost all of the other Young Turk generals consolidating their power at the center, to the corps and division commanders, through the province and district chiefs and their administrations, to the village policeman blackmailing a farmer into paying him a bribe not to report the farmer as a Viet Cong suspect.

The Saigonese form of corruption differed completely in magnitude and nature from the corruption most commonly found in state and local government in the United States. The American variety, while destructive when it grew out of hand, could be a malodorous lubricant for the political machines that got shopping centers and highways and public housing built. Saigonese corruption was incapacitating, a malignancy that poisoned the entire system of government. Graft was the main preoccupation of those on the Saigon side, Vann learned, absorbing more time and thought than any other concern and summoning considerable ingenuity from people who were incompetent at the task they were supposed to perform. At the very time when the Vietnamese on the Saigon side should have been joining together in self-sacrifice and unity to prevent their world from being destroyed, they were hastening its destruction. The greater the peril to their society became, the more viciously they preyed on one another. They seemed to loot with the assumption that they and their families would somehow escape the common disaster at the last moment, or that the Americans would step in and save them. Mostly, Vann observed, their greed was too rapacious to permit any thought of its ultimate consequence.

Hanh gave Vann some of his first lessons on the subject. As province chief, Hanh was entitled to take his meals in his own quarters. Vann and Ramsey began eating with him, rather than with the other province officials, after his arrival near the end of April. Often Hanh invited one or two of his subordinates to join them. Just as frequently there were only the three of them. Eating at the province chief's table was a natural thing for the civilian American advisors in a province to do, and it also fit in with Vann's hope to organize a concerted effort against the Viet Cong in Hau Nghia by managing Hanh. In these early years most American advisors, civilian or military, learned relatively little about the intricacies of corruption in South Vietnam, because they avoided the subject. They knew that corruption was officially regarded as an embarrassment and that reports about it were not welcome at the embassy or at Westmoreland's headquarters. Their Saigonese counterparts also knew this, and while they gossiped about corruption, they did not press confidences on the Americans. Hanh, an exception within his own system, recognized Vann as an American exception. Vann also presented himself as an American with connections in high places who might be able to change things.

One of the initial lessons Hanh taught Vann was that losses and desertions and the difficulty of recruitment did not by themselves explain why Saigon's fighting units were chronically short of men. At Vann's suggestion, Hanh agreed to rotate his Regional Forces troops through a refresher training course. To try to encourage buttressing of the combat units, the Americans had prevailed on the Ministry of Defense to require that a unit meet a minimum strength figure before it could be admitted to a training center. Hanh thought he would have no problem with the first unit he selected because its roster showed approximately 140 men and the training center minimum in this case was about 100. When he mustered the unit he found fifty men. The other ninety names on the roster represented what the Vietnamese called "ghost soldiers" and "potted-tree soldiers." The "ghosts" were men who had been killed or who had deserted. The "potted trees" were men who paid bribes for false discharge or leave papers so that they could return to their families or civilian jobs, hence the allusion to an ornamental tree safely ensconced in a pot. The unit commanders pocketed the monthly pay and allowances for these phantoms and domesticated greenery, dividing the profit with more senior officers who protected them. Instead of looking for incentives to recruit soldiers, the Saigon officer corps had created a disincentive to keeping its units strong enough to fight.

Hanh was aware of the practice, of course, but he had expected to net 100 troops out of a roster that listed 140. He had the ARVN major who was his deputy for military affairs investigate to determine how much the other RF units were understrength. The major came back with an unsettling report. It seemed that the RF commander for Hau Nghia "ate too much," a phrase for a man who was considered greedy even by Saigon standards, and encouraged his subordinates to pad the rolls excessively. Hanh's deputy then made a suggestion. He proposed that he and Hanh cut themselves in on the rakeoff. Hanh decided he had no one on his staff he could trust. He told Vann and Ramsey the story and asked them to start taking pictures of RF and Popular Forces units they encountered on their travels in the province. (The SDC militia had also been renamed and was now called the Popular Forces or PF.) He intended to compare the photographs with the unit rosters to try to find out how many troops he really did have.

Nguyen Tri Hanh was not an exception merely out of personal desire. He had not bought his province chief's job and so did not have to generate graft to pay for the position. Most province and district chiefs in South Vietnam did buy their jobs. Hanh's predecessor, who had been arrested for involvement in the abortive coup in February, was out of jail by late spring but still in trouble for another reason. He had bought the post in 1964 when Hau Nghia had been a somewhat safer place. At the time of his arrest he had not finished paying off his debt to the corps commander who had sold him the province, and the general was pressing him for the money. Hanh had not been asked to pay for the job because so few men had been willing to take Hau Nghia in the spring of 1965 and he had been appointed by a comparatively honest civilian prime minister, who was soon to be forced out by the generals.

Corruption guaranteed incompetence in office, high or low. Professional performance had no bearing on whether men like Chinh held division commands. They kept their positions by their facility at forming corruption alliances with those above them and at creating other corruption alliances with those below in order to channel money upward. (The same pattern of officials generating graft for themselves and higher-ups had prevailed under Diem, with the distinction that the men originally acquired their positions for their loyalty to the Ngo Dinh family.) Lines of authority that needed to function if the country was to be governed rationally and that were already weakened by the influence of family ties and religious and factional connections were undermined entirely by those networks within networks of graft. Hanh had virtually no control, for example, over three of the district chiefs in his province, because they were corruption partners of Chinh and the division commander protected them. Chinh was trying to coerce Hanh into firing the fourth district chief, because the man was independent and competent but would not cooperate sufficiently in graft to please Chinh.

The Saigon regime had, in fact, evolved a system in which no one was permitted to keep his hands clean. For all to be safe, all had to be implicated. As Ramsey was to remark, "The system was designed to ensure that no pot was in a position to call another kettle black." Inflation had undermined salaries during the Diem years, and corruption had negated any incentive to increase them to realistic levels. Salaries were so ludicrously low (Hanh's monthly salary was less than two hundred dollars at the official rate of exchange) that a man had to steal something to support his family and maintain his status. The only way an American could distinguish between honest and dishonest officials was to draw a line between those who embezzled what they needed to

live and those who enriched themselves. Hanh was honest by this cri-
terion, as Vann had noticed Cao to be at 7th Division. It was easier for
an American to discern this line than it was for a Vietnamese who had
begun stealing to hold to it. Corruption fed on itself. Few men who had
bought a job were willing to forgo a profit on their investment and a
bonus in the bargain for the physical risks involved. There was also the
temptation to build a constituency within the system. The province and
district chiefs most popular with their staffs usually were those who
spread the graft around so that everyone got a share.

The system had given rise to a multitude of other distortions that
encouraged corruption. One was the role played by the wives. Madame
General X or Mrs. Colonel Y often acted as agents for their husbands,
frequently dealing with other Madame Generals or Mrs. Colonels. The
women liked the role, because it gave them power. A woman who was
using the shield of her husband's authority to run a graft network acquired a share of that authority in the process. Many of the men also
favored the arrangement, because it freed them from the tedium of
financial details and allowed them to pretend that their wives were just
businesswomen and that they were not crooks. There simply was no
way for a man to remain truly honest and hold a position at a responsible
level. Even if he took only what he needed and kept his wife under
control, he still had to permit corruption to go on around him, and he
often had to embezzle money for payoff demands by his superiors. If
he insisted on honesty to the point of refusing others access to corruption, he became an outsider and was pushed from office. Hanh had so
far been able to escape with moderate payments to Chinh. It was uncertain how long he could continue to get off so lightly.

Vann had already found out prior to Hanh's arrival that corruption
undermined his USOM pacification programs and that Americans were
not beyond its temptation. He discovered that another AID official (not
William Pye, his immediate predecessor) had been allowing the Vietnamese contractor in the province to steal USOM cement and other
building materials in exchange for women. Construction materials were
bringing spectacular prices on the black market in Saigon, because of
the rush of Vietnamese and Chinese speculators to build housing to rent
to the thousands of Americans coming into the country. Cement was
especially golden. The contractor had included his wife among the
women he had provided the AID official. While it might seem difficult
to imagine circumstances in which John Vann would refuse free sex,
sex as bribery was one of them. (Vann did not, of course, renounce sex
because of his assignment to Hau Nghia. He behaved as he had at 7th

Division. He confined his sexual adventures to his trips to Saigon and presented himself as a model of probity while in the province.) The idea that any American would allow himself to be bribed into winking at the theft of government supplies in wartime was also loathsome to Vann. He was outraged at the man and outraged at the contractor for taking advantage of the man's weakness.

The eagerness for graft was sabotaging USOM programs in more subtle ways than outright theft. The hamlet elementary schools USOM financed had an appeal for the peasants, because the farmers wanted their children to be educated. When the Hau Nghia contractor built a school, he put it up as shoddily as possible, and the benches and desks he provided were so poorly fabricated they did not last a year. The AID official had also been induced to look the other way on matters like this, and the province and district officials always ignored the cheating because the contractor was naturally bribing them too. Similarly, USOM funds marked for "Self-Help" projects to stimulate participation by the peasantry ended up going into hamlet and village offices that were subsequently abandoned or wrecked by the Viet Cong. Province officials kept proposing the construction of such buildings because they got a rakeoff on each one. Vann wanted to carry out the original purpose of the program and let the peasants choose what they wanted, probably another school or a clinic, and then give them the cement and roofing and other materials to build it themselves, so that they would take care of it and discourage the guerrillas from harming it. The province officials opposed the idea, because they would be deprived of their graft.

Corruption's biggest customer was the Viet Cong. Corruption gave the guerrillas all sorts of advantages. A "Resources and Population Control" program instigated by the Americans was supposed to restrict the movement of guerrilla sympathizers and to deny the Viet Cong medicines and other useful commodities. Americans new to South Vietnam attributed the persistence of the Saigon regime's complicated edicts and regulations to the influence of French colonialism. They did not understand that each requirement and prohibition served as a pretext for graft. The regulations issued under the control program were an excuse to ask higher prices for contraband goods. The guerrillas did not limit their purchases to such forbidden items as antibiotics and surgical instruments and dry-cell batteries for hand detonators to set off mines. They bought items the Americans had not thought to put on the contraband list, like false identification cards, security clearances for spies seeking jobs with U.S. agencies—almost anything they wanted, simply by paying the requisite prices and bribes.

Corruption in turn raised money to help the Viet Cong finance these purchases and bribes. There was, for example, a large sugar mill in Hau Nghia at Hiep Hoa, northwest of Bau Trai, that processed cane grown by the farmers. The mill was jointly owned by French interests and the Saigon government. The regime's share was leased to Chinese businessmen in Cholon, who split the profits with whoever was in power. The mill was located in the midst of a guerrilla-dominated area, and yet it was never bothered. Vann noticed that the manager and other supervisors felt sufficiently remote from the danger of bullets and explosions to have plate-glass windows in their houses. The mill's trucks were never stopped while hauling processed sugar into Saigon. The Viet Cong obtained annual taxes from the mill of 1.7 million piasters, Vann was told. The Hiep Hoa sugar mill was not unique. Commercial enterprises from which Saigon officials gained profits and the Viet Cong derived taxes existed all over South Vietnam. The guerrilla tax collectors provided signed receipts for the payments stamped with the seal of the National Liberation Front, the Viet Cong's clandestine government.

Trafficking with the guerrillas had a special way of feeding on itself, because it was, at least officially, a crime punishable by death. Once someone on the Saigon side had started down the road, the Communists could enlarge future requests under the threat of blackmail. American intelligence officers sometimes wondered why more guerrilla operatives from district and province committee levels were not captured, accidentally if for no other reason. They were caught on occasion and then frequently bought out of their cells before the Americans could discover that a valuable catch had been made.

The Communists had some problems with corruption in the regime in the North, but the circumstances of the struggle in the South militated against corruption in their organization there. The path to a responsible position in the Viet Cong and then to Party membership was too arduous and dangerous to attract men who were motivated by money. The Communist leaders also took measures to prevent corruption from infecting the guerrilla ranks. They held up the example of its evil on the Saigon side and punished venality whenever they discovered it with a trial and a lengthy term of "reeducation" in a rain-forest labor camp or a bullet in the back of the head.

The Viet Cong were winning the war for a larger reason than this ruinous corruption and these other maladies of the Saigon regime, Vann began to realize. They were leading a social revolution in the South Vietnamese countryside and were harnessing its energy to their cause. Vann could understand this social revolution, because his childhood and youth enabled him to identify with the anger and aspirations of poor Vietnamese. His refusal to abandon the roads gave him an opportunity to see the revolution occurring. Most days he and Ramsey were out among the peasantry—escorting their cargo trucks carrying free American bulgur wheat (the Vietnamese found it inedible and sold it for hog feed and used the money to buy rice), cooking oil, powdered milk, and other supplies to groups of refugees, or trying to move forward one of their programs designed to win the sympathy of the population. When they drove together they went in the canary-yellow International pickup; if they split up they would take turns in their second small vehicle, the slower armored Scout, and Vann would go with an interpreter.

The popularity of the USOM program to build hamlet elementary schools first alerted Vann to the social revolution the Viet Cong were leading. With only six Saigon-controlled hamlets in Hau Nghia, Vann and Ramsey had to build schools in hamlets dominated by the guerrillas if they were to build any at all. The task of building them gave Vann a tangible sense of why the Viet Cong won the Vietnamese peasantry to their side. It took him into that halfway world where the guerrillas were exerting dominance and the majority of the population sympathized with them, but where the Viet Cong's clandestine government had not yet had time to fully organize the community and eradicate every vestige of the Saigon regime and the United States. In areas where they had solidified control, the Viet Cong established their own school system. They tolerated the American school-building program elsewhere, because the farmers were so anxious to have their children educated and many of the peasants also wanted to learn how to read and write and do basic arithmetic in evening classes. The local guerrillas and their children and relatives all benefited. While the teachers were Saigon government employees, the majority were being left undisturbed for the moment as long as they taught from a neutral point of view.

These hamlet elementary schools reminded Vann of the country schools of the Blue Ridge foothills in which he had worked as a teacher's aide while at Ferrum. A single teacher taught all five grades. He was amazed to find 300 children enrolled in one school. The overcrowding in this case was not as much of a problem as it might have been, because this school had no walls. It consisted of a roof of USOM-supplied aluminum sheets spread over support beams. The roof had several holes in it from shrapnel. The teacher taught in three shifts.

Vann made friends right away with the teacher at the hamlet two miles from Bau Trai where the Ranger company had been wiped out. She was a homely middle-aged woman of outgoing temperament. The fact that she was also the Viet Cong medical worker for the hamlet, a place called So Do, did not seem to affect her attitude toward Vann and Ramsey. Vann won her gratitude by repairing her two-room school, which had been damaged in the attack, and also by arranging corrective surgery for several children he noticed there who were afflicted with harelip, a congenital deformity of the upper lip. (The deformity is rarely seen in the United States and other industrialized countries because it is corrected at birth.) These harelip cases Vann encountered at So Do and other hamlets called to mind Gene with his legs bowed by rickets, a senseless curse that modern medicine could banish. Vann started a program to send all such children for treatment to the Filipino and South Korean surgical teams on loan to USOM. Many months later he was to discover that the So Do schoolteacher saved his life and Ramsey's on three occasions by persuading guerrillas who had planted a mine in the road and were waiting for them not to blow them up as they drove by.

John Vann also made friends with a lot of the children. Their bright and eager faces moved him. Vietnamese peasant children had a winning manner, and none more so than the children of the Delta. The diet, protein-rich from fish and vegetables and fruit, made them vigorous. They laughed easily and played hard. In their bare feet and shorts and loose shirts—tending the family water buffalo or shouting and kicking a can for a soccer ball in the dirt of a farmyard because they did not have a real ball or other toys and had to contrive their own fun—they were the children Vann and his brothers had been in their good moments in Norfolk. He learned quickly that the children could protect him. They wanted the American who handed out the candy and gum to return, and they would sometimes warn him when there were guerrillas in a hamlet or farther down a road.

Doug Ramsey was both the perfect subordinate and partner for Vann at this moment and a major influence on Vann's thinking at this time. Ramsey was, like Halberstam, another of the messianic innocents of the 1950s generation, as intense as his fence-rail frame was tall. An only child, he had grown up amid the big firs and ponderosa pines on the fringes of the Grand Canyon and in the desert oasis town of Boulder City, Nevada. Ramsey's father was a minor administrator for the National Park Service, and his mother was chronically ill in a period when the government did not provide virtually limitless medical care to the dependents of civil servants. He had gone through Occidental College in Los Angeles on scholarships and loans, graduating in 1956 as one of the few students in the history of the college to achieve a perfect record, an A in every course for all four years. The State Department had drawn him away from a scholar's life after a year of graduate study at Harvard because it seemed to offer adventure and demanding service. Before he could accept his appointment to the Foreign Service he had to give the Air Force two years, most of the time as a communications intelligence officer, to fulfill a college ROTC obligation he had acquired at Occidental. Ramsey had then found himself assigned to the State Department's Honolulu Reception Center for foreign visitors across from the Royal Hawaiian Hotel in Waikiki.

To rid himself of such comfortable assignments, Ramsey had volunteered for Vietnamese language training and field work in South Vietnam, arriving in May 1963 as the Buddhist crisis was about to begin. He had been given another comfortable assignment, this one as branch public affairs officer for USIS in the mountain resort city of Dalat. Diem and the Nhus had weekend villas at Dalat, and the place was sophisticated and highly politicized. Ramsey's curiosity and his facility with the language had turned his months there into an education in Saigon society. Connections he formed in USIS had also gradually brought him work more to his liking, such as interview surveys of peasants in hamlets along the Central Coast and in the northern Delta to try to pinpoint specific grievances that motivated the farmers to support the Viet Cong. After nearly two years of patience and more volunteering, the State Department had finally given him a job he really wanted—detail to AID and assignment to Hau Nghia in February 1965 as assistant province representative.

Ramsey had known nothing of his new boss when Vann arrived a month later. Vann had introduced himself by giving Ramsey a copy of Halberstam's *Esquire* article. Ramsey was an admirer of Halberstam's reporting on Vietnam in 1962 and 1963. To learn that his new superior had inspired much of that reporting and had been the hero of that miserable tale affected Ramsey deeply. Although it would have been difficult for a young man of Ramsey's inclinations not to have followed Vann, in all that Ramsey was to see of him Vann was never to fall short of Halberstam's heroic portrait. The two men were in tune—in tune in their emotional commitment to the war, in tune in their affection for the country they were struggling to retain. Ramsey was to write afterward of how they would sometimes abandon common sense entirely and go for a spin down a back road at the close of day to watch the falling sun turn the rice fields "to burnished copper in the afterglow."

They would stop for a moment "in some red-tiled or thatched-roof hamlet where the people were settling in for the night as they had for hundreds of years." They would savor the sights and smells of this land "as if we were small city children on the way to camp for the first time."

At night, after dinner with Hanh, Vann and Ramsey would stay up late in their office at the province headquarters (they had electricity and the comfort of fans there) discussing the war and mulling over the events of the day. Ramsey pointed out to Vann that the hunger for education Vann was seeing in the peasant children would, under the Saigon system, end in frustration for those with the most intelligence and initiative. Ramsey had learned enough about South Vietnamese society to know that the educational system set up by the French and perpetuated by the Saigon regime effectively reserved secondary and higher education, and therefore the leadership positions in non-Communist society, for the urban middle and upper classes and for the former landed class of the countryside that had fled to the towns and cities. If a peasant child managed to get through the five years of elementary education, he faced a dead end. The nearest secondary schools were in the district centers. The farm families were usually too poor to send the children to them, and the district schools did not go beyond the initial four years of secondary education in any case.

Virtually the sole route to status in life for a peasant child was to turn to the Viet Cong and their National Liberation Front, as the most talented obviously did. Because they had to draw leaders from the peasantry, the Communists had no rigid educational requirements and tried to further the education of promising cadres within their own system. The commander of the Viet Cong battalion that was killing the most Saigon troops in Hau Nghia (elements of his battalion had annihilated the Rangers at So Do) was a forty-five-year-old native of the abandoned Duc Hue District on the northeast corner of the Plain of Reeds. He was a highly respected man. At the moment he was equivalent in rank to a major in the ARVN. He would soon be equivalent to a lieutenant colonel, as he was expanding his battalion into a regiment. He had worked his way up from the ranks, which meant that he had probably received no more than a few years of elementary education in the Saigon system he was striving to overthrow.

Vann's thoughts during this period were also being influenced by two of Ramsey's friends, who were to become Vann's friends and comrades in the Vietnam enterprise. One was Ev Bumgardner, the psychological-warfare specialist who had witnessed Diem's speech at Tuy Hoa ten years earlier and returned to Vietnam to run the field operations of

USIS. The other was Frank Scotton, Bumgardner's chief operative in the field. Vann had encountered Bumgardner and Scotton during his first year in the country, but had never had an opportunity to become well acquainted. Ramsey introduced him to them. Both were the kind of original men whose spirits attracted Vann.

Frank Scotton was a strapping twenty-seven-year-old in 1965 with a dark complexion and dark brown hair, raised on the lower-middle-class side of a Boston suburb by a conscientious mother after his father, a fireman, enlisted in the Army and was killed during World War II. He was adventurous and friendly and yet a bit rough and wary in manner. His preference in weapons was a 9mm Swedish K submachine gun he had acquired from the Special Forces. His mind was naturally unorthodox, and a fascination with guerrilla warfare and a self-steeping in the writings of Mao Tse-tung and Vo Nguyen Giap had reinforced this trait.

He and Bumgardner were attempting to fight the Vietnamese Communists with their own methods by copying Communist molds and filling them with anti-Communist ideology. A new program to politically indoctrinate and motivate the Saigon militiamen that Vann was enthusiastic about was an outgrowth of an experiment Scotton had conducted the previous year in Quang Ngai Province on the Central Coast. With Bumgardner's encouragement and the help of an imaginative Army major named Robert Kelly and several CIA agents, Scotton had organized forty-five-man commandos that were an imitation of the Viet Cong's armed propaganda teams. Scotton's commandos had not stopped the guerrillas from taking over almost all of Quang Ngai (by May 1965 the regime was considering whether to abandon the province capital itself), but they had performed as no other Saigon units ever had—helping the farmers, propagandizing in guerrilla-dominated sections, laying ambushes that actually did surprise guerrilla bands at night, and sneaking into hamlets to assassinate local Viet Cong leaders.

Bumgardner was at first glance the contrasting mentor that an action-oriented type like Scotton seemed to need, a cerebral and restrained man, diminutive and balding now at forty years. Along with Bumgardner's even temper and self-effacing manner went a capacity to think and behave with the same unorthodoxy Scotton did. The passion in Bumgardner showed in his dogged pursuit of the war and in a zest, concealed from strangers, to put himself in dangerous places and to hear bullets buzz and snap.

Whenever Vann and Ramsey went into Saigon on business together and stayed overnight, they would get together with Bumgardner and Scotton to talk about the war. While Bumgardner and Scotton reflected the same inability as the rest of their countrymen to grasp the nationalist basis of Vietnamese Communism, they were knowledgeable about current social and political conditions in South Vietnam. Both men were fluent in Vietnamese, and Bumgardner had married into a Chinese family that had lived in Vietnam for generations. They were convinced, like Ramsey, that the Viet Cong drew their greatest strength from the conditions that nurtured social revolution. They thought that anti-Communist nationalism was still a viable alternative in the South, but only if there was a complete transformation of the Saigon regime. The United States could not simply take over the regime as Vann's reflex had told him and run the country through Vietnamese front men. The regime had to be somehow changed into an entirely different kind of government that was responsive to the desires of the rural population. Unless a change was made, Bumgardner and Scotton believed, the war could not be won. Even if the U.S. Army were to occupy the whole country and crush the guerrillas, the rebellion would break out again after the American soldiers had gone home.

What Ramsey, Bumgardner, and Scotton said sounded right to Vann because of what he saw in Hau Nghia. By the end of May he had seen and heard enough to express his new and, for Vann, extraordinary appreciation of the war in a letter to General York:

> If it were not for the fact that Vietnam is but a pawn in the larger East-West confrontation, and that our presence here is essential to deny the resources of this area to Communist China, then it would be damned hard to justify our support of the existing government. There is a revolution going on in this country—and the principles, goals, and desires of the *other* side are much closer to what Americans believe in than those of GVN [the Saigon Government]. I realize that ultimately, when the Chinese brand of Communism takes over, that these "revolutionaries" are going to be sadly disappointed—but then it will be too late—for them; and too late for us to win them. I am convinced that, even though the National Liberation Front is Communist-dominated, that the great majority of the people supporting it are doing so because it is their only hope to change and improve their living conditions and opportunities. If I were a lad of eighteen faced with the same choice—whether to support the GVN or the NLF—and a member of a rural community, I would surely choose the NLF.

For eleven years, Vann thought, the United States had been wasting Vietnamese and American lives and hundreds of millions of dollars attempting to preserve the unpreservable old order in South Vietnam. The task before him was so much larger than anything he had envisioned in Denver when he had decided to return to the war. What he had to do was to devise a strategy that was constructive rather than destructive, a strategy that could shape South Vietnam into a nation able to stand with the United States in the global struggle for the underdeveloped lands. After devising that strategy he would have to translate it into a program and then into action by selling the program to those on high. The idealism that Garland Hopkins and Ferrum had instilled in him expressed itself in a desire to Americanize the world. When he looked at these farm youngsters he did not simply see Vietnamese children. He saw potential Vietnamese counterparts of Lansdale's Filipinos—native leaders so infused with American values and so grateful for American help that they would naturally make the cause of the United States their own. "Had we begun eleven years ago," he said in a lecture in Denver while on home leave that fall, "we'd now be having the leaders emerging that we want. I think we can still do it through children like this."

The war was also reaching a juncture that Vann saw as an opportunity to implement a new strategy. By early June 1965, Westmoreland had more than 50,000 American military men in South Vietnam, including nine battalions of Marines and Army paratroops. Although the Johnson administration was being vague in public about the decisions it was reaching, more U.S. battalions were clearly on the way. They were arriving just in time. The Saigon government had been preparing to evacuate all five northern provinces along the Central Coast—the whole of the I Corps zone where the Marines now held the airfield at Phu Bai near the former imperial capital of Hue as well as the port and air base at Da Nang below it. The Saigon generals had even developed a secret plan to move JGS headquarters from the handsome compound de Lattre de Tassigny had built next to Tan Son Nhut to the old French Army school for military orphans on the Vung Tau peninsula (Cap St. Jacques) forty miles southeast of the city. The peninsula was easy to defend, and the generals would be a few minutes from ships and the open sea there. They were uncertain whether they would be able to defend the remnants of the Central Highlands they still held long enough to shift the burden to the Americans. The principal mountain towns of Kontum, Pleiku, and Banmethuot had become fragile islands accessible only by air.

In Hau Nghia there were signs everywhere that the regime would not see 1966 without an American rescue. Minings and ambushes had become so frequent along the main road to Saigon, Route 1, that Vann and Ramsey would pass smashed jeeps and trucks from which no one had yet bothered to remove the bodies. Worse, they occasionally spotted part of a body beside a wreck. On some mornings the guerrillas blew up military vehicles within 200 yards of the police checkpoints at each end of Bau Trai. The policemen stationed in the sentry boxes the night before had probably heard the guerrillas digging the mines into the road or had watched in the moonlight as the Viet Cong had strung the wires to the detonators in the brush nearby, yet they had said nothing. Desertions were also becoming more significant. The chiefs of two hamlets right next to Bau Trai, two of the six supposedly "pacified" hamlets in the province, were no longer willing to depend on the insurance they purchased by assisting the Viet Cong covertly. They deserted openly to the guerrillas. One took his deputy and almost all of the militia platoon in the hamlet with him. Vann and Ramsey had been fond of this PF platoon. Most of its members were local teenagers who would cheer whenever the Americans brought them bulgur wheat or cooking oil to supplement their ridiculous salaries. The happy-go-lucky teenagers shocked their American friends by wiping out part of a pacification team stationed in the neighborhood before deserting.

The nerves of those on the Saigon side who did not desert were so frayed that panic was a flash away. The village center of Duc Lap along the road two miles north of Bau Trai had been attacked several times in recent months. One morning the place was swept by a rumor that a squad of guerrillas—a single squad—was about to arrive. First the regular police, then the heavily armed Combat Police, then a Ranger battalion headquarters and one of its companies fled in terror. They all straggled back after the rumor proved false. Vann and Ramsey would have taken less notice if the panic had occurred at 2:00 A.M. in the predawn darkness when some sort of attack might have been developing. The time had been 10:00 A.M.

Vann had never changed the views he had expressed to Ziegler back in 1962 on the folly of trying to fight the war with American troops. "If the war is to be won," he had written Lodge's assistant from Denver in the spring of 1964, "then it must be done by the Vietnamese—nothing would be more foolhardy than the employment of U.S. (or any other foreign) troops in quantity. We could pour our entire Army into Vietnam—and accomplish nothing worthwhile." He felt the same way roughly a year later as the Marines and Army infantrymen started to arrive.

Not that he was unhappy to see them come. Without them South Vietnam would, he remarked, have "gone down the drain." Their arrival meant an end to the much-feared danger that, as the regime neared collapse, some group of neutralist or pro-Communist politicians would form a government in Saigon and demand that the United States withdraw. Ky and his fellow generals could hold on as long as they had American guns to protect them. The Vietnamese Communists obviously lacked the capacity to eject a large U.S. force that could be supported by sea and air. What troubled Vann was that these American soldiers would now be sent out to fight the Viet Cong and the North Vietnamese regulars of Hanoi's Vietnam People's Army (called the NVA, for North Vietnamese Army, by the U.S. military), who had started to march down the Ho Chi Minh Trail to reinforce the guerrillas. Given the inability of American troops to distinguish friend from foe, the potential for mindless carnage was enormous.

The sensible course, Vann believed, would be to use the American troops to secure Saigon and the ports and airfields and those inland cities and towns that could not, as a matter of prestige, be lost to the Communists. The U.S. soldiers would serve as a garrison and an emergency reserve. They could be employed offensively in those rare instances when a large Viet Cong or NVA unit had been well located, the circumstances favored the Americans, and there was little danger of civilian casualties. The primary if unspoken mission of the American troops would be political. They would provide the muscle to stop the bacchanal of coups and recoups and bring the Saigon generals to heel. Behind the shield of the U.S. Army and the Marine Corps, the United States would take over the regime and gradually turn it into a government whose leaders were not fundamentally corrupt men. The Vietnamese soldiers of the ARVN and the Regional and Popular Forces would do most of the fighting in the countryside, not the American troops. The Saigon forces would have to be reorganized and reformed as they carried the burden of defeating the Viet Cong and beginning the pacification of the hamlets. This goal could be accomplished, Vann felt, by creating a "joint command" in which Americans would issue the orders. He recognized by now that the rank and file of the Saigon forces were as disgusted with their leadership as he was. He was convinced that they would respond to competence and discipline and the success these would bring. Vann began to focus his late-night talks with Ramsey and their discussions in Saigon with Bumgardner and Scotton on the core of a new strategy—the details of a program to attract the peasantry and change the nature of Saigon society.

In the meantime, Vann decided, the place to start changing things was Hau Nghia, and he would begin with an example of corruption he could do something about—the thieving contractor. Vann had been fighting a private guerrilla war with the contractor since his discovery that the man had corrupted another AID official with women. He had a weapon he could use against the crooked builder. USOM regulations required Vann to sign a release before the contractor could be paid for a completed project. Vann made a point of catching the contractor in the theft of aluminum roofing sheets. He drove to a recently finished maternity clinic and to a school, climbed up and counted the number of sheets in the roofs, and checked the records to see how many sheets had been issued to the contractor for the buildings. Vann then refused to sign payment releases until the contractor agreed to reimburse the U.S. government for the missing sheets.

The conflict escalated in the latter part of May when the contractor visited Hanh to offer him the same 10 percent kickback arrangement on contracts that the builder had had with the last province chief. He advised Hanh not to take Vann seriously. The AID official corrupted by the contractor now occupied a staff position at USOM headquarters in Saigon. The contractor said his American friend had informed him that Vann was considered a troublemaker and would be replaced soon. Hanh did not react. That evening he tipped Vann off to what the contractor had told him. Vann asked Hanh to cancel every contract the crooked builder had in the province. Hanh would not commit himself to such drastic action, but he did not seem unwilling if Vann could sufficiently discredit the builder.

A week later the contractor was back to see Hanh. He enlarged his proposition to make it more attractive. The Resources and Population Control program that was supposed to deny the Viet Cong useful commodities required export-import certificates for goods and raw materials, such as sugar, entering or leaving the province. The certificates were commonly sold for graft. The builder had handled the sales for the last province chief. He offered to perform the same service for Hanh, for a percentage, of course. Hanh explicitly declined the offer this time and again repeated the conversation to Vann.

By this point the contractor had learned that Vann was attempting to expel him from Hau Nghia, and he correctly assumed that the new province chief would not be acting so strangely were it not for Vann's encouragement. The Saigonese had become practiced over the years at striking a pose of innocence and injured national pride whenever a genuine interest like corruption was threatened by Americans. The contractor, a member of a prominent Southern Catholic family, was adept at the game. He wrote Vann a letter upbraiding him for behaving like "the French colonial bosses when they dominated our country."

The next move in the game was for the contractor to have his friend at USOM headquarters send a copy of the letter up the chain-of-command ladder to get Vann transferred out of Hau Nghia. Vann guessed this would be the next play. He wrote the contractor a reply laying out the facts of his thievery, but held back the carbon that would normally have gone to USOM headquarters. He suspected that the bribed AID official would divert it or attempt to discredit it. A summons to Saigon soon came, as Vann had expected, from Wilson's deputy, a career civilian AID officer. The deputy immediately began to lecture Vann on how to behave toward Vietnamese. When he was unable to restrain himself any longer, Vann asked whether the deputy wanted to hear his side of the story. The deputy said that he did not, that he was merely trying to help Vann. Unless he could give his side of the story, Vann said, they would have to end the meeting. The deputy grudgingly consented to listen. Vann then described the bribed official's relationship with the contractor and the larger schemes of graft the builder had been running with the last province chief. He gave the deputy a carbon of his reply to the contractor as well as copies of earlier correspondence between them about vanished building materials. Vann could see that Wilson's deputy was unhappy. He apparently feared a scandal. He did say that Vann's account and the full correspondence told a story considerably different from what he had heard.

At noon on June 22, Vann was driving down Route 1 toward Cu Chi, feeling good about his first campaign against corruption in Hau Nghia. The bribed AID official had not stood up well under questioning. Vann had been asked to write a confidential memorandum about the man's relationship with the contractor. The man was in so much hot water at USOM headquarters that he was subsequently to transfer to another country. Wilson's civilian deputy was changing his opinion of Vann and was to become one of Vann's staunchest promoters in AID. Hanh had not yet canceled the last of the builder's contracts, but he seemed about to do so. Vann had become confident enough of victory a week earlier to announce to Hanh and to one of Hanh's deputies that no matter what the official finding of the investigation, he was not going to issue the contractor another bag of cement or a single sheet of roofing as long as he was USOM representative in Hau Nghia.

Vann was alone in the canary-yellow International pickup. He had talked that morning to the district chief at Trang Bang farther up Route 1 about some Self-Help projects and was on his way down to Cu

Chi to meet Hanh. The province chief was also out traveling that morning to present some piglets to farmers participating in the USOM pig raising and corn-growing program. Despite his dislike of convoys, Vann was going to join Hanh's convoy out of courtesy so that they could drive back to Bau Trai together for lunch there with a touring USIA official. Vann had just passed a dangerous spot at a bridge named for the stream it spanned, Suoi Sau (Sau Creek). The province military advisors had nicknamed the bridge Suoi Cide because so many minings and ambushes occurred nearby.

He spotted a group of men a short distance off his side of the two-lane tarmac road. Three of them were armed and dressed in the black pajamalike garb that the peasants, the Viet Cong, and the Saigon militia all wore. They were walking in front of six young men who were stripped to the waist. The three armed men beckoned to Vann to stop. Thinking that they were militia who needed help in some emergency, Vann slowed down. As he did so, one of them raised a rifle and pointed it at him, changing Vann's mind about who was beckoning to him. He slammed in the clutch with his left foot, shoved the gear stick up into second, and began to accelerate away, smiling and waving out the open door window of the truck in the hope that if these men were Viet Cong with prisoners, they might hesitate long enough for him to get away. The man who had been signaling most vigorously for Vann to stop pushed down his companion's rifle, smiled, and waved back.

In a few moments Vann was clear of them and speeding down the potholed tarmac at seventy miles an hour. No guerrillas had ever before signaled to him to stop and behaved so oddly. He was wondering whether they really had been Viet Cong when he heard a volley of shots and the crack of bullets missing the pickup's cab. He ducked instinctively, just in time to keep his eyes from being filled with fragments of glass as more bullets punched holes through the windshield. The little truck careened off to the left into a graveyard that extended down both sides of the road. Vann jerked himself erect to get control of the vehicle and saw his ambushers—about a dozen guerrillas strung out along the left side of the road for the length of a football field. The pickup was headed right for them.

Vann kept his foot pressed on the accelerator to retain every bit of power and speed he could. As the truck fishtailed wildly down the edge of the graveyard and Vann fought the wheel to bring it back up on the road he could see the guerrillas closest to him scatter to avoid being run over. Two of the Viet Cong, both armed with Thompson submachine guns, were calmer than their fellows. They stood where they were and continued to shoot. Vann stared at the second of the two submachine gunners after he had wrestled the truck back to the road and was hurtling through the ambush position. The man did not shoot at the engine or the tires. Instead he looked directly at Vann behind the wheel and kept firing short bursts from the Thompson gun to try to kill him.

The bullets from the last burst as the truck passed the guerrilla came through the open door window in front of Vann's face, one bullet smashing its way back out through a corner of the windshield on the far side of the cab. The truck plunged off the road again into the cemetery on the right, apparently when the guerrillas shot out a tire. Vann fought the vehicle back to the tarmac once more and thought he was free of the ambush when he heard a new burst of firing from behind. He turned to see three more guerrillas shooting at him. They were probably a second element of the ambush party who had been overconfident about the skill of the main group and had relaxed their readiness enough for him to dash past before they could begin firing.

He was still going so fast that he had to brake hard at a police checkpoint three-quarters of a mile down the road. One of the policemen came running up to the truck with a first-aid kit, but as far as Vann could tell his only wounds were scores of tiny cuts from the bits of flying glass on his right arm and hand that had been holding the top of the steering wheel and on his head and on his chest where his open shirt formed a V. He indicated fifteen guerrillas to the policemen by flashing his hands. They nodded. From their sentry box they had been able to see the last three guerrillas shooting at him.

Vann decided to drive the remaining four and a half miles to Cu Chi right away, riding on the rim of the wheel with the blown tire, in the hope of contacting a couple of helicopter gunships that had been over the vicinity late that morning. It took the district advisor half an hour to raise the aircraft on the radio, and the pilots could see nothing when they reached the ambush site. In the meantime Vann described the ambush to Hanh and the district chief and then joined Hanh's convoy to Bau Trai after putting on the spare tire. The ARVN medic at the province headquarters cleaned the glass from the cuts (there were about a hundred of them) and painted them with disinfectant in time for Vann to have lunch with the visiting USIA official.

The ambush had obviously not been a happenstance. There was only one vehicle in Hau Nghia painted canary yellow. The smile and the goodbye wave from the guerrilla who decided to leave Vann to the ambush party and the fact that the ambushers opened fire as soon as they sighted the pickup showed that they had been after him or Ramsey.

He guessed that he was the target because he was the senior man and Hau Nghia was so overpopulated with informers that the guerrillas would have had little trouble learning about his appointments and guessing his likely route that morning. Although he could never prove it, he suspected he had been set up by the contractor or the Cu Chi district chief, whose graft from building materials he had also begun to pinch. He was sure the two men were involved in contraband dealings with the guerrillas or were paying the Viet Cong a percentage of their graft as protection money, or both. It would have been a simple thing for either man to have requested his death. The best surmise is that the request came from the contractor. The man was to play both sides during a subsequent career as a Saigon newspaper publisher and politician and thus probably had better lines to the Viet Cong in Hau Nghia in 1965 than the district chief. He certainly had more reason to want Vann dead. Hanh canceled the last of his contracts the day after the ambush.

John Vann did not change his driving habits, but he did change the color of the pickup. He had it repainted blue. He also began traveling with a carbine slung across his lap and several grenades on the seat beside him. He had lived, he knew, because of the accidental swerve into the ambushers and because they had been such poor shots. He calculated that they had fired 150 to 200 rounds in all, and he could count only four bullet holes through the metal of the truck, including one through the door on his side. A lot more bullets had come through the windshield. The interior of the cab was damaged from bullets ricocheting off the inner roof and sides. Yet the ambushers' overall performance had been bad marksmanship. Even the submachine gunners had fired from the hip in gangster-movie style instead of taking aim.

The little truck had also saved him by proving to be as tough as he was. The mechanics at the USOM motor pool in Saigon discovered while repairing it that every engine mount had snapped in two from the jolt of plunging off the road at high speed, but neither the steering nor the engine power had been affected.

Vann savored besting the guerrillas as much as he did his encounter with mortal danger. He wrote in his diary that night: "Drove thru the ambush—must have been embarrassing to VC—that many men failing to get one vehicle & driver. Close!"

His small victory over the ambushers and the contractor seems to have spurred Vann on toward the development of a formal proposal for the strategy he had been discussing with Ramsey and with Bumgardner and

Scotton. Most of his writing time went into official reports. The absence of diary entries for the month of July indicates the extent to which he was putting what personal writing time he allowed himself into the shaping of a draft. He was also being spurred on by a White House announcement on July 8 that Henry Cabot Lodge would be returning to South Vietnam later in the summer to replace Maxwell Taylor as ambassador. Vann had great expectations of leadership from Lodge and hopes for himself too because of his political and personal acquaint-anceship with the ambassador.

Vann's emotions and those of the three other men were also impelling them to try to devise something better than a higher level of violence with no hope of a meaningful conclusion. The war had reached the point, they agreed, where only blind men could claim that continuing it indefinitely was in the interest of the Vietnamese. As bad as a Com-munist Vietnam would be—and Vann and his friends envisioned it as a place of Maoist agricultural communes where even marital sex would be state-supervised—it would be a lesser evil than torturing these peas-ants with endless war.

One incident in particular stood out for Vann and Ramsey. It occurred at the end of April, on the afternoon of the day the Ranger company was overrun at So Do. A young peasant woman and her two children and two of her friends and their children were cutting sugar cane in a field about a mile away. VNAF and U.S. Air Force fighter-bombers had been called out, as they invariably were after such debacles by the Saigon side, and were over the area with spotter planes looking for the long-gone guerrillas. Two fighter-bombers made a pass over the sugar-cane field. To try to indicate that they were not Viet Cong, the women and her friends and the children did not run. The planes made several more passes and the women and their children kept cutting cane, hoping that their innocence would be recognized. On the next pass the planes dropped napalm. The young woman was the only survivor of the eight in the field. Vann and Ramsey found out what had happened when she walked into Bau Trai for treatment at the dispensary and they questioned her. Both of her arms were burned so badly they were going to have to be amputated. She would never be able to close her eyes to sleep again because her eyelids had been scorched away. She was eight months pregnant with another child, but she was not going to be able to nurse her baby. The nipples of her breasts had been burned off.

The Viet Cong were also becoming less discriminating. Discipline was harder to maintain with the recruiting of more and more men, and bigger and more sophisticated weapons entailed less discrimination. When Bau

Trai was mortared during the attack on the Ranger company, a shell crashed through the roof of the province jail and exploded in its single large cell, killing eight of the prisoners and wounding twenty-six others. Many of the dead and wounded were captured guerrillas. Near the end of July, when Vann was well into the first draft of his strategy proposal, another of those atrocities occurred that revolted him and Ramsey. Eleven civilians, three of them children, were literally blown to pieces when a triwheel Lambretta minibus in which they were riding on the road from Cu Chi to Bau Trai ran over a new type of antitank mine the guerrillas had started to plant. The old-fashioned Viet Cong mine permitted discrimination because it had to be triggered by a man using a hand detonator attached to control wires. This new type was the sort employed by modern armies. It had a pressure detonator, probably American-made and captured or bought from ARVN stocks, that was set off by the weight of a vehicle passing over it. The Viet Cong had intended to blow up an M-113 armored personr   They blew up the Lambretta because, loaded down as it was   eight of the driver and his ten passengers and all of their baggage and farm produce, the vehicle was heavy enough to trigger the detonator. The ferocious twenty kilograms of TNT the guerrillas put into such mines to be certain of demolishing an M-113 ensured that no one would survive. The explosion blasted a crater in the middle of the road seven feet wide and three and a half feet deep.

Vann saw that Hanh exploited the atrocity for propaganda purposes, including the staging of a rally against the Viet Cong in a village center near the scene. The propagandizing was unnecessary. The relatives and friends of the dead spent days searching the swamp around the site to be certain that no part of a body was left unburied. They picked up the twisted remnants of the Lambretta and placed them beside the road as a temporary memorial, arranging the sandals of the victims around the shards of metal and lighting candles there. Later they returned and built a small shrine at the spot and kept a candle lit within it. In a demonstration of the quality of intelligence the farmers could provide when they wanted to, the culprits were caught. They were five turncoat militiamen stationed at an outpost 400 yards farther down the road. The chief of the outpost was one of the traitors. He had supervised the planting of the mine. Hanh had all five court-martialed and shot by a firing squad in the marketplace of the village center.

Despite their conclusion that ordinary Vietnamese would benefit most from a quick end to the war and despite the grisly sights they witnessed daily, Vann and Ramsey, and Bumgardner and Scotton as well, did not want the United States to stop the war and give up the country. While they were concerned with reducing pain and suffering as much as possible, they believed with equal firmness that there was no choice but to sacrifice the Vietnamese peasants for the higher strategic needs of the United States. On this point they were in accord with the leaders in Washington whom they served. John McNaughton, a former Harvard law professor who was McNamara's foreign policy specialist as the assistant secretary of defense for international security affairs, had summarized the Washington view in a memorandum he wrote for McNamara that March. Writing in the efficiency-expert style that was in fashion, McNaughton quantified the reasons that justified sending American soldiers to wage a war in South Vietnam:

70%—To avoid a humiliating U.S. defeat (to our reputation as a guarantor).
20%—To keep SVN (and the adjacent) territory from Chinese hands.
10%—To permit the people of SVN to enjoy a better, freer way of life.

The sacrifice of another people for one's own higher strategic aims is a fearful thing when one is living in the midst of those being sacrificed. To Vann and his friends the sacrifice was too cold-blooded unless the Vietnamese were to receive some benefit in return, some reward to redeem the violence. They also believed wholeheartedly that to disregard the welfare of the Vietnamese peasantry was to disregard the long-term interest of Americans.

Vann had the first draft of the strategy proposal ready by the second week of August. Ramsey and Bumgardner and Scotton approved it, and he distributed the paper to others for comment. The comments and the results of more late-night sessions in Bau Trai and Saigon were incorporated into a final draft of ten pages that he typed and signed a month later. Although Vann did not name his friends as coauthors, he did not claim sole credit either. He said in the introduction that the proposal had a number of authors with "a wide range of backgrounds and expertise" whose "common bond is a combination of field experience in Vietnam and a continuing belief that a viable, non-Communist, democratically oriented government can yet emerge there." The final draft was dated September 10, 1965.

The American ground war in the South was beginning in earnest. The Viet Cong had launched their campaign to finish off the Saigon regime with an offensive in the southern Highlands and along the Central Coast in late spring. By early summer they were annihilating ARVN battalions as a blast furnace consumes coke. By mid-July the survival of the regime had become so precarious that Johnson granted a request from Westmoreland for nearly 200,000 U.S. troops to hold on to the country. McNamara came out to Saigon to learn how many more men the general thought he would need to win a war against the guerrillas and the reinforcements they had begun to receive from Hanoi's regulars, the NVA. Westmoreland estimated that he would require another 100,000. He reserved the right to ask for additional troops later should further need arise. Johnson said that Westmoreland could have these 100,000 men too. Army, Marine Corps, and Air Force units were arriving as fast as they could be dispatched. More Navy carriers steamed into position off the southern coast to lend the support of their fighter-bombers. They were dubbed the "Dixie Station" carriers to distinguish them from the carriers already on "Yankee Station" in the Gulf of Tonkin above the 17th Parallel to bomb the North. By Christmas 1965, Westmoreland was to have almost 185,000 Americans in South Vietnam.

In the latter half of August, a week after Vann completed his initial draft, the Marines fought the first battle of this new American war. They took on the 1st Viet Cong Regiment in a warren of fortified hamlets and rice paddies boxed by hedgerows and bamboo thickets on the Central Coast in northern Quang Ngai, the home province of Ho's disciple, Pham Van Dong. The guerrilla regulars had moved into the area to attack an expeditionary airfield the Marines had built on a stretch of beach just across the border in adjacent Quang Tin Province. (Victor Krulak, now wearing three stars as commanding general of the Fleet Marine Force Pacific, had picked the site for the airfield the previous year in a bit of forethought. He had also given it a name after discovering that the beach had none. He had named it with a souvenir of his years as a lieutenant in Shanghai, calling it Chu Lai, the phonetics of the Chinese characters for his name.) Two battalions of Marines assaulted from the sea and landed behind the guerrillas from helicopters. They went after the Viet Cong with tanks mounting conventional cannon and flamethrowers, armored amphibian tractors, and another tracked killer known as the Ontos with four 106mm recoilless cannon on its armored hull.

At a word over the radio, the 5-inch guns of the Seventh Fleet destroyers *Orleck* and *Prichett* and the 8-inchers in the turrets of the cruiser *Galveston* shattered the horizon. The Marine howitzers and the big mortars ashore also responded to the calls. The barrels burned from hurling thousands of shells. The air overhead was never empty of fighter-bombers from five Marine squadrons, because Marine riflemen, the "grunts" as they called themselves in these Vietnam years, do not depend for air support on the vagaries of the Air Force or on the regular Navy planes from the carriers. The Marines have their own air force, and Marine aviators are masters at blasting a way for the infantry. The A-4 Skyhawks and F-4 Phantom jets flashed in "on the deck"—Viet Cong machine guns be damned—the pilots laying the bombs and napalm on target and rocketing and strafing within 200 feet of their brothers in need.

Most of those guerrillas who could still do so slipped out between the Marine positions after dark on the first day. All organized resistance ceased by the evening of the second. One battalion of the 1st Viet Cong Regiment had been reduced to a frightened remnant and another battalion badly hurt. The Marines claimed to have killed 614 guerrillas and to have captured 109 weapons. The price was 51 Marines dead and 203 wounded. Three amtraks (armored amphibious tractors) and two tanks were knocked out by recoilless cannons and grenades, and a number of others were damaged. The helicopters had lots of bullet holes.

I got back to South Vietnam in time to fly up to the battlefield the day after the fighting. I had left the UPI after my first two years in Vietnam, gone to work for the New York Times, and been sent to Indonesia as the paper's correspondent there. Charlie Mohr, who had resigned from Henry Luce's Time magazine in 1963 after it attacked the resident Vietnam correspondents, had become Saigon bureau chief for the Times in the summer of 1965. He asked me to return to cover the war with him. R. W. "Johnny" Apple, Jr., joined us later. The Marines spoke with amazement of the stamina of their new enemy. There was a brigadier general at the battlefield command post, a short man with a pencil mustache named Frederick Karch, a veteran of Saipan and Iwo Jima and other islands of World War II. I asked him if he had been surprised. "I thought that once they ran up against our first team they wouldn't stand and fight," he said. "I made a miscalculation."

Vann thought that with the blood of American soldiers about to be shed in large quantities, their leaders in Saigon and Washington might feel compelled to face up at last to the failings of the Saigon regime and to the U.S. "mistakes of the past twenty years," as he said in his proposal for a new strategy. He entitled the ten-page proposal "Harnessing the Revolution in South Vietnam." The idea was to gain the sympathy of the peasants by capturing the social revolution from the Communists and harnessing it to the American cause. The short-range goal was to utilize this peasant support to destroy the Viet Cong. The long-range goal was to foster the creation of a different kind of government in Saigon, "a national government . . . responsive to the dynamics of the social revolution," a South Vietnamese government that could endure after the American soldiers had fought and the living had gone home.

U.S. policy in South Vietnam had been blind and destructive, Vann said, because, ironically, Americans had been inhibited by their image of themselves as a people who opposed colonialism and championed self-determination. "Apparently, for fear of tarnishing our own image, we have refused to become overtly involved in the internal affairs of governing to the extent necessary to insure the emergence of a government responsive to a majority of its people," he wrote. "It is a scathing indictment of our political awareness that we have sat idly by while many patriotic and non-Communist Vietnamese were literally forced to ally themselves with a Communist-dominated movement in the belief that it was their only chance to secure a better government."

Vann then laid out a program to start an American-stimulated process of social change, a "positive alternative" that could appeal to the majority of the peasantry and gradually split off from the guerrilla movement "the true patriots and revolutionaries now allied to it." He presented the program as an experiment, because he hoped that moving into the strategy with a step rather than a leap might help overcome resistance to the thought of behaving like a colonial power.

The experiment would begin in January 1966, when three or more provinces would be selected and isolated from the warlordism of the Saigon side. A separate chain of command would be set up directly from Saigon to the chiefs of the experimental provinces, bypassing the corps and division commanders. The province chief would become supreme in his domain. The civilian ministries and the armed forces would send him qualified personnel to serve as district chiefs and to staff the province and district governments, but he could dismiss anyone at any time and choose a replacement. He would control all funds and material aid that entered the province and administer them through flexible and simplified procedures that would be drawn up for the experimental provinces. He would also control all military units stationed in his province, including regular ARVN. The division and corps commanders could give him orders only during interprovincial operations, and care would be taken to see that these did not disrupt pacification programs.

The chiefs of the experimental provinces were to be granted independence from the Saigon warlords so that their American advisors could direct them from behind the scenes. The advisory effort was to be drastically reorganized, too, in order to be certain that the direction given was effective. The confusion and lack of common sense in the pacification programs of the Saigon ministries were mirrored in the behavior of the different American agencies in South Vietnam. In theory, AID had primary responsibility for the civilian pacification program. In fact, the CIA and USIS ran their own uncoordinated programs. Westmoreland's MACV headquarters in turn administered a separate military pacification effort. Vann wanted a unified advisory structure in the test provinces. All of the American advisors, whether civilian or military, were to be pulled together into a team under a team leader who would be the senior American advisor for the province and the counterpart of the province chief. He could be either a civilian or a military man, Vann said, but he should be selected with a care equal to the importance of his position. Given the control he would exercise over the province chief, the senior American advisor would be the real governor of the province.

In another ploy to try to gain acceptance by promoting his scheme as an experiment, Vann suggested a three-year test for the strategy in the three or more provinces selected "with the hope that highly successful results might dictate expansion sooner." He was personally convinced progress would be so rapid that the program would soon be applied all over South Vietnam. With the material benefits it could offer, the United States could generate an astonishing reaction from the peasantry once corruption was eliminated and the American millions were getting down to the poor instead of being siphoned into the feeding trough of the Saigon hogs.

Vann and his friends thought there was still time for the United States to steal the social revolution from the Communists because they had been struck by how shallow Viet Cong domination was in many parts of the countryside. This "thinness of control," as Vann referred to it, was the major reason he and Ramsey were able to move around Hau Nghia with such relative freedom. Bumgardner and Scotton had often been surprised by the same thing elsewhere. The guerrillas had progressed so rapidly since 1963 that in large areas they had not yet had an opportunity to train enough village and hamlet administrators and to indoctrinate the population sufficiently to solidify their rule. Vann and Ramsey noticed the difference when they went into the old rubber-plantation sections of Cu Chi District, where there had been Communist organizing among the plantation workers before World War II and the Viet Minh had found a ready base against the French. No children laughed and shouted for gum and candy in these hamlets. Everyone, adult and child, had a cold look. Vann and Ramsey never dared to stay more than a few minutes. These peasants were as sensitive to Americans being their enemies as they had been to the French. As Ramsey was to put it, the pattern of struggle under Party leadership had gone on "long enough for what was in the mold to set."

In much of the rest of Hau Nghia, the population did not seem so strongly bonded to the Viet Cong that they could not be weaned away with the right program of opportunity and material incentives. However antagonistic they might be to the Saigon soldiery and other representatives of the regime, and whatever they might think of the United States as a nation, they were friendly to individual Americans. They seemed to regard Americans as decent people of good intentions. At a minimum they were ambivalent, like the schoolteacher at So Do. Vann and Ramsey had sometimes found this to be true even of young men they knew were local guerrillas.

Vann made a plea in his paper to leave the Vietnamese peasants in their homes and on the land they cherished so that their allegiance could be won by bettering their lives and the countryside reconquered through them. His experience with the Strategic Hamlet Program in 1962 and 1963 had taught him that forced relocation was a cruel folly. He was alarmed by a tendency among the American military to think, like Colonel Chinh, the commander of the 25th Division in Hau Nghia, that a quicker and more certain method was to empty the countryside by driving the peasants into refugee camps around the district towns, in effect simply to blow away Mao Tse-tung's sea of the people in which the guerrilla "fish" swam.

To Vann's dismay, Chinh, with the support of the 25th Division advisors, had declared several populated sections of Cu Chi District "free-bombing zones" in August. A helicopter equipped with a loudspeaker flew over them telling the peasants to move out or face the consequences. Vann called the action "idiocy" in his monthly report to USOM headquarters. There were already 8,200 refugees in Hau Nghia surviving on handouts from USOM because the Saigon authorities would do nothing substantial for most of them.

Rollen Anthis had devised the free-bombing-zone system in 1962 as yet another way to generate targets and keep his pilots busy. The corps and division commanders and the province chiefs were encouraged to delineate specific zones of guerrilla dominance in which anything that moved could be killed and anything that stood could be leveled. (The zones were also called "free-strike zones" and "free-fire zones," because they were open to unrestricted artillery and mortar fire and strafing by helicopter machine gunners once they had been marked for free bombing.) By the summer of 1965 the system was being exploited to achieve a measure of destruction Anthis had probably not imagined, expanding constantly as more and more Viet Cong-held regions were marked off with red lines on the maps. Anthis had usually contented himself with sparsely populated areas. Now, as in Cu Chi, well-populated sections were among those being condemned.

Moreover, the free-bombing zones were only an indication of what was occurring. Many other guerrilla-controlled areas were being treated in virtually the same way, even though they had not yet been officially condemned, through the "preplanned strike" system for "interdiction" bombing that Anthis had also put in place. At the end of August 1965, the U.S. Air Force announced it had destroyed 5,349 "structures" in South Vietnam that month and damaged 2,400 others. In August, USOM headquarters had transferred Ramsey temporarily to Binh Dinh, the most heavily populated province on the Central Coast, to help with the mass of refugees flowing out of the countryside there. Of an estimated 850,000 people in the province, about 85,000 had fled their homes, primarily to escape the bombing and shelling. Ramsey had written Vann that he was running into stories of air strikes in Binh Dinh "which make anything in Hau Nghia pale into insignificance."

The official explanation in Washington was that the homeless were "refugees from Communism" who were "voting with their feet." Some, mainly Catholics and the families of militiamen, were fleeing the Viet Cong. The talk in the upper levels of the embassy and MACV and USOM was that while the flow of refugees was a temporary embarrassment, the refugees were a long-term "asset" because they were now under Saigon's "control." They could be cared for and indoctrinated and someday sent back to rebuild their homes as loyal citizens, or given vocational training and jobs in small industrial parks that could be built on the sites of the shanty-town camps that were springing up. Ramsey had written Vann that he disagreed. "No one is about to convince me that such conglomerations of demoralized people are an asset under any conditions of amelioration USOM has brought itself to accept," he said.

Wholesale dislocation of the peasantry would only worsen the problems the United States faced in South Vietnam, Vann warned in his strategy proposal, and it was profoundly unjust. "We . . . have naively expected an unsophisticated, relatively illiterate, rural population to recognize and oppose the evils of Communism, even when it is cleverly masked by front organizations," he wrote. "We have damned those who did not give wholehearted support to GVN without seriously questioning whether GVN was so constituted or motivated that it could expect loyalty and support from its people." As an example of the unthinking cruelty reflected in the American attitude, Vann quoted a remark by one of the 25th Division advisors to justify Chinh's action in Cu Chi District. "If these people want to stay there and support the Communists, then they can expect to be bombed," the advisor had said.

With the commitment of the American soldier, such ignorance entailed cruelty to Americans too. To persist in it was to risk the unacceptable, that "a successful military venture will be negated by a continued failure of GVN to win its own people." The American soldier was merely buying time, Vann warned. "The major challenge now facing the U.S. in Vietnam" was to use that time to break the Communist monopoly on social revolution. The United States therefore had the right to act as a benevolent colonial power and push the current regime aside precisely because the need for change was so imperative. "Every effort should be made to 'sell' " the Saigon generals and politicians on the wisdom of the program he was proposing and enlist their cooperation in reforming their society, Vann wrote, but "if this cannot be done without compromising the principal provisions of the proposal, then GVN must be forced to accept U.S. judgment and direction. The situation is now too critical and the investment too great for us to longer tolerate a directionless and floundering effort that is losing the population, hence the war."

Undaunted by the impenetrable fantasies of Paul Harkins, by Maxwell Taylor's lack of curiosity at the lunch, by the canceled briefing for the Joint Chiefs, John Vann set out once more to persuade those he served to fight the war in Vietnam his way. He got some encouragement this time from men in influential positions. He had come a distance from the Army lieutenant colonel at My Tho. Although he was still a small figure in the world of public men, he was a personality in Vietnam, thanks to Halberstam. He represented forthrightness and integrity even to those in the bureaucracy who also regarded him as an obsessed maverick. His reputation and his continuing exploits naturally attracted the newsmen, and, having learned the advantages of access to the press at 7th Division, he did not turn them away.

I was just one of a number of his reporter friends from My Tho days who had returned to the war. Mert Perry, who had resigned from *Time* in 1963 along with Charlie Mohr, was back in the country reporting for

Newsweek when Vann was ambushed in June. He went out to Bau Trai shortly afterward. The result was a four-column feature in *Newsweek* in late July captioned "This Is All Bad News Country," with photographs of Hanh, of a lanky Ramsey striding down the dirt street of Bau Trai, and of Vann in front of a thatched cottage in a hamlet, his features set in an earnest look. The major-league columnists who arrived to write about this new American war began to make Vann a regular stop on their itineraries. Scotty Reston of the *Times* came to spend a day with him in August. Bernard Fall, the Franco-American scholar of Vietnam who was to be killed there two years later, spent three days with him, and they became friends.

Newsmen were drawn to Vann, partly because with him there was always the possibility of the unexpected. Edward Morgan of ABC News was interviewing him on camera one morning in front of a new school at the south end of Bau Trai where a teacher-training program was in progress. Mortar fire and bombing could be heard in the distance. Morgan, harking for action, called attention to the explosions. Vann had just begun to explain that the teachers and pupils weren't disturbed, because the sounds of war were part of life in Hau Nghia, when three Viet Cong snipers decided to harass the policemen at the road checkpoint 200 feet or so away. Incoming bullets snapped by the school, the policemen and several soldiers fired back, and a howitzer crew at the artillery park farther into town—whose state of nerves was typical of the Saigon soldiery—started wildly shooting off their 105mm gun. Teachers, pupils, Morgan, and Vann took cover. The cameramen took cover too, but filmed all they could without getting shot. Morgan and his crew were delighted at their "good luck" in acquiring some real war footage to enliven a documentary on pacification.

Some of Vann's superiors in USOM frowned on his freewheeling relationship with the press and let him know it. Their disapproval convinced him to cultivate the relationship all the more. He had decided that he could never again depend on any bureaucracy for his rise as he had depended on the Army. He had made himself an outsider by leaving the Army. His climb would therefore have to be a singular one. He would have to take risks that other men were unwilling to take, because he would have to defeat the system in order to scale it. The news media were an ally in this simultaneous struggle to advance himself and to sell his ideas. His easy access to the reporters might make the bureaucrats jealous of the limelight they were afraid to seek and arouse their distrust for fear that he might leak something embarrassing, but it also intimidated them and gave him the kind of independence and protection he had unwittingly gained against Harkins. Publicity brought prestige, lent him a certain cachet. It made important people willing to listen to him whether they accepted what he had to say at the moment or not.

He was offered a supervisory post on the staff at USOM headquarters in July. He turned it down and also talked his way out of a promotion to deputy director for the whole of the Mekong Delta that summer, because the jobs would have hidden him behind a desk. "The field," he wrote to a friend in Denver, ". . . happens to be the element I am most at home in, and the one place I will attract the most attention."

Vann hoped to sell "Harnessing the Revolution in South Vietnam" through the contacts he had been building up over the past two years. Westmoreland had been cordial to him, inviting Vann that summer to come to Saigon and pass along his impressions on returning to Vietnam. Vann had done so at the beginning of July, briefing Westmoreland and his deputy, Lt. Gen. John Throckmorton, for well over an hour at MACV headquarters. Nevertheless, Vann decided that, given the radical nature of his proposal, he would be better off if someone high in Westmoreland's headquarters did his selling for him. He had in mind Westmoreland's new chief of staff, Gen. (then Maj. Gen.) William Rosson, who had a long acquaintance with Vietnam.

Rosson had first seen Saigon in the year of the French defeat as a lieutenant colonel and principal aide to the head of the MAAG in 1954, Lt. Gen. John "Iron Mike" O'Daniel. He had cooperated with Lansdale when Lansdale had installed Diem as America's fresh beginning. He and Vann had met at the Pentagon in 1963 while Rosson was concluding an assignment as head of Special Warfare for the Army. Rosson had been one of the generals in the building who had listened to Vann, because he had been incredulous at Harkins's pronouncements. They had renewed acquaintance when Vann had called on him after briefing Westmoreland in July. Vann had mentioned some of the ideas on pacification he was developing in Hau Nghia. As the new chief of staff at MACV, Rosson was under extreme pressure, but he had promised to take a helicopter out for a visit as soon as he could break away for a couple of hours.

In the second week of August, right after the first draft of his strategy paper was completed, Vann sent a copy to Rosson. He received a note from Rosson at the end of the month. "Be alert to receipt of expressions of interest from important quarters," Rosson said. Vann took the "important quarters" to mean that Rosson was attempting to sell his ideas to Westmoreland. Rosson also urged him to submit the proposal formally through USOM channels, which Vann did as soon as the final draft was finished on September 10.

For a proposal submitted by a man who was officially just a province representative, the paper also reached some unusually senior people on the civilian side. An acquaintance at AID Washington to whom Vann mailed the first draft for comment passed a copy up to Rutherford Poats, a former United Press International newsman and executive who had become AID chief for the Far East. Poats in turn sent copies to William Bundy, who had succeeded Roger Hilsman as assistant secretary of state for Far Eastern affairs, and to Leonard Unger, Bundy's deputy and head of the Vietnam Task Force, the Washington committee to coordinate the work of the various government departments involved in the war. Poats said in a letter, a carbon of which he was kind enough to send Vann, that the paper gave the Viet Cong "more credit for a legitimate social objective than I would" and that he was not recommending "the proposed pilot 'solution.' " Just the same, Poats said, Vann's analysis "strikes me as a good description of the problem" and the proposal contained "some useful ideas." Vann was not discouraged by this kind of reaction. To him it meant that the door was at least not barred.

Of all his high-level connections, Vann was counting most on Lodge, who arrived at Tan Son Nhut on August 20, 1965, to replace Taylor and begin his second round as the president's representative in Saigon. The Henry Cabot Lodge whom Vann had gotten to know after he organized a "Lodge for President" movement in Colorado was a public man with a highly personal *modus operandi* who delegated unusual authority to a subordinate he trusted. The most recent recipient of that authority had been another brilliant Army officer of Vann's generation and a friend and classmate at the Command and General Staff College at Fort Leavenworth, Lt. Col. John Michael Dunn.

Mike Dunn was an Irishman in the Robert Kennedy image—a smile that is supposed to connote an altar boy and a pair of brass knuckles in his pocket. He was a Harvard graduate who had been drawn to an Army career by the challenge of the post–World War II American adventure. He had won his combat credentials in Korea with a Silver Star for Gallantry and had earned his intellectual credentials at Princeton with a Ph.D in international relations. When Lodge had come to Saigon in 1963 on his first tour as ambassador he had brought Dunn along to be his personal assistant. He had given Dunn power and all the latitude to exercise it that Dunn could handle, which was a great deal indeed, during the maneuvers to overthrow Diem and in the tussles afterward to see that Lodge continued to have his way against Harkins. Dunn had been such a formidable executor of Lodge's wishes that after Lodge had gone home in 1964 and Dunn had returned to Washington and the Army, Harkins had started proceedings against him for a general court-martial.

Westmoreland had also taken umbrage at a lieutenant colonel feisty enough to unhorse a general for a civilian superior. He had joined Harkins in the accusations. One charge was the equivalent of making false reports. Lodge had stood by Dunn. He had said he would testify that Dunn's every act had been performed on his authority, and if the proceedings went forward, he was going to insist on bringing the entire matter out in public. Harold Johnson, by then chief of staff of the Army, had summoned Dunn to his office and told him to regard the proceedings, which were being dropped, as a misunderstanding. He was not to think that Harkins and Westmoreland were being vindictive, Johnson had said. They had merely been overzealous in seeking to protect the interests of the Army.

Vann assumed that during his second turn at the ambassadorship, Lodge was going to emulate his first year in Vietnam and take an individual and imaginative approach to the war. Vann wanted to be the Mike Dunn of that enterprise. He had written Lodge in July, shortly after the White House announcement that Lodge would be returning, and given the ambassador a careful summary of his learning experience in Hau Nghia. He had proposed that Lodge create a special Field Liaison Office. Its purpose would be to keep the ambassador accurately informed on pacification and military operations by enabling him to get his information "*without* the interpretations of many intervening echelons." The office would consist of just one or two men. They would have the authority to go anywhere Lodge designated, observe and ask questions, and report directly to him. Vann proposed that he head the office, citing his "unique combination of both military and civilian experience" in Vietnam and his conviction that he could serve "as a practical sounding board for [Lodge's] ideas and programs." The Field Liaison Office would, in short, be John Vann and an assistant.

While noncommittal, Lodge's reply was friendly and heartening to Vann:

Dear John:
    I am glad to get your letter, which gives me much to think about. I look forward to seeing you when I return and talking it all over.
    With warm regards,

Sincerely yours,
Henry Cabot Lodge

If Lodge did not accept his "Harnessing the Revolution" strategy or some variation of it as the course to be adopted right away, Vann thought, the ambassador might still offer him the special assistant's job he had proposed, because he was so well qualified for it. He would then have an opportunity to gradually sell his strategy ideas to Lodge in the course of keeping him informed of what was happening on the battlefield and in the hamlets. He waited for a call from the embassy with great impatience after Lodge's arrival on August 20.

A bureaucratic ban on Lansdale's presence in South Vietnam had also been lifted as a result of Lodge's return, and Lansdale came back at the beginning of September for another attempt to save the country he had brought into being ten years before. He visited Vann in Bau Trai a couple of days after arriving and brought along the team he had assembled to help him in his renewed endeavor. One member was a thirty-four-year-old Defense Department intellectual and former Marine named Daniel Ellsberg. Lansdale's charter was vague. He and his team were officially supposed to act as a special liaison group between the embassy and the Saigon government's Rural Reconstruction Council, a body that in theory coordinated the pacification programs of all the ministries.

Vann had been alerted to expect an invitation to join the Lansdale team. Lansdale did not extend the offer that day, and in any case Vann thought he would decline the invitation when it was extended. His aspirations had outgrown Lansdale, and he was uncertain how much influence Lansdale was going to have in this South Vietnam of September 1965. For all his crusading and egocentricity, Vann had a keen sense of the realities of government. Lansdale would have no agency under his control with money and manpower to lend him weight in a world where bureaucracies and the men who ran them were going to compete and clash. Lodge had real power, with which Vann could accomplish something if he could gain a role in wielding it. "I'll have to know one helluva lot more about what Lansdale's plans are before I tie in with him," he wrote a friend in Denver on the night of Lansdale's visit. "I am still waiting for a call from Lodge, and I'm not about to jump until I find out what his ideas may be."

The call came in a few days. Vann put on a suit and tie for the occasion, quite a contrast to the blue jeans and short-sleeved sports shirt that had become his working garb. He also had a freshly typed copy of the final draft of "Harnessing the Revolution" in his hand when he took the elevator up to Lodge's office on the sixth floor of the embassy. The building had been refurbished and fitted with shatterproof windows since the huge car bomb Vann had missed by ten minutes on his last visit five and a half months and a lot of learning ago. The blast had also shattered the official unwillingness to show fear and given the embassy more resemblance to one of the regime's ministries. The traffic on the busy Saigon riverfront streets was now kept a block away in all directions by barricades of barbed wire stretched across welded iron frames.

Lodge was friendly and seemed pleased to see Vann, but apologized that they would have to keep the visit short because his schedule was still so crowded with the business of his return. After the pleasantries Vann had time only to hand Lodge the proposal and explain that he and his friends had devised this strategy to win the war from their collective experience in the field and that he hoped Lodge would find what he had written persuasive. Lodge said that he was glad to have the paper and would read it. Vann mentioned his Field Liaison Office idea. Lodge was again noncommittal. He promised Vann a "lengthy chat" soon and said that in the meantime Vann should hold down the risks he was taking in Hau Nghia, that he was too valuable a man to lose.

Later that week Vann ran into two political officers from the embassy. Lodge had sent the paper to the political section for comment. The two political officers told Vann that he was "out of line" as a USOM province representative to be handing papers on grand strategy to the ambassador. What did they think of the ideas in the proposal? Vann asked. They refused to say.

Vann was not upset. Theirs was the attitude he expected from bureaucrats. "I make nearly all the professional staff people in there [Saigon] damned uneasy," he said in another of his letters to a friend at home. He would wait for his serious talk with Lodge. "Someone must be a catalyst if our policies are to be even remotely dynamic," he wrote to an acquaintance at the Pentagon.

General Rosson kept his promise to break away for a couple of hours from his duties as Westmoreland's chief of staff and flew out to Bau Trai for a briefing by Vann. He restated his approval of the ideas in Vann's proposal. James Killen was being replaced as head of USOM in Vietnam by Charles Mann, who had been running AID operations in Laos. Mann was due in Bau Trai for a visit the third weekend of September. Vann hoped to make a convert of him.

He also won what he called "a small but significant victory" in the first half of September. He got unobserved artillery and mortar fire banned in Hau Nghia. Unless the shells were being directed onto a specific target by a ground or air spotter or an outpost or unit was under attack and calling for protective fire, the guns could not shoot. As random firing accounted for most of the firing, there was a sudden and unusual quiet much of the time in Bau Trai and the district centers. Vann had apparently complained about the shelling when he briefed Westmoreland in July, pointing out that it violated a directive forbidding unobserved fire in the provinces around Saigon that Westmoreland had designated for priority pacification. Westmoreland seems to have responded to Vann's complaint by having JGS issue an order forbidding unobserved shelling in Hau Nghia. Colonel Chinh was in a rage over it. He somehow got the idea that Hanh was the instigator and was angrier at him than he was at Vann. The order did not apply to sections that had been declared free-bombing or free-fire zones, and the preplanned air strikes were continuing. John Vann the pragmatist saw half an evil eliminated.

Vann was in trouble in his war on corruption in the province, but he was fighting gamely. Over dinner with Hanh one Sunday evening toward the end of July, about a week after Lyndon Johnson decided to give Westmoreland 200,000 American soldiers to save South Vietnam, he learned that he had a new problem bigger than the crooked contractor. Hanh said he had just been put on notice that he was going to have to start conforming to the generate-the-graft pattern or lose his province-chief job.

The military government presided over by Air Marshal Ky was consolidating its position and turning on the pressure. Hanh's patron in the regime was understandably a fellow Catholic, Nguyen Van Thieu, who had become the chief of state. (Ky held the executive power as prime minister.) Hanh had been told that to remain province chief of Hau Nghia he would have to contribute 250,000 piasters to the "High Command." Hanh told Vann he did not know what was happening in the coastal provinces of Central Vietnam and in the Highlands, but that the squeeze for more graft was occurring all over the IV Corps zone that encompassed the Delta and in III Corps, which included Hau Nghia and the other provinces around the capital. The district chiefs were being dunned for amounts ranging from 100,000 to 300,000 piasters, depending on the wealth of the district.

As usual, the generals' wives were overseeing the transactions. The wife of the IV Corps commander, a rotund brigadier general named Dang Van Quang who was a close ally of Thieu's, had flown up from Can Tho the past week and laid down payment conditions to district chiefs' wives who were living in Saigon. Hanh had been advised that he could embezzle up to 750,000 piasters on this occasion. He was to share the additional 500,000 piasters with the Hau Nghia district chiefs to help them meet their obligations. It was suggested that he submit phony bills for materials provided free by the Americans or hand in budget requests for nonexistent projects.

Hanh wanted Vann to get the demand stopped, naturally without letting on that Hanh was the informant. The next day, Vann had typed up a memorandum listing the main points of the conversation. He had stated that Hanh was the source of the information, to lend the memorandum credibility, but had marked it "Personal and Confidential" and handed it to Wilson after giving him an account of the dinner. He had asked Wilson to pass the memorandum to Killen and to Taylor, still the ambassador at the time, so that the Saigon generals could be told the United States government knew about their games and would no longer tolerate this filth. Wilson was concerned about corruption too. He had said he would pass the memorandum along. Vann had not heard of any action by the time of his brief call on Lodge in early September. He was determined to bring the matter to Lodge's attention himself if he did not hear soon. In the meantime he was encouraging Hanh to stall on embezzling the money.

In late September he flew home to Littleton for a two-week leave. Mary Jane and the children did not see much of him, because he found it difficult to resist invitations to speak about the war. When he wasn't lecturing on the war he tended to be on the phone about it to someone in Washington or to one of his newspaper contacts.

As soon as he returned to Vietnam in October, Charles Mann, the new USOM director, told him that he would be leaving Hau Nghia at the end of the month. He had not, during Mann's weekend visit, converted Mann to his main thesis, but Mann was a practical-minded individual who liked a number of the ideas in Vann's paper. He also liked Vann's dynamism and knowledge and ability to work with the Vietnamese. He was promoting Vann to a more important field position as USOM representative and advisor on civilian affairs to Maj. Gen. (soon to be Lt. Gen.) Jonathan Seaman, the commander of all U.S. forces in the III Corps area. Seaman was in the process of bringing the 1st Infantry Division into South Vietnam. He was going to put "the Big Red One" together with the 173rd Airborne Brigade, which had already arrived, to start forming a U.S. Army corps to subdue the Viet Cong in the eleven-province region. Vann's job would be to advise Seaman on anything affecting the population and to act as a liaison officer in dealing with the province governments and the USOM advisors in each province.

While the promotion was flattering, Vann was sad to leave Hau Nghia. The struggle for the province and its people had become an unfulfilled commitment. He found himself hoping that he could someday return and finish what he had started during the seven months since he had arrived. He had also formed ties of affection. Ramsey was no longer an assistant and interpreter with impressive educational credentials. He was a fondly regarded companion and protégé. Vann's friendship with Hanh had grown into a friendship with Hanh's family too. Whenever he was driving back from Saigon, Vann would offer Mrs. Hanh a ride to Bau Trai so that she could visit her husband. The Hanhs had invited him to meals at their home in the city. He brought candy and trinkets from the PX to the Hanh children so often that they called him Uncle John. The homely schoolteacher at So Do was another of the figures attaching him to Hau Nghia. The school building, the stopping of the unobserved shellfire, the progress so far in his war on corruption had all given him a sense that his perseverance was beginning to result in tangible gain.

Ramsey remembered Vann's last day as province representative. It was November 1, 1965, the anniversary of the overthrow of Diem, which the succeeding Saigon governments had adopted as the country's National Day. Vann had been in Saigon for meetings to prepare for his new job. He drove to Bau Trai for the National Day ceremonies. Ramsey was surprised to see him appear in the white summer dress uniform of a lieutenant colonel. Because the day was a special one, Vann said, he had obtained permission to take the uniform out of his old Army footlocker that he used as a storage trunk. He had his medals pinned on too. Ramsey recalled a few evenings at the office when they had not been lost in a discussion of the war. Vann would find a tape he had of Douglas MacArthur's farewell address to the corps of cadets at West Point and play it on a portable recorder. He would sit and listen reverently as MacArthur spoke of "faint bugles" and "far drums," of "the strange, mournful mutter of the battlefield," of "Duty, Honor, Country." MacArthur's rhetoric and the dress whites said to Ramsey that John Vann would never leave the U.S. Army. Vann had arranged for Ramsey to be designated acting province representative rather than fully succeeding to his job just in case he might be able to return in a few months. That afternoon he packed his belongings, exchanged the white dress uniform for jeans and a sport shirt again, and set off for the 1st Infantry Division's temporary encampment in a city of tents beside the highway near Bien Hoa.

His gains of seven months started to fade within weeks of his departure. The first to go was Hanh's self-respect. When no action had occurred to block the graft demands by the generals, Vann had sent a copy of his memorandum directly to Lodge. But Lodge, apparently after raising the matter with Ky and getting no response, had taken the attitude that this sort of venality was to be expected in South Vietnam and was not worth a ruckus with a government that continued to be fragile. Ramsey and Vann had agreed that if Vann was unable to get the demand stopped, they would have to let Hanh embezzle the money. Ramsey was accordingly on the lookout for a suspicious appropriation. Not long after Vann left the province, a supplemental request for 750,000 piasters for the education program, an amount that matched the graft scheme, came across Ramsey's desk from Hanh's office. The program for the current fiscal year was already fully funded, because of the special effort they had been putting into it. Hanh had also not mentioned to Ramsey that he would be submitting a supplemental. Ramsey picked up the request and walked over to ask Hanh about it. He encountered the province chief on the way. He waved the paper suspiciously and moved it across Hanh's line of vision slowly so that the province chief could read it. Hanh lowered his eyes. Neither man said a word. Ramsey allowed the supplemental to go through without objection. He felt that he and Vann and the U.S. government had let Hanh down and there was nothing else to be done. "We failed him," Ramsey said.

Chinh then succeeded in getting the ban on unobserved shellfire in Hau Nghia lifted. Vann tried to use his connections to have it reimposed and failed. The U.S. commanders wanted to shoot unobserved artillery in Hau Nghia, so-called harassing and interdiction fire, and the privilege could therefore not be denied to the ARVN. The sole permanent result of the ban was to weaken Hanh's position by giving Chinh another grudge to hold against him. Chinh also continued to be irritated with Hanh's performance on kickbacks. Despite having embezzled the 750,000 piasters, Hanh was still refusing to steal enough to satisfy the 25th Division commander.

Worst of all, Vann did not get the promised "lengthy chat" with Lodge, nor could he interest anyone else in high authority in his strategy. "Harnessing the Revolution in South Vietnam" was to become an important document in the history of the war. Many of the individual ideas it contained, such as drawing all the advisors in a province, whether civilian or military, into a single province team under one senior advisor, were to be slowly accepted and incorporated into the pacification effort over subsequent years. The men with the power to set policy showed no interest in Vann's central concept—to behave like a benevolent colonial power and win the war by winning the Vietnamese peasantry through an American-sponsored social revolution.

Vann had misread the note from Lodge that had heartened him. He did not understand the strengths and limitations of Henry Cabot Lodge. He had also misinterpreted the complimentary remarks on his proposal by Rutherford Poats and Poats's move in sending copies of the paper to men like William Bundy and Leonard Unger. He had read things General Rosson had not intended into Rosson's encouraging words. He and Ramsey and Scotton and Bumgardner had a flawed perception of the priorities of those who led them and had altogether miscalculated the effect of full-scale U.S. military intervention. Instead of creating urgency for political and social action, sending American soldiers removed whatever incentive the U.S. government might have had for reform of the Saigon regime.

To Vann and his friends, the resort to American ground combat units was a fateful but inconclusive act in a conflict of steadily diminishing alternatives. They saw it as an opportunity to start a process of political and social change that had to be seized before time and events diminished and then foreclosed it. As U.S. casualties grew, the American public would tire of this war as the public had tired of Korea. Domestic pressure for a negotiated settlement with the Communists would mount. International pressure for negotiations would increase too, they felt, as the level of destruction rose in South and North Vietnam and Washington's allies became less tolerant of American conduct. Accepting the political and social status quo at this point might make it far more difficult, if not impossible, to undertake a subsequent program of radical reform when the lives of many thousands of American soldiers had been spent and reform was most desperately needed for the long-term survival of the South.

To Lyndon Johnson, Robert McNamara, Dean Rusk, and almost every other major figure of the day, the dispatch of the American infantryman was a conclusive step, a solution in itself. Johnson had approached this step with utmost reluctance, delaying it as long as he dared because of the cost in blood and money and the economic competition a war would entail for the social welfare measures of his Great Society program. Once the step had been taken, however, he and the men whose judgment he relied on had no doubt that the invincibility of American arms on the ground in the South, coupled with the air war against the North, would ensure the destruction of their Vietnamese enemy. (The eloquent secret warning to the contrary of George Ball, the under secretary of state, seems ironically to have confirmed the president in the belief that his judgment was correct. Johnson told himself he had heard the most intelligent argument possible against what he was doing and that Ball was wrong.) Even Lodge, who had reason to be wiser, was carried away during the critical opening phase of his second turn in Saigon by the euphoria that all problems would yield to the arrival of the U.S. Army.

The statesmen of the Kennedy-Johnson years had written off the Korean experience as a combination of rashness by MacArthur and unpreparedness. They did not consider themselves rash men, and the nation's armed forces had never been better prepared in a time of technical peace than they were in 1965. These American statesmen could not conceive of going to war and then being forced into negotiations against their advantage. "U.S. killed-in-action might be in the vicinity of five hundred a month by the end of the year," McNamara had told the President in his July 1965 memorandum, but "United States public opinion will support the course of action because it is a sensible and courageous military-political program designed and likely to bring about a success in Vietnam."

As the Pentagon Papers were to reveal, what McNamara meant by political action was a campaign of public relations and diplomacy unrelated to political and social conditions in South Vietnam. The public relations element was designed to maintain support for the war at home and among Washington's allies by giving them the impression that the U.S. government was interested in negotiating a compromise "political settlement." In the meantime, behind-the-curtain diplomacy was to convince Ho and his associates that the United States would not stop bombing North Vietnam and killing Vietnamese Communists and their followers in the South until the Viet Cong laid down their arms and went to the North and all North Vietnamese Army elements sent to reinforce them were withdrawn too.

Westmoreland and his generals reflected still more markedly this attitude of "Worry no longer, the American soldier has come." Vann had deliberately confined the military aspect of his strategy paper to the handling of forces within a province, omitting his ideas for a "joint command" and other steps to transform the Saigon military as a whole. He was not alone in holding these ideas, of course, and he assumed Westmoreland might listen more receptively if they came from a respected figure like General York, whom Vann was encouraging to promote them. York had written Vann in June from the Dominican Republic, where he was leading the 82nd Airborne Division in the U.S. intervention under Bruce Palmer, to say he agreed that a "joint command or something similar to what we had in Korea" was "our only hope now" of turning the Saigon troops into an effective force. By the time of Vann's home leave in the fall, York had finished his tour at the head of the 82nd and become commandant of the Infantry School at Fort Benning. They discussed the subject further when York invited Vann down to tell the class of captains, many of them bound for Vietnam as company commanders, what he had learned in Hau Nghia.

As soon as York could, in early 1966, he flew out to Saigon and attempted to persuade Westmoreland to impose a joint command, integrating U.S. officers into all of the Saigon echelons from JGS to the field. In this fashion Westmoreland could achieve quick control over the hundreds of thousands of men Saigon possessed, start to employ them usefully, and multiply his fighting power rapidly. York was worried that if Westmoreland relied solely on American soldiers, Hanoi would checkmate the United States by putting in enough men from its regular army in the North to offset them. The Saigon regime claimed to have 679,000 men under arms, including the RF and PF, in 1965. Allowing an average of a third off for "ghost soldiers" and "potted-tree" warriors still meant roughly 450,000 potential fighters who were currently being squandered.

York also urged Westmoreland to form mixed American-Vietnamese units. He took the idea from an expedient MacArthur had resorted to at the outset of the Korean War. Because trained men from the United States had simply not been available, MacArthur had fed South Korean conscripts, known as KATUSAs (for Korean Augmentation to the U.S. Army), into several of his divisions. Each KATUSA had been assigned to an American "buddy." The language barrier had been overcome relatively quickly, because a soldier needs to know only about 100 words of whatever language is spoken in the army in which he is serving to function as an infantryman. The Army in Korea had developed a pidgin of English, Korean, and Japanese. (A few words of it carried over into Vietnam. For example, any building from a wattle hut to a modern frame structure was called a "hootch," a derivative of a Japanese word for "house," *uchi*.) After seasoning, the units with KATUSAs, some up to 50 percent Korean in the rifle squads, had done nearly as well as the all-American ones.

The acquisition of cheap Asian cannon fodder was not the purpose of York's variation on the KATUSA system. His objective was to lay the basis for a Saigon armed forces worthy of the name by producing Vietnamese officers, noncoms, and soldiers molded in the professionalism of the U.S. Army. He suggested that Westmoreland start with mixed companies in which one of the three platoons would be Vietnamese. The deputy company commander might also be a Vietnamese officer. Keeping the Vietnamese together in a platoon, rather than spreading them through the company as individuals, had the advantage of permitting their officers and noncoms to learn while leading their own troops. Mixed units would be tangible evidence of Vietnamese and Americans fighting side by side against a common enemy, York said, and they would lessen abuse of the peasantry because the Saigon troops could be taught the importance of treating their people properly. The U.S. Army could have an important moral effect on the Saigon soldier and young officer, York felt, an effect that might help to reduce the corruption pervading the Saigon side. For the first time these Vietnamese would live and fight in an army free of graft. They might be different people with different attitudes when they were eventually formed into units all their own.

Westmoreland listened and disregarded everything York said. In his memoirs Westmoreland was to say the major reason he did not create a joint command was that "in the final analysis, I had the leverage to influence the South Vietnamese and they knew it, and both sides exercised a rare degree of tact." Westmoreland did have this potential leverage over his Saigon allies, and he exercised a rare degree of tact. He refrained from using his influence to correct incompetence and corruption so gross that even he acknowledged their existence. He did virtually nothing about these evils for the same reason he did not form a joint command or organize the mixed units York urged him to create. He and nearly all of his generals wanted as little as possible to do with the Vietnamese on their side. Rather than taking over the ARVN and the RF and PF and reforming them, as Vann had hoped he would, in order to have Vietnamese fight a Vietnamese war in the countryside, Westmoreland was intent on shunting the Saigon forces out of the way so that he could win the war with the U.S. Army.

The institutional habits and motivations of the Army of the 1960s were at work. Westmoreland showed them in his response to a further suggestion by York that he economize on American manpower by employing Vietnamese soldiers in such service roles as truck drivers. No, Westmoreland said, he had to have American truck drivers; a U.S. Army unit could not depend on Vietnamese to move its supplies. The draft had been a fixture of American life since the Korean War brought it back in 1950. Generals like Westmoreland were accustomed to an uninterrupted flow of healthy and patriotic American conscripts, or young men who volunteered for the Army because they were going to be drafted sooner or later anyway. Why invest time and energy in dealing with Vietnamese when one had a readily available source of manpower whose quality could be trusted?

There was another motivation too. Unlike his French and British predecessors in Asia, a U.S. Army officer could not win acclaim at the head of native troops. For him, glory and professional fulfillment could come only by leading American soldiers in war. The one Army organization in Vietnam that employed a large number of native troops was the Special Forces. Significantly, the commander of the Special Forces was always a colonel rather than a general, even though he controlled the equivalent in riflemen of two infantry divisions while the Special Forces were at peak strength—42,000 local mercenaries led by approximately 2,650 American officers, sergeants, and other U.S. enlisted specialists. (Fred Ladd, Vann's friend and colleague in the Mekong Delta, was to command the Special Forces at the height of the war from mid-1967 to mid-1968.) In regular Army formations a brigade of 3,500 men required a colonel to lead it.

Westmoreland's intention was to gradually return the country to the Saigon regime after he had wiped out the Viet Cong and decimated the NVA units sent to the South. He felt no great need for his Saigon allies to accomplish this task. He wanted to use the best of the Saigon soldiery, the paratroops and the marines, and occasionally one of the ordinary ARVN divisions, as adjuncts to the operations of his U.S. troops. Otherwise he cared little about them.

Rosson had not been attempting to sell "Harnessing the Revolution" to Westmoreland. He was a reserved man who distinguished carefully between his personal opinions and what he considered his duty. The chief of staff responds to the wishes of the commander. Westmoreland had instructed Rosson to concentrate on building a logistic structure to support a U.S. expeditionary corps, and that was what Rosson was doing. Although he did not say so to Vann, Rosson considered Vann's central thesis of taking over the Saigon system beyond the possible. He thought the paper valuable just the same, because of the ideas it contained for pacification. Rosson assumed that Lodge was going to use Lansdale to design and launch a major new pacification program. They were the "important quarters" to whom he had been referring when he told Vann to be alert for "expressions of interest."

The commanding general did receive a copy of Vann's proposal, apparently when Charles Mann, the new head of USOM, circulated the final draft. Westmoreland did not react favorably to Vann's main argument. "No one better understood the Vietnamese than John Vann," Westmoreland was to write in his memoirs, "but he had an affinity for sounding off to the press, particularly on the theory that the United States should assume overall command in the manner of the French." Nor did the general perceive any current usefulness in the individual ideas in Vann's proposal.

Westmoreland was fixed like a bore-sighted cannon on the deployment of his U.S. expeditionary force. Men of limited imagination who rise as high as Westmoreland had tend to play blindly to their strength, no matter what its relevance to the problem at hand. Westmoreland's strength was military action. Political and social action, which Vann was talking about and York had been getting at obliquely and which were the crux of pacification, were areas that did not attract the general, because he did not understand them. His interest in pacification had always been low, and it sank lower after Lyndon Johnson said he could have 300,000 Americans.

Vann thought he was pushing on a door that was stuck and might be open . . . He had his shoulder against a wall. He was appealing to an ethic that . . . most American statesmen and military leaders lacked, and he was asking them to discard an anticolonial myth that they found indispensable. Vann, Ramsey, Bumgardner, and Scotton might be at one with the statesmen and generals who led them in seeing the containment of China and other strategic objectives as a justification for the war. They and their leaders parted over the importance attached to the welfare of ordinary Vietnamese. McNaughton's 70/20/10 percent quantification for McNamara was more than a mere ranking of the reasons that the leaders of the United States were going to war in South Vietnam. It also accurately reflected the 10 percent priority they assigned, in McNaughton's words, to bringing "the people of SVN . . . a better, freer way of life."

The British imperial statesman or military leader of the nineteenth century had felt a responsibility to give the native peoples of his empire decent government. His fulfillment of that responsibility had been decidedly imperfect, but what he did achieve was due to the fact that he felt it. The system of spreading empire through surrogate regimes had permitted his American successors to escape this sense of moral obligation. The American wanted to improve the lot of the impoverished populations in his overseas system. Programs like Kennedy's Alliance for Progress in Latin America were an expression of this desire. When progress failed to occur because of institutionalized social injustice and the predatory nature of the surrogate regime, the American had no ethic that compelled him to use the many tools of persuasion and coercion at his disposal on behalf of the downtrodden. He overcame what guilt he did feel by sheltering in the myth that he was dealing with a "sovereign state" and that his ideals of anticolonialism and self-determination forbade him to meddle in internal affairs. The myth became a kind of holy water that washed his expediency clean.

Moreover, the experience in the Caribbean and Central America had created the impression in the American mind that one could employ a surrogate with the vices of the Saigon government and still keep the country in question within the U.S. sphere. The collapse of the Batista regime in Havana in 1958 and the coming of Fidel Castro and the Cuban Communists had not changed this attitude. The impression had a basis in reality in the Caribbean and Central America. Spanish colonialism had left a landed class of some vitality which viewed the exploitation of its Indian, and former black slave, and mestizo peasantry as a divine right. The creole class was willing to cooperate with a big foreign power to maintain that exploitation.

Vann and his friends were sufficiently steeped in the realities of Vietnam to understand that the Saigonese were a socially depraved group with no capacity to reform or sustain themselves. American leaders in Saigon and Washington saw the generals of the junta and the residue of French collaborators and anti-Communist nationalists through the perspective of their sordid Latin surrogates and assumed that these Tory Vietnamese must have some kind of substance. Henry Cabot Lodge, Dean Rusk, and Lyndon Johnson convinced themselves that Nguyen Cao Ky, who had had himself named prime minister by his fellow generals, really was a prime minister of sorts, and that Nguyen Van Thieu, who had connived his way into being appointed chief of state, represented something besides himself and his title. These people might not be the most attractive of allies, but they would prove a serviceable political tool in the struggle with the Communists. Bolstered by the tool of force that the U.S. military constituted, they would suffice.

The new year did not begin well. Hanh was fired in February for continued reluctance to satisfy Chinh's corruption demands. He was made the staff officer for pacification at III Corps headquarters, not much of a job by ARVN standards.

Before that, something worse had happened. Doug Ramsey was captured by the Viet Cong because he tried to carry on the John Vann image in Hau Nghia. He was caught late in the afternoon of January 17, 1966, shortly before the customary cease-fire at Tet, the Vietnamese Lunar New Year holiday, while attempting to hurry a truckload of rice and other emergency food to refugees created by one of the initial operations of the U.S. 1st Infantry Division. The refugees were located at the village center of Trung Lap in the formidable rubber-plantation area of Cu Chi District. A brigade of the 1st Division had established a command post in the ARVN Ranger training camp there.

The four-mile access road to Trung Lap, a dirt affair that ran off Route 1, was considered the most hazardous stretch of road in Hau Nghia, which probably made it the most dangerous road in the whole III Corps region. Hanh told Ramsey that the shipment could wait until the next morning, when travel would be safer. Ramsey was afraid the refugees might be hungry, and he wanted to get the chore out of the way. He had been working by himself in the two and a half months since Vann had left the province, because USOM headquarters had not yet sent him an assistant, and he was behind in a schedule he tended to overload in Vann fashion. He could have sent the Vietnamese driver alone in the five-ton Chevy cargo truck, as he and Vann had commonly done to expedite deliveries. (The USOM drivers had never been harmed and seemed to pay protection money to the Viet Cong as the commercial truck drivers did.) Ramsey wanted to look into the plight of the refugees at Trung Lap, and he had other considerations he thought pressing at the moment, all of them Vann-like, which persuaded him to "ride shot-gun" in the seat beside the driver.

He was ambushed by four local guerrillas less than a mile from the village center and the U.S. command post. The Vietnamese driver took a bullet in the leg, lost his nerve, and stalled the truck. Ramsey might still have shot his way out of the ambush. He was carrying one of the new fully automatic AR-15 rifles (the commercial version of the M-16 that the Army was then beginning to adopt), two clips of ammunition for it, and a couple of grenades. He didn't know what to do. He had never had any infantry training. He fired back ineffectively from the window of the truck, wasting critical moments and the clip in the rifle. A bullet from the guerrillas punctured a five-gallon can of diesel oil at his feet and sent a jet of the oil into his face, half blinding him.

Ramsey grasped at the one thing he knew how to use—his Vietnam-ese. *"Toi dau hang!"* ("I surrender!"), he shouted, then dropped the rifle and climbed out of the truck, an overly tall man who looked even taller with his hands stretched high above his head. The driver was released. His leg injury was a simple flesh wound, and he made his way back to Bau Trai that evening to report Ramsey's capture.

Doug Ramsey's captors, farmers in their twenties, were so pleased with their catch they were almost friendly. They asked him how to say *dau hang* in English. To get Ramsey out of sight behind a tree line, the guerrillas led him to the nearest hamlet. The farm folk there had a different attitude toward him. Their hamlet had been put to the torch by troops from Chinh's 25th Division who were participating in the operation. Ramsey had seen burned-out hamlets before. He had always seen them days or weeks after the burning when the places had acquired an archaeological look, abandoned by their disheartened inhabitants, the blackened ruins cold.

The rubble of this hamlet was still smoking, and it was obvious that these people had returned only a short time before to discover what had happened to their homes. Children were whimpering. A couple of old people were standing and looking, shaking their heads in a trance of disbelief. Women were poking through the smoldering debris of the houses trying to salvage cooking utensils and any other small possessions that might have escaped the flames. Ramsey could tell from the conversations he was overhearing that these peasants had lost virtually everything. They had had neither time nor warning to remove any household furnishings. The soldiers had also burned all of the rice that had not been buried or hidden elsewhere and had shot the buffalo and other livestock and thrown the carcasses down the wells to poison the water supply. Tet, the week-long holiday that to the Vietnamese is Christmas and Easter, New Year's and Thanksgiving celebrated in one, was a night and two days away. The peasants were asking each other how they were going to celebrate their Tet.

Had Ramsey still been a free man, the scene might have severed him from this war. His predicament rendered such thoughts of conscience academic, but he thought them just the same. He felt sick and infuriated, betrayed and yet also responsible. During a briefing on the operation two weeks earlier at 25th Division headquarters he had expressed concern about civilian casualties and unnecessary damage to homes. The Army lieutenant colonel who was Chinh's senior advisor had assured him there would be no wanton destruction of hamlets. Chinh had sat nearby without a word of contradiction. Ramsey had had enough. If this was to be the price of preserving the American way of life, he did not want to be one of those exacting it.

Ramsey was also frightened. A number of the farmers from the hamlet had gathered around and were demanding the right to kill him. The four guerrillas stopped them. They quoted the National Liberation Front's announced policy of "lenient and humane" treatment for prisoners. Ramsey sensed that they wanted to protect their prize, but they also seemed to be conscientious men who took seriously the preaching of their movement. They reprimanded an old man who spat at Ramsey. The guerrillas said that Ramsey was not a soldier who might have been involved in the destruction of the hamlet. He was a civilian who had been captured while escorting a truckload of rice to refugees. A middle-aged farmer in the group asked Ramsey what agency he worked for.

"AID," Ramsey said. The Vietnamese acronym for the Agency for International Development conveys the same meaning as the initials in English.

"AID!" the farmer cried. "Look about you," he said to Ramsey. He pointed, sweeping his finger from one charred remembrance of a home to another. "Here is your American AID!" The farmer spat on the ground and walked away.

Vann happened to be in the CIA office at the embassy that evening. The job for which he had left Hau Nghia at the end of October, USOM representative to the American forces in the III Corps region, had proved to be a two-month interlude. He had just been given a more important assignment as USOM project manager of a new program to train specialized teams of Vietnamese pacification workers who were to be sent to hamlets all over the country. USOM was to share responsibility for the program with the CIA. He was in the midst of an argument with his CIA counterpart over how to organize the teams and run a national training center when there was a phone call for him. The blood drained from his face.

He drove to Bau Trai at first light, reconstructed what had happened by interrogating the driver and going to the ambush site to examine the gutted truck (the guerrillas had set fire to it), and then organized the best rescue effort he could under the circumstances. Frank Scotton, whose ability to speak Vietnamese was exceedingly useful in an emergency like this, came out to help. Vann told him there was hardly any chance of success, but he wanted to try, because they might be lucky. Through Charles Mann, Vann arranged to have a helicopter from the CIA's Air America fleet put on standby alert just in case he found an opportunity to use it. He got Lodge's authorization to have a Catholic priest in Cu Chi with guerrilla contacts send a letter to the Viet Cong district committee there offering to pay a ransom for Ramsey's release.

Once the three-and-a-half-day cease-fire began on January 20, the first day of Tết, Vann and Scotton were able to roam the province seeking information about Ramsey with a recklessness that not even Vann would have dared at any other time. Vann drove his personal car, a little Triumph sedan he had owned in Colorado and that AID had shipped to Vietnam for him (the privilege of a civilian official), because he knew that it would not be recognized as a USOM or military vehicle. He was struck by how the Communists were consolidating their hold on Hau Nghia. Viet Cong flags were flying everywhere, and there were banners along all the roads, including the main Route 1, with anti-American slogans. In many of the hamlets where he and Scotton stopped to inquire about Ramsey, farmers and women and children who had been friendly to Vann in the past looked away and did not respond to his greeting. A number of those who did answer warned him that he and his friend were taking an enormous risk, despite the fact that the cease-fire had been proclaimed by both sides.

Vann sent one of his appeals to a village chief whom he suspected of conniving with the guerrillas. He and Ramsey had had a fine relationship with the village chief on school-building and other social welfare projects, and Vann was hoping the man might help out of regard for Ramsey. When Vann and Scotton drove to the hamlet where the village center was located to see if the appeal had produced any results, they found the village chief in a restaurant. He was sitting at a table talking to two men who were eating fruit. Scotton was certain that both were Viet Cong cadres. Other men who were unmistakably guerrillas were lounging around outside the restaurant. Vann and Scotton sat down at the table and exchanged Tet pleasantries with the village chief. The two cadres went on eating their fruit. The village chief slid a handwritten note across the table. Vann stuck it in his shirt pocket, and then he and Scotton said goodbye with deliberate slowness and got up and walked briskly to the car, not looking back or sideways in order not to give the guerrillas any second thoughts. Scotton translated the note, which had no signature, as soon as they sped away. "I have heard that the American is alive," the handwriting said. "He will be released later when it is quiet."

Not every guerrilla was as restrained as those with the village chief. Vann made up his mind to drive next to the sugar mill at Hiep Hoa to talk to someone there. On the way he and Scotton passed through So Do hamlet. The Viet Cong had erected a triumphal arch of bamboo and cloth over the road at an open area that served as a hamlet common. Big letters across the top of the arch predicted victory for the National Liberation Front in the Year of the Horse. (Vietnamese and Chinese lunar years follow a cycle in which each year is marked by a different animal symbol.) A group of Viet Cong were taking their ease near the arch. Scotton noticed that two of them were apparently regulars who had been given Tet leave. They were wearing green uniforms and the so-called Ho Chi Minh sandals made by cutting the soles from used tires. Vann and Scotton would have to return to Bau Trai by this same road; there was no alternate route. The contact at Hiep Hoa proved useless, and so Vann decided to stop and question his schoolteacher friend in So Do on the way back.

When he pulled up to her house she screamed out at him that he was about to be killed. He spun the Triumph back into the road and started down through the hamlet, gathering speed but not accelerating to the full, because he and Scotton wanted to try to spot the ambush. Scotton bet that it would be at the arch. He picked up a grenade from several that Vann had been keeping handy on the seat between them. Scotton won his bet. Four guerrillas were waiting just beyond the arch on Vann's side of the road, two of them the regulars. They were holding their weapons and motioning to Vann to stop. He gunned the engine, at the same instant bracing himself in the seat and locking his arms on the wheel so that he could keep it steady longer if he was wounded. The two regulars raised their rifles to fire point-blank. Before they could get off a shot, Scotton reached out his window and looped the grenade over the top of the little car. The surprise of the familiar round missile suddenly sailing toward them scattered the Viet Cong, and Vann and Scotton raced free.

The schoolteacher came to Bau Trai the next morning and warned Vann not to go near So Do for a long time, because the guerrillas there were in a rage for vengeance. None of the four Viet Cong had been hurt. They had managed to run far enough before the grenade exploded to avoid the fragments. Their pride and that of their comrades had been wounded. They had been boasting to the population that they were going to capture or kill the American imperialists when they returned. Now old ladies were laughing at them and making jokes.

John Vann went back to Saigon the same day, forced to admit that further search was useless for the moment. (The cease-fire also expired late that day.) He was disconsolate, despite his realistic assessment of the prospects at the outset. A few days later he received the response from the NLF to the ransom offer he had made through the Catholic priest in Cu Chi. "The American in question is still in good health," the letter of reply said, but ransom was not acceptable. "Money, even dollars or anything else cannot redeem crimes if they have been committed," the letter said. Although the Viet Cong occasionally released American prisoners for propaganda purposes, those let go so far had been Army enlisted men who were considered of negligible value by the Vietnamese Communists. Scotton also observed that the phrase in the note from the village chief—"when it is quiet"—could mean when the war was over. The capture of Ramsey was one of the few episodes in Vann's life when the guilt would not leave him. He was to show it in years to come by his refusal to be discouraged from the hope of somehow, someday bringing Ramsey freedom.

Vann would have been more disconsolate still had he known that by the time his rescue effort had seriously begun, Ramsey was already far beyond his reach at the edge of the Annamite rain forest that was to be Ramsey's purgatory for the next seven years. The day after his capture, Ramsey had been turned over to a three-man liaison team. That evening they had started marching him toward the camp for important prisoners at the region headquarters in War Zone C in northern Tay Ninh Province, the Duong Minh Chau redoubt of the French war that Bumgardner had explored in his jeep when it had been deserted in the interlude of 1955. Except for rest stops, they marched all night. Ramsey slept the next day fettered in leg irons in a bomb shelter under a guerrilla communications hut until they could resume the march in the evening. At midnight he saw fireworks in the distance and thought he might be witnessing the opening of the Tet festivities at Trang Bang in Hau Nghia. The round mass of Nui Ba Den, the Black Virgin Mountain, rising out of the Tay Ninh plain at dawn told him they had been moving northwest at a much faster pace than he had thought. The fireworks he had seen had probably been at Tay Ninh City. They kept marching that morning, the twentieth, because it was the first day of the cease-fire and the guerrillas felt safe from air attack. By noon Ramsey was walking toward the great wall of trees that marks the end of the cultivated lowlands and the beginning of the rain forest and the foothills of the Annamite chain.

Ahead of Ramsey lay the torment of the rain-forest prison camps—the chills and fevers of the two varieties of ordinary malaria and the convulsions and coma of the killer type that attacks the brain, the painful muscle cramps and swelling of the limbs brought on by beriberi, the dysentery, the leeches, the cobras that were to curl for the night under the bunk of his cage, the forced marches whenever the exigencies of the conflict required a shifting of the camp, the terror of the B-52 strikes by his own Air Force, the guards who stole food the prisoners needed to survive because they were hungry themselves, the hideously cruel interrogators who were embittered toward all white men by too many years of war and fugitive jungle existence. Ramsey had no premonition of any of this when the group halted at a creek not far inside the forest to have a swim and eat a midday meal. The guerrillas untied Ramsey to let him swim with them. An attempt at escape did not seem practical, so he relaxed and enjoyed the coolness of the water after the long march. The three members of the liaison team had treated him with humanity, even kindness, given the fact that he was a prisoner of war. The cadre in charge, an older and experienced man, had bought him some sweetened rice cakes, a Tet treat, the previous evening, and early that morning they had stopped at an isolated farmhouse so that Ramsey could rest and share in the Tet feasting that had begun there.

Ramsey had been most impressed by the junior member of the team, a sixteen-year-old farm boy. The youth was tall for a Vietnamese, high-spirited, and clearly enjoying the life of a guerrilla soldier. Shortly after they entered the trees he spotted a hawk perched on a branch and shot it for their dinner that evening. His pride in his prowess as a hunter amused Ramsey. The boy appeared to have little in the way of formal education, but he was bright, and the clearly extensive political indoctrination he had received had not repressed a nature that was curious and friendly. He had become so talkative with Ramsey at one point on the march that the cadre had reprimanded him for crossing the line and being too familiar with a prisoner. Ramsey had remarked to himself as the youth was temporarily silenced that the cadre did not realize what an advertisement the boy was to an American who had encountered too many elitist Saigon University students, teenage street hooligans, and drunken young ARVN irresponsibles.

When they were all resting on the creek bank after the swim, the young man asked Ramsey why the Americans were making war in Vietnam. Ramsey gave the most common reason—the containment of an expansionist China—because he assumed it was the one a sixteen-year-old Vietnamese peasant could most easily understand. He explained that while the war was against the immediate best interests of the Vietnamese people, the United States was benefiting the Vietnamese in the long run by preventing China from taking over all of their country and the other nations of Southeast Asia.

Doug Ramsey's explanation seemed to irritate and arouse the boy. He said that it didn't make sense to him. If the Americans hated or feared the Chinese so much, why didn't they go to China and make war? There were no Chinese soldiers in Vietnam. The only foreign soldiers in Vietnam were Americans and foreign allies of the Americans like the South Koreans, he said. (The first of the South Korean divisions to fight in Vietnam under an arrangement between Seoul and Washington arrived in late 1965.) In fact, the last people to bring Chinese troops into Vietnam had been the Americans. They had let the Chinese Nationalists occupy the North after World War II. Now the Americans were talking again about possibly bringing Chiang Kai-shek's troops from Taiwan to fight for them in the South. The Vietnamese would never permit foreign troops to occupy their soil. "We have no fear that the present Chinese regime will attack us or attempt to take us over," the youth said, "but if things changed in the future and a new government ever dared to try . . ." He began to describe how the Vietnamese had smashed invading armies from China in centuries past.

Ramsey started to explain further why Americans saw the Vietnamese Communists as pawns of the Chinese. The cadre and the other guerrilla broke in. Ramsey was wrong, they said. Just because China had become a socialist country did not mean that it could dominate Vietnam. The Vietnamese would not tolerate any foreign domination, regardless of the ideology of the foreigner. Least of all, they said, would they tolerate Chinese domination. The two older men and the youth brought Ramsey into the historical world of the Vietnamese Communists. He was fascinated that these products of a Communist movement, which denounced modern vestiges of "feudalism," could identify so passionately with the figures of their feudal past. Their nationalism was fervid, quite different from the attitude he had become accustomed to on the Saigon side.

They were glad in a way that the task of defeating the United States had fallen to Vietnamese of their time, the guerrillas said. After the Americans had despaired and gone home, potential menaces closer at hand—they implied they had China uppermost in mind—would not dare to attempt what the most powerful capitalist nation in history had failed to achieve. They were confident they would be able to emulate their ancestors in their war against the United States.

That afternoon they resumed the march deeper into the Duong Minh Chau forest toward the prison camp. The geopolitical rationale that the United States was containing China by frustrating her Vietnamese pawn had been "reduced to ashes" for Ramsey. It occurred to him that Americans need look no further than this Vietnamese Communist enemy for the best possible native barrier against Chinese expansion into Southeast Asia.

Westmoreland's plan to destroy the Vietnamese Communists was essentially a replica of Harkins's war-of-attrition strategy, with American soldiers and the lethal technology that came with them substituted for the ARVN. The similarities extended to details. Both plans had preparatory Phases I and II during which a killing machine was to be put together and the early battles fought, followed by a victorious Phase III when the machine would shift into its highest gear and mince the Vietnamese enemy. The reflex adoption of a war-of-attrition approach demonstrated once more how rotelike the American military mind of the 1960s had become. William DePuy, Westmoreland's chief of operations, who had drawn up this plan that Westmoreland then made his own, was a distinguished infantryman and a highly intelligent officer who was regarded as one of the best thinkers in the U.S. Army. Yet he held the same skewed perspective on World War II that Harkins had—the belief that all a general need do to win was to build a killing machine and turn it loose on his opponent. He gave his "We are going to stomp them to death" prediction in a conversation with Keyes Beech of the *Chicago Daily News* as the buildup was getting underway in 1965. He added, Beech thought in a kind of confession, "I don't know any other way."

Harkins had predicted victory in a year and a half and been instructed by a McNamara who was attempting to be conservative to extend his vision. Westmoreland was more cautious in his scheduling. He allowed three to three and a half years. The time period seems to have been chosen because it would bring clearcut or sufficiently obvious success by the November 1968 presidential election and because, in the atmosphere of Westmoreland's Saigon headquarters in the summer of 1965, it appeared a reasonable length for an American war. The defeat of Nazi Germany had taken slightly less than three and a half years, the destruction of Japan not much more. The stalemated Korean conflict had lasted three years and a month.

Westmoreland said that he would "halt the losing trend by the end of 1965" through defensive measures and limited offensive thrusts called "spoiling attacks" to disrupt the enemy's campaign. He would start his Phase II, his preparing-to-win phase, in the first half of 1966 by going over to the offensive "in high priority areas" with "search and destroy operations" against Main Force Viet Cong units and the North Vietnamese Army regulars who were joining them. During this phase he would bring into the South the rest of the 300,000 Americans he had requested thus far and whatever additional reinforcements he might need. He would also construct the ports, jet-capable airfields, supply and repair depots, base camps, hospitals, communications systems, and other elements of the elaborate support structure the machine required.

He was vague about the amount of time he would need for Phase II, giving himself some margin for the unexpected here. He implied that he could finish it by the end of 1966 or in the first half of 1967. If the Viet Cong and Hanoi had not acquired wisdom and given up the struggle by then, he said, he would launch his Phase III. It would be a full-scale, nationwide offensive to complete "the defeat and destruction of the remaining enemy forces and base areas." This victory phase would take "a year to a year and a half," i.e., until mid-1968 or the end of the year. With this three-to-three-and-a-half-year timetable, McNamara the statistician had thus been projecting a price for South Vietnam of possibly 18,000 American dead when he had told the president in his July memorandum that U.S. killed in action might reach 500 a month by the end of 1965. McNamara could still recommend approval of Westmoreland's plan. The schedule enabled him to assure Lyndon Johnson that the course they were following stood "a good chance of achieving an acceptable outcome within a reasonable time."

The three guerrillas had told Ramsey that they and their comrades would fight harder and die more willingly than the American soldiers because they were defending their homeland. They were wrong about the U.S. Army of 1965 that Westmoreland was given. Its senior leadership might be wanting, but the officers at brigade and battalion and company level and the soldiers who followed them into harm's way were the finest army the United States had ever fielded straight from the training camps of America to a foreign battleground. Colonel and rifleman shared a faith. The president said that if the Communists were not stopped in Vietnam, they would have to be stopped in Honolulu or on the beaches of California. Colonel and rifleman believed him. This was an army that shared a confidence too in its weapons and in its combat skills. The world was a tactical map to these men. They were prepared to fight any enemy at any grid coordinate.

This U.S. Army of 1965 was the fruit of Maxwell Taylor's admonition that the neglected Army of the Eisenhower era had to be reforged into an effective instrument for the "brushfire wars" that were inherent in American foreign policy. McNamara and his secretary of the Army and subsequent deputy, Cyrus Vance, had been at the task for the past four years. They had spared neither care nor expense. The crown of their accomplishment was the 1st Cavalry Division (Airmobile)—the first military organization in history to take full advantage of the helicopter as a vehicle to maneuver troops and bring firepower to bear. The Air Cav, as the officers and men unofficially renamed their division, was to the jeep-and-truck-borne divisions of World War II and Korea what those mechanized formations had been to their predecessors dependent on horses and mules and foot power. The troops of the Air Cav flew to the assault point in agile transport versions of the Huey gunships that had sought to protect the cumbersome old H-21 Flying Bananas of Vann's initial year in Vietnam. There were "escort gunships" to shepherd these "slick ships" carrying the assault force and other "aerial rocket" Hueys with dozens of rockets in side-mounted pods to back up the riflemen once they were on the ground. Each battalion had an Air Force lieutenant attached as a forward air controller to put the heavier ordnance of the fighter-bombers where it would count. A large new cargo helicopter, the CH-47 Chinook, lifted the artillery to wherever the guns were needed. The Chinooks could move an entire battery of six 105mm howitzers twenty miles over roadless country and have the battery firing again within an hour after the first gun had been picked up. Advanced navigational systems enabled the Chinooks to keep the artillery and the troops supplied with almost unlimited quantities of ammunition and other sustenance of war at night or in bad weather.

Intangible things had also been invested in the creation of the Air Cav. The troops and their sergeants and officers knew and trusted one another. Most had organized and trained together for more than a year at Fort Benning as the experimental 11th Air Assault Division. The pilots of the different helicopter formations had learned to play their individual roles and to synchronize their movements in a complicated ballet. When Johnson had said yes to Westmoreland in July 1965, the experimental division had been given the colors of the regular 1st Cavalry Division and additional battalions to bring it up to strength and sent to Vietnam in September, establishing an immense base camp for its three brigades and 435 helicopters in the An Khe Valley on the eastern side of the mountains not far from the Central Vietnamese port of Qui Nhon.

I heard about the first big battle between the Air Cav and Hanoi's regulars of the NVA in mid-November 1965 while I was in Central Vietnam to research a story on refugees. I had found five hamlets behind a stretch of beach in Quang Ngai Province that had comprised a prosperous fishing village of about 15,000 people until the previous summer. The houses had not been the common thatch and wattle. They had been homes of thick-walled brick, the achievement of generations of saving from the labor of the sea. All had been reduced to rubble or grotesque skeletons by two months of bombardment from aircraft and point-blank shelling by the 5-inch guns of Seventh Fleet destroyers. The village had been declared a Viet Cong base and razed simply because it had been in a guerrilla-controlled area. Officials from the district center said their inquiries showed that more than 180 civilians had been killed before most of the inhabitants had fled. Other estimates that seemed reasonable ran to 600. The young officers at the province military advisory detachment said they knew of at least ten more hamlets that had been leveled just as thoroughly on the same vague reasoning and twenty-five others that had been severely damaged. The pattern of destruction was widening, they said.

That evening I called the *Times* office in Saigon to describe the story I would be writing. Charlie Mohr, the bureau chief, told me that it would have to wait. A major fight had just started with the NVA near Pleiku, the principal town in the center of the Highlands, and I had better get there as fast as I could.

An obliging captain drove me out to the province airstrip, and late into the night I hitchhiked rides on planes down the coast to Qui Nhon and then over the mountains to Pleiku. I was accustomed to the desultory quality of an ARVN command post after sunset. At Pleiku the night was alive and roaring. The radios were raucous with requests and orders and reports. The big, boxy Chinooks clattered down, loaded up with artillery shells, and lifted away again to feed the howitzers that reverberated through the flare-broken darkness off to the southwest where the battle was taking place.

Two weeks before Thanksgiving, Col. Thomas "Tim" Brown, a scion of a military family (his brother, George, an Air Force general, became chairman of the Joint Chiefs in the mid-1970s), was at ARVN II Corps headquarters on a hill beside Pleiku being briefed by the corps intelligence officer. Brown commanded the 3rd Brigade of the Air Cav. His executive officer was Lt. Col. Edward "Shy" Meyer, the first of the Vietnam generation of officers to become chief of staff of the Army at the end of the 1970s. The 3rd Brigade had been dispatched to the Highlands earlier in November to find two NVA regiments that had attempted to seize a Special Forces camp at the Montagnard village of Plei Me about twenty-five miles south of the town. Brown's three battalions had searched south and southeast of the camp itself for several days without success, and he had exhausted his intelligence. Westmoreland had sent word through Maj. Gen. Harry Kinnard, the division commander, that he wanted Brown to search west toward the Cambodian border, but Brown didn't know where in the west to begin. He had come to II Corps headquarters hoping for a lead.

Brown was thinking that the ARVN intelligence officer had little to offer when he noticed a red star drawn on the briefing map near the Cambodian border southwest of Pleiku. The star called attention to a massif, a cluster of peaks and ridges covered with double-canopy rain forest, that rose suddenly out of the Drang River Valley west of the Plei Me camp and extended back over the border six to seven miles farther to the west. Brown had seen the massif from the air. It looked forbidding. It was called the Chu Prong (Prong Mountain), after the highest peak within it.

"What does that red star signify?" Brown asked.

"That's a VC secret base, sir," the intelligence officer answered.

"What's in there?" Brown asked.

"We don't know, sir, we've never been in there," the intelligence officer replied.

The Chu Prong, Brown decided, was as good a place as any to begin. He instructed his best battalion commander, Lt. Col. Harold "Hal" Moore, Jr., forty-three, a West Point graduate from a small town near Fort Knox in western Kentucky, to select a landing zone near the massif and explore its edge. Moore was not to penetrate the Chu Prong in any depth, as the terrain would engulf a battalion. Brown also cautioned him to keep his companies within supporting distance of each other. For all their training, the men of Moore's 1st Battalion, 7th Cavalry, and the other two battalions of the 3rd Brigade had yet to be tested in combat. The troops had seen only a few skirmishes during their two months in Vietnam. Brown was concerned about the shock of a battalion suddenly encountering a large North Vietnamese force.

Thirty-five minutes after landing without opposition on a Sunday morning, November 14, 1965, a platoon from Moore's lead company caught a North Vietnamese soldier who was trying to hide in a clump of brush. The man was dressed in a dirty khaki shirt and trousers and was unarmed, carrying only an empty canteen. Moore questioned him through an interpreter. He turned out to be a deserter. He said he had been living on bananas for the past five days. Moore asked him if there were any North Vietnamese troops in the vicinity. Yes, he said. He pointed toward the Chu Prong. The first ridge, a finger that jutted out into the valley, loomed about 200 yards from the clearing Moore was using as a landing zone. There were three battalions in the Chu Prong, the deserter said, and they were eager to kill Americans.

* * *

"X-Ray," as Moore had code-named the landing zone, was not hard to distinguish from the air on Monday morning. It was an island in a sea of red-orange napalm and exploding bombs and shells. Peter Arnett and I watched in awe from 2,500 feet, filled with fear at the imminent prospect of going down there. We had caught a ride on a "slick ship" Huey making an ammunition supply run from the artillery position six miles to the east; we were waiting for a pair of jets to finish a strike so that we could land.

The Huey plummeted, and the pilots dashed in over the trees to minimize exposure, then "flared" the helicopter as soon as we reached the clearing, braking in the air like a parachute popping open. The ammunition was tossed out and stretchers with a couple of wounded hoisted aboard as a bullet thwacked into the fuselage and others buzzed through the open doors. Arnett and I leaped down and ran at a crouch for the partial shelter of a huge anthill nearby where Moore had established his command post.

Moore was a tall man with blue eyes and craggy features, his emotions soaring in the relief and exhilaration of having just broken a three-and-a-quarter-hour assault on the southern and western sides of the perimeter by another North Vietnamese battalion. "By God, they sent us over here to kill Communists and that's what we're doing," he shouted.

Many of the North Vietnamese survivors of this latest attack had turned themselves into snipers. They were all around and would not quit. They had climbed into the tops of the trees on the valley floor, dug "spider holes" amid the scrub brush and stands of five-foot-high elephant grass, and burrowed into the tops and sides of the strange, gargantuan anthills, some considerably taller than a man, that were interspersed everywhere. The dry season had begun in the Highlands. The loose-fitting khaki fatigues of the NVA blended well with the brownish yellow of the elephant grass and other parched vegetation, and they camouflaged themselves with branches. Whenever a helicopter landed or someone moved, one of them would cut loose with a Soviet-designed AK-47 automatic assault rifle and often another of Moore's men would be killed or wounded before the sniper could be silenced.

The battalion's entire perimeter was only 300 yards across, and the clearing itself where helicopters could land was much smaller. It would have been quiet and strewn with American corpses had Hal Moore not been such a superlative fighter, a daring but canny man who had served his apprenticeship in Korea. His intuition and a line of field telephone wire a Cav scout helicopter had spotted strung along a trail north of the clearing (the NVA were not well equipped with tactical radios and used field telephones extensively) had convinced Moore on Sunday that the deserter was not lying. He had immediately understood that if the North Vietnamese rushed a force down off the ridge and got right next to the clearing, they could stop him from landing any more helicopters and slaughter those men he did have on the ground. He had to stiff-arm his enemy away from the clearing until he could bring in all or most of his battalion.

Without waiting for the rest of his second company to arrive, Moore had directed his first company to move up the ridge. He acted not a moment too soon. The three North Vietnamese battalions in the Chu Prong numbered about 1,700 men to Moore's 450. Two of the battalions were from a regiment that had arrived only at the beginning of November; the third was a composite of survivors from one of the regiments that had unsuccessfully besieged the Plei Me camp. The NVA commander was readying one of the battalions as fast as he could, and its lead troops were about to launch a pell-mell assault down the ridge to try to reach the clearing. The men of the two armies met among the trees where the rain forest began.

A pitiless struggle started, Vietnamese and Americans killing each other within yards. The close quarters deprived Moore's men of the advantage of air and artillery, and the Vietnamese did all they could to keep the killing on an infantry-against-infantry basis by staying as close to the Americans as possible, a tactic they called "clinging to the belt." Had Moore's men not been superbly armed themselves with the new M-16 automatic rifle and a quick-loading grenade launcher called the M-79 that looked and worked like a single-barrel shotgun, many more of them would have died.

Tim Brown had been proved right in his concern about a large NVA unit, but he need not have worried about a shock effect on his unseasoned troops. These Americans were as eager as their opponents—too eager in the case of one platoon. The second lieutenant in command fell for a Vietnamese trick: the lure. He carried his men out ahead of the rest of the company in pursuit of an NVA squad that seemed to be fleeing. The lieutenant and his platoon were soon enveloped and cut off on the crest of the ridge.

Moore had already guessed that the NVA would attempt an envelopment of his whole first company, because that is what he would have tried if he had been the enemy commander. He stopped it by rushing his second company to the flank of the first—and into another remorseless action at a dry creek bed near the base of the ridge—as soon as the next helicopter lift arrived with the remainder of this second company's troops. He then blocked one more end run against the second company by positioning the men of his third company on the flank of the second as fast as they landed. To do so he had to leave the rear side of the clearing unprotected, because the rest of his battalion—his weapons company with the 81mm mortars and his reconnaissance platoon—were still being shuttled by the helicopters from the assembly point at the Plei Me camp. He assumed correctly that the NVA commander would not think to hook around that far. Moore's third company spotted the NVA flankers of this last envelopment approaching through the more open terrain close to the valley floor. They hit the Vietnamese with volleys of rifle fire and shattered them with artillery and fighter-bombers and salvos from the aerial-rocket Hueys.

Hal Moore now ordered the first and second companies to assault up the ridge and rescue the surrounded platoon. They were stymied almost immediately and took heavy losses. Second Lt. Walter Marm, Jr., won the Congressional Medal of Honor by single-handedly destroying a Vietnamese machine gun and killing the eight NVA soldiers manning and protecting the weapon before he was felled with a bullet wound in the face. Brown then reinforced Moore with a rifle company from another battalion late Sunday afternoon when the firing slackened enough to risk landing helicopters again and Moore pulled his troops into a perimeter for the night.

Shortly after daybreak on Monday the ordeal passed to Moore's third company, C ("Charlie") Company, which had managed to keep the Vietnamese at arm's length through Sunday and had escaped with minor casualties. It had been assigned the south and southwest sides of the perimeter. The company commander had not requested volunteers to man forward listening posts during the night. He decided that they would be blinded by the thick elephant grass in front and that he could get by with artillery concentrations brought to within 100 yards of his line. At dawn, Moore ordered a local reconnaissance by all companies, a standard precaution. C Company's commander told each of his platoon leaders to send out a squad. The Americans walked right into the soldiers of a fresh NVA battalion creeping toward them on hands and knees. Men died in the long grass as they sought to fall back firing. Others died running out to try to help comrades. The Vietnamese surged into a general assault on C Company, hoping to overrun it quickly and crack open the perimeter.

The company commander asked Moore for the battalion reserve, the reconnaissance platoon. Moore refused. He had to hold the reserve as a last resort. In the confusion of battle he could not know whether C Company was receiving the main blow or a diversion, and shortly afterward an adjacent company also came under attack. C Company's commander was shot in the back and gravely wounded as he stood up to throw a grenade at two NVA soldiers who had penetrated his line. Moore then did try to reinforce with a platoon from another company. They could not reach C Company and lost two killed and two wounded in the attempt. The Vietnamese were laying sheets of bullets across the perimeter—low enough to catch a crawling man—from machine guns and the Soviet equivalent of BARs they had set up around the anthills on the south and southwest sides. Soon all of C Company's officers and most of its noncoms were dead or as seriously injured as the company commander. The attack on the adjacent company worsened.

The air and artillery seemed to be having no effect. In desperation, Moore radioed all units to toss colored smoke grenades and ordered the supporting fire brought right up to the edge of the perimeter. Several artillery shells landed inside it, and an Air Force F-105 Thunderchief jet dropped two canisters of napalm near the anthill where Moore's command post was located, burning some of the men there, "cooking off" a stack of M-16 ammunition, and nearly exploding a pile of hand grenades.

Moore finally had to commit his reconnaissance platoon reserve to prevent the company next to C from cracking. In the meantime a probing attack began against a third section of the perimeter. Moore formed an emergency reserve by withdrawing a platoon from a sector not yet threatened and asked Brown to lift another rifle company to him when the punishment the NVA battalion had been receiving began to tell at last and the volume of fire started to diminish.

C Company had ceased to exist as a unit by the time the assault lost momentum after two hours and then gradually ebbed through the next hour. Of the approximately 100 men who had seen the first light of Monday, fewer than forty were unwounded. There were great gaps in the line where the dead and injured lay. Not enough North Vietnamese ever got through to seriously threaten the battalion position, because the untested men of Charlie Company, 1st Battalion, 7th Cavalry, held and the many who died took as many of their opponents with them as they could. A second lieutenant who had led one of the platoons was dead in his foxhole. Around him were the bodies of five Vietnamese. Out in the elephant grass a Vietnamese and an American who had shot each other lay side by side. The American died with his hands gripped around the throat of the Vietnamese.

When Arnett and I arrived at X-Ray at midmorning on Monday, Moore still had the artillery and air strikes going full-tilt, because he was afraid the third North Vietnamese battalion the deserter had reported might be about to assault and he was trying to break it up before it could attack. The artillery had fired nearly 4,000 rounds in twenty-four hours, and the fighter-bomber sorties were approaching 300.

The survivors of the platoon that had been cut off on the ridge were finally rescued early Monday afternoon when the 2nd Battalion, 5th Cavalry, reached Moore's perimeter by marching from another landing zone two miles away. A three-company sortie worked its way to the platoon slowly, because of the sniper fire. A captain from the reinforcing battalion was shot in the chest. Seven men from the platoon walked back unscathed to the clearing where twenty-seven had landed the day before. Most of the twelve wounded survivors had to be carried in litters improvised out of ponchos. The overly eager lieutenant was among the eight dead brought back that way. Those who returned owed their lives to the soldierly skills and battle sense of Staff Sgt. Clyde Savage, twenty-two, from Birmingham, Alabama, a squad leader and the only senior noncom to walk out in one piece. He had seized the artillery radio after the observer was shot in the throat and erected a barricade of shrapnel and high explosive around the tiny perimeter the survivors formed on the ridge, calling the shells to within twenty-five yards without dropping one among his frayed band. The survivors managed to beat back three attacks during the night with this powerful assistance. The NVA seem to have then forgotten the lonesome platoon in the confusion of their battle.

The third assault Moore anticipated came before dawn on Tuesday. It was weaker than the others, staged by perhaps two companies and once more against the south and southwest sides. C Company had been replaced there by a full-strength rifle company, and this time the attackers were detected and decimated before most of them could get near the foxholes. The riflemen finished off those who did get close with grenades and well-placed bursts from their M-16s.

Moore would not leave on Tuesday afternoon without three of his sergeants. They were from C Company, and he thought they were still out in the elephant grass where they had disappeared the day before. His troops were being relieved by elements of a second fresh battalion.

The artillery and air strikes had been suspended to facilitate the flight pattern of the helicopters. One of the relieving battalion commanders was nervous that the NVA might take advantage of the lull to bring mortars into action from the ridges of the Chu Prong. He wanted Moore to hurry up. Moore refused.

He had not slept in forty-eight hours. He was the victor. The bodies of hundreds of Vietnamese soldiers lay on the ridge and before the foxholes on the valley floor. The Vietnamese had died in such lavish numbers because they had made themselves the attackers and had assaulted without the assistance of any heavy weapons. They had also died because of the worth of Moore's American soldiers, and now that the fight was over the cost of his victory came home to Moore. Seventy-nine Americans were dead and 121 were wounded. Most of them were men whom Moore had schooled and led for a year and a half. The bodies of the three sergeants from C Company had actually been found earlier on Tuesday and evacuated. Through an error, Moore had not been informed. The thought of abandoning their bodies in this strange place, or the even darker possibility, however remote, that one or all of them might still be out there wounded, was more than he could bear. "I won't leave without my NCOs," he shouted, weeping and shaking his rifle with a clenched fist. "I won't leave without them," he cried. He ordered the search continued. A rifleman turned out to be missing. Moore held up the movement until the man's body was discovered and Hal Moore was convinced that he was not leaving any of his soldiers behind.

When I stopped off at Tim Brown's forward command post at a tea plantation south of Pleiku on Tuesday evening, he told me that he wanted to pull out of the valley of the Drang. His mission was to find the North Vietnamese and to kill as many of them as possible. Moore's battalion and the reinforcements Brown had sent him had fulfilled that task manyfold. To hang around in the same area and try for more right away was to play too dangerous a game, Brown said. The NVA seemed to be infiltrating across the border rapidly. Where Moore had encountered one new regiment, more might be hiding. Brown, who had flown into X-Ray several times to stay in touch with the battle and get a grasp of the terrain and the enemy, wanted to lift out all of his troops and probe carefully before seeking battle again.

"Then why don't you pull out?" I asked.

"General Westmoreland won't let me," Brown said. "He says that if we withdraw, the newspapers will make it look like we retreated."

The next day one of the battalions that relieved Moore's, the 2nd Battalion, 7th Cavalry, was ambushed and destroyed as a fighting unit while moving up the valley about two and a half miles north of X-Ray. Its commander was not as canny as Moore and made the mistake of having his troops advance in a column. He also neglected to put out flank security. One element of an NVA battalion quickly formed a classic U-shaped ambush which his two lead companies walked into, while another element struck his third company as it was strung out in the elephant grass and trees. The men of the 2nd of the 7th resisted gallantly, and many Vietnamese also perished in the hand-to-hand fighting that lasted the better part of an afternoon. The two lead companies were grievously hurt, and the third company was massacred; 151 Americans were killed, 121 were wounded, and 4 were missing in action. The 7th Cavalry had been Custer's regiment at the Little Big Horn. On November 17, 1965, "history repeated itself," one of the survivors of the third company said.

McNamara was shaken by the casualties. The Battle of the Ia Drang—as Moore's fight and the ambush came to be known; *ia*, meaning "river" in the language of a local Montagnard tribe, was not translated in the reports of the time—had taken 230 American lives in four days. (The four missing men were also later determined to be dead.) McNamara was shaken by something else the following week—a request from Westmoreland for an additional 41,500 U.S. troops. The general cited as his reason unexpectedly high NVA infiltration. Westmoreland's troop requirements had already been creeping upward since July, and this latest one would mean putting 375,000 Americans into South Vietnam. McNamara had anticipated Westmoreland asking for more men, but not this soon. He flew to Saigon from a NATO meeting in Paris for a thirty-hour visit to reassess the war.

His November 30, 1965, memorandum to the president was a contrast to the easy confidence of his July report. Westmoreland was going to request even more American troops than he had so far done officially—approximately 400,000 to be sent by the end of 1966. The general might then ask for further deployments, "perhaps exceeding 200,000," in 1967. Sending Westmoreland the 400,000 men he would definitely ask for "will not guarantee success," McNamara said. "U.S. killed-in-action can be expected to reach 1,000 a month and the odds are even that we will be faced in early 1967 with a 'no-decision' at an even higher level." The administration could try to negotiate some sort of "compromise solution" and hold the dispatch of any more Americans "to a minimum" in the meantime, McNamara said, but he advised against it. He wanted "to stick with our stated objectives and with the war and provide what it takes in men and matériel."

As his "overall evaluation . . . the best chance of achieving our stated objectives," he recommended a threefold course of action. Hanoi should be given another opportunity to yield. If Ho and his associates again proved stubborn, the air war against the North should then be escalated and Westmoreland should be sent the 400,000 men. The new opportunity to yield would be proffered in "a three- or four-week pause" in the bombing of the North. Johnson had suspended Operation Rolling Thunder for five days in May 1965 and nothing had happened. McNamara's feeling was that five days had been too short a time for Hanoi to reflect. The longer pause he was now recommending was also designed to further the campaign of public relations and diplomacy he had mentioned in his July memorandum. Before taking any more escalatory steps, he told the president, "we must lay a foundation in the minds of the American public and in world opinion for such an enlarged phase of the war and . . . we should give NVN a face-saving chance to stop the aggression."

On Christmas Eve 1965, Johnson suspended the bombing as Mc-Namara wanted. Hanoi was as unyielding after thirty-seven days as it had been after five. The president resumed the bombing on January 31, 1966. By this time Westmoreland's troop requirements for his war of attrition had risen to 459,000 men. At Johnson's instruction, McNamara was engaged in a complicated game of bureaucratic haggling to hold down Westmoreland's demands while giving him most of the American soldiers he wanted.

The men of the Air Cav who had fought in the wilderness of the mountain valley were sent next to the rice-growing hamlets of the Bong Son Plain on the coast above Qui Nhon, one of the most densely populated sections of Central Vietnam and another of the Viet Minh strongholds during the French war. The operation began near the end of January 1966 and was code-named Masher. (Lyndon Johnson bridled at the taste of his generals and soon had the name changed to White Wing after the white-winged dove.) Tim Brown's term as 3rd Brigade commander had ended in December. Hal Moore, who had been promoted to full colonel, was rewarded with command of the brigade for his victory at the Chu Prong. The brigade's hard-luck battalion, the 2nd of the 7th Cavalry, caught the worst of the battle again, especially its third company, which had been rebuilt since the massacre with replacements from the United States.

The countervailing monsoon season was far advanced on this eastern side of the Annamites, and the paddies were flooded. The stretch of sand the battalion commander chose as a landing zone for the third company was zeroed in by NVA machine gunners reinforced by Viet Cong and hidden in fortified positions within groves of coconut palms on two flanks. The company was pinned down as soon as the men jumped from the helicopters and was progressively savaged through a long day of dying. The troops of another company from the battalion managed to fight their way across the paddies and close to their stranded comrades during the night, but it took a larger relief force led by Moore to complete the rescue the next morning. The dead, wrapped in their ponchos, looked forlorn on the rain-beaten sand.

A North Vietnamese regiment from the NVA's 3rd or "Yellow Star" Division had marched down the Ho Chi Minh Trail to the Bong Son Plain earlier in 1965 and had also infiltrated by sea. The Northerners had joined up with a regiment of Viet Cong regulars who had previously cleansed the area of almost all vestiges of the Saigon regime. With the help of the peasants the Communist soldiery turned every hamlet into a bastion. The approaches across the paddies and other open spaces were meticulously covered by interlocking fields of fire from automatic weapons housed in bunkers that had layers of packed earth for protection overhead. The bunkers were constructed by tearing up the abandoned railroad along the coast and using the steel rails and stout wooden ties as supports for the layers of earth. The camouflaged foxholes in the canal dikes had a thoughtful improvement—a little chamber hollowed out off to one side in which a soldier could huddle during an air or artillery bombardment and get the same kind of protection as the fighters in the bunkers. There were also zigzag communication trenches so that the Communist commanders could reinforce, resupply ammunition, and evacuate wounded in the midst of battle. They had plenty of time to arrange their dispositions before the men of the Air Cav arrived. Had their spies in the ARVN not kept them informed, the preparatory movements of their opponents would have done so. Masher had been in planning for forty-five days. It was the southern wing of an offensive involving more than 20,000 American, Saigon, and South Korean troops, the largest action on the Central Coast since the ambitious offensive by the French high command, Operation Atlante, in the winter and spring of 1954.

Moore and his subordinates and the leaders of the ARVN airborne battalions that were the other strike element of the southern wing could hardly be blamed for conserving the lives of their men by calling on every bit of firepower at their disposal. The valley of the Drang had shown that in spite of the unprecedented technology behind him, the American soldier was still subject to the rain forest and the ridges, the elephant grass and the other equalizers of Vietnam's mountains, the moment he got out of his helicopter. This battle on the Bong Son Plain illustrated that he was also not exempt from the equalizers of the low-lands that the ARVN had encountered once the Viet Cong had been allowed to grow strong in the Mekong Delta. Brig. Gen. Howard Eggleston, an odd-man-out engineer who had been one of Charlie Timmes's deputies in 1963, had an engineer's appreciation for water and mud. He observed that no matter how many helicopters an army possessed, "you don't have much mobility in a full rice paddy." To have taken these hamlets chiefly by infantry assault across the flooded paddies would have meant massive casualties. The punishment of the first couple of days (the ARVN paratroops were also initially hurt trying to show the Americans they were not cowards) had a sobering effect. The commanders began to settle for pummeling a hamlet with shellfire and air strikes until the enemy abandoned it.

At the end of four days the Viet Cong regulars and the NVA gave up their last bastions and retreated over the nearest mountains into the narrow An Lao Valley to the west and then further into the Annamite range, generally refusing to give battle when the Air Cav pursued. The Communists left behind several hundred dead and fifty-five weapons. It was impossible to determine from the American side how many of the dead were Viet Cong regulars and NVA and how many were local guerrillas whose surviving comrades had gone to ground temporarily in hideouts in the vicinity. Whatever the precise Communist casualties, they were not serious enough to keep either regiment out of action for long.

While the North Vietnamese and their Viet Cong allies had done a lot less dying on this occasion than the NVA had in the valley of the Drang, Operation Masher had been appropriately named. The peasants were mashed. Fifteen hamlets were torn up. About 1,000 houses were blown apart or burned down in the three hamlets I was able to reach most easily, because they were along the main coastal road, Route 1. The Army captain who drove me to them was the advisor to the nearest district chief at the town of Bong Son about ten miles away at the southern end of the plain. Bong Son town had been the only community remaining in Saigon's hands at the start of the operation. The captain had seen most of the other dozen hamlets fought over, and he and the officials at the district headquarters said these had been savaged just as badly. Bomb craters—the ones from the 500-pounders were ten feet deep by twenty feet across—pockmarked the hamlets and the landscapes around them.

The U.S. Army, like the ARVN, would accept no responsibility for the civilian wounded. The casualties had been substantial among the civilians, if not nearly as severe as the physical damage indicated. The old people and the women and children had for the most part fled or been saved by the bomb shelters the Viet Cong had taught them to dig under their houses. At least 100 people were estimated to have died, however, in Tam Quan, a town near the northern end of the plain that had formerly been a Saigon district headquarters and then the Communist one at the time of the battle. The Air Cav medics and field surgeons and the ARVN airborne medics treated and released hundreds of lightly wounded civilians who came to them. The seriously wounded who lived long enough to be brought to someone's attention were another matter. The Cav medical personnel would do nothing for them other than to give them preliminary treatment and have them evacuated to the province hospital at Qui Nhon. As Saigon government military hospitals were reserved for the ARVN, so U.S. military hospitals were for American soldiers and civilians and so-called third-country nationals, such as the Koreans and Filipinos who were working for the United States in Vietnam. (Exceptions were sometimes made for Vietnamese, but the number was small.)

About ninety seriously injured civilians from the Bong Son hamlets were evacuated to the Qui Nhon hospital. The Humane Society would have had the place closed down had it been an animal hospital in the United States. USOM had started renovating the old French-built hospital in 1963. The usual corruption had prevented the work from ever being completed. The latrines were unfinished. There were no showers or tubs. Patients who could walk relieved themselves in the yard. The hospital was understaffed, and the majority of the Vietnamese doctors and nurses theoretically on duty were lazy and venal. They looked after patients who paid. The poor depended on their families to nurse them and to fan away the flies. Most of the surgery and skilled medical care was performed by two New Zealand surgeons and an anesthetist on a medical mission financed by their government. What two doctors and a medical technician can accomplish when their sense of duty is high can be heroic, but it cannot be miraculous. The scenes as the wounded old people and the women and children were crowded in from Masher were ghastly even by the standard of the Qui Nhon hospital.

I asked Maj. Gen. Stanley Larsen, the commander of the U.S. Army corps that was being formed for the Central Coast and the Highlands,

what plans he had to follow up the operation and pacify the Bong Son
Plain. "Swede" Larsen was an affable man whose ideas fit him comfortably into the Army hierarchy of the day. He was about to be awarded
the third star of a lieutenant general. We talked when I hitched a ride
back down the coast on his plane. He said that he had no pacification
plans. After the pursuit phase of the operation was completed, he was
going to pull out the Air Cav and look for another battlefield. The
ARVN airborne would also be withdrawn.

His answer astonished me. It had never occurred to me that an American general would get so many of his own soldiers killed and inflict
such horror simply to walk away. Why had he gone into those hamlets
in the first place if he had not intended to stay and achieve something
permanent? I asked. Larsen said he did not have enough American
troops to tie any down protecting pacification teams. The best he could
do was to keep the Viet Cong and the NVA off balance by mauling
them in "spoiling attacks," as Masher had been, while the American
buildup went forward as fast as possible. Then what about using the
ARVN? Larsen said he had spoken to his counterpart, Brig. Gen. Vinh
Loc, the ARVN II Corps commander at Pleiku. Loc said he had no
troops to spare either. All Loc would agree to shift to the Bong Son
area was a regiment.

I discovered later that the real explanation for Larsen's attitude was
that he was not interested in pacification. Like most Army generals, he
subscribed to the attrition theory of Harkins and Westmoreland that
repeated confrontations would wear down and eventually consume the
guerrillas and the North Vietnamese. I had heard these American generals speak of a war of attrition, but its meaning for the people and the
country of South Vietnam had not registered with me. Did Larsen realize
that the Viet Cong and the NVA were going to move right back into
those hamlets? I asked. "Then we'll go back and kill more of the sons
of bitches," he said.

The Bong Son Plain was noted for its fine groves of coconut palms.
Many of the farmers depended on selling the dried meat, called copra,
from which coconut oil is extracted, and on peddling fresh coconuts as
produce. Moore's 3rd Brigade and the ARVN airborne had drawn part
of their fire support from Seventh Fleet destroyers. Naval shells are shot
in a relatively flat trajectory. In just one of the hamlets I walked through
along Route 1, hundreds of coconut trees had been snapped in half by
the 5-inch projectiles. The district chief and the U.S. Army captain
advising him said that the regiment Vinh Loc was sending would be
fortunate to be able to defend its compound. The previous hostility of

the population in the area was going to seem mild in retrospect. Hardly any of the children in Tam Quan would smile, and when questioned they stared at one in silence. Vinh Loc might not know how to find troops for pacification, but he and a relative he had recently appointed province chief did know how to take advantage of the temporary security along Route 1 bought by the sacrifice of more of Moore's soldiers and the ARVN paratroops. The corps commander and his relative had Chinese middlemen buying copra from the farmers and running it down to Qui Nhon by the truckload to sell there. Although Vinh Loc regularly traded in copra, he could make more money while the security lasted. Normally, he had to share his profit with the Viet Cong.

Thousands of refugees were camped in the open beside the road and in Bong Son town. Other thousands who had lost their homes were still in their hamlets living on the temporary charity of relatives or friends. These newly homeless of the Bong Son Plain were one of the brooks feeding a river of the uprooted in South Vietnam. There were well over half a million refugees in the country, and the number was rising each month. The USOM representatives from Qui Nhon and their Vietnamese staff and some workers the district chief provided were passing out emergency supplies of bulgur wheat and cooking oil. They also had some bolts of cloth and sewing kits to give away. These ran out quickly, because there were only a few hundred in stock. During a handout of bulgur wheat and cooking oil in one of the hamlets, several psychological-warfare representatives distributed leaflets on Viet Cong bomb atrocities in Saigon. An old lady wailed that the planes had demolished her house and the big guns had cut down forty-seven of the fifty coconut trees she needed for her livelihood. The captain advising the district chief had Vann's sense of irony. He opened a leaflet. Some of the photographs showed American victims of Viet Cong terrorism. "I'll bet these people look at those pictures and think, 'Bully for the Viet Cong,' " he said.

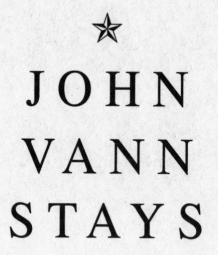

BOOK SEVEN

JOHN
VANN
STAYS

Kennedy exploited in the 1960 election against Nixon, apparently thinking it was true—was a fable. The Soviets' humiliation in the Cuban missile crisis, which was to goad them into a full-fledged nuclear buildup, had not yet occurred. American intelligence showed they had four ICBMs and fewer than 200 intercontinental bombers. The U.S. Air Force generals and Navy admirals had, on the other hand, prepared a thermonuclear blitzkrieg with scores of land-based and submarine-launched missiles and thousands of aircraft. The Joint Chiefs' plan envisioned killing approximately 325 million people in the Soviet Union and China. When deaths from strikes in Eastern Europe and from radioactive fallout in countries on the periphery like Finland and Pakistan and Japan were counted in, along with the number of deaths the Russians would be able to inflict on the United States before they were obliterated, the total fatalities would exceed half a billion. The American military leaders would make Hitler's Holocaust look like a misdemeanor, Ellsberg thought. He attributed the JCS plan to a "mad dog" mentality within the military leadership, especially the Air Force generals who subscribed to the Douhet Theory (named after its originator, the Italian general Giulio Douhet) of waging total war from the air. The solution, Ellsberg decided, was firmer and wiser civilian control.

When the intellectuals came into their reward in 1960 with the election of John Kennedy (when, as Henry Kissinger put it wryly, "professors for the first time moved from advisory to operational responsibilities"), Ellsberg's career flourished. Kennedy did want tighter control of the military. Ellsberg's special knowledge and presumed expertise, the coin of influence for a government intellectual, put him in demand at the top. Rand sent him to Washington on permanent detail to the new administration. He wrote memoranda for McGeorge Bundy and McNamara recommending changes in the Joint Strategic Capabilities Plan, and a number of his recommendations were adopted. When the Cuban missile crisis occurred in October 1962, he worked on the crisis-management teams that Paul Nitze formed at the Pentagon and Walt Rostow organized at State. By 1964, Ellsberg had acquired sufficient stature to be appointed special assistant to John McNaughton, the former Harvard law professor who had recently been named McNamara's deputy for foreign affairs. He left Rand and formally entered government at the highest possible Civil Service level, the "supergrade" rank of a GS-18.

As his professional fortunes were rising, Ellsberg's private life was disintegrating. His wife told him that she didn't love him and insisted on a divorce. The Ellsbergs had two children. The dissolution of his

THE FIRST Vietnamese peasant homes to be burned by U.S. troops were put to the torch by the Marines in several hamlets near Da Nang on August 3, 1965. Morley Safer of CBS filmed the burnings and shocked millions of Americans who watched the network's evening news. "If this is to be our policy," Vann wrote Bob York, "then I want no part of it and will not be associated with such an effort. Am waiting until Lodge arrives and indicates the direction we go."

About a year later John Vann had a chance to leave Vietnam. He was offered the post of chief of the Asian Division in McNamara's brain trust in the Pentagon—the Office of Systems Analysis. Dan Ellsberg helped him get the offer, and McNamara approved his appointment. The job had a future. It was an opportunity to enter the elite world of intellectuals and military men who form a subgovernment within the executive branch. In the year since the first outrage, the Marine generals had, with some lapses, enforced a ban on informal house burnings. Westmoreland and most of the Army generals had taken a more permissive attitude. "Zippo jobs" on Vietnamese hamlets by American soldiers had become so common that television audiences in the United States were no longer scandalized by them. Vann was also no longer writing to York about them. He used the Pentagon job offer as leverage to ensure his promotion to a post he wanted—director of the whole civilian pacification effort for the III Corps region.

Ellsberg had taken the place in Vann's life that Ramsey had held, and he and Vann became more intimate friends than Vann and Ramsey had been. Vann and Ellsberg were the odd couple, difficult men from different worlds satisfying complementary needs in each other. When Ellsberg was five his mother had set out to make him a renowned concert pianist. She started him practicing four hours every day after school and eight hours on Saturday. To keep him from hurting his hands she prevented him from playing any sport, even pickup baseball. If she found him interested in a book she would take it away and hide it to keep him from being diverted from music. When he was fifteen his father, a structural engineer of Russian-Jewish heritage who earned a modest living, first in Chicago where Ellsberg was born and then in Detroit, apparently fell asleep at the wheel of the family car. Ellsberg suffered a head injury that put him in a coma for thirty-six hours and a broken knee. His father was not injured seriously. His mother and sister were killed in the crash. His mother's regimen kept Ellsberg at the piano for a time after she died. Then he stopped. Later when he became a famous man his entry in *Who's Who in America* was to show an extraordinarily rare omission. He listed his father's name; he left out the name of his mother.

He arrived at Harvard in 1948, the year the Cold War became a grim morality play as the Czech Communist Party seized power in Prague and Stalin staged the Berlin Blockade. The Harvard that Ellsberg entered was a place where ambitious intellectuals were beginning to see scholarship as a road to high office in the new American state. World War II had given intellectuals a turn in the action-oriented atmosphere of government, and many liked it. The Cold War perpetuated a cause and a crisis and encouraged the rationale that intellectuals could provide an expertise lacking among the corporation lawyers, investment bankers, and businessmen who had traditionally monopolized the senior appointive posts. Arthur Schlesinger, Jr., the historian, and John Kenneth Galbraith, the economist, both to serve in the Kennedy administration, were teaching at Harvard when Ellsberg entered. McGeorge Bundy, the first academic to hold the office of special assistant to the president for national security affairs, initially to John Kennedy and subsequently to Lyndon Johnson, was on his way to Harvard after a stint as a foreign policy advisor to Thomas Dewey, the Republican presidential candidate in 1948. The intellectual who was to outclimb all of his peers, Henry Kissinger, had had his education delayed by Army service during World War II. He was a junior at Harvard when Ellsberg enrolled as a freshman. Ellsberg majored in economics and graduated third in his class. After his year of postgraduate study in England at King's College, Cambridge, he did something that spoke of Ellsberg.

Proving one's prowess at arms was not a necessity in the world he was entering. He could have fulfilled his military service obligation in these years of the draft with six months of active duty in the Army and reserve status. Instead he joined the Marines for two years and drove

himself to excel at every attribute of a Marine officer. To attain singular distinction of Expert Marksman from both right and left with the .45 caliber pistol, he strengthened his pianist's hands and arms by holding the heavy pistol in the air with arm outstretched hours on end as he read. He learned that the pistol's hammer w knock a pencil several feet if one stuck the eraser end of the pe down the barrel when the .45 was empty and pulled the trigger. Ellsb pasted a bull's-eye on a wall and shot a pencil at it night after ni He achieved a trigger pull so perfectly smooth that the pistol ne wavered off target out on the firing range. Other lieutenants in the Marine Division at Camp Lejeune obtained acting company comman but had to surrender their companies in a few weeks to captains w outranked them. Lieutenant Ellsberg kept the company command got, because under his leadership the company won more awards th any other in the battalion and was foremost in inspections and maneuvers.

When Ellsberg's enlistment was expiring in mid-1956 and he was abou to return to Harvard for the dream of an apprentice intellectual, doctor work as a junior member of the renowned Society of Fellows, Nasse seized the Suez Canal. Ellsberg's battalion was ordered to the Sixth Fleet in the Mediterranean. He wrote a distinguished professor at Harvard that the Society of Fellows would have to wait and extended his Marine enlistment for eight months. Eisenhower disappointed Ellsberg by not intervening.

In 1959 he left Harvard for the Rand Corporation, the civilian research institute the Air Force had established in Santa Monica, California, drawn by what he believed to be the momentous task of his time—preventing nuclear war by deterring the Soviet Union from a surprise attack on the United States. He was given clearances beyond Top Secret—clearances designated by code words that were themselves secret—so that he could analyze intelligence from U-2 spy aircraft and other esoteric sources. He studied the U.S. "command and control" procedures through which the planes with the hydrogen bombs were to be sent on their way to Russia and the intercontinental ballistic missiles launched, and he wrote ultrasecret memoranda on how to improve them. At the Pentagon he read the most closely guarded secrets of all in the central nuclear war plan of the nation, the Joint Strategic Capabilities Plan.

Ellsberg was dismayed by what he learned. The Soviets were hardly in a position to make a surprise attack. The claim that the Russians ha a big advantage in intercontinental missiles—the so-called missile g marriage pushed Ellsberg into despondency. He had become involved with the war in Vietnam through his work for John McNaughton. He probably would have gone off to the conflict sooner or later anyway, whatever the state of his private life, out of the same romanticism and desire to prove himself that had led him to extend his service in the Marines. His dejection made his longing for confrontation and a new cause that much more acute. After the buildup began in mid-1965 he inquired about assignment to Vietnam as a Marine company commander. He was warned that because of his civilian credentials the Marine Corps might assign him to a staff job, which did not interest Ellsberg. He asked Lansdale to take him on as a member of his team, and Lansdale, ever open to verve and intelligence, welcomed him. McNaughton did not attempt to dissuade him from going. He was becoming skittish about Ellsberg. A need to boast about what he knew made Ellsberg somewhat indiscreet under normal circumstances. His emotional distress was making his indiscretion worse. Although appropriate reticence is a matter of survival in any bureaucracy, the lack of it could bring unusually swift ruin in McNamara's Pentagon.

Vann's name was on a "must" list of people to see that Ellsberg carried with him to Vietnam. He followed up his initial visit to Hau Nghia with Lansdale at the beginning of September 1965 by coming out again in mid-October to spend the better part of three days talking to Vann and roaming the province with him. The trip converted Ellsberg to fervid enthusiasm for Vann's social-revolution strategy.

The egocentricity that often grated on Ellsberg's colleagues in the high-stakes-competition world of the government intellectual was muted in his relationship with Vann. These years in Vietnam brought out the zest for adventure and the compassion and sensitivity that were also mixed into Ellsberg's complex personality. He was an appealing figure at thirty-four, with his lithe build, the occasional ironic smile in the slim face, the blue-gray eyes electric with curiosity, the teasing sense of humor. There was no feeling of competition between the two men. To Ellsberg, Vann was supreme in the realm of action. To Vann, Ellsberg was the brightest man he had ever met. Vann was to say to Halberstam that Ellsberg had "the most brilliant mind ever exposed to the realities of Vietnam." He showed his poor-Southern-boy inferiority in the way he expressed his esteem for Ellsberg's academic accomplishment. To third parties who were not mutual friends he would invariably refer to Ellsberg as "Dr. Dan Ellsberg." Converting a man like Ellsberg to his ideas flattered Vann. He hoped that Ellsberg might succeed someday in promoting them and him. After all, Ellsberg actually was on a first-name basis with those who sat next to power in Washington. But Vann's liking for Dan Ellsberg went beyond calculations of self-interest. He enjoyed Ellsberg's company, and Ellsberg was prepared to go wherever John Vann would take him.

Ellsberg discovered what a true companion spirit he had found one weekend in December 1965, during a drive with Vann to two of the more remote province capitals in the III Corps region. It was not the first weekend expedition for Ellsberg. Vann had decided to explore the entire eleven-province area methodically at the end of October when Charles Mann had promoted him out of Hau Nghia to be civilian affairs advisor to Jonathan Seaman, the commanding general of U.S. forces in III Corps. He announced his plan to Ellsberg, saying it was the only way to find out who owned what. Ellsberg immediately asked to join him.

Previous trips had been to provinces relatively close to Saigon. For this one they were going to leave early on Saturday morning, because their first destination, Xuan Loc, deep in the rubber-plantation country, was about sixty road miles northeast of Saigon. They would then have another seventy-five to eighty road miles farther to go before they reached their final goal, the capital of Binh Tuy Province, a forlorn little place near the coast called Ham Tan. Vann intended to arrive in Xuan Loc by noon, have a quick lunch and chat with the advisors there, and proceed right on to Ham Tan in order to get there before dark. They would spend the night in Ham Tan and drive back to Saigon by the same route on Sunday.

That Friday evening he and Ellsberg happened to mention the forthcoming expedition to one of the young Foreign Service officers at the embassy. The man was a field political reporter whose job was to go to the countryside and report on political attitudes and security conditions. Like almost all American officials, he now did his traveling by plane and helicopter. It had been ages since he had gotten out of Saigon, he said, and still longer since he had had an opportunity to assess security conditions realistically by looking at them from the ground. He would love to go along. Vann said fine.

After the turn at Bien Hoa just north of Saigon, the road became lonely. The embassy field political reporter noticed the rows of fence stakes with the bits of chopped barbed wire dangling from them. He looked at the burned militia outposts. He saw the ragged strips of dirt bisecting the asphalt. The strips marked the spots where the Saigon side had hastily filled in ditches the Viet Cong had cut across the road by blasting a culvert to stop all movement during an attack or ambush. "John, I'm really not supposed to be doing this," he said. "Political reporters are not supposed to be out on the roads. We have orders not to get captured. I think I'd better try to catch a helicopter." Vann stopped at an ARVN camp and left him in the care of the advisors to the unit. The embassy man was waiting for Vann and Ellsberg as they drove into the province advisory compound at Xuan Loc. The advisors at the camp had managed to summon a helicopter for him. He looked a bit sheepish. During lunch at Xuan Loc the advisors there treated Vann and Ellsberg with the respect military men accord the daring. They were full of questions about what these two civilians had observed along the road. The reception accorded Vann and Ellsberg rekindled the enthusiasm of the embassy political reporter. "To hell with it," he said when it was time to press on. "I'm going with you."

The three men had a lively conversation underway in the armored Scout as they set off for Ham Tan. Vann had selected the Scout for this trip because of its four-wheel-drive capability; they might have to leave the road to negotiate an obstacle. He was at the steering wheel. Ellsberg was in the passenger seat beside him. The embassy man was in the middle of the little bench seat just behind them where he had been riding in the morning.

A short way out of Xuan Loc the road began to pass through some of the densest rain forest Ellsberg was ever to see in Vietnam. He knew precisely what to do. Vann had trained him during their previous expeditions. He glanced down at his side to be sure a grenade was handy and lifted the carbine he had been cradling in his lap so that he could immediately open fire out the window. Vann started driving with one hand. With the other he raised the M-16 automatic he now customarily carried to be ready to shoot out his side. Ellsberg wondered how they were going to shoot if they did encounter guerrillas. The years of neglect from the war had allowed the rain forest to encroach until the road was only wide enough for one vehicle to pass. The forest was so dense Ellsberg had the feeling that if he stuck his arm out the window, he wouldn't be able to get it back; the undergrowth would snatch it. Then the road began to twist through blind curves. Ellsberg decided that if his seven-year-old daughter had an automatic weapon she could ambush a whole regiment on this one-way track through the jungle.

As the road worsened and they made these preparations for action, Vann and Ellsberg kept up the conversation. Keeping up the conversation was important to them. They were enjoying the self-control and sharpening of the senses they felt in the presence of danger.

The embassy political reporter did not say a word for quite a while.

About twenty minutes out of Xuan Loc, he suddenly found his voice again. "John, how's the security on this road?" he asked.

"Bad," Vann replied.

"Well, I think I'd better go back, John," the embassy man said.

Vann found a place to turn around. He did not recover his temper sufficiently to do more than curse until he had returned to Xuan Loc and had the Scout back out on the one-way track through the rain forest, now with both hands on the wheel, wrenching the vehicle through the turns to try to make up for the lost time. "You know," he said to Ellsberg, "I didn't think he'd have guts enough to get out a second time."

Ellsberg smiled. "Well, dammit, John, why did you say that about the security?" he asked.

"What could I say?" Vann said. He laughed and let go of the steering wheel for a second and swept his hands up toward the jungle that menaced from every side. "Look at it!"

At Ham Tan there was a final moment to savor. They pulled up in front of the building where the province military advisors lived and went in and introduced themselves. One of the young officers noticed the Scout parked outside. He did a double take. He looked at Vann and Ellsberg, at the vehicle, and then back at Vann and Ellsberg again.

"Did you people drive here?" he asked. They said yes as casually as they could.

"Is that road open?" another advisor asked, astounded.

"Well, it is now," Vann said.

They were the first Americans to drive to Ham Tan in nearly a year.

Sex, like danger, was another shared interest that helped make the friendship between Vann and Ellsberg intimate. Ramsey had never displayed much interest in this subject that was of such immense concern to Vann, so Vann had pretended, as he did with men like Ramsey, that his girl hunting in Saigon was just the temporary larking of an overseas bachelor and that he was a serious family man who cared for Mary Jane and was concerned about the upbringing of their children. Ellsberg lacked Vann's insatiable need for women, but his sexual life mattered to him and he was relatively open about it. When Vann found a friend who regarded sex with some of the importance he did, he interpreted the attitude as an invitation to confide the details of his exploits, which he liked to do. He was also inclined to be more candid about other personal relationships and about his past. "I'm only married in name," he explained to Ellsberg. He said that while he respected Mary Jane, he had no special feeling for her, that they had nothing in common anymore. He also told Ellsberg about the statutory-rape episode and how, despite his victory over the lie detector, the accusation would have barred him forever from promotion to general.

The coincidence of having houses in Saigon next door to each other further reinforced the friendship. Although Vann slept most nights during the fall of 1965 in a tent at General Seaman's headquarters or at some other spot in the countryside, he was entitled to quarters in Saigon under his AID contract. He had begun sharing a house on Tran Quy Cap Street not far from Westmoreland's villa with another close friend acquired through the war, Col. George Jacobson. Jake, as he was known to his friends, was once called "the consummate staff officer" by Vann. No derision was intended, as Jacobson had seen a lot of action in an armored cavalry reconnaissance unit in France and Germany. He was a tall and well-proportioned man of innate dignity, fifty years old in 1965, with a mustache, a baritone voice, and a warm and genuinely considerate manner. He had earned his living as a professional magician and master of ceremonies prior to volunteering for the Army early in World War II. George Jacobson had disciplined himself during his twenty-four years in the Army to study the character and mindset of a superior in order to avoid futile clashes with idiosyncrasies and preconceptions. Troubles that the boss should not be bothered with, or would not listen to, Jake settled himself or deflected as temporarily insoluble. He then used the credit built up by his tactful efficiency to try to get the boss to confront other important problems he might be capable of resolving.

Jacobson had first come to Vietnam in 1954 as a lieutenant colonel on Iron Mike O'Daniel's staff. He returned as a colonel in the 1960s, and by 1962 headed the organization and training division of the MAAG under General Timmes. He had been profoundly admiring of Vann's performance at 7th Division and had attempted to persuade a friend, Maj. Gen. William Yarborough, then commander of the Army's Special Warfare Center at Fort Bragg, to have Vann assigned there on his return to the United States. Jacobson's initiative might have kept Vann in the Army had it succeeded. In 1965, Jake had decided that he was sufficiently committed to the war himself to go into the pacification business and had arranged a transfer to AID on detail from the Army. He was officially Vann's immediate superior as a deputy director of field operations and unofficially Vann's chief protector at AID's Saigon headquarters.

The relationship was again one of ease, because it was complementary,

Vann being Jacobson's touchstone with reality in the countryside. There was also a personal reason that the two men got along sharing a house. Jacobson was moderate in his womanizing, not compulsive like Vann, but he regarded the pursuit of the opposite sex as the best of hobbies. Ellsberg had no roommate in the house he had been assigned next door. His rank (his Civil Service rating had been converted to the highest rank in the Foreign Service Reserve, FSR-1, when he went to Vietnam) entitled him to a house of his own. He gave Vann a key and free run of the place. Vann found Ellsberg's house especially useful when he had an assignation at some hour that might inconvenience Jacobson.

Prior to 1965 the presence of American wives and children had enforced convention among middle- and upper-ranking U.S. officials. The benefit of life in a poor Asian country with an uncommon number of attractive women had been reserved for enlisted men and younger officers and civilians. Some men with responsible positions had, of course, still indulged in hanky-panky. To protect their careers they had to be discreet, as Vann had been in 1962 and 1963 by taking his pleasure in Saigon or at the beach resort of Vung Tau (Cap St. Jacques) on the occasional weekend he could fly there. When the families had been evacuated at the beginning of 1965 to "clear the decks," in Dean Rusk's phrase, for the bombing of the North, convention departed with them. American men in South Vietnam became sexually privileged males. One well-known civilian kept his mistress at his villa and brought her to official social functions where the diplomatic corps and the wives of high-ranking Vietnamese were present. Disapproval of his conduct was mixed with envy. His Vietnamese paramour was a young woman of remarkable beauty. After his assignment ended and he returned to the United States and his wife, she slept her way higher up the ladder of U.S. authority until she found a lover powerful enough to arrange an escape to Paris when it was time for him to leave as well.

Claiming that a mistress was a housekeeper, however, or bringing a woman to one's quarters in the evening, or carrying on after hours with the Vietnamese secretaries from the office (the women had no choice but to submit if they wished to retain their jobs), was considered perfectly normal. The custom became acceptable even for men who had their wives and children living in the "safe havens" of Bangkok and the Philippines in order to visit their families monthly. (Vann preferred the excuse the war offered to hold Mary Jane and her brood at the safer distance of Colorado.) Men who worked hard were entitled to relaxation. As Ellsworth Bunker, an upright man who was fond of salacious jokes, put it: "There's a lot of plain and fancy screwing going on around here, but I suppose it's all in the interest of the war effort."

In this atmosphere Vann could indulge his proclivity with an abandon that would have been impossible in the United States or on any normal foreign assignment without destroying himself professionally. Ellsberg was not alone among Vann's friends in noticing that when Vann was in Saigon he often made love to two or three different young women a day. This repeated sexual jousting that would have exhausted most men seemed to invigorate Vann. After his last assignation in the evening he would settle down to the night's work of reading reports and writing memos, concentrating well and writing quickly into the early hours of the morning.

In addition to these innumerable casual romps, Vann formed enduring liaisons with two Vietnamese women and managed, with considerable agility, to keep each woman ignorant of the other for most of the years to come. He spotted Lee, the nickname he gave his first mistress, on a Friday afternoon in November 1965 about three weeks after he left Hau Nghia. She was standing on the sidewalk in front of her family's house on a main thoroughfare in Saigon, waiting to hail a cab for the afternoon and evening teaching sessions of an English-language school she had started. He was on his way to the new 1st Infantry Division command post at Di An just north of the city. He stopped his car about ten yards from where she was standing and got out to scrape a piece of gum off the sole of one of his shoes. (He had just stuck it on, one of his many tricks.) He was then genuinely surprised, after he offered her a ride and she accepted, to discover that she spoke fluent English. He had thought she was a student. She was dressed simply and wore her long black hair down over her shoulders. She was five days short of twenty-one at the time, about two years older than his daughter, Patricia. He was forty-one. During the short drive to her school he asked if she would like to have dinner with him on Sunday night. She saw the wedding ring on his hand. She said yes anyway. They would have to meet in front of the school, she said, because her family would object to her dating an American and the neighbors would talk. They set the time for 7:30. Vann kept his weekend trip to a province with Ellsberg short so as not to be late.

The wedding ring was gone when he met her Sunday evening. He was wearing only the Rutgers class ring that he never took off. She was not to see the wedding ring again. Over dinner and dancing at a fashionable nightclub she asked how many children he had. None, he said, his wife had never been able to have any. He said that he and his wife had separated four years ago and he was looking for someone to fall in love with and marry. She asked his age. He said he was thirty-six. Her twenty-first birthday was that Wednesday, and she intended to take the day off to celebrate. He said he would take the day off. They went to a swimming pool near a billet for American officers in Cholon. She wore a bikini. When he saw her figure he said that until that moment he had not realized how truly lucky he had been to meet her. After dinner that evening they made love in his bedroom in the house he shared with George Jacobson.

Lee's family was one that had prospered in French Cochinchina. Her grandfather had been a finance minister in the Bao Dai years and again under Diem and had headed the National Bank for a while. Her father had served in the Sûreté Générale before 1954 and had then taken a position at the bank. He and her mother kept their French citizenship and passports. At her father's suggestion she had studied English as her second language for half a dozen years at the French schools in Saigon where she had been educated. She had also taken the courses USIS offered through the Vietnamese-American Association. (She learned to speak a Frenchified Vietnamese at home and later had to teach herself how to read and write the language of her people.) Her father had wanted her to go to Saigon University or to France to study pharmacy or medicine, but while Lee was intelligent, she was not intellectual, and she was tired of books. She wanted some financial independence and was enterprising. The teaching of English was becoming a major industry. It seemed as if every young man who could avoid conscription into the ARVN and every young woman who could pay the tuition wanted to learn enough English to get a job with the Americans. When Lee met Vann she had about fifty full-time students at her small school and was earning an excellent living.

Although Lee was a pleasant-looking woman, she did not have one of those slim Vietnamese figures that turned American heads. She was buxom for a Vietnamese, with a rounded figure not unlike Mary Jane's when she and Vann had met at Critic's ice cream parlor. Vann had an eye for women who were, as Lee said in the American slang she quickly learned, "well padded." She was also a physical challenge to him. He told Dan Ellsberg that no matter how many times he made love to her of an evening, she was always prepared for more. Her command of English, her intelligence, and her feisty personality made her a good companion as well.

Their trysts grew into a full-fledged affair after Vann was appointed AID's manager of the new program to train specialized teams of Vietnamese pacification workers near the end of 1965. The job required Vann to divide his time between Saigon and the training camp for the teams at Vung Tau, and on many days when he was at the camp, he flew back to Saigon in the evening. He would pick Lee up at her school after she had taught her last class. The two would have a late supper at his house (he and Jacobson kept a cook) and then make love before he drove her home and returned to tackle his paperwork. On weekends he would treat her to dinner at a French or Chinese restaurant or to dancing at a nightclub, and on an occasional Sunday they would drive to Vung Tau to sun and swim. Vann had an ARVN engineer captain he became friendly with forge a set of French license plates for his car, and Lee was not alarmed by grenades on the seat. She had been ready for an affair with an exciting American, hoping to maneuver the affair into marriage, because she had made up her mind in her teens that she did not want to marry a Vietnamese. She felt that with too few exceptions, Vietnamese men tended to treat their wives crudely and to victimize them. Her father had confirmed her impression. He had taken a second wife and split his spare time between her mother's household and a house he maintained for the other woman. Lee did not intend to share her mother's fate.

She began to suspect after a while that Vann might be cheating on her. On days when he was in Saigon he often picked her up early so that they could make love at the end of the afternoon. He would drive her back to the school afterward for her evening teaching session. He sometimes showered and put on dress slacks and a fresh white shirt and tie before he did. A shirt and tie were acceptable wear for a dinner date at a Saigon restaurant, because even if the restaurant was air-conditioned, a jacket became oppressive as soon as one went outside. About a month after they first made love, he had also put a wrinkle in the initial impression he gave her that he was unencumbered by confessing to the existence of his children. She had been slightly upset as well to discover through her inevitable questions that she was so close in age to Patricia. He then acknowledged being a bit older than he had first told her. He wanted her so much, he said, that he couldn't stop himself from lying. She forgave him the lie about the children and the trimming of his age. He had assured her again that he and Mary Jane were separated and that he was going to ask for a divorce as soon as he went on his next home leave. Whenever she now showed suspicion that he was putting on a shirt and tie to date someone else, he fobbed her off by telling her that he had an important meeting for which he had to dress up.

Lee's suspicion was correct. In the spring of 1966 Vann was starting an affair with the young woman who was to become his second Vietnamese mistress and eventually the mother of his child. He brought to his avocation the same resourcefulness he did to his vocation. The Good Samaritan who happened to be driving by on a rainy night and offered a ride, the nonchalant American who stopped on a sunny afternoon to scrape a piece of gum off the sole of his shoe, also scouted places where Vietnamese girls regularly gathered. One such place was the Vietnamese-American Association when English classes were being held. He found "Annie" there right after the evening session on Saturday, April 2, 1966.

She was a romantically inclined seventeen-year-old with a problem that was not unusual for a girl of her age. She was acquainted with a lot of boys in Dalat, where she had just finished her junior year at the Lycée Yersin, but none of them had ever shown any romantic interest in her. She had yet to go out on her first date. She was back home in Saigon for the annual three-month vacation and had decided to take advantage of her spare time to improve her rudimentary English.

Vann had a practiced eye for loneliness. He walked over to her and said that she was pretty and complimented her on her clothes. He said he had come to the VAA to see an Army captain who was a friend and one of the volunteer English instructors. (The captain did teach there, and the pretense of visiting him was another of Vann's ploys.) Vann said that he wished he had a friend like her to teach him Vietnamese. (Vann was unable to learn foreign languages with any proficiency, because he was tone-deaf. He had dropped out of an AID course in Vietnamese for this reason.) She smiled and said she wished she had an American friend so that she could practice her English. She accepted his offer of a ride home.

In the car she too heard the Vietnam variation of the infallible line that the weeping German girl had recited to Mary Jane in Heidelberg a decade earlier. There was a whit more truth in the separated-from-wife and seeking-new-woman-to-love-and-marry yarn he told Annie than in the one he had given Lee. He no longer felt it necessary to lie about his children. He asked her for a date. She declined, saying that she was too busy at the moment. "Okay, I'll wait," he said. After her next class at the VAA, she found him waiting to drive her home. She gave him her phone number. He called several times and cajoled until she accepted his invitation to dinner at a good French restaurant near the Saigon River. She remembered him as "an ideal man, very kind, very tender, very gentle, and always very patient." After dinner he drove her to his house and asked her to come in and see where he lived. Not this time, she said.

He was surprised when, a number of French and fancy Chinese restaurants later, she did let him take her to bed. He used Ellsberg's house for the occasion, as Jacobson apparently had visitors that evening. He assumed, because of the ease with which she had let him pick her up on the first night at the VAA, that she had some experience and was being coy. She was a virgin.

She went back to the lycée at Dalat in July, but she couldn't study. She was too preoccupied with Vann. She wrote him ardent letters, and he responded. To her surprise, he even flew up to Dalat to see her one weekend. Her parents first learned that something was wrong when her grades, which had been fair, fell drastically. She came home in September for the funeral of a grandmother and refused to return to Dalat. She announced that she was going to find a job in Saigon. Her father, a well-educated man, was devastated. She was his first child, and he was ambitious for her. Hers was also a family of means, Chinese on the father's side, Vietnamese on the mother's. Vann called her by a diminutive of the French first name she had informally acquired at the lycée, where the teachers made the students choose French names for roll call. Her father had studied business and economics in France and in Britain. He had lived abroad for twelve years, mostly in France, before returning after World War II and serving as an economics advisor in the Bao Dai regime. Later he had gone into the export-import and insurance businesses in a modest way. She had passed the first part of the baccalaureate examination shortly after her junior year in Dalat. Her father had planned to send her to Paris to study medicine or chemistry as soon as she had completed senior year and succeeded at the second part.

Vann encouraged her to quit school and stay in Saigon. Everything he said and did reinforced her conviction that he fully returned her love. She was a contrast to Lee in many ways. Her figure was shapely, but slim. While loving, she was not aggressive. Nor was she the bantering companion that Lee was. She was never to develop Lee's command of the English language. Annie was a softly restrained young woman, cheerful in a quiet way. Lee appealed to Vann because she was an adventure each time he bedded her and was one of those rare women to whom he could talk. For a man like Vann, however, there would always be an element of threat in a relationship with a woman like Lee. He wanted Annie precisely because of her contrasting qualities.

When the sudden change in Annie alerted her father to what was happening, he had Vann investigated and learned that he was a womanizer with a wife and family. He waited for Vann and Annie to return to her house one evening. As Vann got out of the car, her father walked over and slapped Vann across the face. "What's wrong with you?" Annie's father shouted. "Don't you have any sense of responsibility? Don't you know you can be sued for seducing a teenager?" Vann made no attempt to defend himself physically. He said that he wanted to explain. "There's nothing to explain," Annie's father said. "You stay away from my daughter!" He slapped Annie across the face and ordered her into the house.

Vann behaved as he never would have dared in the United States. He kept seeing Annie and making love to her. He avoided getting his face slapped again by dropping her off a block from the house. Whenever he called to set up a rendezvous and Annie's father happened to pick up the phone, he would curse at Vann—to no avail. Annie's father was too ashamed to take the only practical recourse open to him of complaining to Lodge. He tried reasoning with his daughter. He explained to Annie that Vann had no intention of marrying her and was too old for her in any case. Vann was just taking advantage of her gullibility. She was destroying her future, depriving herself of both a career and a chance someday to have a decent husband and family.

Reason had no effect. The father turned to physical measures. Their house, like those of other upper-class Saigonese, was surrounded by a wall. Annie's father locked the gate and took away her key to force her to stay home at night. She climbed over the wall. Vann would be waiting outside to lift her down to the street. The tryst had been arranged earlier by phone or note. In his rage and despair, Annie's father started to beat her when she came back. As soon as she could arrange another tryst with Vann, she would climb over the wall again and return to take her beating. Her apparent submissiveness masked a headstrong nature, and at this stage of her life she was a spoiled young woman accustomed to having her way. Above all, she was transfixed by her reverie of romance. She saw Vann's defiance of her father as further evidence of his devotion.

After Vann returned from his mid-1966 home leave, he told Lee that he had tried to persuade Mary Jane to grant him a divorce so that they could marry, but she was unwilling and had set prohibitive conditions. He would have to beggar himself with huge alimony and child-support payments. Lee said she would wait, that Mary Jane might later change her mind. The conversation with Mary Jane had not taken place. Had Vann asked her for a divorce during the first few years after his return to Vietnam, she would have refused, but he had decided not to ask. Maintaining the form of an American marriage and family was as important as ever to Vann's self-image of respectability, and he thought the appearance enhanced his AID personnel record. Mary Jane had become equally important to him as the perfect excuse. An indissoluble marriage in America facilitated sexual freedom in Vietnam.

Annie got pregnant in late 1966 and wanted to have the baby. Vann said his career would be hurt if it was known that he had fathered an illegitimate child and talked her into an abortion. She reluctantly agreed. The abortion was physically and emotionally painful for her. She told Vann she did not want to go through another one. He did not encourage her to adopt contraceptive measures. Lee had two abortions as a result of their affair before she began to practice contraception on her own initiative. Vann appears to have assumed that he would persuade Annie to have another abortion should she get pregnant again. Pregnancy was the woman's problem as far as he was concerned. His attitude seems to have been another manifestation of the urge to use and abuse all women that Myrtle had implanted in him.

Myrtle's son fashioned a victory of sorts over his mother in the fall of 1966. Late one September afternoon the Norfolk police found Myrtle lying in a semicoherent state down by the beachfront. She was living alone there in a furnished room. She stank of alcohol and was clutching an unopened bottle of wine she had presumably bought earlier in the day. The police assumed she was just drunk again and locked her in the tank, a communal cell for alcoholics. It was 4:00 A.M. the next morning before anyone noticed that she had sunk into a coma and might be suffering from something besides wine. She died in the hospital that evening. A sadist had apparently beaten her while she was drunk, fracturing her skull, breaking her ankle, and inflicting numerous minor injuries. Her alcoholism had worsened as she had grown older, with more frequent and prolonged bouts of drinking. The disease had sufficiently weakened her body at sixty-one years so that the doctors could not save her.

By the end, except for what she could beg or chisel, the son to whom she had been cruelest was Myrtle's sole means of financial support. Vann had been sending his mother a check every month for years, much to the resentment of Mary Jane, whom he never ceased holding to the tightest of budgets. He raised the payments in the early 1960s when Myrtle divorced the Navy chief petty officer for whom she left Frank Vann. The petty officer was a rough man. He knocked out Myrtle's left eye by throwing a beer can at her during a fight. She wore a glass eye in its place. Myrtle called her sailor husband Arkie because he was from Gravelly, Arkansas. They went there to live when he retired from the Navy. Arkie was then arrested in his home state for bootlegging and grand larceny. Myrtle took that opportunity to leave him and move back to Norfolk, quickly drinking up the modest property settlement she received in the divorce. By the time she died Vann was sending her a couple of hundred dollars a month.

He also paid for her funeral. He didn't want his mother going to her grave in one of those pine boxes they had used to bury their dead back on the farm in North Carolina. When his first brother, Frank Junior, put through an emergency call to tell Vann of Myrtle's death, he said he was flying home right away and to arrange a respectable funeral and make sure that she had a nice coffin. He would pay for everything.

The funeral was something of a family reunion. Frank Junior had taken up his father's trade of carpentry in Norfolk after a stint in the Army as a paratrooper and two combat jumps during the Korean War. Dorothy Lee had also settled there. She lived in the never-ending desperation of trying to be a good mother to five children with a husband, also a petty officer, who was a drinker and a gambler. She had married him when Myrtle and Frank Vann were breaking up. She had wanted a home of her own and had not discerned her sailor's habits until after they were married. Frank Vann was staying with her. He had retired from his carpenter's job at the Norfolk naval base at the end of 1963 because of high blood pressure. He had not remarried, and he had not lost his attachment to Myrtle. She would often come to him for money to pay her rent or to buy more liquor when she ran through the check John sent. Frank Vann would give her the money. He also nursed her back to a semblance of health after several bad drunks. Gene had successfully escaped into the military, like the older brother he idolized. He had also made a solid marriage. He was far advanced in his career as a super mechanic in the Air Force, soon to be promoted to senior master sergeant. He was able to fly home from the air base in California where he was currently stationed in time to help Frank Junior and Dorothy Lee with the funeral arrangements.

They laid Myrtle out in a fine gray metal casket at the Holloman-Brown Funeral Home and scheduled visiting hours in the evening. Dorothy Lee's two closest friends knew that she could not afford to buy her mother a burial dress, so they pooled their own money and bought Myrtle a lovely blue linen outfit trimmed with lace. The morticians tinted her hair in the color of her prime, a reddish brown, and set it gracefully. When Frank Vann came to see her he said she looked "as pretty as the day I met her." Mollie came from Long Island. Her younger son, Melvin, who had gone with Vann to the recruiting station at Richmond in 1943 to join the Air Corps and had ended up spending World War II in the Marines, drove her down. At Vann's request, Mollie, who was now a widow, had tried to give Myrtle a home, but she had been forced to put Myrtle on a bus back to Norfolk. Myrtle had gotten drunk and vomited on the wall-to-wall carpets in Mollie's large and immaculate house. Dorothy Lee had next tried to keep her mother at her home, with a similar result. Myrtle had then gone alone to the furnished room. Lillian and Roxie, Myrtle's two other sisters, also came to the funeral. Although not alcoholics like Myrtle, they had both become heavy drinkers. They got tipsy during one evening's visiting hours, obtained a white-covered Bible from the funeral home, and placed it in Myrtle's right hand. Frank Junior thought that was going too far. He removed the Bible and put back the lace handkerchief the morticians had originally set in his mother's hand. The Holloman-Brown firm had broken with tradition and no longer used black hearses. Myrtle was driven to her grave on the afternoon of the burial in a hearse painted baby blue.

Vann reached Norfolk that morning, in time to see his mother at the funeral home before the casket was closed. He set out to achieve his dubious victory over her soon after the burial. Myrtle had kept the name of her sailor husband after their divorce. Vann's first move was to bring his mother back into the family. The name he intended to have carved on her headstone (he said he was paying for the headstone too) was one she had not borne for the past seventeen years—Myrtle Lee Vann. Dorothy Lee objected. This was hypocrisy, she said. If their mother had wanted to change her name back to Vann she would have done so. Dorothy Lee was convinced Myrtle had kept the name of her sailor husband because she had still cared for her Arkie, despite having left him. Frank Junior and Gene overruled her by siding with John. They couldn't bear to have the name of that man on their mother's grave.

John then announced what he intended to have inscribed on the headstone. Dorothy Lee thought his inscription even more hypocritical. She did not object again because she realized it was useless. Frank Junior and Gene would have been satisfied with a name and the dates of their mother's birth and death, but they were willing to go along with whatever John wanted. Vann made Myrtle in death the mother she had refused to be to him in life. He had the stone carver chisel into the gray marble: "Myrtle Lee Vann . . . Beloved Mother of John, Dorothy, Frank & Gene."

As Myrtle moved toward her end, John Vann had been rising in the American bureaucracy in Vietnam, although not without his customary perilous scrapes. His appointment as AID's manager for the program to create teams of pacification workers got him into a tussle with the CIA station chief and the ranking CIA officer involved in the project that almost sent him home ahead of his time.

The new program was the biggest single effort to pacify the countryside since Diem's Strategic Hamlet Program. The core manpower for the teams already existed in mass-produced replicas of the armed propaganda teams Frank Scotton had formed with CIA help in Quang Ngai in 1964. The Agency had been so impressed with Scotton's innovation that later that year it had built a large camp at Vung Tau to turn out similar forty-man commandos. They were called Political Action Teams, or PATs for short. By the beginning of 1966 the CIA had trained roughly 16,000 Vietnamese as PATs. The Vung Tau camp had sufficient barracks and other facilities to handle 5,000 men at a time. It was now to serve as the national training center for the pacification workers, with the 16,000 Vietnamese already trained there as PATs to be utilized as pacification team members. The goal, which Vann expected to be revised upward, was to field a force of about 45,000 pacification workers, approximately 30,000 of them by the end of 1966. They were to be dressed in the black-pajama garb of the peasants and to be called "cadres," officially Revolutionary Development (RD) cadres, in yet another American attempt to imitate the Vietnamese Communists.

The CIA station chief in Saigon, Gordon Jorgenson, and his subordinate officer in charge of the PAT project, Tom Donohue, were under the misimpression that the PATs they had already trained and fielded were doing serious damage to the Viet Cong. In fact, the special quality of Scotton's innovation had been lost as soon as it was mass-produced. After training, the PATs were also given to the province and district chiefs to employ against the guerrillas. The CIA officers who worked in the provinces usually did not accompany the teams on operations. They depended on the province and district chiefs to tell them how effective the PATs were, and these Saigonese officials, eager for more CIA money and armed manpower to protect themselves, were engaged in the usual confidence game.

Jorgenson and Donohue viewed pacification as a largely repressive task of identifying and eliminating the cadres of the clandestine Viet Cong government and wiping out the local guerrillas. Their misimpression about the effectiveness of their commandos led them to think the PATs were ideal for this mission. They wanted to keep the PAT training program and forty-man team makeup virtually unaltered and merely give the PATs a new name and use them in a pacification role.

Vann had no quarrel with the repressive aspect of pacification; he took it for granted. With his newly acquired ideas on social revolution, he did not think it was enough. He felt there had to be an element of social and economic change too in order to gain the cooperation of the peasantry and wanted to expand the teams into eighty-man groups to include enough specialists for better village and hamlet government and for health, education, and agricultural improvement work. Expanding the teams to meet these goals would naturally require altering the training program at the Vung Tau camp as well.

Ironically, the CIA officials also found themselves embroiled with the Vietnamese officer they had selected to head the Saigon side of the program, Lt. Col. Tran Ngoc Chau. He in turn had been responsible for bringing Vann into the project and was to become Vann's closest Vietnamese friend.

Tran Ngoc Chau was one of those extremely rare ARVN officers who had actually fought against the French in the Viet Minh, in Chau's case for almost four years. He was from a venerable family of Hue mandarins who had shared the common disgrace of their class by collaborating with the colonizers, yet always uneasily. During World War II, Chau and two of his brothers joined the Viet Minh. Chau proved himself an able Viet Minh fighter, rising from squad leader to acting battalion commander. His dilemma was that he was too temperamental to endure the self-effacement and group discipline the Vietnamese Communist Party demanded of its cadres but too ambitious not to want to keep rising in the world. His two brothers had no difficulty making the career progression from member of the Viet Minh to member of the Party. Chau couldn't bring himself to join the Party. In 1949 he deserted and soon afterward entered Bao Dai's French-sponsored army.

Chau's American friends saw his virtues and never questioned him closely enough to understand why he had parted with the Communists. They interpreted the reasons he did give as politics and principle rather than temperament and character. To Vann, to Dan Ellsberg, who also became his friend, and to Bumgardner and others, Chau was the epitome of a "good" Vietnamese. He had winning qualities. Like Vann, he could be astonishingly candid when he was not trying to manipulate. He was honest by Saigon standards, because though advancement and fame interested him, money did not. He was sincere in his desire to improve the lives of the peasantry, even if the system he served did not permit him to follow through in deed, and his nearly four years in the Viet Minh and his highly intelligent and complicated mind enabled him to discuss guerrilla warfare, pacification, the attitude of the rural population, and the flaws in Saigon society with insight and wit. The difficulty with the Saigonese, he would say, was that they were "Vietnamese-foreigners."

Chau and Vann had first met at Ben Tre in mid-1962 when Diem had appointed Chau chief of Kien Hoa, then the most troubled province in the northern Delta. The relationship had been a quarrelsome one during Vann's first year, because Chau, flattered by the attention and promotions his president was giving him, was an ardent Diemist at the time. Still, the two men had said goodbye with respect, and after Vann's return in 1965 the friendship grew. In Kien Hoa Chau had also formed his connection with the CIA. While he was no more successful when the results were counted than other province chiefs (it was from Chau's strategic hamlets that the Viet Cong recruited most of the 2,500 volunteers they raised in Kien Hoa for new battalions in the spring of 1963 after Ap Bac), Chau was an exception in that he seriously tried to pacify his province. The CIA officers involved in pacification had been drawn to him by this attitude and by the same qualities that attracted Vann. The Agency had financed several experimental programs Chau had started, including one to eliminate members of the clandestine Viet Cong government in the hamlets with squads of gunmen akin to the CIA's assassination squads, the so-called Counter Terror Teams. By the end of 1965, when Gordon Jorgenson, the station chief, and Tom Donohue, his officer in charge of the PATs, needed a Vietnamese director for the pacification-worker project they were supposed to run jointly with AID, Chau was the logical choice. Chau had then brought Vann into the project by requesting that he be appointed Chau's AID advisor, in effect the manager of the AID side.

By March 1966, when a compromise was finally reached over the nature and size of the pacification teams and they were set at fifty-nine men each, the dispute had become so heated that Jorgenson and Donohue wondered why they had ever thought so highly of Chau. Vann and Donohue decided they liked each other despite their differences, but Jorgenson had had enough of the pesky Vann. William Porter, Lodge's deputy ambassador, had just been given supervision over all civilian pacification activities as a result of another strategy conference convened in Honolulu in February by President Johnson. Jorgenson complained to Porter that Vann was a rash empire-builder who was disrupting a marvelous program to try to gain control of it. Porter, fifty-one years old in 1966 and a thirty-year veteran of the Foreign Service, was new to Vietnam and Asia. He was one of the State Department's senior Middle East specialists. His previous overseas post had been as ambassador to Algeria. He might have taken the word of a CIA station

chief had Vann not learned that something unusual was going on at the
Vung Tau camp.

Richard Holbrooke, the fledgling of 1963 who had wanted to hide as
Halberstam banged his fist on the restaurant table and shouted for a
firing squad for Harkins, had been made an assistant to Porter, because
he was one of the few Foreign Service officers with field experience in
pacification. He had spent the better part of a year between 1963 and
the summer of 1964 as AID representative in Ba Xuyen Province in the
lower Delta. Holbrooke couldn't believe what he was hearing when
Vann suddenly appeared in Porter's outer office one day and started to
tell him what was happening at Vung Tau. Porter's other aide was Frank
Wisner II, the eldest son of the famous chief of clandestine operations
at CIA. Young Wisner had chosen not to follow his father into the
Agency and instead to seek his career with the State Department. He
had been assigned to Saigon in 1964 and was by now accustomed to
surprises. He also found Vann's story too fantastic to credit.

The CIA's commando training program had been "captured," Vann
said, by an adherent of an obscurantist Vietnamese political sect and
was being used as a cover to secretly spread the anti-Communist but
also anti-Saigon doctrines of the sect. The sect adherent was the commandant and chief of instruction at the Vung Tau camp, a captain in
the ARVN signal corps named Le Xuan Mai. He had been an employee
of the CIA since the late 1950s. Mai was propagandizing all of the
trainees through the political instruction course that was part of the
curriculum and was also planting cells of four men indoctrinated with
the ideas of his sect in each of the PAT teams graduating from the camp.
He was carrying on right under the noses of Jorgenson and Donohue
and their subordinates. None of the CIA staff at the camp spoke Vietnamese, and neither Jorgenson nor anyone beneath him had ever
been curious enough to have the political lessons translated. Chau
had discovered what was occurring and alerted Vann after they had
gone to Vung Tau to begin reorganizing the camp for its pacification
mission.

Holbrooke and Wisner checked out the story. When they discovered
it was true, they scheduled an appointment for Vann with Porter. A
previous meeting they had set up for Vann to explain his side of the
pacification team dispute to Porter had not gone well for Vann. The
deputy ambassador had heard a great deal about Vann from Jorgenson
beforehand, and all of it had been bad. This second meeting was the
last appointment of Porter's day. About half an hour after it started,
Porter emerged from his inner office and announced to Holbrooke and

Wisner that he was going to his residence. Vann followed the deputy ambassador out the main office door, talking all the while.

Porter came back to the embassy the next morning amused and amazed. He said that Vann had gone down in the elevator with him and out the street entrance to the limousine, still talking. Vann had asked Porter if he could ride along to tell him some more, and when Porter said yes, Vann had climbed into the backseat beside him and kept talking. Vann hadn't stop talking until they had gotten stuck in one of Saigon's ever more tangled traffic jams. He had then abruptly said, "Thank you very much, Mr. Ambassador," and disappeared out the limousine door into the exhaust and bumper-to-bumper vehicles. Porter began to perceive the man and his worth beyond the eccentricities.

Dan Ellsberg's friendship and admiration counted for Vann in this touch-and-go time. Lansdale left Ellsberg relatively free to decide how to use his time and energy, because Lansdale's second mission to Vietnam was already a manifest failure by early 1966. The principal if unannounced purpose for which Lansdale had returned—to reform the Saigon regime from the top through persuasion and the magnetic ideals of the American Revolution—had been silly. Westmoreland could get the ear of Ky and Thieu and the other Saigon leaders, because he had resources they could funnel into graft. Lodge could get their attention, because he had power they could manipulate to further their personal political ambitions. Lansdale commanded neither trading commodity on this second visitation, and so the Saigonese gave the back of the hand to him and his sermons. The announced mission of Lansdale and his team—to act as liaison between the embassy and the regime's Rural Construction Council, now upgraded to a Ministry of Rural Construction with general responsibility for pacification on the Saigon side—had been superseded by the decision of the February Honolulu conference to have Porter oversee civilian pacification programs. Lansdale was in the ill-defined and therefore bureaucratically doomed position of being an advisor on pacification and related matters to Lodge and Porter. The most constructive thing he could do in the circumstances was to use what influence he retained in the U.S. mission to sway opinion on specific issues. The team's charter permitted Ellsberg to poke into the pacification-team dispute and the running of the Vung Tau camp, and poke he did. His reports to Lansdale were colorful and articulate briefs for Vann. Lansdale was persuaded and took Vann's side. Porter also saw the reports and was impressed.

Despite the ludicrousness of the situation, it took months—until June

1966—to get rid of Mai, the sect leader at the camp. Jorgenson simply refused to accept the loss of face involved in admitting that he and the intelligence service he represented had been hoodwinked by such a trusted employee, and he had enough independence as chief of the Saigon CIA station to get his way.

Vann was afraid he had become a marked man. He had been promoted to chief of plans and projects for field operations in April, with supervisory authority over all other counterinsurgency programs in addition to AID's role in the pacification-team training. Nevertheless, he feared that Jorgenson's friends in the Agency would complain loudly enough about him to AID headquarters in Washington to spoil his hope of continued advancement. When he learned through the grapevine that this was indeed occurring, he made up his mind to seek some alternative other than a dreaded return to Martin Marietta in Colorado.

As part of his effort to gain control over the armed services, McNamara had created a small civilian brain trust in the Pentagon to provide him with independent analyses of weapons programs and strategy. It was called the Office of Systems Analysis and was staffed by "whiz kid" government intellectuals like Ellsberg. Its chief in 1966, Alain Enthoven, and his deputy, Fred Hoffman, were both friends of Ellsberg's. Enthoven and Ellsberg had been contemporaries at the Rand Corporation. Prior to 1966, Systems Analysis had avoided Vietnam, concentrating instead on nuclear strategy and the NATO alliance in Europe. McNamara wanted his brain trust to begin evaluating the conduct of the war, and Enthoven and Hoffman were eager to make a contribution. They were looking for a man with an unorthodox mind, field experience in Vietnam, and the intellectual training to do quantitative analysis. (The analytical methods used by Systems Analysis relied heavily on statistics.) Another friend of theirs who had met Vann in Saigon that spring thought he might be the perfect candidate.

In May, Hoffman wrote Vann suggesting that he come to the Pentagon during his next home leave in June to talk over the possibility of heading the Asian Division that Systems Analysis was forming. Vann replied positively and had Ellsberg write Hoffman a letter of recommendation, which Ellsberg did in three single-spaced pages of extraordinary and convincing praise. The job would give Vann a channel to McNamara and allow him to continue to devote himself to the subject that meant most to him, and as a member of the elite who served the power managers in Washington, he might be able to work his way back to Vietnam someday in an important capacity. With Mary Jane and the children settled in Colorado, he might also be able to avoid bringing them to Washington.

He was interviewed by both Hoffman and Enthoven in June and did his best to communicate the impression he thought they were seeking. Enthoven emphasized that the free rein McNamara allowed Systems Analysis obligated those who joined it to respect the secretary's confidence should they ever leave out of disagreement with policy. Vann promised discretion and silence. He regarded the Systems Analysis post even more as his best alternative after he had returned to Vietnam and an acquaintance wrote from Washington in July that Rutherford Poats, AID's chief for the Far East, had become dubious about him because of CIA complaints and was thinking of ordering him sidetracked to a staff position where he would have no executive authority.

It was a tribute to how far Vann's reputation for truth telling, moral courage, and willingness to serve had gone within the system that Enthoven, with the approval of McNamara, did offer him the job. By the time Enthoven made up his mind and wrote Vann with a firm offer at the end of September, however, Vann's primary interest in the Systems Analysis post had shifted. A little perspective and some embarrassing publicity (which Vann helped to promote with leaks) had vindicated him and made Jorgenson and the CIA look foolish. Jorgenson had in the meantime finished his tour and departed. While some ill will lingered, the pacification-team dispute was history to the new CIA station chief. Vann's position in Vietnam had thus become steadily stronger, strong enough that he now thought he could weather the complaints to Poats and others in Washington. At the beginning of October, right after his return from Myrtle's funeral, his Foreign Service Reserve rank was raised a grade to FSR-2 and he was promoted to deputy director of AID operations for III Corps.

Vann knew that a major reorganization of the pacification effort was under consideration in Washington; the president and McNamara were dissatisfied with the rate of progress. One proposal was to give Westmoreland complete responsibility for pacification. Another was to keep civilian and military activities separate, but to unify the civilian agencies by merging all AID, CIA, and USIS programs into a single umbrella organization headed by Porter. A corps directorship in this umbrella organization would clearly amount to a much bigger job than being a regional director for AID alone. Vann had his eye on the job. He had a particularly well-placed advocate now in Ellsberg. Lansdale's team was starting to break up. Ellsberg had gone to work for Porter and was soon to be appointed his special assistant. The quality of his running reports to Lansdale had gained Ellsberg the position with Porter. What he wrote was full of the grist of the war. Having been taught by Vann that physical risk brought a unique reward in information along with emotional fulfillment, Ellsberg kept venturing into the countryside on his own or with Scotton or Bumgardner when Vann was not available. They accepted him as they had accepted Vann, as another in the small band of Americans who cared and dared.

John Vann also knew that the course of least bureaucratic resistance in such reorganizations was to give the senior jobs to noncontroversial men. To fortify his chances he turned the Systems Analysis offer into a look-who-wants-me ploy. He wrote back to Enthoven that he certainly would enjoy leading Enthoven's new Asian Division. Enthoven started the formal appointment process. Vann then made sure that everyone who mattered in Saigon learned of his attractive alternative and also wrote about it to AID headquarters in Washington to try to have his employment converted from temporary to permanent career status. As he said in a letter to a friend in Denver, "I am using the appointment offer to do a little blackmail with USAID."

Porter probably liked Vann well enough to have taken the courageous course anyway. Washington decided on the second alternative—keeping military and civilians separate, but unifying the civilians in an umbrella organization. When the creation of the Office of Civil Operations (OCO) was announced at the end of November 1966, Porter, with Lodge's consent, gave Vann a choice of III or IV Corps. The Mekong Delta had become a backwater of the war. Vann chose III Corps, because it suited him perfectly for professional and personal reasons. His office in Bien Hoa would be only half an hour's drive from downtown Saigon. He would thus be staying at center stage with access to the courts of power in the embassy and Westmoreland's headquarters, to the visiting politicians and other important tourists coming out to see the war, and to his connections in the press.

His appointment got considerable notice. Ward Just of the *Washington Post* wrote in a front-page story that Porter had selected "one of the legendary Americans in Vietnam." He would suffer no inconvenience in his captain's paradise affair with Annie and Lee, nor would he be deprived of the unparalleled variety of one-night stands that Saigon offered. Yet he would also have an arena of action in the eleven provinces around the capital. He would be establishing his headquarters in a modest office compound that AID had just constructed near Bien Hoa Air Base and the ARVN III Corps headquarters, which had been moved out of Saigon in the coup-rocking year of 1964. Jonathan Seaman's nascent U.S. Army corps of Vann's Hau Nghia days had grown to the equivalent of four American divisions and a 4,500-man Australian Army task force with a small New Zealand contingent. It was called II Field Force and had its headquarters in a huge new base being built at a place called Long Binh right down the road.

The III Corps directorship of OCO was Vann's first grasp of substantial authority in Vietnam since 7th Division, and he was thrilled with it. His official letter of appointment from Porter said that he was "the senior U.S. civilian in his region" and as such "will direct, supervise and coordinate all U.S. regional civil activities." The formal appointment to the Systems Analysis job occurred simultaneously with Porter's decision. Vann wrote his regrets to Enthoven, saying that Porter's selection of him had come as a surprise. He purchased some insurance for the future by adding that the experience in III Corps would better prepare him for a Pentagon position later on. Because of Westmoreland's lack of interest in pacification but waiting game to obtain control of it, OCO was merely the civilian half of what Vann had advocated in "Harnessing the Revolution," and a half solely in organizational terms, devoid of the essentials of an American takeover and social reform. The civilian advisors in a province would at last begin working together in a team under a province senior advisor (he could be from any of the agencies) who would represent all of them in dealings with the Saigon province chief. Keeping the province military advisors in a separate chain of command, however, meant that the security elements indispensable to pacification—the Regional Forces and the militia, or PF— would continue to be advised by Americans from a different team.

The shortcomings of OCO and his consciousness of its flaws did not lessen Vann's joy at having the closest equivalent to a field command he could get on the civilian side. When he counted the members of his headquarters and the province advisors and their staffs, he had 330 Americans, nearly 100 Filipinos and South Korean staffers (the so-called third country nationals), and more than 550 Vietnamese employees under him. General Seaman, who was fond of him, welcomed him to the commanding general's mess at II Field Force, gave him the run of the headquarters, and extended him the perquisite of an important man—use whenever he wished of one of the H-23 Raven helicopters the Army kept for observation and liaison flying. The little helicopter (there was room in the Plexiglas bubble cockpit for just the pilot and one passenger alongside) enabled Vann to cover the eleven provinces in the corps in a week in December. He met for half a day with the civilian advisors in each, briefing them on his plans, taking questions and questioning them, and picking out the men who would be his province senior advisors. The following week he gave Seaman and the II Field Force staff a formal briefing on the new civilian pacification organization and what he wanted to accomplish. Then he briefed Seaman's division commanders and their staffs. It was exhilarating to be addressing men with stars on their shoulders again. "Needless to state, I am absolutely delighted with my new job," he wrote to Bob York.

Vann did not lose his perspective. "Regrettably, I cannot report to you any significant progress since our discussion last spring," he said in the same December 23, 1966, letter to York. "I am still optimistic about what can be done in Vietnam, but I continue to be distressed at how little is actually being done." Momentous events were occurring as Vann wrote. General Westmoreland had 385,000 U.S. troops in the South and was far advanced into Phase II, the preparing-to-win phase, of his war of attrition. Vann did not see how any of the violence was contributing to the establishment of a Saigon government and society that could endure. "I am very much afraid that we will never find out if we could have been successful in South Vietnam," he said in another letter home. "It appears relatively certain to me that this [war] will be escalated to a point where we will force North Vietnam to negotiate and then, at the negotiating table, we will throw away all that has been purchased at the cost of U.S. and Vietnamese lives, not to mention the many billions of dollars of U.S. taxpayers' money." He was an angry John Vann whenever I saw him that year, angry at the unnecessary pain being inflicted on the Vietnamese peasantry, angry at the American-fostered corruption, angry at the neglect of the ARVN, angry at the ugly transformation of this country in which he had invested so much emotion.

The river of the uprooted had swelled to more than 2 million refugees from the many brooks of homeless like the one I had seen flowing from the Bong Son Plain. The civilian casualties, the majority from "friendly action," amounted by conservative estimate to about 25,000 dead a year, an average of sixty-eight men, women, and children every day. Approximately 50,000 noncombatants a year were being seriously wounded. Abandoned hamlets and barren rice fields were becoming a common sight in the countryside. As much as a third of the riceland had been forsaken in several provinces along the Central Coast. Free-fire zones proliferated so rapidly with new red lines on maps for laying waste that it was no longer possible to keep track of their number and the total area they encompassed. (They had been given the official euphemism of Specified Strike Zones, but everyone still called them free-fire or free-strike or free-bombing zones except in formal reports.) The B-52s of the Strategic Air Command, which struck under the code name Arc Light, were restricted to bombing suspected Communist bases in relatively uninhabited sections, because their potency approached that of a tactical nuclear weapon. The eight-engine jets had been converted into monster flying bomb platforms, each capable of lofting in excess of twenty tons. A formation of six B-52s, dropping their bombs from 30,000 feet, could "take out," in the language of the airmen, almost everything within a "box" approximately five-eighths of a mile wide by about two miles long. For example, the length of a box would encompass the national monuments of the United States from the Lincoln Memorial and the Vietnam Veterans Memorial, which was to be dedicated in 1982, to the Washington Monument, to the Smithsonian Institution complex with its Air and Space Museum and other museums and galleries, to the National Gallery of Art, and on to the smaller Reflecting Pool just below the Capitol. The width of a target box would extend the destruction up through the State Department, Interior, Commerce, Internal Revenue, Justice, the National Archives, the Federal Bureau of Investigation, and a number of other important institutions to the back lawn of the White House. Whenever Arc Light struck in the predawn anywhere in the vicinity of Saigon, the city woke from the tremor.

The B-52s delivered only a third of the bomb tonnage. Two-thirds was delivered by the fighter-bombers, and they were under no such restriction. By the end of 1966, fighter-bomber sorties were up to 400 a day. Each day, if one included the B-52s, about 825 tons of bombs and other air munitions were let loose on a country the size of the state of Washington. From the window of an airplane or the open door of a helicopter the big brown blotches of the bomb craters disfigured the beauty of the Vietnamese landscape in every direction.

The planes dropped more than bombs. In 1966 specially equipped C-123 transports of Operation Ranch Hand destroyed nearly 850,000 acres of forest and crops by spraying them with chemical herbicides, also called defoliants. The spraying had begun in the early 1960s as another of John Kennedy's mistakes, urged on him by Diem in his cruelty and by McNamara in his search for technological solutions. With the arrival of the U.S. armed forces in 1965 the defoliation had, like everything else, expanded geometrically. By 1967, 1.5 million acres a year of forest and crops were being destroyed in an effort to deny the Communist soldiers food and places to hide. Leaky spray nozzles on the C-123s, wind drift, and vaporization of the herbicides from the high temperatures also wilted fruit trees and killed large sections of crops that were not officially targeted. Eighteen million gallons of the herbicides were to be sprayed over 20 percent of the forest land of the South. The most commonly used defoliant, Agent Orange, contained minute amounts of dioxin, a highly poisonous substance. The dioxin accumulated from the repeated spraying, lingering in the silt of the streambeds and entering the eco-system of South Vietnam. After the war scientific tests indicated that the Vietnamese of the South had levels of dioxin in their bodies three times higher than inhabitants of the United States.

The tonnage of high explosive and shrapnel detonating from howitzers and mortars roughly equaled that of bombs, for whereas the ARVN fired thousands, the U.S. Army fired tens of thousands of shells on its "search-and-destroy operations" against the Viet Cong and the North Vietnamese regulars. The rates of expenditure far exceeded those the logisticians had established on the basis of experience in World War II and Korea. DePuy was rewarded by Westmoreland in the spring of 1966 with command of the 1st Infantry Division, and a second star for his work in planning the war of attrition. He shot off so much artillery in the rubber-plantation region that Seaman (1st Division was part of his corps) started rationing the supply of shells to him. "The solution in Vietnam is more bombs, more shells, more napalm . . . till the other side cracks and gives up," DePuy told Ellsberg over lunch at his tent command post.

Army Field Manual 27-10, "The Law of Land Warfare," which in-terprets the Hague and Geneva conventions that are legally binding on the U.S. military, enjoins officers to "conduct hostilities with regard for the principles of humanity and chivalry." As in Operation Masher at Bong Son, the American leaders in Vietnam looked away. The peasant victims were left to what AID might provide. A compassionate Air Force surgeon, Maj. Gen. James Humphreys, on detail to AID as its chief of public health in Vietnam, tried. He asked for two transport planes and five helicopters to evacuate civilian wounded to the province hospitals and to transfer patients in need of more specialized treatment to the better civilian hospitals in Saigon. Gravely injured victims who did not have the good luck to be put on a military helicopter were dying before they could reach help, and a long, bumpy ride in an ambulance to a Saigon hospital was sometimes enough to finish off a severe head-wound case. In a country that was to hold squadrons of U.S. transport planes, 2,000 helicopters by the end of 1966, and more than 3,000 by the end of 1967, General Humphreys was told that military necessity precluded sparing any for regular evacuation of civilians.

Humphreys devised a plan to have three U.S. military hospitals built for the treatment of civilian wounded. He calculated that the toll of wounded civilians might soon rise to about 75,000 a year. (It was to approximate 85,000 during 1968.) Senator Edward Kennedy, the only political figure in Washington to take a consistent interest in the plight of the Vietnamese civilians through his Senate Judiciary Subcommittee to Investigate Problems Connected with Refugees and Escapees, arranged for Humphreys to brief the president on his plan at another strategy conference at Guam in March 1967. Lyndon Johnson approved.

The hospitals could have been built in ninety days. The Army medical bureaucracy did not want the responsibility and sought to sabotage the proposal by delay. A medical survey team of distinguished American physicians headed by the executive vice-president of the American Medical Association, sent to South Vietnam in the summer of 1967 by AID, also opposed the idea. Among other objections, the team was afraid the Army would draft more doctors to staff the hospitals. Under badgering from Kennedy, the Army allotted 300 beds in its existing hospitals to civilian casualties in October 1967, adding another 200 in December. The first two of the three military hospitals to treat civilians finally opened in the spring of 1968 and the third in the middle of that year. They handled roughly 10 percent of the civilian casualties before they closed in 1971. Humphreys and his successor gradually obtained surgical teams for all of the province hospitals from the U.S. military and from allies of the United States in Vietnam like Australia and South Korea. AID also sent out volunteer American physicians recruited by the AMA for two-month tours. None of these efforts ever raised the province hospitals above the level of charnel houses.

Vann was convinced that this "generating" of refugees and its concomitant toll in civilian casualties was not an accidental outgrowth of an attempt to bludgeon the enemy, but a policy deliberately fostered by the high command. Whenever we talked about it he would get as mad as he had at the 25th Division advisor who had reasoned that if the peasants were willing to live with the Communists "then they can expect to be bombed." His neck and face would redden to that hue of rage peculiar to Vann, and his side of the conversation would become a staccato of curses.

In all probability, Westmoreland had not set out with the intention of causing a massive movement of population and civilian casualties on the scale that was occurring. Rather, he apparently began with the thought that came as a reflex to him and DePuy to "stomp" the enemy to death. There appears to be no doubt that once he saw the collateral effects of his strategy, he decided to reap what seemed to him an advantage and that he was conscious—as were those in authority above and below him—of what he was doing. Westmoreland is a courteous man, and he was forthcoming with the press during these early years of the American war. Before a resident correspondent left for reassignment elsewhere he was given the privilege of a day in the field with the commanding general on one of Westmoreland's regular trips by helicopter to visit American units. I took advantage of the privilege shortly before leaving for the Washington bureau of the *Times* in August 1966. At one point in the trip I asked the general if he was worried about the large number of civilian casualties from the air strikes and the shelling. He looked at me carefully. "Yes, Neil, it is a problem," he said, "but it does deprive the enemy of the population, doesn't it?"

The destruction was not confined to the physical. The building of the killing machine had become an end in itself. In this small country with a simple agrarian economy, Westmoreland proceeded to construct as fast as he could four new jet air bases (the Air Force soon pressured him into making it five) to add to the three he had at Tan Son Nhut, Bien Hoa, and Da Nang before the buildup started (he was enlarging these as well); six new deep-water ports with twenty-eight deep-draft unloading berths for freighters to end his dependence on the port of Saigon and the single pier then in existence at Cam Ranh Bay; four central supply and maintenance depots; twenty-six permanent base camps for combat and support troops; seventy-five new tactical airfields long enough to handle four-engine C-130 Hercules transports (he already had nineteen such airfields in 1965, but the objective was to put as many points as possible in South Vietnam within quick reach of a good runway); twenty-six hospitals with 8,280 beds; and a new two-story, prefabricated headquarters for himself next to Tan Son Nhut with air-conditioned office and work space for 4,000 people. Everything was to be connected by the latest in secure electronic data and teletype circuits and by a direct-dial telephone network called the Southeast Asia Automatic Telephone System—220 communications facilities in all, with 13,900 circuits.

Each of the jet air bases was a panoramic installation. There was a 10,000-foot runway, a parallel taxiway, high-speed turnoffs, and tens of thousands of square yards of apron for parking and moving aircraft—initially laid with aluminum matting that was later replaced by concrete—along with hangars, repair shops, offices and operations buildings, barracks, mess halls, and the sundry other structures that go with airfields of this size. Many of the base camps were small cities. Long Binh, Seaman's headquarters just northeast of Saigon and down the road from Vann's office compound, was literally to grow to the status of a city. It was selected as the site of one of the four central supply and maintenance depots and then additionally as the headquarters for U.S. Army Vietnam, USARV, the chief administrative and support command under Westmoreland's MACV. Long Binh covered twenty-five square miles and was inhabited by about 43,000 Americans at its height.

Another arsenal city rose on the peninsula that forms the upper reach of Cam Ranh Bay on the Central Coast 185 miles northeast of Saigon. Cam Ranh is considered the finest natural harbor in the world after Sydney, Australia, but the region has always been sparsely populated, because the dark green of the rain-forested Annamites touches the emerald green of the South China Sea there and what level land exists around the bay is either sand or sandy. The French had built a small naval station and airstrip that the Saigon navy had kept up. Big floating piers were now towed from the East Coast of the United States around the tip of South America and across the Pacific to create the largest of the new ports, with ten unloading berths for deep-draft vessels. The empty sands in the middle of the Cam Ranh peninsula were suddenly occupied by warehouses, ammunition storage areas, and tank farms filled with aviation fuel and other petroleum supplies, called POL, for petroleum, oil, and lubricants, by the military: Cam Ranh was the logical place to construct the second of the four central supply and maintenance depots. (The third and fourth depots were located farther north at Qui Nhon and Da Nang.) A 10,000-foot runway of gray aluminum matting for one of the new jet air bases cut across the upper end of the peninsula where the neck begins to narrow and curve back toward the mainland.

The construction program Westmoreland set in motion with maximum speed all over South Vietnam entailed 10.4 million square feet of warehousing, 5.4 million square feet of ammunition storage, enough tank-farm capacity to hold 3.1 million barrels of POL, 39 million cubic meters of dredging, about 2,550 miles of new hardtop road, and 434,000 acres of land clearing.

The panoply included transporting to South Vietnam the amenities of American civilization. These began for the enlisted men with base camps that had well-ventilated wooden barracks on concrete-slab foundations, hot water in the showers, and flushing toilets, and for the generals and colonels at Long Binh with courts of air-conditioned trailers that had lawns and flower beds tended by Vietnamese. To serve hundreds of thousands of men in a tropical country 10,000 miles away three meals a day of fresh fruit, vegetables, meat, and dairy products nearly identical to those on the Army's U.S. Continental Master Menu requires an extraordinary number of cold-storage lockers, but the Army quartermasters began accomplishing the feat by early 1966. The task of furnishing dairy products eased as early as December 1965 when Foremost Dairy opened a milk-recombining plant the Army had paid the company to build and operate in Saigon. Meadowgold Dairies was subsequently given a contract to construct and run two other plants at Cam Ranh Bay and Qui Nhon. To be sure the troops got enough ice cream, the Army also installed forty small ice cream plants at less accessible locations. Although the men of the fighting units still had to face C rations along with the hardship and danger of campaigning, they frequently ate "A ration" meals cooked at the kitchens in the base camps, placed in insulated containers to keep the food hot, and flown to them by helicopter.

With the senior officers at the higher headquarters setting an example of climatized living, everybody else who could do so put air-conditioners in their living quarters, mess halls, and offices. Given the other electricity demands of the U.S. military, the local generating capacity was immediately overwhelmed. Power had to be shut down on alternating days in different sections of Saigon. Tactical generators proved inadequate. The Army bought more than 1,300 commercial generators in the U.S. and Japan and rushed them to South Vietnam while it withdrew World War II tankers from the Maritime Reserve Fleet and hired the Vinnell Corporation to convert the ships into floating generator barges and to build high-voltage central systems at the inland bases.

The amenities were completed by constructing an additional air-conditioned world of PXs, movie theaters, bowling alleys, and service clubs generously supplied with soft drinks, beer, whiskey, plenty of ice cubes to keep the drinks cold, milk shakes, hamburgers, hot dogs, and steaks, all at giveaway prices. The PXs were not mere canteens where a soldier could buy cigarettes, shaving articles, and candy. They were emporia that offered him a proper assortment of the fine things to which Americans have become accustomed—radios, tape recorders, hi-fis, watches, slacks and sport shirts to wear on his rest-and-recreation leave (R&R) if he survived the first six months of his one-year tour, and cosmetics to help raise the living standard of Vietnamese women. (It was difficult for the PX managers to keep hair spray in stock.) Should the soldier want an electric fan, a toaster, a percolator, a television set, a room air-conditioner, or perhaps a small refrigerator that the PX did not have in stock, he could pick it out of a catalogue and have it sent to him by a mail-order service. The official theory was that giving the American military man access to this consumer's paradise would reduce spending on the local market and thus hold down inflation in South Vietnam.

The theory may have had some validity. Inflation was held to between 50 and 60 percent a year, mainly by more than doubling the commodity imports AID financed for the South Vietnamese economy ($650 million in 1966) and by shipping millions of tons of American rice to a country that had been able to export rice as recently as 1964. Given the magnitude of the social and moral catastrophe, what points the theory gained against the inflation index could not have made much difference. The Vietnamese of the South found themselves in a world turned upside down. Hundreds of thousands started to earn their livelihood by serving the profligate foreigners. When one counted the families of these Vietnamese, other hundreds of thousands began to live off the Americans by proxy. The sanitation services collapsed in Saigon, because the workers quit en masse and rushed away to labor at the base construction sites for much higher salaries than the municipality could pay.

Prior to 1965, two prominent American construction firms, Raymond International and Morrison-Knudsen, had formed a partnership to build bases in South Vietnam under the military assistance program. To take advantage of the cost-plus-a-fixed-fee windfall, they subsequently pooled resources with two other big firms in the industry, Brown & Root and J. A. Jones, and created a consortium known as RMK-BRJ. In mid-1966, during the most labor-intensive phase of the base-construction program, RMK-BRJ had about 50,000 Vietnamese on its payroll. The Army engineers, the Navy Seabees and Marine engineer battalions, and the Air Force developed their own Vietnamese labor forces. The Army Engineer Command, for example, had 8,500 Vietnamese workers in 1967. Pacific Architects and Engineers (PA&E), another big company that the Army paid on a cost-plus-a-fixed-fee basis to maintain facilities once they were completed, employed many thousands more. The U.S. military also required domestic help. There were Vietnamese "housemaids" and "houseboys" to do laundry, shine boots, and clean the barracks, waitresses for the clubs and mess halls, and scullery workers to perform the menial chores in the kitchens. (Enlisted men were freed of KP duty at most base camps.) Counting the PA&E staff, more than 20,000 Vietnamese were to work at Long Binh alone.

Other Vietnamese among these hundreds of thousands were employed in the business of amusing the foreigners. The Saigon newspapers published cartoons of a new social hierarchy ranked by its importance to the Americans. The prostitutes stood at the top, followed by their pimps, and then by the taxi drivers who carried the Americans to and from their pleasures. (The drivers no longer wanted Vietnamese passengers, because they could not overcharge them.) GI culture in bars with names like A-Go-Go and Chicago and The Bunny (after Hugh Hefner's creation), cheap tailor shops, and "Turkish Bath" and "Massage Parlor" bordellos proliferated in Saigon, Qui Nhon, Da Nang, and the other cities and in the shanty towns thrown up overnight outside bases in the once sparsely populated regions like Cam Ranh Bay. Saigon itself was to acquire 56,000 *registered* prostitutes; this figure did not, of course; include the amateurs. The bar girls were the elite among the prostitutes. They received a percentage from the drinks of colored water, called "Saigon tea," that the soldiers had to buy them to enjoy their company and dance to the rock 'n' roll music that blared from the bars. After-hours sex cost extra. The bar girls and their less fortunate sisters who worked the brothels and the streets were pathetic creatures. They flaunted themselves in makeup and clothes they did not know how to wear and swelled their Vietnamese breasts with injections of silicone to attract the bosom-conscious Americans. Some had their eyelids Westernized by cosmetic surgery, an operation that was also becoming popular among young upper-class Saigonese women.

Many of the prostitutes were farm girls, for another collateral effect of the physical destruction in the countryside was to help fulfill American needs for labor and entertainment. Refugees crowded into the already crowded warrens of shacks that were the working-class quarters of Saigon and the other cities and raised new slums around towns and urban centers everywhere. One noticed the new slums quickly, because some of the shacks had a novel construction that reflected the Vietnamese talent for coping. The refugees scavenged empty beer and soda cans discarded at the American dumps, cut the cans open, pounded them flat, and nailed them to strips of scrap wood to make metal sheets for walls.

Not everyone could find a job serving the Americans, or live off someone who did; not everyone had a daughter old enough to sell herself. South Vietnam had always had some beggars. On Saigon's Rue Catinat a small number of regulars, most of them crippled unfortunates, had occupied the same sidewalk spots day after day, nodding a greeting to regular passersby and seeming to subsist on many tiny handouts. Widows, orphans, and amputees begging from Americans now became a ubiquitous element of urban life. The children, filthy in a nation where the poor traditionally valued personal cleanliness, their legs covered with sores, would call "Hey, you!" or "Hey, GI!" and shout obscenities if they were not given money. They formed gangs to pick pockets and steal.

The garbage, rarely collected because the municipal workers had deserted to the higher salaries at the base sites and the regime did not care enough to recruit replacements from among the refugees, piled up in Saigon until the stacks were half a block long. Late at night after curfew when the streets were still, the tops of the stacks would move as one walked by. The feeding rats would be disturbed by the sound of approaching footsteps and scurry about. One day I saw words in Vietnamese chalked in large letters on the pavement in front of a pile of garbage. I asked a Vietnamese reporter who was with me to translate them. The words said: "This is the fruit of American aid."

The generals and the Madame Generals, their friends the Mrs. Colonels, the Chinese middlemen in Cholon, and all the lesser crooks in the Saigon regime had laid before them an unprecedented feast of corruption, gargantuan in scale. Thieu and his wife made so many millions that eventually they acquired control of a bank of their own to funnel their graft. Saigonese happenstance explained why so many of the buildings the Americans decided to rent as living quarters, offices, and supplementary warehousing turned out to belong to the families of people in the regime or people connected to it. With the U.S. Army paying more than $24 million in leases in 1966, the by-chance owners had good luck indeed. The Chinese and rich Vietnamese clamored with bribes for permits to put up more apartments and hotels to rent to the Americans. All new construction required permits, because cement, steel reinforcing bars, and other building materials were supposedly being rationed for the war effort and critical social needs like refugee housing. The hundreds of millions of dollars of increased AID-financed commodities coming into the country to try to hold down inflation meant a lot more graft from the sale of import licenses.

Given the thirst of the American soldier, franchises to distribute Filipino and Japanese beer were also particularly lucrative. In addition to the forty ice cream plants, the U.S. Army shipped forty ice-making plants to South Vietnam, mainly to keep the mess halls and clubs in ice cubes. It seemed, however, that the Americans could never get enough ice and bought all they could locally. Brig. Gen. Pham Quoc Thuan, the commander of the 5th ARVN Division at Ben Cat in the rubber-plantation country, responded to the need of his allies. He had his division engineers construct an ice plant, went into the ice-peddling business, and was henceforth known as the Icehouse General.

Bao Dai and his Binh Xuyen friend Bay Vien and their cronies had considered themselves fortunate to enjoy the time-honored rake-off from prostitution and associated entertainment. The rake-off of their successors was magnified by these galaxies of prostitutes attracted by the armed forces of the most powerful nation on earth, whose soldiers were wealthy men compared to the French troops and the Foreign Legionnaires and North African mercenaries of the Expeditionary Corps. An entrepreneurial spirit also need not be confined to such traditional rackets as prostitution rake-off, because new rackets kept appearing that were peculiar to the American style of war. The brass business was an example. The historic expenditure of ammunition caused a worldwide shortage of brass. The empty brass shell casings were collected and shipped out of the country to scrap-metal dealers at premium prices.

One of the new sources of wealth that appeared with the Americans was sinister—narcotics. Opium addiction was not uncommon in Southeast Asia, and, as Vann had discovered, the ARVN soldiers had turned to marijuana and alcohol as means of escape from their hopelessness in 1965. Heroin users were rare among the native peoples. The Americans were different. Many of them brought to South Vietnam the craving for marijuana and heroin that had been increasing gradually in the United States since the latter half of the 1950s.

The Corsican gangsters who had traditionally run opium out of Indochina, refining it into heroin in Marseilles and then selling the heroin in Europe and the United States, couldn't take advantage of the sudden appearance of a major American market right in South Vietnam. There were too few of them; they lacked networks with sufficient span. The big-time Chinese racketeers in Cholon could handle the business. They had plenty of capital, networks of brothers and cousins and in-laws all over Southeast Asia, and lots of lesser Chinese at their beckoning to run the distribution system in the South. The Corsicans continued to buy what opium they could in Laos and send it to Marseilles, but most of the Southeast Asian opium was now bought by other hands and refined into heroin in secret laboratories in Burma and Thailand. Marijuana, previously grown on a small scale as a cash crop by the farmers of the region, was also planted much more widely and began to come into South Vietnam by the ton. The soldiers of the Air Cav learned that in the shanty town outside their base camp at An Khe in the middle of nowhere they could buy all of the "grass" they could smoke as well as cheap heroin that gave them a fast high because it was not diluted like the dope being sold for far more money on the streets back home. Huge payoffs were necessary to protect a business as profitable and sensitive as this one. The Chinese traffickers did not have to pay every Saigon general, only those powerful enough to assure protection in return for the money.

With the exception of the airborne battalions and the Saigon marines whom Westmoreland employed on his search-and-destroy operations, the regular ARVN avoided combat assiduously after 1965. "I consider the performance of the ARVN to be more disgraceful than ever," Vann wrote in the December 23, 1966, letter to York in which he said that while delighted with his new job as director of OCO for III Corps, he could not see any significant progress in the war. He laid out the statistics on small-unit operations reported by the three ARVN divisions in III Corps for the previous five days. The 25th Division under Vann's acquaintance in Hau Nghia, Phan Trong Chinh, who had struck up an alliance with Ky and got himself promoted to brigadier general; the 5th Division under "Icehouse" Thuan; and the 18th ARVN Division at Xuan Loc claimed to have conducted 5,237 patrols and other small-unit operations over the five-day period. They reported making contact with the enemy thirteen times. "I can easily establish more enemy contacts on a daily basis myself," Vann wrote.

As Westmoreland kept raising his demands for more American troops to fight his war of attrition, he came under increasing pressure to end the nonperformance of the ARVN. By early 1967 Lyndon Johnson had agreed to give him 470,000 Americans. In March the general then informed Washington that he had to have another 80,576 for a "Minimum Essential Force" of about 550,500 men "as soon as possible but not later than 1 July 1968." He said he would prefer to have an additional 207,838 Americans for an "Optimum Force" of about 678,000 men. The president admonished him to "make certain we are getting value received from the South Vietnamese troops" and to try experiments to save U.S. manpower like the KATUSAs in Korea.

The general responded by pressing his latest request for more Americans while taking steps to protect himself against the accusation that he might be neglecting Vietnamese soldiers. Westmoreland had his staff draw up a program and reproduce it in a thick booklet marked "Secret." The booklet described forty-four subprograms for more equipment, better training, and more advisors for the Saigon forces. Westmoreland gave the Saigon forces 3,000 more advisors. He also issued instructions that senior advisors were to accentuate, whenever possible, "the positive combat accomplishments of the South Vietnamese Army," and to play down the failings of the Saigon troops. He made speeches praising them. His chief public affairs officer said that the general wanted to "improve the image" of the ARVN. Westmoreland also began several experiments in the use of Vietnamese soldiers. The most serious, the mating of an ARVN Ranger group with the U.S. 199th Light Infantry Brigade, was to be terminated before the end of the year.

Most of the soldiers in the regular ARVN divisions might be able to escape for the moment; the men in the Regional Forces and the PF could not, because they continued to be frittered away in the outposts and in ambushes. On the Saigon side, 11,953 men perished in 1966, approximately 2 for each of the 6,053 Americans who died in Vietnam that year; 12,716 Vietnamese soldiers were to be killed on the Saigon side in 1967, the year the Americans almost caught up to them in dying.

With his penchant for gallows humor, Vann would have appreciated the irony had he known that at this moment at the end of 1966 when he was writing York that nothing had changed on the Saigon side, his nemesis of three and a half years earlier, Victor Krulak of the Marine Corps, was as frustrated and as angry as Vann had ever been. The singular quality of Brute Krulak's intellect and his gift for his craft had finally brought him abreast of the war. He had acquired the distinction of becoming an American military leader who understood the minds of the men in Hanoi.

As a good lawyer is impelled to approach each case as unique, the beginning of the American war in 1965 had inspired Krulak to look at the war in Vietnam anew. The attrition strategy of Westmoreland and DePuy that he had accepted so unquestioningly in Harkins's time no longer made sense to him, particularly in view of the terrain and population features of the five northernmost provinces on the Central Coast (I Corps) where the Marines were being deployed. Krulak also happened to be in Vietnam on another of his frequent trips there as Commanding General Fleet Marine Force Pacific, when the first hard fight occurred in August 1965. Watching the battle with the 1st Viet Cong Regiment in which fifty-one of his Marines died amid the hedgerows and bamboo thickets near the airfield that bore the Chinese phonetics of his name and then studying the reports of Moore's fight and the destruction of the other Air Cav battalion in the valley of the Drang in November made him reflect more carefully still. By December 1965 his mind was made up. He had been expounding ideas as they occurred to him since the previous spring in memoranda and letters to McNamara and others and had not been obtaining the response he wanted. He decided to bring all of his thoughts together into one paper that would arouse the attention he needed. It was plain that Hanoi was not going to buckle under the gradually escalating air raids against the North and that the ground conflict in the South was passing the point of no return. Krulak wanted to get the war under control and on a winning course while there was still time.

He wrote his paper in his office on the mountain overlooking Pearl Harbor where he now held the place of Holland Smith. He took a week to write it, drafting the sentences in pencil on a large pad of lined paper as he did all of his important letters and memoranda. The finished product ran to seventeen typed pages; Krulak went into each of his arguments in detail, even drawing diagrams to illustrate his main points. The paper was full of the standard American misconceptions about the Vietnamese and ignorance of their history. That Krulak could find his way to the dynamics of the war despite this mental bric-a-brac was another demonstration of the originality of his mind.

Attrition would fail, Krulak wrote, because attrition was the enemy's game. In a reference to the fighting in the valley of the Drang that had taken 233 American lives in four days, he warned that the Vietnamese Communists were "seeking to attrit U.S. forces through the process of violent, close-quarters combat which tends to diminish the effectiveness of our supporting arms," i.e., artillery and air power. The Hanoi leaders believed that if they killed and wounded enough American soldiers over a period of time they would "erode our national will and cause us to cease our support of the GVN." Vo Nguyen Giap "was sure that if the cost in casualties and francs was high enough, the French would defeat themselves in Paris. He was right. It is likely that he feels the same about the U.S.A."

Krulak did the arithmetic of attrition to prove that Hanoi had far more people to spend at this macabre game than the United States did. The Vietnamese Communists had at their disposal in the North and through the Viet Cong in the South a probable military manpower pool of about 2.5 million men. If one accepted the current official "kill ratio" of one American or Saigon soldier for 2.6 Viet Cong or North Vietnamese—an exchange of corpses that Krulak thought might be "optimistic"—and the proportional share of dying in 1965 between the American and the Saigon troops, 10,000 Americans and 165,000 Saigon soldiers would have to die in order "to reduce the enemy [manpower] pool by only a modest 20 percent."

Brute Krulak laid out his plan to win. In a further irony Vann would have appreciated, Krulak's plan was similar to his. Krulak also wanted to adopt a strategy of pacification that would seek the support of the Vietnamese peasantry through a generous program of land reform and other social and economic benefits and change. To accomplish it he too advocated a level of U.S. influence that would amount to a takeover of the Saigon regime. He explained that a strategy of pacification and social and economic reform was the only way to succeed. Attrition was "peripheral" to the real struggle. The big-unit fighting with the Main Force Viet Cong and the NVA "could move to another planet today, and we would still not have won the war" because "the Vietnamese people are the prize." Without the sustenance they provided through the local guerrillas and the clandestine Viet Cong government, the Communist regulars could not exist. The United States therefore had to employ its troops to shield the populated areas while it pacified by earning "the trust and loyalty of the people."

The Main Force Viet Cong and the NVA were not to be left entirely at peace in their rain-forest and mountain fastnesses. Krulak wanted to track them by every possible means of intelligence and to "attack them continuously by air." He was willing to join battle in these sparsely inhabited regions when the intelligence promised "benefits . . . overwhelmingly in our favor, and when to do so will not consume forces needed for protection of cleared areas." But the United States must not march to the enemy's plan by reacting to Communist "initiatives or seek them out just to do battle." The choice of strategies was a choice of outcomes. Pacification and social and economic reform were "a design for victory." Attrition was "the route to defeat."

This was no renegade lieutenant colonel buttonholing generals in the Pentagon, no USOM province representative peddling a brainstorm. This was the third-ranking general in the Marine Corps and a man whose influence had, in any case, always outreached his rank. Furthermore, Krulak had two senior allies in the military hierarchy. The first was his superior in Hawaii, Adm. Ulysses S. Grant Sharp, who had been a destroyer commander during World War II and had replaced Harry Felt as Commander-in-Chief Pacific in 1964. "Oley" Sharp had decided many months before, when Krulak had begun developing his ideas, that his was the logical way to proceed in Vietnam. Krulak's second ally was his like-preaching bishop, the commandant of the Marine Corps, Gen. Wallace Greene, Jr., another slightly built man, with a gravelly voice and a deliberate way of speaking. Krulak sent Greene a copy of his memorandum as soon as he passed one to Sharp. "Wally" Greene and Brute Krulak had been professional acquaintances since Krulak's days as a lieutenant with the 4th Marine Regiment in Shanghai, where Greene had been a captain and company commander. Greene was no more hesitant than any other American military leader of the 1960s to go to war in Vietnam. He wanted to mobilize the reserves and put 500,000 men in South Vietnam as fast as possible, but he did not want to see American soldiers and Marines used as Westmoreland intended. There was a school of pacification strategists within the upper ranks of the Marine Corps because of its institutional history. The decades of pre–World War II pacifying in Central America and the Caribbean, codified in the Corps' *Small Wars Manual*, were a strategic precedent which ruled that wars like Vietnam were wars of pacification. The Marines had adopted an approach that emphasized pacification over big-unit battles almost from the outset of their buildup in I Corps. While Krulak had been the guiding intellect, taking account of the special conditions of the Vietnamese war and grafting social and economic reform onto the strategy the Marines had followed in those earlier decades of pacifying, Greene and other senior Marine officers believed just as firmly in the concept.

Westmoreland was the obstacle. Greene had vainly attempted to talk him into a simpler version of the pacification approach during a visit to South Vietnam on the eve of the buildup in April 1965. Sharp had sought to persuade him, and Krulak had argued with him repeatedly. Krulak's scheme was to go over Westmoreland's head, exploit the relationship he had formed with McNamara during the Kennedy years, and use his paper to convert the secretary to the strategy. Sharp and Greene approved. Krulak flew to Washington and saw McNamara in mid-January 1966. The secretary was struck by Krulak's mathematics of futility—175,000 lives for 20 percent of Hanoi's manpower reserves. "I think you ought to talk to the president about this," he said. In the meantime he suggested that Krulak see Averell Harriman to discuss thoughts Krulak had also expressed in his memorandum about the air war against the North, thoughts McNamara did not like. Krulak warned that it was foolish to try to interdict Soviet and Chinese war matériel once the weapons and supplies were flowing to the South down the roads and rail lines of the North. To be effective, he said, the air campaign had to stop the matériel from entering the North by bombing and mining Haiphong and the other ports and attacking the North Vietnamese railroads from China.

"Do you want war with the Soviet Union or the Chinese?" Harriman lectured during the soup course at lunch at his Georgetown home. He waved a heavy sterling-silver spoon in Krulak's face as he spoke. Krulak has a prominent nose and felt uncomfortable having a big spoon waved at it. McNamara did not follow up his implied promise to arrange a meeting with the president. Krulak did not realize at the time that although he could catch McNamara's attention momentarily, he could not hold it. Despite the fright McNamara had received from the fighting in the valley of the Drang, he was still too captivated by Westmoreland and the other Army generals to heed logic and simple arithmetic.

Wally Greene tried to bring his fellow members of the Joint Chiefs of Staff around to the Marine point of view in hope of persuading them to order Westmoreland to adopt the strategy. He had a separate study done by his staff at Marine Corps headquarters. It confirmed Krulak's estimate of the manpower available to the Vietnamese Communists. Greene briefed his colleagues on its findings and argued for the Marine approach to the war. None of his peers were won over. No one disputed the manpower estimate and the calculations that followed. "You couldn't challenge the figures," Greene was to recall from retirement. Greene's peers reacted as Westmoreland did. They avoided coming to grips with the numbers and the logical implication the numbers had for strategy. The Army generals, Earle Wheeler, now chairman of the Joint Chiefs, and Harold Johnson, the chief of staff, rallied to their Army commander in the field. Gen. John McConnell, who had taken Curtis LeMay's place as chief of staff of the Air Force, and Adm. David McDonald, the current chief of naval operations, saw no reason to side with Greene against their Army colleagues. The Air Force and the Navy were obtaining their share of the action in Indochina through the air war.

Unlike Vann, Krulak was prominent enough in the system to appeal to the highest tribunal. He did have to wait months for his audience with the president, until Greene could arrange it in the summer of 1966. Krulak sent a copy of his paper over to the White House ahead of time for Johnson to read and carried another in his hand into the Oval Office to refer to while he briefed. Johnson's opening question indicated that he had not read the paper. "What is it going to take to win?" he asked. Krulak proceeded to tell him. Johnson did not rush Krulak. He gave him forty minutes. He asked few additional questions, and Krulak had the impression that everything he was saying was going "seven leagues" over the president's head. When Krulak finally switched from pacification to mining Haiphong, Johnson suddenly "looked like he'd sat on a tack." He stood up, put his arm around Krulak's shoulder, and told him he was a great general as he escorted him to the door.

* * *

Brute Krulak was not accustomed to being stymied. He was determined to have the Marines demonstrate the merits of the strategy. Westmoreland might then have no choice but to accept it for the whole of South Vietnam. The I Corps region assigned to the Marines was also a geographical model for Krulak's plan. There were about 2.6 million people in the five northernmost provinces of the Central Coast from Quang Ngai up to Quang Tri at the Demilitarized Zone. More than 98 percent of them lived within twenty-five miles of the sea (most considerably closer) and on less than a quarter of the land, on the coastal littoral of small rice deltas pressed between the Annamites and the South China Sea. The remaining three-quarters of the territory provided formidable rain-forest and mountain redoubts for the Main Force Viet Cong and the NVA troops who had infiltrated into the South, but barely enough rice to feed the sparse numbers of tribal people who normally inhabited it. The Marines had established three base zones: around Chu Lai on the border of Quang Ngai and Quang Tin provinces, in and around the port and air base at Da Nang, and north across the Hai Van Pass around the airfield at Phu Bai just below Hue. The idea was to reach out in both directions from the three base zones, slowly bringing more and more of the population under control until the whole of the littoral was joined into one pacified zone. It would not matter then how many thousands of Viet Cong regulars were out in the mountains. Their battalions would wither without the sustaining flow of food, recruits, and intelligence from the peasantry, and Hanoi would have to truck down food for every NVA soldier who marched into I Corps.

Krulak had no operational authority over the Marines in Vietnam. As chief for the theater, he controlled directly only the Marine reserve troops and support units in the Pacific. His formal responsibility toward Vietnam was to see that the Marines there in the III Marine Amphibious Force (III MAF) were adequately supplied, equipped, and trained. He nevertheless had an enthusiastic collaborator for a while in the man Greene had selected to lead the Marines in Vietnam, Lewis Walt, the most junior major general in the Corps at the time of his appointment in mid-1965.

Walt did not collaborate out of diffidence to Krulak. He was every bit his own man. Greene had chosen him over half a dozen more senior candidates because he considered Walt the premier fighter and finest troop leader in the Marines. Lew Walt had won the Navy Cross twice. He had started in the first Marine counteroffensive of World War II at Guadalcanal, gone to Cape Gloucester on New Britain Island, where a ridge he had wrested from the Japanese had been named after him, then to Peleliu to help clear the route for MacArthur's reconquest of the Philippines. The son of a Kansas rancher, he had played football and worked his way through Colorado State University before joining the Marines. At fifty-two years of age in 1965 he still looked the lineman, tall, with brawler hands and arms, sturdy shoulders, and a big head. In the formal chain of command, Walt and the Marines of III MAF were under the operational control or "opcon" of Westmoreland; Walt was theoretically one of Westmoreland's corps commanders. In practice, no Marine is beyond the Corps, and Walt shared the belief in pacification of Krulak and Greene. Krulak was in Vietnam constantly to observe and pass along ideas. He was to make forty-five trips there during his four years as Commanding General Fleet Marine Force Pacific. He and Walt also talked frequently over the secure telephone connection between Da Nang and Pearl Harbor. Both kept Greene informed, and he gave them moral encouragement.

Lew Walt devoted about a third of his effort to fighting the Main Force Viet Cong and the NVA in order to chase them out of the populated deltas and to punish them by joining battle in the hinterland whenever the intelligence indicated he could do so on advantageous terms like those Krulak had described in his plan. Walt's principal effort, fully half the time of the Marine battalions, was invested in a painstaking campaign to rid the hamlets of the guerrillas and the political cadres, and not merely by killing or capturing them. A year and three months before AID and the other civilian agencies made a start toward a unified field arrangement and Vann was appointed III Corps director of the Office of Civil Operations, Walt used his authority to bring the sundry pacification programs in I Corps under Marine guidance. He formed a coordinating council of the regional heads of the civilian agencies and the senior Army advisor to the ARVN, now one of Walt's subordinates, and persuaded the Saigon corps commander, Brig. Gen. Nguyen Chanh Thi, to lend the council his authority by appointing a Vietnamese representative. Walt's deputy became the council chairman.

To acquire armed Vietnamese manpower and expand control at the village and hamlet levels, Walt began integrating Marine rifle squads into PF platoons. The Marine sergeant commanding the squad became the militia platoon leader, and the Vietnamese platoon leader became his deputy. The pattern of a Marine in charge and a Vietnamese deputy was repeated in the squads of the platoon. Several of these Combined Action Platoons would then be pulled together into a Combined Action Company under a Marine officer and a Vietnamese deputy. The plan was to gradually integrate Marines into virtually every militia platoon in the five provinces. The regular Marine battalions combined their thousands of day and night patrols and ambushes (they were conducting 7,000 platoon- and squad-size patrols and 5,000 night ambushes a month by April 1966) with a full-scale civic action program among the peasantry.

Walt and Krulak were soon as embattled with the powerful of Saigon and Washington as the Marine riflemen were with the Vietnamese enemy. Westmoreland harried Walt to leave the pacification business and the local guerrillas and political cadres to the civilians and the ARVN. He wanted the Marine battalions out in the foothills and the mountains on a search-and-destroy campaign of attrition every day possible. The pressure came in talks with Walt, in suggestions for specific operations followed by threats to issue orders if they were not performed, and in the rebound effect of complaints to McNamara and other important men in Washington that coddling peasants was not going to win the war, that the Marines were behaving timidly and letting the Army carry the burden of combat. The pressure extended to bureaucratic needles. One of the statistical devices Westmoreland used to measure the efficiency of his commanders was called "Battalion Days in the Field." The Marine battalions got credit only for days spent on search-and-destroy operations. Days and nights on pacification were not acceptable to the MACV computer.

Krulak was driven into a defensive struggle to try to relieve the pressure on Walt and stop Westmoreland from coercing the Marines into fighting the war his way. During a trip to Washington at the beginning of May 1966 he found McNamara willing to listen, as McNamara always did out of respect for Krulak, but no longer even fleetingly open to Krulak's main argument. The Marine strategy was too slow, McNamara told him. It would take too many men too long to win the war. Back in Hawaii, Krulak wrote the secretary a five-page, single-spaced letter attempting to explain that the Marines were not "bemused with handing out soap or bushwhacking guerrillas at the expense of attacking the main force units." The question of who held what in the mountains was "meaningless because there is nothing of value there," Krulak said. He cited for McNamara safer roads and more secure hamlets and other signs that the Marines were beginning to obtain some hold where it mattered. These signs, while "harder to quantify," were a better measure of progress than Westmoreland's body count. "The raw figure of VC killed . . . can be a dubious index of success since, if their killing is accompanied by devastation of friendly areas, we may end up having done more harm than good."

As Vann had already discovered, the men who directed American policy were not overly concerned with devastation. Two months later, in July 1966, Paul Nitze, then secretary of the Navy, visited South Vietnam. He got an earful from Westmoreland, whom he admired, and on his way back through Hawaii gave Krulak an earful. Krulak seethed at the lecture. He had just returned from another trip to Vietnam himself and had said in a letter of thanks to Walt: "Everywhere I turned in III MAF I saw progress." He called Walt's attention to a remark by an Army general that the United States was "winning militarily" in Vietnam, noting how "meaningless" the statement was. "You cannot win militarily," Krulak said. "You have to win totally, or you are not winning at all."

The Marines had not made as much progress in pacification by the summer of 1966 as Krulak thought. The clandestine Viet Cong organization had been hurt but remained intact deep within Marine lines. Saigon village and hamlet officials were still being assassinated on occasion in the outskirts of Da Nang. Lodge had set Walt back substantially in the spring and early summer of 1966 with the mistake of permitting Ky to oust the I Corps commander, Nguyen Chanh Thi, in a political squabble. Thich Tri Quang, the most ambitious of the Buddhist leaders who had brought down Diem, had leaped at the opportunity to assert himself, and three months of turmoil followed—demonstrations, strikes, and a week of civil war in Da Nang between ARVN units loyal to Tri Quang and Thi and paratroops and South Vietnamese marines Ky flew up from Saigon. (Vann's old acquaintance, Huynh Van Cao, redeemed himself during the crisis. The other generals forced him to accept command of I Corps because none of them wanted the job. Ky's police chief then demanded that Cao assault the pagoda the Buddhists and ARVN dissidents were using as their headquarters in Da Nang. Attacking a Buddhist pagoda was a sacrilege Cao declined to commit. He refused to issue the order. The police chief had one of his thugs put a pistol to Cao's head. Cao prepared to die. An American advisor walked into the room and saved him before the thug could pull the trigger. Ky threw Cao out of the ARVN by forcing him to retire. Cao subsequently went into politics as a representative of the Catholic community, a calling to which he was better suited than soldiering in any case.)

Nevertheless, despite the setback, Walt had started to see the dimensions of the task before him, and he was increasing his control in the countryside with the Combined Action militia units and other techniques like the organization of hamlet and village intelligence networks.

While the majority of the peasantry in Central Vietnam supported the cause of Ho Chi Minh, the Communists had plenty of enemies there too, and not every Vietnamese peasant cherished independence enough to resist forever the combination of coercion and blandishment the Marines were applying. With time and persistence Walt might well have subdued the populated coastal strip, at least temporarily. However many regulars Hanoi was able to maintain in the mountains through supply from the North could not decide the issue then. The regulars would be crushed by the Marines when they exposed themselves by venturing into the lower ground. Walt, who had been awarded the third star of a lieutenant general, had 55,000 men in his III Marine Amphibious Force in mid-1966. They were formed into two reinforced divisions, the 1st Marines with a command post at Chu Lai and the 3rd Marines operating out of Da Nang. He had a Marine air wing in support. His strength was to rise to about 70,000 men by the end of the year, when he would begin to approach the limit of Marine manpower. Lew Walt would never have enough Marines to fight both a war of attrition against the big Communist units and a pacification campaign.

The men in Hanoi settled the argument, with Westmoreland in the role of their unwitting cat's paw. They thrust a division, the 324B, across the Demilitarized Zone in the summer of 1966. Marine reconnaissance teams began to encounter the NVA troops in June near the large district center of Cam Lo northwest of the province capital of Quang Tri, where the old French road that traverses the Annamites into Laos, Route 9, starts to climb up into the foothills. By July, Marine intelligence officers had learned from prisoners and captured documents that their patrols were skirmishing with the advance elements of a force of at least 5,000 and perhaps the entire division of 10,000 to 12,000 men. Westmoreland ran for the lure as eagerly as Moore's lieutenant had in the valley of the Drang. He flew to Da Nang and encouraged Walt to go after the North Vietnamese with 8,000 Marines. The NVA held long enough to engage vigorously, then withdrew. In August they came back and challenged from a bit farther west in the mountains. Westmoreland sent Walt after them again.

The Demilitarized Zone and northern I Corps were an ideal battleground for the Vietnamese to bring to bear against the Americans the process of wearing down that their ancestors had worked to grim effect on the Mongols and the Ming and that they had previously brought to bear against the French. Their lines of supply and reinforcement were obviously shortest along the Demilitarized Zone, and whenever a Vietnamese unit needed to break off a fight it could easily gain sanctuary across the DMZ or over the adjacent border in Laos. The land lent itself perfectly to the Vietnamese strategy. It is broken even along the coast, with hills, stretches of sand dunes, and swamps interspersed among the rice fields. The foothills and the jungle start within about a dozen miles of the sea, and the mountains beyond are among the wildest on earth—a primeval confusion of lonesome peaks, steep ridges, winding valleys, and hidden ravines. One can conceal an army in just a bit of this immensity. Where there are no thickets of bamboo and fields of elephant grass, there is broadleaf, evergreen rain forest with canopy trees sixty feet high, pole trees in a second layer, and undergrowth so dense that visibility is often limited to five to ten yards.

The rainy season in the northern I Corps region brings chills and influenza when the temperature falls to 45 degrees in the dankness of the night, but the weather was another rough friend to the Vietnamese soldier on the Communist side. The northeast monsoon that sweeps into Central Vietnam from October to May has a different pattern than does the southwest monsoon that reaches the Mekong Delta and the Central Highlands from May to October. The rainy season in the Mekong Delta and the Central Highlands normally means an afternoon downpour and days at the height of the monsoon when fog is heavy but usually patchy. The northeast monsoon blows a light, steady, cold rain at its height called the *crachin* from the French word for "drizzle." The rain often lasts two to three days at a time and is frequently accompanied by a blanketing fog that stops close air support and also makes artillery hard to adjust when the fog is thick enough. Northern I Corps happens to be the place where the northeast monsoon is most intense. It is the rainiest place in Vietnam. The average rainfall for Hue is 128 inches, compared to 77 for Saigon.

Lew Walt became the man in the middle, caught between West-moreland pushing him into the NVA and Krulak hammering at him to continue to resist. Wally Greene tried to help during another trip to Vietnam that August. As always, he and Westmoreland did their serious talking alone after dinner in the villa on Tran Quy Cap that West-moreland had inherited from Harkins. For Greene to have argued with Westmoreland in front of any of the MACV staff would have been unseemly. On this occasion, Greene remembered, he pointed out to Westmoreland that the tactics of attrition made no more sense than the strategy. He had read a report of an Army unit fighting its way to the top of a jungled ridge only to have to fight its way back down again. This was not a sound expenditure of American soldiers, Greene said.

He got no further than he had on past occasions. These Marine generals forgot that for Westmoreland to have conceded they were right would have been to deny himself the war he wanted to wage of mass troop movements, artillery barrages, skies filled with helicopters and fighter-bombers, and the thunder of B-52s.

In September 1966, Westmoreland announced that he was ordering the Seabees to turn a little dirt airstrip in the far northwest corner of South Vietnam into an aluminum-matted field capable of handling C-130 transports. He told Walt to put a battalion of Marines there. In another of the lesser ironies of this war, Krulak had first heard about the spot twenty-nine years earlier. His battalion commander in Shanghai had gone to Indochina to hunt tiger and had returned with tales of a picturesque mountain valley called Khe Sanh and with photographs, which Krulak still had, showing the Bru tribal people and some of the French planters of coffee who lived there. The tribal people and the Frenchmen had crowded around the slain tiger in the photographs in order to have their picture taken too.

Krulak flew to Vietnam to try to talk Westmoreland out of his plan. They arranged to meet at Chu Lai aboard Westmoreland's twin-engine executive jet. One battalion of Marines would not suffice, Krulak argued. At least another battalion would have to be sent to occupy the hills that dominated the small plateau in the valley where the French had built the airstrip. A major helicopter commitment would then have to be made to supply the troops on the hills. Men and resources would be withdrawn from the pacification campaign to no useful purpose.

Westmoreland saw the purpose as useful. He gave Krulak several reasons for wanting a solitary airfield six miles from Laos and fifteen miles below the Demilitarized Zone. One was its possible future use as a jumping-off point (Route 9 went through the Khe Sanh Valley) should he ever receive permission for a thrust into Laos to cut the Ho Chi Minh Trail. (The president, McNamara, Rusk, and most other leading members of the administration were opposed to a move into Laos for fear that it might bring China into the war. Westmoreland also placed a curiously low priority on it, given the fact that depriving the Viet Cong of reinforcements and supplies from the North would seem to be a sine qua non of any attrition approach to the war. He was to say in his memoirs that he did not think he would be able to spare enough American troops to attempt a Laos thrust until 1968 and did not plan to lobby hard for the operation until that time. He already had a Special Forces camp at Khe Sanh in 1966 and could, of course, have waited to secure the place with Marines until he actually needed the airfield for a cutting of the Trail.)

As Westmoreland talked, Krulak could see that his overriding motive for sending Marines to Khe Sanh was the hope that a Marine base isolated in the mountains would attract thousands of North Vietnamese troops who presumably could be pulverized by U.S. firepower. Krulak flew back to Pearl Harbor, the Seabees and a battalion of Marines went to Khe Sanh, and Westmoreland, more determined than ever to bring Walt to heel, turned up the pressure. He soon had five additional battalions of Marines maneuvering full-time in northern Quang Tri Province in search of fights with the NVA.

Krulak appealed to Walt to defy folly. He sent him a cable at the end of the first week of October marked "SPECAT [Special Category] EXCLUSIVE FOR LTGEN WALT FROM LTGEN KRULAK/MARINE CORPS EYES ONLY." The cable was one of those supersensitive messages between generals that are called "back channels" because they are transmitted by the intelligence communications men over their separate circuits for greater secrecy. "If I were the enemy," Krulak said, he would regard pacification, and particularly the Marine demonstration that pacification could succeed, "as the greatest threat to my aspirations on the Indochina Peninsula." There was a way to remove that threat. It was to divert the Marines by "applying Mao's tactical doctrine, 'Uproar in the East, Strike in the West.' " Diversion had been the mission of the 324B Division. "Additionally, the northern battlefield is his [the enemy's] choice and to his liking." The fury in Krulak showed when he moved to his conclusion. "Our current actions in Quang Tri are probably agreeable to the NVN. I believe they are glad we have a battalion invested in the defense of Khe Sanh, and that we have five other battalions operating in the inhospitable jungle which might otherwise be engaged in Revolutionary Development Support [the official term for pacification]. . . . We may expect him [the enemy] to hang on to our forces in Quang Tri as long as he can."

Westmoreland and the Vietnamese Communists had eliminated Walt's room to maneuver. The issue had been narrowed to simple obedience to a military superior. If Walt kept resisting as Krulak was goading him to do, Westmoreland would have him relieved. Getting himself relieved on principle would not allow Walt to affect strategy, nor would his defiance be widely understood. Lyndon Johnson was not the only American who had confidence in William Westmoreland. The general was popular with the press and the public. He had already been on the cover of *Time* once and in his second appearance at the end of 1966 was *Time*'s Man of the Year. Walt does not seem to have had Krulak's acute perception that if Westmoreland had his way, Marines would die from that day forth for the benefit of the enemy. He seems to have rationalized that he could continue pacification at a reduced level while fighting a war of attrition along the DMZ.

Lew Walt was not the kind of Marine who would wage permanent guerrilla warfare against an Army superior with whom he disagreed. And he was the kind of Marine who in the end makes his decisions for reasons that are not subject to logic. It had turned out afterward that the Japanese forces on Cape Gloucester and Peleliu could not have seriously interfered with MacArthur's advance to the Philippines. They could have been left to curse and starve as Japanese were on many bypassed Pacific islands. The valor of Walt and his fellow Marines at Cape Gloucester and Peleliu had been as unnecessary as that much-better-known epic of superfluous Marine courage at Tarawa. But those Marines of World War II had died without knowing that their sacrifice was not needed, and in the end victory had redeemed it. Somehow the sacrifice of Marines would be redeemed in this war too.

Walt gave in and withdrew the 3rd Marine Division from the Da Nang area in October, shifting it north of the Hai Van Pass. Westmoreland had him establish a series of strongpoints along the DMZ. Those on the east were right on the edge of the zone at Gio Linh and Con Thien. Another series farther back moved west with Route 9 toward Khe Sanh: Cam Lo; Camp Carroll (named for a Marine captain who died to seize a nearby ridge); a humplike mound still farther west, just twelve miles from Khe Sanh, that more Marines died to possess and that they dubbed "the Rockpile"; and a place not far down the road called Ca Lu.

Westmoreland sent Walt Army artillery batteries of 175mm guns to install in the strongpoints. The "Long Toms" could throw a 147-pound shell twenty miles, covering Khe Sanh and beyond almost to the Laotian border, or all the way across the DMZ into North Vietnam. This "strong-point obstacle system," Westmoreland explained in his memoirs, was "designed to channel the enemy into well-defined corridors where we might bring air and artillery to bear and then hit him with mobile ground reserves." The 1st Marine Division was extended now from Chu Lai to Da Nang. Westmoreland formed a provisional Army division of three brigades, called Task Force Oregon and subsequently to be named the Americal after a provisional division MacArthur had organized during World War II, and dispatched it to I Corps in April 1967, to take over responsibility for Quang Ngai Province and the Chu Lai sector. The 1st Marines were obviously stretched too thin, and he also wanted to dilute the Marine monopoly in I Corps. He planned to move more Army divisions into the war there as they became available. Walt did not abandon his pacification program. It shriveled.

Krulak watched from Pearl Harbor in the position Vann had known in 1963. He could see the catastrophe coming and was helpless to stop it. The system might provide a hearing to a man of his rank and accomplishments; a rational response was another matter. Greene could do no more, and Admiral Sharp, Commander in Chief Pacific, had long since ceased to be of help. Under pressure from the Joint Chiefs to support Westmoreland in his perpetual wrestling with McNamara for more troops, Oley Sharp had developed a tendency simply to affirm whatever Westmoreland wanted. Westmoreland looked with satisfaction at the escalating combat along the DMZ. "We'll just go on bleeding them until Hanoi wakes up to the fact that they have bled their country to the point of national disaster for generations," he announced as he sent the first Army division to I Corps.

Ten days after Westmoreland's boast, on April 24, 1967, a five-man Marine forward observer party from Khe Sanh was ambushed in a grove of bamboo on Hill 861 northwest of the airstrip. One Marine survived. The first and the cruelest struggle at Khe Sanh, the "Hill Fights," began.

Krulak had been right that to hold Khe Sanh the Marines would have to garrison the hills that dominated the valley. The Vietnamese understood this and seized the hills. A regiment from the NVA's 325C Division marched in through the fog and under the low clouds of the monsoon and occupied Hill 861 and the two hills beyond it—881 South and 881 North. A second regiment from the division hid itself in a reserve position behind the hills. It was subsequently discovered that North Vietnamese combat engineer troops had probably been at work on the three hills for months without being detected by the Marines before the main body of NVA infantry arrived. (Walt had reduced the Marine battalion originally stationed at Khe Sanh in September to a reinforced company in February, because the battalion had been unable to find any North Vietnamese worth mentioning.) Westmoreland wanted to keep the airstrip. The Marines therefore had to drive the Vietnamese from the heights. They did not know the strength of the enemy they faced, nor did they suspect the nature of the battleground the Vietnamese had prepared.

For three days two companies of Marines—initially the company stationed at Khe Sanh, quickly followed by a second company under a battalion command group sent to take charge—attempted to clear Hill 861. The word "hill" is field shorthand for what is properly called a "hill mass" in military terminology. Hill 861 and Hills 881 South and 881

North were clusters of intertwining ridges, the highest ridge forming the crest that gave the hill mass its designation by height in meters. (Hills 881 South and 881 North happened to be the same height and so were differentiated by the fact that one was north of the other.)

The Vietnamese on Hill 861 let the Marines climb the ridges to within fifteen to twenty yards, then raked the Americans with fusillades from positions concealed in the undergrowth. Shells hurled by 82mm mortars from unseen pits somewhere back in the ridgelines crashed into the Marines, killing and wounding more of them. Counterfire by the Marine mortars, salvos of high explosive and white phosphorus from the howitzers at the airstrip, strafing and rocket runs by Huey gunships, and bombs and napalm from the jets of the 1st Marine Aircraft Wing interrupted but did not silence the enemy mortars or discourage the NVA infantry. When the Marines tried to disengage, the Vietnamese would not let go. They followed the Americans, harrying them with automatic-weapons fire. The Marines could not evacuate their wounded. Whenever they called in a helicopter the Vietnamese would plaster the landing zone with mortar shells.

The two companies were separated. The Khe Sanh company was on the northwest side of Hill 861, the company with the battalion command group was on the south. The battalion commander told the Khe Sanh company to link up with the company to which he was attached. The captain leading the Khe Sanh company replied that after three days of combat he did not have enough able-bodied men left to carry the dead and wounded that far. Marines abhor abandoning their dead because of the mystical comradeship of the Corps. Leave the dead, the battalion commander ordered. The captain answered that he still would not have enough able-bodied Marines to carry out the wounded, and wounded Marines cannot be abandoned under any circumstances. He said he was pulling into a nearby bank of fog to hide from the mortars and "fight until it was over" against the NVA infantry he was certain would follow.

The artillery officer back at the airstrip had his batteries walk shells to the company through the fog. He circled the beleaguered men with shrapnel, as Sergeant Savage had done to save Moore's lost platoon, until a platoon from a third Marine company flown to Khe Sanh as reinforcements could infiltrate to them at dusk. Litters for the wounded were improvised out of ponchos; the dead were slung in ponchos to be carried too; and the Marines gathered up all of the rifles and equipment. When the column set out to march back through the darkness and rain and a fog that thickened with the lowering temperatures of the night, only the men at the point and the rear guard walked without burdens.

The periodic downpours turned the dirt of the trails into slippery mud. The days had become hotter now toward the end of the rainy season, and the corpses had deteriorated and bloated. Many times during the night the Marines carrying one of the dead stumbled and the body fell out of the poncho and rolled down the slope. The column halted. The body was retrieved and laid in the poncho again, and the march resumed. When the Marines reached safety at dawn they had left none of their comrades behind.

The second company also disengaged with the help of the reinforcements. The two depleted companies were replaced, and the Marines built up their forces at Khe Sanh to two battalions under a regimental command post while the 105s and the 155s at the airstrip, Westmoreland's 175s firing from one of the strongpoints back across the mountains, and the Marine fighter-bombers battered and burned Hill 861 for a day and a night. A battalion then assaulted the hill. The Vietnamese were gone. They had apparently withdrawn to the next hill, 881 South, possibly soon after the fight with the two companies and before the worst of the bombardment had begun. They left many of their dead behind. Otherwise, as the Marine regimental after-action report noted, "the battle area was extremely well policed by the enemy; virtually no equipment or information of intelligence value remained." The Marines did count twenty-five bunkers on Hill 861, and they found 400 foxholes on and around it and mortar pits on the back slopes. The overhead cover on a number of the bunkers was six feet high in layers of bamboo and packed earth and grass, thick enough to protect the NVA troops inside from a direct hit by the artillery. The bunkers should have made the Marine regimental and battalion commanders suspicious.

The battalion that launched another headlong assault against Hill 881 South after another day and night of battering and burning attacked right into a man trap. The Vietnamese held fire once more until the lead platoons were fifteen to twenty yards from the bunkers in the undergrowth and the opening volley would have maximum killing effect. Snipers hidden in trees not yet knocked down by bombs and shells picked out radio operators and machine gunners and killed them carefully with a single shot through the head or the chest. At the same moment, salvos of 82mm mortar shells again exploded among the Marines. The NVA did not seem to mind calling mortar fire so close that they were, in effect, bringing it down on their own positions.

Marines are unsurpassed as assault troops, and these Marines pressed forward with the classic aggressiveness instilled by the Corps. They discovered that the farther they fought their way into the Vietnamese position, the more resistance they encountered and the worse their situation became. Soon those men still capable of fighting were unable to go forward or back. The fire from the bunkers, foxholes, and trenches in front was withering. Meanwhile, Vietnamese in bunkers the Marines had fought their way past were back in action behind them and had cut off their retreat.

Krulak's warning in his strategy paper that the Vietnamese Communists wanted "violent, close-quarters combat" because it "tends to diminish the effectiveness" of air and artillery was turning out to be something of an understatement. The Marines on 881 South were feeling the extent of the diminishment. While Westmoreland had been thinking about ports and warehouses for his attrition machine, the Vietnamese had been learning better ways to fight the Americans. There were not twice as many bunkers on 881 South as the Marines had found on Hill 861, there were ten times as many, and the approximately 250 bunkers on this hill were astonishingly rugged. The smaller ones, apparently two- or three-man affairs, had been constructed with roofs consisting of two layers of logs topped by five feet of dirt. Larger four-man bunkers had still better protection overhead and, before the battle, had served as fairly comfortable living quarters. They were fitted with storage shelves, bamboo-mat floors, and a drainage system to keep them dry. The largest bunkers, clearly the command posts, had roofs with four to eight layers of logs and then four feet of packed earth above the logs. Field telephone wire had been strung throughout the bunker complex so that the NVA battalion, company, and platoon commanders could talk to each other during the battle and they and the forward observers could adjust the mortars by calling instructions to the crews in the pits on the rear slopes.

The day-and-night bombardment of the hill that had seemed so awesomely destructive to the watching Marines had been mainly fireworks. The rockets detonated on the branches or the overhead cover of the bunkers, and the machine-gun bullets and 20mm cannon shells didn't penetrate anything either. Most of the napalm burned in the trees. The howitzer shells did give the Vietnamese in the bunkers headaches. The bombs were more frightening, extremely difficult to bear. The concussion from them gave some of the Vietnamese bleeding noses and ears, but the bombs usually did not kill or disable either.

Prior to the assault on the morning of April 30, the fighter-bombers had dropped no 750-pounders and only a small number of 1,000- and 2,000-pound bombs on Hill 881 South. Almost all of the bombs had been the 250- and 500-pound "Snake-eye" type preferred by the Marine pilots and their Navy and Air Force counterparts. Snake-eye bombs have large tail fins that unfold after release to retard descent so that the bomb can be launched from low altitude in a slow, parabolic trajectory that allows the aircraft time to fly clear of the blast and fragmentation. Jets can bomb accurately from a low, relatively flat approach and Vietnamese weather also encouraged the use of Snake-eyes. Navy and Air Force pilots had to be prepared to fly anywhere. With one part of the country or the other always in a monsoon, they frequently encountered low cloud ceilings. At Khe Sanh in late April and early May 1967, the ceiling was often 1,000 feet or less. To drop the heavier 750-, 1,000-, and 2,000-pound bombs accurately and escape the blast and fragments, a pilot had to take a high-angle approach akin to dive-bombing and pull away at a good height. An approach like this was dangerous when the clouds were down and the air space around a target was crowded. The Vietnamese had also observed this practice of the American aviators. The bunkers were sturdy enough to withstand anything but a direct or close hit by a 250- or 500-pound Snake-eye bomb, infrequent in practice.

Rain-forest bunker complexes served the Vietnamese for both offensive and defensive purposes. During the early stages of a battle, as in the fighting for Hill 861, the Vietnamese could sortie out and employ their flanking and envelopment tactics to advantage. They knew the terrain intimately, because they had been living in the area secretly for quite a while during the last phase of bunker construction. Later, when the battle was approaching a high point, as in the assault on Hill 881 South, the Vietnamese could wait out the bombardment in the shelter of the bunkers.

In the end, bombs and shells would exact their toll. Those Vietnamese who were ordered to hold their positions or to expose themselves in counterattacks would die, as they were to die by the hundreds during the two and a half weeks of the Hill Fights. By planning carefully, by fortifying in advance, and by designing a battlefield that enticed the Americans into becoming victims of their own stylized methods of fighting, the Vietnamese could accomplish what was most important to them: they could prolong the combat and make any American infantry sent against them suffer grievously. Merely to strip away the top layer of canopy trees, the second layer of pole trees, and finally the underbrush so that one could see the bunkers to attack them with precision consumed days of this standard bombardment with artillery and 250- and 500-pound bombs. Despite all of the preparatory bombing and shelling of Hill 881 South, the Marines could not see the bunkers until they were almost on top of them, and there were plenty of trees left standing to give the snipers leafy perches.

Lew Walt cared about the lives of his Marines. He flew to Khe Sanh the moment he received a report of the bloodletting on the hill, took a squad of riflemen, and crawled forward to find out for himself what was happening. Peleliu in the fall of 1944 had been the first of the Pacific islands where the Japanese had avoided foolish banzai charges and holed up in caves and pillboxes of steel-reinforced concrete and coral. Walt had been sent back to the Marine Corps Schools at Quantico, Virginia, after that battle and put in charge of the attack section, which developed a special course on how to overcome a fortified position. He therefore understood the limits of conventional bombardment against bunkers like the ones he now saw on Hill 881 South and the rashness of sending infantry to seize them. He ordered all of the Marines withdrawn from the hill and instructed the air wing to switch to 750-, 1,000-, and 2,000-pound bombs with delay fuses. The delay fusing meant that the bomb penetrated the earth before exploding. A miss was still effective, because the subterranean shock waves tended to collapse the bunkers from beneath. The concussion from the big bombs was disabling in itself (lethal when the hit was close enough), and the delay also gave the pilot time to fly clear.

Walt intervened too late. The death toll in the Hill Fights was already ninety-nine. Close to half of the men had just been killed in this impetuous attack on 881 South, and this time the Marines were forced to abandon their dead in order to extricate the living. When they returned two days later to recover the bodies of their comrades and occupy the wasteland of cratered ridges littered with splintered trees, fifty of the bunkers were still intact and the Vietnamese were gone again. The survivors of the 18th NVA Regiment that had borne the battle until this point had retreated to Hill 881 North, where, unbeknownst to the Americans, they had been relieved by fresh troops of the 95th Regiment, which the NVA division commander had been holding in reserve.

Lew Walt had also put his 1st Marine Aircraft Wing to work on Hill 881 North with heavy bombs, but 2,000-pounders could not blow away the perverse weather of this land. As the lead Marine company neared the top of that hill late on the same afternoon that 881 South was occupied, the men encountered brisk sniper fire. The Marines thought they could handle the snipers. They could not handle the tropical storm that enveloped them with forty-mile-per-hour winds and blinding rain. The battalion commander had to order a retreat. It was too dangerous to allow his Marines to plunge ahead into who knew what.

The Vietnamese took advantage of the hiatus to launch a counterattack that night by two reinforced companies. The NVA troops broke through the perimeter of one Marine company and seized some previously unoccupied bunkers in a tree line. There, with automatic weapons and grenades, they traded their lives through most of the next day in a fight to the death bunker by bunker. More dying followed on subsequent days. By the time the two and a half weeks of fighting for the hills had ended, the bodies of 155 Marines had been carried to the graves registration point at Khe Sanh airstrip and 425 had been wounded, the worst Marine losses for any single battle of the war thus far.

As quickly as they let it ebb in the west, the Vietnamese shifted the fighting to the eastern side of the DMZ, striking the Marine base at Con Thien with two battalions in early May. The shelling became the worst curse of this DMZ war, worse than the infantry assaults, worse than the ambushes of the supply convoys, worse than the raids by the sappers (a term Americans applied to NVA and Viet Cong commando-type troops) who stripped to their undershorts and crawled through the barbed wire to toss satchel charges into bunkers and artillery revetments. The shelling was worse because it was equally lethal but harder on the nerves. It too began to get serious in May when nearly 4,200 rounds fell on the Marine positions. The Vietnamese brought to bear all manner of artillery in the Soviet-designed arsenal—85mm, 100mm, 122mm, and 130mm guns; 120mm mortars that burst in an extremely large fragmentation pattern; and 122mm Katyusha rockets nine feet long. By July they were shooting 152mm guns at the Marines. The duds from these penetrated four feet into the earth.

The Marines tried all manner of counterbattery measures to silence their opponents. Their batteries, Westmoreland's Long Toms, and the guns of the Seventh Fleet cruisers and destroyers fired hundreds of thousands of shells. The A-4 Skyhawks and F-8 Crusaders precision-dive-bombed, and the B-52s and the Marine and Navy A-6 Intruder bombers, which lofted a respectable seven tons each, laid carpets in the tens of thousands of tons. Nothing gave more than a respite from these Asian artillerymen who counted in their intellectual heritage the seventeenth-century French genius of artillery and siegecraft Sebastien de Vauban, and who had had so much practice at digging and disguising against his direct military heirs who had forgotten his teachings.

The Vietnamese built phony gun positions for the interpreters of the aerial photographs to find. They set off harmless explosive charges to simulate muzzle flashes for the Marine observers. They hid the real guns and mortars and rocket launchers in deep pits and in tunnels, fired the weapons at irregular intervals, and pulled the camouflage back over the weapon and its emplacement after each shot. A favorite time to shoot was in the late afternoon when the muzzle flashes were hardest to spot. A technique for the heavy mortars was to burrow a narrow shaft far down into the slope of a hill or ridge that looked toward a Marine position. Chambers were hollowed out at the bottom of the shaft for the mortar and its crew so that weapon and men would have the whole of the earth above as protection. The fired mortar round flew up and out the camouflaged opening of the shaft. A variation of the technique was often used for the howitzers. Gun and mortar and rocket-launching sites were found, of course, and the weapons and the crews smothered in bombs and shells. The arsenals of the Soviet Union, China, and the Eastern European countries produced a plentitude of artillery to resupply the Vietnamese, and Hanoi did not stint at replacing the crews. Soon, if one counted in the smaller 82mm mortars, half of the Marine casualties were resulting from shellfire and rockets.

When Lew Walt went home in June 1967, at the end of two years, he took with him the lesson in how to deal with the bunker complexes. The lesson had to be relearned on almost every occasion by trial and error in American lives. The American military system of the 1960s provided for the unlearning rather than the learning of lessons. The one-year tour that Westmoreland had decided to carry over from the advisory era because he thought it would help morale meant that all ranks from colonel to private first class left the country by the time they were beginning to acquire some experience and perspective. The turnover was twice as fast, every six months, at the operating levels of battalion and brigade (regiment was the equivalent of brigade in the Marine Corps), where experienced leadership was needed most. The officer spent the other six months of his tour in a staff job or as an executive officer at a higher level. There were few exceptions, and only rarely could a man hold a command longer than six months by volunteering to extend his tour. (Often the turnover was faster than six months because the officer became a casualty or got sick.)

The Army personnel bureaucracy tended to view Vietnam as an educational exercise and rationalized the six-month rule as a way of seasoning more officers for the "big war" yet to come with the Soviets in Europe and for more of these "brushfire wars." The real reason, which held true for the Marine Corps too and which explained why the practice was derisively called "ticket-punching," was a mechanistic promotion process and the bureaucratic impetus this created. To win eagles a lieutenant colonel had to punch a battalion command on his record. To gain a star a colonel had to punch on command of a brigade or a regiment. To keep an officer in a battalion or brigade or regimental command longer than six months was regarded as unfair to his contemporaries. Much the same system of ticket-punching held true for the general officers, although they were on eighteen-month tours. A general was seldom permitted to hold a division or corps command for more than a year, because so many other generals were waiting in line to qualify for another star. Walt had been an exception, because he was the senior Marine. The Vietnamese could thus count on their American opponents to behave according to pattern.

More than half of all American servicemen who died in combat in Vietnam from 1967 onward, 52 percent, were to die in I Corps. Of this 52 percent, 25 percent were to perish along or close to the DMZ itself in the two northernmost I Corps provinces of Quang Tri and Thua Thien. The remaining 27 percent were to die in the three lower provinces of I Corps, because these quickly reverted to big-unit warfare after Westmoreland forced Walt and Krulak to abandon their pacification strategy. Westmoreland's success had the effect of uncovering the Marines' rear and permitting the Viet Cong regulars and the NVA to operate freely once more in the populated rice deltas close to the coast.

The same summer of 1966 that they lured Westmoreland to the DMZ, the Vietnamese moved the focus of their second border front in the Central Highlands where Moore had fought his battle. They drew the Americans farther north to the remote mountains of upper Kontum Province, right next to the terminus of the Ho Chi Minh Trail supply line and another region where the Annamites are at their most rugged. In 1967 the Hanoi leaders were able to open a third border front in III Corps along the Cambodian frontier. The Chinese made an arrangement with Sihanouk to ship the Vietnamese thousands of tons of arms, ammunition, medicine, and other supplies (more than 26,600 metric tons by the end of 1969) through the port of Sihanoukville. The Cambodian army received a small share of the weaponry, and Sihanouk and his generals were bribed. One of Sihanouk's wives owned the trucking company that was paid to haul the weapons from the port to the Vietnamese depots.

The statistics on where Americans died invariably demonstrated the extent to which Westmoreland convenienced his enemy. Nearly four-fifths of all Americans killed in action in Vietnam from 1967 onward, 77 percent, died in just ten of the country's forty-four provinces. Five of the provinces were those constituting I Corps. Three others were the border provinces of Kontum, Tay Ninh, and Hau Nghia of Vann's memory. The ninth province was Binh Duong, in between Tay Ninh and Hau Nghia and thus part of the Cambodian border front. The sole exception to the border pattern was the tenth province, Binh Dinh on the Central Coast, and Binh Dinh has its own mountainous interior that reaches back into the Highlands.

Krulak found it hard to look at the casualty lists a secretary laid on his desk each morning in his office on the mountain overlooking Pearl Harbor. He had a memory for names and faces and was familiar with many of the company commanders and platoon leaders and with the noncoms and the "grunts" from his visits to the units. His three sons had followed him into the Corps. His oldest, an Episcopal clergyman, had chosen a military ministry as a chaplain; his two younger sons were regular Marine officers, company commanders. Their choice of a vocation gave a grim edge to his ordeal. At one point all three of his sons were in Vietnam together. His youngest, Charles Krulak, served two tours in I Corps as a company commander and won a Silver Star for Gallantry and three Bronze Stars for Valor. He was wounded twice, the second time on the same ridge where Capt. James Carroll, after whom Camp Carroll was named, died three years earlier.

Had John Kennedy lived, Krulak thought, the war might have gone differently. Kennedy's fascination with counterinsurgency and the lessons he would have learned by 1965 would have enabled him to grasp the importance of what Krulak was saying when Krulak had gone to the Oval Office with his strategy paper in hand. The president would have forced the Army generals to fight the war intelligently.

If Krulak was right about Kennedy, if there was any substance to his musing, it was another of the many might-have-beens of Vietnam. In this war, 14,691 Marines were to die, three times as many as had died in Korea, a weighty loss in lives, a loss that weighed more heavily than the 24,511 Marines who had been lost during World War II. For Brute Krulak was to know, before most of these Marines of Vietnam had died, that all of them were to die in vain.

As the Vietnamese Communists were shifting the focus of combat to the eastern side of the DMZ in May 1967, John Vann was engaged in a bureaucratic battle to help Robert Komer create the pacification organization that was to be known by the acronym CORDS, for Civil Operations and Revolutionary Development Support. The battle was one of the few bureaucratic contests of Vann's career that turned into a relatively easy victory, because Westmoreland saw that it was not in his interest to resist and overruled his own staff. Komer's bravado broke any further resistance.

The U.S. Army MPs who protected Westmoreland's headquarters didn't believe in the beginning that this slightly balding man of forty-five in a bow tie and a three-button suit was the first civilian general. Komer convinced them, as he was to convince others, in Komer fashion. When Komer arrived at the MACV gate for the first time in the status symbol Westmoreland had provided him, one of three black Chrysler Imperials in Saigon (Westmoreland and his new military deputy, Gen. Creighton Abrams, rode around in the other two), the MP on duty threw up the back of his hand in a halt signal. Komer was sitting in the backseat behind his Vietnamese civilian police driver and a Vietnamese police bodyguard. The MP walked over to the rear door of the Chrysler. Komer rolled down the window.

"Sir, who are you?" the MP asked.

"I'm the high panjandrum of pacification," Komer said, and then identified himself.

"Yes sir, I'll look you up," the MP said. He walked back to the guard post and read down his list of VIPs. He picked up the phone and called inside.

The Vietnamese driver and bodyguard started to talk. Komer could tell that they were discussing the delay and that he was losing face. There were more important people in Saigon with whom Robert Komer was determined not to lose face. Komer spoke loudly whether his ever-present pipe was in or out of his mouth. He had laughed with satisfaction when he learned in 1966 while quarterbacking pacification from the White House that Lodge had nicknamed him "the Blowtorch" because of the heat he generated for progress. This morning, as the military policeman was embarrassing him, Komer had on his mind an article that Ward Just, the correspondent for the *Washington Post*, had written a few days earlier. Just had said that Komer might think he was tough in Washington, but he would discover things were different in the military aviary of Saigon. Komer was now a pullet among chicken hawks, Just implied, and the generals and colonels on Westmoreland's staff were going to have him for lunch.

Komer decided he was going to make Just a false prophet. He had noticed that the MP who stopped him had given an instant wave-through and a snap to attention and salute to a plain olive-green sedan that was ahead of his Imperial. The sedan displayed red plates with the two white stars of a major general.

"That's it, that does it," Komer shouted to his assistant, Col. Robert

Montague, as soon as he entered his office in the headquarters. "I want four stars put on my car. Westy has four stars. Abe"—the nickname of Creighton Abrams—"has four stars. I want four stars. Tell the chief of staff to put four-star plates on my car." Montague picked up the phone and relayed Komer's instructions.

William Rosson was no longer the chief of staff at MACV. He had gone to Quang Ngai to command the provisional division Westmoreland had formed there. Maj. Gen. Walter Kerwin, Jr., an energetic artillery-man with a sense of the orthodox akin to a regimental striped tie, had taken Rosson's place. "Dutch" Kerwin spared himself the humiliation of dealing with Komer on this occasion and sent a deputy, an Air Force general.

"Sir, we've got a problem, we can't put four-star plates on your car," the Air Force general said.

"Why not?" Komer boomed.

The general explained that according to the regulations only a military man of four-star rank was entitled to a four-star plate.

"Those regulations were written before anyone ever thought we'd be fighting a war like this. Put four stars on my car," Komer said.

The Air Force general had the temerity to suggest that the regulations ought to be taken seriously. He got a further browbeating from Komer. The exchange ended with the general backing out the door saying, "Yes, sir."

He returned in an hour. "Sir, I think we've got a solution to the problem," he said.

"What is it?" Komer demanded.

"We're going to design a special plate for you. It has an eagle in the middle and four stars on it, one in each corner. It's just like the plate the secretary of the Army has." He looked at Komer and smiled tentatively.

"Fine, put it on," Komer said.

"Yes, sir," the Air Force general said with a less tentative smile.

If the MPs at the MACV gate still had to puzzle at the oddball plate, they were awfully quick to give the wave-through and the snap to attention and salute, and in a short time they didn't need to see an eagle and stars. They knew that the man in the back in the bow tie was Komer.

When Lyndon Johnson had initially appointed him the White House watchman of the "other war" in Vietnam in the spring of 1966, Robert Komer knew virtually nothing about East Asia. It was the one part of the world he had never studied and where he had never traveled during a twenty-two-year career in government, begun in Italy during World War II as a corporal in Army intelligence. Komer, the son of a prosperous Midwestern family, had graduated from Harvard *magna cum laude* in 1942, returned right after the war to take an M.B.A. at Harvard Business School, and then decided that intelligence, not business, was his calling. As a senior analyst in the Office of National Estimates at the CIA, he had headed staffs on Western Europe, on the Middle East, and on the Soviet Union. After John Kennedy's election and the offer of a job on the National Security Council staff from McGeorge Bundy, he had served as the White House man for the Middle East. Africa had later been added to his responsibilities, and he had risen to become Bundy's deputy.

Komer warned Kennedy's successor that he was ignorant on Vietnam. That did not trouble Lyndon Johnson. He subscribed to the notion of the day that a smart American, especially an American with an Ivy League education, could accomplish anything. The cultural inferiority complex of the Texan tended to magnify Johnson's faith in men with fancy Eastern educations. "You Harvards," was how he put it to Komer on occasion. Komer also had much more going for him with the president than his Eastern education. The brassy, ruthless, work-and-ambition-driven qualities in him appealed to Johnson. Bob Komer was a man of the system and yet he was not of the system. He would not hesitate to take a hammer to some bureaucrat's sacred mold.

Much of what Komer subsequently learned about Vietnam and pacification he learned from Vann and from those who had been influenced by Vann, like Dan Ellsberg and Richard Holbrooke. Komer tapped Ellsberg as a source of information soon after Johnson put him to work on pacification in 1966, because they were acquainted through the fraternity of high-powered government intellectuals. Holbrooke, after leaving Porter's Saigon embassy staff to return home, had been recruited by Komer to be his civilian assistant at the White House. Ellsberg and Holbrooke had both told Komer how valuable Vann was. Holbrooke then arranged for Vann to come to the White House and talk to Komer while Vann was in Washington on leave in June 1966 to explore the Office of Systems Analysis job at the Pentagon. The talk lasted three hours. Komer found Vann "devastating because he was so knowledgeable" and "terribly embittered" by his years of fruitless preaching. He was struck by the duality in what Vann had said. Victory was a mirage the way the war was currently being run, but "if we did it the right way, we could win." Ever quick to cultivate a contact who had power or influence, Vann had continued to see Komer on Komer's frequent trips to South Vietnam and stayed in touch in between with letters and memos.

Although the limitations common to American statesmen kept President Johnson from reaching for the kind of fundamentally different approach that Vann and Krulak advocated, he did want a pacification program that would complement Westmoreland's war of attrition. The attempt to achieve it at the end of November 1966 by unifying the civilian agencies in the Office of Civil Operations had proved useful chiefly as an organizing exercise on the civilian side. Vann progressed further than any of the other OCO regional directors in forming his III Corps advisors into a working team, but he too was hampered by continued rivalry between AID, CIA, and USIS and by the decision to leave the province military advisors in Westmoreland's separate chain of command. In the spring of 1967, Westmoreland's waiting game paid off. The president decided to formally assign all responsibility for pacification to him. Johnson also decided to send Komer out to South Vietnam that May to manage the effort under Westmoreland. The pacification army that Komer then proceeded to form in the entity known as Civil Operations and Revolutionary Development Support, or CORDS, lacked Vann's central concept of an American takeover of the Saigon side and social reform. Otherwise CORDS owed its command system and organizational structure largely to Vann's thinking.

Johnson granted Komer the personal rank of ambassador for protocol purposes and he was addressed as Ambassador Komer, but his duties in Saigon were hardly those of a diplomat. He was also not a member of Westmoreland's staff or a special assistant to the general. Bob Komer was *the* deputy commander for pacification, officially "Deputy to COMUSMACV for CORDS." The distinction was important in a military universe, because it meant that Komer had direct authority over everyone who worked for him and direct access to Westmoreland. He ranked third at MACV after Creighton Abrams, Westmoreland's military deputy. Everyone else at the headquarters had to report to Westmoreland through Dutch Kerwin, the chief of staff.

Vann had warned Komer that if he arrived with less authority and access, he would be eaten by the chicken hawks. Komer therefore drew up his charter beforehand in a memorandum he showed the president and gave Westmoreland during an earlier trip to Saigon that spring, telling Westmoreland the president approved the deputy commander arrangement. Komer assured the general that Westmoreland had everything to gain. If Komer failed, the president would blame Komer, because he was the president's choice. "Westy, it'll be my head," Komer said. If he succeeded, Westmoreland would succeed at pacification too, because Komer would be his deputy. Komer added a fillip he hoped would appeal to the pride Westmoreland took in his ability as a manager.

He reminded the general that they were both graduates of Harvard Business School. (Westmoreland had been sent there for a thirteen-week course while a brigadier general at the Pentagon back in the 1950s.) A direct line of authority and responsibility was the Harvard Business School solution, Komer said.

The fillip was unnecessary. William Westmoreland wanted to fulfill the wishes of the president when he thought he could do so at no cost to himself, and whereas he might lack astuteness at war, a shrewdness for the politics of bureaucracy was one of the principal reasons he had risen so far. He saw Komer's point immediately. Furthermore, his empire was being extended to all of pacification and at the same time he was being relieved of the burden of it. He could get on with his big-unit war and leave the problem to Komer. When the question of a staff car later came up he offered Komer the big Chrysler.

The CORDS structure established below Komer was a unique civil-military command that amounted to a special pacification service within the U.S. forces in Vietnam. A new American deputy commander for pacification was appointed in each of the four corps regions. The corps deputy for pacification had the same relationship with the American commanding general at corps level that Komer had with Westmoreland and bore the same abbreviated title Komer did, Dep/CORDS. The corps deputies also reported to Komer and were, in effect, his corps commanders. Under the corps deputies were the fully unified province teams that Vann had proposed two years earlier in his "Harnessing the Revolution." The RF and PF and other province military advisors were merged with the civilian advisors into a single team led by a PSA—a province senior advisor.

Vann's friend and former superior as chief of AID's pacification program, Col. Sam Wilson, made a significant contribution to the formation of CORDS by volunteering to go to Long An Province in the fall of 1966 and run an experimental province team unified like this. He proved that military and civilian could work harmoniously together, and his team now became the model for those being created in every province. Some of the PSAs were military men, others were from the civilian agencies. While there was bureaucratic log-rolling to be sure that all agencies got a share, the PSAs were ideally chosen on the basis of talent and experience. The PSA reported directly to the Dep/CORDS in his corps. At Vann's urging, Komer established an efficiency-report system to help instill discipline, and orders were issued within CORDS just as they were within the military.

*   *   *

Vann was fortunate that the new commander of U.S. forces in III Corps, Maj. Gen. Fred Weyand, worried about being too conventional in his thinking and valued unconventional men who gave him insights he would not acquire on his own. Otherwise Komer might have had to find another corps not of Vann's choosing where he could serve as Dep/CORDS. Westmoreland indicated to Weyand that Vann was a hair shirt Weyand did not have to accept. Weyand thought differently. He had gained two stars and was about to gain his third by adapting to the world of the U.S. Army; his ease within it sometimes made him feel uncomfortable. Weyand's conventional side would, in fact, have done him out of stars had he not waked up after a long, slow start.

He had obtained his commission in the Coast Artillery on the eve of World War II through ROTC at the University of California at Berkeley. The Coast Artillery was a branch of the Army that did not understand it had been rendered obsolete by the airplane and modern amphibious warfare. It supposedly protected the nation's harbors with long-range guns installed in concrete forts. Weyand drifted in this anachronism through the first part of World War II and then volunteered for Combat Intelligence School, hoping to put to good use in Europe a respectable amount of German he had learned in high school and college. Instead the Army posted him to the staff of Gen. Joseph Stilwell in the China-Burma-India Theater as the officer in charge of deriving intelligence from broken Japanese codes. "Vinegar Joe" Stilwell was one of the most accomplished infantrymen in the history of the U.S. Army, but despite the experience of working for him, Weyand drifted again in intelligence after the war. Finally, while a thirty-two-year-old lieutenant colonel in Hawaii, he encountered a general who gave him advice he heeded: to move up, move out to the cutting edge.

Fred Weyand transferred to the infantry and graduated from the Advanced Course at Fort Benning as Kim Il Sung's tanks were crossing the 38th Parallel. He found his métier practicing the "Follow Me!" motto of the Infantry School. In January 1951 he was given a battalion of the 3rd Infantry Division, reduced to 162 men by MacArthur's debacle in North Korea. He built it back up with replacements, many of them KATUSAs, reorganized it, and then trained on the march as he led his battalion in the counteroffensives to drive the Chinese back up the peninsula and reestablish a line along the Parallel. "Those were the days when you commanded your battalion from the lead platoon," Weyand said with nostalgia. "If you succeeded, it was because you were there."

He won a Silver Star for Gallantry and the Bronze Star for Valor. Maj. Gen. Frank Milburn, the commander of I Corps, had singled out Weyand's battalion as the finest in the corps.

His performance in Korea was the flint striking steel to light Weyand's career. Afterward he was able to get the kind of assignments a non–West Pointer needs to give him an advantage—military assistant to the secretary of the Army, commander of a battle group in Berlin, and for two years in the early 1960s the sensitive post of chief liaison officer to Congress. His physical appearance helped. He was six feet four inches and handsome. So did his manner. He could be reasonably open and honest while also being deft, and he was an informal and friendly man. Weyand shortened his classy name of Frederick Carlton to Fred C. in official correspondence. He did not wait for junior officers and enlisted men to salute him. He saluted them first.

Weyand and Vann had met in Hau Nghia not much more than a year before the formation of CORDS. Vann had been on another of his periodic expeditions to try to get information about where the Viet Cong were keeping Ramsey captive. Weyand had just brought the headquarters of the 25th Infantry Division he was then commanding to Vietnam from Hawaii and was in the midst of setting up a base camp at Cu Chi. Ramsey's last reports to AID and a comprehensive description he had written of Hau Nghia gave Weyand a lot of practical information, but he lacked anything precise on the Viet Cong forces in the province, what is called order of battle intelligence in the military. The G-2 section at MACV and Seaman's staff at II Field Force, as the U.S. corps-level command for III Corps was called, had nothing useful.

Fred Weyand considered himself a lucky soldier when a walking intelligence file on Hau Nghia suddenly appeared and introduced himself as John Vann. The two men got to know each other better on Vann's subsequent expeditions and after he was appointed III Corps director for OCO near the end of 1966. Vann would stop at Weyand's headquarters on a Saturday or a Sunday for a late-afternoon volleyball game and stay for the night so that he and Weyand could talk over dinner and into the evening.

Some regular Army officers tended in these years to look askance at John Vann as a kind of renegade lieutenant colonel. Weyand tested what Vann told him and noticed that Vann was right far more often than he was wrong. Weyand admired Vann's moral courage. He was fascinated by the detail Vann gathered from the myriad of friends and acquaintances he had built up among Vietnamese on the Saigon side and from his forays down questionable roads and his nights spent in hamlets and militia outposts. Weyand was not in a position to do that sort of thing, and he didn't know anyone else who did it. Bruce Palmer, Vann's old commanding officer and patron in the 16th Infantry Regiment in Germany, became II Field Force commander in March 1967, after Seaman rotated home. Weyand moved up from the division to be Palmer's deputy. Westmoreland then decided, to Palmer's unhappiness, that he needed Palmer to run the main support and administrative command, U.S. Army Vietnam. Weyand got the corps. When Westmoreland indicated to him that Vann might be troublesome as a Dep/CORDS, Weyand was fully aware that John Vann meant trouble. What he received in exchange was what mattered to Weyand.

Vann did not have to shift his office from the former OCO compound near ARVN III Corps headquarters on the outskirts of Bien Hoa when he became the Dep/CORDS for II Field Force in June 1967. His job simply got bigger, and he added a building in the compound for more staff. After the inaugural session at II Field Force Headquarters at the Long Binh base, Weyand asked if there was anything special he could do for his new deputy. "Yes, I'd like to have a military aide," Vann said. Did he have any particular young officer in mind, Weyand asked. "No, any lieutenant or warrant officer will do as long as he brings his helicopter with him," Vann said.

The access Seaman had given Vann to one of the corps' little H-23 Raven helicopters whenever Vann wished had been a perquisite to cherish (and one that Palmer and Weyand had continued), but a pilot and a helicopter of one's own made one feel considerably more like a general. Vann's new "aide" appeared shortly afterward with his two-seater Plexiglas-bubble flying machine. Vann had concrete helicopter pads laid next to his office compound and beside the house nearby that AID had rented for him as living quarters in Bien Hoa. He arranged for the pilot to live in an aviation compound across the road. No spot in the eleven provinces in the corps was beyond an hour's flight. Vann now had almost 800 Americans working for him on his staff and in the unified province teams, the majority military men. When he added the Filipino and South Korean help and the Vietnamese employees, he had about 2,225 people under him. American soldiers—lieutenant colonels, majors, captains, lieutenants, sergeants—were once again taking orders from John Vann. "I am back in the military fold and I am in command," he said in a round-robin letter to his friends.

He had read a letter from Ramsey that February. It was written on tissue paper in a minute hand with a ball-point pen and smuggled out of a jungle prison camp by Pfc. Charles Crafts, one of two captured American soldiers released by the Viet Cong as a propaganda act during the 1967 Tet or Lunar New Year holiday. The letter was from Ramsey to his parents in Boulder City, Nevada. Crafts hid it in his eyeglass case and turned it over to the U.S. Army intelligence officers who questioned him right after his release. Vann was called to the embassy, where the letter went for forwarding. He had stayed in touch with Ramsey's parents, occasionally sending them whatever fragments of information he could obtain. (At one point he was to offer them financial help, which they thanked him for and said they did not need.) He immediately wrote to alert them and to give them a summary of the letter's contents. The embassy kept the original for the special file maintained on a prisoner, but sent Ramsey's parents an exact typescript.

Ramsey, the only child, told his parents, "It is the thought of seeing you again and the memories of home which are keeping me above water at present." He hoped to survive, "but we must be realistic." He wanted the letter to serve as testimony that "I was still alive as of the 13th of January [1967]," the day he completed it, so his parents could collect his back pay to that date "without undue difficulty" should he perish. Ramsey tried, nevertheless, to be encouraging. He had endured a bout with ordinary malaria and then come through an assault by the falciparum variety "said to be 90 percent fatal in this region." (Falciparum is the so-called "killer malaria" that attacks the brain.) "If I can survive something like that I am now completely confident of my ability to survive any of the lesser diseases I have seen in this area—with no sweat," he said. The Viet Cong "medical treatment is quite good, given jungle conditions. . . . As to protection from U.S. artillery, bombs, rockets, etc., you mustn't fret yourselves either." They had deep foxholes in the camp and were in the process of digging underground sleeping quarters. A similarly constructed camp had recently been hit by B-52s and "only one person [was] slightly wounded."

Vann could read between the lines, and he had the information supplied by Pfc. Crafts and Sgt. Sammie Womach, the other prisoner released, to give him a more realistic vision of Ramsey's captivity. He still could not imagine it. No one could have imagined Ramsey's corner of Purgatory.

The two Viet Cong interrogators at the first prison camp to which Ramsey had been taken near the Cambodian border in northwestern Tay Ninh Province had decided right away that he was a CIA agent. In their frame of reference any American with Ramsey's specialized language training who was traveling around the countryside in civilian clothes armed with an AR-15 and carrying a lot of money had to be engaged in spying and clandestine operations. He had about 31,000 piastres on him when captured, money owed to a new local contractor for some office construction. The interrogators assumed that he was out paying salaries to the CIA's assassination teams in Hau Nghia. Ramsey's denials and his attempts to explain what he really did only angered them. They thought that his AID job was a cover. To the guerrillas, a CIA agent was a loathsome species of American. The Agency's sponsorship since the 1950s of the Saigon regime's intelligence and security services, including the Sûreté, now called the Special Branch, its involvement in the terror of Diem's Denunciation of Communists Campaign, and its role in the Strategic Hamlet Program and in so many other acts the Viet Cong considered crimes gave it a mythical aura of evil in their eyes.

Physical torture was apparently regarded by these interrogators as unproductive. Psychological torture was another matter. They turned the guards on Ramsey. To vent their hatred of what they thought he represented and to amuse themselves in the evening, the guards began to compose skits about Ramsey. The skits became elaborate. Ramsey was portrayed as the archetypal U.S. aggressor who "has the blood of thousands of Vietnamese on his hands." The skit format acquired a triumphant ending: the dedication of a monument to the demise of this CIA agent in humanitarian cloak, "Mr. USOM Ramsey." The monument was to be dedicated with Ramsey's blood by executing him and burying him underneath it. Each guard participating in the skit would propose a fitting demise for Ramsey: shooting after a public trial, lynching, beating to death by the peasants. The rain-forest prison compound was small, and Ramsey could not avoid seeing and hearing the skits. His cell was a large wooden cage. He was kept isolated from the three other American prisoners in the compound, prevented from speaking or having any sort of contact with them. A guard lived above his cell to watch him. At night a kerosene lamp inside the cell was lit so that he could also be watched from the nearby guard shack.

The two interrogators soon sensed Ramsey's guilty conscience over the killing of civilians and the razing of hamlets like the one he had seen at his capture. They harped on these atrocities in the frequent examination sessions. One of his inquisitors was an older Viet Cong officer, irascible and embittered. Ramsey later discovered that the other prisoners had nicknamed him Grandpa. He would rail at Ramsey, accusing him of all sorts of heinous acts, shouting that the crimes of a civilian were far worse than those of a military man because the soldier at least came in uniform with an announced mission. The other inquisitor, a younger but higher-ranking cadre nicknamed Alex, was quieter and more chilling in his threats. He claimed to have the authority to kill a prisoner. He said that he had selected the prisoners shot in 1965 to avenge the firing-squad execution in the main Saigon marketplace of a young Viet Cong named Nguyen Van Troi who had tried to blow up McNamara's car during one of the secretary's trips to Vietnam. He hoped, Alex said, that he would not have to select Ramsey or any of the three other Americans currently in his charge for like retribution on some future occasion.

The interrogation hut was also in the compound, and so the guards heard all of the sessions and the fury of Grandpa and Alex when Ramsey would protest that he could not give them the names of secret Vietnamese agents of the CIA and similar information they demanded. Ramsey's seeming obstinacy made the guards hate him all the more. They petitioned the regional headquarters, which was apparently adjacent to the prison, for permission to erect the monument and execute him. When the request was denied, they petitioned neighboring commands for support. Some of the skits were broadcast over the Viet Cong's youth radio frequency for the Tay Ninh area. Couriers and other guerrillas stationed at the headquarters came to see the monster Ramsey in his cage.

Fear, isolation, guilt, and vilification building month upon month pushed Ramsey close to hysteria. The guards taunted him more brutally when they saw that he was losing control, apparently hoping that if they could drive him insane, his potential usefulness would be gone and they could kill him; perhaps he might assist them by committing suicide. Alex and Grandpa were clearly willing to risk killing him on the chance that he might instead break down and give them the CIA secrets they thought he had. If he remained unresponsive, they warned, "it would not be the way to life."

The difficulty of sleeping at night further weakened Ramsey's nerves. The advisors who had lived with ARVN battalions in the Delta in the early 1960s had lost a lot of weight on a good Vietnamese diet. Americans require more calories and protein than Vietnamese. The diet on which prisoners and guards subsisted in these rain-forest camps was usually poor by Vietnamese standards, especially in protein and vitamin B1. It initially caused Ramsey's body to break out in boils. His bed was a crude bench fashioned from pole trees with bamboo slats laid on top. These were in turn covered with a woven reed mat. The slats protruded up through the thin mat and irritated the boils. He got painful cramps in his leg muscles from an incipient case of beriberi, a vitamin-B1-

deficiency disease. The light of the kerosene lamp in the cell sometimes kept him awake. The lamp sat in a big tin can that had been cut open on one side to let the light shine out. Whenever the guards heard an aircraft engine they covered the light by pulling on a vine to manipulate a shutter on the side of the can. The clattering of the shutter back and forth was another robber of sleep. Ramsey started to have nightmares when he did fall asleep and to cry out. The guards threatened to shoot him if he did not keep quiet. He became afraid to fall asleep.

One night in August 1966, after nearly seven months of torment, Ramsey's emotions suddenly crested. Some of the guards were saying that he ought be disposed of in any case, because he was too weak to make a difficult march to a new camp. The Viet Cong had decided to move the prisoners because the U.S. Army's operations in III Corps had started to penetrate the Duong Minh Chau redoubt. Ramsey resolved to fight back. He requested permission, which was granted, to work at milling rice and at the other manual chores the prisoners did around the camp. He began exercising vigorously in his cell. When representatives of the Viet Cong's "Red Cross" came around soliciting statements against the war for "Liberation Radio," Ramsey agreed to provide one. He filled the statement with slogans so that it would strike an American as ridiculous and read it into the tape recorder in a tremolo voice in the hope of rendering it useless for broadcast. Alex and Grandpa didn't seem to notice. They eased up a bit and let him talk to the other prisoners on occasion and do calisthenics with them.

A fourteen-day trek at the end of October into the jungle of upper Binh Duong Province north of Saigon took Ramsey from psychological to physical torment. The Viet Cong initially regarded the new camp as a bivouac until they could march the prisoners farther north to a hiding place just inside Cambodia in the mountains of the lower Central Highlands. They were instead to stay in this camp for a year, and in their desire for concealment the guerrillas had chosen one of the most inhospitable places in Vietnam. The site was so inaccessible that even the guides got lost during the last part of the trek. The country around it was cut by innumerable ravines that one crossed on log bridges set at crazy angles and covered with slime from the trees. These trails were too rugged for porters to carry in enough food to meet the camp's needs. Poor soil in the area and early and heavy rains in 1967 prevented the prisoners and the guards from growing much in the way of vegetables. The guards hunted for wild pigs and deer and other game and couldn't find any. A nest of rats they discovered one day provided a rare bit of fresh meat and protein. Usually there was nothing to eat but manioc boiled in salted water, poor-quality rice, and bamboo shoots, and not a great deal of that.

The mundane variety of malaria hit Ramsey a week after his arrival and laid him out with nineteen days of fever, 105 degrees or higher. For four days he could eat nothing and could hold down only thin rice soup most of the other days. The falciparum came on Christmas Eve as he was helping his fellow prisoners prepare a service. He fell to the ground with cerebral convulsions. The camp doctor found a weak pulse and injected a heart stimulant, but the Viet Cong then debated whether they ought to deplete their short supply of quinine and chloroquinine on Ramsey. They too were being struck with the malaria, of course. A senior cadre happened to be visiting the camp. Being a CIA agent could also be a saving grace—a valuable prisoner for some possible future exchange. The senior cadre said to try to keep Ramsey alive. Ramsey awoke from the coma sixty hours later in the thatched hut that served as the camp hospital. He noticed that his skin was absolutely white. His superficial blood vessels had closed from the excessive doses of chloroquinine the doctor had been forced to use to bring him back from the shadows.

The early and torrential rains of the 1967 monsoon raised the water table and flooded the underground bunkers in which the prisoners were supposed to sleep. Nor could they stay dry in their aboveground cells during the downpours, because the thatch roofs got saturated and turned into sieves. The ground became so water-soaked that the roots of several big trees let loose. The trees toppled over and smashed huts in the camp. No one was hurt, but it was terrifying. Thumb-size leeches thrived in the green wetness. They bit into the legs to feed. The bites became infected. Periodically the fever of the ordinary malaria returned and stayed with Ramsey for a week or longer. The doctor had him put on a special diet of chicken broth and protein supplements for a short time after the falciparum. He and the other prisoners received vitamins in pill and injection form fairly regularly, but nothing approaching what they would have needed to compensate for the malnutrition. The beriberi appeared in full viciousness. Ramsey's skin lost its elasticity. Some of his hair fell out. His left thigh swelled to twice its normal size. Both of his feet and legs also swelled grotesquely. The pain was dreadful.

One of the prisoners at the Tay Ninh camp, an Army major who had been in captivity longer than Ramsey, had died from the combined effects of beriberi, malaria, and malnutrition. Everyone in the little compound had listened to his death rattle. Ramsey wanted to be encouraged as well as to sound encouraging when he wrote his mother and father at the beginning of the year. He knew as 1967 wore on that his life was like a candle in the wind.

His captors would have taken him out of this place and measurably improved his chance of survival had he been willing to say publicly and at length and repeatedly what he now truly thought about the war. His honor would not permit him to be used as a tool against his countrymen. The truth he felt could not ease his suffering. He could tell it only in secret to his parents. "We are all hoping that peace will come about soon," he wrote of himself and his fellow prisoners, "and I personally [hope] that our leaders have no illusions . . . that they do not entertain ambitions going beyond a minimum face-saving roll-back which will permit our withdrawal without undue loss of military prestige. Anything more is wishful thinking, and any attempt to achieve it would be to compound past folly with future folly."

Vann liked Robert Komer a great deal and his affection for Komer as a person was to grow, but by the late summer of 1967 he was writing Ellsberg that "Komer has been a big disappointment to me." Ellsberg had gone back to the Rand Corporation in Santa Monica, California, at the end of May, saved by hepatitis from getting himself wounded or killed. He was discouraged by his inability to persuade anyone in power to adopt the radical measures he and Vann thought necessary and was disheartened by the continued failures of his private life. The trauma of his divorce had been worsened by a complicated and unhappy affair with a Eurasian woman, the mistress of a Corsican restaurant owner in Saigon. A romance with Patricia Marx, a radio journalist who was the daughter of the toy manufacturer Louis Marx, had also come to naught. One of the reasons for the breakup was that they had quarreled over the war, which Patricia Marx opposed. Ellsberg was in such low spirits by the end of 1966 that he conceived a scheme to attach himself as an observer and participate in combat with one U.S. infantry unit after another from the upper Mekong Delta to the DMZ. The hepatitis caught him before a bullet could. He had not given up on the war. He intended to promote more studies on Vietnam at Rand while he recovered his health and tried to sort out his life and to exercise what influence on policy he could through memos and visits to his well-placed network of friends and acquaintances in Washington.

The amphetaminelike effect on Vann of his elevation to Dep/CORDS for III Corps had worn off over the summer of 1967, and reality was crowding in on him again in the latter days of August. The ARVN would not perform its assigned role of providing security for the pacification teams in the hamlets. The Regional Forces and the militia were ever-lastingly deplorable despite the better training Vann was now providing for those in III Corps. The pacification teams he and Tran Ngoc Chau had struggled so hard to design and to establish a training course for at Vung Tau were often composed of time-servers and street punks who joined to avoid being drafted into the ARVN. But had the teams been composed of anti-Communist fanatics and saints they could not have offset the damage done by most of the district and province chiefs from whom they had to take orders.

The trouble with Komer was that he thought the managerial razzle-dazzle he had learned at Harvard Business School had some magical efficacy in itself. He did not realize that its limits would be determined by the worthiness or lack of worthiness of what he was managing. For all of his high and unorthodox intelligence, he was also another believer in the "sheer weight and mass" delusion of his time. "Wastefully, ex-pensively, but nonetheless indisputably, we are winning the war in the South," he had told the president in February 1967, in a report after one of his earlier periodic trips to Vietnam. "We are grinding the enemy down by sheer weight and mass." Despite his subsequent move from the White House to Saigon to shift some of that weight and mass into pacification and to do so with the efficiency on which he prided himself, he had not changed his judgment that the United States would win by might alone. He did not yet understand that one could apply might and double the might and "square the error," as Sir Robert Thompson, the British counterrevolutionary strategist, once observed of American be-havior in Vietnam.

Komer made sorties in the proper direction. Westmoreland caught him trying to send a back-channel message to the president asking John-son to instruct Westmoreland to force the replacement of incompetent ARVN commanders. Komer's secretary mistakenly gave the "Eyes Only" message to the special communications officer at MACV instead of sending it over to the CIA station in the embassy for transmission. The back channel to the president got no further than Westmoreland's desk, and he called Komer in for a chat. Komer soon learned to avoid such quixotic behavior. He had never accepted Vann's argument that control and reform of the Saigon regime were a *sine qua non* of victory. He was one more American abroad who could not bear to think of himself as an imperialist in the nineteenth-century sense. He saw virtue in the latitude the U.S. government gave Ky and Thieu and the other Saigon generals and regarded Vann's "colonialist" bent as a flaw. Komer's energy and enthusiasm and style, his organizational brilliance, his saber slashes through bureaucratic knots were failing to achieve anything that mattered. The unique civil-military pacification service he had created on the American side was working briskly in a void. Nothing was changing, except for the worse, among the Vietnamese on the Saigon side.

The intimacy of their friendship and the feeling that he was speaking to someone who truly understood led Vann to write more candidly to Ellsberg than to anyone else of his disillusion with Komer and his despondency over the course the United States was following in Vietnam. "I think we are on the road to doom and that we must change direction and change soon," he wrote on August 19, 1967. "I have, quite frankly, never been so discouraged as I am now because the American community appears to be operating at cross purposes and flying out in every direction," Vann said. "What is desperately needed is a strong, dynamic, ruthless, colonialist-type ambassador with the authority to relieve generals, mission chiefs and every other bastard who does not follow a stated, clear-cut policy which, in itself, at a minimum, involves the U.S. in the hiring and firing of Vietnamese leaders."

Lodge had relinquished the ambassadorship and gone home in April, escaping a second time before the war could make a serious casualty of his reputation. His successor, Ellsworth Bunker, was less inclined still to behave like the proconsul Vann wanted.

The president had rebuffed an attempt by Westmoreland to have himself declared a theater commander and a civilian deputy appointed to fulfill an ambassador's functions. Truman's confrontation with MacArthur during the Korean War had convinced Lyndon Johnson that it was imprudent to allow a general to become an El Supremo. Johnson did think that Westmoreland was going to drain the will to fight from the Vietnamese Communists with his war of attrition, and the president wanted to achieve the corollary political success: legitimizing the rule of Washington's Saigon protégés with the formalities of constitutional government.

The legitimization process was being facilitated by the blessing-in-disguise concessions that Ky had been forced to make during the political turmoil of 1966—a constituent assembly and then elections for a president and vice-president and a new national assembly. The election for the constituent assembly had been duly held in September 1966, and the delegates had met in Saigon and drawn up another constitution by March 1967. The elections for the presidency and vice-presidency and the upper house of the assembly were to take place in September. The election for the lower house was to follow in October. (Communists and "neutralists," a category that covered pro-Communists and anyone else suspected of serious opposition to the American presence and the Saigon system, were formally barred from participating.)

Ellsworth Bunker was the perfect man to oversee the legitimization process. His performance as pacifier in the Dominican Republic crisis in 1965 had been a kind of dress rehearsal for the role now assigned to him in Saigon. He had shown in the Dominican Republic that he could work deftly with the military, as he had with Bruce Palmer, the commanding general there, and use the physical stability and influence American guns gave him to sort out the local political factions and shape a government acceptable to the United States. He had arrived in Saigon just in time to exercise his talent for imposing calm, because in May, Thieu had suddenly upset Ky's plans by announcing that he was going to run for president. Although some of the civilian fixtures on the Saigon political scene intended to campaign for president too, it was foreordained that the armed forces would continue to run the country and that the president would be a military man.

Bunker invited Thieu, Ky, and Cao Van Vien, the chief of the Joint General Staff, to lunch at his residence and warned them that he would tolerate no power plays, that they and the other generals would have to argue the issue out among themselves. He probably did not mean to throw the decision to Thieu, but his restricting of the dispute to scheming and to shouting contests in the council of generals had this effect. Thieu was better at that game than Ky was, and although a number of his colleagues thought he was as egocentric as Ky and cold-blooded to boot, he had the virtue Ky lacked of being predictable. A man interested in exercising power and amassing wealth with a minimum of fuss is less likely to disrupt the same pursuit by others who gain his favor. Ky had been coerced into agreeing to run for the vice-presidency, and Thieu had plans for him and his clique after the election.

Had Bunker come to Vietnam much earlier in his life, he might have been able to think for himself. His father, a cofounder and later head of the National Sugar Refining Company, had initiated his heir apparent as a laborer on the dock unloading 100-pound bags of raw sugar and put Bunker through nearly every manual job in the refinery before he was given authority. The calloused-hands expertise helped Bunker to become a creative businessman. He transformed National Sugar from a refinery on the Hudson River at Yonkers, New York, where he was born in 1894, into the second-largest American refining concern, with extensive interests in Cuba, Puerto Rico, Mexico, and elsewhere in Latin

America, making himself a millionaire many times over in the process. He was equally thoughtful in his politics. His business associates were content to recite the Republican catechism that Franklin Roosevelt was a traitor to his class and the New Deal an offspring of Bolshevism. Bunker decided that Roosevelt was a wise man and that the country needed the New Deal. He changed his party affiliation and became an active Democrat.

In 1951, Truman's secretary of state and Bunker's Yale classmate of 1916, Dean Acheson, started Bunker on a second career by convincing him that the job of ambassador to Argentina, caught in the era of the Yankee-baiting fascist dictator Juan Perón, would be more interesting than chairman of the board. The ambassadorship to Italy followed, and later that of India after another old associate who was Eisenhower's secretary of state, John Foster Dulles, decided Bunker was too valuable to sit out a Republican administration as president of the American National Red Cross. Bunker proved a rare American statesman in India, gaining the trust of the haughty Indo-Anglo aristocrat prime minister, Jawaharlal Nehru. Then in 1962 at President Kennedy's behest he averted a small war in the South Pacific by persuading the Dutch to see reason and surrender Netherlands New Guinea (the western half of the island of New Guinea), a useless souvenir of their lost Asian empire, to Indonesia.

Ellsworth Bunker was two weeks from his seventy-third birthday when he reached Saigon. He had become a bit quaint, a thrifty millionaire who, after the pants had worn out, saved the coat of a suit to wear it as a sport jacket. His shoes were Brooks Brothers' best English make, but there were lots of cracks in the leather under the gleam of the polish, because Bunker had the shoes resoled until the tops wore out. He had maple syrup from his Vermont dairy farm flown over in the diplomatic pouch to serve as topping on the ice cream at official dinners. There was nothing unalert about him physically or mentally, however, no stoop in the shoulders of this six-foot-two-inch Yankee cornstalk. The white hair, the narrow face, the blue eyes behind the amber-rimmed glasses lent themselves to the aplomb of the patrician, an aplomb that was fortified by Bunker's natural reserve and a discretion he cultivated. The Saigonese quickly nicknamed him Mr. Refrigerator, not knowing that the reserve hid forebearance and a man who was a raconteur and wit of the first order in private company.

The rub was that after thirty-four years in the sugar business and all that implied in acquired attitudes toward Latin America, and after his second and more satisfying career in the service of the American state, the furniture of Ellsworth Bunker's mind had settled into place. It was impossible for him not to see Vietnam in the perspective of the Caribbean and Central America. Nor was it possible, after so much time as a successful man in a successful system, for him to question the judgment of generals like Westmoreland. Lodge had become increasingly worried about the reliance on Westmoreland's war of attrition. His fundamental doubt was so simple and personal that he did not put it in the cables. He recalled it afterward while in semiretirement as special envoy to the Vatican. Maj. George Patton and the other Army regulars he made friends with as a reservist in the 1930s had said that the mistake of the European generals had been to fight World War I as if it were a musket-and-muzzle-loading-cannon war of the nineteenth century. Every war was different, they said, and if they had a turn to lead they would remember the lesson. Westmoreland seemed to Lodge to be trying to refight World War II in Vietnam. Bunker had no reason for such doubt.

Vann tried to talk to Bunker about the war and was somewhat intimidated. Where an extroverted patrician like Lodge tended to bring out the boldness in Vann, a reserved one like Bunker aroused his sense of social inferiority. By the late summer of 1967, Vann also knew that he could not hope for anything from the new ambassador. His friend and former housemate George Jacobson had become mission coordinator, the embassy official responsible for handling the agenda of the Mission Council, the U.S. executive committee that consisted of Bunker, Westmoreland, and the heads of the different American agencies in Vietnam. Jacobson was "very alarmed," Vann wrote Ellsberg in his August 19 letter, over the extent to which Bunker was an intellectual prisoner of Westmoreland. The rapidity with which Westmoreland responded to any inquiry from Bunker with a concise memorandum composed by the MACV staff, the confidence the general communicated in briefings and private conversations, and the deference he showed the older man all had a reinforcing effect. "Westy is the best damned subordinate that Bunker has ever had," Vann quoted Jacobson as saying. Westmoreland had so thoroughly convinced Bunker he was grinding up the Viet Cong and the NVA and that there had been "substantial improvement" in the Saigon forces that Jacobson indicated he could "no longer afford to push the opposite viewpoint" in reports and staff papers he gave the ambassador. He had warned Vann to "tone down" his criticism of the ARVN when Vann was around Bunker.

John Vann had difficulties of his own making too. Annie got pregnant again at the beginning of April 1967, and refused to have a second

abortion. She told Vann she could not face the trauma she had endured
after the first one. She said that people in love should accept the consequences of their love: the consequence of theirs was a baby. Vann
tried as hard as he could to persuade her to abort the child. He repeated
the argument he had resorted to on the first occasion that fathering an
illegitimate child would damage his career if the secret became known.
When she responded that her pregnancy was an opportunity for him to
do what he said he wanted to do—turn the legal separation he claimed
to have from Mary Jane into a divorce so that he could remarry a woman
he loved—she received the line he had composed for Lee on how he
was financially chained to Mary Jane.

Annie's parents inadvertently became Vann's allies. Her father had
learned about and reluctantly approved of her first abortion, hoping
that it would cure her of Vann or at least teach her to be more careful
about getting pregnant. He and her mother were beside themselves when
she announced that she was pregnant again and was going to keep the
baby this time. They pleaded with her to get another abortion and then
to renounce Vann. She was only eighteen and was about to ruin herself
for life. No respectable Vietnamese man would ever marry her and give
her the proper love and family that she ought to want. Her parents
found out just how willful the daughter they had pampered could be.
Annie said that she was in love with John and he with her. She said
that even if John abandoned her now because of his career, she still
would not surrender the child.

Vann did try to abandon Annie, but her father wouldn't let him. He
telephoned Vann at his headquarters in Bien Hoa and asked Vann to
meet him so that they could discuss the problem. Vann fobbed him off
and did not call back. Annie's father then drove out to Bien Hoa and
confronted Vann right in his office. He coerced Vann into an arrangement that Annie wanted. It was the best her father could obtain for her
under the circumstances. If Vann would promise to rent a house for
Annie and to support her and the child in the circumstances to which she
was accustomed, her father would not complain to Bunker. Vann would
also have to go through a ceremony with her in front of the family to
lend the union a semblance of respectability. Vann agreed. He did not
blame himself; rather, he saw himself as having been blackmailed.

Annie decided to have the ceremony on her nineteenth birthday, July
15, 1967, at the family's home in the European quarter of Saigon. The
ceremony was a melange of traditional Vietnamese engagement and
wedding ceremonies, Westernized by the touch of a ring. Vann dressed
decorously in a suit and tie. Annie told him what to bring and how to

play his part. He gave her a pair of gold earrings, which a Vietnamese girl receives at her engagement and again on her wedding day. He gave her a small box filled with other pieces of jewelry too to show that she was allying herself to a prosperous man. He did not bring the most important gift that the groom must carry to the bride's home on the wedding day, because Annie thought that as a foreigner he might not understand. She had already bought it herself and had placed it on the family altar. It was a brightly painted box of betel leaves and areca nuts. The rust-colored nuts of the graceful areca palm, wrapped in leaves from the betel vine that is planted to curl up around the trunk of the tree, are chewed by elderly peasant women in Vietnam for the mildly stimulating effect the combination gives. The two are also the Vietnamese symbols of unity and faithfulness, and no wedding takes place without betel leaves and areca nuts on the altar to the ancestors. The ornate brass urn on the altar in Annie's home had been burnished for this occasion, and the altar had been decorated with freshly lit candles, offerings of fruit, rice alcohol and tea, and burning joss sticks that were giving off incense. Vann put the ring on Annie's finger. He took a smoldering joss stick in his hands, knelt beside her before the altar, and bent low to her ancestors. Her father then formally introduced him to the other members of the family and they all sat down to a celebratory meal. There were no guests.

Vann did not have to pay the rent for the house. An obliging AID administrator passed the bill along to the American taxpayers. Vann was legally entitled to a house. He and Wilbur ("Coal Bin Willie") Wilson, the salty former paratroop colonel who had been his superior at the Ranger Training Command at Fort Benning in 1951 and a corps senior advisor during the Harkins years, had been saving money for the taxpayers by sharing the house at Bien Hoa. Under AID regulations they could have declined to share a house and demanded separate quarters. (Wilson had retired from the Army after his outspokenness had denied him stars. Vann had persuaded him to go to work for AID and then to become Vann's deputy in the spring of 1967.) Shortly after the ceremony at Annie's home, Vann approached one of the senior AID executives in Saigon and, requesting confidence, confessed his need for additional housing.

The executive took a tolerant view. While Vann's position would have been hurt had the secret got out, the fathering of illegitimate Amerasian children was becoming another common by-product of war. Many thousands were to be born, and mother and child were almost always casually abandoned when the man went home. AID had also acquired an interest in protecting Vann. Every agency was under pressure to demonstrate its contribution to the war effort. Vann had become AID's house expert on pacification and its star performer in the field. The Washington headquarters had taken an exceptional administrative action in June to finally grant his request for conversion from temporary employee to permanent career officer. He need no longer worry about having to return to Martin Marietta in Colorado should it ever be necessary for him to leave Vietnam. The Saigon AID executive simply placed the Bien Hoa house in Wilbur Wilson's name and leased a separate house for Vann in Gia Dinh town on the north side of Saigon.

Gia Dinh town was both the capital of the province surrounding the city and a contiguous suburb of Saigon. AID and other civilian agencies and the construction firms had taken to renting houses there, because of the shortage in Saigon itself. Vann's rank brought Annie a comfortable home—a two-story place with three bedrooms upstairs, living room, dining room, and kitchen on the ground floor, and an adjacent garage, the whole surrounded by the inevitable stuccoed brick wall topped by barbed wire. AID also refurbished the house and provided the basic furniture. Annie moved into it in August. Vann gave her money for living expenses and to hire a maid who would cook and keep house. He protected himself with the bureaucracy by having her sign a contract stating that she was his cook and housekeeper.

Annie became none the wiser about Lee and Lee none the wiser about Annie. Nothing changed that Lee would have noticed. Vann and Wilbur Wilson continued to share the Bien Hoa house, where Lee often slept in Vann's bedroom. Wilson was an ascetic bachelor who restricted his relationships with women to gruffly polite dealings at the office. Otherwise he shunned their company and would carefully ignore Lee as she traipsed about the house in a dressing gown. It amused her that a man as eager to cavort as Vann would choose to share a house with another man who, as she put it, "lived like a monk" amid the sexual cornucopia of an American's Vietnam.

Lee was Vann's public mistress, the one he took to diplomatic receptions in Saigon and to other social occasions as the official attitude toward bringing Vietnamese paramours to these events gradually relaxed. (While Vann had been sufficiently rash in the initial excitement of the affair to fetch Annie at her lycée in Dalat, he had been careful not to flaunt her in Saigon. He had held the restaurant and nightclub outings there to the minimum necessary to seduce her and then to keep her content. After her second pregnancy and the arrangement with her father, he never let himself be seen in public with her. Only his close friends like Ellsberg and George Jacobson, some of his senior subordinates like Wilson, and his American secretary, Frenchy Zois, knew about her.) Lee's sophistication and her command of colloquial English rendered her the natural choice for the public role. Vann was reasonably generous to her. She had virtually full-time use of a Toyota sedan he bought in 1967 to replace the little Triumph he had shipped from Colorado. The Toyota turned out to be superfluous, as Vann preferred a livelier Ford Mustang that AID provided him.

Although money was not Lee's motive, she did profit from the affair. She obtained a concession for a souvenir boutique at the Saigon USO club. Vann did not intervene to get the concession for her or do anything else that was corrupt. Being his mistress brought her the necessary connections. She sold her English-language school and took up the more pleasant livelihood of running the boutique and managing a Saigon restaurant for its Corsican owner. Lee in turn tried to make herself useful to Vann. She constantly did personal errands for him, and on the occasions when he had to entertain a VIP at his Bien Hoa residence she would act as hostess and see that the drinks went around and that the lunch or dinner was properly cooked and served.

Vann spoke to McNamara alone for the first time that July when the secretary flew out to bargain Westmoreland down on his most recent troop request. The day that he saw McNamara was, Vann wrote Ellsberg, "a red letter day" of VIP meetings. Nicholas Katzenbach, who had replaced George Ball as under secretary of state the previous fall, spent two and a half hours questioning him. That evening David McGiffert, the under secretary of the Army, came to Bien Hoa to have dinner at Vann's house, passed the night talking late, and then traveled around III Corps with him all the next day. Vann spoke to McNamara for only half an hour, but the fact that the secretary would seek Vann's opinion was an indication of what the war had been doing to McNamara. Robert McNamara had, to his credit, become frightened.

The failure of the air war against the North first opened McNamara's eyes. The bombs of Rolling Thunder did not stop or substantially reduce the flow of men and equipment from the North into the South any more than they weakened the will of the Vietnamese. Rather, as the bombs hardened Vietnamese will, so they goaded the Vietnamese into building a transportation system that each year could carry more and that each year was less vulnerable to air attack. The Ho Chi Minh Trail that the CIA cartographers sketched at the beginning of 1965 was a faint skein of Montagnard trails and washed-out dirt roads from the colonial era, only parts of it drivable and then only in the dry season. Eight years later the Agency's map of the Trail was to show thousands of miles of all-weather roads, surfaced with crushed rock and laterite or corduroyed with logs where the local soil could not be compacted enough to hold, bridged at the creeks and rivers. The roads swirled from the North down through the mountains of Laos and into the South in double loops and triple bypasses, a rain-forest highway grid that the Vietnamese called the Truong Son Strategic Supply Route after their name for the Annamite mountain range.

For the better part of two years during World War II the American and British air forces vainly sought to stop supplies and reinforcements from reaching the German army in Italy through just a few mountain passes. Operation Strangle in Korea, a more ambitious effort to interdict a stream of troops and supplies moving along roads and railways, was a fiasco. Senior aviators are the most unfailingly forgetful of military men, for if they reminded themselves and others of the limits of their flying machines, civilian leaders might be less willing to let them lavish money and blood in the use of them.

U. S. Grant Sharp, Commander in Chief Pacific, might be a seafaring warrior, but he believed in air power, and the air campaign against the North was his war. (Westmoreland did not control air operations outside of South Vietnam.) In the flush of March 1965 the admiral described how aerial interdiction would master the Vietnamese in an "LOC cut program" he and his air staff devised for the "Panhandle" section of North Vietnam from the 20th Parallel down to the DMZ. LOC is the military abbreviation for lines of communication, i.e., roads, rail lines, and waterways. The planes were going to bomb "choke points"— bridges, ferry crossings, and spots where the roads and rails curved around slopes and headed through passes. Repeat strikes and free-ranging "armed reconnaissance" round-the-clock, at night by flares, would prevent the Vietnamese from making adequate repairs. "All targets selected are extremely difficult or impossible to bypass," Sharp said in a cable to the Joint Chiefs. "LOC network cutting in this depth will degrade tonnage arrivals at the main 'funnels' and will develop a broad series of new targets such as backed-up convoys, off-loaded matériel dumps, and personnel staging areas at one or both sides of cuts."

In 1965, in 1966, in 1967, and in the years of the air war to follow, the planes of the U.S. Air Force and the Navy did not destroy more than 20 to 25 percent of the trucks rolling down the Panhandle and along the Trail through Laos to sustain the battlegrounds of the South.

The Vietnamese also managed to keep their railroads operating, although at times they had to resort to using sections of the lines as cargo shuttles for the trucks. If one decided that this tally of trucks destroyed was too conservative and added another 10 percent, the Vietnamese still got two-thirds of the weapons and ammunition and other provender of war to its destination, a satisfactory "through-put" rate, in the jargon of the logisticians. The average loss to aircraft of troops sent to the South was much less than 20 to 25 percent, because the men marched through the most dangerous areas to better avoid the planes. An infiltration group tended to lose about 10 to 20 percent of its men along the way, but mainly from sickness and desertion.

Airmen have never been able to wage a successful interdiction campaign, because they are confronted with an insoluble dilemma. It is composed of time and distance compounded by weather, antiaircraft defenses, and the ingenuity and determination of those other human beings on the ground whom they are trying to kill. If Italy and Korea exposed the dilemma, Vietnam illuminated it with unprecedented drama, because the dimensions of the challenge were so much greater there. The insurmountability of time and distance starts with the practical consideration that the number of planes is always limited and so is the time they can stay in the air. In 1967, when Admiral Sharp had his war in full flight, the United States could put about 300 strike aircraft over North Vietnam and Laos on an average day and keep each there an average of approximately half an hour. The Vietnamese transportation network ran all the way down from the China border. With a limited number of planes and a limited time to strike, it was impossible to subject enough of the roads and rail lines to surveillance and attack a sufficient number of hours in twenty-four to have a decisive impact. A lot of the trucks escaped simply because no aircraft happened to be overhead while they were moving. Indochinese weather worsened the time and distance problem by forcing planes to sit idle at airfields and on the decks of carriers when they should have been striking, and then often limited what the pilots could see when they were on the attack. The weather hampered the Vietnamese too. For a number of years they lacked enough all-weather roads to keep the Trail open during the Laos monsoon season from May to October.

The Vietnamese further degraded American air power with the superlative air defenses they established with Soviet-supplied early-warning radars, antiaircraft cannons, and SA-2 missiles (surface-to-air, called SAMs by the pilots), and by passing out semiautomatic and automatic weapons to everyone in the countryside able to shoot at a plane. To survive, the pilots had to bomb and strafe from higher altitudes where they were less accurate. They had to waste precious "time over target" dodging missiles. The defenses also did not have to shoot down fighter-bombers to effectively reduce the number. Planes that might have been hitting transportation targets were instead absorbed in going after the SAM sites and antiaircraft batteries in order to try to protect their bomb-laden fellows. More than 40 percent of the sorties flown over North Vietnam and Laos were consumed in such "flak suppression" missions and other escort duties.

What the Vietnamese did with head and hand was the greatest com-pounder of the time and distance problem. The Communist leaders marshaled a force of 300,000 men and women to labor full-time at repairing the roads and rails and bridges and at continuously expanding the network. Another 200,000 North Vietnamese peasants worked in what time could be spared from the fields. The Chinese came to the assistance of the Vietnamese with roughly 40,000 engineer and antiair-craft troops to help keep open the two rail lines from the border to Hanoi. The Russians provided bulldozers for the road crews. The prin-cipal earth-moving equipment was a type more familiar in Vietnam—pick and shovel, a wheelbarrow that rolls better than the American model because it has bicycle wheels on the sides, and if no wheelbarrow was available to move earth, then two baskets, one slung at each end of a pole balanced on the shoulder.

An American thinks of a road or trail as a line going from Point A to Point B, curving only as necessary to accommodate terrain. The Vietnamese wanted a "chokeproof" road system, so they built six or eight or ten different routes from A to B, often with pontoon bridges at the crossing points which were removed at dawn and towed back into place at dusk. When the planes cut a road by cratering it with bombs or knocked out a bridge, the trucks shifted to an alternate route while repairs were carried out. The multiplicity of routes also permitted the convoys to make themselves scarcer targets by dispersing. The drivers camouflaged their trucks with foliage, of course, and there were pull-off points everywhere in which they could hide at an aircraft alert. The Vietnamese camouflaged long stretches of road too. They tied the trees together overhead or suspended big trellises of bamboo covered with brush and freshly cut boughs.

The pilots exacted punishment. Driving a truck year in year out with 20 to 25 to perhaps 30 percent odds of mortality was not a military occupation conducive to retirement on pension. A man or woman on a road crew could have an assignment as dangerous as an infantryman's.

To keep the roads open, the crews had to stay close to them, closest of all to the segments most frequently bombed. Bombs that missed trucks and bridges hit people. The crews were caught in the flares of night raids. It was impossible for them to do their job and shift as often as they should have to avoid the carpets laid by the B-52s in Laos and the Panhandle of North Vietnam. The memorial cemetery to those who died for the Ho Chi Minh Trail was to cover almost forty acres and to hold the headstones of 10,306 Vietnamese men and women. Their names had been recorded. Thousands of others who died for the Trail were to remain where they perished, unnoted in the confusion of war.

To punish was not to prevail. Each double loop and triple bypass in this ever enlarging whirligig of roads that must have been difficult to keep track of after a while even at the transport center in Hanoi meant more road mileage the American pilots had to cover. The Ho Chi Minh Trail was the best example of the achievement of the Vietnamese. The straight-line length of the Laos corridor from the Mu Gia Pass at the top to the triborder point at the bottom where Laos, Cambodia, and South Vietnam meet is about 250 miles. The Vietnamese estimated that when finished the Trail comprised about 9,600 miles of all-weather and secondary roadway. The biggest portion of the web work was within this 250-mile corridor.

Oley Sharp and the Joint Chiefs told McNamara and the president that they could stop the trucks by shutting off most of the gasoline. All they had to do was to bomb the principal tank farm at the port of Haiphong and the other bulk POL storage facilities, mainly in the Hanoi-Haiphong area. Walt Rostow, who replaced McGeorge Bundy as Johnson's special assistant for national security affairs in 1966, was also enthusiastic about the scheme from his World War II experience recommending targets for the strategic bombing of Germany.

The sky was clear over Haiphong on June 29, 1966. The pilots left the receiving facilities and the tank farm in flames. Within a month, nearly 80 percent of the known bulk POL (petroleum, oil, and lubricants) storage capacity of North Vietnam was gone, including a number of small sites that were harder to hit. As far as can be determined, not a single truck ran out of gas. Rather, the number of Russian-model trucks supplied to the Vietnamese by the Soviet Union, the Eastern European countries, and China kept rising through 1966 and by the end of the year there were twice as many as in 1965. The Vietnamese, who produced no oil and refined no gasoline themselves, anticipated the raids and long before had dispersed enough gasoline, diesel fuel, and lubricating oil to meet their needs in underground tanks and in concealed stacks of barrels. In the future they had the Russians ship them much of the POL poured into barrels ahead of time so that they could disperse it immediately on arrival. To facilitate refueling the trucks, they began the construction of two pipelines down the Panhandle and into Laos, with spur lines branching off as useful. Three of the spurs were eventually to reach into South Vietnam, one down the A Shau Valley in the mountains west of Hue. One of the commemorative statues in the memorial cemetery of the Ho Chi Minh Trail was to be a figure of a woman operating a gasoline pump.

Krulak showed prescient wit when he warned in his December 1965 strategy paper that trying to interdict columns of men and supplies moving to the South "can be likened to fighting an alligator by chewing on his tail." That Sharp and the carrier admirals and Air Force generals under him would consent to preside over this phantasmic enterprise was a study in how obsession and ambition can warp judgment. The "truck kill" was the central measure of the effectiveness of interdiction in the air war. Year after year, Sharp and his senior air commanders traded complicated jets that, depending on the type, cost the American taxpayers from $1 to $4 million each (the rough equivalent of $3 to $12 million in 1985 dollars), and brave airmen in whom hundreds of thousands of dollars and the faith of the nation had been invested, for the Russian version of two-and-half-ton trucks and Vietnamese drivers who were born with their courage and whose education in plane dodging was acquired on the job. A number of trucks destroyed for every plane shot down over the North did not improve the exchange. The trucks cost about $6,000 apiece to make, in the estimate of the Defense Intelligence Agency, and were one of the items the heavy industry of the Soviet Union and Eastern Europe happened to produce in abundance, and that China also manufactured in sizable quantity. It was a comparatively minor expense to replace every truck lost and to oblige the Vietnamese by simultaneously increasing the convoy fleet. In a report to the Joint Chiefs at the end of 1967, Sharp made an admission that was remarkably honest under the circumstances. He admitted that after another year of bombing there were just as many trucks in December as there had been in January. There probably were more. The number of trucks sighted in Laos during 1967 showed a 165 percent increase over those seen during 1966. Robert McNamara estimated in 1967 that the Vietnamese had 10,000 to 12,000 trucks coursing the roads.

The solution did not lie in closing Haiphong and the other ports of the North with mines and bombs, as Krulak and Greene thought and as Sharp and Greene's fellow members of the Joint Chiefs now increas-

ingly clamored to do. Closing the ports appeared to be the answer
because, except for food and lives, practically all the essentials of the
war came from Russia and Hanoi's other Communist allies; the bulk
arriving by sea. Freighters just happened to be the most convenient
means of transport. China was willing, with its foreign-policy goals of
the moment, to permit the Soviets to transship equipment and supplies
to the Vietnamese on Chinese railways. Had the ports been shut the
Vietnamese would have brought the weapons and other essentials down
from the China border by rail and truck, as they were to do after Nixon
belatedly closed their ports in 1972. They made arrangements for such
transshipment in the spring of 1967, and some Soviet supplies began
coming through China by rail that year.

The foolish expectations of the POL raids in the summer of 1966 upset
McNamara so much that he was able to discern the truth. He warned
Johnson that the only way they could achieve decisive results with the
air war was to target the people of North Vietnam. "To bomb the North
sufficiently to make a radical impact upon Hanoi's political, economic
and social structure, would require an effort which we could make but
which would not be stomached either by our own people or by world
opinion; and it would involve a serious risk of drawing us into open war
with China," he told the president in a memorandum that October.

Dan Ellsberg helped to disabuse McNamara of his illusions about the
ground war in the South. Ellsberg remembered the moment as "the
height of my bureaucratic career." It occurred that same October of
1966 aboard a "McNamara Special" bound for Saigon, one of those
windowless KC-135 jet tankers the Air Force had fitted out for long-
distance VIP travel and that the secretary used on his frequent shuttles.
Nicholas Katzenbach was along on his first trip to Vietnam as the new
under secretary of state. Porter had sent Ellsberg to Washington to brief
Katzenbach and to travel with him as his escort officer.

The seats in the nonsleeping section (there were separate compart-
ments with cots so that the VIPs could arrive refreshed) were arranged
around desk-tables at which one could eat a meal or work. Ellsberg
happened to be seated across the aisle from his former Pentagon
superior, John McNaughton, McNamara's deputy for foreign affairs.
McNamara was sitting on the opposite side of the table from Mc-
Naughton. Not without calculation, Ellsberg had brought along a briefcase full of his best memos, more than 200 pages of them, including a
vivid account of the three days he had spent with Vann in Hau Nghia

in the fall of 1965. As soon as the plane lifted off from Andrews Air Force Base he opened the briefcase and passed a memo to McNaughton with the suggestion that he might find the reading interesting enough to while away flight time. McNaughton glanced through the memorandum and handed it to McNamara, who looked at it and then began to read. Ellsberg fetched another memorandum from the briefcase for McNaughton, who started to read carefully too.

McNamara and McNaughton were both swift readers, and Ellsberg had emptied his briefcase before the plane had gone far toward Saigon. McNaughton called him aside a bit later and said that McNamara wanted a copy of the Hau Nghia memo, the best official writing Ellsberg was to do in Vietnam, rich in detail of the moral depravity and buffoonery of the Saigon side. McNamara had another request, McNaughton said. In the interest of maintaining civilian-military relations, would Ellsberg please not show this memorandum to General Wheeler.

Disaffection, once begun, acquires a momentum of its own, and by now more than the failure of the air campaign was at work on Robert McNamara. The sudden receptivity to realities he had ignored for years was what apparently led him that fall of 1966 to approve the proposal by Alain Enthoven, the chief of his Pentagon brain trust, the Office of Systems Analysis, to hire Vann as the head of the new Asian Division that Systems Analysis was forming. McNamara's report to the president on his October 1966 trip to Vietnam was a watershed. The McNamara of just a year earlier could absorb the shock of 230 Americans dead in four days of fighting in the valley of the Drang and urge the president to "stick with" Westmoreland's war and "provide what it takes in men and matériel." Now he wanted to put a clamp on Westmoreland, to end "the spectre of apparently endless escalation of U.S. deployments." The general should be told he could have a total of 470,000 men and no more. Where the air war in the North was concerned, McNamara no longer had any stomach for the blackmail of bombing pause and ultimatum and escalation. He wanted Johnson to try to coax the Vietnamese Communists into negotiations by halting the bombing in all of North Vietnam, or if the president thought that too generous, in the northeast quadrangle—the Hanoi-Haiphong region up to the China border. The Joint Chiefs made it clear they would revolt if the president did anything of the kind.

McNamara was beginning to learn, and the more he learned the more disturbed he became. Although Enthoven had been unable to hire Vann, he did hire as an analyst in 1966 a young statistician named Thomas Thayer who had spent two and a half years in South Vietnam working for the Pentagon's Advanced Research Projects Agency. McNamara started to get a stream of what he understood, numbers, and these were the right numbers about the war, the kind McNamara had not been in a mood to heed when Krulak had earlier sought to rouse him with them. Thayer's own experience in Vietnam had taught him what mattered, and he was wise enough to test his statistical findings against the reflections of canny fighters whose analyses had been distilled from the battlefield. He interviewed Hal Moore after Moore relinquished command of the 3rd Brigade of the Air Cav and came to Washington in the fall of 1966 to serve as a staff assistant to McNaughton. Moore was convinced that one of the reasons the Vietnamese had struck the Cav so boldly and repeatedly at the Drang and had resisted so ferociously at Bong Son was that they had been intent on learning how to fight the Americans. They had learned, Moore said, and moreover had got the Americans to fight the war their way. They were leading the Army and the Marine Corps by the nose.

In the spring of 1967, when the insatiable general in Saigon wanted still more troops, this time his "Minimum Essential Force" of 550,500 Americans by mid-1968, or an "Optimum Force" of 678,000 if the president wished to hasten victory, Thayer was ready. He and a staff of analysts he had assembled within Systems Analysis in a special Southeast Asia Office had done sufficient research to demonstrate that Westmoreland's war of attrition was an absurdity. Enthoven transmitted the findings to McNamara with his memoranda urging the secretary to oppose any troop increase beyond the ceiling of 470,000 men.

A study of fifty-six representative engagements in 1966 from platoon-size to multibattalion showed that the Viet Cong and the NVA had *initiated* the action in about 85 percent of the clashes, either by attacking the American unit or by choosing to stand and fight from fortified positions. The enemy also had an element of surprise in his favor nearly 80 percent of the time. In only about 5 percent of the cases did the U.S. commander have "reasonably accurate knowledge of enemy positions and strength" before the shooting started. Thayer had confirmed his results by checking them against the mass of after-action reports submitted by the field commanders and against an earlier study of a different set of engagements in late 1965 and the beginning of 1966. This earlier study had found that the Viet Cong and the NVA started the shooting 88 percent of the time.

To make attrition work in his favor, a military leader must be able to force his enemy to fight, as Grant could force Lee to fight when he had Lee locked into a defense of the Confederate capital of Richmond in the last year of the Civil War and as the American and British armies could make Hitler's Wehrmacht do after the landing at Normandy in 1944. Thayer's findings proved that Westmoreland was unable to force his enemy to fight, because the Vietnamese had an overwhelming grasp of the initiative. The Vietnamese controlled their own rate of attrition. Furthermore, because of Westmoreland's insistence on giving battle whenever and wherever the Vietnamese appeared, they controlled his rate of loss to a significant degree as well. They could raise or lower U.S. casualties by their willingness to sacrifice their own people.

Even if one set aside this determining factor of who held the initiative, and if one gave Westmoreland all the American soldiers he wanted and accepted the most indulgent projections, Thayer's analysis showed that the general's strategy still did not make sense. With 678,000 Americans to do the killing and the Vietnamese getting themselves killed at roughly twice the average rate, Hanoi would be losing about 400 men per week beyond what its manpower pool enabled it to replace. "In theory, we'd then wipe them out in ten years," Enthoven wrote McNamara.

Robert McNamara, the technocratic manager extraordinary who had run out of solutions, performed an act of abundant moral courage in May of 1967. He gave the president of the United States a memorandum saying that the president could not win the war in Vietnam and ought to negotiate an unfavorable peace.

John McNaughton, who shared McNamara's anguish because he shared his high responsibility for the bloodshed, drafted the memorandum for him. They did not state baldly that the war could not be won; that would have been too impolitic in the circumstances of the moment. McNamara and McNaughton let this conclusion become apparent from the actions they proposed and the peace they described. They wanted the president to abandon the officially engraved goals of defeating the Vietnamese Communists and establishing "an independent, non-Communist South Vietnam" and to issue a secret policy directive setting out new "minimum objectives." These amounted to a fig-leaf political settlement in the South that would enable the United States to gradually disengage from Vietnam. This "circumscription of the U.S. commitment . . . may cause a 'rush for the exits' in Thailand, in Laos, and especially inside South Vietnam," the memorandum acknowledged, but its pains were "fewer and smaller than the difficulties of any other approach." McNamara and McNaughton urged the president to start moving toward this settlement by holding Westmoreland to another 30,000 troops and no more and by halting the bombing of North Vietnam above the 20th Parallel, i.e., confining the air raids to the infiltration routes that ran down the Panhandle.

What McNamara had done so much to set in motion he could no longer influence. Lyndon Johnson had invested close to 11,000 American lives and his place in history in the Vietnamese war by the time of McNamara's awakening, and he was listening to other men like Komer and Rostow and Rusk who did not see what McNamara saw. The president continued to employ McNamara as a foil against the military. He had no intention of providing the 678,000 men for Westmoreland's "Optimum Force," because this would require mobilizing the reserves, an act that would destroy Johnson's Great Society legislation and profoundly exacerbate domestic dissent over the war. Nor did he intend to provide all of the 550,500 men for the general's "Minimum Essential Force," because Westmoreland did not convince him during a trip to Washington in April that this many Americans were essential to win. The president had come to see Westmoreland's troop demands more as bargaining parameters than genuine needs. He sent McNamara to South Vietnam again in July, when Vann saw him alone for the first time, to haggle the general down. Westmoreland finally agreed that he could make do with an additional 55,000 troops beyond the previous ceiling to give him 525,000 men by the middle of 1968.

Running an errand for the president was not to be confused with enjoying his trust. Lyndon Johnson began to put Robert McNamara at a distance.

McNamara lost his friend and confidant John McNaughton to a midair collision between a small private plane and a commercial aircraft over a North Carolina airport that July. McNaughton's wife and an eleven-year-old son also died on the airliner. The loss must have been difficult for McNamara, because he had started to show his emotions. He had let the President glimpse them in a description of the bombing of the North in the memorandum in May. "The picture of the world's greatest superpower killing or seriously injuring 1,000 noncombatants a week, while trying to pound a tiny backward nation into submission on an issue whose merits are hotly disputed, is not a pretty one."

More troubled him than bloodshed. Another associate who worked closely with him in 1967 remembered how ashamed McNamara had become of all the bad advice he had given two presidents in earlier years, ashamed of what he saw as his failure at the most important task of his life. In June he commissioned the Pentagon Papers, the top-secret inquiry into U.S. involvement in Indochina from its origins in the French era, an inquiry that was to burgeon into a forty-three-volume archive of the war, more than 7,000 pages and two and a half million words of classified history and documents. He gave Leslie Gelb, who was to direct the project, a list of about a hundred questions he wanted the study to answer. One of the first questions on McNamara's list condemned as unnecessary everything he had brought to pass: "Was Ho Chi Minh an Asian Tito?"

Perhaps in part because he paid so little attention before, he was now willing to subject himself to the details of the killing and destruction. In the fall of 1967, Jonathan Schell, then a twenty-four-year-old writer for *The New Yorker,* had just finished an account of what Task Force Oregon, the provisional Army division Westmoreland had formed and sent to Chu Lai in the spring to replace the Marines, was doing in Quang Ngai Province and in the southern end of Quang Tin. Schell had spent several weeks during the summer observing the operations of the division, most of the time from a vantage that gave him a panoramic view of the havoc—the rear seat of one of the Air Force L-19 spotter planes that controlled the air strikes.

The damage to rural society and the killing of civilians in Quang Ngai had become serious two years earlier, as I had learned in November 1965, when I found the five hamlets on the coast in which hundreds had perished under bombs and naval gunfire. During 1966 the Marines had staged a number of operations in Quang Ngai that turned brutal because of the resistance they encountered from the Viet Cong, an unyielding peasantry who stood behind the guerrillas, and NVA troops who infiltrated down the Annamites to reinforce. The pacification strategy Krulak and Walt had been attempting to implement acted as something of a checkrein on the local Marine commanders. The inhibition disappeared in the spring of 1967 with the arrival of Task Force Oregon. The Army, with its corpse-exchange strategy, was not interested in securing hamlets and protecting ground. The machine was freed of all restraint, and the ravaging expanded geometrically.

Where I had learned that at least ten other hamlets had been flattened as thoroughly as the five along the coast and a further twenty-five heavily damaged, Schell discovered that fully 70 percent of the estimated 450 hamlets in Quang Ngai had been destroyed. Except for a narrow strip of hamlets along Route 1, which was patrolled after a fashion, the destruction was proceeding apace. Day after day from the back of the spotter plane Schell watched the latest smashing and burning in bombings and shellings and rocket runs by the helicopter gunships and in the meandering progress of flames and smoke from houses set afire by the

American infantry. He tallied up the previous destruction from the traces of the houses and, going to the military maps, carefully checked his estimates with the L-19 pilots, officers of Task Force Oregon, members of the CORDS team in Quang Ngai, and several local Saigon officials.

A lot of the peasants had returned to the shards of their homes, even though many of the communities had been officially condemned in free-fire zones, and were living in underground bomb shelters. They preferred to chance an existence from their cratered rice fields and to endure the peril of being frequently blasted and shot at rather than accept the certainty of hunger and filth and disease in the refugee camps. The province hospital had been admitting an average of thirty wounded civilians a day since Task Force Oregon had arrived. A volunteer British doctor who had been working in Quang Ngai for more than three years gave Schell an estimate that put the total civilian casualties for the province, including the dead and the lightly wounded, at a current annual rate of about 50,000. (A conservative formula worked out by Tom Thayer of Systems Analysis from hospital admissions throughout the country would have given a figure of about 33,000 civilian casualties a year for Quang Ngai.)

Schell happened to tell Jerome Wiesner, the provost of the Massachusetts Institute of Technology, what he had witnessed. Wiesner was a scientist who had lent his talent to the U.S. military ever since he helped to perfect radar at MIT's Radiation Laboratory during World War II. He had been Kennedy's science adviser and was a friend of McNamara's. He arranged for Schell to see the secretary in his big office over the River Entrance to the Pentagon.

Jonathan Schell had gained considerable notoriety from an earlier *New Yorker* article on the forced evacuation by the Army in January 1967 of 6,100 guerrilla family members and sympathizers from the so-called Iron Triangle northwest of Saigon and the razing of Ben Suc and several other hamlets in which they had lived. Although Vann did not believe in forced relocation, because of his experience with the Strategic Hamlet Program, he had handled their resettlement in his first major task as OCO Director for III Corps and had gotten into a spectacular row with DePuy, who wanted his 1st Infantry Division to have complete charge. Vann had thought Schell's reporting of the event accurate, despite Schell's personal opposition to the war.

McNamara had not turned away visitors like Schell when friends sent them in the past. He liked to give the impression that he had an open mind. In a short time the visitor would notice that the secretary was fretting and glancing at the clock on the wall opposite his desk. An assistant would walk in and hand him a message or there would be a telephone call of overriding importance and the visitor would have to leave the office so that the secretary could speak freely. When the visitor returned, McNamara would be on his feet beside his desk, and who could continue to impose on such a harried public servant?

Schell was not interrupted. He still got the impression that he was imposing on a bristlingly busy man, but McNamara made no attempt to hurry Schell. He listened intently with a poker face, asking few questions. When Schell was through, McNamara took him over to a map and asked him to point out the districts of Quang Ngai he had been describing. "Can you put something in writing? We've got to have something in writing," McNamara said. Schell said that he had a manuscript in longhand. McNamara summoned an assistant and told him to arrange for Schell to dictate the manuscript. Schell thanked the secretary for listening to him and left.

McNamara did not ask Schell how long his article was. It was the length of a short book. Schell spent the next three days reading it into a dictaphone in the office of a general who was away. A secretary sent the recordings one after another down to the Pentagon typing pool. McNamara's assistant also arranged for Schell to eat his meals in a Pentagon mess reserved for high-ranking officers and civilian officials. Schell had several conversations there that struck him as "weird." He left at the end of three days with a typed copy of the manuscript he could submit to *The New Yorker*. McNamara never contacted him afterward to let him know what happened to the copy left at the Pentagon. When Schell next encountered McNamara in an airport fifteen years later, McNamara seemed "a haunted man" and Schell thought it unkind to ask.

Robert McNamara sent the manuscript straight to Bunker. The ambassador showed it to Westmoreland and, with the general's consent, ordered a secret inquiry. "The descriptions of destruction by the author are overdrawn but not to such a degree as to discredit his statements. . . . Mr. Schell's estimates are substantially correct," the report of the investigation said. "There are some very important political and military reasons for the scope of the destruction in this area," the report continued. "The population is totally hostile towards the GVN and is probably nearly in complete sympathy with the NLF movement." The Viet Cong also refused to accept American rules and insisted on fortifying hamlets and organizing the entire population to resist. "For the Viet Cong there isn't any distinction; the Viet Cong *are* the people." (The emphasis is in the original report.) In a display of the moral obtuseness that had become so characteristic of U.S. officialdom, the report tried to explain away everything Schell had written.

Less than four months after this exercise in exculpation was submitted, on the morning of March 16, 1968, a massacre occurred in the village of Son My on the South China Sea about seven miles northeast of Quang Ngai town. The largest killing took place at a hamlet called My Lai and was directed by a second lieutenant named William Calley, Jr., a platoon leader in the 23rd Infantry Division (Americal), which Task Force Oregon had been formally designated. The criminal investigation division of the Military Police subsequently concluded that 347 people perished at My Lai. The CID reports indicated that about another ninety unarmed Vietnamese were killed at a second hamlet of the village by soldiers from a separate company the same morning. The monument that was erected to the victims after the war was to list the names of 504 inhabitants of Son My.

Some of the troops refused to participate in the massacre; their refusal did not restrain their fellows. The American soldiers and junior officers shot old men, women, boys, girls, and babies. One soldier missed a baby lying on the ground twice with a .45 pistol as his comrades laughed at his marksmanship. He stood over the child and fired a third time. The soldiers beat women with rifle butts and raped some and sodomized others before shooting them. They shot the water buffalos, the pigs, and the chickens. They threw the dead animals into the wells to poison the water. They tossed satchel charges into the bomb shelters under the houses. A lot of the inhabitants had fled into the shelters. Those who leaped out to escape the explosives were gunned down. All of the houses were put to the torch.

Lieutenant Calley, who herded many of his victims into an irrigation ditch and filled it with their corpses, was the only officer or soldier to be convicted of a crime. He was charged with personally killing 109 Vietnamese. A court-martial convicted him of the premeditated murder of at least twenty-two, including babies, and sentenced him to life in prison at hard labor. President Nixon intervened for him. Calley was confined for three years, most of the time under house arrest in his apartment at Fort Benning with visitation rights for a girlfriend.

The officers of the court-martial acted correctly in seeking to render justice in the case of Calley, and Richard Nixon shamed himself in frustrating them. Calley appears to have been a sadist, but his personality alone does not explain the massacre. What Calley and others who participated in the massacre did that was different was to kill hundreds of unarmed Vietnamese in two hamlets in a single morning and to kill point-blank with rifles, pistols, and machine guns. Had they killed just as many over a larger area in a longer period of time and killed impersonally with bombs, shells, rockets, white phosphorus, and napalm, they would have been following the normal pattern of American military conduct. The soldier and the junior officer observed the lack of regard his superiors had for the Vietnamese. The value of Vietnamese life was systematically cheapened in his mind. Further brutalized by the cycle of meaningless violence that was Westmoreland's war of attrition, and full of hatred because his comrades were so often killed and wounded by mines and booby traps set by the local guerrillas and the peasants who helped them, he naturally came to see all Vietnamese of the countryside as vermin to be exterminated. The massacre at Son My was inevitable. The military leaders of the United States, and the civilian leaders who permitted the generals to wage war as they did, had made the massacre inevitable.

McNamara tried again to convince the president at the beginning of November 1967. He stated his case fervidly at the weekly White House planning session on Vietnam on October 31, called the Tuesday Luncheon because Johnson always held it during the Tuesday noon meal. The next day he gave the president a memorandum elaborating his dissent. The memorandum predicted the course of the war over the next fifteen months if Johnson held to the strategy they were pursuing until the end of his current term of office on Inauguration Day in late January 1969. By that time, McNamara said, Lyndon Johnson would have on his conscience "between 24,000 and 30,000" Americans killed in action. (The number was to exceed 31,000.) The president would have nothing of substance to show for the dead. The public would be crying out for withdrawal from Vietnam. Simultaneously, the military leaders and the hawks in Congress who supported them would be pushing hard to mine the ports and bomb the population centers of the North and to widen the ground war by thrusting into the Communist sanctuaries in Cambodia, cutting the Ho Chi Minh Trail through Laos, and invading North Vietnam above the DMZ.

In May, McNamara had wanted the president to try to induce Hanoi to negotiate by limiting the bombing to the 20th Parallel. Now he wanted Johnson to halt the bombing in all of North Vietnam and to do so by the end of the year. The evening of the day he handed the president this latest unpleasantness, McNamara told a secret gathering of elder statesmen and close advisers whom Johnson had convened in Washington that he was afraid everything he and Dean Rusk had done since 1961 to further the war effort might turn out to be a failure.

Lyndon Johnson was perplexed by the change in McNamara. Rusk, whom McNamara had included in his gloomy remark, certainly did not share his feelings, nor did anyone else whose opinion the president respected. The group McNamara spoke to was dubbed "the Wise Men" within the bureaucracy, because it was a constellation of American statecraft and military experience that included Dean Acheson and Omar Bradley, the surviving five-star general of the Army from World War II. (President Eisenhower was technically another, but he had surpassed the distinction by becoming a commander in chief.) They were briefed the same evening by Earle Wheeler, who addressed Westmoreland's operations and the air war, and by George Carver, the CIA's ranking specialist on Vietnam, who evaluated Komer's pacification program.

Walt Rostow sent Johnson a report on the briefings just before the Wise Men arrived at the White House the following morning to give the president their counsel. "I found the briefings impressive," Rostow said, "especially Carver who hit just the right balance between the progress we have made and the problems we still confront. . . . There was hardly a word spoken that could not be given directly to the press. You may wish to consider a full leadership meeting of this kind, introduced by yourself, after which you could put the whole thing on television. . . ."

During the midmorning discussion and then lunch with the president, one of the Wise Men, George Ball, the original in-house opponent of the war who was currently chairman of the Lehman Brothers investment banking firm in New York, told Johnson he no longer favored getting out of Vietnam. The briefings had been "very reassuring," Ball said.

The president took the precaution of soliciting written comments on McNamara's November 1, 1967, memorandum from Rostow, Maxwell Taylor, and two of his confidants—Justice Abe Fortas, the distinguished constitutional lawyer he had placed on the Supreme Court; and Clark Clifford, prized by Harry Truman for his political insights as a youthful White House assistant, who in 1967 was perhaps the shrewdest lawyer in Washington and certainly the most influential. All urged Johnson to pay no heed to McNamara's views.

In his "Top Secret Literally Eyes Only" comment, Rostow said they did not have to stop the bombing to induce negotiations. He noted that at a time when they were bombing the North harder than ever, their latest secret contact with the other side had opened up. The contact had been initiated in August by the head of the Party organization for the Saigon area through an emissary in Cambodia to attempt an exchange of prisoners. It was to result in the release of two American enlisted men in December 1967, and might have brought the freeing of Ramsey or others had the administration been seriously interested in prisoner exchanges. Rostow read a much larger purpose into the contact than an exchange of captives. He said he detected this purpose "in the full flow of intelligence." Hanoi had abandoned hope of taking over South Vietnam within the foreseeable future. To try to save the Viet Cong from being destroyed, the Hanoi leaders were probing to see what sort of legal status they might be able to negotiate for the Southern Communists "in a time of peace." He drew a parallel for the president with the Korean War negotiations at Panmunjom. "If this is right, we are already in a kind of Panmunjom stage; that is, their military operations are designed not to produce victory but to improve their position in a negotiation which is, in a sense, already under way."

At the end of November, McNamara learned through a press leak of his appointment as the new president of the World Bank. Johnson decided that his secretary of defense, who had been at the Pentagon for the better part of seven years, had come unstrung from too many years of carrying the burden of the war. The man had deteriorated into "an emotional basket case," the president told his press secretary, George Christian. Johnson liked McNamara. Despite his worship of the Kennedys, McNamara had served Johnson with self-effacing loyalty. But the president could not afford to keep him. The antiwar wing of the Democratic Party had started a "Dump Johnson" movement and were soon to acquire a candidate in Senator Eugene McCarthy of Minnesota to try to unseat Johnson at the 1968 Democratic National Convention.

The serious menace, from Johnson's point of view, was Robert Kennedy, now a senator from New York, waiting to step in at the most propitious moment. If McNamara was to crack utterly and resign during the forthcoming election year, Kennedy could exploit him too. The president suspected that McNamara was, in his distress, already confiding in his friend. He was right. There were rumors in Washington, where I was now working in the *New York Times* bureau, that McNamara had turned against the war. I asked Robert Kennedy if they were true. He said they were and described McNamara's feelings in detail. I was reluctant to believe him at the time. A transformed McNamara seemed to fit too conveniently into Robert Kennedy's ambition to inherit his brother's office.

Quietly during November, without telling McNamara, Lyndon Johnson arranged his appointment to the presidency of the bank. On a couple
of occasions in the past, they had discussed the possibility of McNamara's
taking the job someday. Robert McNamara wanted to think of himself
as a man who did good. When he had waged war in Vietnam in earlier
years, he had thought he was doing good. The World Bank, technically
called the International Bank for Reconstruction and Development,
worked at raising the economies of the underdeveloped countries. The
President reasoned that if he gave McNamara this opportunity,
McNamara would go quietly and keep his silence.

Johnson's instinct was to prove surer than he could have known. The
high moral courage that Robert McNamara could summon up within
the secrecy of the American state he could not summon up outside of
it to denounce what the American state was doing. In all the years of
the war that lay ahead he was never to speak publicly against it. His
guilt and shame may have contributed to an inability to confront what
he had done. When the Pentagon Papers he commissioned were published, he declined to read them.

Vo Nguyen Giap explained how and why the Hanoi leaders had enticed
the American forces to the borders of the South in an extended two-
part article published in mid-September 1967 by *Military People's Daily*
(*Quan Doi Nhan Dan*), the Vietnamese Communist equivalent of the
U.S. armed forces newspaper, *Stars & Stripes*. The article, entitled "Big
Victory, Gigantic Task," was meant as a primer for the officers and men
of the Viet Cong and the NVA. Radio Hanoi broadcast the full text.
The CIA translated and distributed the article through its public sub-
sidiary, the Foreign Broadcasting Information Service. Giap cited the
fighting along the DMZ and in the Central Highlands as principal examples of Hanoi's strategy at work.

When William Westmoreland's preconceptions were challenged, he
paid as little heed to his enemies as he did to Krulak and York and
other would-be helpmates. It has been a historical characteristic of generals like Westmoreland that whatever they are given—keen soldiers,
innovative weapons, timely intelligence, discerning counsel, published
primers on an opponent's strategy—they will waste. They expect their
enemies to behave stupidly, and they perceive their own behavior as
farsighted generalship. Westmoreland had disposed of the "border battles" in his mind before the publication of Giap's article. During a
background session with the press at his Saigon headquarters in the

latter half of August 1967, he claimed to have inflicted so much damage on his opponents that "major efforts" by the Viet Cong and the NVA "are now largely limited to the periphery of South Vietnam."

A reporter took issue with him. "The enemy has pulled us to the borders and is bleeding us," the reporter said.

"He has not pulled us to the borders," Westmoreland replied. "Rather, he can only mount large actions from the borders. . . . We are bleeding him a great deal more than he is bleeding us."

The question of who was bleeding whom soon became still more definitively settled in Westmoreland's mind. The public affairs section of his headquarters kept a record of his background briefings for the newsmen. The briefings reflect his thinking well, because he spoke informally, there was give and take, and what he had to say was no more optimistic than the content of his classified reports. He was, in fact, more cautious with the newsmen than he was with the president in announcing the approach of the all-important breakthrough, the "crossover point," in his war of attrition. The crossover point was the moment when the machine would start to kill Viet Cong and NVA troops faster than replacements could be recruited in the South or sent down from the North, a kind of crossing of the bar toward enfeeblement and defeat for the Vietnamese Communists. When Westmoreland had flown home at the end of April for a White House meeting to present the case for his Minimum Essential and Optimum forces, he told the president that "it appears that last month we reached the crossover point in areas excluding the two northern provinces." When a reporter asked at the end of June if the crossover point was approaching, Westmoreland said he thought it had "perhaps been reached but frankly we just don't know." During the background briefings in the latter half of August the general was more positive but remained careful on this issue. Communist "armed strength is falling," he said, "not spectacularly and not mathematically provable, but every indication suggests this. . . . There is evidence that we may have reached the crossover point." Three months later, in the middle of November 1967, William Westmoreland had the mathematical proof that he had sent his enemy crossing over to perdition.

These November briefings, the most elaborate of the war, were held at "Pentagon East," the neatly laid-out complex of two-story prefabricated metal office buildings, air-conditioned for 4,000 officers and enlisted staff, that Westmoreland had recently opened as his new headquarters near Tan Son Nhut. The newsmen were briefed by Westmoreland, by his assistant chiefs of staff for intelligence and operations, and by a colonel from the intelligence section who specialized in enemy morale. What they and Westmoreland said could be attributed, as was the custom, to U.S. military officials.

The president had ordered the briefings as the overture to a public relations campaign. Domestic support for the war was being undermined by the pathos of American soldiers and Marines dying on ridges in the rain forest of nowhere and amid bomb-scarred rice fields and the ruins of thatch-and-mud-wattle hamlets in which no American would want to live, dying for no visible purpose and with no conclusion in sight. Opinion polls showed that by late October 1967, the number of voters who wanted to pull out of Vietnam had doubled from 15 to 30 percent. Johnson, who was being reminded of how quickly the public had turned against the Korean War, was seriously concerned. The minority who opposed the war on moral grounds had also grown large enough to mount fearsome protests. Fifty thousand demonstrators marched on the Pentagon on October 21, 1967. McNamara had watched from a special command post on the roof, listening to the chants of "Hey, hey, LBJ, how many kids did you kill today!" He was not accustomed to mobs, and the experience had further frayed his nerves.

Acheson and the other Wise Men advised the president to launch the public relations campaign. They felt that if he could impart to the public the progress they had learned of in the secret briefings, he would be able to slow down the erosion of support. The president's appointments secretary, who kept the record of the Wise Men's meeting, summed up the advice of McGeorge Bundy, currently president of the Ford Foundation and a member of the group: "Emphasize the 'light at the end of the tunnel' instead of battles, deaths, and danger."

Westmoreland didn't have to lie to help the president. In a celebrated libel case after the war, the general sued CBS for accusing him of conspiring to deceive the president on the strength of the enemy. The general did not win his libel suit, but he did not conspire either. As Vann explained to Ellsberg, "It was massive self-delusion." In the pattern of his predecessor, Paul Harkins, Westmoreland and the military system of which he too was so representative had foreordained his conquest when Johnson told him in July 1965 that he could have his first 200,000 American troops. He presided over the same self-fulfilling process with the same freedom from doubt that Harkins exhibited, sending home or drumming into line anyone who seemed to be predicting rain for the parade. When his intelligence chief in the spring of 1967, Maj. Gen. Joseph McChristian, informed him that he was underestimating the enemy in the South by a couple of hundred thousand, he replaced

McChristian with another intelligence chief who thought like West-moreland. When the CIA's specialist on the Viet Cong, Samuel Adams, a descendant of the Adamses of the Revolution, sought to raise an alarm that summer and fall, Westmoreland had him muffled as well. The general's staff officers manipulated body counts and kill ratios and reports of desertion and falling morale among the enemy to gradually compile these proofs of imminent victory he now displayed to the newsmen in these November briefings.

The general was especially proud, when describing his accomplishment, of the management skill he had shown in building so many ports, airfields, POL tank farms, and arsenals throughout South Vietnam, "the physical infrastructure that was required in this underdeveloped country." Westmoreland dwelt on the "logistic island concept" he had designed in locating his major depots in the Saigon area and at Cam Ranh Bay, Qui Nhon, and Da Nang. Although the construction program was still incomplete, in two short years "the support base . . . has been capitalized," he said. His staff had prepared a billboard row of multicolored charts to assist him as he briefed. One chart he pointed to illustrated how his port capacity had sextupled from five deep-draft unloading berths in September 1965 to thirty-two by September 1967. On another chart he turned to, the bar graphs representing airfields rose from twenty-two, three of them jet-capable, to sixty-eight, including eight jet bases, over the same two years. He had fallen somewhat but not too far behind in the three-phase plan he had submitted to McNamara and the president in July 1965. He explained that only since the fall of 1966, when his force reached 350,000 Americans, had he possessed "enough troops and had the physical infrastructure and logistics . . . to progressively apply pressure" on the enemy.

The charts kept by Harkins's intelligence section had proved how the strength of the Viet Cong withered once his war of attrition got going full-bore in mid-1963, the ranks of the guerrillas falling from a peak of 124,000 men in January 1963 to possibly as low as 102,000 by early that summer. The single year of pressure since the autumn of 1966 was having a similar effect on the Viet Cong and the North Vietnamese Army of Westmoreland's war. He pointed to other multicolored bar graphs on what he called his "attrition charts." Viet Cong and NVA killed in action had more than doubled since 1965 and since 1966 had increased again by half. During the April-through-October monsoon season of 1966 the average monthly count of bodies had been 4,903. The average had risen to 7,315 bodies a month for the rainy season of 1967. This attainment of the crossover point was inexorably draining away the fighting power of the Vietnamese Communists. One of Westmoreland's charts traced their decline from a pinnacle of 285,000 men in South Vietnam during the third quarter of 1966 to a total current strength of 242,000. Harkins had thought that the morale of the Viet Cong was deteriorating under the hammering he was giving them and that many of the Communist soldiers were sick and hungry. His successor had identical thoughts. Some of the Viet Cong and NVA units in the Central Highlands "are almost starving to death," Westmoreland said, "and even just north of Saigon, the units in War Zone D are having rice problems." Of the 163 Main Force Viet Cong and NVA battalions, almost half, fully 76, were "not combat-effective" from the combined impact of casualties, bad morale, desertion, hunger, and disease.

The pacification war was also being won as Harkins had won his. The Vietnamese peasant, Harkins's "common man of the Orient," ever respectful of the strong, had once more looked about him, observed who was winning, and was changing sides. Komer had obtained the proof this time with a computer. He had put together an elaborate procedure, called HES for Hamlet Evaluation System, that involved the filling out and filing of many thousands of computer-programmed forms every month. The computer scanned the forms and announced who controlled each hamlet.

Komer was, like Krulak, too canny a man to remain forever stupid about the war. Years later he was to write a perceptive study of what went wrong, aptly entitled *Bureaucracy Does Its Thing*. At this time, however, he was caught up in the hubris that McNamara had formerly personified. He sat in the briefing room lending credibility as Westmoreland informed the newsmen what this "scientifically developed" with "certain very precise criteria . . . and . . . automated" HES had discovered. The Viet Cong controlled a mere 17 percent of the population. Another 16 percent were "in the contested category." So 67 percent of the estimated 16.9 million people in South Vietnam were living under the control of the Saigon government in the cities and in "relatively secure" hamlets in the countryside. Harkins had claimed in 1963 that 67 percent of the rural population were secured in Saigon's strategic hamlets. When Vann described HES in a letter to a friend who was then teaching at the University of Denver, Vincent Davis, Davis wrote back that HES would undoubtedly become "the body count of pacification."

The recurrence of this apparently magical 67 percent was and was not a coincidence. Whether the men who ran this system had at their disposal staff officers with adding machines and pencils or civilian consultants with academic pedigrees and computers, those who served them knew what they wanted, and the answer always came out as they desired. The wish-think that drove the pencil programmed the computer too.

Lyndon Johnson might have lost his credibility; his general was still believed. The president called Westmoreland home for a major speech and a round of press conferences and television appearances. Acheson and several of the other Wise Men had suggested that he bring Bunker home. In Johnson's line of work one learned the public relations value of stars and a uniform. Barry Zorthian, a shrewd publicist who headed the USIA operations in South Vietnam and who less shrewdly believed at the moment that Westmoreland was right about the war, had also been pressing for some time for a morale-fortifying expedition by the general on the home front. He had been struck by Westmoreland's talent for publicity and by his credibility with Congress and the public during the general's trip to Washington for the troop discussions at the end of April. Johnson had had Westmoreland address a joint session of Congress then. The speech had been a great success, and Westmoreland had provided the perfect finale. He had come to attention, turned around, and saluted the presiding officers, Vice-President Hubert Humphrey and Speaker of the House John McCormack, and then turned front again and saluted the assembled legislators on both sides of the aisle. They had still been applauding as he left the chamber.

Zorthian was also certain that Westmoreland would welcome a platform in the United States for a reason of his own. He had detected in the general an ambition that the Army was too small to satisfy. Westmoreland was not scheming with any political faction, nor was he doing anything else that was improper. He was simply allowing himself to be put in position so that later, should he choose to do so, he might take advantage of the American tradition that had begun with George Washington and most recently sent Dwight Eisenhower to the White House. Johnson did bring Bunker home in November to appear jointly with Westmoreland on NBC's Sunday-morning television interview program, *Meet the Press*. He also summoned Komer back to promote the cause in private background sessions with the Washington press corps and in appearances of his own. The president put Westmoreland at the center of the stage.

"We have reached an important point when the end begins to come into view," the general said in his speech at the National Press Club in Washington on November 21, 1967. The beginning of the end was the start of "Phase III," his victory phase, which would accelerate to all-out thrust with the onset of 1968. He gave the country a summary of the Saigon briefings, explaining again how he had built his ports and airfields, achieved the crossover point by raising the enemy's "losses above his input capacity," and harried the Viet Cong regulars and the NVA to the frontiers of South Vietnam. He did not place a specific time frame on his victory phase as he had in 1965 in telling McNamara and Johnson it would take "a year to a year and a half." He conveyed that impression by saying that "we have already entered parts of Phase III" and by hastening forward to a new phase that had not existed in his 1965 plan, "Phase IV—the final phase," the mopping up of the Vietnamese Communists. "That period will see the conclusion of our plan to weaken the enemy and strengthen our friends until we become progressively superfluous." (In answer to a question afterward that was reported and televised along with the speech, the general said "it is conceivable to me that within two years or less" Phase IV would have advanced sufficiently to begin withdrawing American troops, "at the outset . . . token, but hopefully progressive, and certainly we are preparing our plans to make it progressive.") Westmoreland concluded by exhorting his fellow Americans to have faith in him:

> We are making progress. We know you want an honorable and early transition to the fourth and last phase.
> So do your sons and so do I.
> It lies within our grasp—the enemy's hopes are bankrupt. With your support we will give you a success that will impact not only on South Vietnam, but on every emerging nation in the world.

Vann left Saigon on November 14, 1967, for the longest leave he had ever taken—nearly eight weeks. His discouragement had become so severe that for the first time in Vietnam he had been finding his work a burden. He could distract himself from his frustration during the day by staying out in the field. At night it closed in on him as he confronted the papermill in his office in Bien Hoa. Vann tolerated paperwork well when he thought the effort was furthering his cause. Now the task seemed without purpose, and the burden had increased manyfold with the new CORDS organization and his added responsibilities.

The paperwork had grown to the point where it was interfering with his sex life, which irritated him the more. Lt. Col. David Farnham, a former reservist who had become disenchanted with academic life at Boston University and abandoned his pursuit of a doctorate in philosophy to volunteer for active duty, was the executive secretary of the

Bien Hoa headquarters in 1967. He would stack the paperwork on Vann's desk in three piles of descending priority, Absolutely Critical, Critical, and Necessary (which could be postponed for a few nights and invariably was), and would watch the anger build in Vann as he became more and more intolerant of what duty was requiring him to do. By 10:30 or 11:00 P.M. Vann would look at his watch again and say that he couldn't bear one more letter, one more memo, one more form. If he didn't have Lee waiting for him at the Bien Hoa house, he would announce that he was leaving for Saigon or for the house in Gia Dinh where he was keeping Annie. Farnham would remonstrate to no avail that the Viet Cong were going to get curious about who drove a blue Ford Mustang late down the Bien Hoa Highway four to five nights a week or that Vann was going to get himself shot by the nervous and trigger-happy troopers of a U.S. armored cavalry regiment who were forced to patrol the road in the darkness in tanks and M-113s. Annie never knew which night he would arrive. Some weeks he appeared twice, others three times, waking her at midnight or at 1:00 A.M., on occasion at 4:00 A.M.

He flew from Saigon to Europe, ostensibly to brief the embassy staff in Rome and Paris on the war and actually to spend several days on the Riviera and in Paris with Lee, who had preceded him to France for a holiday. Then he flew on to Washington. Komer let him stay there for a couple of days while Komer was in town with Westmoreland and Bunker and could keep Vann under at least a modicum of surveillance. Vann managed just the same to give a few closed briefings at AID and at the Pentagon and the State Department for insiders like Holbrooke, briefings that contradicted what Westmoreland and Bunker and Komer were saying. He went to Littleton for Thanksgiving with Mary Jane and the children and tried to arrange an audience with the president through Palmer Hoyt, the editor and publisher of the *Denver Post*.

Vann got as far as Walt Rostow's office in the White House basement. The meeting began at 2:00 P.M. on December 8, 1967. Rostow is a warm and enthusiastic man. He welcomed Vann and sat down next to him on the office couch. Ambassador William Leonhart, Rostow's assistant, and George Christian, the president's press secretary, were also there. Vann had decided on a dilute-the-vinegar approach. He started out by listing the positive aspects he could think of, like the organizational accomplishments of CORDS. Rostow smiled. He slapped Vann on the knee. "That's great!" he said. Vann gradually shifted to the unpleasantries. Rostow left the couch, sat down behind his desk, and riffled the papers on the desktop. He interrupted Vann. Didn't Vann agree, despite these flaws he claimed to see, that the United States would be over the worst of the war in six months?

Restraint deserted Vann. "Oh hell no, Mr. Rostow," he said. "I'm a born optimist. I think we can hold out longer than that."

Rostow remarked that a man with Vann's attitude should not be working for the U.S. government in Vietnam. It was close to 2:30 P.M. Rostow had another appointment.

Vann's Vietnamese daughter was born the day after Christmas while he was once more in Littleton with Mary Jane and his American family. The baby was not supposed to arrive until shortly after his return to Vietnam in early January, but Annie slipped on the stairs of the Gia Dinh house and the mishap brought on labor. Her maternal grandmother had recently moved into the house to watch over her. They took a taxi to her parents' home in Saigon, and her parents then drove her to the Clinique St. Paul, a small lying-in hospital run by an order of French nuns. Her obstetrician, an elderly French doctor, delivered the child at 11:30 on the morning of December 26, 1967. To keep the bargain with Vann, the space for the name of the father was left blank on the child's birth certificate. Annie alluded to him in the Vietnamese name she decided to give the baby on the certificate, Thuy Van, a name she also chose because it is that of the daughter who leads a happy life in the famous Vietnamese narrative poem *The Tale of Kieu*. The allusion was more direct in the informal European name she gave the little girl, the name by which his daughter was always to be called. Vann had left Annie an address in Littleton to which she could send letters. He said it was the address of an uncle, that he didn't live at home during his visits because of the legal separation he claimed to have from Mary Jane. The address was the home of a former secretary at Martin Marietta with whom he remained friendly. Annie's father cabled the news to him there. Mary Jane was another woman in Vann's life who was for the moment none the wiser.

He got back to Bien Hoa on January 7, 1968, after a stopover in Santa Monica to see Dan Ellsberg, and found Fred Weyand a worried corps commander. Westmoreland's 1968 campaign plan was based on the assumption that the Viet Cong and the NVA were no longer capable of sustained attacks within the interior of South Vietnam. The central provinces of III Corps were scheduled to be turned over to the ARVN by July 1. The 1968 campaign was to get under way with a series of assaults, starting with a spectacular parachute drop into the wilds of northeastern Phuoc Long Province in the upper corner of the corps area 110 miles above Saigon, a region sufficiently remote so that the Viet

Cong had been marching Ramsey to it when he had been caught in the horror of the interim camp. If Weyand positioned his troops for this and other planned border operations, he would have most of his forty-three infantry and armor battalions (they included the 4,500-man Australian task force with its small New Zealand contingent and a separate battalion of Thais) in the rain forests out along the Cambodian frontier by the Tet or Lunar New Year holiday at the end of January.

Weyand did not share Westmoreland's view of the war. His disinclination to join in the contentment of the high command was due in considerable measure to the influence of Vann, which Weyand was the first to acknowledge. Like Vann, Weyand did not see a crippled enemy, nearly half of whose battalions were "not combat-effective." The 600-to-700-man knockout battalions the Viet Cong had fielded at their zenith in 1965 had been ground down over two years of resisting the Americans and were struggling to maintain a day-to-day strength of 400 to 500 men. Westmoreland's policy of driving the peasantry into urban slums and refugee camps to "deprive the enemy of the population" had also shrunk the guerrillas' recruiting base in the South. One of the three Communist divisions in the corps was a regular NVA division, the 7th. The other two divisions, the 5th and the 9th Viet Cong, were about half filled with North Vietnamese replacements. The mix of Northerners and Southerners was working, however; a roll call of 400 to 500 men was respectable for fighting battalions, and what was impressive was that the Communists were able to sustain this strength despite high casualties and the high desertion rate brought on by the danger and hardship of the war against the Americans.

The Communist leadership had also greatly enhanced the firepower of all of the Viet Cong battalions, not just the regulars. One after another during the summer and fall of 1967 the twenty-nine regional or provincial battalions in III Corps, now called "local force" battalions by U.S. intelligence, had marched over to the sanctuaries in Cambodia, where weapons shipped in Chinese freighters through Sihanoukville had been cached. They turned in their semiautomatic M-1 Garands and other captured American arms and were reequipped and trained in the use of fully automatic AK-47 assault rifles, B-40 rocket-propelled grenade launchers (an antitank weapon that served equally as a hand-held cannon with lots of blast and penetration), and the rest of the Soviet-designed infantry arsenal employed by the NVA.

A further complaint of Weyand's was that Westmoreland's intelligence officers were not paying enough attention to the threat posed by the genuine local guerrillas in the district companies, village platoons, and hamlet squads. He did a study on his own and discovered when he added up all of those in III Corps that they constituted the equivalent in rifle strength of roughly another forty battalions.

Weyand had been opposed to Westmoreland's campaign plan since the previous fall. "It's a great plan but it won't work," he told the MACV colonel who came out from Pentagon East to brief him on the latest version around the time Vann was going on leave. His particular worry by Vann's return, which he described to Vann right away, was that while he was under orders to move out to the Cambodian border, the enemy was apparently moving into the interior of South Vietnam. The intelligence indicated firmly that the three divisions, and the three separate Main Force Viet Cong regiments in III Corps, were shifting out of their bases near or across the frontier and infiltrating down into the populated provinces closer to Saigon. Weyand was fearful that as soon as he stripped the interior provinces of American troops, the Communist regulars would team up with the local force battalions and the true local guerrillas and lay waste the cadre teams working in the hamlets, the newly trained RF and PF units, and the other pacification projects in which he and Vann had invested so much effort.

He was thinking of going to Saigon to see Westmoreland. Vann urged him to do so. Weyand started with Creighton Abrams, Westmoreland's deputy, as that seemed the most prudent approach. Abrams listened, said that Weyand had a good argument, and took him into Westmoreland's office. Weyand laid out his intelligence once more for the commanding general and summed up at the map. "I can see these guys moving inward. They're not staying in their base areas," he said. His hand was up along the Cambodian border. "We're going to be in the base areas and they're going to be down here somewhere." He pointed to the Saigon–Bien Hoa area. "I don't know what they've got in mind, but there's an attack coming." Weyand wanted to postpone the opening of the whole 1968 campaign plan in III Corps.

Westmoreland tended to be ad hoc in the latitude he gave local commanders. Weyand had amassed a lot of evidence, and he was asking Westmoreland to postpone, not to cancel. Westmoreland agreed. He thought he had a bigger worry of his own at the moment. The Vietnamese Communists seemed to be attempting to achieve a second Dien Bien Phu at Khe Sanh.

Hanoi was moving two infantry divisions, each bristling with a regiment of artillery, roughly 20,000 men in all, into the ridges around the airstrip in the Khe Sanh Valley and the hill positions above it that the Marines had clung to after the ghastly struggle for them in April and May of 1967. The 325C Division, two of whose regiments had fought the Marines for the hills, was coming back. The other division, the 304th, an original regular formation of the Viet Minh, had Dien Bien Phu emblazoned on one of its battle streamers. The opinion of the Marine generals as to the wisdom of possessing Khe Sanh had not changed since Lowell English, the assistant commander of the 3rd Marine Division in 1966, had observed: "When you're at Khe Sanh, you're not really anywhere." Robert Cushman, Jr., who had succeeded Walt, and his subordinate commanders had kept their peace and done Westmoreland's bidding. Krulak, still in Hawaii as Commanding General Fleet Marine Force Pacific, and less able than ever to influence events, was vitriolic, hiding his scorn only from newsmen. (Lyndon Johnson had just denied him the commandancy of the Marine Corps. The rancor he had aroused against himself by his opposition to Westmoreland's strategy had been one of the contributing factors.) In December, as the scud clouds and fog and *crachin* rain of the northeast monsoon shrouded Khe Sanh and the enemy activity around it quickened, Cushman had reinforced the caretaker battalion and a regimental headquarters garrisoning the base with a second Marine battalion.

The anticipated confrontation was both nerve-racking and welcome to Westmoreland. It held out promise of fulfillment on a grand scale of the scheme he had presented to Krulak during their argument at Chu Lai in the fall of 1966 when Westmoreland had first decided to cast Marines as bait at Khe Sanh. He had also never ceased to be convinced, and had said publicly a number of times that at some point in the war Hanoi would try to stage a second Dien Bien Phu. Hanoi's ambition was Westmoreland's opportunity; he would achieve a Dien Bien Phu in reverse. He would bury Hanoi's divisions under a cascade of bombs and shells. Five days before Weyand came to see him in January he issued instructions for the initial phase, the silent phase, of his plan, code-named Niagara after the famous honeymooners' waterfall on the Canadian-American border where John Vann and Mary Jane had gone on their wedding trip. No intelligence means—ground reconnaissance teams, aerial photography, airborne infrared and side-looking radar, communications and signal intercept, electronic sensors sown from aircraft along likely approach routes—was to be spared to pinpoint the NVA troops and their heavy weapons enveloping Khe Sanh.

Westmoreland did not intend to rely solely on planes and artillery for this climactic battle. As January lengthened and the forays from the base encountered more and more resistance from the NVA closing in and Cushman strengthened the garrison with a third Marine battalion, Westmoreland ordered the entire Air Cav division to shift from the Central Coast to northern I Corps. With the Air Cav he could reinforce rapidly and massively at Khe Sanh should the need arise. He instructed his staff to organize a new higher headquarters for I Corps. It was to be called the MACV Forward Command Post and would outrank Cushman's III MAF. Creighton Abrams was to be put in charge of it. Westmoreland wanted to tighten his control over the Marines and the additional Army forces, besides the Air Cav, that he planned to send north as soon as he could. He had a further worry. He feared that the Vietnamese Communists would couple an assault on Khe Sanh with a conventional-style invasion across the DMZ to try to seize most of the two northernmost provinces of Quang Tri and Thua Thien in order to set up an NLF regime in a "liberated zone." By the end of January he had concentrated in I Corps, if one counted the Marines, 40 percent of all the infantry and armor battalions he had in South Vietnam.

An NVA lieutenant showed up outside the barbed wire around the Khe Sanh airstrip perimeter early on the afternoon of January 20, carrying an AK-47 in one hand and a white flag in the other. He said that he commanded an antiaircraft machine gun company and wanted to defect because he had been passed over for promotion. He was cooperative with the Marine interrogators, describing an elaborate plan for the seizure of the base. It was to commence that night with the capture of two key hill outposts that were to be used as mortar and recoilless cannon positions to support further diversionary attacks on the airfield perimeter. The main assault, by a full regiment of the 304th Division, was to come during Tet, when the U.S. and Saigon side had scheduled a thirty-six-hour cease-fire and the Communists had proclaimed seven days of no shooting for the entire holiday period.

The events of the night of January 20 and the next day seemed to corroborate the lieutenant's information. Not long after midnight the better part of an NVA battalion struck one of the hill outposts and was repulsed after penetrating a section of the defenses. No attack materialized against the second hill the lieutenant had named, but the assault force could have been broken up by a preemptive artillery barrage. Then, at 5:30 in the morning, the NVA artillerymen announced their arrival. All manner of artillery pieces, rockets, and mortars opened fire on the airstrip and the principal Marine positions in the valley. Hundreds of 122mm rockets streaked into the air from the slopes of Hill 881 North, the one hill mass bought so dearly in the spring that the Marines had judged too far forward to defend. The biggest ammunition dump at the base was set off by some of the first NVA shells. The repeated explosions shook the Marines' bunkers with mini-earthquakes, threatening to collapse them, and scattered burning mortar and artillery shells all over the place, many of which in turn blew up on impact and created further havoc. Another NVA shell hit a cache of sensitive material—tear gas. Clouds of the stuff drifted through the airstrip, dosing Marines who had laid aside their gas masks.

Westmoreland turned loose Niagara. Every three hours around the clock, six B-52s from the Strategic Air Command bases in Guam and Thailand obliterated a "box" with 162 tons of bombs. In between, a fighter-bomber struck on the average of nearly every five minutes. Flights of Marine, Navy, and Air Force jets were stacked up as high as 36,000 feet over Khe Sanh awaiting their turn. Forty-six Marine howitzers in sandbagged revetments around the airstrip and the Army 175mm cannon at Camp Carroll and the Rockpile contributed no small flow to the cascade. The Marine artillery was to fire almost 159,000 rounds. Westmoreland airlifted in more Marine infantry and a battalion of ARVN Rangers to show the flag for the Saigon side until he had 6,680 men in the fortifications at the airstrip and the outposts on the hills. The Marines demonstrated their confidence in their Vietnamese ally by placing the Rangers in front of a line of Marines who would be shooting Rangers and NVA if the Rangers did not hold. And as always, nothing silenced the NVA artillery and rockets and mortars, and nothing stopped NVA machine gunners from shooting up transport planes landing in the valley and helicopters trying to resupply the hill outposts and evacuate wounded Marines. The weather is so bad at Khe Sanh at the height of the rainy season that on a good day one is fortunate to get 500 feet of ceiling for a few hours. Despite the massive intelligence-collection effort, most of the time the planes were bombing grid coordinates where someone merely suspected the enemy to be and the artillery was firing blind in the same way.

Where the commanding general places his standard, the newsmen focus and the nation follows. The images in the newspaper and magazine photographs and on the television evening news programs were the begrimed and haggard faces of Marines in peril. The staunchness of the Marines in these miserable circumstances (another 205 were to die in this second battle in the far northwest corner of South Vietnam) could not relieve the sadness of Khe Sanh nor dispel the public's anxiety for an American garrison besieged in such a forlorn place.

The anxiety was shared by a man who was supposedly better informed than ordinary Americans. Lyndon Johnson had a sand-table model of Khe Sanh built and placed in the Situation Room in the White House basement so that Walt Rostow could describe the course of the battle to him. He made Earle Wheeler give him a memorandum from the Joint Chiefs explaining how Khe Sanh could be defended successfully.

Fred Weyand and John Vann were too concerned with the threat in III Corps to be preoccupied with Khe Sanh. The closer the calendar got to the Tet holiday at the end of January, the more Weyand got the feeling that "something was coming that was going to be pretty goddam bad and it wasn't going to be up on the Laotian border somewhere, it was going to be right in our backyard." The Viet Cong attacked all over the corps in the first three weeks of the month. They overran Bau Trai when the province chief denuded the place of ARVN troops one day during an operation, and on the night of January 19 they raided the Chieu Hoi (Open Arms) Center for defectors in Bien Hoa.

Vann wrote to York that the Communists seemed to be "making a maximum effort to try and go into the Tet cease-fire with an appearance of military strength." The guerrillas then contradicted Vann's theory. Their attacks dwindled. Yet the intelligence picture grew steadily more ominous. The trackers in the sky of Vann's advisory year at 7th Division—the technicians of the 3rd Radio Research Unit who had eavesdropped on the Viet Cong radio operators from their single-engine Otter aircraft—had become the large and sophisticated communications-intercept establishment the U.S. Army fielded. The radio direction-finding analysis told Weyand and Vann that the three Communist divisions were arraying themselves in an arc to the north and northwest of Saigon and Bien Hoa. Two regiments of the 5th Viet Cong Division were about seven miles away, "pointing in like a dagger," as Vann put it, toward Bien Hoa. Gleanings from the intercepts of the radio traffic and agent reports indicated a big assault on Bien Hoa Air Base, which was, along with Tan Son Nhut, one of the two major air complexes necessary for the support of both III and IV Corps.

Attacks on Weyand's headquarters and on a nearby prisoner-of-war camp to liberate the Communist POWs there were also apparently being planned. Weyand sent for Rome Plows, bulldozers with pointed and sharpened blades that had been brought to Vietnam to employ as forest killers in the guerrilla base zones, and stripped away all of the vegetation around his headquarters. The POW camp was in the middle of a former rubber plantation across the Bien Hoa Highway about half a mile away.

He had the plows slice down and remove all of the rubber trees too. To be able to react at night with speed and mass, Weyand put his armored cavalry squadrons on full alert.

The thirty-six-hour cease-fire declared by the United States and the Saigon side began at 6:00 P.M. on January 29, Tet Eve, except in the two northernmost provinces, where Westmoreland had it canceled out of fear for Khe Sanh. George Jacobson, who continued to serve as mission coordinator, gave a party that evening on the lawn of the house where he was currently living. It was behind the new U.S. Embassy a few blocks down wide Thong Nhat Boulevard from the garish Independence Palace that Diem had begun and in which Thieu now resided. Vann went to the party and took Lee with him. The new seat of American power was a rectangular six-story fortress that had been completed in September. The embassy building was encased on all four sides by a concrete shield against bomb blast and rocket and shell fire and was set well back from the street behind the lower protective wall of a guarded compound. The house to which Jake had managed to get himself assigned was a pre–World War II French one that had been incorporated into the back of the compound.

Vann was struck by what a bizarre contrast the party was to the atmosphere at Weyand's headquarters less than twenty miles away. The latest intelligence Weyand had was that the attacks would come on the night of January 30 to 31. The officers in his Tactical Operations Center had formed a betting pool as to precisely when the Viet Cong would strike. The bettor had a choice of fifteen-minute intervals beginning with darkness on the 30th. All of the money was being laid on intervals between midnight and 5:00 A.M.

Jake had hired a band, and Bunker was among the guests, along with a goodly representation of others who counted in the American and Vietnamese establishment in Saigon. In the midst of the evening a twenty-three-foot string of Chinese firecrackers, hanging from a tree, was lit off to drive away the evil spirits for the New Year. The firecrackers were a present from Nguyen Van Loc, the prime minister of the cabinet Thieu had formed since his election as president in September. Ky, who had been elected vice-president, was a ram waiting to be dehorned. With 492,900 American servicemen in the country, the regime felt secure enough to authorize the traditional firecrackers at Tet, a custom that had been forbidden for a number of years to prevent the Viet Cong from using the firecrackers as a cover for gunfire. Vann talked to the ambassador and discovered that Bunker had not heard about the anticipated assaults at Bien Hoa and Long Binh. Westmoreland's headquarters, which was kept informed, had apparently not bothered to pass on the information. Nothing that Vann told the ambassador seemed to alarm him. Vann interpreted his serenity as a reflection of Bunker's assumption that Westmoreland had the war in hand.

Weyand moved the usual 5:00 P.M. briefing up to 3:00 the next afternoon, January 30, the first day of Tet, in order to clear for action. He was plying his old trade of intelligence officer and said the assaults against Bien Hoa Air Base and his headquarters and the POW compound would probably come at 3:00 A.M. on the 31st. A report from Westmoreland's headquarters raised the tension. It said that installations in Da Nang, Qui Nhon, Nha Trang, Ban Me Thuot, Kontum, and Pleiku had been hit during the predawn and on the morning of the 30th.

Despite these attacks and all of the intelligence, Vann found it hard to believe that the Viet Cong would engage in major combat during the first couple of days of Tet. Although there had been violations in the past, the cease-fires had always been honored in the main long enough to permit a decent celebration. He let caution guide him just the same. He had David Farnham, the executive secretary of his headquarters, dispatch a teletype message to the CORDS teams in every province capital in the corps warning of the intelligence indicators and ordering "maximum alert posture . . . especially during hours of darkness, throughout the Tet period." When Farnham said that encoding the message would delay it several hours, Vann replied: "Send it in the clear." He was not going to let the tension interfere with his own Tet, and he assumed that the Viet Cong would do nothing until their favorite wee hours. He drove the Ford Mustang into Saigon, picked up Lee and took her to dinner, and then drove back to the house in Bien Hoa. They made love and went to sleep not long after midnight, early for Vann.

Bunker's Marine guards woke him shortly after 3:00 A.M. in his bedroom on the second floor of the ambassador's residence. "Saigon is under attack," they said. The Viet Cong were assaulting the embassy four blocks away. The residence might be hit at any moment. The Marines had brought an armored personnel carrier to the house. They had orders to drive Bunker in it to the home of the chief of embassy security, where they thought he might be safer. He was not to argue, they said, and there was no time for him to dress. The Marines told him to just put his bathrobe on over his pajamas.

The ambassador's study on the ground floor of the villa was filled with smoke from burning secret documents. Bunker had a small safe there in which he kept documents for his night reading. The Marines had opened and emptied the safe and were burning everything in case the guards who were to stay behind were killed and the house was captured. In the confusion they scorched two holes through the leather on the top of Bunker's Brooks Brothers briefcase. He had left the briefcase on his desk when he went to bed.

Ellsworth Bunker was not a man who would resist Marines attempting to do their duty. He climbed into the M-113. The armored machine rumbled off into the darkness hauling the ambassador of the United States in bathrobe and pajamas through the streets of the capital of a country where 67 percent of the citizenry were supposed to be living in American-conferred security. Tet firecrackers still being lit by the un-witting were muffling the gunfire. Fifteen Viet Cong battalions, ap-proximately 6,000 Communist troops, had moved into Saigon and its suburbs. Bunker kept the scorched briefcase and carried it around af-terward in remembrance of the night.

Khe Sanh was the biggest lure of the war. The Vietnamese Com-munists had no intention of attempting to stage a second Dien Bien Phu there. The objective of the siege was William Westmoreland, not the Marine garrison. The siege was a ruse to distract Westmoreland while the real blow was prepared. The men in Hanoi had long ago decided that it was impossible to repeat Dien Bien Phu against the Americans. The French Expeditionary Corps had been a polyglot colonial army of a European nation enfeebled by defeat and occupation during World War II. The Vietnamese could gradually build an army that outweighed its French opponent, as the Viet Minh of 1954 clearly did. Giap had more artillery at Dien Bien Phu than the French. The French also had little in the way of transport planes and fighter-bombers and no heavy bomber aircraft. Gen. Henri Navarre lacked the means to sustain or relieve the garrison he placed in the mountains 185 miles from the nearest French stronghold at Hanoi.

The United States had too much raw military power for the Vietnam-ese to hope for a literal repetition of their earlier triumph. A serious attempt to overwhelm 6,000 troops as solid as the Marines in the face of U.S. firepower would have entailed an insane number of casualties, far more than the thousands of Vietnamese who were to die at Khe Sanh to maintain the false appearance of this threat, and the effort would certainly have ended in failure, because the siege could always be bro-ken. Khe Sanh was less than thirty miles from the landing docks on the Viet Estuary (Cua Viet) just in from the coast near Dong Ha, and the road was usable as far as the artillery base at Ca Lu ten miles to the rear. If the Air Cav did not suffice to relieve Khe Sanh, West-moreland could line up a couple of other divisions and blast his way through. These conditions were not unique to Khe Sanh. The Vietnam-ese realized that the essentials of this military equation would always prevail in their war with the United States. Yet to turn the war decisively in their favor they had to achieve a masterstroke that would have the will-breaking effect on the Americans that Dien Bien Phu had had on the French. The masterstroke was Tet, 1968.

For the most desperate battle in the history of their nation they reached back to the bold Nguyen Hue who had caught the Manchus at Dong Da during that Tet 179 years before and conceived a plan that in its breadth and daring was beyond the imagination of foreigners and Vietnamese who served foreigners. In cities and towns all across South Vietnam, tens of thousands of Communist troops were launching what the chief of Westmoreland's operations center, Brig. Gen. John Chais-son of the Marine Corps, called a "panorama of attacks." The bulk of an NVA division, guided by local guerrillas, stormed into Hue and occupied nearly the whole city and the imperial citadel. The gold-starred banner of the Viet Cong was raised to the top of the immense flagpole at the Zenith Gate where the like-starred banner of the first Viet Minh had been unfurled during Bao Dai's abdication in 1945. Military camps and command posts, police stations, administrative headquarters, pris-ons, and radio stations in more than half of the forty-four province capitals and in all of the autonomous cities in the country were under assault in the predawn hours of January 31, 1968, or were soon to be hit. Scores of district centers and ARVN bases in the countryside were being struck. Tan Son Nhut, Bien Hoa, and a number of other air bases were under ground attack or shelling to try to prevent air support or helicopter reinforcement for endangered garrisons.

In Saigon, the Viet Cong were also attempting to seize Independence Palace (Thieu was not inside; he had gone to My Tho to celebrate Tet there with his wife's family), the Navy headquarters, the Joint General Staff compound, and the radio station. With the exception of the em-bassy, a target of grandstand propaganda value that could not be ig-nored, and the air bases that were jointly held, the Communist troops were generally seeking to bypass the Americans and to concentrate on their Saigonese allies. The goal was to collapse the Saigon regime with these military blows and with a revolt patterned on the August Revo-lution of 1945. The revolt was to be fomented by Viet Cong cadres among the population in the urban areas being occupied by the Com-munist fighters. Ho Chi Minh and his confederates hoped to knock the prop out from under the American war, force the United States to open negotiations under disadvantageous conditions, and begin the process of wedging the Americans out of their country. Khe Sanh was one of the few places in South Vietnam where, except for more miserable shelling, nothing was taking place.

The ruse of Khe Sanh did not by itself enable the Vietnamese Communists to achieve a surprise on this scale. The American style of war had created a vacuum in South Vietnam in which the Communists could move freely. A massive shift of population had been brought about by Westmoreland's generating of refugees and by the economic attraction of the base-building and other extravagances of the U.S. military machine to poor and war-impoverished Vietnamese. No one knew how many Vietnamese had become refugees. The staff of Edward Kennedy's subcommittee put the number at 3 million by the end of 1967. A South Vietnam that had been overwhelmingly rural, with 85 percent of its people in the countryside when Vann arrived in 1962, had become substantially urban. The population of greater metropolitan Saigon had grown from about 1.4 million in 1962 to between 3.5 and 4 million, an extraordinary change given a population of about 17 million for the whole of the South. Samuel Huntington, a professor of government at Harvard and a consultant to AID and the State Department, coined the term "forced-draft urbanization and modernization" for what had been wrought. "In an absentminded way the United States in Vietnam may well have stumbled upon the answer to 'wars of national liberation,' " he said.

The crowding of so many people in and around the cities and towns was deceptive. It gave an appearance of increased Saigon government control while, in reality, there was less control than ever because of the social and economic chaos and the unprecedented corruption. The police had no desire to venture into the new slums that had risen in response to American needs. They feared the gangs of hoodlums and ARVN deserters in these warrens. With everyone so busy at the feast of loot there was scant security in many better sections. The official ARVN history of the Tet Offensive, by and large an intellectually honest account, was to acknowledge that assassinations and other acts of terrorism had been common in the northern Saigon suburb of Go Vap during 1967 and that the guerrillas had frequently established roadblocks on outlying streets in Cholon and attacked police posts there and in adjacent Phu Lam. "Enemy soldiers had reached the doors of the city," the history said.

Annie and her grandmother became friendly with several of the neighbors around the house AID had rented for Vann in the other Saigon suburb of Gia Dinh. The neighbors pointed to the homes of a number of families who were known to be guerrilla sympathizers or who had family members or close relatives in the Viet Cong. Vann's new daughter was five weeks old by the end of January. When Annie woke early on the morning of the 31st to feed the baby she heard shouts of "Let's get out of here!" from the street. She and her grandmother ran outside and saw people hurrying from their houses with as many of their belongings as they could carry to flee the shooting that was about to begin. A group of Viet Cong had taken up positions in a Buddhist pagoda a few hundred yards away. Weeks before with the collusion of the monks the guerrillas had dug a bunker under the pagoda and stashed weapons and ammunition there.

The majority of the Viet Cong battalions that penetrated the western side of Saigon to attack Tan Son Nhut and other targets came through Tan Binh District. Vann had learned the previous summer that the district chief of Tan Binh was collecting pay for 582 RF and PF troops when he actually had 150. One of the RF battalions presumed to be defending the west side of Saigon was called "the Chinese Battalion." The names on its roll were mostly shopkeepers and other Chinese who never left their businesses in Cholon. William Westmoreland thought that he possessed South Vietnam. What he owned was a lot of American islands where his soldiers stood.

Vann woke at the first thunderclaps of the 122mm rockets and 82mm mortars slamming into Bien Hoa Air Base almost exactly at 3:00 A.M. He dressed in a frenzy, telling Lee that he had to go to the CORDS compound and she could not come with him. The house was the safest place for her, he said. She should stay in the bedroom and hide in the wardrobe if any Viet Cong broke inside. He ran out the door to his car with Wilbur Wilson, his deputy, who had also awaked and dressed in an instant.

The concussion from an ammunition dump at Long Binh detonated by sappers who sneaked into the base blew the fluorescent light bulbs out of their fixtures and tossed furniture around the Quonset hut where Fred Weyand had his Tactical Operations Center. Weyand wasn't hurt. He put on his helmet and flak jacket as the duty officers and enlisted staff recovered from the shock and lit emergency gasoline lanterns. Weyand hadn't been able to sleep and had gotten out of bed and gone to the TOC an hour earlier to wait. The helicopter gunships he had placed on strip alert were taking off, some to search for the rocket and mortar positions, others to wait for the Communist infantry. The night was confusion, flash, and din. More 122mm rockets and mortars crashed around Weyand's headquarters as the Viet Cong sought to knock out his command post with a bombardment rather than a ground assault. The generators kept feeding power to the radios and teletypes and the phones kept working fine, and Weyand was amazed at the reports coming in from Saigon and the ring of installations around the capital.

A U.S. unit near the TOC began wildly shooting .50 caliber machine guns. The big bullets cracking through the Quonset hut were at the least a hindrance to concentration. Weyand sent the colonel who was his G-1 off in a jeep with two MPs to tell the unit to cease fire. The man was back in a few minutes. He was in a daze. "The VC are right across the street," he said. The jeep had been shot to pieces.

Weyand's G-1 and the MPs had encountered the two companies of Viet Cong assigned to liberate the POW camp. The Viet Cong had been told they would find the camp in a rubber plantation, and when they couldn't find the plantation, because Weyand had removed it, they got lost. They were milling around in a hamlet of ARVN widows and orphans opposite Weyand's headquarters.

Fred Weyand gave an order. M-113s from the 9th Division and infantrymen from the 199th Light Infantry Brigade laid the bodies of these guerrillas out in windrows.

The lead Viet Cong assault groups from another battalion had penetrated the bunkers around the eastern end of Bien Hoa Air Base and were dashing for a line of hangars. The pilots of the helicopter gunships swooped, scattering the running figures with machine guns and rockets. More M-113s from the 9th Division drove into guerrillas farther back who were still trying to fight their way through the bunkers. Other Viet Cong attacking the ARVN III Corps headquarters near Vann's CORDS compound soon found themselves in a similarly unequal struggle with still more armored personnel carriers and American infantry.

Weyand rescued Tan Son Nhut with a flying column of tanks and APCs from the armored cavalry squadron of the U.S. 25th Infantry Division at Cu Chi. To skirt possible ambushes and the shooting at Hoc Mon, where the Viet Cong were endeavoring to block Route 1, the squadron commander circled above the column in a helicopter, dropping flares and guiding it along cross-country detours.

Throughout the night and into the morning, as Weyand set thousands of U.S. fighting men in motion, he was a fire chief afraid he was going to run out of engine companies. He never did. He had prepared better than he could have known for a battle he could never have anticipated.

He kept the air and land lines to Saigon open, and he delivered or readied enough counterblows to deprive the Communists of the momentum they needed to win the city.

Vann became so preoccupied with rallying his CORDS teams in the provinces that he did not take his helicopter to Gia Dinh to rescue Annie and his infant daughter until the afternoon. By that time the house was ringed with shooting between the Viet Cong from the pagoda and the province RF. He had the pilot circle low over the house. Annie did not signal to him. Vann assumed she was hiding inside. The pilot dropped him at the province headquarters, and, armed with an M-16, Vann slipped through the guerrillas. He instructed the pilot to orbit above the house and be prepared at his signal to plummet down and snatch up Annie and her grandmother and the child. Vann found the house empty. No one answered his shouts. Stray bursts from automatic weapons were ripping through the windows on the second floor. On his way back to the province center he and a guerrilla bumped into each other. Vann killed the man.

Annie's parents had beaten Vann to the rescue. Frightened for their daughter and granddaughter and for the grandmother, they drove to Gia Dinh at first light, were forced to leave the car at a roadblock the police and RF had thrown up near the central market, and walked the further mile and a quarter to the house. They arrived as Annie, her grandmother, and the maid were about to flee on their own. Annie had prepared an extra bottle for the baby and wrapped her in a blanket while her grandmother and the maid were gathering a few belongings.

It took the family most of the day to reach her parents' home in Saigon. Many streets were mobbed with others attempting to escape the fighting. They were stopped at one roadblock after another by police and RF fearful of more infiltrators and had to show their papers and permit the car to be searched. The troops fired their weapons into the air to try to control the crowds.

Vann learned that Annie and the child were safe when he reached her parents' home shortly after the family got there. He was relieved to know they were all right, but Annie could tell he was also miffed that she and the baby had not been in Gia Dinh to be saved. "I tried to rescue you and I almost got shot," he said, telling her what had occurred.

"Well, John, I had a baby to worry about, I couldn't wait," she said.

As with Peter at the Children's Hospital in Boston nine years before, Vann wanted to be the hero of the hour, and so he was. In the story he told to friends, he spirited Annie and the baby away amid guerrilla gunfire. Annie did not contradict him when she heard the tale.

Although Weyand was not given to boasting, he was convinced afterward, as was Vann, that Saigon would have fallen had he not objected to sending his troops up to the Cambodian frontier. "It would have been absolute disaster, because there's no doubt in my mind Saigon would have been taken," Weyand said. There were only eight ARVN infantry battalions in the metropolitan area at the time of the attack, none at more than 50 percent strength because of Tet leaves and some considerably weaker. The best two, paratroop battalions, were still in the city merely by chance. A staff officer at JGS had become so absorbed in a holiday game of mah-jongg the day before that he had forgotten to request transport planes to fly them to northern I Corps. The paratroopers were supposed to have been flown there on the 30th as part of the ARVN contribution to Westmoreland's buildup over Khe Sanh. The closest approximation to an American combat unit in the city was a battalion of MPs. In his mood of confidence, Westmoreland had handed responsibility for the defense of Saigon to the ARVN in December, withdrawing the U.S. 199th Light Infantry Brigade from the Capital Military District and giving the brigade back to Weyand.

The fifteen Viet Cong battalions assigned to the initial assault, most of them local force battalions, because they knew the vicinity of the capital best (one was a sapper battalion of 250 men who had been living in the city, working at such lowly jobs as taxi and pedicab drivers), had orders to seize their objectives and hold in place until additional regular battalions could join them from outside. Many of the assaults went awry. To safeguard surprise, the precise attack orders were not issued to the battalions until seventy-two to forty-eight hours before, insufficient time for reconnaissance, particularly for a rural army operating in an urban environment for the first time. The thinly manned ARVN battalions reacted bravely after overcoming dismay. Their backs were to the wall; a lot of the soldiers had wives and children in Saigon. The RF troops scattered around the city and its suburbs also acquitted themselves well in many instances. Nevertheless, had American fighting units not been available to intervene right away, the Communist regulars would have arrived on the heels of the local force battalions and the outnumbered and outclassed defenders would have faced more than they could have withstood. The thousands of U.S. and ARVN staff officers and enlisted staff and support troops in the city, unorganized, untrained, lightly armed, could not have constituted more than an annoyance.

Fred Weyand, and John Vann to the extent he had encouraged Weyand to hold back his troops, might have saved Saigon from capture. What could not be saved was the war. Westmoreland had lost it. The ultimate result of Weyand's generalship in crisis was, ironically, to prolong an unwinnable conflict. More than 20,000 Americans had died in Vietnam and more than 50,000 had been wounded seriously enough to be hospitalized by the time a small Peugeot truck and a battered little taxicab turned the corner of Mac Dinh Chi Street onto Thong Nhat Boulevard about 2:45 A.M. on January 31, 1968, and a platoon of sappers leaped out and blew a hole through the wall of the new U.S. Embassy compound.

"The Green Machine," as the American soldier had come to so aptly name the Army of this war, had demanded and been given 841,264 draftees by Christmas 1967, and the draft call in January 1968 was for 33,000 more young men. The financial cost of the war had reached $33 billion a year, provoking an inflation that was beginning to seriously disturb the economy of the United States. The college and university campuses were in turmoil. Prior to 1967 the sons of the white middle class had largely avoided the war through the escape hatch of a college deferment. By 1967 the needs of the Green Machine were such that the draft had begun to take significant numbers of them as they graduated. The threat of being conscripted for a war that was the object of widespread moral revulsion made marchers and shouters out of young men who might otherwise have been less concerned over the victimization of an Asian people and the turning into cannon fodder of farm boys and the sons of the working class and the minorities. The appeal of the cause aroused women students in equal number and with equal passion.

The majority of Americans, as credulous as other peoples, were tolerating this pain only because the authority figures in whom they had faith had assured them it was necessary for the safety of the nation and that victory and an end to the pain were at hand. American society had been stressed to the point where its will could be snapped. The financial and human costs of Westmoreland's war of attrition were so high that when the Tet 1968 Offensive exposed it as a fiasco, the inevitable result was a psychological collapse and a domestic political crisis of historic proportions. Westmoreland had brought about the kind of catastrophe MacArthur had perpetrated when he had sent an American army into the mountains of North Korea in the winter of 1950, but on a scale magnified many times by the extravagance of the failure in Vietnam.

It did not matter to the American public that the platoon of sappers did not actually break into and seize the embassy building, although they had plenty of B-40 rockets and explosives with which to do so. The sappers apparently became confused after their leaders were killed in an opening exchange and simply occupied the interior of the compound around the building and shot it out for nearly six and a half hours until they were all killed or wounded. Toward the end of the battle an MP tossed a gas mask and a pistol through a window to George Jacobson so that he could shoot a wounded sapper who was climbing the stairs inside his house to get away from tear gas. Jake, who had retired from the Army, thought that as a diplomat he would not need a weapon and had been trapped all night on the second floor of the house with just a grenade he found in a desk drawer.

It did not matter in the United States that the Vietnamese Communists failed to topple the Saigon regime and foment a rebellion by the urban population. The Hanoi leadership miscalculated the rapidity with which American military power could bolster the regime, as Weyand did with his counterstrokes, and they did not understand the tumbleweed mentality of the new "forced-draft" urban dwellers. While some did actively assist the Communist forces and the majority were sufficiently antagonistic to the Americans and the regime to give no warning as tens of thousands of armed men moved through their midst, they were people too confused by loss of home and place and the corrosion of family and social values to be committed to any cause or to rebel against anyone.

What mattered to the American public was that this defeated enemy could attack anywhere and was attacking everywhere more fiercely than ever before. The winning of the war was not coming "into view." The war in Vietnam was never going to be won. Nothing had been achieved by the outpouring of lives and treasure and the rending of American society. The assurances the public had been given were the lies and vaporings of foolish men.

Everything Americans saw as the offensive unfolded reinforced this impression. The Viet Cong holed up in the Phu Tho section of western Saigon and in Cholon and Phu Lam and resisted block by block. They did the same in other cities and towns where they could. To have prohibited the use of heavy weapons and aircraft would have meant a high cost in the lives of U.S. and ARVN soldiers (the infantry was to pay dearly in any case), but not even minimal restrictions were imposed, and the saving of the soldiers' lives was not the principal reason for the lack of restraint. It was more in the nature of a reflex to turn loose on the urban centers the "stomp-them-to-death" firepower that had brutalized the Vietnamese countryside.

Serious fighting went on in Saigon for two weeks. Americans watched the country they were supposed to be rescuing being burned down and blown apart on television—in color. "Although no accurate statistics are available," the official ARVN history said of the toll throughout South Vietnam, "there were approximately 14,300 [civilians] killed, 24,000 wounded, 72,000 homes destroyed, and 627,000 persons made homeless." In Saigon and its suburbs, approximately 6,300 civilians died, 11,000 were wounded, 206,000 became refugees, and 19,000 houses were smashed. The spectacle broadened opposition to the war and made it a profoundly moral concern, not just for students and intellectuals, but also for a large segment of the middle class who had no sons of draft age. The mad logic seemed to be epitomized by the remark of an American major to Peter Arnett after much of Ben Tre had been turned into broken bricks and cinders: "It became necessary to destroy the town to save it."

Westmoreland contributed by playing as ever into the hands of his enemy. He drove to the embassy on the morning of the 31st, inspected the damage, and then gave a press conference amid the bodies of the sappers and the MPs, announcing that this raid and the whole offensive was a diversion for an intended main thrust at Khe Sanh and across the DMZ. The man who thought he was baiting was unable to understand that he had been baited. He kept shipping American fighting men north until he had fully half of his maneuver battalions in I Corps. He had a cot set up in the Combined Operations Center at Pentagon East so that he could watch over Khe Sanh day and night. He personally approved B-52 strikes. Dutch Kerwin, his chief of staff, became so concerned about Westmoreland's lack of sleep that he asked Katherine "Kitsy" Westmoreland to get on a medical evacuation plane returning to Saigon from the Philippines so that the general would have to spend a few nights in his own bed at his villa.

While the Vietnamese Communists held Westmoreland mesmerized by Khe Sanh, they prolonged the struggle for the prize of Hue, quietly withdrawing a regiment from each of the two divisions encircling the Marines and sending them over the mountains to join the battle for the former imperial capital. Unlike Saigon, Hue is a small city, with a population in 1968 of about 140,000. The least harmful alternative where a place of so much historic and political significance was concerned would have been to regain the initiative immediately by driving the NVA troops out before they could consolidate. Westmoreland had the force available in two brigades of the Air Cav standing by about fourteen miles north of the city, but he was afraid to commit them because he thought he might need the Cav to relieve Khe Sanh. He abandoned the battle to the ARVN and a couple of reinforced battalions of Marines.

It was twenty-five days before the flag of the Viet Cong was hauled down and the yellow-and-red-striped banner of the Saigon side hoisted again over the Zenith Gate. The Thai Hoa Palace of the emperors and the other monuments were grievously scarred. Enough homes were destroyed or seriously damaged to render 90,000 of the 140,000 inhabitants of Hue refugees in their own city. The local Viet Cong took advantage of the occupation to settle scores. They rounded up current and retired officials, civil servants, police officers, anyone connected to the regime or a known sympathizer, and killed them. Most of the victims were shot; some were beheaded; others were buried alive. The number of victims is impossible to establish with precision. One careful estimate put the toll at 3,000. The killings were as stupid as they were cruel. The massacre gave substance to the fear that a bloodbath would occur should the Communists ever win the war in the South.

By the end of March 1968, the effect of Tet was apparent in the United States. Senator Eugene McCarthy had come within three hundred votes of beating Lyndon Johnson for the Democratic Party nomination in the New Hampshire primary, an unprecedented challenge to an incumbent president. (McCarthy won by a slight majority after the write-in votes were counted.) Robert Kennedy then pounced and was running for president too. His act was not entirely opportunistic. He had genuinely turned against the war. With his popularity and the ghost of his revered brother to help him, he seemed assured of appropriating McCarthy's antiwar cause and inflicting the ultimate humiliation on Johnson.

Westmoreland had finally undone himself by letting Wheeler use him in an unsuccessful scheme to try to force the president to mobilize the reserves and give Westmoreland another 206,756 men. Bunker, disillusioned with Westmoreland and angry at him for setting them up for such a hard fall at Tet, warned him against asking for the troops. He explained to the general that it was now politically impossible for the president to mobilize the reserves for Vietnam, even if Johnson wanted to do so, which was also more unlikely than ever. Bunker did not yet realize the complete extent of the psychological victory the Vietnamese Communists had won in the United States, but he sensed that the Tet Offensive had broken the will of the administration in the same way it had the public will. He could tell that nothing he and Westmoreland said was believed in Washington anymore. Rusk, normally the most restrained of men, was constantly on the phone to him with questions. Westmoreland did not heed the ambassador. The president suddenly announced on March 22 that he was bringing Westmoreland home to be chief of staff of the Army. "Westy, of course, was kicked upstairs," Bunker said with his wry laugh after the war was over.

Bunker was correct in sensing a break of will within the administration. After the president arranged McNamara's departure to the World Bank, he said to his press secretary, George Christian: "The one man in this war I never need to worry about is Dean Rusk. He's as tough as a Georgia pine knot." The pine knot from Cherokee County, Georgia, had cracked. In early March, Rusk began circulating among senior members of the administration one of the proposals for which McNamara had been fired. It was to suspend indefinitely the bombing of North Vietnam except in the infiltration corridor below the 19th Parallel, what Rusk called "the area associated with the battle zone," as a step toward the possible opening of negotiations. Rusk was not hopeful that Hanoi would respond positively, at least not right away. Not knowing the Vietnamese, he did not understand the import of a speech by Nguyen Duy Trinh, the foreign minister in the North, that had been publicized with care as part of the preparations for Tet. On prior occasions the Hanoi leadership had said that it "could" negotiate with the United States if the bombing ceased. In his speech at the end of December 1967, Trinh had said that his government "will hold talks" if all bombing was halted unconditionally. Rusk wanted to try just the same. Clark Clifford, the enthusiastic war hawk who had been sobered by Tet and the responsibility of confronting the war as the new secretary of defense, favored the proposal. Moreover, although the president was not committed to accepting it, Rusk was circulating the proposal with his permission, because something had cracked in Lyndon Johnson too.

The Wise Men made up the president's mind. Johnson convened a second meeting of his senior counselors at the end of March. The group that assembled at the White House on the morning of March 26, 1968, had received briefings at the State Department on the evening of the 25th that were quite different from the briefings of November. Most of those present were changed men too. A memorandum prepared by McGeorge Bundy to summarize their views explained why: "When we last met we saw reasons for hope." Cyrus Vance, who had been forced to give up the post of deputy secretary of defense in 1967 because of complications from back surgery, was one of the newcomers to the group, but he had worked for Johnson since the president's days in the Senate. "Unless we do something quick, the mood in this country may lead us to withdrawal," he warned.

In one of the greater ironies of the war, it was left to Dean Acheson to pronounce the death sentence on the venture that he had been so responsible for commencing. He had spoken the previous evening after the briefings at the State Department. McGeorge Bundy had written down Acheson's words because they summed up the views of the majority. He read them to the president and the gathering: "We can no longer do the job we set out to do in the time we have left and we must begin to take steps to disengage." Justice Fortas now sought to argue with Acheson. He was in the minority who wanted to hold firm. Acheson put him down: "The issue is not that stated by Fortas. The issue is can we do what we are trying to do in Vietnam. I do not think we can. . . . Can we by military means keep the North Vietnamese off the South Vietnamese. I do not think we can. They can slip around and end-run them and crack them up."

Five days later, on March 31, 1968, Lyndon Johnson gave his televised speech to the nation restricting the bombing of North Vietnam and renouncing any possibility of another term as president in order to hold the country together in the time he had left. Three days later, on April 3, 1968, the Vietnamese surprised the president and his secretary of state again. Radio Hanoi announced that they would negotiate with the Americans.

John Vann could not accept the death of the war. He could not admit that Tet had written a finis to it. His inability to do so was to transform him in the years that lay ahead.

Tet gave him something to grasp at as a rationalization to continue. The price of the political and psychological victory the Vietnamese Communists achieved was the destruction of the Viet Cong. Except in northern I Corps and parts of the Central Highlands, the guerrillas were the force employed at Tet, because they could most easily maneuver into the cities and towns. The result was that tens of thousands perished during the original Tet attacks and in a second offensive into the urban centers the Hanoi leaders ordered in May to keep the pressure on the Johnson administration. The army of Southern peasants that the Viet Minh survivors had first raised in fighting bands during the winter of Diem's terror, which had grown into regiments and divisions from the ordeal of Ap Bac, was as torn as the country it would have won had American soldiers not denied it victory in 1965. By late June 1968, Vann estimated that the Communist forces in III Corps had suffered more than 20,000 killed.

The replacements were almost all North Vietnamese. The clandestine Viet Cong government could not possibly replace losses this rapidly from its shrunken recruiting base, and demoralization was widespread within the guerrilla movement that remained. The Viet Cong fighters did not see the will-breaking effect their sacrifice had in the United

States. They saw only the loss of their comrades on missions that had become so unrealistic in military terms by May that they were suicidal.

Where Tet savaged the reputations of men like Komer and Westmoreland, it vindicated Vann's realism of the fall. His credibility within the bureaucracy and among the journalists rose higher than ever. A friend sent him a sample of the remarks being made in the upper reaches of the Pentagon and the State Department about his November briefings: "Nothing that John said turned out to be an exaggeration." Tet thrust Vann into his element too. He had once said to Ellsberg in Hau Nghia that he harped on the failings of the ARVN and the Saigon regime "because everyone else is singing a merry tune. If they were all discouraged, I would be saying, 'Look, it's not hopeless; here's what can be done.' " He was appalled by the turning loose of American firepower on the cities and towns. Twitchy-fingered ARVN and U.S. soldiers doubled the risk of driving the roads and flying in and out of province and district centers at night, yet bullets from any direction put Vann that much more into his element. He was all over the corps, encouraging his CORDS teams, reorganizing, preparing to hit back. As early as the third week of February he sent a pep-talk memo around to his teams:

> Now is the time, quite literally, to separate the men from the boys. I have been disappointed in several instances to find advisors who are obviously feeling sorry for themselves and mentally wringing their hands. . . . Get your counterparts and their troops out from behind their barbed wire and aggressively on the offensive, both day and night. The enemy has never been more vulnerable to effective military action than he is today.

Komer bore Vann no grudge. He was generous enough to accept the vindication of another man despite the cost to himself. He demanded in a cable to AID's Washington headquarters in April that Vann be promoted to FSR-1, the highest Foreign Service Reserve grade. James Grant, the assistant administrator for Vietnam, was happy to oblige. Komer was also not yet ready to give up on the war, and he too saw possibilities of rebound in the destruction of the Viet Cong. His unwillingness to accept the logical consequences of Tet was symptomatic of the attitude of many senior figures within the American power structure. Having come to maturity in a system that had usually had its way in international affairs, they resisted conceding that this time they would not prevail. The thought of what they had invested in the war made them more inclined to resist. As the shock of Tet receded they looked around for alternatives.

Vann seized on the decimation of the guerrillas as the turn that could bring victory to the United States and the Saigon side. He quickly convinced himself that the North Vietnamese Army could not take up the share of the burden the guerrillas had been carrying and win the war by itself. In his judgment the long-term threat to the existence of the Saigon regime was the Viet Cong, with its capacity for political and military action. He tended to view the NVA as a physical force that could be contained. The guerrilla movement had now been so severely weakened that he decided it could be ground down further and contained too.

What most impressed Vann about the Viet Cong losses was not the number—ordinary soldiers could be replaced with a bit of time—but the loss of the company- and battalion-level officers and the seasoned NCOs. These men were the fruit of years. The mix of North Vietnamese and Southerners in the Viet Cong units in III Corps had worked well prior to Tet because most of the NVA had been common soldiers. Southerners had continued to hold the leadership positions. The majority of Southern company and battalion officers and NCOs had then died at Tet and during the "May Tet" attacks. Northerners had arrived to take their places. About 70 percent of all officers and men in the regular and local force battalions in III Corps were North Vietnamese by late June. The Northerners were too conventionally trained to adapt to guerrilla warfare, Vann concluded, and they would never master the necessary political rapport with the Southern peasantry. The regional differences simply could not be overcome. "In fact, they [the NVA] are nearly as alien in this country as are our U.S. forces and receive only that support and assistance from the population that they are able to coerce through fear," he wrote to Bob York.

On the basis of these assumptions, Vann devised a new plan to win the war. He wanted to "pacify the main stream of the American public" with "a phased reduction" of U.S. forces while gradually transferring to the ARVN responsibility for combat with the NVA and the Viet Cong regulars who remained. The number of U.S. servicemen in South Vietnam reached 536,000 in May 1968 and was to peak at 543,000 in April 1969, because of a token increase Johnson had included in his March 31 speech to try to mollify the generals. Vann thought that large withdrawals could be made quickly just by choosing to live more leanly and eliminating a lot of the base camps and the "almost unbelievable layering of headquarters and the proliferation of many nice-to-have (but not essential) units and activities" that Westmoreland had insisted on having. "I consider it entirely feasible to phase down our troop involvement here to a level of 200,000 by mid-1971," he said in an April 1968 letter to Edward Kennedy, one of the first political figures to whom he tried to sell his plan, because he was upset by Robert Kennedy's antiwar statements.

Tet also made his plan feasible, Vann persuaded himself, because the blow must have shaken many within the Saigon government into realizing that they could not continue to tolerate the extent of the regime's corruption and incompetence. The Communists had inadvertently created an atmosphere in which American pressure to curb these ills might at last have an effect. A phased reduction of U.S. troops "would provide the necessary stimulus to the GVN" to move seriously in this direction, Vann told Edward Kennedy.

John Vann did not want to withdraw all American military men. He wanted to keep a residual force of about 100,000 in South Vietnam for the foreseeable future, mostly advisors, technical personnel, and helicopter and fixed-wing aviation units to support the Saigon troops. The ARVN was at last receiving M-16 rifles in quantity, and M-16s were soon to be distributed to the RF and PF too. Vann felt that a better-armed, better-led ARVN, backed by B-52s and the fighter-bombers of the U.S. Air Force and the Navy, could handle the NVA.

He failed to convince Dan Ellsberg. They had long discussions about the Tet Offensive and Vann's new plan when he was in the United States for three weeks in July on regular home leave and to recuperate from abdominal surgery. Lee had found him unconscious in a puddle of blood on the bathroom floor of the Bien Hoa house on the night of May 30. Wilbur Wilson, awakened by her screams, summoned a helicopter to rush him to the Long Binh hospital. The Army surgeons assumed he had a bleeding ulcer and nearly killed him pumping ice water into his intestines through his nostrils for ten hours to try to stop the bleeding before they decided to operate. They discovered he had suffered a rare accident called a Mallory-Weiss syndrome. While vomiting from nausea caused by a series of booster vaccination shots against typhoid and the other nineteenth-century diseases still common in countries like Vietnam, he had torn a gash in his esophagus at the point where it reaches the stomach. The exceptional stomach muscles he had built up from so many years of gymnastics had given him the strength to rip himself apart. The surgeons clipped several of the muscles so that he couldn't do it again. He lost and received fourteen pints of blood.

Tet had brought despair rather than hope of renewal to Ellsberg. The shock had provoked him into a reexamination of the war, an intellectual journey complicated by emotions as turbulent as those he had known in Vietnam. He had started psychoanalysis to try to cope with a case of writer's block that was interfering with his work at Rand, and he was experimenting with the sexual freedom fashionable in California in the 1960s. An Australian pacification specialist working in Vietnam had lectured at Rand in May and spoken of the "opportunities" the grave weakening of the Viet Cong had opened for the United States and the Saigon regime. "My own attitude about such matters now," Ellsberg had written Vann, "is that the VC are right to bet that the GVN and U.S. will fail to exploit any such 'opportunities' and fanatics like you, me (before), [and] our friends were always wrong to imagine otherwise."

Vann took it as a good omen that important men in Washington did welcome his reasons for being encouraged. He called Harry McPherson, President Johnson's chief speech writer, soon after reaching the house in Littleton in July. They had met when McPherson visited South Vietnam during the summer of 1967. McPherson was so impressed by Vann's heartening words over the phone that he typed up a memorandum of their conversation and gave it to the president.

Lyndon Johnson had become immobilized after his March 31 speech, gripped by the same resistance that was affecting Komer and so many others. He was seeking to salvage through his negotiators in Paris, Harriman and Vance, what his general had lost in the field. He let Westmoreland linger on in Vietnam too as a kind of lame-duck commander. Creighton Abrams did not take charge until mid-June. Johnson wanted to negotiate a mutual withdrawal of the NVA and the U.S. forces, persuading himself this was compromise. The Vietnamese Communists were prepared to discuss the conditions of an American withdrawal. Mutual withdrawal did not interest them. They sat down for the years of haggling they had known might ensue until the course of the war and the continued alienation of the American public could settle the issue. At the end of October they were to trade Johnson unwritten, indefinite assurances of de-escalation along the DMZ and around Saigon and the other major cities for an end to all bombing of the North and admission to the talks of a delegation from the National Liberation Front.

This concession by the United States put the Saigon regime and the Viet Cong on an equal footing. While this arranging of the chairs around the table in Paris dawdled along, 14,589 Americans fell in battle in Vietnam during 1968, more than half again as many as in 1967, the highest for any year of the war. Although Lyndon Johnson was not interested in a withdrawal of American troops during what was left of his administration, because this did not fit into his negotiating strategy, he obviously had reason to be looking for cheer in July when he received McPherson's memo on the phone call from Vann. He was glad to have someone tell him that time might be on the side of the United States and the Saigon regime. He read the memorandum to a meeting of his cabinet. Vann was thrilled at the compliment.

He then nearly got thrown out of South Vietnam while promoting his strategy. Peter Arnett stopped by his office in Bien Hoa one evening about a month after his return. Arnett was doing an article on the possibility of future U.S. troop withdrawals, what is called a "think piece" in the trade. Vann had known Arnett for six years. He provided lots of thought on the subject of withdrawals. He gave Arnett permission to quote him by name on his optimistic remarks, such as the consequences of what had happened to the Viet Cong at Tet. He assumed Arnett would protect him on everything else by paraphrasing or quoting without attribution. His remarks might be recognized in Saigon as Vann-isms, as they so often were, but he could disclaim them, as he never hesitated to do. This time Arnett changed the rules, without informing Vann. The article was caustic, at times mocking, in its portrait of the U.S. military machine. Among the direct quotes was one in which Vann explained why there would be no difficulty sending home the first 100,000 men:

> "The first 100,000 Americans to leave would be for free," Vann
> declared. "They are the clerks, the laundrymen, the engineer battalions
> building officers' clubs throughout the country. So many extraneous
> things are soaking up people not essential."

The Associated Press released the article on its news wire at the end of the first week of September. Komer got a warning call at 7:00 in the morning while he was still at his house. He phoned Vann. "You stupid son of a bitch," he shouted. "You're in deep trouble."

Someone had already called Vann too, because he knew why Komer was shouting at him. "Bob, let me tell you what happened," he said.

"Don't bother to tell me how it happened. I keep telling you every six weeks to keep your yap shut," Komer yelled.

Vann persisted. Komer had never heard him sound so crestfallen. "You'd better listen to me, Bob," he said. Komer did and then he cursed Vann again and hung up.

At 8:30 A.M. precisely, the moment each day that General Abrams reached his desk at MACV headquarters, the intercom in Komer's office said: "Bob, I'd like to see you right away." Creighton Abrams was a tanker, according to George Patton the meanest tanker the Germans had faced in the whole U.S. Third Army, and he had a temper that matched the fearsome machines he loved. He assumed that no reporter would quote John Vann without his permission, that the article was a deliberate affront. "Have you seen . . ." he started to say as Komer walked into his office and shut the door.

Komer interrupted in an attempt to gain the high ground. "I have seen and it's inexcusable. I've called Vann and reamed him out. I read him the riot act," Komer said.

Abrams's roughhewn features flushed and his eyes bulged. "I don't care if you read him the riot act. I won't stand for it," he screamed, his voice twisting up into a squeaky pitch as he choked on his words. "It isn't that Vann criticized the U.S. Army. It isn't that Vann criticized me personally. It isn't any of that shit. What gets me is that the dirty son of a bitch did it in quotes." He raged on while Komer stood silent, assuming it was futile at this stage to try to explain. "I want that man fired," Abrams said as soon as his rage had sufficiently abated for him to form the sentence.

"Now Abe, we can't do that," Komer said.

"Fire that man!" Abrams screeched. "That is a direct order!" He got so red in the face Komer was afraid he was going to asphyxiate himself.

"Look, Abe. He screwed up. He's screwed up before. I have no doubt he will screw up again. He seems terribly accident-prone on this question of talking to the press, but that goes back to the battlefield of Ap Bac in 1963. There's nothing we can do about it now. John Vann is the one indispensable man I've got in all of the four regions. As a matter of fact, if I had three more John Vanns, we could cut the length of the war in half. I'm not about to give up my best guy because he said something to a correspondent."

Abrams stared at Komer in disbelief. "You don't understand. I said fire that man. That is a direct order!" he screeched again.

Komer decided he would need a large bazooka to stop the tank. He knew that Abrams was frightened of newsmen. Abrams had watched the reporters maul Westmoreland after Tet, and he dreaded the possibility that they might turn on him. He had so far enjoyed a friendly press, because he was new in command; he looked like a different general with his short, rugged figure, and events did not contradict his words, because he took a lesson from Westmoreland's misfortune and rarely said anything of substance to the newsmen.

"If you give me a direct order to fire John Vann, I'm going to fire John Vann," Komer said, "but I want to tell you what's going to happen. I will not have been in my office and have talked to John more than five minutes when every correspondent in Saigon will be on the phone to me asking why John Vann was fired. And within an hour, half the reporters in the United States will be calling out here. . . . When they ask me the direct question 'Was he fired on your recommendation?' I will say, 'No, I was ordered to fire him.' When they ask, 'Who fired him?' I will say, 'It was General Abrams, personally.' They will ask, 'Did you, Bob Komer, concur in the firing?' I'm going to tell them that you did it over my violent protest. The firing of John Vann is going to be such a *cause célèbre* to his friends"—Komer rattled off the name of every reporter he could think of who knew Vann, beginning with Halberstam—"that I am not going to take the rap for it. This is really going to be something, Abe. You'll be fighting a second war that's much worse than the one against the NVA." For maximum effect, Komer spun around and ignored the insult Abrams screamed at him as he cleared the door.

Abrams never mentioned the matter again. Komer punished Vann by letting him hang on the edge for a full twenty-four hours before calling him back. Then he told Vann he might be able to rescue him from the firing squad, but he wasn't sure. He wanted to keep Vann contrite as long as he could. Not until years later did he regale Vann with the whole tale.

The outcome was worth the scare. Vann discovered he had a new president with whom he was in tune. His taste in American politicians had become somewhat catholic after his return to South Vietnam in 1965. He tended to overlook behavior he would otherwise have found objectionable as long as the politician in question backed the war and promoted John Vann and his ideas.

One of his most enthusiastic supporters was a character named Sam Yorty, whose gift for public relations and appeals to racism were to gain him three four-year terms as mayor of Los Angeles and enough voter tolerance for absenteeism to permit frequent trips to the Far East and other places. He and Vann had met during Yorty's first visit to the war in November 1965, and they invariably got together on subsequent occasions. Yorty sent a copy of Arnett's article to his fellow California Republican Richard Nixon, who thanked him for it in a letter dated a week and a half before the 1968 presidential election. By the time Vann received a copy of the letter from Yorty, Richard Nixon was president-elect of the United States.

A process of elimination had helped to elect him. Robert Kennedy had been killed in Los Angeles in June by an Arab fanatic. Eugene McCarthy had then been denied the Democratic nomination at the convention in Chicago in August by the party regulars. They conferred it on Hubert Humphrey, Johnson's vice-president. Humphrey campaigned with the wound of Vietnam. The wide distrust of Nixon still made it hard for him to defeat the weakest of his potential opponents. He won narrowly by giving the public the impression that he had a secret plan to end the war.

Nixon admitted in his old age that he never had any such plan. His letter to Yorty alerted Vann to the quite different plan he did have. He intended to do what Vann wanted—purchase time from the American public with U.S. troop withdrawals while continuing the war by using the Vietnamese on the Saigon side to fight it. After saying that he found Vann's ideas "most interesting" and had referred the clip to "my research and policy staff," Nixon went on to explain the similarity of his own ideas:

> As you undoubtedly know, it has been my position that the de-Americanization of the war must proceed with all deliberate speed. The [Johnson] Administration appears to have recognized this only as a consequence of the Tet Offensive, and even now does not seem to place the necessary trust in the Vietnamese and their capacity to assume a greater share of the war's burden.

Vann immediately composed a six-and-a-half-page letter, addressed to Yorty and written for Nixon. He described his phased reduction plan in detail and made a bid to temporarily join the new administration as a high-level advisor to supervise implementation of the strategy. "The old problems of corruption, nepotism, and nonresponsiveness to rural needs . . . are as much with us as ever," Vann said, but he indicated that he had changed his mind about their importance. They did not matter as much because of the altered circumstances brought about by Tet. In one flourish of self-salesmanship he enclosed a copy of McPherson's memorandum to Johnson and mentioned how "the memo was read by the President to his Cabinet." In another he trotted out the glory he had been unable to resist stealing. He put himself once more into Ralph Puckett's foxhole on the hill in North Korea on the night in November 1950 when the Chinese had attacked. That night, he said, he had first learned the folly of trading American soldiers for Asian ones "in the overpopulated Orient." Using Vietnamese soldiers to fight would also help calm the American public, because they were far cheaper in dollars, Vann said. Most of the $33 billion annual cost of the war was being consumed by the U.S. forces. "I think we could be eminently successful in South Vietnam at a cost of around five billion a year by 1975," he wrote.

Yorty forwarded the letter to the president-elect, but Vann received no inquiries about joining the Nixon administration as a high-level advisor. Exuberance and his search for his star occasionally led him to flights of fancy about his eligibility for exalted Washington office. He dreamed of one day being rewarded for his Vietnam service with the post of secretary of the Army so that he could settle scores with the institution he felt had rejected him. Vann nevertheless did contribute to the formulation of the Nixon strategy through the letter, the Arnett article, and the fact that Henry Kissinger, who was chosen that November to be Nixon's special assistant for national security affairs, was familiar with his ideas. Vann managed to convey them to Kissinger during an earlier attempt in 1968 to further himself and his war. He had offered to join Nelson Rockefeller's campaign as its Vietnam expert. His overture became moot with Rockefeller's defeat by Nixon at the Republican National Convention, but in the meantime Kissinger had received copies of Vann's letters to Edward Kennedy and others.

The Nixon strategy was soon to emerge under a catchier term than the de-Americanization one Nixon had used in the letter to Yorty. It was to be called Vietnamization. Kissinger was to pay Vann an exaggerated compliment on the extent of his contribution. "It's your policy," he was to say. Despite the lack of an invitation to come to Washington, John Vann was content for the moment. He believed he had at last found a way to win the war that put him at one with the men of power who made victory and advancement possible.

He became a touchstone of optimism and progress for his fellow seekers of this other way. Komer passed Vann to his successor, William Colby, when Komer decided to accept Johnson's farewell gift of the ambassadorship to Turkey and left Vietnam in November 1968. Colby had returned to Saigon from CIA headquarters shortly after Tet at Komer's behest to serve as his deputy. By the time Komer left, Colby held Vann in the same regard. CORDS did seem to be pacifying the South Vietnamese countryside. Under pressure from Johnson, the Saigon regime widened the military manpower pool in 1968 by lowering the draft age with a new General Mobilization Law. The law was to bring an additional 200,000 Vietnamese into uniform by the end of 1969 and to permit a major expansion of the ARVN and, more important for pacification, of the RF and PF.

Komer and Colby, with Vann encouraging them, also persuaded Thieu to put his authority behind a special program to capture or kill the cadres of the clandestine Viet Cong government, the so-called VCI, for Viet Cong Infrastructure. The program was given the English name Phoenix, a compromise translation for the Vietnamese name Phung Hoang, a mythical bird that could fly anywhere. The rival intelligence and police agencies on the Saigon side were forced to pool their information so that dossiers and blacklists could be drawn up and cadres targeted. The CIA's assassination squads, the former Counter Terror Teams that were now known as Provincial Reconnaissance Units (PRUs), constituted the action arm, with the RF and PF employed too when convenient. Technically, no cadres were marked for assassination, only for arrest, because a prisoner led to others when he or she talked. In practice, the PRUs anticipated resistance in disputed areas and shot first. People taken prisoner were usually men and women denounced and arrested in Saigon-held zones, picked up at checkpoints, or captured in combat and later identified as VCI. Cadres who did not wish to risk the PRUs or jail had the choice any guerrilla had of defecting. Komer set a quota for all of South Vietnam. He wanted 3,000 VCI "neutralized" every month. He launched the first Accelerated Pacification Campaign just before he departed.

Tet had drained the Viet Cong of the armed strength the guerrillas needed to shield their cadres and to contest the Saigon side for physical control of the hamlets. Vann confirmed this supposition during the final months of 1968 in III Corps and after he was transferred to Can Tho in February 1969 to be chief of pacification for the Mekong Delta (IV Corps). Komer had wanted to shift him there during the summer of 1968, because he felt Vann had set standards and built a CORDS team in III Corps that could be passed on to someone else and because the Viet Cong had traditionally drawn so much of their manpower, tax revenues, and other resources from the Delta. Vann had resisted surrendering the III Corps position and all that it meant to him, sending Wilbur Wilson to Can Tho in his place. He had eventually given in to pressure from Colby.

He discovered that many of the 2,100 hamlets the HES listed as under Viet Cong ownership in IV Corps in February 1969 (another 2,000 hamlets were listed in varying degrees of Saigon control) were actually held by half a dozen guerrillas. The district companies and regional battalions that had once been on the qui vive to back up the locals and punish intrusions by the Saigon side had more dead heroes than keen-for-battle fighters on their rolls. Moreover, those on the Saigon side sensed the change. The atmosphere was the reverse of the days of panic and intimidation in Hau Nghia in 1965 when Viet Cong commandos could barge into Cu Chi town and chase recalcitrant members of the district intelligence squad down dirt lanes and across rooftops for hours undisturbed. The province and district chiefs were willing to tackle their enemy when prodded to do so by Americans like Vann. His methodical recruiting of more RF and PF to form garrisons and his establishment of hamlet and village administrations through the RD Cadre teams enabled him to quickly penetrate reaches of the Delta that had known no Saigon presence since Diem.

Saigon officialdom saw the glitter of extortionist gold in the Phoenix Program, blackmailing innocents and taking bribes not to arrest those they should have arrested. In the rush to fill quotas they posthumously elevated lowly guerrillas killed in skirmishes to the status of VC hamlet and village chiefs. The Phoenix bird was a predator nonetheless. After all of these years, the identity of many hamlet, village, and district cadres was common knowledge in their neighborhoods. Thousands died or vanished into Saigon's prisons. Colby was to state in 1971 that 28,000 VCI had been captured in the whole of South Vietnam under the program, 20,000 had been killed, and another 17,000 had defected.

The Viet Cong did not disappear, of course, nor did the fighting cease, but the guerrillas were forced into a period of relative quiesence. They managed to retain strongholds south of the Bassac in the U Minh Forest of Ca Mau, in Kien Giang and Chuong Thien provinces, and in Chau Doc along the Cambodian border, and they clung to smaller bases in the northern Delta. To accomplish this, Hanoi had to infiltrate four NVA regiments into IV Corps. A lot of the cadres who survived had to hide in the swamps and jungles or pose as Saigon officials. Large sections of the Delta acquired a tranquillity that was spoiled only once in a while by shooting. Bridges were repaired and long-closed roads and canals reopened. The farmers who had stayed on the land or who re-turned to it thrived. Television was one of the gifts of a technological civilization that the U.S. military had brought in its baggage train, to broadcast tapes of American programs for the troops and to create a Saigon network that could propagandize for the regime. From his hel-icopter Vann noticed television antennas appearing on the roofs of the bigger farmhouses.

He acquired friends he would not have made before. "You and I

. . . such unlikely companions," Joseph Alsop, the Establishment newspaper columnist who was one of them, remarked in a letter to Vann in
the fall of 1969. Alsop and Vann had met once before, in the fall of
1967, at Alsop's request and under duress from Komer. Vann had at
first refused to see Alsop, because he looked on him then with the scorn
of Halberstam and Vann's other reporter friends. Komer had said that
one could not refuse to talk to Joe Alsop, that Komer would order Vann
to do so if Vann persisted. Vann had relented, and Alsop had satisfied
his curiosity. "I am not at all sure that we see the Vietnamese situation
from the same angle of vision," Alsop had said afterward in a rare
instance of understatement in his note thanking Vann for the meeting.
Vann got no mention in Alsop's column. Two years later, Alsop's hope
in Westmoreland was a memory, but he was as much in search as ever
of proof that the United States could achieve victory in Vietnam. With
Vann's new angle of vision, he was the touchstone Alsop needed.

That fall of 1969, Alsop spent the better part of a week touring the
Delta and wrote several columns celebrating the experience of being in
"John Vann's country." If Vann, "in the long past . . . Vietnam's super-
pessimist," said the United States and the Saigon side were currently
winning, then it had to be true. " 'Not too far down the road,' John
Vann told me, 'I'm confident that 90 percent of the Delta population
will be under solid government control.' " John Vann was "an infinitely
patriotic, intelligent, and courageous and magnificent leader." The sincerity in the friendship that developed came from Alsop, a man who,
when he gave his affection, gave it generously. Vann outwardly returned
the friendship, accepted the advertising and the increased respectability
Alsop provided him, and explained that he was nice to Joe because Joe
was "the president's journalist."

Respectability opened the door of the Oval Office. Colby received a
cable from Washington during the second week of December 1969. The
president wished to see Vann on December 22 at 11:00 A.M. Vann was
due to be in the United States then for Christmas leave and had hoped
to meet Kissinger. He had written for an appointment. Another of his
newly acquired friends, Sir Robert Thompson, transformed a prospective meeting with the president's special assistant into the ultimate compliment. He suggested to Kissinger that the president talk to Vann.

Sir Robert's opinion of whether the United States would prevail in
Vietnam had fluctuated over the years, depending on whose ideas were
being pursued. He was perceptive in analyzing Westmoreland's. As with
so many men of affairs, his critical faculties were daunted by his own.
Richard Nixon was a student of Thompson's writings and had invited

him to the White House that October. Thompson had told the president that the Vietnamization strategy could put the essentials of victory in place within two years. (He was more cautious in a book he published in 1969, giving a three-to-five-year estimate.) Nixon then hired Thompson as a consultant and sent him to South Vietnam to validate his judgment. Thompson, another man in need of a touchstone, chose Vann as his validator.

Vann escorted him around the Delta for three days at the beginning of November. They were together to hear Nixon's watershed speech on Vietnam on November 3, 1969, listening to it over the radio in a district headquarters in Ba Xuyen Province, a former guerrilla bastion below the Bassac. Nixon had already ordered the withdrawal of 60,000 American troops to appease public opinion, and there was general expectation that he would use the occasion to announce a program for quick withdrawal of most of the rest and perhaps a cease-fire too. He instead appealed to "the great silent majority of my fellow Americans" for their patience and support while he prosecuted the war until he could obtain "peace with honor." The withdrawals would continue, but at a measured pace to permit the strengthening of the Saigon forces. Vann was elated by the speech, because it meant, he wrote a friend, that Nixon had decided "to tell the demonstrators to go to hell." Fortified by his days with Vann, Thompson reported back to Nixon that the Saigon side held a "winning position."

The president was standing beside his desk, looking out the French door toward the Rose Garden, when Vann entered his office. The hour of the appointment had been changed. The time was five minutes past noon. Nixon turned and stepped forward in greeting. Kissinger introduced Vann with unstinting praise. The president had cleared his desk to listen, his habitual courtesy to visitors, but he seemed genuinely to want to listen to what Vann had come to tell him. "I will not be the first president of the United States to lose a war," Nixon said to the Republican congressional leaders that fall. He talked with Vann for nearly an hour. After Vann briefed him on pacification in the Delta, Nixon questioned Vann on how he had seen the war change over the years, seeking to learn why Vann had arrived at his current opinions. "He appeared to accept with some confidence the judgments I gave him as to the now favorable situation," Vann said in his memorandum of the conversation. Vann assured the president that with the advantage of heavy weapons and U.S. airpower the ARVN would be able to handle the NVA when they someday faced off. The worst that could occur, he said, was that the Saigon regime "would have to give up some territory and some population if an all-out conventional invasion took place," but the "invasion would be contained as the enemy extended his supply lines and became vulnerable to bombardment by air and artillery." The president thanked Vann for his service and instructed him to return to Vietnam and keep up the good work. He gave Vann a fountain pen and an autographed golf ball as souvenirs of their meeting.

Success did not tame John Vann easily. He almost got himself fired again for attempting to save his best Vietnamese friend, Tran Ngoc Chau, from jail. After the dispute with the CIA over the pacification teams, and simultaneous trouble he had had with Ky's minister for pacification, Chau decided he had spoiled his chance for further promotion in the ARVN. He took a leave of absence from the army and transferred his ambition to politics, winning the seat from Kien Hoa in the lower house of the National Assembly during the October 1967 elections. He did well in the Assembly, managing to get himself elected secretary-general of the Lower House. The Tet Offensive then propelled him into a high-stakes maneuver. He sought to make himself the go-between in the peace talks, utilizing one of his brothers who had stayed loyal to Ho Chi Minh as a secret channel to the other side. This brother, Tran Ngoc Hien, was a senior agent in Hanoi's intelligence service and had been back in the South since 1965, posing as a traveling salesman of pharmaceuticals. To further his plan, Chau had turned on an old ARVN friend and a former political ally, Nguyen Van Thieu, and attacked him by denouncing his bag man in the Assembly, a wealthy pharmacist named Nguyen Cao Thang whose task was to bribe delegates to vote as Thieu desired. Chau was not motivated entirely by ambition. Tet had convinced him that it was wrong to inflict on the Vietnamese people a war "without any end in sight," and he thought that the Saigon side had a chance of surviving if it negotiated a peace in time.

Chau's brother was arrested in the spring of 1969. A policeman at a checkpoint had the wit to notice that Tran Ngoc Hien's Central Vietnamese accent did not accord with the place of origin on the identity card he was currently using. Hien behaved with the shrewdness of a good intelligence officer. To avoid being tortured into revealing his important espionage networks, he deflected his interrogators. Chau was his means of deflection. He threw Chau to Thieu by telling the police about their meetings. Secret contacts between family members were common in South Vietnam. They were also illegal.

Vann did not approve of Chau's negotiating maneuver, and Bunker had warned him to stay clear of the affair the previous summer after Vann intervened to try to defuse the quarrel between Thieu and Chau. Bunker prized Thieu for the stability of his rule. He suspected that Chau was a Communist or a Communist agent, in any case a dangerous troublemaker who seemed to be attempting to gain a place for himself in a coalition government with the other side. The ambassador had called Vann to the embassy and administered "a polite but very steely asschewing," as Vann later described the session. "John, you're getting involved in politics. That's my business," Bunker said. "You tend to the pacification of the Delta and I'll tend to the politics of South Vietnam. Don't let it happen again."

By the time Vann returned in early January 1970 from his holiday leave and the exhilaration of his talk with President Nixon, Thieu, who had been moving slowly but surely toward vengeance, was about to arrest and imprison Chau for the secret meetings with his brother. He was bribing other deputies to sign a petition to strip Chau of immunity as a member of the National Assembly. Vann submitted a request through Colby asking that Chau be flown out of the country on a U.S. plane and granted asylum in the United States in consideration for past services. Chau could not leave South Vietnam legally, because Thieu had revoked his passport. Ev Bumgardner, who was back in Saigon working as an assistant to Colby, joined in the request. Bunker refused.

John Vann couldn't bear to give up Chau. It was not simply a matter of friendship. Chau still represented to Vann "the good Vietnamese" of his earlier vision, a symbol of the decent, progressive society that he and Bumgardner, Doug Ramsey, Frank Scotton, and Dan Ellsberg had wanted to create in South Vietnam. He knew that Chau was not a Communist or a Communist agent, no matter how much Chau might try to use Hien, as Hien might try to use Chau in this war in which brother exploited brother. Bumgardner felt the same way. Vann proceeded to concoct a plan to smuggle Chau to Cambodia. Chau could make his way from there to France or the United States. Vann had learned to fly a helicopter by having his pilots give him lessons. He was going to fly Chau to the nearest Cambodian fishing village up the Gulf of Siam coast and hover just offshore while Chau climbed into a rubber raft and paddled to the village.

Vann obtained the raft, one of the instantly inflatable types the Air Force issued to pilots, and rehearsed the flight by taking his helicopter out alone. At a prearranged time, Bumgardner drove Chau to the helicopter pad at the trash dump at Newport, the military port Westmoreland had built on the Saigon River. Vann met them and flew Chau to

Can Tho. Another close friend from III Corps, Dr. Merrill "Bud" Shutt, who was currently serving as Vann's public health officer for IV Corps, agreed to shelter Chau in his apartment in one of the CORDS compounds in Can Tho.

Had Chau let Vann go through with the plan, Vann's career in Vietnam certainly would have been terminated. Thieu would have been so angry at being cheated of vengeance that he would have demanded Vann's expulsion. The police tailed Bumgardner and Chau as far as the entrance to the Newport dump and saw Bumgardner drive out alone. Knowing the friendships, it was not difficult to surmise what was going on. After days of hesitation and reflection, Chau decided that if he fled, he would be implicitly admitting Thieu's accusation that he was a Communist. If he stayed and denied the charge and went to jail, he would become a martyr and retain a political future in South Vietnam. He and Vann got into a tumultuous argument in the apartment in Can Tho. Vann told Chau he was being a fool, that Thieu would endure a long time, because the United States was behind him, and he would keep Chau locked up for years. Chau followed his star. He had Vann fly him back to Saigon to hide for a while. Then he went to his office in the building where the Lower House met, the same place where Diem's National Assembly had met, the Saigon Opera House of the French time, to wait for the police to arrest him.

Bunker called Vann to the embassy again after he learned that Vann had been hiding Chau. The old man was cold on this occasion, as glacially cold as Ellsworth Bunker could be when he was enraged. "If it were anyone but you, John, you'd already be out of the country," he said. "I warned you once, and now it has happened again. There cannot be a third time. If there is, you'll have to leave, no matter how outstanding a job you have done, and you have done an outstanding job here."

George Jacobson had never seen anyone intimidate John Vann before. Vann was ashen when he came out of Bunker's office. "It is not part of my game plan to be fired at this point," he said to Jake.

The thought that he might be caught in the syndrome of self-fulfilling prophecy for which he had mocked Harkins and Westmoreland seems never to have occurred to Vann. Dan Ellsberg teased him about his meeting with Nixon. "You finally had some good news to give the president, John," he said. Vann did not appreciate the ironic humor.

He and Ellsberg remained best personal friends. They were able to argue about the war for hours during Vann's visits to the United States without alienating each other, but they were at opposite poles. Ellsberg's personal life was on the mend. In 1970 he was to marry Patricia Marx, the woman with whom he had quarreled over the war in Saigon.

As far as the war was concerned, Ellsberg's metamorphosis was complete. The experience of reading the still-top-secret Pentagon Papers, the forty-three-volume inquiry into the origins and history of the conflict that McNamara had commissioned and that was completed in January 1969 (Ellsberg, being Ellsberg, read all forty-three), convinced him that the American cause in Indochina was now and had always been wrong-headed and futile. The Vietnamization policy was thus a "bloody, hopeless, uncompelled, hence surely immoral prolongation of U.S. involvement in this war," Ellsberg wrote an official of the Carnegie Endowment for International Peace that September. Opinions may change; zealotry is a constant in the character of a man. Ellsberg, once Vann's most impassioned convert in the pursuit of the war, became a force to be reckoned with in the struggle to stop it. Ellsberg discussed the Pentagon Papers with his friend. He told Vann that Vann too might alter his opinion if he ever had time to read some of them. He did not tell his friend that during the fall of 1969 he began slipping the Rand Corporation copy of the Pentagon Papers, several volumes at a time, past the security guards at the front door and photocopying them.

Vann came to regard his trips to the United States as triumphs. Lee taught him to dress better for them. She persuaded him to buy dark, custom-tailored suits in Hong Kong and to wear soberly striped ties. His lectures at the Army War College and other service schools were treated as major occasions. He did not get to see the president again, but he regularly briefed Melvin Laird, Nixon's secretary of defense. Laird was the most enthusiastic advocate of Vietnamization within the Administration and was lavishing equipment on the Saigon forces— artillery of all kinds, armored personnel carriers, hundreds of tanks, squadrons of jet fighter-bombers, more than 500 Huey and Chinook helicopters. Vann would also call at the chief of staff's office to talk to Westmoreland, who was eager for an outcome that would vindicate what he had spent. Bruce Palmer, currently the vice-chief of staff, was always on Vann's list to visit. Palmer had been discouraged by Tet. He had then taken heart again because Vann assured him that he could.

While many of the reporters Vann knew no longer agreed with his conclusions about the war, he retained a special credibility with the press because of all he had put in the bank in the past and because he could still be frank about the flaws on the Saigon side. He kept his credibility within the lower levels of the bureaucracy for the same reasons. His friendship with Halberstam survived in a strained way. Halberstam was in the midst of writing *The Best and the Brightest*, his indictment of the generation of American leaders who had led the country into Vietnam. He argued to Vann that American society was being torn to serve a foreign war of no importance to it; Vann ought to look at the social divisions and other costs the war was exacting at home. "I'm not interested in that," Vann said.

John Vann didn't see some of his old Vietnam friends anymore, because his life had passed them by. Bob York was one. Although York had been awarded his third star and command of Fort Bragg and the XVIIIth Airborne Corps, he had retired from the Army in mid-1968 a disillusioned man.

Vann's visits with his aunt Mollie Tosolini were happy occasions. He would telephone her when he happened to be passing through the New York area and go out to her big house on Long Island. She loved to see him come, carrying a briefcase and looking like a diplomat. They would reminisce about Norfolk and he would tell her how he wished she had been his mother. He would tell her about the men in Washington who were listening to Myrtle's child. "You and me, Aunt Mollie, we're going places," he would say.

The move to Can Tho caused no trouble in his captain's paradise. Rather, it enhanced his amusement at keeping two women ignorant of each other. He adopted a variation of the III Corps gambit. He had CORDS lease, renovate, and furnish a house in Can Tho, where he installed Annie and the child and where he slept himself on nights when he was not out in one of the provinces or districts or in Saigon. The place was not listed as his official residence. He officially slept in the second bedroom of a bungalow assigned to Wilbur Wilson in the main CORDS housing compound in Can Tho, nicknamed Palm Springs because the bungalows were built around a swimming pool. He kept a set of clothes in the closet there and toilet articles beside the bed and photographs on the walls to give the room a lived-in look. When Lee came to Can Tho for an occasional visit, that was where they slept.

Annie was not a danger to the game, because she remained naive about him and did not ask questions. Lee was the inquisitive sort to begin with, and by this time she understood that Vann was constantly unfaithful to her. He instructed his driver, his interpreter, and his helicopter pilot to parry her questions. His secretary, Frenchy Zois; Wilbur Wilson's secretary, Tess Johnston; and the rest of the American and Vietnamese office staff at CORDS headquarters protected him too. Lee frequently telephoned him from Saigon. They made sure she did not accidentally obtain the number at the house if she called while he happened to be there. Lee never suspected that his unfaithfulness consisted of anything but transitory romping. (The bungalow bedroom was handy for this too.)

Vann also stood beside Lee before her ancestors in 1970. She had been bringing him home with her at night when he was in Saigon, and she would lose all face with her family if he made no gesture toward her. She pressed him into an engagement ceremony on her twenty-sixth birthday at the home of her grandfather, who had served in cabinets of Bao Dai and Diem and had later run the national bank. She lied to her grandfather, telling the old man that Vann was divorced. Because it was just an engagement, the ceremony was less elaborate than the one Vann had undergone with Annie. He presented Lee with the symbolic engagement earrings and several other pieces of jewelry. Her grandfather formally introduced him to her uncle and aunt and the rest of the family members who assembled and to the spirit of Lee's grandmother, whose portrait was on the ancestral altar. Vann clasped his hands and bowed his head while Lee prayed. Everyone sat down to a meal and champagne. Again there were no American guests.

Richard Nixon's "de-Americanization . . . with all deliberate speed" was not proving cheap in American lives. During 1969, 11,527 U.S. servicemen perished in Vietnam. During 1970, another 6,065 were to die. In all, nearly 21,000 Americans were killed in Vietnam during Nixon's presidency and about 53,000 seriously wounded, more than a third of the total U.S. casualties.

Nixon's troop withdrawals did have an unanticipated benefit. They prevented the Army in Vietnam from disintegrating. The riflemen who had fought with Hal Moore in the valley of the Drang and at Bong Son would not have recognized the U.S. Army of 1969. It was an Army in which men escaped into marijuana and heroin and other men died because their comrades were "stoned" on these drugs that profited the Chinese traffickers and the Saigon generals. It was an Army whose units in the field were on the edge of mutiny, whose soldiers rebelled against the senselessness of their sacrifice by assassinating officers and noncoms in "accidental" shootings and "fraggings" with grenades. The signs of demoralization were evident by the time of Westmoreland's departure in mid-1968. They worsened under Creighton Abrams because, while he attempted new tactics, he continued Westmoreland's attrition strategy and kept pushing American soldiers into the bunker-complex killing grounds the NVA prepared. In a notorious example in May 1969, fifty-five men of the 101st Airborne Division died to seize a fortified ridgeline on the edge of the wild A Shau Valley in the mountains west of Hue. The troops named the ridge "Hamburger Hill." The sad idiom of the American soldier in Vietnam reflected the futility of his war. A man was not killed there. He was "wasted." He was "blown away."

The ARVN did not get better as Vann had persuaded himself it would. The venerable bungler Phan Trong Chinh had at last been deprived of command of the 25th Division on the eve of Tet, but his removal had not been complicated by any question of competence. It had been one of those periodic shuffles motivated by personal relationships and graft and politics. As if to prove the point, Lam Quang Tho, the province chief at My Tho in 1963, Vann's "goddam poltroon" who had sabotaged every attempt to unhinge the Viet Cong flank at Ap Bac, rose to general and was given command of a division by Thieu. Westmoreland's failure to reform the Saigon forces and provide them with sound leadership while there was time meant grisly casualties now that they were being pushed into border battles with the NVA and fights with the remaining Viet Cong regulars. The Saigon troops had suffered nearly 28,000 killed in action during the year of Tet, almost half of all U.S. dead for the war. Their killed declined to about 22,000 in 1969, but the toll was running roughly twice as high as in pre-Tet years. In 1970 they were to lose more than 23,000 men.

Nor did Vann find himself working with the kind of province and district chiefs he had originally hoped Tet would shock the Saigon regime into appointing. Most were not stolid and well-meaning men like Hanh, or men like Chau in whom ambition was mixed with some idealism. The best-known province chief in the Mekong Delta in 1970 was Lt. Col. Hoang Duc Ninh. His first cousin, the president of the Republic, Nguyen Van Thieu, gave him Bac Lieu Province in the lower Delta. Ninh was boundless in his rapacity. He levied tribute on almost every commodity sold in the province from gasoline to cigarettes; he sold government supplies, too, and had his troops steal back some of the government gasoline he sold so that he could sell it a second time; flower and potted-tree soldiers bloomed on his muster rolls; no one retained a safe assignment in Bac Lieu town or in one of the district centers without a fee to Ninh; his artillery batteries kept the countryside awake with harassing and interdiction fire so that he could flog off additional thousands of brass shell casings; he extorted unusually large payments from innocent people he blackmailed under the Phoenix Program and let real Viet Cong out of jail for twice the price. No opportunity to make money escaped his attention. He even broke holes in a coastal dike that had been built with U.S. funds to keep the salt seawater out of farmers' rice fields and sold fishermen the privilege of erecting nets at the breaks to catch fish when the tide rose. The farmers had to endure the ruin of their paddies. Ninh was as brazen as he was greedy. Warren Parker, a former lieutenant colonel in the Special Forces who joined AID after retirement and was Vann's province senior advisor in Bac Lieu, tried to restrain Ninh by warning that corruption this extreme might provoke a scandal in the press. "I'm not afraid of American or Vietnamese newspapermen," Ninh said. Every time Ninh made a speech he boasted of "my cousin, the president."

Komer had started a secret program to fight corruption, and Colby carried it forward and regularized it in his methodical way. Bumgardner supervised the program for him. Dossiers were compiled on province and district chiefs and other provincial officials who were more egregiously corrupt than their fellows. Colby would deliver the dossiers to Thieu's prime minister with a request for removal and punishment. Bunker would follow up by raising the case with Thieu. That the program continued year after year was as much a measure of the capacity of senior American officials for meaningless ritual as it was of the corruption of the Saigonese. Bunker kept count of the occasions on which he saw Thieu on corruption cases. He did it seventy-eight times. (The dossier eventually submitted on Ninh was a tribute to his entrepreneurship at graft. It was about thirty pages long in single-spaced type.) Hardly anyone was punished. Ninh was promoted to full colonel in 1971. Pressure sometimes resulted in the removal of an individual, but Bumgardner discovered this was a trick. The man would be put in a staff job for a while and then given another province or district. Bumgardner named this dodge "the Lazy Susan." No Saigon official was taken off the wheel of corruption. He revolved on it.

The John Vann of years past had known that a Saigon government led by moral bankrupts and a Saigon armed forces commanded by thieving incompetents were doomed. He had raged against those who spent Vietnamese and American lives in the false hope of perpetuating them. The John Vann of years past would deceive himself and others without limit to satisfy his cravings. The deceptions had never affected his professional integrity. He had always kept professional truth in a separate compartment of his life, and he had preserved inviolate this central truth about the war. His willingness to hew to this truth had been one of the qualities that had made him stand out morally and intellectually from the other major figures of the war. He had never fooled himself about it nor fooled those he served. His crusades in Hau Nghia against corruption and for a strategy of social revolution and reform might have been quixotic, but they had been sincerely motivated by the knowledge that to wage war for the status quo was wrong and would fail.

The new John Vann's proposed solution to the corruption of Ninh was, incredibly, to try to have Ninh made a regimental commander. He went to see a contact he had recently acquired at the presidential palace in Saigon, Hoang Duc Nha, Ninh's younger brother. Nha had spent his lycée years living in Thieu's household before going to college in the United States. Thieu regarded him as a son. He was ostensibly commissioner general for information; he was actually a confidant whom Thieu relied on for advice on how to deal with the Americans. Vann invited Nha to dinner at La Cave, at this time the favorite French restaurant of the American community. He told Nha that his brother's military talents were being wasted in a province chief's job, that Ninh ought to be put at the head of a regiment. Nha was flattered that Vann would think so highly of his brother, as was Ninh when he heard what Vann had said. "He'll steal less with a regiment," Vann later explained to Warren Parker. The ploy didn't work. Ninh was left in Bac Lieu to continue enriching himself. When he was later given a special interprovincial command, considerably more important than a regiment, his entrepreneurship was to mature accordingly. He was to sell artillery barrages to imperiled garrisons; no bribe, no artillery when the Communists attacked.

Dan Ellsberg and David Halberstam were not the only old friends to notice that Vann had lost his compass. Col. Sam Wilson was hardly a man to become an antiwar dissenter. He was to complete his career in the 1970s as a lieutenant general and director of the Pentagon's Defense Intelligence Agency. Despite the organizational success of his Long An experiment and its contribution to the founding of CORDS, he had no faith that the United States would win by the time he came home in mid-1967. He kept his peace and kept soldiering, because the Army was his life; he commanded the 6th Special Forces Group at Fort Bragg and then the Military Assistance School there. Fort Bragg was one of Vann's regular lecture stops when he was on home leave. Wilson would watch with fascination as Vann, wearing a neck microphone, paced back and forth across the platform, enthralled himself and seeking to enthrall, melding anecdote and statistic and opinion and emotion into a performance that was more a stream of consciousness than a formal lecture. Many of his listeners were swayed. Wilson was not. Nothing Vann said convinced Wilson that anything essential had changed in South Vietnam.

Wilson decided Vann had invested so much of John Vann in the war that he had talked himself into believing he had to be winning. "John, you're there and I'm not and I'd like to agree with you," Wilson said after one performance, "but this tells me I can't." He tapped at his stomach.

The John Vann his old friends had known had disappeared into the war. Each year South Vietnam had become a more perfect place for him. The war satisfied him so completely that he could no longer look at it as something separate from himself. He had finally bent the truth about the war as he had bent other and lesser truths in the past.

Vann got his stars through Fred Weyand and a Saigon general of ordinary venality who thought that he could benefit from Vann's talents and was willing to be manipulated. Nixon's decision to send the U.S. Army and the ARVN into Cambodia at the end of April 1970 set Vann on his way.

The character of Norodom Sihanouk, the hereditary ruler of Cambodia, triggered the destruction of his country. He was a mercurial man, fond of intrigue for its own sake. Although he and his cronies were being well compensated for the use of Sihanoukville as a supply port, and the Vietnamese Communists publicly recognized the French-established frontiers of Cambodia, which the Saigon regime refused to do, and privately assured Sihanouk they would depart as soon as the war was over, his temperament would not permit him to wait. After Nixon began secret B-52 bombing of the Vietnamese sanctuaries in Cambodia in March 1969, Sihanouk tacitly encouraged the raids. He also incited right-wingers in his regime to demand that the Vietnamese evacuate the country. The first and most ironic result was a series of events that provoked Sihanouk's overthrow by his own prime minister, Gen. Lon Nol. Nixon then moved, hoping that a war in Cambodia would divert Hanoi's energies from the battle for South Vietnam. He encouraged Lon Nol, who had a poorly led wisp of an army, to go to war against the Vietnamese, a lunatic enterprise where the welfare of the Cambodian people was concerned and one that Lon Nol was witless enough to undertake. At the same moment, Nixon sought to buy additional time for Vietnamization by ordering U.S. and Saigon forces across the Cambodian frontier to tear up the Vietnamese sanctuaries and seize as much as possible of the arms and ammunition stockpiled there.

Cambodia was to suffer the cruelest consequences of the American war in Indochina. Sihanouk shifted to the left, installing himself in

Peking and forming a national front with Pol Pot and other leaders of the formerly insignificant Cambodian Communist movement. The Vietnamese had never encouraged the Cambodian Communists, known as the Khmer Rouge, because Cambodian bases were essential to the struggle for the South and they had no wish to disturb their arrangement with Sihanouk, who previously had persecuted his own Communists. Hanoi proceeded to train and equip a Cambodian Communist army to assume the burden of fighting Lon Nol. Sihanouk provided his name to rouse the masses.

Hundreds of thousands of Cambodians died in the subsequent civil war, in which the United States sustained Lon Nol with arms and lavish airpower, particularly B-52s. The Vietnamese soon lost control of the Khmer Rouge army they formed when China became its supplier. The Hanoi leaders discovered they had created a monster that would one day make war on Vietnam. Pol Pot and his adherents turned out to be zealots of an extremist form of Communism. They were to rule Cambodia after their victory in 1975 with a homicidal mysticism akin to that of Hitler. They emptied Phnom Penh and the other cities and towns by driving the inhabitants into the countryside, banned the national religion of Buddhism and murdered the monks, and killed educated persons as a group, including most of the country's doctors. The surviving urban dwellers and peasants were herded into labor camps to dig irrigation canals and till the rice fields. An estimated 1 to 1.5 million persons out of a population of roughly 7 million perished under Pol Pot from famine, forced labor, disease, and unremitting executions with hoes and axes.

While these consequences could not be foreseen in 1970, many found the casting of another nation into the furnace morally abhorrent. Laos had already been sacrificed for the sake of the Vietnam venture. The sections where the Ho Chi Minh Trail ran were not the only parts of Laos to feel American bombs. The towns and villages of Communist-held northern Laos were a desolation. The CIA had enticed the Hmong tribal people of the Laotian mountains, also called the Meo, to fight the Vietnamese and the Laotian Communists, the Pathet Lao, and killed off a quarter of the tribe in the process. The United States was sending twelve-year-old boys into battle in Laos. Three members of Kissinger's staff, William Watts, Roger Morris, and Anthony Lake, who had served in Vietnam as an aide to Lodge and as consul in Hue, resigned to protest the addition of Cambodia. Kissinger probably would have been dismissed had he too been opposed and resisted strongly, but he favored what Nixon was doing. Lake made a last plea on humanitarian grounds. "No one has a monopoly on compassion, Tony," Kissinger replied.

John Vann had once disapproved of cross-border marches as a diversion from the real problem. "If we go across the border, there will always be one more sanctuary just beyond the one we clean out," he told Philip Geyelin, the editorial-page editor of the *Washington Post*, in December 1967. With his new perspective he enthusiastically approved of Nixon's thrust into Cambodia, because he now also viewed it as a worthy purchase of time for the war in Vietnam.

Had Vann known the effect of the cross-border venture on Ramsey, his reaction would have been more complicated. He suspected that Ramsey was dead from disease or a bombing raid. He had been unable to obtain any firm information on Ramsey since the smuggled letter in February 1967 and a fragmentary report shortly afterward. He was careful not to convey his suspicion in the letters he sent once or twice a year to Ramsey's parents to encourage them.

Ramsey was in Cambodia, chained to a tree in a patch of jungle where he and seven other prisoners in his group had been marched by their captors to evade the American troops crossing the frontier. He was so weak from a two-thirds reduction in rations, from diarrhea, and from a renewed onslaught of beriberi that he could hardly raise his arms above his head to adjust the plastic sheeting that was his only shelter. He had survived "the Hell Hole," as he had named the bivouac camp in northern Binh Duong, he had beaten the worst of the beriberi and trekked to new camps astride the Cambodian border in the mountains of the lower Central Highlands, and he had escaped B-52s in the fall of 1969 that had driven the guards to yet another camp a few miles inside Cambodia—three consecutive days and nights of Arc Light strikes on the ridges and in the valleys all around him, fifteen raids in one night of trembling earth and thunder and huge fireballs, again three weeks later with no warning in darkness and rain, the bombs marching right up to the edge of a low ridge behind the prison compound, the concussion deafening, the shattered tree limbs and debris whirling through the camp—only to come to this hiding place with his captors to avoid the advancing American soldiers, having to dodge infantry firefights and artillery barrages and helicopter gunships on strafing and rocket runs as they fled. He was kept chained to the tree in the patch of jungle for five weeks, unshackled just to relieve himself and for a rare washing, before the guards felt secure enough to return to the camp.

By that time, Ramsey no longer had access to the chloroquinine tablets he had been taking to control the recurring malaria, and he had a fever. He was dizzy too, because the starvation diet had affected the balance mechanism in his inner ears, and he had night blindness. The moon did not look its normal color to him. It shone a bloody red. The march back to camp took fifteen hours. The guards had to lead him after darkness came. He fell six times in the last quarter of a mile.

Ngo Dzu, the ARVN general who was to help Vann gain his stars, had never expected to become a corps commander himself. A pleasant, round-faced man with a bit of a puckish manner, he had standard credentials for an ARVN officer. He was a Catholic born in Qui Nhon, the son of a province finance official in the colonial administration, and had been educated by French priests at a boys' school in Hue. Dzu was intelligent and enjoyed hard work, despite a mild heart condition. He was not a courageous man, and he was not particularly greedy or adept at scheming. He had not gained a reputation as one of the rare fighting generals in the ARVN, like Du Quoc Dong, a Southerner from Kien Hoa who led the paratroop division, or Ngo Quang Truong, Dong's former deputy, who was currently 1st Division commander at Hue. Nor had he cultivated sufficient ties of political cronyism and corruption to place himself on the common road to senior command. During the latter years of Dzu's career he had served in a series of staff jobs at JGS, rising by his industriousness to the most important, deputy chief of staff for operations. As such, he had supervised ARVN planning for the push into Cambodia. When Brig. Gen. Nguyen Viet Thanh, the IV Corps commander, an unusual man whom Vann liked because he was relatively free of corruption, was killed in a midair helicopter collision two days after the operation began, Creighton Abrams put pressure on Thieu to replace him with the general most familiar with the plan. Ngo Dzu went to IV Corps as acting commanding general.

After Dzu had been in command for a month, Vann pointed out that if he wished to keep the corps, he would have to do more than supervise a charge into Cambodia. He was going to have to make a name for himself quickly by demonstrating that he could get on with the pacification of the Mekong Delta and do so with style. Dzu had met Vann and learned to respect him back in 1967 when Dzu had been the JGS staff officer for pacification. Vann had a scheme to crack one of the remaining Viet Cong strongholds in the northern Delta, a section of Kien Hoa Province, by putting a regiment right into the middle of it. Dzu accepted the scheme without a quibble. Vann had another scheme to break up the Communist bases in the rugged Seven Mountains region in the far-western Delta. It combined B-52 strikes with air-dropped tear gas and night infantry assaults. Dzu bought that idea too.

Vann and Dzu began spending their evenings laying out the details at the corps commander's house in Can Tho and the next day in the field executing their plans. Dzu's wife and eleven children had stayed in Saigon, and he appreciated having something with which to keep busy at night. Aside from the benefits he hoped to derive, he liked working with an American who was direct and informal and who treated him as an individual. Dzu was passing most of his time with Vann rather than with the officer who was officially Dzu's senior advisor—Dzu's counterpart and Vann's superior, Maj. Gen. Hal McCown, the commanding general of the Delta Military Assistance Command. This was precisely what Vann wanted, because there was a motive behind his campaign to capture Ngo Dzu.

A civilian official had never in American history assumed the position of a general and commanded U.S. military forces in the field in wartime. Komer had been a civilian general, but he had not controlled U.S. Army and Air Force units. Vann intended to become the exception. His game was to have Dzu request that he become Dzu's senior advisor when McCown's tour ended in the spring of 1971. Vann then hoped to convince Abrams that as senior advisor to the ARVN commander he should have authority over all American activities in IV Corps, including the U.S. aviation and other support elements assigned to the Delta Military Assistance Command, with the chief of DMAC serving as one of his deputies. Vann's objective encompassed more than control of the dwindling number of U.S. military men in IV Corps. He planned, through the hold he was acquiring over Dzu, to also exercise behind-the-curtain control of the Saigon forces there. In effect, John Vann would become the commanding general of the Mekong Delta.

The plan went awry when Thieu shuffled corps commanders in late August 1970. Vann had made Dzu look good enough so that Abrams was after Thieu to let him keep IV Corps, but for reasons of his own, Thieu did not want to leave Dzu in the Delta. He sent him to Pleiku to be the II Corps commander. Now Vann had to contrive a way to get himself transferred to the Central Highlands and the Central Coast provinces of II Corps and take the place of the U.S. Army general who was Dzu's counterpart and senior advisor there.

The return to the war in the fall of 1970 of Vann's friend and admirer Fred Weyand made Vann's audacious scheme possible and gave him an opportunity for glory he would never have had in the Delta. Weyand had himself twice escaped professional oblivion in the two years since he had completed his tour at II Field Force and gone home in August 1968. Westmoreland, as Army chief of staff, had not rewarded him with the position others like Bunker thought Weyand had earned for saving Saigon at Tet. Rather than giving Weyand one of the mainline Army staff positions that lead to advancement, Westmoreland had designated him chief of the Office of Reserve Components, the active-duty general who oversees the National Guard and the Army Reserve. Lodge had rescued Weyand after he had been appointed Nixon's negotiator at the peace talks in January 1969. Philip Habib, Lodge's deputy in Paris and former political counselor in Saigon, had suggested they bring Weyand to Paris to serve in the newly created post of military advisor to the delegation. That job had played out too after Lodge resigned in frustration. Nixon was offering the Vietnamese the same proposition Johnson had, mutual withdrawal, and Lodge got no further than Harriman and Vance did. The death of Ho Chi Minh in September 1969 caused no weakening in the Vietnamese stance. The collective leadership Ho had spent so many years preparing to succeed him carried on as if he were still among them. For public relations purposes, Nixon eventually replaced Lodge with another elder statesman, David Bruce, but began to rely on the secret talks Kissinger started in Paris with Le Duc Tho, Hanoi's chief negotiator. By the summer of 1970, Weyand was back in Washington in another post of no promise. Unlike Westmoreland, Abrams had taken due note of Weyand's performance at Tet, perhaps in part because it in no way reflected on his own. The two men had also discovered they liked each other during the year when Abrams had been Westmoreland's deputy. The personalities were complementary, the calm Weyand looking up to and yet not easily thrown off balance by the quick-tempered Abrams. Creighton Abrams needed a new deputy in a hurry in the fall of 1970. To his surprise, Weyand suddenly found himself with orders for Saigon, and Vann had a patron among the kingmakers in his time of need.

Vann met Dzu secretly in Dalat in early 1971. The Army general who was Dzu's counterpart in II Corps was scheduled to end his tour in May. Vann told Dzu to simply confirm, if anyone asked, that Dzu wanted Vann to be his new senior advisor. Vann said that he would handle the rest from his end. Dzu could think of nothing better and was delighted to be in on the plot.

Weyand was not a man to tilt at bureaucratic windmills. That he agreed to act as Vann's advocate was a measure of how much Vann's stature had grown and of how much the circumstances of the war had changed. As Weyand presented Vann's case to Abrams in April 1971, the moment was approaching with disquieting swiftness when the Saigon side would have to stand and hold against a full-scale NVA offensive and American help would be limited to advisors, Army helicopter units, and the fixed-wing airpower of the Air Force and the Navy. Nixon's withdrawals had reduced the number of U.S. military men in South Vietnam by half, to about 270,000, from the April 1969 peak of 543,500.

The thrust into Cambodia had bought some time. This widening of the war had lit such a bonfire of antiwar protest, however, that Nixon had had no choice but to accelerate the rate of withdrawal. By April 1972, there were to be fewer than 70,000 Americans in the South, virtually all advisors and aviation and support personnel. The Vietnamese Communists were rebuilding and enlarging their Cambodian border bases. The antiwar protests had forced Nixon to pull the American troops out of Cambodia after a couple of months, and the NVA and the newly created Khmer Rouge guerrillas had chased Lon Nol's little army into the interior.

Hanoi was also overcoming the loss of Sihanoukville as a supply port by lengthening the road webwork of the Ho Chi Minh Trail. Johnson's 1968 halt in the bombing of the North had not affected raids on the southeast Laos corridor where the Trail ran, and air attacks on it had intensified during 1969 and 1970. The Air Force had raised the "truck kill" in the corridor by combining a system of sensors McNamara had created with C-119 Stinger and C-130 Spectre gunships carrying 40mm Bofors cannons and extremely rapid-fire 20mm Vulcan guns that spewed out 2,500 rounds a minute. The planes still could not get enough trucks to make a difference. In the hope of postponing the showdown for at least two more years, Abrams sent the ARVN into Laos along Route 9 from Khe Sanh in February 1971 to seize the road center at Tchepone and sever the Trail. The result was ominous, a debacle in which more than 3,000 Saigon soldiers died. The showdown could not be put off much longer.

All of these circumstances were auspicious for Vann. He would not be ruffling cocky major generals who had just got a division and were playing for a third star. The number of Americans in II Corps had been drawn down to the point where the U.S. Field Force headquarters for the region was being reduced to a military assistance command under a two-star general. Abrams's opinion of Vann had sufficiently altered and he was open-minded enough to listen when Weyand spoke up for his friend, but the question arose of how military men would react to taking orders from a renegade lieutenant colonel turned civilian. Weyand remembered that the question had arisen in III Corps in 1967 when CORDS was established and the military and civilian advisors were merged. He had noticed then that the doubt disappeared as soon as

Vann took charge as Dep/CORDS. The good officers responded to his leadership. Weyand assured Abrams that the same thing would happen in II Corps.

The most important argument Weyand could make for Vann was his influence over Dzu and his unparalleled experience with the Saigon forces. Abrams and others at the top believed the forthcoming NVA offensive would have two focal points. The first would be the natural one of the DMZ region. The second would be the Central Highlands where Dzu now commanded, because the Highlands were far up the Communist supply network at the original terminus of the Ho Chi Minh Trail. Everything possible had to be done to pacify II Corps and ready the ARVN units there for the big battle. What American had better prepared himself for this task than John Vann?

On May 15, 1971, the renegade lieutenant colonel left Can Tho to become Creighton Abrams's general over the mountains of the Highlands and the old Viet Minh redoubts in the rice deltas of the Central Coast. In keeping with his new dignity he added a tie to the short-sleeved sport shirt and slacks that were his working uniform. He could not literally be called a general, even though he held a major general's place and had two metaphorical stars on his shoulders, and so he was called director. The Second Regional Assistance Command (SRAC) he was to direct was redesignated Second Regional Assistance Group (SRAG). The change was necessary to avoid controversy and to get around the legal question of whether a civilian official can exercise command. Only a military man can wield court-martial authority, the legal power to enforce orders. For the same reasons, Vann was given a "deputy for military functions" who bore the title of Commanding General U.S. Army Forces Military Region 2. (Military Region 2 was the alternate designation for II Corps.) Vann initially hoped to acquire a major general as a deputy. He could then have awarded himself a third star. He had to settle for a brigadier.

However many stars Vann possessed, he was the boss at last. He had a letter of instruction from Abrams saying that he was. The language was a bit vague, once more for bureaucratic reasons, but John Vann would see that it was interpreted his way.

The civilian general was to be tested before he had long to enjoy his stars. When he went home for Christmas in mid-December 1971, he arranged with Weyand and George Jacobson, who had come into his own reward by succeeding Colby as head of CORDS, to send him an alert message in January so that he would have an excuse to cut short his leave. He expected the NVA to attack in February, and he wanted to be ready.

For the first time in his six years of coming home to visit he did not sleep at the house in Littleton. He ate his meals there with Mary Jane and the family and naturally went there for the Christmas celebration, but he slept at the nearby home of Mary Allen and Doris Moreland, Mary Jane's mother and sister, who were both widows by this time and had moved to Littleton some years before.

Vann and Mary Jane had been divorced, at her request, in October 1971. Logically there was no more reason for Mary Jane to want to divorce John Vann in 1971 than there had been in most other years of their quarter century of marriage. He had never ceased to support her and the children, if always stingily, and her prospects of remarriage were not good. She had also known about his Vietnamese daughter since 1968, when he had, probably deliberately, left a letter from Annie which mentioned the child at the Littleton house. Mary Jane's response had been to offer to adopt the little girl if he would give up the war and return. The accumulated weight of anger and frustration and a feeling that divorce was the only way she could lash out at him had finally driven her to demand one. He had opposed the divorce at first, because the form of a marriage he had with Mary Jane suited him so well. He had then decided he would be better off with his legal freedom from her in exchange for his share of the house, modest alimony, and child-support payments for Tommy, seventeen, and Peter, sixteen, who were still living at home.

He remained a man who wanted a wife. He was planning to marry Annie. He did not, however, intend to give up Lee. She was shamed and disappointed when he told her of his new marriage plans and of the existence of the child. He was gradually taming her to accept second place as a permanent mistress. He continued to succeed in keeping Annie ignorant of Lee.

His relationship with Dan Ellsberg had become increasingly compli-cated. He had been enraged at Ellsberg after the publication of the Pentagon Papers in June 1971, cursing him to mutual acquaintances and shouting that Ellsberg, who was being prosecuted by the Nixon admin-istration for conspiracy, theft, and a violation of the espionage statute, ought to be thrown into jail for treason. Vann was not angry at Ellsberg's wholesale breach of security regulations. He was incensed at the assault Ellsberg was attempting on his war. Yet he did not want to forsake the friendship. "Can't say I'm in agreement with your way of making your point—but you sure as hell created a stir," he wrote Ellsberg that fall. Six different investigators from four agencies had come to his head-quarters in Pleiku to question him, he said, and he had seen to it that none of them "made his trip worthwhile." He was lying. He apparently cooperated with the investigators. He also passed tips to Kissinger on how the administration ought to proceed against Ellsberg.

On his way home to Littleton for this Christmas of 1971, he landed in Los Angeles so that he could see his brother Gene, who was living in nearby Redlands, California. He called Ellsberg on the phone from Gene's house, and they had a long talk. Ellsberg described for Vann in confidence the defense strategy his lawyers had developed for Ellsberg's forthcoming trial in Los Angeles. Later in this holiday leave, when Vann flew from Colorado to Washington for his usual round of calls, he stopped at the Pentagon office of J. Fred Buzhardt, then the general counsel of the Defense Department and subsequently one of Nixon's lawyers in the Watergate affair. Buzhardt was gathering information for the prosecution of Ellsberg. Vann spent an hour and a half passing along Ellsberg's defense strategy and suggesting how the administration might defeat it.

Vann did not intend the game to end as the betrayal of a friend. After the message from Weyand and Jacobson came in January and Vann was on his way back to South Vietnam and to battle, he stopped in San Francisco. He and Ellsberg met there for several hours to talk about the war and Ellsberg's trial. Ellsberg asked Vann to testify for him, because Vann would carry such credibility with a jury. "I'll say anything you want," Vann replied. The promise was one he undoubtedly meant to keep, but he would not have known what he was going to say until just before he sat down in the witness chair.

John Vann planned to defeat his enemy as he had seen Walton Walker defeat the North Koreans in the Pusan Perimeter. He would not throw away infantry as Westmoreland had done in sending men against fortified positions in the wilderness. The roles had been reversed. To win the war, the Vietnamese Communists had to come to him, and when they advanced out of the mountains, he would break them on his strong-points. The apparent objective of the NVA offensive in II Corps was Kontum, a garrison and trading center with a population of about 25,000, the capital of the province of the same name and the northernmost town of substance in the Highlands. Kontum was guarded to the north by the regimental base at Tan Canh on a plateau near the district headquarters of Dak To twenty-five miles up the ascending asphalt ribbon of Route 14. Just below Tan Canh and to the west of it, a series of ridgelines ran in a north-south direction, parallel to Route 14 and back down toward Kontum. These were known collectively as Rocket Ridge because they had been the recipients over the years of so many of the NVA's 122mm rockets. The U.S. Army had built a string of fortified artillery positions, called fire support bases or fire bases for short, down Rocket Ridge to shield the road and the northwest approaches to Kontum and had bequeathed these to the ARVN. Before the Vietnamese Communists could attack Kontum, they first had to overrun Tan Canh or crack the firebase line along Rocket Ridge.

Hanoi gathered about 35,000 men for the showdown under one of its best generals, Hoang Minh Thao, a protégé of Giap's who was destined to become chief of staff of the Vietnamese Army. Thao had commanded the B-3 Front, the NVA corps for the Highlands, since 1966. He was given two regular infantry divisions, one of which had just infiltrated from the North at the turn of the year, and he had the equivalent of a third infantry division in independent regiments. The infantry were assisted by other regiments of sappers and combat engineers and backed by artillery regiments equipped with captured American 105mm guns, Soviet-model 130mm guns, 120mm mortars, the formidable rockets, and an array of antiaircraft weapons.

Thao marshaled his troops in the triborder area beyond Tan Canh and Rocket Ridge where Laos, Cambodia, and Vietnam meet. The region was another of those primeval fastnesses of the Annamites that the NVA had transformed into a bastion they called Base Area 609. It was a place of dread for the Saigon soldiers, as it had become for their American predecessors. On Hill 875 and neighboring precipitous ridges in Base Area 609, 287 men of the 173rd Airborne Brigade and the 4th Infantry Division had died and more than 1,000 had been wounded in a gruesome border battle in November 1967 while Westmoreland was proclaiming victory in Washington. The Plei Trap Valley farther south had been the scene of so many ambushes that only an intrepid few from the Special Forces and the long-range patrols of the ARVN Airborne would venture there anymore.

When the offensive did not begin in February, Vann mistakenly thought he might have forestalled it with dozens of B-52 strikes he was laying along the approach routes and by incessant bombardment with tactical jets. The Hanoi leadership wanted to coordinate the attacks in II Corps with the focal points of the offensive in other corps regions, and the preparations for all required time.

The NVA made their preparations boldly on this occasion. Sound travels far in the mountains at night, and light can be seen a long way off. The advisors on the fire bases could hear the bulldozers of the NVA engineers widening the old French tracks and cutting new roads, and they could see the headlights of the trucks hauling food and ammunition and towing artillery into position. The 2nd NVA Division closed on Tan Canh from the northwest while the 320th Division maneuvered from the west against Rocket Ridge, the Communist infantry sheltering as they came in the great massif of Chu Mom Ray (Mom Ray Mountain) that the American soldiers had named, not with affection, Big Mama.

On March 30, 1972, in the general assault the Americans called the Easter 1972 Offensive because Easter Sunday came three days later, NVA troops led by tanks surged out of the Demilitarized Zone against Camp Carroll and the other positions the Marines had won in I Corps and turned over to the ARVN there. By that time several of the fire bases in Vann's area along Rocket Ridge were under siege. A few days later, there was an assault where no one expected an attack. Vann's old acquaintances in III Corps, the 5th and 9th VC divisions and the 7th NVA, appeared out of Cambodia, overran the district headquarters of Loc Ninh in the rubber-plantation country at the top of Route 13, one of the main roads to Saigon, and moved down on the province town of An Loc sixty miles from the South Vietnamese capital. They too were led by tanks.

Vann's plan worked to perfection in the beginning. Hoang Minh Thao tried to unhinge the Rocket Ridge line by knocking out the strongest position near the bottom of it, Fire Base Delta, manned by a battalion of ARVN paratroops from one of two airborne brigades Dzu had obtained from the Joint General Staff as reinforcements. Thao encountered the lieutenant who had kept the riflemen in the fight on the lonely hilltops beyond Masan, Korea, in September 1950. "Rogue's Gallery" (Vann's radio call sign in II Corps) happened to arrive over Delta at the break of dawn on April 3, 1972, with a flight of three slick-ship Hueys and two Cobra gunship helicopters. The NVA attackers had just overwhelmed the paratroops in the northern part of the base and were battling their way down trench lines to conquer the rest of it. The Cobra was a slimmed-down advance on the Huey, roughly twice as fast and built to carry firepower. Pods on stubby wings held dozens of rockets, an extremely rapid-fire 7.62mm "Minigun" shot streams of bullets, and an automatic launcher hurled 40mm grenades. Vann had come to rescue the crew of a Chinook that had been shot down while resupplying Delta four days earlier. In an instant he turned rescue of crew into rescue of fire base.

He sent the Cobras slashing into the follow-on groups of Communist infantry who were running through the wire to help their comrades already inside. He took charge of the artillery at the brigade command post back at Vo Dinh on Route 14, of the Stinger and Spectre fixed-wing gunships with the Bofors cannons and Vulcan guns, and of the fighter-bombers arriving from the carriers off the coast and from the Air Force squadrons that had been shifted to fields in Thailand. While the Saigon paratroops counterattacked, Vann destroyed every attempt by the NVA to reinforce the couple of hundred assault troops who had fought their way inside.

Lt. Huynh Van Cai, Vann's ARVN aide who was flying with him, had seen combat. He had been an infantry platoon leader with the regiment at Tan Canh for eight months. He had never seen a battle from a helicopter before. He was fascinated by the scene below of men rushing forward and being tossed into the air by bombs and shells, and falling as the bullets cut them down.

The NVA inside Delta were wiped out by the afternoon, but the base was still going to have to be abandoned soon for lack of ammunition, water, and medical supplies. Vann announced that he personally would resupply it. The paratroop battalion commander, despite his need, radioed that Vann would be killed. The NVA had sited 12.7mm and electrically rotated 14.5mm antiaircraft machine guns around Delta and had a flak cannon whose shells burst in the air with a black puff. That Vann's helicopter had not been shot down while dancing high above the base since dawn to direct the artillery and air strikes was already a sufficient miracle for the day. The airborne brigade commander at Vo Dinh and his advisor, Maj. Peter Kama, the tall Hawaiian who had been one of Vann's captains at My Tho, told him he was being foolhardy. "I'm experienced at this," Vann said.

The model helicopter Vann now used was the latest Scout type the Bell Aircraft Corporation had produced for the Army, officially designated the OH-58 Kiowa and commonly known as the Ranger from its commercial name, JetRanger. The Ranger was a sleek little craft with a swept-back fuselage and a nose shaped like the snout of a shark, the perfect helicopter for Vann because it combined the speed of a Huey with the agility of a small machine. There were two seats in front for pilot and copilot and a space behind, with separate side doors, for cargo or two passengers. Vann always rode in the copilot's seat so that he could fly when he wanted or take the controls if the pilot was hit. The pilot flying him that day was a brave Cajun from Louisiana, Chief Warrant Officer Paul Arcement. Vann also had Cai to help with the resupply. Vann had decided when he came to II Corps that an ARVN aide who spoke English would be more appropriate than a U.S. Army aide and he could then dispense with an interpreter. Dzu had selected Cai, the son of a shopkeeper in Duc Hoa in Hau Nghia. The post-Tet mobilization had caught him because he had flunked out of the Saigon College of Pharmacy in grief over the death of his mother and he was too poor to buy false exemption papers. Cai was honest, without fear, and devoted to Vann. Where Vann went, he went too.

Vann supervised the loading of the supplies into the Ranger at the airborne brigade command post at Vo Dinh. He had noted the positions of the NVA machine guns earlier in the day. He showed Arcement a path to take in and out across the treetops that would present the most elusive target. As soon as the Ranger flashed over the barbed wire of the perimeter, Vann and Cai pitched out the cases of M-16 ammunition, grenades, claymore mines, flares, canisters of water, and medical supplies for the scores of wounded paratroopers. Then Arcement tossed the helicopter into a steep climbing turn and twisted away back over the trees to Vo Dinh for another load.

When the duty officers in the II Corps Tactical Operations Center down at Pleiku figured out what was going on, they alerted Dzu and Vann's staff. The underground bunker next to the headquarters building on the hill above the town filled with officers listening to the voices over the radio as the little Ranger loaded again and again at Vo Dinh and ran the gauntlet of machine guns to the fire base, six times before dark. "No Vietnamese general would do that," Dzu said. "Not even a U.S. general would do that." Fire Base Delta had enough sustenance to hold out through the night, and the next day relieving airborne battalions broke the siege.

Vann's continuing ability to manage Dzu was a major source of his confidence that he would defeat the NVA. He had put Dzu in unique debt to him the previous summer by rescuing Dzu from an accusation of heroin trafficking. The ARVN general whom Dzu had replaced had sought revenge for losing his job by concocting a dossier purporting to prove that Dzu was a narcotics smuggler. He palmed the dossier off on a visiting American congressman, who subsequently announced at a congressional hearing in Washington that Ngo Dzu was one of the heroin lords of South Vietnam. The accusation came at a time when narcotics peddling to American soldiers had burst into a notorious scandal and Thieu was being squeezed by Bunker to take some action. He decided Dzu would make a fine goat to sacrifice to the American public and its politicians and was going to relieve and disgrace him.

John Vann had not been about to part with his investment. Dzu also swore to him that dope was not among his sources of graft. Vann believed him. As Vann explained to George Jacobson, narcotics was such a jealously guarded racket that the senior generals and their Chinese businessmen partners would never have let anyone as far down the ladder as Dzu chisel in on the profits. Vann saved Dzu by organizing a press campaign for him to refute the charges. He drafted a statement for Dzu to issue and coached him on how to answer questions. He set up a televised press conference, arranged subsequent interviews to keep up the momentum, and made statements on Dzu's behalf himself. Dzu was astounded at Vann's ability to assemble reporters and amazed that any American would protect him like this. "He acted as if he was my brother," Dzu said. His feeling of obligation to Vann tended to reinforce his original belief that he could promote himself through Vann's talents. Dzu did not always do what Vann wanted, but he did so enough of the time that members of Dzu's staff who did not like him mocked him as "the slave of John Paul Vann."

Vann's victory at Fire Base Delta raised his confidence to a sense of near infallibility. He dictated a four-and-a-half-page "Memorandum For: My Friends" to Frenchy Zois and had her make copies and mail them to Sir Robert Thompson and Joe Alsop, to other important men in Washington like Melvin Laird, and to friends elsewhere. He prophesied disaster for the NVA on all fronts in South Vietnam, not just on his own, and said that by the time the offensive was over the position of the Vietnamese Communists would be weakened in Laos and Cambodia too. In his December 1969 meeting with Nixon he had been prudent enough to warn that the Saigon side might "have to give up some territory and some population" in the face of an all-out offensive. He eschewed caution now, publicly committing himself not to give ground. The struggle on his front in II Corps was "going to be a difficult fight and a lot of soldiers are yet to die," he said, but "we expect to hold our major positions, to include Dak To District . . . and Tan Canh." The Saigon side would also retain "the hard-won pacification gains in Binh Dinh" on the Central Coast, where Vann had concentrated since the summer of 1971 on liquidating the Viet Cong and firming the regime's hold over the unruly northern districts. "I stand ready to be challenged on the foregoing analysis by the events that take place subsequent to this date," he said in conclusion. His memorandum was dated April 12, 1972. The challenge had begun three days before.

The trouble started in that other battleground of II Corps over on the Central Coast, in those old Viet Minh strongholds in the narrow rice deltas of northern Binh Dinh that Vann boasted of pacifying in his memorandum. The place seemed insignificant, and Vann thought he had the situation under control. The spot was a former fire support base of the Air Cav called Landing Zone Pony near the western end of the serpentine Hoai An Valley that coils back into the mountains about forty miles northwest of Qui Nhon. Pony was garrisoned by a battalion of RF. The base came under bombardment and ground assault on April 9 and fell the next day. The attackers, not yet fully identified by Vann, contradicted his belief that North Vietnamese troops would find themselves as alien in South Vietnam as American soldiers had been. They were a regiment of the 3rd NVA or "Yellow Star" Division, the same amalgam of NVA infantry and Viet Cong regulars that Hal Moore's 3rd Brigade of the Air Cav had fought in 1966 on this same battleground. The Yellow Star Division was the real phoenix of Binh Dinh, destroyed and risen more times than the intelligence officers on the Saigon and U.S. side would have wanted to know.

First one and then two battalions of the 40th ARVN Regiment from Landing Zone English near Bong Son town to the north, reinforced by a company of M-113s, were sent down to recapture Pony and prevent the NVA from advancing up the valley to Hoai An District headquarters. Vann flew to Hoai An on April 11 and spent the night in the district compound. In January he had managed to have an acquaintance of many years, Col. Nguyen Van Chuc, an eccentric ARVN engineer who practiced yoga and went about his work with the vigor of an ambitious American, installed as province chief of Binh Dinh. Chuc flew up from Qui Nhon, the province capital. Vann liked the 40th Regiment commander, Col. Tran Hieu Duc, who set up a command post in the district compound to direct the counterattack. Duc had been an enthusiastic participant in the pacification campaign and seemed a good organizer. General Dzu had just obtained a promotion for him in March at Vann's urging. There were briefings that night and a planning session. Vann encouraged the ARVN officers and their American advisors and left the next morning feeling good.

Duc would not fight. He made no attempt to regain Pony or to hold any of the high ground farther down the valley. Instead, he let his battalions keep falling back toward the district center. His advisor, Lt. Col. David Schorr, could put no spine into him. Chuc, who had been given control over all ARVN and territorial troops in the province at Vann's insistence on unity of command, could do nothing with Duc either. Vann returned to Hoai An twice, landing under mortar fire, each time to no avail. There were twenty-nine PF platoons in the district. They were deserting.

Nor was there tranquillity in other parts of Binh Dinh. This province in which pacification had supposedly progressed so far suddenly became hostile. Two and possibly three battalions of NVA sappers moved down from Quang Ngai and raised havoc under the guidance of the local Viet Cong. The northernmost district headquarters of Tam Quan was struck. Bridges were blown up hither and yon, two right outside Qui Nhon, and outposts were attacked and harassed everywhere. RF and PF began to desert in other districts besides Hoai An.

On April 18, a week after the encouraging council of war, Duc had no more high ground to give away to the NVA. He announced that night that he was abandoning Hoai An. "Friendly troops may bug out at any time. Request guidance. If friendlies bug out before guidance arrives, will bug out with them," Maj. Gary Hacker, the acting district advisor (he was filling in for another officer on leave), radioed to Qui Nhon. During the day, Duc had let the Communist soldiery have the district police station on a hill about 500 yards from the hill where the headquarters compound was located. With the compound under full observation, the NVA were belting it in leisurely fashion with mortars and recoilless rifles. The place stank of dead ARVN soldiers no one would bury.

When every attempt to persuade Duc to stay failed, Vann had Dzu authorize a withdrawal for noon on April 19. He preferred to have Duc leave in organized fashion rather than bolt. The NVA were interdicting the secondary road from the district center back to Route 1, but not enough to prevent a breakout. The plan was to have the armored personnel carriers lead the column, with the trucks and jeeps and marching infantry behind. There were about forty wounded from the two battalions and the district forces. They were to be carried out in the M-113s. A pair of Cobra gunships would orbit the column, strafing and rocketing, while a command-and-control Huey would hover higher overhead to guide protective artillery and fighter-bomber strikes.

Vann could not come down from the Highlands to supervise the evacuation, because he was starting to have trouble with Rocket Ridge. The NVA had switched from attempting to unhinge the fire-base line to cracking the middle of it and had partially succeeded. They had conquered a position called Fire Base Charlie by alternating artillery barrages with infantry assaults until the ARVN paratroops had run so low on ammunition they had been forced to break out, leaving their seriously wounded behind in the bunkers as they went. Of the 471 ARVN officers and men in the defending airborne battalion, only about half got back to Vo Dinh, and half of these were walking wounded.

Vann explained the Hoai An withdrawal plan over the radio on the morning of the 19th to Lt. Col. Jack Anderson, who was to fly the command and control Huey.

About half an hour before the noon departure time, a couple of mortar rounds exploded near the convoy assembly point below the district compound. Most of the wounded had still not been loaded into the armored personnel carriers. Duc jumped into the nearest APC with his staff and took off up the road. The rest of the M-113s and trucks and jeeps raced after him. The district chief, an ARVN major, raced off in his jeep too after kicking his deputy for administration out of the vehicle to make room for his refrigerator. Some NVA were waiting in ambush in a nearby hamlet, but Duc's M-113 and the district chief's jeep were among the vehicles that crashed through.

Colonel Schorr could have left with Duc, but he did not want to abandon Major Hacker and Lt. Thomas Eisenhower, the assistant district advisor, who had been conscientiously burning their classified documents and destroying the radio and other equipment up at the compound. He waited for them to run down the hill. They fled east over the paddy dikes toward Route 1. All around them, ARVN soldiers were reverting to instant peasants, tossing away M-16 rifles and helmets and combat web gear and stripping off boots and uniforms to run across the paddies in bare feet and undershorts. The advisors had not gone far when Schorr fell with a bullet in the leg from the NVA who were chasing them. While Eisenhower gave him first aid, Hacker and two Kit Carson Scouts, Viet Cong defectors who had originally been hired as mercenaries by the U.S. Army and were now serving as bodyguards for the advisors, tried to fend off their pursuers. With so many ARVN undressed, Hacker had difficulty telling friend from foe. He began shooting at any Vietnamese approaching him with a weapon who was not wearing an ARVN uniform. Some of the NVA soldiers started to crawl forward while their companions laid down covering fire.

Colonel Anderson in the command-and-control Huey had been listening to what was happening on the ground; as he flew toward Hoai An up a neighboring valley, he had tuned his radio to the frequency of the portable radio Schorr was carrying. The Cobra gunships would not arrive until noon, too late for the advisors. If Anderson attempted a rescue and was shot down, he and his copilot and crew would also be killed or captured.

The aviation units were the sole combat element of the U.S. Army that did not come apart under the stress of the war in Vietnam. Nearly 6,000 helicopter pilots and crew members perished, but the Army airmen never cracked. Whether it was the oneness of man and acrobatic flying machine, whether it was the equally shared risk of officer pilot and enlisted crew member, whatever the reason, the men of the helicopters kept their discipline and their spirit. As the French parachutists became the paladins of that earlier war, so the U.S. Army aviators became the dark knights of this one. Almost all career aviators served two tours in Vietnam. Anderson was on his second. He was a tall, big-boned Westerner, the commanding officer of the 7th Squadron of the 17th (Air) Cavalry, and his radio call sign befitted him: it was Ruthless Six. He raised Schorr on the radio and asked for the advisors' position. He told his copilot and gunners over the intercom that they were going down.

Anderson started to draw fire as soon as he began his descent; he was fifty to seventy-five feet above the rice fields before he spotted the little band, despite a smoke grenade one of the advisors set off to guide him. The helicopter vibrated from the thumping recoil of the .50 caliber machine guns Anderson had installed for his door gunners to replace the 7.62mm guns a Huey normally carried. He was glad he had decided to mount the great machine guns. His gunners knew how to handle them. If they got in and out on this trip, Anderson thought, it would be because the .50s spoke with such authority. He hovered on a dike while Eisenhower helped Schorr aboard and Hacker and the two Kit Carson Scouts then vaulted inside. A couple of mud-covered ARVN in their skivvies appeared out of the paddy and scrambled aboard too. The door gunners were killing NVA soldiers twenty-five yards away.

When they reached the airstrip at Landing Zone English near Bong Son town, they counted the bullet holes in the aircraft. There were only nine. The crew chief, who served as one of the gunners, had several pieces of shrapnel in his leg from a round that had struck an ammunition box and exploded a .50 caliber shell.

Over the next twelve days the two larger districts of Bong Son and Tam Quan went in the same wretched way Hoai An had. The whole of northern Binh Dinh, where 200,000 people lived, fell to the Communists. Vann took time he could not spare from the battle for the Highlands to fly down to the coast and exhort: another Canute vainly commanding the waves to stand still. Thousands of RF and PF deserted. The two remaining battalions of the 40th Regiment would not even defend their home base at LZ English. The ARVN military police forced the wounded to die on the airstrip at English while they sold seats on the VNAF medical evacuation helicopters to deserters. They split the proceeds with the VNAF pilots before the helicopters took off.

* * *

All the while, a bigger crash was in the making in the Highlands. Dzu had, with Vann's encouragement, invested the equivalent of an ARVN division, roughly 10,000 men, in the defense of Tan Canh. He and Vann had placed the headquarters of the 22nd Division with two of its infantry regiments there and reinforced them with separate infantry battalions, the 22nd's own armored cavalry regiment, and most of a second independent regiment of armor. Because Tan Canh was the most forward position, the alignment was a gamble of the highest order. If the Rocket Ridge line broke and Route 14 running south from Tan Canh to Kontum was cut, these forces around Tan Canh with their accompanying artillery, tanks, APCs, trucks, and other fighting gear would be enveloped and isolated. If the Tan Canh defenses themselves cracked, it would be impossible with troops as unsteady as the ARVN to conduct an orderly retreat down a single mountain road. The division would disintegrate. More was at risk than an ARVN division. If either eventuality occurred, the forces needed to hold Kontum would be lost.

Vann's military deputy, Brig. Gen. George Wear, told him he was courting a catastrophe. His chief of staff, Col. Joseph Pizzi, a shrewd soldier who had tried to warn of the Chinese peril in North Korea in 1950 while serving as the estimating officer in Eighth Army intelligence, said the same thing. The prudent course would have been to organize a battlefield in depth and seek to exhaust the offensive by withdrawing to successive lines of defense, punishing the NVA for each one. This would have meant giving up Tan Canh and nearby Dak To District headquarters at some point with the hope of later regaining them. Vann was not in a mood to listen. "The sons of bitches will have to fight or die," he said of the ARVN. Wear and Pizzi persisted. Vann said he would raise their fear at his next Saigon strategy meeting with Abrams.

On his return, he said the answer was no, that Tan Canh and Dak To had to be held for political reasons. The evidence is that he deceived Wear and Pizzi and never did state their case with conviction because he had already committed himself privately to retaining Tan Canh and Dak To and was about to commit himself publicly in his April 12 memorandum. When Abrams came to Pleiku on a rare visit, Wear argued emotionally in a meeting with Vann and Dzu and the commanding general. He told Abrams the Tan Canh position was "a pending disaster." Vann, who was fond of Wear and was attempting to get him his second star, suggested with irritation that they discuss the matter in private afterward. Abrams was also displeased. He seemed to regard such fears as defeatist.

The gamble at Tan Canh was rendered yet more uncomfortable by the division commander there, Col. Le Duc Dat, whom Vann had helped to get fired for excessive graft when he had been a province chief in III Corps in 1967. Dat had been vulnerable at the time, because although he had a high corruption connection, Ky's power was waning and Thieu's waxing and Dat had not kept his political alliances adjusted to changing times. He had subsequently recouped and in 1970 had been appointed deputy commander of the 22nd Division. Vann had just managed to rid himself of the previous 22nd Division commander, a lazy man, in February 1972. He had sought then to block Dat's elevation to full command and to substitute a candidate of his own, but Dzu had been unable to object to Dat, whose corruption connection was too high for Dzu to risk offense. Dat, a slim, intense, excitable man, was a heavy smoker of a brand of English cigarettes called Craven "A." They came in little red packages of ten. He did not carry the cigarettes himself. When he wanted one he flicked his hand and an aide put a cigarette in his fingers and gave him a light.

On April 20, the Joint General Staff notified Dzu that they were depriving him of the second airborne brigade and the field headquarters of the Airborne Division that had been guiding the two brigades in the fight for Rocket Ridge. Dzu and Vann would have to hold the line, weakened in the middle by the loss of Fire Base Charlie on the 14th, with the remaining paratroop brigade and a depleted Ranger group Dzu was to be given. The brigade being withdrawn and the Airborne Division headquarters were to be flown to I Corps to defend Hue. Despite Vann's prediction of disaster for the Vietnamese Communists on all fronts in his April 12 memorandum, the NVA in I Corps were in the process of conquering the whole of Quang Tri Province below the DMZ and were also threatening Hue from the A Shau Valley to the west.

If the former imperial capital fell, Thieu would fall with it, and so difficult choices had to be made. The frayed Ranger group Dzu was being sent were the only troops that could be spared. The other major element of Saigon's general reserve, the marine division, was already fully engaged in I Corps. The last of the reserve, the third brigade of the airborne, was caught in battle too on the Cambodian front of the offensive at the province capital of An Loc sixty miles northwest of Saigon. An Loc was under full-scale assault and might well succumb. The 21st ARVN Division had been brought up from the Delta to try to prevent the Communists from advancing down Route 13 any closer to Saigon if An Loc did go under.

On April 21, while Vann was in Saigon for another strategy conference with Abrams, Fire Base Delta, the bottom hinge point of Rocket Ridge, was overrun. The NVA pressure was proving to be more than the airborne could handle. The situation was becoming as grim at Tan Canh as it was on Rocket Ridge. Vann's plan to break the NVA on his strongpoints had not envisioned the ARVN simply sitting and waiting in foxholes and bunkers. He had wanted them to sortie out and make contact in order to bring artillery and air to bear as the NVA moved forward, to establish themselves on key ridges, and to counterattack and retake high ground when it was lost. Instead, Dat occupied some of the high ground around Tan Canh and sat. He would not maneuver, nor would he marshal reinforcements and relieve one of his battalions when it was attacked. The infantry of the 2nd NVA Division were steadily fragmenting his defenses by working their way in between the ARVN positions, each time closer to the former regimental compound where Dat's command bunker was located.

When Dat's advisor, Col. Phillip Kaplan, would tell him that he had to maneuver and fight, Dat would explain that North Vietnamese soldiers were superior to South Vietnamese soldiers and you could not maneuver against the NVA. If you tried, they would surround and destroy you. Kaplan, a keen and robust airborne officer who had served under Bob York in the Dominican Republic, held his temper with Dat as best he could and kept coaching in the positive way of the American military man. He did not realize that the attitude expressed by Dat, a Northerner himself (he was from a Tonkinese family of substance and had taken his baccalaureate at the Lycée Albert Sarraut in Hanoi), had nothing to do with the fact that Dat's opponents were North Vietnamese, but was rather the ingrained inferiority complex toward the Viet Minh of a Vietnamese who had fought with the French. Dat was behaving as most ARVN commanders would have in the circumstances. He was sheltering in his bunker and assuming his troops would hang on until U.S. air power persuaded his enemy to go away.

A successful defense of Tan Canh entailed a slugging match of blow and counterblow in difficult terrain, a battle the ARVN was incapable of fighting. Vann had placed this army he was trying to use for his ends in a contest beyond its strength. He sought to goad Dat into becoming the leader he wanted him to be. They were standing in the briefing room of the bunker late one afternoon in front of the situation map with its ominous indications. Vann jabbed at the map, curtly describing in his harsh, nasal twang the actions Dat had to take to survive. "Colonel Dat, you are going to be the first division commander in the ARVN to lose your division, because you are going to be overrun and destroyed if you do not . . ."

"Oh, that won't happen," Dat replied.

* * *

It started to happen on the morning of Sunday, April 23, 1972. An ARVN infantry battalion was engaged with the NVA not far from the Tan Canh compound. The shelling, which had been building gradually since Friday, had increased to about a round a minute of mortar, artillery, and 122mm rockets. The bombardment was sufficiently accurate to indicate that smaller groups of NVA had infiltrated to within hundreds of yards and had the compound under good observation. Phil Kaplan, the division senior advisor, received a report that a tank had been knocked out at the main gate. He and his deputy, Lt. Col. Terrence McClain, left the command bunker to investigate, making their way to the gate along a ditch to avoid the bombardment. An ARVN soldier who spoke English told Kaplan he had seen a missile fly through the air and hit the tank. The wire-guided antitank missile, a unique weapon because it can be sent to its target with precision from a considerable distance, had been invented in the 1950s by a French air force officer. The Soviets had developed a powerful version during the 1960s called the Sagger. None had ever appeared in Vietnam. As Kaplan was continuing to question the soldier, a Sagger sailed overhead with a high-pitched warbling noise and in a flash and roar knocked out another tank inside the compound about sixty to seventy yards away.

The command bunker was next, a bit later in the morning. Something that could be shot in a straight line, probably another Sagger, penetrated the sandbag wall at a weak point near a fresh-air vent and exploded in the radio room, setting the supporting timbers of the bunker on fire. The timbers had been treated with creosote or a similar wood preservative. Smoke billowed from them. No one had thought to stock fire extinguishers, and there was no water line to the bunker. Kaplan was about to toss a plastic container of water the advisors kept for making coffee at the blaze when he realized he was being foolish. In moments men would be suffocating and trampling each other in a stampede for the exits. "Get everybody out of here!" he ordered.

The 22nd Division headquarters soon became a pile of smoldering sandbags, the timbers of the bunker collapsing as they were consumed by the flames. An alternative command post was set up in a much smaller bunker the advisors had beside their living quarters, and the wounded were evacuated by helicopter in the afternoon. Kaplan had only a superficial scalp wound from the explosion and Colonel Dat had not been hurt, but the operations advisor, Maj. Jon Wise, had been more seriously injured in the head and arm. Eight to ten members of Dat's staff had also been hurt, and there were forty or so ARVN from elsewhere in the compound who had been wounded by the bombardment. Vann flew up from Pleiku and supervised the evacuation, a nerve-racking business for the helicopter crews and the wounded because of the incoming shells. Vann would not duck from them himself. Kaplan told him, before he returned to Pleiku, that if the worst came the advisors would assemble for a pickup at an alternative helicopter pad next to the minefield on the west side of the compound. The Cobra gunships had used it as a parking spot in quieter times.

The NVA kept shooting the Saggers at the ARVN tanks around the Tan Canh compound throughout Sunday. There were eight operational in the morning. By Sunday afternoon there was only one left. Dat took to sitting in a chair and staring. As the night approached he looked at Kaplan and said: "We will be overrun tomorrow."

Around 10:00 P.M. they received a report from Dak To District that the PF at a Montagnard hamlet near Route 14 northwest of the district center could hear tanks. Route 14 ran north past Tan Canh, continued up past the district headquarters, and turned west into country that was now, except for PF platoons at the Montagnard hamlets, controlled by the NVA. A battalion positioned on a ridge high enough to overlook the road radioed next that they could hear tanks and then that they could see the lights of a tank column. Kaplan asked the air operations center at Pleiku for a C-130 Spectre gunship. The Spectres had night-vision devices and infrared sensors. "There are eleven tanks down there," the Spectre pilot told Kaplan. The tanks were driving east along the road toward the turn down for Dak To District. Capt. Richard Cassidy, the assistant district advisor, ran to the front gate of the district compound. He saw the hooded blackout headlights military vehicles are equipped with about half a mile away. The Spectre dropped a flare, and Cassidy saw the tanks coming toward him in a staggered column. "They're shooting at us," he yelled in panic before he caught himself. The tanks were not shooting. Cassidy had no immediate cause for fear. The tankers had orders to disregard the district headquarters. They drove past the compound without firing a shot.

The NVA were engaged in a maneuver the Vietnamese call "striking the head of the snake." The idea is one of those oft-used schemes of war that are forever new when executed with surprise. The Vietnamese were ignoring Fire Bases Five and Six near Tan Canh and all of the battalion positions around it and going straight for Dat's headquarters. There were actually fifteen tanks coming down the road. They were Soviet-built T-54s, medium tanks of late-1950s vintage that were attached to the 2nd NVA Division. The North Vietnamese tankers had driven their T-54s down the Ho Chi Minh Trail in February, towing additional ammunition and diesel fuel behind them in trailers. They had waited in Laos for a month and crossed into South Vietnam about two weeks earlier. For the past few days they had been hiding their tanks above Tan Canh, apparently in some gullies off a dirt track that connected with Route 14.

An irrational skepticism Vann had been displaying over the presence of NVA tanks in II Corps contributed to this surprise. It was logical that if the NVA were employing tanks in I Corps and had managed to drive them down to III Corps, they would use them in II Corps as well. There had also been plenty of evidence of tanks before the opening of the offensive and during the prior weeks of fighting in the Highlands. Prisoners and defectors had spoken of tanks. The Special Forces and the long-range patrols from the ARVN Airborne had found tank tracks in Laos and in the Plei Trap Valley west of Rocket Ridge. Another battalion of T-54s was attached to the 320th NVA Division, and they seem to have entered South Vietnam earlier.

The habit of personally verifying reports had become a form of arrogance in Vann, to the point where he tended to disregard what he could not confirm. Every time he received a report of tanks he had flown out to look for them and had found none. He had decided the reports were the exaggerations of spooked men or sightings of PT-76s, light amphibious tanks the NVA occasionally brought into play which were not a major threat because of their thin armor. Just two days before, the 320th had used three of its T-54s in the final assault on Fire Base Delta, but Vann had been at the Saigon strategy conference then and had not paid attention to the report on return. When Kaplan now called him on the radiophone to say that the Spectre confirmed the vehicles were tanks, he got the customary gallows humor mixed with self-defensiveness: "Well, if they are, congratulations," Vann said, "because these are the first positive tanks that anybody has found in II Corps."

A surprise gained is not a battle won. There was a lot of time in which to stop the tanks and a lot of weaponry with which to destroy them. The T-54s were not accompanied by NVA infantry, and tanks alone are vulnerable to opposing infantry with antitank weapons, particularly at night when the infantry can more easily wait in ambush or approach unseen. Despite his skepticism, Vann had made certain that the 22nd Division troops and the Dak To District forces were equipped with hundreds of M-72 LAWs (light antitank weapons), the Vietnam-era successor to the bazooka, just in case. The troops had been instructed in how to fire the LAW, and tank-killer teams had been formed in the companies. One of the division's 106mm recoilless cannons, lethal against tanks, happened to be sited along the road, and the crew had been issued antitank rounds. There was also the regular division artillery, and Dat still had tanks to counter the NVA's. While the North Vietnamese with the Saggers had eliminated the ARVN tanks around the Tan Canh compound to facilitate the arrival of their own, more tanks were stationed at the main Dak To airfield a couple of miles away, called Dak To II to distinguish it from an older and shorter airstrip next to the compound.

The PF militia at the first bridge the tanks had to cross had LAWs. They were ordered to ambush the T-54s. They ran away. "Yes, we'll do it," Dat said when Kaplan told him to dispatch ARVN tank-killer teams. The teams didn't leave their foxholes. "We've already given those orders," Dat replied when Kaplan told him to summon the tanks from Dak To II. They didn't come. The crew of the 106mm recoilless cannon sited along the road does not seem to have fired a round.

The Spectre had in the meantime been trying to do the job for the ARVN. Ingenious Air Force technicians had mounted a 105mm howitzer in the C-130. The cannon shot pinpoint, because it was hooked up to a digital fire-control computer that was fed data by the sensors. Six times the pilot radioed Kaplan that he had "hit" a tank. The difficulty was that, not having been forewarned, the Spectre had no antitank ammunition aboard, only high explosive. The T-54 is a sturdy tank. The three-man crews were undoubtedly being given something worse than headaches, but only one crew abandoned its tank near a hamlet just below Dak To District center. The PF there captured the driver, an eighteen-year-old North Vietnamese, and brought him to the district headquarters. A small group of NVA then came down the road, chased away the PF around the tank, and drove it off to join the others still moving toward Dat's command post.

Kaplan resorted to the artillery batteries at Tan Canh, with the Spectre acting as his spotter. The tanks scattered at the first salvos. The NVA observers around the compound, who had registered their artillery during the day, then called for counterbattery, and the ARVN gunners ran back to their bunkers at the incoming shells.

"Colonel, the artillery must fire!" Terry McClain, Kaplan's deputy, shouted at Dat.

"The artillery is firing, Colonel," Dat replied.

* * *

John Vann wrote his will in the helicopter speeding toward Tan Canh early on the morning of April 24, 1972. The last time he had visited Norfolk, his oldest brother, Frank Junior, had asked him if he wasn't afraid of dying in Vietnam. "Hell, no," he said. He had survived so many scrapes that he was sure the war would never claim him. The odds did not apply to him, he said. After the offensive intensified, he had started to wonder. The antiaircraft fire was getting so bad, he wrote Dan Ellsberg, that he might not come through this fight.

On several occasions he had told Annie that he had made a provision for the support of his child in the event something happened to him. In fact, he had made no provision for his Vietnamese daughter. His estate was small. The dual expense of his women and the family in Littleton kept him from saving anything substantial. He had some life insurance policies worth about $85,000, and if he left a widow she would receive his combined military and AID pension. The way his affairs stood, Annie could not claim the pension and she and the child would have a tenuous claim at best to any of the insurance benefits. With the offensive on his mind, Vann had not even taken the preliminary step, during one of his trips to Saigon, of filling out a declaration to marry Annie at the consular section of the embassy. She and his daughter were currently living in a house in Nhatrang on the coast. Vann had decided to leave the CORDS component of II Corps in the former Field Force headquarters in Nhatrang, and the house there was his official residence. His most recent will, drawn up at the time of his abdominal surgery in mid-1968 when the child was about six months old, left everything to Mary Jane and his American children. It had been duly registered in Colorado and remained in effect.

When he went to bed in his room at Pleiku around 2:00 A.M. that morning, it was clear there was nothing he could do to stop the tanks and that he would need some sleep for the day to come. The Tactical Operations Center woke him a little before 6:30 and said that Kaplan wanted him at Tan Canh right away. He had his pilot roused while he pulled on his clothes, and they ran to the helicopter pad and took off for Tan Canh in the little Bell Ranger. He might succeed in snatching a bunch of advisors from a compound with tanks bursting into the place. He might not.

Vann carried a three-by-five-inch spiral note pad in his shirt pocket to jot down whatever he wanted to remember of a day. He took it out as he flew toward Tan Canh, marked the time, 0700, and the date at the top right corner of the lined page, printed "LAST WILL & TESTAMENT," and wrote underneath: "My wife, . . . , and my

772][A BRIGHT SHINING LIE

daughter, . . . , are to share equally in my estate. All my possessions in SVN are to be sold and the proceeds also given to my wife, ..." He signed, "John P. Vann," and put the note pad back in his pocket. He apparently thought that if it was found on his body, he would have provided for Annie and his Vietnamese daughter.

He didn't tell the pilot beside him, Chief Warrant Officer Robert Richards, what he had written. Richards was a skinny, friendly redneck from South Georgia, a former NCO who had become an officer and a gentleman because of the Army's sudden need for helicopter pilots in 1966. He had learned harum-scarum flying during his first tour in Vietnam as a scout pilot for the 1st Infantry Division and had become Vann's regular pilot in the Delta in 1970 because he was deft with a helicopter in dangerous spots and would take risks Vann's previous pilots had refused. Ordinary men have to draw on their fortitude for brave deeds. Since the beginning of the offensive, Vann had been draining the courage out of Richards faster than Richards could replace it. Richards had once liked to drink at night for fun. Now he was looking for valor in whiskey. Vann knew how tattered Richards's nerves were. "We'll make it, Bob," he said. "We always make it."

The scud clouds of the oncoming monsoon, morning haze, and smoke from fires lit by the NVA bombardment obscured Tan Canh. Richards saw there were enough holes in the clouds so that he would be able to get underneath them. Another Ranger piloted by Capt. Dolph Todd of Tacoma, Washington, was right behind Vann and Richards's aircraft. Todd had volunteered the day before to be Vann's backup pilot on the 24th. He liked hazardous flying but had not known then what he would face.

Vann began talking on the radio to Kaplan, McClain, and seven other Americans from the division advisory team. Kaplan had despaired of stimulating any resistance and ordered his team to abandon the substitute command bunker shortly after dawn. He made sure when they left it that two of his advisors were carrying portable radios so that they would be able to communicate with helicopters. Dat and his staff had followed the Americans out of the bunker and then, in a few minutes, returned to its seeming safety. To keep their opponents intimidated while the tanks drew near, the NVA had quickened the bombardment to three to four rounds of mortar, artillery, and rockets every minute. Vann, and Richards and Todd, who were monitoring the radio conversation, learned they were going to face the additional risk of detonating mines when the helicopters landed. The advisors said they were in the middle of the minefield where it curved around the west side of the Tan Canh compound.

Kaplan's original escape plan had proved impractical. By the time he led his advisors to the Cobra parking place next to the minefield where he had told Vann to pick them up, two tanks had rolled in through the front of the compound, the NVA infantry were starting to follow, and a third tank had pulled up beneath a tall concrete water tower not far away at the west front corner, threatening their position. Capt. Kenneth Yonan, a twenty-three-year-old West Pointer who was a deputy regimental advisor, had climbed to the top of the water tower with his ARVN counterpart to call in jets on the tanks. He hadn't been able to do so because of the clouds and haze, and the tanks had then trapped him and the ARVN officer on the water tower. Yonan was never seen again.

Staff Sgt. Walter Ward, the team's administrative NCO, spotted a way to get through the minefield and gain some distance from the tank under the water tower. About 900 of the nearly 1,200 ARVN officers and men stationed at the Tan Canh headquarters were signal, engineer, and other service personnel. When the tanks came in through the front of the compound, these service troops panicked and burst out through the barbed wire and the minefield that encircled the rest of Tan Canh, many blowing themselves up on their own mines as they ran. Ward suggested that the team follow, walking in the footsteps of those ARVN soldiers who had escaped unhurt so as not to step on a mine. The advisors stopped at an old road that ran through a slight dip about midpoint in the minefield. Kaplan thought the fold in the ground there would partially shield a helicopter from the tank when it landed. The Americans lay down to hide while they waited. Lying around them were terrified ARVN soldiers also hoping for life.

Bob Richards didn't see any sheltering fold in the ground. All he saw was the 100mm gun in the turret of the T-54 under the water tower pointed right at the spot where the advisors were lying and where he was about to put his helicopter. "I'm coming in to land and I'm looking at that big son of a bitch and I'm thinking, 'I ain't going to make it, this is the end of me,' " Richards said. "That barrel looked to me like I could have flown the helicopter down it."

Mines or no mines, Richards came in "hot," the skids striking hard, the rotor guard at the end of the tail boom bouncing against the ground. Todd darted in after him. Kaplan sent three of the advisors scrambling into each machine. He did not want to risk a crash by overloading the Rangers; neither did Vann. Kaplan and McClain, as the senior officers, would wait for the next pickup, along with Capt. David Stewart, the division signal advisor, who had one of the portable radios. Richards stared at the big gun again when he lifted away. To his surprise it did not explode, and no one else seemed to be shooting at them with anything of smaller bore.

Two of the ARVN in the minefield grabbed hold of the radio antennas on the sides of Vann and Richards's helicopter when they took off with the advisors in the back, and a couple of other Saigon soldiers clung to the skids. Vann could also see several ARVN dangling from the outside of Todd's aircraft. He had originally intended to ferry the advisors to the former Special Forces camp at Ben Het a dozen miles to the west, one of the few islands still held by the Saigon side. along the Laotian border and relatively safe because it was not under threat of imminent assault. The Rangers could bear the weight of the ARVN clinging to them once they were aloft, but Vann was afraid the Saigon soldiers would lose their grip during the longer flight to Ben Het and fall to their deaths. He decided to take the advisors instead to the main Dak To airfield, Dak To II, because it was just a couple of miles away. He knew the NVA would soon overrun the airfield too, but he had a Huey on the way that could reach Dak To II before the NVA did. Vann and Richards and Todd dropped the six advisors off at the airfield. He radioed the Huey pilot and ordered him to land there and fly the advisors to Pleiku.

Richards and Vann started back for Kaplan and the two others. They ran out of luck. They were flying contour, because that seemed safest and because of the low clouds. An NVA soldier who knew how to shoot saw them coming. He popped up from behind a bush and raised his AK-47 to rake the front of the cockpit with a burst. Richards "honked" back on the controls, powering the helicopter up into an arc, hoping to escape into one of the scud clouds. The stream of bullets thudded into the Ranger, riddling the FM radio in the console between Richards and Vann and smacking the floor under Vann. He would have been wounded or worse but for Richards's acrobatic maneuver and the fact that the AK-47 fires a bullet that is relatively light and of modest velocity. The rounds that struck under Vann came through the honeycombed aluminum decking of the floor at an angle, tumbled, and lost their force.

Vann raised Todd on an alternate radio and had him go for Kaplan, McClain, and Stewart. Todd picked them up without incident. Vann instructed him to bring them to Pleiku behind him and Richards. The damage to the radio made it imperative for them to return there. The fuel gauge fell with unusual rapidity during the flight. When they landed at the pad beside II Corps Headquarters, Richards climbed out and looked at the fuel cells. The NVA soldier had punched holes in them too. The fuel was running down the fuselage. Richards shook his head.

One tracer bullet would have turned the Ranger into an orange ball.

John Vann paid no attention. He leaped into Todd's machine as soon as Kaplan and the two other advisors got out and headed back to Tan Canh. His ARVN aide, Cai, who had been waiting for him at the headquarters pad, jumped into the rear seat to go with him. Vann had Todd land near Dak To II to rescue an American major, the advisor to an ARVN airborne battalion Dat had been lent a week before in an attempt to stiffen his defenses. The airfield had been overrun by now, and some of the paratroops were in a panic. Vann beat off those who grabbed the skid on his side of the Ranger with his rifle butt as Todd was lifting away with the major and the major's wounded interpreter aboard, but so many clung to Todd's side that the helicopter tipped until a main rotor blade struck the ground and the machine crashed, flipping over twice. Cai was pinned underneath. Vann pulled him free, snatched a portable radio from the wreckage, guided Cobra gunships in strafing runs against the NVA soldiers who immediately started to close, and hammered at them with his M-16. A Huey pilot managed to maneuver down and pluck Vann, Cai, Todd, and the two others from the Communist infantry, his aircraft taking repeated hits as he did so.

Vann left Cai at the Kontum dispensary for treatment of an injured shoulder, got another helicopter, and flew once more toward Tan Canh. The close call reminded him of his will. He stopped at the airborne brigade command post at Vo Dinh, where his former captain at My Tho, Peter Kama, was the brigade advisor. He tore the page out of the note pad, had Kama sign it as a witness, and left the will with him for safekeeping.

John Vann could not sit in the Tactical Operations Center in the bunker at Pleiku and moan with Dzu. He guided jets in strikes against the tanks, he ordered the bombing of the ammunition dumps around Tan Canh to deny the munitions to his enemy, he evacuated other advisors from neighboring fire bases, he picked up Captain Cassidy and the major who was the district senior advisor at Dak To. He had to act, no matter to what avail, amid this calamity he had done so much to bring about.

Those thousands of ARVN soldiers who could get away ran so fast down the road toward Kontum that the Montagnard tribesmen nick-named them "the rabbit soldiers." Dat perished. He finally did leave the bunker, after vainly radioing Dzu to send a helicopter to rescue him at the bunker door, and reached Dak To II airfield, where he was wounded and may have shot himself with his service pistol. Kaplan and McClain were fortunate that rank required them to wait in the minefield, as was Stewart to wait with them. Three of the six advisors Richards and Todd shuttled to Dak To II were killed when the Huey Vann sent to fetch them was shot down while taking off. Sergeant Ward, who had led the way into the minefield, was among the survivors.

Had the NVA possessed a tradition of pursuit, the course of the war would have been different. The collapse at Tan Canh created the classic moment for pursuit, the moment when one's enemy is so demoralized he will keep running from anything, and while the might-have-been's of war can never be more than speculation, the special circumstances of Vietnam posed a unique opportunity. If the NVA commanders had refueled their tanks that night of April 24, 1972, loaded a couple of battalions of infantry into captured jeeps and trucks and armored personnel carriers (they had plenty from which to choose; the ARVN abandoned everything in the Tan Canh area, including more than 200 vehicles), and shot their way down the twenty-five miles of Route 14 to Kontum, the town would have been theirs by morning. If they had not wished to risk a dash, they could have pursued at leisure, pushing down from Tan Canh and Rocket Ridge in a few days, or in a week, or even in ten days, and Kontum "would have fallen apart," Vann acknowledged later.

If Kontum had fallen in 1972, the panic that was always just waiting beneath the surface on the Saigon side would have burst forth in an uncontrollable contagion in II Corps. The Highlands would have been lost, and much of the Central Coast would have become untenable. The panic would have spread there. Binh Dinh was already teetering, because of the collapse of the northern districts. The Communists could have captured the port of Qui Nhon and started to threaten the other major coastal towns after the B-3 Front divisions from the Highlands had linked up with the Yellow Star Division in Binh Dinh. Lack of supplies need not have halted the Communist units. Their opponents would have abandoned enough to sustain them.

The Nixon administration thought it had hired Hessians to guard the coast. At the cost of additional hundreds of millions of dollars in military and economic aid to South Korea, the administration had persuaded the government in Seoul to leave two ROK divisions in place from Nhatrang up through Qui Nhon. The Koreans would not have held on their own with the Saigon side collapsing around them. They would have demanded evacuation. They were already reneging on their Hessian role because of secret instructions from Seoul to avoid casualties. They would not even keep open the road that was II Corps' main supply route from the docks at Qui Nhon to the depots at Pleiku. Two battalions from a regiment of the Yellow Star Division had blocked Route 19 at the An Khe Pass in Binh Dinh in mid-April. Vann had to curse at the Korean generals for two weeks to get them to reopen the road. In the meantime he was dependent on aerial resupply and on a longer overland route from Nhatrang that might also be cut at any moment.

The negotiations in Paris were in the balance too. Nixon had made Kissinger's secret talks there with Le Duc Tho public in January in an attempt to portray the Vietnamese Communists as obstinate. The Vietnamese were obstinate. They had fruitfully waited out Nixon's withdrawal gamble and now, with the battlefield going their way, were more unyielding than ever in their demand that the United States pull out all of its forces unilaterally and dismantle the Thieu regime as well in exchange for a peace agreement. Nixon had resumed regular air raids on the North in response to the offensive, after years of bombing intermittently to try to intimidate the Vietnamese, and was about to mine Haiphong and the other ports. The outcome in the South was what would matter. Kissinger was attempting to bargain a compromise. If the divisions of the NVA were linked from the mountains to the sea and South Vietnam was split in two there would not be a great deal to bargain about.

Joe Pizzi, Vann's chief of staff, saw the incipient panic and realized that Pleiku would disappear in an instant should Kontum go. The population of the town shrank to about a quarter of its pre-offensive level as the ARVN officers and everyone else who could shipped their families and belongings to Saigon or to Nhatrang or another of the towns farther down the coast. A seat on a regular Air Vietnam flight acquired a bribery premium equivalent to several hundred dollars. The VNAF helicopters and transport planes were constantly unavailable for military tasks because the pilots and crews were busy ferrying people and goods to the coast for lesser bribes.

Pizzi came to the office one morning and discovered that so many of the VNAF air traffic controllers had deserted it was going to be difficult to continue manning the tower at the main Pleiku airfield. He ordered a secret plan drawn up to evacuate all Americans from Pleiku by helicopter and by C-130 from the airstrip at Camp Holloway, the U.S. Army helicopter base on the other side of town. Vann accepted the plan because he had no choice. Pizzi immediately began to reduce the number of men who would need to be evacuated by transferring to Nhatrang any American whose presence was not absolutely required in Pleiku.

Vann had Cai smuggle out most of his clothes and other belongings on administrative flights to Nhatrang. He even sent away a wooden footlocker, painted brown, with a padlock on it to which Vann had the only key. He called the footlocker "The Box." He had never parted with it before. It held albums with photographs of him and his sister and brothers in Norfolk, of Johnny Vann doing a backflip in a sand pile at Ferrum, of himself as an Air Corps cadet and a second lieutenant navigating a B-29 called "Lost Weekend," of Mary Jane in Rochester, of her and the children in Japan and Germany. The footlocker held his Army officer's record, his medals and his awards, and the inscribed silver cigarette box Halberstam and I and the other reporters had given him in 1963 for moral heroism and professional integrity, and it held photographs of himself with some of his sexual partners.

"If anything ever happens to me, watch out for that box," he said with a smile.

"What's in the box?" a subordinate asked who did not know him well.

"I'm in the box," Vann said.

Vann's Vietnamese enemy delayed the attack on Kontum for twenty days after the fall of Tan Canh, giving him the time he needed. Armies, like human beings, are not capable of what is not in them. The entire experience of the NVA militated against pursuit and demanded elaborate planning and positioning for each major step of a campaign. Vann needed every day.

Dzu, his instrument, broke in his hands as Cao had ten years earlier. Worse, Dzu schemed against him, secretly plotting to abandon the Highlands. Thieu summoned Dzu to Saigon two days after the Tan Canh debacle and ordered him to hold Kontum at all costs. That evening, after Thieu had released him from the meeting at the palace, Dzu showed up at the home in Cholon of Cao Van Vien, the chief of the Joint General Staff. He was extremely agitated. Kontum and Pleiku were indefensible, Dzu said. The sole alternative left was to abandon both towns and Ban Me Thuot farther south in the mountains and pull all of the Saigon forces down to the coast. Dzu wanted Vien to help him persuade Thieu of the wisdom of wholesale retreat. Forsaking the Highlands was a new American strategy, he said.

Vien said no one had mentioned it to him. He instructed Dzu to return to Pleiku and find a way to defend Kontum. Dzu did not tell Vann of his conversation with Vien. He started telephoning Thieu and

Vien late at night, apparently when his nerves were most jangled and he could not sleep, pleading for permission to withdraw. Thieu wanted to fire him right away, but Vien could not find another ARVN general to accept his place. He called nearly half a dozen two- and three-star generals without commands and, one after another, offered them II Corps. Some said their astrologers had looked at their horoscopes and advised that this was an inauspicious year to take up a new command. Others said they were in poor health. None admitted that they believed the situation in the Highlands was beyond recall.

In the meantime, Dzu concocted a scheme with the Kontum province chief and several of the senior ARVN officers in the town to precipitate a retreat, and he almost succeeded at it, because Vann was confused and downcast himself in the immediate aftermath of Tan Canh. Then he caught on to the gambit and stopped Dzu.

Vann's rage renewed his strength. During one of his arguments with Dan Ellsberg after Tet he had acknowledged that if the regime did not change as the United States reduced its military forces in Vietnam "we [could] get ourselves into a damn tenuous situation where we are kind of surrounded and fighting for our lives." John Vann was surrounded and fighting for his life. The Vietnamese Communists were threatening everything that mattered to him. He had not won his stars to see them become the tarnished stars of a defeated general. He had not prophesied victory to important men to have his prophecies exposed as vainglorious boasting. A cornered man is dangerous; John Vann cornered was dangerous indeed.

Weyand told him he could have any brigadier general he wanted as his deputy to replace George Wear, who had been evacuated. Vann asked Weyand to send Brig. Gen. John Hill, Jr., who was finishing a second tour in Vietnam by closing down the depot at Cam Ranh Bay for lack of something better to do. Hill would fight, Vann said. He and Vann had been contemporaries in the Army. They had met while instructors at ROTC summer camp not long after Korea, where Hill had also served in the Pusan Perimeter and in North Korea as a company commander with the 1st Cavalry Division. A short, slightly stooped man, John Hill was intelligent and resourceful, and liked to fight. He had spent most of his career in mechanized infantry before being selected for helicopter flight school and promotion to brigadier. Vann left Hill free to do what Hill excelled at—organizing the aviation assets and major firepower of a battlefield. Every day, all day, a command-and-control Huey called "the Air Boss ship" began flying over the Kontum area to coordinate Cobras and fighter-bombers on strikes, scout helicopters seeking NVA assembly points for B-52 targeting, C-130's and Chinooks hauling in supplies, artillery registering patterns of defensive fire. Hill's objective was to see that everything meshed and no effort was wasted. The 7th Air Force colonel on Vann's staff wanted to stay in his office in Pleiku. Hill fired him and got a man who would keep track of jets over Kontum.

In Hau Nghia in 1965 Vann had cursed the leaders of the United States for refusing "to take over the command of this operation lock, stock, and barrel." Vann now did precisely that. He abandoned pretense of who was running II Corps and overrode Dzu. He had a Vietnamese officer who was willing to try to defend Kontum. The man was Ly Tong Ba, the commander of the M-113 company at Ap Bac and the object of so much of Vann's wrath on that momentous day. They had been forced to work together during later years of the 1960s when Ba had serve as province chief of Binh Duong in III Corps. Vann had decided that while Ba was hardly a model of combativeness, he was not a crook and was a better soldier than most ARVN officers. Their relationship was a measure of how far Vann had worked himself into the Saigon system, for Ba had no Vietnamese patron. Other ARVN officers referred to him as "Mr. Vann's man." At the end of January 1972, Vann had maneuvered Ba, by this time a full colonel, into command of the 23rd ARVN Division at Ban Me Thuot, responsible for the defense of the southern Highlands. One of its regiments had been shifted north to garrison Kontum in April after the JGS had taken away the second airborne brigade. Vann initially hesitated to risk all of the only remaining division he had in II Corps. He wanted Ba to defend Kontum with a polyglot force consisting of this regiment, what was left of the first airborne brigade, understrength and exhausted from the Rocket Ridge battle, and a Ranger group. The plan didn't make sense, Ba argued. He needed unity to resist. Vann let the airborne and the Rangers go, stripped the southern Highlands of troops, and flew the other two regiments of the 23rd ARVN Division into Kontum.

Vann sent for an advisor whom Ba trusted—Col. R. M. Rhotenberry, a homely, husky Texan. The initials didn't stand for anything. In the Texas of Rhotenberry's birth, some people just gave their children initials. "Rhot" and Vann had first met in the spring of 1962 when they had shared a room in a BOQ in Cholon while both were assigned to Dan Porter's staff at the old III Corps headquarters. Rhotenberry had returned to Vietnam so regularly—four tours as an advisor, one with Ba in Binh Duong, half a tour to command a battalion of the U.S. 9th Infantry Division Vann had obtained for him through Fred Weyand—

that Cao Van Vien called him "Rhotenberry, the soldier of fortune."

A twin-engine Beechcraft was standing by to fly Rhotenberry to Pleiku when he walked down the gangway of an airliner at Tan Son Nhut on the morning of May 14, 1972. The first assault on Kontum had already begun at 5:30 A.M. Vann had airlifted Ba's third regiment into the town only two days before. He was in his Ranger over the battlefield, and so Rhotenberry was able to sleep for a couple of hours at Pleiku before Master Sgt. Edward Black, a Filipino-American NCO who was Vann's administrative assistant, woke him to say that Vann was returning to pick him up and take him to the command post Ba had established in the bunker of a former Special Forces compound on the west side of Kontum.

With the last major unit in II Corps committed, the stakes could not have been higher, and hardly anyone on the Saigon side and few among the American military thought that Kontum would hold. In expectation of new rulers, Qui Nhon was down to half its normal population. Ba's own deputy went AWOL for the first twenty-four hours of the battle, hiding out in Kontum in the hope of escaping. Vann was conscious of these stakes, but they were not uppermost in his mind. "My credibility is at stake, Rhot," he said in the helicopter. "The troop disposition at Tan Canh was mine. I said we could defend there . . . and they didn't hold. Now my career is at stake because I've said we can defend Kontum. If you don't hold it, I no longer have any credibility or career."

The Vietnamese Communist soldiery attacked with an ardor undiminished by the years, but what they faced by the time they assaulted was more than human will could overcome. Kontum is in the valley of the Bla River where it flows west to meet the Poko coming down from Tan Canh and Dak To. To seize Kontum once a defense had been organized, the NVA had to mass in the hills on the edges of the valley and in the valley itself and attack along routes that were under daily observation by the scout helicopters of the air cavalry. Radio intercepts and direction-finding helped follow their movements too.

The circumstances rendered the NVA vulnerable to the B-52s at a moment in the war when experience and technology had perfected the employment of the bombers. The Strategic Air Command had learned during the siege of Khe Sanh that three B-52s provided enough destructive effect to satisfy most ground commanders. SAC now launched the planes in flights of three rather than the original six in order to double the number of Arc Lights. A new radar system named Combat Skyspot made it possible to place the strikes within five-eighths of a mile of friendly positions. (Rhotenberry and Ba did not hesitate to call a strike within 700 yards.) The location of the "box," the target zone that was five-eighths of a mile wide by approximately two miles long, could be changed up to three hours before the bombs were scheduled to fall. Rhotenberry kept a list of every B-52 strike allotted to the battle with the drop time and change time marked in order to switch the box to a new location and catch the NVA in it when an assault was imminent or underway against a sector of the perimeter.

The virtually three-week delay also cost the NVA the advantage of their T-54 tanks. Ba was able to give the tank-killer teams he formed some psychological preparation by having them practice firing the M-72 LAW at junked ARVN tank hulls. The Pentagon had time to respond to an appeal from Abrams and rush out an experimental helicopter-mounted system for the American wire-guided antitank missile, called the TOW for tube-launched, optically tracked, wire-guided. Two Hueys in which the system had been installed were loaded into C-141 jet transports at the Yuma Proving Grounds in Arizona and flown directly to Pleiku. Jeep-mounted versions of the TOW also arrived, but they were not to prove useful. The NVA commanders could use their tanks to lead an assault that began at night. The dimensions of the battle forced them to continue the assault into the day with the tanks maintaining a spearpoint role. Hill would have the Hueys with the TOWs over Kontum at first light, and any T-54 in sight was doomed. One tank crew backed its behemoth into a house to try to hide. The TOW team got the tank by shooting a missile through a window.

Vann made the bombers his personal weapon. He could have left the B-52 targeting to Hill and Rhotenberry and the efficient officers in his G-3, air operations section, but he wanted to do it himself. Brig. Gen. Nguyen Van Toan, whom Cao Van Vien finally recruited to replace Dzu, and the Vietnamese staff at the Pleiku headquarters nicknamed Vann "Mr. B-52." (Toan had been sidelined for excessive graft and a scandal over a girl. Vien had proposed to him that he redeem his career and gain another star by volunteering to take II Corps, and, being a personally courageous man, Toan had accepted. Vien admonished him to listen to Vann.)

The Strategic Air Command was sending Creighton Abrams three-plane flights of B-52s at roughly hourly intervals around the clock from Andersen Air Force Base on Guam and the B-52 base at Sattahip in southern Thailand. By mid-May, when the struggle for Kontum began, the siege of An Loc on the Cambodian front had crested, and it was apparent that the ARVN garrison there would survive. In I Corps, after overrunning all of Quang Tri Province and pressing toward Hue from the west too, the NVA thrusts had also started to falter under the weight of U.S. air power. Hue looked like it was going to stand. Kontum was the last opportunity the Vietnamese Communists had to transform an offensive with important but limited objectives into a spectacular achievement, and it was Abrams's last big worry. He could let Vann have the bombers. Capt. Christopher Scudder, the B-52 control officer on Vann's staff, recalled that on some days at the height of the battle Vann lobbied hard enough to obtain twenty-one of the twenty-five B-52 flights coming into the country every day.

Between May 14 and the end of the first week of June, John Vann laid the best part of 300 B-52 strikes in the environs of Kontum. To increase the safety margin in strikes close to friendly positions, SAC had instructed the bombers to fly one behind the other down the center of the box. This formation didn't give sufficient bomb coverage to satisfy Vann. He persuaded SAC to place the three B-52s in echelon. The first bomber flew right along the safety line to get as close as possible to the ARVN positions and plaster the inner third of the box, the second B-52 flew just behind and beyond it to devastate the middle, and the third came right behind and beyond it to obliterate anything left in the target zone. Vann would circle in his Ranger off a scheduled strike a few minutes before the B-52s arrived and then low-level around the box as soon as the smoke and dust had cleared enough for him to see how many NVA he had killed. He would fire bursts from his M-16 into the bomb craters. There was no danger, he explained to two reporters riding with him one day. Anyone "still living in there is in such a state of shock that he couldn't pull a trigger for thirty minutes." On another day he found forty to fifty NVA who had survived staggering around among the craters. He radioed for Cobra gunships to finish them off.

Larry Stern of the *Washington Post* had met Vann in the mid-1960s through Frank Scotton. He came to Pleiku to interview him and was astonished by the man he found. He had never seen a person so suffused with rage and exaltation. Stern remembered the way Vann's eyes "burned" as he described how he was wielding the bombers. "Anytime the wind is blowing from the north where the B-52 strikes are turning the terrain into a moonscape, you can tell from the battlefield stench that the strikes are effective," Vann said. "Outside Kontum, wherever you dropped bombs, you scattered bodies."

The NVA endured the B-52s. Four regiments of infantry, reinforced with sappers, antiaircraft machine gunners, and the ten or so T-54s that remained of the forty that had come from the North, broke into the east side of Kontum from the north and south ends of the town on the

25th, 26th, and 27th of May. Their goal was to link up, turn west, and crush Ba's reserve and overrun his command post. They almost won. At the height of the battle all that prevented them from linking was two lines of bunkers, one on the upper and the other on the lower edge of the airfield inside the town. The men in the bunkers were Vietnamese too, and on this occasion they upheld the tradition of their people. Ba and Rhotenberry were able to regroup and counterattack, and slowly, despairingly, the Communist soldiers had to give way and withdraw, leaving thousands of their comrades on the battlefield in and around Kontum.

Thieu came on a morale-raising visit on May 30, even though serious shooting was still going on in parts of the town and there was sporadic shelling. Vann carried the president of the Saigon Republic to Ba's command post in his Ranger and flew Thieu back to Pleiku afterward. Ba briefed his president, and Thieu then pinned single stars on the collar tabs of his fatigues. The ARVN had devised a one-star rank to imitate the American insignia for brigadier. The Vietnamese title was "candidate general," but being a general under any title is satisfying. Vann had been told that Ba was to be rewarded and had a pair of stars in his pocket in case Thieu forgot to bring them.

Vann did not see the fallacy in his victory. He did not see that in having to assume total control at the moment of crisis, he had proved the Saigon regime had no will of its own to survive. Nor did it occur to him that he might be playing the role he and Fred Weyand had played at Tet—postponing the end. He had once again been the indispensable man. John Hill had been struck by how necessary Vann was to the victory. Any competent American general could have done what he himself accomplished, Hill said, unfairly denigrating his contribution, but without Vann there would have been no battle at Kontum, because Ba and the other Vietnamese on the Saigon side would not have stayed to fight.

The man who had become so skilled at manipulating Vietnamese for the U.S. government would not have approved the use to which the men he served would put his triumph. Nixon was to take advantage of the respite bought by the victory at Kontum to have Kissinger negotiate a settlement that would doom the Saigon regime when the next crisis occurred. The Paris Agreement of January 1973 removed the advisors and the residual U.S. military forces propping up the Saigon side, while leaving the NVA in the South to finish its task. The exigencies of American domestic politics demanded the settlement. The president was facing reelection, and he had exhausted his capacity to manipulate public opinion on the war. The Vietnamese Communists would not give him a settlement until he agreed to withdraw the last of his forces and leave theirs in place. The farce of mutual withdrawal was at an end. Nixon and Kissinger convinced themselves they were not condemning their Saigon surrogate. They reasoned that they could hold Hanoi at bay with the threat of American air power.

On the morning of June 7, 1972, two days after the last NVA soldier was killed inside Kontum, John Vann spoke to a group of recently arrived advisors assembled at his rear headquarters in Nhatrang. His talk was a periodic event called the Newcomers' Briefing. He said he was "often struck by the widespread belief" that South Vietnam had "suffered immeasurably" from an American war. "In point of fact . . . while South Vietnam is not worth what it has cost the United States in terms of U.S. values, in terms of South Vietnamese values these people are much further ahead today than they would have been either with peace and a non-Communist government or with peace and a Communist government. . . . In 1962 the literacy rate was 15 percent. Today it's over 80 percent." The social revolution he had wanted to capture from the Communists in 1965 "has been achieved," Vann said, "partly by design, but mostly by the accident of the war." He spoke of miracle rice and irrigation equipment, of television sets and Honda motorcycles. Forced urbanization had helped bring the social revolution to pass, he said, by creating a class of "consumers" for the farmers. In the year in which Vann spoke, 39,000 Saigon soldiers died.

On June 9, 1972, Vann flew to Saigon with John Hill for a morning ceremony at which Abrams awarded Hill a Legion of Merit for his contribution to the victory. Vann stayed there for an afternoon strategy conference with Abrams and Weyand and the U.S. Army generals advising the three other ARVN corps commanders. He and Hill returned to Pleiku late in the day with Vann's new deputy, Col. Robert Kingston, who was on the promotion list for brigadier. Hill was going home. He had already postponed his scheduled departure for several weeks to see Vann through the battle. Vann tarried at the Pleiku mess for the farewell dinner for Hill. Wine was served, and there were short speeches. Vann told Pizzi and Hill and others at the head table that he was leaving for Kontum immediately afterward to spend the night with Rhotenberry and Ba. He didn't want to break his record. "I've been in Kontum every day since this thing started." he said. He had the mess stewards wrap some fruit and leftover fresh rolls and took an unopened bottle of wine to bring to Rhotenberry and Ba.

He was in a jubilant mood when his helicopter took off shortly after 9:00 P.M. He had celebrated between the morning ceremony and the afternoon strategy conference by making love to Lee and then to two other Vietnamese women. He had started the official proceedings to marry Annie during an earlier trip to Saigon in May and had just sent her a note with Thomas Barnes, his Dep/CORDS for II Corps, who was flying to Nhatrang that night. He had forgotten all about the will he wrote on the day that Tan Canh fell. Peter Kama had gone off to Hue, where the airborne brigade had been transferred, with the slip of notepaper in his wallet. Vann radioed Rhotenberry and asked for a report on the weather in Kontum. The sky over the town was fairly clear on the night of June 9, but it had been so miserable with rain and fog on recent nights that Rhotenberry could not resist a quip after answering that the weather was fine. "You won't have to reach down with your foot to find the LZ," he said. "Roger that!" Vann replied. "I am fifteen minutes from your location."

Two creeks, one named the Khol and the other the Drou, cross Route 14 about three miles south of the Chu Pao (Pao Mountain) Pass below Kontum near the Montagnard hamlet of Ro Uay. The ARVN soldiers manning a sandbag blockhouse at the bridge there heard a helicopter approaching through the dark sky and then saw the fireball and heard the explosion of a crash. The Army aviators found him. A Cobra pilot spotted the last flames of the wreckage under a grove of tall trees the helicopter had struck. A special Huey gunship called the Night Hawk shone down the beam of its searchlight and located a place where Lt. Col. Jack Anderson, the aviator who had rescued the advisors at Hoai An, could land his Huey. He and a senior aircraft mechanic who had volunteered to go with him, Master Sgt. John Johnson, came upon Vann lying facedown in the grove. He had died instantly from the shock of the crash and his body was broken in many places, but he was not bloodied and the flames had not touched him. His Wellington boots were still on his feet. A patrol of ARVN Rangers who had arrived a few minutes earlier from a nearby fire base exacted payment for the danger of being sent to fetch him at night in an area where they had been fighting with the NVA. They stripped him of his wristwatch and wallet and his Rutgers class of 1954 ring before they carried his body to Anderson's helicopter. "I hate to be the guy to give John Vann his last ride," Anderson said to the copilot who had volunteered to fly with him, Capt. Bernard Ferguson, as they lifted off for the hospital at Pleiku.

Doug Ramsey learned of Vann's death in his seventh and last prison camp, this one near Kratie in Cambodia, where he had been moved in April. He and the other POWs were permitted to listen to Radio Hanoi and to Liberation Radio, the purported voice of the Viet Cong. The Vietnamese Communists paid Vann a reverse tribute by exulting in his end. They gave far more attention to his death than they had to the occasional deaths earlier in the war of ordinary American generals. "Vann committed towering crimes," Liberation Radio said, and his removal "constitutes a stunning blow" for the U.S. and the Saigon side. The NVA newspaper, *Military People's Daily*, published a special commentary, which Radio Hanoi broadcast, on the demise of "this outstanding chief advisor." The Communists claimed to have brought down Vann's helicopter. Radio Hanoi said a message had been sent to the antiaircraft unit responsible congratulating the gunners "for good shooting."

The Vietnamese Communists did not kill John Vann. The ARVN soldiers at the bridge heard no shooting prior to the crash, nor was there any other indication Vann's Ranger had been crippled by bullets before it hit the trees. The force of the impact and the way the whirling rotor blades sheared off tree branches indicated that the helicopter had flown into the grove under power at cruising speed. The technical analysis of the engine and other components recovered from the wreckage confirmed this.

The explanation of the crash did not lie in gunfire. Vann had drained the last of the courage out of his regular pilot, Bob Richards, with the rescue of the advisors at Tan Canh. He had been forced to let Richards stay in Nhatrang in May to try to recover his nerve. Richards had then taken leave in Bangkok and gone AWOL. As a replacement, Vann had recruited a twenty-six-year-old aviator, Lt. Ronald Doughtie. He was a capable and a daring pilot, but he did not have Richards's experience and judgment. While the weather was fine that night in the valley of the Bla River where Kontum is located, it was bad in the Pleiku region south of the Chu Pao Pass, with rain squalls and a lot of haze to hinder visibility. The verdict of the official investigation was that Doughtie may have suddenly found himself in a patch of blinding weather and instead of instantly switching to his instruments for guidance, attempted to continue to fly visually. When a pilot does this he is overcome by vertigo. He may think he is flying level, when actually he is turning and descending steeply in what airmen call "the graveyard spiral." The fact that Doughtie flew into the trees at a 45-degree angle was taken as substantial evidence that this had occurred. Colonel Anderson had guessed at vertigo when he stood amid the wreckage and looked up at the slash marks down through the trees while the Night Hawk ship illuminated them with the searchlight. Doughtie was also killed instantly by the shock of the impact, as was a captain from the Pleiku headquarters who was riding along in the backseat. The captain was interested in becoming a pilot, and Doughtie was going to give him an informal lesson on the way back from Kontum.

Anderson and some of the other aviators wondered why Vann and Doughtie were following the road up to Kontum. It was the hazardous way. One had to fly fairly low to keep the road in sight, and one ran the additional risk of being shot at going through the Chu Pao Pass. A regiment of NVA had occupied bunkers and caves on its ridges in May to prevent overland resupply and reinforcement of Kontum, and despite B-52 strikes, some of them were still there, including the crew of a 12.7mm antiaircraft machine gun who fired at anything flying low. There was a safe route that circled around to the west of Chu Pao. It avoided bullets, and in case of bad weather one could get landing instructions from a U.S. Air Force Ground Control Approach team that had been stationed with its radar equipment at Kontum Airfield to guide C-130s carrying supplies in at night, when there was less danger of shelling. Another senior Army aviator flew to Kontum along this westerly route the same night, leaving Pleiku shortly after Vann did, and he encountered no trouble.

If one understood John Vann, one was not puzzled. The road was the quickest way, and Vann would have preferred it for fun. In his mood of jubilation he would have enjoyed taunting his enemies in the pass as his helicopter raced by them in the dark. Doughtie had either ignored the risks too or had not understood them because of his inexperience, and so he had not resisted Vann as Richards might have done.

Four months after Vann died, on October 9, 1972, I found the grove of trees. I had gone to the Highlands to interview Rhotenberry and Ba and others who had fought his last battle with him, and I felt that I could not leave without seeing the place where his helicopter had crashed. I had read the official reports. I knew by then that official reports were never enough to explain John Vann. There was always more to his story.

The CORDS advisors at Pleiku let me hitch a ride out to the fire base nearest the crash site on the Huey assigned to them. An advisor to the task force of ARVN Rangers there, Capt. Dennis Franson, offered to help me look. We ran across a second lieutenant at a company position down the road who was a Montagnard. He said he knew where a crash like the one I was seeking had occurred. He took a soldier as a bodyguard and led us down a trail toward the hamlet of Ro Uay.

The day was hot and sunny, with a sky of white clouds. One could see for miles in every direction. The grove was just 550 yards off the road on the northwest side of the hamlet and was the only clump of high trees in the whole vicinity. The Montagnards practice the crude system of slash-and-burn agriculture. They kill the trees by cutting around the trunk, burn the undergrowth, and plant crops until the soil is exhausted in three or four years. Then they move on to another section of forest while the original planting renews itself. All of the other trees in the vicinity were lower, second-growth ones coming up in abandoned plantings. It seemed strange that Vann's helicopter had somehow found this one patch of tall trees in the darkness and rain.

The wreckage was scattered around the grove for fifty to sixty yards. The speed at which the machine had hit the trees and the explosion of the fuel cells had shattered the little helicopter. The sole recognizable fragment was the twisted tail boom. The grove was beautiful. The trees were majestic in their natural state. The canopy of their branches gave deep shade. The sun came down in rays of gentled light. I wondered why the tribal people had left this grove of trees untouched.

I saw a small, low square of hewn logs planted upright in the ground nearby and asked the Montagnard lieutenant what it was. "Dead men here," he said. "Dead men here," he repeated, sweeping his hand about.

Then I saw the figures placed around another, larger square of hewn logs farther into the trees. I had not noticed them before, because I had been concentrating on the wreckage. They were carved of wood in the primitive fashion of the Montagnards, an ancient people who migrated into Indochina earlier than the Vietnamese. The figures were squatting, resting their chins on their hands and staring into space. I had seen figures like them at another tribal hamlet not far from this one nearly ten years before, and I knew now why the trees had not been touched. The grove was the hamlet graveyard. The tribal people had left the trees in their natural state to guard the graves and to provide shade for their burial rites.

Now I also knew what had happened on that night. John Vann had come skylarking up the road, mocking death again, unaware that these figures of death were waiting for him in this grove.

* * *

Vann's friend, George Jacobson, stayed until the end. He left on a helicopter from the roof of the embassy not long before dawn on April 30, 1975, to take refuge aboard a Seventh Fleet ship off Vung Tau as the NVA tanks were preparing to move into Saigon. John Vann was not meant to flee to a ship at sea, and he did not miss his exit. He died believing he had won his war.

ACKNOWLEDGMENTS

The research and writing of this book have been like a long voyage of discovery. I would not have completed it without the love and support of my family, the help and encouragement of friends, and the generosity and assistance of those I encountered along the way.

For fellowships to partially defray research costs and living expenses on my sixteen-year odyssey I thank Gordon Ray and The John Simon Guggenheim Memorial Foundation; William Polk, Peter Diamandopoulos, and The Adlai Stevenson Institute of International Affairs; Nicholas Rizopoulos, David Calleo, Lewis Lehrman, and The Lehrman Institute; Leslie Dunbar and the Field Foundation; John Bresnan, Reuben Frodin, and The Ford Foundation; Joel Colton and The Rockefeller Foundation; and James Billington, Peter Braestrup, Michael Lacey, and The Woodrow Wilson International Center for Scholars. Russell Baker, John Fairbank, Leslie Gelb, Brendan Gill, James B. Reston, A. M. Rosenthal, Harrison Salisbury, Arthur Schlesinger, Jr., Roger Stevens, Seymour Topping, Cyrus Vance, and Tom Wicker wrote fellowship recommendations for me.

The Library of Congress gave me space in which to write and access to its unsurpassed research facilities from 1980 onward. I thank Daniel Boorstin, the former Librarian of Congress; John Broderick; Ellen Hahn; Winston Tabb; Christopher Wright; William Sartain; Joseph Brooks; and in particular Suzanne Thorin and Bruce Martin for being so accommodating.

A. M. Rosenthal, Seymour Topping, Max Frankel, James Greenfield, Craig Whitney, Hedrick Smith, and Bill Kovach extended to me the facilities of the New York Times. Vo Tuan Chan and Le Kim Dinh of the Saigon bureau helped with logistics and translation during my research trips to South Vietnam in 1972 and 1973. Sunday Fellows, the librarian of the Washington bureau, always responded to my requests for material from the clip files. Linda Lake of the news research section in New York also located clips for me.

Ambassador Tran Kim Phuong granted me a visa to South Vietnam for my 1972 research trip despite the recommendation of a high-ranking State Department official that he refuse. Hoang Duc Nha, then commissioner-general for information of the Saigon government, gave Ambassador Phuong permission to do so. Ambassador Bui Diem, the former envoy in Washington, urged them to grant me the visa.

For their hospitality during that 1972 trip I thank Craig Whitney, Frenchy Zois McDaniel and Morris McDaniel, John Swango, Maj. Gen. Michael Healy and Col. Jack Matteson, and former Sgt. Major Charles Eatley; Joseph Treaster and Barbara Gluck and Frank Wisner were especially hospitable during my subsequent trip in 1973.

I am also grateful for the hospitality extended to me during research trips in the United States—to Mary Jane Vann and John Allen Vann, Vince and Ann Davis, Carl and Edith Bernard, and Edward Story.

Robert Osgood granted me the use of an office at Washington's School of Advanced International Studies of Johns Hopkins University for the academic year of 1974–75.

James Chace served as chairman of four seminars I gave at The Lehrman Institute in the winter and spring of 1976. The rapporteur was John Lax, a young historian of imagination and brilliance whose life and promise were snuffed out by a drunken driver.

Brig. Gen. E. H. Simmons made me welcome at the Marine Corps Historical Center in the Washington Navy Yard. Jack Shulimson and Keith Fleming guided me in locating the documents I needed. Joyce Bonnett found most of those I requested in her archives.

Vincent Demma, George MacGarrigle, Richard Hunt, William Hammond, and Joel Meyerson of the U.S. Army Center of Military History in Washington were companions along the road, patiently replying to every inquiry.

Col. James Agnew, Col. Donald Shaw, and Dr. Richard Sommers of the U.S. Army Military History Institute at Carlisle Barracks, Pennsylvania, facilitated the declassification of the classified portion of John Vann's papers they held. The Army's Office of the Adjutant General and the Department of Defense responded swiftly and with little quibbling to my other Freedom of Information Act requests. Harry Eisenstadt of the Defense Mapping Agency helped me to purchase the military maps I needed.

The Office of Air Force History in Washington graciously provided publications and general reference assistance.

Harry Middleton, David Humphrey, Charles Corkran, and Sharon Fawcett of the Lyndon Baines Johnson Library in Austin, Texas, were forthcoming with documents from their archives.

Ann Elam of the Fairfax County Police Department located the records of Garland Hopkins's suicide.

Tess Johnston typed large sections of a semifinal draft of the manuscript. Prosser Gifford, deputy director of The Woodrow Wilson International Center for Scholars, and William Dunn, the assistant director for administration, arranged for the typing of other sections by Eloise Doane and Pat Sheridan.

Col. Paul Raisig, Jr., an old comrade from 1962 in the Mekong Delta, consented to read the manuscript for technical military accuracy. If any mistakes remain, however, they are mine.

My friend and agent, Robert Lescher, gave me more than his professional help. He kept faith with me down the years.

Other friends, Mitchell and Sheila Rogovin and Gay Talese, gave me special help when I most needed it.

William Shawn, the former editor of *The New Yorker*, warmly encouraged me and came to my assistance at a critical moment. I am grateful as well to his successor, Robert Gottlieb, for his decision to run four excerpts from the book in the magazine; to John Bennet for editing the excerpts; and to Peter Canby and Hal Espen for checking the excerpts for accuracy.

I am thankful for the friendship of Robert Loomis, my editor at Random House, and for his sensitivity and guidance in shaping the manuscript. I thank Victoria Klose and Edward Johnson for copy editing this book and Barbé Hammer for her assistance. I am fortunate to be published by a house headed by Robert Bernstein, and I thank Jason Epstein, Anthony Schulte (formerly with Random House), Gerald Hollingsworth, and Joni Evans for their support.

My daughters, Maria and Catherine, collated my hundreds of interviews and typed a catalogue of them on three-by-five-inch index cards. They extracted news clippings from microfilm and performed numerous research chores uncomplainingly.

My wife, Susan, edited every draft of the manuscript, typed parts of the semifinal draft, listened to all my discussions of John Vann and the war in Vietnam, talked me through my crises, and gave me the love and the grit to press on.

INTERVIEWS

Interviews were indispensable to the writing of this book. So much that is important in the life of a man and in the history of a war is recorded only in perishable memory. Three hundred and eighty-five persons were interviewed between 1972 and 1988. I made two three-month trips to South Vietnam, the first in 1972 and the second in 1973, in order to interview as many persons as possible before the fragile world of the South came apart. The rank given for military personnel is that held at the time of the initial interview. When there is no indication for retirement (Ret.), the individual was still on active service. Some of the interviews were brief exchanges, verbal or in correspondence. Most were substantial and some lasted for days. Public men under pressure kindly kept finding an hour to spare from their schedules. The late Ellsworth Bunker, for example, let me interview him on eleven occasions from 1974 to 1976 while he was negotiating the Panama Canal Treaty. People also bore with me down the years as I returned for additional information. I interviewed Gen. Fred Weyand in 1974 when he was chief of staff of the Army and in 1985 and 1986 when he was retired in Hawaii. Nearly 170 of the interviews were tape recorded. I accumulated almost 640 cassettes. These proved invaluable because years later, when writing a particular episode, I could listen to the pertinent sections of the tapes and rescue details and insights that had eluded my note taking in the 186 stenographer's pads I also accumulated. The names of many of the interviewees listed below do not appear in the narrative because the book is a distillation of a much larger body of research. Nevertheless, I am as grateful to them as I am to those mentioned in the text. The book is a house built with the contributions of all. If there are flaws in the architecture, they are mine alone.

Samuel Adams
Col. Dwight Adams, USA
George Allen
Mary Allen
T. D. Allman
Joseph Alsop
Pham Xuan An
Tran Van An

Lt. Col. Jack Anderson, USA
"Annie" and her father, mother,
  and sister
Lt. Col. Bob Armentrout, USAF
Peter Arnett
Candidate Gen. Ly Tong Ba,
  ARVN
Gene Bable

William Bader
Thomas Barnes
Richard Barnet
Col. Nguyen Be, ARVN
Keyes Beech
Charles Benoit
Col. George Benson, USA (Ret.)
Lt. Col. John Bergen, USA
Amb. Samuel Berger
2d Lt. Gary Bergtholdt, USA
Col. Carl Bernard, USA
Edith Bernard
Lt. Gen. Sidney Berry, USA
Lt. Col. Le Nguyen Binh, ARVN
Master Sgt. Edward Black, USA
Brig. Gen. Frank Blazey, USA
Joy Blazey
Robert Borosage
Lt. Col. Louis Borum, USA
Sgt. Major Arnold Bowers, USA
  (Ret.)
Capt. John Bozin, USA
Col. Francis Bradley, USA (Ret.)
Maj. Noel Brady, USA
Philip Brady
Peter Braestrup
Henry Brandon
Peter Brownback
Malcolm Browne
Jack Buhl
Everet Bumgardner
Amb. Ellsworth Bunker
David Butler
Fox Butterfield
J. Fred Buzhardt
Dorothy Lee Vann Cadorette
1st Lt. Huynh Van Cai, ARVN
Brig. Gen. Huynh Van Cao,
  ARVN (Ret.)
Maj. Richard Carey, USA
Lt. Col. Verner Carlson, USA
Col. G. Baker Carrington, USA
  (Ret.)
Jerry Carta
Sgt. First Class Bobby Carter, USA

Capt. Richard Cassidy, USA
James Chace
Bryan Chastain
Nguyen Van Chau
Tran Ngoc Chau
Brig. Gen. Ernie Cheatham,
  USMC
George Christian
Candidate Gen. Nguyen Van Chuc,
  ARVN
Maj. Gen. Frank Clay, USA (Ret.)
1st Lt. James Cloninger, USA
William Colby
Tom Coles, Jr.
Donald Colin
Lt. Col. Lucien Conein
Rev. Robert Consolvo
Robert Craig
Edward Crutchfield
Lt. Col. Cleve Cunningham, USA
  (Ret.)
Patrick Dailey
Brig. Gen. Bui Dinh Dam
Greyson Daughtrey
Peter Davis
Prof. Vincent Davis
Alan Dawson
Amb. John Dean
Dale de Haan
Vincent Demma
Lt. Gen. William DePuy, USA
Brig. Gen. Tran Ba Di, ARVN
Amb. Bui Diem
Col. Huynh Ngoc Diep, ARVN
George Dillard
Lillian Dillard
Tran Van Dinh
Brig. Gen. Pham Van Dong,
  ARVN
Tom Donohue
Col. James Drummond, USA
  (Ret.)
Ronnie Dugger
Maj. Gen. John M. Dunn, USA
  (Ret.)

Capt. Walter Dunn, USA
Maj. Gen. Ngo Dzu, ARVN
Sgt. Major Charles Eatley, USA
(Ret.)
Brig. Gen. Howard Eggleston,
USA (Ret.)
1st Lt. Thomas Eisenhower, USA
Daniel Ellsberg
Patricia Marx Ellsberg
Gloria Emerson
George Esper
Eugenia Wilson Evans
John Evans, Jr.
Horst Faas
Lt. Col. David Farnham, USA
Col. Elmer Faust, USA (Ret.)
Myrtle Felton
Capt. Bernard Ferguson, USA
Bea Firman
Frances FitzGerald
Lt. Gen. George Forsythe, USA
(Ret.)
Tom Fox
Matt Franjola
Capt. Dennis Franson, USA
Polly Fritchey
Rev. Harold Fuss
Maj. Frank Gall, Jr., USA
Lt. Col. Norbert Gannon, USA
Lt. Col. George Gaspard, USA
Col. Silas Gassett, USA (Ret.)
Leslie Gelb
Philip Geyelin
Maj. Nguyen Van Giong, ARVN
Gen. Wallace Greene, Jr., USMC
(Ret.)
Lawrence Grinter
Joseph Gulvas
Amb. Philip Habib
Maj. Gary Hacker, USA
David Halberstam
Michael Halberstam, M.D.
Morton Halperin
William Hammond
Nguyen Hieu Hanh

Col. Nguyen Tri Hanh, ARVN
Richard Harrington
Roy Haverkamp
Brig. Gen. Michael Healy, USA
William Heasley
Col. Thomas Henry, USA
Brig. Gen. James Herbert, USA
Seymour Hersh
Capt. John Heslin, USA
Gerald Hickey
Maj. Gen. John Hill, Jr., USA
Richard Holbrooke
Lt. Col. Leslie Holcomb, Jr., USA
(Ret.)
Lt. Gen. Harris Hollis, USA (Ret.)
Margaret Hopkins
Capt. Donald Hudson, USA
Maj. Do Huy Hue, ARVN
Dick Hughes
Nguyen Manh Hung
Richard Hunt
Mark Huss
Maj. Charles Ingram, USA
Vice Adm. Andrew Jackson, USN
(Ret.)
Col. George Jacobson, USA (Ret.)
Robert Joffe
Lt. Col. Harry Johnson, USA
(Ret.)
Ralph Johnson
Tess Johnston
Col. Thomas Jones, USA (Ret.)
Howard Jordan
Robert Josephson
Lt. Col. Peter Kama, USA
Col. Phillip Kaplan, USA
Stanley Karnow
Samuel Katz, M.D.
Col. Francis Kelly, USA (Ret.)
Col. Irvin Kent, USA (Ret.)
Maj. Gen. Le Nguyen Khang,
ARVNAF Marines
Maj. Gen. Tran Thien Khiem,
ARVN
Dang Duc Khoi

Eva Kim
Col. Pham Chi Kim, ARVN
William King
Brig. Gen. Douglas Kinnard, USA
  (Ret.)
Col. Alfred Kitts, USA (Ret.)
Amb. Akitane Kiuchi
Col. Wendell Knowles, USA (Ret.)
Prof. Gabriel Kolko
Amb. Robert Komer
Lt. Col. Albert Kotzebue, USA
  (Ret.)
Maj. Gen. William Kraft, Jr., USA
Col. Charles Krulak, USMC
Lt. Gen. Victor Krulak, USMC
  (Ret.)
Col. Jonathan F. Ladd, USA
  (Ret.)
Prof. Walter LaFeber
W. Anthony Lake
Maj. John Lang, USA
Maj. Gen. Edward Lansdale,
  USAF (Ret.)
John Lax
Lorraine Layne
"Lee" and her sister
Jacques Leslie
John Levinson, M.D.
Thomas Lewis
Capt. John Litsinger, USA
Col. Samuel Loboda, USA (Ret.)
Emily Lodge
Hon. Henry Cabot Lodge, Jr.
Col. Hoang Ngoc Lung, ARVN
Col. Paul Lunsford, USA
John McAlister, Jr.
George McArthur
Daniel McCreadie
Frenchy Zois McDaniel
Morris McDaniel
Capt. Robert McDonald, USA
Lt. Col. George MacGarrigle, USA
  (Ret.)
Col. David MacIsaac, USAF (Ret.)

Amb. Allan McLean
Harry McPherson, Jr.
Joachim Maitre
John Malott
Col. Richard Manion, USA
Charles Mann
Robin Mannock
John Marks
Richard Marks, M.D.
Nora Bowling Martin
Col. Jack Matteson, USA
CWO Russell Maxson, USA
Lt. Col. Robert Mays, USA (Ret.)
Robert Mellen
Robert Mendenhall
Gen. Edward Meyer, USA
Harvey Meyerson
Joel Meyerson
Harry Middleton
Lloyd Miller
William Miller
John Modderno
Charles Mohr
Brig. Gen. Robert Montague, USA
  (Ret.)
Robert Moore
Kenneth Moorfield
Richard Moose
Ron Moreau
Doris Allen Moreland
Maj. Gen. John Murray, USA
Mark Murray
Edmundo Navarro
Amb. John Negroponte
Hoang Duc Nha
Col. Ma Sanh Nhon, ARVN
Robert Odom
Minoru Omori
Maj. Gen. Frank Osmanski, USA
  (Ret.)
Lt. Col. Billy Owen, USMC (Ret.)
Gen. Bruce Palmer, Jr., USA
Lt. Gen. Theodore Parker, USA
  (Ret.)

Lt. Col. Warren Parker, USA (Ret.)
Richard Parkinson
Maj. Gen. George S. Patton III, USA
Mary Payer
Robert Payette
Maj. Donnie Pearce, USA
Robert Pell
Capt. Tim Petropulos, USA
Rufus Phillips
Douglas Pike
Col. Joseph Pizzi, USA
Thomas Polgar
Col. Daniel Boone Porter, Jr., USA (Ret.)
Thomas Pownall
Col. Herbert Prevost, USAF (Ret.)
Lamar Prosser
Jean Puckett
Col. Ralph Puckett, Jr., USA (Ret.)
Kenneth Quinn
Joseph Raby, Jr.
Melvin Raby
Col. Paul Raisig, Jr., USA
Kathleen (Doughtie) Ralston
Douglas Ramsey
Marcus Raskin
J. Donald Rauth
Benjamin Read
James B. Reston
Col. R. M. Rhotenberry, USA
Sgt. First Class (formerly CWO) Robert Richards, USA
John Roberts
Mitchell Rogovin
Lt. Col. James Rose, USA
Gen. William Rosson, USA (Ret.)
Walt Rostow
Hon. Dean Rusk
Anthony Russo
Harrison Salisbury
Willie Saulters

Lt. Col. James Scanlon, USA (Ret.)
Sydney Schanberg
Jonathan Schell
Frank Scotton
Lt. Gen. Brent Scowcroft, USAF
Capt. Christopher Scudder, USA
Lt. Gen. Jonathan Seaman, USA (Ret.)
Brigadier Francis Serong, Australian Army (Ret.)
Theodore Shackley
Robert Shaplen
James Sheldon
Jack Shulimson
Alvin Shuster
Samuel Shuster, M.D.
Merrill Shutt, M.D.
Maj. Gen. Winant Sidle, USA
Richard Silverstein, Esq.
Col. Ivan Slavich, USA (Ret.)
Col. Edward P. Smith, USA
Lt. Col. J. Lapsley Smith, USA
Frank Snepp
Ed Sprague
CWO Clifford Spry, USA (Ret.)
Col. Alfred Earl Spry, USA (Ret.)
John Paul Spry, Jr.
Vaughn Stapleton
Ralph Stavins
Richard Steadman
Laurence Stern
Steve Stibbins
Lt. Gen. Richard Stilwell, USA
Walter Stoneman
Edward Story
Patricia Vann Stromberg
Lt. Col. John Swango, USA (Ret.)
Norman Sweet
2d Lt. Gary Swingle, USA
Lt. Col. William Taylor, Jr., USA
Col. Doan Van Te, ARVN
Thomas Thayer, Jr.
Sir Robert Thompson

Kieu Mong Thu
Lt. Col. Trinh Tieu, ARVN
Maj. Gen. Charles Timmes, USA
 (Ret.)
Jerry Tinker
Maj. Gen. Nguyen Van Toan,
 ARVN
Peter Tomsen
Seymour Topping
Mollie Tosolini
Robert Traister
Archie Treadwell
William Arthur Tripp
Col. John Truby, USA
Amb. William Trueheart
Col. Jack Van Loan, USAF (Ret.)
Aaron Frank Vann, Jr.
Chief Master Sgt. Eugene Vann,
 USAF
Jo Vann
Jesse Vann
John Allen Vann
Mary Jane Vann
Peter Vann
Thomas Vann
1st Lt. Charles Vasquez
Lt. Gen. Cao Van Vien, ARVN

Paul Warnke
William Watts
Lt. Gen. Richard Weede, USMC
 (Ret.)
Yao Wei
Cora Weiss
Gen. William Westmoreland, USA
 (Ret.)
Gen. Fred Weyand, USA
Amb. Charles Whitehouse
Craig Whitney
William Wild
Lt. Gen. Samuel Wilson, USA
Col. Wilbur Wilson, USA (Ret.)
Maj. Jon Wise, USA
Amb. Frank G. Wisner II
Alex Wong
Prof. Alexander Woodside
Lacy Wright
Rev. William Wright, Jr.
Lt. Gen. Robert York, USA (Ret.)
Florence Yonan
Earl Young
Lt. Col. Richard Ziegler, USA
 (Ret.)
Barry Zorthian

DOCUMENTS

John Vann's papers were the primary source of written material for this book. His family turned all of them over to me when they were shipped home from Vietnam after his death. The classified documents and letters among them were culled by a military historian in Saigon and sent separately to the U.S. Army Military History Institute at the Army War College at Carlisle Barracks, Pennsylvania. These were, except for a small number of documents lost by the State Department, declassified by the relevant agencies under a Freedom of Information Act request I submitted and copies were made for me by the institute. Because permission was granted by his family, the Office of The Adjutant General also arranged for the retrieval and release to me of Vann's entire Army record, including that of his enlisted service in World War II. Friends of Vann, such as Prof. Vincent Davis, director of the Patterson School of Diplomacy and International Commerce at the University of Kentucky, added material they held. Davis, for example, had safeguarded all of his correspondence with Vann and had tape recorded the not-for-attribution lectures Vann gave for him each year while on home leave. I had the lectures transcribed. I further supplemented Vann's papers with much that I had gathered in the course of newspapering and with other correspondence and documents given to me by people I interviewed for the book. The result filled the better part of five file cabinets.

The Pentagon Papers were the second major source of documentation for the book. Despite the years that have passed since they were first published in condensed form by the *New York Times* in 1971, they remain the most complete and informative official archive on the Vietnam War. Regrettably, no full edition of the papers has ever been published. The *Times* series was first printed in book form in paperback by Bantam as *The Pentagon Papers*, followed soon afterward in 1971 by a hardcover version by Quadrangle Books. Beacon Press of Boston also published a four-volume edition with a fifth index volume, *The Pentagon Papers: History of United States Decision Making on Vietnam*, Senator Gravel edition, in 1971 and 1972. The most extensive but unfortunately censored version is the one declassified by the Department of Defense and published in a twelve-book set in 1971 by the U.S. Government Printing Office as *United States–Vietnam Relations, 1945–1967*. I relied on the copy of the original, approximately three thousand pages of narrative history and more than four thousand pages of appended documents, that I first obtained for the *Times*. It was reasonably complete except for four sections on the secret negotiations with Hanoi. I later acquired these after they were obtained and made public by Jack Anderson.

The Source Notes for "The Funeral" and Books I–VII that now follow are by no means an exhaustive listing. They are simply an attempt to indicate the principal interviews, correspondence and documents, and published works consulted for the sections cited.

SOURCE NOTES

The Funeral

The experience of going to John Vann's funeral led me to write this book. I drew for this section on my interviews with the members of the Vann family and with the principal public figures who attended the funeral. Col. Samuel Loboda, the commander of the U.S. Army Band in 1972, was extremely helpful in explaining details of the ceremony. Mark Murray, the Department of the Army civilian official in charge of Vann's funeral as operations officer for ceremonies for the Military District of Washington, was equally helpful in this regard. Maj. Charles Ingram, ceremonial officer on the Military District of Washington staff at the time, was of further assistance. Mr. Murray also provided details on the confrontation in the Roosevelt Room at the White House and Lt. Gen. Brent Scowcroft was kind enough to let me interview him on Jesse Vann's attempt to give Richard Nixon half of his draft card.

In this section and elsewhere in the book, conversations are rendered in quotation marks where there is a written record or the memory of the person or persons interviewed seemed precise enough to justify placing the words in quotes.

Book I: Going to War

The most significant interviews for Book I were those with Lt. Col. Le Nguyen Binh, Maj. Gen. Frank Clay, Col. James Drummond, Col. Elmer Faust, Col. Jonathan F. Ladd, Col. Daniel Porter, Jr., Col. Herbert Prevost, and Lt. Col. Richard Ziegler. I am especially grateful to Colonels Drummond, Porter, and Ziegler for the breadth of information they provided and I thank Colonel Porter for speaking with such candor on subjects that were painful to him.

John Vann's papers were the most important source of written material. It was possible to reconstruct much of this period from the reports he wrote while at 7th Division, notes, letters, newspaper clippings, photographs, and an occasional item of surpassing value like the invitation to the September 11, 1962, lunch for Maxwell Taylor and the results of the lunch Vann penned on the back. The transcript of Vann's tape-recorded top-secret interview with an Army historian, Charles von Luttichau, on July 22, 1963, after his return to the United States was also helpful.

Colonel Ziegler provided me with an additional source of written material that supplemented Vann's papers. He had kept copies, complete with map overlays, of a number of the after-action reports, including the report on the July 20, 1962, action on the Plain of Reeds. These reports were missing from Vann's papers and the copies in the official Army records had also been lost. Furthermore, Colonel Ziegler turned his operations journal, one of those old-fashioned cloth-bound eight-by-fourteen-inch ledgers the Army used to issue for record keeping, into a diary of his year at 7th Division, Scotch taping photographs of people and events onto the pages. The diary, and related documents he preserved, was a mine of information on this period with many insights into Vann's thinking.

The carbons of my UPI dispatches proved another valuable archive. David Halberstam's *The Making of a Quagmire* was a useful published source. Here, as elsewhere in the book, I also drew on my memory and my talks with John Vann.

While the behavior of Generals Harkins and Anthis speaks for them on the bombing and shelling of peasant hamlets, the generals did admit in secret that they were aware of what they were doing. The admission came after W. Averell Harriman, then assistant secretary of state for Far Eastern Affairs, attacked the bombing policy in a position paper in March 1963. Ambassador Frederick Nolting replied at the end of April 1963 with a lengthy letter, classified Top Secret, attaching to it a still lengthier top-secret memorandum from Harkins and Anthis. Both had been drafted by Anthis's 2nd Air Division staff. The central argument of the letter and the memorandum was a World War II-derived rationale that any peasant hamlet was fair game if it was in an area believed to be dominated by the Viet Cong. The ambassador said in the letter that the peasants were more likely to blame the Viet Cong for occurrence of the air strikes than the Saigon regime and the Americans for making them. The generals also argued that the strikes would help win the war by putting fear into the peasants. "The common man in the Orient has an inordinate respect for power," they said.

Book II: Antecedents to a Confrontation

Everet Bumgardner, Lt. Col. Lucien Conein, and Col. Alfred Kitts provided the key interviews for Book II.

Maj. Gen. Edward Lansdale's secret history of his mission to Vietnam, which came to me through the Pentagon Papers, was the basic documentary source on his role. Lansdale's book, *In the Midst of Wars: An American's Mission to Southeast Asia*, was also helpful, as were my talks with him over the years.

The Pentagon Papers repeatedly proved to be a valuable archive: on the return of the French in 1945, on Ho Chi Minh's vain appeals for American help, on the so-called Bao Dai solution, and on the origins of the second Indochina war in the birth of the Viet Cong.

I am grateful to Prof. Walter LaFeber for clarifying, in an important monograph, the role of Franklin Roosevelt in the Indochina tragedy. See "Roosevelt, Churchill, and Indochina: 1942–45," *American Historical Review*, December 1975.

Vietnam: The Origins of Revolution, by John McAlister, Jr., is a fine published source on the genesis of the Viet Minh and France's return in 1945. The official history of the U.S. Navy in Vietnam in these early years, *The United States Navy and the Vietnam Conflict*, Volume I: *The Setting of the Stage to 1959*, by Dean Allard and Edwin Hooper, is another source on the circumstances of the French return.

Lucien Bodard, in his *The Quicksand War: Prelude to Vietnam*, is eloquent on the French debacle along Route Coloniale 4 in October 1950, and Bernard Fall provides details in his *The Two Viet-Nams*.

Denis Warner's *The Last Confucian* and Robert Shaplen's writings on Ngo Dinh Diem and his family were a supplement to my own research and my personal experience.

My greatest debt is to Alexander Woodside for discerning the nature of the Vietnamese Communist leadership and much more in his pathfinding book on Vietnamese history and culture: *Community and Revolution in Modern Vietnam*. Professor Woodside placed me further in his debt by reading Book II in manuscript and suggesting a number of changes.

The source for Diem's desecration of the Viet Minh cemeteries and war memorials in the South is Bernard Fall's account of the Battle of Dien Bien Phu, *Hell in a Very Small Place*.

Figures on the growth of the Viet Cong from the start of the insurrection in 1957 until John Kennedy's decision to intervene in November 1961 are taken from U.S. military intelligence reports.

Book III: The Battle of Ap Bac

To write this account of the Battle of Ap Bac, I compared John Vann's exhaustive after-action report with the equally thorough Viet Cong report that was later captured. I expanded on the information in both documents with interviews and with my own observations of the battlefield at the time. My UPI dispatches on Ap Bac stimulated memory as well as adding more material.

Vann's report and the Viet Cong document tended to corroborate each other, a fact of which Vann was proud.

Some nitty-gritty, such as Vann's radio call sign, "Topper Six," and that of the advisors to the M-113 company, "Walrus," again came from the marvelous record keeping of Colonel Ziegler. He saved his pocket notebooks with the jottings he had made during Ap Bac and other actions.

Information on the home areas of the men of the 1st Company of the 261st Main Force Viet Cong Battalion comes from a personnel roster of the unit that was also captured after the battle. Unfortunately, the original copy of the roster, with the names of the ordinary guerrillas and the aliases of the ranking cadres, has been lost and all that remains is an American analysis of it which mentions the places of origin.

The principal interviews for Book III were those with Candidate Gen. Ly Tong Ba, Sgt. Major Arnold Bowers, Lt. Col. Robert Mays, Colonel Porter, Colonel Prevost, Lt. Col. James Scanlon, and Colonel Ziegler.

Book IV: Taking On the System

"Friendly" shelling at Bac and background on General York: personal recollections, carbons of my UPI dispatches, Vann's after-action report on Ap Bac, and interview with Lt. Gen. Robert York.

Harkins wanting to fire Vann right after Ap Bac and subsequently relenting: interview with Maj. Gen. Charles Timmes. The clipping of the Bill Mauldin cartoon with the note by Harkins was in Vann's papers.

Porter's memorandum to Harkins on Ap Bac: Vann preserved a copy of Porter's indorsement on his Ap Bac after-action report by attaching it to the copy of the report in his papers.

July 23, 1962, Honolulu Conference: Where the official documents, such as the record of the conference, are mentioned in the text, I will not cite them again here.

Joint Chiefs' mission to South Vietnam provoked by Ap Bac: The Joint Chiefs' instructions to the team were repeated in the team's subsequent report. The remark by the head of the team summing up its mission—to answer the question "Are we winning or are we losing?"—was made during the "debrief" at the Hawaii headquarters of Commander in Chief Pacific when the team was on its way back to Washington.

"Brute" Krulak's pre-Vietnam career: interview with Lt. Gen. Victor Krulak; sundry Marine Corps sources, including the official history of Marine helicopter development, which recounts Krulak's contribution; and the general's 1984 book on the history of the Corps and his career: *First to Fight*.

Conduct of the JCS investigating team in South Vietnam and the writing of its report: interviews with Colonels Porter and Ladd, General York, General Krulak, and Lt. Gen. George Forsythe, then a colonel and the senior aide to the four-star Army general who led the team. In addition, I questioned Lt. Gen. Theodore Parker, on the team as the Army's deputy chief of staff for operations, and Vice Adm. Andrew Jackson, the senior Navy representative.

Premier Pham Van Dong's skepticism: Ambassador Maneli told me of his exchange with the Hanoi prime minister when I first met Maneli in Saigon in 1963.

The U.S. arms the Viet Cong: The figures on American weapons supplied to the Saigon side, and thus available for capture by the guerrillas, are taken from the records of the Honolulu strategy conferences and other official U.S. documents of the period.

Viet Cong recruiting after Ap Bac: The discovery that the guerrillas recruited 2,500 young farmers in Kien Hoa in the spring of 1963, most right out of the strategic hamlets, was made by Lt. Col. J. Lapsley Smith, then a captain and intelligence advisor for the province.

Smuggling of heavy weapons by sea: Vann and Drummond received information in early 1963 of weapons being landed along the coast of the Mekong Delta by seagoing vessels, but the reports were not taken with sufficient seriousness in Saigon. The details of how the trawlers made their smuggling runs became known later in the war when several were intercepted by U.S. forces.

Halberstam-Vann relationship: interview with David Halberstam; Halberstam-Vann correspondence in Vann papers; personal recollections.

Vann's February 8, 1963, memorandum on the Viet Cong units Cao and Dam refused to attack: Drummond and Ziegler interviews; Vann's tape-recorded interview with the U.S. Army historian Charles von Luttichau; and correspondence in Vann's papers.

Porter's final report: Although Harkins suppressed the report, Porter remembered its general contents. Fred Ladd was also of assistance.

Vann's canceled briefing for the Joint Chiefs: The correspondence and documents in Vann's papers supported his version of the briefing incident. Col. Francis Kelly, Vann's immediate superior in the Directorate of Special Warfare, and Maj. Gen. Frank Clay, who was stationed at the Pentagon at the time and in touch with Vann, remembered Krulak's role. Clay also had friends on the staff of the Joint Chiefs and his brother, Lucius, an Air Force general, was in the Pentagon then and privy to JCS affairs.

The overthrow of the Ngo Dinhs: interviews with the Hon. Henry Cabot Lodge, Jr.; Lucien Conein; and Maj. Gen. John M. Dunn, then a lieutenant colonel and Lodge's executive assistant in Saigon; my UPI carbons; a memorandum written at the time with information from Col. (subsequently ARVN Brig. Gen.) Pham Van Dong, who was privy to the plot; the Pentagon Papers and particularly the secret cable traffic between Lodge and President Kennedy and others in Washington.

Clandestine warfare against the North—"Operation Plan 34A": Krulak interview; the Pentagon Papers and separate official documents. Colby admits the failure of his own smaller program and discusses his opposition to Krulak's scheme and McNamara's rejection of his arguments in his memoirs, *Honorable Men: My Life in the CIA*.

The creation of the second Viet Minh: The strength and level of organization of the Viet Cong army at the end of 1964 is based on retrospective U.S. military intelligence reports. The intelligence officers achieved a realistic estimate by reevaluating the data and utilizing subsequent information. A copy of a captured Viet Cong after-action report on the destruction of the entire company of M-113's on December 9, 1964, was in Vann's papers.

Book V: Antecedents to the Man

John Vann's ancestry: interviews with Mollie Tosolini and William Arthur "Buddie" Tripp; for the Spry side with Lorraine Layne, a younger sister of Johnny Spry, and with John Paul Spry, Jr., Johnny Spry's oldest son. Commonwealth of Virginia, Department of Health, Bureau of Vital Records and Health Statistics for birth, marriage, and death information. For published works consulted see in Bibliography: *Albion's Fatal Tree: Crime and Society in Eighteenth-Century England*, by Douglas Hay et al.; *Convicts and the Colonies*, by A.G.L. Shaw; *The Encyclopedia of Southern History; The Mind of the South*, by W. J. Cash; *Night Comes to the Cumberlands*, by Harry Caudill; *Beaufort County [North Carolina], Two Centuries of Its History*, by C. Wingate Reid; *Sketches of Pitt County [North Carolina], 1704–1910,* by Henry T. King; "Some Colonial History of Beaufort County, North Carolina," by Francis H. Cooper; *North Carolina: An Economic and Social Profile*, by S. Huntington Hobbs, Jr.; *A Sketch of North Carolina; Origins of the New South, 1877–1913,* by C. Vann Woodward.

Character of Myrtle: Mollie Tosolini, Buddie Tripp, Lillian and George Dillard, Dorothy Lee Vann Cadorette, Aaron Frank Vann, Jr.

Character of Johnny Spry and his affair with Myrtle: Mollie Tosolini and John Paul Spry, Jr., the son to whom Johnny Spry talked most freely about his early life. John Paul Spry, Jr., also lent me photographs of his father in his younger years. Two other sons, retired CWO Clifford "Kirby" Spry and Col. Alfred Earl Spry, provided further insights into their father's character and personality.

John Vann's birth and infancy: Mollie Tosolini and Lillian Dillard.

Background of Aaron Frank Vann: Myrtle Felton, one of his sisters.

John Vann's childhood and youth in Norfolk: Dorothy Lee Cadorette and Aaron Frank Vann, Jr., were vital to this section because of the extent of their memories as the older siblings and their willingness to be honest with me. Gene Vann also made valuable contributions. During a research trip to Norfolk in

1981, Dorothy Lee took me on a tour of the Lamberts Point neighborhood which, unlike Atlantic City, had not been torn down for urban renewal. We found houses in which the Vanns had lived, including the house described in the book. Dorothy Lee lent me her mother's photo album, which she had preserved. Frank Junior had kept what few documents his father left behind. Among them were a birth certificate in the original name of John Paul LeGay and the 1943 adoption order by the Circuit Court of Norfolk. Vann's cousins, George Dillard, Joseph Raby, Jr., and Melvin Raby, provided memories of their summer vacations in Norfolk. Rev. Robert Consolvo, a retired Methodist minister whom I originally interviewed because he was a friend of the late Garland Hopkins, had grown up in the Atlantic City neighborhood and was an extremely knowledgeable source on it and the Norfolk of Vann's youth. Reverend Consolvo performed numerous follow-up research tasks for me, such as finding the records of the Boy Scout troops to which Vann had belonged and the news story of the raid on Johnny Spry's bootleg whiskey still on the microfilm of the defunct *Portsmouth Star* in the Portsmouth library. John Paul Spry, Jr., had told me of the raid. Lloyd Miller, a retired police officer who was a contemporary of John Vann in the Atlantic City neighborhood, was another source on life there and on the Vann family. I am indebted to him for leading me to Edward "Gene" Crutchfield. For published works on historic Norfolk and the city of Vann's youth see in the Bibliography: *Through the Years in Norfolk; Norfolk: Historic Southern Port*, by Thomas J. Wertenbaker; *The City by the Sea*; and *Norfolk: A Tricentennial Pictorial History*, by Carroll Walker.

Garland Hopkins: Margaret Hopkins, his former wife; Rev. Robert Consolvo; Rev. William Wright, Jr.; Lloyd Miller; Gene Crutchfield; *Who's Who in America*, 1964–65 edition.

John Vann at Ferrum: Margaret Clark, the assistant registrar in 1981, found Vann's record there for me. When I drove to Ferrum after my research trip to Norfolk she also put me in touch with Nora Bowling Martin, a classmate of Vann's. Mrs. Martin gave me her recollections of Johnny Vann and called a number of classmates to pass along their recollections too.

Vann joins the Army Air Corps: Vann's Army enlisted record, which the Office of The Adjutant General provided me, supplemented by interviews with Melvin Raby and others. Frank Junior discovered Vann's application for flight training with the letters from the teachers at Ferrum among his father's documents.

Mary Jane Allen and Vann's courtship of her: interviews with Mary Jane; Mary Allen, her mother; and Doris Moreland, her sister; news clippings and other memorabilia of her childhood and youth; photos of Vann and Mary Jane during their courtship.

Mary Jane's marriage to John Vann: interviews with her and with Mollie Tosolini and Joseph Raby, Jr.; Mary Jane's photo album of the marriage and the news clippings she had saved.

Japan period: Mary Jane; Vann's Army efficiency reports and other material in his record; a picture of the house on the hill near Osaka and other photos Mary Jane kept.

Vann's aerial resupply of the rifle companies in the Pusan Perimeter: interview with Col. Silas Gassett; recommendation to award Vann the Silver Star submitted in 1958 by Colonel Gassett. Lt. Col. Dudley Parrish, who witnessed the flights as a major and intelligence officer with the 25th Infantry Division, could not be interviewed because he was deceased, but his eyewitness account was attached to the recommendation. Roy Appleman's superb history, *South to the Naktong, North to the Yalu*, was also of help for the general battle situation.

Ralph Puckett's fight on Hill 205: interview with Col. Ralph Puckett, Jr.; news clipping of the encounter found in Vann's papers; S.L.A. Marshall's *The River and the Gauntlet*. The newspaper clipping and Vann's efficiency reports and other notations in his service record alerted me to the fact that he had not been commanding the Ranger company at the time of the fight. Puckett told me of the trouble Vann took to see that Puckett received the Distinguished Service Cross and that a number of the enlisted men were also decorated.

Other Korean War interviews that offered particular insights: Yao Wei; Col. Carl Bernard, a friend of Vann's who won a Distinguished Service Cross as a lieutenant with Task Force Smith, the first American unit to encounter the North Koreans; Col. Joseph Pizzi, who was in Eighth Army intelligence at the time of the Chinese intervention and more than twenty years later served as Vann's chief of staff at II Corps; Fred Ladd, who served as an aide to Douglas MacArthur and then to Lt. Gen. Edward Almond, MacArthur's chief of staff, before managing a transfer to an infantry unit.

Published works consulted for Korean War period: In addition to Appleman and Marshall see Bibliography for Dean Acheson's *Present at the Creation*; Daniel Yergin's *Shattered Peace*; Joseph Goulden's *Korea, the Untold Story of the War*; James Schnabel's *Policy and Direction: The First Year*; Trumbull Higgins's *Korea and the Fall of MacArthur*; J. Robert Moskin's *The Story of the U.S. Marine Corps*; and for Inchon also Krulak's *First to Fight*; William Manchester's biography of MacArthur, *American Caesar; Without Parallel, The American-Korean Relationships Since 1945*, edited by Frank Baldwin; and Edgar Snow's *The Other Side of the River*.

Germany period: Photos given me by Mary Jane and Patricia Vann Stromberg were again of great assistance in portraying family life.

Statutory rape charge: the CID report that the Office of The Adjutant General located for me along with the rest of Vann's record. The seventeen-page account Vann concocted to try to demonstrate his innocence was attached to the report. Interviews with Mary Jane; Brig. Gen. Frank Blazey, an Army friend stationed at West Point at the time in whom Vann confided; Col. Francis Bradley; Lt. Col. David Farnham, the executive secretary of Vann's CORDS headquarters for III Corps in Vietnam to whom he also told the story.

Peter Vann's illness and admission to The Children's Hospital in Boston: I owe the truth of this episode to Samuel Schuster, M.D., who performed the surgery, and Samuel Katz, M.D., then a staff pediatrician at the hospital who was assigned Peter's case. They spoke to me and Dr. Schuster sent me, with Peter's permission, a copy of his hospital record.

John Vann's decision before he went to Vietnam to retire in 1963: Colonel Bradley; Vann's correspondence with Colonel Bradley in his papers; his employment record at Martin Marietta, which the firm kindly provided me.

Suicide of Garland Hopkins: records of the Fairfax County Police Department; Hopkins's will on file in Fairfax County Court House; Mary Jane, to whom Vann described the suicide; Margaret Hopkins; Rev. Robert Consolvo; Rev. William Wright, Jr.

Exact time of John Vann's arrival back in South Vietnam: a diary he kept upon return.

Book VI: A Second Time Around

Reunion dinner with Cao: the diary Vann kept intermittently, in a lined stenographer's pad, during the first six months after his return, hereinafter referred to as Diary. Maj. Gen. Michael Healy, a brigadier general in 1972 and Vann's successor as U.S. commander in II Corps, found the Diary in Vann's former quarters in the advisory compound at Pleiku. He was kind enough to give it to me during my research trip to Vietnam that year.

Embassy bombing: Diary. Account by Peer de Silva, the CIA station chief who nearly lost his eyesight, in his book *Sub Rosa*.

John Vann in Hau Nghia: In addition to the Diary, the major sources of material for this period were my interview with Douglas Ramsey and a copy of an unfinished manuscript he let me have on his experiences in Vietnam and his captivity; Vann's reports to his USOM superiors and similar records in his papers; his correspondence with General York and with Prof. Vincent Davis, Vann's friend who was then teaching at the University of Denver and who subsequently became director of the Patterson School of Diplomacy and International Commerce at the University of Kentucky; a tape-recorded lecture Vann gave for Davis at the University of Denver in October 1965; a twenty-nine-page memorandum by Daniel Ellsberg, entitled "Visit to an Insecure Province," on three days he spent with Vann in Hau Nghia that October. Also helpful were a series of photographs of Vann and Ramsey living and working in Hau Nghia that were taken in 1965 by the late Mert Perry for the article in *Newsweek* that is mentioned in the text. The photographs were in Vann's papers.

Corruption: The Diary contains details and incidents, including Vann's conversation with Hanh on the subject, and his battle with the crooked contractor and the tainting of the former AID official in Hau Nghia. Vann preserved in his papers the file of his correspondence with the crooked contractor. The graft demand levied on Hanh by the military regime presided over by Nguyen Cao Ky is described by Vann in a confidential memorandum dated July 26, 1965. Doug Ramsey was immensely informative on the workings of corruption in Hau Nghia and Ev Bumgardner and Frank Scotton provided further information and understanding on the subject in general. Sam Wilson was also of assistance on Vann's struggle with the contractor and the graft demand placed on Hanh. The tax reportedly paid to the Viet Cong by the Hiep Hoa sugar mill is mentioned in Daniel Ellsberg's memorandum.

Social revolution: Doug Ramsey, Frank Scotton, Ev Bumgardner. Recollections of personal discussions with John Vann in 1965 and 1966.

Ambush of the canary yellow pickup: Diary and an account of the ambush Vann wrote for the senior USOM police advisor in the III Corps region. He also described the ambush to me and showed me photographs of the damaged truck.

John McNaughton's 70%–20%–10% memorandum; Westmoreland's troop requests and his plan to win the war; McNamara's memorandum to Lyndon Johnson and the president's decisions; the Pentagon Papers.

"Harnessing the Revolution in South Vietnam": The drafts of Vann's strategy proposal were among his papers. Interviews with Bumgardner, Ramsey, Scotton, and Gen. William Rosson. General Rosson remembered Westmoreland's returning to MACV headquarters one day with a copy of Vann's proposal, apparently one of those distributed by Charles Mann at a meeting of the mission council.

The Marines meet the 1st Viet Cong Regiment: my dispatches to the *New York Times*; personal recollections; the official Marine history for 1965 by Jack Shulimson and Maj. Charles Johnson, *U.S. Marines in Vietnam: The Landing and the Buildup*.

Vann's hopes for Lodge: Vann's correspondence; Sam Wilson; personal discussions with Vann in 1965 and 1966.

York's recommendations to Westmoreland: Vann-York correspondence; interview with General York.

Capture of Ramsey: Vann's investigation of the ambush and the notes and report in his papers; interview with Ramsey; his unfinished manuscript; a copy, which Ramsey provided me, of his official debriefing on his captivity by the State Department after his release on February 11, 1973.

Vann's attempt to rescue Ramsey: his report to his USOM superior on the rescue endeavor; a copy of the handwritten note from the village chief; the original of the letter of reply from the National Liberation Front, neatly penned in black ink in a tiny Vietnamese hand on both sides of a small piece of graph paper, filed in Vann's papers along with a translation. Also, interviews with Frank Scotton and Tom Donohue, the CIA officer who saw Vann's face when he received the news.

Ramsey's argument with the sixteen-year-old guerrilla and his two older escorts: his unfinished manuscript and my interview with him.

The Battle of the Ia Drang: my dispatches to the *New York Times* and my memories. Tim Brown told me how he noticed the red star over Chu Prong on the ARVN intelligence officer's map during a series of interviews I also did with him and Hal Moore and others right after the battle for a proposed article for the *Times'* Sunday magazine. The article was never written because of the pressure of daily news reporting. An account of Moore's fight at "X-Ray" by Maj. John Cash, published by the U.S. Army's Office of the Chief of Military History in *Seven Firefights in Vietnam*, was of great assistance. The ambush of the 2nd Battalion of the 7th Cavalry north of X-Ray was graphically described by one of the survivors, Specialist Four Jack P. Smith, a son of the television commentator Howard K. Smith, in an article in the *Saturday Evening Post* of January 28, 1967.

"Masher": I am indebted to my colleague R. W. "Johnny" Apple, Jr., for reporting the next ordeal of the 2nd Battalion of the 7th Cavalry on the Bong Son Plain. He covered that battle for the *Times*. I went to Bong Son afterward to do follow-up stories and have drawn on those dispatches and on my memories. Frank Scotton confirmed my memory of Vinh Loc, the ARVN II Corps commander, and his relative, the new province chief of Binh Dinh, taking advantage of Masher to run copra down to Qui Nhon.

Book VII: John Vann Stays

John Vann and Daniel Ellsberg: interview with Daniel Ellsberg; Vann-Ellsberg correspondence; their correspondence with others which casts light on the relationship; sundry notes and memoranda by both men; interviews with a number of acquaintances of both. The skittishness John McNaughton developed about Ellsberg shortly before his departure for Vietnam in 1965 is mentioned in a letter to Vann by a mutual acquaintance who was in the Pentagon at the time.

Vann and "Lee": interviews with Lee and her sister; letters and photographs Lee gave me.

John Vann and "Annie": interviews with Annie and her father, mother, sister. Photographs and letters Annie gave me. Vann talked to friends like Ellsberg and George Jacobson about his relationship with both women.

Death of Myrtle and her funeral: interviews with Dorothy Lee Cadorette and Aaron Frank Vann, Jr. Frank Junior remembered his father's remark on seeing Myrtle at the funeral home. Dorothy Lee took me to her mother's grave during my research trip to Norfolk in 1981.

Pacification teams dispute: interviews with Tran Ngoc Chau, Tom Donohue, Daniel Ellsberg, Richard Holbrooke, and Frank G. Wisner II. Vann's running notebook on the dispute and a memorandum dated March 16, 1966, on his initial meeting with Ambassador Porter. Vann-Porter correspondence. Ellsberg's memoranda to Lansdale. Early on in the dispute Vann told me and Charlie Mohr of the scandal at the training camp and his confrontation with Jorgenson. We decided he would be fired if we wrote the story then and waited until Mai was finally removed, when Mohr recounted the tale in a dispatch published in the July 18, 1966, edition of the *Times*.

Key aspects of Westmoreland's war of attrition and the creation of the killing machine:

(1) Civilian casualties: estimates based on a formula worked out by Thomas Thayer, director of the Southeast Asia Office of Systems Analysis at the Pentagon from 1966 to 1972. See Bibliography for his book-length statistical monograph on the war. He graciously gave me a copy. Also taken into account were figures derived through my own reporting and those compiled by the staff of Edward Kennedy's Subcommittee on Refugees and Escapees. The attempt by Maj. Gen. James Humphreys to ameliorate the lot of the civilian wounded and the effort to establish three U.S. military hospitals to care for them is also drawn from my own reporting and from testimony before Kennedy's subcommittee.

(2) Firepower: Bomb tonnage figures are official ones. Lt. Gen. Jonathan Seaman remembered when I interviewed him how he had been forced to restrict the supply of artillery shells to 1st Infantry Division while General DePuy commanded it. DePuy's call for "more bombs, more shells, more napalm" was quoted in a memorandum from Ellsberg to Ambassador Porter.

(3) Base building and the amenities of American civilization: details primarily from personal observation and from three book-length monographs in a series commissioned by General Westmoreland after he became Chief of Staff and published by the Department of the Army: *Base Development, 1965–1970*, by Lt. Gen. Carroll Dunn; *Logistic Support*, by Lt. Gen. Joseph Heiser, Jr.; and *U.S. Army Engineers, 1965–1970*, by Maj. Gen. Robert Ploger.

(4) Moral and social consequences for the Vietnamese and the unprecedented corruption: wide variety of sources including personal recollection and my reporting (e.g., "Not a Dove, But No Longer a Hawk" in the Sunday, October 9, 1966, edition of *The New York Times Magazine*); my talks with Vann in this period; numerous news clippings in years since; interviews with Ev Bumgardner, Frank Scotton, and others.

Westmoreland's neglect of the ARVN and RF and PF: Vann's constant complaints in his correspondence; news clippings including a particularly helpful one on Westmoreland's public relations approach to the matter by R. W. Apple, Jr., in the *Times* of June 1, 1967. Lyndon Johnson's admonishment of his general is in the Pentagon Papers.

The ordeal of Victor Krulak and the Marines of Vietnam: interviews with General Krulak and with Gen. Wallace Greene, Jr.; papers and correspondence that General Krulak kindly gave me, including his October 7, 1966, back-channel message to General Walt; relevant chapters from his book, *First to Fight*; LBJ Library in Austin, Texas, for records of his August 1, 1966, meeting with Lyndon Johnson; official Marine histories for 1965, and 1967 by Shulimson et al. Also personal recollections and reporting as I was in I Corps frequently in 1965–1966, spent several days with a Marine company attempting to pacify a village south of Da Nang, and covered the minor civil war there between the pro-Ky and pro-Buddhist forces. The after-action report of the 3rd Marine Regiment, preserved in the archives of the Marine Corps Historical Center at the Washington Navy Yard, was indispensable to reconstructing the "Hill Fights" at Khe Sanh. General Walt told me after his return to the United States in 1967 of flying to Khe Sanh in alarm at the casualties and ordering heavy bombs with delay fusing. The records of the 1st Marine Aircraft Wing confirmed his account.

Where Americans died in South Vietnam: The figures are Tom Thayer's from his statistical analysis of the war. Thayer also let me interview him for the book.

Robert Komer and CORDS: interview with Ambassador Komer. Holbrooke-Vann correspondence. Also interviews with Holbrooke; Brig. Gen. Robert Montague, Komer's military assistant; and Lt. Gen. Samuel Wilson.

Fred Weyand and John Vann: interview with General Weyand; news clippings and other biographical material on him. The anecdote about the aide with the flying machine came from Col. Thomas Jones, a friend and senior subordinate of Vann's in III Corps.

Ramsey in captivity: Ramsey gave me a typed copy of his letter to his parents. Also my interview with him; his unfinished manuscript; and his official debriefing on his captivity by the State Department.

Ellsworth Bunker: interview with the late Ambassador Bunker and news clippings and other biographical data. I also requested, with his consent, the declassification of his Vietnam papers, a request the State Department partially fulfilled. Bunker was proud of his performance in the Dominican Republic. The anecdote of how he pressured Ky and Thieu and the other generals into settling the 1967 election dispute among themselves came from my interview with him.

Annie's second pregnancy and the ceremony and arrangement with Vann: interview with Annie. The senior AID administrator mentioned here told me how Vann had approached him and why he decided to give Vann a house for Annie and the child to come.

Awakening of Robert McNamara: McNamara's October 14, 1966, memorandum to the president; Enthoven's memoranda to McNamara on the absurdity of Westmoreland's war of attrition and Thayer's statistics to prove the contention; and the May 19, 1967, memorandum to Johnson from McNamara and John McNaughton are in the Pentagon Papers. Ellsberg interview for the memorandum reading on the flight to Saigon. Interview with Jonathan Schell for the episode with McNamara in the Pentagon. (Schell's *New Yorker* article was republished by Knopf in 1968 as *The Military Half*.) Bunker interview for McNamara's sending the manuscript to the ambassador and the inquiry he ordered. The report of the investigation was among the Bunker papers the State Department declassified for me. LBJ Library for McNamara's November 1, 1967, memorandum to Johnson, which the library had declassified in 1985, and the written comments on it Johnson sought from Walt Rostow, Maxwell Taylor,

Justice Abe Fortas, and Clark Clifford. Interview with George Christian, who was close to the president, for Johnson's personal assessment of the war at this time and his conclusion about the change in McNamara. What Christian had to say was confirmed by others and by the documentary record. Also personal reporting as I did a series of interviews in the fall of 1967 with friends and associates of McNamara's after the rumors began circulating that he had turned against the war. Robert Kennedy was one of those I interviewed.

Bombing of the North and the Ho Chi Minh Trail: While the analysis of the futility of the air war is my own, Col. Jack Van Loan of the Air Force, who was shot down over North Vietnam and imprisoned there, set me on the way with some observations he made when I interviewed him. Much of the material, such as Admiral Sharp's "LOC cut program" and the POL raids in the summer of 1966, came from the Pentagon Papers. The map of the Ho Chi Minh Trail that eight years of bombing produced was provided to me by Dennis Berend of the public affairs office of the CIA. The estimate that the planes destroyed only about 20 to 25 percent of the trucks rolling to the South was originally derived from classified official figures I obtained in the fall of 1968 from Walt Rostow and one of his assistants. Rostow was then President Johnson's special assistant for National Security Affairs. Rostow had had the Air Force and the Navy compile the figures for the president. My research indicated that the estimate held for subsequent years in the bombing of the Laos corridor of the Trail, which never ceased, and in the intermittent and then full-scale resumption of the bombing of the North by President Nixon. I am indebted to William Branigan of the *Washington Post* for a dispatch from Vietnam in the April 23, 1985, edition of the newspaper giving the length of the Trail as estimated by the Vietnamese and a description of the memorial cemetery to those who died for it.

The Wise Men: LBJ Library for the records of the meetings, declassified in 1983 and 1984.

My Lai: See Bibliography for books on the massacres and the court-martial of William Calley by Seymour Hersh and Richard Hammer. Also see the report of the investigating commission headed by Lt. Gen. William Peers.

The eve of Tet: Vann had two extended telephone conversations about the Tet 1968 Offensive and the period preceding it with Dan Ellsberg while on home leave in the United States in July 1968. Ellsberg taped the conversations and had them transcribed at the Rand Corporation. Vann also left behind in his papers pocket notebooks with comments by Weyand as Tet drew near. The transcripts and the notebooks were useful both as a record of what occurred and as a stimulus to the memories of Fred Weyand and others whom I interviewed. Vann described his meeting with Rostow to a number of friends. Rostow did not recall details. A copy of his office record, which he generously let me have, showed the time of the meeting. Westmoreland continued to maintain in his memoirs, *A Soldier Reports*, published in 1976, that the Vietnamese Communists were attempting a second Dien Bien Phu at Khe Sanh. The memoirs were of great assistance in describing his attitudes and actions here and after the offensive unfolded. Also helpful was another of the book-length Department of the Army monographs he commissioned while Chief of Staff, *The War in the Northern Provinces, 1966–1968,* by Lt. Gen. Willard Pearson. For the siege of Khe Sanh itself I found most useful an early Marine history, *The Battle for Khe Sanh,* by Capt. Moyers Shore II, published by the historical branch of the Marine Corps in 1969.

Tet, 1968: Ellsworth Bunker told me the story of his Marine guards waking him and showed me the scorched briefcase when I interviewed him. Lt. Col. Pham Van Son, the chief ARVN military historian, was the first to suspect that Khe Sanh was a lure. Examination demonstrated his suspicion was correct and the analysis that follows here is mine. In addition to the interviews with Bunker, Weyand, George Jacobson, David Farnham, Annie, Lee, and others, I also consulted a number of published works. The three most important were the official ARVN history by Colonel Son et al., *The Viet Cong Tet Offensive, 1968;* Don Oberdorfer's *Tet!;* and *The General Offensives of 1968–69,* by Col. Hoang Ngoc Lung, the former J-2 of the Joint General Staff. Westmoreland's having a cot set up in the Combined Operations Center at Pentagon East and Dutch Kerwin's sending for Katherine Westmoreland is from the general's memoirs. Dean Rusk's change of heart and his initiative to suspend the bombing of the North and open negotiations is from the Pentagon Papers and from my interview with him.

Creighton Abrams orders Vann fired: interview with Robert Komer.

The Phoenix Program: Vann's attitude toward the Phoenix Program is clear from letters and other documents in his papers. The Vietnamese Communists subsequently acknowledged how destructive Phoenix was to what remained of the Viet Cong organization in the post-Tet years.

John Vann reaches the Oval Office: Copies of Nixon's letter to Yorty thanking him for Arnett's article and Vann's six-and-a-half-page letter of reply meant for Nixon were in his papers. Interview with Sir Robert Thompson for his suggestion to Kissinger that the president see Vann. My gratitude to Frenchy Zois, Vann's American secretary, for giving me a copy of his December 22, 1969 memorandum on his meeting with the president during my research trip to Vietnam in 1972. The original was missing from Vann's papers when they reached the United States. Vann also described the meeting to his friend Vincent Davis; to his oldest son, John Allen; and to Daniel Ellsberg. Notes kept by Davis and Ellsberg and John Allen's memory of what his father said were of further assistance.

Chau affair: interviews with Ellsworth Bunker; Tran Ngoc Chau; Ev Bumgardner; Dr. Merrill "Bud" Shutt; George Jacobson; Tom Donohue; Theodore Shackley, the Saigon CIA station chief at the time; and Mrs. Kieu Mong Thu, another member of the lower house of the National Assembly. Richard Moose, also interviewed, heard Bunker call Chau a Communist while on a trip to Vietnam as a staff assistant to the Senate Committee on Foreign Relations. Daniel Ellsberg supplied a file of cables between Bunker and the State Department to which he had been privy and which he had transcribed. Tran Ngoc Hien described his meetings with his brother in a written statement made public during Chau's trial in Saigon in 1970. Shackley, as another intelligence professional, admired the cleverness with which Hien had handled himself after his arrest.

The new John Vann's proposed solution to Ninh: A report in Vann's papers stated that Ninh was "the most blatantly corrupt" province chief in the Mekong Delta and gave some details. Interview with Warren Parker for much fuller details. Tess Johnston, Wilbur Wilson's secretary, remembered the length of the corruption profile compiled on Ninh. Ev Bumgardner on supervising the anticorruption program for Colby. Hoang Duc Nha told me when I interviewed him in 1972 of Vann's proposal to make his brother a regimental commander and his brother's reaction, of course not knowing the real motive. Warren Parker told me the motive.

Bringing Cambodia into the war: Bunker remembered Sihanouk's signaling that he approved the B-52 raids on the Vietnamese sanctuaries. Anthony Lake told me of Kissinger's parting remark to him.

Vann and Dzu: interview with Maj. Gen. Ngo Dzu; his official ARVN biographical record; observations of a wide range of American and Vietnamese acquaintances on the relationship between the two men.

Creighton Abrams makes John Vann one of his generals: Weyand interview; a copy of the letter of instruction, the official term for a letter of authority, from Abrams to Vann and other documents relating to Vann's appointment were in his papers.

Vann's complicated game with Ellsberg after the publication of the Pentagon Papers: There is firm evidence in Vann's correspondence that he was passing tips to Kissinger on how the administration ought to proceed against Ellsberg. Gene Vann remembered his brother's long telephone conversation with Ellsberg and Vann told him how Ellsberg had described his defense strategy. David Farnham was with Vann when he then passed the information to J. Fred Buzhardt at the Pentagon. Vann's meeting with Buzhardt is on his Pentagon schedule for the Christmas 1971 trip.

NVA preparations for the 1972 Offensive and its unfolding: interview with Col. Hoang Ngoc Lung, J-2 of the ARVN Joint General Staff, during my research trip to Vietnam in 1972; interview with Lt. Col. Trinh Tieu, then G-2 at ARVN II Corps headquarters at Pleiku; prisoner interrogation reports and other intelligence information kindly given me by Thomas Polgar, CIA station chief in Saigon in 1972; an early official history of the entire offensive written for the Joint Chiefs of Staff that the Army declassified at my request. The section on the offensive in the Central Highlands was written by 2d Lt. Gary Swingle. Also material in Vann's papers.

Vann's rescue and resupply of Fire Base Delta: interview with Lt. Col. Peter Kama and copy of a recommendation he wrote at the time to award Vann a medal for heroism; interview with 1st Lt. Huynh Van Cai, Vann's ARVN aide, and Cai's diary; interviews with Maj. Frank Gall, Jr., the commander of the

57th Assault Helicopter Company who was flying that day; General Dzu; and Col. Joseph Pizzi, Vann's chief of staff at II Corps. Colonel Kama was also of great assistance in understanding the general struggle for Rocket Ridge because he preserved a chronology of the battles, the after-action report of the fight for Fire Base Charlie, and recommendations for awards for a number of the other advisors, with graphic details of the fighting.

Vann's rescue of Ngo Dzu from the heroin trafficking accusation: correspondence and other material in Vann's papers and what he told George Jacobson and a number of friends. Interviews with General Dzu and with Philip Brady, a friend and former CORDS subordinate of Vann's who was a correspondent for NBC in 1971 and who helped Vann with the press campaign. Brady was expelled from South Vietnam for implying in one of his broadcasts that the traffic could not have continued without at least the tacit consent of Thieu.

Binh Dinh fighting: interviews with Maj. Gary Hacker, 1st Lt. Thomas Eisenhower, Lt. Col. Jack Anderson, with a number of advisors who fought elsewhere in the province, and with Candidate Gen. Nguyen Van Chuc, and General Dzu. In addition, during my research trip in 1972, I spent a week reading and taking notes from the journal maintained by the province Tactical Operations Center in Quinhon. The courtesy was extended to me by John Swango, the PSA for Binh Dinh, and Maj. Richard Carey, the province operations advisor. I also interviewed Major Carey and he gave me further documentary information on the struggle for the province.

Fall of Tan Canh: interviews with Colonel Pizzi, General Dzu, Col. Phillip Kaplan, Maj. Jon Wise, Capt. Richard Cassidy, Lieutenant Cai, and Sgt. First Class (formerly CWO) Robert Richards, Vann's helicopter pilot. Colonel Kaplan, who ultimately retired from the Army as a major general, was extremely patient, giving me several days of interview time. He also drew a map overlay so that I could plot the location of each of the ARVN units involved and did map sketches to illustrate the progress of the battle and the approach route the tanks took. Captain Cassidy learned how the tanks had driven down from the North and the attack orders the NVA tankers had received from the interrogation of the captured driver. Peter Kama and Lt. Col. Trinh Tieu, the G-2 at Pleiku, and General Dzu and Lieutenant Cai were helpful in explaining Vann's irrational skepticism about the presence of NVA tanks in II Corps. Matt Franjola, then a correspondent for the AP, gave me a tape recording of the press conference Vann gave at Pleiku on the night of the day that Tan Canh fell. I also spent days at Pleiku in the fall of 1972, reading and taking notes from the journal of the II Corps Tactical Operations Center in order to get precise times and dates and other valuable data for the fall of Tan Canh and other major events of the offensive. The courtesy was extended to me by Major Wise, who was by this time in charge of the advisory side of the corps TOC.

Rescue of the advisors at Tan Canh: interviews with Colonel Kaplan and SFC Richards, Vann's pilot. A copy of the holographic will Vann wrote in the helicopter was given to me by his oldest son, John Allen Vann.

Overturning of Vann's helicopter by the panicked ARVN paratroopers: interview with Lieutenant Cai and his diary. Vann also told the story to Charlie Mohr, who was in Vietnam to cover the offensive. Mohr's dispatch to the *Times* was not published, but I obtained a copy of it through the kindness of Robert Rosenthal, a former clerk on the foreign news desk.

Dzu panics and schemes to abandon the Highlands: interview in 1972 with Lt. Gen. Cao Van Vien, chief of the ARVN Joint General Staff. Candidate Gen. Ly Tong Ba told me of the plot Dzu concocted to try to precipitate a withdrawal from Kontum.

The Battle of Kontum: interviews with General Ba, Maj. Gen. John Hill, Jr., Col. R. M. Rhotenberry. Reports on the battle written by General Ba's staff and maps and map overlays illustrating the course of the fighting. I also flew to Kontum with General Ba and Colonel Rhotenberry one day when Ba had to visit a 23rd Division regiment still stationed there. Colonel Rhotenberry took me on a tour of the battleground within and around the edges of the town.

John Vann wields the B-52's: Maj. Gen. Nguyen Van Toan mentioned to me when I interviewed him how he and the ARVN staff at Pleiku had nicknamed Vann "Mr. B-52." Interview with Capt. Christopher Scudder for the number of B-52 flights the Strategic Air Command was sending to Creighton Abrams every day, the number of strikes Vann placed in the environs of Kontum, and how Vann persuaded SAC to echelon the B-52's for better bomb coverage of the target zone. Colonel Rhotenberry and General Ba also described for me the echeloning and how the bombers were employed so close to the ARVN lines. Jacques Leslie of the *Los Angeles Times*, whom I interviewed and who gave me his notebooks, was one of the two reporters with Vann when he circled over the bomb craters of a B-52 strike and explained that anyone still alive below would be too dazed to pull a trigger. Vann told Gerald Hickey, the anthropologist and writer who went to Pleiku to request airlift for the evacuation of Montagnard refugees from Kontum, how he had called in Cobra gunships to finish off the forty to fifty NVA who survived on another occasion. There was also an entry in the II Corps TOC journal that seemed to refer to this incident. Interview with Laurence Stern of the *Washington Post* for Vann's rage and exaltation. Vann's remark on the stench from the battlefield is taken from Stern's article in the June 8, 1972, edition of the *Post*.

Vann's last "Newcomers' Briefing": I thank Frenchy Zois and Bryan Chastain, who was on the II Corps CORDS staff at Nhatrang, for the tape recording of the briefing.

The crash: the report of the official Army investigation. Numerous interviews, including those with General Hill; Colonel Pizzi; Lieutenant Cai; Master Sgt. Edward Black, Vann's administrative assistant; General Ba; Colonel Rhotenberry; and Lieutenant Colonel Anderson. Capt. John Heslin, an Army aviator with the helicopter group at Holloway who had a historical bent and was of considerable help, put me in touch with Capt. Bernard Ferguson, who volunteered to fly as Anderson's copilot that night. Capt. Robert McDonald was the Cobra gunship pilot who spotted the last flames of the wreckage under the trees.

BIBLIOGRAPHY

Acheson, Dean. *Present at the Creation: My Years in the State Department.* New York: W. W. Norton & Co., 1969.

Adams, Nina S., and McCoy, Alfred W., eds. *Laos: War and Revolution.* New York: Harper & Row, 1970.

Aftermath of War: Humanitarian Problems of Southeast Asia. Staff Report, Subcommittee to Investigate Problems Connected with Refugees and Escapees, Committee on the Judiciary, U.S. Senate, Ninety-fourth Congress. Washington, D.C.: U.S. Government Printing Office, 1976.

Albright, John, John A. Cash, and Allan W. Sandstrum. *Seven Firefights in Vietnam.* Washington, D.C.: U.S. Army Office of the Chief of Military History, 1970.

Appleman, Roy E. *South to the Naktong, North to the Yalu: United States Army in the Korean War.* Washington, D.C.: U.S. Army Office of the Chief of Military History, 1961.

Archer, Jules. *The Plot to Seize the White House.* New York: Hawthorn Books, 1973.

Armbruster, Frank E., et al. *Can We Win in Vietnam?* New York: Hudson Institute, 1968.

Asprey, Robert B. *War in the Shadows: The Guerrilla in History.* Volumes I and II. New York: Doubleday, 1975.

Austin, Anthony. *The President's War: The Story of the Tonkin Gulf Resolution and How the Nation Was Trapped in Vietnam.* Philadelphia: J. B. Lippincott Company, 1971.

Bain, David Haward. *Sitting in Darkness: Americans in the Philippines.* Boston: Houghton Mifflin, 1984.

Baldwin, Frank, ed. *Without Parallel: The American-Korean Relationships Since 1945.* New York: Pantheon, 1974.

Ball, George W. *The Discipline of Power: Essentials of a Modern World Structure.* Boston: Little, Brown, 1968.

Ballard, Jack S. *Development and Employment of Fixed-Wing Gunships, 1962–1972,* The United States Air Force in Southeast Asia series. Washington, D.C.: Office of Air Force History, U.S. Air Force, 1982.

Bamford, James. *The Puzzle Palace: A Report on America's Most Secret Agency.* Boston: Houghton Mifflin, 1982.

Barnet, Richard J. *The Giants: Russia and America.* New York: Simon and Schuster, 1977.

———. *Real Security: Restoring American Power in a Dangerous Decade.* New York: Simon and Schuster, 1981.

———. *Roots of War: The Men and Institutions Behind U.S. Foreign Policy.* New York: Atheneum, 1972.

Baskir, Lawrence M., and William A. Strauss. *Chance and Circumstance: The Draft, the War, and the Vietnam Generation.* New York: Alfred A. Knopf, 1978.

Blum, John Morton. *V Was for Victory: Politics and American Culture During World War II.* New York: Harcourt Brace Jovanovich, 1976.

Blumenson, Martin. *The Patton Papers, 1885–1940.* Volume I. Boston: Houghton Mifflin, 1972.

———. *The Patton Papers, 1940–1945.* Volume II. Boston: Houghton Mifflin, 1974.

Bodard, Lucien. *The Quicksand War: Prelude to Vietnam.* Boston: Little, Brown, 1967.

Bohlen, Charles E., with the editorial assistance of Robert H. Phelps. *Witness to History 1929–1969.* New York: W. W. Norton & Co., 1973.

Braestrup, Peter. *Big Story: How the American Press and Television Reported and Interpreted the Crisis of Tet 1968 in Vietnam and Washington.* Volume 1. Boulder, Colorado: Westview Press, 1977.

———, ed. *Vietnam as History: Ten Years After the Paris Peace Accords.* Washington, D.C.: University Press of America, 1984.

Brandon, Henry. *Anatomy of Error: The Secret History of the Vietnam War.* London: André Deutsch, 1970.

Bromley, Dorothy Dunbar. *Washington and Vietnam: An Examination of the Moral and Political Issues.* Dobbs Ferry, N.Y.: Oceana Publications, Inc., 1966.

Browne, Malcolm W. *The New Face of War.* Indianapolis: Bobbs-Merrill, 1965.

Buckingham, William A., Jr. *Operation Ranch Hand: The Air Force and Herbicides in Southeast Asia, 1961–1971.* Washington, D.C.: Office of Air Force History, U.S. Air Force, 1982.

Bunting, Josiah. *The Lionheads.* New York: George Braziller, 1972.

Burchett, Wilfred. *My Visit to the Liberated Zones of South Vietnam.* Hanoi: Foreign Languages Publishing House, 1964.

Buttinger, Joseph. *Vietnam: A Dragon Embattled.* Volume I, *From Colonialism to the Vietminh.* Volume II, *Vietnam at War.* New York: Praeger, 1967.

Cameron, Allan W. *Vietnam Crisis: A Documentary History.* Volume 1: 1940–1956. Ithaca: Cornell University Press, 1971.

Caro, Robert A. *The Years of Lyndon Johnson: The Path to Power.* New York: Alfred A. Knopf, 1982.

Cash, Wilbur J. *Mind of the South*. New York: Alfred A. Knopf, 1960.

Caudill, Harry. *Night Comes to the Cumberlands: Biography of a Depressed Area*. Boston: Atlantic Monthly Press, 1963.

Charlton, Michael, and Anthony Moncrieff. *Many Reasons Why: The American Involvement in Vietnam*. New York: Hill and Wang, 1978.

Chester, Lewis, et al. *Watergate: The Full Inside Story*. New York: Ballantine Books, 1973.

Hoang Van Chi. *From Colonialism to Communism: A Case History of North Vietnam*. London: Pall Mall Press, 1964.

Truong Chinh. *The August Revolution*. Hanoi: Foreign Languages Publishing House, 1962.

Chomsky, Noam. *At War with Asia*. New York: Pantheon, 1970.

Colby, William, and Peter Forbath. *Honorable Men: My Life in the CIA*. New York: Simon and Schuster, 1978.

Committee of Concerned Asian Scholars. *The Indochina Story*. New York: Bantam, 1970.

Cooper, Chester L. *The Lost Crusade: America in Vietnam*. New York: Dodd, Mead & Co., 1970.

Cooper, Francis H. "Some Colonial History of Beaufort County, North Carolina." Chapel Hill, N.C.: James Sprunt Historical Publications, North Carolina Historical Society, University of Norh Carolina, Vol. 14, No. 2, 1916.

Corson, William R. *Consequences of Failure*. New York: W. W. Norton & Co., 1974.

Del Vecchio, John M. *The 13th Valley*. New York: Bantam, 1982.

de Silva, Peer. *Sub Rosa: The CIA and the Uses of Intelligence*. New York: Times Books, 1978.

Bui Diem with David Chanoff. *In the Jaws of History*. Boston: Houghton Mifflin, 1987.

Dommen, Arthur J. *Conflict in Laos: The Politics of Neutralization*. New York: Praeger, 1971.

Dos Passos, John. *Mr. Wilson's War*. New York: Doubleday, 1962.

Draper, Theodore. *Abuse of Power*. New York: Viking, 1967.

Nguyen Du. *The Tale of Kieu*. New York: Random House, 1973.

Dudman, Richard. *Forty Days with the Enemy*. New York: Liveright, 1971.

Duffett, John, ed. *Against the Crime of Silence: Proceedings of the International War Crimes Tribunal*. New York: Clarion, 1970.

Duncan, Donald. *The New Legions*. New York: Random House, 1967.

General Van Tien Dung. *Our Great Spring Victory: An Account of the Liberation of South Vietnam*. New York: Monthly Review Press, 1977.

Dunn, Lt. Gen. Carroll H. *Base Development in South Vietnam 1965–1970*. Washington, D.C.: Department of the Army, 1972.

Ellsberg, Daniel. *Papers on the War*. New York: Simon and Schuster, 1972.

Emerson, Gloria. *Winners and Losers: Battles, Retreats, Gains, Losses and Ruins from a Long War*. New York: Random House, 1977.

Esper, George, and the Associated Press. *The Eyewitness History of the Vietnam War, 1961–1975*. New York: Villard Books, 1983.

Ewell, Lt. Gen. Julian J. and Major Gen. Ira A. Hunt, Jr. *Sharpening the Combat Edge: The Use of Analysis to Reinforce Military Judgment*. Washington, D.C.: Department of the Army, 1974.

Fails, Lt. Col. William R. *Marines and Helicopters, 1962–1973*. Washington, D.C.: History and Museums Division, Headquarters, U.S. Marine Corps, 1978.

Fair, Charles. *From the Jaws of Victory*. New York: Simon and Schuster, 1971.

Fall, Bernard. *Hell in a Very Small Place: The Siege of Dien Bien Phu*. Philadelphia: J. B. Lippincott Company, 1967.

———. *Street Without Joy: Insurgency in Indochina, 1946–63*. Harrisburg, Pa.: The Stackpole Company, 1963.

———. *The Two Viet-Nams: A Political and Military Analysis*. London: Pall Mall Press, 1963.

———. *Viet-Nam Witness, 1953–66*. New York: Praeger, 1966.

Fallaci, Oriana. *Interview with History*. Boston: Houghton Mifflin, 1976.

———. *Nothing and So Be It*. New York: Doubleday, 1972.

FitzGerald, Frances. *Fire in the Lake: The Vietnamese and the Americans in Vietnam*. Boston: Little, Brown, 1972.

FitzSimons, Louise. *The Kennedy Doctrine*. New York: Random House, 1972.

Fuchs, Elinor, and Joyce Antler. *Year One of the Empire: A Play of American Politics, War and Protest Taken from the Historical Record*. Boston: Houghton Mifflin, 1973.

Fulton, Maj. Gen. William B. *Riverine Operations 1966–1969*. Washington, D.C.: Department of the Army, 1973.

Galluci, Robert L. *Neither Peace Nor Honor: The Politics of American Military Policy in Viet-Nam*. Baltimore: Johns Hopkins University Press, 1975.

Gelb, Leslie, and Richard Betts. *The Irony of Vietnam: The System Worked*. New York: Brookings, 1979.

Vo Nguyen Giap. *People's War, People's Army: The Viet Cong Insurrection Manual for Underdeveloped Countries*. New York: Praeger, 1964.

Goulden, Joseph C. *Truth Is the First Casualty: The Gulf of Tonkin Affair—Illusion and Reality*. Chicago: Rand McNally, 1969.

———. *Korea: The Untold Story of the War*. New York: Times Books, 1982.

Greene, Graham. *The Quiet American*. New York: Viking, 1956.

Groom, Winston. *Better Time Than These*. New York: Summit Books, 1978.

Gurtov, Melvin. *Southeast Asia Tomorrow: Problems and Prospects for U.S. Policy*. Baltimore: Johns Hopkins University Press, 1970.

Halberstam, David. *The Best and the Brightest*. New York: Random House, 1972.

———. *The Making of a Quagmire*. New York: Random House, 1965.

Halperin, Morton H., et al. *The Lawless State: The Crimes of the U.S. Intelligence Agencies*. New York; Penguin Books, 1976.

Hammer, Ellen J. *The Struggle for Indochina*. Stanford, Calif.: Stanford University Press, 1954.

Hammer, Richard. *The Court-Martial of Lt. Calley*. New York: Coward-McCann, 1971.

———. *One Morning in the War: The Tragedy at Son My*. New York: Coward-McCann, 1970.

Harriss, C. Lowell, ed. *Inflation: Long-term Problems*. New York: The Academy of Political Science, 1975.

Hart, Capt. B. H. Liddell. *The Real War 1914–1918*. Boston: Atlantic Monthly Press, 1930.

Hassler, Alfred. *Saigon, U.S.A.* New York: Richard W. Baron, 1970.

Hatch, Alden. *The Lodges of Massachusetts*. New York: Hawthorn Books, 1973.

Hay, Douglas, et al. *Albion's Fatal Tree: Crime and Society in Eighteenth-Century England*. New York: Pantheon, 1975.

Heinemann, Larry. *Close Quarters*. New York: Farrar, Straus & Giroux, 1977.

Heiser, Jr., Lt. Gen. Joseph M. *Logistic Support*. Washington, D.C.: Department of the Army, 1974.

Herr, Michael. *Dispatches*. New York: Alfred A. Knopf, 1977.

Herring, George C. *America's Longest War: The United States and Vietnam, 1950–1975*. New York: Alfred A. Knopf, 1986.

Hersh, Seymour M. *Cover-Up: The Army's Secret Investigation of the Massacre at My Lai 4*. New York: Random House, 1972.

———. *My Lai 4: A Report on the Massacre and Its Aftermath*. New York: Random House, 1970.

Hewes, James E., Jr. *From Root to McNamara: Army Organization and Administration, 1900–1963*. Washington, D.C.: Center of Military History, 1975.

Hickey, Gerald Cannon. *Village in Vietnam*. New Haven, Conn.: Yale University Press, 1964.

Higgins, Trumbull. *Korea and the Fall of MacArthur: A Precis in Limited War*. New York: Oxford University Press, 1960.

Hilsman, Roger. *To Move a Nation*. New York: Doubleday, 1967.

Hobbs, Jr., S. Huntington. *North Carolina: An Economic and Social Profile*. Chapel Hill, N.C.: University of North Carolina Press, 1958.

Honey, P. J. *Communism in North Vietnam: Its Role in the Sino-Soviet Dispute*. Cambridge, Mass.: M.I.T. Press, 1963.

———. *North Vietnam Today: Profile of a Communist Satellite*. New York: Praeger, 1962.

Hooper, Edwin Bickfard, et al. *The United States Navy and the Vietnam Conflict*, Volume I, *The Setting of the Stage to 1959*. Washington, D.C.: Naval History Division, Department of the Navy (U.S. Government Printing Office), 1976.

Hoopes, Townsend. *The Limits of Intervention (an Inside Account of How the Johnson Policy of Escalation in Vietnam Was Reversed)*. New York: David McKay, 1969.

Hosmer, Stephen T. *Viet Cong Repression and Its Implications for the Future.* Santa Monica, Calif.: Rand Corporation, 1970.

Isaacs, Arnold R. *Without Honor: Defeat in Vietnam and Cambodia.* Baltimore: Johns Hopkins University Press, 1983.

Johnson, Lyndon Baines. *The Vantage Point: Perspectives of the Presidency, 1963–1969.* New York: Holt, Rinehart and Winston, 1971.

Just, Ward. *Military Men.* New York: Alfred A. Knopf, 1970.

———. *To What End: Report from Vietnam.* Boston: Houghton Mifflin, 1968.

Kahin, George McT. *Intervention: How America Became Involved in Vietnam.* New York: Alfred A. Knopf, 1986.

Karnow, Stanley. *Vietnam: A History.* New York: Viking, 1983.

Karsten, Peter. *The Naval Aristocracy: The Golden Age of Annapolis and the Emergence of Modern American Navalism.* New York: The Free Press, 1976.

Kaufmann, William W. *The McNamara Strategy.* New York: Harper & Row, 1964.

Kelly, Col. Francis J. *U.S. Army Special Forces, 1961–1971.* Washington, D.C.: Department of the Army, 1973.

King, Henry T. *Sketches of Pitt County, 1704–1910.* Greenville, N.C.: ERA Press, 1976.

Kinnard, Douglas. *The War Managers.* Hanover, N.H.: University Press of New England, 1977.

Kirk, Donald. *Wider War: The Struggle for Cambodia, Thailand, and Laos.* New York: Praeger, 1971.

Kirkpatrick, Lyman B., Jr. *The U.S. Intelligence Community: Foreign Policy and Domestic Activities.* New York: Hill and Wang, 1973.

Kissinger, Henry. *White House Years.* Boston: Little, Brown, 1979.

Knightley, Phillip. *The First Casualty: From the Crimea to Vietnam: The War Correspondent as Hero, Propagandist, and Myth Maker.* New York: Harcourt Brace Jovanovich, 1975.

———, and Colin Simpson. *The Secret Lives of Lawrence of Arabia.* London: Nelson, 1969.

Knoebl, Kuno. *Victor Charlie: The Face of War in Vietnam.* New York: Praeger, 1967.

Knoll, Erwin, and Judith Nies McFadden, eds. *War Crimes and the American Conscience.* New York: Holt, Rinehart and Winston, 1970.

Kolko, Gabriel. *Anatomy of a War: Vietnam, the United States, and the Modern Historical Experience.* New York: Pantheon, 1986.

Kolpacoff, Victor. *The Prisoners of Quai Dong.* New York: New American Library, 1967.

Komer, R. W. *Bureaucracy Does Its Thing: Institutional Constraints on U.S.-G.V.N. Performance in Vietnam.* Santa Monica, Calif.: Rand Corporation, 1972.

Korb, Lawrence J. *The Joint Chiefs of Staff: The First Twenty-five Years.* Bloomington, Ind.: Indiana University Press, 1976.

Krulak, Victor H. *First to Fight: An Inside View of the U.S. Marine Corps.* Annapolis, Md.: Naval Institute Press, 1984.

Nguyen Cao Ky. *Twenty Years and Twenty Days.* New York: Stein and Day, 1976.

Lacouture, Jean. *Vietnam: Between Two Truces.* New York: Random House, 1966.

LaFeber, Walter. *America, Russia and the Cold War, 1945–1975.* New York: Wiley, 1976.

Lancaster, Donald. *The Emancipation of French Indochina.* London: Oxford University Press, 1961.

Lansdale, Edward G. *In the Midst of Wars; An American's Mission to Southeast Asia.* New York: Harper & Row, 1972.

Law of Land Warfare, The. Field Manual 27-10. Washington, D.C.: Department of the Army, 1956.

Lederer, William J. *Our Own Worst Enemy.* New York: W. W. Norton & Co., 1968.

———, and Eugene Burdick. *The Ugly American.* New York: W. W. Norton & Co., 1958.

Le Hong Linh et al. *Ap Bac: Major Victories of the South Vietnamese Patriotic Forces in 1963 and 1964.* Hanoi: Foreign Languages Publishing House, 1965.

Littauer, Raphael, and Norman Uphoff, eds. *The Air War in Indochina.* Boston: Beacon Press, 1972.

Lodge, Henry Cabot. *The Storm Has Many Eyes: A Personal Narrative.* New York: W. W. Norton & Co., 1973.

Lukas, J. Anthony. *Night-mare: The Underside of the Nixon Years.* New York: Viking, 1976.

Col. Hoang Ngoc Lung. *The General Offensives of 1968–69.* Washington, D.C.: U.S. Army Center of Military History, 1981.

McAlister, John T., Jr. *Viet Nam: The Origins of Revolution.* New York: Alfred A. Knopf, 1969.

———, and Paul Mus. *The Vietnamese and Their Revolution.* New York: Harper & Row, 1970.

McNamara, Robert S. *The Essence of Security: Reflections in Office.* New York: Harper & Row, 1968.

McPherson, Myra. *Long Time Passing: Vietnam and the Haunted Generation.* New York: Doubleday, 1984.

Mailer, Norman. *Armies of the Night.* New York: Signet, 1968.

Manchester, William. *American Caesar: Douglas MacArthur, 1880–1964.* Boston: Little, Brown, 1978.

Maneli, Mieczyslaw. *War of the Vanquished.* New York: Harper & Row, 1971.

Manning, Robert, and Michael Janeway, eds. *Who We Are: An Atlantic Chronicle of the United States and Vietnam.* Boston: Little, Brown, 1969.

Marchetti, Victor, and John D. Marks. *The CIA and the Cult of Intelligence.* New York: Alfred A. Knopf, 1974.

Marines in Vietnam, 1954–1973: An Anthology and Annotated Bibliography, The. Washington, D.C.: History and Museums Division, Headquarters, U.S. Marine Corps, 1974.

Marshall, Samuel Lyman Atwood. *The River and the Gauntlet.* Westport, Conn.: Greenwood Press: 1970.

Mason, Robert. *Chickenhawk.* New York: Penguin Books, 1984.

Mata Handbook for Vietnam. Ft. Bragg, N.C.: U.S. Army Special Warfare School, 1966.

Mecklin, John. *Mission in Torment: An Intimate Account of the U.S. Role in Vietnam.* New York: Doubleday, 1965.

Melman, Seymour, director of research, *In the Name of America* (a study commissioned and published by Clergy and Laymen Concerned About Vietnam). New York: Distributed by E. P. Dutton, 1968.

Miller, William J. *Henry Cabot Lodge.* New York: James H. Heineman, Inc., 1967.

Millett, Allan R. *Semper Fidelis: The History of the U.S. Marines.* New York: Macmillan, 1980.

Morison, Elting E. *Turmoil and Tradition: A Study of the Life and Times of Henry L. Stimson.* New York: Atheneum, 1963.

Morris, George. *CIA and American Labor: The Subversion of the AFL-CIO's Foreign Policy.* New York: International Publishers, 1967.

Moskin, J. Robert. *The Story of the U.S. Marine Corps.* New York: Paddington Press, 1979.

Mrazek, Col. James. *The Art of Winning Wars.* New York: Walker and Company, 1968.

New York Times, The. The Pentagon Papers. New York: Quadrangle Books, 1971.

New York Times, The. The Watergate Hearings. New York: Bantam, 1973.

Nixon, Richard. *The Memoirs of Richard Nixon.* New York: Grosset & Dunlap, 1978.

————. *No More Vietnams.* New York: Arbor House, 1985.

Norfolk Advertising Board. *Through the Years in Norfolk.* Norfolk, Va. 1937.

Norfolk Chamber of Commerce. *The City by the Sea: Facts and Figures About Norfolk, Va.* Norfolk, Va.: 1893.

North Carolina State Department of Agriculture. *A Sketch of North Carolina.* 1902.

Oberdorfer, Don. *Tet!* New York: Doubleday, 1971.

O'Brien, Tim. *If I Die in a Combat Zone: Box Me Up and Ship Me Home.* New York: Delacorte Press, 1973.

O'Connor, John J. *A Chaplain Looks at Vietnam.* Cleveland: World Publishing Co., 1968.

Osgood, Robert Endicott. *Ideals and Self-Interest in America's Foreign Relations: The Great Transformation of the Twentieth Century.* Chicago: University of Chicago Press, 1953.

Page, Tim. *Nam*. New York: Alfred A. Knopf, 1983.

Pearson, Lt. Gen. Willard. *The War in the Northern Provinces, 1966–1968*. Washington, D.C.: Department of the Army, 1975.

Peters, Charles, and Taylor Branch. *Blowing the Whistle: Dissent in the Public Interest*. New York: Praeger, 1972.

Pike, Douglas. *Viet Cong: The Organization and Techniques of the National Liberation Front of South Vietnam*. Cambridge, Mass.: M.I.T. Press, 1966.

Pilger, John. *The Last Day: America's Final Hours in Vietnam*. New York: Random House, 1975.

Ploger, Maj. Gen. Robert R. *U.S. Army Engineers 1965–1970*. Washington, D.C.: Department of the Army, 1974.

Porter, Gareth. *A Peace Denied: The United States, Vietnam, and the Paris Agreement*. Bloomington, Ind.: Indiana University Press, 1975.

Powers, Thomas. *The Man Who Kept the Secrets: Richard Helms and the CIA*. New York: Alfred A. Knopf, 1979.

———. *The War at Home, Vietnam and the American People, 1964–1968*. New York: Grossman Publishers, 1973.

Ransom, Harry Howe. *The Intelligence Establishment*. Cambridge, Mass.: Harvard University Press, 1970.

Rapoport, Daniel. *Inside the House: An Irreverent Guided Tour Through the House of Representatives from the Days of Adam Clayton Powell to Those of Peter Rodino*. Chicago: Follett Publishing Co., 1975.

Rawlins, Lt. Col. Eugene W., and Maj. William J. Sambito, eds. *Marines and Helicopters, 1946–1962*. Washington, D.C.: History and Museums Division, Headquarters, U.S. Marine Corps, 1976.

Rearden, Steven L. *History of the Office of the Secretary of Defense, Volume I, The Formative Years, 1947–1950*, Alfred Goldberg, general ed. Washington, D.C.: Historical Office, Office of the Secretary of Defense, 1984.

Reed, C. Wingate. *Beaufort County: Two Centuries of Its History*. Raleigh, N.C.: Edwards & Broughton, 1962.

Reischauer, Edwin O. *Beyond Vietnam: The United States and Asia*. New York: Alfred A. Knopf, 1967.

Reston, James, Jr. *The Amnesty of John David Herndon*. New York: McGraw-Hill, 1973.

Rogers, Lt. Gen. Bernard William. *Cedar Falls-Junction City: A Turning Point*. Washington, D.C.: Department of the Army, 1974.

Roller, David C., and Robert W. Twyman, eds. *The Encyclopedia of Southern History*. Baton Rouge, La.: Louisiana State University Press, 1979.

Roth, Robert. *Sand in the Wind*. Boston: Little, Brown, 1973.

Roy, Jules. *The Battle of Dienbienphu*. New York: Harper & Row, 1965.

Sack, John. *M*. New York: New American Library, 1967.

Sanders, Ronald. *Lost Tribes and Promised Lands: The Origins of American Racism*. Boston: Little, Brown, 1978.

Santoli, Al. *Everything We Had: An Oral History of the Vietnam War by Thirty-*

three American Soldiers Who Fought It. New York: Random House, 1981.

Schandler, Herbert Y. *The Unmaking of a President: Lyndon Johnson and Vietnam*. Princeton, N.J.: Princeton University Press, 1977.

Schell, Jonathan. *The Military Half: An Account of Destruction in Quang Ngai and Quang Tin*. New York: Alfred A. Knopf, 1968.

———. *The Village of Ben Suc*. New York: Random House, 1967.

Schlesinger, Arthur M., Jr. *The Bitter Heritage: Vietnam and American Democracy, 1941–1966*. Boston: Houghton Mifflin, 1967.

———. *The Imperial Presidency*. Boston: Houghton Mifflin, 1973.

Schnabel, James F. *Policy and Direction: The First Year, United States Army in the Korean War*. Washington, D.C.: Office of the Chief of Military History, U.S. Army, 1972.

Schultz, George F., ed. *Vietnamese Legends*. Rutland, Vt.: Charles E. Tuttle, 1965.

Shaplen, Robert. *Bitter Victory*. New York: Harper & Row, 1986.

———. *A Forest of Tigers*. London: Mayflower Books Ltd., 1965.

———. *A Turning Wheel: Thirty Years of the Asian Revolution by a Correspondent for* The New Yorker. New York: Random House, 1979.

Shaw, A.G.L. *Convicts and the Colonies: A Study of Penal Transportation from Great Britain and Ireland to Australia and Other Parts of the British Empire*. Melbourne, Australia: Melbourne University Press, 1977.

Shawcross, William. *Side-Show: Kissinger, Nixon, and the Destruction of Cambodia*. New York: Pocket Books, 1979.

Sheehan, Susan. *Ten Vietnamese*. New York: Alfred A. Knopf, 1967.

Shepard, Elaine. *The Doom Pussy*. New York: Trident Press, 1967.

Sherwin, Martin J. *A World Destroyed: The Atomic Bomb and the Grand Alliance*. New York: Alfred A. Knopf, 1975.

Shore II, Capt. Moyers S. *The Battle for Khe Sanh*. Washington, D.C.: Historical Branch, G-3 Division, Headquarters, U.S. Marine Corps, 1969.

Shulimson, Jack. *U.S. Marines in Vietnam: An Expanding War, 1966*. Washington, D.C.: History and Museums Division, Headquarters, U.S. Marine Corps, 1982.

———, and Keith Fleming. *U.S. Marines in Vietnam: Fighting the North Vietnamese, 1967*. Washington, D.C.: History and Museums Division, Headquarters, U.S. Marine Corps, 1984.

———, and Maj. Charles M. Johnson. *U.S. Marines in Vietnam: The Landing and the Buildup, 1965*. Washington, D.C.: History and Museums Division, Headquarters, U.S. Marine Corps, 1978.

Sivaram, M. *The Vietnam War: Why?* Rutland, Vt.: Charles E. Tuttle, 1966.

Snepp, Frank. *A Decent Interval: An Insider's Account of Saigon's Indecent End*. New York: Random House, 1977.

Snow, Edgar. *The Other Side of the River: Red China Today*. New York: Random House, 1962.

Lt. Col. Pham Van Son, ed. *The Viet Cong "Tet" Offensive (1968)*. Saigon: Printing and Publications Center (A.G./ Joint General Staff) RVNAF, 1969.

Sorenson, Theodore C. *Kennedy*. New York: Harper & Row, 1965.

Stanton, Shelby L. *The Rise and Fall of an American Army: U.S. Ground Forces in Vietnam, 1965–1973*. Novato, Calif.: Presidio Press, 1985.

Steel, Ronald. *Pax Americana*. New York: Viking, 1967.

Stockwell, John. *In Search of Enemies: A CIA Story*. New York: W. W. Norton & Co., 1978.

Stone, Robert. *Dog Soldiers*. Boston: Houghton Mifflin, 1974.

Sweet, William Warren. *Virginia Methodism: A History*. Richmond, Va.: Whittet & Shepperson, 1960.

Swinson, Arthur. *North-West Frontier: People and Events, 1839–1947*. London: Hutchinson, 1967.

Taylor, Maxwell D. *Swords and Plowshares*. New York: W. W. Norton & Co., 1972.

———. *The Uncertain Trumpet*. New York: Harper, 1960.

Taylor, Telford. *Nuremberg and Vietnam*. Chicago: Quadrangle Books, 1970.

Terzani, Tiziano. *Giai Phong! The Fall and Liberation of Saigon*. New York: St. Martin's Press, 1976.

Thayer, Thomas C. *How to Analyze a War Without Fronts: Vietnam 1965–1972*. Washington, D.C.: Journal of Defense Research, Volume 7B, Number 3, 1975.

Thompson, Sir Robert. *No Exit from Vietnam*. New York: David McKay, 1969.

———. *Peace Is Not at Hand: The American Position in the Post-Vietnam World and the Strategic Weakening of the West*. New York: David McKay, 1974.

Thorne, Christopher. *Allies of a Kind: The United States, Britain, and the War Against Japan, 1941–1945*. New York: Oxford University Press, 1978.

Toland, John. *The Rising Sun: The Decline and Fall of the Japanese Empire, 1936–1945*. New York: Random House, 1977.

Trager, Frank N. *Why Vietnam?* New York: Praeger, 1966.

Trask, Roger R. *The Secretaries of Defense: A Brief History, 1947–1985*. Washington, D.C.: Historical Office, Office of the Secretary of Defense, 1985.

Tregaskis, Richard. *Vietnam Diary*. New York: Holt, Rinehart and Winston, 1963.

Trinquier, Roger. *Modern Warfare: A French View of Counterinsurgency*. New York: Praeger, 1964.

Tuchman, Barbara W. *The March of Folly: From Troy to Vietnam*. New York: Alfred A. Knopf, 1984.

———. *Stilwell and the American Experience in China, 1911–45*. New York: Macmillan, 1970.

———. *The Proud Tower: A Portrait of the World Before the War: 1890–1914*. New York: Macmillan, 1966.

———. *The Guns of August*. New York: Macmillan, 1962.

U.S. Army Area Handbook for Vietnam. Foreign Areas Studies Division, Special Operations Research Office, The American University, Washington, D.C.: U.S. Government Printing Office, 1962.

U.S. Government and the Vietnam War: Executive and Legislative Roles and

Relationships, Part I, 1945–1961, The. Prepared for the Committee on Foreign Relations, U.S. Senate, Congressional Research Service, Library of Congress. Washington, D.C.: U.S. Government Printing Office, 1984.

U.S. Government and the Vietnam War: Executive and Legislative Roles and Relationships, Part II, 1961–1964, The. Prepared for the Committee on Foreign Relations, U.S. Senate, Congressional Research Service, Library of Congress. Washington, D.C.: U.S. Government Printing Office, 1984.

Nguyen Van Thai and Nguyen Van Mung. *A Short History of Viet-Nam.* Saigon: The Times Publishing Co., 1958.

Vietnam: Policy and Prospects, 1970. Hearings Before the Committee on Foreign Relations, U.S. Senate, Ninety-first Congress. Washington, D.C.: U.S. Government Printing Office, 1970.

Walker, Carroll. *Norfolk: A Tricentennial Pictorial History.* Norfolk, Va.: Donning Company, 1981.

Walt, Lewis W. *Strange War, Strange Strategy: A General's Report on Vietnam.* New York: Funk & Wagnalls, 1970.

Walton, Richard J. *Cold War and Counter-Revolution: The Foreign Policy of John F. Kennedy.* New York: Viking, 1972.

Warner, Denis. *The Last Confucian: Vietnam, Southeast Asia, and the West.* Baltimore: Penguin Books, 1964.

Waterhouse, Larry G., and Mariann G. Wizard. *Turning the Guns Around: Notes on the GI Movement.* New York: Praeger, 1971.

Watts, William, and Lloyd A. Free. *State of the Nation, III.* Lexington, Mass.: D. C. Heath and Company, 1978.

Wertenbaker, Thomas J. *Norfolk: Historic Southern Port.* Durham, N.C.: Duke University Press, 1931.

Werth, Alexander. *Russia at War, 1941–1945.* New York: Avon, 1965.

West, F. J. (Bing), Jr. "The Fast Rifles: A Strategy for Grassroots Pacification in Vietnam," in *Public and International Affairs, Volume V, No. 1.* Princeton, N.J.: Woodrow Wilson School, 1967.

West, Morris L. *The Ambassador.* New York: William Morrow, 1965.

Westmoreland, Gen. William C. *A Soldier Reports.* New York: Doubleday, 1976.

————, and U. S. Grant Sharp. *Report on the War in Vietnam.* Washington, D.C.: U.S. Government Printing Office, 1969.

Whitlow, Capt. Robert H. *U.S. Marines in Vietnam: The Advisory & Combat Assistance Era, 1954–1964.* Washington, D.C.: History and Museums Division, Headquarters, U.S. Marine Corps, 1977.

Wicker, Tom. *On Press: A Top Reporter's Life in, and Reflections on, American Journalism.* New York: Viking, 1978.

Windchy, Eugene G. *Tonkin Gulf.* New York: Doubleday, 1971.

Wolfkill, Grant, with Jerry A. Rose. *Reported to Be Alive.* New York: Simon and Schuster, 1965.

Woodside, Alexander B. *Community and Revolution in Modern Vietnam.* Boston: Houghton Mifflin, 1976.

Woodward, C. Vann. *Origins of the New South, 1877–1913*. Baton Rouge, La.: Louisiana State University Press, 1951.

Yergin, Daniel. *Shattered Peace: The Origins of the Cold War and the National Security State*. Boston: Houghton Mifflin, 1977.

Zumwalt, Elmo R. *On Watch: A Memoir*. New York: Quadrangle, 1976.

INDEX

Bruce Chatwin
In Patagonia £3.99

Patagonia – 'the uttermost part of the earth' – at the tip of South America. The name calls to mind giants and outlaws, Magellan's dog-headed monster, natives whose heads steam. This book is a quest, a wonder voyage – about wandering and exile. The narrator's quest for a strange beast is marked by encounters with other people whose stories delay him on his road.

'A brilliant travel book' THE OBSERVER

'Pure pleasure – full of incident and anecdote and the oddest facts imaginable . . . vastly enjoyable' PAUL THEROUX, THE TIMES

Ryszard Kapuściński
The Emperor £3.99

The downfall of an autocrat

'A brilliant portrait of the last days of Haile Selassie and his maniacal, medieval court . . . An unforgettable book' SALMAN RUSHDIE

'Few twentieth-century rulers have reigned with more imperial assurance and panache. A charmer, a demagogue and a despot with an implacable will to power, Haile Selassie contrived for forty-four years to present himself as an enlightened monarch and forward-looking statesman, while his subjects remained in boundless poverty and ignorance. The real subject of this memoir . . . is modern totalitarianism reduced to its primordial elements' TIME

'A stunning exhibit. The interviewed subjects, while the turbulent aftermath of the revolution and its frenzied nationwide *fetashs* raged, enunciated their memories of the days of Selassie with a magical elegance' JOHN UPDIKE, NEW YORKER

'A bone-chilling, brilliant tale' ALVIN TOFFLER

All Pan books are available at your local bookshop or newsagent, or can be ordered direct from the publisher. Indicate the number of copies required and fill in the form below.

Send to: **CS Department, Pan Books Ltd., P.O. Box 40, Basingstoke, Hants.   RG21 2YT.**

or phone: 0256 469551 (Ansaphone), quoting title, author and Credit Card number.

Please enclose a remittance* to the value of the cover price plus: 60p for the first book plus 30p per copy for each additional book ordered to a maximum charge of £2.40 to cover postage and packing.

*Payment may be made in sterling by UK personal cheque, postal order, sterling draft or international money order, made payable to Pan Books Ltd.

Alternatively by Barclaycard/Access:

Card No.

Signature:

Applicable only in the UK and Republic of Ireland.

While every effort is made to keep prices low, it is sometimes necessary to increase prices at short notice. Pan Books reserve the right to show on covers and charge new retail prices which may differ from those advertised in the text or elsewhere.

NAME AND ADDRESS IN BLOCK LETTERS PLEASE:

....

Name

Address

3/87